Literature

of

Western Civilization

LITERATURE
of
WESTERN
CIVILIZATION

SELECTED AND EDITED BY

Louis G. Locke
MARY BALDWIN COLLEGE

John Pendy Kirby
RANDOLPH-MACON WOMAN'S COLLEGE

M. E. Porter
INDIANA UNIVERSITY

◆

IN TWO VOLUMES

VOLUME II

THE RONALD PRESS COMPANY , NEW YORK

Copyright, 1952, by

THE RONALD PRESS COMPANY

___

All Rights Reserved

3

Library of Congress Catalog Card Number: 52–6204

PRINTED IN THE UNITED STATES OF AMERICA

Preface

LITERATURE OF WESTERN CIVILIZATION has been conceived as a basic text for the study of the humane tradition of European and American literatures. In its remarkable continuity of development from its classical origins in Greece and Rome to its infusion with the spirit of Christianity this tradition constitutes the literary heritage of the West. The imaginative literature of the West provides the stable foundation of a common European and American culture, the basic texture of Western civilization which it is—more than ever today—our moral obligation to preserve and transmit to succeeding generations.

Recognition of this responsibility has largely defined the limits of this anthology. Since all aims cannot be equally achieved in a single course in literature, we believe that the primary purpose must be to inculcate in the college student a knowledge of his own Western literary traditions. For this reason, and because their inclusion would seriously limit selections from American literature and from the literature of the Modern World, we have felt that it would be inappropriate and impractical to represent the literatures of the Near and Far East.

In order to define and illustrate the significant philosophic and literary tempers that have historically motivated the literature of the Western world, *Literature of Western Civilization* is organized chronologically into seven main divisions: The Greek World, The Roman World, The Medieval World, The Renaissance World, The Neo-Classical World, The Romantic World, and The Modern World. Within each period, emphasis is placed upon the great and permanent manifestations of the human spirit (such as Classicism) which are revealed in literature as in the other fine arts. The chief stress has been given to the dominant spirit of each period, but divergent tendencies have been represented (e.g., the Goliardic poets), though of course in less space.

Literature alone, however, cannot provide a balanced representation of a culture; there must be a correlation with the other arts, for, as Degas said to Paul Valéry, "All the muses dance together." Since we are fully in accord with the modern humanistic insistence upon a cultural view that will illuminate the interrelations among the several arts, we have sought to present literature in its harmonious relation to painting, sculpture, architecture, music, and, to some extent, the dance (this last, for example, in the account of the origins of Greek drama). Within practical spatial limits, we have attempted in the various period introductions to show that the character and direction of Western civilization have been the product of all the arts, and to trace the parallel development of the arts with literature. The plates were not selected simply as illustrations of the text or as mere ornaments of the book, but rather to reflect the same manifestations of man's spirit in the fine arts that inform the literature of the period. The lists of recordings offer the reader the opportunity to listen to some of the great musical works and to perceive in them the same spirit that dominates the lit erature and plastic arts of their age. In thus giving the student a fuller appreciation of the complementary contributions of all the arts to Western culture, the anthology should at the same time furnish him with a sounder insight—moral, spiritual, and aesthetic—into its literature. Such correlation of the arts also makes this anthology well suited for use in the introductory humanities course.

In this orientation of the student the biographical-critical sketches of the various authors supplement the period introductions. Where the writers are not simply representative of their age, but have more or less directly affected the development of the civilization of their time, the sketch has been somewhat expanded to make this influence clear. Thus, together, the introductions, the biographies, and the selections themselves trace for the student the unfolding story of the development of Western culture.

In winnowing the great bulk of humane Western belles-lettres to select representative literature, we have sought to satisfy several considerations. The chosen material should "cover the ground"; that is, adequately represent Western man's literary achievement. In each of the seven periods, the selections should truly reflect the best writing and the cultural spirit of the age. Furthermore the literature of each period should receive its just proportional emphasis; within each division, the development of national cultures should be reflected in proportion to the importance of their contributions to the wider perspective of Western culture; and the various types of writing should be effectually represented, both in the several parts and in the over-all presentation. Throughout the entire process, our basic criterion of selection has been the value of the work as imaginative literature.

Hence the student can herein study the emergence of national cultures in such significant works as the *Iliad* and *Odyssey,* the *Aeneid,* and the *Song of Roland* and find as well an adequate representation of those figures whose genius and ideals have left their permanent impress upon our cultural tradition: among them Chaucer, Dante, Shakespeare, Rabelais, Cervantes, Milton, Voltaire, Goethe, Emerson, Ibsen, Yeats, and Eliot. Here is offered an extensive survey of lyric poetry, not only as found within each of the major periods, but also as representative of the various national literatures in their different stages of development. The drama is generously represented with ten complete plays. In our presentation of the various Continental literatures, especially Romance, we believe that the reader will find the selections particularly distinctive, both in perspective and balance.

Since English and American contributions to the literature of Western civilization have been so significant, we have sought to give them corresponding recognition. Proud of our American heritage, we believe that inasmuch as American literature has earned a substantial place in world literature, it should receive corresponding consideration in the introductory literature courses; the student should supplement his knowledge of comparative literature through an understanding, as well, of his own national cultural traditions. We have consequently devoted a more equitable space to American literature than is usually found in most anthologies of world literature.

As a consequence of our conviction that the American student should be familiar with antecedent and recent concepts basic to an understanding of the traditions of Western political and social democracy, we have included appropriate selections. Also represented are some works of the most influential philosophers. Both the political and philosophical readings conform to the basic criterion, literary quality.

Within the limits imposed by the anthology, we have kept to a minimum the inclusion of fragments from the longer literary masterpieces, which, when divorced from the whole work, often lose their significance or become misleading. Whenever feasible, we have presented complete works; if, as in the instance of *Don Quixote* and Boswell's *Life of Samuel Johnson, LL.D.*, this was impossible, we have offered complete artistic units of sufficient magnitude to enable the reader to form an intelligent impression of the work as a whole. To assure the reader's getting an integrated impression of the entire work, we have in several instances supplied synopses of omitted material.

No masterpiece, and this is especially true of lyric poetry, is ever translated with total effectiveness. The student's full aesthetic understanding of the subtler aspects of style and form can of course be cultivated only through his knowledge of the original language; but much as we may lament the linguistic inadequacies of the college undergraduate, he does not learn Greek to read Homer, German to read Goethe, French to read Rabelais, and Russian to read Tolstoi. Yet it has never been more timely for the undergraduate to read the seminal books of our culture. We have consequently sought the best translations available. If the best happened to be an old one, we have used it; but whenever there has been a choice we have avoided translations in archaic English (which too often almost need to be translated for students) and have sought instead the most competent translations into modern English. The result, we feel, is a distinguished array of modern, even contemporary, translations. To mention only a few, here are Homer translated by W. H. D. Rouse, Lucretius by William Ellery Leonard, Dante by Laurence Binyon, Cervantes by Samuel Putnam, Montaigne by E. J. Trechmann, and many others. The anthology contains some translations made especially for it, and the translation of Dante incorporates hitherto unpublished corrections by Mr. Binyon. In order that the poetry, especially lyric, may most nearly approximate the quality of the original, we present a wide array of poet-translators; among these are Spenser, Shelley, Longfellow, Swinburne, Rossetti, Dowson, Symons, Housman, Humbert Wolfe, and Stephen Spender. As a consequence of this effort to offer superior translations, a number, such as those by Rouse and Putnam, are here anthologized for the first time.

It is impossible to acknowledge our obligations, which are numerous and great. Professor Ernest Bernbaum has given generously of his extensive knowledge and experience; *Literature of Western Civilization* has benefited richly from his advice. The correlations of literature and arts could never have been made without the advice and assistance of Mr. Huntington Cairns of The National Gallery of Art. Our debt to many colleagues and friends is large; we regret that it is possible to recognize here our obligation to only a few: Professors S. F. Will and H. J. Meesen of Indiana University; Professor John H. Kent of the University of Vermont; Professor William Merriam Gibson of New York University; Professors George Arms, Dane Smith, Joaquin Ortega, Joseph Kuntz, and Kenneth Lash of The University of New Mexico; Professors Mabel K. Whiteside, Herbert C. Lipscomb, and colleagues in the course in the Correlated Arts Professors Beatrice von Keller, Marjorie Harris, Eleanor Struppa, Elaine Dahl, and Pierre Daura, for suggestions growing out of the course at Randolph-Macon Woman's College; Professor Nicholson B. Adams of the University of North Carolina; Professors Herbert S. Turner, Gordon Page, Fletcher Collins, Jr., and Horace Day of Mary Baldwin College; Professor Harry T. Moore of Babson Institute; and Professor James Holly Hanford of Western Reserve University. Where there is virtue in this anthology others deserve much of the credit; where there is error or imperfection, the editors are solely responsible.

L. G. L.
J. P. K.
M. E. P.

February 15, 1952

THE NEO-CLASSICAL WORLD
(Pages 3 to 216)

◆

THE ROMANTIC WORLD

(Pages 219 to 467)

◆

THE MODERN WORLD
(Pages 471 to 810)

xv

THE NEO-CLASSICAL WORLD

The Neo-classical World

Oedipus Answering the Riddle by J. A. D. Ingres.

Fʀᴏᴍ the middle of the seventeenth century to almost the end of the eighteenth, European literature was predominantly Neo-classical. All dates given as termini of literary periods are of course only approximate, and are therefore somewhat false; just as literary categorizing itself, because of the necessity for oversimplification, is false. Yet both periods and categories can be useful to all who remember that they are not to interpret them too literally and strictly, and that all such dates are approximations which may vary even decades. Within these reservations, the last half of the seventeenth century and the first three-quarters of the eighteenth contain the rise, flowering, and gradual decline of Neo-classicism.

Neo-classicism and Romanticism themselves, though useful terms, are nebulous, for both are manifestations of the human spirit, attitudes, and temperaments, and as such they are not tangible, concrete things which can be subjected to laboratory examination and analysis. Thus there have been in all ages Neo-classicists and Romanticists, depending upon the artist's orientation to, and outlook upon, his world. There are Neo-classicists today just as well as there were in the age of Dryden and Voltaire; T. S. Eliot, for example, can be so classified. The only reason for calling the period *ca.* 1640–*ca.* 1785 "The Neo-classical World" is that during this time the Neo-classical mood was more prominent and more widely respected than in other periods.

Temple of Flora at Stourhead Park, Wiltshire.

The Rotunda of the University of Virginia, designed by Thomas Jefferson (late Neo-classical).

Without attempting any hard and fast definition —for the editors of this book eschew formal definitions—the more salient characteristics of Neo-classicism will be described. In the first place, although deriving its name from this interest, it is a great deal more than an admiration and imitation of classical (Greek and Roman) literary models. Of course this choice of models is a significant element in Neo-classicism, but it is only one element. In France and England during the seventeenth and eighteenth centuries, Neo-classical artists, both literary and plastic, chose to imitate Greek and Roman models not because they were Greek and Roman, and hence classic, but because they found in them those qualities with which their spirits felt an affinity, moods which appealed to their moods, and attitudes toward life congenial to their own.

Perhaps the most striking characteristic of the Neo-classic temper, expressed in all the arts, is rationalism. Indeed, if this age which decried excess as fanatical went to any extreme, it was in this deification of Reason—in the unshaken confidence that the intelligence with which every man had been endowed by the Supreme Architect of the Universe would bring about the constant betterment of humanity and of civilized society throughout the world. Much in the manner that we of the twentieth century have looked to Science to give us an earthly paradise, so men in that earlier age looked to Reason—and who can say they were less wise than we? Thus the great emphasis in literature and in the sister arts was on the mind, not the emotions. Indeed it is this emphasis on the intellect with its attendant slighting of the emotions which formerly

led many critics to speak of its coldness. That quality of coldness has been greatly exaggerated, but
in some Neo-classics—Boileau and Racine, for example—there is a modicum of truth in the charge.

Before condemning the Neo-classicists as cold,
however, we should consider some of the other
qualities for which they strove: decorum, restraint,
and good taste. In England and France there has

Courtesy Osvald Sirén, *China and Gardens of Europe*
(copyright, 1950)

The Pheasantry, formerly in Kew Gardens.

always been an ideal of aristocratic reserve. No
gentleman would, publicly at least, give way to his
private emotions in the manner of Shelley, who
could write:

> Oh, lift me from the grass!
> I die! I faint! I fail!
> Let thy love in kisses rain
> On my lips and eyelids pale.
> My cheek is cold and white, alas!
> My heart beats loud and fast;
> Oh! press it close to thine again,
> Where it will break at last.

Among his Neo-classical predecessors such public
utterance, and of course Shelley's poetry was written
for publication, would not have been considered in
good taste. Any similar expression of personal feel-

ing would have met only contempt among English
Cavaliers, the Restoration Beau Monde, or the
Court of Louis Quatorze. No man of quality would
have published these lines above his name for a
handsome estate. Thus the manners of the time
required the exercise of restraint, though it were
folly indeed to think human nature any less passionate in the Age of Reason than in succeeding generations. It is simply that an aristocratic, gentlemanly
distinction between the private and public areas of
life was rigidly maintained.

Particularly in the fashionable architecture of the
time is the Neo-classical quality of decorum evident.
The Palladian style (so-called from the Italian architect Palladio, 1518–1580) was introduced into England by Inigo Jones (1573–1652). It spread rapidly
there, and on the Continent as well. The style is
marked by a strict demand for axial design, an
emphasis on horizontal, rather than vertical lines,
and by the use of classical pediment, columns, and
dome. Throughout the Georgian, or Neo-classic,
architecture there was a strict adherence to form. All
the exuberance and individuality of the Tudor and
Gothic architecture give way in the Palladian to the
rigid requirements of the basic type. No longer is it
possible to introduce a bay window or a spire at
one's caprice. The necessity for maintaining the
strict balance of axial design forbade. The result
was a building of formal grandeur in the best Neo-
classical taste, giving an impression of dignity, simplicity, and serenity—all qualities greatly sought by
the poets and painters as well.

The demands of the new architecture quickly
spread in the mid-seventeenth century to gardens,
where a high degree of formality and perfection was
also achieved. As in the Palladian house, there was
an insistence on axial design, symmetrical balance,
geometrical figures, and exact parterres. Everything
had to be in order to be in the best taste. Here one
could truly find "nature methodised." The gardens
before the middle of the eighteenth century consisted of carefully laid out and strictly geometric
parterres, straight graveled, bordered by neatly
trimmed yews or box; at the end of these walks, or
vistas, there was generally a reproduction of a classic
temple or a Roman bust. Another garden attraction
was the canal, straight and pellucid. Somewhere in
the garden, perhaps at the end of one of the vistas,
one might find a garden house done in the Chinese

Courtesy National Gallery of Art (Kress Collection), Washington, D. C.

The Herdsman by Claude Lorrain.

taste, a part of the eighteenth-century vogue for everything Oriental, a vogue which attests to the strength of the counterclassical or Romantic substratum of the time.

Even as early as 1713, there was some satiric protest against the unnaturalness of the fashionable French or Italian formal garden, for Alexander Pope, quoting his own translation of the *Odyssey*, cites Homer's description of the garden of Alcinous in proof that the ancients practiced a more natural type of gardening. Then he added:

How contrary to this simplicity is the modern practice of gardening? We seem to make it our study to recede from nature, not only in the various tonsure of greens into the most regular and formal shapes, but even in monstrous attempts beyond the reach of art itself. We run into sculpture; and are yet better pleased to have our trees in the most awkward figures of men and animals, than in the most regular of their own.

The emphasis on form and balance in architecture and garden, the elaborate simplicity which was always in good taste, the concomitant restraint, are all equally characteristic of poetry and music, for this was an aristocratic and urbane world. The literature is aristocratic in tone, manner, subject matter, and outlook. Though some authors were not born of aristocratic family (e.g., Molière and Pope), they instinctively identified themselves with the aristocracy, gravitated naturally into the orbit of the Beau Monde, and henceforth expressed its ideals, ideas, prejudices, and fashions. At the beginning of this period the reading public was still small, though it increased rapidly about the turn of the eighteenth century, and literature (excluding the drama) was produced without the slightest intention of making money by gentlemen of quality for the delectation and benefit of other gentlemen. With the gradual extension of the reading public, the aristocratic tone declined, and with it, according to the opinion of some contemporary writers, literature declined also. During the later seventeenth century, a new social class came into prominence in England. The courtier and country squire were being supplanted by the manufacturer and trader. John Dennis, the literary critic, laments in 1702 that conditions are no longer as favorable to literature as they had been during the Restoration because now there are five or six times as many people in trade as formerly. The rising commercial classes were predominantly Whigs in politics and Dissenters in religion. Because of this religious preference, they adhered to a much stricter moral code than that of the fashionable world. According to Dennis's theory, therefore, perhaps the shift from the bawdy Restoration comedy of manners to the slightly less bawdy sentimental comedy of Steele and Cibber may be explained not so much by the Reverend Jeremy Collier's pious blast, *A Short View of the Immorality and Profaneness of the English Stage* (1698), as by the larger proportion of tired businessmen in theater audiences. In any event, as the century became less aristocratic and more middle class, a new definition of wit and a different set of moral values become apparent. But the real Neo-classic viewpoint is aristocratic. Thomas Gainsborough's "Georgiana, Duchess of Devonshire," for example, perfectly expresses the elegance, polish, and poised taste of the world to which she belonged.

Not only was the Neo-classic world urbane; it was also urban. It considered man much more important than landscapes, and cities more interesting than cottages. There was no interest in the actualities of country life, although there was in its literature a great deal of idealization of the country. The attitude was entirely pastoral, not realistic, and was characterized by shepherds and shepherdesses dancing daintily on the green. The pastoral element in literature, incidentally, has a striking counterpart in the delicate unreality of Fragonard and Boucher's paintings, which represent the *fête champêtre* amidst idealized country scenes.

Nature to the Neo-classicist, and his literature is full of allusions to nature, ordinarily meant normal

La Camargo Dancing by Nicolas Lancret.

Promenade of the Chestnut Trees, Versailles.

human nature, as when Pope issued his admonition to aspiring writers, "First follow Nature, and your judgments frame/ By her just standards which are still the same." It does not mean daffodils, skylarks, waterfalls, cascades, and awesome peaks. Indeed the more rugged and awe-inspiring part of nature was not at all appreciated by our early eighteenth-century ancestors. They did not care for views. The part of nature they really found congenial was the part that man's hand had transformed, "nature to advantage dressed," a formal garden or a well-tilled farm, but not the Alps.

Of course nature was sometimes identified with the universe, the conception of which Isaac Newton had vastly transformed and extended by his *Principia* (1687). His discoveries promoted a much grander concept of God than had previously been possible: God now became the master mind of a universe infinitely larger and more complex than that conceived of by His worshipers in earlier ages. Newtonians thus conceived of the universe as they might have a great watch, reflecting unlimited credit on the skill of the watchmaker. They believed that the universe could be comprehended if men would but focus their God-given intelligence upon it and use correct mathematical methods. The essential orderliness of the Newtonian world machine was

carried over into religion, politics, and society, where attempts were made to construct mechanical organisms. Yet there failed to develop a conception of evolution through countless ages. The great development in seventeenth-century thinking followed the slow process of growth from thought processes based upon authority to thought processes based upon reason, experiment, objectivity, and mathematical methods.

In this development the work of four philosophers is of the highest importance: Francis Bacon, René Descartes, Thomas Hobbes, and John Locke. Of Bacon it has been said that no subject he touched remained the same thereafter, and the impetus he gave to experimental science entitles him to be called the spiritual father of the Royal Society of London. The philosophy of Hobbes is logically coherent and completely rationalistic. Descartes sought to establish the basis of understanding with his famous dictum, *"Cogito, ergo sum."* But it is John Locke (1632–1704) who most nearly personifies the thought of the seventeenth and eighteenth centuries. In his great *Essay Concerning Human Understanding* (1690), he carries forward Descartes' work on a theory of knowledge by rejecting belief in innate ideas and propounding the concept of the mind as a blank page (*tabula rasa*) upon which all ideas are to be written by experience alone. Locke also philosophizes on the nature of the state. In his *Two Treatises of Government* (1690) he advances the contract theory and justifies the Glorious Revolution of 1688 in which King James II was supplanted, almost by popular demand, by William and Mary. In his theory Locke makes the individual citizen the basis of the state, with the government (monarch) acting as a sort of trustee for the citizens who have delegated their rights to the monarch for safekeeping.

Although the Neo-classical world was predominantly aristocratic and not in any sense of the word democratic, it provides some very important landmarks in the growth of political democracy, for it was during this time that the groundwork was laid for both modern British and American democracy. A Stuart absolutist ascended the British throne soon after the beginning of the seventeenth century, and at the time of his coronation there existed a rather general belief in the divine right of kings. By poor judgment, stubbornness, and an almost complete lack of political acumen, his son Charles I provoked the rebellion against himself which developed into the English Civil War (1642–1649). The concept of divine right was seriously undermined by the execution of King Charles I. This historical event was destined to have many repercussions in Europe and America. With the Glorious (or Bloodless) Revolution of 1688–1689, the expulsion of James II, and the bringing in of William and Mary to reign, the second mortal blow to the idea of the sacredness of monarchy was struck—which is another way of saying that the idea of the sovereignty of the people, or political democracy, had taken a long step forward. Then, John Locke's *Treatises* provided the philosophical justification for the *fait accompli* and so supplied a firm basis for further democratic development. The founding fathers of the American republic studied Locke; there is, indeed, hardly a phrase in the Declaration of Independence which cannot be traced to his ideas. The French Revolution of 1789 was likewise intimately affected by these seventeenth-century events.

Europe of the seventeenth century witnessed many political and social upheavals, struggles, and civil wars. Finally, the desire for peace and stability led civilized men in all countries to seek a basis upon which order might be established. The philos-ophers Descartes, Spinoza, and Leibnitz were in general accord that the only answer was to be found in the rule of reason. This philosophical concept contributed in an important degree to the stability, both social and political, of the reign of Queen Anne—"the peace of the Augustans." The wars of this period (those between the English Civil War and the French Revolution) while almost constant were not troublesome to the large majority of people either in England or on the Continent, for they were not mass wars in which whole populations were engaged, but small, rather localized wars fought by professional soldiers, who actually constituted a very small percentage of the total population. Thus, though wars were frequent, they were neither too disquieting nor discommoding to eighteenth-century serenity.

The prevailing rationalism also produced developments in religious thought. These developments began by distinguishing between natural and revealed religion. According to this approach, natural religion consisted of that body of religious tenets which could be deduced by reason and the empirical method alone: those matters that required no divine revelation to convince men of their truth, since they had (or so men thought) the universal consent of mankind; Cicero was quoted in support—*"Omnium consensus naturae vox est."* This branch of religion, then, was believed to consist of universal and demonstrable truths. Revealed religion, on the other hand, included those articles of Christianity which could neither be deduced nor demonstrated by the use of reason alone—the sacraments of baptism and communion, for example. But the skeptical seventeenth-century preoccupation with the problem of how we know what we know was carried steadily forward, one major result being a denial of the validity of revealed religion. What then remained was a belief in natural religion, or Deism, perhaps the most generally held religious concept of eighteenth-century intellectuals. Next, the rationalistic searchlight was focused on the validity of Deism itself, with the eventual result being a tremendous growth in atheism. Ever-growing rationalism thus led ultimately to unbelief or, by reaction, to a new sort of religion which, turning its back on reason, took its stand upon faith and intuition alone. Out of this reversion came the Methodist revival.

Courtesy Philadelphia Museum of Art

Room from Tower Hill, London.

One of the most important developments in the Neo-classical world is the beginning of modern science. Bacon, with his insistence on the experimental method for discovering physical truth, gave the scientific movement its first and probably greatest impetus. Though the nucleus of the Royal Society of London can be traced back at least to 1645, the Society itself was not formally chartered by King Charles II until 1662. Its members were not for the most part professional scientists. They were intelligent nobility and gentlemen drawn from many professions, for an interest in experimental science was one of the fashions of the time. Poets like Cowley and Dryden, prominent divines like Bishop Sprat, Bishop Wilkins, and Dr. Tillotson were members, and, incredibly enough, Samuel Pepys sat in the presidential chair in the year that Newton published his *Principia* (1687). Even the blasé Charles set up a chemistry laboratory in Whitehall Palace. Though many of the experiments performed and papers read before the Society seem naïve today, it is to this source that we must trace the wonders of our modern technological world.

The scientific spirit, itself a manifestation of the prevailing rationalism of the times, forced a change in English prose style. From the sonorous, balanced, ornate periods of Milton, Browne, Taylor, and Donne, rich in Latinate diction and farfetched but brilliant conceits, prose shifted in the third quarter of the seventeenth century to the plain, lucid, unadorned style required of its members by the Royal Society. In a word, modern prose had been created. The new plain style was utilized by Dryden, Swift, and Addison and Steele, all of whom have in this medium never been surpassed. In fact their brilliant prose is no doubt responsible for Matthew Arnold's dubbing the Augustan the "age of prose and reason."

It is manifestly impossible in an essay of this length to deal with the events of a century and a half of European and American history. A few broad, general statements are nevertheless appropriate. During this period Britain became an empire, outgrowing the little England of Shakespeare's day. London was of course a much larger and more significant fact in English life then than now, for the great cities of the North hardly existed. All the changes implied in the phrase "Industrial Revolution" were just then beginning. Scotland was not really a part of England, for she long remained loyal to the Pretender after the Act which made her formally and legally united with England. Political conditions in the American colonies were quiet, or fairly quiet, until the very eve of the Revolution. The acquisition of Canada from the French was of course one of the prominent evidences that the French star of empire was beginning to set. Trade with newly acquired India boomed. In fact, despite her notorious mismanagement of the American problem, England handled her possessions abroad better than any other imperial power in the eighteenth century. Her colonial philosophy, which held that the colonies should contribute as much as possible to the prosperity of the mother country, is nevertheless unacceptable to twentieth-century minds. Trade with the colonies was one of the most important activities of both England and France during the eighteenth century, and it produced the greatest fashion of the day—a mania for oriental *objets d'art*, tea, coffee, lacquer ware, cot-

A Midnight Modern Conversation by William Hogarth.

tons, and chintzes. The import of exotic goods from the East was accompanied by a new and unparalleled era of luxurious living.

The influence of the Town on all phases of fashion, and on artistic tastes as well, was tremendous. In England the Town meant London; that is, the fashionable West End of London, and such extensions as the watering place, Bath. Here prominent noblemen always spent the season in their great town houses, retiring to their estates in the country only during the summer. To be carried off to the country was a potent threat always held over the heads of frivolous wives, for the country was banishment indeed. In the country were no balls and assemblies, no gay theater parties, no midnight games of ombre for stakes that sometimes ran perilously high, none of the excitement of the Town. There was nothing but visiting back and forth with neighboring ladies, and even this simple,

dull pastime was largely denied during the winter months when the roads became virtually impassable.

London and Paris, however, were another matter. Here were assembled brilliant and gay societies, the Beau Monde, the people who set fashion and determined taste. Here were infinite diversions: here was the world. Little wonder that the great Doctor Johnson could say, "When a man is tired of London he is tired of life." Metropolises though they were, they were yet vastly different from the London and Paris that we know. In Restoration London, for example, only a few streets were paved with cobblestones, the others very often being muddy; open ditches served for sewers; and until fairly late in the eighteenth century there was no street lighting. The earliest attempt at lighting required householders to burn a penny candle in the street windows along principal thoroughfares. The fondness of ladies and gentlemen of quality for their coaches and sedan chairs, under these circumstances, is quite understandable. Nor will the modern reader consider their linkboys and torchbearers merely ostentatious displays of wealth.

Inside the houses there was more comfort and even luxury than had ever been known before. Beautiful new furniture, today highly esteemed by the public and by antiquarians alike, was being designed and produced. A good deal of Chinese lacquer furniture was also imported in trade with the East, as were Indian screens, calicoes, and chintzes. The introduction of the new luxury drinks of tea and coffee wrought profound changes in the social life of the aristocracy. And to drink tea required porcelain cups, at first fabulously expensive, to be brought from China. The fashionable custom of

keeping a pet monkey accorded poorly with the veritable feminine mania for collecting china. In a day when servants were extremely plentiful, and so cheap they seem to us almost free, it was customary to deduct china breakage from the maids' wages, so that it often happened that a careless maid would end the year owing her employer money. Unfortunately this garnishee could not be attached to my lady's monkey.

Our ancestors in the Neo-classical world did not eat what we now consider a balanced diet: it consisted of many different courses of meat—fish, game, roasts, fowl—and of many different kinds of wines, cordials, and brandies. (The lower classes were demoralized for a time by the introduction of gin.) Fruits, berries, and vegetables were eaten in sea-

Courtesy Metropolitan Museum of Art, New York

Marriage à la Mode (Plate IV) by William Hogarth.

son, but in winter the gentry lapsed back to meat, alcohol, and rich pastry. Gout and "strokes" were prevalent. Our ancestors, however, must have developed a considerable tolerance for alcohol, for in the eighteenth century it was customary to give each newborn baby a dram of brandy, and the eighteenth century was well along before tea and coffee became cheap enough to replace ale as the usual breakfast drink.

Surgery still belonged for the most part to the blood-letting-and-cupping barbers, and the practice of medicine to quacks. Molière detested all doctors, whom he considered to be nothing but quacks—as indeed they probably were—and wrote several satiric comedies about them, notably *The Doctor in Spite of Himself* and *The Imaginary Invalid.* Dr. Levett, whom Dr. Johnson befriended, for example, had acquired his knowledge of medicine from being a waiter in a Parisian coffee house much frequented by physicians; and although Dr. Johnson knew the source of his professional training, he still trusted his skill more than that of the more orthodoxly educated doctors. How people in the seventeenth and eighteenth centuries lived to mature years, considering their diet, the absence of sanitation, and the complete lack of scientific medical practice is something of a mystery; but the answer unquestionably is contained in the old phrase, "survival of the fittest."

No picture of life in the age of reason would be complete without mention of the coffee houses, more than three thousand of which were operating in London in 1705. Although originally open to the public, many gradually became known for the particular groups that congregated in them (for example, Will's was generally resorted to by the literati, and it was here that John Dryden kept his chair by the fire), and eventually developed into private clubs. For the price of a cup of coffee, a gentleman could sit and talk all morning with his friends, attend to his correspondence, hear the news, and read the papers to which the proprietor subscribed. They served as clearinghouses for gossip, fashions, news, and ideas.

Although the morals of middle-class citizens were probably as high as ever, public morality and the moral tone of fashionable life as set by the aristocracy were notably low. For example, love was thought to be completely impossible in marriage, and marriage itself was quite usually based on social and financial considerations. Keeping a mistress was practically obligatory for a gentleman who wanted to cut a figure in society, so common was the practice. Drunkenness and gambling were the twin vices of the age. In fact more than one play had as its central situation a beautiful young heroine who had lost all stakes but one at the gaming table. Duelling, the third curse of the times, survived long after laws were enacted making it illegal.

But the Neo-classical world was a civilized world. There was generally a free exchange of ideas between countries and complete freedom of travel about Europe unknown in recent decades of the twentieth century. For this was before the era of the supernationalistic states. Cultivated Frenchmen and Englishmen thought of themselves not exclusively as Frenchmen and Englishmen, but as men of the world. Ideas flourished and by interchange gained the widest possible currency.

The Neo-classical movement had its inception in France, but spread a short generation later to England and Germany and the rest of Europe. Neo-classical literature is primarily a French and English literature. Boileau codified the Neo-classical tenets, which were taken over and given expression in Alexander Pope's *Essay of Criticism,* and Molière taught the English Restoration dramatists how to write the comedy of manners. German literature is not represented in "The Neo-classical World" because there is no German literature in this period worthy of inclusion. Evidently the Germanic spirit is essentially Romantic. Likewise, there is little Italian or Spanish literature of permanent worth in this period. Spain has frequently failed to become a full participant in European cultural movements, for Spain usually appears to be idiosyncratic. Indeed, when Spain does take over a cultural movement from beyond her borders, the new force is so rapidly transmuted into something typically Spanish that it is soon almost unrecognizable.

Throughout the Neo-classical world, the quality of universality in art was generally recognized as the great objective. Thus the emphasis was not on the individual, but on the type. As Dr. Johnson said: "The business of a poet . . . is to examine, not the individual but the species; to remark general properties and large appearances; he does not number the streaks of the tulip, or describe the different shades in the verdure of the forest. He is to exhibit in his portraits of nature such prominent and striking features as recall the original to every mind, and must neglect the minuter discriminations, which one may have remarked and another neglected.

Courtesy National Gallery of Art (Kress Collection), Washington, D. C.

Allegory of Victory by Germain Pilon.

lected, for those characteristics which are alike obvious to vigilance and carelessness." This striving for universality naturally had the effect of curbing subjectivity and individuality of all sorts. It likewise set a rather low value on the imagination and on originality, for the goal, as Pope expressed it,

was "What oft was thought, but ne'er so well expressed." The emphasis was on polish and perfection, not on striking originality.

Neo-classic painting and sculpture exhibit the same general characteristics found in literature: form, balance, decorum, serenity, dignity, and good taste. But perhaps the general insistence on universality may have in some degree been detrimental to the plastic arts, for they reflect a marked effort toward regularization. Sir Peter Lely (1618–1680), the fashionable court artist who painted portraits of all of Charles the Second's mistresses as well as of other aristocratic ladies, so regularized the faces of his beauties that they look like sisters. Of course when one knows that Lely practically operated a portrait factory, where the body, draperies, and all but the heads were painted into a standard Lely pose by his assistants, one has a partial explanation. Yet the sameness even of the faces is striking. Perhaps a good deal of this similarity springs from the Neo-classical emphasis upon the general at the expense of the particular. Not only did Dr. Johnson insist upon the examination of the species rather than the individual, his good friend Sir Joshua Reynolds, in his *Discourses on Painting* also makes a strong case for the universal in painting: "He, therefore, who is acquainted with the works which have pleased different ages and different countries, and has formed his opinion on them, has more materials, and more means of knowing what is analogous to the mind of man, than he who is conversant only with the works of his own age and country. What has pleased, and continues to please, is likely to please again: hence are derived the rules of art, and on this immovable foundation they must ever stand." When one has such a pronouncement from the President of the Royal Academy, there is little reason to marvel at the lack of originality in the portraits, the conversation pieces, and commemorative pieces of the period. Yet it must be said in behalf of Reynolds and his contemporary artists, that stylized though their work may be, it yet lives. And it probably lives because they succeeded in putting into it this universal element that Reynolds so highly commends. Reynolds' "Lady Elizabeth Compton," for example, though no doubt commissioned by a doting husband and painted for a fee, brings across the centuries to us the charm, serenity, and polite hauteur of Neo-classic life,

Courtesy National Gallery of Art
(Chester Dale Collection), Washington, D. C.

Madame Hamelin by Jacques Louis David.

though it does not give us much insight into what Lady Elizabeth was really like as a person.

The lofty and aristocratic tone of much of the later Neo-classic art was set by Lorenzo Bernini (1598–1680), whose bust of Louis XIV is magnificently regal. And the predilection of Neo-classical painters for classical themes is amply illustrated in Ingres' (1780–1867) "Oedipus," as it also is in Pilon's (*ca.* 1537–*ca.* 1590) "Allegory of Victory." The rather formalized amusements of the Neo-classical world of fashion are depicted by Nicolas Lancret (1690–1743) in his "La Camargo Dancing," a painting of a lovely, vanished world. In Claude Lorrain's (1600–1682) "The Herdsman" the pastoral is so perfectly idyllic as to seem completely unreal. The composure and serenity of Jacques Louis David's (1748–1825) "Madame Hamelin" are authentically in the Neo-classic spirit.

The Neo-classical conception of the purpose of art, either literary or plastic, was that it was intended to please and to instruct. Perhaps the requirement that it instruct may go a long way to-

ward explaining the popularity of satire. Genuine satire always has a moral purpose; that is, it seeks to correct or improve conditions which are capable of amendment or amelioration. When one thinks of the array of brilliant satirists which this period produced, certainly the greatest aggregation of satirists in any period of Western civilization—Molière, Dryden, Swift, Pope, Voltaire, and Hogarth—the relationship of satire to the Neo-classical conception of art becomes evident. The moralizing, satiric spirit is nowhere more apparent than in the high good humor of William Hogarth (1697–1764). The inspiration of the lively conversation pieces which he invented was neither Greek nor Roman, but native and insular. His "Rake's Progress" and "Marriage à la Mode" have not only charmed generation after generation, but have also provided us with a true insight into the realities of life in the eighteenth century. His eye for significant and revealing detail was infallible.

The quality of moderation was also greatly sought after by the Neo-classicists, who took Aristotle's Golden Mean for their own. Abstention from excess was their cardinal rule, and all infractions were regarded as "enthusiastic," or, as we would say today, "fanatical."

A great deal has been said about "the rules" in connection with this age. The regard for ancient literary and artistic authority is simply an expression of the conservative belief that it is possible for intelligent people to learn from the past. The rules were not blindly worshiped simply because they were "the rules." Alexander Pope makes a very important and valid distinction when he tells aspiring authors to give due regard to "Those rules of old discovered, not devised." For the rules are not statutes enacted by the whims of ancient writers: they are artistic truths which they discovered empirically. No doubt the French Neo-classicists observed the dramatic unities and other rules much more punctiliously than ever they were observed in England. For while Pope and Dr. Johnson recommended compliance, both granted authors the right to break any rule in order to "catch a grace beyond the reach of art." In other words, the Neo-classicists were not so completely regimented as they are often said to be.

The preference of the age for certain literary forms is particularly evident. The heroic couplet, for example, was the approved medium for poetic expression, and its almost universal use all but superseded such older forms as the sonnet, blank verse, ballad stanza, or Spenserian stanza. However, odes in some quantity might reasonably be expected in a period which revered the classic past, and the actuality well justifies this expectation. Certain poetic genres were also prominent. Since the Neo-classicists held that it is the purpose of literature to please and to instruct, it is not at all remarkable that there was a profusion of didactic poetry as well as a great wealth of satire. In emulation of Greek and Roman literature, there was a considerable body of pastoral poetry.

In the drama, tragedies were modeled closely on Greco-Roman patterns, with an often successful effort made to observe the Aristotelian unities of action, time, and place. The French dramatists Molière and Racine were particularly adept in their close observance of the rules; and John Dryden revamped Shakespeare's *Antony and Cleopatra* into *All for Love,* a veritable paragon of Neo-classic tragedy which many students of literature consider at least equal to the original. But Neo-classical tragedy, even the most successful, was derivative; the greatest original dramatic contributions were in the comedy of manners, so greatly admired by the fashionable world. It is in this particular literary genre that the brilliance and wit of the Neo-classic world appear at their best. We have only to mention the incomparable Molière along with Wycherley, Etherege, Congreve, Vanbrugh, and Farquhar to establish the late seventeenth century as the greatest age of the comedy of manners. This is a truly literary comedy, pure comedy, in contradistinction to comedy of situation, humours comedy, or romantic comedy.

Although the beginnings of modern fiction occur at this time—as well as a very considerable development of the novel, particularly the imaginary voyage as developed by Voltaire and Swift—the most important prose type is the essay. Originally a French importation, for the word "essay" is from the French *essai,* a gentlemanly attempt upon a subject, this genre accorded closely with the aristocratic, urbane, moderate spirit of the times. It came to have substantial vogue throughout the seventeenth and eighteenth centuries, for beginning with Montaigne and Bacon the essay progressed steadily in public popularity, developing at least two well-known specialized types: the character essay as written by La Bruyère, and the periodical essay of the Addison and Steele variety. Both of these specialized types of essays contributed greatly to the development of longer prose fiction in the novel.

The Neo-classical world developed a special diction for its poetry, which was often several steps removed from the language of everyday use. This was characterized by stock epithets, particularly compound epithets and epithets ending in -y, personifications of abstract nouns, and periphrases, such

Louis XIV by Lorenzo Bernini.

as "the scaly breed" and "the woolly kind." These periphrases, which so irritated Wordsworth and the Romantic poets, were devised partly to meet the necessity which poets felt (since they regarded poetry as an art) to elevate poetry above the vulgarity of common speech, partly to satisfy their desire to make elegant variations, and perhaps even more to conform with their school training in the composition of Latin poetry. At any event, much of the poetry of the period is written in a specialized poetic medium, no doubt much admired by the contemporary readers of fashion, no matter how bitterly excoriated it was by later critics who had developed a different taste.

Georgiana, Duchess of Devonshire, by Thomas Gainsborough.

It is a mistake, however, to think that there was only one poetic diction in which all Neo-classical poetry was written. There undoubtedly were several which the careful student can distinguish. For example, Pope's contemporaries unquestionably drew a distinction between poetic types, for "the epistle" always appears much more informal than "the essay." Striking the level of diction appropriate to the specific type was thus a part of the general decorum expected of a polite author.

The music of the Neo-classical world, with some striking exceptions, generally manifests the same qualities that appear in the other arts. During the seventeenth century the focal point in music was opera and the *stile rappresentativo*, i.e., dramatic music in general. Instrumental music had not yet attained the importance it was to gain in the next century, but it did nevertheless make considerable gains. Many new forms, such as the concerto grosso, the fugue, the sonata ("chamber," "church," and "solo"), and the overture were developed. Another important development was the establishment of the "suite," grouping together several dances into a larger entity held together by common tonality. The most important keyboard instruments were the organ and harpsichord, known generically as clavier. The two always go together, for in the seventeenth century every harpsichordist was an organist.

In Italy, Monteverdi (1567–1643) wrote several volumes of utterly bold madrigals, but after his conversion to the new dramatic style his output centered around opera and grandiose concerted church music. Another Italian, Corelli (1653–1713), composed great chamber and orchestral music. In England there is only one great composer during the seventeenth century, Henry Purcell (1659–1695). He wrote *Dido and Aeneas,* an opera in the Neo-classic taste, and much instrumental and church music. In France, the greatest name is that of Jean Baptiste Lully (*ca.* 1633?–1687), who wrote opera expressing the contemporary taste for entertainment in the grand manner. It is actually the musical counterpart of the impressive but impersonal architecture, just as surely as it is also the musical equivalent of the somewhat cold formality of Racine. In the Protestant North, the new faith produced great music in the works of a legion of cantors, i.e., choirmasters and organists at municipal churches. Perhaps the greatest among these were Heinrich Schütz (1585–1672), a truly Biblical composer, and Dietrich Buxtehude (1637–1707) who was greatly admired by Bach.

The two greatest figures in music between 1700 and 1750 are Bach and Handel, and though by time-honored custom they are generally treated together, there is practically no similarity in their work. Bach, for example, is remarkably isolated from the cultural and artistic fashions of his own time, a sort of throwback to the Reformation in the ardor of his Protestantism, while on the other hand Handel enthusiastically embraced his milieu. Much has been made of the cold, mathematical quality in Bach, but this emphasis is an exaggeration; for though his craftsmanship is always magnificently and meticulously sure, this is no reason to say that he is less emotionally warm than other musicians. But there is in Bach's fugues the convincing power of logic, which is always tremendously powerful. Yet at the same time there is a religious fervor in Bach which can only be described as Baroque, and which completely removes him from direct participation in the Neo-classical *zeitgeist*. Here again is a divergent element in the dominant spirit of the times. In his Passion music and other religious compositions, he exploits the mysticism and fervor of his own personality in a manner less than consonant with the purely musical logic of his other compositions.

Handel's greatest mastery lay in vocal compositions, unlike Bach's, whose genius found consummate expression in instrumental music. One must bear in mind, however, that eighteenth-century composers were at home in every type of music. Though remembered chiefly today for his great oratorio *The Messiah*, Handel was not primarily a religious composer. He spent the major part of his life, broke his heart, and impaired his fortunes, trying to please the capricious London aristocracy with forty-three operatic compositions before he finally turned his attention toward the more solid and devout middle classes, who proved receptive to his cantatas and oratorios. These works, based upon familiar Biblical themes, succeed in embodying a great deal of universality, a fact which perhaps goes far in explaining their perennial popularity. But they are, nevertheless, British to the core, for they express especially the spirit of Anglican Christianity.

The transition from the High Baroque of Bach and Handel produced a style known as the "style galant," more popularly called the Rococo. The tremendous tonal architecture of the great fugues and vast choral works was dissolved into garlands of surface ornaments. This was the era of the minuets and little harpsichord pieces, and of operas without convincing dramatic force but of enchanting melodic freshness. The various tendencies coalesced into what we call the symphonic era, the so-called Viennese School led by Haydn and Mozart and crowned by Beethoven.

Perhaps the greatest contribution of Haydn and Mozart to music was the development of the sonata-idea which created the symphony, the string quartet, other forms of chamber music, and the keyboard solo sonata. Haydn represents the epitome of Neo-classicism in music, and the same characteristic qualities which mark the temper in the other arts may be heard in his music: polish, restraint, ornamentation, good taste, and cheerfulness, for example, are all evident in Haydn's "Clock" Symphony. Although viewed with parochial condescension by the Romanticists, Haydn has never been excelled: Brahms could not get away from

Courtesy National Gallery of Art (Mellon Collection),
Washington, D. C.

Lady Elizabeth Compton by Sir Joshua Reynolds.

the shadow of Haydn's quartets; Beethoven reached a crisis that silenced him for ten years when he realized he could not go beyond Haydn; and Mozart quit writing quartets and turned to quintets for the same reason.

Haydn and Mozart should not be compared; rather they complement each other. For though Haydn conforms much more closely to the Neo-classical pattern, Mozart is more dramatic, and possibly a bit more versatile, for he had dramatic

Courtesy National Gallery of Art (Widener Collection),
Washington, D. C.

A Woman Weighing Gold by Jan Vermeer.

insight into human nature (the Countess in *Figaro*), he knew how to represent demoniac passions, as in *Don Giovanni*, or even otherworldly religiosity, as in Sarastro (in *The Magic Flute*); nor is he above a low-grade buffoonery at times. It is indicative of Mozart's stature that beneath the formality and balance and lightness of his symphonies and chamber music, one senses the eternal note of sadness, occasioned perhaps by his realization of the ephemeralness of the gay world he represents.

The Neo-classical world was by no means completely Neo-classical. In any literary or artistic

movement, there are always divergent trends, and in this age there was always a strong subcurrent of Romanticism which was never entirely absent, even at the very apex of the Neo-classical movement. When one thinks of Pope sitting in his grotto, or of his *Eloisa to Abelard*, or of Blaise Pascal's *Pensées*, for example, or of Pre-romantics like Gray and Thomson, or of some of Gainsborough's wind-swept paintings, one realizes that the two moods are frequently concurrent. It is simply a question of which is in the ascendancy.

Above all, students should remember that Neo-classicism is not faulty Romanticism. These were not authors, or painters, or composers who tried to be Romantic and failed; they were attempting something entirely different. To appreciate their work intelligently we must judge their achievement within the framework of their intentions.

LIST OF RECORDINGS

SEVENTEENTH- AND EIGHTEENTH-CENTURY MUSIC

1. Victor Masterworks Album 496 contains an excellent selection from the works of Claudio Monteverdi (1567–1643), the first of the great baroque composers.
2. *Madrigals*, by Claudio Monteverdi, Vox Long Playing record 6670.
3. *O Sacrum Convivium*, by Lodovico Grossi da Viadana (1564–1627), performed by the Strasbourg Choir on Columbia record RFX-56.
4. *Gagliarda*, by Girolamo Frescobaldi (1583–1643), performed on the harpsichord by Alice Ehlers, Decca record 23089.
5. *Fiori Musicali*, by Girolamo Frescobaldi, Allegro Long Playing record AL-111.
6. Gramophone Shop (New York) record GSC-5, 6 contains a magnificent collection of cantatas by the great Saxon master Heinrich Schütz (1585–1672). His *St. John Passion*, performed by the Stuttgart Choral Society, appears on Renaissance Long Playing record X-26.
7. *Donzelle Fuggite*, by Francesco Cavalli (1602?–1676), performed by Ezio Pinza and Fritz Kitzinger, Victor record 17915.
8. *Courante*, by Jean Baptiste Lully (1633?–1687), performed by Alice Ehlers, harpsichord, Decca record 23089.
9. Overture to Molière's *Amour Médecin*, by John Baptiste Lully, performed by the Paris Conservatory Orchestra, French Boîte à Musique record 22.
10. Incidental music for Molière's *Bourgeois Gentilhomme*, by Jean Baptiste Lully, on Gramophone record P-809.
11. Incidental music for Molière's *Médecin malgré lui*, by Jean Baptiste Lully, in Gramophone record set L-994/7.
12. *Concerto Grosso No. 8* ("Christmas Concerto"), by Arcangelo Corelli (1653–1713), performed by the London Symphony Orchestra, in Victor Masterworks set 600, and by the Munich Symphony on Vox Long Playing record 6250.

13. *Se Florindo è Fedele,* from *Pirro e Demetrio,* by Alessandro Scarlatti (1659–1725), performed by Marian Anderson and K. Vehanen, Victor record 17257.

14. *Ah, How Pleasant 'tis to Love,* by Henry Purcell (ca. 1658–1695), with text from Milton's *L'Allegro,* on Decca record M-550.

15. *Dido and Aeneas* (complete opera), by Henry Purcell, in Gramophone Masterworks set 389 and Decca set X-101-107.

16. Selected works by François Couperin (1668–1733) have been recorded for the Couperin Society on the harpsichord by Wanda Landowska. Other collections: (a) by Marcelle Meyer, harpsichord, Discophiles Français Album A-16; (b) by Claude Jean Chiasson, Lyrichord Long Playing record LL-12.

17. *Concerto in C Major* ("Per la Solennità di S. Lorenzo"), by Antonio Vivaldi (ca. 1680–1743), performed by the La Scala Orchestra, on Italian Durium record SA-106/7, 2.

18. A collection of shorter Vivaldi items is presented on Period Long Playing record 514.

19. *Brandenburg Concertos,* by Johann Sebastian Bach (1685–1750), performed by the Busch Chamber Players, in Columbia Masterworks set 249 and 250, and by Pablo Casals with the Prades Festival Orchestra on Columbia Long Playing records 4345 and 4346.

20. *C Major Fugue* ("Fanfare"), by Johann Sebastian Bach, performed by E. Power Biggs, Organ, Victor record 11-9146.

21. *Partita in B Flat Major,* by Johann Sebastian Bach, performed by Wanda Landowska, harpsichord, on Gramophone records DB-4995-6; and by Rosalyn Tureck, piano, on Allegro Long Playing record AL-18.

22. Toccatas and Fugues by Johann Sebastian Bach, complete recordings by Carl Weinrich, Musicraft Albums 36-37.

23. *Well-Tempered Clavier,* by Johann Sebastian Bach, performed by Wanda Landowska, harpsichord, on Victor Long Playing records 1017, 1107, 1136.

24. *The Messiah,* oratorio, by George Frederick Handel (1685–1759), performed by the Luton Choral Society in Victor Masterworks Set 1194-95. There is an abridged version in Columbia set DX 630-7. A complete presentation is made by the Huddersfield Choral Society in Columbia Long Playing set SL-151.

25. *The Water Music,* by George Frederick Handel, performed by the London Philharmonic Orchestra, Decca record ED-38, and by Bales with the National Gallery Orchestra on WCFM Long Playing record LP-2.

26. *La Serva Padrona,* by Giovanni Pergolesi (1710–1736), complete opera on Cetra-Soria (Italian) Long Playing record 50036.

27. *Orpheus and Eurydice,* by Christoph Willibald Gluck (1714–1787), abridged version, on Vox Long Playing record PL-6780.

28. *Symphony No. 94 in G Major* ("Surprise"), by Franz Joseph Haydn (1732–1809), performed by the Boston Symphony Orchestra in Victor Masterworks set 1155, and on Victor Long Playing record LM-28.

29. *Symphony No. 101 in G Major* ("Clock"), by Franz Joseph Haydn, performed by the New York Philharmonic Orchestra in Victor Masterworks set 37 and on Victor Long Playing record LM-1038.

30. *Quartet in D Major for Strings* ("Lark"), by Franz Joseph Haydn, performed by the Budapest String Quartet on Columbia Long Playing record ML-4216.

31. *The Creation Oratorio,* by Franz Joseph Haydn, based on a text by Lidley and derived from Milton's *Paradise Lost,* in Haydn Society Long Playing set HSLP-2005; excerpts on the following Columbia records: LX1011, 71450D, DX1052, DX1392, DX1407, 71450D, 11830D, and on the following Victor records: 11-8405, 11-960, 11-8406, 11-9430, 1015.

32. *Don Giovanni,* complete opera by Wolfgang Amadeus Mozart (1756–1791), in Haydn Society Long Playing set HSLP-2030, and in Victor Masterworks sets 423-424-425.

33. *Symphony No. 35 in D Major* ("Haffner"), by Wolfgang Amadeus Mozart, performed by the New York Philharmonic Orchestra in Victor Masterworks set 65, and on Victor Long Playing record LM-1038.

34. *Adagio and Fugue in C Minor,* by Wolfgang Amadeus Mozart, performed by the Paris Conservatory Orchestra on French Oiseau Lyre record 93 and by the Vienna Philharmonic Orchestra on Columbia Long Playing record ML-4370.

35. *Symphony No. 38 in D Major* ("Prague"), by Wolfgang Amadeus Mozart, performed by the Vienna Philharmonic Orchestra, in Victor Masterworks set 457, and by the Royal Philharmonic Orchestra under Sir Thomas Beecham on Columbia Long Playing record ML-4313.

36. *Symphony No. 41 in C Major* ("Jupiter"), by Wolfgang Amadeus Mozart, performed by the NBC Symphony Orchestra in Victor Masterworks set 1080, and on Victor Long Playing record LM-1030.

English Lyric Poetry

GEORGE HERBERT

1593–1633

George Herbert, Anglican rector of Bemerton in Wiltshire, came of the noble family of Herberts. His brother was Lord Herbert of Cherbury, the famous Cambridge Platonist. He was educated at Trinity College, Cambridge. His poems, consisting exclusively of religious lyrics often dealing with his own inner conflicts, were collected and published posthumously in 1633 as *The Temple*. His biographer, Izaak Walton, called him "holy Mr. Herbert."

A metaphysical poet of the school of Donne, his use of the conceit is nevertheless not so startling as Donne's. His imagery is rich and the emotion of his poems is profoundly moving. Beyond question, the best devotional poetry in all English literature was written in the seventeenth century, and in this literary genre Herbert is surpassed by no one. Even the Puritans respected his deep Anglican mysticism. It is doubtful if there is more powerful devotional poetry than his in any language.

FURTHER READING

HUTCHINSON, F. E., ed. *The Works of George Herbert* (Oxford, 1941).
KNIGHTS, L. C., "George Herbert," *Scrutiny*, XII (Spring, 1944).

Virtue

Sweet day, so cool, so calm, so bright,
  The bridal of the earth and sky!
The dew shall weep thy fall to-night;
  For thou must die.

Sweet rose, whose hue, angry and brave,
  Bids the rash gazer wipe his eye,
Thy root is ever in its grave,
  And thou must die.

Sweet spring, full of sweet days and roses,
  A box where sweets compacted lie,
My music shows ye have your closes,
  And all must die.

Only a sweet and virtuous soul,
  Like seasoned timber, never gives;
But though the whole world turn to coal,
  Then chiefly lives.

The Pulley

When God at first made man,
Having a glass of blessings standing by,
  "Let us," said he, "pour on him all we can.
Let the world's riches, which dispersed lie,
  Contract into a span."

So Strength first made a way;
Then Beauty flowed; then Wisdom, Honor, Pleasure.
  When almost all was out, God made a stay,
Perceiving that alone, of all his treasure,
  Rest in the bottom lay.

"For if I should," said he,
"Bestow this jewel also on my creature,
  He would adore my gifts instead of me,
And rest in Nature, not the God of Nature;
  So both should losers be.

"Yet let him keep the rest,
But keep them with repining restlessness;
  Let him be rich and weary, that at least,
If goodness lead him not, yet weariness
  May toss him to my breast."

ROBERT HERRICK

1591–1674

Herrick, born a Londoner, spent most of his mature life in Devonshire where he was rector of Dean Prior. Educated at Cambridge, he entered the Church in 1627, and bade farewell to a gay London life of taverns and wits in his poem, "Farewell to Poetry." Though it is likely that at first he detested Devonshire, this Cavalier of the Cloth found much poetic material in the rural life around him. In fact in his *Hesperides,* a collection of twelve hundred lyrics, we can trace the pleasant round of the country year with its harvest festivals, maypoles, and weddings; he states his theme in these lines:

> I sing of brooks, of blossoms, birds, and bowers,
> Of April, May, of June, and July flowers;
> I sing of maypoles, hock-carts, wassails, wakes,
> Of bridegrooms, brides, and of their bridal-cakes.

And in celebrating all these aspects of his Devonshire environment, Herrick proved himself one of the greatest lyric poets in any literature. Some of his lyrics, which seem almost to sing themselves, were set to music by Henry Lawes.

He was deprived of his living at Dean Prior by the Long Parliament in 1647, and very little is known about his life for the next dozen years. His living was restored in 1662 by the Royalists, but where Herrick was and what he did in the interval is not clear.

Herrick's poetry follows the distinguished tradition of Anacreon, Horace, Catullus, and Ben Jonson. Though the metaphysical style of Donne, striving for admiration with sometimes tortured conceits, was then in vogue, Herrick did not follow the new fashion but preferred rather to write in the older tradition of classical lyricism.

Whether his Julias, Antheas, Corinnas, and Electras were flesh-and-blood mistresses of the Anglican rector is extremely doubtful, unconventional though he must have seemed to his parishioners, but no reader can doubt the poetic genuineness of Julia in silks.

FURTHER READING

Moorman, F. W. *Robert Herrick, a Biographical and Critical Study* (Oxford, 1910).
Tuve, Rosemond. *Elizabethan and Metaphysical Imagery* (Chicago, 1947).

To the Virgins, to Make Much of Time

Gather ye rosebuds while ye may,
  Old Time is still a-flying;
And this same flower that smiles to-day,
  To-morrow will be dying.

The glorious lamp of heaven, the sun,
  The higher he's a-getting,
The sooner will his race be run,
  And nearer he's to setting.

That age is best which is the first,
  When youth and blood are warmer;
But being spent, the worse, and worst
  Times, still succeed the former.

Then be not coy, but use your time,
  And while ye may, go marry;
For, having lost but once your prime,
  You may forever tarry.

Upon Julia's Clothes

Whenas in silks my Julia goes,
Then, then, methinks, how sweetly flows
The liquefaction of her clothes.

Next, when I cast mine eyes, and see
That brave vibration, each way free,
O, how that glittering taketh me!

———◆———

SIR JOHN SUCKLING

1609–1642

Sir John Suckling is perhaps the most typical of all the Cavalier poets. A soldier, a Royalist, a gambler, a profligate spender, a wit and a poet, he represents the Cavalier ideal to perfection. Poetry with him was not a profession, but a gentlemanly accomplishment, the sort of thing one might expect of a man of parts from an old Norfolk family. He was educated at Trinity College, Cambridge, and he made the grand tour of the Continent. He inherited vast ancestral estates and, in 1630, was knighted by the King. At the outbreak of the Civil War he became a leader in the Royalist forces, raised a troop of horse and lavishly outfitted his men at his own expense, and then courageously led them on many fields of honor. D'Avenant, a contemporary, says that he was the greatest wit and gallant of the day. He was a great lover of practical jokes; he invented the game of cribbage; and, if the gossipy antiquarian John Aubrey may be relied upon, having wasted his great fortune, he died in Paris a very poor man.

He wrote several plays, the best of which is *The Goblins*, but his solid reputation as a minor poet rests on such delightfully graceful lyrics as "Why So Pale and Wan, Fond Lover?" and "The Constant Lover," which in themselves are sufficient warrant for his abiding fame.

FURTHER READING

THOMPSON, A. P., ed. *The Works of Sir John Suckling* (London, 1910).

Why So Pale and Wan?

Why so pale and wan, fond lover?
　Prithee, why so pale?
Will, when looking well can't move her,
　Looking ill prevail?
　Prithee, why so pale?

Why so dull and mute, young sinner?
　Prithee, why so mute?
Will, when speaking well can't win her,
　Saying nothing do 't?
　Prithee, why so mute?

Quit, quit for shame! This will not move;
　This cannot take her.
If of herself she will not love,
　Nothing can make her:
　The devil take her!

The Constant Lover

Out upon it, I have loved
　Three whole days together!
And am like to love thee more,
　If it prove fair weather.

Time shall moult away his wings
　Ere he shall discover
In the whole wide world again
　Such a constant lover.

But the spite on't is, no praise
　Is due at all to me:
Love with me had made no stays,
　Had it any been but she.

Had it any been but she,
　And that very face,
There had been at least ere this
　A dozen dozen in her place.

RICHARD LOVELACE

1618–1658

Lovelace, reputed to have been one of the handsomest Englishmen who ever lived, came of a wealthy Kentish family. Educated at Charterhouse School and at Oxford, he espoused the King's cause and served him well. He sat in Parliament, but was arrested and imprisoned because of his loyalty to the Crown; it was in the Gatehouse Prison, Westminster, that he composed the immortal "To Althea." He fought for the King, and afterwards lived for a while in France. Upon his return, he was again imprisoned, and during this time he prepared his *Lucasta* (1649). After the King's execution he was freed, but broken in fortune and in body he died in 1658.

His name is generally coupled with Suckling's in the annals of English poetry, but though both were gay, dashing Cavalier poets, Lovelace is more sober and sincere in his attitude toward women. Though many of his poems are of uneven quality, in his best he blends with consummate skill the best lyric quality of Ben Jonson with the cleverness of Donne and the other Metaphysicals. A minor poet, he nevertheless has left us two immortal lyrics, both as nearly perfect as the mind can imagine.

FURTHER READING

WILKINSON, C. H., ed. *The Poems of Richard Lovelace* (Oxford, 1925).

To Althea, from Prison

When Love with unconfinéd wings
　Hovers within my gates,
And my divine Althea brings
　To whisper at the grates;
When I lie tangled in her hair
　And fettered to her eye,
The birds that wanton in the air
　Know no such liberty.

When flowing cups run swiftly round
　With no allaying Thames,
Our careless heads with roses bound,
　Our hearts with loyal flames;

When thirsty grief in wine we steep,
  When healths and draughts go free,
Fishes that tipple in the deep
  Know no such liberty.

When, like committed linnets, I
  With shriller throat will sing
The sweetness, mercy, majesty,
  And glories of my king;
When I shall voice aloud how good
  He is, how great should be,
Enlargèd winds, that curl the flood,
  Know no such liberty.

Stone walls do not a prison make,
  Nor iron bars a cage;
Minds innocent and quiet take
  That for an hermitage;
If I have freedom in my love
  And in my soul am free,
Angels alone, that soar above,
  Enjoy such liberty.

To Lucasta, Going to the Wars

Tell me not, sweet, I am unkind,
  That from the nunnery
Of thy chaste breast and quiet mind
  To war and arms I fly.

True, a new mistress now I chase,
  The first foe in the field;
And with a stronger faith embrace
  A sword, a horse, a shield.

Yet this inconstancy is such
  As thou too shalt adore;
I could not love thee, dear, so much,
  Loved I not honor more.

———◆———

EDMUND WALLER

1606–1687

Though the decasyllabic couplet had been used, and perhaps invented, by Chaucer, Dryden gave Waller credit for refining it. Without doubt the smoothness and exactness of Waller's self-contained couplets gave a mighty impetus to the popularity of the form which for almost two centuries remained the dominant English poetic medium.

Waller came of a prominent Buckinghamshire family from whom he inherited his estate, Beaconsfield. His early education was received at Eton, from whence he proceeded to King's College, Cambridge. He was married in 1631 to an heiress who died three years later. Upon his entrance to Parliament he allied himself with the Puritan party, but soon changed his allegiance to the Royalists, among whom he became an ardent partisan. In fact, so eager was he in behalf of the King, that in 1643 he was arrested as leader of "Waller's Plot," an attempt to seize London for Charles I. He was imprisoned, fined 10,000 pounds, banished by the government, and escaped execution only by turning government witness. By 1651 he had placated the anger of Cromwell, and was allowed to return. Upon the Restoration, he not only made his peace with the Royalists, but very soon won the King's favor.

Much of his poetry is addressed to "Sacharissa," Lady Dorothy Sidney, whom he unsuccessfully wooed after the death of his first wife. There is in Waller's best poetry a deceptive ease of expression which is very difficult to imitate. If he had written nothing but "Go, Lovely Rose" he would be a great minor poet, for as Logan Pearsall Smith has said, "he joined three words so happily together that he left his name to float down through time on the wings of a phrase and a flower."

FURTHER READING

DRURY, G. THORNE, ed. *The Poems of Edmund Waller* (London, 1893).

Go, Lovely Rose!

Go, lovely Rose!
Tell her that wastes her time and me,
That now she knows,
When I resemble her to thee,
How sweet and fair she seems to be.

Tell her that's young,
And shuns to have her graces spied,
That hadst thou sprung
In deserts where no men abide,
Thou must have uncommended died.

Small is the worth
Of beauty from the light retired;
Bid her come forth,
Suffer herself to be desired,
And not blush so to be admired.

Then die! that she
The common fate of all things rare
May read in thee:
How small a part of time they share,
That are so wondrous sweet and fair!

On a Girdle

That which her slender waist confined,
Shall now my joyful temples bind;
No monarch but would give his crown,
His arms might do what this has done.

It was my heaven's extremest sphere,
The pale which held that lovely deer;
My joy, my grief, my hope, my love,
Did all within this circle move!

A narrow compass! and yet there
Dwelt all that's good, and all that's fair;
Give me but what this ribband bound,
Take all the rest the sun goes round!

———◆———

HENRY VAUGHAN

1622–1695

Henry Vaughan was born in Brecknockshire, Wales, the ancient Roman province of Siluria, and because he always retained a great love for his native region he is known as "the Silurist." He was educated at Jesus College, Oxford, studied law in London and medicine in Wales, where, after the conclusion of the Civil War, he practiced medicine. His collections of devotional lyrics are *Silex Scintillans* (1650 and 1655) and *Thalia Rediviva* (1678).

Vaughan, a member of the metaphysical school of poets, was particularly under the influence of George Herbert. Though not quite so skilful in the handling of complicated metrical forms as Herbert, he is just as ecstatically mystical. Some of his devotional poems are marked by an even more magnifi-

cent mystical vision than those of his devout contemporaries. It is also interesting to note that in his warm love of nature and in his philosophy of childhood (e.g., "The Retreat") he anticipates Wordsworth and the other Romantic poets.

FURTHER READING

BLUNDEN, EDMUND. *On the Poems of Henry Vaughan* (London, 1927).
WHITE, H. C. *The Metaphysical Poets* (New York, 1936).

Peace

My soul, there is a country
    Far beyond the stars,
Where stands a wingèd sentry
    All skilful in the wars.
There, above noise and danger,
    Sweet Peace sits crowned with smiles,
And One born in a manger
    Commands the beauteous files.
He is thy gracious friend,
    And—O my soul, awake!—
Did in pure love descend
    To die here for thy sake.
If thou canst get but thither,
    There grows the flower of peace,
The rose that cannot wither,
    Thy fortress and thy ease.
Leave, then, thy foolish ranges;
    For none can thee secure
But One who never changes,
    Thy God, thy life, thy cure.

The Retreat

Happy those early days, when I
Shined in my angel-infancy!
Before I understood this place
Appointed for my second race,
Or taught my soul to fancy aught
But a white, celestial thought;
When yet I had not walked above
A mile or two from my first love,
And looking back at that short space,
Could see a glimpse of his bright face;
When on some gilded cloud or flower
My gazing soul would dwell an hour,
And in those weaker glories spy
Some shadows of eternity;
Before I taught my tongue to wound

My conscience with a sinful sound,
Or had the black art to dispense,
A several sin to every sense,
But felt through all this fleshly dress
Bright shoots of everlastingness.
    O, how I long to travel back,
And tread again that ancient track,
That I might once more reach that plain,
Where first I felt my glorious train;
From whence the enlightened spirit sees
That shady city of palm trees.
But ah! my soul with too much stay
Is drunk, and staggers in the way!
Some men a forward motion love,
But I by backward steps would move;
And when this dust falls to the urn,
In that state I came, return.

The World

I saw Eternity the other night,
Like a great ring of pure and endless light,
    All calm, as it was bright;
And round beneath it, Time, in hours, days, years,
    Driven by the spheres,
Like a vast shadow moved, in which the world
    And all her train were hurled.
The doting lover in his quaintest strain
    Did there complain;
Near him, his lute, his fancy, and his flights,   10
    Wit's sour delights,
With gloves, and knots, the silly snares of pleasure,
    Yet his dear treasure,
All scattered lay, while he his eyes did pour
    Upon a flower.

The darksome statesman, hung with weights and
        woe,
Like a thick midnight-fog, moved there so slow,
    He did not stay, nor go;
Condemning thoughts, like sad eclipses scowl
    Upon his soul,   20
And clouds of crying witnesses without
    Pursued him with one shout.
Yet digged the mole, and, lest his ways be found,
    Worked under ground,
Where he did clutch his prey. But one did see
    That policy:
Churches and altars fed him; perjuries
    Were gnats and flies;
It rained about him blood and tears, but he
    Drank them as free.

The fearful miser on a heap of rust
Sat pining all his life there, did scarce trust
    His own hands with the dust,
Yet would not place one piece above, but lives
    In fear of thieves.
Thousands there were as frantic as himself,
    And hugged each one his pelf:
The downright epicure placed heaven in sense,
    And scorned pretence;
While others, slipped into a wide excess,   40
    Said little less;
The weaker sort, slight, trivial wares enslave,
    Who think them brave;
And poor, despised Truth sat counting by
    Their victory.

Yet some, who all this while did weep and sing,
And sing and weep, soared up into the ring;
    But most would use no wing.
"O fools," said I, "thus to prefer dark night
    Before true light!   50
To live in grots and caves, and hate the day
    Because it shows the way,
The way, which from this dead and dark abode
    Leads up to God;
A way where you might tread the sun, and be
    More bright than he!"
But, as I did their madness so discuss,
    One whispered thus:
"This ring the Bridegroom did for none provide,
    But for his bride."   60

————◆————

ANDREW MARVELL

1621–1678

    The urbane Puritan, Andrew Marvell, came of
a Yorkshire family and was educated at Trinity
College, Cambridge. After spending four years on
the Continent, he became tutor to Mary Fairfax,
daughter of Lord Fairfax, at Nun Appleton, Yorkshire. Here he wrote some of his best poems and
here, amidst delightful surroundings, his interest in
gardens began to develop. In 1653 he became tutor
to a ward of Oliver Cromwell, and four years later
became John Milton's assistant in the Latin Secre-
taryship. He entered Parliament in 1659.
    A man of moderation, he led a happy life even
in the midst of intestine political upheavals, and

although closely associated with the leaders of the Puritan regime, he wrote a poem, "To His Coy Mistress," more cavalier in spirit than the Cavaliers ever wrote. After the Restoration he re-entered Parliament, where he habitually attacked the new regime with tracts and verse satires which, however, were not published until much later. A great admirer of Milton, with whom he had worked in close association, he wrote verses in praise of *Paradise Lost* at a time when the public did not highly regard the poem.

The literary reputation of Andrew Marvell has never been higher than at present, for of all the seventeenth-century poets he, along with Donne, seems to speak most directly to the twentieth century. His deep love and close observation of nature has, for example, been greatly admired by Edith Sitwell, who says that "The Garden" is "one of the loveliest short poems in our language. Its green and leafy summer of rich sun and richer shade will live while our language still lives." No poet in all English literature has demonstrated a greater power of making a particular incident universal than Marvell: all of the transiency of life, the shortness of man's allotted span, and the sureness of death are expressed in the indelible couplet:

> But at my back I always hear
> Time's wingèd chariot hurrying near;

and all of the terrible urgency felt by all lovers in all ages has been embodied in the words,

> The grave's a fine and private place,
> But none, I think, do there embrace.

FURTHER READING

Bradbrook, M. C., and Thomas, M. G. Lloyd. *Andrew Marvell* (Cambridge, 1940).
Margoliouth, H. M., ed. *The Poems and Letters of Andrew Marvell* (Oxford, 1927).

To His Coy Mistress

Had we but world enough, and time,
This coyness, Lady, were no crime.
We would sit down and think which way
To walk and pass our long love's day.
Thou by the Indian Ganges' side
Shouldst rubies find; I by the tide
Of Humber would complain. I would

Love you ten years before the Flood,
And you should, if you please, refuse
Till the conversion of the Jews.   10
My vegetable love should grow
Vaster than empires, and more slow;
An hundred years should go to praise
Thine eyes and on thy forehead gaze;
Two hundred to adore each breast,
But thirty thousand to the rest;
An age at least to every part,
And the last age should show your heart.
For, Lady, you deserve this state,
Nor would I love at lower rate.   20
    But at my back I always hear
Time's wingèd chariot hurrying near;
And yonder all before us lie
Deserts of vast eternity.
Thy beauty shall no more be found,
Nor, in thy marble vault, shall sound
My echoing song; then worms shall try
That long preserved virginity,
And your quaint honor turn to dust,
And into ashes all my lust: 30
The grave's a fine and private place,
But none, I think, do there embrace.
    Now therefore, while the youthful hue
Sits on thy skin like morning dew,
And while thy willing soul transpires
At every pore with instant fires,
Now let us sport us while we may,
And now, like amorous birds of prey,
Rather at once our time devour
Than languish in his slow-chapped power.   40
Let us roll all our strength and all
Our sweetness up into one ball,
And tear our pleasures with rough strife
Thorough the iron gates of life:
Thus, though we cannot make our sun
Stand still, yet we will make him run.

The Garden

How vainly men themselves amaze,
To win the palm, the oak, or bays,
And their incessant labors see
Crowned from some single herb or tree,
Whose short and narrow-verged shade
Does prudently their toils upbraid,
While all the flowers and trees do close
To weave the garlands of repose!

Fair Quiet, have I found thee here,
And Innocence, thy sister dear?   10

Mistaken long, I sought you then
In busy companies of men.
Your sacred plants, if here below,
Only among the plants will grow;
Society is all but rude
To this delicious solitude.

No white nor red was ever seen
So amorous as this lovely green.
Fond lovers, cruel as their flame,
Cut in these trees their mistress' name.   20
Little, alas! they know or heed
How far these beauties hers exceed!
Fair trees! wheres'e'r your barks I wound,
No name shall but your own be found.

When we have run our passion's heat,
Love hither makes his best retreat.
The gods, that mortal beauty chase,
Still in a tree did end their race;
Apollo hunted Daphne so,
Only that she might laurel grow;   30
And Pan did after Syrinx speed,
Not as a nymph, but for a reed.

What wondrous life is this I lead!
Ripe apples drop about my head;
The luscious clusters of the vine
Upon my mouth do crush their wine;
The nectarine and curious peach
Into my hands themselves do reach;
Stumbling on melons, as I pass,
Ensnared with flowers, I fall on grass.   40

Meanwhile the mind, from pleasure less,
Withdraws into its happiness;
The mind, that ocean where each kind
Does straight its own resemblance find;
Yet it creates, transcending these,
Far other worlds, and other seas,
Annihilating all that's made
To a green thought in a green shade.

Here at the fountain's sliding foot,
Or at some fruit-tree's mossy root,   50
Casting the body's vest aside,
My soul into the boughs does glide;
There, like a bird, it sits and sings,
Then whets and combs its silver wings,
And, till prepared for longer flight,
Waves in its plumes the various light.

Such was that happy garden-state,
While man there walked without a mate;
After a place so pure and sweet,
What other help could yet be meet!   60

But 'twas beyond a mortal's share
To wander solitary there:
Two paradises 'twere in one,
To live in paradise alone.

How well the skilful gardener drew
Of flowers and herbs this dial new!
Where, from above, the milder sun
Does through a fragrant zodiac run,
And, as it works, the industrious bee
Computes its time as well as we!   70
How could such sweet and wholesome hours
Be reckoned, but with herbs and flowers?

RICHARD CRASHAW

1612?–1649

Crashaw was educated at the Charterhouse and at Pembroke Hall, Cambridge. Though he came of an ardent Protestant family—his father was an Anglican clergyman celebrated for his vigorous attacks on Catholicism—he was converted to the Roman Church about the time of the Civil War. He therefore left England and resided for a time in Paris, where he met Queen Henrietta Maria who introduced him to Cardinal Pallotto. The Cardinal, who was governor of Rome, took Crashaw into his retinue as his private secretary, and in 1649 procured for him a benefice in the Church of Our Lady of Loretto. He died a short time later.

His collection of devotional lyrics, *Steps to the Temple* appeared in 1646, and his *Carmen Deo Nostro* in 1652. A follower of the metaphysical school of Donne and Herbert, he is the greatest English mystical poet before Blake. The burning intensity of his devotion to the Virgin and to St. Teresa is the dominant emotion of his poetry. His imagery, often drawing upon almost rash conceits, is mostly original and always of the most powerful intensity.

FURTHER READING

MARTIN, L. C., ed. *The Poems of Richard Crashaw* (Oxford, 1927).
WARREN, A. *Richard Crashaw: A Study in Baroque Sensibility* (University of Louisiana, 1939).

A Hymn to the Name and Honor of the Admirable Saint Teresa

Foundress of the Reformation of the Discalced Carmelites, both men and women. A woman for angelical height of speculation, for masculine courage of performance, more than a woman; who yet a child outran maturity, and durst plot a martyrdom.

Love, thou art absolute sole lord
Of life and death. To prove the word,
We'll now appeal to none of all
Those thy old soldiers, great and tall,
Ripe men of martyrdom, that could reach down
With strong arms their triumphant crown;
Such as could with lusty breath
Speak loud into the face of death
Their great Lord's glorious name; to none
Of those whose spacious bosoms spread a throne   10
For Love at large to fill. Spare blood and sweat,
And see Him take a private seat,
Making His mansion in the mild
And milky soul of a soft child.
  Scarce has she learnt to lisp the name
Of martyr, yet she thinks it shame
Life should so long play with that breath
Which spent can buy so brave a death.
She never undertook to know
What death with Love should have to do;   20
Nor has she e'er yet understood
Why to show love she should shed blood;
Yet though she cannot tell you why,
She can love and she can die.
Scarce has she blood enough to make
A guilty sword blush for her sake;
Yet has she a heart dares hope to prove
How much less strong is death than Love.
  Be Love but there, let poor six years
Be posed with the maturest fears   30
Man trembles at, you straight shall find
Love knows no nonage, nor the mind.
'Tis Love, not years or limbs, that can
Make the martyr or the man.
  Love touched her heart, and lo it beats
High, and burns with such brave heats,
Such thirsts to die, as dares drink up
A thousand cold deaths in one cup.
Good reason, for she breathes all fire,
Her weak breast heaves with strong desire   40
Of what she may with fruitless wishes
Seek for amongst her mother's kisses.
  Since 'tis not to be had at home,
She'll travel to a martyrdom.
No home for hers confesses she
But where she may a martyr be.
  She'll to the Moors, and trade with them
For this unvalued diadem.
She'll offer them her dearest breath,
With Christ's name in 't, in change for death.   50
She'll bargain with them, and will give
Them God, teach them how to live
In Him; or, if they this deny,
For Him she'll teach them how to die.
So shall she leave amongst them sown
Her Lord's blood, or at least her own.
  Farewell then, all the world, adieu!
Teresa is no more for you.
Farewell, all pleasures, sports, and joys,
Never till now esteemèd toys;   60
Farewell, whatever dear may be,
Mother's arms, or father's knee;
Farewell house and farewell home,
She's for the Moors and martyrdom!
  Sweet, not so fast! lo, thy fair Spouse
Whom thou seek'st with so swift vows
Calls thee back, and bids thee come
T' embrace a milder martyrdom.
  Blest powers forbid thy tender life
Should bleed upon a barbarous knife;   70
Or some base hand have power to rase
Thy breast's chaste cabinet, and uncase
A soul kept there so sweet; oh no,
Wise Heav'n will never have it so:
Thou art Love's victim, and must die
A death more mystical and high;
Into Love's arms thou shalt let fall
A still surviving funeral.
His is the dart must make the death
Whose stroke shall taste thy hallowed breath;   80
A dart thrice dipped in that rich flame
Which writes thy Spouse's radiant name
Upon the roof of Heav'n, where aye
It shines, and with a sovereign ray
Beats bright upon the burning faces
Of souls which in that name's sweet graces
Find everlasting smiles. So rare,
So spiritual, pure, and fair
Must be th' immortal instrument
Upon whose choice point shall be sent   90
A life so loved; and that there be
Fit executioners for thee,
The fair'st and first-born sons of fire,
Blest seraphim, shall leave their choir
And turn Love's soldiers, upon thee
To exercise their archery.

Oh, how oft shalt thou complain
Of a sweet and subtle pain,
Of intolerable joys,
Of a death in which who dies   100
Loves his death, and dies again,
And would for ever so be slain,
And lives and dies, and knows not why
To live, but that he thus may never leave to die!
   How kindly will thy gentle heart
Kiss the sweetly killing dart!
And close in his embraces keep
Those delicious wounds, that weep
Balsam to heal themselves with. Thus
When these thy deaths, so numerous,   110
Shall all at last die into one,
And melt thy soul's sweet mansion;
Like a soft lump of incense, hasted
By too hot a fire, and wasted
Into perfuming clouds, so fast
Shalt thou exhale to Heav'n at last
In a resolving sigh; and then,
Oh, what? Ask not the tongues of men;
Angels cannot tell; suffice,
Thyself shall feel thine own full joys   120
And hold them fast for ever. There
So soon as thou shalt first appear,
The moon of maiden stars, thy white
Mistress, attended by such bright
Souls as thy shining self, shall come
And in her first ranks make thee room;
Where 'mongst her snowy family
Immortal welcomes wait for thee.
   Oh, what delight when revealed life shall stand
And teach thy lips heav'n with his hand,   130
On which thou now mayst to thy wishes
Heap up thy consecrated kisses.
What joys shall seize thy soul when she,
Bending her blessed eyes on thee,
Those second smiles of heaven, shall dart
Her mild rays through thy melting heart!
   Angels, thy old friends, there shall greet thee,
Glad at their own home now to meet thee.
   All thy good works which went before
And waited for thee at the door   140
Shall own thee there, and all in one
Weave a constellation
Of crowns, with which the King, thy Spouse,
Shall build up thy triumphant brows.
   All thy old woes shall now smile on thee,
And thy pains sit bright upon thee;
All thy sorrows here shall shine,
All thy sufferings be divine;
Tears shall take comfort and turn gems,

And wrongs repent to diadems.   150
Even thy deaths shall live, and new
Dress the soul that erst they slew;
Thy wounds shall blush to such bright scars
As keep account of the Lamb's wars.
   Those rare works where thou shalt leave writ
Love's noble history, with wit
Taught thee by none but Him, while here
They feed our souls, shall clothe thine there.
Each heav'nly word by whose hid flame
Our hard hearts shall strike fire, the same   160
Shall flourish on thy brows, and be
Both fire to us and flame to thee,
Whose light shall live bright in thy face
By glory, in our hearts by grace.
   Thou shalt look round about and see
Thousands of crowned souls throng to be
Themselves thy crown; sons of thy vows,
The virgin-births with which thy sovereign Spouse
Made fruitful thy fair soul, go now
And with them all about thee, bow   170
To Him. "Put on," He'll say, "put on,
My rosy love, that thy rich zone
Sparkling with the sacred flames
Of thousand souls whose happy names
Heav'n keeps upon thy score. Thy bright
Life brought them first to kiss the light
That kindled them to stars." And so
Thou with the Lamb, thy Lord, shalt go,
And whereso'er He sets His white
Steps, walk with Him those ways of light   180
Which who in death would live to see
Must learn in life to die like thee.

Charitas Nimia; or, the Dear Bargain

Lord, what is man? why should he cost Thee
So dear? what had his ruin lost Thee?
Lord, what is man, that Thou hast over-bought
So much a thing of naught?

Love is too kind, I see, and can
Make but a simple merchant-man.
'Twas for such sorry merchandise
Bold painters have put out his eyes.

Alas, sweet Lord! what were't to Thee
If there were no such worms as we?   10
Heav'n ne'er the less still Heav'n would be,
    Should mankind dwell
     In the deep hell.
What have his woes to do with Thee?

Let him go weep
O'er his own wounds;
Seraphims will not sleep,
Nor spheres let fall their faithful rounds.

Still would the youthful spirits sing,
And still Thy spacious palace ring;   20
Still would those beauteous ministers of light
Burn all as bright,
And bow their flaming heads before Thee;
Still thrones and dominations would adore Thee.
Still would those ever-wakeful sons of fire
Keep warm Thy praise
Both nights and days,
And teach Thy loved name to their noble lyre.

Let froward dust then do its kind,
And give itself for sport to the proud wind.   30
Why should a piece of peevish clay plead shares
In the eternity of Thy old cares?
Why shouldst Thou bow Thy awful breast to see
What mine own madnesses have done with me?

Should not the king still keep his throne
Because some desperate fool's undone?
Or will the world's illustrious eyes
Weep for every worm that dies?

Will the gallant sun
E'er the less glorious run?
Will he hang down his golden head,   40
Or e'er the sooner seek his western bed,
Because some foolish fly
Grows wanton, and will die?

If I were lost in misery,
What was it to Thy heaven and Thee?
What was it to Thy precious blood
If my foul heart called for a flood?

What if my faithless soul and I
Would needs fall in   50
With guilt and sin;
What did the Lamb that He should die?
What did the Lamb that He should need,
When the wolf sins, Himself to bleed?

If my base lust
Bargained with death and well-beseeming dust,
Why should the white
Lamb's bosom write
The purple name
Of my sin's shame?   60
Why should His unstained breast make good
My blushes with His own heart-blood?

O my Saviour, make me see
How dearly Thou hast paid for me;
That, lost again, my life may prove,
As then in death, so now in love.

———◆———

THOMAS CAREW

1598?–1639?

Thomas Carew was one of the most brilliant of
Cavalier poets, ranking perhaps next to Herrick.
Like Herrick, he also was one of the "sons of Ben,"
a follower of Jonsonian poetic traditions. Educated
at Oxford, he traveled widely on the Continent,
and was for a time secretary to Sir Dudley Carleton
at Venice and later at The Hague. He became a
favorite of King Charles I and of Queen Henrietta
Maria; and while Oxford served as the King's pro-
visional capital, he lived in the royal household.

He was indubitably one of the brightest ornaments of a court generally regarded as brilliant. His
genius lay in the love lyric, but not in the abandoned, cynical lyric of the kind that his friend
Suckling wrote. Lawes set many of his poems to
music, and the troubled monarch probably found
gentle solace in hearing them sung. Though a
minor poet, he is the author of several lyrics that
will last with the language. For his incomparable
"Ask Me No More Where Jove Bestows" there is
only one word, and that word is perfection.

FURTHER READING

VINCENT, A., ed. *The Poems of Thomas Carew* (London, 1905).

Disdain Returned

He that loves a rosy cheek,
   Or a coral lip admires,
Or from starlike eyes doth seek
   Fuel to maintain his fires,
As old Time makes these decay,
So his flames must waste away.

But a smooth and steadfast mind,
   Gentle thoughts and calm desires,
Hearts with equal love combined,
   Kindle never-dying fires.

Where these are not, I despise
Lovely cheeks or lips or eyes.

No tears, Celia, now shall win
　My resolved heart to return;
I have searched thy soul within,
　And find naught but pride and scorn;
I have learned thy arts, and now
　Can disdain as much as thou.
Some power, in my revenge, convey
　That love to her I cast away.

Song

Ask me no more where Jove bestows,
When June is past, the fading rose;
For in your beauty's orient deep
These flowers, as in their causes, sleep.

Ask me no more whither do stray
The golden atoms of the day;
For, in pure love, heaven did prepare
Those powders to enrich your hair.

Ask me no more whither doth haste
The nightingale when May is past;
For in your sweet dividing throat
She winters and keeps warm her note.

Ask me no more where those stars light
That downwards fall in dead of night;
For in your eyes they sit, and there
Fixed become as in their sphere.

Ask me no more if east or west
The Phoenix builds her spicy nest;
For unto you at last she flies,
And in your fragrant bosom dies.

BLAISE PASCAL

1623–1662

One of the world's great writers and thinkers, Pascal was a distinguished physicist, mathematician, and philosopher who at the age of sixteen composed an erudite treatise on conics and at nineteen invented a mechanical calculator. His *Lettres Provinciales* (1656), justly celebrated during the seventeenth century, was written in defense of the Jansenists, a sect which held the unorthodox view that man is by nature depraved and can achieve salvation only through divine grace. In spite of the fact that this work is a monument of clarity, logic, and brilliant style, interest in it has diminished because it was concerned so directly with purely contemporary matters. Of much greater regard today are his *Thoughts,* a series of random notes intended as prolegomena for a vast treatise in defense of Christianity which he did not live to compose. The *Thoughts* touch on many philosophical problems which have always and always will beset humanity. Pascal, who calls himself a Pyrrhonist, believed that human reason, while highly effective in its own sphere, is still totally incapable of solving man's spiritual problems, and that the only recourse possible in these matters is a complete, mystical faith in Christian revelation.

FURTHER READING

CAILLIET, E. *The Clue to Pascal* (Philadelphia, 1943).
STEWART, H. F. *The Heart of Pascal* (Cambridge, Eng., 1945).
STEWART, H. F. *The Living Thoughts of Pascal Presented by François Mauriac* (New York, 1940).

Pensées *

IF WE must not act save on a certainty, we ought not to act on religion, for it is not certain. But how many things we do on an uncertainty, sea voyages, battles! I say then we must do nothing at all, for nothing is certain, and that there is more certainty in religion than there is as to whether we may see to-morrow; for it is not certain that we may see to-morrow, and it is certainly possible that we may not see it. We cannot say as much about religion. It is not certain that it is; but who will venture to say that it is certainly possible that it is not? Now when we work for to-morrow, and so on an uncertainty, we act reasonably; for we ought to work for

* Translated by William F. Trotter. From *Pensées* by Blaise Pascal, Everyman's Library edition. By permission of E. P. Dutton & Co., Inc., and J. M. Dent & Sons, Ltd.

an uncertainty according to the doctrine of chance which was demonstrated above.

Saint Augustine has seen that we work for an uncertainty, on sea, in battle, etc. But he has not seen the doctrine of chance which proves that we should do so. Montaigne has seen that we are shocked at a fool, and that habit is all-powerful; but he has not seen the reason of this effect.

All these persons have seen the effects, but they have not seen the causes. They are, in comparison with those who have discovered the causes, as those who have only eyes are in comparison with those who have intellect. For the effects are perceptible by sense, and the causes are visible only to the intellect. And although these effects are seen by the mind, this mind is, in comparison with the mind which sees the causes, as the bodily senses are in comparison with the intellect.

. . .

The heart has its reasons, which reason does not know. We feel it in a thousand things. I say that the heart naturally loves the Universal Being, and also itself naturally, according as it gives itself to them; and it hardens itself against one or the other at its will. You have rejected the one, and kept the other. Is it by reason that you love yourself?

It is the heart which experiences God, and not the reason. This, then, is faith: God felt by the heart, not by the reason.

Faith is a gift of God; do not believe that we said it was a gift of reasoning. Other religions do not say this of their faith. They only gave reasoning in order to arrive at it, and yet it does not bring them to it.

The knowledge of God is very far from the love of Him.

We know truth, not only by the reason, but also by the heart, and it is in this last way that we know first principles; and reason, which has no part in it, tries in vain to impugn them. The sceptics, who have only this for their object, labor to no purpose. We know that we do not dream, and however impossible it is for us to prove it by reason, this inability demonstrates only the weakness of our reason, but not, as they affirm, the uncertainty of all our knowledge. For the knowledge of first principles, as space, time, motion, number, is as sure as any of those which we get from reasoning. And reason must trust these intuitions of the heart, and must base them on every argument. (We have intuitive knowledge of the tri-dimensional nature of space, and of the infinity of number, and reason

then shows that there are no two square numbers one of which is double of the other. Principles are intuited, propositions are inferred, all with certainty, though in different ways.) And it is as useless and absurd for reason to demand from the heart proofs of her first principles, before admitting them, as it would be for the heart to demand from reason an intuition of all demonstrated propositions before accepting them.

This inability ought, then, to serve only to humble reason, which would judge all, but not to impugn our certainty, as if only reason were capable of instructing us. Would to God, on the contrary, that we had never need of it, and that we knew everything by instinct and intuition! But nature has refused us this boon. On the contrary, she has given us but very little knowledge of this kind; and all the rest can be acquired only by reasoning.

Therefore, those to whom God has imparted religion by intuition are very fortunate, and justly convinced. But to those who do not have it, we can give it only by reasoning, waiting for God to give them spiritual insight, without which faith is only human, and useless for salvation.

. . .

"Why do you kill me? What! do you not live on the other side of the water? If you lived on this side, my friend, I should be an assassin, and it would be unjust to slay you in this manner. But since you live on the other side, I am a hero, and it was just."

. . .

It is right that what is just should be obeyed; it is necessary that what is strongest should be obeyed. Justice without might is helpless; might without justice is tyrannical. Justice without might is gainsaid, because there are always offenders; might without justice is condemned. We must then combine justice and might, and for this end make what is just strong, or what is strong just.

Justice is subject to dispute; might is easily recognized and is not disputed. So we cannot give might to justice, because might has gainsaid justice, and has declared that it is she herself who is just. And thus being unable to make what is just strong, we have made what is strong just.

. . .

I can well conceive a man without hands, feet, head (for it is only experience which teaches us that the head is more necessary than feet). But I cannot conceive man without thought; he would be a stone or a brute.

The arithmetical machine produces effects which approach nearer to thought than all the actions of animals. But it does nothing which would enable us to attribute will to it, as to the animals.

Reason commands us far more imperiously than a master; for in disobeying the one we are unfortunate, and in disobeying the other we are fools.

Thought constitutes the greatness of man.

Man is but a reed, the most feeble thing in nature; but he is a thinking reed. The entire universe need not arm itself to crush him. A vapor, a drop of water suffices to kill him. But, if the universe were to crush him, man would still be more noble than that which killed him, because he knows that he dies and the advantage which the universe has over him; the universe knows nothing of this.

All our dignity consists, then, in thought. By it we must elevate ourselves, and not by space and time which we cannot fill. Let us endeavor, then, to think well; this is the principle of morality.

.   .   .

What astonishes me most is to see that all the world is not astonished at its own weakness. Men act seriously, and each follows his own mode of life, not because it is in fact good to follow since it is the custom, but as if each man knew certainly where reason and justice are. They find themselves continually deceived, and by a comical humility think it is their own fault, and not that of the art which they claim always to possess. But it is well there are so many such people in the world, who are not sceptics for the glory of scepticism, in order to show that man is quite capable of the most extravagant opinions, since he is capable of believing that he is not in a state of natural and inevitable weakness, but, on the contrary, of natural wisdom.

Nothing fortifies scepticism more than that there are some who are not sceptics; if all were so, they would be wrong.

.   .   .

When we are too young, we do not judge well; so, also, when we are too old. If we do not think enough, or if we think too much on any matter, we get obstinate and infatuated about it. If one considers one's work immediately after having done it, one is entirely prepossessed in its favor; by delaying too long, one can no longer enter into the spirit of it. So with pictures seen from too far or too near; there is but one exact point which is the

true place wherefrom to look at them: the rest are too near, too far, too high, or too low. Perspective determines that point in the art of painting. But who shall determine it in truth and morality?

.   .   .

We know the existence and nature of the finite, because we also are finite and have extension. We know the existence of the infinite, and are ignorant of its nature, because it has extension like us, but not limits like us. But we know neither the existence nor the nature of God, because He has neither extension nor limits.

But by faith we know His existence; in glory we shall know His nature. Now, I have already shown that we may well know the existence of a thing without knowing its nature.

Let us now speak according to natural lights.

If there is a God, He is infinitely incomprehensible, since, having neither parts nor limits, He has no affinity to us. We are then incapable of knowing either what He is or if He is. This being so, who will dare to undertake the decision of the question? Not we, who have no affinity to Him.

Who then will blame Christians for not being able to give a reason for their belief, since they profess a religion for which they cannot give a reason? They declare, in expounding it to the world, that it is a foolishness, *stultitiam*; and then you complain that they do not prove it! If they proved it, they would not keep their word; it is in lacking proofs, that they are not lacking in sense. "Yes, but although this excuses those who offer it as such, and takes away from them the blame of putting it forward without reason, it does not excuse those who receive it." Let us then examine this point, and say: "God is, or He is not." But to which side shall we incline? Reason can decide nothing here. There is an infinite chaos which separates us. A game is being played at the extremity of this infinite distance where heads or tails will turn up. What will you wager? According to reason, you can do neither the one thing nor the other; according to reason, you can defend neither of the propositions.

Do not then reprove for error those who have made a choice; for you know nothing about it. "No, but I blame them for having made, not this choice, but a choice; for again both he who chooses heads and he who chooses tails are equally at fault, they are both in the wrong. The true course is not to wager at all."

Yes; but you must wager. It is not optional. You

are embarked. Which will you choose then? Let us see. Since you must choose, let us see which interests you least. You have two things to lose, the true and the good; and the two things to stake, your reason and your will, your knowledge and your happiness; and your nature has two things to shun, error and misery. Your reason is no more shocked in choosing one rather than the other, since you must of necessity choose. This is one point settled. But your happiness? Let us weigh the gain and the loss in wagering that God is. Let us estimate these two chances. If you gain, you gain all; if you lose, you lose nothing. Wager, then, without hesitation that He is. "That is very fine. Yes, I must wager; but I may perhaps wager too much." Let us see. Since there is an equal risk of gain and of loss, if you had only to gain two lives, instead of one, you might still wager. But if there were three lives to gain, you would have to play (since you are under the necessity of playing), and you would be imprudent, when you are forced to play, not to chance your life to gain three at a game where there is an equal risk of loss and gain. But there is an eternity of life and happiness. And this being so, if there were an infinity of chances, of which one only would be for you, you would still be right in wagering one to win two, and you would act stupidly, being obliged to play, by refusing to stake one life against three at a game in which out of an infinity of chances there is one for you, if there were an infinity of an infinitely happy life to gain. But there is here an infinity of an infinitely happy life to gain, a chance of gain against a finite number of chances of loss, and what you stake is finite. It is all divided; wherever the infinite is and there is not an infinity of chances of loss against that of gain, there is no time to hesitate, you must give all. And thus, when one is forced to play, he must renounce reason to preserve his life, rather than risk it for infinite gain, as likely to happen as the loss of nothingness.

For it is no use to say it is uncertain if we will gain, and it is certain that we risk, and that the infinite distance between the *certainty* of what is staked and the *uncertainty* of what will be gained, equals the finite good which is certainly staked against the uncertain infinite. It is not so, as every player stakes a certainty to gain an uncertainty, and yet he stakes a finite certainty to gain a finite uncertainty, without transgressing against reason. There is not an infinite distance between the certainty staked and the uncertainty of the gain; that is untrue. In truth, there is an infinity between the certainty of gain and the certainty of loss. But the uncertainty of the gain is proportioned to the certainty of the stake according to the proportion of the chances of gain and loss. Hence it comes that, if there are as many risks on one side as on the other, the course is to play even; and then the certainty of the stake is equal to the uncertainty of the gain, so far is it from fact that there is an infinite distance between them. And so our proposition is of infinite force, when there is the finite to stake in a game where there are equal risks of gain and of loss, and the infinite to gain. This is demonstrable; and if men are capable of any truths, this is one.

"I confess it, I admit it. But, still, is there no means of seeing the faces of the cards?" Yes, Scripture and the rest, etc. "Yes, but I have my hands tied and my mouth closed; I am forced to wager, and am not free. I am not released, and am so made that I cannot believe. What, then, would you have me do?"

True. But at least learn your inability to believe, since reason brings you to this, and yet you cannot believe. Endeavour then to convince yourself, not by increase of proofs of God, but by the abatement of your passions. You would like to attain faith, and do not know the way; you would like to cure yourself of unbelief, and ask the remedy for it. Learn of those who have been bound like you, and who now stake all their possessions. These are people who know the way which you would follow, and who are cured of an ill of which you would be cured. Follow the way by which they began; by acting as if they believed, taking the holy water, having masses said, etc. Even this will naturally make you believe, and deaden your acuteness. "But this is what I am afraid of." And why? What have you to lose?

But to show you that this leads you there, it is this which will lessen the passions, which are your stumbling-blocks.

The end of this discourse.—Now, what harm will befall you in taking this side? You will be faithful, honest, humble, grateful, generous, a sincere friend, truthful. Certainly you will not have those poisonous pleasures, glory and luxury; but will you not have others? I will tell you that you will thereby gain in this life, and that, at each step you take on this road, you will see so great certainty of gain, so much nothingness in what you risk, that you will at last recognise that you have wagered for something certain and infinite, for which you have given nothing.

"Ah! This discourse transports me, charms me," etc.

If this discourse pleases you and seems impressive, know that it is made by a man who has knelt, both before and after it, in prayer to that Being, infinite and without parts, before whom he lays all he has, for you also to lay before Him all you have for your own good and for His glory, that so strength may be given to lowliness.

———◆———

JEAN RACINE

1639–1699

The figure who most adequately epitomizes the spirit of French Neo-classicism is the tragedian Racine. He has unfortunately always been somewhat unattractive to the majority of English and American audiences, though to the French he has been the object of almost universal admiration, even veneration, for he represents to perfection many of the habits of thought and taste characteristic of the French temperament. The plays of Racine contain an action taken at its crisis and treated under the dictates of the rule of the unities of time, place, action, and tone. The scene is nearly always one locality, usually one room, and the duration of the action is not normally longer than that of the play itself. Never is a subsidiary action introduced, for then the unity of action would be violated. Racine's plays are highly concentrated: every word, every phrase serves a definite purpose. There is not a word too much and no word can be omitted. There are no irrelevancies, nothing unusual, nothing unexpected, nothing odd, nothing extra.

Racine was not only a very great dramatic poet. He was also a great psychologist, infusing into his work all the varied subtleties of character and passion which produce an impression of vigorous life. He particularly excels in painting the profundities, agonies, and triumphs of passionate love.

In *Phaedra* (1677) his genius appears at its best. *Phaedra* contains one of the most overwhelming studies of passion in all the literature of the world. The leading role increases in intensity as the play progresses, and horror is poured upon horror. Into this play Racine placed the entire wealth of his poetic and dramatic powers, making of it one of the greatest tragedies ever written.

(In French classical drama a new scene begins with the entrance of a new character. Exit signs are not given.)

FURTHER READING

BAILLY, A. *Racine* (Paris, 1949, in French).
CLARK, A. F. B. *Jean Racine* (Cambridge, Eng., 1939).
TILLEY, A. *Three French Dramatists: Racine, Marivaux, Musset* (Cambridge, Eng., 1933).
TURNELL, MARTIN. *The Classical Moment; Studies of Corneille, Molière, and Racine* (New York, 1946).

Phaedra *
(PHÈDRE)

CHARACTERS OF THE DRAMA

THESEUS, *son of Aegeus and King of Athens*
PHAEDRA, *wife of Theseus and daughter of Minos and Pasiphae*
HIPPOLYTUS, *son of Theseus and the Queen of the Amazons*
ARICIA, *captive princess of the blood royal of Athens*
OENONE, *nurse of Phaedra*
THERAMENES, *tutor of Hippolytus*
ISMENE, *bosom friend of Aricia*
PANOPE, *waiting-woman of Phaedra*
GUARDS

SCENE—Troezen, a town of the Peloponnesus.
TIME—Before 1200 B.C.

ACT I

SCENE 1. HIPPOLYTUS, THERAMENES

HIPPOLYTUS. My mind is settled, dear Theramenes,
And I can stay no more in lovely Troezen.
In doubt that racks my soul with mortal anguish,
I grow ashamed of such long idleness.
Six months and more my father has been gone,
And what may have befallen one so dear
I know not, nor what corner of the earth
Hides him.
    THERAMENES. And where, prince, will you look for him?

* Translation by R. B. Boswell (1890).

Already, to content your just alarm,
Have I not crossed the seas on either side   10
Of Corinth, asked if aught were known of Theseus
Where Acheron is lost among the Shades,
Visited Elis, doubled Tenarus,
And sail'd into the sea that saw the fall
Of Icarus? Inspir'd with what new hope,
Under what favor'd skies think you to trace
His footsteps? Who knows if the King, your father,
Wishes the secret of his absence known?
Perchance, while we are trembling for his life,
The hero calmly plots some fresh intrigue,   20
And only waits till the deluded fair—
HIP. Cease, dear Theramenes, respect the name
Of Theseus. Youthful errors have been left
Behind, and no unworthy obstacle
Detains him. Phaedra long has fix'd a heart
Inconstant once, nor need she fear a rival.
In seeking him I shall but do my duty,
And leave a place I dare no longer see.
THER. Indeed! When, prince, did you begin to
        dread
These peaceful haunts, so dear to happy child-
        hood,   30
Where I have seen you oft prefer to stay,
Rather than meet the tumult and the pomp
Of Athens and the court? What danger shun you,
Or shall I say what grief?
HIP.   That happy time
Is gone, and all is chang'd, since these shores
The gods sent Phaedra.
THER.   I perceive the cause
Of your distress. It is the queen whose sight
Offends you. With a step-dame's spite she schem'd
Your exile soon as she set eyes on you.
But if her hatred is not wholly vanish'd,   40
It has at least taken a milder aspect.
Besides, what danger can a dying woman,
One too who longs for death, bring on your head?
Can Phaedra, sick'ning of a dire disease
Of which she will not speak, weary of life
And of herself, form any plots against you?
HIP. It is not her vain enmity I fear:
Another foe alarms Hippolytus.
I fly, it must be own'd, from young Aricia,
The sole survivor of an impious race.[1]   50
THER. What! You become her persecutor too!
The gentle sister of the cruel sons
Of Pallas shared not in their perfidy;
Why should you hate such charming innocence?
HIP. I should not need to fly, if it were hatred.

[1] Aricia's brothers, the Pallantids, sons of Theseus' uncle, Pallas, had conspired to get the throne of Athens.

THER. May I then learn the meaning of your
        flight?
Is this the proud Hippolytus I see,
Than whom there breathed no fiercer foe to love
And to that yoke which Theseus has so oft
Endured? And can it be that Venus, scorn'd   60
So long, will justify your sire at last?
Has she, then, setting you with other mortals,
Forced e'en Hippolytus to offer incense
Before her? Can you love?
HIP.   Friend, ask me not.
You, who have known my heart from infancy
And all its feelings of disdainful pride,
Spare me the shame of disavowing all
That I profess'd. Born of an Amazon,
The wildness that you wonder at, I suck'd
With mother's milk. When come to riper age   70
Reason approved what Nature had implanted.
Sincerely bound to me by zealous service,
You told me then the story of my sire,
And know how oft, attentive to your voice,
I kindled when I heard his noble acts,
As you describ'd him bringing consolation
To mortals for the absence of Alcides,
The highways clear'd of monsters and of robbers,
Procrustes, Cercyon, Sciro, Sinnis slain,
The Epidaurian giant's bones dispersed,   80
Crete reeking with the blood of Minotaur.
But when you told me of less glorious deeds,
Troth plighted here and there and everywhere,
Young Helen stolen from her home at Sparta,
And Periboea's tears in Salamis,
With many another trusting heart deceived,
Whose very names have 'scaped his memory,
Forsaken Ariadne to the rocks
Complaining, last this Phaedra, bound to him
By better ties,—you know with what regret   90
I heard and urged you to cut short the tale,
Happy had I been able to erase
From my remembrance that unworthy part
Of such a splendid record. I, in turn,
Am I too made the slave of love, and brought
To stoop so low? The more contemptible
That no renown is mine such as exalts
The name of Theseus, that no monsters quell'd
Have given me a right to share his weakness.
And if my pride of heart must needs be hum-
        bled,   100
Aricia should have been the last to tame it.
Was I beside myself to have forgotten
Eternal barriers of separation
Between us? By my father's stern command
Her brethren's blood must ne'er be reinforced

By sons of hers; he dreads a single shoot
From stock so guilty, and would fain with her
Bury their name, that, even to the tomb
Content to be his ward, for her no torch
Of Hymen may be lit. Shall I espouse   110
Her rights against my sire, rashly provoke
His wrath, and launch upon a mad career—

    THER. The gods, dear prince, if once your hour is
      come,
Care little for the reasons that should guide us.
Wishing to shut your eyes, Theseus unseals them;
His hatred, stirring a rebellious flame
Within you, lends his enemy new charms.
And, after all, why should a guiltless passion
Alarm you? Dare you not essay its sweetness,
But follow rather a fastidious scruple?   120
Fear you to stray where Hercules has wander'd?
What heart so stout that Venus has not vanquish'd?
Where would you be yourself, so long her foe,
Had your own mother, constant in her scorn
Of love, ne'er glow'd with tenderness for Theseus?
What boots it to affect a pride you feel not?
Confess it, all is changed; for some time past
You have been seldom seen with wild delight
Urging the rapid car along the strand,
Or, skilful in the art that Neptune taught,   130
Making th' unbroken steed obey the bit;
Less often have the woods return'd our shouts;
A secret burden on your spirits cast
Has dimm'd your eye. How can I doubt you love?
Vainly would you conceal the fatal wound.
Has not the fair Aricia touched your heart?

    HIP. Theramenes, I go to find my father.

    THER. Will you not see the queen before you
      start,
My prince?

    HIP.   That is my purpose; you can tell her.
Yes, I will see her; duty bids me do it.   140
But what new ill vexes her dear Oenone?

SCENE 2. HIPPOLYTUS, OENONE, THERAMENES

    OENONE. Alas, my lord, what grief was e'er like
      mine?
The queen has almost touched the gates of death.
Vainly close watch I keep by day and night;
E'en in my arms a secret malady
Slays her, and all her senses are disorder'd.
Weary yet restless from her couch she rises,
Pants for the outer air, but bids me see
That no one on her misery intrudes.
She comes.

    HIP. Enough. She shall not be disturb'd,
Nor be confronted with a face she hates.   10

SCENE 3. PHAEDRA, OENONE

    PHAEDRA. We have gone far enough. Stay, dear
      Oenone;
Strength fails me, and I needs must rest awhile.
My eyes are dazzled with this glaring light
So long unseen; my trembling knees refuse
Support. Ah, me!

    OEN.   Would Heaven that our tears
Might bring relief!

    PHA.   Ah, how these cumbrous gauds,
These veils, oppress me! What officious hand
Has tied these knots, and gather'd o'er my brow
These clustering coils? How all conspires to add
To my distress!

    OEN.   What is one moment wish'd,   10
The next, is irksome. Did you not just now,
Sick of inaction, bid us deck you out,
And, with your former energy recall'd,
Desire to go abroad, and see the light
Of day once more? You see it, and would fain
Be hidden from the sunshine that you sought.

    PHA. Thou glorious author of a hapless race,
Whose daughter 'twas my mother's boast to be,
Who well may'st blush to see me in such plight,
For the last time I come to look on thee,   20
O Sun!

    OEN. What! Still are you in love with death?
Shall I ne'er see you, reconciled to life,
Forgo these cruel accents of despair?

    PHA. Would I were seated in the forest's shade!
When may I follow with delighted eye,
Thro' glorious dust flying in full career,
A chariot—

    OEN.   Madam?

    PHA.   Have I lost my senses?
What said I, and where am I? Whither stray
Vain wishes? Ah! The gods have made me mad.
I blush, Oenone, and confusion covers   30
My face, for I have let you see too clearly
The shame and grief that, in my own despite,
O'erflow these eyes of mine.

    OEN.   If you must blush,
Blush at a silence that inflames your woes.
Resisting all my care, deaf to my voice,
Will you have no compassion on yourself,
But let your life be ended in mid course?
What evil spell has drain'd its fountain dry?
Thrice have the shades of night obscured the
    heav'ns
Since sleep has enter'd thro' your eyes, and thrice   40
The dawn has chased the darkness thence, since
    food

Pass'd your wan lips, and you are faint and languid.
To what dread purpose is your heart inclined?
How dare you make attempts upon your life,
And so offend the gods who gave it you,
Prove false to Theseus and your marriage vows,
Ay, and betray your most unhappy children,
Bending their necks yourself beneath the yoke?
That day, be sure, which robs them of their mother,
Will give high hopes back to the stranger's son,   50
To that proud enemy of you and yours,
To whom an Amazon gave birth, I mean
Hippolytus—

    PHA.   Ye gods!

    OEN.   Ah, this reproach
Moves you!

    PHA.   Unhappy woman, to what name
Gave your mouth utterance?

    OEN.   Your wrath is just.
'Tis well that that ill-omen'd name can rouse
Such rage. Then live. Let love and duty urge
Their claims. Live, suffer not this son of Scythia,
Crushing your children 'neath his odious sway,
To rule the noble offspring of the gods,   60
The purest blood of Greece. Make no delay;
Each moment threatens death; quickly restore
Your shatter'd strength, while yet the torch of life
Holds out, and can be fann'd into a flame.

    PHA. Too long have I endur'd its guilt and shame!

    OEN. Why? What remorse gnaws at your heart?
      What crime
Can have disturb'd you thus? Your hands are not
Polluted with the blood of innocence?

    PHA. Thanks be to Heav'n, my hands are free
      from stain.
Would that my soul were innocent as they!   70

    OEN. What awful project have you then con-
      ceived,
Whereat your conscience should be still alarm'd?

    PHA. Have I not said enough? Spare me the rest.
I die to save myself a full confession.

    OEN. Die then, and keep a silence so inhuman;
But seek some other hand to close your eyes.
Tho' but a spark of life remains within you,
My soul shall go before you to the Shades.
A thousand roads are always open thither;
Pain'd at your want of confidence, I'll choose   80
The shortest. Cruel one, when has my faith
Deceiv'd you? Think how in my arms you lay
New born. For you, my country and my children
I have forsaken. Do you thus repay
My faithful service?

    PHA.   What do you expect
From words so bitter? Were I to break silence,

Horror would freeze your blood.

    OEN.   What can you say
To horrify me more than to behold
You die before my eyes?

    PHA.   When you shall know
My crime, my death will follow none the less,   90
But with the added stain of guilt.

    OEN.   Dear Madam,
By all the tears that I have shed for you,
By these weak knees I clasp, relieve my mind
From torturing doubt.

    PHA.   It is your wish. Then rise.

    OEN. I hear you. Speak.

    PHA.   Heav'ns! How shall I begin?

    OEN. Dismiss vain fears; you wound me with dis-
      trust.

    PHA. O fatal animosity of Venus!
Into what wild distractions did she cast
My mother!

    OEN.   Be they blotted from remembrance,
And for all time to come buried in silence.   100

    PHA. My sister Ariadne, by what love
Were you betray'd to death, on lonely shores
Forsaken!

    OEN.   Madam, what deep-seated pain
Prompts these reproaches against all your kin?

    PHA. It is the will of Venus, and I perish,
Last, most unhappy of a family
Where all are wretched.

    OEN.   Do you love?

    PHA.   I feel
All love's mad fever.

    OEN.   Ah, for whom?

    PHA.   Hear now
The crowning horror. Yes, I love—my lips
Tremble to say his name!

    OEN.   Whom?

    PHA.   Know you him,   110
Son of the Amazon, whom I've oppress'd
So long?

    OEN. Hippolytus? Great gods!

    PHA.   'Tis you
Have named him.

    OEN.   All the blood within my veins
Seems frozen. O despair! O cursèd race!
Ill-omen'd journey! Land of misery!
Why did we ever reach thy dangerous shores?

    PHA. My wound is not so recent. Scarce had I
Been bound to Theseus by the marriage yoke,
And happiness and peace seem'd well secur'd,
When Athens showed me my proud enemy.   120
I look'd, alternately turn'd pale and blush'd
To see him, and my soul grew all distraught;

A mist obscur'd my vision, and my voice
Falter'd, my blood ran cold, then burn'd like fire;
Venus I felt in all my fever'd frame,
Whose fury had so many of my race
Pursued. With fervent vows I sought to shun
Her torments, built and deck'd for her a shrine,
And there, 'mid countless victims did I seek
The reason I had lost; but all for naught,   130
No remedy could cure the wounds of love!
In vain I offered incense on her altars;
When I invoked her name my heart adored
Hippolytus, before me constantly;
And when I made her altars smoke with victims,
'Twas for a god whose name I dar'd not utter.
I fled his presence everywhere, but found him—
Oh, crowning horror!—in his father's features.
Against myself, at last, I raised revolt,
And stirr'd my courage up to persecute   140
The enemy I lov'd. To banish him
I wore a step-dame's harsh and jealous carriage,
With ceaseless cries I clamor'd for his exile,
Till I had torn him from his father's arms.
I breath'd once more, Oenone; in his absence
My days flow'd on less troubled than before,
And innocent. Submissive to my husband,
I hid my grief, and of our fatal marriage
Cherish'd the fruits. Vain caution! Cruel Fate!
Brought hither by my spouse himself, I saw   150
Again the enemy whom I had banish'd,
And the old wound too quickly bled afresh.
No longer is it love hid in my heart,
But Venus in her might seizing her prey.
I have conceiv'd just terror for my crime;
I hate my life, and hold my love in horror.
Dying, I wish'd to keep my fame unsullied,
And bury in the grave a guilty passion;
But I have been unable to withstand
Tears and entreaties. I have told you all;   160
Content, if only, as my end draws near,
You do not vex me with unjust reproaches,
Nor with vain efforts seek to snatch from death
The last faint lingering sparks of vital breath.

SCENE 4. PHAEDRA, OENONE, PANOPE

  PANOPE. Fain would I hide from you tidings so
    sad,
But 'tis my duty, madam, to reveal them.
The hand of death has seized your peerless hus-
    band,
And you are last to hear of this disaster.
  OEN. What say you, Panope?
  PAN.   The queen, deceived
By a vain trust in Heav'n, begs safe return

For Theseus, while Hippolytus, his son,
Learns of his death from vessels that are now
In port.
  PHA. Ye gods!
  PAN.   Divided counsels sway
The choice of Athens; some would have the
    prince,   10
Your child, for master; others, disregarding
The laws, dare to support the stranger's son.
'Tis even said that a presumptuous faction
Would crown Aricia and the house of Pallas.
I deemed it right to warn you of this danger.
Hippolytus already is prepared
To start, and should he show himself at Athens,
'Tis to be feared the fickle crowd will all
Follow his lead.
  OEN.   Enough! The queen who hears you
By no means will neglect this timely warning.   20

SCENE 5. PHAEDRA, OENONE

  OEN. Dear lady, I had almost ceas'd to urge
The wish that you should live, thinking to follow
My mistress to the tomb, from which my voice
Had fail'd to turn you; but this new misfortune
Alters the aspect of affairs, and prompts
Fresh measures. Madam, Theseus is no more,
You must supply his place. He leaves a son,
A slave if you should die, but if you live,
A King. On whom has he to lean but you?
No hand but yours will dry his tears. Then live   10
For him, or else the tears of innocence
Will move the gods, his ancestors, to wrath
Against his mother. Live! Your guilt is gone.
No blame attaches to your passion now.
The king's decease has freed you from the bonds
That made the crime and horror of your love.
Hippolytus no longer need be dreaded,
Him you may see henceforth without reproach.
It may be that, convinc'd of your aversion,
He means to head the rebels. Undeceive him,   20
Soften his callous heart, and bend his pride.
King of this fertile land, in Troezen here
His portion lies; but as he knows, the laws
Give to your son the ramparts that Minerva
Built and protects. A common enemy
Threatens you both; unite then to oppose
Aricia.
  PHA. To your counsel I consent.
Yes, I will live, if life can be restored,
If my affection for a son has pow'r
To rouse my sinking heart at such a dangerous
    hour.   30

ACT II

SCENE I. ARICIA, ISMENE

ARICIA. Hippolytus request to see me here!
Hippolytus desire to bid farewell!
Is't true, Ismene? Are you not deceived?
　ISMENE. This is the first result of Theseus' death.
Prepare yourself to see from every side
Hearts turn toward you that have been kept away
By Theseus. Mistress of her lot at last,
Aricia soon shall find all Greece fall low,
To do her homage.
　ARI. 　　　　'Tis not then, Ismene,
An idle tale? Am I no more a slave? 　　　　10
Have I no enemies?
　ISM. 　　　　The gods oppose
Your peace no longer, and the soul of Theseus
Is with your brothers.
　ARI. 　　　　Does the voice of fame
Tell how he died?
　ISM. 　　　　Rumors incredible
Are spread. Some say that, seizing a new bride,
The faithless husband by the waves was swallow'd.
Others affirm, and this report prevails,
That with Pirithoüs to the world below
He went, and saw the shores of dark Cocytus,
Showing himself alive to the pale ghosts; 　　　　20
But that he could not leave those gloomy realms
Where whoso enters once abides forever.
　ARI. Shall I believe that ere his destined hour
A mortal may descend into the gulf
Of Hades? What attraction could o'ercome
Its terrors?
　ISM. 　　　He is dead, and you alone
Doubt it. The men of Athens mourn his loss;
Troezen already hails Hippolytus
As King. And Phaedra, fearing for her son,
Asks counsel of the friends who share her
　　trouble, 　　　　30
Here in this palace.
　ARI. 　　　　Will Hippolytus,
Think you, prove kinder than his sire, make light
My chains, and pity my misfortunes?
　ISM. 　　　　　　Yes,
I think so, Madam.
　ARI. 　　　　Ah, you know him not—
Or you would never deem so hard a heart
Can pity feel, or me alone except
From the contempt in which he holds our sex.
Has he not long avoided every spot
Where we resort?
　ISM. 　　　I know what tales are told
Of proud Hippolytus, but I have seen 　　　　40

Him near you, and have watch'd with curious eye
How one esteem'd so cold would bear himself.
Little did his behavior correspond
With what I look'd for; in his face confusion
Appear'd at your first glance; he could not turn
His languid eyes away, but gazed on you.
Love is a word that may offend his pride,
But what the tongue disowns, looks can betray.
　ARI. How eagerly my heart hears what you say,
Tho' it may be delusion, dear Ismene! 　　　　50
Did it seem possible to you, who know me,
That I, sad sport of a relentless Fate,
Fed upon bitter tears by night and day,
Could ever taste the maddening draught of love?
The last frail offspring of a royal race,
Children of Earth, I only have survived
War's fury. Cut off in the flow'r of youth,
Mown by the sword, six brothers have I lost,
The hope of an illustrious house, whose blood
Earth drank with sorrow, near akin to his 　　　　60
Whom she herself produced. Since then, you know
How thro' all Greece no heart has been allow'd
To sigh for me, lest by a sister's flame
The brother's ashes be perchance rekindled.
You know, besides, with what disdain I view'd
My conqueror's suspicions and precautions,
And how, oppos'd as I have ever been
To love, I often thank'd the King's injustice
Which happily confirm'd my inclination.
But then I never had beheld his son. 　　　　70
Not that, attracted merely by the eye,
I love him for his beauty and his grace,
Endowments which he owes to Nature's bounty,
Charms which he seems to know not or to scorn.
I love and prize in him riches more rare,
The virtues of his sire, without his faults.
I love, as I must own, that generous pride
Which ne'er has stoop'd beneath the amorous yoke.
Phaedra reaps little glory from a lover
So lavish of his sighs; I am too proud 　　　　80
To share devotion with a thousand others,
Or enter where the door is always open.
But to make one who ne'er has stoop'd before
Bend his proud neck, to pierce a heart of stone,
To bind a captive whom his chains astonish,
Who vainly 'gainst a pleasing yoke rebels,—
That piques my ardor, and I long for that.
'Twas easier to disarm the god of strength
Than this Hippolytus, for Hercules
Yielded so often to the eyes of beauty, 　　　　90
As to make triumph cheap. But, dear Ismene,
I take too little heed of opposition
Beyond my pow'r to quell, and you may hear me,

Humbled by sore defeat, upbraid the pride
I now admire. What! Can he love? And I
Have had the happiness to bend—
   ISM.   He comes.
Yourself shall hear him.

SCENE 2. HIPPOLYTUS, ARICIA, ISMENE

   HIP.   Lady, ere I go,
My duty bids me tell you of your change
Of fortune. My worst fears are realized;
My sire is dead. Yes, his protracted absence
Was caus'd as I foreboded. Death alone,
Ending his toils, could keep him from the world
Conceal'd so long. The gods at last have doom'd
Alcides' friend, companion, and successor.
I think your hatred, tender to his virtues,
Can hear such terms of praise without resent-
    ment,   10
Knowing them due. One hope have I that soothes
My sorrow: I can free you from restraint.
Lo, I revoke the laws whose rigour moved
My pity; you are at your own disposal,
Both heart and hand. Here, in my heritage,
In Troezen, where my grandsire Pittheus reign'd
Of yore and I am now acknowledg'd King,
I leave you free, free as myself,—and more.
   ARI. Your kindness is too great, 'tis overwhelming.
Such generosity, that pays disgrace   20
With honor, lends more force than you can think
To those harsh laws from which you would release
    me.
   HIP. Athens, uncertain how to fill the throne
Of Theseus, speaks of you, anon of me,
And then of Phaedra's son.
   ARI.   Of me, my lord?
   HIP. I know myself excluded by strict law:
Greece turns to my reproach a foreign mother.
But if my brother were my only rival,
My rights prevail o'er his clearly enough
To make me careless of the law's caprice. 30
My forwardness is check'd by juster claims:
To you I yield my place, or, rather, own
That it is yours by right, and yours the sceptre,
As handed down from Earth's great son, Erech-
    theus.
Adoption placed it in the hands of Aegeus:
Athens, by him protected and increased,
Welcomed a king so generous as my sire,
And left your hapless brothers in oblivion.
Now she invites you back within her walls;
Protracted strife has cost her groans enough, 40
Her fields are glutted with your kinsmen's blood
Fatt'ning the furrows out of which it sprung

At first. I rule this Troezen; while the son
Of Phaedra has in Crete a rich domain.
Athens is yours. I will do all I can
To join for you the votes divided now
Between us.
   ARI.   Stunn'd at all I hear, my lord,
I fear, I almost fear a dream deceives me.
Am I indeed awake? Can I believe
Such generosity? What god has put it   50
Into your heart? Well is the fame deserved
That you enjoy! That fame falls short of truth!
Would you for me prove traitor to yourself?
Was it not boon enough never to hate me,
So long to have abstain'd from harboring
The enmity—
   HIP.   To hate you? I, to hate you?
However darkly my fierce pride was painted,
Do you suppose a monster gave me birth?
What savage temper, what envenom'd hatred
Would not be mollified at sight of you?   60
Could I resist the soul-bewitching charm—
   ARI. Why, what is this, Sir?
   HIP.   I have said too much
Not to say more. Prudence in vain resists
The violence of passion. I have broken
Silence at last, and I must tell you now
The secret that my heart can hold no longer.
You see before you an unhappy instance
Of hasty pride, a prince who claims compassion.
I, who, so long the enemy of Love,
Mock'd at his fetters and despised his captives, 70
Who, pitying poor mortals that were shipwreck'd,
In seeming safety view'd the storms from land,
Now find myself to the same fate exposed,
Toss'd to and fro upon a sea of troubles!
My boldness has been vanquish'd in a moment,
And humbled is the pride wherein I boasted.
For nearly six months past, ashamed, despairing,
Bearing where'er I go the shaft that rends
My heart, I struggle vainly to be free
From you and from myself; I shun you, present; 80
Absent, I find you near; I see your form
In the dark forest depths; the shades of night,
Nor less broad daylight, bring back to my view
The charms that I avoid; all things conspire
To make Hippolytus your slave. For fruit
Of all my bootless sighs, I fail to find
My former self. My bow and javelins
Please me no more, my chariot is forgotten,
With all the Sea God's lessons; and the woods
Echo my groans instead of joyous shouts 90
Urging my fiery steeds. Hearing this tale
Of passion so uncouth, you blush perchance

At your own handiwork. With what wild words
I offer you my heart, strange captive held
By silken jess! But dearer in your eyes
Should be the offering, that this language comes
Strange to my lips; reject not vows express'd
So ill, which but for you had ne'er been form'd.

SCENE 3. HIPPOLYTUS, ARICIA, THERAMENES,
    ISMENE

THER. Prince, the Queen comes. I herald her ap-
    approach.
'Tis you she seeks.
HIP.   Me?
THER.   What her thought may be
I know not. But I speak on her behalf.
She would converse with you ere you go hence.
HIP. What shall I say to her? Can she expect—
ARI. You cannot, noble Prince, refuse to hear her,
Howe'er convinced she is your enemy:
Some shade of pity to her tears is due.
HIP. Shall we part thus? And will you let me go,
Not knowing if my boldness has offended   10
The goddess I adore? Whether this heart,
Left in your hands—
ARI.   Go, Prince; pursue the schemes
Your generous soul dictates. Make Athens own
My scepter. All gifts you offer me
Will I accept, but this high throne of empire
Is not the one most precious in my sight.

SCENE 4. HIPPOLYTUS, THERAMENES

HIP. Friend, is all ready? But the Queen ap-
    proaches!
Go; see the vessel in fit trim to sail.
Haste; bid the crew aboard, and hoist the signal.
Then soon return, and so deliver me
From interview most irksome.   20

SCENE 5. PHAEDRA, HIPPOLYTUS, OENONE

PHA. (to OENONE)   There I see him!
My blood forgets to flow, my tongue to speak
What I am come to say.
OEN.   Think of your son,
How all his hopes depend on you.
PHA. (to HIPPOLYTUS)   I hear
You leave us, and in haste. I come to add
My tears to your distress, and for a son
Plead my alarm. No more has he a father,
And at no distant day my son must witness
My death. Already do a thousand foes
Threaten his youth. You only can defend him.   10
But in my secret heart remorse awakes,
And fear lest I have shut your ears against

His cries. I tremble lest your righteous anger
Visit on him ere long the hatred earn'd
By me, his mother.
HIP.   No such base resentment,
Madam, is mine.
PHA.   I could not blame you, Prince,
If you should hate me. I have injur'd you:
So much you know, but could not read my heart.
T'incur your enmity has been mine aim.
The self-same borders could not hold us both;   20
In public and in private I declared
Myself your foe, and found no peace till seas
Parted us from each other. I forbade
Your very name to be pronounced before me,
And yet if punishment should be proportion'd
To the offense, if only hatred draws
Your hatred, never woman merited
More pity—less deserv'd your enmity.
HIP. A mother jealous of her children's rights
Seldom forgives the offspring of a wife   30
Who reigned before her. Harassing suspicions
Are common sequels of a second marriage.
Of me would any other have been jealous
No less than you, perhaps more violent.
PHA. Ah, Prince, how Heav'n has from the gen-
    eral law
Made me exempt, be that same Heav'n my witness!
Far different is the trouble that devours me!
HIP. This is no time for self-reproaches, Madam.
It may be that your husband still beholds
The light, and Heav'n may grant him safe re-
    turn,   40
In answer to our prayers. His guardian god
Is Neptune, ne'er by him invoked in vain.
PHA. He who has seen the mansions of the dead
Returns not thence. Since to those gloomy shores
Theseus is gone, 'tis vain to hope that Heav'n
May send him back. Prince, there is no release
From Acheron's greedy maw; and yet, methinks,
He lives and breathes in you. I see him still
Before me, and to him I seem to speak—
My heart—Oh! I am mad; Do what I will,   50
I cannot hide my passion.
HIP.   Yes, I see
The strange effects of love. Theseus, tho' dead,
Seems present to your eyes, for in your soul
There burns a constant flame.
PHA.   Ah, yes, for Theseus
I languish and I long, not as the Shades
Have seen him, of a thousand different forms
The fickle lover, and of Pluto's bride
The would-be ravisher, but faithful, proud
E'en to a slight disdain, with youthful charms

Attracting every heart, as gods are painted,   60
Or like yourself. He had your mien, your eyes,
Spoke and could blush like you, when to the isle
Of Crete, my childhood's home, he cross'd the
        waves,
Worthy to win the love of Minos' daughters.
What were you doing then? Why did he gather
The flow'r of Greece, and leave Hippolytus?
Oh, why were you too young to have embark'd
On board the ship that brought thy sire to Crete?
At your hands would the monster then have per-
        ish'd,
Despite the windings of his vast retreat.   70
To guide your doubtful steps within the maze
My sister would have arm'd you with the clue.
But no, therein would Phaedra have forestall'd her,
Love would have first inspir'd me with the thought;
And I it would have been whose timely aid
Had taught you all the labyrinth's crooked ways.
What anxious care a life so dear had cost me!
No thread had satisfied your lover's fears:
I would myself have wish'd to lead the way,
And share the peril you were bound to face;   80
Phaedra with you would have explored the maze,
With you emerged in safety, or have perish'd.

    HIP. Gods! What is this I hear? Have you for-
        gotten
That Theseus is my father and your husband?

    PHA. Why should you fancy I have lost remem-
        brance
Thereof, and am regardless of mine honor?

    HIP. Forgive me, Madam. With a blush I own
That I misconstrued words of innocence.
For very shame I cannot bear your sight
Longer. I go—

    PHA.   Ah! cruel Prince, too well   90
You understand me. I have said enough
To save you from mistake. I love. But think not
That at the moment when I love you most
I do not feel my guilt; no weak compliance
Has fed the poison that infects my brain.
The ill-starr'd object of celestial vengeance,
I am not so detestable to you
As to myself. The gods will bear me witness,
Who have within my veins kindled this fire,
The gods, who take a barbarous delight   100
In leading a poor mortal's heart astray.
Do you yourself recall to mind the past:
'Twas not enough for me to fly; I chas'd you
Out of the country, wishing to appear
Inhuman, odious; to resist you better,
I sought to make you hate me. All in vain!
Hating me more, I lov'd you none the less:

New charms were lent to you by your misfortunes.
I have been drown'd in tears, and scorch'd by fire;
Your own eyes might convince you of the truth,   110
If for one moment you could look at me.
What is 't I say? Think you this vile confession
That I have made is what I meant to utter?
Not daring to betray a son for whom
I trembled, 'twas to beg you not to hate him
I came. Weak purpose of a heart too full
Of love for you to speak of aught besides!
Take your revenge, punish my odious passion;
Prove yourself worthy of your valiant sire,
And rid the world of an offensive monster!   120
Does Theseus' widow dare to love his son?
The frightful monster! Let her not escape you!
Here is my heart. This is the place to strike.
Already prompt to expiate its guilt,
I feel it leap impatiently to meet
Your arm. Strike home. Or, if it would disgrace
        you
To steep your hand in such polluted blood,
If that were punishment too mild to slake
Your hatred, lend me then your sword, if not
Your arm. Quick, give 't.

    OEN.   What, Madam, will you do?   130
Just gods! But someone comes. Go, fly from shame,
You cannot 'scape if seen by any thus.

SCENE 6. HIPPOLYTUS, THERAMENES

    THER. Is that the form of Phaedra that I see
Hurried away? What mean these signs of sorrow?
Where is your sword? Why are you pale, confused?

    HIP. Friend, let us fly. I am, indeed, confounded
With horror and astonishment extreme.
Phaedra—but no! Gods, let this dreadful secret
Remain forever buried in oblivion.

    THER. The ship is ready if you wish to sail.
But Athens has already giv'n her vote;
The leaders have consulted all her tribes;   10
Your brother is elected; Phaedra wins.

    HIP. Phaedra?

    THER.   A herald, charged with a commission
From Athens, has arrived to place the reins
Of power in her hands. Her son is King.

    HIP. Ye gods who know her, do ye thus reward
Her virtue?

    THER.   A faint rumor meanwhile whispers
That Theseus is not dead, but in Epirus
Has shown himself. However, since my search,
I know too well—

    HIP.   Let nothing be neglected.
This rumor must be trac'd back to its source.   20
If it be found unworthy of belief,

Let us set sail, and cost whate'er it may,
To hands deserving trust the sceptre's sway!

ACT III

SCENE 1. PHAEDRA, OENONE

    PHA. Ah, let them take elsewhere the worthless honors
They bring me! Why so urgent I should see them?
What flattering balm can soothe my wounded heart?
Far rather hide me; I have said too much.
My madness has burst forth like streams in flood,
And I have utter'd what should ne'er have reach'd
His ear. Gods! How he heard me! How reluctant
To catch my meaning, dull and cold as marble,
And eager only for a quick retreat!
How oft his blushes made my shame the deeper! 10
Why did you turn me from the death I sought?
Ah, when his sword was pointed to my bosom,
Did he grow pale, or try to snatch it from me?
That I had touch'd it was enough for him
To render it forever horrible,
Leaving defilement in the hand that holds it.
    OEN. Thus brooding on your bitter disappointment,
You only fan a fire that must be stifled.
Would it not be more worthy of the blood
Of Minos to find peace in nobler cares, 20
And, in defiance of a wretch who flies
From what he hates, reign, mount the proffer'd throne?
    PHA. I reign! Shall I the rod of empire sway,
When reason reigns no longer o'er myself?
When I have lost control of all my senses?
When 'neath a shameful yoke I scarce can breathe?
When I am dying?
    OEN.   Fly!
    PHA.   I cannot leave him!
    OEN. Dare you not fly from him you dared to banish?
    PHA. The time for that is past. He knows my frenzy.
I have o'erstepp'd the bounds of modesty, 30
And blazon'd forth my shame before his eyes.
Hope stole into my heart against my will.
Did you not rally my declining pow'rs?
Was it not you yourself recall'd my soul
When fluttering on my lips, and with your counsel,
Lent me fresh life, and told me I might love him?
    OEN. Blame me or blame me not for your misfortunes,
Of what was I incapable, to save you?

But if your indignation, e'er was rous'd
By insult, can you pardon his contempt? 40
How cruelly his eyes, severely fix'd,
Survey'd you almost prostrate at his feet!
How hateful then appear'd his savage pride!
Why did not Phaedra see him then as I
Beheld him?
    PHA.   This proud mood that you resent
May yield to time. The rudeness of the forests
Where he was bred, inured to rigorous laws,
Clings to him still; love is a word he ne'er
Had heard before. It may be his surprise
Stunn'd him, and too much vehemence was shown 50
In all I said.
    OEN.   Remember that his mother
Was a barbarian.
    PHA.   Scythian tho' she was,
She learnt to love.
    OEN.   He has for all the sex
Hatred intense.
    PHA.   Then in his heart no rival
Shall ever reign. Your counsel comes too late.
Oenone, serve my madness, not my reason.
His heart is inaccessible to love;
Let us attack him where he has more feeling.
The charms of sovereignty appear'd to touch him;
He could not hide that he was drawn to Athens; 60
His vessels' prows were thither turn'd already,
All sail was set to scud before the breeze.
Go you on my behalf; to his ambition
Appeal, and let the prospect of the crown
Dazzle his eyes. The sacred diadem
Shall deck his brow, no higher honour mine
Than there to bind it. His shall be the pow'r
I cannot keep; and he shall teach my son
How to rule men. It may be he will deign
To be to him a father. Son and mother 70
He shall control. Try ev'ry means to move him;
Your words shall find more favour than can mine.
Urge him with groans and tears; show Phaedra dying,
Nor blush to use the voice of supplication.
In you is my last hope; I'll sanction all
You say; and on the issue hangs my fate.

SCENE 2. PHAEDRA

Venus implacable, who seest me shamed
And sore confounded, have I not enough
Been humbled? How can cruelty be stretch'd
Further? Thy shafts have all gone home, and thou
Hast triumph'd. Would'st thou win a new renown?
Attack an enemy more contumacious;

Hippolytus neglects thee, braves thy wrath,
Nor ever at thine altars bow'd the knee.
Thy name offends his proud, disdainful ears.
Our interests are alike: avenge thyself,   10
Force him to love—
           But what is this? Oenone
Return'd already? He detests me then,
And I will not hear you.

SCENE 3. PHAEDRA, OENONE

OEN.   Madam, you must stifle
A fruitless love. Recall your former virtue:
The king who was thought dead will soon appear
Before your eyes. Theseus has just arrived,
Theseus is here. The people flock to see him
With eager haste. I went by your command
To find the prince, when with a thousand shouts
The air was rent—
PHA.   My husband is alive—   10
That is enough, Oenone. I have own'd
A passion that dishonours him. He lives:
I ask to know no more.
OEN.   What?
PHA.   I foretold it,
But you refus'd to hear. Your tears prevail'd
Over my just remorse. Dying this morn,
I had deserved compassion; your advice
I took, and die dishonoured.
OEN.   Die?
PHA.   Just Heav'ns!
What have I done today? My husband comes,
With him his son: and I shall see the witness
Of my adulterous flame watch with what face   20
I greet his father, while my heart is big
With sighs he scorn'd, and tears that could not move
    him
Moisten mine eyes. Think you that his respect
For Theseus will induce him to conceal
My madness, nor disgrace his sire and king?
Will he be able to keep back the horror
He has for me? His silence would be vain.
I know my treason, and I lack the boldness
Of those abandon'd women who can taste
Tranquillity in crime, and show a forehead   30
All unabash'd. I recognize my madness,
Recall it all. These vaulted roofs, methinks,
These walls can speak, and, ready to accuse me,
Wait but my husband's presence to reveal
My perfidy. Death only can remove
This weight of horror. Is it such misfortune
To cease to live? Death causes no alarm
To misery. I only fear the name
That I shall leave behind me. For my sons

How sad a heritage! The blood of Jove   40
Might justly swell the pride that boasts descent
From Heav'n, but heavy weighs a mother's guilt
Upon her offspring. Yes, I dread the scorn
That will be cast on them with too much truth,
For my disgrace. I tremble when I think
That, crush'd beneath that curse, they'll never dare
To raise their eyes.
OEN.   Doubt not I pity both;
Never was fear more just than yours. Why then
Expose them to this ignominy? Why
Will you accuse yourself? You thus destroy   50
The only hope that's left; it will be said
That Phaedra, conscious of her perfidy,
Fled from her husband's sight. Hippolytus
Will be rejoiced that, dying, you should lend
His charge support. What can I answer him?
He'll find it easy to confute my tale,
And I shall hear him with an air of triumph
To every open ear repeat your shame.
Sooner than that may fire from heav'n consume me!
Deceive me not. Say, do you love him still?   60
How look you now on this contemptuous prince?
PHA. As on a monster frightful to mine eyes.
OEN. Why yield him then an easy victory?
You fear him. Venture to accuse him first,
As guilty of the charge which he may bring
This day against you. Who can say 'tis false?
All tells against him: in your hands his sword
Happily left behind, your present trouble,
Your past distress, your warnings to his father,
His exile which your earnest pray'rs obtain'd.   70
PHA. What! Would you have me slander inno-
    cence?
OEN. My zeal has need of naught from you but
    silence.
Like you I tremble, and am loath to do it;
More willingly I'd face a thousand deaths.
But since without this bitter remedy
I lose you, and to me your life outweighs
All else, I'll speak. Theseus, howe'er enraged,
Will do no worse than banish him again.
A father, when he punishes, remains
A father, and his ire is satisfied   80
With a light sentence. But if guiltless blood
Should flow, is not your honour of more moment?
A treasure far too precious to be risk'd?
You must submit, whatever it dictates;
For, when your reputation is at stake,
All must be sacrificed—conscience itself.
But someone comes. 'Tis Theseus.
PHA.   And I see
Hippolytus, my ruin plainly written

In his stern eyes. Do what you will; I trust
My fate to you. I cannot help myself.   90

SCENE 4. THESEUS, HIPPOLYTUS, PHAEDRA, OENONE,
    THERAMENES

    THES. Fortune no longer fights against my wishes,
Madam, and to your arms restores—
    PHA.   Stay, Theseus!
Do not profane endearments that were once
So sweet, but which I am unworthy now
To taste. You have been wrong'd. Fortune has
    prov'd
Spiteful, nor in your absence spared your wife.
I am unfit to meet your fond caress.
How I may bear my shame my only care
Henceforth.

SCENE 5. THESEUS, HIPPOLYTUS, THERAMENES

    THES.   Strange welcome for your father this!
What does it mean, my son?
    HIP.   Phaedra alone
Can solve this mystery. But if my wish
Can move you, let me never see her more;
Suffer Hippolytus to disappear
Forever from the home that holds your wife.
    THES. You, my son! Leave me?
    HIP.   'Twas not I who sought her:
'Twas you who led her footsteps to these shores.
At your departure you thought meet, my lord,
To trust Aricia and the Queen to this   10
Troezenian land, and I myself was charged
With their protection. But what cares henceforth
Need keep me here? My youth of idleness
Has shown its skill enough o'er paltry foes
That range the woods. May I not quit a life
Of such inglorious ease, and dip my spear
In nobler blood? Ere you had reach'd my age,
More than one tyrant, monster more than one,
Had felt the weight of your stout arm. Already,
Successful in attacking insolence,   20
You had removed all dangers that infested
Our coasts to east and west. The traveler fear'd
Outrage no longer. Hearing of your deeds,
Already Hercules relied on you,
And rested from his toils, while I, unknown
Son of so brave a sire, am far behind
Even my mother's footsteps. Let my courage
Have scope to act, and if some monster yet
Has 'scaped you, let me lay the glorious spoils
Down at your feet; or let the memory   30
Of death faced nobly keep my name alive,
And prove to all the world I was your son.

    THES. Why, what is this? What terror has pos-
    sess'd
My family to make them fly before me?
If I return to find myself so fear'd,
So little welcome, why did Heav'n release me
From prison? My sole friend, misled by passion,
Was bent on robbing of his wife the tyrant
Who ruled Epirus. With regret I lent
The lover aid; but Fate had made us blind,   40
Myself as well as him. The tyrant seized me
Defenseless and unarm'd. Pirithoüs
I saw with tears cast forth to be devour'd
By savage beasts that lapp'd the blood of men.
Myself in gloomy caverns he inclosed,
Deep in the bowels of the earth, and nigh
To Pluto's realms. Six months I lay ere Heav'n
Had pity, and I 'scaped the watchful eyes
That guarded me. Then did I purge the world
Of a foul foe, and he himself has fed   50
His monsters. But, when with expectant joy
To all that is most precious I draw near
Of what the gods have left me, when my soul
Looks for full satisfaction in a sight
So dear, my only welcome is a shudder,
Embrace rejected, and a hasty flight.
Inspiring, as I clearly do, such terror,
Would I were still a prisoner in Epirus!
Phaedra complains that I have suffer'd outrage.
Who has betray'd me? Speak. Why was I not   60
Avenged? Has Greece, to whom my arm so oft
Brought useful aid, shelter'd the criminal?
You make no answer. Is my son, mine own
Dear son, confederate with mine enemies?
I'll enter. This suspense is overwhelming.
I'll learn at once the culprit and the crime,
And Phaedra must explain her troubled state.

SCENE 6. HIPPOLYTUS, THERAMENES

    HIP. What do these words portend, which seem'd
    to freeze
My very blood? Will Phaedra, in her frenzy,
Accuse herself and seal her own destruction?
What will the king say? Gods! What fatal poison
Has love spread over all his house! Myself,
Full of a fire his hatred disapproves,
How changed he finds me from the son he knew!
With dark forebodings is my mind alarm'd,
But innocence has surely naught to fear.
Come, let us go, and in some other place   10
Consider how I best may move my sire
To tenderness, and tell him of a flame
Vex'd but not vanquish'd by a father's blame.

ACT IV

SCENE 1. THESEUS, OENONE

THES. Ah! What is this I hear? Presumptuous
    traitor!
And would he have disgraced his father's honour?
With what relentless footsteps Fate pursues me!
Whither I go I know not, nor where now
I am. O kind affection ill repaid!
Audacious scheme! Abominable thought!
To reach the object of his foul desire
The wretch disdain'd not to use violence.
I know this sword that served him in his fury,
The sword I gave him for a nobler use.   10
Could not the sacred ties of blood restrain him?
And Phaedra,—was she loath to have him punish'd?
She held her tongue. Was that to spare the culprit?
    OEN. Nay, but to spare a most unhappy father.
O'erwhelm'd with shame that her eyes should have
    kindled
So infamous a flame and prompted him
To crime so heinous, Phaedra would have died.
I saw her raise her arm, and ran to save her.
To me alone you owe it that she lives;
And, in my pity both for her and you,   20
Have I against my will interpreted
Her tears.
    THES.   The traitor! He might well turn pale.
'Twas fear that made him tremble when he saw me.
I was astonish'd that he show'd no pleasure;
His frigid greeting chill'd my tenderness.
But was this guilty passion that devours him
Declared already ere I banish'd him
From Athens?
    OEN.   Sire, remember how the Queen
Urged you. Illicit love caus'd all her hatred.
    THES. And then this fire broke out again at
    Troezen?   30
    OEN. Sire, I have told you all. Too long the
    Queen
Has been allow'd to bear her grief alone.
Let me now leave you and attend her.

SCENE 2. THESEUS, HIPPOLYTUS

THES. Ah! There he is! Great gods! That noble
    mien
Might well deceive an eye less fond than mine!
Why should the sacred stamp of virtue gleam
Upon the forehead of an impious wretch?
Ought not the blackness of a traitor's heart
To show itself by sure and certain signs?
    HIP. My father, may I ask what fatal cloud
Has troubled your majestic countenance?

Dare you not trust this secret to your son?
    THES. Traitor, how dare you show yourself before
    me?   10
Monster, whom Heaven's bolts have spar'd too long!
Survivor of that robber crew whereof
I cleansed the earth. After your brutal lust
Scorn'd even to respect my marriage bed,
You venture—you, my hated foe—to come
Into my presence, here, where all is full
Of your foul infamy, instead of seeking
Some unknown land that never heard my name.
Fly, traitor, fly! Stay not to tempt the wrath
That I can scarce restrain, nor brave my hatred. 20
Disgrace enough have I incurr'd forever
In being father of so vile a son,
Without your death staining indelibly
The glorious record of my noble deeds.
Fly, and unless you wish quick punishment
To add you to the criminals cut off
By me, take heed this sun that lights us now
Ne'er see you more set foot upon this soil.
I tell you once again,—fly, haste, return not,
Rid all my realms of your atrocious presence. 30
To thee, to thee, great Neptune, I appeal;
If erst I clear'd thy shores of foul assassins,
Recall thy promise to reward those efforts,
Crown'd with success, by granting my first pray'r.
Confined for long in close captivity,
I have not yet call'd on thy pow'rful aid,
Sparing to use the valued privilege
Till at mine utmost need. The time is come,
I ask thee now. Avenge a wretched father!
I leave this traitor to thy wrath; in blood   40
Quench his outrageous fires, and by thy fury
Theseus will estimate thy favor tow'rds him.
    HIP. Phaedra accuses me of lawless passion!
This crowning horror all my soul confounds;
Such unexpected blows, falling at once,
O'erwhelm me, choke my utterance, strike me
    dumb.
    THES. Traitor, you reckon'd that in timid silence
Phaedra would bury your brutality.
You should not have abandon'd in your flight
The sword that in her hands helps to condemn
    you;   50
Or rather, to complete your perfidy,
You should have robb'd her both of speech and
    life.
    HIP. Justly indignant at a lie so black,
I might be pardon'd if I told the truth;
But it concerns your honor to conceal it.
Approve the reverence that shuts my mouth;
And, without wishing to increase your woes,

Examine closely what my life has been.
Great crimes are never single, they are link'd
To former faults. He who has once transgress'd　60
May violate at last all that men hold
Most sacred; vice, like virtue, has degrees
Of progress; innocence was never seen
To sink at once into the lowest depths
Of guilt. No virtuous man can in a day
Turn traitor, murderer, an incestuous wretch.
The nursling of a chaste, heroic mother,
I have not proved unworthy of my birth.
Pittheus, whose wisdom is by all esteem'd,
Deign'd to instruct me when I left her hands.　70
It is no wish of mine to vaunt my merits,
But, if I may lay claim to any virtue,
I think beyond all else I have display'd
Abhorrence of those sins with which I'm charged.
For this Hippolytus is known in Greece,
So continent that he is deem'd austere.
All know my abstinence inflexible;
The daylight is not purer than my heart.
How then could I, burning with fire profane—
　　THES. Yes, dastard, 'tis that very pride condemns
　　　　you.　　　　　　　　　　　　　　　　　　　80
I see the odious reason of your coldness:
Phaedra alone bewitch'd your shameless eyes;
Your soul, to others' charms indifferent,
Disdain'd the blameless fires of lawful love.
　　HIP. No, father, I have hidden it too long,
This heart has not disdain'd a sacred flame.
Here at your feet I own my real offense:
I love, and love in truth where you forbid me;
Bound to Aricia by my heart's devotion,
The child of Pallas has subdued your son.　90
A rebel to your laws, her I adore,
And breathe forth ardent sighs for her alone.
　　THES. You love her? Heav'ns! But no, I see the
　　　　trick.
You feign a crime to justify yourself.
　　HIP. Sir, I have shunn'd her for six months, and
　　　　still
Love her. To you yourself I came to tell it,
Trembling the while. Can nothing clear your mind
Of your mistake? What oath can reassure you?
By heav'n and earth and all the pow'rs of nature—
　　THES. The wicked never shrink from perjury.　100
Cease, cease, and spare me irksome protestations,
If your false virtue has no other aid.
　　HIP. Tho' it to you seem false and insincere,
Phaedra has secret cause to know it true.
　　THES. Ah! How your shamelessness excites my
　　　　wrath!
　　HIP. What is my term and place of banishment?

　　THES. Were you beyond the Pillars of Alcides,
Your perjured presence were too near me yet.
　　HIP. What friends will pity me, when you forsake
And think me guilty of a crime so vile?　110
　　THES. Go, look you out for friends who hold in
　　　　honour
Adultery, and clap their hands at incest—
Low, lawless traitors, steep'd in infamy,
The fit protectors of a knave like you.
　　HIP. Are incest and adultery the words
You cast at me? I hold my tongue. Yet think
What mother Phaedra had; too well you know
Her blood, not mine, is tainted with those horrors.
　　THES. What! Does your rage before my eyes lose
　　　　all
Restraint? For the last time—out of my sight!　120
Hence, traitor! Wait not till a father's wrath
Force thee away 'mid general execration.

SCENE. 3. THESEUS (alone).

Wretch! Thou must meet inevitable ruin.
Neptune has sworn by Styx—to gods themselves
A dreadful oath—and he will execute
His promise. Thou canst not escape his vengeance.
I loved thee; and, in spite of thine offense,
My heart is troubled by anticipation
For thee. But thou hast earn'd thy doom too well.
Had father ever greater cause for rage?
Just gods, who see the grief that overwhelms me,
Why was I cursed with such a wicked son?　10

SCENE 4. PHAEDRA, THESEUS

　　PHA. My lord, I come to you, fill'd with just
　　　　dread.
Your voice rais'd high in anger reach'd mine ears,
And much I fear that deeds have follow'd threats.
Oh, if there yet is time, spare your own offspring,
Respect your race and blood, I do beseech you.
Let me not hear that blood cry from the ground;
Save me the horror and perpetual pain
Of having caus'd his father's hand to shed it.
　　THES. No, Madam, from that stain my hand is
　　　　free.
But, for all that, the wretch has not escap'd me.　10
The hand of an Immortal now is charged
With his destruction. 'Tis a debt that Neptune
Owes me, and you shall be avenged.
　　PHA.　　　　　　　　　　A debt
Ow'd you? Pray'rs made in anger—
　　THES.　　　　　　　　　　Never fear
That they will fail. Rather join yours to mine.
In all their blackness paint for me his crimes,
And fan my tardy passion to white heat.

But yet you know not all his infamy:
His rage against you overflows in slanders;
Your mouth, he says, is full of all deceit, 20
He says Aricia has his heart and soul—
That her alone he loves.

PHA. Aricia?

THES. Ay,
He said it to my face—an idle pretext!
A trick that gulls me not! Let us hope Neptune
Will do him speedy justice. To his altars
I go, to urge performance of his oaths.

SCENE 5. PHAEDRA (alone).

Ah, he is gone! What tidings struck mine ears?
What fire, half smother'd, in my heart revives?
What fatal stroke falls like a thunderbolt?
Stung by remorse that would not let me rest,
I tore myself out of Oenone's arms,
And flew to help Hippolytus with all
My soul and strength. Who knows if that repent-
ance
Might not have mov'd me to accuse myself?
And, if my voice had been choked with shame,
Perhaps I had confess'd the frightful truth. 10
Hippolytus can feel, but not for me!
Aricia has his heart, his plighted troth.
Ye gods, when, deaf to all my sighs and tears,
He arm'd his eye with scorn, his brow with threats,
I deem'd his heart, impregnable to love,
Was fortified 'gainst all my sex alike;
And yet another has prevail'd to tame
His pride, another has secured his favour.
Perhaps he has a heart easily melted;
I am the only one he cannot bear! 20
And shall I charge myself with his defense?

SCENE 6. PHAEDRA, OENONE

PHA. Know you, dear nurse, what I have learn'd
just now?

OEN. No; I come, but in truth, with trembling
limbs.
I dreaded with what purpose you went forth,
The fear of fatal madness made me pale.

PHA. Who would have thought it, Nurse? I had
a rival.

OEN. A rival?

PHA. Yes, he loves. I cannot doubt it.
This wild untamable Hippolytus,
Who scorn'd to be admired, whom lovers' sighs
Wearied, this tiger, whom I fear'd to rouse,
Fawns on a hand that has subdued his pride: 10
Aricia has found entrance to his heart.

OEN. Aricia?

PHA. Ah! anguish as yet untried!
For what new tortures am I still reserved?
All I have undergone, transports of passion,
Longings and fears, the horrors of remorse,
The shame of being spurn'd with contumely,
Were feeble foretastes of my present torments.
They love each other! By what secret charm
Have they deceived me? Where, and when, and
how
Met they? You knew it all. Why was I cozen'd? 20
You never told me of those stolen hours
Of amorous converse. Have they oft been seen
Talking together? Did they seek the shades
Of thickest woods? Alas! Full freedom had they
To see each other. Heav'n approved their sighs;
They lov'd without the consciousness of guilt;
And every morning's sun for them shone clear,
While I, an outcast from the face of Nature,
Shunn'd the bright day, and sought to hide myself.
Death was the only god whose aid I dared 30
To ask: I waited for the grave's release.
Water'd with tears, nourish'd with gall, my woe
Was all too closely watch'd; I did not dare
To weep without restraint. In mortal dread
Tasting this dangerous solace, I disguised
My terror 'neath a tranquil countenance,
And oft had I to check my tears, and smile.

OEN. What fruit will they enjoy of their vain
love?
They will not see each other more.

PHA. That love
Will last forever. Even while I speak, 40
Ah, fatal thought, they laugh to scorn the madness
Of my distracted heart. In spite of exile
That soon must part them, with a thousand oaths
They seal yet closer union. Can I suffer
A happiness, Oenone, which insults me?
I crave your pity. She must be destroy'd.
My husband's wrath against a hateful stock
Shall be reviv'd, nor must the punishment
Be light: the sister's guilt passes the brother's.
I will entreat him in my jealous rage. 50
What am I saying? Have I lost my senses?
Is Phaedra jealous, and will she implore
Theseus for help? My husband lives, and yet
I burn. For whom? Whose heart is this I claim
As mine? At every word I say, my hair
Stands up with horror. Guilt henceforth has pass'd
All bounds. Hypocrisy and incest breathe
At once thro' all. My murderous hands are ready
To spill the blood of guileless innocence.
Do I yet live, wretch that I am, and dare 60
To face this holy Sun from whom I spring?

My father's sire was king of all the gods;
My ancestors fill all the universe.
Where can I hide? In the dark realms of Pluto?
But there my father holds the fatal urn;
His hand awards th' irrevocable doom:
Minos is judge of all the ghosts in hell.
Ah! How his awful shade will start and shudder
When he shall see his daughter brought before
    him,
Forced to confess sins of such varied dye,   70
Crimes it may be unknown to hell itself!
What wilt thou say, my father, at a sight
So dire? I think I see thee drop the urn,
And, seeking some unheard-of punishment,
Thyself become my executioner.
Spare me! A cruel goddess has destroyed
Thy race; and in my madness recognize
Her wrath. Alas! My aching heart has reap'd
No fruit of pleasure from the frightful crime
The shame of which pursues me to the grave,   80
And ends in torment, life-long misery.
    OEN. Ah, Madam, pray dismiss a groundless
      dread;
Look less severely on a venial error.
You love. We cannot conquer destiny.
You were drawn on as by a fatal charm.
Is that a marvel without precedent
Among us? Has love triumph'd over you,
And o'er none else? Weakness is natural
To man. A mortal, to a mortal's lot
Submit. You chafe against a yoke that others   90
Have long since borne. The dwellers on Olympus,
The gods themselves, who terrify with threats
The sins of men, have burn'd with lawless fires.
    PHA. What words are these I hear? What counsel
      this
You dare to give me? Will you to the end
Pour poison in mine ears? You have destroy'd
    me.
You brought me back when I should else have
    quitted
The light of day, made me forget my duty
And see Hippolytus, till then avoided.
What hast thou done? Why did your wicked
    mouth   100
With blackest lies slander his blameless life?
Perhaps you've slain him and the impious pray'r
Of an unfeeling father has been answer'd.
No, not another word! Go, hateful monster,
Away; and leave me to my piteous fate!
May Heav'n with justice pay you your deserts!
And may your punishment forever be
A terror to all those who would, like you,

Nourish with artful wiles the weaknesses
Of princes, push them to the brink of ruin   110
To which their hearts incline, and smooth the path
Of guilt. Such flatterers doth the wrath of Heav'n
Bestow on kings as its most fatal gift!   (*Exit.*)
    OEN. (*alone*). O gods! to serve her what I have
      not done?
This is the true reward that I have won!

ACT V

SCENE I. HIPPOLYTUS, ARICIA

    ARI. Can you keep silent in this mortal peril?
Your father loves you. Will you leave him thus
Deceived? If in your cruel heart you scorn
My tears, content to see me nevermore,
Go, part from poor Aricia!—But at least,
Going, secure the safety of your life.
Defend your honour from a shameful stain,
And force your father to recall his pray'rs.
There is yet time. Why out of mere caprice
Leave the field free to Phaedra's calumnies?   10
Let Theseus know the truth.
    HIP.   Could I say more,
Without exposing him to dire disgrace?
How should I venture, by revealing all,
To make a father's brow grow red with shame?
The odious mystery to you alone
Is known. My heart has been outpour'd to none
Save you and Heav'n. I could not hide from you
(Judge if I love you!) all I fain would hide
E'en from myself. But think under what seal
I spoke. Forget my words, if that may be;   20
And never let so pure a mouth disclose
This dreadful secret. Let us trust to Heav'n
My vindication, for the gods are just;
For their own honour will they clear the guiltless;
Sooner or later punish'd for her crime,
Phaedra will not escape the shame she merits.
I ask no other favour than your silence;
In all besides I give my wrath free scope.
Make your escape from this captivity,
Be bold to bear me company in flight;   30
Linger not here on this accursèd soil,
Where virtue breathes a pestilential air.
To cover your departure, take advantage
Of this confusion caused by my disgrace.
The means of flight are ready, be assured;
You have as yet no other guards than mine.
Pow'rful defenders will maintain our quarrel;
Argos spreads open arms, and Sparta calls us.
Let us appeal for justice to our friends,

Nor suffer Phaedra, in a common ruin 40
Joining us both, to hunt us from the throne,
And aggrandize her son by robbing us!
Embrace this happy opportunity!
What fear restrains? You seem to hesitate.
Your interest alone prompts me to urge
Boldness. When I am all on fire, how comes it
That you are ice? Fear you to follow, then,
A banish'd man?

ARI.   Ah, dear to me would be
Such exile! With what joy, my fate to yours
United, could I live, by all the world 50
Forgotten! But not yet has that sweet tie
Bound us together. How then can I steal
Away with you? I know the strictest honour
Forbids me not out of your father's hands
To free myself; this is no parent's home,
And flight is lawful when one flies from tyrants.
But you, Sir, love me; and my virtue shrinks—

HIP. No, no, your reputation is to me
As dear as to yourself. A nobler purpose
Brings me to you. Fly from your foes, and follow 60
A husband. Heav'n, that sends us these misfor-
    tunes,
Sets free from human instruments the pledge
Between us. Torches do not always light
The face of Hymen. At the gates of Troezen,
'Mid ancient tombs where princes of my race
Lie buried, stands a temple ne'er approach'd
By perjurers, where mortals dare not make
False oaths, for instant punishment befalls
The guilty. Falsehood knows no stronger check
Than what is present there—the fear of death 70
That cannot be avoided. Thither, then,
We'll go, if you consent, and swear to love
Forever, take the guardian god to witness
Our solemn vows, and his paternal care
Entreat. I will invoke the name of all
The holiest Pow'rs: chaste Dian, and the Queen
Of Heav'n, yea, all the gods who know my heart
Will guarantee my sacred promises.

ARI. The king draws near. Depart!—Make no
    delay.
To mask my flight, I linger yet one moment. 80
Go you, and leave with me some trusty guide,
To lead my timid footsteps to your side.

SCENE 2. THESEUS, ARICIA, ISMENE

THES. Ye gods, throw light upon my troubled
    mind.
Show me the truth that I am seeking here.

ARI. (*aside to* ISMENE). Get ready, dear Ismene,
    for our flight.

SCENE 3. THESEUS, ARICIA

THES. Your colour comes and goes, you seem con-
    fused,
Madam! What business had my son with you?

ARI. Sire, he was bidding me farewell forever.

THES. Your eyes, it seems, can tame that stubborn
    pride;
And the first sighs he breathes are paid to you.

ARI. I can't deny the truth; he has not, Sire,
Inherited your hatred and injustice;
He did not treat me like a criminal.

THES. That is to say, he swore eternal love.
Do not rely on that inconstant heart; 10
To others he has sworn as much before.

ARI. He, Sire?

THES.   You ought to check his roving taste.
How could you bear a partnership so vile?

ARI. And how can you endure that vilest slanders
Should make a life so pure as black as pitch?
Have you so little knowledge of his heart?
Do you so ill distinguish between guilt
And innocence? What mist before your eyes
Blinds them to virtue so conspicuous?
Ah, 'tis too much to let false tongues defame him! 20
Repent; call back your murderous wishes, Sire;
Fear, fear lest Heav'n in its severity
Hate you enough to hear and grant your pray'rs.
Oft in their wrath the gods accept our victims,
And oftentimes chastise us with their gifts.

THES. No, vainly would you cover up his guilt;
Your love is blind to his depravity.
But I have witness irreproachable:
Tears have I seen, true tears that may be trusted.

ARI. Take heed, my lord. Your hands invinci-
    ble 30
Have rid the world of monsters numberless;
But all are not destroy'd; one have you left
Alive—Your son forbids me to say more.
Knowing with what respect he still regards you,
I should too much distress him if I dared
Complete my sentence. I will imitate
His reverence, and, to keep silence, leave you.

SCENE 4. THESEUS (*alone*).

What is there in her mind? What meaning lurks
In speech begun but to be broken short?
Would both deceive me with a vain pretence?
Have they conspired to put me to the torture?
And yet, despite my stern severity,
What plaintive voice cries deep within my heart?
A secret pity troubles and alarms me.
Oenone shall be questioned once again;

I must have clearer light upon this crime.
Guards, bid Oenone come, and come alone.   10

SCENE. 5. THESEUS, PANOPE

PANOPE. I know not what the Queen intends to
    do,
But from her agitation, dread the worst.
Fatal despair is painted on her features;
Death's pallor is already in her face.
Oenone, sham'd and driven from her sight,
Has cast herself into the ocean depths.
None knows what prompted her to deed so rash;
And now the waves hide her from us forever.
    THES. What say you?
    PAN.   Her sad fate seems to have added
Fresh trouble to the Queen's tempestuous soul.   10
Sometimes, to soothe her secret pain, she clasps
Her children close, and bathes them with her tears;
Then suddenly, the mother's love forgotten,
She thrusts them from her with a look of horror.
She wanders to and fro with doubtful steps;
Her vacant eye no longer knows us. Thrice
She wrote, and thrice did she, changing her mind,
Destroy the letter ere 'twas well begun.
Vouchsafe to see her, Sire: vouchsafe to help her.
    THES. Heav'ns! Is Oenone dead, and Phaedra
        bent   20
On dying too? Oh, call me back my son!
Let him defend himself, and I am ready
To hear him. Be not hasty to bestow
Thy fatal bounty, Neptune; let my pray'rs
Rather remain ever unheard. Too soon
I lifted cruel hands, believing lips
That may have lied! Ah! What despair may follow!

SCENE 6. THESEUS, THERAMENES

    THES. Theramenes, is 't thou? Where is my son?
I gave him to thy charge from tenderest childhood.
But whence these tears that overflow thine eyes?
How is it with my son?
    THER.   Concern too late!
Affection vain! Hippolytus is dead.
    THES. Gods!
    THER.   I have seen the flow'r of all mankind
Cut off, and I am bold to say that none
Deserv'd it less.
    THES.   What! My son dead! When I
Was stretching out my arms to him, has Heav'n
Hasten'd his end? What was this sudden stroke?   10
    THER. Scarce had we pass'd out of the gates of
        Troezen,
He silent in his chariot, and his guards,
Downcast and silent too, around him ranged;

To the Mycenian road he turn'd his steeds,
Then, lost in thought, allow'd the reins to lie
Loose on their backs. His noble chargers, erst
So full of ardour to obey his voice,
With heads depress'd and melancholy eye
Seem'd now to mark his sadness and to share it.
A frightful cry, that issues from the deep,   20
With sudden discord rends the troubled air;
And from the bosom of the earth a groan
Is heard in answer to that voice of terror.
Our blood is frozen at our very hearts;
With bristling manes the list'ning steeds stand still.
Meanwhile upon the watery plain there rises
A mountain billow with a mighty crest
Of foam, that shoreward rolls, and, as it breaks,
Before our eyes vomits a furious monster.
With formidable horns its brow is arm'd,   30
And all its body cloth'd with yellow scales,
In front a savage bull, behind a dragon
Turning and twisting in impatient rage.
Its long continued bellowings make the shore
Tremble; the sky seems horror-struck to see it;
The earth with terror quakes; its poisonous breath
Infects the air. The wave that brought it ebbs
In fear. All fly, forgetful of the courage
That cannot aid, and in a neighbouring temple
Take refuge—all save bold Hippolytus.   40
A hero's worthy son, he stays his steeds,
Seizes his darts, and, rushing forward, hurls
A missile with sure aim that wounds the monster
Deep in the flank. With rage and pain it springs
E'en to the horses' feet, and, roaring, falls,
Writhes in the dust, and shows a fiery throat
That covers them with flames, and blood, and
        smoke.
Fear lends them wings; deaf to his voice for once;
And heedless of the curb, they onward fly.
Their master wastes his strength in efforts vain;   50
With foam and blood each courser's bit is red.
Some say a god, amid this wild disorder,
Is seen with goads pricking their dusty flanks.
O'er jaggèd rocks they rush, urged on by terror;
Crash! goes the axle-tree. Th' intrepid youth
Sees his car broken up, flying to pieces;
He falls himself entangled in the reins.
Pardon my grief. That cruel spectacle
Will be for me a source of endless tears.
I saw thy hapless son, I saw him, Sire,   60
Dragg'd by the horses that his hands had fed,
Pow'rless to check their fierce career, his voice
But adding to their fright, his body soon
One mass of wounds. Our cries of anguish fill
The plain. At last they slacken their swift pace,

Then stop, not far from those old tombs that mark
Where lie the ashes of his royal sires.
Panting I thither run, and after me
His guard, along the track stain'd with fresh blood
That reddens all the rocks; caught in the briers   70
Locks of his hair hang dripping, gory spoils!
I come, I call him. Stretching forth his hand,
He opes his dying eyes, soon closed again.
"The gods have robb'd me of a guiltless life,"
I hear him say: "Take care of sad Aricia
When I am dead. Dear friend, if e'er my father
Mourn, undeceiv'd, his son's unhappy fate
Falsely accused; to give my spirit peace,
Tell him to treat his captive tenderly,
And to restore—" With that the hero's breath   80
Fails, and a mangled corpse lies in my arms,
A piteous object, trophy of the wrath
Of Heav'n—so chang'd, his father would not know
    him.
    THES. Alas, my son! Dear hope forever lost!
The ruthless gods have served me but too well.
For what a life of anguish and remorse
Am I reserved!
    THER.   Aricia at that instant,
Flying from you, comes timidly, to take him
For husband, there, in presence of the gods.
Thus drawing nigh, she sees the grass all red   90
And reeking, sees (sad sight for lover's eye!)
Hippolytus stretch'd there, pale and disfigured.
But, for a time doubtful of her misfortune,
Unrecogniz'd the hero she adores,
She looks, and asks, "Where is Hippolytus?"
Only too sure at last that he lies there
Before her, with sad eyes that silently
Reproach the gods, she shudders, groans, and falls,
Swooning and all but lifeless, at his feet.
Ismene, all in tears, kneels down beside her,   100
And calls her back to life—life that is naught
But sense of pain. And I, to whom this light
Is darkness now, come to discharge the duty
The hero has imposed on me, to tell thee
His last request—a melancholy task.
But hither comes his mortal enemy.

SCENE 7. THESEUS, PHAEDRA, THERAMENES, PANOPE,
    GUARDS

    THES. Madam you've triumph'd, and my son is
        kill'd!
Ah, but what room have I for fear! How justly
Suspicion racks me that in blaming him
I err'd! But he is dead; accept your victim,
Rightly or wrongly slain. Let your heart leap
For joy. My eyes shall be forever blind.

Since you accuse him, I'll believe him guilty.
His death affords me cause enough for tears,
Without a foolish search for further light
Which, pow'rless to restore him to my grief,   10
Might only serve to make me more unhappy.
Far from this shore and far from you I'll fly,
For here the image of my mangled son
Would haunt my memory and drive me mad.
From the whole world I fain would banish me,
For all the world seems to rise up in judgment
Against me; and my very glory weights
My punishment; for, were my name less known,
'Twere easier to hide me. All the favours
The gods have granted me I mourn and hate,   20
Nor will I importune them with vain pray'rs
Henceforth forever. Give me what they may,
What they have taken will all else outweigh.
    PHA. Theseus, I cannot hear you and keep silence:
I must repair the wrong that he has suffer'd—
Your son was innocent!
    THES.   Unhappy father!
And it was on your word that I condemn'd him!
Think you such cruelty can be excus'd—
    PHA. Moments to me are precious; hear me
        Theseus.
'Twas I who cast an eye of lawless passion   30
On chaste and dutiful Hippolytus.
Heav'n in my bosom kindled baleful fire,
And vile Oenone's cunning did the rest.
She fear'd Hippolytus, knowing my madness,
Would make that passion known which he regarded
With horror; so advantage of my weakness
She took, and hasten'd to accuse him first.
For that she has been punish'd, tho' too mildly;
Seeking to shun my wrath, she cast herself
Beneath the waves. The sword ere now had cut   40
My thread of life, but slander'd innocence
Made its cry heard, and I resolv'd to die
In a more lingering way, confessing first
My penitence to you. A poison, brought
To Athens by Medea, runs thro' my veins.
Already in my heart the venom works,
Infusing there a strange and fatal chill;
Already as thro' thickening mists I see
The spouse to whom my presence is an outrage.
Death, from mine eyes veiling the light of heav'n,   50
Restores its purity that they defiled.
    PAN. She dies, my lord!
    THES.   Would that the memory
Of her disgraceful deed could perish with her!
Ah, disabused too late! Come, let us go,
And with the blood of mine unhappy son
Mingle our tears, clasping his dear remains,

In deep repentance for a pray'r detested.
Let him be honour'd as he well deserves;
And, to appease his sore offended ghost,
Be her near kinsmen's guilt whate'er it may,   60
Aricia shall be held my daughter from today!

———◆———

MOLIÈRE

1622–1673

Jean Baptiste Poquelin, known as Molière, was the celebrated writer of comedy during the Golden Age of French Literature. Son of a Parisian upholsterer, he occupies a pre-eminent place not only in French but also in world literature. His was a universal genius which rose above the limits of time and place. His work consequently has always been as pleasing to English-speaking audiences as to French. Molière was a realist in the strictly classical sense, highly selective in his subject matter and dealing in generalizations which are valid for all time because they concern fundamental human nature. His work has the incompleteness and imperfections which are totally lacking in that of Racine. He has no hesitation in using language to fit his character, in spite of the law of unity of tone, and we find in his work the wildest buffoonery of the farce together with the subtlest wit and cutting satire of the sophisticated comedy of manners. Molière did not have Racine's mastery of form, and probably did not desire to have it. He was careless, throwing his work together in a most perfunctory fashion. His language and style have many faults, but his work contains a note of humanity that has never been surpassed.

Molière lived and died a professional entertainer, always managing his troop of actors and taking, himself, the leading role. His life was a constant struggle against numerous enemies who were motivated largely by jealousy, and against the frivolity of his beautiful young actress wife whom he adored. Unfortunately he did not live long enough to reap the rewards of his work, for he died at the age of fifty-one, immediately after a performance in the title role of the *Imaginary Invalid*.

Molière raised French comedy to the dignity of a serious literary genre. His material is rich and varied, drawn from the failings and foibles of all mankind. Portrayal of character rather than incident is the thing to look for in the plays of Molière, for the action is intended to heighten the impression produced by the character. Ordinarily he was highly successful in going straight to the essential qualities of the type of person he was portraying, and the result is unforgettable in its vividness.

Molière's genius probably reaches its height in *The Misanthrope* (1666). The plot incidents are few and unimportant, yet we understand completely the people portrayed. Alceste is rather a sensitive man than a misanthrope, for he, of the group of frivolous ladies and gentlemen, is the only one capable of true feeling. Only he really knows love and suffering; only he has understanding. The character of Alceste may be at least partly a portrayal of Molière himself. Alceste's disillusionment is occasioned by the unfashionableness of "plain-dealing" in social intercourse; in this respect his plight reminds us how closely high and serious comedy may come to tragic implication.

FURTHER READING

ASHTON, H. *Molière* (New York, 1930).
CHAPMAN, P. A. *The Spirit of Molière* (Princeton, 1940).
CHATFIELD-TAYLOR, H. C. *Molière, a Biography* (New York, 1906).
DOUMIC, R. *Le Misanthrope de Molière, étude et analyse* (Paris, 1945).
TURNELL, M. *The Classical Moment* (New York, 1946).

———◆———

The Misanthrope *

(LE MISANTHROPE)

DRAMATIS PERSONAE

ALCESTE, *in love with Célimène*
PHILINTE, *his friend*
ORONTE, *in love with Célimène*
CÉLIMÈNE, *beloved by Alceste*
ÉLIANTE, *her cousin*
ARSINOÉ, *Célimène's friend*
ACASTE, *marquis*

* Original translation by Henri van Laun, revised by the editors.

CLITANDRE, *marquis*
BASQUE, *servant to Célimène*
DUBOIS, *servant to Alceste*
AN OFFICER OF THE MARÉCHAUSSÉE

SCENE—*At Paris, in* CÉLIMÈNE'S *house.*

ACT I

SCENE I. PHILINTE, ALCESTE

PHILINTE. What is the matter? What ails you?

ALCESTE (*seated*). Leave me, I pray.

PHILINTE. But, once more, tell me what strange whim . . .

ALCESTE. Leave me, I tell you, and get out of my sight.

PHILINTE. But you might at least listen to people without getting angry.

ALCESTE. I choose to get angry, and I do not choose to listen.

PHILINTE. I do not understand you in these abrupt moods, and although we are friends, I am the first . . .

ALCESTE (*rising quickly*). I, your friend? Take my name off your list. I have until now professed to be so; but after what I have just seen of you, I tell you candidly that I am such no longer; I have no wish to occupy a place in a corrupt heart.

PHILINTE. I am then very much to be blamed from your point of view, Alceste?

ALCESTE. To be blamed? You ought to die from very shame; there is no excuse for such behavior, and every man of honor must be disgusted at it. I see you almost smother a man with caresses, show him the most ardent affection, and overwhelm him with protestations, offers and vows of friendship, and when I ask you who that man is, you can scarcely tell me his name; your feelings for him, the moment you have turned your back, suddenly cool; you speak of him most indifferently to me. Hang it! I call it unworthy, base, and infamous, so far to lower one's self as to act contrary to one's own feelings. If, by some mischance, I had done such a thing, I should hang myself at once out of sheer vexation.

PHILINTE. I do not see that it is a hanging matter at all; and I beg of you not to think it amiss if I ask you to show me some mercy and not to hang me, if it is all the same to you.

ALCESTE. That is a sorry joke.

PHILINTE. But, seriously, what would you have people do?

ALCESTE. I would have people be sincere and, like honorable men, speak no word which does not come from the heart.

PHILINTE. When a man comes and embraces you joyously, you must pay him back in his own coin, respond as best you can to his show of feeling, and return offer for offer, and vow for vow.

ALCESTE. Not so. I cannot bear such a base method as your fashionable people generally affect; there is nothing I detest so much as the contortions of those great time and lip servers, those affable dispensers of meaningless embraces, those obliging utterers of empty words, who view every one in civilities, and treat the man of worth and the fop alike. What good does it do if a man heaps endearments on you, vows that he is your friend, that he believes in you, is full of zeal for you, esteems and loves you, and lauds you to the skies, when he rushes to do the same to the first rascal he meets? No, no; no heart with the least self-respect cares for esteem so prostituted; he will hardly relish it, even when openly expressed, when he finds that he shares it with the whole universe. Preference must be based on esteem, and to esteem every one is to esteem no one. Since you abandon yourself to the vices of the times, heavens above! you are not the man for me. I decline this over-complacent kindness, which uses no discrimination. I like to be distinguished; and, to make matters short, the friend of all mankind is no friend of mine.

PHILINTE. But when we are in high society, we must conform to the outward civilities which custom demands.

ALCESTE. I deny it. We ought to punish pitilessly that shameful pretence of friendship. I like a man to be a man, and to show on all occasions the bottom of his heart in his discourse. Let that be the thing to speak, and never let our feelings be hidden beneath vain compliments.

PHILINTE. There are many cases in which plain speaking would be ridiculous, and intolerable. And, with all due allowance for your unbending honesty, it is as well to conceal your feelings sometimes. Would it be right or fitting to tell thousands of people what we think of them? And when we meet with some one whom we hate or who displeases us, must we tell him so openly?

ALCESTE. Yes.

PHILINTE. What! Would you tell old Emilia that it ill becomes her to play the coquette at her age, and that the paint she uses disgusts everyone?

ALCESTE. Undoubtedly.

PHILINTE. Or Dorilas, that he is a bore, and that there is no one at court who is not sick of hearing him boast of his courage, and the lustre of his family?

ALCESTE. Certainly.

PHILINTE. You are joking.

ALCESTE. I am not joking at all, and I would not spare any one in that respect. It offends my eyes too much; and whether at Court or in town, I behold nothing that does not provoke my anger. I become quite melancholy and grieved to see men behave to each other as they do. Everywhere I find nothing but base flattery, injustice, selfishness, deceit, roguery. I can not bear it any longer; I am furious; and my intention is to break with all mankind.

PHILINTE. This philosophical irritability is somewhat too savage. I can not help laughing to see you in these gloomy fits, and I fancy that I perceive in us two, brought up together, the two brothers described in *The School for Husbands*, who . . .

ALCESTE. Good Heavens! drop your insipid comparisons.

PHILINTE. Nay, seriously, leave off those violent outbursts. The world is not going to change for all your meddling. And as plain speaking has such charms for you, I shall tell you frankly that this ill humor of yours is as good as a play wherever you go, and that such anger against the manners of the age make you a laughing stock to many people.

ALCESTE. So much the better, damn it! so much the better. That is just what I want. It is a very good sign, and I rejoice in it. All men are so odious to me, that I should be sorry to appear rational in their eyes.

PHILINTE. But do you wish harm to all mankind?

ALCESTE. Yes. I have conceived a terrible hatred for them.

PHILINTE. Shall all poor mortals, without exception, be included in this aversion? There are some, even in the age in which we live . . .

ALCESTE. No, they are all alike, and I hate all men: some, because they are wicked and maleficent; others because they are complacent toward the wicked, and have not that healthy contempt with which vice ought to inspire all virtuous minds. You can see how unjustly and excessively complacent people are to that bare-faced scoundrel with whom I am at law. You may plainly perceive the traitor through his mask; and he is well known everywhere in his true colors. His rolling eyes and his honeyed tones fool only those who do not know him. People are aware that this low-bred fellow who deserves to be pilloried has made his way in the world only by the dirtiest intrigues. The splendid position

he has acquired makes merit groan and virtue blush. Yet whatever dishonorable epithets may be launched against him everywhere, nobody defends his wretched honor. Call him a rogue, an infamous wretch, a damned scoundrel if you like: all the world will say "yea," and no one will contradict you. But for all that, his bowing and scraping are welcome everywhere. He is received, smiled upon. He insinuates himself into all kinds of society, and, if any appointment is to be secured by intriguing, he will carry the day over a man of the greatest worth. Good heavens! these are mortal stabs to me, to see vice tolerated; and sometimes I feel suddenly inclined to fly into a wilderness far from the approach of men.

PHILINTE. Great heavens! let us torment ourselves a little less about the vices of the age, and be a little more lenient to human nature. Let us not scrutinize it with the utmost severity, but look with some indulgence at its failings. In society we need virtue to be more pliable. If we are too wise, we may be equally to blame. Good sense avoids all extremes, and requires us to be soberly rational. This unbending and virtuous stiffness of ancient times shocks too much the ordinary customs of our own. It requires too great perfection from us mortals. We must yield to the times without being too stubborn. It is the height of folly to busy ourselves in correcting the world. Both of us notice a thousand things every day which might be better managed, but whatever I may discover at any moment, people do not see me in a rage like you. I take men quietly just as they are; I accustom my mind to bear with what they do; and I believe that at Court, as well as in the city, my phlegm is as philosophical as your bile.

ALCESTE. But this phlegm, good sir, you who reason so well, could it not be disturbed by anything? And if perchance a friend should betray you, if he forms a subtle plot to get hold of what is yours, if people should try to spread evil reports about you, would you tamely submit to all this without flying into a rage?

PHILINTE. Yes. I look upon all these faults of which you complain as vices inseparably connected with human nature. In short, my mind is no more shocked at seeing a man a rogue, unjust, or selfish, than at seeing vultures eager for prey, mischievous apes, or raging wolves.

ALCESTE. What! I should see myself deceived, torn to pieces, robbed, without being . . . Heavens! I shall say no more about it. All this reasoning is beside the point!

PHILINTE. Upon my word, you would do well to keep silence. Rail a little less at your opponent, and attend a little more to your suit.

ALCESTE. That I shall not do; that was settled long ago.

PHILINTE. But whom then do you expect to represent you?

ALCESTE. Whom? Reason, my just right, equity.

PHILINTE. Aren't you going to visit any of the judges?

ALCESTE. No. Is my cause unjust or doubtful?

PHILINTE. I am agreed on that, but you know what harm intrigues do, and . . .

ALCESTE. No. I am resolved not to stir a step. I am either right or wrong.

PHILINTE. Do not trust to that.

ALCESTE. I shall not budge an inch.

PHILINTE. Your opponent is powerful, and by his underhand work, may induce . . .

ALCESTE. It does not matter.

PHILINTE. You will be making a mistake.

ALCESTE. Be it so. I wish to see the end of it.

PHILINTE. But . . .

ALCESTE. I shall have the satisfaction of losing my suit.

PHILINTE. But after all . . .

ALCESTE. I shall see by this trial whether men have sufficient impudence, are wicked, villainous, and perverse enough to do me this injustice in the face of the whole world.

PHILINTE. What a strange fellow!

ALCESTE. I could wish, were it to cost me ever so much, that, for the fun of the thing, I lost my case.

PHILINTE. But people will really laugh at you, Alceste, if they hear you go on in this fashion.

ALCESTE. So much the worse for those who will.

PHILINTE. But this uprightness which you exact so carefully in every case, this absolute integrity in which you entrench yourself, do you perceive it in the lady you love? As for me, I am astonished that, appearing to be at war, as you are, with the whole human race, you have chosen from it the person who pleases you most. And what surprises me still more is the strange choice your heart has made. The sincere Éliante has a liking for you, the prude Arsinoé gives you soulful looks, yet your heart does not respond to their passion: you wear the chains of Célimène, who sports with you and whose coquettish humor and malicious wit seems to accord so well with the manner of the times. How does it happen that, hating these things as mortally as you do, you stand so much of them in that lady? Are they no longer faults in so sweet a charmer? Don't you perceive them, or, if you do, do you excuse them?

ALCESTE. Not at all. The love I feel for this young widow does not make me blind to her faults, and, notwithstanding the great passion which she has inspired in me, I am the first to see, as well as to condemn, them. But for all this, do what I will, I confess my weakness: she has the art of pleasing me. In vain I see her faults—I may even blame them, but in spite of all, she makes me love her. Her charms conquer everything. No doubt my sincere love will purify her heart of the vices of our times.

PHILINTE. If you accomplish that, it will be no small achievement. Do you think she loves you?

ALCESTE. Yes, certainly! I would not love her at all if I did not think so.

PHILINTE. But if her love for you is so apparent, how does it happen that your rivals cause you so much uneasiness?

ALCESTE. It is because a heart, deeply smitten, claims all to itself. I come here only with the intention of telling her what my feelings dictate on this subject.

PHILINTE. If I had only to consult my wishes, her cousin Éliante would have all my love. Her heart, which values yours, is stable and sincere; and this more compatible choice would have suited you better.

ALCESTE. That is true—my good sense tells me so every day, but good sense does not always rule love.

PHILINTE. Well, I fear greatly for your affections, and the hope which you cherish may perhaps . . .

SCENE II. ORONTE, ALCESTE, PHILINTE

ORONTE (to ALCESTE). I have been informed yonder that Éliante and Célimène have gone shopping. But as I heard that you were here, I came to tell you most sincerely that I have conceived a boundless regard for you, and that for a long time this regard has inspired me with the most ardent wish to be reckoned among your friends. Yes, I like to do homage to merit, and I am most eager that a bond of friendship should unite us. I suppose that a zealous friend, and one of my standing, is not altogether to be rejected. (All this time ALCESTE has been musing, and seems not to be aware that ORONTE is addressing him. He looks up only when ORONTE says to him)—It is to you, if you please, that this speech is addressed.

ALCESTE. To me, sir?

ORONTE. To you. Is it in any way offensive to you?

ALCESTE. Not in the least. But my surprise is very great; and I did not expect that honor.

ORONTE. The esteem in which I hold you ought not to astonish you: you can claim just as much from everybody.

ALCESTE. Sir . . .

ORONTE. Our whole kingdom contains nothing above the dazzling merit which people discover in you.

ALCESTE. Sir . . .

ORONTE. Yes. For my part, I prefer you to the most important person in it.

ALCESTE. Sir . . .

ORONTE. May Heaven strike me dead, if I lie! And, to convince you on this very spot of my feelings, allow me, sir, to embrace you with all my heart, and to solicit a place in your friendship. Your hand, if you please. Will you promise me your friendship?

ALCESTE. Sir . . .

ORONTE. What! you refuse me?

ALCESTE. Sir, you do me too much honor. But friendship is a sacred thing, and to lavish it on every occasion is surely to profane it. Judgment and choice should preside at such a compact. We ought to know more of each other before engaging ourselves, and it may happen that our dispositions are such that we may both of us repent of our bargain.

ORONTE. Upon my word! that is wisely said, and I esteem you all the more for it. Let us therefore leave it to time to form such a pleasing bond, but meanwhile, I am entirely at your disposal. If you have any business at Court, everyone knows how well I stand with the King. I have his private ear, and, upon my word, he treats me in everything with the utmost intimacy. In short, I am yours in every emergency, and, as you are a man of brilliant parts, and to inaugurate our charming amity, I have come to read you a sonnet which I wrote a little while ago, and to find out whether it is good enough for publication.

ALCESTE. I am not fit, sir, to decide such a matter. You will therefore excuse me.

ORONTE. Why so?

ALCESTE. I have the failing of being a little more sincere in those things than is necessary.

ORONTE. The very thing I ask. And I would have reason to complain if you should deceive me and disguise anything from me after I have risked asking your frank opinion.

ALCESTE. If that is the case, sir, I am perfectly willing.

ORONTE. *Sonnet* . . . It is a sonnet . . . *Hope* . . . It is to a lady who flattered my passion with some hope. *Hope* . . . They are not long, pompous verses, but sweet, tender and melting little lines. (*At every one of these interruptions he looks at* ALCESTE.)

ALCESTE. We shall see.

ORONTE. *Hope* . . . I do not know whether the style will strike you as sufficiently clear and easy, and whether you will approve of my choice of words.

ALCESTE. We shall soon see, sir.

ORONTE. Besides, you must know that I was only a quarter of an hour in composing it.

ALCESTE. Let us hear, sir. The time means nothing.

ORONTE (*reads*).   *Hope, it is true, oft gives relief,*
　　　　　　　　Rocks for a while our tedious
　　　　　　　　　　pain,
　　　　　　　　But what a poor advantage,
　　　　　　　　　　Phillis,
　　　　　　　　When nought remains, and all
　　　　　　　　　　is gone!

PHILINTE. I am already charmed with this little bit.

ALCESTE (*softly to* PHILINTE). What! do you mean to tell me that you like that stuff?

ORONTE.   *You once showed some complacence,*
　　　　　　But less would have sufficed,
　　　　　　You should not take that trouble
　　　　　　To give me nought but hope.

PHILINTE. In what pretty terms these thoughts are put!

ALCESTE. What! you vile flatterer, you praise that rubbish!

ORONTE.   *If I must wait eternally,*
　　　　　　My passion, driven to extremes,
　　　　　　Will fly to death.
　　　　　　Your tender cares cannot prevent this,
　　　　　　Fair Phillis, aye we're in despair,
　　　　　　When we must hope for ever.

PHILINTE. The conclusion is pretty, amorous, admirable.

ALCESTE (*softly, and aside to* PHILINTE). A plague on the conclusion! I wish you had concluded to break your neck, you devilish poisoner!

PHILINTE. I have never heard verses more skilfully turned.

ALCESTE (*softly, and aside*). Gad! . . .

ORONTE (*to* PHILINTE). You flatter me, and you are under the impression perhaps . . .

PHILINTE. No, I am not flattering at all.

ALCESTE (*softly, and aside*). What else are you doing, you wretch?

ORONTE (*to* ALCESTE). But for you, you know our agreement. Speak to me, I pray, in all sincerity.

ALCESTE. These matters, Sir, are always more or less delicate, and every one is fond of being praised for his wit. But I was saying one day to a certain person, who shall be nameless, when he showed me some of his verses, that a gentleman ought at all times to exercise a great control over that itch for writing which sometimes attacks us, and should keep a tight rein over the strong propensity which people have for taking part in such amusements, and that, in the frequent eagerness to show their productions people frequently expose themselves to acting very foolishly.

ORONTE. Do you wish to convey to me by this that I am wrong in desiring . . .

ALCESTE. I do not say that exactly. But I told him that writing without warmth is a bore, that only this weakness is needed to bring disgrace on a man, that we view people from their worst sides even if they have a great many good qualities.

ORONTE. Do you find anything objectionable in my sonnet?

ALCESTE. I do not say that. But, to keep him from writing I showed him how, nowadays, the desire to do so has spoiled a great many very worthy people.

ORONTE. Do I write badly? Am I like them in any way?

ALCESTE. I do not say that. But I said to him in short: Who in the devil drives you into print? If we can pardon the sending into the world of a badly written book, it will be only in those unfortunate men who write for their livelihood. Believe me, resist your temptations, keep these effusions from the public, and do not, however much you may be asked, forfeit the reputation which you enjoy at court of being a man of sense and a gentleman in order to take from the hands of a greedy printer the reputation of being a ridiculous and wretched author. That is what I tried to make him understand.

ORONTE. This is all well and good, and I seem to understand you. But I should like to know what there is in my sonnet to . . .

ALCESTE. Candidly, you had better put it in your desk and leave it there. You have been following bad models, and your expressions are not at all natural. Pray what is—*Rocks for a while our tedious pain?* And what, *When nought remains, and all is gone?* What, *You should not take that trouble to give me nought but hope?* And what, *Phillis, aye we're in despair when we must hope for ever?* This figurative style, that people are so vain of, is beside all good taste and truth; it is only a play upon words, sheer affectation, and it is not thus that nature speaks. The wretched taste of the age is what I dislike in this. Our forefathers, unpolished as they were, had a much better one; and I value all that is admired nowadays far less than an old song which I am going to repeat to you:

> *"Had our great monarch granted me*
> *His Paris large and fair;*
> *And I straightway must quit for aye*
> *The love of my true dear;*
> *Then would I say, King Hal, I pray,*
> *Take back your Paris fair,*
> *I love much mo my dear, I trow,*
> *I love much mo my dear."*

This versification is not rich, and the style is antiquated; but do you not see that it is far better than all those trumpery trifles against which good sense revolts, and that in this, passion speaks from the heart?

> *"Had our great monarch granted me*
> *His Paris large and fair;*
> *And I straightway must quit for aye*
> *The love of my true dear;*
> *Then would I say, King Hal, I pray,*
> *Take back your Paris fair,*
> *I love much mo my dear, I trow,*
> *I love much mo my dear."*

This is what a really loving heart would say. (*To* PHILINTE, *who is laughing*.) Yes, master wag, in spite of all your wit, I care more for this than for all the florid pomp and the tinsel which everybody is admiring nowadays.

ORONTE. And I, I maintain that my verses are very good.

ALCESTE. Doubtless you have your reasons for thinking them so; but you will allow me to have mine, which, with your permission, will remain independent.

ORONTE. It is enough for me that others prize them.

ALCESTE. That is because they know how to dissemble, which I do not.

ORONTE. Do you really believe that you have such a great share of wit?

ALCESTE. If I praised your verses, I should have more.

ORONTE. I shall do very well without your approval.

ALCESTE. You will have to do without it, if it is all the same to you.

ORONTE. I should very much like to see you compose some on the same subject, just to have a sample of your style.

ALCESTE. I might happen to make some just as bad,—but I should take good care not to show them to anyone.

ORONTE. You are mighty positive, and this great sufficiency . . .

ALCESTE. Please seek someone else to flatter you, and not me.

ORONTE. But, my little Sir, drop that haughty tone.

ALCESTE. In truth, my big Sir, I shall do as I like.

PHILINTE (*coming between them*). Stop, gentlemen! That is carrying the matter too far. Cease, I pray.

ORONTE. Ah! I am wrong, I confess; and I leave the field to you. I am your servant, Sir, most heartily.

ALCESTE. And I, Sir, am your most humble servant.

SCENE III. PHILINTE, ALCESTE

PHILINTE. Well! you see. By being too sincere, you have got a nice affair on your hands; I saw that Oronte, in order to be flattered . . .

ALCESTE. Do not talk to me.

PHILINTE. But . . .

ALCESTE. No more society for me.

PHILINTE. Is it too much . . .

ALCESTE. Leave me alone.

PHILINTE. If I . . .

ALCESTE. Not another word.

PHILINTE. But what . . .

ALCESTE. I will hear no more.

PHILINTE. But . . .

ALCESTE. Again?

PHILINTE. People insult . . .

ALCESTE. Ah! Gad! this is too much. Do not dog my steps.

PHILINTE. You are making fun of me; I shall not leave you.

ACT II

SCENE I. ALCESTE, CÉLIMÈNE

ALCESTE. Will you let me speak candidly to you, madam? Well, then, I am very much dissatisfied with your behavior. I am very angry when I think about it, and I perceive that we shall have to break with each other. Yes, I should only deceive you were I to speak otherwise. Sooner or later we will undoubtedly break, and if I were to promise the contrary a thousand times, I should not be able to bear all of this any longer.

CÉLIMÈNE. Oh, I see! it is to quarrel with me that you wished to conduct me home?

ALCESTE. I am not quarreling. But your disposition, madam, is too ready to give the first comer an entrance into your heart. Too many admirers are besieging you, and my temper can not put up with that.

CÉLIMÈNE. Am I to blame for having too many admirers? Can I prevent people from thinking me attractive? Am I to take a stick to drive them away every time they try so sweetly to visit me?

ALCESTE. No, madam, there is no need for a stick, but only a heart less yielding and less melting at their love-tales. I am aware that your good looks accompany you wherever you go. But your reception retains those whom your eyes attract, and that gentleness, accorded to those who surrender their arms, finishes on their hearts the sway which your charms began. The too agreeable expectation which you offer them increases their assiduities towards you; and your complacency, a little less extended, would drive away the great crowd of so many admirers. But, tell me, at least, madam, by what good fortune Clitandre has the happiness of pleasing you so mightily? Upon what basis of merit and sublime virtue do you ground the honor of your regard for him? Is it by the long nail on his little finger that he has acquired the esteem which you display for him? Are you, like all the rest of the fashionable world, fascinated by the dazzling merit of his fair wig? Do his fashionable hose make you love him? Do his many ribbons charm you? Is it by the attraction of his great German breeches that he has conquered your heart, while at the same time he pretended to be your slave? Or have his manner of smiling, and his falsetto voice found out the secret of stimulating your emotions?

CÉLIMÈNE. How unjustly you take umbrage at him! Do you not know why I countenance him? He has promised to interest all his friends in my lawsuit.

ALCESTE. Lose your lawsuit, madam, with patience, and do not countenance a rival whom I detest.

CÉLIMÈNE. But you are getting jealous of the whole world.

ALCESTE. It is because the whole world is so kindly received by you.

MOLIÈRE

CÉLIMÈNE. That is the very thing to calm your frightened mind. Because my goodwill is given to everybody, you would have more reason to be offended if you saw me entirely occupied by one.

ALCESTE. But as for me, whom you accuse of too much jealousy, what have I more than any of them, madam, pray?

CÉLIMÈNE. The happiness of knowing that you are beloved.

ALCESTE. And what grounds has my love-sick heart for believing it?

CÉLIMÈNE. I think that, as I have taken the trouble to tell you so, such a declaration ought to satisfy you.

ALCESTE. But who will assure me that you may not, at the same time, say as much to everybody else perhaps?

CÉLIMÈNE. Certainly for a lover that is a pretty amorous speech, and you make me out a very nice lady. Well! to remove such a suspicion, I retract this moment everything I have said; and no one but yourself shall for the future impose upon you. Will that satisfy you?

ALCESTE. Gad! why do I love you so! Ah! if ever I get heart-whole out of your hands, I shall bless Heaven for that rare good fortune. I make no secret of it: I am doing all that I can to tear this unfortunate attachment from my heart. Hitherto my greatest efforts have been of no avail, and it is for my sins that I love you thus.

CÉLIMÈNE. It is very true that your affection for me is unequalled.

ALCESTE. As for that, I can challenge the whole world. No one can conceive of my love for you. Never, madam, has any man loved as I do.

CÉLIMÈNE. Your method, however, is entirely new, for you love people only to quarrel with them. It is in peevish expressions alone that you express your love. No one ever saw such a grumbling swain.

ALCESTE. But it lies with you alone to dissipate this ill-humor. For mercy's sake, let's make an end of all this bickering, deal openly with each other, and try to put a stop . . .

SCENE II. CÉLIMÈNE, ALCESTE, BASQUE

CÉLIMÈNE. What is the matter?
BASQUE. Acaste is below.
CÉLIMÈNE. Very well! have him come up.

SCENE III. CÉLIMÈNE, ALCESTE

ALCESTE. What! can one never have a little private conversation with you? You are always ready to receive company. You can not for a single instant make up your mind to be "not at home."

CÉLIMÈNE. Do you wish me to quarrel with Acaste?

ALCESTE. You have such regard for people, which I by no means like.

CÉLIMÈNE. He is a man who would never forgive me if he knew that his presence might annoy me.

ALCESTE. And what is it to you, to inconvenience yourself so . . .

CÉLIMÈNE. But, Heavens above! the good will of such people is important. They are a kind of people who in some way or other have acquired the right to be heard at Court. They take their part in every conversation. They can do you no good, but they may do you harm, and whatever support one may find elsewhere, it will never do to be on bad terms with these big talkers.

ALCESTE. In short, whatever people may say or do, you always find reasons to bear with every one of them; and your very careful judgment . . .

SCENE IV. ALCESTE, CÉLIMÈNE, BASQUE

BASQUE. Clitandre is here too, madam.
ALCESTE. Exactly so. (*Wishes to go.*)
CÉLIMÈNE. Where are you running to?
ALCESTE. I am going.
CÉLIMÈNE. Stay.
ALCESTE. For what?
CÉLIMÈNE. Stay.
ALCESTE. I cannot.
CÉLIMÈNE. I wish it.
ALCESTE. I will not. These conversations only weary me; and it is too bad of you to wish me to endure them.
CÉLIMÈNE. I wish it, I wish it.
ALCESTE. No, it is impossible.
CÉLIMÈNE. Very well, then. Go, begone. You can do as you like.

SCENE V. ÉLIANTE, PHILINTE, ACASTE, CLITANDRE, ALCESTE, CÉLIMÈNE, BASQUE

ÉLIANTE (*to* CÉLIMÈNE). Here are the two marquises coming up with us. Has anyone told you?

CÉLIMÈNE. Yes. (*To* BASQUE.) Place chairs for everyone. (BASQUE *places chairs and goes out.*) (*To* ALCESTE.) You are not gone?

ALCESTE. No; but I am determined, madam, to have you make up your mind either for them or for me.

CÉLIMÈNE. Hold your tongue.

ALCESTE. This very day you shall explain yourself.

CÉLIMÈNE. You are losing your senses.

ALCESTE. Not at all. You shall declare yourself.

CÉLIMÈNE. Indeed!

ALCESTE. You must take your stand.

CÉLIMÈNE. You are joking, I believe.

ALCESTE. Not so. But you must choose. I have been too patient.

CLITANDRE. Gad! I have just come from the Louvre where Cléonte, at the levee, made himself very ridiculous. Has he not some friend who could charitably enlighten him upon his manners?

CÉLIMÈNE. To tell the truth, he compromises himself a great deal in society. Everywhere he carries himself with an air that is noticed at first sight, and when after a short absence you meet him again, he is still more absurd than ever.

ACASTE. What! Talk of absurd people, I have just now endured one of the most tedious ones: that contentious Damon kept me, if you please, for a full hour in the broiling sun away from my sedan chair.

CÉLIMÈNE. He is a strange talker, and one who always finds the means of telling you nothing with a great flow of words. There is no sense at all in his tittle-tattle, and all that we hear is nothing but noise.

ÉLIANTE (to PHILINTE). This beginning is not bad. The conversation is taking a sufficiently agreeable turn against our neighbors.

CLITANDRE. Timante, too, Madam, is another original.

CÉLIMÈNE. He is a complete mystery from top to bottom. He is a man who casts upon you as you pass a bewildered glance, who is always busy without having anything to do. Whatever he says is accompanied by grimaces. He stuns people with his mannerisms. To interrupt a conversation, he always has a secret to whisper to you, and that secret turns out to be nothing. Of the merest molehill he makes a mountain, and whispers everything in your ear, even to a "good morning."

ACASTE. And Géralde, Madam?

CÉLIMÈNE. That tiresome story-teller! He never comes down from his nobleman's pedestal. He continually mixes with the best society, and never quotes any one of lower rank than a duke, prince or princess. Rank is his hobby, and his conversation is of nothing but horses, carriages, and dogs. He *thee's* and *thou's* persons of the highest standing, and the word *Sir* is quite obsolete with him.

CLITANDRE. It is said that he is on the best of terms with Bélise.

CÉLIMÈNE. Poor silly woman, and the dreariest company! When she comes to visit me, I suffer martyrdom. One has to rack one's brain perpetually to find out what to say to her; and the sterility of her expression is always killing the conversation. In vain do you try to overcome her stupid silence by talking about the most commonplace topics. Even the fine weather, the rain, the heat and the cold are subjects which, with her, are soon exhausted. Yet for all that, her calls, which are unbearable enough, are prolonged to an insufferable length; and you may consult the clock or yawn twenty times: she stirs no more than a log of wood.

ACASTE. What do you think of Adraste?

CÉLIMÈNE. Oh! What excessive pride! He is a man positively puffed up with conceit. His self-importance is never satisfied with the Court, against which he inveighs daily. And whenever an office, a position, or a living is bestowed on another, he is sure to think himself unjustly treated.

CLITANDRE. But young Cléon, whom the most respectable people go to see, what do you say of him?

CÉLIMÈNE. That it is to his cook that he owes his distinction and to his table that people pay visits.

ÉLIANTE. He takes pains to provide the most dainty dishes.

CÉLIMÈNE. True; but I should be very glad if he would not dish up himself. His foolish person is a very bad dish which, to my thinking, spoils every entertainment which he gives.

PHILINTE. His uncle Damis is very much esteemed; what do you say about him, Madam?

CÉLIMÈNE. He is one of my friends.

PHILINTE. I think him a perfect gentleman and quite sensible.

CÉLIMÈNE. True, but he pretends to too much wit, which annoys me. He is always upon stilts, and, in all his conversations, one sees him laboring to say smart things. Since he took it into his head to be clever, he is so difficult to please that nothing suits him. He tries to find mistakes in everything that one writes, and thinks that to bestow praise does not become a wit, that to find fault shows learning, that only fools admire and laugh, and that, by not approving of anything in the works of our time, he is superior to all other people. Even in conversations he finds something to cavil at, the subjects are too trivial for him to condescend to them; and, with arms crossed on his breast, he looks down from the height of his intellect with pity on what everyone says.

ACASTE. Damn it! That's a perfect picture of him.

CLITANDRE (*to* CÉLIMÈNE). You have an admirable knack of portraying people to the life.

ALCESTE. Excellent! Go on, my fine courtly friends. You spare no one, and everyone will have his turn. Nevertheless, let but any one of those persons appear, and we shall see you rush to meet him, offer him your hand, and, with a flattering kiss, give weight to your protestations of being his servant.

CLITANDRE. Why blame us? If what is said offends you, the reproach must be addressed to this lady.

ALCESTE. No, by Heaven! it concerns you, for your assenting smiles draw from her wit all these slanderous remarks. Her satirical vein is incessantly fed by your false flattery; and her mind would find fewer charms in raillery if she discovered that no one applauded her. Thus it is that to flatterers we ought everywhere to impute the vices which are sown among mankind.

PHILINTE. But why do you take so great an interest in those people? You would condemn the very things that are blamed in them.

CÉLIMÈNE. And is not this gentleman bound to contradict? Would you have him subscribe to the general opinion? Must he not everywhere display the spirit of contradiction with which Heaven has endowed him? Other people's sentiments can never please him. He always supports a contrary idea, and he would think himself too much of the common herd if he were observed to be of any one's opinion but his own. The honor of contradicting has so many charms for him, that he very often takes up arms against himself. He combats his own sentiments as soon as he hears them from other folks' lips.

ALCESTE. In short, madam, the laughers are on your side; and you may launch your satire against me.

PHILINTE. But it is very true, too, that you always take up arms against everything that is said, and that your avowed malice can not bear people to be praised or blamed.

ALCESTE. Malice against mankind is always seasonable, because man is never in the right. I see that, in all their dealings, they either praise impertinently or censure rashly.

CÉLIMÈNE. But . . .

ALCESTE. No, madam, no. Though I were to die

for saying so, you have pastimes which I can not tolerate. People are very wrong to encourage in you that great attachment to the very faults which they blame in you.

CLITANDRE. As for myself, I do not know, but I openly acknowledge that hitherto I have thought this lady faultless.

ACASTE. I see that she is endowed with charms and attractions. The faults which she has have not struck me.

ALCESTE. They have struck me all the more. Far from my denying them, she knows that I take care to reproach her with them. The more we love anyone, the less we ought to flatter her. True love shows itself by overlooking nothing. If I were a lady, I would banish all those mean-spirited lovers who agree with everything I say and whose mild complacencies encourage at every moment my vagaries.

CÉLIMÈNE. In short, if love were governed by you, we, in order to love well, would have to relinquish all tenderness and make it the highest aim of perfect attachment to insult the persons we love.

ÉLIANTE. Love, generally speaking, is not very apt to accept those decrees, and lovers are always observed to extol their choice. Their passion never sees anything to blame, and in the beloved all things become loveable. They think their sweetheart's faults are perfections, and they invent sweet terms to call them by. The pale one vies with the jasmine in fairness; another, dark enough to frighten people, becomes an adorable brunette; the lean one has a good shape and is lithe; the stout one has a portly and majestic bearing; the slattern, who has few charms, passes under the name of a careless beauty; the giantess seems a very goddess in their sight; the dwarf is an epitome of all the wonders of Heaven; the proud one has a soul worthy of a diadem; the artful brims with wit; the silly one is good-natured; the chatter-box is good-tempered; and the silent one modest and reticent. Thus a passionate swain loves even the very faults of those of whom he is enamored.

ALCESTE. And I maintain that . . .

CÉLIMÈNE. Let us drop the subject, and take a turn or two in the gallery. What! are you going, gentlemen?

CLITANDRE *and* ACASTE. No, no, madam.

ALCESTE. The fear that they will depart troubles you very much. Go when you like, gentlemen, but I tell you beforehand that I shall not leave until you leave.

ACASTE. Unless it inconveniences this lady, I have nothing to call me elsewhere the whole day.

CLITANDRE. I, provided I am present when the King retires, have no other matter to call me away.

CÉLIMÈNE (*to* ALCESTE). You are only joking, I suppose.

ALCESTE. Not at all. We shall soon see whether I am the one you want to depart.

SCENE VI. ALCESTE, CÉLIMÈNE, ÉLIANTE, ACASTE, PHILINTE, CLITANDRE, BASQUE

BASQUE (*to* ALCESTE). There is a man down stairs, sir, who wishes to speak to you on business which can not be postponed.

ALCESTE. Tell him that I have no urgent business.

BASQUE. He wears a jacket with large plaited skirts embroidered with gold.

CÉLIMÈNE (*to* ALCESTE). Go and see who it is, or else let him come in.

SCENE VII. ALCESTE, CÉLIMÈNE, ÉLIANTE, ACASTE, PHILINTE, CLITANDRE, A GUARD OF THE MARÉCHAUSSÉE

ALCESTE (*going to meet the guard*). What may be your pleasure? Come in, sir.

GUARD. I would have a few words privately with you, sir.

ALCESTE. You may speak aloud, sir, so as to let me know.

GUARD. The Marshals of France, whose commands I bear, hereby summon you to appear before them immediately, sir.

ALCESTE. Whom? Me, sir?

GUARD. Yourself.

ALCESTE. And for what?

PHILINTE (*to* ALCESTE). It is that ridiculous affair between you and Oronte.

CÉLIMÈNE (*to* PHILINTE). What do you mean?

PHILINTE. Oronte and he have been insulting each other just now about some trifling verses which he did not like; and the Marshals wish to nip the affair in the bud.

ALCESTE. Well, I shall never basely submit.

PHILINTE. But you must obey the summons. Come, get ready.

ALCESTE. How will they settle this between us? Will the edict of these gentlemen oblige me to approve of the verses which are the cause of our quarrel? I will not retract what I have said. I think them abominable.

PHILINTE. But with a little milder tone . . .

ALCESTE. I will not retract one word. The verses are execrable.

PHILINTE. You ought to show a more tractable spirit. Come along.

ALCESTE. I shall go, but nothing will induce me to retract.

PHILINTE. Go and show yourself.

ALCESTE. Unless an express order from the King himself commands me to approve of the verses which have caused all the trouble, I shall continue to maintain that they are bad, and that a fellow deserves hanging for making them. (*To* CLITANDRE *and* ACASTE *who are laughing.*) Hang it! gentlemen, I did not think I was so amusing.

CÉLIMÈNE. Go quickly where you are wanted.

ALCESTE. I am going, madam, but I shall come back here to finish our discussion.

ACT III

SCENE I. CLITANDRE, ACASTE

CLITANDRE. My dear marquis, you appear mightily pleased with yourself; everything amuses you, and nothing discomposes you. But really and truly, do you think, without flattering yourself, that you have good reasons for appearing so joyful?

ACASTE. Gad, I do not find, on looking at myself, any matter to be sorrowful about. I am wealthy, I am young and am descended from a family which, with some appearance of truth, may be called noble; and I think that, by the rank which my lineage confers upon me, there are very few offices to which I might not aspire. As for courage, which we ought especially to value, it is well known—this without vanity—that I do not lack it; and people have seen me carry on an affair of honor in a manner sufficiently vigorous and brisk. As for wit, I have some, no doubt; and as for good taste, to judge and reason upon everything without study. At "first nights," of which I am very fond, I am clever enough to take my place as a critic upon the stage, to give my opinion as a judge, to applaud, and point out the best passages by repeated bravoes. I carry myself well, and am good-looking, have particularly fine teeth and a good figure. I believe, without flattering myself, that, as for dressing in good taste, a person would be ill-advised to dispute with me about it. I find myself treated with every possible consideration, very much beloved by the fair sex; and I stand very well with the King. With all that, I think, dear marquis, that one might be satisfied with oneself anywhere.

CLITANDRE. True, but finding so many easy conquests elsewhere, why do you come here to utter fruitless sighs?

ACASTE. I? The idea! I have neither the wish nor the disposition to put up with the indifference of any woman. I leave it to awkward and ordinary people to burn constantly for cruel fair maidens, to languish at their feet, and to bear with their severities, to invoke the aid of sighs and tears, and to endeavor, by long and persistent assiduities, to obtain what is denied to their little merit. But men of my stamp, marquis, are not made to love on trust and be at all the expenses themselves. Be the merit of the fair ever so great, I think, thank Heaven, that we have our value as well as they, that it is not reasonable to enthrall a heart like mine without its costing them anything and that, weighing everything justly, the advances should be reciprocal.

CLITANDRE. Then you think that you are well received here, marquis?

ACASTE. I have some reason to think so, marquis.

CLITANDRE. Believe me, divest yourself of that great mistake: you are flattering and deceiving yourself, dear friend.

ACASTE. It is true. I am flattering and deceiving myself.

CLITANDRE. But what causes you to judge your happiness so complete?

ACASTE. I am flattering myself.

CLITANDRE. Upon what do you ground your belief?

ACASTE. I am deceiving myself.

CLITANDRE. Have you any sure proofs?

ACASTE. I am mistaken, I tell you.

CLITANDRE. Has Célimène made you any secret avowal of her inclinations?

ACASTE. No, I am very badly treated by her.

CLITANDRE. Answer me, I pray.

ACASTE. I meet with nothing but rebuffs.

CLITANDRE. A truce to your raillery; and tell me what hope she has held out to you.

ACASTE. I am the rejected, and you are the lucky one. She has a great aversion to me, and one of these days I shall have to hang myself.

CLITANDRE. Nonsense. Shall we, marquis, make a compact together so that we may adjust our love affairs? Whenever one of us is able to show a certain proof of having a greater share in Célimène's heart, the other shall leave the field free to the supposed winner, and by that means rid him of an obstinate rival.

ACASTE. Gad! you please me with these words.

I agree to that from the bottom of my heart. But, hush.

SCENE II. CÉLIMÈNE, ACASTE, CLITANDRE

CÉLIMÈNE. What! here still?

CLITANDRE. Love, madam, detains us.

CÉLIMÈNE. I hear a carriage below. Do you know whose it is?

CLITANDRE. No.

SCENE III. CÉLIMÈNE, ACASTE, CLITANDRE, BASQUE

BASQUE. Arsinoé, madam, is coming up to see you.

CÉLIMÈNE. What does that woman want with me?

BASQUE. Éliante is down stairs talking to her.

CÉLIMÈNE. What is she thinking about, and what brings her here?

ACASTE. She has everywhere the reputation of being a consummate prude, and her fervent zeal...

CÉLIMÈNE. Pshaw, downright humbug. In her inmost soul she is as worldly as any. Her every nerve is strained to hook some one, but she is, however, never successful. All she can do is to look with envious eyes on the accepted lovers of others; and in her wretched condition, forsaken by all, she is forever railing against the blindness of the age. She endeavors to hide the dreadful isolation of her home under a false cloak of prudishness, and to save the credit of her feeble charms, she brands as criminal the power which they do not have. Yet a swain would please her very much: she even shows a certain tenderness for Alceste. She regards every attention he pays me as a theft committed by me. Her jealous spite, which she can hardly hide, breaks out against me at every opportunity and in an underhand manner. In short, I think I have never seen anything so stupid. She is impertinent to the last degree...

SCENE IV. ARSINOÉ, CÉLIMÈNE, CLITANDRE, ACASTE

CÉLIMÈNE. Ah! what happy chance brings you here, madam. I was really getting uneasy about you.

ARSINOÉ. I have come to give you some advice as a matter of duty.

CÉLIMÈNE. How very glad I am to see you!

(*Exeunt* CLITANDRE *and* ACASTE, *laughing.*)

SCENE V. ARSINOÉ, CÉLIMÈNE

ARSINOÉ. They could not have left at a more convenient opportunity.

CÉLIMÈNE. Shall we sit down?

ARSINOÉ. It is not necessary. Friendship, madam, must show itself above all in matters which may be of consequence to us. As there are none of greater importance than honor and decorum, I have come to prove to you on a matter which closely concerns your reputation, the friendship which I feel for you. Yesterday I was with some people of rare merit where the conversation turned upon you; and there your conduct, which is causing some stir, was, madam, unfortunately far from being commended. That crowd of people, whose visits you permit, your intrigues and the talk that they start, were criticised rather more freely and more severely than I could have wished. You can easily imagine whose part I took. I did all I could to defend you. I exonerated you, and vouched for the purity of your heart and the honesty of your intentions. But you know there are things in life which one can not well defend, although one may have the greatest wish to do so; and I was finally obliged to confess that the way in which you live does some harm, that it has a doubtful look in the eyes of the world, that there is no story so ill-natured as not to be told about it, and that, if you liked, your behavior might well give less cause for censure. Not that I believe that decency is in any way outraged—Heaven forbid that I should harbor such a thought! But the world is so ready to give credit to the faintest shadow of a crime, and it is not enough to live blameless one's self. Madam, I believe you to be too sensible not to take in good part this useful counsel, and not to attribute it solely to the inner promptings of an affection that feels an interest in your welfare.

CÉLIMÈNE. Madam, I have a great many thanks to return to you. Such counsel lays me under an obligation. Far from taking it amiss, I intend this very moment to repay the favor by giving you some advice which closely concerns your reputation. As I see you prove yourself my friend by acquainting me with the stories that are current about me, I shall follow such a fine example by informing you of what is said about you. In a house where I paid a visit the other day, I met some people of exemplary merit who, while talking of the proper duties of a well spent life, turned the topic of conversation upon you, madam. There your prudishness and your too fervent zeal were not at all cited as a good example. Your affectation of a grave demeanor, your eternal conversations on wisdom and honor, your mincings and mouthings at the slightest shadow of indecency which an innocent though ambiguous word may convey, that lofty esteem in which you hold yourself, and those pitying glances which you cast upon everybody, your frequent lectures and your acrid censures on things which are pure and harmless,—all this, madam, if I may speak frankly to you, was blamed unanimously. What is the good, said they, of that modest mien and that prudent exterior, both of which are belied by the rest? She says her prayers with the utmost exactness, but she beats her servants and pays them no wages. She displays great fervor in every place of devotion, but she paints and wishes to appear beautiful. She covers up nudity in her pictures, but loves the reality. As for me, I undertook your defence against everyone, and positively assured them that it was nothing but slander. The general opinion went against me, as they came to the conclusion that you would do well to concern yourself less about the actions of others and take a little more pains with your own, that one ought to look a long time at one's self before thinking of condemning other people, that when we wish to correct others, we ought to add the weight of a blameless life, and that, even then, it would be better to leave it to those whom Heaven has ordained for the task. Madam, I also believe you to be too sensible not to take in good part this useful counsel, and not to ascribe it solely to the inner promptings of an affection that feels an interest in your welfare.

ARSINOÉ. To whatever we may be exposed when we reprove, I did not expect this retort, madam, and, by its very sting, I see how my sincere advice has hurt your feelings.

CÉLIMÈNE. On the contrary, madam. If we were wise, these mutual counsels would be put in effect. If honestly made use of, they would destroy that great blindness which people have of themselves. It depends entirely on you whether we shall continue this trustworthy practice with equal zeal, and whether we shall take great care to tell each other confidentially what we hear, you of me and I of you.

ARSINOÉ. Ah! Madam, I can hear nothing said of you. It is in me that people find so much to reprove.

CÉLIMÈNE. Madam, it is easy, I believe, to blame or praise everything. Everyone may be right according to his age and taste. There is a time for gallantry—there is one also for prudishness. One may prudently take to it when youthful attractions have faded away. It sometimes serves to hide vexatious ravages of time. I do not say that I shall not follow your example one of these days. Those things come with old age, but twenty, as everybody knows, is not an age to play the prude.

ARSINOÉ. You certainly pride yourself upon a very weak advantage, and you boast terribly of your age. Whatever difference there may be between your years and mine, there is no occasion to make such a tremendous fuss about it. I am at a loss to know, madam, why you should get so angry and what makes you goad me in this manner.

CÉLIMÈNE. And I, madam, am at an equal loss to know why one hears you inveigh so bitterly against me everywhere. Must you always blame me for your sorrows? Can I help it if people refuse to pay you any attentions? If a man insists on falling in love with me and on offering me each day those attentions of which you would like to see me deprived, I cannot alter it: it is not my fault. You have a free field—I am not preventing you from having charms to attract them.

ARSINOÉ. Alas! Do you think that I would trouble myself about the crowd of lovers of which you are so proud and that it is not very easy to judge at what price they may be attracted nowadays? Do you wish to have it believed that, seeing what is going on, it is your merit alone which attracts this crowd? Are you trying to get people to think that their affection for you is strictly honest and that it is for nothing but your virtue that they are paying you their court? People are not blinded by such empty pretenses: the world is not duped in that way. I see many ladies who are capable of inspiring a tender feeling, yet who do not succeed in attracting a crowd of beaux. From that fact we may conclude that those conquests are not altogether made without some great advances, that no one cares to sigh for us, for our beauty only, and that the attentions bestowed on us are generally dearly bought. Do not therefore puff yourself up with vainglory at the trifling advantages of a poor victory. Moderate slightly the pride in your good looks instead of looking down upon people on account of them. If I were at all envious of your conquests, I dare say that I might manage like other people, be under no restraint, and thus show plainly that one may have lovers when one wishes them.

CÉLIMÈNE. Go ahead and have some then, madam. Let us see you try it. Endeavor to please by that extraordinary secret . . .

ARSINOÉ. Let us break off this conversation, madam. It might excite too much both your temper and mine. I would have already taken my leave if I had not been obliged to wait for my carriage.

CÉLIMÈNE. Please stay as long as you like. Do not hurry yourself on that account, madam. But instead of wearying you longer with my presence, I am going to give you more pleasant company. This gentleman, who comes very opportunely, will better entertain you.

SCENE VI. ALCESTE, CÉLIMÈNE, ARSINOÉ

CÉLIMÈNE. Alceste, I have to write a short note which I can not well delay. Please stay with this lady. She will then be so kind enough as to pardon my rudeness.

SCENE VII. ALCESTE, ARSINOÉ

ARSINOÉ. You see, I am left here to entertain you until my coach comes around. She could have devised no more charming treat for me than such a conversation. Indeed, people of exceptional merit attract the esteem and love of everyone, and yours has undoubtedly some secret charm which makes me feel interested in all your doings. I could wish that the Court, with a real regard to your merits, would do you more justice. You have reason to complain. It vexes me to see that day after day nothing is done for you.

ALCESTE. For me, madam? And by what right would I have pretensions to anything? What service have I rendered to the State? Pray, what have I done, if you please, so brilliant in itself, for me to complain of the Court doing nothing for me?

ARSINOÉ. Not everyone whom the State delights to honor has rendered signal services. There must be an opportunity as well as the ability, and the merit which you allow us to see ought . . .

ALCESTE. For Heaven's sake, let us have no more about my abilities, I beg of you. What would you have the Court do? It would have enough to do, and have its hands full, to discover the merits of people.

ARSINOÉ. Sterling merit discovers itself. A great deal is made of yours in certain places. Let me tell you that, not later than yesterday, you were highly spoken of in two distinguished circles by people of very great standing.

ALCESTE. As for that, madam, everyone is praised nowadays, and very little discrimination is shown. Everything is equally endowed with great merit, so that it is no longer an honor to be praised. People are smothered with praise, they throw it at one's head. Even my valet is put in the Gazette.

ARSINOÉ. As for me, I could wish that, in order to bring yourself into greater notice, some place at Court might tempt you. If you will only give me a hint that you seriously think about it, a great many machinations might be set in motion to serve you. I know some people whom I could employ on your behalf and who would manage the matter smoothly enough.

ALCESTE. And what would I do when I got there, madam? My disposition rather prompts me to keep away from it. Heaven, when ushering me into the world, did not give me a mind suited to the atmosphere of a Court. I do not have the qualifications necessary for success or for making my fortune there. To be open and candid is my chief talent. I do not have the art of deceiving people in conversation, and he who has not the gift of concealing his thoughts ought not to stay long in those places. When not at Court, one doubtless has not that standing, and the advantage of those honorable titles which it bestows nowadays. But on the other hand, one has not the vexation of playing the silly fool. One does not have to bear a thousand galling rebuffs. One is not forced, as it were, to praise the verses of Mister So-and-So, to laud Madam Such and Such, and to put up with the whims of an ingenious marquis.

ARSINOÉ. Since you wish it, let us drop the subject of the Court. But I can not help grieving for your amours. To tell you frankly my opinion on that score, I could heartily wish that your affections were better bestowed. You certainly deserve a much happier fate. She who has fascinated you is unworthy of you.

ALCESTE. In saying that, madam, remember, I pray, that this lady is your friend.

ARSINOÉ. True. But really my conscience revolts at the thought of longer enduring the wrong which is being done to you. The position in which I see you afflicts my very soul. I caution you that your affections are being betrayed.

ALCESTE. That is certainly showing me a great deal of good feeling, madam. Such information is very welcome to a lover.

ARSINOÉ. Yes. Even though Célimène is my friend, I do not hesitate to call her unworthy of possessing the heart of a man of honor. Hers has for you only a feigned affection.

ALCESTE. That is very possible, madam. One can not look into the heart. But your charitable feelings might well have refrained from awakening such a suspicion as mine.

ARSINOÉ. Nothing is easier than to say no more about it, if you do not wish to be undeceived.

ALCESTE. Just so. But whatever may be openly said on this subject is not half so annoying as hints thrown out; and I for one would prefer to be plainly told only that which can be clearly proved.

ARSINOÉ. Very well! and that is sufficient. I can

fully enlighten you on that subject. I will have you believe nothing but what your own eyes see. Only have the kindness to escort me as far as my house. I will give you undeniable proof of the faithlessness of your fair one's heart. If, after that, you can find charms in anyone else, we will perhaps find you some consolation.

ACT IV

SCENE I. ÉLIANTE, PHILINTE

PHILINTE. No, never have I seen so obstinate a mind, nor a reconciliation more difficult to effect. In vain was Alceste tried on all sides, but it was not possible to drag him from his stand. Never, I believe, has a more curious dispute engaged the attention of those gentlemen. "No, gentlemen," exclaimed he, "I will not retract, and I will agree with you on every point except that one. At what is Oronte offended? With what does he reproach me? Does it reflect upon his honor that he can not write well? What to him is my opinion which he has altogether wrongly construed? One may be a perfect gentleman and still write bad verses. Those things have nothing to do with honor. I take him to be a gallant man in every respect: a man of standing, of merit, and courage, anything you like, but he is a wretched author. I shall praise, if you wish, his mode of living, his lavishness, his skill in riding, in fencing, in dancing; but as to praising his verses, I am his humble servant. If one has not the gift of composing better, one ought to leave off rhyming altogether unless condemned to it on forfeit of one's life." In short, all the modification they could with difficulty obtain from him, was to say, in what he thought was a much gentler tone— "I am sorry, sir, to be so difficult to please. Out of regard to you, I could wish, with all my heart, to have found your sonnet a little better." And they compelled them to settle the dispute quickly with an embrace.

ÉLIANTE. He is very eccentric in his doings; but I must confess that I think a great deal of him. The candor upon which he prides himself has something noble and heroic about it. It is a rare virtue nowadays, and I, for one, should not be sorry to meet with it everywhere.

PHILINTE. As for me, the more I see of him, the more I am amazed at that passion to which his whole heart is devoted. I can not conceive how, with a disposition like his, he has taken it into his head to love at all. Still less can I understand how your cousin happens to be the person to whom his feelings are inclined.

ÉLIANTE. That shows that love is not always produced by compatibility of temper. In this case, all the pretty theories of gentle sympathies are belied.

PHILINTE. But do you think him beloved in return, judging from what we see?

ÉLIANTE. That is a point not easily decided. How can we judge whether it be true she loves? Her own heart is not so very sure of what it feels. It sometimes loves, without being quite aware of it, and at other times thinks it does, without the least grounds.

PHILINTE. I think that our friend will have more trouble with that cousin of yours than he imagines. To tell you the truth, if he were of my mind, he would bestow his affections elsewhere. By a better choice, we should see him, madam, profit by the kind feelings which your heart evinces for him.

ÉLIANTE. As for me, I do not mince matters. I think that in such cases we ought to act with sincerity. I am not opposed to his tender feelings; on the contrary, I feel interested in them. If it depended only on me, I would unite him to the object of his love. But if, as it may happen in love affairs, his affections should receive a check, and if Célimène should respond to the love of someone else, I could easily be prevailed upon to listen to his addresses, and I should have no repugnance whatever to them on account of their rebuff elsewhere.

PHILINTE. Nor do I, from my side, oppose the tender feelings which you entertain for him. He himself, if he wished, might inform you what I have taken care to say to him on that score. But if, by the union of those two, you should be prevented from accepting his attentions, all mine would endeavor to gain that great favor which your kind feelings are offering to him. I would be, madam, only too happy to have them transferred to myself, if his heart could not respond to yours.

ÉLIANTE. You are in a joking humor, Philinte.

PHILINTE. Not so, madam, I am speaking my inmost feelings. I am only waiting for the opportunity to offer myself openly, and am wishing most anxiously to hurry its advent.

SCENE II. ALCESTE, ÉLIANTE, PHILINTE

ALCESTE. Ah, madam! obtain justice for me for an offense which triumphs over all my constancy!

ÉLIANTE. What ails you? What disturbs you?

ALCESTE. So much ails me that it is death to me to think about it. The upheaving of all creation would less overwhelm me. It is all over with me . . . My love . . . I can not speak.

ÉLIANTE. Try to get a hold on yourself.

ALCESTE. O, just Heaven! Can the odious vices of the basest minds be joined to such beauty?

ÉLIANTE. But, once more, what can have . . .

ALCESTE. Alas! All is ruined! I am! I am betrayed! I am stricken to death! Célimène . . . would you believe it! Célimène is betraying me!

ÉLIANTE. Have you just grounds for believing so?

PHILINTE. Perhaps it is just a suspicion, rashly conceived; your jealous temper often harbors fancies.

ALCESTE. Ah! Certainly not! Please mind your own business, sir. (To ÉLIANTE.) Her treachery is but too certain, for I have in my pocket a letter in her own handwriting. Yes, Madam, a letter, intended for Oronte, has showed me my misfortune and her shame; Oronte, whose advances I thought she was avoiding and whom, of all my rivals, I feared the least.

PHILINTE. A letter may deceive by appearances and is often not so culpable as may be thought.

ALCESTE. Once more, sir, leave me alone, if you please. Trouble yourself only about your own concerns.

ÉLIANTE. You should moderate your passion. The insult . . .

ALCESTE. You must be left to do that, madam. It is to you that my heart has recourse today to free itself from this goading pain. Avenge me on an ungrateful and perfidious relative who basely deceives such faithful love. Avenge me for an act that ought to fill you with horror.

ÉLIANTE. I avenge you? How?

ALCESTE. By accepting my heart. Take it, madam, instead of the false one. It is in this way that I can avenge myself upon her. I shall punish her by the sincere attachment and profound love, the respectful cares, the eager devotions, the ceaseless attentions which this heart will henceforth offer to you.

ÉLIANTE. I certainly sympathize with you in your sufferings and I do not despise your proffered heart. But the wrong done may not be so great as you think, and you might wish to forego this desire for revenge. When the injury proceeds from a beloved object, we form many designs which we never execute. We may find as powerful a reason as we like to break off the connection, but we soon find that the guilty charmer is innocent. All the harm we wish for her quickly vanishes, and we know what a lover's anger means.

ALCESTE. No, no, madam, no. The offense is too cruel. There will be no relenting—I have done with her. Nothing shall change the resolution I have taken, and I should hate myself for ever loving her again. Here she comes. My anger increases at her approach. I shall taunt her with her black guilt, completely put her to the blush, and, after that, bring you a heart wholly freed from her deceitful attractions.

SCENE III. CÉLIMÈNE, ALCESTE

ALCESTE (aside). Grant, O Heaven, that I may control my temper.

CÉLIMÈNE (aside). Ah! (To ALCESTE.) What is all this trouble that I see you in, and what mean those long-drawn sighs and those black looks which you are casting at me?

ALCESTE. That all the wickedness of which a heart is capable is not to be compared to your faithlessness, that neither fate, Hell, nor Heaven in its wrath ever produced anything so wicked as you are.

CÉLIMÈNE. Those are certainly pretty compliments. I admire them very much.

ALCESTE. Do not joke. This is no time for laughing. Blush rather: you have cause to do so. I have undeniable proof of your treachery. That is what the agitations of my mind anticipated. It was not without cause that my love took alarm. By those frequent suspicions, which were hateful to you, I was trying to discover the misfortune which my eyes have finally beheld. In spite of all your care and all your skill in dissembling, I foresaw what I had to fear. But do not imagine that I will bear unavenged this slight of being insulted. I know that we have no command over our inclinations, that love will everywhere spring up spontaneously, that there is no entering a heart by force, and that every soul is free to name its conqueror. I should thus have no reason to complain, if you had spoken to me without dissembling, and rejected my advances from the very beginning. My heart would then have been justified in blaming fortune alone. But to see my love encouraged by a deceitful avowal on your part is an action so treacherous and perfidious that it can not meet with too great a punishment, and I can allow my resentment to do anything. Yes, after such an outrage, you may fear the worst. I am no longer myself: I am mad with rage. My senses, struck by the deadly blow with which you are killing me, are no longer governed by

reason. I give way to the outbursts of a just wrath, and am no longer responsible for what I may do.

CÉLIMÈNE. Whence comes, I pray, such a passion? Speak! Have you lost your senses?

ALCESTE. Yes, yes, I lost them when, to my misfortune, I first beheld you and thus took the poison which is killing me, and when I thought to meet with some sincerity in those treacherous charms that bewitched me.

CÉLIMÈNE. Of what treachery have you to complain?

ALCESTE. Ah! how double-faced she is! How well she knows how to dissemble! But I am fully prepared with the means of driving her to extremities. Cast your eyes here and recognize your writing. This note which I have picked up is sufficient to confound you; such proof can not easily be refuted.

CÉLIMÈNE. So that, then, is what has been troubling you?

ALCESTE. You are not blushing to see this writing?

CÉLIMÈNE. And why should I blush?

ALCESTE. What! You add boldness to trickery! Will you disown this note because it bears no name?

CÉLIMÈNE. Why should I disown it, since I wrote it?

ALCESTE. And you can look at it without becoming confused at the crime of which its style accuses you!

CÉLIMÈNE. You are, in truth, a very eccentric man.

ALCESTE. What! You thus out-brave this convincing proof? And you think that the contents which are so full of tenderness for Oronte have nothing in them to outrage me or to shame you?

CÉLIMÈNE. Oronte! Who told you that this letter is for him?

ALCESTE. The people who put it into my hands this morning. But I will even suppose that it is for someone else. Has my heart any less cause to complain? Will you, in fact, be any less guilty toward me for that?

CÉLIMÈNE. But if it is a woman to whom this letter is addressed, how can it hurt you, or what is there culpable in it?

ALCESTE. Ah! The prevarication is ingenious and the excuse is excellent. I must own that I did not expect this turn. Nothing but that was wanting to convince me. Do you dare to have recourse to such crude tricks? Do you think that people are entirely destitute of common sense? Come, let us see a little by what subterfuge, with what manner you can

MOLIÈRE

support so palpable a falsehood. How can you apply to a woman every word of this note which evinces so much tenderness? Reconcile, if you can, in order to hide your perfidiousness, what I am going to read.

CÉLIMÈNE. I do not care to do so. I think it ridiculous that you should take so much upon yourself, daring to tell me that to my face!

ALCESTE. No, no, without flying into a rage, take a little trouble to explain to me these words.

CÉLIMÈNE. No, I shall do nothing of the kind. It matters very little to me what you think about it.

ALCESTE. I pray you, show me, and I shall be satisfied, if this letter can be explained as meant for a woman.

CÉLIMÈNE. Not at all. It is for Oronte. I will have you believe it. I accept all his attentions gladly. I admire what he says. I like him and I shall agree to whatever you please. Do as you like, and act as you think proper. Let nothing hinder you and do not harass me any longer.

ALCESTE (aside). Heavens! Can anything more cruel be conceived? Was ever a heart treated like mine? What! I am justly angry with her. I come to complain, and I am quarrelled with instead! My grief and my suspicions are excited to the utmost. I am allowed to believe everything. She boasts of everything. And yet my heart is so weak that it can not break the bonds which hold it fast, and arm itself with a great contempt for the ungrateful object of which it is too much enamored. (To CÉLIMÈNE.) Perfidious woman, you know well how to take advantage of my great weakness and how to employ for your own purposes that excessive, astonishing, and fatal love which your treacherous looks have inspired! Defend yourself at least from this crime that overwhelms me. Stop pretending to be guilty. Show me, if you can, that this letter is innocent—my affection will even consent to assist you. At any rate try to appear faithful, and I shall strive to believe that you are.

CÉLIMÈNE. Come, you are mad with your jealous frenzies and do not deserve the love which I have for you. I should like very much to know what could compel me to stoop to the baseness of dissembling. I should like to know why, if my heart were disposed to another, I should not say so candidly. What! Does the kind assurance of my sentiments towards you not defend me sufficiently against all your suspicions? Ought they to possess any weight at all with such a guarantee? Is it not insulting to me even to listen to them? And since it is with the utmost difficulty that we can resolve to confess our love, since the strict honor of our sex, hostile to our passion, strongly opposes such a confession, ought a lover who sees such an obstacle overcome for his sake, doubt with impunity our avowal? And is he not greatly to blame in not assuring himself of the truth of that which is never said except after a severe struggle with oneself? Come, such suspicions deserve my anger. You are not worthy of being worried about. I am silly and I am annoyed at my own simplicity in still preserving any kindness at all for you. I ought to place my affections elsewhere and really give you cause for complaint.

ALCESTE. Ah! you traitress! My love is incomprehensible to you. Those tender expressions are doubtless meant only to deceive me. But it matters little. I must submit to my fate. My very soul is wrapped up in you. I will see to the bitter end how you will act towards me and whether you will be wicked enough to betray me.

CÉLIMÈNE. No, you do not love me as you ought to.

ALCESTE. Indeed! Nothing can be compared to my exceeding love. And, in its eagerness to show itself to the whole world, it goes even so far as to form wishes against you. Yes, I could wish that no one thought you loveable, that you were reduced to a miserable existence, that Heaven had bestowed nothing upon you at your birth, that you had no rank, no nobility, no wealth, so that I might openly proffer my heart, and thus make amends to you for the injustice of such a lot. I could wish that, this very day, I might have the joy and the glory of seeing you owe everything to my love.

CÉLIMÈNE. That is a strange way to wish me well! Heaven grant that you may never have occasion . . . But here comes Monsieur Dubois dressed up in a ridiculous manner.

SCENE IV. CÉLIMÈNE, ALCESTE, DUBOIS

ALCESTE. What do that strange attire and that frightened look mean? What is the matter with you?

DUBOIS. Sir . . .

ALCESTE. Well?

DUBOIS. The most mysterious event.

ALCESTE. What is it?

DUBOIS. Our affairs are turning out badly, sir.

ALCESTE. What?

DUBOIS. Shall I speak out?

ALCESTE. Yes, do, and quickly.

DUBOIS. Isn't there someone there?

ALCESTE. Curse your trifling! Will you speak?

DUBOIS. Sir, we must beat a retreat.

ALCESTE. What do you mean?

DUBOIS. We must steal away quietly from all of this.

ALCESTE. And why?

DUBOIS. I tell you that we must leave this place.

ALCESTE. The reason?

DUBOIS. You must go, sir, without staying to say goodbye.

ALCESTE. But why are you saying such things to me?

DUBOIS. Because, sir, we must pack our baggage.

ALCESTE. I am certainly going to break your head, fool, if you do not explain yourself more clearly.

DUBOIS. Sir, a fellow black both in dress and in mien got as far as the kitchen and left us a paper scribbled over in such a fashion that Satan himself could not read it. It is about your law-suit, I have no doubt, but the devil himself could not make head or tail out of it.

ALCESTE. Well, then what? What has the paper got to do with the going away that you are talking about, you scoundrel?

DUBOIS. I must tell you, sir, that about an hour afterwards a gentleman who often calls came and asked for you quite eagerly and, not finding you at home, he told me quietly, knowing how attached I am to you, to let you know . . . Wait a moment, what *is* his name?

ALCESTE. Never mind his name, you scoundrel. Tell me what he told you.

DUBOIS. He is one of your friends—that is enough. He told me that your peril is very great here and that you are threatened with arrest.

ALCESTE. What! Didn't he specify anything?

DUBOIS. No. He asked me for ink and paper and wrote you a note from which you can, I think, get to the bottom of the mystery.

ALCESTE. Hand it over then.

CÉLIMÈNE. What does all this mean?

ALCESTE. I do not know, but I am anxious to get it cleared up. Will you please get through with this, you stupid fool?

DUBOIS (*after fumbling for some time trying to find the note*). For Heaven's sake, sir, I have left it on your table!

ALCESTE. I do not know what keeps me from . . .

CÉLIMÈNE. Do not fly into a passion. Go and unravel this perplexing business.

ALCESTE. It seems that fate, whatever I may do, has sworn to prevent my having a conversation with you. But, to get the better of her, allow me to see you again, madam, before the end of the day.

ACT V

SCENE I. ALCESTE, PHILINTE

ALCESTE. I tell you, my mind is made up about it.

PHILINTE. But, whatever this blow may be, does it compel you . . .

ALCESTE. You can talk and argue until doomsday, if you like, but nothing can keep me from doing what I have said. The age we are living in is too wicked. I am determined to withdraw completely from association with people. What! when honor, probity, decency and the laws are all against my opponent; when the equity of my claim is recognized everywhere; when my mind is at rest as to the justice of my cause, I still see myself betrayed by its issue! What! I have justice on my side and I still lose my case! A wretch, whose scandalous background is well known, wins through the blackest falsehoods! All good faith yields to his treachery! By cutting my throat he finds the means of being in the right! His cunning dissimulation upsets right and turns justice aside. He has even obtained a court decree to crown his villainy. And, not content with the wrong he has already done me, he is circulating in society an abominable book, one of which the very reading is to be condemned, one which deserves the greatest severity, and the scoundrel has had the impudence to proclaim me the author of it. With reference to this, you can see Oronte murmur something, trying wickedly to support the imposture: he who holds an honorable position at Court, to whom I have done nothing except be sincere and candid when he came to ask my opinion of some of his verses! Because I treat him honestly and will not betray either him or the truth, he tries to overwhelm me with a trumped-up crime. Now he is my greatest enemy! I shall never obtain his pardon for having found that his sonnet was not good! Heavens! To think that mankind is made thus! The thirst for fame brings them to such actions. That is the good faith, the virtuous zeal, the justice and the honor that is to be found among them! Let us begone. It is too much to endure the annoyances which they are creating for us. Let us get out of this woods, this den of cut-throats. Since one can live among men only like real wolves and traitors, you will never see me around here again as long as I live.

PHILINTE. I think that you are acting somewhat hastily. The harm which has been done is not as great as you would make out. Whatever your opponent has dared to impute to you has not been enough to cause your arrest. We see his false reports defeating themselves. This is an action which might well hurt him.

ALCESTE. He does not mind the scandal of such tricks as these. He is permitted to be an arrant knave. His action, far from damaging his position, will obtain for him an even better standing tomorrow.

PHILINTE. In short, it is certain that little notice has been taken of the report which he has maliciously spread against you. You have nothing to fear from it. And as for your law-suit, of which you certainly have reason to complain, it will be easy for you to get a new trial.

ALCESTE. No, I shall leave it as it is. Whatever wrong the verdict has inflicted on me, I shall take particular care not to have it set aside. It is only too clear how justice has been maltreated in it. I wish to go down to posterity as a signal proof, as a notorious testimony of the wickedness of the men of our age. It may indeed cost me twenty thousand francs, but at that cost I shall have the right to rail against the wickedness of human nature, and of preserving an undying hatred of it.

PHILINTE. But after all . . .

ALCESTE. But after all, you are wasting your efforts. What can you, sir, say about the matter? Would you have the effrontery to excuse to my face the horror of all that is happening?

PHILINTE. No, I agree with you in all that you say. Everything proceeds through intrigue and selfishness. Nothing but trickery can win out in this day and time. Men ought to act differently, but is their lack of fairness a reason for wishing to withdraw from their society? All human failings give us, in life, the means of exercising our philosophy. That is the finest use which virtue can find. If honesty reigned everywhere, if all hearts were candid, just and tractable, most of our virtues would be useless to us, since their function is to bear the injustice caused us by others. Just in the same way as a heart full of virtue . . .

ALCESTE. I know, sir, that you are a most excellent speaker, and that you always abound in fine arguments, but you are wasting your time with all your splendid speeches. Reason tells me to retire for my own good. I do not have sufficient power over my tongue. I can not answer for what I might say and I would probably get myself into a hundred scrapes. Let me, without further discussion, wait for Célimène. She must consent to the plan which has brought me here. I shall see whether her heart

has any love for me; it is this moment which will prove it to me.

PHILINTE. Let us go upstairs to Éliante and wait until she comes.

ALCESTE. No, my mind is too harassed. You go and see her, and leave me in this little dark corner with my deep trouble.

PHILINTE. That is strange company to leave you with. I will persuade Éliante to come down.

SCENE II. CÉLIMÈNE, ORONTE, ALCESTE

ORONTE. Yes, madam, it remains for you to consider whether, by ties so dear, you care to make me yours. I must be absolutely sure of your affection: a lover does not like to be held in suspense upon such a subject. If the ardor of my affection has been able to move your feelings, you ought not to hesitate to let me see it. The proof, after all, which I ask of you, is not to allow Alceste to wait upon you any longer, to sacrifice him to my love, and, in short, to banish him from your house this very day.

CÉLIMÈNE. But why are you so incensed against him; you, whom I have so often heard speak of his merits?

ORONTE. There is no need, madam, of explaining that. The question is, what are your feelings? Please choose between us: my resolution depends entirely on yours.

ALCESTE (coming out of his corner). Yes, this gentleman is right, madam. You must make a choice. His request agrees perfectly with mine. I am equally eager, and the same desire brings me here. My love desires an assurance from you. Things can no longer go as they have been going: the moment has arrived for explaining your feelings.

ORONTE. I have no wish, sir, to disturb at all by an untimely affection, your good fortune.

ALCESTE. And I have no wish, sir, jealous or not, to share any of her heart with you.

ORONTE. If she prefers your affection to mine . . .

ALCESTE. If she has the slightest inclination towards you . . .

ORONTE. I swear henceforth not to pretend to it again.

ALCESTE. I absolutely swear never to see her again.

ORONTE. Madam, it remains with you now to speak openly.

ALCESTE. Madam, you can explain yourself without fear.

ORONTE. You have only to tell us where your feelings are attached.

ALCESTE. You have only to cut the matter short and choose between us.

ORONTE. What! your heart still wavers, and appears uncertain!

CÉLIMÈNE. Good Heavens! How out of place this persistence is and how unreasonable you both are! It is not that I do not know whom I prefer, nor is it my heart that wavers. It is not at all in doubt between you two. Nothing could be more quickly accomplished than the choice between you. But to tell the truth, I feel too confused to pronounce such an avowal before you. I think that disobliging words ought not to be spoken in people's presence, that a heart can give sufficient proof of its attachment without going so far as to break with everyone. Gentler intimations suffice to inform a lover of the ill success of his suit.

ORONTE. No, no, I do not fear a frank avowal; for my part I consent to it.

ALCESTE. And I demand it. It is just that very publicity which I claim, and I do not wish you to spare my feelings in the least. Your great study has always been to keep friends with everyone. But no more trifling, no more uncertainty. You must explain yourself clearly, or I shall take your refusal as a decision. I shall know, for my part, how to interpret your silence, and shall consider it as a confirmation of the worst.

ORONTE. I owe you many thanks, sir, for that wrath, and I say in every respect as you do.

CÉLIMÈNE. How you weary me with such a whim! Is there any justice in what you demand? Have I not told you what motive prevents me? I will be judged by Éliante who is just coming.

SCENE III. ÉLIANTE, PHILINTE, CÉLIMÈNE, ORONTE, ALCESTE

CÉLIMÈNE. Good cousin, I am being persecuted here by people who appear to have joined together to do so. They both demand heatedly that I should declare which of them my heart has chosen, and that, by a decision which I must give to their very faces, I should forbid one of them to pay further attention to me. Tell me if such a thing is ever done.

ÉLIANTE. Please do not consult me on such a matter: you might be addressing yourself to a wrong person, for I am decidedly in favor of people who speak their minds.

ORONTE. Madam, it is useless for you to refuse.

ALCESTE. All your evasions will be poorly seconded here.

ORONTE. You must speak, you must, and no longer waver.

ALCESTE. You need do no more than remain silent.

ORONTE. I desire but one word to end our discussions.

ALCESTE. To me your silence will convey as much as speech.

SCENE IV. ARSINOÉ, CÉLIMÈNE, ÉLIANTE, ALCESTE, PHILINTE, ACASTE, CLITANDRE, ORONTE

ACASTE (to CÉLIMÈNE). We have both come, by your leave, madam, to clear up a certain small matter.

CLITANDRE (to ORONTE and ALCESTE). It is a good thing that you are here, for this matter concerns you also.

ARSINOÉ (to CÉLIMÈNE). You are probably surprised to see me here, madam, but these gentlemen have caused me to come. They both came to see me and complained of a proceeding which I could not credit. I have too high an opinion of the kindness of your heart ever to believe you capable of such a crime. My eyes even refused to give credence to their strongest proofs, and, forgetting trivial disagreements out of the friendship which I have for you, I have been induced to accompany them here to hear you refute the slander.

ACASTE. Yes, madam, let us see with composure how you will manage to bear this out. Was this letter written by you to Clitandre?

CLITANDRE. And did you address this tender epistle to Acaste?

ACASTE (to ORONTE and ALCESTE). This handwriting is not at all unknown to you, gentlemen, and I have no doubt that her courtesy has before now made you familiar with her hand. But this is well worth the trouble of reading.

You are a strange man to condemn my gaiety and to reproach me that I am never so merry as when I am not with you. Nothing could be more unjust, and if you do not come very quickly to beg my pardon for that offense, I shall never forgive you as long as I live. Our big booby of a Viscount . . .

He ought to be here.

Our big booby of a Viscount, by whom you begin your complaints, is a man who could not possibly appeal to me. Ever since I watched him for a full three-quarters of an hour spitting in a well to make circles in the water, I have never been able to have a good opinion of him. As for the little Marquis . . .

That is I myself, ladies and gentlemen, be it said without the slightest vanity.

As for the little Marquis, who held my hand a long time yesterday, I think that there is nothing so delicate as his whole person, and his sole merit consists in his cloak and sword. As to the man with the green ribbons . . .

(*to* ALCESTE). It is your turn now, sir.

As to the man with the green ribbons, he amuses me sometimes with his bluntness and his peevish irritability, but there are hundreds of times when I think him the biggest bore in the world. And as to the man with the waistcoat . . .

(*to* ORONTE). This is your share.

As to the man with the waistcoat who has gone in for wit in a big way and who is trying to become an author in spite of everybody, I can not bear to listen to what he says. His prose tires me as much as his verse. Be assured that I do not always have as good a time as you think, that I miss you more than I would like at all the parties to which I am dragged, and that the presence of those we love seasons marvelously well the pleasures which we have.

CLITANDRE. Now for me.

Your Clitandre, whom you mention to me and who always has such a quantity of tender expressions at his command, is the last man for whom I could feel any affection. He is foolish to persuade himself that I love him, and you are so too in thinking that I do not love you. You ought to change your fancies to his, and come and see me as often as you can in order to help me bear the annoyance of being pestered by him.

That is the model of a very beautiful character, madam, and do you know what that is called? That is enough: we are both going to display this faithful portrait of your heart everywhere.

ACASTE. I might also have something to say to you, and the matter is tempting, but I do not regard you as worthy of my anger. I shall show you that a little marquis can find a more worthy heart than yours with which to console itself.

SCENE V. CÉLIMÈNE, ÉLIANTE, ARSINOÉ, ALCESTE, ORONTE, PHILINTE

ORONTE. What! Am I to be pulled to pieces this way after all you have written me? And does your

heart, adorned with all its semblance of love, promise itself to every member of mankind in turn? Come, I have been a dupe, but I shall be one no longer. You have done me a service in showing yourself for what you are. I am the richer by a heart which you thus restore to me, and I find my revenge in what you are losing. (*To* ALCESTE.) Sir, I shall no longer be an obstacle to your love. You can settle affairs with this lady.

SCENE VI. CÉLIMÈNE, ÉLIANTE, ARSINOÉ, ALCESTE, PHILINTE

ARSINOÉ (*to* CÉLIMÈNE). That is certainly one of the blackest deeds I have ever seen. I can no longer keep silent. I feel quite upset. Has anyone ever seen conduct like yours? I do not concern myself much with the affairs of other people, but should a gentleman who has staked all of his happiness on you, who worshipped you to madness, an honorable and deserving man . . .

ALCESTE. Please leave me, madam, to manage my own affairs. Do not trouble yourself with those unnecessary cares. It does no good for you to take my side in this quarrel, you will not be repaid for it. If I ever seek to avenge myself by making another choice, it will not be you whom I shall select.

ARSINOÉ. Ah, do you think, sir, that I have ever had that thought or that I am so anxious to get you? I find that you are indeed vain to flatter yourself with such an idea. Célimène's leavings are a commodity of which no one needs be very enamored. Pray, undeceive yourself, and do not act in such a high-handed manner. It is not people like me that you need: you will do well to keep sighing after her. I long to see so fine a union.

SCENE VII. CÉLIMÈNE, ÉLIANTE, ALCESTE, PHILINTE

ALCESTE (*to* CÉLIMÈNE). Well! I have held my tongue in spite of what I have seen, and I have let everyone have his say before me. Have I controlled myself long enough? May I now? . . .

CÉLIMÈNE. Yes, you may say what you like. You are justified in complaining and you may reproach me with whatever you please. I confess that I am in the wrong, and I am not trying to lessen it by any vain excuse. I scorn the anger of the others, but I admit my guilt toward you. Doubtless your resentment is just. I know how guilty I must appear to you. I know that everything speaks of my treachery to you and that, in short, you have reason to hate me. Do so, I consent to it.

ALCESTE. But can I do so, you traitress? Can I thus overcome all my love for you? Although I wish with all my soul to hate you, can I find within my breast a heart ready to obey me? (*To* ÉLIANTE *and* PHILINTE.) You see what an unworthy passion can do. I call both of you as witnesses to my infatuation. Nor, to tell the truth, is that all: you will see me carry it out to the bitter end. I will show you that it is wrong to call us wise, and that in all hearts there remains still something of the man. (*To* CÉLIMÈNE.) Yes, faithless creature, I am willing to forget your crimes. I can find in my own heart an excuse for all your doings. I hide them under the name of a weakness into which the vices of the age betrayed your youth, if you will agree to the purpose which I have formed of avoiding all human creatures and make up your mind to follow me without delay into the solitude where I have vowed to pass the rest of my days. It is by that only, that, in everyone's opinion, you can repair the harm done by your letters, and that, after the scandal which every noble heart must abhor, it may still be possible for me to love you.

CÉLIMÈNE. I give up the world before I grow old and bury myself in your desert!

ALCESTE. If your affection responds to mine what does the rest of the world need mean to you? Am I not sufficient for you?

CÉLIMÈNE. Solitude is frightful to a person of twenty. I do not feel strong enough to make up my mind to adopt such a plan. If the gift of my hand can satisfy your wishes, I might be induced to tie such bonds; and the marriage . . .

ALCESTE. No. My heart loathes you now: that refusal alone does more than all the rest. As you are not disposed, within such sweet ties, to find all you desire in me as I would in you, begone—I refuse your offer, and this painful insult frees me forever from your unworthy fetters.

SCENE VIII. ÉLIANTE, ALCESTE, PHILINTE

ALCESTE (*to* ÉLIANTE). Madam, your beauty is adorned by many virtues, and I have never seen anything in you that was not sincere. For a long time I have thought very highly of you. Allow me to esteem you thus forever: suffer my heart in its various troubles not to offer itself for the honor of your acceptance. I feel too unworthy, and I begin to perceive that Heaven did not intend me for the marriage bond. The remainder of a heart unworthy of you would not be sufficient homage. In short . . .

ÉLIANTE. You may pursue that thought. I am not at all lacking in opportunity for marriage: here is your friend who, without giving me much trouble, might possibly accept my hand if I asked him.

PHILINTE. Ah! madam, I ask for nothing better than that honor. I would sacrifice my blood and my life for it.

ALCESTE. May you taste true contentment by preserving forever those feelings towards each other! Deceived on all sides, overwhelmed with injustice, I will fly from this abyss where vice is triumphant, and seek out some small secluded spot on earth where one may enjoy the freedom of being an honest man.

PHILINTE. Come, madam, let us leave nothing untried to deter him from the purpose on which he has set his heart.

————◆————

LA ROCHEFOUCAULD

1613–1680

François VI Duc de la Rochefoucauld, Prince de Marsillac, French prose writer, member of a very ancient and very noble family, began his court life at the age of sixteen. Shortly afterward he began to frequent the famous literary salons which flourished in the Paris of his time, and there he developed a taste for letters. Like Racine he was a consummate master of concise expression and, like Molière, he was a profound psychologist. His little book of about five hundred maxims, each as finely cut as a gem, contains the observations of a lifetime. The theme which runs through them constantly is the vanity of all mankind, man's petty self-love. The success and fame of the *Maxims* perhaps rests less upon what they say than how they say it.

FURTHER READING

GRANDSAIGNES D'HAUTERIVE, R. *Le Pessimisme de La Rochefoucauld* (Paris, 1914).

Maxims *

WHAT we term virtue is often but a mass of various actions and divers interests, which fortune, or our own industry, manage to arrange; and it is not always from valor or from chastity that men are brave, and women chaste.

Self-love is the greatest of flatterers.

* Translator anonymous.

Passion often renders the most clever man a fool, and even sometimes renders the most foolish man clever.

Great and striking actions which dazzle the eyes are represented by politicians as the effect of great designs, instead of which they are commonly caused by the temper and the passions. Thus the war between Augustus and Antony, which is set down to the ambition they entertained of making themselves masters of the world, was probably but an effect of jealousy.

Passions often produce their contraries: avarice sometimes leads to prodigality, and prodigality to avarice; we are often obstinate through weakness and daring through timidity.

Whatever care we take to conceal our passions under the appearances of piety and honour, they are always to be seen through these veils.

Our self-love endures more impatiently the condemnation of our tastes than of our opinions.

Men are not only prone to forget benefits and injuries; they even hate those who have obliged them, and cease to hate those who have injured them. The necessity of revenging an injury or of recompensing a benefit seems a slavery to which they are unwilling to submit.

The clemency of princes is often but policy to win the affections of the people.

This clemency, of which they make a merit, arises oftentimes from vanity, sometimes from idleness, oftentimes from fear, and almost always from all three combined.

The moderation of those who are happy arises from the calm which good fortune bestows upon their temper.

Moderation is caused by the fear of exciting the envy and contempt which those merit who are intoxicated with their good fortune; it is a vain display of our strength of mind, and in short the moderation of men at their greatest height is only a desire to appear greater than their fortune.

We have all sufficient strength to support the misfortunes of others.

The constancy of the wise is only the talent of concealing the agitation of their hearts.

Those who are condemned to death affect sometimes a constancy and contempt for death which is only the fear of facing it; so that one may say that this constancy and contempt are to their mind what the bandage is to their eyes.

Philosophy triumphs over past evils and future evils; but present evils triumph over it.

Few people know death, we only endure it, usu-

ally from determination, and even from stupidity and custom; and most men only die because they know not how to prevent dying.

When great men permit themselves to be cast down by the continuance of misfortune, they show us that they were only sustained by ambition, and not by their mind; so that *plus* a great vanity, heroes are made like other men.

We need greater virtues to sustain good than evil fortune.

Neither the sun nor death can be looked at without winking.

People are often vain of their passions, even of the worst, but envy is a passion so timid and shamefaced that no one ever dare avow her.

Jealousy is in a manner just and reasonable, as it tends to preserve a good which belongs, or which we believe belongs to us; on the other hand envy is a fury which cannot endure the happiness of others.

The evil that we do does not attract to us so much persecution and hatred as our good qualities.

We have more strength than will; and it is often merely for an excuse we say things are impossible.

If we had no faults we should not take so much pleasure in noting those of others.

Jealousy lives upon doubt; and comes to an end or becomes a fury as soon as it passes from doubt to certainty.

Pride indemnifies itself and loses nothing even when it casts away vanity.

If we had no pride we should not complain of that of others.

Pride is much the same in all men, the only difference is the method and manner of showing it.

It would seem that nature, which has so wisely ordered the organs of our body for our happiness, has also given us pride to spare us the mortification of knowing our imperfections.

Pride has a larger part than goodness in our remonstrances with those who commit faults, and we reprove them not so much to correct as to persuade them that we ourselves are free from faults.

We promise according to our hopes; we perform according to our fears.

Interest speaks all sorts of tongues and plays all sorts of characters; even that of disinterestedness.

Interest blinds some and makes some see.

Those who apply themselves too closely to little things often become incapable of great things.

We have not enough strength to follow all our reason.

A man often believes himself leader when he is

led; as his mind endeavours to reach one goal, his heart insensibly drags him towards another.

Strength and weakness of mind are misnamed; they are really only the good or happy arrangement of our bodily organs.

The caprice of our temper is even more whimsical than that of Fortune.

The attachment or indifference which philosophers have shown to life is only the style of their self-love, about which we can no more dispute than of that of the palate or of the choice of colours.

Whatever difference there appears in our fortunes, there is nevertheless a certain compensation of good and evil which renders them equal.

Whatever great advantages Nature may give, it is not she alone, but Fortune also that makes the hero.

The contempt of riches in philosophers was only a hidden desire to avenge their merit upon the injustice of fortune, by despising the very goods of which fortune had deprived them; it was a secret to guard themselves against the degradation of poverty, it was a back way by which to arrive at that distinction which they could not gain by riches.

The hate of favourites is only a love of favour. The envy of *not* possessing it consoles and softens its regrets by the contempt it evinces for those who possess it, and we refuse them our homage, not being able to detract from them what attracts that of the rest of the world.

To establish ourselves in the world we do everything to appear as if we were established.

Although men flatter themselves with their great actions, they are not so often the result of a great design as of chance.

It would seem that our actions have lucky or unlucky stars to which they owe a great part of the blame or praise which is given them.

Our temper sets a price upon every gift that we receive from fortune.

Happiness is in the taste, and not in the things themselves; we are happy from possessing what we like, not from possessing what others like.

We are never so happy or so unhappy as we suppose.

Those who think they have merit persuade themselves that they are honoured by being unhappy, in order to persuade others and themselves that they are worthy to be the butt of fortune.

Nothing should so much diminish the satisfaction which we feel with ourselves as seeing that we disapprove at one time of that which we approve of at another.

It is difficult to define love; all we can say is that in the soul it is a desire to rule, in the mind it is a sympathy, and in the body it is a hidden and delicate wish to possess what we love—*plus* many mysteries.

If there is a pure love, exempt from the mixture of our other passions, it is that which is concealed at the bottom of the heart and of which even ourselves are ignorant.

There is no disguise which can long hide love where it exists, nor feign it, where it does not.

There are few people who would not be ashamed of being beloved when they love no longer.

If we judge of love by the majority of its results, it rather resembles hatred than friendship.

We may find women who have never indulged in an intrigue, but it is rare to find those who have intrigued but once.

There is only one sort of love, but there are a thousand different copies.

We often persuade ourselves to love people who are more powerful than we are, yet interest alone produces our friendships; we do not give our hearts away for the good we wish to do, but for that we expect to receive.

Our distrust of another justifies his deceit.

There is real love just as there are real ghosts; every person speaks of it, few persons have seen it.

Love lends its name to an infinite number of engagements (*commerces*) which are attributed to it, but with which it has no more concern than the Doge has with all that is done in Venice.

The love of justice is simply in the majority of men the fear of suffering injustice.

Silence is the best resolve for him who distrusts himself.

What renders us so changeable in our friendship is that it is difficult to know the qualities of the soul, but easy to know those of the mind.

We can love nothing but what agrees with us, and we can only follow our taste or our pleasure when we prefer our friends to ourselves; nevertheless, it is only by that preference that friendship can be true and perfect.

Reconciliation with our enemies is but a desire to better our condition, a weariness of war, the fear of some unlucky accident.

What men term friendship is merely a partnership with a collection of reciprocal interests and an exchange of favours—in fact, it is but a trade in which self-love always expects to gain something.

It is more disgraceful to distrust than to be deceived by our friends.

Men would not live long in society were they not the dupes of each other.

Self-love increases or diminishes for us the good qualities of our friends, in proportion to the satisfaction we feel with them, and we judge of their merit by the manner in which they act towards us.

Every one blames his memory, no one blames his judgment.

In the intercourse of life, we please more by our faults than by our good qualities.

The largest ambition has the least appearance of ambition when it meets with an absolute impossibility in compassing its object.

To awaken a man who is deceived as to his own merit is to do him as bad a turn as that done to the Athenian madman, who was happy in believing that all the ships touching at that port belonged to him.

Old men delight in giving good advice as a consolation for the fact that they can no longer set bad examples.

Great names degrade instead of elevating those who know not how to sustain them.

The test of extraordinary merit is to see those who envy it the most yet obliged to praise it.

A man is perhaps ungrateful, but often less chargeable with ingratitude than his benefactor is.

We are deceived if we think that mind and judgment are two different matters: judgment is but the extent of the light of the mind. This light penetrates to the bottom of matters; it remarks all that can be remarked, and perceives what appears imperceptible. Therefore we must agree that it is the extent of the light in the mind that produces all the effects which we attribute to judgment.

Every one praises his heart, none dare praise their understanding.

Politeness of mind consists in thinking chaste and refined thoughts.

Gallantry of mind is saying the most empty things in an agreeable manner.

Ideas often flash across our minds more complete than we could make them after much labour.

The head is ever the dupe of the heart.

Those who know their minds do not necessarily know their hearts.

Men and things have each their proper perspective; to judge rightly of some it is necessary to see them near, of others we can never judge rightly but at a distance.

A man for whom accident discovers sense, is not a rational being. A man only is so who understands, who distinguishes, who tests it.

To understand matters rightly we should understand their details, and as that knowledge is almost infinite, our knowledge is always superficial and imperfect.

We become so accustomed to disguise ourselves to others that at last we are disguised to ourselves.

We often act treacherously more from weariness than from a fixed motive.

We frequently do good to enable us with impunity to do evil.

If we conquer our passions it is more from their weakness than from our strength.

If we never flattered ourselves we should have but scant pleasure.

The most deceitful persons spend their lives in blaming deceit, so as to use it on some great occasion to promote some great interest.

The daily employment of cunning marks a little mind; it generally happens that those who resort to it in one respect to protect themselves lay themselves open to attack in another.

Cunning and treachery are the offspring of incapacity.

The true way to be deceived is to think oneself more knowing than others.

If it were not for the company of fools, a witty man would often be greatly at a loss.

We often boast that we are never bored, but yet we are so conceited that we do not perceive how often we bore others.

As it is the mark of great minds to say things in a few words, so it is that of little minds to use many words to say nothing.

It is oftener by the estimation of our own feelings that we exaggerate the good qualities of others than by their merit, and when we praise them we wish to attract their praise.

We do not like to praise, and we never praise without a motive. Praise is flattery, artful, hidden, delicate, which gratifies differently him who praises and him who is praised. The one takes it as the reward of merit, the other bestows it to show his impartiality and knowledge.

We often select envenomed praise which, by a reaction upon those we praise, shows faults we could not have shown by other means.

Usually we praise only to be praised.

Few are sufficiently wise to prefer censure which is useful to praise which is treacherous.

Some reproach praise; some praise reproach.

The refusal of praise is only the wish to be praised twice.

The desire which urges us to deserve praise

strengthens our good qualities, and praise given to wit, valor, and beauty tends to increase them.

It is easier to govern others than to prevent being governed.

If we never flattered ourselves the flattery of others would not hurt us.

Nature makes merit, but fortune sets it to work.

Fortune cures us of many faults that reason could not.

There are some persons who only disgust with their abilities; there are persons who please even with their faults.

There are persons whose only merit consists in saying and doing stupid things at the right time, and who ruin all if they change their manners.

The fame of great men ought always to be estimated by the means used to acquire it.

Flattery is base coin to which only our vanity gives currency.

It is not enough to have great qualities, we should also have the management of them.

However brilliant an action it should not be esteemed great unless the result of a great motive.

A certain harmony should be kept between actions and ideas if we desire to estimate the effects that they produce.

The art of using moderate abilities to advantage wins praise, and often acquires more reputation than real brilliancy.

Numberless arts appear foolish whose secret motives are most wise and weighty.

It is much easier to seem fitted for posts we do not fill than for those we do.

Ability wins us the esteem of the true men, luck that of the people.

The world oftener rewards the appearance of merit than merit itself.

Avarice is more opposed to economy than to liberality.

However deceitful Hope may be, yet she carries us on pleasantly to the end of life.

Idleness and fear keep us in the path of duty, but our virtue often gets the praise.

If one acts rightly and honestly, it is difficult to decide whether it is the effect of integrity or skill.

As rivers are lost in the sea, so are virtues in self.

If we thoroughly consider the varied effects of indifference, we find we miscarry more in our duties than in our interests.

There are different kinds of curiosity: one springs from interest, which makes us desire to know everything that may be profitable to us; another from pride, which springs from a desire of knowing what others are ignorant of.

It is far better to accustom our mind to bear the ills we have than to speculate on those which may befall us.

Constancy in love is a perpetual inconstancy which causes our heart to attach itself to all the qualities of the person we love in succession, sometimes giving the preference to one, sometimes to another. This constancy is merely inconstancy fixed and limited to the same person.

There are two kinds of constancy in love, one arising from incessantly finding in the loved one fresh objects to love, the other from regarding it as a point of honour to be constant.

Perseverance is not deserving of blame or praise, as it is merely the continuance of tastes and feelings which we can neither create nor destroy.

— ◆ —

JEAN DE LA FONTAINE

1621–1695

Member of the famous generation of 1660, La Fontaine was born at Château-Thierry. He first intended to enter the Church, but changed to law and made his literary debut with a translation from the Latin dramatist Terence. Receiving a pension from Fouquet, finance minister to Louis XIV, and from other patrons, he was able to devote his time to literary production. His work exhibits a remarkable power of observation, the ability to perceive and convey the humor of a situation, and a most effective technique of portraying the human through the animal. His fables are miniature dramas, serious but at the same time playful, joyous, reflective. He was a great master of the language and of all its poetic resources. His style is concise, like that of Racine, but highly expressive. He differs fundamentally from preceding fabulists in that he takes the moral as his point of departure, as the excuse for telling his story, instead of using the story to present the moral.

FURTHER READING

BAILLY, A. *La Fontaine* (Paris, 1937).
HAMEL, F. *Jean de La Fontaine* (New York, 1912).
A new translation of the fables by Margaret Wise Brown was published in New York and London, 1940.

The Cock and the Fox *

Upon a tree there mounted guard
  A veteran cock, adroit and cunning;
When to the roots a fox up running
  Spoke thus, in tones of kind regard:—
"Our quarrel, brother, 's at an end;
  Henceforth I hope to live your friend;
    For peace now reigns
    Throughout the animal domains.
  I bear the news. Come down, I pray,
And give me the embrace fraternal;   10
  And please, my brother, don't delay:
So much the tidings do concern all,
  That I must spread them far to-day.
Now you and yours can take your walks
Without a fear or thought of hawks;
And should you clash with them or others,
In us you'll find the best of brothers;—
    For which you may, this joyful night,
    Your merry bonfires light.
    But, first, let's seal the bliss   20
    With one fraternal kiss."
"Good friend," the cock replied, "upon my word,
A better thing I never heard;
    And doubly I rejoice
    To hear it from your voice:
And, really, there must be something in it,
  For yonder come two greyhounds, which, I flatter
  Myself, are couriers on this very matter;
They come so fast, they'll be here in a minute.
  I'll down, and all of us will seal the blessing   30
  With general kissing and caressing."
    "Adieu," said the Fox, "my errand's pressing;
    I'll hurry on my way,
    And we'll rejoice some other day."
So off the fellow scampered, quick and light,
To gain the fox-holes of a neighboring height,—
Less happy in his stratagem than flight.
  The cock laughed sweetly in his sleeve;—
  'Tis doubly sweet deceiver to deceive.

The Wolf and the Dog

A prowling wolf, whose shaggy skin
(So strict the watch of dogs had been)
  Hid little but his bones,
Once met a mastiff dog astray.
A prouder, fatter, sleeker Tray,
  No human mortal owns.

* This and the two following fables were translated by Elizur Wright.

Sir Wolf in famish'd plight
  Would fain have made a ration
  Upon his fat relation;
But then he first must fight;   10
  And well the dog seem'd able
  To save from wolfish table
His carcass snug and tight.
  So, then, in civil conversation
  The wolf express'd his admiration
Of Tray's fine case. Said Tray, politely,
Yourself, good sir, may be as sightly,
  Quit but the woods, advised by me.
  For all your fellows here, I see,
Are shabby wretches, lean and gaunt,   20
Belike to die of haggard want.
With such a pack, of course it follows,
One fights for every bit he swallows.
    Come, then, with me, and share
    On equal terms our princely fare.
    But what with you
    Has one to do?
Inquires the wolf. Light work indeed,
Replies the dog; you only need
  To bark a little now and then,   30
  To chase off duns and beggar men,
To fawn on friends that come or go forth,
Your master please, and so forth;
  For which you have to eat
  All sorts of well-cook'd meat—
Cold pullets, pigeons, savoury messes—
Besides unnumber'd fond caresses.
  The wolf, by force of appetite
  Accepts the terms outright,
  Tears glistening in his eyes,   40
  But faring on, he spies
    A gall'd spot on the mastiff's neck.
What's that? he cries. O, nothing but a speck.
A speck? Ay, ay; 'tis not enough to pain me;
Perhaps the collar's mark by which they chain me.
  Chain! chain you! What! run you not, then,
  Just where you please, and when?
    Not always, sir; but what of that?
    Enough for me, to spoil your fat!
    It ought to be a precious price   50
    Which could to servile chains entice;
    For me, I'll shun them while I've wit.
    So ran Sir Wolf, and runneth yet.

The Cat and the Old Rat

A story-writer of our sort
Historifies, in short,

Of one that may be reckoned
A Rodilard the Second,—
The Alexander of the cats,
The Attila, the scourge of rats,
    Whose fierce and whiskered head
    Among the latter spread,
    A league around, its dread;
    Who seemed, indeed, determined   10
    The world should be unvermined.
The planks with props more false than slim,
    The tempting heaps of poisoned meal,
    The traps of wire and traps of steel,
Were only play, compared with him.
    At length, so sadly were they scared,
    The rats and mice no longer dared
        To show their thievish faces
        Outside their hiding-places,
    Thus shunning all pursuit; whereat   20
    Our crafty General Cat
Contrived to hang himself, as dead,
Beside the wall, with downward head,—
Resisting gravitation's laws
By clinging with his hinder claws
        To some small bit of string.
        The rats esteemed the thing
    A judgment for some naughty deed,
        Some thievish snatch,
        Or ugly scratch;   30
And thought their foe had got his meed
By being hung indeed.
    With hope elated all
    Of laughing at his funeral,
They thrust their noses out in air;
And now to show their heads they dare,
Now dodging back, now venturing more;
At last, upon the larder's store
They fall to filching, as of yore.
A scanty feast enjoyed these shallows;   40
Down dropped the hung one from his gallows,
        And of the hindmost caught.
"Some other tricks to me are known,"
Said he, while tearing bone from bone,
    "By long experience taught;
The point is settled, free from doubt,
That from your holes you shall come out."
His threat as good as prophecy
Was proved by Mr. Mildandsly;
For, putting on a mealy robe,   50
He squatted in an open tub,
And held his purring and his breath;—
Out came the vermin to their death.
On this occasion, one old stager,
A rat as gray as any badger,

Who had in battle lost his tail,
Abstained from smelling at the meal;
And cried, far off, "Ah! General Cat,
I much suspect a heap like that;
Your meal is not the thing, perhaps,   60
For one who knows somewhat of traps;
Should you a sack of meal become,
I'd let you be, and stay at home."

Well said, I think, and prudently,
By one who knew distrust to be
The parent of security.

JEAN DE LA BRUYÈRE

1645–1696

La Bruyère's *Characters*, modeled on a book of similar title by Theophrastus, has as its declared purpose the observation of manners and customs of his time. It is remarkable for vividness of expression, for its realism, and for its classic balance. La Bruyère's style is perhaps more like that of Montaigne than that of La Rochefoucauld. His work is justly celebrated for the portraits or caricatures with which it abounds and which are based upon his observation of well-known people of the time. He attacks certain aspects of society: fortune hunters, tax collectors, patrons, misers, the self-interest of courtiers; and he manifests a certain pessimism and disillusionment to be found in other works of the later years of the reign of Louis XIV.

FURTHER READING

The Characters of Jean de la Bruyère, translated by Henri Van Laun with an introduction, biographical memoir, and notes (London, 1929).
TAVERA, F. *L'Idéal Moral et l'Idée Religieuse dans les Caractères de La Bruyère* (Paris, 1940).

The Characters *

OF PERSONAL MERIT

(1) What man is not convinced of his inefficiency, though endowed with the rarest talents and the most extraordinary merit, when he considers that at his death he leaves a world that will not feel

* Translated by Henri Van Laun.

his loss, and where so many people are ready to supply his place?

(2) All the worth of some people lies in their name; upon a closer inspection it dwindles to nothing, but from a distance it deceives us.

(3) Though I am convinced that those who are selected to fill various offices, every man according to his talents and his profession, perform their duties well, yet I venture to say that perhaps there are many men in this world, known or unknown, who are not employed, and would perform those duties also very well. I am inclined to think so from the marvellous success of certain people, who through chance alone obtained a place, and from whom until then no great things were expected.

How many admirable men, of very great talent, die without ever being talked about! And how many are there living yet of whom one does not speak, nor ever will speak!

(4) A man without eulogists and without a set of friends, who is unconnected with any clique, stands alone, and has no other recommendations but a good deal of merit, has very great difficulty in emerging from his obscurity and in rising as high as a conceited noodle who has a good deal of influence!

(5) No one hardly ever thinks of the merit of others, unless it is pointed out to him. Men are too engrossed by themselves to have the leisure of penetrating or discerning character, so that a person of great merit and of greater modesty may languish a long time in obscurity.

(6) Genius and great talents are often wanting, but sometimes only opportunities. Some people deserve praise for what they have done, and others for what they would have done.

(7) It is not so uncommon to meet with intelligence as with people who make use of it, or who praise other persons' intelligence and employ it.

(8) There are more tools than workmen, and of the latter more bad than good ones. What would you think of a man who would use a plane to saw, and his saw to plane?

(9) There is no business in this world so troublesome as the pursuit of fame: life is over before you have hardly begun your work.

(10) What is to be done with Egesippus who solicits some employment? Shall he have a post in the finances or in the army? It does not matter much, and interest alone can decide it, for he is as able to handle money or to make up accounts as to be a soldier. "He is fit for anything," say his friends, which always means that he has no more talent for one thing than for another, or, in other words, that he is fit for nothing. Thus it is with most men; in their youth they are only occupied with themselves, are spoiled by idleness or pleasure, and then wrongly imagine, when more advanced in years, that it is sufficient for them to be useless or poor for the commonwealth to be obliged to give them a place or to relieve them. They seldom profit by that important maxim, that men ought to employ the first years of their lives in so qualifying themselves by their studies and labour, that the commonwealth itself, needing their industry and their knowledge as necessary materials for its building up, might be induced, for its own benefit, to make their fortune or improve it. It is our duty to labour in order to make ourselves worthy of filling some office: the rest does not concern us, but is other people's business.

(11) To make the most of ourselves through things which do not depend on others, but on ourselves alone, or to abandon all ideas of making the most of ourselves, is an inestimable maxim and of infinite advantage when brought into practice, useful to the weak, the virtuous, and the intelligent, whom it renders masters of their fortune or their ease; hurtful to the great, as it would diminish the number of their attendants, or rather of their slaves, would abate their pride, and partly their authority, and would almost reduce them to the pleasures of the table and the splendour of their carriages; it would deprive them of the pleasure they feel in being entreated, courted, solicited; of allowing people to dance attendance on them, or of refusing any request; of promising and not performing; it would thwart the disposition they sometimes have of bringing fools forward and of depressing merit when they chance to discern it; it would banish from courts plots, parties, trickery, baseness, flattery, and deceit; it would make a court, full of agitation, bustle, and intrigue, resemble a comedy, or even a tragedy, where the wise are only spectators; it would restore dignity to the several conditions of men, serenity to their looks, enlarge their liberty, and awaken in them their natural talents as well as a habit for work and for exercise; it would excite them to emulation, to a desire for renown, a love for virtue; and instead of vile, restless, useless courtiers, often burdensome to the commonwealth, would make them clever administrators, exemplary heads of families, upright judges or good financiers, great commanders, orators, or philosophers; and all the inconvenience any of them would suffer through this

would be, perhaps, to leave to their heirs less treasures, but excellent examples.

(27) You tell me that Philemon's clothes blaze with gold, but that metal also shone when they were in the tailor's shop. His clothes are made of the finest materials; but are those same materials less fine in the warehouse or in the whole piece? But then the embroidery and trimmings make them still more magnificent. I praise, therefore, the skill of his tailor. Ask him what o'clock it is, and he pulls out a watch, a masterpiece of workmanship; the handle of his sword is an onyx, and on his finger he wears a large diamond which dazzles our eyes and has no flaw. He wants none of all those curious nicknacks which are worn more for show than service, and is as profuse with all kinds of ornaments as a young fellow who has married a wealthy old lady. Well, at last you have excited my curiosity: I should, at least, like to see all this finery: send me Philemon's clothes and jewels; but I do not wish to see him.

You are mistaken, Philemon, if you think you will be esteemed a whit the more for your showy coach, the large number of rogues who follow you, and those six horses that draw you along; we mentally remove all splendour which is not properly yours, to reach you personally, and find you to be a mere conceited noodle.

Not but that a man is sometimes to be forgiven who, on account of his splendid retinue, his rich clothes, and his magnificent carriage, thinks himself of more noble descent and more intelligent than he really is; for he sees this opinion expressed on the countenances and in the eyes of those who speak to him.

(40) Menippus is a bird decked in various feathers which are not his. He neither says nor feels anything, but repeats the feelings and sayings of others; it is so natural for him to make use of other people's minds that he is the first deceived by it, and often believes he speaks his own mind or expresses his own thoughts when he is but the echo of some man he just parted with. He is bearable for a quarter of an hour, but a moment after he flags, degenerates, loses the little polish his shallow memory gives him, and shows he has nothing more left. He alone ignores how very far he is from the sublime and the heroic; and having no idea of the extent of his intelligence, ingenuously believes that he possesses as much as it is possible for any man to have, and accordingly assumes the air and manners of one who has nothing more to wish for nor to envy any one. He often soliloquises, and so

little conceals it, that the passers-by see him and think he is always making up his mind, or is finally deciding some matter or other. If you bow to him at a certain time, you perplex him as to whether he has to return the bow or not; and, whilst he is deliberating, you are already out of his sight. His vanity, which has made him a gentleman, has raised him above himself, and made him what naturally he is not. When you behold him, you can judge he has nothing to do but to survey himself, so that he may perceive everything he wears suits him, and that his dress is not incongruous; he fancies all men's eyes are upon him, and that people come to look on him one after another.

OF SOCIETY AND OF CONVERSATION

A fool is always troublesome, a man of sense perceives when he pleases or is tiresome; he goes away the very minute before it might have been thought he stayed too long.

(3) Mischievous wags are a kind of insect which is in everybody's way and plentiful in all countries. Real wit is rarely to be met with, and even if it be innate in a man, it must be very difficult to maintain a reputation for it during any length of time; for, commonly, he that makes us laugh does not stand high in our estimation.

(6) We meet with persons who, in their conversation, or in the little intercourse we have with them, disgust us with their ridiculous expressions, the novelty, and, if I may say so, the impropriety of the phraseology they use, as well as by linking together certain words which never came together but in their mouths, and were never intended by their creators to have the meaning they give to them. In their conversation they neither follow reason nor custom, but only their own eccentricity; and their desire always to jest, and perhaps to shine, gradually changes it into a peculiar sort of dialect which at last becomes natural to them; they accompany this extraordinary language by affected gesticulations and a conceited kind of pronunciation. They are all highly delighted with themselves, and with their pleasant wit, of which, indeed they are not entirely destitute; but we pity them for the little they have, and, what is worse, we suffer through it.

(9) Arrias has read and seen everything, at least he would lead you to think so; he is a man of universal knowledge, or pretends to be, and would rather tell a falsehood than be silent or appear to be ignorant of something. Some person is talking

at meal-time in the house of a man of rank of a northern court; he interrupts and prevents him from telling what he knows; he goes hither and thither in that distant country as if he were a native of it; he discourses about the habits of its court, the native women, the laws and customs of the land; he tells many little stories which happened there, thinks them very entertaining, and is the first to laugh loudly at them. Somebody presumes to contradict him, and clearly proves to him that what he says is untrue. Arrias is not disconcerted; on the contrary, he grows angry at the interruption, and exclaims: "I aver and relate nothing but what I know on excellent authority; I had it from Sethon, the French ambassador at that court, who only a few days ago came back to Paris, and is a particular friend of mine; I asked him several questions, and he replied to them all without concealing anything." He continues his story with greater confidence than he began it, till one of the company informs him that the gentleman whom he has been contradicting was Sethon himself, but lately arrived from his embassy.

(11) Any one who is infatuated with himself and quite convinced he is very clever, only shows that he has but very little intelligence or none at all. It is a misfortune for a man to listen to the conversation of such a person. What a great many affected phrases he has to endure! How many of those fanciful words which appear of a sudden, live for a short time, and then are never heard again! If such a person relates some trifling event, it is not so much to give some information to his hearers, as merely for the honour of telling it and of telling it cleverly. He amplifies it till it becomes a romance; he makes the people connected with it think as he does; he puts his own trivial expressions in their mouths, and renders them like himself, very talkative; he falls then into some parentheses which may pass for episodes, and by which speaker and hearers forget what the story really was about. It is difficult to say what might have become of them, had not somebody fortunately come in to break up the company and put an end to the narrative.

(15) Some men speak one moment before they think; others tediously study everything they say, and in conversation bore us as painfully as was the travail of their mind; they are, as it were, made up of phrases and quaint expressions, whilst their gestures are as affected as their behaviour. They call themselves "purists" and do not venture to say the most trifling word not in use, however expressive it may be. Nothing comes from them worth remembering, nothing is spontaneous and unrestrained; they speak correctly, but they are very tiresome.

(16) The true spirit of conversation consists more in bringing out the cleverness of others than in showing a great deal of it yourself; he who goes away pleased with himself and his own wit is also greatly pleased with you. Most men rather please than admire you; they seek less to be instructed, and even to be amused, than to be praised and applauded; the most delicate of pleasures is to please another person.

(32) Politeness does not always produce kindness of heart, justice, complacency, or gratitude, but it gives to a man at least the appearance of it, and makes him seem externally what he really should be.

We may define all the essentials of politeness, but we cannot determine how and where they should be used; they depend on ordinary habits and customs, are connected with times and places, and are not the same in both sexes nor indifferent ranks of life; intelligence alone cannot find this out; politeness is acquired and perfected by imitation. Only some persons are naturally disposed to be polite, as others are in acquiring great talents and solid virtue. Politeness tends, undoubtedly, to advance merit and to render it agreeable; a man must have very eminent qualities to hold his own without being polite.

The very essence of politeness seems to be to take care that by our words and actions we make other people pleased with us as well as with themselves.

(64) Advice which is necessary in all matters of business, is sometimes hurtful in social affairs to those who give it, and useless to the persons to whom it is given. You observe, perhaps, faults in manners and morals which are either not acknowledged, or, perhaps, considered virtues; you blot out some passages in a composition which please the author most, and in which he thinks he has surpassed himself. By those means you lose the confidence of your friend without making him better or wiser.

(76) Profound ignorance makes a man dogmatical; he who knows nothing thinks he can teach others what he just now has learned himself; whilst he who knows a great deal can scarcely imagine anyone should be unacquainted with what he says, and, therefore, speaks with more indifference.

THE ABSENT-MINDED MAN *

Menalcas comes down stairs, opens his door to go out, and then shuts it; he perceives that he has his night-cap on, and on looking more closely he finds that he is only half shaved, that his sword is hung on the right-hand side, that his hose are wrinkled down upon his heels, and that his shirt is outside his breeches.

As he walks down the street, he receives a buffet in the stomach or in the face; he has not the remotest idea what it may be until he opens his eyes and, emerging from sleep, finds himself in front of a long carriage-shaft or behind a long building-board carried by a workman. We see him colliding with a blind man, getting tangled up in his legs, and both of them falling over backwards. Many a time he has suddenly come nose to nose with a prince, and looking about him carefully has found that he has time enough only to plaster himself against the wall in order to make way for him.

He searches frantically, he upsets everything, he shouts, he get into a temper, he calls his servants one after the other; everything is gone; everything is lost. He asks for his gloves when they are on his own hands, like the lady who took occasion to ask for her mask when she had it on her face already. He enters a room at court and walks under a chandelier; his wig catches upon it and remains hanging. All the court see it and laugh; Menalcas sees it and laughs harder than anybody else. He casts his eyes over the whole assembly to see whose ears are showing or who else has lost his wig.

If he goes out through the city, after he has walked a little way he thinks himself lost. He grows excited; he asks passers-by where he is, and is told exactly the name of the street. He finally goes into his house, and then comes running out again, thinking he has made a mistake.

He comes out of the Palace of Justice and, finding at the foot of the steps a carriage, he takes it for his own and seats himself in it. The coachman whips up, thinking he is taking his own master home. Menalcas gets out at the gate, crosses the courtyard, mounts the stairs, walks through the ante-chamber, the drawing-room, the study. Everything is familiar: nothing is strange to him. He sits down; he rests himself; he is at home. The master of the house appears. Menalcas arises to receive him; he treats him with great civility; he begs him to be seated, and thinks he is doing the honors of his own house. He talks; he meditates;

* Translator anonymous.

he resumes conversation. The master of the house is bored, but he lingers on amazed. Menalcas is no less bored, but he does not say what he thinks: that he has to do with a bore, or an idler, who he hopes finally will withdraw. At last when night comes Menalcas is with great difficulty apprised of his mistake.

On another occasion he pays a visit to a lady and, convincing himself that it is he that is receiving her, he seats himself in a chair without the slightest idea of leaving it. It seems to him after a time that the lady is making rather a long visit and begins to expect at every moment that she will get up and leave him to himself. When the visit prolongs itself well into the night and he is growing hungry, he finally invites her to have supper. The lady laughs so heartily that she awakes him.

He marries in the morning, forgets it by evening, and stays out all night. Some years later he loses his wife; she dies in his arms, and he assists at the obsequies. The next day, when dinner is announced, he asks if his wife is ready and if she has been informed.

At another time he loses at play all the money in his purse; he goes to his study, opens his safe, brings out his money chest, takes from it what he needs, and returns it to the safe. Then he hears a sound of yelping from the safe. Astonished at this prodigy he opens the safe again and bursts into laughter to find that he has locked up his dog instead of his money. When he is playing at trick-track [1] he calls for a drink. It is brought to him as it is his turn to play. He holds the dice-box in one hand and the drink in the other, and, being very thirsty, he downs the dice and almost the dice-box as well and throws the glass of water on the trick-track board, drenching his opponent.

In a bed-chamber where he was familiarly received he spit on the bed and threw his hat on the floor, thinking that he was doing just the opposite.

As he is walking along the bank he asks what time it is. A watch is handed to him and he has hardly received it when he forgets both the time and the watch and throws the timepiece into the water to get it out of his way.

Menalcas is going down the steps of the Louvre and meets another man coming up. "You're the one I'm looking for," he says. He takes him by the hand and makes him walk back down with him. He crosses several courts, goes into the rooms, comes out again, goes one way, and retraces his steps; and at last he happens to look at the man he

[1] backgammon.

has been leading about for a quarter of an hour and is astonished that he should be there. He has nothing to say to him; he lets go his hand and turns away.

He often asks you a question and is far away before you can answer; or he asks you in passing how your father does, and when you reply that he is very ill he exclaims that he is very glad to hear it. He encounters you on the street; he is delighted to see you, for he was just coming to talk to you about something. Then he looks at your hand. "You have a beautiful ruby there," he says, "is it a balas?" [2]—and he leaves you and continues on his way. So much for the important matter about which he wished to speak with you.

He finds himself in the country and says to someone that he considers him fortunate to have been able to slip away and spend on his country estate the time when the court is being held at Fontainebleau. He passes on and talks variously with other people; then he comes back to the same person and says to him, "No doubt you had a pleasant time at Fontainebleau; you must have had plenty of hunting." Then he begins a story which he forgets to finish; he laughs to himself; he roars out at something that with him passes for cleverness; he replies aloud to his own thoughts, sings between his teeth, whistles, throws himself into a chair, gives a complaining whine, yawns—he thinks he is alone.

When he is at dinner the bread keeps piling up on his plate; it is true his neighbors are going without it as well as without knives and forks, for he cannot refrain from playing with them. There has been invented a great soup ladle to facilitate serving. He takes it, plunges it into his dish, fills it, carries it to his mouth, and cannot get over his astonishment at seeing spattered over his clothing the soup that he thinks he has just swallowed. He forgets to drink all through the dinner, or if he does remember it and finds he has been given too much wine, he dashes half of it into the face of the diner at his right. He drinks the rest tranquilly and cannot understand why everybody bursts out laughing just because he has thrown on the ground the superfluous quantity.

He is taken to Chartres. There he is shown a cloister adorned with works all from the hand of an excellent painter. The monk who explains it speaks of St. Bruno and tells a long tale of the saint's adventure with the canon, and shows it to him in one of the pictures. Menalcas, who during the recital is out of the cloister and far away, at

[2] Persian spinel (variety of ruby).

last comes to himself and asks of the monk whether it was Bruno or the canon that was damned.

He finds himself by chance in the company of a young widow; he speaks of the departed husband and asks how he died. The woman, in whom grief was renewed by this remark, weeps, sobs, and goes into all the details of her husband's malady from the beginning of the fever to the death-agony. "Madame," asks Menalcas, who has apparently listened with great attention, "was he the only one you had?"

———◆———

PIERRE DE CORNEILLE

1606–1684

Corneille was the forerunner of the great Neoclassic dramatists of the Golden Age in France. His play *Le Cid* (1636) paved the way for the appearance of Racine. In addition to his plays, Corneille left a certain amount of lyric verse in the sophisticated tone of the seventeenth century.

FURTHER READING

TURNELL, M. *The Classical Moment* (New York, 1946).

Stanzas to the Marquise

Lady fair, if on the page
Of my face traits elderly
Show, remember, at my age,
Yours will little better be.

Time to all that is most fair
Loves to offer his affront;
He your roses will not spare,
As he furrowed hath my front.

The same course of star and star
Rules the days of you and me:
Folk have seen me what you are;
And what I am you will be.

None the less, I have some charm,
Enough puissant, anydele,
For me not o'er much alarm
At Time's ravages to feel.

Charms you have, that men adore;
But this other, that you scorn,
Well may last, when yours of yore
Have been long ago outworn.

I the glory of your eyes
Can preserve for ages new
And cause races yet to rise
What I choose believe of you.

'Midst the newborn nations, where
I shall in some credit be,
You will only pass for fair,
Inasmuch as pleases me.

So bethink you, fair Marquise:
Though a greybeard fright the eye,
He is worth the pains to please,
When he fashioned is as I.

(trans. by John Payne)

———————◆———————

VOLTAIRE

1694–1778

The life of François Arouet, better known by his pen name, Voltaire, epitomizes the Age of Reason in France. Prose writer, poet, dramatist, philosopher, satirist, scientist, pamphleteer, the greatest wit in an age of great wits, his work embraced almost the totality of the intellectual activity of his period. From his prolific pen came a hundred volumes containing every known literary type: tragedies, comedies, lengthy epic and didactic poems; volumes of history and biography; novels and tales in prose and verse; treatises, essays, and tracts on a multitude of subjects; countless letters and innumerable shorter poems, epigrams, and maxims. The perennial state of chronic ill-health in which he lived seems not to have disturbed in any manner the tremendous productivity of the man or to have shortened his life or lessened his vitality to the slightest degree.

Born into a respectable bourgeois family in Paris, the son of a notary, young François was sent to study law, but instead spent his time participating in the nonconformist activity of a group of freethinkers which flourished at the time. In 1726, forced to flee as a consequence of a quarrel with the stupid Chevalier de Rohan-Chabot, Voltaire spent two years in England where he established highly fruitful contacts with the leading writers, philosophers, and scientists of that country. When he returned to France, his thought had been channeled into the domains of skeptical philosophy and cosmopolitan criticism and he was most interested in pub-

licizing the liberal parliamentary institutions he had found among the English. This he did in his famous *Lettres Philosophiques*; as a consequence of their critical nature he was again forced to flee. This time he went to Cirey, a château in Lorraine which belonged to one Madame du Châtelet, one of the first women of her time in intellect. There, assisted by his hostess, he devoted himself wholeheartedly to scientific, philosophical, and literary activity, as well as to the interminable series of literary and philosophical quarrels which he perpetually carried on with his contemporaries.

After a long correspondence, and plagued at home by continual persecution from the forces of religious and governmental orthodoxy, Voltaire accepted the oft-repeated invitation of Frederick the Great to come to Prussia. For a time he was the leading figure of that enlightened monarch's brilliant court, but, as is almost inevitable when two such strong wills come together, a rift developed. The result was that, less than three years after his arrival, Voltaire was again forced to flee. This time it was difficult to find a home, since he was a *persona non grata* not only to French officialdom, which he had unremittingly lampooned in countless inflammatory pamphlets and other writings, but also to authorities in any predominantly Catholic country because of his relentless thrusts at the intolerance and authoritarianism of the eighteenth-century Church. He finally purchased the splendid estate of Ferney in Burgundy near enough to the Swiss border so that in case of need he could slip across it to another dwelling which he owned on the other side. So, at the age of sixty when most men are retiring, Voltaire settled down in comparative security from persecution to begin the most productive period of his long life.

It is impossible to summarize in a brief space the vast scope of Voltaire's literary activity. Suffice it to say that it is in the lighter genres—the epistles, tales, and occasional verse—that his gaiety, ready wit, grace, and talent were allowed full sway, and that it is precisely these works that are more attractive to the modern reader. His serious works tend to follow too closely the slavish subjection to those Neo-classic rules which are characteristic of the writers of his period with the result that they have an unpleasant dullness, absence of warmth, and stiltedness. Composed largely in the tradition of the oriental apologue so popular in the eighteenth century, his philosophical tales, such as *Candide, Zadig,* and "The Way the World Goes," are characterized by rapidity of action, brilliant sprightliness of style, shrewd philosophical concept, and an incomparable display of wit in its most graceful form. They usually involve a personage with a strange name who travels through exotic lands, or else visitors with equally strange names who come to Paris (Persepolis in our story) from their distant homelands, and the tale presents one or more of the principles dear to the eighteenth-century *philosophes,* usually to the detriment of the existing regime.

In all his work, Voltaire placed himself squarely in the stream of skepticism which runs from Montaigne through Molière into the French Revolution. He pleaded, among other things, for religious and civil tolerance, free speech, abolition of slavery, civil liberty of the person, separation of Church and State, proportional taxation, and inviolability of property. His political ideal was an enlightened monarchy, one perhaps nearer to benevolent despotism than to liberalism. No democratic reformer in the modern sense, like Rabelais he had no confidence in the judgment of the masses. While he was a great humanitarian, as his treatment of the peasants on his estate at Ferney adequately proves, and while he was the implacable enemy of all forms of tyranny and authoritarianism, he gave no support to any cause resembling equalitarianism in government. Voltaire had no desire to overthrow the French monarchy or to foment a revolution; he merely hoped that his writings might stimulate the government into improving itself and thereby into improving the conditions of life in France.

"The Way the World Goes" might be considered not only as an Oriental apologue, but also as a variant of the very popular imaginary voyage literature to which *Gulliver's Travels* also belongs. Through observation or apparent criticism of a distant government, the institutions of contemporary France are attacked in characteristic Voltairian fashion. It was this sort of thing which, despite lack of intent on Voltaire's part, accelerated the movement toward the French Revolution and the consequent fall of the Old Regime in France. The story is indicative of the philosophy and manner of treatment which we find in many of Voltaire's longer and perhaps more important works.

FURTHER READING

ALDINGTON, R. *Voltaire* (London and New York, 1925).
BRAILSFORD, H. *Voltaire* (London, 1935).
MAUROIS, A. *Voltaire,* translated by Hamish Miles (London, 1935).
TORREY, N. L. *The Spirit of Voltaire* (New York, 1938).
TORREY, N. L. *Voltaire and the English Deists* (New Haven and London, 1930).

The Way the World Goes *

AMONG the genii who preside over the empires of the world, Ithuriel holds one of the first places, and has the province of Upper Asia. He came down one morning, entered the dwelling of Babouc, a Scythian who lived on the banks of the Oxus, and addressed him thus:

"Babouc, the follies and disorders of the Persians have drawn down upon them our wrath. An assembly of the genii of Upper Asia was held yesterday to consider whether Persepolis should be punished or utterly destroyed. Go thither, and make full investigation; on thy return inform me faithfully of all, and I will decide according to thy report either to chastise the city or to root it out."

"But, my lord," said Babouc humbly, "I have never been in Persia, and know no one there."

"So much the better," said the angel, "thou wilt be the more impartial. Heaven has given thee discernment, and I add the gift of winning confidence. Go, look, listen, observe, and fear nothing; thou shalt be well received everywhere."

Babouc mounted his camel, and set out with his servants. After some days, on approaching the plains of Sennah, he fell in with the Persian army, which was going to fight with the army of India. He first accosted a soldier whom he found at a distance from the camp, and asked him what was the cause of the war.

"By all the gods," said the soldier, "I know nothing about it; it is no business of mine; my trade is to kill and be killed to get a living. It makes no odds to me whom I serve. I have a great mind to pass over to-morrow into the Indian camp, for I hear that they are giving their men half a copper drachma a day more than we get in this cursed service of Persia. If you want to know why we are fighting, speak to my captain."

Babouc gave the soldier a small present, and entered the camp. He soon made the captain's acquaintance, and asked him the cause of the war.

"How should I know?" said he; "such grand mat-

* Translated by Robert Bruce Boswell.

ters are no concern of mine. I live two hundred leagues away from Persepolis; I hear it said that war has been declared; I immediately forsake my family, and go, according to our custom, to make my fortune or to die, since I have nothing else to do."

"But surely," said Babouc, "your comrades are a little better informed than yourself?"

"No," replied the officer, "hardly anybody except our chief satraps has any very clear notion why we are cutting each other's throats."

Babouc, astonished at this, introduced himself to the generals, and they were soon on intimate terms. At last one of them said to him:

"The cause of this war, which has laid Asia waste for the last twenty years, originally sprang out of a quarrel between a eunuch belonging to one of the wives of the great King of Persia, and a custom-house clerk in the service of the great King of India. The matter in dispute was a duty amounting to very nearly the thirtieth part of a daric. The Indian and Persian prime ministers worthily supported their masters' rights. The quarrel grew hot. They sent into the field on both sides an army of a million troops. This army has to be recruited every year with more than 400,000 men. Massacres, conflagrations, ruin, and devastation multiply; the whole world suffers, and their fury still continues. Our own as well as the Indian prime minister often protest that they are acting solely for the happiness of the human race; and at each protestation some towns are always destroyed and some province ravaged."

The next day, on a report being spread that peace was about to be concluded, the Persian and Indian generals hastened to give battle; and a bloody one it was. Babouc saw all its mistakes and all its abominations; he witnessed stratagems carried on by the chief satraps, who did all they could to cause their commander to be defeated; he saw officers slain by their own troops; he saw soldiers despatching their dying comrades in order to strip them of a few blood-stained rags, torn and covered with mud. He entered the hospitals to which they were carrying the wounded, most of whom died through the inhuman negligence of those very men whom the King of Persia paid handsomely to relieve them.

"Are these creatures men," cried Babouc, "or wild beasts? Ah! I see plainly that Persepolis will be destroyed."

Occupied with this thought he passed into the camp of the Indians, and found there as favourable a reception as in that of the Persians, just as he had been led to expect; but he beheld there all the same abuses that had already filled him with horror.

"Ah!" said he to himself, "if the angel Ithuriel resolves to exterminate the Persians, then the angel of India must destroy the Indians as well."

Being afterwards more particularly informed of all that went on in both camps, he was made acquainted with acts of generosity, magnanimity, and humanity that moved him with astonishment and delight.

"Unintelligible mortals!" he exclaimed, "how is it that ye can combine so much meanness with so much greatness, such virtues with such crimes?"

Meanwhile peace was declared. The commanders of both armies, neither of whom had gained the victory, but who had caused the blood of so many of their fellow-men to flow, only to promote their own interests, began to solicit rewards at their respective courts. The peace was extolled in public proclamations which announced nothing less than the return of virtue and happiness to earth.

"God be praised!" said Babouc, "Persepolis will be the abode of purified innocence. It will not be destroyed, as those rascally genii wished: let us hasten without delay to this capital of Asia."

On his arrival he entered that immense city by the old approach, which was altogether barbarous, and offended the eye with its hideous want of taste. All that part of the city bore witness to the time at which it had been built; for, in spite of men's obstinate stupidity in praising ancient at the expense of modern times, it must be confessed that in every kind of art first attempts are always rude.

Babouc mingled in a crowd of people composed of all the dirtiest and ugliest of both sexes, who with a dull and sullen air were pouring into a vast and dreary building. From the constant hum of voices and the movements that he remarked, from the money that some were giving to others for the privilege of sitting down, he thought that he was in a market where straw-bottomed chairs were on sale; but soon, when he observed several women drop upon their knees, pretending to look fixedly before them, but giving sidelong glances at the men, he became aware that he was in a temple. Grating voices, harsh, disagreeable, and out of tune, made the roof echo with ill-articulated sounds, which produced much the same effect as the braying of wild asses on the plains of the Pictavians, when they answer the summons of the cow-herd's horn. He shut his ears; but he was yet more anxious to shut his eyes and nose, when he saw workmen entering this temple with crowbars and spades, who removed a large stone and threw up the earth to right and left, from which there issued a most offensive smell. Then people came and laid a dead body in the opening, and the stone was put back above it.

"What!" cried Babouc, "these folk bury their dead in the same places where they worship the Deity, and their temples are paved with corpses! I am no longer surprised at those pestilential diseases which often consume Persepolis. The air, tainted with the corruption of the dead and by so many of the living gathered and crammed together in the same place, is enough to poison the whole earth. Oh, what an abominable city is this Persepolis! It would seem that the angels intend to destroy it in order to raise up a fairer one on its site, and to fill it with cleaner inhabitants, and such as can sing better. Providence may be right after all; let us leave it to take its own course."

Meanwhile the sun had almost reached the middle of its course. Babouc was to dine at the other end of the town with a lady for whom he had letters from her husband, an officer in the army. He first took several turns in and about Persepolis, where he saw other temples better built and more tastefully adorned, filled with a refined congregation, and resounding with harmonious music. He observed public fountains, which, badly paced though they were, struck the eye by their beauty; open spaces, where the best kings who had governed Persia seemed to breathe in bronze, and others where he heard the people exclaiming: "When shall we see our beloved master here?" He admired the magnificent bridges that spanned the river, the splendid and serviceable quays, the palaces built on either side, and especially an immense mansion where thousands of old soldiers, wounded in the hour of victory, daily returned thanks to the God of armies. At last he entered the lady's house, where he had been invited to dine with a select company. The rooms were elegant and handsomely furnished, the dinner delicious, the lady young, beautiful, clever, and charming, the company worthy of their hostess; and Babouc kept saying to himself every moment: "The angel Ithuriel must set the opinion of the whole world at defiance, if he thinks of destroying a city so delightful."

As time went on he perceived that the lady, who had begun by making tender inquiries after her husband, was, towards the end of the repast, speaking more tenderly still to a young magian. He saw a magistrate who, in his wife's presence, was bestowing the liveliest caresses upon a widow; and that indulgent widow kept one hand round the

magistrate's neck, while she stretched out the other to a handsome young citizen whose modesty seemed equal to his good looks. The magistrate's wife was the first to leave the table, in order to entertain in an adjoining chamber her spiritual director, who had been expected to dine with them but arrived too late; and the director, a man of ready eloquence, addressed her in that chamber with such vigour and unction that the lady, when she came back, had her eyes moist and her cheeks flushed, an unsteady step, and a stammering utterance.

Then Babouc began to fear that the genius Ithuriel was in the right. The gift that he possessed of winning confidence let him into the secrets of his fair hostess that very day; she owned to him her partiality for the young magian, and assured him that in all the houses at Persepolis he would find the same sort of behaviour as he had witnessed in hers. Babouc came to the conclusion that such a society could not long hold together; that jealousy, discord, and revenge were bound to make havoc in every household; that tears and blood must be shed daily; that the husbands would assuredly kill or be killed by the lovers of their wives; and, finally, that Ithuriel would do well to destroy immediately a city given up to continual dissensions.

He was brooding over these doleful thoughts, when there appeared at the door a man of grave countenance, clad in a black cloak, who humbly entreated a word with the young magistrate. The latter, without getting up or even looking at him, gave him some papers with a haughty and absent air, and then dismissed him. Babouc asked who the man was. The mistress of the house said to him in a low tone:

"That is one of the ablest counsellors we have in this city, and he has been studying the laws for fifty years. The gentleman yonder, who is but twenty-five years of age, and who was made a satrap of the law two days ago, has employed him to draw up an abstract of a case on which he has to pronounce judgment to-morrow, and which he has not yet examined."

"This young spark acts wisely," said Babouc, "in asking an old man's advice, but why is not that old man himself the judge?"

"You must be joking," was the reply; "those who have grown old in toilsome and inferior employments never attain positions of great dignity. This young man enjoys a high office because his father is rich, and because the right of administering justice is bought and sold here like a farm."

"O unhappy city, to have such customs!" cried

Babouc; "that is the coping-stone of confusion. Doubtless those who have purchased the right of dispensing justice sell their judgments; I see nothing here but unfathomable depths of iniquity."

As he thus testified his sorrow and surprise, a young warrior, who had that very day returned from the campaign, addressed him in the following terms:

"Why should you object to judicial appointments being made matter of purchase? I have myself paid a good price for the right of facing death at the head of two thousand men under my command; it has cost me forty thousand gold darics this year to lie on the bare ground in a red coat for thirty nights together, and to be twice wounded by an arrow pretty severely, of which I still feel the smart. If I ruin myself to serve the Persian emperor whom I have never seen, this gentleman who represents the majesty of the law may well pay something to have the pleasure of giving audience to suitors."

Babouc in his indignation could not refrain from condemning in his heart a country where the highest offices of peace and war were put up to auction; he hastily concluded that there must be among such people a total ignorance of legal and military affairs, and that even if Ithuriel should spare them they would be destroyed by their own detestable institutions.

His bad opinion was further confirmed by the arrival of a fat man, who, after giving a familiar nod to all the company, approached the young officer, and said to him:

"I can only lend you fifty thousand gold darics; for to tell you the truth, the imperial taxes have not brought me in more than three hundred thousand this year."

Babouc inquired who this man might be who complained of getting so little, and was informed that there were in Persepolis forty plebeian kings, who held the Persian empire on lease and paid the monarch something out of what they made.

After dinner he went into one of the grandest temples in the city, and seated himself in the midst of a crowd of men and women who had come there to pass away the time. A magian appeared in a structure raised above their heads, and spoke for a long time about virtue and vice. This magian divided under several heads what had no need of division; he proved methodically what was perfectly clear, and taught what everybody knew already. He coolly worked himself into a passion, and went away perspiring and out of breath. Then all the congregation awoke, and thought that they had been listening to an edifying discourse. Babouc said:

"There is a man who has done his best to weary two or three hundred of his fellow-citizens; but his intention was good, there is no reason in that for destroying Persepolis."

On leaving this assembly, he was taken to witness a public entertainment, which was exhibited every day in the year. It was held in a sort of hall, at the further end of which appeared a palace. The fairest part of the female population of Persepolis and the most illustrious satraps, seated in orderly ranks, formed a spectacle so brilliant that Babouc imagined at first that there was nothing more to be seen. Two or three persons, who seemed to be kings and queens, soon showed themselves at the entrance of the palace; their language was very different from that of the people; it was measured, harmonious, and sublime. No one slept, but all listened in profound silence, which was only interrupted by expressions of feeling and admiration on the part of the audience. The duty of kings, the love of virtue, and the dangerous nature of the passions were set forth in terms so lively and touching that Babouc shed tears. He had no doubt that those heroes and heroines, those kings and queens whom he had just heard, were the preachers of the empire. He even proposed to himself to persuade Ithuriel to come and hear them, quite convinced that such a spectacle would reconcile him for ever to the city.

As soon as the entertainment was over, he was anxious to see the principal queen, who had delivered such pure and noble sentiments of morality in that beautiful palace. He procured an introduction to her majesty, and was led up a narrow staircase to the second storey, and ushered into a badly furnished apartment, where he found a woman meanly clad, who said to him with a noble and pathetic air:

"This calling of mine does not afford me enough to live upon; one of the princes whom you saw has got me into the family way, and I shall soon be brought to bed; I am in want of money, and one cannot lie in without that."

Babouc gave her a hundred gold darics, saying to himself:

"If there were nothing worse than this in the city, I think Ithuriel would be wrong in being so angry."

After that he went, under the escort of an intelligent man with whom he had become acquainted, to pass the evening in the shops of those who dealt in objects of useless ostentation. He bought whatever took his fancy, and everything was sold him in the most polite manner at far more than it was worth. His friend, on their return to his house, explained to him how he had been cheated, and Babouc made a note of the trades-man's name, in order to have him specially marked out by Ithuriel on the day when the city should be visited with punishment. As he was writing, a knock was heard at the door; it was the shopkeeper himself come to restore his purse, which Babouc had left by mistake on his counter.

"How comes it to pass," cried Babouc, "that you can be so honest and generous, after having had the face to sell me a lot of trumpery for four times as much as it is worth?"

"There is no merchant of any note in this city," answered the shopkeeper, "who would not have brought you back your purse; but whoever told you that you paid four times its proper value for what you bought from me, has grossly deceived you; my profit was ten times as much; and so true is this, that if you wish to sell the articles again in a month's time, you will not get even that tenth part. But nothing is fairer; it is men's passing fancy which settles the price of such gewgaws; it is that fancy which affords a livelihood to the hundred workmen whom I employ; it is that which provides me with a fine house, a comfortable carriage, and horses; it is that which stimulates industry, and promotes taste, traffic, and plenty. I sell the same trifles to neighbouring nations at a much dearer rate than to you, and in that way I am useful to my country."

Babouc, after a moment's reflection, scratched the man's name out of his pocket-book.

"For after all," said he, "the arts that minister to luxury multiply and flourish in a country only when all the necessary arts are also practised, and the nation is numerous and wealthy. Ithuriel seems to me a little too severe."

Babouc, much puzzled as to what opinion he ought to have of Persepolis, determined to visit the magi and men of letters; for, inasmuch as the former devote themselves to religion and the latter to wisdom, he had great hopes that they would obtain pardon for the rest of the people. So next morning he repaired to a college of the magi. The archimandrite acknowledged that he had an income of a hundred thousand crowns for having taken a vow of poverty, and that he exercised a very exten-sive dominion in virtue of his profession of humil-ity; after which he left Babouc in the hands of a brother of low degree, who did the honours of the place.

Whilst this brother was showing him all the magnificence of that home of penitence, a rumour spread that he was come to reform all those religious houses. He immediately began to receive memorials from each of them, all of which were substantially to this effect: "Preserve us, and destroy all the others."

To judge by the arguments that were used in self-defence, these societies were all absolutely nec-essary; if their mutual accusations were to be be-lieved, they all alike deserved extinction. He mar-velled how there was not one of them but wished to govern the whole world in order to enlighten it. Then a little fellow, who was a demi-magian, came forward and said to him:

"I see clearly that the work is going to be accom-plished; for Zerdust has returned to earth; little girls prophesy, getting themselves pinched in front and whipped behind. It is evident that the world is coming to an end; could you not, before the final catastrophe, protect us from the grand lama?"

"What nonsense!" said Babouc. "From the grand lama? From the pontiff-king who resides in Thibet?"

"Yes," said the little demi-magian, with a decided air; "against him, and none else."

"Then you wage war on him, and have armies?" asked Babouc.

"No," said the other, "but we have written three or four thousand books against him, that nobody reads, and as many pamphlets, which are read by women at our direction. He has hardly ever heard us spoken of, he has only pronounced sentence against us, as a master might order the trees in his garden to be cleared of caterpillars."

Babouc shuddered at the folly of those men who made a profession of wisdom; the intrigues of those who had renounced the world; the ambition, greed, and pride of those who taught humility and un-selfishness; and he came to the conclusion that Ithuriel had very good reason for destroying the whole brood.

On his return to his lodging, he sent for some new books in order to soothe his indignation; and he invited some literary men to dinner for the sake of cheerful society. Twice as many came as he had asked, like wasps attracted by honey. These para-sites were as eager to speak as they were to eat; two classes of persons were the objects of their praise, the dead and their own selves—never their contem-poraries, the master of the house excepted. If one of them happened to make a clever remark, the countenances of all the others fell, and they gnawed their lips for vexation that it was not they who had said it. They did not disguise their real feelings so much as the magi, because their ambition was not pitched so high. There was not one of them but was soliciting some petty post or another, and at the same time wishing to be thought a great man. They said to each other's face the most insulting things, which they took for flashes of wit. Having some knowledge of Babouc's mission, one of them begged him in a whisper to annihilate an author who had not praised him as much as he thought proper, five years ago; another entreated the ruin of a citizen for having never laughed at his comedies; and a third desired the abolition of the Academy, because he himself had never succeeded in gaining admission. When the meal was finished, each went out by himself, for in all the company there were not two men who could endure or even speak a civil word to each other, outside the houses of those rich patrons who invited them to their table. Babouc deemed that it would be no great loss if all that breed of vermin were to perish in the general destruction.

As soon as he was rid of them, he began to read some of the new books, and recognized in them the same temper as his guests had shown. He saw with special indignation those gazettes of slander, those records of bad taste, which are dictated by envy, baseness, and abject poverty; those cowardly satires in which the vulture is treated with respect while the dove is torn to pieces; and those novels, destitute of imagination, in which are displayed so many portraits of women with whom the author is totally unacquainted.

He threw all those detestable writings into the fire, and went out to take an evening stroll. He was introduced to an old scholar who had not made one of his late company of parasites, for he always avoided the crowd. Knowing men well, he made good use of his knowledge, and was careful to whom he gave his confidence. Babouc spoke to him with indignation of what he had read and what he had seen.

"You have been reading poor contemptible stuff," said the learned sage; "but at all times, in all countries, and in every walk of life, the bad swarm and the good are rare. You have entertained the mere scum of pedantry, for in all professions alike those who least deserve to appear always obtrude themselves with most effrontery. The men of real wisdom live a quiet and retired life; there are still among us some men and books worthy of your attention."

While he was speaking thus another man of letters joined them; and their conversation was so agreeable and instructive, so superior to prejudice and conformable to virtue, that Babouc confessed he had never heard anything like it before.

"Here are men," he said to himself, "whom the angel Ithuriel will not dare to touch, or he will be ruthless indeed."

Reconciled as he now was to the men of letters, Babouc was still enraged with the rest of the nation.

"You are a stranger," said the judicious person who was talking to him; "abuses present themselves to your eyes in a mass, and the good which is concealed, and which sometimes springs out of these very abuses, escapes your observation."

Then he learned that among the men of literature there were some who were free from envy, and that even among the magi virtuous men were to be found. He understood at last that these great societies, which seemed by their mutual collisions to be bringing about their common ruin, were in the main beneficial institutions; that each community of magi was a check upon its rivals; that if they differed in some matters of opinion, they all taught the same principles of morality, instructed the people, and lived in obedience to the laws; like tutors who watch over the son of the house, while the master watches over them. Becoming acquainted with several of these magi, he saw souls of heavenly disposition. He found that even among the simpletons who aspired to make war on the grand lama there had been some very great men. He began to suspect that the character of the people of Persepolis might be like their buildings, some of which had seemed to him deplorably bad, while others had ravished him with admiration.

Said Babouc to his literary friend:

"I see clearly enough that these magi, whom I thought so dangerous, are in reality very useful, especially when a wise government prevents them from making themselves too indispensable. But you will at least acknowledge that your young magistrates, who buy a seat on the bench as soon as they have learned to mount a horse, must needs display in your courts of law the most ridiculous incompetence and the most perverse injustice; it would undoubtedly be better to give these appointments gratuitously to those old lawyers who have passed all their lives in weighing conflicting arguments."

The man of letters made reply:

"You saw our army before your arrival at Persepolis; you know that our young officers fight very well, although they have purchased their commissions; perhaps you will find that our young magistrates do not pronounce wrong judgments, in spite of having paid for the positions they occupy."

He took Babouc the next day to the High Court of Judicature, where an important decision was to be delivered. The case was one that excited universal interest. All the old advocates who spoke about it were uncertain in their opinions; they quoted a hundred laws, not one of which had any essential bearing upon the question; they regarded the matter from a hundred points of view, none of which presented it in its true light. The judges were quicker in giving their decision than the advocates in raising doubts; their judgment was almost unanimous; and their sentence was just, because they followed the light of reason, whereas the others went astray in their opinions, because they had only consulted their books.

Babouc came to the conclusion that abuses often entail very good results. He had an opportunity of seeing that very day how the riches of the farmers of the revenue, which had given him so much offence, might produce an excellent effect, for the emperor being in want of money, obtained in an hour by their means a sum that he would not have been able to procure in six months through the ordinary channels; he saw that those big clouds, swollen with the dews of earth, restored to it in rain all that they received from it. Moreover, the children of those self-made men, often better educated than those of the most ancient families, were sometimes of much greater value to their country; for there is nothing to hinder a man from making a good judge, a brave soldier, or a clever statesman, in the circumstance of his having had a good accountant for his father.

By degrees Babouc forgave the greed of the farmers of the revenue, who are not in reality more greedy than other men, and who are necessary to the welfare of the state. He excused the folly of those who impoverished themselves in order to be a judge or a soldier, a folly which creates great magistrates and heroes. He pardoned the envy displayed by the men of letters, among whom were to be found men who enlightened the world; he became reconciled to the ambitious and intriguing magi, among whom eminent virtues outweighed petty vices. But there remained behind abundant matter of offence, above all, the love affairs of the ladies; and the ruin which he felt sure must follow filled him with disquietude and alarm.

As he wished to gain an insight into human life under all conditions, he procured an introduction to a minister of state, but on his way he was trembling all the time lest some wife should be assassinated by her husband before his eyes. On arriving at the statesman's house, he had to wait two hours in the antechamber before he was announced, and two hours more after that had been done. He fully made up his mind during that interval to report to the angel Ithuriel both the minister and his insolent lackeys. The antechamber was filled with ladies of every degree, with magi of all shades of opinion, with judges, tradesmen, officers, and pedants; all found fault with the minister. The misers and usurers said: "That fellow plunders the provinces, there's no doubt about it." The capricious reproached him with being eccentric. The libertines said: "He thinks of nothing but his pleasures." The factious flattered themselves that they should soon see him ruined by a cabal. The women hoped that they might ere long have a younger minister.

Babouc heard their remarks, and could not help saying:

"What a fortunate man this is! He has all his enemies in his antechamber; he crushes under his heel those who envy him; he sees those who detest him grovelling at his feet."

At last he was admitted, and saw a little old man stooping under the weight of years and business, but still brisk and full of energy.

He was pleased with Babouc, who thought him a worthy man, and their conversation became interesting. The minister confessed that he was very unhappy; that he passed for rich, but was really poor; that he was believed to be all powerful, yet was being constantly thwarted; that almost all his favours had been conferred on the ungrateful; and that amid the continual labours of forty years he had scarcely had a moment's peace. Babouc was touched with compassion, and thought that if this man had committed faults and the angel Ithuriel wished to punish him, he had no need to destroy him; it would be enough to leave him where he was.

While the minister and he were talking together, the fair dame with whom Babouc had dined hastily entered; and in her eyes and on her forehead were seen symptoms of vexation and anger. She burst out into reproaches against the statesman; she shed tears; she complained bitterly that her husband had been refused a post to which his birth allowed him to aspire, and to which his services and his wounds entitled him. She expressed herself so forcibly, she made her complaints with so much grace, she overcame objections with such skill, and reinforced her arguments with such eloquence, that ere she left the room she had made her husband's fortune.

Babouc held out his hand, and said:

"Is it possible, madam, that you can have given yourself all this trouble for a man whom you do not love, and from whom you have everything to fear?"

"A man whom I do not love!" she cried. "My husband, let me tell you, is the best friend I have in the world; there is nothing that I would not sacrifice for him, except my lover, and he would do anything for me, except giving up his mistress. I should like you to know her; she is a charming woman, full of wit, and of an excellent disposition; we sup together this evening with my husband and my little magian; come and share our enjoyment."

The lady took Babouc home with her. The husband, who had arrived at last, overwhelmed with grief, saw his wife again with transports of delight and gratitude; he embraced by turns his wife, his mistress, the little magian, and Babouc. Unity, cheerfulness, wit, and elegance were the soul of the repast.

"Learn," said the fair dame at whose house he was supping, "that those who are sometimes called women of no virtue have almost always merits as genuine as those of the most honourable man; and to convince yourself of it come with me to-morrow and dine with the fair Theona. There are some old vestals who pick her to pieces, but she does more good than all of them together. She would not commit even a trifling act of injustice to promote her own interests, however important; the advice she gives her lover is always noble; his glory is her sole concern; he would blush to face her if he had neglected any occasion of doing good; for a man can have no greater encouragement to virtuous actions than to have for a witness and judge of his conduct a mistress whose good opinion he is anxious to deserve."

Babouc did not fail to keep the appointment. He saw a house where all the pleasures reigned, with Theona at their head, who knew how to speak in the language of each. Her natural good sense put others at their ease; she made herself agreeable without an effort, for she was as amiable as she was generous, and, what enhanced the value of her good qualities, she was beautiful.

Babouc, Scythian though he was, and though a genius had sent him on his mission, perceived that, if he stayed any longer at Persepolis, he should forget Ithuriel for Theona. He felt fond of a city whose inhabitants were polite, good-humoured, and

kind, however frivolous they might be, greedy of scandal, and full of vanity. He feared that the doom of Persepolis was sealed; he dreaded, too, the report he would have to give.

This was the method he adopted for making that report. He gave instructions to the best founder in the city to cast a small image composed of all kinds of metals, earth, and stones, alike the most precious and the most worthless. He brought it to Ithuriel, and said:

"Wilt thou break this pretty little image, because it is not all gold and diamonds?"

Ithuriel understood his meaning before the words were out of his mouth, and determined that he would not think of punishing Persepolis, but would let the world go on in its own way; "for," said he, "if everything is not as it should be, there is nothing intolerably bad." So, Persepolis was allowed to remain unharmed, and Babouc was very far from uttering any complaint like Jonah, who was angry because Nineveh was not destroyed. But when a man has been three days in a whale's belly, he is not so good-tempered as after a visit to the opera or to the play, or after having supper in good company.

———◆———

JOHN DRYDEN

1631–1700

John Dryden, in many respects the first professional English man of letters, was born in Northamptonshire and educated at Westminster and at Trinity College, Cambridge, where he took his B.A. in 1654. His literary career, which dominates English literature during the last half of the seventeenth century, comprises several changes of allegiance in both religion and politics. Although it was formerly fashionable to deprecate Dryden as a turncoat, modern scholars now take a more kindly attitude toward the great man of letters whose fate it was to live amidst the many vicissitudes of a turbulent period of English history.

His career began with a poem entitled "Heroic Stanzas on the Death of Oliver Cromwell" (1658), for Dryden apparently came of a family of Puritan sympathies. Barely two years later, however, he celebrated the restoration of monarchy and the return of Charles II from his Continental exile with *Astræa Redux,* "A Poem on the Happy Restoration

& Return of His Sacred Majesty Charles the Second." Yet of his change it can be said, as Dr. Johnson pointed out in his *Life of Dryden,* that if Dryden was guilty of shifting allegiance at the time of the Restoration, most of the English nation changed with him. His next occasional poem of note, *Annus Mirabilis* (1666), was evoked by the momentous events of 1665–1666: the naval war with the Dutch, the great London Fire, and the last terrible visitation of the plague.

Dryden, now a staunch Church of England man, found royal favor and was made Poet Laureate. Seriously concerned with the great religious problems and controversies of his time, he wrote in *Religio Laici* (1683) a statement of his own religious position and a justification of the Anglican Church as the best of churches because it followed a moderate, middle way between the superstition of Catholicism on one hand and the excesses of Protestant fanaticism on the other. Even in this poem, however, Dryden is obviously searching for an authority upon which his faith might solidly rest. And the discerning reader may find in it anticipations of *The Hind and the Panther* (1687), a work in which he reveals his conversion to the Roman Catholic Church and defends the Catholic as the one true Church. His conversion might not have occasioned so much misunderstanding had it not coincided so closely with a great political change, for in 1685 the Catholic Duke of York, Charles II's brother, succeeded to the throne as James II. When, however, James II fled in 1688, and was replaced by William and Mary, ardent Protestant monarchs, Dryden vindicated the sincerity of his previous change by remaining Catholic, giving up his Laureateship, pension, and honors, and continuing to the end of his life in reduced circumstances.

Dryden excelled in all branches of literature. But perhaps his satires are more widely read today than most of his other poetry. His *Absalom and Achitophel* (1681), a satire against the treasonable attempt of the Whigs to supplant Charles II with his own bastard son, the Duke of Monmouth, is a brilliant piece of political satire. In it Dryden first perfected the satiric portrait. The same technique is employed in *Mac Flecknoe,* a satire largely occasioned by politics but containing more literary criticism than the former. Students may observe that Dryden's satires, although trenchantly effective, are still gentlemanly enough in tone to be classified as Horatian rather than Juvenalian.

Much of Dryden's creative energy went into dramatic composition. He wrote many plays—comedies, tragicomedies, heroic plays, and one great tragedy, *All for Love.* In fact it was probably from the theater that he received most of his income.

Dryden is likewise celebrated as a writer of prose, for he was one of the first to write in the new plain style which is essentially modern. Always easy, clear, and in the natural rhythms of cultivated conversation, his essays are models of style never surpassed. The subject matter of most of his prose is literary criticism, as, for example, his two most celebrated essays, *The Essay of Dramatic Poesy* (1666) and *The Preface to the Fables* (1700), either of which would suffice to prove Dryden the greatest literary critic of his era.

In his poetry, Dryden perfected the use of the heroic couplet, and made of it a remarkably sensitive and flexible medium of poetic expression. Though his accomplishments as a poet were much belittled by the Romantics and by the Romantic critical tradition which obtained throughout the nineteenth century, under the leadership of T. S. Eliot his literary reputation has been largely rehabilitated during the past three decades.

FURTHER READING

BREDVOLD, L. I. *The Intellectual Milieu of John Dryden* (Ann Arbor, Mich., 1934).
ELIOT, T. S. *Selected Essays* (New York, 1932).
SMITH, DAVID NICHOL. *John Dryden* (Cambridge, 1950).
VAN DOREN, MARK. *John Dryden, a Study of His Poetry* (New York, 1946).

Bad, dull poet

Mac Flecknoe

OR, A SATIRE UPON THE TRUE-BLUE-PROTESTANT POET

[*Thomas Shadwell* (1642?–1692) *was a Whig dramatist and poet, who replaced Dryden as Poet Laureate after the Glorious Revolution of 1688. Shadwell's plays* (The Sullen Lovers, Epsom Wells, *and others) were considerably better than Dryden here represents them. Shadwell was not a fool. Dryden had formerly been friendly with him, despite the bitterness of this satire. The original cause of their quarrel is not clear.*]

Compared
liking
although
he is
dull
radon

All human things are subject to decay,
And when Fate summons, monarchs must obey.
This Flecknoe found, who, like Augustus, young
Was call'd to empire, and had govern'd long;
In prose and verse, was own'd, without dispute,
Through all the realms of Nonsense, absolute.
This aged prince, now flourishing in peace,
And blest with issue of a large increase;
Worn out with business, did at length debate
To settle the succession of the State; plot   10
And, pond'ring which of all his sons was fit
To reign, and wage immortal war with wit,
Cried, " 'Tis resolv'd; for nature pleads, that he
Should only rule, who most resembles me:
Sh—— alone my perfect image bears,
Mature in dullness from his tender years;
Sh—— alone, of all my sons, is he
Who stands confirm'd in full stupidity.
The rest to some faint meaning make pretence,
But Sh—— never deviates into sense.   20
Some beams of wit on other souls may fall,
Strike through, and make a lucid interval;
But Sh——'s genuine might admits no ray,
His rising fogs prevail upon the day:
Besides, his goodly fabric fills the eye,
And seems design'd for thoughtless majesty:
Thoughtless as monarch oaks that shade the plain,
And, spread in solemn state, supinely reign.
Heywood and Shirley were but types of thee,
Thou last great prophet of tautology: 30
Even I, a dunce of more renown than they,
Was sent before but to prepare thy way;
And, coarsely clad in Norwich drugget, came
To teach the nations in thy greater name.
My warbling lute, the lute I whilom strung,
When to King John of Portugal I sung,
Was but the prelude to that glorious day,
When thou on silver Thames didst cut thy way,
With well-tim'd oars before the royal barge,
Swell'd with the pride of thy celestial charge;   40
And big with hymn, commander of an host,
The like was ne'er in Epsom blankets toss'd.
Methinks I see the new Arion sail,
The lute still trembling underneath thy nail.
At thy well-sharpen'd thumb from shore to shore
The treble squeaks for fear, the basses roar;
Echoes from Pissing Alley Sh—— call,
And Sh—— they resound from Aston Hall.
About thy boat the little fishes throng,
As at the morning toast that floats along.   50
Sometimes, as prince of thy harmonious band,
Thou wield'st thy papers in thy threshing hand.
St. André's feet ne'er kept more equal time,

Not ev'n the feet of thy own *Psyche's* rhyme,
Though they in number as in sense excel;
So just, so like tautology, they fell,
That, pale with envy, Singleton forswore
The lute and sword, which he in triumph bore,
And vow'd he ne'er would act Villerius more."
Here stopp'd the good old sire, and wept for joy   60
In silent raptures of the hopeful boy.
All arguments, but most his plays, persuade.
That for anointed dullness he was made.
    Close to the walls which fair Augusta bind,
(The fair Augusta much to fears inclin'd,)
An ancient fabric rais'd t' inform the sight,
There stood of yore, and Barbican it hight:
A watchtower once; but now, so fate ordains,
Of all the pile an empty name remains.
From its old ruins brothel-houses rise,   70
Scenes of lewd loves, and of polluted joys,
Where their vast courts the mother-strumpets keep,
And, undisturb'd by watch, in silence sleep.
Near these a Nursery erects its head,
Where queens are form'd, and future heroes bred;
Where unfledg'd actors learn to laugh and cry,
Where infant punks their tender voices try,
And little Maximins the gods defy.
Great Fletcher never treads in buskins here,
Nor greater Jonson dares in socks appear;   80
But gentle Simkin just reception finds
Amidst this monument of vanish'd minds:
Pure clinches the suburban Muse affords,
And Panton waging harmless war with words.
Here Flecknoe, as a place to fame well known,
Ambitiously design'd his Sh——'s throne.
For ancient Dekker prophesied long since,
That in this pile should reign a mighty prince,
Born for a scourge of wit, and flail of sense;
To whom true dullness should some *Psyches*
    owe,   90
But words of *Misers* from his pen should flow;
Humorists and hypocrites it should produce,
Whole Raymond families, and tribes of Bruce.
    Now Empress Fame had publish'd the renown
Of Sh——'s coronation through the town.
Rous'd by report of Fame, the nations meet,
From near Bunhill, and distant Watling Street.
No Persian carpets spread th' imperial way,
But scatter'd limbs of mangled poets lay;
From dusty shops neglected authors come,   100
Martyrs of pies, and relics of the bum.
Much Heywood, Shirley, Ogleby there lay,
But loads of Sh—— almost chok'd the way.
Bilk'd stationers for yeomen stood prepar'd,
And Herringman was captain of the guard.

Nursery theatre - place where young
actors were trained.

The hoary prince in majesty appear'd,
High on a throne of his own labours rear'd.
At his right hand our young Ascanius sate,
Rome's other hope, and pillar of the State.
His brows thick fogs, instead of glories, grace, 110
And lambent dullness play'd around his face.
As Hannibal did to the altars come,
Sworn by his sire, a mortal foe to Rome;
So Sh—— swore, nor should his vow be vain,
That he till death true dullness would maintain;
And, in his father's right, and realm's defence,
Ne'er to have peace with wit, nor truce with sense.
The king himself the sacred unction made,
As king by office, and as priest by trade.
In his sinister hand, instead of ball, 120
He plac'd a mighty mug of potent ale;
Love's Kingdom to his right he did convey,
At once his sceptre and his rule of sway;
Whose righteous lore the prince had practis'd young,
And from whose loins recorded *Psyche* sprung. ·
His temples, last, with poppies were o'erspread,
That nodding seem'd to consecrate his head.
Just at that point of time, if fame not lie,
On his left hand twelve reverend owls did fly.
So Romulus, 'tis sung, by Tiber's brook, 130
Presage of sway from twice six vultures took.
Th' admiring throng loud acclamations make,
And omens of his future empire take.
The sire then shook the honours of his head,
And from his brows damps of oblivion shed
Full on the filial dullness: long he stood,
Repelling from his breast the raging god;
At length burst out in this prophetic mood:
  "Heavens bless my son, from Ireland let him reign
To far Barbadoes on the western main; 140
Of his dominion may no end be known,
And greater than his father's be his throne;
Beyond *Love's Kingdom* let him stretch his pen!"
He paus'd, and all the people cried, "Amen."
Then thus continued he: "My son, advance
Still in new impudence, new ignorance.
Success let others teach, learn thou from me
Pangs without birth, and fruitless industry.
Let *Virtuosos* in five years be writ;
Yet not one thought accuse thy toil of wit. 150
Let gentle George in triumph tread the stage,
Make Dorimant betray, and Loveit rage;
Let Cully, Cockwood, Fopling, charm the pit,
And in their folly show the writer's wit.
Yet still thy fools shall stand in thy defence,
And justify their author's want of sense.
Let 'em be all by thy own model made
Of dullness, and desire no foreign aid;

That they to future ages may be known,
Not copies drawn, but issue of thy own. 160
Nay, let thy men of wit too be the same,
All full of thee, and differing but in name.
But let no alien S—dl—y interpose,
To lard with wit thy hungry *Epsom* prose.
And when false flowers of rhetoric thou wouldst cull,
Trust nature, do not labour to be dull;
But write thy best, and top; and, in each line,
Sir Formal's oratory will be thine:
Sir Formal, though unsought, attends thy quill,
And does thy northern dedications fill. 170
Nor let false friends seduce thy mind to fame,
By arrogating Jonson's hostile name.
Let father Flecknoe fire thy mind with praise,
And uncle Ogleby thy envy raise.
Thou art my blood, where Jonson has no part:
What share have we in nature, or in art?
Where did his wit on leaning fix a brand,
And rail at arts he did not understand?
Where made he love in Prince Nicander's vein,
Or swept the dust in *Psyche's* humble strain? 180
Where sold he bargains, "whip-stitch, kiss my arse,"
Promis'd a play and dwindled to a farce?
When did his Muse from Fletcher scenes purloin,
As thou whole Eth'rege dost transfuse to thine?
But so transfus'd as oils on waters flow,
His always floats above, thine sinks below.
This is thy province, this thy wondrous way,
New humours to invent for each new play:
This is that boasted bias of thy mind,
By which one way, to dullness, 'tis inclin'd; 190
Which makes thy writings lean on one side still,
And, in all changes, that way bends thy will.
Nor let thy mountain belly make pretence
Of likeness; thine's a tympany of sense.
A tun of man in thy large bulk is writ,
But sure thou'rt but a kilderkin of wit.
Like mine, thy gentle numbers feebly creep;
Thy tragic Muse gives smiles, thy comic sleep.
With whate'er gall thou sett'st thyself to write,
Thy inoffensive satires never bite. 200
In thy felonious heart though venom lies,
It does but touch thy Irish pen, and dies.
Thy genius calls thee not to purchase fame
In keen iambics, but mild anagram.
Leave writing plays, and choose for thy command
Some peaceful province in Acrostic Land.
There thou may'st wings display and altars raise,
And torture one poor word ten thousand ways.
Or, if thou wouldst thy diff'rent talents suit,
Set thy own songs, and sing them to thy lute." 210

He said: but his last words were scarcely heard;
For Bruce and Longvil had a trap prepar'd,
And down they sent the yet declaiming bard.
Sinking he left his drugget robe behind,
Borne upwards by a subterranean wind.
The mantle fell to the young prophet's part,
With double portion of his father's art.

To the Pious Memory of the Accomplished Young Lady, Mrs. Anne Killigrew

EXCELLENT IN THE TWO SISTER-ARTS OF POESY AND PAINTING

AN ODE

[*Anne Killigrew (1660–1685), poetess and painter, was drowned in the Thames. Dr. Johnson declared this ode to be "the finest in the language." The fourth stanza has autobiographical significance: here Dryden confesses his (and his contemporaries') licentiousness in the Restoration drama and begs divine forgiveness.*]

I

Thou youngest virgin daughter of the skies,
Made in the last promotion of the blest;
Whose palms, new pluck'd from paradise,
In spreading branches more sublimely rise,
Rich with immortal green above the rest:
Whether, adopted to some neighbouring star,
Thou roll'st above us, in thy wand'ring race,
   Or, in procession fix'd and regular,
    Mov'd with the heavens' majestic pace;
   Or, call'd to more superior bliss,   10
Thou tread'st, with seraphims, the vast abyss—
Whatever happy region is thy place,
Cease thy celestial song a little space;
(Thou wilt have time enough for hymns divine,
   Since heav'n's eternal year is thine.)
Hear then a mortal Muse thy praise rehearse,
    In no ignoble verse;
But such as thy own voice did practise here,
When thy first fruits of poesy were giv'n,
To make thyself a welcome inmate there;   20
    While yet a young probationer,
     And candidate of heav'n.

II

If by traduction came thy mind,
Our wonder is the less to find
A soul so charming from a stock so good;
Thy father was transfus'd into thy blood:
So wert thou born into the tuneful strain,
(An early, rich, and inexhausted vein.)
   But if thy pre-existing soul
    Was form'd, at first, with myriads more,   30
It did through all the mighty poets roll,
    Who Greek or Latin laurels wore,
And was that Sappho last, which once it was before.
   If so, then cease thy flight, O heav'n-born mind!
   Thou hast no dross to purge from thy rich ore;
   Nor can thy soul a fairer mansion find,
   Than was the beauteous frame she left behind:
Return, to fill or mend the choir of thy celestial kind.

III

   May we presume to say, that at thy birth
New joy was sprung in heav'n, as well as here on
    earth?   40
For sure the milder planets did combine
On thy auspicious horoscope to shine,
And ev'n the most malicious were in trine.
Thy brother angels at thy birth
   Strung each his lyre, and tun'd it high,
   That all the people of the sky
Might know a poetess was born on earth.
   And then, if ever, mortal ears
   Had heard the music of the spheres!
And if no clust'ring swarm of bees   50
On thy sweet mouth distill'd their golden dew,
   'Twas that such vulgar miracles
   Heav'n had not leisure to renew;
For all the blest fraternity of love
Solemniz'd there thy birth, and kept thy holiday
    above.

IV

   O gracious God! how far have we
Profan'd thy heav'nly gift of poesy!
Made prostitute and profligate the Muse,
Debas'd to each obscene and impious use,
Whose harmony was first ordain'd above   60
For tongues of angels, and for hymns of love!
O wretched we! why were we hurried down
   This lubric and adult'rate age,
(Nay, added fat pollutions of our own,)
   T' increase the steaming ordures of the stage?
What can we say t' excuse our second fall?
Let this thy vestal, Heav'n, atone for all:
Her Arethusian stream remains unsoil'd,
Unmix'd with foreign filth, and undefil'd;
Her wit was more than man, her innocence a
    child!   70

V

Art she had none, yet wanted none;
For nature did that want supply:
So rich in treasures of her own,
She might our boasted stores defy:
Such noble vigour did her verse adorn
That it seem'd borrow'd, where 'twas only born.
Her morals too were in her bosom bred,
By great examples daily fed,
What in the best of books, her father's life, she read.
And to be read herself she need not fear;   80
Each test, and ev'ry light, her Muse will bear,
Though Epictetus with his lamp were there.
Ev'n love (for love sometimes her Muse express'd)
Was but a lambent flame which play'd about her
      breast,
Light as the vapours of a morning dream:
So cold herself, whilst she such warmth express'd,
'Twas Cupid bathing in Diana's stream.

VI

Born to the spacious empire of the Nine,
One would have thought she should have been con-
      tent
To manage well that mighty government;   90
But what can young ambitious souls confine?
   To the next realm she stretch'd her sway,
   For Painture near adjoining lay,
A plenteous province, and alluring prey.
   A chamber of dependences was fram'd,
(As conquerors will never want pretence,
   When arm'd, to justify th' offence,)
And the whole fief in right of poetry she claim'd.
The country open lay without defence;
For poets frequent inroads there had made,   100
   And perfectly could represent
   The shape, the face, with ev'ry lineament;
And all the large domains which the Dumb Sister
      sway'd,
   All bow'd beneath her government;
   Receiv'd in triumph wheresoe'er she went.
Her pencil drew whate'er her soul design'd,
And oft the happy draught surpass'd the image in
      her mind.
   The sylvan scenes of herds and flocks,
   And fruitful plains and barren rocks,
   Of shallow brooks that flow'd so clear   110
   The bottom did the top appear;
   Of deeper too and ampler floods,
   Which, as in mirrors, show'd the woods;
   Of lofty trees, with sacred shades,
   And perspectives of pleasant glades,

Where nymphs of brightest form appear,
And shaggy satyrs standing near,
Which them at once admire and fear:
The ruins too of some majestic piece,
Boasting the pow'r of ancient Rome, or
      Greece,   120
Whose statues, friezes, columns broken lie,
And, though defac'd, the wonder of the eye:
What nature, art, bold fiction, e'er durst frame,
Her forming hand gave feature to the name.
So strange a concourse ne'er was seen before,
But when the peopled ark the whole creation bore.

VII

The scene then chang'd: with bold erected look
Our martial king and sight with reverence strook;
For, not content t' express his outward part,
Her hand call'd out the image of his heart: 130
His warlike mind, his soul devoid of fear,
His high-designing thoughts were figur'd there,
As when, by magic, ghosts are made appear.
   Our Phoenix queen was portray'd too so bright,
Beauty alone could beauty take so right:
Her dress, her shape, her matchless grace,
Were all observ'd, as well as heav'nly face.
With such a peerless majesty she stands,
As in that day she took the crown from sacred
      hands;
Before a train of heroines was seen,   140
In beauty foremost, as in rank the queen.
Thus nothing to her genius was denied,
   But like a ball of fire the farther thrown,
   Still with a greater blaze she shone,
And her bright soul broke out on ev'ry side.
What next she had design'd, Heaven only knows;
To such immod'rate growth her conquest rose
That fate alone its progress could oppose.

VIII

Now all those charms, that blooming grace,
The well proportion'd shape, and beauteous face, 150
Shall never more be seen by mortal eyes:
In earth the much-lamented virgin lies!
   Not wit, nor piety could fate prevent;
   Nor was the cruel destiny content
   To finish all the murder at a blow,
   To sweep at once her life and beauty too;
But, like a harden'd felon, took a pride
   To work more mischievously slow,
And plunder'd first, and then destroy'd.
Oh double sacrilege on things divine,   160
To rob the relic, and deface the shrine!
   But thus Orinda died:

Heav'n, by the same disease, did both translate;
As equal were their souls, so equal was their fate.

IX

Meantime her warlike brother on the seas
    His waving streamers to the winds displays,
And vows for his return, with vain devotion, pays.
        Ah, generous youth, that wish forbear,
        The winds too soon will waft thee here!
    Slack all thy sails, and fear to come,   170
Alas, thou know'st not thou art wreck'd at home!
No more shalt thou behold thy sister's face;
Thou hast already had her last embrace.
But look aloft, and if thou kenn'st from far
Among the Pleiads a new-kindled star;
If any sparkles than the rest more bright,
'Tis she that shines in that propitious light.

X

When in mid air the golden trump shall sound,
    To raise the nations under ground;
    When in the Valley of Jehosaphat   180
The judging God shall close the book of fate,
    And there the last assizes keep
    For those who wake and those who sleep;
    When rattling bones together fly
    From the four corners of the sky;
When sinews o'er the skeletons are spread,
Those cloth'd with flesh, and life inspires the dead;
The sacred poets first shall hear the sound,
And foremost from the tomb shall bound,
For they are cover'd with the lightest ground;   190
And straight, with inborn vigour, on the wing,
Like mounting larks, to the new morning sing.
There thou, sweet saint, before the choir shalt go,
As harbinger of heav'n, the way to show,
The way which thou so well hast learn'd below.

Preface to Fables Ancient and Modern

TRANSLATED INTO VERSE FROM HOMER, OVID, BOCCACE, AND CHAUCER

'Tis with a poet, as with a man who designs to build, and is very exact, as he supposes, in casting up the cost beforehand; but, generally speaking, he is mistaken in his account, and reckons short of the expense he first intended. He alters his mind as the work proceeds, and will have this or that conveni-

ence more, of which he had not thought when he began. So has it happened to me; I have built a house where I intended but a lodge; yet with better success than a certain nobleman, who, beginning with a dog-kennel, never lived to finish the palace he had contrived.

From translating the first of Homer's *Iliads* (which I intended as an essay to the whole work), I proceeded to the translation of the Twelfth Book of Ovid's *Metamorphoses,* because it contains, among other things, the causes, the beginning, and ending, of the Trojan War. Here I ought in reason to have stopped; but the speeches of Ajax and Ulysses lying next in my way, I could not balk 'em. When I had compassed them, I was so taken with the former part of the Fifteenth Book (which is the masterpiece of the whole *Metamorphoses*), that I enjoined myself the pleasing task of rendering it into English. And now I found, by the number of my verses, that they began to swell into a little volume, which gave me an occasion of looking backward on some beauties of my author in his former books: there occurred to me the *Hunting of the Boar, Cinyras and Myrrha,* the good-natured story of *Baucis and Philemon,* with the rest, which I hope I have translated closely enough, and given them the same turn of verse which they had in the original; and this, I may say, without vanity, is not the talent of every poet. He who has arrived the nearest to it is the ingenious and learned Sandys, the best versifier of the former age; if I may properly call it by that name, which was the former part of this concluding century. For Spenser and Fairfax both flourished in the reign of Queen Elizabeth; great masters in our language, and who saw much further into the beauties of our numbers than those who immediately followed them. Milton was the poetical son of Spenser, and Mr. Waller of Fairfax; for we have our lineal descents and clans as well as other families. Spenser more than once insinuates that the soul of Chaucer was transfused into his body, and that he was begotten by him two hundred years after his decease. Milton has acknowledged to me that Spenser was his original; and many besides myself have heard our famous Waller own that he derived the harmony of his numbers from *Godfrey of Bulloign,* which was turned into English by Mr. Fairfax.

But to return: having done with Ovid for this time, it came into my mind that our old English poet, Chaucer, in many things resembled him, and that with no disadvantage on the side of the modern author, as I shall endeavour to prove when I compare them; and as I am, and always have been, studious to promote the honour of my native country, so I soon resolved to put their merits to the trial, by turning some of the *Canterbury Tales* into our language, as it is now refined; for by this means, both the poets being set in the same light, and dressed in the same English habit, story to be compared with story, a certain judgment may be made betwixt them by the reader, without obtruding my opinion on him. Or, if I seem partial to my countryman and predecessor in the laurel, the friends of antiquity are not few; and, besides many of the learned, Ovid has almost all the beaux, and the whole fair sex, his declared patrons. Perhaps I have assumed somewhat more to myself than they allow me, because I have adventured to sum up the evidence; but the readers are the jury, and their privilege remains entire, to decide according to the merits of the cause; or, if they please, to bring it to another hearing before some other court. In the mean time, to follow the thread of my discourse (as thoughts, according to Mr. Hobbes, have always some connection), so from Chaucer I was led to think on Boccace, who was not only his contemporary, but also pursued the same studies; wrote novels in prose, and many works in verse; particularly is said to have invented the octave rhyme, or stanza of eight lines, which ever since has been maintained by the practice of all Italian writers who are, or at least assume the title of heroic poets. He and Chaucer, among other things, had this in common, that they refined their mother-tongues; but with this difference, that Dante had begun to file their language, at least in verse, before the time of Boccace, who likewise received no little help from his master Petrarch; but the reformation of their prose was wholly owing to Boccace himself, who is yet the standard of purity in the Italian tongue, though many of his phrases are become obsolete, as in process of time it must needs happen. Chaucer (as you have formerly been told by our learned Mr. Rymer) first adorned and amplified our barren tongue from the Provençal, which was then the most polished of all the modern languages; but this subject has been copiously treated by that great critic, who deserves no little commendation from us his countrymen. For these reasons of time, and resemblance of genius, in Chaucer and Boccace, I resolved to join them in my present work; to which I have added some original papers of my own, which whether they are equal or inferior to my other poems, an author is the most improper judge; and therefore I leave them wholly to the mercy of the reader. I will hope the best, that

they will not be condemned; but if they should, I have the excuse of an old gentleman, who, mounting on horseback before some ladies, when I was present, got up somewhat heavily, but desired of the fair spectators that they would count four-score and eight before they judged him. By the mercy of God, I am already come within twenty years of his number; a cripple in my limbs, but what decays are in my mind, the reader must determine. I think myself as vigorous as ever in the faculties of my soul, excepting only my memory, which is not impaired to any great degree; and if I lose not more of it, I have no great reason to complain. What judgment I had increases rather than diminishes; and thoughts, such as they are, come crowding in so fast upon me that my only difficulty is to choose or to reject, to run them into verse, or to give them the other harmony of prose: I have so long studied and practised both that they are grown into a habit, and become familiar to me. In short, though I may lawfully plead some part of the old gentleman's excuse, yet I will reserve it till I think I have greater need, and ask no grains of allowance for the faults of this my present work but those which are given of course to human frailty. I will not trouble my reader with the shortness of time in which I writ it, or the several intervals of sickness. They who think too well of their own performances are apt to boast in their prefaces how little time their works have cost them, and what other business of more importance interfered; but the reader will be as apt to ask the question, why they allowed not a longer time to make their works more perfect, and why they had so despicable an opinion of their judges as to thrust their indigested stuff upon them, as if they deserved no better.

With this account of my present undertaking, I conclude the first part of this discourse; in the second part, as at a second sitting, though I alter not the draught, I must touch the same features over again, and change the dead-colouring of the whole. In general I will only say that I have written nothing which savours of immorality or profaneness; at least, I am not conscious to myself of any such intention. If there happen to be found an irreverent expression, or a thought too wanton, they are crept into my verses through my inadvertency; if the searchers find any in the cargo, let them be staved or forfeited, like counterbanded goods; at least let their authors be answerable for them, as being but imported merchandise, and not of my own manufacture. On the other side, I have endeavoured to choose such fables, both ancient and modern, as contain in each of them some instructive moral; which I could prove by induction, but the way is tedious, and they leap foremost into sight, without the reader's trouble of looking after them. I wish I could affirm, with a safe conscience, that I had taken the same care in all my former writings; for it must be owned that, supposing verses are never so beautiful or pleasing, yet, if they contain anything which shocks religion or good manners, they are at best what Horace says of good numbers without good sense, *Versus inopes rerum, nugaeque canorae.*[1] Thus far, I hope, I am right in court, without renouncing to my other right of self-defence, where I have been wrongfully accused, and my sense wiredrawn into blasphemy or bawdry, as it has often been by a religious lawyer, in a late pleading against the stage; in which he mixes truth and falsehood, and has not forgotten the old rule of calumniating strongly, that something may remain.

I resume the thread of my discourse with the first of my translations, which was the first *Iliad* of Homer. If it shall please God to give me longer life, and moderate health, my intentions are to translate the whole *Ilias*; provided still that I meet with those encouragements from the public which may enable me to proceed in my undertaking with some cheerfulness. And this I dare assure the world beforehand that I have found by trial, Homer a more pleasing task than Virgil, though I say not the translation will be less laborious; for the Grecian is more according to my genius than the Latin poet. In the works of the two authors we may read their manners, and natural inclinations, which are wholly different. Virgil was of a quiet, sedate temper; Homer was violent, impetuous, and full of fire. The chief talent of Virgil was propriety of thoughts, and ornament of words: Homer was rapid in his thoughts, and took all the liberties, both of numbers and of expressions, which his language, and the age in which he lived, allowed him. Homer's invention was more copious, Virgil's more confined; so that if Homer had not led the way, it was not in Virgil to have begun heroic poetry; for nothing can be more evident than that the Roman poem is but the second part of the *Ilias*; a continuation of the same story, and the persons already formed. The manners of Aeneas are those of Hector, superadded to those which Homer gave him. The adventures of Ulysses in the *Odysseis* are imitated in the first six books of Virgil's *Aeneis*; and though the accidents are not the same (which would have argued him of a servile

copying, and total barrenness of invention), yet the seas were the same in which both the heroes wandered; and Dido cannot be denied to be the poetical daughter of Calypso. The six latter books of Virgil's poem are the four-and-twenty *Iliads* contracted: a quarrel occasioned by a lady, a single combat, battles fought, and a town besieged. I say not this in derogation to Virgil, neither do I contradict anything which I have formerly said in his just praise; for his episodes are almost wholly of his own invention, and the form which he has given to the telling makes the tale his own, even though the original story had been the same. But this proves, however, that Homer taught Virgil to design; and if invention be the first virtue of an epic poet, then the Latin poem can only be allowed the second place. Mr. Hobbes, in the preface to his own bald translation of the *Ilias* (studying poetry as he did mathematics, when it was too late), Mr. Hobbes, I say, begins the praise of Homer where he should have ended it. He tells us that the first beauty of an epic poem consists in diction; that is, in the choice of words, and harmony of numbers. Now the words are the colouring of the work, which, in the order of nature, is last to be considered. The design, the disposition, the manners, and the thoughts are all before it: where any of those are wanting or imperfect, so much wants or is imperfect in the imitation of human life, which is in the very definition of a poem. Words, indeed, like glaring colours, are the first beauties that arise and strike the sight; but, if the draught be false or lame, the figures ill disposed, the manners obscure or inconsistent, or the thoughts unnatural, then the finest colours are but daubing, and the piece is a beautiful monster at the best. Neither Virgil nor Homer were deficient in any of the former beauties; but in this last, which is expression, the Roman poet is at least equal to the Grecian, as I have said elsewhere: supplying the poverty of his language by his musical ear, and by his diligence.

But to return: our two great poets being so different in their tempers, one choleric and sanguine, the other phlegmatic and melancholic; that which makes them excel in their several ways is that each of them has followed his own natural inclination, as well in forming the design as in the execution of it. The very heroes show their authors: Achilles is hot, impatient, revengeful—

Impiger, iracundus, inexorabilis, acer,[2] etc.,

Aeneas patient, considerate, careful of his people,

---

[1] "Verses without content and melodious trifles."
　　　　　　　　　　　　　　　　　　　　　(Horace)

[2] Tireless, passionate, unyielding, fierce.

and merciful to his enemies; ever submissive to the will of heaven—

> . . . *quo fata trahunt retrahuntque, sequamur.*[3]

I could please myself with enlarging on this subject, but am forced to defer it to a fitter time. From all I have said, I will only draw this inference, that the action of Homer, being more full of vigour than that of Virgil, according to the temper of the writer, is of consequence more pleasing to the reader. One warms you by degrees; the other sets you on fire all at once, and never intermits his heat. 'Tis the same difference which Longinus makes betwixt the effects of eloquence in Demosthenes and Tully; one persuades, the other commands. You never cool while you read Homer, even not in the second book (a graceful flattery to his countrymen); but he hastens from the ships, and concludes not that book till he has made you an amends by the violent playing of a new machine. From thence he hurries on his action with variety of events, and ends it in less compass than two months. This vehemence of his, I confess, is more suitable to my temper; and, therefore, I have translated his first book with greater pleasure than any part of Virgil; but it was not a pleasure without pains. The continual agitations of the spirits must needs be a weakening of any constitution, especially in age; and many pauses are required for refreshment betwixt the heats; the *Iliad* of itself being a third part longer than all Virgil's works together.

This is what I thought needful in this place to say of Homer. I proceed to Ovid and Chaucer; considering the former only in relation to the latter. With Ovid ended the Golden Age of the Roman tongue; from Chaucer the purity of the English tongue began. The manners of the poets were not unlike. Both of them were well-bred, well-natured, amorous, and libertine, at least in their writings; it may be also in their lives. Their studies were the same, philosophy and philology. Both of them were knowing in astronomy; of which Ovid's books of the *Roman Feasts*, and Chaucer's *Treatise of the Astrolabe*, are sufficient witnesses. But Chaucer was likewise an astrologer, as were Virgil, Horace, Persius, and Manilius. Both writ with wonderful facility and clearness; neither were great inventors: for Ovid only copied the Grecian fables, and most of Chaucer's stories were taken from his Italian contemporaries, or their predecessors. Boccace his *Decameron* was first published, and from thence our Englishman has borrowed many of his *Canterbury Tales*:

[3] Whither the fates draw us back and forth, let us follow.

yet that of *Palamon and Arcite* was written, in all probability, by some Italian wit, in a former age, as I shall prove hereafter. The tale of *Grizild* was the invention of Petrarch; by him sent to Boccace, from whom it came to Chaucer. *Troilus and Cressida* was also written by a Lombard author, but much amplified by our English translator, as well as beautified; the genius of our countrymen, in general, being rather to improve an invention than to invent themselves, as is evident not only in our poetry, but in many of our manufactures. I find I have anticipated already, and taken up from Boccace before I come to him: but there is so much less behind; and I am of the temper of most kings, who love to be in debt, are all for present money, no matter how they pay it afterwards: besides, the nature of a preface is rambling, never wholly out of the way, nor in it. This I have learned from the practice of honest Montaigne, and return at my pleasure to Ovid and Chaucer, of whom I have little more to say.

Both of them built on the inventions of other men; yet since Chaucer had something of his own, as *The Wife of Bath's Tale*, *The Cock and the Fox*, which I have translated, and some others, I may justly give our countryman the precedence in that part; since I can remember nothing of Ovid which was wholly his. Both of them understood the manners; under which name I comprehend the passions, and in a larger sense, the descriptions of persons, and their very habits. For an example, I see Baucis and Philemon as perfectly before me as if some ancient painter had drawn them; and all the Pilgrims in the *Canterbury Tales*, their humours, their features, and the very dress, as distinctly as if I had supped with them at the Tabard in Southwark. Yet even there, too, the figures of Chaucer are much more lively, and set in a better light; which though I have not time to prove, yet I appeal to the reader, and am sure he will clear me from partiality. The thoughts and words remain to be considered, in the comparison of the two poets, and I have saved myself one-half of the labour by owning that Ovid lived when the Roman tongue was in its meridian, Chaucer in the dawning of our language; therefore, that part of the comparison stands not on an equal foot, any more than the diction of Ennius and Ovid, or of Chaucer and our present English. The words are given up, as a post not to be defended in our poet, because he wanted the modern art of fortifying. The thoughts remain to be considered; and they are to be measured only by their propriety; that is, as they flow more or less naturally from the persons described, on such and such occasions. The vulgar judges, which are nine parts in ten of all nations, who call conceits and jingles wit, who see Ovid full of them, and Chaucer altogether without them, will think me little less than mad for preferring the Englishman to the Roman. Yet, with their leave, I must presume to say that the things they admire are only glittering trifles, and so far from being witty, that in a serious poem they are nauseous, because they are unnatural. Would any man, who is ready to die for love, describe his passion like Narcissus? Would he think of *inopem me copia fecit*,[4] and a dozen more of such expressions, poured on the neck of one another, and signifying all the same thing? If this were wit, was this a time to be witty, when the poor wretch was in the agony of death? This is just John Littlewit, in *Bartholomew Fair*, who had a conceit (as he tells you) left him in his misery, a miserable conceit. On these occasions the poet should endeavour to raise pity; but, instead of this, Ovid is tickling you to laugh. Virgil never made use of such machines when he was moving you to commiserate the death of Dido: he would not destroy what he was building. Chaucer makes Arcite violent in his love, and unjust in the pursuit of it; yet, when he came to die, he made him think more reasonably: he repents not of his love, for that had altered his character; but acknowledges the injustice of his proceedings, and resigns Emilia to Palamon. What would Ovid have done on this occasion? He would certainly have made Arcite witty on his deathbed; he had complained he was further off from possession, by being so near, and a thousand such boyisms, which Chaucer rejected as below the dignity of the subject. They who think otherwise would, by the same reason, prefer Lucan and Ovid to Homer and Virgil, and Martial to all four of them. As for the turn of words, in which Ovid particularly excels all poets, they are sometimes a fault, and sometimes a beauty, as they are used properly or improperly; but in strong passions always to be shunned, because passions are serious, and will admit no playing. The French have a high value for them; and, I confess, they are often what they call delicate, when they are introduced with judgment; but Chaucer writ with more simplicity, and followed nature more closely than to use them. I have thus far, to the best of my knowledge, been an upright judge betwixt the parties in competition, not meddling with the design nor the disposition of it; because the design was not their own; and in the disposing of it they were equal.

[4] "Plenty has made me poor." (OVID)

It remains that I say somewhat of Chaucer in particular.

In the first place, as he is the father of English poetry, so I hold him in the same degree of veneration as the Grecians held Homer, or the Romans Virgil. He is a perpetual fountain of good sense; learned in all sciences; and, therefore, speaks properly on all subjects. As he knew what to say, so he knows also when to leave off; a continence which is practised by few writers, and scarcely by any of the ancients, excepting Virgil and Horace. One of our late great poets is sunk in his reputation because he could never forgive any conceit which came in his way; but swept like a drag-net, great and small. There were plenty enough, but the dishes were ill sorted; whole pyramids of sweetmeats for boys and women but little of solid meat for men. All this proceeded not from any want of knowledge, but of judgment. Neither did he want that in discerning the beauties and faults of other poets, but only indulged himself in the luxury of writing; and perhaps knew it was a fault, but hoped the reader would not find it. For this reason, though he must always be thought a great poet, he is no longer esteemed a good writer; and for ten impressions, which his works have had in so many successive years, yet at present a hundred books are scarcely purchased once a twelvemonth; for, as my last Lord Rochester said, though somewhat profanely, "not being of God, he could not stand."

Chaucer followed Nature everywhere, but was never so bold to go beyond her; and there is a great difference of being *poeta* and *nimis poeta*,[5] if we may believe Catullus, as much as betwixt a modest behaviour and affectation. The verse of Chaucer, I confess, is not harmonious to us; but 'tis like the eloquence of one whom Tacitus commends, it was *auribus istius temporis accommodata*:[6] they who lived with him, and some time after him, thought it musical; and it continues so, even in our judgment, if compared with the numbers of Lydgate and Gower, his contemporaries; there is the rude sweetness of a Scotch tune in it, which is natural and pleasing, though not perfect. 'Tis true, I cannot go so far as he who published the last edition of him; for he would make us believe the fault is in our ears, and that there were really ten syllables in a verse where we find but nine: but this opinion is not worth confuting; 'tis so gross and obvious an error that common sense (which is a rule in everything but matters of faith and revelation) must convince

[5] "A poet and too much of a poet." (MARTIAL)
[6] Suited to the ears of that time.

the reader that equality of numbers, in every verse which we call *heroic*, was either not known, or not always practised, in Chaucer's age. It were an easy matter to produce some thousands of his verses which are lame for want of half a foot, and sometimes a whole one, and which no pronunciation can make otherwise. We can only say that he lived in the infancy of our poetry, and that nothing is brought to perfection at the first. We must be children before we grow men. There was an Ennius and in process of time a Lucilius and a Lucretius, before Virgil and Horace; even after Chaucer there was a Spenser, a Harrington, a Fairfax, before Waller and Denham were in being; and our numbers were in their nonage till these last appeared. I need say little of his parentage, life, and fortunes; they are to be found at large in all the editions of his works. He was employed abroad, and favoured, by Edward the Third, Richard the Second, and Henry the Fourth, and was poet, as I suppose, to all three of them. In Richard's time, I doubt, he was a little dipped in the rebellion of the Commons; and being brother-in-law to John of Gaunt, it was no wonder if he followed the fortunes of that family; and was well with Henry the Fourth when he had deposed his predecessor. Neither is it to be admired that Henry, who was a wise as well as a valiant prince, who claimed by succession, and was sensible that his title was not sound, but was rightfully in Mortimer, who had married the heir of York; it was not to be admired, I say, if that great politician should be pleased to have the greatest wit of those times in his interests, and to be the trumpet of his praises. Augustus had given him the example, by the advice of Maecenas, who recommended Virgil and Horace to him; whose praises helped to make him popular while he was alive, and after his death have made him precious to posterity. As for the religion of our poet, he seems to have some little bias towards the opinions of Wiclif, after John of Gaunt, his patron; somewhat of which appears in the tale of *Piers Plowman*; yet I cannot blame him for inveighing so sharply against the vices of the clergy in his age: their pride, their ambition, their pomp, their avarice, their worldly interest deserved the lashes which he gave them, both in that, and in most of his *Canterbury Tales*. Neither has his contemporary Boccace spared them: yet both those poets lived in much esteem with good and holy men in orders; for the scandal which is given by particular priests reflects not on the sacred function. Chaucer's Monk, his Canon, and his Friar took not from the character of his Good Parson. A satirical poet is the check of the laymen on bad priests. We are only to take care that we involve not the innocent with the guilty in the same condemnation. The good cannot be too much honoured, nor the bad too coarsely used, for the corruption of the best becomes the worst. When a clergyman is whipped, his gown is first taken off, by which the dignity of his order is secured. If he be wrongfully accused, he has his action of slander; and 'tis at the poet's peril if he transgress the law. But they will tell us that all kind of satire, though never so well deserved by particular priests, yet brings the whole order into contempt. Is then the peerage of England anything dishonoured when a peer suffers for his treason? If he be libelled, or any way defamed, he has his *scandalum magnatum* to punish the offender. They who use this kind of argument seem to be conscious to themselves of somewhat which has deserved the poet's lash, and are less concerned for their public capacity than for their private; at least there is pride at the bottom of their reasoning. If the faults of men in orders are only to be judged among themselves, they are all in some sort parties; for, since they say the honour of their order is concerned in every member of it, how can we be sure that they will be impartial judges? How far I may be allowed to speak my opinion in this case, I know not; but I am sure a dispute of this nature caused mischief in abundance betwixt a King of England and an Archbishop of Canterbury; one standing up for the laws of his land, and the other for the honour (as he called it) of God's Church; which ended in the murder of the prelate, and in the whipping of his Majesty from post to pillar for his penance. The learned and ingenious Dr. Drake has saved me the labour of inquiring into the esteem and reverence which the priests have had of old; and I would rather extend than diminish any part of it; yet I must needs say that when a priest provokes me without any occasion given him, I have no reason, unless it be the charity of a Christian, to forgive him: *prior laesit* [7] is justification sufficient in the civil law. If I answer him in his own language, self-defence, I am sure, must be allowed me; and if I carry it further, even to a sharp recrimination, somewhat may be indulged to human frailty. Yet my resentment has not wrought so far but that I have followed Chaucer in his character of a holy man, and have enlarged on that subject with some pleasure; reserving to myself the right, if I shall think fit hereafter, to describe another sort of priests, such as are more easily to be found than the Good Parson; such as have given the last blow

[7] He struck first.

to Christianity in this age, by a practice so contrary to their doctrine. But this will keep cold till another time. In the meanwhile, I take up Chaucer where I left him.

He must have been a man of a most wonderful comprehensive nature, because, as it has been truly observed of him, he has taken into the compass of his *Canterbury Tales* the various manners and humours (as we now call them) of the whole English nation in his age. Not a single character has escaped him. All his pilgrims are severally distinguished from each other; and not only in their inclinations, but in their very physiognomies and persons. Baptista Porta could not have described their natures better, than by the marks which the poet gives them. The matter and manner of their tales, and of their telling, are so suited to their different educations, humours, and callings that each of them would be improper in any other mouth. Even the grave and serious characters are distinguished by their several sorts of gravity: their discourses are such as belong to their age, their calling, and their breeding; such as are becoming of them, and of them only. Some of his persons are vicious, and some virtuous; some are unlearned, or (as Chaucer calls them) lewd, and some are learned. Even the ribaldry of the low characters is different: the Reeve, the Miller, and the Cook are several men, and distinguished from each other as much as the mincing Lady Prioress and the broad-speaking, gaptoothed Wife of Bath. But enough of this; there is such a variety of game springing up before me that I am distracted in my choice, and know not which to follow. 'Tis sufficient to say, according to the proverb, that "here is God's plenty." We have our forefathers and great-grand-dames all before us, as they were in Chaucer's days: their general characters are still remaining in mankind, and even in England, though they are called by other names than those of Monks, and Friars, and Canons, and Lady Abbesses, and Nuns; for mankind is ever the same, and nothing lost out of nature, though everything is altered. May I have leave to do myself the justice (since my enemies will do me none, and are so far from granting me to be a good poet that they will not allow me so much as to be a Christian, or a moral man), may I have leave, I say, to inform my reader that I have confined my choice to such tales of Chaucer as savour nothing of immodesty. If I had desired more to please than to instruct, the Reeve, the Miller, the Shipman, the Merchant, the Summoner, and, above all, the Wife of Bath, in the Frologue to her Tale, would have procured me as many friends and readers as there are beaux and ladies of pleasure in the town. But I will no more offend against good manners: I am sensible as I ought to be of the scandal I have given by my loose writings; and make what reparation I am able, by this public acknowledgment. If anything of this nature, or of profaneness be crept into these poems, I am so far from defending it that I disown it. *Totum hoc indictum volo.*[8] Chaucer makes another manner of apology for his broad speaking, and Boccace makes the like; but I will follow neither of them. Our countryman, in the end of his Characters, before the *Canterbury Tales,* thus excuses the ribaldry, which is very gross in many of his novels—

> But firste, I pray you, of your courtesy,
> That ye ne arrete it nought my villany,
> Though that I plainly speak in this mattere,
> To tellen you her words, and eke her chere:
> Ne though I speak her words properly,
> For this ye knowen as well as I,
> Who shall tellen a tale after a man,
> He mote rehearse as nye as ever he can:
> Everich word of it ben in his charge,
> All speke he, never so rudely, ne large:
> Or else he mote tellen his tale untrue,
> Or feine things, or find words new:
> He may not spare, altho he were his brother,
> He mote as wel say o word as another.
> Crist spake himself ful broad in holy Writ,
> And well I wote no villany is it.
> Eke Plato saith, who so can him rede,
> The words mote been cousin to the dede.

Yet if a man should have enquired of Boccace or of Chaucer what need they had of introducing such characters, where obscene words were proper in their mouths, but very undecent to be heard; I know not what answer they could have made; for that reason, such tales shall be left untold by me. You have here a specimen of Chaucer's language, which is so obsolete that his sense is scarce to be understood; and you have likewise more than one example of his unequal numbers, which were mentioned before. Yet many of his verses consist of ten syllables, and the words not much behind our present English: as for example, these two lines, in the description of the Carpenter's young wife—

> Wincing she was, as is a jolly colt,
> Long as a mast, and upright as a bolt.

I have almost done with Chaucer, when I have answered some objections relating to my present

[8] I wish all this unsaid.

work. I find some people are offended that I have turned these tales into modern English, because they think them unworthy of my pains, and look on Chaucer as a dry, old-fashioned wit, not worth reviving. I have often heard the late Earl of Leicester say that Mr. Cowley himself was of that opinion; who, having read him over at my Lord's request, declared he had no taste of him. I dare not advance my opinion against the judgment of so great an author; but I think it fair, however, to leave the decision to the public. Mr. Cowley was too modest to set up for a dictator; and being shocked perhaps with his old style, never examined into the depth of his good sense. Chaucer, I confess, is a rough diamond, and must first be polished ere he shines. I deny not likewise that, living in our early days of poetry, he writes not always of a piece; but sometimes mingles trivial things with those of greater moment. Sometimes also, though not often, he runs riot, like Ovid, and knows not when he has said enough. But there are more great wits besides Chaucer, whose fault is their excess of conceits, and those ill sorted. An author is not to write all he can, but only all he ought. Having observed this redundancy in Chaucer (as it is an easy matter for a man of ordinary parts to find a fault in one of greater), I have not tied myself to a literal translation; but have often omitted what I judged unnecessary, or not of dignity enough to appear in the company of better thoughts. I have presumed farther, in some places, and added somewhat of my own where I thought my author was deficient, and had not given his thoughts their true lustre, for want of words in the beginning of our language. And to this I was the more emboldened, because (if I may be permitted to say it for myself) I found I had a soul congenial to his, and that I had been conversant in the same studies. Another poet, in another age, may take the same liberty with my writings; if at least they live long enough to deserve correction. It was also necessary sometimes to restore the sense of Chaucer, which was lost or mangled in the errors of the press. Let this example suffice at present: in the story of *Palamon and Arcite*, where the temple of Diana is described, you find these verses in all the editions of our author:—

> There saw I Danè turned unto a tree,
> I mean not the goddess Diane,
> But Venus daughter, which that hight Danè.

Which, after a little consideration, I knew was to be reformed into this sense, that Daphne, the daughter of Peneus, was turned into a tree. I durst not

make thus bold with Ovid, lest some future Milbourne should arise and say I varied from my author because I understood him not.

But there are other judges who think I ought not to have translated Chaucer into English, out of a quite contrary notion: they suppose there is a certain veneration due to his old language, and that it is little less than profanation and sacrilege to alter it. They are farther of opinion that somewhat of his good sense will suffer in this transfusion, and much of the beauty of his thoughts will infallibly be lost, which appear with more grace in their old habit. Of this opinion was that excellent person, whom I mentioned, the late Earl of Leicester, who valued Chaucer as much as Mr. Cowley despised him. My Lord dissuaded me from this attempt (for I was thinking of it some years before his death) and his authority prevailed so far with me, as to defer my undertaking while he lived, in deference to him: yet my reason was not convinced with what he urged against it. If the first end of a writer be to be understood, then, as his language grows obsolete, his thoughts must grow obscure—

Multa renascentur, quae nunc cecidere; cadentque
Quae nunc sunt in honore vocabula, si volet usus,
Quen penes arbitrium est et jus et norma loquendi.[9]

When an ancient word, for its sound and significancy, deserves to be revived, I have that reasonable veneration for antiquity to restore it. All beyond this is superstition. Words are not like landmarks, so sacred as never to be removed; customs are changed, and even statutes are silently repealed, when the reason ceases for which they were enacted. As for the other part of the argument, that his thoughts will lose of their original beauty by the innovation of words; in the first place, not only their beauty, but their being is lost, where they are no longer understood, which is the present case. I grant that something must be lost in all transfusion, that is, in all translations; but the sense will remain, which would otherwise be lost, or at least be maimed, when it is scarce intelligible, and that but to a few. How few are there who can read Chaucer so as to understand him perfectly? And if imperfectly, then with less profit, and no pleasure. It is not for the use of some old Saxon friends that I have taken these pains with him: let them neglect my version, because they have no need of it. I made it for their sakes,

[9] "Full many a word, now lost, again shall rise,
And many a word shall droop which now we prize,
As shifting fashion stamps the doom of each,
Sole umpire, arbitress, and guide of speech."

(HORACE)

who understand sense and poetry as well as they, when that poetry and sense is put into words which they understand. I will go farther, and dare to add, that what beauties I lose in some places, I give to others which had them not originally: but in this I may be partial to myself; let the reader judge, and I submit to his decision. Yet I think I have just occasion to complain of them, who because they understand Chaucer, would deprive the greater part of their countrymen of the same advantage, and hoard him up, as misers do their grandam gold, only to look on it themselves, and hinder others from making use of it. In sum, I seriously protest that no man ever had, or can have, a greater veneration for Chaucer than myself. I have translated some part of his works, only that I might perpetuate his memory, or at least refresh it, amongst my countrymen. If I have altered him anywhere for the better, I must at the same time acknowledge that I could have done nothing without him. *Facile est inventis addere* [10] is no great commendation; and I am not so vain to think I have deserved a greater. I will conclude what I have to say of him singly, with this one remark: a lady of my acquaintance, who keeps a kind of correspondence with some authors of the fair sex in France, has been informed by them that Mademoiselle de Scudéry, who is as old as Sibyl, and inspired like her by the same god of poetry, is at this time translating Chaucer into modern French. From which I gather that he has been formerly translated into the old Provençal; for how she should come to understand old English, I know not. But the matter of fact being true, it makes me think that there is something in it like fatality; that, after certain periods of time, the fame and memory of great wits should be renewed, as Chaucer is both in France and England. If this be wholly chance, 'tis extraordinary; and I dare not call it more, for fear of being taxed with superstition.

Boccace comes last to be considered, who, living in the same age with Chaucer, had the same genius, and followed the same studies. Both writ novels, and each of them cultivated his mother tongue. But the greatest resemblance of our two modern authors being in their familiar style and pleasing way of relating comical adventures, I may pass it over, because I have translated nothing from Boccace of that nature. In the serious part of poetry, the advantage is wholly on Chaucer's side, for though the Englishman has borrowed many tales from the Italian, yet it appears that those of Boccace were not generally of his own making, but taken from authors of

[10] It is easy to add to something already invented.

former ages, and by him only modelled; so that what there was of invention, in either of them, may be judged equal. But Chaucer has refined on Boccace, and has mended the stories which he has borrowed, in his way of telling; though prose allows more liberty of thought, and the expression is more easy when unconfined by numbers. Our countryman carries weight, and yet wins the race at disadvantage. I desire not the reader should take my word; and, therefore, I will set two of their discourses, on the same subject, in the same light, for every man to judge betwixt them. I translated Chaucer first, and, amongst the rest, pitched on *The Wife of Bath's Tale*; not daring, as I have said, to adventure on her Prologue, because 'tis too licentious. There Chaucer introduces an old woman, of mean parentage, whom a youthful knight, of noble blood, was forced to marry, and consequently loathed her. The crone being in bed with him on the wedding-night, and finding his aversion, endeavours to win his affection by reason, and speaks a good word for herself (as who could blame her?) in hope to mollify the sullen bridegroom. She takes her topics from the benefits of poverty, the advantages of old age and ugliness, the vanity of youth, and the silly pride of ancestry and titles, without inherent virtue, which is the true nobility. When I had closed Chaucer, I returned to Ovid, and translated some more of his fables; and, by this time, had so far forgotten *The Wife of Bath's Tale*, that, when I took up Boccace, unawares I fell on the same argument, of preferring virtue to nobility of blood and titles, in the story of *Sigismonda*; which I had certainly avoided, for the resemblance of the two discourses, if my memory had not failed me. Let the reader weigh them both; and, if he thinks me partial to Chaucer, 'tis in him to right Boccace.

I prefer, in our countryman, far above all his other stories, the noble poem of *Palamon and Arcite*, which is of the epic kind, and perhaps not much inferior to the *Ilias*, or the *Aeneis*. The story is more pleasing than either of them, the manners as perfect, the diction as poetical, the learning as deep and various, and the disposition full as artful: only it includes a greater length of time, as taking up seven years at least; but Aristotle has left undecided the duration of the action; which yet is easily reduced into the compass of a year, by a narration of what preceded the return of Palamon to Athens. I had thought, for the honour of our narration, and more particularly for his, whose laurel, though unworthy, I have worn after him, that his story was of English growth, and Chaucer's own: but I was undeceived by Boccace; for, casually looking on the end of his seventh *Giornata,* I found Dioneo (under which name he shadows himself), and Fiametta (who represents his mistress, the natural daughter of Robert, King of Naples), of whom these words are spoken: *Dioneo e Fiametta gran pezza cantarono insieme d'Arcita, e di Palemone;* [11] by which it appears that this story was written before the time of Boccace; but the name of its author being wholly lost, Chaucer is now become an original; and I question not but the poem has received many beauties, by passing through his noble hands. Besides this tale, there is another of his own invention, after the manner of the Provençals, called *The Flower and the Leaf,* with which I was so particularly pleased, both for the invention and the moral, that I cannot hinder myself from recommending it to the reader.

As a corollary to this preface, in which I have done justice to others, I owe somewhat to myself; not that I think it worth my time to enter the lists with one M——, and one B——, but barely to take notice that such men there are, who have written scurrilously against me, without any provocation. M——, who is in orders, pretends, amongst the rest, this quarrel to me, that I have fallen foul on priesthood: if I have, I am only to ask pardon of good priests, and am afraid his part of the reparation will come to little. Let him be satisfied that he shall not be able to force himself upon me for an adversary. I contemn him too much to enter into competition with him. His own translations of Virgil have answered his criticisms on mine. If (as they say, he has declared in print) he prefers the version of Ogilby to mine, the world has made him the same compliment, for 'tis agreed, on all hands, that he writes even below Ogilby. That, you will say, is not easily to be done; but what cannot M—— bring about? I am satisfied, however, that, while he and I live together, I shall not be thought the worst poet of the age. It looks as if I had desired him underhand to write so ill against me; but upon my honest word I have not bribed him to do me this service, and am wholly guiltless of his pamphlet. 'Tis true, I should be glad if I could persuade him to continue his good offices, and write such another critique on anything of mine; for I find, by experience, he has a great stroke with the reader, when he condemns any of my poems, to make the world have a better opinion of them. He has taken some pains with my poetry; but nobody will be persuaded to take the

[11] Dioneo and Fiametta sang together for a good while of Arcite and of Palamon.

same with his. If I had taken to the Church, as he affirms, but which was never in my thoughts, I should have had more sense, if not more grace, than to have turned myself out of my benefice, by writing libels on my parishioners. But his account of my manners and my principles are of a piece with his cavils and his poetry; and so I have done with him for ever.

As for the City Bard, or Knight Physician, I hear his quarrel to me is that I was the author of *Absalom and Achitophel,* which, he thinks, is a little hard on his fanatic patrons in London.

But I will deal the more civilly with his two poems, because nothing ill is to be spoken of the dead; and therefore peace be to the *manes* of his *Arthurs.* I will only say that it was not for this noble knight that I drew the plan of an epic poem on King Arthur, in my preface to the translation of Juvenal. The Guardian Angels of kingdoms were machines too ponderous for him to manage; and therefore he rejected them, as Dares did the whirlbats of Eryx when they were thrown before him by Entellus: yet from that preface, he plainly took his hint; for he began immediately upon the story, though he had the baseness not to acknowledge his benefactor, but instead of it, to traduce me in a libel.

I shall say the less of Mr. Collier, because in many things he has taxed me justly; and I have pleaded guilty to all thoughts and expressions of mine which can be truly argued of obscenity, profaneness, or immorality, and retract them. If he be my enemy, let him triumph; if he be my friend, as I have given him no personal occasion to be otherwise, he will be glad of my repentance. It becomes me not to draw my pen in the defence of a bad cause, when I have so often drawn it for a good one. Yet it were not difficult to prove that in many places he has perverted my meaning by his glosses, and interpreted my words into blasphemy and bawdry, of which they were not guilty. Besides that, he is too much given to horseplay in his raillery, and comes to battle like a dictator from the plough. I will not say, "The zeal of God's house has eaten him up"; but I am sure it has devoured some part of his good manners and civility. It might also be doubted whether it were altogether zeal which prompted him to this rough manner of proceeding; perhaps it became not one of his functions to rake into the rubbish of ancient and modern plays: a divine might have employed his pains to better purpose than in the nastiness of Plautus and Aristophanes, whose examples, as they excuse not me, so it might be possibly supposed that he read them not without some pleasure. They who have written commentaries on those poets, or on Horace, Juvenal, and Martial, have explained some vices, which, without their interpretation, had been unknown to modern times. Neither has he judged impartially betwixt the former age and us. There is more bawdry in one play of Fletcher's, called *The Custom of the Country,* than in all ours together. Yet this has been often acted on the stage, in my remembrance. Are the times so much more reformed now than they were five-and-twenty years ago? If they are, I congratulate the amendment of our morals. But I am not to prejudice the cause of my fellow poets, though I abandon my own defence: they have some of them answered for themselves; and neither they nor I can think Mr. Collier so formidable an enemy that we should shun him. He has lost ground, at the latter end of the day, by pursuing his point too far, like the Prince of Condé, at the battle of Senneph: from immoral plays to no plays, *ab abusu ad usum, non valet consequentia.*[12] But, being a party, I am not to erect myself into a judge. As for the rest of those who have written against me, they are such scoundrels that they deserve not the least notice to be taken of them. B—— and M—— are only distinguished from the crowd by being remembered to their infamy:

> . . . *Demetri, teque, Tigelli,*
> *Discipulorum inter jubeo plorare cathedras.*[13]

———◆———

JONATHAN SWIFT

1667–1745

Jonathan Swift, one of the great satirists in all literature, was born of English parents in Dublin, where he received his education at Trinity College. After his graduation he went to England (1688), and became secretary to Sir William Temple. It was at the Temple estate, Moor Park, Surrey, that Swift first met Esther Johnson, a little girl of eight, who was perhaps the natural daughter of Sir William. Swift was placed in charge of her education, a task which he seems to have enjoyed, for she re-

[12] No logical conclusion about the use of anything is to be drawn from its misuse.
[13] "Demetrius and you, Tigellus, I bid weep among your scholars' chairs." (HORACE)

mained his lifelong, intimate friend. During his years at Moor Park, Swift wrote several unimportant poems and began his career as a prose writer with *A Tale of a Tub,* a brilliant allegorical satire on the chief divisions of European Christianity—Roman, Anglican, and Presbyterian—and *The Battle of the Books,* a mock-heroic satire in prose. Written perhaps at the instigation of Sir William, it is a defense of the ancient classical writers in the controversy then raging over the *Epistles* of Phalaris and the larger debate over the relative merits of ancient and modern writers.

In 1694 Swift returned to Ireland and took orders as an Anglican clergyman, after which he was for a while a parish priest. He then returned to Moor Park for a brief period, but after the death of Temple in 1699 he returned to Ireland, where he was given a prebend in St. Patrick's, Dublin, and the living of Larcor. But during the course of frequent visits to London he became acquainted with Addison, Steele, Halifax, and renewed his college acquaintance with Congreve, the great comic dramatist. From 1708 to 1714, he lived mostly in London, where, in the vain attempt to gain ecclesiastical preferment, he lent his satiric pen to the Tory ministry of Oxford and Bolingbroke. The ministry was grateful to Swift, but never in a very tangible way. Although he had every right to expect the reward of a bishopric, for at one time he may have been the most influential man in England, the reward was constantly postponed and never actually produced. It may be true that Queen Anne, who is reported to have been displeased by the coarseness and levity of *A Tale of a Tub,* considered him an improper person to be made a bishop. The only reward he ever received for his brilliant political writing in *The Examiner,* and this after many promises and disappointments, was the deanship of St. Patrick's in Dublin.

Swift looked upon his Irish residence as a kind of exile, and there is no doubt that he missed Pope, Gay, Arbuthnot, Congreve, and Bolingbroke, his creative coterie of friends in London. But he kept up his friendships by voluminous correspondence and frequent visits.

During his London years he wrote constantly to Esther Johnson, a correspondence published under the title of *Journal to Stella.* Also during his London sojourn, he met a beautiful young lady of twenty named Hester van Homrigh, who fell madly in love with him, followed him to Ireland, and there, after being repulsed by the Dean, died practically of a broken heart. Swift's relationship with Stella (Esther Johnson) is an enigma: the two were constant companions in Dublin and may have been secretly married; but if there was a marriage, they never lived together as man and wife. A great deal has been written about Swift's alleged marriage, but the evidence is insufficient either to prove or to disprove it.

Swift sympathized deeply with the economic and political oppression which the Irish had to endure. For their cause he wrote the *Drapier's Letters*, a series of pamphlets which put a price on their author's head. The Irish knew their benefactor and refused to supply evidence. Instead, they treated Dean Swift as the first citizen of Ireland, and his popularity in his adopted land was boundless. One other pamphlet was written in the Irish cause, *A Modest Proposal*, a masterpiece of ironic prose in which Swift proposed that the British, having devoured the Irish economy, turn cannibal and eat Irish babies.

Swift's greatest masterpiece is, as everybody knows, the work that he entitled *Travels into Several Remote Nations of the World* (London, 1726) but that generations of delighted readers have persisted in calling *Gulliver's Travels*.

For many years Swift suffered from vertigo and increasing deafness. In his seventy-fifth year his mind had so deteriorated that guardians had to be appointed. He lived three more years completely bereft of his reason, and died in 1745, leaving the bulk of his estate to found an insane asylum in Dublin. He is buried beside his beloved Stella in St. Patrick's Cathedral, as his Latin epitaph says, "where fierce indignation cannot further lacerate his heart."

Many writers have seized upon the phrase *saeva indignatio* in his inscription and in an act of clever simplification have proclaimed it the key to Swift's whole personality. Without a doubt indignation— against the wrongness of the world and all of its institutions, indignation against the failure of man to use his God-given powers of reason, indignation against men who live with the brutality of beasts, indignation against all sorts and conditions of abuses in human life—is the key to the greater half of Swift's work. But it is not the key to all of Swift, for it leaves completely out of account all of his humorous, sprightly, jocular, whimsical writings such as *The Predictions for the Year 1708* . . . by Isaac Bickerstaff. Though Swift himself confessed to being a misanthrope—in a letter to Pope he said, "I heartily love John, Peter, Thomas, and so forth . . . I hate and detest that animal called man. . . . Upon this great foundation of misanthropy . . . the whole building of my Travels is erected"—it is a queer kind of misanthropy that spends a man's entire life in an unsparing crusade to improve his fellow men. The desire to reform mankind is actually the mainspring of Swift's greatest works, including *Gulliver*. The furious indignation which lacerated Swift was the result of a perfectly rational realization that mankind was not going to be reformed in spite of all his efforts. Coarseness there is in Swift, too, but it is never mere vulgarity; rather it is coarseness used in a desperate attempt to reform by *disgusting* people, since it could not be done any other way.

Gulliver's Travels is in every way a classic: that is to say, it can be read and enjoyed on various levels. It is even read by children, who particularly enjoy the Lilliputians of Book I and the giant Brobdingnagians of Book II, little suspecting that they are reading the greatest prose satire in world literature. On another level it is most trenchant political satire. Book IV, which the editors print here in its entirety, has been called Swift's libel against the human race. Actually, it is this book, somewhat less familiar to most students than the first two books, which carries the heart of Swift's teachings; for it is here that he acidly delineates the contrast between the ideal rational life that men could lead, if only they would lead it (the Houyhnhnms), and the brutality and disgusting ugliness of human life as it actually exists, exaggerated for satiric purpose to some degree (the yahoos). Often regarded as the height of Swift's misanthropy, properly interpreted Book IV is the highest evidence of his love of his fellow men. *Gulliver* is written in impeccable prose, simple, and clear, and right. It perfectly conforms to Swift's own definition of good writing: "proper words in the proper places." Better prose is hard to imagine

FURTHER READING

CASE, A. E. *Four Essays on Gulliver's Travels* (Princeton, 1945).

DAVIS, HERBERT. *The Satire of Jonathan Swift* (New York, 1947).

QUINTANA, RICARDO. *The Mind and Art of Jonathan Swift* (New York, 1936).

TOBIN, J. E. *Jonathan Swift: A List of Critical Studies Published 1895 to 1945* (New York, 1945).

VAN DOREN, CARL. *Swift* (New York, 1930).

Gulliver's Travels *

PART IV

A VOYAGE TO THE COUNTRY OF THE HOUYHNHNMS

CHAPTER I

The author sets out as captain of a ship. His men conspire against him, confine him a long time to his cabin, set him on shore in an unknown land. He travels up in the country. The yahoos, a strange sort of animal, described. The author meets two Houyhnhnms.

I CONTINUED at home with my wife and children about four months in a very happy condition, if I could have learned the lesson of knowing when I was well. I left my poor wife big with child, and accepted an advantageous offer made me to be captain of the *Adventure*, a stout merchantman of 350 tons: for I understood navigation well, and being grown weary of a surgeon's employment at sea, which however I could exercise upon occasion, I took a skilful young man of that calling, one Robert Purefoy, into my ship. We set sail from Portsmouth upon the second day of August, 1710; on the fourteenth, we met with Captain Pocock of Bristol, at Tenariff,[1] who was going to the bay of Campechy,[2] to cut logwood. On the sixteenth, he was parted from us by a storm; I heard since my return that his ship foundered, and none escaped, but one cabin-boy. He was an honest man, and a good sailor, but a little too positive in his own opinions, which was the cause of his destruction, as it hath been of sev-

eral others. For if he had followed my advice, he might have been safe at home with his family at this time, as well as myself.

I had several men died in my ship of calentures,[3] so that I was forced to get recruits out of Barbadoes, and the Leeward Islands, where I touched by the direction of the merchants who employed me, which I had soon too much cause to repent; for I found afterwards that most of them had been buccaneers. I had fifty hands on board, and my orders were, that I should trade with the Indians, in the South Sea, and make what discoveries I could. These rogues whom I had picked up debauched my other men, and they all formed a conspiracy to seize the ship and secure me; which they did one morning, rushing into my cabin, and binding me hand and foot, threatening to throw me overboard, if I offered to stir. I told them, I was their prisoner, and would submit. This they made me swear to do, and then they unbound me, only fastening one of my legs with a chain near my bed, and placed a sentry at my door with his piece charged, who was commanded to shoot me dead, if I attempted my liberty. They sent me down victuals and drink, and took the government of the ship to themselves. Their design was to turn pirates, and plunder the Spaniards, which they could not do, till they got more men. But first they resolved to sell the goods in the ship, and then go to Madagascar for recruits, several among them having died since my confinement. They sailed many weeks, and traded with the Indians, but I knew not what course they took, being kept a close prisoner in my cabin, and expecting nothing less than to be murdered, as they often threatened me.

Upon the ninth day of May, 1711, one James Welch came down to my cabin; and said he had orders from the captain to set me ashore. I expostulated with him, but in vain; neither would he so much as tell me who their new captain was. They forced me into the longboat, letting me put on my best suit of clothes, which were as good as new, and a small bundle of linen, but no arms except my hanger; and they were so civil as not to search my pockets, into which I conveyed what money I had, with some other little necessaries. They rowed about a league, and then set me down on a strand. I desired them to tell me what country it was. They all swore, they knew no more than myself, but said, that the captain (as they called him) was resolved, after they had sold the lading, to get rid of me in the first place where they could discover land. They

---

* By permission from *Swift: Gulliver's Travels*, edited by Arthur E. Case. Copyright, 1938, by The Ronald Press Company.

[1] Teneriffe, the largest of the Canary Islands.

[2] In the Gulf of Mexico.

[3] Sunstrokes or tropical fevers.

pushed off immediately, advising me to make haste, for fear of being overtaken by the tide, and so bade me farewell.

In this desolate condition I advanced forward, and soon got upon firm ground, where I sate down on a bank to rest myself, and consider what I had best to do. When I was a little refreshed I went up into the country, resolving to deliver myself to the first savages I should meet, and purchase my life from them by some bracelets, glass rings, and other toys, which sailors usually provide themselves with in those voyages, and whereof I had some about me: the land was divided by long rows of trees, not regularly planted, but naturally growing; there was great plenty of grass, and several fields of oats. I walked very circumspectly for fear of being surprised, or suddenly shot with an arrow from behind or on either side. I fell into a beaten road, where I saw many tracks of human feet, and some of cows, but most of horses. At last I beheld several animals in a field, and one or two of the same kind sitting in trees. Their shape was very singular, and deformed, which a little discomposed me, so that I lay down behind a thicket to observe them better. Some of them coming forward near the place where I lay, gave me an opportunity of distinctly marking their form. Their heads and breasts were covered with a thick hair, some frizzled and others lank; they had beards like goats, and a long ridge of hair down their backs, and the fore-parts of their legs and feet, but the rest of their bodies were bare, so that I might see their skins, which were of a brown buff colour. They had no tails, nor any hair at all on their buttocks, except about the anus; which, I presume, nature had placed there to defend them as they sate on the ground; for this posture they used, as well as lying down, and often stood on their hind feet. They climbed high trees, as nimbly as a squirrel, for they had strong extended claws before and behind, terminating in sharp points, and hooked. They would often spring, and bound, and leap with prodigious agility. The females were not so large as the males; they had long lank hair on their heads, but none on their faces, nor any thing more than a sort of down on the rest of their bodies, except about the anus, and pudenda. Their dugs hung between their fore-feet, and often reached almost to the ground as they walked. The hair of both sexes was of several colours, brown, red, black, and yellow. Upon the whole, I never beheld in all my travels so disagreeable an animal, nor one against which I naturally conceived so strong antipathy. So that thinking I

had seen enough, full of contempt and aversion, I got up and pursued the beaten road, hoping it might direct me to the cabin of some Indian. I had not gone far when I met one of these creatures full in my way, and coming up directly to me. The ugly monster, when he saw me, distorted several ways every feature of his visage, and stared as at an object he had never seen before; then approaching nearer, lifted up his forepaw, whether out of curiosity or mischief, I could not tell. But I drew my hanger, and gave him a good blow with the flat side of it, for I durst not strike him with the edge, fearing the inhabitants might be provoked against me, if they should come to know that I had killed or maimed any of their cattle. When the beast felt the smart, he drew back, and roared so loud, that a herd of at least forty came flocking about me from the next field, howling and making odious faces; but I ran to the body of a tree, and leaning my back against it, kept them off, by waving my hanger. Several of this cursed brood getting hold of the branches behind leapt up in the tree, from whence they began to discharge their excrements on my head: however, I escaped pretty well, by sticking close to the stem of the tree, but was almost stifled with the filth, which fell about me on every side.

In the midst of this distress, I observed them all to run away on a sudden as fast as they could, at which I ventured to leave the tree, and pursue the road, wondering what it was that could put them into this fright. But looking on my left hand, I saw a horse walking softly in the field: which my persecutors having sooner discovered, was the cause of their flight. The horse started a little when he came near me, but soon recovering himself, looked full in my face with manifest tokens of wonder: he viewed my hands and feet, walking round me several times. I would have pursued my journey, but he placed himself directly in the way, yet looking with a very mild aspect, never offering the least violence. We stood gazing at each other for some time; at last I took the boldness to reach my hand towards his neck, with a design to stroke it, using the common style and whistle of jockeys when they are going to handle a strange horse. But this animal, seeming to receive my civilities with disdain, shook his head, and bent his brows, softly raising up his right forefoot to remove my hand. Then he neighed three or four times, but in so different a cadence, that I almost began to think he was speaking to himself in some language of his own.

While he and I were thus employed, another

horse came up; who applying himself to the first in a very formal manner, they gently struck each other's right hoof before, neighing several times by turns, and varying the sound, which seemed to be almost articulate. They went some paces off, as if it were to confer together, walking side by side, backward and forward, like persons deliberating upon some affair of weight, but often turning their eyes towards me, as it were to watch that I might not escape. I was amazed to see such actions and behaviour in brute beasts, and concluded with myself, that if the inhabitants of this country were endued with a proportionable degree of reason, they must needs be the wisest people upon earth. This thought gave me so much comfort, that I resolved to go forward until I could discover some house or village, or meet with any of the natives, leaving the two horses to discourse together as they pleased. But the first, who was a dapple grey, observing me to steal off, neighed after me in so expressive a tone, that I fancied myself to understand what he meant; whereupon I turned back, and came near him, to expect his farther commands. But concealing my fear as much as I could, for I began to be in some pain, how this adventure might terminate; and the reader will easily believe I did not much like my present situation.

The two horses came up close to me, looking with great earnestness upon my face and hands. The grey steed rubbed my hat all round with his right fore-hoof, and discomposed it so much, that I was forced to adjust it better, by taking it off, and settling it again; whereat both he and his companion (who was a brown bay) appeared to be much surprised; the latter felt the lappet of my coat, and finding it to hang loose about me, they both looked with new signs of wonder. He stroked my right hand, seeming to admire the softness, and colour; but he squeezed it so hard between his hoof and his pastern, that I was forced to roar; after which they both touched me with all possible tenderness. They were under great perplexity about my shoes and stockings, which they felt very often, neighing to each other, and using various gestures, not unlike those of a philosopher, when he would attempt to solve some new and difficult phaenomenon.

Upon the whole, the behaviour of these animals was so orderly and rational, so acute and judicious, that I at last concluded, they must needs be magicians, who had thus metamorphosed themselves upon some design, and seeing a stranger in the way, were resolved to divert themselves with him; or

perhaps were really amazed at the sight of a man so very different in habit, feature, and complexion from those who might probably live in so remote a climate. Upon the strength of this reasoning, I ventured to address them in the following manner: "Gentlemen, if you be conjurers, as I have good cause to believe, you can understand any language; therefore I make bold to let your Worships know, that I am a poor distressed English man, driven by his misfortunes upon your coast, and I entreat one of you, to let me ride upon his back, as if he were a real horse, to some house or village, where I can be relieved. In return of which favour, I will make you a present of this knife and bracelet" (taking them out of my pocket). The two creatures stood silent while I spoke, seeming to listen with great attention; and when I had ended, they neighed frequently towards each other, as if they were engaged in serious conversation. I plainly observed, that their language expressed the passions very well, and the words might with little pains be resolved into an alphabet more easily than the Chinese.

I could frequently distinguish the word *"yahoo,"* which was repeated by each of them several times; and although it was impossible for me to conjecture what it meant, yet while the two horses were busy in conversation, I endeavoured to practise this word upon my tongue; and as soon as they were silent, I boldly pronounced *"yahoo"* [4] in a loud voice, imitating, at the same time, as near as I could, the neighing of a horse; at which they were both visibly surprised, and the grey repeated the same word twice, as if he meant to teach me the right accent, wherein I spoke after him as well as I could, and found myself perceivably to improve every time, though very far from any degree of perfection. Then the bay tried me with a second word, much harder to be pronounced; but reducing it to the English orthography, may be spelt thus, *"Houyhn-hnm."* [5] I did not succeed in this so well as the former, but after two or three farther trials, I had better fortune; and they both appeared amazed at my capacity.

After some farther discourse, which I then conjectured might relate to me, the two friends took their leaves, with the same compliment of striking each other's hoof; and the grey made me signs that

[4] Morley suggested that "yahoo" was compounded from two expressions of disgust, "yah" and "ugh" (or "hoo"), common in the eighteenth century.
[5] This word is an obvious imitation of the whinny of a horse.

I should walk before him, wherein I thought it prudent to comply, till I could find a better director. When I offered to slacken my pace, he would cry "Hhuun, hhuun"; I guessed his meaning, and gave him to understand, as well as I could, that I was weary, and not able to walk faster; upon which he would stand a while to let me rest.

CHAPTER II

The author conducted by a Houyhnhnm to his house. The house described. The author's reception. The food of the Houyhnhnms. The author in distress for want of meat, is at last relieved. His manner of feeding in this country.

Having travelled about three miles, we came to a long kind of building, made of timber stuck in the ground, and wattled across; the roof was low and covered with straw. I now began to be a little comforted, and took out some toys, which travellers usually carry for presents to the savage Indians of America and other parts, in hopes the people of the house would be thereby encouraged to receive me kindly. The horse made me a sign to go in first; it was a large room with a smooth clay floor, and a rack and manger extending the whole length on one side. There were three nags, and two mares, not eating, but some of them sitting down upon their hams, which I very much wondered at; but wondered more to see the rest employed in domestic business. They seemed but ordinary cattle; however, this confirmed my first opinion, that a people who could so far civilize brute animals must needs excel in wisdom all the nations of the world. The grey came in just after, and thereby prevented any ill treatment which the others might have given me. He neighed to them several times in a style of authority, and received answers.

Beyond this room there were three others, reaching the length of the house, to which you passed through three doors, opposite to each other, in the manner of a vista; we went through the second room towards the third; here the grey walked in first, beckoning me to attend:[6] I waited in the second room, and got ready my presents for the master and mistress of the house: they were two knives, three bracelets of false pearl, a small looking-glass and a bead necklace. The horse neighed three or four times, and I waited to hear some answers in a human voice, but I observed no other returns than in the same dialect, only one or two a little shriller than his. I began to think that this

[6] Wait without.

house must belong to some person of great note among them, because there appeared so much ceremony before I could gain admittance. But that a man of quality should be served all by horses was beyond my comprehension. I feared my brain was disturbed by my sufferings and misfortunes: I roused myself, and looked about me in the room where I was left alone; this was furnished like the first, only after a more elegant manner. I rubbed my eyes often, but the same objects still occurred. I pinched my arms and sides, to awake myself, hoping I might be in a dream. I then absolutely concluded, that all these appearances could be nothing else but necromancy and magic. But I had no time to pursue these reflections; for the grey horse came to the door, and made me a sign to follow him into the third room, where I saw a very comely mare, together with a colt and foal,[7] sitting on their haunches, upon mats of straw, not unartfully made, and perfectly neat and clean.

The mare, soon after my entrance, rose from her mat, and coming up close, after having nicely observed my hands and face, gave me a most contemptuous look; then turning to the horse, I heard the word "yahoo" often repeated betwixt them; the meaning of which word I could then comprehend, although it were the first I had learned to pronounce; but I was soon better informed, to my everlasting mortification: for the horse beckoning to me with his head, and repeating the word "Hhuun, hhuun," as he did upon the road, which I understood was to attend him, led me out into a kind of court, where was another building at some distance from the house. Here we entered, and I saw three of these detestable creatures, whom I first met after my landing, feeding upon roots, and the flesh of some animals, which I afterwards found to be that of asses and dogs, and now and then a cow dead by accident or disease. They were all tied by the neck with strong withes, fastened to a beam; they held their food between the claws of their forefeet, and tore it with their teeth.

The master horse ordered a sorrel nag, one of his servants, to untie the largest of these animals, and take him into the yard. The beast and I were brought close together, and our countenances diligently compared, both by master and servant, who thereupon repeated several times the word "yahoo." My horror and astonishment are not to be described, when I observed, in this abominable animal, a per-

[7] Swift evidently intends to differentiate between male and female by these words: they do not ordinarily bear the meanings implied.

fect human figure; the face of it indeed was flat and broad, the nose depressed, the lips large and the mouth wide. But these differences are common to all savage nations, where the lineaments of the countenance are distorted by the natives suffering their infants to lie grovelling on the earth, or by carrying them on their backs, nuzzling with their face against the mother's shoulders. The forefeet of the yahoo differed from my hands in nothing else but the length of the nails, the coarseness and brownness of the palms, and the hairiness on the backs. There was the same resemblance between our feet, with the same differences, which I knew very well, though the horses did not, because of my shoes and stockings; the same in every part of our bodies, except as to hairiness and colour, which I have already described.

The great difficulty that seemed to stick with the two horses, was to see the rest of my body so very different from that of a yahoo, for which I was obliged to my clothes, whereof they had no conception: the sorrel nag offered me a root, which he held (after their manner, as we shall describe in its proper place) between his hoof and pastern; I took it in my hand, and having smelt it, returned it to him again as civilly as I could. He brought out of the yahoo's kennel a piece of ass's flesh, but it smelt so offensively that I turned from it with loathing: he then threw it to the yahoo, by whom it was greedily devoured. He afterwards showed me a wisp of hay, and a fetlock full of oats; but I shook my head, to signify, that neither of these were food for me. And indeed, I now apprehended, that I must absolutely starve, if I did not get to some of my own species: for as to those filthy yahoos, although there were few greater lovers of mankind, at that time, than myself, yet I confess I never saw any sensitive being so detestable on all accounts; and the more I came near them, the more hateful they grew, while I stayed in that country. This the master horse observed by my behaviour, and therefore sent the yahoo back to his kennel. He then put his fore-hoof to his mouth, at which I was much surprised, although he did it with ease, and with a motion that appeared perfectly natural, and made other signs to know what I would eat; but I could not return him such an answer as he was able to apprehend; and if he had understood me, I did not see how it was possible to contrive any way for finding myself nourishment. While we were thus engaged, I observed a cow passing by, whereupon I pointed to her, and expressed a desire to let me go and milk her. This had its effect;

for he led me back into the house, and ordered a mare-servant to open a room, where a good store of milk lay in earthen and wooden vessels, after a very orderly and cleanly manner. She gave me a large bowl full, of which I drank very heartily, and found myself well refreshed.

About noon I saw coming towards the house a kind of vehicle drawn like a sledge by four yahoos. There was in it an old steed, who seemed to be of quality; he alighted with his hind feet forward, having by accident got a hurt in his left forefoot. He came to dine with our horse, who received him with great civility. They dined in the best room, and had oats boiled in milk for the second course, which the old horse eat warm, but the rest cold. Their mangers were placed circular in the middle of the room, and divided into several partitions, round which they sate on their haunches upon bosses of straw. In the middle was a large rack with angles answering to every partition of the manger. So that each horse and mare eat their own hay, and their own mash of oats and milk, with much decency and regularity. The behaviour of the young colt and foal appeared very modest, and that of the master and mistress extremely cheerful and complaisant to their guest. The grey ordered me to stand by him, and much discourse passed between him and his friend concerning me, as I found by the stranger's often looking on me, and the frequent repetition of the word "yahoo."

I happened to wear my gloves, which the master grey observing, seemed perplexed, discovering signs of wonder what I had done to my forefeet; he put his hoof three or four times to them, as if he would signify, that I should reduce them to their former shape, which I presently did, pulling off both my gloves, and putting them into my pocket. This occasioned farther talk, and I saw the company was pleased with my behaviour, whereof I soon found the good effects. I was ordered to speak the few words I understood, and while they were at dinner, the master taught me the names for oats, milk, fire, water, and some others; which I could readily pronounce after him, having from my youth a great facility in learning languages.

When dinner was done, the master horse took me aside, and by signs and words made me understand the concern that he was in, that I had nothing to eat. Oats in their tongue are called "hlunnh." This word I pronounced two or three times; for although I had refused them at first, yet upon second thoughts, I considered that I could contrive to make of them a kind of bread, which might be sufficient with milk to keep me alive, till I could make my escape to some other country, and to creatures of my own species. The horse immediately ordered a white mare-servant of his family to bring me a good quantity of oats in a sort of wooden tray. These I heated before the fire as well as I could, and rubbed them till the husks came off, which I made a shift to winnow from the grain; I ground and beat them between two stones, then took water, and made them into a paste or cake, which I toasted at the fire, and eat warm with milk. It was at first a very insipid diet, though common enough in many parts of Europe, but grew tolerable by time; and having been often reduced to hard fare in my life, this was not the first experiment I had made how easily nature is satisfied. And I cannot but observe, that I never had one hour's sickness, while I stayed in this island. 'Tis true, I sometimes made a shift to catch a rabbit, or bird, by springes [8] made of yahoos' hairs, and I often gathered wholesome herbs, which I boiled, or eat as salads with my bread, and now and then, for a rarity, I made a little butter, and drank the whey. I was at first at a great loss for salt; but custom soon reconciled the want of it; and I am confident that the frequent use of salt among us is an effect of luxury, and was first introduced only as a provocative to drink; except where it is necessary for preserving of flesh in long voyages, or in places remote from great markets. For we observe no animal to be fond of it but man: [9] and as to myself, when I left this country, it was a great while before I could endure the taste of it in anything that I eat.

This is enough to say upon the subject of my diet, wherewith other travellers fill their books, as if the readers were personally concerned whether we fared well or ill. However, it was necessary to mention this matter, lest the world should think it impossible that I could find sustenance for three years in such a country, and among such inhabitants.

When it grew towards evening, the master horse ordered a place for me to lodge in; it was but six yards from the house, and separated from the stable of the yahoos. Here I got some straw, and covering myself with my own clothes, slept very sound. But I was in a short time better accommodated, as the reader shall know hereafter, when I come to treat more particularly about my way of living.

[8] Snares.
[9] A very inaccurate statement, as Scott observed: many animals including horses, are extremely fond of salt.

CHAPTER III

The author studious to learn the language, the Houyhnhnm his master assists in teaching him. The language described. Several Houyhnhnms of quality come out of curiosity to see the author. He gives his master a short account of his voyage.

My principal endeavour was to learn the language, which my master (for so I shall henceforth call him) and his children, and every servant of his house were desirous to teach me. For they looked upon it as a prodigy that a brute animal should discover such marks of a rational creature. I pointed to every thing, and enquired the name of it, which I wrote down in my journal-book when I was alone, and corrected my bad accent, by desiring those of the family to pronounce it often. In this employment, a sorrel nag, one of the under servants, was very ready to assist me.

In speaking, they pronounce through the nose and throat, and their language approaches nearest to the High Dutch or German, of any I know in Europe; but is much more graceful and significant. The Emperor Charles V made almost the same observation, when he said, that if he were to speak to his horse, it should be in High Dutch.[10]

The curiosity and impatience of my master were so great, that he spent many hours of his leisure to instruct me. He was convinced (as he afterwards told me) that I must be a yahoo, but my teachableness, civility and cleanliness astonished him; which were qualities altogether so opposite to those animals. He was most perplexed about my clothes, reasoning sometimes with himself, whether they were a part of my body; for I never pulled them off till the family were asleep, and got them on before they waked in the morning. My master was eager to learn from whence I came, how I acquired those appearances of reason which I discovered in all my actions, and to know my story from my own mouth, which he hoped he should soon do by the great proficiency I made in learning and pronouncing their words and sentences. To help my memory, I formed all I learned into the English alphabet, and writ the words down with the translations. This last, after some time, I ventured to do in my master's presence. It cost me much trouble to explain to him what I was doing;

[10] The original epigram was hardly complimentary either to horses or to the German language: Charles is supposed to have said that he would address his God in Spanish, his mistress in Italian, and his horse in German.

for the inhabitants have not the least idea of books or literature.

In about ten weeks time I was able to understand most of his questions, and in three months could give him some tolerable answers. He was extremely curious to know from what part of the country I came, and how I was taught to imitate a rational creature, because the yahoos (whom he saw I exactly resembled in my head, hands and face, that were only visible), with some appearance of cunning, and the strongest disposition to mischief, were observed to be the most unteachable of all brutes. I answered, that I came over the sea, from a far place, with many others of my own kind, in a great hollow vessel made of the bodies of trees. That my companions forced me to land on this coast, and then left me to shift for myself. It was with some difficulty, and by the help of many signs, that I brought him to understand me. He replied, that I must needs be mistaken, or that I "said the thing which was not." (For they have no word in their language to express lying or falsehood.) He knew it was impossible that there could be a country beyond the sea, or that a parcel of brutes could move a wooden vessel whither they pleased upon water. He was sure no Houyhnhnm alive could make such a vessel, nor would trust yahoos to manage it.

The word *"Houyhnhnm,"* in their tongue, signifies "a horse," and in its etymology, "the perfection of nature." I told my master, that I was at a loss for expression, but would improve as fast as I could; and hoped in a short time I should be able to tell him wonders: he was pleased to direct his own mare, his colt and foal, and the servants of the family to take all opportunities of instructing me, and every day for two or three hours he was at the same pains himself: several horses and mares of quality in the neighbourhood came often to our house upon the report spread of a wonderful yahoo, that could speak like a Houyhnhnm, and seemed in his words and actions to discover some glimmerings of reason. These delighted to converse with me; they put many questions, and received such answers as I was able to return. By all these advantages, I made so great a progress, that in five months from my arrival I understood whatever was spoke, and could express myself tolerably well.

The Houyhnhnms who came to visit my master, out of a design of seeing and talking with me, could hardly believe me to be a right yahoo, because my body had a different covering from others of my kind. They were astonished to observe me without the usual hair or skin except on my head, face, and hands; but I discovered that secret to my master, upon an accident, which happened about a fortnight before.

I have already told the reader, that every night, when the family were gone to bed, it was my custom to strip and cover myself with my clothes: it happened one morning early, that my master sent for me, by the sorrel nag, who was his valet; when he came, I was fast asleep, my clothes fallen off on one side, and my shirt above my waist. I awaked at the noise he made, and observed him to deliver his message in some disorder; after which he went to my master, and in a great fright gave him a very confused account of what he had seen: this I presently discovered; for going, as soon as I was dressed, to pay my attendance upon his Honour, he asked me the meaning of what his servant had reported, that I was not the same thing when I slept as I appeared to be at other times; that his valet assured him, some part of me was white, some yellow, at least not so white, and some brown.

I had hitherto concealed the secret of my dress, in order to distinguish myself as much as possible from that cursed race of yahoos; but now I found it in vain to do so any longer. Besides, I considered that my clothes and shoes would soon wear out, which already were in a declining condition, and must be supplied by some contrivance from the hides of yahoos or other brutes; whereby the whole secret would be known: I therefore told my master, that in the country from whence I came those of my kind always covered their bodies with the hairs of certain animals prepared by art, as well for decency, as to avoid the inclemencies of air both hot and cold; of which, as to my person, I would give him immediate conviction, if he pleased to command me; only desiring his excuse, if I did not expose those parts that nature taught us to conceal. He said my discourse was all very strange, but especially the last part; for he could not understand why nature should teach us to conceal what nature had given. That neither himself nor family were ashamed of any parts of their bodies; but however I might do as I pleased. Whereupon, I first unbuttoned my coat, and pulled it off. I did the same with my waistcoat; I drew off my shoes, stockings, and breeches. I let my shirt down to my waist, and drew up the bottom, fastening it like a girdle about my middle to hide my nakedness.

My master observed the whole performance with great signs of curiosity and admiration. He took up all my clothes in his pastern, one piece after another, and examined them diligently; he then stroked my body very gently and looked round me several times, after which he said, it was plain I must be a perfect yahoo; but that I differed very much from the rest of my species, in the softness, and whiteness, and smoothness of my skin, my want of hair in several parts of my body, the shape and shortness of my claws behind and before, and my affectation of walking continually on my two hinder feet. He desired to see no more, and gave me leave to put on my clothes again, for I was shuddering with cold.

I expressed my uneasiness at his giving me so often the appellation of *"yahoo,"* an odious animal, for which I had so utter an hatred and contempt; I begged he would forbear applying that word to me, and take the same order in his family, and among his friends whom he suffered to see me. I requested likewise, that the secret of my having a false covering to my body might be known to none but himself, at least as long as my present clothing should last; for as to what the sorrel nag his valet had observed his Honour might command him to conceal it.

All this my master very graciously consented to, and thus the secret was kept till my clothes began to wear out, which I was forced to supply by several contrivances, that shall hereafter be mentioned. In the mean time, he desired I would go on with my utmost diligence to learn their language, because he was more astonished at my capacity for speech and reason than at the figure of my body, whether it were covered or no; adding, that he waited with some impatience to hear the wonders which I promised to tell him.

From thenceforward he doubled the pains he had been at to instruct me; he brought me into all company, and made them treat me with civility, because as he told them privately, this would put me into good humour, and make me more diverting.

Every day when I waited on him, beside the trouble he was at in teaching, he would ask me several questions concerning myself, which I answered as well as I could; and by these means he had already received some general ideas, though very imperfect. It would be tedious to relate the several steps by which I advanced to a more regular conversation: but the first account I gave of myself in any order and length, was to this purpose:

That I came from a very far country, as I already had attempted to tell him, with about fifty more of my own species; that we travelled upon the seas, in a great hollow vessel made of wood, and larger than his Honour's house. I described the ship to him in the best terms I could, and explained by the help of my handkerchief displayed, how it was driven forward by the wind. That upon a quarrel among us, I was set on shore on this coast, where I walked forward without knowing whither, till he delivered me from the persecution of those execrable yahoos. He asked me, who made the ship, and how it was possible that the Houyhnhnms of my country would leave it to the management of brutes? My answer was, that I durst proceed no farther in my relation, unless he would give me his word and honour that he would not be offended, and then I would tell him the wonders I had so often promised. He agreed; and I went on by assuring him, that the ship was made by creatures like myself, who in all the countries I had travelled, as well as in my own, were the only governing, rational animals; and that upon my arrival hither, I was as much astonished to see the Houyhnhnms act like rational beings, as he or his friends could be in finding some marks of reason in a creature he was pleased to call a yahoo, to which I owned my resemblance in every part, but could not account for their degenerate and brutal nature. I said farther, that if good fortune ever restored me to my native country, to relate my travels hither, as I resolved to do, every body would believe that I "said the thing which was not"; that I invented the story out of my own head; and with all possible respect to himself, his family and friends, and under his promise of not being offended, our countrymen would hardly think it probable, that a Houyhnhnm should be the presiding creature of a nation, and a yahoo the brute.

CHAPTER IV

The Houyhnhnms' notion of truth and falsehood. The author's discourse disapproved by his master. The author gives a more particular account of himself, and the accidents of his voyage.

My master heard me with great appearance of uneasiness in his countenance, because *doubting* or *not believing,* are so little known in this country, that the inhabitants cannot tell how to behave themselves under such circumstances. And I remember in frequent discourses with my master concerning the nature of manhood, in other parts of the world, having occasion to talk of "lying" and "false representation," it was with much difficulty that he comprehended what I meant, although he had otherwise a most acute judgment. For he argued thus; that the use of speech was to make us understand one another, and to receive information of facts; now if any one "said the thing which was not," these ends were defeated; because I cannot properly be said to understand him, and I am so far from receiving information, that he leaves me worse than in ignorance, for I am led to believe a thing *black* when it is *white,* and *short* when it is *long.* And these were all the notions he had concerning that faculty of *lying,* so perfectly well understood among human creatures.

To return from this digression; when I asserted that the yahoos were the only governing animals in my country, which my master said was altogether past his conception, he desired to know, whether we had Houyhnhnms among us, and what was their employment: I told him, we had great numbers, that in summer they grazed in the fields, and in winter were kept in houses, with hay and oats, where yahoo servants were employed to rub their skins smooth, comb their manes, pick their feet, serve them with food, and make their beds. "I understand you well," said my master, "it is now very plain, from all you have spoken, that whatever share of reason the yahoos pretend to, the Houyhnhnms are your masters; I heartily wish our yahoos would be so tractable." I begged his Honour would please to excuse me from proceeding any farther, because I was very certain that the account he expected from me would be highly displeasing. But he insisted in commanding me to let him know the best and the worst: I told him, he should be obeyed. I owned, that the Houyhnhnms among us, whom we called horses, were the most generous [11] and comely animal we had, that they excelled in strength and swiftness; and when they belonged to persons of quality, employed in travelling, racing, or drawing chariots, they were treated with much kindness and care, till they fell into diseases, or became foundered in the feet; and then they were sold, and used to all kind of drudgery till they died; after which their skins were stripped and sold for what they were worth, and their bodies left to be devoured by dogs and birds of prey. But the common race of horses had not so good fortune, being kept by farmers and carriers and other mean people, who put them to greater labour, and fed them worse. I described, as well as I could, our way of riding, the shape and use of a bridle, a saddle, a spur, and a whip, of harness and wheels. I added, that we fastened plates of a certain hard substance called "iron" at the bottom of their feet, to preserve their hoofs from being broken by the stony ways on which we often travelled.

My master, after some expressions of great indig-

11 Noble.

nation, wondered how we dared to venture upon a Houyhnhnm's back, for he was sure that the weakest servant in his house would be able to shake off the strongest yahoo, or by lying down, and rolling on his back, squeeze the brute to death. I answered, that our horses were trained up from three or four years old to the several uses we intended them for; that if any of them proved intolerably vicious, they were employed for carriages; that they were severely beaten while they were young, for any mischievous tricks; that the males, designed for common use of riding or draught, were generally "castrated" about two years after their birth, to take down their spirits, and make them more tame and gentle; that they were indeed sensible of rewards and punishments; but his Honour would please to consider, that they had not the least tincture of reason any more than the yahoos in this country.

It put me to the pains of many circumlocutions to give my master a right idea of what I spoke; for their language doth not abound in variety of words, because their wants and passions are fewer than among us. But it is impossible to represent his noble resentment at our savage treatment of the Houyhnhnm race, particularly after I had explained the manner and use of "castrating" horses among us, to hinder them from propagating their kind, and to render them more servile. He said, if it were possible there could be any country where yahoos alone were endued with reason, they certainly must be the governing animal, because reason will in time always prevail against brutal strength. But, considering the frame of our bodies, and especially of mine, he thought no creature of equal bulk was so ill contrived for employing that reason in the common offices of life; whereupon he desired to know whether those among whom I lived resembled me or the yahoos of his country. I assured him, that I was as well shaped as most of my age: but the younger and the females were much more soft and tender, and the skins of the latter generally as white as milk. He said, I differed indeed from other yahoos, being much more cleanly, and not altogether so deformed, but in point of real advantage he thought I differed for the worse. That my nails were of no use either to my fore or hinder feet; as to my forefeet, he could not properly call them by that name, for he never observed me to walk upon them; that they were too soft to bear the ground; that I generally went with them uncovered, neither was the covering I sometimes wore on them of the same shape or so strong as that on my feet behind. That I could not walk with any security, for if either of my hind feet slipped, I must inevitably fall. He then began to find fault with other parts of my body, the flatness of my face, the prominence of my nose, my eyes placed directly in front, so that I could not look on either side without turning my head: that I was not able to feed myself without lifting one of my forefeet to my mouth: and therefore nature had placed those joints to answer that necessity. He knew not what could be the use of those several clefts and divisions in my feet behind; that these were too soft to bear the hardness and sharpness of stones without a covering made from the skin of some other brute; that my whole body wanted a fence against heat and cold, which I was forced to put on and off every day with tediousness and trouble. And lastly, that he observed every animal in this country naturally to abhor the yahoos, whom the weaker avoided, and the stronger drove from them. So that supposing us to have the gift of reason, he could not see how it were possible to cure that natural antipathy which every creature discovered against us; nor consequently, how we could tame and render them serviceable. However, he would (as he said) debate that matter no farther, because he was more desirous to know my own story, the country where I was born, and the several actions and events of my life before I came hither.

I assured him how extremely desirous I was that he should be satisfied in every point; but I doubted much, whether it would be possible for me to explain myself on several subjects whereof his Honour could have no conception, because I saw nothing in his country to which I could resemble them. That however, I would do my best, and strive to express myself by similitudes, humbly desiring his assistance when I wanted proper words; which he was pleased to promise me.

I said, my birth was of honest parents, in an island called England, which was remote from this country as many days' journey as the strongest of his Honour's servants could travel in the annual course of the sun. That I was bred a surgeon, whose trade it is to cure wounds and hurts in the body, got by accident or violence; that my country was governed by a female man, whom we called a "queen." That I left it to get riches, whereby I might maintain myself and family when I should return. That in my last voyage I was commander of the ship, and had about fifty yahoos under me, many of which died at sea, and I was forced to supply them by others picked out from several nations. That our ship was twice in danger of being sunk; the first time by a great storm, and the second, by striking

against a rock. Here my master interposed, by asking me, how I could persuade strangers out of different countries to venture with me, after the losses I had sustained, and the hazards I had run. I said, they were fellows of desperate fortunes, forced to fly from the places of their birth, on account of their poverty or their crimes. Some were undone by lawsuits; others spent all they had in drinking, whoring, and gaming; others fled for treason; many for murder, theft, poisoning, robbery, perjury, forgery, coining false money, for committing rapes or sodomy, for flying from their colours, or deserting to the enemy, and most of them had broken prison; none of these durst return to their native countries for fear of being hanged, or of starving in a jail; and therefore were under a necessity of seeking a livelihood in other places.

During this discourse, my master was pleased to interrupt me several times; I had made use of many circumlocutions in describing to him the nature of the several crimes, for which most of our crew had been forced to fly their country. This labour took up several days' conversation before he was able to comprehend me. He was wholly at a loss to know what could be the use or necessity of practising those vices. To clear up which I endeavoured to give him some ideas of the desire of power and riches, of the terrible effects of lust, intemperance, malice and envy. All this I was forced to define and describe by putting of cases, and making of suppositions. After which, like one whose imagination was struck with something never seen or heard of before, he would lift up his eyes with amazement and indignation. Power, government, war, law, punishment, and a thousand other things had no terms wherein that language could express them, which made the difficulty almost insuperable to give my master any conception of what I meant. But being of an excellent understanding, much improved by contemplation and converse, he at last arrived at a competent knowledge of what human nature in our parts of the world is capable to perform, and desired I would give him some particular account of that land which we call Europe, but especially of my own country.

CHAPTER V

The author, at his master's commands, informs him of the state of England. The causes of war among the princes of Europe. The author begins to explain the English constitution.

The reader may please to observe, that the following extract of many conversations I had with my

THE NEO-CLASSICAL WORLD

master contains a summary of the most material points which were discoursed at several times for above two years; his Honour often desiring fuller satisfaction as I farther improved in the Houyhnhnm tongue. I laid before him, as well as I could, the whole state of Europe; I discoursed of trade and manufactures, of arts and sciences; and the answers I gave to all the questions he made, as they arose upon several subjects, were a fund of conversation not to be exhausted. But I shall here only set down the substance of what passed between us concerning my own country, reducing it into order as well as I can, without any regard to time or other circumstances, while I strictly adhere to truth. My only concern is, that I shall hardly be able to do justice to my master's arguments and expressions, which must needs suffer by my want of capacity, as well as by a translation into our barbarous English.

In obedience therefore to his Honour's commands, I related to him the Revolution under the Prince of Orange; the long war with France entered into by the said prince, and renewed by his successor the present queen, wherein the greatest powers of Christendom were engaged, and which still continued: I computed, at his request, that about a million of yahoos might have been killed in the whole progress of it, and perhaps a hundred or more cities taken, and thrice as many ships burnt or sunk.[12]

He asked me what were the usual causes or motives that made one country go to war with another. I answered they were innumerable, but I should only mention a few of the chief. Sometimes the ambition of princes, who never think they have land or people enough to govern: sometimes the corruption of ministers, who engage their master in a war in order to stifle or divert the clamour of the subjects against their evil administration. Difference in opinions hath cost many millions of lives: for instance, whether *flesh* be *bread*, or *bread* be *flesh*; whether the juice of a certain *berry* be *blood* or *wine*; whether *whistling* be a vice or a virtue; whether it be better to *kiss a post*, or throw it into the fire; what is the best colour for a *coat*, whether *black, white, red,* or *gray*; and whether it should be *long* or *short, narrow* or *wide, dirty* or *clean,*[13] with many more. Neither are any wars so furious and bloody, or of so long continuance, as those occasioned by difference in opinion, especially if it be in things indifferent.[14]

Sometimes the quarrel between two princes is to decide which of them shall dispossess a third of his dominions, where neither of them pretend to any right. Sometimes one prince quarrelleth with another, for fear the other should quarrel with him. Sometimes a war is entered upon, because the enemy is too *strong*, and sometimes because he is too *weak*. Sometimes our neighbours *want* the things which we *have*, or *have* the things which we *want*; and we both fight, till they take ours or give us theirs. It is a very justifiable cause of war to invade a country after the people have been wasted by famine, destroyed by pestilence, or embroiled by factions among themselves. It is justifiable to enter into war against our nearest ally, where one of his towns lies convenient for us, or a territory of land, that would render our dominions round and complete. If a prince sends forces into a nation where the people are poor and ignorant, he may lawfully put half of them to death, and makes slaves of the rest, in order to civilize and reduce them from their barbarous way of living. It is a very kingly, honourable, and frequent practice, when one prince desires the assistance of another to secure him against an invasion, that the assistant, when he hath driven out the invader, should seize on the dominions himself, and kill, imprison or banish the prince he came to relieve. Alliance by blood or marriage is a sufficient cause of war between princes, and the nearer the kindred is, the greater is their disposition to quarrel: *poor* nations are *hungry*, and *rich* nations are *proud*, and pride and hunger will ever be at variance. For these reasons, the trade of a "soldier" is held the most honourable of all others: because a "soldier" is a yahoo hired to kill in cold blood as many of his own species, who have never offended him, as possible he can.

There is likewise a kind of beggarly princes in Europe, not able to make war by themselves, who hire out their troops to richer nations, for so much a day to each man; of which they keep three fourths to themselves, and it is the best part of their maintenance; such as those in Germany and other northern parts of Europe.[15]

"What you have told me," said my master, "upon the subject of war, does indeed discover most admirably the effects of that reason you pretend to:

[12] Swift exaggerates the losses in the War of the Spanish Succession.
[13] The first two controversies were concerned with the doctrine of transubstantiation, the third with the use of music in church services, the fourth with the use of the crucifix, and the others with various quarrels about ecclesiastical vestments.
[14] Unimportant.
[15] George I, as King of Hanover, had been involved in this traffic.

however, it is happy that the *shame* is greater than the *danger*; and that nature hath left you utterly uncapable of doing much mischief.

"For your mouths lying flat with your faces, you can hardly bite each other to any purpose, unless by consent. Then as to the claws upon your feet before and behind, they are so short and tender, that one of our yahoos would drive a dozen of yours before him. And therefore in recounting the numbers of those who have been killed in battle, I cannot but think that you have 'said the thing which is not'."

I could not forbear shaking my head and smiling a little at his ignorance. And being no stranger to the art of war, I gave him a description of cannons, culverins, muskets, carabines, pistols, bullets, powder, swords, bayonets, battles, sieges, retreats, attacks, undermines, countermines, bombardments, sea-fights; ships sunk with a thousand men, twenty thousand killed on each side; dying groans, limbs flying in the air, smoke, noise, confusion, trampling to death under horses' feet; flight, pursuit, victory; fields strewed with carcases left for food to dogs, and wolves, and birds of prey; plundering, stripping, ravishing, burning and destroying. And to set forth the valor of my own dear countrymen, I assured him, that I had seen them blow up a hundred enemies at once in a siege; and as many in a ship, and beheld the dead bodies come down in pieces from the clouds, to the great diversion of the spectators.

I was going on to more particulars, when my master commanded me silence. He said, whoever understood the nature of yahoos might easily believe it possible for so vile an animal to be capable of every action I had named, if their strength and cunning equalled their malice. But as my discourse had increased his abhorrence of the whole species, so he found it gave him a disturbance in his mind, to which he was wholly a stranger before. He thought his ears being used to such abominable words, might by degrees admit them with less detestation. That although he hated the yahoos of this country, yet he no more blamed them for their odious qualities, than he did a *gnnayh* (a bird of prey) for its cruelty, or a sharp stone for cutting his hoof. But when a creature pretending to reason could be capable of such enormities, he dreaded lest the corruption of that faculty might be worse than brutality itself. He seemed therefore confident, that instead of reason, we were only possessed of some quality fitted to increase our natural vices; as the reflection from a troubled stream returns the images of an ill-shapen body, not only *larger*, but more *distorted*.

He added, that he had heard too much upon the subject of war, both in this and some former discourses. There was another point which a little perplexed him at present. I had informed him, that some of our crew left their country on account of being ruined by "law"; that I had already explained the meaning of the word; but he was at a loss how it should come to pass, that the "law" which was intended for *every* man's preservation, should be any man's ruin. Therefore he desired to be farther satisfied what I meant by "law," and the dispensers thereof according to the present practice in my own country; because he thought nature and reason were sufficient guides for a reasonable animal, as we pretended to be, in showing us what we ought to do, and what to avoid.

I assured his Honour, that law was a science wherein I had not much conversed, further than by employing advocates in vain, upon some injustices that had been done me: however, I would give him all the satisfaction I was able.

I said, there was a society of men among us, bred up from their youth in the art of proving by words multiplied for the purpose, that white is black, and black is white, according as they are paid. To this society all the rest of the people are slaves. For example, if my neighbour hath a mind to my cow, he hires a lawyer to prove, that he ought to have my cow from me. I must then hire another to defend my right, it being against all rules of law that any man should be allowed to speak for himself. Now in this case, I who am the right owner lie under two great disadvantages. First, my lawyer, being practised almost from his cradle in defending falsehood, is quite out of his element when he would be an advocate for justice, which as an office unnatural, he always attempts with ill will. The second disadvantage is, that my lawyer must proceed with great caution, or else he will be reprimanded by the judges, and abhorred by his brethren, as one that would lessen the practice of the law. And therefore I have but two methods to preserve my cow. The first is to gain over my adversary's lawyer with a double fee, who will then betray his client by insinuating that he hath justice on his side. The second way is for my lawyer to make my cause appear as unjust as he can, by allowing the cow to belong to my adversary; and this, if it be skilfully done, will certainly bespeak the favour of the bench. Now, your Honour is to know that these judges are persons appointed to decide all controversies of property, as well as for the trial of criminals, and picked out from the most dextrous lawyers who are grown old or lazy, and, having been biassed all their lives against truth and equity, are under such a fatal necessity of favouring fraud, perjury, and oppression, that I have known several of them refuse a large bribe from the side where justice lay, rather than injure the faculty [16] by doing any thing unbecoming their nature or their office.

It is a maxim among these lawyers, that whatever hath been done before may legally be done again: and therefore they take special care to record all the decisions formerly made against common justice and the general reason of mankind. These, under the name of "precedents," they produce as authorities, to justify the most iniquitous opinions; and the judges never fail of decreeing accordingly.

In pleading, they studiously avoid entering into the *merits* of the cause, but are loud, violent, and tedious in dwelling upon all *circumstances* which are not to the purpose. For instance, in the case already mentioned; they never desire to know what claim or title my adversary hath to my *cow*, but whether the said *cow* were red or black, her horns long or short; whether the field I graze her in be round or square, whether she was milked at home or abroad, what diseases she is subject to, and the like; after which they consult "precedents," adjourn the cause from time to time, and in ten, twenty, or thirty years come to an issue.

It is likewise to be observed that this society hath a peculiar cant and jargon of their own, that no other mortal can understand, and wherein all their laws are written, which they take special care to multiply; whereby they have wholly confounded the very essence of truth and falsehood, of right and wrong; so that it will take thirty years to decide whether the field left me by my ancestors for six generations belongs to me or to a stranger three hundred miles off.

In the trial of persons accused for crimes against the state the method is much more short and commendable: the judge first sends to sound the disposition of those in power, after which he can easily hang or save the criminal, strictly preserving all due forms of law.

Here my master, interposing, said it was a pity, that creatures endowed with such prodigious abilities of mind as these lawyers, by the description I gave of them, must certainly be, were not rather encouraged to be instructors of others in wisdom and knowledge. In answer to which I assured his Honour, that in all points out of their own trade they were the most ignorant and stupid generation

[16] Profession.

among us, the most despicable in common conversation, avowed enemies to all knowledge and learning, and equally disposed to pervert the general reason of mankind in every other subject of discourse, as in that of their own profession.

CHAPTER VI

A continuation of the state of England. The character of a first minister.

My master was yet wholly at a loss to understand what motives could incite this race of lawyers to perplex, disquiet, and weary themselves, and engage in a confederacy of injustice, merely for the sake of injuring their fellow-animals; neither could he comprehend what I meant in saying they did it for "hire." Whereupon I was at much pains to describe to him the use of "money," the materials it was made of, and the value of the metals; that when a yahoo had got a great store of this precious substance, he was able to purchase whatever he had a mind to, the finest clothing, the noblest houses, great tracts of land, the most costly meats and drinks, and have his choice of the most beautiful females. Therefore since "money" alone was able to perform all these feats, our yahoos thought they could never have enough of it to spend or to save, as they found themselves inclined from their natural bent either to profusion or avarice. That the rich man enjoyed the fruit of the poor man's labour, and the latter were a thousand to one in proportion to the former. That the bulk of our people were forced to live miserably, by labouring every day for small wages to make a few live plentifully. I enlarged myself much on these and many other particulars to the same purpose: but his Honour was still to seek,[17] for he went upon a supposition that all animals had a title to their share in the productions of the earth, and especially those who presided over the rest.[18] Therefore he desired I would let him know what these costly meats were, and how any of us happened to want [19] them. Whereupon I enumerated as many sorts as came into my head, with the various methods of dressing them, which could not be done without sending vessels by sea to every part of the world, as well for liquors to drink, as for sauces, and innumerable other conveniences. I assured him, that

[17] At a loss to understand.
[18] The meaning is "especially that species which presided over the rest."
[19] Lack.

this whole globe of earth must be at least three times gone round, before one of our better female yahoos could get her breakfast, or a cup to put it in. He said, that must needs be a miserable country which cannot furnish food for its own inhabitants. But what he chiefly wondered at was how such vast tracts of ground as I described should be wholly without *fresh water*, and the people put to the necessity of sending over the sea for drink. I replied, that England (the dear place of my nativity) was computed to produce three times the quantity of food more than its inhabitants are able to consume, as well as liquors extracted from grain, or presssed out of the fruit of certain trees, which made excellent drink, and the same proportion in every other convenience of life. But in order to feed the luxury and intemperance of the males, and the vanity of the females, we sent away the greatest part of our necessary things to other countries, from whence in return we brought the materials of diseases, folly, and vice, to spend among ourselves. Hence it follows of necessity that vast numbers of our people are compelled to seek their livelihood by begging, robbing, stealing, cheating, pimping, forswearing, flattering, suborning, forging, gaming, lying, fawning, hectoring, voting, scribbling, star-gazing, poisoning, whoring, canting, libelling, free-thinking, and the like occupations: every one of which terms, I was at much pains to make him understand.

That "wine" was not imported among us from foreign countries to supply the want of water or other drinks, but because it was a sort of liquid which made us merry, by putting us out of our senses; diverted all melancholy thoughts, begat wild extravagant imaginations in the brain, raised our hopes, and banished our fears, suspended every office of reason for a time, and deprived us of the use of our limbs, till we fell into a profound sleep; although it must be confessed, that we always awaked sick and dispirited, and that the use of this liquor filled us with diseases, which made our lives uncomfortable and short.

But beside all this, the bulk of our people supported themselves by furnishing the necessities or conveniences of life to the rich, and to each other. For instance, when I am at home and dressed as I ought to be, I carry on my body the workmanship of an hundred tradesmen; the building and furniture of my house employ as many more, and five times the number to adorn my wife.

I was going on to tell him of another sort of people, who get their livelihood by attending the sick, having upon some occasions informed his Honour that many of my crew had died of diseases. But here it was with the utmost difficulty that I brought him to apprehend what I meant. He could easily conceive that a Houyhnhnm grew weak and heavy a few days before his death, or by some accident might hurt a limb. But that Nature, who works all things to perfection, should suffer any pains to breed in our bodies, he thought it impossible, and desired to know the reason of so unaccountable an evil. I told him, we fed on a thousand things which operated contrary to each other; that we eat when we were not hungry, and drank without the provocation of thirst; that we sate whole nights drinking strong liquors without eating a bit, which disposed us to sloth, enflamed our bodies, and precipitated or prevented digestion. That prostitute female yahoos acquired a certain malady, which bred rottenness in the bones of those who fell into their embraces; that this and many other diseases were propagated from father to son, so that great numbers come into the world with complicated maladies upon them; that it would be endless to give him a catalogue of all diseases incident to human bodies; for they could not be fewer than five or six hundred, spread over every limb and joint; in short, every part, external and intestine, having diseases appropriated to them. To remedy which, there was a sort of people bred up among us, in the profession or pretence of curing the sick. And because I had some skill in the faculty, I would, in gratitude to his Honour, let him know the whole mystery and method by which they proceed.

Their fundamental is, that all diseases arise from *repletion*, from whence they conclude that a great *evacuation* of the body is necessary, either through the natural passage, or upwards at the mouth. Their next business is, from herbs, minerals, gums, oils, shells, salts, juices, seaweed, excrements, barks of trees, serpents, toads, frogs, spiders, dead men's flesh and bones, birds, beasts and fishes, to form a composition for smell and taste the most abominable, nauseous and detestable they can possibly contrive, which the stomach immediately rejects with loathing; and this they call a "vomit"; or else from the same storehouse, with some other poisonous additions, they command us to take it at the orifice *above* or *below* (just as the physician then happens to be disposed) a medicine equally annoying and disgustful to the bowels, which, relaxing the belly, drives down all before it, and this they call a "purge" or a "glyster." For nature (as the physicians allege) having intended the superior anterior orifice only for the intromission of solids and liquids, and the inferior posterior for ejection, these artists ingeniously considering that in all diseases Nature is forced out of her seat, therefore to replace her in it, the body must be treated in a manner directly contrary, by interchanging the use of each orifice, forcing solids and liquids in at the anus, and making evacuations at the mouth.

But besides real diseases we are subject to many that are only imaginary, for which the physicians have invented imaginary cures; these have their several names, and so have the drugs that are proper for them, and with these our female yahoos are always infested.

One great excellency in this tribe is their skill at "prognostics," wherein they seldom fail; their predictions in real diseases, when they rise to any degree of malignity, generally portending *death,* which is always in their power, when recovery is not: and therefore, upon any unexpected signs of amendment, after they have pronounced their sentence, rather than be accused as false prophets, they know how to approve [20] their sagacity to the world by a seasonable dose.

They are likewise of special use to husbands and wives who are grown weary of their mates, to eldest sons, to great ministers of state, and often to princes.

I had formerly upon occasion discoursed with my master upon the nature of "government" in general, and particularly of our own "excellent constitution," deservedly the wonder and envy of the whole world. But having here accidentally mentioned a "minister of state," he commanded me some time after to inform him, what species of yahoo I particularly meant by that appellation.

I told him that a "first" or "chief minister of state," who was the person I intended to describe, was a creature wholly exempt from joy and grief, love and hatred, pity and anger; at least made use of no other passions but a violent desire of wealth, power, and titles; that he applies his words to all uses, except to the indication of his mind; that he never tells a *truth,* but with an intent that you should take it for a *lie;* nor a *lie,* but with a design that you should take it for a *truth;* that those he speaks worst of behind their backs are in the surest way to preferment; and whenever he begins to praise you to others or to yourself, you are from that day forlorn. The worst you can receive is a *promise,* especially when it is confirmed with an oath; after which every wise man retires, and gives over all hopes.

There are three methods by which a man may rise to be chief minister: the first is, by knowing

[20] Prove.

how with prudence to dispose of a wife, a daughter, or a sister: the second, by betraying or undermining his predecessor: and the third is, by a *furious zeal* in public assemblies against the corruptions of the court. But a wise prince would rather choose to employ those who practise the last of these methods; because such zealots prove always the most obsequious and subservient to the will and passions of their master. That these "ministers" having all employments at their disposal, preserve themselves in power by bribing the majority of a senate or great council; and at last, by an expedient called an "act of indemnity" [21] (whereof I described the nature to him) they secured themselves from after reckonings, and retired from the public, laden with the spoils of the nation.

The palace of a "chief minister" is a seminary to breed up others in his own trade: the pages, lackeys, and porter, by imitating their master, become "ministers of state" in their several districts, and learn to excel in the three principal *ingredients,* of *insolence, lying,* and *bribery.* Accordingly, they have a *subaltern* court paid to them by persons of the best rank, and sometimes by the force of dexterity and impudence arrive through several gradations to be successors to their lord.

He is usually governed by a decayed wench or favourite footman, who are the tunnels through which all graces are conveyed, and may properly be called, *in the last resort,* the governors of the kingdom.

One day in discourse my master, having heard me mention the "nobility" of my country, was pleased to make me a compliment which I could not pretend to deserve: that he was sure I must have been born of some noble family, because I far exceeded in shape, colour, and cleanliness, all the yahoos of his nation, although I seemed to fail in strength and agility, which must be imputed to my different way of living from those other brutes, and besides, I was not only endowed with the faculty of speech, but likewise with some rudiments of reason, to a degree that with all his acquaintance I passed for a prodigy.

He made me observe, that among the Houyhnhnms, the *white,* the *sorrel,* and the *iron-grey,* were not so exactly shaped as the *bay,* the *dapple-grey,* and the *black;* nor born with equal talents of the mind, or a capacity to improve them; and therefore continued always in the condition of servants, with-

[21] An act of this sort was usually passed at each session of Parliament, to protect holders of public office from the possible consequences of any official acts done illegally but in good faith.

out ever aspiring to match out of their own race, which in that country would be reckoned monstrous and unnatural.

I made his Honour my most humble acknowledgments for the good opinion he was pleased to conceive of me; but assured him at the same time that my birth was of the lower sort, having been born of plain honest parents, who were just able to give me a tolerable education: that "nobility" among us was altogether a different thing from the idea he had of it; that our young "noblemen" are bred from their childhood in idleness and luxury; that as soon as years will permit, they consume their vigor and contract odious diseases among lewd females; and when their fortunes are almost ruined, they marry some woman of mean birth, disagreeable person, and unsound constitution, merely for the sake of money, whom they hate and despise. That the productions of such marriages are generally scrofulous, rickety, or deformed children, by which means the family seldom continues above three generations, unless the wife takes care to provide a healthy father among her neighbours or domestics, in order to improve and continue the breed. That a weak diseased body, a meager countenance, and sallow complexion are the true marks of noble blood; and a healthy robust appearance is so disgraceful in a man of quality, that the world concludes his real father to have been a *groom*, or a *coachman*. The imperfections of his mind run parallel with those of his body, being a composition of spleen, dulness, ignorance, caprice, sensuality, and pride.

Without the consent of this *illustrious body* no law can be made, repealed, or altered, and these have the decision of all our possessions without appeal.

Chapter VII

The author's great love of his native country. His master's observations upon the constitution and administration of England, as described by the author, with parallel cases and comparisons. His master's observations upon human nature.

The reader may be disposed to wonder how I could prevail on myself to give so free a representation of my own species, among a race of mortals who were already too apt to conceive the vilest opinion of human kind from that entire congruity betwixt me and their yahoos. But I must freely confess, that the many virtues of those excellent *quadrupeds*, placed in opposite view to human corruptions, had

so far opened my eyes and enlarged my understanding, that I began to view the actions and passions of man in a very different light, and to think the honour of my own kind not worth managing; [22] which, besides, it was impossible for me to do before a person of so acute a judgment as my master, who daily convinced me of a thousand faults in myself, whereof I had not the least perception before, and which among us would never be numbered even among human infirmities: I had likewise learned from his example an utter detestation of all falsehood or disguise; and *truth* appeared so amiable to me, that I determined upon sacrificing every thing to it.

Let me deal so candidly with the reader as to confess, that there was yet a much stronger motive for the freedom I took in my representation of things. I had not been a year in this country before I contracted such a love and veneration for the inhabitants, that I entered on a firm resolution never to return to human kind, but to pass the rest of my life among these admirable Houyhnhnms in the contemplation and practice of every virtue; where I could have no example or incitement to vice. But it was decreed by Fortune, my perpetual enemy, that so great a felicity should not fall to my share. However, it is now some comfort to reflect, that in what I said of my countrymen I *extenuated* their faults as much as I durst before so strict an examiner, and upon every article gave as *favourable* a turn as the matter would bear. For, indeed, who is there alive that will not be swayed by his bias and partiality to the place of his birth?

I have related the substance of several conversations I had with my master, during the greatest part of the time I had the honour to be in his service, but have indeed for brevity sake omitted much more than is here set down.

When I had answered all his questions, and his curiosity seemed to be fully satisfied, he sent for me one morning early, and commanding me to sit down at some distance (an honour which he had never before conferred upon me), he said, he had been very seriously considering my whole story, as far as it related both to myself and my country: that he looked upon us as a sort of animals to whose share, by what accident he could not conjecture, some small pittance of *reason* had fallen, whereof we made no other use than by its assistance to aggravate our *natural* corruptions, and to acquire new ones which Nature had not given us. That we disarmed ourselves of the few abilities she had bestowed, had

[22] Treating with care.

been very successful in multiplying our original wants, and seemed to spend our whole lives in vain endeavours to supply them by our own inventions. That as to myself, it was manifest I had neither the strength or agility of a common yahoo, that I walked infirmly on my hinder feet, had found out a contrivance to make my claws of no use or defence, and to remove the hair from my chin, which was intended as a shelter from the sun and the weather. Lastly, that I could neither run with speed, nor climb trees like my "brethren" (as he called them) the yahoos in this country.

That our institutions of "government" and "law" were plainly owing to our gross defects in *reason*, and by consequence, in *virtue*; because *reason* alone is sufficient to govern a *rational* creature; which was therefore a character we had no pretence to challenge, even from the account I had given of my own people, although he manifestly perceived, that in order to favour them I had concealed many particulars, and often "said the thing which was not."

He was the more confirmed in this opinion, because he observed, that as I agreed in every feature of my body with other yahoos, except where it was to my real disadvantage in point of strength, speed and activity, the shortness of my claws, and some other particulars where nature had no part; so from the representation I had given him of our lives, our manners, and our actions, he found as near a resemblance in the disposition of our minds. He said the yahoos were known to hate one another more than they did any different species of animals; and the reason usually assigned was the odiousness of their own shapes, which all could see in the rest, but not in themselves. He had therefore begun to think it not unwise in us to *cover* our bodies, and, by that invention, conceal many of our own deformities from each other, which would else be hardly supportable. But he now found he had been mistaken, and that the dissensions of those brutes in his country were owing to the same cause with ours, as I had described them. "For if," said he, "you throw among five yahoos as much food as would be sufficient for fifty, they will, instead of eating peaceably, fall together by the ears, each single one impatient to *have all to itself*"; and therefore a servant was usually employed to stand by while they were feeding abroad, and those kept at home were tied at a distance from each other; that if a cow died of age or accident, before a Houyhnhnm could secure it for his own yahoos, those in the neighbourhood would come in herds to seize it, and then would ensue such a battle as I had described, with terrible

wounds made by their claws on both sides, although they seldom were able to kill one another, for want of such convenient instruments of death as we had invented. At other times the like battles have been fought between the yahoos of several neighbourhoods without any visible cause: those of one district watching all opportunities to surprise the next before they are prepared. But if they find their project hath miscarried, they return home, and, for want of enemies, engage in what I call a civil war among themselves.

That in some fields of his country there are certain *shining stones* of several colours, whereof the yahoos are violently fond, and when part of these *stones* is fixed in the earth, as it sometimes happeneth, they will dig with their claws for whole days to get them out, then carry them away, and hide them by heaps in their kennels; but still looking round with great caution, for fear their comrades should find out their treasure. My master said, he could never discover the reason of this unnatural appetite, or how these *stones* could be of any use to a yahoo; but now he believed it might proceed from the same principle of "avarice" which I had ascribed to mankind; that he had once, by way of experiment, privately removed a heap of these *stones* from the place where one of his yahoos had buried it: whereupon the sordid animal, missing his treasure, by his loud lamenting brought the whole herd to the place, there miserably howled, then fell to biting and tearing the rest, began to pine away, would neither eat, nor sleep, nor work, till he ordered a servant privately to convey the *stones* into the same hole and hide them as before; which when his yahoo had found, he presently recovered his spirits and good humour, but took care to remove them to a better hiding-place, and hath ever since been a very serviceable brute.

My master farther assured me, which I also observed myself, that in the fields where these *shining stones* abound, the fiercest and most frequent battles are fought, occasioned by perpetual inroads of the neighbouring yahoos.

He said, it was common, when two yahoos discovered such a *stone* in a field, and were contending which of them should be the proprietor, a third would take the advantage, and carry it away from them both; which my master would needs contend to have some kind of resemblance with our "suits at law"; wherein I thought it for our credit not to undeceive him; since the decision he mentioned was much more equitable than many decrees among us: because the plaintiff and defendant there lost nothing beside the *stone* they contended for, whereas our *courts of equity* would never have dismissed the cause while either of them had any thing left.

My master, continuing his discourse, said, there was nothing that rendered the yahoos more odious than their undistinguishing appetite to devour every thing that came in their way, whether herbs, roots, berries, the corrupted flesh of animals, or all mingled together: and it was peculiar in their temper, that they were fonder of what they could get by rapine or stealth at a greater distance, than much better food provided for them at home. If their prey held out, they would eat till they were ready to burst, after which Nature had pointed out to them a certain *root* that gave them a general evacuation.

There was also another kind of *root* very *juicy*, but somewhat rare and difficult to be found, which the yahoos sought for with much eagerness, and would suck it with great delight; and it produced in them the same effects that wine hath upon us. It would make them sometimes hug, and sometimes tear one another; they would howl and grin, and chatter, and reel, and tumble, and then fall asleep in the dirt.

I did indeed observe, that the yahoos were the only animals in this country subject to any diseases; which, however, were much fewer than horses have among us, and contracted not by any ill treatment they meet with, but by the nastiness and greediness of that sordid brute. Neither has their language any more than a general appellation for those maladies, which is borrowed from the name of the beast, and called *"hnea-yahoo,"* or the *"yahoo's evil,"* and the cure prescribed is a mixture of *their own dung* and *urine* forcibly put down the yahoo's throat. This I have since often known to have been taken with success, and do freely recommend it to my countrymen, for the public good, as an admirable specific against all diseases produced by repletion.

As to learning, government, arts, manufactures, and the like, my master confessed he could find little or no resemblance between the yahoos of that country and those in ours. For he only meant to observe what parity there was in our natures. He had heard indeed some curious Houyhnhnms observe, that in most herds there was a sort of ruling yahoo (as among us there is generally some leading or principal stag in a park), who was always more *deformed* in body, and *mischievous in disposition*, than any of the rest. That this *leader* had usually a favourite as *like himself* as he could get, whose employment was to *lick his master's feet and pos-*

teriors, and drive the female yahoos to his kennel; for which he was now and then rewarded with a piece of ass's flesh. This "favorite" is hated by the whole herd, and therefore, to protect himself, keeps always *near the person of his leader*. He usually continues in office till a worse can be found; but the very moment he is discarded, his successor, at the head of all the yahoos in that district, young and old, male and female, come in a body, and discharge their excrements upon him from head to foot. But how far this might be applicable to our "courts" and "favourites," and "ministers of state," my master said I could best determine.

I durst make no return to this malicious insinuation, which debased human understanding below the sagacity of a common *hound*, who has judgment enough to distinguish and follow the cry of the *ablest dog in the pack*, without being ever mistaken.

My master told me, there were some qualities remarkable in the yahoos, which he had not observed me to mention, or at least very slightly, in the accounts I had given him of human kind; he said, those animals, like other brutes, had their females in common; but in this they differed, that the she-yahoo would admit the male while she was pregnant, and that the hees would quarrel and fight with the females as fiercely as with each other. Both which practices were such degrees of brutality, that no other sensitive creature ever arrived at.

Another thing he wondered at in the yahoos was their strange disposition to nastiness and dirt, whereas there appears to be a natural love of cleanliness in all other animals. As to the two former accusations, I was glad to let them pass without any reply, because I had not a word to offer upon them in defence of my species, which otherwise I certainly had done from my own inclinations. But I could have easily vindicated human kind from the imputation of singularity upon the last article, if there had been any *swine* in that country (as unluckily for me there were not), which, although it may be a *sweeter quadruped* than a yahoo, cannot, I humbly conceive, in justice pretend to more cleanliness; and so his Honour himself must have owned, if he had seen their filthy way of feeding, and their custom of wallowing and sleeping in the mud.

My master likewise mentioned another quality which his servants had discovered in several yahoos, and to him was wholly unaccountable. He said, a fancy would sometimes take a yahoo to retire into a corner, to lie down and howl, and groan, and spurn away all that came near him, although he were young and fat, wanted neither food nor water; nor did the servants imagine what could possibly ail him. And the only remedy they found was to set him to hard work, after which he would infallibly come to himself. To this I was silent out of partiality to my own kind; yet here I could plainly discover the true seeds of *spleen*,[23] which only seizeth on the *lazy*, the *luxurious*, and the *rich*; who, if they were forced to undergo the *same regimen*, I would undertake for the cure.

His Honour had farther observed, that a female yahoo would often stand behind a bank or a bush, to gaze on the young males passing by, and then appear, and hide, using many antic gestures and grimaces, at which time it was observed, that she had a most *offensive smell*; and when any of the males advanced, would slowly retire, looking often back, and with a counterfeit show of fear, run off into some convenient place where she knew the male would follow her.

At other times if a female stranger came among them, three or four of her own sex would get about her, and stare and chatter, and grin, and smell her all over, and then turn off with gestures that seemed to express contempt and disdain.

Perhaps my master might refine a little in these speculations, which he had drawn from what he observed himself, or had been told him by others: however, I could not reflect without some amazement, and much sorrow, that the rudiments of *lewdness*, *coquetry*, *censure*, and *scandal*, should have place by instinct in womankind.

I expected every moment that my master would accuse the yahoos of those unnatural appetites in both sexes, so common among us. But Nature, it seems, hath not been so expert a schoolmistress; and these politer pleasures are entirely the productions of art and reason, on our side of the globe.

Chapter VIII

The author relates several particulars of the yahoos. The great virtues of the Houyhnhnms. The education and exercise of their youth. Their general assembly.

As I ought to have understood human nature much better than I supposed it possible for my master to do, so it was easy to apply the character he gave of the yahoos to myself and my countrymen, and I believed I could yet make farther discoveries

[23] Hypochondria.

from my own observation. I therefore often begged his favour to let me go among the herds of yahoos in the neighbourhood, to which he always very graciously consented, being perfectly convinced that the hatred I bore those brutes would never suffer me to be corrupted by them; and his Honour ordered one of his servants, a strong sorrel nag, very honest and good-natured, to be my guard, without whose protection I durst not undertake such adventures. For I have already told the reader how much I was pestered by those odious animals upon my first arrival. And I afterwards failed very narrowly three or four times of falling into their clutches, when I happened to stray at any distance without my hanger. And I have reason to believe they had some imagination that I was of their own species, which I often assisted myself, by stripping up my sleeves, and showing my naked arms and breast in their sight, when my protector was with me. At which times they would approach as near as they durst, and imitate my actions after the manner of monkeys, but ever with great signs of hatred, as a tame *jackdaw*, with cap and stockings, is always persecuted by the wild ones, when he happens to be got among them.

They are prodigiously nimble from their infancy; however, I once caught a young male of three years old, and endeavoured by all marks of tenderness to make it quiet; but the little imp fell a squalling, and scratching, and biting with such violence, that I was forced to let it go, and it was high time, for a whole troop of old ones came about us at the noise, but finding the cub was safe (for away it ran), and my sorrel nag being by, they durst not venture near us. I observed the young animal's flesh to smell very rank, and the stink was somewhat between a *weasel* and a *fox*, but much more disagreeable. I forgot another circumstance (and perhaps I might have the reader's pardon if it were wholly omitted) that while I held the odious vermin in my hands, it voided its filthy excrements of a yellow liquid substance, all over my clothes; but by good fortune there was a small brook hard by, where I washed myself as clean as I could, although I durst not come into my master's presence, until I were sufficiently aired.

By what I could discover, the yahoos appear to be the most unteachable of all animals, their capacities never reaching higher than to draw or carry burthens. Yet I am of opinion this defect ariseth chiefly from a perverse, restive disposition. For they are cunning, malicious, treacherous and revengeful. They are strong and hardy, but of a cowardly spirit, and by consequence insolent, abject, and cruel. It is observed, that the *red-haired* of both sexes are more libidinous and mischievous than the rest, whom yet they much exceed in strength and activity.

The Houyhnhnms keep the yahoos for present use in huts not far from the house; but the rest are sent abroad to certain fields, where they dig up roots, eat several kinds of herbs, and search about for carrion, or sometimes catch weasels and *luhimuhs* (a sort of wild rat), which they greedily devour. Nature hath taught them to dig deep holes with their nails on the side of a rising ground, wherein they lie by themselves, only the kennels of the females are larger, sufficient to hold two or three cubs.

They swim from their infancy like frogs, and are able to continue long under water, where they often take fish, which the females carry home to their young. And upon this occasion, I hope the reader will pardon my relating an odd adventure.

Being one day abroad with my protector the sorrel nag, and the weather exceeding hot, I entreated him to let me bathe in a river that was near. He consented, and I immediately stripped myself stark naked, and went down softly into the stream. It happened that a young female yahoo, standing behind a bank, saw the whole proceeding, and enflamed by desire, as the nag and I conjectured, came running with all speed, and leaped into the water within five yards of the place where I bathed. I was never in my life so terribly frighted; the nag was grazing at some distance, not suspecting any harm. She embraced me after a most fulsome manner; I roared as loud as I could, and the nag came galloping towards me, whereupon she quitted her grasp, with the utmost reluctancy, and leaped upon the opposite bank, where she stood gazing and howling all the time I was putting on my clothes.

This was matter of diversion to my master and his family, as well as of mortification to myself. For now I could no longer deny that I was a real yahoo in every limb and feature, since the females had a natural propensity to me as one of their own species: neither was the hair of this brute of a red colour (which might have been some excuse for an appetite a little irregular) but black as a sloe, and her countenance did not make an appearance altogether so hideous as the rest of the kind; for, I think, she could not be above eleven years old.

Having lived three years in this country, the reader I suppose will expect that I should, like other travellers, give him some account of the manners and customs of its inhabitants, which it was indeed my principal study to learn.

As these noble Houyhnhnms are endowed by nature with a general disposition to all virtues, and have no conceptions or ideas of what is evil in a rational creature, so their grand maxim is, to cultivate *reason,* and to be wholly governed by it. Neither is *reason* among them a point problematical as with us, where men can argue with plausibility on both sides of a question; but strikes you with immediate conviction; as it must needs do where it is not mingled, obscured, or discoloured by passion and interest. I remember it was with extreme difficulty that I could bring my master to understand the meaning of the word "opinion," or how a point could be disputable; because *reason* taught us to affirm or deny only where we are certain; and beyond our knowledge we cannot do either. So that controversies, wranglings, disputes, and positiveness in false or dubious propositions are evils unknown among the Houyhnhnms. In the like manner, when I used to explain to him our several systems of "natural philosophy," he would laugh that a creature pretending to *reason* should value itself upon the knowledge of other people's conjectures, and in things where that knowledge, if it were certain, could be of no use. Wherein he agreed entirely with the sentiments of Socrates, as Plato delivers them; which I mention as the highest honour I can do that prince of philosophers. I have often since reflected what destruction such a doctrine would make in the libraries of Europe, and how many paths to fame would be then shut up in the learned world.

Friendship and *benevolence* are the two principal virtues among the Houyhnhnms, and these not confined to particular objects, but universal to the whole race. For a stranger from the remotest part is equally treated with the nearest neighbour, and wherever he goes, looks upon himself as at home. They preserve *decency* and *civility* in the highest degrees, but are altogether ignorant of *ceremony.* They have no fondness [24] for their colts or foals, but the care they take in educating them proceeds entirely from the dictates of *reason.* And I observed my master to show the same affection to his neighbour's issue that he had for his own. They will have it that *Nature* teaches them to love the whole species, and it is *reason* only that maketh a distinction of persons, where there is a superior degree of virtue.

[24] Foolish tenderness.

When the matron Houyhnhnms have produced one of each sex, they no longer accompany with their consorts, except they lose one of their issue by some casualty, which very seldom happens: but in such a case they meet again, or when the like accident befalls a person whose wife is past bearing, some other couple bestow him one of their own colts, and then go together again till the mother is pregnant. This caution is necessary to prevent the country from being overburthened with numbers. But the race of inferior Houyhnhnms bred up to be servants is not so strictly limited upon this article; these are allowed to produce three of each sex, to be domestics in the noble families.

In their marriages they are exactly careful to choose such colours as will not make any disagreeable mixture in the breed. *Strength* is chiefly valued in the male, and *comeliness* in the female, not upon the account of *love,* but to preserve the race from degenerating; for where a female happens to excel in *strength,* a consort is chosen with regard to *comeliness.* Courtship, love, presents, jointures, settlements, have no place in their thoughts, or terms whereby to express them in their language. The young couple meet and are joined, merely because it is the determination of their parents and friends: it is what they see done every day, and they look upon it as one of the necessary actions of a rational being. But the violation of marriage, or any other unchastity, was never heard of: and the married pair pass their lives with the same friendship and mutual benevolence that they bear to all others of the same species who come in their way; without jealousy, fondness, quarrelling, or discontent.

In educating the youth of both sexes, their method is admirable, and highly deserves our imitation. These are not suffered to taste a grain of *oats,* except upon certain days, till eighteen years old; nor *milk,* but very rarely; and in summer they graze two hours in the morning, and as long in the evening, which their parents likewise observe, but the servants are not allowed above half that time, and a great part of their grass is brought home, which they eat at the most convenient hours, when they can be best spared from work.

Temperance, industry, exercise and *cleanliness,* are the lessons equally enjoined to the young ones of both sexes: and my master thought it monstrous in us to give the females a different kind of education from the males, except in some articles of domestic management; whereby, as he truly observed, one half of our natives were good for nothing but bringing children into the world: and to trust the care of our children to such useless animals, he said, was yet a greater instance of brutality.

But the Houyhnhnms train up their youth to strength, speed, and hardiness, by exercising them in running races up and down steep hills, and over hard stony grounds, and when they are all in a sweat, they are ordered to leap over head and ears into a pond or a river. Four times a year the youth of a certain district meet to show their proficiency in running and leaping, and other feats of strength and agility, where the victor is rewarded with a song made in his or her praise. On this festival the servants drive a herd of yahoos into the field, laden with hay, and oats, and milk for a repast to the Houyhnhnms; after which these brutes are immediately driven back again, for fear of being noisome to the assembly.

Every fourth year, at the *vernal equinox,* there is a representative council of the whole nation, which meets in a plain about twenty miles from our house, and continues about five or six days. Here they enquire into the state and condition of the several districts; whether they abound or be deficient in hay or oats, or cows or yahoos. And wherever there is any want (which is but seldom) it is immediately supplied by unanimous consent and contribution. Here likewise the regulation of children is settled: as for instance, if a Houyhnhnm hath two males, he changeth one of them with another that hath two females: and when a child hath been lost by any casualty, where the mother is past breeding, it is determined what family in the district shall breed another to supply the loss.

Chapter IX

A grand debate at the general assembly at the Houyhnhnms, and how it was determined. The learning of the Houyhnhnms. Their buildings. Their manner of burials. The defectiveness of their language.

One of these grand assemblies was held in my time, about three months before my departure, whither my master went as the representative of our district. In this council was resumed their old debate, and indeed, the only debate which ever happened in that country; whereof my master after his return gave me a very particular account.

The question to be debated was, whether the yahoos should be exterminated from the face of the earth. One of the members for the affirmative offered several arguments of great strength and weight, alleging, that as the yahoos were the most filthy, noisome, and deformed animal which nature ever produced, so they were the most restive and indocible, mischievous and malicious: they would privately suck the teats of the Houyhnhnms' cows, kill and devour their cats, trample down their oats and grass, if they were not continually watched, and commit a thousand other extravagancies. He took notice of a general tradition, that yahoos had not been always in that country: but that many ages ago two of these brutes appeared together upon a mountain, whether produced by the heat of the sun upon corrupted mud and slime, or from the ooze and froth of the sea, was never known. That these yahoos engendered, and their brood in a short time grew so numerous as to overrun and infest the whole nation. That the Houyhnhnms, to get rid of this evil, made a general hunting, and at last enclosed the whole herd; and destroying the elder, every Houyhnhnm kept two young ones in a kennel, and brought them to such a degree of tameness, as an animal so savage by nature can be capable of acquiring; using them for draught and carriage. That there seemed to be much truth in this tradition, and that those creatures could not be *ylnhniamshy* (or *aborigines* of the land) because of the violent hatred the Houyhnhnms, as well as all other animals, bore them; which although their evil disposition sufficiently deserved, could never have arrived at so high a degree, if they had been *aborigines*, or else they would have long since been rooted out. That the inhabitants taking a fancy to use the service of the yahoos, had very imprudently neglected to cultivate the breed of asses, which were a comely animal, easily kept, more tame and orderly, without any offensive smell, strong enough for labour, although they yield to the other in agility of body; and if their braying be no agreeable sound, it is far preferable to the horrible howling of the yahoos.

Several others declared their sentiments to the same purpose, when my master proposed an expedient to the assembly, whereof he had indeed borrowed the hint from me. He approved of the tradition, mentioned by the "honourable member" who spoke before, and affirmed, that the two yahoos said to be first seen among them had been driven thither over the sea; that coming to land, and being forsaken by their companions, they retired to the mountains, and degenerating by degrees, became in process of time much more savage than those of their own species in the country from whence these two originals came. The reason of his assertion was, that he had now in his possession a certain wonder-

ful yahoo (meaning myself) which most of them had heard of, and many of them had seen. He then related to them how he first found me; that my body was all covered with an artificial composure of the skins and hairs of other animals: that I had a language of my own, and had thoroughly learned theirs: that I had related to him the accidents which brought me thither: that when he saw me without my covering, I was an exact yahoo in every part, only of a whiter colour, less hairy, and with shorter claws. He added, how I had endeavoured to persuade him, that in my own and other countries the yahoos acted as the governing, rational animal, and held the Houyhnhnms in servitude: that he observed in me all the qualities of a yahoo, only a little more civilized by some tincture of reason, which however was in a degree as far inferior to the Houyhnhnm race as the yahoos of their country were to me: that, among other things, I mentioned a custom we had of "castrating" Houyhnhnms when they were young, in order to render them tame; that the operation was easy and safe; that it was no shame to learn wisdom from brutes, as industry is taught by the ant, and building by the swallow. (For so I translate the word *lyhannh*, although it be a much larger fowl.) That this invention might be practised upon the younger yahoos here, which, besides rendering them tractable and fitter for use, would in an age put an end to the whole species without destroying life. That in the mean time the Houyhnhnms should be *exhorted* to cultivate the breed of asses, which, as they are in all respects more valuable brutes, so they have this advantage, to be fit for service at five years old, which the others are not till twelve.

This was all my master thought fit to tell me at that time of what passed in the grand council. But he was pleased to conceal one particular, which related personally to myself, whereof I soon felt the unhappy effect, as the reader will know in its proper place, and from whence I date all the succeeding misfortunes of my life.

The Houyhnhnms have no letters, and consequently their knowledge is all traditional. But there happening few events of any moment among a people so well united, naturally disposed to every virtue, wholly governed by reason, and cut off from all commerce with other nations, the historical part is easily preserved without burthening their memories. I have already observed, that they are subject to no diseases, and therefore can have no need of physicians. However, they have excellent medicines composed of herbs, to cure accidental bruises and cuts in the pastern or frog of the foot by sharp stones, as well as other maims and hurts in the several parts of the body.

They calculate the year by the revolution of the sun and the moon, but use no subdivisions into weeks. They are well enough acquainted with the motions of those two luminaries, and understand the nature of *eclipses*; and this is the utmost progress of their *astronomy*.

In *poetry* they must be allowed to excel all other mortals; wherein the justness of their similes, and the minuteness, as well as exactness of their descriptions, are indeed inimitable. Their verses abound very much in both of these, and usually contain either some exalted notions of friendship and benevolence, or the praises of those who were victors in races and other bodily exercises. Their buildings, although very rude and simple, are not inconvenient, but well contrived to defend them from all injuries of cold and heat. They have a kind of tree, which at forty years old loosens in the root, and falls with the first storm; they grow very straight, and being pointed like stakes with a sharp stone (for the Houyhnhnms know not the use of iron), they stick them erect in the ground about ten inches asunder, and then weave in oat-straw, or sometimes wattles betwixt them. The roof is made after the same manner, and so are the doors.

The Houyhnhnms use the hollow part between the pastern and the hoof of their forefeet as we do our hands, and this with greater dexterity than I could at first imagine. I have seen a white mare of our family thread a needle (which I lent her on purpose) with that joint. They milk their cows, reap their oats, and do all the work which requires hands, in the same manner. They have a kind of hard flints, which, by grinding against other stones, they form into instruments, that serve instead of wedges, axes, and hammers. With tools made of these flints they likewise cut their hay, and reap their oats, which there groweth naturally in several fields: the yahoos draw home the sheaves in carriages, and the servants tread them in certain covered huts, to get out the grain, which is kept in stores. They make a rude kind of earthen and wooden vessels, and bake the former in the sun.

If they can avoid casualties, they die only of old age, and are buried in the obscurest places that can be found, their friends and relations expressing neither joy nor grief at their departure; nor does the dying person discover the least regret that he is leaving the world, any more than if he were upon returning home from a visit to one of his neighbours; I remember my master having once made an appointment with a friend and his family to come to his house upon some affair of importance; on the day fixed, the mistress and her two children came very late; she made two excuses, first for her husband, who, as she said, happened that very morning to *shnuwnh*. The word is strongly expressive in their language, but not easily rendered into English; it signifies, "to retire to his first mother." Her excuse for not coming sooner was, that her husband dying late in the morning, she was a good while consulting her servants about a convenient place where his body should be laid; and I observed she behaved herself at our house as cheerfully as the rest, and died about three months after.

They live generally to seventy or seventy-five years, very seldom to fourscore: some weeks before their death they feel a gradual decay, but without pain. During this time they are much visited by their friends, because they cannot go abroad with their usual ease and satisfaction. However, about ten days before their death, which they seldom fail in computing, they return the visits that have been made them by those who are nearest in the neighbourhood, being carried in a convenient sledge drawn by yahoos, which vehicle they use, not only upon this occasion, but when they grow old, upon long journeys, or when they are lamed by any accident. And therefore when the dying Houyhnhnms return those visits, they take a solemn leave of their friends, as if they were going to some remote part of the country, where they designed to pass the rest of their lives.

I know not whether it may be worth observing, that the Houyhnhnms have no word in their language to express any thing that is *evil*, except what they borrow from the deformities or ill qualities of the yahoos. Thus they denote the folly of a servant, an omission of a child, a stone that cuts their feet, a continuance of foul or unseasonable weather, and the like, by adding to each the epithet of *"yahoo."* For instance, *"hhnm yahoo," "whnaholm yahoo," "ynhmndwihlma yahoo,"* and an ill-contrived house *"ynholmhnmrohlnw yahoo."*

I could with great pleasure enlarge farther upon the manners and virtues of this excellent people; but intending in a short time to publish a volume by itself expressly upon that subject, I refer the reader thither. And in the mean time, proceed to relate my own sad catastrophe.

Chapter X

The author's oeconomy and happy life among the Houyhnhnms. His great improvement in virtue, by conversing with them. Their conversations. The author has notice given him by his master that he must depart from the country. He falls into a swoon for grief, but submits. He contrives and finishes a canoe, by the help of a fellow-servant, and puts to sea at a venture.

I had settled my little oeconomy to my own heart's content. My master had ordered a room to be made for me after their manner, about six yards from the house, the sides and floors of which I plaistered with clay, and covered with rush mats of my own contriving; I had beaten hemp, which there grows wild, and made of it a sort of ticking: this I filled with the feathers of several birds I had taken with springes made of yahoos' hairs, and were excellent food. I had worked two chairs with my knife, the sorrel nag helping me in the grosser and more laborious part. When my clothes were worn to rags, I made myself others with the skins of rabbits, and of a certain beautiful animal about the same size, called *nnuhnoh*, the skin of which is covered with a fine down. Of these I likewise made very tolerable stockings. I soled my shoes with wood which I cut from a tree, and fitted to the upper leather, and when this was worn out, I supplied it with the skins of yahoos dried in the sun. I often got honey out of hollow trees, which I mingled with water, or eat with my bread. No man could more verify the truth of these two maxims, "That nature is very easily satisfied"; and "That necessity is the mother of invention." I enjoyed perfect health of body and tranquillity of mind; I did not find the treachery or inconstancy of a friend, nor the injuries of a secret or open enemy. I had no occasion of bribing, flattering or pimping to procure the favour of any great man or of his minion. I wanted no fence against fraud or oppression; here was neither physician to destroy my body, nor lawyer to ruin my fortune; no informer to watch my words and actions, or forge accusations against me for hire; here were no gibers, censurers, backbiters, pickpockets, highwaymen, housebreakers, attorneys, bawds, buffoons, gamesters, politicians, wits, splenetics, tedious talkers, controvertists, ravishers, murderers, robbers, virtuosos; no leaders or followers of party and faction; no encouragers to vice, by seducement or examples; no dungeon, axes, gibbets, whipping-posts, or pillories; no cheating shopkeepers or mechanics; no

pride, vanity, or affectation; no fops, bullies, drunkards, strolling whores, or poxes; no ranting, lewd, expensive wives; no stupid, proud, pedants; no importunate, overbearing, quarrelsome, noisy, roaring, empty, conceited, swearing companions: no scoundrels raised from the dust for the sake of their vices, or nobility thrown into it on account of their virtues; no lords, fiddlers, judges or dancing-masters.

I had the favour of being admitted to several Houyhnhnms, who came to visit or dine with my master; where his Honour graciously suffered me to wait in the room, and listen to their discourse. Both he and his company would often descend to ask me questions, and receive my answers. I had also sometimes the honour of attending my master in his visits to others. I never presumed to speak, except in answer to a question, and then I did it with inward regret, because it was a loss of so much time for improving myself: but I was infinitely delighted with the station of an humble auditor in such conversations, where nothing passed but what was useful, expressed in the fewest and most significant words: where the greatest *decency* was observed, without the least degree of ceremony; where no person spoke without being pleased himself, and pleasing his companions: where there was no interruption, tediousness, heat, or difference of sentiments. They have a notion, that when people are met together, a short silence doth much improve conversation: this I found to be true; for during those little intermissions of talk, new ideas would arise in their thoughts, which very much enlivened the discourse. Their subjects are generally on friendship and benevolence, or order and oeconomy, sometimes upon the visible operations of nature, or ancient traditions, upon the bounds and limits of virtue, upon the unerring rules of reason, or upon some determinations to be taken at the next great assembly, and often upon the various excellencies of poetry. I may add without vanity, that my presence often gave them sufficient matter for discourse, because it afforded my master an occasion of letting his friends into the history of me and my country, upon which they were all pleased to descant in a manner not very advantageous to human kind; and for that reason I shall not repeat what they said; only I may be allowed to observe, that his Honour, to my great admiration, appeared to understand the nature of yahoos in all countries much better than myself. He went through all our vices and follies, and discovered many which I had never mentioned to him, by only supposing what qualities a yahoo of their country, with a small proportion of reason, might be capable of exerting; and concluded, with too much probability, how vile as well as miserable such a creature must be.

I freely confess, that all the little knowledge I have of any value was acquired by the lectures I received from my master, and from hearing the discourses of him and his friends; to which I should be prouder to listen, than to dictate to the greatest and wisest assembly in Europe. I admired the strength, comeliness, and speed of the inhabitants; and such a constellation of virtues in such amiable persons produced in me the highest veneration. At first, indeed, I did not feel that natural awe which the yahoos and all other animals bear towards them; but it grew upon me by degrees, much sooner than I imagined, and was mingled with a respectful love and gratitude, that they would condescend to distinguish me from the rest of my species.

When I thought of my family, my friends, my countrymen, or human race in general, I considered them as they really were, yahoos in shape and disposition, only a little more civilized, and qualified with the gift of speech, but making no other use of reason than to improve and multiply those vices whereof their brethren in this country had only the share that nature allotted them. When I happened to behold the reflection of my own form in a lake or a fountain, I turned away my face in horror and detestation of myself, and could better endure the sight of a common yahoo, than of my own person. By conversing with the Houyhnhnms, and looking upon them with delight, I fell to imitate their gait and gesture, which is now grown into an habit, and my friends often tell me in a blunt way that I "trot like a horse"; which, however, I take for a great compliment: neither shall I disown, that in speaking I am apt to fall into the voice and manner of the Houyhnhnms, and hear myself ridiculed on that account without the least mortification.

In the midst of all this happiness, and when I looked upon myself to be fully settled for life, my master sent for me one morning a little earlier than his usual hour. I observed by his countenance that he was in some perplexity, and at a loss how to begin what he had to speak. After a short silence, he told me, he did not know how I would take what he was going to say; that in the last general assembly, when the affair of the yahoos was entered upon, the representatives had taken offence at his keeping a yahoo (meaning myself) in his family more like a Houyhnhnm than a brute animal. That he was known frequently to converse with me, as if he could receive some advantage or pleasure in

my company: that such a practice was not agreeable to reason or nature, nor a thing ever heard of before among them. The assembly did therefore *exhort* him, either to employ me like the rest of my species, or command me to swim back to the place from whence I came. That the first of these expedients was utterly rejected by all the Houyhnhnms who had ever seen me at his house or their own; for they alleged, that because I had some rudiments of reason, added to the natural pravity of those animals, it was to be feared, I might be able to seduce them into the woody and mountainous parts of the country, and bring them in troops by night to destroy the Houyhnhnms' cattle, as being naturally of the ravenous kind, and averse from labour.

My master added, that he was daily pressed by the Houyhnhnms of the neighbourhood to have the assembly's *exhortation* executed, which he could not put off much longer. He doubted it would be impossible for me to swim to another country, and therefore wished I would contrive some sort of vehicle resembling those I had described to him, that might carry me on the sea, in which work I should have the assistance of his own servants, as well as those of his neighbours. He concluded, that for his own part he could have been content to keep me in his service as long as I lived, because he found I had cured myself of some bad habits and dispositions, by endeavouring, as far as my inferior nature was capable, to imitate the Houyhnhnms.

I should here observe to the reader, that a decree of the general assembly in this country is expressed by the word *hnhloayn*, which signifies an "exhortation," as near as I can render it: for they have no conception how a rational creature can be *compelled*, but only advised or *exhorted*, because no person can disobey reason, without giving up his claim to be a rational creature.

I was struck with the utmost grief and despair at my master's discourse, and being unable to support the agonies I was under, I fell into a swoon at his feet; when I came to myself he told me, that he concluded I had been dead. (For these people are subject to no such imbecilities of nature.) I answered, in a faint voice, that death would have been too great an happiness; that although I could not blame the assembly's *exhortation*, or the urgency of his friends, yet, in my weak and corrupt judgment, I thought it might consist with reason to have been less rigorous. That I could not swim a league, and probably the nearest land to theirs might be distant above an hundred; that many materials, necessary for making a small vessel to carry me off, were wholly wanting in this country, which, however, I would attempt in obedience and gratitude to his Honour, although I concluded the thing to be impossible, and therefore looked on my self as already devoted [25] to destruction. That the certain prospect of an unnatural death was the least of my evils: for, supposing I should escape with life by some strange adventure, how could I think with temper [26] of passing my days among yahoos, and relapsing into my old corruptions, for want of examples to lead and keep me within the paths of virtue? That I knew too well upon what solid reasons all the determinations of the wise Houyhnhnms were founded, not to be shaken by arguments of mine, a miserable yahoo; and therefore, after presenting him with my humble thanks for the offer of his servants' assistance in making a vessel, and desiring a reasonable time for so difficult a work, I told him I would endeavour to preserve a wretched being; and, if ever I returned to England, was not without hopes of being useful to my own species, by celebrating the praises of the renowned Houyhnhnms, and proposing their virtues to the imitation of mankind.

My master in a few words made me a very gracious reply, allowed me the space of two months to finish my boat; and ordered the sorrel nag, my fellow-servant (for so at this distance I may presume to call him) to follow my instructions, because I told my master, that his help would be sufficient, and I knew he had a tenderness for me.

In his company my first business was to go to that part of the coast where my rebellious crew had ordered me to be set on shore. I got upon a height, and looking on every side into the sea, fancied I saw a small island, towards the northeast: I took out my pocket-glass, and could then clearly distinguish it about five leagues off, as I computed; but it appeared to the sorrel nag to be only a blue cloud: for as he had no conception of any country beside his own, so he could not be as expert in distinguishing remote objects at sea as we who so much converse in that element.

After I had discovered this island, I considered no farther; but resolved it should, if possible, be the first place of my banishment, leaving the consequence to fortune.

I returned home, and consulting with the sorrel nag, we went into a copse at some distance, where I with my knife, and he with a sharp flint fastened

very artificially [27] after their manner, to a wooden handle, cut down several oak wattles about the thickness of a walking-staff, and some larger pieces. But I shall not trouble the reader with a particular description of my own mechanics; let it suffice to say that in six weeks' time, with the help of the sorrel nag, who performed the parts that required most labour, I finished a sort of Indian canoe, but much larger, covering it with the skins of yahoos well stitched together, with hempen threads of my own making. My sail was likewise composed of the skins of the same animal; but I made use of the youngest I could get, the older being tough and thick, and I likewise provided myself with four paddles. I laid in a stock of boiled flesh, of rabbits and fowls, and took with me two vessels, one filled with milk, and the other with water.

I tried my canoe in a large pond near my master's house, and then corrected in it what was amiss; stopping all the chinks with yahoos' tallow, till I found it staunch, and able to bear me and my freight. And when it was as complete as I could possibly make it, I had it drawn on a carriage very gently by yahoos to the seaside, under the conduct of the sorrel nag and another servant.

When all was ready, and the day came for my departure, I took leave of my master and lady, and the whole family, my eyes flowing with tears, and my heart quite sunk with grief. But his Honour, out of curiosity, and perhaps (if I may speak it without vanity) partly out of kindness, was determined to see me in my canoe, and got several of his neighbouring friends to accompany him. I was forced to wait above an hour for the tide, and then observing the wind very fortunately bearing towards the island, to which I intended to steer my course, I took a second leave of my master: but as I was going to prostrate myself to kiss his hoof, he did me the honour to raise it gently to my mouth. I am not ignorant how much I have been censured for mentioning this last particular. For my detractors are pleased to think it improbable, that so illustrious a person should descend to give so great a mark of distinction to a creature so inferior as I. Neither have I forgot how apt some travellers are to boast of extraordinary favours they have received. But if these censurers were better acquainted with the noble and courteous disposition of the Houyhnhnms, they would soon change their opinion.

I paid my respects to the rest of the Houyhnhnms in his Honour's company; then getting into my canoe, I pushed off from shore.

[25] Doomed.
[26] Equanimity.
[27] Ingeniously.

Chapter XI

The author's dangerous voyage. He arrives at New Holland, hoping to settle there. Is wounded with an arrow by one of the natives. Is seized and carried by force into a Portuguese ship. The great civilities of the captain. The author arrives at England.

I began this desperate voyage on February 15, 1714-5, at 9 o'clock in the morning. The wind was very favourable; however, I made use at first only of my paddles, but considering I should soon be weary, and that the wind might chop about, I ventured to set up my little sail; and thus with the help of the tide I went at the rate of a league and a half an hour, as near as I could guess. My master and his friends continued on the shore till I was almost out of sight; and I often heard the sorrel nag (who always loved me) crying out, *"Hnuy illa nyha majah yahoo,"* "Take care of thyself, gentle yahoo."

My design was, if possible, to discover some small island uninhabited, yet sufficient by my labour to furnish me with the necessaries of life, which I would have thought a greater happiness than to be first minister in the politest court of Europe; so horrible was the idea I conceived of returning to live in the society and under the government of yahoos. For in such a solitude as I desired, I could at least enjoy my own thoughts, and reflect with delight on the virtues of those inimitable Houyhnhnms, without any opportunity of degenerating into the vices and corruptions of my own species.

The reader may remember what I related when my crew conspired against me, and confined me to my cabin. How I continued there several weeks, without knowing what course we took, and when I was put ashore in the long-boat, how the sailors told me with oaths, whether true or false, that they knew not in what part of the world we were. However, I did then believe us to be about ten degrees southward of the Cape of Good Hope, or about 45 degrees southern latitude, as I gathered from some general words I overheard among them, being I supposed to the southeast in their intended voyage to Madagascar. And although this were but little better than conjecture, yet I resolved to steer my course eastward, hoping to reach the southwest coast of New Holland, and perhaps some such island as I desired, lying westward of it. The wind was full west, and by six in the evening I computed I had gone eastward at least eighteen leagues, when I spied a very small island about half a league off, which I soon reached. It was nothing but a

rock, with one creek, naturally arched by the force of tempests. Here I put in my canoe, and climbing up a part of the rock, I could plainly discover land to the east, extending from south to north. I lay all night in my canoe, and repeating my voyage early in the morning, I arrived in seven hours to the southeast point of New Holland. This confirmed me in the opinion I have long entertained, that the maps and charts place this country at least three degrees more to the east than it really is; which thought I communicated many years ago to my worthy friend Mr. Herman Moll,[28] and gave him my reasons for it, although he hath rather chosen to follow other authors.

I saw no inhabitants in the place where I landed, and being unarmed, I was afraid of venturing far into the country. I found some shellfish on the shore, and eat them raw, not daring to kindle a fire, for fear of being discovered by the natives. I continued three days feeding on oysters and limpets, to save my own provisions, and I fortunately found a brook of excellent water, which gave me great relief.

On the fourth day, venturing out early a little too far, I saw twenty or thirty natives upon a height, not above five hundred yards from me. They were stark naked, men, women, and children, round a fire, as I could discover by the smoke. One of them spied me, and gave notice to the rest; five of them advanced towards me, leaving the women and children at the fire. I made what haste I could to the shore, and getting into my canoe, shoved off: the savages observing me retreat, ran after me; and before I could get far enough into the sea, discharged an arrow, which wounded me deeply on the inside of my left knee (I shall carry the mark to my grave). I apprehended the arrow might be poisoned, and paddling out of the reach of their darts (being a calm day), I made a shift to suck the wound, and dress it as well as I could.

I was at a loss what to do, for I durst not return to the same landing-place, but stood to the north, and was forced to paddle; for the wind, though very gentle, was against me, blowing northwest. As I was looking about for a secure landing-place, I saw a sail to the north-northeast, which appearing every minute more visible, I was in some doubt, whether I should wait for them or no; but at last my detestation of the yahoo race prevailed, and turning my canoe, I sailed and paddled together to the south, and got into the same creek from whence I set out in the morning, choosing rather to trust myself

[28] A famous eighteenth-century map-maker.

among these barbarians, than live with European yahoos. I drew up my canoe as close as I could to the shore, and hid myself behind a stone by the little brook, which, as I have already said, was excellent water.

The ship came within a half a league of this creek, and sent out her long-boat with vessels to take in fresh water (for the place it seems was very well known) but I did not observe it till the boat was almost on shore, and it was too late to seek another hiding-place. The seamen at their landing observed my canoe, and rummaging it all over, easily conjectured that the owner could not be far off. Four of them well armed searched every cranny and lurking-hole, till at last they found me flat on my face behind the stone. They gazed a while in admiration at my strange uncouth dress, my coat made of skins, my wooden-soled shoes, and my furred stockings; from whence, however, they concluded I was not a native of the place, who all go naked. One of the seamen in Portuguese bid me rise, and asked who I was. I understood that language very well, and getting upon my feet, said, I was a poor yahoo, banished from the Houyhnhnms, and desired they would please to let me depart. They admired to hear me answer them in their own tongue, and saw by my complexion I must be an European; but were at a loss to know what I meant by yahoos and Houyhnhnms, and at the same time fell a laughing at my strange tone in speaking, which resembled the neighing of a horse. I trembled all the while betwixt fear and hatred: I again desired leave to depart, and was gently moving to my canoe; but they laid hold on me, desiring to know, what country I was of, whence I came, with many other questions. I told them I was born in England, from whence I came about five years ago, and then their country and ours were at peace. I therefore hoped they would not treat me as an enemy, since I meant them no harm, but was a poor yahoo, seeking some desolate place where to pass the remainder of his unfortunate life.

When they began to talk, I thought I never heard or saw any thing so unnatural; for it appeared to me as monstrous as if a dog or a cow should speak in England, as a yahoo in Houyhnhnmland. The honest [29] Portuguese were equally amazed at my strange dress, and the odd manner of delivering my words, which however they understood very well. They spoke to me with great humanity, and said they were sure their captain would carry me *gratis* to Lisbon, from whence I might return to

[29] Ingenuous, simple.

my own country; that two of the seamen would go back to the ship, inform the captain of what they had seen, and receive his orders; in the mean time, unless I would give my solemn oath not to fly, they would secure me by force. I thought it best to comply with their proposal. They were very curious to know my story, but I gave them very little satisfaction; and they all conjectured, that my misfortunes had impaired my reason. In two hours the boat, which went loaden with vessels of water, returned with the captain's commands to fetch me on board. I fell on my knees to preserve my liberty; but all was in vain, and the men having tied me with cords, heaved me into the boat, from whence I was taken into the ship, and from thence into the captain's cabin.

His name was Pedro de Mendez; he was a very courteous and generous person; he entreated me to give some account of myself, and desired to know what I would eat or drink; said, I should be used as well as himself, and spoke so many obliging things, that I wondered to find such civilities from a yahoo. However, I remained silent and sullen; I was ready to faint at the very smell of him and his men. At last I desired something to eat out of my canoe; but he ordered me a chicken and some excellent wine, and then directed that I should be put to bed in a very clean cabin. I would not undress myself, but lay on the bed-clothes, and in half an hour stole out, when I thought the crew was at dinner, and getting to the side of the ship was going to leap into the sea, and swim for my life, rather than continue among yahoos. But one of the seamen prevented me, and having informed the captain, I was chained to my cabin.

After dinner Don Pedro came to me, and desired to know my reason for so desperate an attempt: assured me he only meant to do me all the service he was able, and spoke so very movingly, that at last I descended to treat him like an animal which had some little portion of reason. I gave him a very short relation of my voyage, of the conspiracy against me by my own men, of the country where they set me on shore, and of my three years' residence there. All which he looked upon as if it were a dream or a vision; whereat I took great offence; for I had quite forgot the faculty of lying, so peculiar to yahoos in all countries where they preside, and, consequently, the disposition of suspecting truth in others of their own species. I asked him, whether it were the custom in his country to "say the thing that was not." I assured him I had almost forgot what he meant by falsehood, and if I had lived a thousand years in Houyhnhnmland, I should never have heard a lie from the meanest servant; that I was altogether indifferent whether he believed me or no; but however, in return for his favours, I would give so much allowance to the corruption of his nature as to answer any objection he would please to make, and then he might easily discover the truth.

The captain, a wise man, after many endeavours to catch me tripping in some part of my story, at last began to have a better opinion of my veracity, and the rather because he confessed, he met with a Dutch skipper, who pretended to have landed with five others of his crew upon a certain island or continent south of New Holland, where they went for fresh water, and observed a horse driving before him several animals exactly resembling those I described under the name of yahoos, with some other particulars, which the captain said he had forgot; because he then concluded them all to be lies. But he added, that since I professed so inviolable an attachment to truth, I must give him my word of honour to bear him company in this voyage without attempting any thing against my life, or else he would continue me a prisoner till we arrived in Lisbon. I gave him the promise he required; but at the same time protested that I would suffer the greatest hardships rather than return to live among yahoos.

Our voyage passed without any considerable accident. In gratitude to the captain I sometimes sate with him at his earnest request, and strove to conceal my antipathy to human kind, although it often broke out, which he suffered to pass without observation. But the greatest part of the day, I confined myself to my cabin, to avoid seeing any of the crew. The captain had often entreated me to strip myself of my savage dress, and offered to lend me the best suit of clothes he had. This I would not be prevailed on to accept, abhorring to cover myself with anything that had been on the back of a yahoo. I only desired he would lend me two clean shirts, which having been washed since he wore them, I believed would not so much defile me. These I changed every second day, and washed them myself.

We arrived at Lisbon, Nov. 5, 1715. At our landing the captain forced me to cover myself with his cloak, to prevent the rabble from crowding about me. I was conveyed to his own house, and, at my earnest request, he led me up to the highest room backwards.[30] I conjured him to conceal from all persons what I had told him of the Houyhnhnms,

[30] At the rear of the house.

because the least hint of such a story would not only draw numbers of people to see me, but probably put me in danger of being imprisoned, or burnt by the Inquisition. The captain persuaded me to accept a suit of clothes newly made, but I would not suffer the tailor to take my measure; however, Don Pedro being almost of my size, they fitted me well enough. He accoutred me with other necessaries all new, which I aired for twenty-four hours before I would use them.

The captain had no wife, nor above three servants, none of which were suffered to attend at meals, and his whole deportment was so obliging, added to very good *human* understanding, that I really began to tolerate his company. He gained so far upon me, that I ventured to look out of the back window. By degrees I was brought into another room, from whence I peeped into the street, but drew my head back in a fright. In a week's time he seduced me down to the door. I found my terror gradually lessened, but my hatred and contempt seemed to encrease. I was at last bold enough to walk the street in his company, but kept my nose well stopped with rue, or sometimes with tobacco.

In ten days Don Pedro, to whom I had given some account of my domestic affairs, put it upon me as a matter of honour and conscience, that I ought to return to my native country, and live at home with my wife and children. He told me, there was an English ship in the port just ready to sail, and he would furnish me with all things necessary. It would be tedious to repeat his arguments, and my contradictions. He said it was altogether impossible to find such a solitary island as I had desired to live in; but I might command in my own house, and pass my time in a manner as recluse as I pleased.

I complied at last, finding I could not do better. I left Lisbon the 24th day of November, in an English merchantman, but who was the master I never enquired. Don Pedro accompanied me to the ship, and lent me twenty pounds. He took kind leave of me, and embraced me at parting, which I bore as well as I could. During the last voyage I had no commerce with the master or any of his men, but pretending I was sick kept close in my cabin. On the fifth of December, 1715, we cast anchor in the Downs about nine in the morning, and at three in the afternoon I got safe to my house at Rotherhith.

My wife and family received me with great surprise and joy, because they concluded me certainly dead; but I must freely confess the sight of them filled me only with hatred, disgust and contempt, and the more by reflecting on the near alliance I had to them. For although, since my unfortunate exile from the Houyhnhnm country, I had compelled myself to tolerate the sight of yahoos, and to converse with Don Pedro de Mendez, yet my memory and imaginations were perpetually filled with the virtues and ideas of those exalted Houyhnhnms. And when I began to consider, that by copulating with one of the yahoo species I had become a parent of more, it struck me with the utmost shame, confusion, and horror.

As soon as I entered the house, my wife took me in her arms, and kissed me, at which, having not been used to the touch of that odious animal for so many years, I fell in a swoon for almost an hour. At the time I am writing it is five years since my last return to England: during the first year I could not endure my wife or children in my presence, the very smell of them was intolerable, much less could I suffer them to eat in the same room. To this hour they dare not presume to touch my bread, or drink out of the same cup, neither was I ever able to let one of them take me by the hand. The first money I laid out was to buy two young stone-horses,[31] which I keep in a good stable, and next to them the groom is my greatest favourite; for I feel my spirits revived by the smell he contracts in the stable. My horses understand me tolerably well; I converse with them at least four hours every day. They are strangers to bridle or saddle; they live in great amity with me, and friendship to each other.

Chapter XII

The author's veracity. His design in publishing this work. His censure of those travellers who swerve from the truth. The author clears himself from any sinister ends in writing. An objection answered. The method of planting colonies. His native country commended. The right of the crown to those countries described by the author is justified. The difficulty of conquering them. The author takes his last leave to the reader, proposeth his manner of living for the future, gives good advice, and concludes.

Thus, gentle reader, I have given thee a faithful history of my travels for sixteen years, and above seven months, wherein I have not been so studious of ornament as truth. I could perhaps like others

[31] Stallions.

have astonished thee with strange improbable tales; but I rather chose to relate plain matter of fact in the simplest manner and style, because my principal design was to inform, and not to amuse thee.

It is easy for us who travel into remote countries, which are seldom visited by Englishmen or other Europeans, to form descriptions of wonderful animals both at sea and land. Whereas a traveller's chief aim should be to make men wiser and better, and to improve their minds by the bad as well as good example of what they deliver concerning foreign places.

I could heartily wish a law was enacted, that every traveller, before he were permitted to publish his voyages, should be obliged to make oath before the Lord High Chancellor that all he intended to print was absolutely true to the best of his knowledge; for then the world would no longer be deceived as it usually is, while some writers, to make their works pass the better upon the public, impose the grossest falsities on the unwary reader. I have perused several books of travels with great delight in my younger days; but having since gone over most parts of the globe, and been able to contradict many fabulous accounts from my own observation, it hath given me a great disgust against this part of reading, and some indignation to see the credulity of mankind so impudently abused. Therefore since my acquaintance were pleased to think my poor endeavours might not be unacceptable to my country, I imposed on myself as a maxim, never to be swerved from, that I would *strictly adhere to truth*; neither indeed can I be ever under the least temptation to vary from it, while I retain in my mind the lectures and example of my noble master, and the other illustrious Houyhnhnms, of whom I had so long the honour to be an humble hearer.

—— Nec si miserum Fortuna Sinonem
Finxit, vanum etiam mendacemque improba finget.[32]

I know very well how little reputation is to be got by writings which require neither genius nor learning, nor indeed any other talent, except a good memory or an exact journal. I know likewise, that writers of travels, like *dictionary-makers*, are sunk into oblivion by the weight and bulk of those who come after, and therefore lie uppermost. And it is highly probable, that such travellers who shall hereafter visit the countries described in this work of mine, may, by detecting my errors (if there be any),

[32] "Nor has Fortune, although she has created Sinon an unfortunate man, been so harsh as to fashion him untrustworthy and lying as well." (Vergil, Æneid, 2.79, 80.)

and adding many new discoveries of their own, justle me out of vogue, and stand in my place, making the world forget that I was ever an author. This indeed would be too great a mortification if I wrote for fame: but, as my sole intention was the PUBLIC GOOD, I cannot be altogether disappointed. For who can read of the virtues I have mentioned in the glorious Houyhnhnms, without being ashamed of his own vices, when he considers himself as the reasoning, governing animal of his country? I shall say nothing of those remote nations where yahoos preside, amongst which the least corrupted are the Brobdingnagians, whose wise maxims in morality and government it would be our happiness to observe. But I forbear descanting farther, and rather leave the judicious reader to his own remarks and applications.

I am not a little pleased that this work of mine can possibly meet with no censurers: for what objections can be made against a writer who relates only plain facts that happened in such distant countries, where we have not the least interest with respect either to trade or negotiations? I have carefully avoided every fault with which common writers of travels are often too justly charged. Besides, I meddle not the least with any *party*, but write without passion, prejudice, or ill-will against any man or number of men whatsoever. I write for the noblest end, to inform and instruct mankind, over whom I may, without breach of modesty, pretend to some superiority from the advantages I received by conversing so long among the most accomplished Houyhnhnms. I write without any view towards profit or praise. I never suffer a word to pass that may look like reflection, or possibly give the least offence even to those who are most ready to take it. So that I hope I may with justice pronounce myself an author perfectly blameless, against whom the tribe of answerers, considerers, observers, reflecters, detecters, remarkers, will never be able to find matter for exercising their talents.

I confess, it was whispered to me that I was bound in duty, as a subject of England, to have given in a memorial to a secretary of state, at my first coming over; because, whatever lands are discovered by a subject belong to the crown. But I doubt whether our conquests in the countries I treat of would be as easy as those of Ferdinando Cortez over the naked Americans. The Lilliputians, I think, are hardly worth the charge of a fleet and army to reduce them, and I question whether it might be prudent or safe to attempt the Brobdingnagians. Or whether an English army would be much at their ease with the Flying Island over their heads. The Houyhnhnms, indeed, appear not to be so well prepared for war, a science to which they are perfect strangers, and especially against missive weapons. However, supposing myself to be a minister of state, I could never give my advice for invading them. Their prudence, unanimity, unacquaintedness with fear, and their love of their country would amply supply all defects in the military art. Imagine twenty thousand of them breaking into the midst of an European army, confounding the ranks, overturning the carriages, battering the warriors' faces into mummy,[33] by terrible yerks[34] from their hinder hoofs. For they would well deserve the character given to Augustus; *"Recalcitrat undique tutus."*[35] But instead of proposals for conquering that magnanimous nation, I rather wish they were in a capacity or disposition to send a sufficient number of their inhabitants for civilizing Europe, by teaching us the first principles of honour, justice, truth, temperance, public spirit, fortitude, chastity, friendship, benevolence, and fidelity. The *names* of all which virtues are still retained among us in most languages, and are to be met with in modern as well as ancient authors; which I am able to assert from my own small reading.

But I had another reason which made me less forward to enlarge his Majesty's dominions by my discoveries. To say the truth, I had conceived a few scruples with relation to the distributive justice of princes upon those occasions. For instance, a crew of pirates are driven by a storm they know not whither, at length a boy discovers land from the topmast, they go on shore to rob and plunder, they see an harmless people, are entertained with kindness, they give the country a new name, they take formal possession of it for their king, they set up a rotten plank or a stone for a memorial, they murder two or three dozen of the natives, bring away a couple more by force for a sample, return home, and get their pardon. Here commences a new dominion acquired with a title by *divine right*. Ships are sent with the first opportunity, the natives driven out or destroyed, their princes tortured to discover their gold, a free licence given to all acts of inhumanity and lust, the earth reeking with the blood of its inhabitants: and this execrable crew of butchers employed in so pious an expedition, is a *modern colony* sent to convert and civilize an idolatrous and barbarous people.

[33] Pulpy mass.
[34] Kicks.
[35] "He kicks backward, invulnerable on every side." (Horace, *Satires*, 2.1.20.)

But this description, I confess, doth by no means affect the British nation, who may be an example to the whole world for their wisdom, care, and justice in planting colonies; their liberal endowments for the advancement of religion and learning; their choice of devout and able pastors to propagate Christianity; their caution in stocking their provinces with people of sober lives and conversations from this the mother kingdom; their strict regard to the distribution of justice, in supplying the civil administration through all their colonies with officers of the greatest abilities, utter strangers to corruption; and to crown all, by sending the most vigilant and virtuous governors, who have no other views than the happiness of the people over whom they preside, and the honour of the king their master.

But, as those countries which I have described do not appear to have any desire of being conquered, and enslaved, murdered or driven out by colonies, nor abound either in gold, silver, sugar or tobacco; I did humbly conceive they were by no means proper objects of our zeal, our valour, or our interest. However, if those whom it more concern think fit to be of another opinion, I am ready to depose, when I shall be lawfully called, that no European did ever visit these countries before me. I mean, if the inhabitants ought to be believed; unless a dispute may arise about the two yahoos, said to have been seen many ages ago on a mountain in Houyhnhnmland, from whence the opinion is, that the race of those brutes hath descended; and these, for any thing I know, may have been English, which indeed I was apt to suspect from the lineaments of their posterity's countenances, although very much defaced. But, how far that will go to make out a title, I leave to the learned in colony-law.

But as to the formality of taking possession in my sovereign's name, it never came once into my thoughts; and if it had, yet as my affairs then stood, I should perhaps, in point of prudence and self-preservation, have put it off to a better opportunity.

Having thus answered the only objection that can ever be raised against me as a traveller, I here take a final leave of all my courteous readers, and return to enjoy my own speculations in my little garden at Redriff, to apply those excellent lessons of virtue which I learned among the Houyhnhnms, to instruct the yahoos of my own family as far as I shall find them docible animals, to behold my figure often in a glass, and thus if possible habituate myself by time to tolerate the sight of a human creature: to lament the brutality of Houyhnhnms in my own country, but always treat their persons with respect, for the sake of my noble master, his family, his friends, and the whole Houyhnhnm race, whom these of ours have the honour to resemble in all their lineaments, however their intellectuals came to degenerate.

I began last week to permit my wife to sit at dinner with me, at the farthest end of a long table, and to answer (but with the utmost brevity) the few questions I ask her. Yet the smell of a yahoo continuing very offensive, I always keep my nose well stopped with rue, lavender, or tobacco leaves. And although it be hard for a man late in life to remove old habits, I am not altogether out of hopes in some time to suffer a neighbour yahoo in my company without the apprehensions I am yet under of his teeth or his claws.

My reconcilement to the yahoo-kind in general might not be so difficult if they would be content with those vices and follies only which nature hath entitled them to. I am not in the least provoked at the sight of a lawyer, a pickpocket, a colonel, a fool, a lord, a gamester, a politician, a whoremaster, a physician, an evidence, a suborner, an attorney, a traitor, or the like; this is all according to the due course of things: but when I behold a lump of deformity and diseases both in body and mind, smitten with *pride,* it immediately breaks all the measures of my patience; neither shall I be ever able to comprehend how such an animal and such a vice could tally together. The wise and virtuous Houyhnhnms, who abound in all excellencies that can adorn a rational creature, have no name for this vice in their language, which hath no terms to express any thing that is evil, except those whereby they describe the detestable qualities of their yahoos, among which they were not able to distinguish this of pride, for want of thoroughly understanding human nature, as it showeth itself in other countries, where that animal presides. But I, who had more experience, could plainly observe some rudiments of it among the wild yahoos.

But the Houyhnhnms, who live under the government of reason, are no more proud of the good qualities they possess, than I should be for not wanting a leg or an arm, which no man in his wits would boast of, although he must be miserable without them. I dwell the longer upon this subject from the desire I have to make the society of an English yahoo by any means not insupportable, and therefore I here entreat those who have any tincture of this absurd vice, that they will not presume to come in my sight.

———◆———

JOSEPH ADDISON and

1672–1719

SIR RICHARD STEELE

1672–1729

Joseph Addison and Sir Richard Steele, though both Whigs and literary collaborators in *The Tatler* and *The Spectator*, actually enjoyed quite separate literary careers. Addison wrote "The Campaign," a poem in heroic couplets on the victory at Blenheim, and *Cato*, a wooden, blank-verse tragedy, very stoical in its philosophy and quite popular in its day. Steele, who at this distance appears much less stuffy and far more human than Addison, wrote sentimental comedies like *The Conscious Lovers* and *The Tender Husband*. Always fighting his own personal battle with the vices against which he campaigned in public, he wrote *The Christian Hero*, one may surmise, as much for his own edification as for the reader's.

Both Addison and Steele attempted to reform the vices and the viciousness of the eighteenth-century society in which they moved, particularly the worst of them—gambling, drunkenness, and duelling. But applying the lighter touch, they also loved to satirize the various foibles and fashions of the aristocracy.

The Tatler, the first essay-type periodical of consequence, began publication in 1709 and continued until 1711. Addison began his participation in the eighteenth number. Its general editorial policy was "to recommend truth, honor, and virtue as the chief ornaments of life." No crusaders, Addison and Steele tried to laugh vices out of fashion.

The sound moral and critical taste of *The Spectator* (1711–1713) enabled it to extend and popularize urbanity and good sense in thought and conduct. In a delightful style, it catered to the tastes of the mercantile classes. Striking a medium between the sort of criticism written by Jeremy Collier and the pointed wit of the comic dramatists, its avowed purpose was "to enliven morality with wit and to temper wit with morality." The name "Spectator" indicates aloofness, detachment, and lack of the crusading spirit. The members of the Spectator Club were chosen with thought, for they are representative of the various segments of the population (e.g., Sir Roger stands for the country gentry, and Sir Andrew Freeport for the merchants). There is in *The Spectator* a whole set of carefully wrought schemes for the semifictional treatment of matters which cannot tactfully be handled as fact. The purpose was generally to deal with the absurd, not with the wicked, and to vanquish folly by laughing at it. Thus mild forms of vice are made to seem unfashionable rather than wicked.

FURTHER READING

GRAHAM, W. J. *The Beginnings of English Literary Periodicals* (New York, 1926).
MARR, G. S. *The Periodical Essayists of the Eighteenth Century* (New York, 1924).

The Tatler

BY

ISAAC BICKERSTAFF, ESQ.

No. 1. TUESDAY, APRIL 12, 1709 [STEELE] [1]

Quicquid agunt homines——
nostri est farrago libelli.
                                    —Juv.

THO' the other Papers, which are published for the Use of the good People of *England*, have certainly very wholesome Effects, and are laudable in their particular Kinds, they do not seem to come up to the main Design of such Narrations, which, I humbly presume, should be principally intended for the Use of politick Persons, who are so publick-spirited as to neglect their own Affairs to look into Transactions of State. Now these Gentlemen, for the most part, being Persons of strong Zeal, and weak Intellects, it is both a charitable and necessary Work to offer something, whereby such worthy and well-affected Members of the Commonwealth may be instructed after their Reading, *what to think*; which shall be the End and Purpose of this my Paper, wherein I shall, from Time to Time, report and consider all Matters of what kind soever that shall occur to me, and publish such my Advices and Reflections every *Tuesday, Thursday*, and *Saturday*, in the Week, for the Convenience of the Post. I resolve to have something which may be of Entertainment to the Fair Sex, in Honour of whom I have invented the Title

[1] This and the following paper follow the spelling and capitalization of the first collected edition. In the other numbers the text has been modernized.

of this Paper. I therefore earnestly desire all Persons, without Distinction, to take it in for the present *Gratis,* and hereafter at the Price of one Penny, forbidding all Hawkers to take more for it at their Peril. And I desire all Persons to consider, that I am at a very great Charge for proper Materials for this Work, as well as that before I resolved upon it, I had settled a Correspondence in all Parts of the known and knowing World. And forasmuch as this Globe is not trodden upon by mere Drudges of Business only, but that Men of Spirit and Genius are justly to be esteemed as considerable Agents in it, we shall not, upon a Dearth of News, present you with musty Foreign Edicts, or dull Proclamations, but shall divide our Relation of the Passages which occur in Action or Discourse throughout this Town, as well as elsewhere, under such Dates of Places as may prepare you for the Matter you are to expect in the following Manner.

All accounts of *Gallantry, Pleasure,* and *Entertainment,* shall be under the Article of *White's Chocolate-house; Poetry,* under that of *Will's Coffee-house;* Learning, under the title of *Grecian; Foreign* and Domestick News, you will have from *St. James's Coffee-house;* and what else I have to offer on any other subject shall be dated from my own Apartment.

I once more desire my Reader to consider, That as I cannot keep an ingenious Man to go daily to *Will's* under Two-pence each Day, merely for his Charges; to *White's* under Six-pence; nor to the *Grecian,* without allowing him some plain *Spanish,* to be as able as others at the Learned Table; and that a good Observer cannot speak with even *Kidney* at *St. James's* without clean Linen; I say, these Considerations will, I hope, make all Persons willing to comply with my humble Request (when my *Gratis* Stock is exhausted) of a Penny a-piece; especially since they are sure of some proper Amusement, and that it is impossible for me to want Means to entertain them, having, besides the Force of my own Parts, the Power of Divination, and that I can, by casting a Figure, tell you all that will happen before it comes to pass.

But this last Faculty I shall use very sparingly, and speak but of few Things until they are passed, for fear of divulging Matters which may offend our Superiors.

White's Chocolate-house, April 7

The deplorable Condition of a very pretty Gentleman, who walks here at the Hours when Men of Quality first appear, is what is very much lamented.

His History is, That on the 9th of *September* 1705, being in his one-and-twentieth Year, he was washing his Teeth at a Tavern Window in *Pall-Mall,* when a fine Equipage passed by, and in it a young Lady who look'd up at him; away goes the Coach, and the young Gentleman pull'd off his Night-Cap, and instead of rubbing his Gums, as he ought to do, out of the Window until about four a-clock, sits him down and spoke not a Word till twelve at Night; after which he began to enquire if any Body knew the Lady?—The Company asked, What Lady? but he said no more, till they broke up at six in the Morning. All the ensuing Winter he went from Church to Church every Sunday, and from Playhouse to Play-house every Night in the Week; but could never find the Original of the Picture which dwelt in his Bosom. In a Word, his Attention to any Thing but his Passion was utterly gone. He has lost all the Money he ever play'd for, and been confuted in every Argument he has entered upon, since the Moment he first saw her. He is of a noble Family, has naturally a very good Air, and is of a frank honest Temper: But this Passion has so extreamly mauled him, that his Features are set and uninformed, and his whole Visage is deaden'd, by a long Absence of Thought. He never appears in any Alacrity, but when raised by Wine; at which Time he is sure to come hither, and throw away a great Deal of Wit on Fellows who have no Sense farther than just to observe, That our poor Lover has most Understanding when he is drunk, and is least in his Senses when he is sober.

Will's Coffee-house, April 8

On *Thursday* last was acted, for the Benefit of Mr. *Betterton,* the celebrated Comedy called *Love for Love.* Those excellent Players, Mrs. *Barry,* Mrs. *Bracegirdle,* and Mr. *Dogget,* though not at present concerned in the House, acted on that Occasion. There has not been known so great a Concourse of Persons of Distinction as at that Time; the Stage itself was cover'd with Gentlemen and Ladies, and when the Curtain was drawn, it discovered even there a very splendid Audience. This unusual Encouragement, which was given to a Play for the Advantage of so great an Actor, gives an undeniable Instance, that the true Relish for manly Entertainments and rational Pleasures is not wholly lost. All the Parts were acted to Perfection: The Actors were careful of their Carriage, and no one was Guilty of the Affectation to insert Witticisms of his own; but a due Respect was had to the Audience, for encouraging this accomplished Player. It is not now doubted but Plays will revive, and take their usual Place in the Opinion of Persons of Wit and Merit, notwithstanding their late Apostacy in Favour of Dress and Sound. This Place is very much altered since Mr. *Dryden* frequented it; where you used to see *Songs, Epigrams,* and *Satires,* in the Hands of every Man you met, you have now only a Pack of Cards; and instead of the Cavils about the Turn of the Expression, the Elegance of the Stile, and the like, the Learned now dispute only about the Truth of the Game. But however the Company is alter'd, all have shewn a great Respect for Mr. *Betterton*: And the very Gaming Part of this House have been so much touched with a Sense of the Uncertainty of Human Affairs (which alter with themselves every Moment) that in this Gentleman they pitied *Mark Antony* of *Rome, Hamlet* of *Denmark, Mithridates* of *Pontus, Theodosius* of *Greece,* and *Henry* the Eighth of *England.* It is well known, he has been in the Condition of each of those illustrious Personages for several Hours together, and behaved himself in those high Stations, in all the Changes of the Scene, with suitable Dignity. For these Reasons, we intend to repeat this Favour to him on a proper Occasion, lest he, who can instruct us so well in personating feigned Sorrows, should be lost to us by suffering under real ones. The Town is at present in very great Expectation of seeing a Comedy now in Rehearsal, which is the 25th Production of my honoured Friend Mr. *Thomas D'Urfey*; who, besides his great Abilities in the Dramatick, has a peculiar Talent in the Lyrick way of Writing, and that with a Manner wholly new and unknown to the ancient *Greeks* and *Romans,* wherein he is but faintly imitated in the Translations of the modern *Italian* Opera's.

St. *James's Coffee-house, April 11*

Letters from the *Hague* of the 16th say, That Major General *Cadogan* was gone to *Brussels,* with Orders to disperse proper Instructions for assembling the whole Force of the Allies in *Flanders,* in the Beginning of the next Month. The late Offers concerning Peace were made in the Stile of Persons who think themselves upon equal Terms: But the Allies have so just a Sense of their present Advantages, that they will not admit of a Treaty, except *France* offers what is more suitable to her present Condition. At the same Time we make Preparations, as if we were alarmed by a greater Force than that which we are carrying into the Field. Thus this Point seems now to be argued Sword in Hand. This was what a Great General alluded to, when being

asked the Names of those who were to be Plenipotentiaries for the ensuing Peace, he answered with a serious Air, *There are about an hundred thousand of us.* Mr. *Kidney,* who has the Ear of the greatest Politicians that come hither, tells me, There is a Mail come in to-day with Letters, dated *Hague, April* 19, N.S. which say, a Design of bringing Part of our Troops into the Field, at the latter End of this Month, is now altered to a Resolution of marching towards the Camp about the 20th of the next. [Prince *Eugene* was then returned thither from *Amsterdam.* He sets out from *Brussels* on *Tuesday*: the greater Number of the General Officers at the *Hague* have Orders to go at the same Time. The Squadron at *Dunkirk* consists of seven Vessels.] There happened t' other Day, in the Road of *Scheveling,* an Engagement between a Privateer of *Zeeland* and one of *Dunkirk.* The *Dunkirker,* carrying 33 Pieces of Cannon, was taken and brought into the *Texel.* It is said the Courier of Monsieur *Rouille* is returned to him from the Court of *France.* Monsieur *Vendosme,* being re-instated in the Favour of the Dutchess of *Burgundy,* is to command in *Flanders.*

Mr. *Kidney* added, that there were Letters of the 17th from *Ghent,* which give an Account, That the Enemy had formed a Design to surprize two Battalions of the Allies which lay at *Alost*: but those Battalions received Advice of their March, and retired to *Dendermond.* Lieutenant General *Wood* appeared on this Occasion at the Head of 5000 Foot and 1000 Horse; upon which the Enemy withdrew, without making any farther Attempt.

From my own Apartment

I am sorry I am obliged to trouble the Publick with so much Discourse upon a Matter which I at the very first mentioned as a Trifle, *viz.* the Death of Mr. *Partridge,* under whose Name there is an Almanack come out for the Year 1709, in one Page of which it is asserted by the said *John Partridge,* That he is still living, and not only so, but that he was also living some Time before, and even at the Instant when I writ of his Death. I have in another Place, and in a Paper by itself, sufficiently convinced this Man that he is dead, and, if he has any Shame, I don't doubt but that by this Time he owns it to all his Acquaintance: For though the Legs and Arms and whole Body of that Man may still appear, and perform their animal Functions; yet since, as I have elsewhere observed, his Art is gone, the Man is gone. I am, as I said, concerned, that this little Matter should make so much Noise; but since I am engaged, I take myself obliged in Honour to go on in my Lucubrations, and by the Help of these Arts of which I am Master, as well as my Skill in Astrological Speculations, I shall, as I see Occasion, proceed to confute other dead Men, who pretend to be in Being, although they are actually deceased. I therefore give all Men fair Warning to mend their Manners; for I shall from Time to Time print Bills of Mortality; and I beg the Pardon of all such who shall be named therein, if they who are good for nothing shall find themselves in the Number of the Deceased.

No. 95. THURSDAY, NOVEMBER 17, 1709 [STEELE]

Interea dulces pendent circum oscula nati,
Casta pudicitiam servant domus——
—VIRG.

From my own Apartment, November 16

There are several Persons who have many Pleasures and Entertainments in their Possession, which they do not enjoy. It is, therefore, a kind and good Office to acquaint them with their own Happiness, and turn their Attention to such Instances of their good Fortune as they are apt to overlook. Persons in the married State often want such a Monitor; and pine away their Days, by looking upon the same Condition in Anguish and Murmur, which carries with it in the Opinion of others a Complication of all the Pleasures of Life, and a Retreat from its Inquietudes.

I am led into this Thought by a Visit I made an old Friend, who was formerly my School-Fellow. He came to Town last Week with his Family for the Winter, and yesterday Morning sent me Word his Wife expected me to Dinner. I am as it were at Home at that House, and every Member of it knows me for their Well-wisher. I cannot indeed express the Pleasure it is, to be met by the Children with so much Joy as I am when I go thither: The Boys and Girls strive who shall come first, when they think it is I that am knocking at the Door; and that Child which loses the Race to me runs back again to tell the Father it is Mr. *Bickerstaff*. This Day I was led in by a Pretty Girl, that we all thought must have forgot me; for the Family has been out of Town these two Years. Her knowing me again was a mighty Subject with us, and took up our Discourse at the first Entrance. After which, they began to rally me upon a Thousand little Stories they heard in the Country, about my Marriage to one of my Neighbour's Daughters. Upon which the Gentle-

man, my Friend, said, "Nay, if Mr. *Bickerstaff* marries a Child of any of his old Companions, I hope mine shall have the Preference; there's Mrs. *Mary* is now Sixteen, and would make him as fine a Widow as the best of them. But I know him too well; he is so enamoured with the very Memory of those who flourished in our Youth, that he will not so much as look upon the modern Beauties. I remember, old Gentleman, how often you went Home in a Day to refresh your Countenance and Dress, when *Teraminta* reigned in your Heart. As we came up in the Coach, I repeated to my Wife some of your Verses on her." With such Reflections on little Passages which happened long ago, we passed our Time, during a chearful and elegant Meal. After Dinner, his Lady left the Room, as did also the Children. As soon as we were alone, he took me by the Hand; Well, my good Friend, says he, I am heartily glad to see thee; I was afraid you would never have seen all the Company that dined with you to-Day again. Do not you think the good Woman of the House a little altered, since you followed her from the Playhouse, to find out who she was, for me? I perceived a Tear fall down his Cheek as he spoke, which moved me not a little. But to turn the Discourse, said I, She is not indeed quite that Creature she was, when she returned me the Letter I carried from you; and told me, she hoped, as I was a Gentleman, I would be employed no more to trouble her, who had never offended me; but would be so much the Gentleman's Friend, as to disswade him from a Pursuit which he could never succeed in. You may remember, I thought her in earnest; and you were forced to employ your Cousin *Will*, who made his Sister get acquainted with her, for you. You cannot expect her to be for ever Fifteen.—Fifteen! replied my good Friend: Ah! you little understand, you that have lived a Batchelor, how great, how exquisite a Pleasure there is, in being really beloved! It is impossible, that the most beauteous Face in Nature should raise in me such pleasing Ideas, as when I look upon that excellent Woman. That Fading in her Countenance is chiefly caused by her watching with me, in my Fever. This was followed by a Fit of Sickness, which had like to have carried her off last Winter. I tell you sincerely, I have so many Obligations to her, that I cannot, with any sort of Moderation, think of her present State of Health. But as to what you say of Fifteen, she gives me every Day Pleasures beyond what I ever knew in the Possession of her Beauty, when I was in the Vigour of Youth. Every Moment of her Life brings me fresh Instances of her Complacency to my Inclinations, and her Prudence in Regard to my Fortune. Her Face is to me much more beautiful than when I first saw it; there is no Decay in any Feature, which I cannot trace, from the very Instant it was occasioned by some anxious Concern for my Welfare and Interests. Thus, at the same Time, methinks, the Love I conceived towards her for what she was, is heightened by my Gratitude for what she is. The Love of a Wife is as much above the idle Passion commonly called by that Name, as the loud Laughter of Buffoons is inferior to the elegant Mirth of Gentlemen. Oh! she is an inestimable Jewel. In her Examination of her Household Affairs, she shews a certain Fearfulness to find a Fault, which makes her Servants obey her like Children; and the meanest we have has an ingenuous Shame for an Offence, not always to be seen in Children in other Families. I speak freely to you, my old Friend; ever since her Sickness, Things that gave me the quickest Joy before, turn now to a certain Anxiety. As the Children play in the next Room, I know the poor Things by their Steps, and am considering what they must do, should they lose their Mother in their tender Years. The Pleasure I used to take in telling my Boy Stories of Battle, and asking my Girl Questions about the Disposal of her Baby, and the Gossiping of it, is turned into inward Reflection and Melancholy.

He would have gone on in this tender Way, when the good Lady entered, and with an inexpressible Sweetness in her Countenance told us, she had been searching her Closet for something very good, to treat such an old Friend as I was. Her Husband's Eyes sparkled with Pleasure at the Chearfulness of her Countenance; and I saw all his Fears vanish in an Instant. The Lady, observing something in our Looks which shewed we had been more serious than ordinary, and seeing her Husband receive her with great Concern under a forced Chearfulness, immediately guessed at what we had been talking of; and applying herself to me, said with a Smile, Mr. *Bickerstaff*, don't believe a Word of what he tells you, I shall live to have you for my Second, as I have often promised you, unless he takes more Care of himself than he has done since his coming to Town. You must know, he tells me, That he finds *London* is a much more healthy Place than the Country; for he sees several of his old Acquaintance and School-fellows are here young Fellows with fair full-bottom'd Periwigs. I could scarce keep him this Morning from going out open-breasted. My Friend, who is always extremely delighted with her agreeable Humour, made her sit

down with us. She did it with that Easiness which is peculiar to Women of Sense; and to keep up the good Humour she had brought in with her, turned her Raillery upon me: Mr. *Bickerstaff*, you remember you followed me one Night from the Playhouse; Supposing you should carry me thither to-morrow Night, and lead me into the Front-Box. This put us into a long Field of Discourse about the Beauties who were Mothers to the present, and shined in the Boxes twenty Years ago. I told her, I was glad she had transferred so many of her Charms, and I did not question but her eldest Daughter was within Half a Year of being a Toast.

We were pleasing ourselves with this fantastical Preferment of the young Lady, when on a sudden we were alarmed with the Noise of a Drum, and immediately entered my little God-son to give me a Point of War. His Mother, between Laughing and Chiding, would have put him out of the Room; but I would not part with him so. I found, upon Conversation with him, though he was a little noisy in his Mirth, that the Child had excellent Parts, and was a great Master of all the Learning on t'other Side Eight Years old. I perceived him a very great Historian in *Aesop's* Fables: But he frankly declared to me his Mind, That he did not delight in that Learning, because he did not believe they were true; for which Reason I found he had very much turned his Studies, for about a Twelvemonth past, into the Lives and Adventures of Don *Bellianis* of *Greece*, *Guy* of *Warwick*, the *Seven Champions*, and other historians of that Age. I could not but observe the Satisfaction the Father took in the Forwardness of his Son; and, that these Diversions might turn to some Profit, I found the Boy had made Remarks, which might be of Service to him during the Course of his whole Life. He would tell you the Mismanagements of *John Hickathrift*, find Fault with the passionate Temper in *Bevis* of *Southampton*, and loved St. *George* for being the Champion of *England*; and by this Means had his Thoughts insensibly moulded into the Notions of Discretion, Virtue, and Honour. I was extolling his Accomplishments, when the Mother told me, That the little Girl who led me in this Morning was in her Way a better Scholar than he: Betty (says she) deals chiefly in Fairies and Sprights; and sometimes in a Winter-Night will terrify the Maids with her Accounts, till they are afraid to go up to Bed.

I sat with them until it was very late, sometimes in merry, sometimes in serious Discourse, with this particular Pleasure, which gives the only true Relish to all Conversation, a Sense that every one of us liked each other. I went Home, considering the different Conditions of a married Life and that of a Batchelor: and I must confess it struck me with a secret Concern, to reflect, that whenever I go off, I shall leave no Traces behind me. In this pensive Mood I returned to my Family; that is to say, to my Maid, my Dog, and my Cat, who only can be the better or worse for what happens to me.

No. 158. Thursday, April 13, 1710 [Addison]

Faciunt nae intelligendo, ut nihil intelligant.—Ter.

Tom Folio is a broker in learning, employed to get together good editions, and stock the libraries of great men. There is not a sale of books begins until Tom Folio is seen at the door. There is not an auction where his name is not heard, and that too in the very nick of time, in the critical moment, before the last decisive stroke of the hammer. There is not a subscription goes forward in which Tom is not privy to the first rough draught of the proposals; nor a catalogue printed, that doth not come to him wet from the press. He is an universal scholar, so far as the title-page of all authors; knows the manuscripts in which they were discovered, the editions through which they have passed, with the praises or censures which they have received from the several members of the learned world. He has a greater esteem for Aldus and Elzevir, than for Virgil and Horace. If you talk of Herodotus, he breaks out into a panegyric upon Harry Stephens. He thinks he gives you an account of an author, when he tells you the subject he treats of, the name of the editor, and the year in which it was printed. Or if you draw him into farther particulars, he cries up the goodness of the paper, extols the diligence of the corrector, and is transported with the beauty of the letter. This he looks upon to be sound learning and substantial criticism. As for those who talk of the fineness of style, and the justness of thought, or describe the brightness of any particular passages; nay, though they themselves write in the genius and spirit of the author they admire; Tom looks upon them as men of superficial learning, and flashy parts.

I had yesterday morning a visit from this learned *idiot*, for *that* is the light in which I consider every pedant, when I discovered in him some little touches of the coxcomb, which I had not before observed. Being very full of the figure which he makes in the republic of letters, and wonderfully satisfied with his great stock of knowledge, he gave me broad intimations, that he did not believe in all points as his forefathers had done. He then communicated to me a thought of a certain author upon a passage of Virgil's account of the dead, which I made the subject of a late paper. This thought hath taken very much among men of Tom's pitch and understanding, though universally exploded by all that know how to construe Virgil, or have any relish of antiquity. Not to trouble my reader with it, I found, upon the whole, that Tom did not believe a future state of rewards and punishments, because Aeneas, at his leaving the empire of the dead, passed through the gate of ivory, and not through that of horn. Knowing that Tom had not sense enough to give up an opinion which he had once received, that I might avoid wrangling, I told him "that Virgil possibly had his oversights as well as another author." "Ah! Mr. Bickerstaff," says he, "you would have another opinion of him, if you would read him in Daniel Heinsius's edition. I have perused him myself several times in that edition," continued he; "and after the strictest and most malicious examination, could find but two faults in him; one of them is in the Aeneids, where there are two commas instead of a parenthesis; and another in the third Georgic, where you may find a semi-colon turned upside down." "Perhaps," said I, "these were not Virgil's faults, but those of the transcriber." "I do not design it," says Tom, "as a reflection on Virgil; on the contrary, I know that all the manuscripts declaim against such a punctuation. Oh! Mr. Bickerstaff," says he, "what would a man give to see one simile of Virgil writ in his own hand?" I asked him which was the simile he meant; but was answered, any simile in Virgil. He then told me all the secret history in the commonwealth of learning; of modern pieces that had the names of ancient authors annexed to them; of all the books that were now writing or printing in the several parts of Europe; of many amendments which are made, and not yet published, and a thousand other particulars, which I would not have my memory burdened with for a Vatican.

At length, being fully persuaded that I thoroughly admired him, and looked upon him as a prodigy of learning, he took his leave. I know several of Tom's class, who are professed admirers of Tasso, without understanding a word of Italian: and one, in particular, that carries a *Pastor Fido* in his pocket, in which, I am sure, he is acquainted with no other beauty but the clearness of the character.

There is another kind of pedant, who, with all Tom Folio's impertinences, hath greater superstructures and embellishments of Greek and Latin; and is still more insupportable than the other, in the same degree as he is more learned. Of this kind very often are editors, commentators, interpreters, scholiasts, and critics; and, in short, all men of deep learning without common sense. These persons set a greater value on themselves for having found out the meaning of a passage in Greek, than upon the author for having written it; nay, will allow the passage itself not to have any beauty in it, at the same time that they would be considered as the greatest men of the age, for having interpreted it. They will look with contempt on the most beautiful poems that have been composed by any of their contemporaries; but will lock themselves up in their studies for a twelvemonth together, to correct, publish, and expound such trifles of antiquity, as a modern author would be contemned for. Men of the strictest morals, severest lives, and the gravest professions, will write volumes upon an idle sonnet, that is originally in Greek or Latin; give editions of the most immoral authors; and spin out whole pages upon the various readings of a lewd expression. All that can be said in excuse for them is that their works sufficiently show they have no taste of their authors; and that what they do in this kind, is out of their great learning, and not out of any levity or lasciviousness of temper.

A pedant of this nature is wonderfully well described in six lines of Boileau, with which I shall conclude his character:

> Un Pédant enyuré de sa vaine science,
> Tout herissé de Grec, tout bouffi d'arrogance;
> Et qui de mille auteurs retenus mot pour mot,
> Dans sa tête entassés n'a souvent fait qu'un sot,
> Croit qu'un livre fait tout, et que sans Aristote
> La raison ne voit goute, et le bon sens radote.

Brim-full of learning see that pedant stride,
Bristling with horrid Greek, and puffed with pride!
A thousand authors he in vain has read,
And with their maxims stuffed his empty head;
And thinks that without Aristotle's rule,
Reason is blind, and common sense a fool.

The Spectator

No. 1. THURSDAY, MARCH 1, 1711 [ADDISON]

*Non fumum ex fulgore, sed ex fumo dare lucem
Cogitat, ut speciosa dehinc miracula promat.*
—HORACE.

I have observed that a reader seldom peruses a book with pleasure till he knows whether the writer of it be a black or a fair man, of a mild or choleric disposition, married or a bachelor, with other particulars of the like nature that conduce very much to the right understanding of an author. To gratify this curiosity, which is so natural to a reader, I design this paper and my next as prefatory discourses to my following writings, and shall give some account in them of the several persons that are engaged in this work. As the chief trouble of compiling, digesting, and correcting will fall to my share, I must do myself the justice to open the work with my own history. I was born to a small hereditary estate, which, according to the tradition of the village where it lies, was bounded by the same hedges and ditches in William the Conqueror's time that it is at present, and has been delivered down from father to son whole and entire, without the loss or acquisition of a single field or meadow, during the space of six hundred years. There runs a story in the family, that when my mother was gone with child of me about three months, she dreamed that she was brought to bed of a judge: whether this might proceed from a lawsuit which was then depending in the family, or my father's being a justice of the peace, I cannot determine; for I am not so vain as to think it presaged any dignity that I should arrive at in my future life, though that was the interpretation which the neighborhood put upon it. The gravity of my behavior at my very first appearance in the world, and all the time that I sucked, seemed to favor my mother's dream: for, as she has often told me, I threw away my rattle before I was two months old, and would not make use of my coral till they had taken away the bells from it.

As for the rest of my infancy, there being nothing in it remarkable, I shall pass it over in silence. I find that, during my nonage, I had the reputation of a very sullen youth, but was always a favorite of my schoolmaster, who used to say *that my parts were solid and would wear well.* I had not been long at the University before I distinguished myself by a most profound silence; for during the space of eight years, excepting in the public exercises of the college, I scarce uttered the quantity of an hundred words; and indeed do not remember that I ever spoke three sentences together in my whole life. Whilst I was in this learned body, I applied myself with so much diligence to my studies that there are very few celebrated books, either in the learned or the modern tongues, which I am not acquainted with.

Upon the death of my father I was resolved to travel into foreign countries, and therefore left the University with the character of an odd, unaccountable fellow, that had a great deal of learning if I would but show it. An insatiable thirst after knowledge carried me into all the countries of Europe in which there was anything new or strange to be seen; nay, to such a degree was my curiosity raised, that having read the controversies of some great men concerning the antiquities of Egypt, I made a voyage to Grand Cairo, on purpose to take the measure of a pyramid; and as soon as I had set myself right in that particular, returned to my native country with great satisfaction.

I have passed my latter years in this city, where I am frequently seen in most public places, though there are not above half a dozen of my select friends that know me; of whom my next paper shall give a more particular account. There is no place of general resort wherein I do not often make my appearance; sometimes I am seen thrusting my head into a round of politicians at Will's, and listening with great attention to the narratives that are made in those little circular audiences. Sometimes I smoke a pipe at Child's, and whilst I seem attentive to nothing but *The Postman,* overhear the conversation of every table in the room. I appear on Sunday nights at St. James's Coffee-house, and sometimes join the little committee of politics in the Inner Room, as one who comes there to hear and improve. My face is likewise very well known at the Grecian, the Cocoa-Tree, and in the theatres both of Drury Lane and the Hay-Market. I have been taken for a merchant upon the Exchange for above these ten years, and sometimes pass for a Jew in the assembly of stock-jobbers at Jonathan's. In short, wherever I see a cluster of people, I always mix with them, though I never open my lips but in my own club.

Thus I live in the world rather as a SPECTATOR of mankind than as one of the species; by which means I have made myself a speculative statesman, soldier, merchant, and artisan, without ever meddling with any practical part in life. I am very well versed in the theory of an husband or a father, and can discern the errors in the economy, business, and diversion of others better than those who are engaged in them; as standers-by discover blots which are apt to escape those who are in the game. I never espoused any party with violence, and am resolved to observe an exact neutrality between the Whigs and Tories, unless I shall be forced to declare myself by the hostilities of either side. In short, I have acted in all the parts of my life as a looker-on, which is the character I intend to preserve in this paper.

I have given the reader just so much of my history and character as to let him see I am not altogether unqualified for the business I have undertaken. As for other particulars in my life and adventures, I shall insert them in following papers as I shall see occasion. In the meantime, when I consider how much I have seen, read, and heard, I begin to blame my own taciturnity: and since I have neither time nor inclination to communicate the fullness of my heart in speech, I am resolved to do it in writing, and to print myself out, if possible, before I die. I have been often told by my friends that it is a pity so many useful discoveries which I have made, should be in the possession of a silent man. For this reason, therefore, I shall publish a sheetful of thoughts every morning for the benefit of my contemporaries; and if I can in any way contribute to the diversion or improvement of the country in which I live, I shall leave it, when I am summoned out of it, with the secret satisfaction of thinking that I have not lived in vain.

There are three very material points which I have not spoken to in this paper, and which, for several important reasons, I must keep to myself, at least for some time: I mean, an account of my name, my age, and my lodgings. I must confess, I would gratify my reader in anything that is reasonable; but, as for these three particulars, though I am sensible they might tend very much to the embellishment of my paper, I cannot yet come to a resolution of communicating them to the public. They would indeed draw me out of that obscurity which I have enjoyed for many years, and expose me in public places to several salutes and civilities which have been always very disagreeable to me; for the greatest pain I can suffer is the being talked to and being stared at. It is for this reason, likewise, that I keep my complexion and dress as very great secrets, though it is not impossible but I may make discoveries of both in the progress of the work I have undertaken.

After having been thus particular upon myself, I shall in to-morrow's paper give an account of those gentlemen who are concerned with me in this work; for, as I have before intimated, a plan of it is laid and concerted (as all other matters of importance are) in a club. However, as my friends have engaged me to stand in the front, those who have a mind to correspond with me may direct their letters *To The Spectator, at Mr. Buckley's, in Little Britain.* For I must further acquaint the reader that, though our club meets only on Tuesdays and Thursdays, we have appointed a committee to sit every night for the inspection of all such papers as may contribute to the advancement of the public weal.

No. 2. Friday, March 2, 1711 [Steele]

—*Haec alii sex*
Vel plures uno conclamant ore.
—Juvenal.

The first of our society is a gentleman of Worcestershire, of ancient descent, a baronet, his name Sir Roger de Coverley. His great-grandfather was inventor of that famous country-dance which is called after him. All who know that shire are very well acquainted with the parts and merits of Sir Roger. He is a gentleman that is very singular in his behavior, but his singularities proceed from his good sense, and are contradictions to the manners of the world only as he thinks the world is in the wrong. However, this humor creates him no enemies, for he does nothing with sourness of obstinacy; and his being unconfined to modes and forms, makes him but the readier and more capable to please and oblige all who know him. When he is in town, he lives in Soho Square. It is said he keeps himself a bachelor by reason he was crossed in love by a perverse, beautiful widow of the next county to him. Before this disappointment, Sir Roger was what you call a fine gentleman, had often supped with my Lord Rochester and Sir George Etherege, fought a duel upon his first coming to town, and kicked Bully Dawson in a public coffee-house for calling him "youngster." But being ill-used by the above-mentioned widow, he was very serious for a year and a half; and though, his temper being naturally jovial, he at last got over it, he grew careless of himself, and never dressed afterward. He continues to wear a coat and doublet of the same cut that were in fashion at the time of his repulse, which, in his merry humors, he tells us, has been in and out twelve times since he first wore it. 'Tis said Sir Roger grew humble in his desires after he had forgot this cruel beauty; insomuch that it is reported he has frequently offended in point of chastity with beggars and gypsies; but this is looked upon by his friends rather as matter of raillery than truth. He is now in his fifty-sixth year, cheerful, gay, and hearty; keeps a good house in both town and country; a great lover of mankind; but there is such a mirthful cast in his behavior that he is rather beloved than esteemed. His tenants grow rich, his servants look satisfied, all the young women profess love to him, and the young men are glad of his company; when he comes into a house, he calls the servants by their names, and talks all the way up stairs to a visit. I must not omit that Sir Roger is a justice of the quorum; that

he fills the chair at a quarter-session with great abilities; and, three months ago, gained universal applause by explaining a passage in the Game Act.

The gentleman next in esteem and authority among us is another bachelor, who is a member of the Inner Temple; a man of great probity, wit, and understanding; but he has chosen his place of residence rather to obey the direction of an old humorsome father, than in pursuit of his own inclinations. He was placed there to study the laws of the land, and is the most learned of any of the house in those of the stage. Aristotle and Longinus are much better understood by him than Littleton or Coke. The father sends up, every post, questions relating to marriage-articles, leases, and tenures, in the neighborhood; all which questions he agrees with an attorney to answer and take care of in the lump. He is studying the passions themselves, when he should be inquiring into the debates among men which arise from them. He knows the argument of each of the orations of Demosthenes and Tully, but not one case in the reports of our own courts. No one ever took him for a fool; but none, except his intimate friends, know he has a great deal of wit. This turn makes him at once both disinterested and agreeable; as few of his thoughts are drawn from business, they are most of them fit for conversation. His taste of books is a little too just for the age he lives in; he has read all, but approves of very few. His familiarity with the customs, manners, actions, and writings of the ancients makes him a very delicate observer of what occurs to him in the present world. He is an excellent critic, and the time of the play is his hour of business; exactly at five he passes through New Inn, crosses through Russell Court, and takes a turn at Will's till the play begins; he has his shoes rubbed and his periwig powdered at the barber's as you go into the Rose. It is for the good of the audience when he is at a play, for the actors have an ambition to please him.

The person of next consideration is Sir Andrew Freeport, a merchant of great eminence in the city of London, a person of indefatigable industry, strong reason, and great experience. His notions of trade are noble and generous, and (as every rich man has usually some sly way of jesting which would make no great figure were he not a rich man) he calls the sea the British Common. He is acquainted with commerce in all its parts, and will tell you that it is a stupid and barbarous way to extend dominion by arms; for true power is to be got by arts and industry. He will often argue that if this part of our trade were well cultivated, we should gain from one nation; and if another, from another. I have heard him prove that diligence makes more lasting acquisitions than valor, and that sloth has ruined more nations than the sword. He abounds in several frugal maxims, among which the greatest favorite is, "A penny saved is a penny got." A general trader of good sense is pleasanter company than a general scholar; and Sir Andrew having a natural unaffected eloquence, the perspicuity of his discourse gives the same pleasure that wit would in another man. He has made his fortunes himself, and says that England may be richer than other kingdoms by as plain methods as he himself is richer than other men; though at the same time I can say this of him, that there is not a point in the compass but blows home a ship in which he is an owner.

Next to Sir Andrew in the club-room sits Captain Sentry, a gentleman of great courage, good understanding, but invincible modesty. He is one of those that deserve very well, but are very awkward at putting their talents within the observation of such as should take notice of them. He was some years a captain, and behaved himself with great gallantry in several engagements and at several sieges; but having a small estate of his own, and being next heir to Sir Roger, he has quitted a way of life in which no man can rise suitably to his merit who is not something of a courtier as well as a soldier. I have heard him often lament that in a profession where merit is placed in so conspicuous a view, impudence should get the better of modesty. When he has talked to this purpose, I never heard him make a sour expression, but frankly confess that he left the world because he was not fit for it. A strict honesty and an even, regular behavior are in themselves obstacles to him that must press through crowds who endeavor at the same end with himself —the favor of a commander. He will, however, in this way of talk, excuse generals for not disposing according to men's desert, or inquiring into it, "For," says he, "that great man who has a mind to help me, has as many to break through to come at me as I have to come at him"; therefore he will conclude that the man who would make a figure, especially in a military way, must get over all false modesty, and assist his patron against the importunity of other pretenders by a proper assurance in his own vindication. He says it is a civil cowardice to be backward in asserting what you ought to expect, as it as a military fear to be slow in attacking when it is your duty. With this candor

does the gentleman speak of himself and others. The same frankness runs through all his conversation. The military part of his life has furnished him with many adventures, in the relation of which he is very agreeable to the company; for he is never overbearing, though accustomed to command men in the utmost degree below him; nor ever too obsequious from an habit of obeying men highly above him.

But that our society may not appear a set of humorists unacquainted with the gallantries and pleasures of the age, we have among us the gallant Will Honeycomb, a gentleman who, according to his years, should be in the decline of his life, but having ever been very careful of his person, and always had a very easy fortune, time has made but very little impression either by wrinkles on his forehead or traces in his brain. His person is well turned and of a good height. He is very ready at that sort of discourse with which men usually entertain women. He has all his life dressed very well, and remembers habits as others do men. He can smile when one speaks to him, and laughs easily. He knows the history of every mode, and can inform you from which of the French king's wenches our wives and daughters had this manner of curling their hair, that way of placing their hoods; whose frailty was covered by such a sort of petticoat, and whose vanity to show her foot made that part of the dress so short in such a year. In a word, all his conversation and knowledge has been in the female world. As other men of his age will take notice to you what such a minister said upon such and such an occasion, he will tell you when the Duke of Monmouth danced at court such a woman was then smitten, another was taken with him at the head of his troop in the Park. In all these important relations, he has ever about the same time received a kind glance or a blow of a fan from some celebrated beauty, mother of the present Lord Such-a-one. If you speak of a young commoner that said a lively thing in the House, he starts up: "He has good blood in his veins; Tom Mirabell begot him; the rogue cheated me in that affair; that young fellow's mother used me more like a dog than any woman I ever made advances to." This way of talking of his very much enlivens the conversation among us of a more sedate turn; and I find there is not one of the company but myself, who rarely speak at all, but speaks of him as of that sort of man who is usually called a well-bred, fine gentleman. To conclude his character, where women are not concerned, he is an honest, worthy man.

I cannot tell whether I am to account him whom I am next to speak of as one of our company, for he visits us but seldom; but when he does, it adds to every man else a new enjoyment of himself. He is a clergyman, a very philosophic man, of general learning, great sanctity of life, and the most exact good breeding. He has the misfortune to be of a very weak constitution, and consequently cannot accept of such cares and business as preferments in his function would oblige him to; he is therefore among divines what a chamber-counselor is among lawyers. The probity of his mind and the integrity of his life create him followers, as being eloquent or loud advances others. He seldom introduces the subject he speaks upon; but we are so far gone in years that he observes, when he is among us, an earnestness to have him fall on some divine topic, which he always treats with much authority, as one who has no interest in this world, as one who is hastening to the object of all his wishes and conceives hope from his decays and infirmities. These are my ordinary companions.

No. 10. MONDAY, MARCH 12, 1711 [ADDISON]

Non aliter quam qui adverso vix flumine lembum
Remigiis subigit, si bracchia forte remisit,
Atque illum praeceps prono rapit alveus amni.
             —VERGIL, *Georg.* I. 201

So the boat's brawny crew the current stem,
And slow advancing, struggle with the stream:
But if they slack their hands, or cease to strive,
Then down the flood with headlong haste they drive.
             —DRYDEN

It is with much satisfaction that I hear this great city inquiring day by day after these my papers, and receiving my morning lectures with a becoming seriousness and attention. My publisher tells me that there are already three thousand of them distributed every day: so that if I allow twenty readers to every paper, which I look upon as a modest computation, I may reckon about threescore thousand disciples in London and Westminster, who I hope will take care to distinguish themselves from the thoughtless herd of their ignorant and unattentive brethren. Since I have raised to myself so great an audience, I shall spare no pains to make their instruction agreeable, and their diversion useful. For which reasons I shall endeavor to enliven morality with wit, and to temper wit with morality, that my readers may, if possible, both ways find their account in the speculation of the day. And to the end that their virtue and discretion may not

be short, transient, intermitting starts of thought, I have resolved to refresh their memories from day to day, till I have recovered them out of that desperate state of vice and folly into which the age is fallen. The mind that lies fallow but a single day sprouts up in follies that are only to be killed by a constant and assiduous culture. It was said of Socrates, that he brought philosophy down from heaven, to inhabit among men; and I shall be ambitious to have it said of me that I have brought philosophy out of closets and libraries, schools and colleges, to dwell in clubs and assemblies, at tea-tables and in coffee-houses.

I would, therefore, in a very particular manner recommend these my speculations to all well-regulated families, that set apart an hour in every morning for tea and bread and butter; and would earnestly advise them for their good to order this paper to be punctually served up, and to be looked upon as a part of the tea equipage.

Sir Francis Bacon observes that a well-written book, compared with its rivals and antagonists, is like Moses's serpent, that immediately swallowed up and devoured those of the Egyptians. I shall not be so vain as to think that where the *Spectator* appears the other public prints will vanish; but shall leave it to my reader's consideration, whether is it not much better to be let into the knowledge of one's self, than to hear what passes in Muscovy or Poland; and to amuse ourselves with such writings as tend to the wearing out of ignorance, passion, and prejudice, than such as naturally conduce to inflame hatreds and make enmities irreconcilable?

In the next place, I would recommend this paper to the daily perusal of those gentlemen whom I cannot but consider as my good brothers and allies; I mean the fraternity of spectators who live in the world without having anything to do in it, and either by the affluence of their fortunes, or laziness of their dispositions, have no other business with the rest of mankind but to look upon them. Under this class of men are comprehended all contemplative tradesmen, titular physicians, fellows of the Royal Society, Templars that are not given to be contentious, and statesmen that are out of business; in short, everyone that considers the world as a theatre, and desires to form a right judgment of those who are the actors on it.

There is another set of men that I must likewise lay a claim to, whom I have lately called the blanks of society, as being altogether unfurnished with ideas till the business and conversation of the day has supplied them. I have often considered these poor souls with an eye of great commiseration, when I have heard them asking the first man they have met with, whether there was any news stirring? and by that means gathering together materials for thinking. These needy persons do not know what to talk of till about twelve o'clock in the morning; for by that time they are pretty good judges of the weather, know which way the wind sits, and whether the Dutch mail be come in. As they lie at the mercy of the first man they meet, and are grave or impertinent all the day long, according to the notions which they have imbibed in the morning, I would earnestly entreat them not to stir out of their chambers till they have read this paper, and do promise them that I will daily instill into them such sound and wholesome sentiments, as shall have a good effect on their conversation for the ensuing twelve hours.

But there are none to whom this paper will be more useful than to the female world. I have often thought there has not been sufficient pains taken in finding out proper employments and diversions for the fair ones. Their amusements seem contrived for them, rather as they are women, than as they are reasonable creatures; and are more adapted to the sex than to the species. The toilet is their great scene of business, and the right adjusting of their hair the principal employment of their lives. The sorting of a suit of ribbons is reckoned a very good morning's work; and if they make an excursion to a mercer's, or a toy-shop, so great a fatigue makes them unfit for anything else all the day after. Their more serious occupations are sewing and embroidery, and their greatest drudgery the preparation of jellies and sweetmeats. This, I say, is the state of ordinary women; though I know there are multitudes of those of a more elevated life and conversation, that move in an exalted sphere of knowledge and virtue, that join all the beauties of the mind to the ornaments of dress, and inspire a kind of awe and respect, as well as love, into their male beholders. I hope to increase the number of these by publishing this daily paper, which I shall always endeavor to make an innocent, if not an improving, entertainment, and by that means at least divert the minds of my female readers from greater trifles. At the same time, as I would fain give some finishing touches to those which are already the most beautiful pieces in human nature, I shall endeavor to point out all those imperfections that are the blemishes, as well as those virtues which are the embellishments, of the sex. In the meanwhile I hope these my gentle readers, who have so much

time on their hands, will not grudge throwing away a quarter of an hour in a day on this paper, since they may do it without any hindrance to business.

I know several of my friends and well-wishers are in great pain for me, lest I should not be able to keep up the spirit of a paper which I oblige myself to furnish every day; but to make them easy in this particular, I will promise them faithfully to give it over as soon as I grow dull. This I know will be matter of great raillery to the small wits; who will frequently put me in mind of my promise, desire me to keep my word, assure me that it is high time to give over, with many other little pleasantries of the like nature, which men of a little smart genius cannot forbear throwing out against their best friends, when they have such a handle given them of being witty. But let them remember that I do hereby enter my caveat against this piece of raillery.

No. 267. SATURDAY, JANUARY 5, 1712 [ADDISON]

Cedite Romani scriptores, cedite Graii.
　　—PROPERT[IUS, *Elegies*, II, 34, 65. (III, 26, 65)

Give place, ye Roman authors; give place, ye Greek.]

There is nothing in nature so irksome as general discourses, especially when they turn chiefly upon words. For this reason I shall waive the discussion of that point which was started some years since, whether Milton's *Paradise Lost* may be called an heroic poem. Those who will not give it that title, may call it (if they please) a divine poem. It will be sufficient to its perfection if it has in it all the beauties of the highest kind of poetry; and as for those who allege it is not an heroic poem, they advance no more to the diminution of it than if they should say Adam is not Aeneas, nor Eve Helen.

I shall therefore examine it by the rules of epic poetry, and see whether it falls short of the *Iliad* or *Aeneid*, in the beauties which are essential to that kind of writing. The first thing to be considered in an epic poem is the fable, which is perfect or imperfect, according as the action which it relates is more or less so. This action should have three qualifications in it. First, it should be but one action. Secondly, it should be an entire action; and thirdly, it should be a great action. To consider the action of the *Iliad, Aeneid,* and *Paradise Lost,* in these three several lights, Homer to preserve the unity of his action hastens into the midst of things, as Horace has observed: had he gone up to Leda's egg, or begun much later, even at the rape of Helen, or the investing of Troy, it is manifest that the story of the poem would have been a series of several actions. He therefore opens his poem with the discord of his princes, and with great art interweaves in the several succeeding parts of it, an account of everything material which relates to them, and had passed before that fatal dissension. After the same manner, Aeneas makes his first appearance in the Tyrrhene seas, and within sight of Italy, because the action proposed to be celebrated was that of his settling himself in Latium. But because it was necessary for the reader to know what had happened to him in the taking of Troy, and in the preceding parts of his voyage, Virgil makes his hero relate it by way of episode in the second and third books of the *Aeneid*. The contents of both which books come before those of the first book in the thread of the story, though for preserving of this unity of action, they follow them in the disposition of the poem. Milton, in imitation of these two great poets, opens his *Paradise Lost* with an infernal council plotting the fall of man, which is the action he proposed to celebrate; and as for those great actions which preceded, in point of time, the battle of the angels, and the creation of the world, (which would have entirely destroyed the unity of his principal action, had he related them in the same order that they happened) he cast them into the fifth, sixth, and seventh books by way of episode to this noble poem.

Aristotle himself allows that Homer has nothing to boast of as to the unity of his fable, though at the same time that great critic and philosopher endeavors to palliate this imperfection in the Greek poet, by imputing it in some measure to the very nature of an epic poem. Some have been of opinion that the *Aeneid* labors also in this particular, and has episodes which may be looked upon as excrescencies rather than as parts of the action. On the contrary, the poem which we have now under our consideration hath no other episodes than such as naturally arise from the subject, and yet is filled with such a multitude of astonishing incidents that it gives us at the same time a pleasure of the greatest variety, and of the greatest simplicity.

I must observe also, that as Virgil in the poem which was designed to celebrate the original of the Roman Empire has described the birth of its great rival, the Carthaginian commonwealth, Milton, with the like art in his poem on the fall of man, has related the fall of those angels who are his professed enemies. Besides the many other beauties

in such an episode, its running parallel with the great action of the poem hinders it from breaking the unity so much as another episode would have done, that had not so great an affinity with the principal subject. In short, this is the same kind of beauty which the critics admire in *The Spanish Friar, or the Double Discovery*, where the two different plots look like counterparts and copies of one another.

The second qualification required in the action of an epic poem is that it should be an entire action; an action is entire when it is complete in all its parts; or, as Aristotle describes it, when it consists of a beginning, a middle, and an end. Nothing should go before it, be intermixed with it, or follow after it that is not related to it. As on the contrary, no single step should be omitted in that just and regular process which it must be supposed to take from its original to its consummation. Thus we see the anger of Achilles in its birth, its continuance and effects; and Aeneas's settlement in Italy, carried on through all the oppositions in his way to it both by sea and land. The action in Milton excels (I think) both the former in this particular; we see it contrived in hell, executed upon earth, and punished by Heaven. The parts of it are told in the most distinct manner, and grow out of one another in the most natural method.

The third qualification of an epic poem is its greatness. The anger of Achilles was of such consequence that it embroiled the kings of Greece, destroyed the heroes of Troy, and engaged all the gods in factions. Aeneas's settlement in Italy produced the Caesars and gave birth to the Roman Empire. Milton's subject was still greater than either of the former; it does not determine the fate of single persons or nations, but of a whole species. The united powers of hell are joined together for the destruction of mankind, which they effected in part, and would have completed, had not Omnipotence itself interposed. The principal actors are man in his greatest perfection, and woman in her highest beauty. Their enemies are the fallen angels, the Messiah their friend, and the Almighty their protector. In short, everything that is great in the whole circle of being, whether within the verge of nature, or out of it, has a proper part assigned it in this noble poem.

In poetry, as in architecture, not only the whole, but the principal members and every part of them, should be great. I will not presume to say that the book of games in the *Aeneid* or that in the *Iliad* are not of this nature, nor to reprehend Virgil's simile of the top, and many other of the same nature in the *Iliad,* as liable to any censure in this particular; but I think we may say, without derogating from those wonderful performances, that there is an unquestionable magnificence in every part of *Paradise Lost,* and indeed a much greater than could have been formed upon any pagan system.

But Aristotle, by the greatness of the action does not only mean that it should be great in its nature, but also in its duration, or, in other words, that it should have a due length in it, as well as what we properly call greatness. The just measure of the kind of magnitude he explains by the following similitude. An animal no bigger than a mite cannot appear perfect to the eye because the sight takes it in at once, and has only a confused idea of the whole, and not a distinct idea of all its parts; if on the contrary you should suppose an animal of ten thousand furlongs in length, the eye would be so filled with a single part of it that it could not give the mind an idea of the whole. What these animals are to the eye, a very short or a very long action would be to the memory. The first would be, as it were, lost and swallowed up by it; and the other difficult to be contained in it. Homer and Virgil have shown their principal art in this particular; the action of the *Iliad* and that of the *Aeneid* were in themselves exceeding short, but are so beautifully extended and diversified by the invention of episodes, and the machinery of gods, with the like poetical ornaments, that they make up an agreeable story sufficient to employ the memory without overcharging it. Milton's action is enriched with such a variety of circumstances that I have taken as much pleasure in reading the contents of his books as in the best invented story I ever met with. It is possible that the traditions on which the *Iliad* and *Aeneid* were built had more circumstances in them than the history of the fall of man, as it is related in Scripture. Besides it was easier for Homer and Virgil to dash the truth with fiction as they were in no danger of offending the religion of their country by it. But as for Milton, he had not only a very few circumstances upon which to raise his poem, but was also obliged to proceed with the greatest caution in everything that he added out of his own invention. And, indeed, notwithstanding all the restraints he was under, he has filled his story with so many surprising incidents which bear so close an analogy with what is delivered in Holy Writ that it is capable of pleasing the most delicate reader, without giving offense to the most scrupulous.

The modern critics have collected from several hints in the *Iliad* and *Aeneid* the space of time which is taken up by the action of each of those poems; but as a great part of Milton's story was transacted in regions that lie out of the reach of the sun and the sphere of day, it is impossible to gratify the reader with such a calculation, which indeed would be more curious than instructive, none of the critics, either ancient or modern, having laid down rules to circumscribe the action of an epic poem with any determined number of years, days, or hours.

This piece of criticism on Milton's *Paradise Lost* shall be carried on in the following Saturdays' papers.

❖

ALEXANDER POPE

1688–1744

Alexander Pope, the greatest English satiric and didactic poet, was born in London, the son of a Roman Catholic linen draper. Because his religion denied admission to private schools and universities (and later to any public position), he was educated by competent private tutors. Even as a precocious child he was poetically inclined, or, as he himself expressed it, he "lisped in numbers, for the numbers came." Perhaps the happiest years of his life were those spent at Binfield, an estate near Windsor Forest, to which his father retired after having made a competence in business. Here Pope read widely, with his tutors and independently, in English, French, Italian, Latin, and Greek authors.

Though normal at birth, Pope suffered a terrible disease at the age of twelve from which he emerged misshapen and crippled in body. Hunchbacked and only about four-and-a-half feet tall, he grew up to be almost a caricature of a man. After the age of twelve, it is doubtful if Pope ever enjoyed a well day in his life; in fact, he refers to "this long disease, my life." Much of Pope's venom and misanthropy may perhaps be extenuated by some understanding of his physical suffering and its attendant frustrations. None can deny that Pope had personal faults, such as disingenuousness, vindictiveness, deceit, a general furtiveness of mind which delighted in mystification and obfuscation. Yet it is very easy to overdo the "wasp of Twickenham" side of his nature; on the other side of the ledger, it should be written that he had as his intimate friends some of the most aristocratic and talented men of his time—noblemen and bishops, as well as writers like Swift, Gay, and Arbuthnot. Certainly a man without personal warmth and charm of personality could not have won and held the friendship of the celebrities of his day. Although there are aspects of Pope's character and incidents in his behavior which even the most charitable critic could hardly condone because of his ill-health, the man's tremendous achievement in literature is the important thing, not his private personality, whether pleasant or unpleasant.

The *Pastorals* (1709) was Pope's first publication, and his quarrel with Addison may be traced back to this occasion, for Addison in a wrong-headed manner insisted on praising the pastorals of Ambrose Philips as superior. Two years later Pope published his *Essay on Criticism*. Based rather directly on Boileau's *L'Art Poétique* and indirectly and ultimately on Horace's *Ars Poetica,* it was nevertheless a most remarkable accomplishment for a young man. It offers the modern reader perhaps the best succinct statement of the principles of Neo-classicism.

Pope's collected *Poems,* which appeared in 1717, included his *Pastorals, Windsor Forest,* and two Romantic poems of great sentiment: "Verses to the Memory of an Unfortunate Lady," and "Eloisa to Abelard." Anyone who thinks that the greatest of the English Neo-classicists was cold and devoid of sentiment ought by all means to read the latter. The 1717 collection also included "The Rape of the Lock," Pope's most charming and urbane poem. Perhaps the best example of Pope's consummate artistry, it is the greatest mock-heroic poem in all English literature. In its crystalline case are beautifully displayed the wares of Neo-classic art: wit, humor, taste, urbanity, sophistication, didacticism, skill, and polish.

In 1713 Pope had begun to translate Homer's *Iliad,* which he issued in a number of volumes between then and 1720. No sooner had he published the first of this series than Thomas Tickell published his own translation of *Iliad,* I. The breach

between Addison and Pope was widened by Tickell's act, for Pope supposed, and in all likelihood correctly so, that Addison had instigated the Tickell translation. Pope allowed his wrath to smolder for some years before he took vengeance on Addison in his caustic satiric portrait of "Atticus" (Addison), which found its way into the "Epistle to Dr. Arbuthnot" (1735). Pope's *Iliad* and later his *Odyssey* are estimated to have brought him about nine thousand pounds, a considerable fortune in the eighteenth century, which by careful investment made Pope a man of independent means for the rest of his life. This, together with a small paternal legacy, enabled Pope to buy his famous estate at Twickenham on the Thames, far, far away from the garrets of Grub Street, where his detractors eked out their days.

In 1725 he published his edition of Shakespeare, in which his faulty scholarship led to the disapproval of Lewis Theobald, whom Pope was later to pillory as the first hero in *The Dunciad* (1728). The latter work was his most vitriolic and personal satire—a sort of general paying-off of old scores against his enemies, as well as a lavish crusade against sham and shoddy art.

Pope's *Essay on Man* (1733–1734) is a philosophical and didactic poem, certainly along with Lucretius' *De Rerum Natura* one of the most successful poems in this genre in any literature. Though a good many of its ethical and philosophical ideas may seem outmoded today, it is practically a compendium of the ideas of Pope's contemporaries, and it does assay very high in quotable lines.

Under the Romantic bias of Wordsworth and his nineteenth-century followers, who still cast their shadow over our time, it has long been fashionable to disparage the poetry of Pope as "rhymed prose" and to deplore the artificiality of his poetic diction. The tide during the last several decades has, however, at last begun to turn, and once again Pope is recognized as a great poetic artist. With a development of greater catholicity in literary taste in our own time, there has come an increased appreciation of Neo-classical art as well as a realization that Dr. Johnson had no intention of being facetious when he said, "If Pope be not poetry, pray where is poetry?" Within the restrictions of the heroic couplet which he imposed on himself, he has chiseled out gemlike lines of subtle beauty and pungent truth which are more widely quoted by English-speaking people than the work of any other poet except Shakespeare. He brought the satiric portrait, originated by his master John Dryden, to perfection, and as George Sherburn, the greatest American authority on Pope, has said, "a studied ease is his great achievement."

FURTHER READING

Root, Robert K. *The Poetical Career of Alexander Pope* (Princeton, 1938).

Sherburn, George. *The Early Career of Alexander Pope* (Oxford, 1934).

Spence, Joseph. *Anecdotes* (London, 1820).

Tobin, J. E. *Alexander Pope: A List of Critical Studies Published 1895–1944* (New York, 1945).

The Rape of the Lock

AN HEROI-COMICAL POEM

Nolueram, Belinda, tuos violare capillos;
Sed juvat, hoc precibus me tribuisse tuis.[1]
—Mart. [*Epigr.* xii. 84.]

TO MRS. ARABELLA FERMOR

Madam,

It will be in vain to deny that I have some regard for this piece, since I dedicate it to You. Yet you may bear me witness, it was intended only to divert a few young Ladies, who have good sense and good humour enough to laugh not only at their sex's little unguarded follies, but at their own. But as it was communicated with the air of a Secret, it soon found its way into the world. An imperfect copy having been offer'd to a Bookseller, you had the good-nature for my sake to consent to the publication of one more correct: This I was forc'd to, before I had executed half my design, for the Machinery was entirely wanting to compleat it.

The Machinery, Madam, is a term invented by the Critics, to signify that part which the Deities, Angels, or Daemons are made to act in a Poem: For

the ancient Poets are in one respect like many modern Ladies: let an action be never so trivial in itself, they always make it appear of the utmost importance. These Machines I determined to raise on a very new and odd foundation, the Rosicrucian doctrine of Spirits.

I know how disagreeable it is to make use of hard words before a Lady; but 't is so much the concern of a Poet to have his works understood, and particularly by your Sex, that you must give me leave to explain two or three difficult terms.

The Rosicrucians are a people I must bring you acquainted with. The best account I know of them is in a French book call'd *Le Comte de Gabalis,* which both in its title and size is so like a Novel, that many of the Fair Sex have read it for one by mistake. According to these Gentlemen, the four Elements are inhabited by Spirits, which they call Sylphs, Gnomes, Nymphs, and Salamanders. The Gnomes or Daemons of Earth delight in mischief; but the Sylphs, whose habitation is in the Air, are the best condition'd creatures imaginable. For they say, any mortals may enjoy the most intimate familiarities with these gentle Spirits, upon a condition very easy to all true Adepts, an inviolate preservation of Chastity.

As to the following Canto's, all the passages of them are as fabulous, as the Vision at the beginning, or the Transformation at the end; (except the loss of your Hair, which I always mention with reverence). The Human persons are as fictitious as the airy ones; and the character of Belinda, as it is now manag'd, resembles you in nothing but in Beauty.

If this Poem had as many Graces as there are in your Person, or in your Mind, yet I could never hope it should pass thro' the world half so Uncensur'd as You have done. But let its fortune be what it will, mine is happy enough, to have given me this occasion of assuring you that I am, with the truest esteem, Madam,

Your most obedient, Humble Servant,

A. Pope.

CANTO I

What dire offence from am'rous causes springs,
What mighty contests rise from trivial things,
I sing—This verse to Caryl, Muse! is due:
This, ev'n Belinda may vouchsafe to view:
Slight is the subject, but not so the praise,
If She inspire, and He approve my lays.
Say what strange motive, Goddess! could compel
A well-bred Lord t' assault a gentle Belle?

---

[1] "I did not wish, Belinda, to do violence to your locks, but I am glad to grant this much at your request." Pope substitutes Belinda's name for the one in Martial. The implication of the quotation is of course that Miss Fermor asked Pope to write the poem. The Fermors are said to have approved it in manuscript, but to have resented some of the double-entendres they detected in the printed version. The baron is Lord Petre.

O say what stranger cause, yet unexplor'd,
Could make a gentle Belle reject a Lord? 10
In tasks so bold, can little men engage,
And in soft bosoms dwells such mighty Rage?

   Sol thro' white curtains shot a tim'rous ray,
And oped those eyes that must eclipse the day:
Now lap-dogs give themselves the rousing shake,
And sleepless lovers, just at twelve, awake:
Thrice rung the bell, the slipper knock'd the ground,
And the press'd watch return'd a silver sound.
Belinda still her downy pillow prest
Her guardian Sylph prolong'd the balmy rest: 20
'T was He had summon'd to her silent bed
The morning-dream that hover'd o'er her head;
A Youth more glitt'ring than a Birth-night Beau,
(That ev'n in slumber caus'd her cheek to glow)
Seem'd to her ear his winning lips to lay,
And thus in whispers said, or seem'd to say.

   "Fairest of mortals, thou distinguish'd care
Of thousand bright Inhabitants of Air!
If e'er one vision touch'd thy infant thought,
Of all the Nurse and all the Priest have taught; 30
Of airy Elves by moonlight shadows seen,
The silver token, and the circled green,
Or virgins visited by Angel-pow'rs,
With golden crowns and wreaths of heav'nly flow'rs;
Hear and believe! thy own importance know,
Nor bound thy narrow views to things below,
Some secret truths, from learned pride conceal'd,
To Maids alone and Children are reveal'd:
What tho' no credit doubting Wits may give?
The Fair and Innocent shall still believe. 40
Know, then, unnumber'd Spirits round thee fly,
The light Militia of the lower sky:
These, tho' unseen, are ever on the wing,
Hang o'er the Box, and hover round the Ring.
Think what an equipage thou hast in Air,
And view with scorn two Pages and a Chair.
As now your own, our beings were of old,
And once enclos'd in Woman's beauteous mould;
Thence, by a soft transition, we repair
From earthly Vehicles to these of air. 50
Think not, when Woman's transient breath is fled
That all her vanities at once are dead;
Succeeding vanities she still regards,
And tho' she plays no more, o'erlooks the cards.
Her joy in gilded Chariots, when alive,
And love of Ombre,[2] after death survive.
For when the Fair in all their pride expire,
To their first Elements their Souls retire:
The Sprites of fiery Termagants in Flame
Mount up, and take a Salamander's name. 60

  [2] Ombre was a favourite game of the ladies.

Soft yielding minds to Water glide away,
And sip, with Nymphs, their elemental Tea.
The graver Prude sinks downward to a Gnome,
In search of mischief still on Earth to roam.
The light Coquettes in Sylphs aloft repair,
And sport and flutter in the fields of Air.

   "Know further yet; whoever fair and chaste
Rejects mankind, is by some Sylph embrac'd:
For Spirits, freed from mortal laws, with ease
Assume what sexes and what shapes they please. 70
What guards the purity of melting Maids,
In courtly balls, and midnight masquerades,
Safe from the treach'rous friend, the daring spark,
The glance by day, the whisper in the dark,
When kind occasion prompts their warm desires,
When music softens, and when dancing fires?
'T is, but their Sylph, the wise Celestials know,
Tho' Honour is the word with Men below.

   "Some nymphs there are, too conscious of their
     face
For life predestin'd to the Gnomes' embrace. 80
These swell their prospects and exalt their pride,
When offers are disdain'd, and love deny'd:
Then gay Ideas crowd the vacant brain,
While Peers, and Dukes, and all their sweeping
     train,
And Garters, Stars, and Coronets appear,
And in soft sounds, Your Grace salutes their ear.
'T is these that early taint the female soul,
Instruct the eyes of young Coquettes to roll,
Teach Infant-cheeks a bidden blush to know,
And little hearts to flutter at a Beau. 90

   "Oft, when the world imagine women stray,
The Sylphs thro' mystic mazes guide their way,
Thro' all the giddy circle they pursue,
And old impertinence expel by new.
What tender maid but must a victim fall
To one man's treat, but for another's ball?
When Florio speaks what virgin could withstand,
If gentle Damon did not squeeze her hand?
With varying vanities, from ev'ry part,
They shift the moving Toyshop of their heart; 100
Where wigs with wigs, with sword-knots sword-
     knots strive,
Beaux banish beaux, and coaches coaches drive.
This erring mortals Levity may call;
Oh blind to truth! the Sylphs contrive it all.

   "Of these am I, who thy protection claim,
A watchful sprite, and Ariel is my name.
Late, as I rang'd the crystal wilds of air,
In the clear Mirror of thy ruling Star
I saw, alas! some dread event impend,
Ere to the main this morning sun descend, 110

But heav'n reveals not what, or how, or where:
Warn'd by the Sylph, oh pious maid, beware!
This to disclose is all thy guardian can:
Beware of all, but most beware of Man!"
   He said; when Shock, who thought she slept too
     long,
Leap'd up, and wak'd his mistress with his tongue.
'T was then, Belinda, if report say true,
Thy eyes first open'd on a Billet-doux;
Wounds, Charms, and Ardors were no sooner read,
But all the Vision vanish'd from thy head.   120
   And now, unveil'd, the Toilet stands display'd,
Each silver Vase in mystic order laid.
First, rob'd in white, the Nymph intent adores,
With head uncover'd, the Cosmetic pow'rs.
A heav'nly image in the glass appears,
To that she bends, to that her eyes she rears;
Th' inferior Priestess, at her altar's side,
Trembling begins the sacred rites of Pride.
Unnumber'd treasures ope at once, and here
The various off'rings of the world appear;   130
From each she nicely culls with curious toil,
And decks the Goddess with the glitt'ring spoil.
This casket India's glowing gems unlocks,
And all Arabia breathes from yonder box.
The Tortoise here and Elephant unite,
Transform'd to combs, the speckled, and the white.
Here files of pins extend their shining rows,
Puffs, Powders, Patches, Bibles, Billet-doux.
Now awful Beauty puts on all its arms;
The fair each moment rises in her charms,   140
Repairs her smiles, awakens ev'ry grace,
And calls forth all the wonders of her face;
Sees by degrees a purer blush arise,
And keener lightnings quicken in her eyes.
The busy Sylphs surround their darling care,
These set the head, and those divide the hair,
Some fold the sleeve, whilst others plait the gown;
And Betty 's prais'd for labours not her own.

CANTO II

Not with more glories, in th' etherial plain,
The Sun first rises o'er the purpled main,
Than, issuing forth, the rival of his beams
Launch'd on the bosom of the silver Thames.
Fair Nymphs, and well-drest Youths around her
    shone,
But ev'ry eye was fix'd on her alone.
On her white breast a sparkling Cross she wore,
Which Jews might kiss, and Infidels adore.
Her lively looks a sprightly mind disclose,
Quick as her eyes, and as unfix'd as those: 10

Favours to none, to all she smiles extends;
Oft she rejects, but never once offends.
Bright as the sun, her eyes the gazers strike,
And, like the sun, they shine on all alike.
Yet graceful ease, and sweetness void of pride,
Might hide her faults, if Belles had faults to hide:
If to her share some female errors fall,
Look on her face, and you 'll forget 'em all.
   This Nymph, to the destruction of mankind,
Nourish'd two Locks, which graceful hung be-
    hind   20
In equal curls, and well conspir'd to deck
With shining ringlets the smooth iv'ry neck.
Love in these labyrinths his slaves detains,
And mighty hearts are held in slender chains.
With hairy springes we the birds betray,
Slight lines of hair surprise the finny prey,
Fair tresses man's imperial race ensnare,
And beauty draws us with a single hair.
   Th' advent'rous Baron the bright locks admir'd;
He saw, he wish'd, and to the prize aspir'd.   30
Resolv'd to win, he meditates the way,
By force to ravish, or by fraud betray;
For when success a Lover's toil attends,
Few ask, if fraud or force attain'd his ends.
   For this, ere Phoebus rose, he had implor'd
Propitious heav'n, and ev'ry pow'r ador'd,
But chiefly Love—to Love an Altar built,
Of twelve vast French Romances, neatly gilt.
There lay three garters, half a pair of gloves;
And all the trophies of his former loves;   40
With tender Billet-doux he lights the pyre,
And breathes three am'rous sighs to raise the fire.
Then prostrate falls, and begs with ardent eyes
Soon to obtain, and long possess the prize:
The pow'rs gave ear, and granted half his pray'r,
The rest, the winds dispers'd in empty air.
   But now secure the painted vessel glides,
The sun-beams trembling on the floating tides:
While melting music steals upon the sky,
And soften'd sounds along the waters die;   50
Smooth flow the waves, the Zephyrs gently play,
Belinda smil'd, and all the world was gay.
All but the Sylph—with careful thoughts opprest,
Th' impending woe sat heavy on his breast.
He summons strait his Denizens of air;
The lucid squadrons round the sails repair:
Soft o'er the shrouds aërial whispers breathe,
That seem'd but Zephyrs to the train beneath.
Some to the sun their insect-wings unfold,
Waft on the breeze, or sink in clouds of gold;   60
Transparent forms, too fine for mortal sight,
Their fluid bodies half dissolv'd in light,

Loose to the wind their airy garments flew,
Thin glitt'ring textures of the filmy dew,
Dipt in the richest tincture of the skies,
Where light disports in ever-mingling dyes,
While ev'ry beam new transient colours flings,
Colours that change whene'er they wave their
    wings.
Amid the circle, on the gilded mast,
Superior by the head, was Ariel place'd;   70
His purple pinions op'ning to the sun,
He rais'd his azure wand, and thus begun.
    "Ye Sylphs and Sylphids, to your chief give ear!
Fays, Fairies, Genii, Elves, and Daemons, hear!
Ye know the spheres and various tasks assign'd
By laws eternal to th' aërial kind.
Some in the fields of purest Aether play,
And bask and whiten in the blaze of day.
Some guide the course of wand'ring orbs on high,
Or roll the planets thro' the boundless sky.   80
Some less refin'd, beneath the moon's pale light
Pursue the stars that shoot athwart the night,
Or suck the mists in grosser air below,
Or dip their pinions in the painted bow,
Or brew fierce tempests on the wintry main,
Or o'er the glebe distil the kindly rain.
Others on earth o'er human race preside,
Watch all their ways, and all their actions guide:
Of these the chief the care of Nations own,
And guard with Arms divine the British Throne. 90
    "Our humbler province is to tend the Fair,
Not a less pleasing, tho' less glorious care;
To save the powder from too rude a gale,
Nor let th' imprison'd essences exhale;
To draw fresh colours from the vernal flow'rs;
To steal from rainbows e'er they drop in show'rs
A brighter wash; to curl their waving hairs,
Assist their blushes, and inspire their airs;
Nay oft, in dreams, invention we bestow,
To change a Flounce, or add a Furbelow.   100
    "This day, black Omens threat the brightest Fair,
That e'er deserv'd a watchful spirit's care;
Some dire disaster, or by force, or slight;
But what, or where, the fates have wrapt in night.
Whether the nymph shall break Diana's law,
Or some frail China jar receive a flaw;
Or stain her honour or her new brocade;
Forget her pray'rs, or miss a masquerade;
Or lose her heart, or necklace, at a ball;
Or whether Heav'n has doom'd that Shock must
    fall.   110
Haste, then, ye spirits! to your charge repair:
The flutt'ring fan be Zephyretta's care;
The drops to thee, Brillante, we consign;

And, Momentilla, let the watch be thine;
Do thou, Crispissa, tend her fav'rite Lock;
Ariel himself shall be the guard of Shock.
    "To fifty chosen Sylphs, of special note,
We trust th' important charge, the Petticoat:
Oft have we known that seven-fold fence to fail,
Tho' stiff with hoops, and arm'd with ribs of
    whale;   120
Form a strong line about the silver bound,
And guard the wide circumference around.
    "Whatever spirit, careless of his charge,
His post neglects, or leaves the fair at large,
Shall feel sharp vengeance soon o'ertake his sins,
Be stopp'd in vials, or transfix'd with pins;
Or plung'd in lakes of bitter washes lie,
Or wedg'd whole ages in a bodkin's eye:
Gums and Pomatums shall his flight restrain,
While clogg'd he beats his silken wings in vain; 130
Or Alum styptics with contracting pow'r
Shrink his thin essence like a rivel'd flow'r:
Or, as Ixion fix'd, the wretch shall feel
The giddy motion of the whirling Mill,
In fumes of burning Chocolate shall glow,
And tremble at the sea that froths below!"
    He spoke; the spirits from the sails descend;
Some, orb in orb, around the nymph extend;
Some thrid the mazy ringlets of her hair;
Some hang upon the pendants of her ear: 140
With beating hearts the dire event they wait,
Anxious, and trembling for the birth of Fate.

CANTO III

Close by those meads, for ever crown'd with flow'rs,
Where Thames with pride surveys his rising tow'rs,
There stands a structure of majestic frame,
Which from the neighb'ring Hampton takes its
    name.
Here Britain's statesmen oft the fall foredoom
Of foreign Tyrants and of Nymphs at home;
Here thou, great Anna! whom three realms obey,
Dost sometimes counsel take—and sometimes Tea.
    Hither the heroes and the nymphs resort,
To taste awhile the pleasures of a Court;   10
In various talk th' instructive hours they past,
Who gave the ball, or paid the visit last;
One speaks the glory of the British Queen,
And one describes a charming Indian screen;
A third interprets motions, looks, and eyes;
At ev'ry word a reputation dies.
Snuff, or the fan, supply each pause of chat,
With singing, laughing, ogling, *and all that.*

Mean while, declining from the noon of day,
The sun obliquely shoots his burning ray; 20
The hungry Judges soon the sentence sign,
And wretches hang that jury-men may dine;
The merchant from th' Exchange returns in peace,
And the long labours of the Toilet cease.
Belinda now, whom thirst of fame invites,
Burns to encounter two advent'rous Knights,
At Ombre singly to decide their doom;
And swells her breast with conquests yet to come.
Straight the three bands prepare in arms to join,
Each band the number of the sacred nine. 30
Soon as she spreads her hand, th' aërial guard
Descend, and sit on each important card:
First Ariel perch'd upon a Matadore,
Then each, according to the rank they bore;
For Sylphs, yet mindful of their ancient race,
Are, as when women, wondrous fond of place.

Behold, four Kings in majesty rever'd,
With hoary whiskers and a forky beard;
And four fair Queens whose hands sustain a flow'r,
Th' expressive emblem of their softer pow'r; 40
Four Knaves in garbs succinct, a trusty band,
Caps on their heads, and halberts in their hand;
And particolour'd troops, a shining train,
Draw forth to combat on the velvet plain.

The skilful Nymph reviews her force with care:
Let Spades be trumps! she said, and trumps they
    were.
Now move to war her sable Matadores,
In show like leaders of the swarthy Moors.
Spadillo³ first, unconquerable Lord!
Led off two captive trumps, and swept the board. 50
As many more Manillio⁴ forc'd to yield,
And march'd a victor from the verdant field.
Him Basto⁵ follow'd, but his fate more hard
Gain'd but one trump and one Plebeian card.
With his broad sabre next, a chief in years,
The hoary Majesty of Spades appears,
Puts forth one manly leg, to sight reveal'd,
The rest, his many-colour'd robe conceal'd.
The rebel Knave, who dares his prince engage,
Proves the just victim of his royal rage. 60
Ev'n mighty Pam,⁶ that Kings and Queens o'er-
    threw
And mow'd down armies in the fights of Lu,
Sad chance of war! now destitute of aid,
Falls undistinguish'd by the victor spade!

³ The ace of spades, the first trump at Ombre.
⁴ The deuce of trumps when trumps are black, the seven
when red.
⁵ The ace of clubs.
⁶ The knave of clubs.

Thus far both armies to Belinda yield;
Now to the Baron fate inclines the field.
His warlike Amazon her host invades,
Th' imperial consort of the crown of Spades.
The Club's black Tyrant first her victim dy'd,
Spite of his haughty mien, and barb'rous pride: 70
What boots the regal circle on his head,
His giant limbs, in state unwieldly spread;
That long behind he trails his pompous robe,
And, of all monarchs, only grasps the globe?

The Baron now his Diamonds pours apace;
Th' embroider'd King who shows but half his face,
And his refulgent Queen, with pow'rs combin'd
Of broken troops an easy conquest find
Clubs, Diamonds, Hearts, in wild disorder seen,
With throngs promiscuous strow the level green. 80
Thus when dispers'd a routed army runs,
Of Asia's troops, and Afric's sable sons,
With like confusion different nations fly,
Of various habit, and of various dye,
The pierc'd battalions dis-united fall,
In heaps on heaps; one fate o'erwhelms them all.

The Knave of Diamonds tries his wily arts,
And wins (oh shameful chance!) the Queen of
    Hearts.
At this, the blood the virgin's cheek forsook,
A livid paleness spreads o'er all her look; 90
She sees, and trembles at th' approaching ill,
Just in the jaws of ruin, and Codille.⁷
And now (as oft in some distemper'd State)
On one nice Trick depends the gen'ral fate.
An Ace of Hearts steps forth: The King unseen
Lurk'd in her hand, and mourn'd his captive
    Queen:
He springs to Vengeance with an eager pace,
And falls like thunder on the prostrate Ace.
The nymph exulting fills with shouts the sky;
The walls, the woods, and long canals reply. 100

Oh thoughtless mortals! ever blind to fate,
Too soon dejected, and too soon elate.
Sudden, these honours shall be snatch'd away,
And curs'd for ever this victorious day.

For lo! the board with cups and spoons is crown'd,
The berries crackle, and the mill turns round;
On shining Altars of Japan they raise
The silver lamp, the fiery spirits blaze:
From silver spouts the grateful liquors glide,
While China's earth receives the smoking tide: 110
At once they gratify their scent and taste,
And frequent cups prolong the rich repast.
Straight hover round the Fair her airy band;
Some, as she sipp'd the fuming liquor fann'd,

⁷ A term in Ombre.

Some o'er her lap their careful plumes display'd,
Trembling, and conscious of the rich brocade.
Coffee, (which makes the politician wise,
And see thro' all things with his half-shut eyes)
Sent up in vapours to the Baron's brain
New Stratagems, the radiant Lock to gain.   120
Ah cease, rash youth! desist ere 't is too late,
Fear the just Gods, and think of Scylla's Fate!
Chang'd to a bird, and sent to flit in air,
She dearly pays for Nisus' injur'd hair!
    But when to mischief mortals bend their will,
How soon they find fit instruments of ill!
Just then, Clarissa drew with tempting grace
A two-edg'd weapon from her shining case:
So Ladies in Romance assist their Knight,
Present the spear, and arm him for the fight.   130
He takes the gift with rev'rence, and extends
The little engine on his fingers' ends;
This just behind Belinda's neck he spread,
As o'er the fragrant steams she bends her head.
Swift to the Lock a thousand Sprites repair,
A thousand wings, by turns, blow back the hair;
And thrice they twitch'd the diamond in her ear;
Thrice she look'd back, and thrice the foe drew near.
Just in that instant, anxious Ariel sought
The close recesses of the Virgin's thought;   140
As on the nosegay in her breast reclin'd,
He watch'd th' Ideas rising in her mind,
Sudden he view'd, in spite of all her art,
An earthly Lover lurking at her heart.
Amaz'd, confus'd, he found his pow'r expir'd,
Resign'd to fate, and with a sigh retir'd.
    The Peer now spreads the glitt'ring Forfex wide,
T' inclose the Lock; now joins it, to divide.
Ev'n then, before the fatal engine clos'd,
A wretched Sylph too fondly interpos'd;   150
Fate urg'd the shears, and cut the Sylph in twain,
(But airy substance soon unites again)
The meeting points the sacred hair dissever
From the fair head, for ever, and for ever!
    Then flash'd the living lightning from her eyes,
And screams of horror rend th' affrighted skies.
Not louder shrieks to pitying heav'n are cast,
When husbands, or when lap-dogs breathe their last;
Or when rich China vessels fall'n from high,
In glitt'ring dust and painted fragments lie!   160
    "Let wreaths of triumph now my temples twine
(The victor cry'd) the glorious Prize is mine!
While fish in streams, or birds delight in air
Or in a coach and six the British Fair,
As long as Atalantis shall be read,
Or the small pillow grace a Lady's bed,
While visits shall be paid on solemn days,

When num'rous wax-lights in bright order blaze,
While nymphs take treats, or assignations give,
So long my honour, name, and praise shall live!"   170
    What Time would spare, from Steel receives its
          date,
And monuments, like men, submit to fate!
Steel could the labour of the Gods destroy,
And strike to dust th' imperial tow'rs of Troy;
Steel could the works of mortal pride confound,
And hew triumphal arches to the ground.
What wonder then, fair nymph! thy hairs should
          feel,
The conqu'ring force of unresisted steel?

CANTO IV

But anxious cares the pensive nymph oppress'd,
And secret passions labour'd in her breast.
Not youthful kings in battle seiz'd alive,
Not scornful virgins who their charms survive,
Not ardent lovers robb'd of all their bliss,
Not ancient ladies when refus'd a kiss,
Not tyrants fierce that unrepenting die,
Not Cynthia when her manteau 's pinn'd awry,
E'er felt such rage, resentment, and despair,
As thou, sad Virgin! for thy ravish'd Hair.   10
    For, that sad moment, when the Sylphs withdrew
And Ariel weeping from Belinda flew,
Umbriel, a dusky, melancholy sprite,
As ever sully'd the fair face of light,
Down to the central earth, his proper scene,
Repair'd to search the gloomy Cave of Spleen.
    Swift on his sooty pinions flits the Gnome,
And in a vapour reach'd the dismal dome.
No cheerful breeze this sullen region knows,
The dreaded East is all the wind that blows.   20
Here in a grotto, shelter'd close from air,
And screen'd in shades from day's detested glare,
She sighs for ever on her pensive bed,
Pain at her side, and Megrim at her head.
    Two handmaids wait the throne: alike in place,
But diff'ring far in figure and in face.
Here stood Ill-nature like an ancient maid,
Her wrinkled form in black and white array'd;
With store of pray'rs, for mornings, nights, and
          noons,
Her hand is fill'd; her bosom with lampoons.   30
    There Affectation, with a sickly mien,
Shows in her cheek the roses of eighteen,
Practis'd to lisp, and hang the head aside,
Faints into airs, and languishes with pride,
On the rich quilt sinks with becoming woe,
Wrapt in a gown, for sickness, and for show.

The fair ones feel such maladies as these,
When each new night-dress gives a new disease.

A constant Vapour o'er the palace flies;
Strange phantoms rising as the mists arise;   40
Dreadful, as hermit's dreams in haunted shades,
Or bright, as visions of expiring maids.
Now glaring fiends, and snakes on rolling spires,
Pale spectres, gaping tombs, and purple fires:
Now lakes of liquid gold, Elysian scenes,
And crystal domes, and angels in machines.

Unnumber'd throngs on every side are seen,
Of bodies chang'd to various forms by Spleen.
Here living Tea-pots stand, one arm held out,
One bent; the handle this, and that the spout: 50
A Pipkin there, like Homer's Tripod walks;
Here sighs a Jar, and there a Goose-pie talks;
Men prove with child, as pow'rful fancy works,
And maids turn'd bottles, call aloud for corks.

Safe past the Gnome thro' this fantastic band,
A branch of healing Spleenwort in his hand.
Then thus address'd the pow'r: "Hail, wayward
      Queen!
Who rule the sex to fifty from fifteen:
Parent of vapours and of female wit,
Who give th' hysteric, or poetic fit,   60
On various tempers act by various ways,
Make some take physic, others scribble plays;
Who cause the proud their visits to delay,
And send the godly in a pet to pray.
A nymph there is, that all thy pow'r disdains,
And thousands more in equal mirth maintains.
But oh! if e'er thy Gnome could spoil a grace,
Or raise a pimple on a beauteous face,
Like Citron-waters matrons cheeks inflame,
Or change complexions at a losing game;   70
If e'er with airy horns I planted heads,
Or rumpled petticoats, or tumbled beds,
Or caus'd suspicion when no soul was rude,
Or discompos'd the head-dress of a Prude,
Or e'er to costive lap-dog gave disease,
Which not the tears of brightest eyes could ease:
Hear me, and touch Belinda with chagrin,
That single act gives half the world the spleen."

The Goddess with a discontented air
Seems to reject him, tho' she grants his pray'r.   80
A wond'rous Bag with both her hands she binds,
Like that where once Ulysses held the winds;
There she collects the force of female lungs,
Sighs, sobs, and passions, and the war of tongues.
A Vial next she fills with fainting fears,
Soft sorrows, melting griefs, and flowing tears.
The Gnome rejoicing bears her gifts away.
Spreads his black wings, and slowly mounts to day.

Sunk in Thalestris' arms the nymph he found,
Her eyes dejected and her hair unbound.   90
Full o'er their heads the swelling bag he rent,
And all the Furies issu'd at the vent.
Belinda burns with more than mortal ire,
And fierce Thalestris fans the rising fire.
"O wretched maid!" she spread her hands, and cry'd,
(While Hampton's echoes, "Wretched maid!"
      reply'd)
"Was it for this you took such constant care
The bodkin, comb, and essence to prepare?
For this your locks in paper durance bound,
For this with tort'ring irons wreath'd around?   100
For this with fillets strain'd your tender head,
And bravely bore the double loads of lead?
Gods! shall the ravisher display your hair,
While the Fops envy, and the Ladies stare!
Honour forbid! at whose unrivall'd shrine
Ease, pleasure, virtue, all our sex resign.
Methinks already I your tears survey,
Already hear the horrid things they say,
Already see you a degraded toast,
And all your honour in a whisper lost!   110
How shall I, then, your helpless fame defend?
'T will then be infamy to seem your friend!
And shall this prize, th' inestimable prize,
Expos'd thro' crystal to the gazing eyes,
And heighten'd by the diamond's circling rays,
On that rapacious hand for ever blaze?
Sooner shall grass in Hyde-park Circus grow,
And wits take lodgings in the sound of Bow;
Sooner let earth, air, sea, to Chaos fall,
Men, monkeys, lap-dogs, parrots, perish all!"   120

She said; then raging to Sir Plume repairs,
And bids her Beau demand the precious hairs:
(Sir Plume of amber snuff-box justly vain,
And the nice conduct of a clouded cane)
With earnest eyes, and round unthinking face,
He first the snuff-box open'd, then the case,
And thus broke out—"My Lord, why, what the
      devil?
Z—ds! damn the lock! 'fore Gad, you must be
      civil!
Plague on 't! 't is past a jest—nay prithee, pox!
Give her the hair"—he spoke, and rapp'd his box. 130

"It grieves me much" (reply'd the Peer again)
"Who speaks so well should ever speak in vain.
But by this Lock, this sacred Lock I swear,
(Which never more shall join its parted hair;
Which never more its honours shall renew,
Clipp'd from the lovely head where late it grew)
That while my nostrils draw the vital air,
This hand, which won it, shall for ever wear."

He spoke, and speaking, in proud triumph spread
The long-contended honours of her head.   140

    But Umbriel, hateful Gnome! forbears not so;
He breaks the Vial whence the sorrows flow.
Then see! the nymph in beauteous grief appears,
Her eyes half-languishing, half-drown'd in tears;
On her heav'd bosom hung her drooping head,
Which, with a sigh, she rais'd; and thus she said.

    "For ever curs'd be this detested day,
Which snatch'd my best, my fav'rite curl away!
Happy! ah ten times happy had I been,
If Hampton-Court these eyes had never seen!   150
Yet am not I the first mistaken maid,
By love of Courts to num'rous ills betray'd.
Oh had I rather un-admir'd remain'd
In some lone isle, or distant Northern land;
Where the gilt Chariot never marks the way,
Where none learn Ombre, none e'er taste Bohea!
There kept my charms conceal'd from mortal eye,
Like roses, that in deserts bloom and die.
What mov'd my mind with youthful Lords to roam?
Oh had I stay'd, and said my pray'rs at home!   160
'T was this, the morning omens seem'd to tell,
Thrice from my trembling hand the patch-box fell;
The tott'ring China shook without a wind,
Nay, Poll sat mute, and Shock was most unkind!
A Sylph too warn'd me of the threats of fate,
In mystic visions, now believ'd too late!
See the poor remnants of these slighted hairs!
My hands shall rend what ev'n thy rapine spares:
These in two sable ringlets taught to break,
Once gave new beauties to the snowy neck;   170
The sister-lock now sits uncouth, alone,
And in its fellow's fate foresees its own;
Uncurl'd it hangs, the fatal shears demands,
And tempts once more thy sacrilegious hands.
Oh hadst thou, cruel! been content to seize
Hairs less in sight, or any hairs but these!"

CANTO V

She said: the pitying audience melt in tears.
But Fate and Jove had stopp'd the Baron's ears.
In vain Thalestris with reproach assails,
For who can move when fair Belinda fails?
Not half so fix'd the Trojan could remain,
While Anna begg'd and Dido rag'd in vain.
Then grave Clarissa graceful wav'd her fan;
Silence ensu'd, and thus the nymph began.

    "Say why are Beauties prais'd and honour'd most,
The wise man's passion, and the vain man's toast?   10
Why deck'd with all that land and sea afford,
Why Angels call'd, and Angel-like ador'd?

Why round our coaches crowd the white-glov'd
    Beaux,
Why bows the side-box from its inmost rows;
How vain are all these glories, all our pains,
Unless good sense preserve what beauty gains:
That men may say, when we the front-box grace:
'Behold the first in virtue as in face!'
Oh! if to dance all night, and dress all day,
Charm'd the small-pox, or chas'd old-age away;   20
Who would not scorn what housewife's cares pro-
    duce,
Or who would learn one earthly thing of use?
To patch, nay ogle, might become a Saint,
Nor could it sure be such a sin to paint.
But since, alas! frail beauty must decay,
Curl'd or uncurl'd, since Locks will turn to grey;
Since painted, or not painted, all shall fade,
And she who scorns a man, must die a maid;
What then remains but well our pow'r to use,
And keep good-humour still whate'er we lose?   30
And trust me, dear! good-humour can prevail,
When airs, and flights, and screams, and scolding
    fail.
Beauties in vain their pretty eyes may roll;
Charms strike the sight, but merit wins the soul."

    So spoke the Dame, but no applause ensu'd;
Belinda frown'd, Thalestris call'd her Prude.
"To arms, to arms!" the fierce Virago cries,
And swift as lightning to the combat flies.
All side in parties, and begin th' attack;
Fans clap, silks rustle, and tough whalebones
    crack;   40
Heroes' and Heroines' shouts confus'dly rise,
And bass, and treble voices strike the skies.
No common weapons in their hands are found,
Like Gods they fight, nor dread a mortal wound.

    So when bold Homer makes the Gods engage,
And heav'nly breasts with human passions rage;
'Gainst Pallas, Mars; Latona, Hermes arms;
And all Olympus rings with loud alarms:
Jove's thunder roars, heav'n trembles all around,
Blue Neptune storms, the bellowing deeps re-
    sound: 50
Earth shakes her nodding tow'rs, the ground gives
    way,
And the pale ghosts start at the flash of day!

    Triumphant Umbriel on a sconce's height
Clapp'd his glad wings, and sate to view the fight:
Propp'd on their bodkin spears, the Sprites survey
The growing combat, or assist the fray.

    While thro' the press enrag'd Thalestris flies,
And scatters death around from both her eyes,
A Beau and Witling perish'd in the throng,

One died in metaphor, and one in song. 60
"O cruel nymph! a living death I bear,"
Cry'd Dapperwit, and sunk beside his chair.
A mournful glance Sir Fopling upwards cast,
"Those eyes are made so killing"—was his last.
Thus on Maeander's flow'ry margin lies
Th' expiring Swan, and as he sings he dies.

When bold Sir Plume had drawn Clarissa down,
Chloe stepp'd in, and kill'd him with a frown;
She smil'd to see the doughty hero slain,
But, at her smile, the Beau reviv'd again. 70

Now Jove suspends his golden scales in air,
Weighs the Men's wits against the Lady's hair;
The doubtful beam long nods from side to side;
At length the wits mount up, the hairs subside.

See, fierce Belinda on the Baron flies,
With more than usual lightning in her eyes:
Nor fear'd the Chief th' unequal fight to try,
Who sought no more than on his foe to die.
But this bold Lord with manly strength endu'd,
She with one finger and a thumb subdu'd: 80
Just where the breath of life his nostrils drew,
A charge of Snuff the wily virgin threw;
The Gnomes direct, to ev'ry atom just,
The pungent grains of titillating dust.
Sudden, with starting tears each eye o'erflows,
And the high dome re-echoes to his nose.

"Now meet thy fate," incens'd Belinda cry'd,
And drew a deadly bodkin from her side.
(The same, his ancient personage to deck,
Her great great grandsire wore about his neck, 90
In three seal-rings; which after, melted down,
Form'd a vast buckle for his widow's gown:
Her infant grandame's whistle next it grew,
The bells she jingled, and the whistle blew;
Then in a bodkin grac'd her mother's hairs,
Which long she wore, and now Belinda wears.)

"Boast not my fall" (he cry'd) "insulting foe!
Thou by some other shalt be laid as low,
Nor think, to die dejects my lofty mind:
All that I dread is leaving you behind! 100
Rather than so, ah let me still survive,
And burn in Cupid's flames—but burn alive."

"Restore the Lock!" she cries; and all around
"Restore the Lock!" the vaulted roofs rebound.
Not fierce Othello in so loud a strain
Roar'd for the handkerchief that caus'd his pain.
But see how oft ambitious aims are cross'd,
And chiefs contend 'till all the prize is lost!
The Lock, obtain'd with guilt, and kept with pain,
In ev'ry place is sought, but sought in vain: 110
With such a prize no mortal must be blest,
So heav'n decrees! with heav'n who can contest?

Some thought it mounted to the Lunar sphere,
Since all things lost on earth are treasur'd there.
There Heros' wits are kept in pond'rous vases,
And beaux', in snuff-boxes and tweezer-cases.
There broken vows and death-bed alms are found,
And lovers' hearts with ends of riband bound,
The courtier's promises, and sick man's pray'rs,
The smiles of harlots, and the tears of heirs, 120
Cages for gnats, and chains to yoke a flea,
Dry'd butterflies, and tomes of casuistry.

But trust the Muse—she saw it upward rise,
Tho' mark'd by none but quick, poetic eyes:
(So Rome's great founder to the heav'ns withdrew,
To Proculus alone confess'd in view)
A sudden Star, it shot thro' liquid air,
And drew behind a radiant trail of hair.
Not Berenice's Locks first rose so bright,
The heav'ns bespangling with dishevell'd light. 130
The Sylphs behold it kindling as it flies,
And pleas'd pursue its progress thro' the skies.

This the Beau monde shall from the Mall survey,
And hail with music its propitious ray.
This the blest Lover shall for Venus take,
And send up vows from Rosamonda's lake.
This Partridge soon shall view in cloudless skies,
When next he looks thro' Galileo's eyes;
And hence th' egregious wizard shall foredoom
The fate of Louis, and the fall of Rome. 140

Then cease, bright Nymph! to mourn thy ravish'd
hair,
Which adds new glory to the shining sphere!
Not all the tresses that fair head can boast,
Shall draw such envy as the Lock you lost.
For, after all the murders of your eye,
When after millions slain, yourself shall die:
When those fair suns shall set, as set they must,
And all those tresses shall be laid in dust,
This Lock, the Muse shall consecrate to fame,
And 'midst the stars inscribe Belinda's name. 150

Epistle to Dr. Arbuthnot,

BEING THE

PROLOGUE TO THE SATIRES

P. Shut, shut the door, good John! fatigu'd, I said,
Tie up the knocker, say I 'm sick, I 'm dead.
The Dog-star rages! nay 't is past a doubt,
All Bedlam, or Parnassus, is let out:
Fire in each eye, and papers in each hand,
They rave, recite, and madden round the land.

What walls can guard me, or what shade can hide?
They pierce my thickets, thro' my Grot they glide;
By land, by water, they renew the charge;
They stop the chariot, and they board the barge. 10
No place is sacred, not the Church is free;
Ev'n Sunday shines no Sabbath-day to me;
Then from the Mint walks forth the Man of rhyme,
Happy to catch me just at Dinner-time.

Is there a Parson, much bemus'd in beer,
A maudlin Poetess, a rhyming Peer,
A Clerk, foredoom'd his father's soul to cross,
Who pens a Stanza, when he should *engross*?
Is there, who, lock'd from ink and paper, scrawls
With desp'rate charcoal round his darken'd walls? 20
All fly to Twit'nam, and in humble strain
Apply to me, to keep them mad or vain.
Arthur, whose giddy son neglects the Laws,
Imputes to me and my damn'd works the cause:
Poor Cornus sees his frantic wife elope,
And curses Wit, and Poetry, and Pope.

Friend to my Life! (which did not you prolong,
The world had wanted many an idle song)
What *Drop* or *Nostrum* can this plague remove?
Or which must end me, a Fool's wrath or love? 30
A dire dilemma! either way I 'm sped,
If foes, they write, if friends, they read me dead.
Seiz'd and tied down to judge, how wretched I!
Who can't be silent, and who will not lie.
To laugh, were want of goodness and of grace,
And to be grave, exceeds all Pow'r of face.
I sit with sad civility, I read
With honest anguish, and an aching head;
And drop at last, but in unwilling ears,
This saving counsel, "Keep your piece nine years." 40

"Nine years!" cries he, who high in Drury-lane,
Lull'd by soft Zephyrs thro' the broken pane,
Rhymes ere he wakes, and prints before *Term* ends,
Oblig'd by hunger, and request of friends:
"The piece, you think, is incorrect? why, take it,
I'm all submission, what you 'd have it, make it."

Three things another's modest wishes bound,
My Friendship, and a Prologue, and ten pound.
Pitholeon sends to me: "You know his Grace,
I want a Patron; ask him for a Place." 50
'Pitholeon libell'd me,'—'but here 's a letter
Informs you, Sir, 't was when he knew no better.
Dare you refuse him? Curll invites to dine,
He 'll write a *Journal*, or he 'll turn Divine."

Bless me! a packet.—"'T is a stranger sues,
A Virgin Tragedy, an Orphan Muse."
If I dislike it, "Furies, death and rage!"

If I approve, "Commend it to the Stage."
There (thank my stars) my whole Commission ends,
The Play'rs and I are, luckily, no friends, 60
Fir'd that the house reject him, "'Sdeath I'll print it,
And shame the fools——Your Int'rest, Sir, with Lintot!"
'Lintot, dull rogue! will think your price too much:'
"Not, sir, if you revise it, and retouch."
All my demurs but double his Attacks;
At last he whispers, "Do; and we go snacks."
Glad of a quarrel, straight I clap the door,
Sir, let me see your works and you no more.

'T is sung, when Midas' Ears began to spring,
(Midas, a sacred person and a king) 70
His very Minister who spy'd them first,
(Some say his Queen) was forc'd to speak, or burst.
And is not mine, my friend, a sorer case,
When ev'ry coxcomb perks them in my face?
A. Good friend, forbear! you deal in dang'rous things.
I 'd never name Queens, Ministers, or Kings;
Keep close to Ears, and those let asses prick;
'T is nothing— P. Nothing? if they bite and kick?
Out with it, Dunciad! let the secret pass,
That secret to each fool, that he 's an Ass: 80
The truth once told (and wherefore should we lie?)
The Queen of Midas slept, and so may I.

You think this cruel? take it for a rule,
No creature smarts so little as a fool.
Let peals of laughter, Codrus! round thee break,
Thou unconcern'd canst hear the mighty crack:
Pit, Box, and gall'ry in convulsions hurl'd,
Thou stand'st unshook amidst a bursting world.
Who shames a Scribbler? break one cobweb thro',
He spins the slight, self-pleasing thread anew: 90
Destroy his fib or sophistry, in vain,
The creature 's at his dirty work again,
Thron'd in the centre of his thin designs,
Proud of a vast extent of flimsy lines!
Whom have I hurt? has Poet yet, or Peer,
Lost the arch'd eye-brow, or Parnassian sneer?
And has not Colley still his Lord, and whore?
His Butchers Henley, his free-masons Moore?
Does not one table Bavius still admit?
Still to one Bishop Philips seem a wit? 100
Still Sappho— A. Hold! for God's sake—you 'll offend,
No Names!—be calm!—learn prudence of a friend!
I too could write, and I am twice as tall;
But foes like these— P. One Flatt'rer 's worse than all.

Of all mad creatures, if the learn'd are right,
It is the slaver kills, and not the bite.
A fool quite angry is quite innocent:
Alas! 't is ten times worse when they *repent.*

   One dedicates in high heroic prose,
And ridicules beyond a hundred foes: 110
One from all Grubstreet will my fame defend,
And more abusive, calls himself my friend.
This prints my *Letters,* that expects a bribe,
And others roar aloud, "Subscribe, subscribe."

   There are, who to my person pay their court:
I cough like *Horace,* and, tho' lean, am short,
Ammon's great son one shoulder had too high,
Such *Ovid's* nose, and "Sir! you have an Eye"—
Go on, obliging creatures, make me see
All that disgrac'd my Betters, met in me.   120
Say for my comfort, languishing in bed,
"Just so immortal *Maro* held his head:"
And when I die, be sure you let me know
Great *Homer* died three thousand years ago.

   Why did I write? what sin to me unknown
Dipt me in ink, my parents', or my own?
As yet a child, nor yet a fool to fame,
I lisp'd in numbers, for the numbers came.
I left no calling for this idle trade,
No duty broke, no father disobey'd.   130
The Muse but serv'd to ease some friend, not Wife,
To help me thro' this long disease, my Life,
To second, Arbuthnot! thy Art and Care,
And teach the Being you preserv'd, to bear.

   But why then publish? *Granville* the polite,
And knowing *Walsh,* would tell me I could write;
Well-natur'd *Garth* inflam'd with early praise;
And *Congreve* lov'd, and *Swift* endur'd my lays;
The Courtly *Talbot, Somers, Sheffield,* read;
Ev'n mitred *Rochester* would nod the head,   140
And *St. John's* self (great *Dryden's* friends before)
With open arms receiv'd one Poet more.
Happy my studies, when by these approv'd!
Happier their author, when by these belov'd!
From these the world will judge of men and books,
Not from the *Burnets, Oldmixons,* and *Cookes.*

   Soft were my numbers; who could take offence,
While pure Description held the place of Sense?
Like gentle *Fanny's* was my flow'ry theme,
A painted mistress, or a purling stream.   150
Yet then did *Gildon* draw his venal quill;—
I wish'd the man a dinner, and sat still.
Yet then did *Dennis* rave in furious fret;
I never answer'd,—I was not in debt.
If want provok'd, or madness made them print,
I wag'd no war with *Bedlam* or the *Mint.*

   Did some more sober Critic come abroad;

If wrong, I smil'd; if right, I kiss'd the rod.
Pains, reading, study, are their just pretence,
And all they want is spirit, taste, and sense.   160
Commas and points they set exactly right,
And 't were a sin to rob them of their mite.
Yet ne'er one sprig of laurel grac'd these ribalds,
From slashing *Bentley* down to pidling *Tibalds:*
Each wight, who reads not, and but scans and
    spells,
Each Word-catcher, that lives on syllables,
Ev'n such small Critics some regard may claim,
Preserv'd in *Milton's* or in *Shakespeare's* name.
Pretty! in amber to observe the forms
Of hairs, or straws, or dirt, or grubs, or worms!   170
The things, we know, are neither rich nor rare,
But wonder how the devil they got there.

   Were others angry: I excus'd them too;
Well might they rage, I gave them but their due.
A man's true merit 'tis not hard to find;
But each man's secret standard in his mind,
That Casting-weight pride adds to emptiness,
This, who can gratify? for who can *guess?*
The Bard whom pilfer'd Pastorals renown,
Who turns a Persian tale for half a Crown,   180
Just writes to make his barrenness appear,
And strains, from hard-bound brains, eight lines a
    year;
He, who still wanting, tho' he lives on theft,
Steals much, spends little, yet has nothing left:
And He, who now to sense, now nonsense leaning,
Means not, but blunders round about a meaning:
And He, whose fustian's so sublimely bad,
It is not Poetry, but prose run mad:
All these, my modest Satire bade *translate,*
And own'd that nine such Poets made a *Tate.*   190
How did they fume, and stamp, and roar, and chafe!
And swear, not Addison himself was safe.

   Peace to all such! but were there One whose fires
True Genius kindles, and fair Fame inspires;
Blest with each talent and each art to please,
And born to write, converse, and live with ease:
Should such a man, too fond to rule alone,
Bear, like the Turk, no brother near the throne.
View him with scornful, yet with jealous eyes,
And hate for arts that caus'd himself to rise;   200
Damn with faint praise, assent with civil leer,
And without sneering, teach the rest to sneer;
Willing to wound, and yet afraid to strike,
Just hint a fault, and hesitate dislike;
Alike reserv'd to blame, or to commend,
A tim'rous foe, and a suspicious friend;
Dreading ev'n fools, by Flatterers besieg'd,
And so obliging, that he ne'er oblig'd;

Like *Cato*, give his little Senate laws,
And sit attentive to his own applause;   210
While Wits and Templars ev'ry sentence raise,
And wonder with a foolish face of praise:——
Who but must laugh, if such a man there be?
Who would not weep, if Atticus [1] were he?
    What tho' my Name stood rubric on the walls
Or plaister'd posts, with claps, in capitals?
Or smoking forth, a hundred hawkers' load,
On wings of winds came flying all abroad?
I sought no homage from the Race that write;
I kept, like *Asian* Monarchs, from their sight: 220
Poems I heeded (now be-rhym'd so long)
No more than thou, great George! a birth-day song.
I ne'er with wits or witlings pass'd my days,
To spread about the itch of verse and praise;
Nor like a puppy, daggled thro' the town,
To fetch and carry sing-song up and down;
Nor at Rehearsals sweat, and mouth'd, and cry'd,
With handkerchief and orange at my side;
But sick of fops, and poetry, and prate,
To *Bufo* [2] left the whole *Castalian* state.   230
    Proud as *Apollo* on his forked hill,
Sat full-blown *Bufo,* puff'd by ev'ry quill;
Fed with soft Dedication all day long,
Horace and he went hand in hand in song.
His Library (where busts of Poets dead
And a true *Pindar* stood without a head,)
Receiv'd of wits an undistinguish'd race,
Who first his judgment ask'd, and then a place:
Much they extoll'd his pictures, much his seat,
And flatter'd ev'ry day, and some days eat: 240
Till grown more frugal in his riper days,
He paid some bards with port, and some with praise;
To some a dry rehearsal was assign'd,
And others (harder still) he paid in kind.
Dryden alone (what wonder?) came not nigh,
Dryden alone escap'd this judging eye:
But still the *Great* have kindness in reserve,
He help'd to bury whom he help'd to starve.
    May some choice patron bless each gray goose quill!
May ev'ry *Bavius* have his *Bufo* still!   250
So, when a Statesman wants a day's defence,
Or Envy holds a whole week's war with Sense,
Or simple pride for flatt'ry makes demands,
May dunce by dunce be whistled off my hands!
Blest be the *Great!* for those they take away,
And those they left me; for they left me Gay; [3]
Left me to see neglected Genius bloom,

Neglected die, and tell it on his tomb:
Of all thy blameless life the sole return   210
My Verse, and Queensb'ry weeping o'er thy urn.   260
    Oh let me live my own, and die so too!
(To live and die is all I have to do:)
Maintain a Poet's dignity and ease,
And see what friends, and read what books I please;
Above a Patron, tho' I condescend
Sometimes to call a minister my friend.
I was not born for Courts or great affairs;
I pay my debts, believe, and say my pray'rs;
Can sleep without a Poem in my head;
Nor know, if *Dennis* be alive or dead.   270
    Why am I ask'd what next shall see the light?
Heav'ns! was I born for nothing but to write?
Has Life no joys for me? or, (to be grave)
Have I no friend to serve, no soul to save?
"I found him close with *Swift*"—'Indeed? no doubt,'
(Cries prating *Balbus*) 'something will come out.'
'T is all in vain, deny it as I will.
'No, such a Genius never can lie still;'
And then for mine obligingly mistakes
The first Lampoon Sir *Will.* or *Bubo* makes.   280
Poor guiltless I! and can I choose but smile,
When ev'ry Coxcomb knows me by my *Style?*
    Curst be the verse, how well soe'er it flow,
That tends to make one worthy man my foe,
Give Virtue scandal, Innocence a fear,
Or from the soft-eyed Virgin steal a tear.
But he who hurts a harmless neighbour's peace,
Insults fall'n worth, or Beauty in distress,
Who loves a Lie, lame Slander helps about,
Who writes a Libel, or who copies out: 290
That Fop, whose pride affects a patron's name,
Yet absent, wounds an author's honest fame:
Who can *your* merit *selfishly* approve,
And show the *sense* of it without the *love*;
Who has the vanity to call you friend,
Yet wants the honour, injur'd, to defend;
Who tells whate'er you think, whate'er you say,
And, if he lie not, must at least betray:
Who to the *Dean*, and *silver bell* can swear,
And sees at *Canons* what was never there;   300
Who reads, but with a lust to misapply,
Make Satire a Lampoon, and Fiction, Lie.
A lash like mine no honest man shall dread,
But all such babbling blockheads in his stead.
    Let *Sporus* [4] tremble— A. What? that thing of silk,
Sporus, that mere white curd of Ass's milk?
Satire or sense, alas! can *Sporus* feel?

[1] I.e., Addison.
[2] A literary patron, perhaps the Earl of Halifax.
[3] John Gay, author of *The Beggar's Opera.*
[4] I.e., Lord Harvey.

Who breaks a butterfly upon a wheel?
P. Yet let me flap this bug with gilded wings,
This painted child of dirt, that stinks and stings; 310
Whose buzz the witty and the fair annoys,
Yet wit ne'er tastes, and beauty ne'er enjoys:
So well-bred spaniels civilly delight
In mumbling of the game they dare not bite.
Eternal smiles his emptiness betray,
As shallow streams run dimpling all the way.
Whether in florid impotence he speaks,
And, as the prompter breathes, the puppet squeaks;
Or at the ear of *Eve*, familiar Toad,
Half froth, half venom, spits himself abroad,   320
In puns, or politics, or tales, or lies,
Or spite, or smut, or rhymes, or blasphemies.
His wit all see-saw, between *that* and *this,*
Now high, now low, now master up, now miss,
And he himself one vile Antithesis.
Amphibious thing! that acting either part.
The trifling head or the corrupted heart,
Fop at the toilet, flatt'rer at the board,
Now trips a Lady, and now struts a Lord.
Eve's tempter thus the Rabbins have exprest,   330
A Cherub's face, a reptile all the rest;
Beauty that shocks you, parts that none will trust;
Wit that can creep, and pride that licks the dust.

  Not Fortune's worshipper, nor fashion's fool,
Not Lucre's madman, nor Ambition's tool,
Not proud, or servile;—be one Poet's praise,
That, if he pleas'd, he pleas'd by manly ways:
That Flatt'ry, ev'n to Kings, be held a shame,
And thought a Lie in verse or prose the same.
That not in Fancy's maze he wander'd long,   340
But stoop'd to Truth, and moraliz'd his song:
That not for Fame, but Virtue's better end,
He stood the furious foe, the timid friend,
The damning critic, half approving wit,
The coxcomb hit, or fearing to be hit;
Laugh'd at the loss of friends he never had,
The dull, the proud, the wicked, and the mad;
The distant threats of vengeance on his head,
The blow unfelt, the tear he never shed;
The tale reviv'd, the lie so oft o'erthrown,   350
Th' imputed trash, and dulness not his own;
The morals blacken'd when the writings scape,
The libell'd person, and the pictur'd shape;
Abuse, on all he lov'd, or lov'd him, spread,
A friend in exile, or a father, dead;
The whisper, that to greatness still too near,
Perhaps, yet vibrates on his Sov'reign's ear:
Welcome for thee, fair *Virtue!* all the past;
For thee, fair *Virtue!* welcome ev'n the *last!*
  A. But why insult the poor, affront the great? 360

P. A knave 's a knave, to me, in ev'ry state:
Alike my scorn, if he succeed or fail,
Sporus at court, or *Japhet* in a jail,
A hireling scribbler, or a hireling peer,
Knight of the post corrupt, or of the shire;
If on a Pillory, or near a Throne,
He gain his Prince's ear, or lose his own.
  Yet soft by nature, more a dupe than wit,
Sappho can tell you how this man was bit;
This dreaded Sat'rist *Dennis* will confess   370
Foe to his pride, but friend to his distress:
So humble, he has knock'd at *Tibbald's* door,
Has drunk with *Cibber,* nay has rhym'd for *Moore.*
Full ten years slander'd, did he once reply?
Three thousand suns went down on *Welsted's* lie.
To please a Mistress one aspers'd his life;
He lash'd him not, but let her be his wife.
Let *Budgel* charge low *Grubstreet* on his quill,
And write whate'er he pleas'd, except his Will;
Let the two *Curlls* of Town and Court, abuse   380
His father, mother, body, soul, and muse.
Yet why? that Father held it for a rule,
It was a sin to call our neighbour fool:
That harmless Mother thought no wife a whore:
Hear this, and spare his family, *James Moore!*
Unspotted names, and memorable long!
If there be force in Virtue, or in Song.
  Of gentle blood (part shed in Honour's cause,
While yet in *Britain* Honour had applause)
Each parent sprung— A. What fortune, pray?—   390
              P. Their own,
And better got, than *Bestia's* from the throne.
Born to no Pride, inheriting no Strife,
Nor marrying Discord in a noble wife,
Stranger to civil and religious rage,
The good man walk'd innoxious thro' his age.
Nor Courts he saw, no suits would ever try,
Nor dar'd an Oath, nor hazarded a Lie.
Un-learn'd, he knew no schoolman's subtle art,
No language, but the language of the heart.
By Nature honest, by Experience wise,   400
Healthy by temp'rance, and by exercise;
His life, tho' long, to sickness past unknown,
His death was instant, and without a groan.
O grant me, thus to live, and thus to die!
Who sprung from Kings shall know less joy than I.
  O Friend! may each domestic bliss be thine!
Be no unpleasing Melancholy mine:
Me, let the tender office long engage,
To rock the cradle of reposing Age,
With lenient arts extend a Mother's breath,   410
Make Languor smile, and smooth the bed of Death,
Explore the thought, explain the asking eye,

And keep a while one parent from the sky!
On cares like these if length of days attend,
May Heav'n, to bless those days, preserve my friend,
Preserve him social, cheerful, and serene,
And just as rich as when he serv'd a Queen.
A. Whether that blessing be deny'd or giv'n,
Thus far was right, the rest belongs to Heav'n.

◆

JAMES BOSWELL

1740–1795

James Boswell, the greatest English biographer and autobiographer, was born in Scotland, son of the Laird of Auchinleck, and, as he liked to boast, the descendant of nine belted earls. Educated in law at the universities of Edinburgh and Utrecht, he made a success of his legal practice in Scotland before he gave it up to his stronger aspiration to be a famous London lawyer. Boswell always was interested in celebrities; he therefore sought out and became acquainted with some of the most distinguished people in Europe: General Paoli, Voltaire, Rousseau, Sir Joshua Reynolds, and others, in addition to his famous friendship with Dr. Johnson. But Boswell was no insignificant toady, as many have mistakenly thought. A distinguished aristocrat, a *bon vivant* with considerable social charm, great men were thoroughly appreciative of his company. The personality of Boswell is fascinating and paradoxical, for as Frederick A. Pottle, the celebrated Boswellian scholar has said, he was "a sincerely religious man with an unusual capacity for worship, and he was also a notable fornicator. He savored as few others have the delights of intellectual conversation, and he was a sensualist. He was weak of will, and he sat up all night through four nights in one week to record Johnson's conversation. He loved Scotland deeply, and he preferred to live in England. He was inordinately proud of his ancestry and his status as a gentleman, and he associated with the lowest of low people. He was an affectionate husband, painfully dependent on his wife, and he was unfaithful to her. . . . He was dissipated and restless, and he carried on an extensive legal practice. He was often gloomy to

the point of suicide, and Mrs. Thrale gave him a perfect score for good humor."[1] His two great weaknesses were alcohol and women, for he was a social drunkard, though not a solitary alcoholic, and a consorter with prostitutes. His whole neurotic personality exhibits the striking inconsistencies and paradoxes that often characterize the Romantic temperament, and indeed, in an age less dominated by powerful Neo-classic minds, it is almost certain that Boswell would have been a thorough-going Romantic writer. A man of sound intellect, though he often played the fool, he nevertheless was no fool.

It is one of the curiosities of literature that the author of *The Life of Samuel Johnson, LL.D.*, generally conceded to be one of the ten greatest works in English prose, should not be called a great writer. Yet it surely follows that the author of a great book must be a great author, no matter what the foibles and follies of his private life may have been. At the beginning of his *Life of Johnson*, Boswell asserted, "I will now venture to say that he will be seen in this work more completely than any man who has ever yet lived." This promise he fulfilled; and Dr. Johnson has for generations been better known (and, by more than a few, better loved) than any other character in history or literature. For Boswell was no mere reporter, notebook in hand, jotting down the conversations of the great. He was a highly imaginative writer, with the gift of almost total recall, who knew how to select and focus his material into a genuine work of art, and who also knew how to manufacture material by leading and eliciting interesting conversations. These are the qualities which make his *Life of Johnson* the greatest biography ever written, for from it we not only learn what Johnson said and did, but we even know how he would react to a new situation and what he would probably do or say under almost any circumstance.

The discovery of Boswell's own private *Journal*, which covers with frankness and almost perfect completeness his whole adult life from 1761 to 1794, now bids fair to make Boswell succeed Johnson as the best known man who ever lived. Covering a large segment of the eighteenth century in thoroughly complete detail, it will almost certainly

[1] Frederick A. Pottle, "The Life of Boswell," *The Yale Review*, XXXV (March, 1946), 455.

supersede Pepy's *Diary* as the greatest English work of this sort. With the addition of the vast new Boswell papers, estimated at forty-five volumes, the once depreciated Boswell is destined to assume his rightful place among the greatest English writers of prose.

FURTHER READING

POTTLE, F. A., ed. *Boswell in Holland: 1763–64* (New York, 1952).
POTTLE, F. A., ed. *Boswell's London Journal* (New York, 1950).
POTTLE, F. A., ed. *The Literary Career of James Boswell* (Oxford, 1929).
SCOTT, GEOFFREY, and POTTLE, F. A. *The Private Papers of James Boswell from Malahide Castle* (Mt. Vernon, N. Y., 1928–34).

The Life of Samuel Johnson, LL.D.

THE YEAR 1763

THIS is to me a memorable year; for in it I had the happiness to obtain the acquaintance of that extraordinary man whose memoirs I am now writing; an acquaintance which I shall ever esteem as one of the most fortunate circumstances in my life. Though then but two-and-twenty, I had for several years read his works with delight and instruction, and had the highest reverence for their authour, which had grown up in my fancy into a kind of mysterious veneration, by figuring to myself a state of solemn elevated abstraction, in which I supposed him to live in the immense metropolis of London. Mr. Gentleman, a native of Ireland, who passed some years in Scotland as a player, and as an instructor in the English language, a man whose talents and worth were depressed by misfortunes, had given me a representation of the figure and manner of DICTIONARY JOHNSON as he was then generally called; and during my first visit to London, which was for three months in 1760, Mr. Derrick the poet, who was Gentleman's friend and countryman, flattered me with hopes that he would introduce me to Johnson, an honour of which I was very ambitious. But he never found an opportunity; which made me doubt that he had promised to do what was not in his power; till Johnson some years afterwards told me, "Derrick, Sir, might very well have introduced you. I had a kindness for Derrick, and am sorry he is dead." . . .

Mr. Thomas Davies the actor, who then kept a bookseller's shop in Russel-street, Covent-garden,[1] told me that Johnson was very much his friend, and came frequently to his house, where he more than once invited me to meet him: but by some unlucky accident or other he was prevented from coming to us.

Mr. Thomas Davies was a man of good understanding and talents, with the advantage of a liberal education. Though somewhat pompous, he was an entertaining companion; and his literary performances have no inconsiderable share of merit. He was a friendly and very hospitable man. Both he and his wife, (who has been celebrated for her beauty,) though upon the stage for many years, maintained an uniform decency of character; and Johnson esteemed them, and lived in as easy an intimacy with them as with any family which he used to visit. Mr. Davies recollected several of Johnson's remarkable sayings, and was one of the best of the many imitators of his voice and manner, while relating them. He increased my impatience more and more to see the extraordinary man whose works I highly valued, and whose conversation was reported to be so peculiarly excellent.

At last, on Monday the 16th of May, when I was sitting in Mr. Davies's back-parlour, after having drunk tea with him and Mrs. Davies, Johnson unexpectedly came into the shop;[2] and Mr. Davies having perceived him through the glass-door in the room in which we were sitting, advancing towards us,—he announced his awful approach to me, somewhat in the manner of an actor in the part of Horatio, when he addresses Hamlet on the appearance of his father's ghost, "Look, my Lord, it comes." I found that I had a very perfect idea of Johnson's figure, from the portrait of him painted by Sir

[1] No. 8.—The very place where I was fortunate enough to be introduced to the illustrious subject of this work, deserves to be particularly marked. I never pass by it without feeling reverence and regret.
[2] Mr. Murphy in his "Essay on the Life and Genius of Dr. Johnson," has given an account of this meeting considerably different from mine, I am persuaded without any consciousness of errour. His memory, at the end of near thirty years, has undoubtedly deceived him, and he supposes himself to have been present at a scene, which he has probably heard inaccurately described by others. In my note *taken on the very day*, in which I am confident I marked every thing material that passed, no mention is made of this gentleman; and I am sure, that I should not have omitted one so well known in the literary world. It may easily be imagined that this my first interview with Dr. Johnson, with all its circumstances, made a strong impression on my mind, and would be registered with peculiar attention.

Joshua Reynolds soon after he had published his Dictionary, in the attitude of sitting in his easy chair in deep meditation; which was the first picture his friend did for him, which Sir Joshua very kindly presented to me, and from which an engraving has been made for this work. Mr. Davies mentioned my name, and respectfully introduced me to him. I was much agitated; and recollecting his prejudice against the Scotch, of which I had heard much, I said to Davies, "Don't tell where I come from."—"From Scotland," cried Davies, roguishly. "Mr. Johnson, (said I) I do indeed come from Scotland, but I cannot help it." I am willing to flatter myself that I meant this as light pleasantry to soothe and conciliate him, and not as an humiliating abasement at the expense of my country. But however that might be, this speech was somewhat unlucky; for with that quickness of wit for which he was so remarkable, he seized the expression "come from Scotland," which I used in the sense of being of that country; and, as if I had said that I had come away from it, or left it, retorted, "That, Sir, I find is what a very great many of your countrymen cannot help." This stroke stunned me a good deal; and when we had sat down, I felt myself not a little embarrassed, and apprehensive of what might come next. He then addressed himself to Davies: "What do you think of Garrick? He has refused me an order for the play for Miss Williams, because he knows the house will be full, and that an order would be worth three shillings." Eager to take any opening to get into conversation with him, I ventured to say, "O, Sir, I cannot think Mr. Garrick would grudge such a trifle to you." "Sir, (said he, with a stern look,) I have known David Garrick longer than you have done: and I know no right you have to talk to me on the subject." Perhaps I deserved this check; for it was rather presumptuous in me, an entire stranger, to express any doubt of the justice of his animadversion upon his old acquaintance and pupil.[3] I now felt myself much mortified, and began to think, that the hope which I had long indulged of obtaining his acquaintance was blasted. And, in truth, had not my ardour been uncommonly strong, and my resolution uncom-

monly persevering, so rough a reception might have deterred me for ever from making any further attempts. Fortunately, however, I remained upon the field not wholly discomfited; and was soon rewarded by hearing some of his conversation, of which I preserved the following short minute, without marking the questions and observations by which it was produced.

"People (he remarked) may be taken in once, who imagine that an authour is greater in private life than other men. Uncommon parts require uncommon opportunities for their exertion.

"In barbarous society, superiority of parts is of real consequence. Great strength or great wisdom is of much value to an individual. But in more polished times there are people to do every thing for money; and then there are a number of other superiorities, such as those of birth and fortune, and rank, that dissipate men's attention, and leave no extraordinary share of respect for personal and intellectual superiority. This is wisely ordered by Providence, to preserve some equality among mankind."

"Sir, this book ('The Elements of Criticism,' which he had taken up,) is a pretty essay, and deserves to be held in some estimation, though much of it is chimerical."

Speaking of one who with more than ordinary boldness attacked publick measures and the royal family, he said, "I think he is safe from the law, but he is an abusive scoundrel; and instead of applying to my Lord Chief Justice to punish him, I would send half a dozen footmen and have him well ducked."

"The notion of liberty amuses the people of England, and helps to keep off the *tedium vitae*. When a butcher tells you that *his heart bleeds for his country*, he has, in fact, no uneasy feeling."

"Sheridan will not succeed at Bath with his oratory. Ridicule has gone down before him, and I doubt, Derrick is his enemy.[4]

"Derrick may do very well, as long as he can outrun his character; but the moment his character gets up with him, it is all over."

It is, however, but just to record, that some years afterwards, when I reminded him of this sarcasm, he said, "Well, but Derrick has now got a character that he need not run away from."

I was highly pleased with the extraordinary vigour of his conversation, and regretted that I was

---

[3] That this was a momentary sally against Garrick there can be no doubt; for at Johnson's desire he had, some years before, given a benefit-night at his theatre to this very person, by which she had got two hundred pounds. Johnson indeed, upon all other occasions, when I was in his company, praised the very liberal charity of Garrick. I once mentioned to him, "It is observed, Sir, that you attack Garrick yourself, but will suffer nobody else to do it." JOHNSON (smiling), "Why, Sir, that is true."

[4] Mr. Sheridan was then reading lectures upon Oratory at Bath, where Derrick was Master of the Ceremonies; or, as the phrase is, KING.

drawn away from it by an engagement at another place. I had, for a part of the evening, been left alone with him, and had ventured to make an observation now and then, which he received very civilly; so that I was satisfied that though there was a roughness in his manner, there was no ill-nature in his disposition. Davies followed me to the door, and when I complained to him a little of the hard blows which the great man had given me, he kindly took upon him to console me by saying, "Don't be uneasy. I can see he likes you very well."

A few days afterwards I called on Davies, and asked him if he thought I might take the liberty of waiting on Mr. Johnson at his chambers in the Temple. He said I certainly might, and that Mr. Johnson would take it as a compliment. So on Tuesday the 24th of May, after having been enlivened by the witty sallies of Messieurs Thornton, Wilkes, Churchill, and Lloyd, with whom I had passed the morning, I boldly repaired to Johnson. His chambers were on the first floor of No. 1, Inner-Temple-lane, and I entered them with an impression given me by the Reverend Dr. Blair, of Edinburgh, who had been introduced to him not long before, and described his having "found the Giant in his den"; an expression which, when I came to be pretty well acquainted with Johnson, I repeated to him, and he was diverted at this picturesque account of himself. Dr. Blair had been presented to him by Dr. James Fordyce. At this time the controversy concerning the pieces published by Mr. James Macpherson, as translations of Ossian, was at its height. Johnson had all along denied their authenticity; and, what was still more provoking to their admirers, maintained that they had no merit. The subject having been introduced by Dr. Fordyce, Dr. Blair, relying on the internal evidence of their antiquity, asked Dr. Johnson whether he thought any man of a modern age could have written such poems? Johnson replied, "Yes, Sir, many men, many women, and many children." Johnson at this time, did not know that Dr. Blair had just published a Dissertation, not only defending their authenticity, but seriously ranking them with the poems of Homer and Virgil; and when he was afterwards informed of this circumstance, he expressed some displeasure at Dr. Fordyce's having suggested the topick, and said, "I am not sorry that they got thus much for their pains. Sir, it was like leading one to talk of a book, when the author is concealed behind the door."

He received me very courteously: but, it must be confessed, that his apartment, and furniture, and morning dress, were sufficiently uncouth. His brown suit of cloaths looked very rusty: he had on a little old shrivelled unpowdered wig, which was too small for his head; his shirt-neck and knees of his breeches were loose; his black worsted stockings ill drawn up; and he had a pair of unbuckled shoes by way of slippers. But all these slovenly particularities were forgotten the moment that he began to talk. Some gentlemen, whom I do not recollect, were sitting with him; and when they went away, I also rose; but he said to me, "Nay, don't go."—"Sir, (said I), I am afraid that I intrude upon you. It is benevolent to allow me to sit and hear you." He seemed pleased with this compliment, which I sincerely paid him, and answered, "Sir, I am obliged to any man who visits me."—I have preserved the following short minute of what passed this day.

"Madness frequently discovers itself merely by unnecessary deviation from the usual modes of the world. My poor friend Smart showed the disturbance of his mind, by falling upon his knees, and saying his prayers in the street, or in any other unusual place. Now although, rationally speaking, it is greater madness not to pray at all, than to pray as Smart did, I am afraid there are so many who do not pray, that their understanding is not called in question."

Concerning this unfortunate poet, Christopher Smart, who was confined in a mad-house, he had, at another time, the following conversation with Dr. Burney.—BURNEY. "How does poor Smart do, Sir; is he likely to recover?" JOHNSON. "It seems as if his mind had ceased to struggle with the disease; for he grows fat upon it." BURNEY. "Perhaps, Sir, that may be from want of exercise." JOHNSON. "No, Sir; he has partly as much exercise as he used to have, for he digs in the garden. Indeed, before his confinement, he used for exercise to walk to the alehouse; but he was *carried* back again. I did not think he ought to be shut up. His infirmities were not noxious to society. He insisted on people praying with him; and I'd as lief pray with Kit Smart as any one else. Another charge was, that he did not love clean linen; and I have no passion for it."

Johnson continued. "Mankind have a great aversion to intellectual labour; but even supposing knowledge to be easily attainable, more people would be content to be ignorant than would take even a little trouble to acquire it.

"The morality of an action depends on the motive from which we act. If I fling half a crown to a beggar with intention to break his head, and he picks it up and buys victuals with it, the physical effect is good; but, with respect to me, the action is very wrong. So, religious exercises, if not performed with an intention to please GOD, avail us nothing. As our Saviour says of those who perform them from other motives, 'Verily they have their reward.'"

"The Christian religion has very strong evidences. It, indeed, appears in some degree strange to reason; but in History we have undoubted facts, against which, in reasoning *à priori*, we have more arguments than we have for them; but then, testimony has great weight and casts the balance. I would recommend to every man whose faith is yet unsettled, Grotius,—Dr. Pearson,—and Dr. Clarke."

Talking of Garrick, he said, "He is the first man in the world for sprightly conversation."

When I rose a second time, he again pressed me to stay, which I did.

He told me, that he generally went abroad at four in the afternoon, and seldom came home till two in the morning. I took the liberty to ask if he did not think it wrong to live thus, and not make more use of his great talents. He owned it was a bad habit. On reviewing, at the distance of many years, my journal of this period, I wonder how, at my first visit, I ventured to talk to him so freely, and that he bore it with so much indulgence.

Before we parted, he was so good as to promise to favour me with his company one evening at my lodgings: and, as I took my leave, shook me cordially by the hand. It is almost needless to add, that I felt no little elation at having now so happily established an acquaintance of which I had been so long ambitious.

My readers will, I trust, excuse me for being thus minutely circumstantial, when it is considered that the acquaintance of Dr. Johnson was to me a most valuable acquisition, and laid the foundation of whatever instruction and entertainment they may receive from my collections concerning the great subject of the work which they are now perusing. . . .

My next meeting with Johnson was on Friday the 1st of July, when he and I and Dr. Goldsmith supped at the Mitre. I was before this time pretty well acquainted with Goldsmith, who was one of the brightest ornaments of the Johnsonian school. Goldsmith's respectful attachment to Johnson was then at its height; for his own literary reputation had not yet distinguished him so much as to excite a vain desire of competition with his great Master. He had increased my admiration of the goodness of Johnson's heart, by incidental remarks in the course of conversation, such as, when I mentioned Mr. Levet, whom he entertained under his roof, "He is poor and honest, which is recommendation enough to Johnson"; and when I wondered that he was very kind to a man of whom I had heard a very bad character, "He is now become miserable, and that insures the protection of Johnson."

Goldsmith attempting this evening to maintain, I suppose from an affectation of paradox, "that knowledge was not desirable on its own account, for it often was a source of unhappiness." JOHNSON. "Why, Sir, that knowledge may in some cases produce unhappiness, I allow. But, upon the whole, knowledge, *per se,* is certainly an object which every man would wish to attain, although, perhaps, he may not take the trouble necessary for attaining it."

Dr. John Campbell, the celebrated political and biographical writer, being mentioned, Johnson said, "Campbell is a man of much knowledge, and has a good share of imagination. His 'Hermippus Redivivus' is very entertaining, as an account of the Hermetick philosophy, and as furnishing a curious history of the extravagances of the human mind. If it were merely imaginary, it would be nothing at all. Campbell is not always rigidly careful of truth in his conversation; but I do not believe there is any thing of this carelessness in his books. Campbell is a good man, a pious man. I am afraid he has not been in the inside of a church for many years; [5] but he never passes a church without pulling off his hat. This shews that he has good principles. I used to go pretty often to Campbell's on a Sunday evening till I began to consider that the shoals of Scotchmen who flocked about him might probably say, when any thing of mine was well done, 'Ay, ay, he has learnt this of CAWMELL!'" . . .

[5] I am inclined to think that he was misinformed as to this circumstance. I own I am jealous of my worthy friend Dr. John Campbell. For though Milton could without remorse absent himself from public worship, I cannot. On the contrary, I have the same habitual impressions upon my mind, with those of a truly venerable Judge, who said to Mr. Langton, "Friend Langton, if I have not been at church on Sunday, I do not feel myself easy." Dr. Campbell was a sincerely religious man. Lord Macartney, who is eminent for his variety of knowledge, and attention to men of talents, and knew him well, told me, that when he called on him in a morning, he found him reading a chapter in the Greek New Testament, which he informed his Lordship was his constant practice. The quantity of Dr. Campbell's composition is almost incredible, and his labours brought him large profits. Dr. Joseph Warton told me that Johnson said of him, "He is the richest authour that ever grazed the common of literature."

Let me here apologize for the imperfect manner in which I am obliged to exhibit Johnson's conversation at this period. In the early part of my acquaintance with him, I was so wrapt in admiration of his extraordinary colloquial talents, and so little accustomed to his peculiar mode of expression, that I found it extremely difficult to recollect and record his conversation with its genuine vigour and vivacity. In progress of time, when my mind was, as it were, *strongly impregnated with the Johnsonian aether,* I could with much more facility and exactness, carry in my memory and commit to paper the exuberant variety of his wisdom and wit.

At this time *Miss* Williams, as she was then called, though she did not reside with him in the Temple under his roof, but had lodgings in Bolt-court, Fleet-street, had so much of his attention, that he every night drank tea with her before he went home, however late it might be, and she always sat up for him. This, it may be fairly conjectured, was not alone a proof of his regard for *her,* but of his own unwillingness to go into solitude, before that unseasonable hour at which he had habituated himself to expect the oblivion of repose. Dr. Goldsmith, being a privileged man, went with him this night, strutting away, and calling to me with an air of superiority, like that of an esoterick over an exoterick disciple of a sage of antiquity, "I go to see Miss Williams." I confess, I then envied him this mighty privilege, of which he seemed so proud; but it was not long before I obtained the same mark of distinction.

On Tuesday the 5th of July, I again visited Johnson. He told me he had looked into the poems of a pretty voluminous writer, Mr. (now Dr.) John Ogilvie, one of the Presbyterian ministers of Scotland, which had lately come out, but could find no thinking in them. BOSWELL. "Is there not imagination in them, Sir?" JOHNSON. "Why, Sir, there is in them what *was* imagination, but it is no more imagination in *him,* than sound is sound in the echo. And his diction too is not his own. We have long ago seen *white-robed innocence,* and *flower-bespangled meads.*"

Talking of London, he observed, "Sir, if you wish to have a just notion of the magnitude of this city, you must not be satisfied with seeing its great streets and squares, but must survey the innumerable little lanes and courts. It is not in the showy evolutions of buildings, but in the multiplicity of human habitations which are crowded together, that the wonderful immensity of London consists."—I have often amused myself with thinking how different

a place London is to different people. They, whose narrow minds are contracted to the consideration of some one particular pursuit, view it only through that medium. A politician thinks of it merely as the seat of government in its different departments; a grazier, as a vast market for cattle; a mercantile man, as a place where a prodigious deal of business is done upon 'Change; a dramatick enthusiast, as the grand scene of theatrical entertainments; a man of pleasure, as an assemblage of taverns, and the great emporium for ladies of easy virtue. But the intellectual man is struck with it, as comprehending the whole of human life in all its variety, the contemplation of which is inexhaustible.

On Wednesday, July 6, he was engaged to sup with me at my lodgings in Downing-street, Westminster. But on the preceding night my landlord having behaved very rudely to me and some company who were with me, I had resolved not to remain another night in his house. I was exceedingly uneasy at the awkward appearance I supposed I should make to Johnson and the other gentlemen whom I had invited, not being able to receive them at home, and being obliged to order supper at the Mitre. I went to Johnson in the morning, and talked of it as of a serious distress. He laughed, and said, "Consider, Sir, how insignificant this will appear a twelvemonth hence."—Were this consideration to be applied to most of the little vexatious incidents of life, by which our quiet is too often disturbed, it would prevent many painful sensations. I have tried it frequently with good effect. "There is nothing (continued he) in this mighty misfortune; nay, we shall be better at the Mitre." I told him that I had been at Sir John Fielding's office, complaining of my landlord, and had been informed, that though I had taken my lodgings for a year, I might, upon proof of his bad behaviour, quit them when I pleased, without being under an obligation to pay rent for any longer time than while I possessed them. The fertility of Johnson's mind could shew itself even upon so small a matter as this. "Why, Sir, (said he,) I suppose this must be the law, since you have been told so in Bow-street. But, if your landlord could hold you to your bargain, and the lodgings should be yours for a year, you may certainly use them as you think fit. So, Sir, you may quarter two life-guardmen upon him; or you may send the greatest scoundrel you can find into your apartments; or you may say that you want to make some experiments in natural philosophy, and may burn a large quantity of assafoetida in his house."

THE NEO-CLASSICAL WORLD

I had as my guests this evening at the Mitre tavern, Dr. Johnson, Dr. Goldsmith, Mr. Thomas Davies, Mr. Eccles, an Irish gentleman, for whose agreeable company I was obliged to Mr. Davies, and the Reverend Mr. John Ogilvie,[6] who was desirous of being in company with my illustrious friend, while I in my turn, was proud to have the honour of shewing one of my countrymen upon what easy terms Johnson permitted me to live with him.

Goldsmith, as usual, endeavoured, with too much eagerness, to *shine*, and disputed very warmly with Johnson against the well known maxim of the British constitution, "the King can do no wrong"; affirming, that, "what was morally false could not be politically true; and as the King might, in the exercise of his regal power, command and cause the doing of what was wrong, it certainly might be said, in sense and in reason, that he could do wrong." JOHNSON. "Sir, you are to consider, that in our constitution, according to its true principles, the King is the head, he is supreme: he is above every thing, and there is no power by which he can be tried. Therefore, it is, Sir, that we hold the King can do no wrong; that whatever may happen to be wrong in government may not be above our reach, by being ascribed to Majesty. Redress is always to be had against oppression, by punishing the immediate agents. The King, though he should command, cannot force a Judge to condemn a man unjustly; therefore it is the Judge whom we prosecute and punish. Political institutions are formed upon the consideration of what will most frequently tend to the good of the whole, although now and then exceptions may occur. Thus it is better in general that a nation should have a supreme legislative power, although it may at times be abused. And then, Sir, there is this consideration, that *if the abuse be enormous, Nature will rise up, and claiming her original rights, overturn a corrupt political system.*" I mark this animated sentence with peculiar pleasure, as a noble instance of that truly dignified spirit of freedom which ever glowed in his heart, though he was charged with slavish tenets by superficial observers; because he was at all times indignant against that false patriotism, that pretended love of freedom,

that unruly restlessness which is inconsistent with the stable authority of any good government.

This generous sentiment, which he uttered with great fervour, struck me exceedingly, and stirred my blood to that pitch of fancied resistance, the possibility of which I am glad to keep in mind, but to which I trust I never shall be forced.

"Great abilities (said he) are not requisite for an Historian; for in historical composition, all the greatest powers of the human mind are quiescent. He has facts ready to his hand, so there is no exercise of invention. Imagination is not required in any high degree; only about as much as is used in the lower kinds of poetry. Some penetration, accuracy, and colouring, will fit a man for the task, if he can give the application which is necessary."

"Bayle's Dictionary is a very useful work for those to consult who love the biographical part of literature, which is what I love most."

Talking of the eminent writers in Queen Anne's reign, he observed, "I think Dr. Arbuthnot the first man among them. He was the most universal genius, being an excellent physician, a man of deep learning, and a man of much humour. Mr. Addison was, to be sure, a great man; his learning was not profound; but his morality, his humour, and his elegance of writing, set him very high."

Mr. Ogilvie was unlucky enough to choose for the topick of his conversation the praises of his native country. He began with saying, that there was very rich land around Edinburgh. Goldsmith, who had studied physick there, contradicted this, very untruly, with a sneering laugh. Disconcerted a little by this, Mr. Ogilvie then took a new ground, where, I suppose, he thought himself perfectly safe; for he observed, that Scotland had a great many noble wild prospects. JOHNSON. "I believe, Sir, you have a great many. Norway, too, has noble wild prospects; and Lapland is remarkable for prodigious noble wild prospects. But, Sir, let me tell you, the noblest prospect which a Scotchman ever sees, is the high road that leads him to England!" This unexpected and pointed sally produced a roar of applause. After all, however, those who admire the rude grandeur of Nature, cannot deny it to Caledonia.

On Saturday, July 9, I found Johnson surrounded with a numerous levee, but have not preserved any part of his conversation. On the 14th we had another evening by ourselves at the Mitre. It happening to be a very rainy night, I made some common-place observations on the relaxation of nerves and depression of spirits which such weather

---

[6] The Northern bard mentioned [above]. When I asked Dr. Johnson's permission to introduce him, he obligingly agreed; adding, however, with a sly pleasantry, "but he must give us none of his poetry." It is remarkable that Johnson and Churchill, however much they differed in other points, agreed on this subject. See Churchill's "Journey." It is, however, but justice to Dr. Ogilvie to observe, that his "Day of Judgment" has no inconsiderable share of merit.

occasioned; adding, however, that it was good for the vegetable creation. Johnson, who, as we have already seen, denied that the temperature of the air had any influence on the human frame, answered, with a smile of ridicule, "Why, yes, Sir, it is good for vegetables, and for the animals who eat those vegetables, and for the animals who eat those animals." This observation of his aptly enough introduced a good supper; and I soon forgot, in Johnson's company, the influence of a moist atmosphere.

Feeling myself now quite at ease as his companion, though I had all possible reverence for him, I expressed a regret that I could not be so easy with my father, though he was not much older than Johnson, and certainly however respectable had not more learning and greater abilities to depress me. I asked him the reason of this. Johnson. "Why, Sir, I am a man of the world. I live in the world, and I take, in some degree, the colour of the world as it moves along. Your father is a Judge in a remote part of the island, and all his notions are taken from the old world. Besides, Sir, there must always be a struggle between a father and son, while one aims at power and the other at independence." I said, I was afraid my father would force me to be a lawyer. Johnson. "Sir, you need not be afraid of his forcing you to be a laborious practising lawyer; that is not in his power. For as the proverb says, 'One man may lead a horse to the water, but twenty cannot make him drink.' He may be displeased that you are not what he wishes you to be; but that displeasure will not go far. If he insists only on your having as much law as is necessary for a man of property, and then endeavours to get you into Parliament, he is quite in the right."

He enlarged very convincingly upon the excellence of rhyme over blank verse in English poetry. I mentioned to him that Dr. Adam Smith, in his lectures upon composition, when I studied under him in the College of Glasgow, had maintained the same opinion strenuously, and I repeated some of his arguments. Johnson. "Sir, I was once in company with Smith, and we did not take to each other; but had I known that he loved rhyme as much as you tell me he does, I should have HUGGED him."

Talking of those who denied the truth of Christianity, he said, "It is always easy to be on the negative side. If a man were now to deny that there is salt upon the table, you could not reduce him to an absurdity. Come, let us try this a little further. I deny that Canada is taken, and I can support my denial by pretty good arguments. The French are a much more numerous people than we; and it is not likely that they would allow us to take it. 'But the ministry have assured us, in all the formality of the Gazette, that it is taken.'—Very true. But the ministry have put us to an enormous expence by the war in America, and it is their interest to persuade us that we have got something for our money.—'But the fact is confirmed by thousands of men who were at the taking of it.'—Ay, but these men have still more interest in deceiving us. They don't want that you should think the French have beat them, but that they have beat the French. Now suppose you should go over and find that it really is taken, that would only satisfy yourself; for when you come home we will not believe you. We will say, you have been bribed.—Yet, Sir, notwithstanding all these plausible objections, we have no doubt that Canada is really ours. Such is the weight of common testimony. How much stronger are the evidences of the Christian religion?"

"Idleness is a disease which must be combated; but I would not advise a rigid adherence to a particular plan of study. I myself have never persisted in any plan for two days together. A man ought to read just as inclination leads him; for what he reads as a task will do him little good. A young man should read five hours in a day, and so may acquire a great deal of knowledge."

To a man of vigorous intellect and ardent curiosity like his own, reading without a regular plan may be beneficial; though even such a man must submit to it, if he would attain a full understanding of any of the sciences.

To such a degree of unrestrained frankness had he now accustomed me, that in the course of this evening I talked of the numerous reflections which had been thrown out against him on account of his having accepted a pension from his present Majesty. "Why, Sir, (said he, with a hearty laugh,) it is a mighty foolish noise that they make.[7] I have accepted of a pension as a reward which has been thought due to my literary merit; and now that I have this pension, I am the same man in every respect that I have ever been; I retain the same principles. It is true, that I cannot now curse (smiling) the House of Hanover; nor would it be decent for me to drink King James's health in the

---

[7] When I mentioned the same idle clamour to him several years afterwards, he said, with a smile, "I wish my pension were twice as large, that they might make twice as much noise."

wine that King George gives me money to pay for. But, Sir, I think that the pleasure of cursing the House of Hanover, and drinking King James's health, are amply overbalanced by three hundred pounds a year."

There was here, most certainly, an affectation of more Jacobitism than he really had; and indeed an intention of admitting, for the moment, in a much greater extent than it really existed, the charge of disaffection imputed to him by the world, merely for the purpose of shewing how dexterously he could repel an attack, even though he were placed in the most disadvantageous position; for I have heard him declare, that if holding up his right hand would have secured victory at Culloden to Prince Charles's army, he was not sure he would have held it up; so little confidence had he in the right claimed by the House of Stuart, and so fearful was he of the consequences of another revolution on the throne of Great-Britain; and Mr. Topham Beauclerk assured me, he had heard him say this before he had his pension. At another time he said to Mr. Langton, "Nothing has ever offered, that has made it worth my while to consider the question fully." He, however, also said to the same gentleman, talking of King James the Second, "It was become impossible for him to reign any longer in this country." He no doubt had an early attachment to the House of Stuart; but his zeal had cooled as his reason strengthened. Indeed, I heard him once say, "that after the death of a violent Whig, with whom he used to contend with great eagerness, he felt his Toryism much abated." [8] I suppose he meant Mr. Walmsley.

Yet there is no doubt that at earlier periods he was wont often to exercise both his pleasantry and ingenuity in talking Jacobitism. My much respected friend, Dr. Douglas, now Bishop of Salisbury, has favoured me with the following admirable instance from his Lordship's own recollection. One day when dining at old Mr. Langton's, where Miss Roberts, his niece, was one of the company, Johnson, with his usual complacent attention to the fair sex, took her by the hand and said, "My dear, I hope you are a Jacobite." Old Mr. Langton, who, though a high and steady Tory, was attached to the present Royal Family, seemed offended, and asked Johnson, with great warmth, what he could mean by putting such a question to his niece! "Why, Sir, (said Johnson) I meant no offence to your niece, I meant her a great compliment. A Jacobite, Sir, be-

lieves in the divine right of Kings. He that believes in the divine right of Kings believes in a Divinity. A Jacobite believes in the divine right of Bishops. He that believes in the divine right of Bishops believes in the divine authority of the Christian religion. Therefore, Sir, a Jacobite is neither an Atheist nor a Deist. That cannot be said of a Whig; for *Whiggism is a negation of all principle.*" [9]

He advised me when abroad to be as much as I could with the Professors in the Universities, and with the Clergy; for from their conversation I might expect the best accounts of every thing in whatever country I should be, with the additional advantage of keeping my learning alive.

It will be observed, that when giving me advice as to my travels, Dr. Johnson did not dwell upon cities, and palaces, and pictures, and shows, and Arcadian scenes. He was of Lord Essex's opinion, who advises his kinsman Roger Earl of Rutland, "rather to go a hundred miles to speak with one wise man, than five miles to see a fair town." [10]

I described to him an impudent fellow from Scotland, who affected to be a savage, and railed at all established systems. JOHNSON. "There is nothing surprising in this, Sir. He wants to make himself conspicuous. He would tumble in a hogstye, as long as you looked at him and called to him to come out. But let him alone, never mind him, and he'll soon give it over."

I added that the same person maintained that there was no distinction between virtue and vice. JOHNSON. "Why, Sir, if the fellow does not think as he speaks, he is lying; and I see not what honour he can propose to himself from having the character of a lyar. But if he does really think that there is no distinction between virtue and vice, why, Sir, when he leaves our houses let us count our spoons."

Sir David Dalrymple, now one of the Judges of Scotland by the title of Lord Hailes, had contributed much to increase my high opinion of Johnson, on account of his writings, long before I attained to a personal acquaintance with him; I, in return, had informed Johnson of Sir David's eminent character for learning and religion; and John-

[8] *Journal of a Tour to the Hebrides,* 3d ed., p. 402 (Nov. 10).

[9] He used to tell, with great humour, from my relation to him, the following little story of my early years, which was literally true: "Boswell, in the year 1745, was a fine boy, wore a white cockade, and prayed for King James, till one of his uncles (General Cochrane) gave him a shilling on condition that he would pray for King George, which he accordingly did. So you see (says Boswell) that *Whigs of all ages are made the same way.*"

[10] Letter to Rutland on Travel, 16mo., 1596.

son was so much pleased, that at one of our evening meetings he gave him for his toast. I at this time kept up a very frequent correspondence with Sir David; and I read to Dr. Johnson to-night the following passage from the letter which I had last received from him:

"It gives me pleasure to think that you have obtained the friendship of Mr. Samuel Johnson. He is one of the best moral writers which England has produced. At the same time, I envy you the free and undisguised converse with such a man. May I beg you to present my best respects to him, and to assure him of the veneration which I entertain for the author of the Rambler and of Rasselas? Let me recommend this last work to you; with the Rambler you certainly are acquainted. In Rasselas you will see a tender-hearted operator, who probes the wound only to heal it. Swift, on the contrary, mangles human nature. He cuts and slashes, as if he took pleasure in the operation, like the tyrant who said, *Ita feri ut se sentiat emori.*" [11] Johnson seemed to be much gratified by this just and well-turned compliment.

He recommended to me to keep a journal of my life, full and unreserved. He said it would be a very good exercise, and would yield me great satisfaction when the particulars were faded from my remembrance. I was uncommonly fortunate in having had a previous coincidence of opinion with him upon this subject, for I had kept such a journal for some time; and it was no small pleasure to me to have this to tell him, and to receive his approbation. He counselled me to keep it private, and said I might surely have a friend who would burn it in case of my death. From this habit I have been enabled to give the world so many anecdotes, which would otherwise have been lost to posterity. I mentioned that I was afraid I put into my journal too many little incidents. JOHNSON. "There is nothing, Sir, too little for so little a creature as man. It is by studying little things that we attain the great art of having as little misery and as much happiness as possible."

Next morning Mr. Dempster happened to call on me, and was so much struck even with the imperfect account which I gave him of Dr. Johnson's conversation, that to his honour be it recorded, when I complained that drinking port and sitting up late with him, affected my nerves for some time after, he said, "One had better be palsied at eighteen than not keep company with such a man."

[11] "I kill him in such a way that he may know he is dying."

On Tuesday, July 18, I found tall Sir Thomas Robinson sitting with Johnson. Sir Thomas said, that the King of Prussia valued himself upon three things;—upon being a hero, a musician, and an author. JOHNSON. "Pretty well, Sir, for one man. As to his being an author, I have not looked at his poetry; but his prose is poor stuff. He writes just as you may suppose Voltaire's foot-boy to do, who has been his amanuensis. He has such parts as the valet might have, and about as much of the colouring of the style as might be got by transcribing his works." When I was at Ferney, I repeated this to Voltaire, in order to reconcile him somewhat to Johnson, whom he, in affecting the English mode of expression, had previously characterised as "a superstitious dog"; but after hearing such a criticism on Frederick the Great, with whom he was then on bad terms, he exclaimed, "An honest fellow!"

But I think the criticism much too severe; for the "Memoirs of the House of Brandenburgh" are written as well as many works of that kind. His poetry, for the style of which he himself makes a frank apology, *"Jargonnant un François barbare,"* though fraught with pernicious ravings of infidelity, has, in many places, great animation, and in some a pathetick tenderness.

Upon this contemptuous animadversion on the King of Prussia, I observed to Johnson, "It would seem then, Sir, that much less parts are necessary to make a King, than to make an Author: for the King of Prussia is confessedly the greatest King now in Europe, yet you think he makes a very poor figure as an Author."

Mr. Levet this day showed me Dr. Johnson's library, which was contained in two garrets over his Chambers, where Lintot, son of the celebrated bookseller of that name, had formerly his warehouse. I found a number of good books, but very dusty and in great confusion. The floor was strewed with manuscript leaves, in Johnson's own handwriting which I beheld with a degree of veneration, supposing they perhaps might contain portions of the Rambler, or of Rasselas. I observed an apparatus for chymical experiments, of which Johnson was all his life very fond. The place seemed to be very favourable for retirement and meditation. Johnson told me, that he went up thither without mentioning it to his servant when he wanted to study, secure from interruption; for he would not allow his servant to say he was not at home when he really was. "A servant's strict regard for truth, (said he) must be weakened by such a practice. A philosopher may know that it is merely a form of denial; but few servants are such nice distinguishers. If I accustom a servant to tell a lie for *me*, have I not reason to apprehend that he will tell many lies for *himself*." I am, however, satisfied that every servant, of any degree of intelligence, understands saying his master is not at home, not at all as the affirmation of a fact, but as the customary words, intimating that his master wishes not to be seen; so that there can be no bad effect from it.

Mr. Temple, now vicar of St. Gluvias, Cornwall, who had been my intimate friend for many years, had at this time chambers in Farrar's-buildings, at the bottom of Inner Temple-lane, which he kindly lent me upon my quitting my lodgings, he being to return to Trinity Hall, Cambridge. I found them particularly convenient for me, as they were so near Dr. Johnson's.

On Wednesday, July 20, Dr. Johnson, Mr. Dempster, and my uncle Dr. Boswell, who happened to be now in London, supped with me at these Chambers. JOHNSON. "Pity is not natural to man. Children are always cruel. Savages are always cruel. Pity is acquired and improved by the cultivation of reason. We may have uneasy sensations for seeing a creature in distress, without pity; for we have not pity unless we wish to relieve them. When I am on my way to dine with a friend, and finding it late, have bid the coachman make haste, if I happen to attend when he whips his horses, I may feel unpleasantly that the animals are put to pain, but I do not wish him to desist. No, Sir, I wish him to drive on."

Mr. Alexander Donaldson, bookseller, of Edinburgh, had for some time opened a shop in London, and sold his cheap editions of the most popular English books, in defiance of the supposed common-law right of *Literary Property*. Johnson, though he concurred in the opinion which was afterwards sanctioned by a judgment of the House of Lords, that there was no such right, was at this time very angry that the Booksellers of London, for whom he uniformly professed much regard, should suffer from an invasion of what they had ever considered to be secure; and he was loud and violent against Mr. Donaldson. "He is a fellow who takes advantage of the law to injure his brethren; for notwithstanding that the statute secures only fourteen years of exclusive right, it has always been understood by the *trade*, that he, who buys the copyright of a book from the authour, obtains a perpetual property; and upon that belief, numberless bargains are made to transfer that property after the expiration of the statutory term. Now Donaldson, I say, takes advantage here, of people who have really an equitable title from usage; and if we consider how few of the books, of which they buy the property, succeed so well as to bring profit, we should be of opinion that the term of fourteen years is too short; it should be sixty years." DEMPSTER. "Donaldson, Sir, is anxious for the encouragement of literature. He reduces the price of books, so that poor students may buy them." JOHNSON (laughing), "Well, Sir, allowing that to be his motive, he is no better than Robin Hood, who robbed the rich in order to give to the poor."

It is remarkable, that when the great question concerning Literary Property came to be ultimately tried before the supreme tribunal of this country, in consequence of the very spirited exertions of Mr. Donaldson, Dr. Johnson was zealous against a perpetuity; but he thought that the term of the exclusive right of authors should be considerably enlarged. He was then for granting a hundred years.

The conversation now turned upon Mr. David Hume's style. JOHNSON. "Why, Sir, his style is not English; the structure of his sentences is French. Now the French structure and the English structure may, in the nature of things, be equally good. But if you allow that the English language is established, he is wrong. My name might originally have been Nicholson, as well as Johnson; but were you to call me Nicholson now, you would call me very absurdly."

Rousseau's treatise on the inequality of mankind was at this time a fashionable topick. It gave rise to an observation by Mr. Dempster, that the advantages of fortune and rank were nothing to a wise man, who ought to value only merit. JOHNSON. "If man were a savage, living in the woods by himself, this might be true; but in civilized society we all depend upon each other, and our happiness is very much owing to the good opinion of mankind. Now, Sir, in civilized society, external advantages make us more respected. A man with a good coat upon his back meets with a better reception than he who has a bad one. Sir, you may analyse this, and say what is there in it? But that will avail you nothing, for it is a part of a general system. Pound St. Paul's church into atoms, and consider any single atom; it is, to be sure, good for nothing: but, put all these atoms together, and you have St. Paul's church. So it is with human felicity, which is made up of many ingredients, each of which may be shewn to be very insignificant. In civilized society, personal merit will not serve you so much as money will. Sir, you may make the experiment. Go into the street, and give one man a lecture on morality, and another a shilling, and see which will respect you most. If you wish only to support nature, Sir William Petty fixed your allowance at three pounds a year; but as times are much altered, let us call it six pounds. This sum will fill your belly, shelter you from the weather, and even get you a strong lasting coat, supposing it to be made of good bull's hide. Now, Sir, all beyond this is artificial, and is desired in order to obtain a greater degree of respect from our fellow-creatures. And, Sir, if six hundred pounds a year procure a man more consequence, and, of course, more happiness than six pounds a year, the same proportion will hold as to six thousand, and so on, as far as opulence can be carried. Perhaps he who has a large fortune may not be so happy as he who has a small one; but that must proceed from other causes than from his having the large fortune: for, *coeteris paribus*, he who is rich in a civilized society, must be happier than he who is poor; as riches, if properly used, (and it is a man's own fault if they are not,) must be productive of the highest advantages. Money, to be sure, of itself is of no use; for its only use is to part with it. Rousseau, and all those who deal in paradoxes, are led away by a childish desire of novelty. When I was a boy, I used always to choose the wrong side of a debate, because most ingenious things, that is to say, most new things, could be said upon it. Sir, there is nothing for which you may not muster up more plausible arguments, than those which are urged against wealth and other external advantages. Why, now, there is stealing; why should it be thought a crime? When we consider by what unjust methods property has been often acquired, and that what was unjustly got it must be unjust to keep, where is the harm in one man's taking the property of another from him? Besides, Sir, when we consider the bad use that many people make of their property, and how much better use the thief may make of it, it may be defended as a very allowable practice. Yet, Sir, the experience of mankind has discovered stealing to be so very bad a thing, that they make no scruple to hang a man for it. When I was running about this town a very poor fellow, I was a great arguer for the advantages of poverty; but I was, at the same time, very sorry to be poor. Sir, all the arguments which are brought to represent poverty as no evil, shew

it to be evidently a great evil. You never find people labouring to convince you that you may live very happily upon a plentiful fortune.—So you hear people talking how miserable a King must be; and yet they all wish to be in his place."

It was suggested that Kings must be unhappy, because they are deprived of the greatest of all satisfactions, easy and unreserved society. JOHNSON. "That is an ill-founded notion. Being a King does not exclude a man from such society. Great Kings have always been social. The King of Prussia, the only great King at present, is very social. Charles the Second, the last King of England who was a man of parts, was social; and our Henrys and Edwards were all social."

Mr. Dempster having endeavoured to maintain that intrinsick merit *ought* to make the only distinction amongst mankind. JOHNSON. "Why, Sir, mankind have found that this cannot be. How shall we determine the proportion of intrinsick merit? Were that to be the only distinction amongst mankind, we should soon quarrel about the degrees of it. Were all distinctions abolished, the strongest would not long acquiesce, but would endeavour to obtain a superiority by their bodily strength. But, Sir, as subordination is very necessary for society, and contentions for superiority very dangerous, mankind, that is to say, all civilized nations, have settled it upon a plain invariable principle. A man is born to hereditary rank; or his being appointed to certain offices, gives him a certain rank. Subordination tends greatly to human happiness. Were we all upon an equality, we should have no other enjoyment than mere animal pleasure."

I said, I considered distinction of rank to be of so much importance in civilized society, that if I were asked on the same day to dine with the first Duke in England, and with the first man in Britain for genius, I should hesitate which to prefer. JOHNSON. "To be sure, Sir, if you were to dine only once, and it were never to be known where you dined, you would choose rather to dine with the first man for genius; but to gain most respect, you should dine with the first Duke in England. For nine people in ten that you meet with, would have a higher opinion of you for having dined with a Duke; and the great genius himself would receive you better, because you had been with the great Duke."

He took care to guard himself against any possible suspicion that his settled principles of reverence for rank and respect for wealth were at all owing to mean or interested motives; for he asserted his own independence as a literary man. "No man (said he) who ever lived by literature, has lived more independently than I have done." He said he had taken longer time than he needed to have done in composing his Dictionary. He received our compliments upon that great work with complacency, and told us that the Academy *della Crusca* could scarcely believe that it was done by one man.

Next morning I found him alone, and have preserved the following fragments of his conversation. Of a gentleman who was mentioned, he said, "I have not met with any man for a long time who has given me such general displeasure. He is totally unfixed in his principles, and wants to puzzle other people." I said his principles had been poisoned by a noted infidel writer, but that he was, nevertheless, a benevolent good man. JOHNSON. "We can have no dependence upon that instinctive, that constitutional goodness which is not founded upon principle. I grant you that such a man may be a very amiable member of society. I can conceive him placed in such a situation that he is not much tempted to deviate from what is right; and as every man prefers virtue, when there is not some strong incitement to transgress its precepts, I can conceive him doing nothing wrong. But if such a man stood in need of money, I should not like to trust him; and I should certainly not trust him with young ladies, for *there* there is always temptation. Hume, and other sceptical innovators, are vain men, and will gratify themselves at any expence. Truth will not afford sufficient food to their vanity; so they have betaken themselves to errour. Truth, Sir, is a cow which will yield such people no more milk, and so they are gone to milk the bull. If I could have allowed myself to gratify my vanity at the expence of truth, what fame might I have acquired. Every thing which Hume has advanced against Christianity had passed through my mind long before he wrote. Always remember this, that after a system is well settled upon positive evidence, a few partial objections ought not to shake it. The human mind is so limited, that it cannot take in all the parts of a subject, so that there may be objections raised against any thing. There are objections against a *plenum,* and objections against a *vacuum*; yet one of them must certainly be true."

I mentioned Hume's argument against the belief of miracles, that it is more probable that the witnesses to the truth of them are mistaken, or speak falsely, than that the miracles should be true. JOHNSON. "Why, Sir, the great difficulty of proving miracles should make us very cautious in believing them. But let us consider; although GOD has made Nature to operate by certain fixed laws, yet it is not unreasonable to think that he may suspend those laws, in order to establish a system highly advantageous to mankind. Now the Christian Religion is a most beneficial system, as it gives us light and certainty where we were before in darkness and doubt. The miracles which prove it are attested by men who had no interest in deceiving us; but who, on the contrary, were told that they should suffer persecution, and did actually lay down their lives in confirmation of the truth of the facts which they asserted. Indeed, for some centuries the heathens did not pretend to deny the miracles; but said they were performed by the aid of evil spirits. This is a circumstance of great weight. Then, Sir, when we take the proofs derived from prophecies which have been so exactly fulfilled, we have most satisfactory evidence. Supposing a miracle possible, as to which, in my opinion, there can be no doubt, we have as strong evidence for the miracles in support of Christianity, as the nature of the thing admits."

At night, Mr. Johnson and I supped in a private room at the Turk's Head coffee-house, in the Strand. "I encourage this house (said he,) for the mistress of it is a good civil woman, and has not much business."

"Sir, I love the acquaintance of young people; because, in the first place, I don't like to think myself growing old. In the next place, young acquaintances must last longest, if they do last; and then, Sir, young men have more virtue than old men; they have more generous sentiments in every respect. I love the young dogs of this age, they have more wit and humour and knowledge of life than we had; but then the dogs are not so good scholars. Sir, in my early years I read very hard. It is a sad reflection but a true one, that I knew almost as much at eighteen as I do now. My judgment, to be sure, was not so good; but, I had all the facts. I remember very well, when I was at Oxford, an old gentleman said to me, 'Young man, ply your book diligently now, and acquire a stock of knowledge; for when years come upon you, you will find that poring upon books will be but an irksome task.'"

This account of his reading, given by himself in plain words, sufficiently confirms what I have already advanced upon the disputed question as to his application. It reconciles any seeming inconsistency in his way of talking upon it at different times; and shews that idleness and reading hard were with him relative terms, the import of which, as used by him, must be gathered from a comparison with what scholars of different degrees of ardour and assiduity have been known to do. And let it be remembered, that he was now talking spontaneously, and expressing his genuine sentiments; whereas at other times he might be induced, from his spirit of contradiction, or more properly from his love of argumentative contest, to speak lightly of his own application to study. It is pleasing to consider that the old gentleman's gloomy prophecy as to the irksomeness of books to men of an advanced age, which is too often fulfilled, was so far from being verified in Johnson, that his ardour for literature never failed, and his last writings had more ease and vivacity than any of his earlier productions.

He mentioned to me now, for the first time, that he had been distrest by melancholy, and for that reason had been obliged to fly from study and meditation, to the dissipating variety of life. Against melancholy he recommended constant occupation of mind, a great deal of exercise, moderation in eating and drinking, and especially to shun drinking at night. He said melancholy people were apt to fly to intemperance for relief, but that it sunk them much deeper in misery. He observed, that labouring men who work hard, and live sparingly, are seldom or never troubled with low spirits.

He again insisted on the duty of maintaining subordination of rank. "Sir, I would no more deprive a nobleman of his respect, than of his money. I consider myself as acting a part in the great system of society, and I do to others as I would have them to do to me. I would behave to a nobleman as I should expect he would behave to me, were I a nobleman and he Sam. Johnson. Sir, there is one Mrs. Macaulay [12] in this town, a great republican. One day when I was at her house, I put on a very grave countenance, and said to her, 'Madam, I am now become a convert to your way of thinking. I am convinced that all mankind are upon an equal footing; and to give you an unquestionable proof, Madam, that I am in earnest, here is a very sensible, civil, well-behaved fellow-citizen, your footman; I desire that he may be allowed to sit down and dine with us.' I thus, Sir, shewed her the absurdity of

the levelling doctrine. She has never liked me since. Sir, your levellers wish to level *down* as far as themselves; but they cannot bear levelling *up* to themselves. They would all have some people under them; why not then have some people above them?" I mentioned a certain authour who disgusted me by his forwardness, and by shewing no deference to noblemen into whose company he was admitted. JOHNSON. "Suppose a shoemaker should claim an equality with him, as he does with a Lord: how he would stare. 'Why, Sir, do you stare? (says the shoemaker,) I do great service to society. 'Tis true, I am paid for doing it; but so are you, Sir: and I am sorry to say it, better paid than I am, for doing something not so necessary. For mankind could do better without your books, than without my shoes.' Thus, Sir, there would be a perpetual struggle for precedence, were there no fixed invariable rules for the distinction of rank, which creates no jealousy, as it is allowed to be accidental."

He said, Dr. Joseph Warton was a very agreeable man, and his "Essay on the Genius and Writings of Pope," a very pleasing book. I wondered that he delayed so long to give us the continuation of it. JOHNSON. "Why Sir, I suppose he finds himself a little disappointed, in not having been able to persuade the world to be of his opinion as to Pope."

We have now been favoured with the concluding volume, in which, to use a parliamentary expression, he has *explained,* so as not to appear quite so adverse to the opinion of the world, concerning Pope, as was at first thought; and we must all agree, that his work is a most valuable accession to English literature.

A writer of deserved eminence being mentioned, Johnson said, "Why, Sir, he is a man of good parts, but being originally poor, he has got a love of mean company and low jocularity; a very bad thing, Sir. To laugh is good, and to talk is good. But you ought no more to think it enough if you laugh, than you are to think it enough if you talk. You may laugh in as many ways as you talk; and surely *every* way of talking that is practised cannot be esteemed."

I spoke of Sir James Macdonald as a young man of most distinguished merit, who united the highest reputation at Eton and Oxford, with the patriarchal spirit of a great Highland Chieftain. I mentioned that Sir James had said to me, that he had never seen Mr. Johnson, but he had a great respect for him, though at the same time it was mixed with

[12] This *one* Mrs. Macaulay was the same personage who afterwards made herself so much known as "the celebrated female historian."

some degree of terrour. JOHNSON. "Sir, if he were to be acquainted with me, it might lessen both."

The mention of this gentleman led us to talk of the Western Islands of Scotland, to visit which he expressed a wish that then appeared to be a very romantick fancy, which I little thought would be afterwards realised. He told me, that his father had put Martin's account of those islands into his hands when he was very young, and that he was highly pleased with it; that he was particularly struck with the St. Kilda man's notion that the high church of Glasgow had been hollowed out of a rock; a circumstance to which old Mr. Johnson had directed his attention. He said, he would go to the Hebrides with me, when I returned from my travels, unless some very good companion should offer when I was absent, which he did not think probable; adding, "There are few people whom I take so much to, as you." And when I talked of my leaving England, he said with a very affectionate air, "My dear Boswell, I should be very unhappy at parting, did I think we were not to meet again."— I cannot too often remind my readers, that although such instances of his kindness are doubtless very flattering to me, yet I hope my recording them will be ascribed to a better motive than to vanity; for they afford unquestionable evidence of his tenderness and complacency, which some, while they were forced to acknowledge his great powers, have been so strenuous to deny.

He maintained that a boy at school was the happiest of human beings. I supported a different opinion, from which I have never yet varied, that a man is happier: and I enlarged upon the anxiety and sufferings which are endured at school. JOHNSON. "Ah! Sir, a boy's being flogged is not so severe as a man's having the hiss of the world against him. Men have a solicitude about fame; and the greater share they have of it, the more afraid they are of losing it." I silently asked myself, "Is it possible that the great SAMUEL JOHNSON really entertains any such apprehension, and is not confident that his exalted fame is established upon a foundation never to be shaken?"

He this evening drank a bumper to Sir David Dalrymple, "as a man of worth, a scholar, and a wit." "I have (said he) never heard of him, except from you; but let him know my opinion of him: for as he does not shew himself much in the world, he should have the praise of the few who hear of him."

On Tuesday, July 26, I found Mr. Johnson alone.

It was a very wet day, and I again complained of the disagreeable effects of such weather. JOHNSON. "Sir, this is all imagination, which physicians encourage; for man lives in the air, as a fish lives in water, so that if the atmosphere press heavy from above, there is an equal resistance from below. To be sure, bad weather is hard upon people who are obliged to be abroad; and men cannot labour so well in the open air in bad weather, as in good: but, Sir, a smith or a taylor, whose work is within doors, will surely do as much in rainy weather, as in fair. Some very delicate frames, indeed, may be affected by wet weather; but not common constitutions."

We talked of the education of children; and I asked him what he thought was best to teach them first. JOHNSON. "Sir, it is no matter what you teach them first, any more than what leg you shall put into your breeches first. Sir, you may stand disputing which is best to put in first, but in the mean time your breech is bare. Sir, while you are considering which of two things you should teach your child first, another boy has learnt them both."

On Thursday, July 28, we again supped in private at the Turk's Head coffee-house. JOHNSON. "Swift has a higher reputation than he deserves. His excellence is strong sense; for his humour, though very well, is not remarkably good. I doubt whether the 'Tale of a Tub' be his; for he never owned it, and it is much above his usual manner." [13]

"Thomson, I think, had as much of the poet about him as most writers. Everything appeared to him through the medium of his favourite pursuit. He could not have viewed those two candles burning but with a poetical eye."

"Has not —— a great deal of wit, Sir?" JOHNSON. "I do not think so, Sir. He is, indeed, continually attempting wit, but he fails. And I have no more pleasure in hearing a man attempting wit and failing, than in seeing a man trying to leap over a ditch and tumbling into it."

He laughed heartily when I mentioned to him a saying of his concerning Mr. Thomas Sheridan, which Foote took a wicked pleasure to circulate. "Why, Sir, Sherry is dull, naturally dull; but it must have taken him a great deal of pains to become what we now see him. Such an excess of stupidity, Sir, is not in Nature."—"So (said he,) I allowed him all his own merit."

[13] This opinion was given by him more at large at a subsequent period. See *Journal of a Tour to the Hebrides*, 3d ed., p. 32 (Aug. 16).

He now added, "Sheridan cannot bear me. I bring his declamation to a point. I ask him a plain question, 'What do you mean to teach?' Besides, Sir, what influence can Mr. Sheridan have upon the language of this great country, by his narrow exertions? Sir, it is burning a farthing candle at Dover, to shew light at Calais."

Talking of a young man who was uneasy from thinking that he was very deficient in learning and knowledge, he said, "A man has no reason to complain who holds a middle place, and has many below him; and perhaps he has not six of his years above him;—perhaps not one. Though he may not know any thing perfectly, the general mass of knowledge that he has acquired is considerable. Time will do for him all that is wanting."

The conversation then took a philosophical turn. JOHNSON. "Human experience, which is constantly contradicting theory, is the great test of truth. A system, built upon the discoveries of a great many minds, is always of more strength, than what is produced by the mere workings of any one mind, which, of itself, can do little. There is not so poor a book in the world that would not be a prodigious effort were it wrought out entirely by a single mind, without the aid of prior investigators. The French writers are superficial, because they are not scholars, and so proceed upon the mere power of their own minds; and we see how very little power they have."

"As to the Christian Religion, Sir, besides the strong evidence which we have for it, there is a balance in its favour from the number of great men who have been convinced of its truth, after a serious consideration of the question. Grotius was an acute man, a lawyer, a man accustomed to examine evidence, and he was convinced. Grotius was not a recluse, but a man of the world, who certainly had no bias to the side of religion. Sir Isaac Newton set out an infidel, and came to be a very firm believer."

He this evening again recommended to me to perambulate Spain.[14] I said it would amuse him to get a letter from me dated at Salamancha. JOHNSON. "I love the University of Salamancha; for when the Spaniards were in doubt as to the lawfulness of their conquering America, the University of Salamancha gave it as their opinion that it was

[14] I fully intended to have followed advice of such weight; but having staid much longer both in Germany and Italy than I proposed to do, and having also visited Corsica, I found that I had exceeded the time allowed me by my father, and hastened to France in my way homewards.

not lawful." He spoke this with great emotion, and with that generous warmth which dictated the lines in his "London," against Spanish encroachment. . . .

I again begged his advice as to my method of study at Utrecht. "Come, (said he) let us make a day of it. Let us go down to Greenwich and dine, and talk of it there." The following Saturday was fixed for this excursion.

As we walked along the Strand to-night, arm in arm, a woman of the town accosted us, in the usual enticing manner. "No, no, my girl, (said Johnson) it won't do." He, however, did not treat her with harshness; and we talked of the wretched life of such women, and agreed, that much more misery than happiness, upon the whole, is produced by illicit commerce between the sexes.

On Saturday, July 30, Dr. Johnson and I took a sculler at the Temple-stairs, and set out for Greenwich. I asked him if he really thought a knowledge of the Greek and Latin languages an essential requisite to a good education. JOHNSON. "Most certainly, Sir; for those who know them have a very great advantage over those who do not. Nay, Sir, it is wonderful what a difference learning makes upon people even in the common intercourse of life, which does not appear to be much connected with it." "And yet, (said I) people go through the world very well, and carry on the business of life to good advantage, without learning." JOHNSON. "Why, Sir, that may be true in cases where learning cannot possibly be of any use; for instance, this boy rows us as well without learning, as if he could sing the song of Orpheus to the Argonauts, who were the first sailors." He then called to the boy, "What would you give, my lad, to know about the Argonauts?" "Sir, (said the boy) I would give what I have." Johnson was much pleased with his answer, and we gave him a double fare. Dr. Johnson then turning to me, "Sir, (said he) a desire of knowledge is the natural feeling of mankind; and every human being, whose mind is not debauched, will be willing to give all that he has, to get knowledge."

We landed at the Old Swan, and walked to Billingsgate, where we took oars and moved smoothly along the silver Thames. It was a very fine day. We were entertained with the immense number and variety of ships that were lying at anchor, and with the beautiful country on each side of the river.

I talked of preaching, and of the great success

which those called methodists [15] have. JOHNSON. "Sir, it is owing to their expressing themselves in a plain and familiar manner, which is the only way to do good to the common people, and which clergymen of genius and learning ought to do from a principle of duty, when it is suited to their congregations; a practice, for which they will be praised by men of sense. To insist against drunkenness as a crime, because it debases reason, the noblest faculty of man, would be of no service to the common people; but to tell them that they may die in a fit of drunkenness, and shew them how dreadful that would be, cannot fail to make a deep impression. Sir, when your Scotch clergy give up their homely manner, religion will soon decay in that country." Let this observation, as Johnson meant it, be ever remembered.

I was much pleased to find myself with Johnson

[15] All who are acquainted with the history of religion, (the most important, surely, that concerns the human mind,) know that the appellation of *Methodists* was first given to a society of students in the University of Oxford, who about the year 1730, were distinguished by an earnest and *methodical* attention to devout exercises. This disposition of mind is not a novelty, or peculiar to any sect, but has been, and still may be found, in many Christians of every denomination. Johnson himself was in a dignified manner, a Methodist. In his Rambler, No. 110, he mentions with respect "the whole discipline of regulated piety"; and in his "Prayers and Meditations," many instances occur of his anxious examination into his spiritual state. That this religious earnestness, and in particular an observation of the influence of the Holy Spirit, has sometimes degenerated into folly, and sometimes been counterfeited for base purposes, cannot be denied. But it is not, therefore, fair to decry it when genuine. The principal argument in reason and good sense against methodism is, that it tends to debase human nature, and prevent the generous exertions of goodness, by an unworthy supposition that God will pay no regard to them; although it is positively said in the Scriptures, that he "will reward every man according to his works." But I am happy to have it in my power to do justice to those whom it is the fashion to ridicule, without any knowledge of their tenets; and this I can do by quoting a passage from one of their best apologists, Mr. Milner, who thus expresses their doctrine upon this subject: "Justified by faith, renewed in his faculties, and constrained by the love of Christ, their believer moves in the sphere of love and gratitude, and all his *duties* flow more or less from this principle. And though *they are accumulating for him in heaven a treasure of bliss proportioned to his faithfulness and activity, and it is by no means inconsistent with his principles to feel the force of this consideration,* yet love itself sweetens every duty to his mind; and he thinks there is no absurdity in his feeling the love of GOD as the grand commanding principle of his life." *Essay on several religious Subjects, &c., by Joseph Milner, A.M. Master of the Grammar School of Kingston-upon-Hull,* 1789, p. 11.

at Greenwich, which he celebrates in his "London" as a favourite scene. I had the poem in my pocket, and read the lines aloud with enthusiasm:

On Thames's banks in silent thought we stood,
Where Greenwich smiles upon the silver flood:
Pleas'd with the seat which gave ELIZA birth,
We kneel, and kiss the consecrated earth.

He remarked that the structure of Greenwich hospital was too magnificent for a place of charity, and that its parts were too much detached, to make one great whole.

Buchanan, he said, was a very fine poet; and observed, that he was the first who complimented a lady, by ascribing to her the different perfections of the heathen goddesses; but that Johnson improved upon this, by making his lady, at the same time, free from their defects.

He dwelt upon Buchanan's elegant verses to Mary, Queen of Scots, *Nympha Caledoniae,* &c. and spoke with enthusiasm of the beauty of Latin verse. "All the modern languages (said he) cannot furnish so melodious a line as

Formosam resonare doces Amarillida silvas."

Afterwards he entered upon the business of the day, which was to give me his advice as to a course of study. And here I am to mention with much regret, that my record of what he said is miserably scanty. I recollect with admiration an animating blaze of eloquence, which roused every intellectual power in me to the highest pitch, but must have dazzled me so much, that my memory could not preserve the substance of his discourse; for the note which I find of it is no more than this:—"He ran over the grand scale of human knowledge; advised me to select some particular branch to excel in, but to acquire a little of every kind." The defect of my minutes will be fully supplied by a long letter upon the subject, which he favoured me with, after I had been some time at Utrecht, and which my readers will have the pleasure to peruse in its proper place.

We walked in the evening in Greenwich Park. He asked me I suppose, by way of trying my disposition, "Is not this very fine?" Having no exquisite relish of the beauties of Nature, and being more delighted with "the busy hum of men," I answered, "Yes, Sir; but not equal to Fleet-street." JOHNSON. "You are right, Sir."

I am aware that many of my readers may censure my want of taste. Let me, however, shelter myself under the authority of a very fashionable Baronet [16] in the brilliant world, who, on his attention being called to the fragrance of a May evening in the country, observed, "This may be very well; but for my part, I prefer the smell of a flambeau at the play-house."

We staid so long at Greenwich, that our sail up the river, in our return to London, was by no means so pleasant as in the morning; for the night air was so cold that it made me shiver. I was the more sensible of it from having sat up all the night before recollecting and writing in my Journal what I thought worthy of preservation; an exertion, which, during the first part of my acquaintance with Johnson, I frequently made. I remember having sat up four nights in one week, without being much incommoded in the day time.

Johnson, whose robust frame was not in the least affected by the cold, scolded me, as if my shivering had been a paltry effeminacy, saying, "Why do you shiver?" Sir William Scott, of the Commons, told me, that when he complained of a head-ach in the post-chaise, as they were travelling together to Scotland, Johnson treated him in the same manner: "At your age, Sir, I had no head-ach." It is not easy to make allowance for sensations in others, which we ourselves have not at the time. We must all have experienced how very differently we are affected by the complaints of our neighbours, when we are well and when we are ill. In full health, we can scarcely believe that they suffer much; so faint is the image of pain upon our imagination: when softened by sickness, we readily sympathize with the sufferings of others.

We concluded the day at the Turk's Head coffee-house very socially. He was pleased to listen to a particular account which I gave him of my family, and of its hereditary estate, as to the extent and population of which he asked questions, and made calculations; recommending, at the same time, a liberal kindness to the tenantry, as people over whom the proprietor was placed by Providence. He took delight in hearing my description of the romantick seat of my ancestors. "I must be there, Sir, (said he) and we will live in the old castle; and if there is not a room in it remaining, we will build one."

[16] My friend Sir Michael Le Fleming. This gentleman, with all his experience of sprightly and elegant life, inherits, with the beautiful family domain, no inconsiderable share of that love of literature, which distinguished his venerable grandfather, the Bishop of Carlisle. He one day observed to me, of Dr. Johnson, in a felicity of phrase, "There is a blunt dignity about him on every occasion."

I was highly flattered, but could scarcely indulge a hope that Auchinleck would indeed be honoured by his presence, and celebrated by a description, as it afterwards was, in his "Journey to the Western Islands."

After we had again talked of my setting out for Holland, he said, "I must see thee out of England; I will accompany you to Harwich." I could not find words to express what I felt upon this unexpected and very great mark of his affectionate regard.

Next day, Sunday, July 31, I told him I had been that morning at a meeting of the people called Quakers, where I had heard a woman preach. JOHNSON. "Sir, a woman's preaching is like a dog's walking on his hind legs. It is not done well; but you are surprised to find it done at all."

On Tuesday, August 2, (the day of my departure from London having been fixed for the 5th,) Dr. Johnson did me the honour to pass a part of the morning with me at my Chambers. He said, that "he always felt an inclination to do nothing." I observed, that it was strange to think that the most indolent man in Britain had written the most laborious work, *The English Dictionary*.

I mentioned an imprudent publication, by a certain friend of his, at an early period of life, and asked him if he thought it would hurt him. JOHNSON. "No, Sir; not much. It may, perhaps, be mentioned at an election."

I had now made good my title to be a privileged man, and was carried by him in the evening to drink tea with Miss Williams, whom, though under the misfortune of having lost her sight, I found to be agreeable in conversation; for she had a variety of literature, and expressed herself well; but her peculiar value was the intimacy in which she had long lived with Johnson, by which she was well acquainted with his habits, and knew how to lead him on to talk.

After tea he carried me to what he called his walk, which was a long narrow paved court in the neighbourhood, overshadowed by some trees. There we sauntered a considerable time; and I complained to him that my love of London and of his company was such, that I shrunk almost from the thought of going away even to travel, which is generally so much desired by young men. He roused me by manly and spirited conversation. He advised me, when settled in any place abroad, to study with an eagerness after knowledge, and to apply to Greek an hour every day; and when I was moving about, to read diligently the great book of mankind. . . .

Having stopped at night at Colchester, Johnson talked of that town with veneration, for having stood a siege for Charles the First. The Dutchman alone now remained with us.[17] He spoke English tolerably well; and thinking to recommend himself to us by expatiating on the superiority of the criminal jurisprudence of this country over that of Holland, he inveighed against the barbarity of putting an accused person to the torture, in order to force a confession. But Johnson was as ready for this, as for the Inquisition. "Why, Sir, you do not, I find, understand the law of your own country. To torture in Holland is considered as a favour to an accused person; for no man is put to the torture there, unless there is as much evidence against him as would amount to conviction in England. An accused person among you, therefore, has one chance more to escape punishment, than those who are tried among us."

At supper this night he talked of good eating with uncommon satisfaction. "Some people (said he,) have a foolish way of not minding or pretending not to mind, what they eat. For my part, I mind my belly very studiously, and very carefully; for I look upon it, that he who does not mind his belly, will hardly mind any thing else." He now appeared to me *Jean Bull philosophe,* and he was for the moment, not only serious, but vehement. Yet I have heard him, upon other occasions, talk with great contempt of people who were anxious to gratify their palates; and the 206th number of his Rambler is a masterly essay against gulosity. His practice, indeed, I must acknowledge, may be considered as casting the balance of his different opinions upon this subject; for I never knew any man who relished good eating more than he did. When at table, he was totally absorbed in the business of the moment; his looks seemed rivetted to his plate; nor would he, unless when in very high company, say one word, or even pay the least attention to what was said by others, till he had satisfied his appetite: which was so fierce, and indulged with such intenseness, that while in the act of eating, the veins of his forehead swelled, and generally a strong perspiration was visible. To those whose sensations were delicate, this could not but be disgusting; and it was doubtless not very suitable to the character of a philosopher, who should be distinguished by self-command. But it must be owned, that Johnson, though he could be rigidly *abstemious,* was not a *temperate* man either in eating or drinking. He could refrain,

[17] A young man whom they had met in the Harwich coach.

but he could not use moderately. He told me, that he had fasted two days without inconvenience, and that he had never been hungry but once. They who beheld with wonder how much he eat upon all occasions, when his dinner was to his taste, could not easily conceive what he must have meant by hunger; and not only was he remarkable for the extraordinary quantity which he eat, but he was, or affected to be, a man of very nice discernment in the science of cookery. He used to descant critically on the dishes which had been at table where he had dined or supped, and to recollect very minutely what he had liked. I remember when he was in Scotland, his praising *"Gordon's palates,"* (a dish of palates at the Honourable Alexander Gordon's) with a warmth of expression which might have done honour to more important subjects. "As for Maclaurin's imitation of a *made dish,* it was a wretched attempt." He about the same time was so much displeased with the performances of a nobleman's French cook, that he exclaimed with vehemence, "I'd throw such a rascal into the river;" and he then proceeded to alarm a lady at whose house he was to sup, by the following manifesto of his skill: "I, Madam, who live at a variety of good tables, am a much better judge of cookery, than any person who has a very tolerable cook, but lives much at home; for his palate is gradually adapted to the taste of his cook: whereas, Madam, in trying by a wider range, I can more exquisitely judge." When invited to dine, even with an intimate friend, he was not pleased if something better than a plain dinner was not prepared for him. I have heard him say on such an occasion, "This was a good dinner enough, to be sure: but it was not a dinner to *ask* a man to." On the other hand, he was wont to express, with great glee, his satisfaction when he had been entertained quite to his mind. One day when he had dined with his neighbour and landlord, in Bolt-court, Mr. Allen, the printer, whose old housekeeper had studied his taste in every thing, he pronounced this eulogy: "Sir, we could not have had a better dinner, had there been a *Synod of Cooks.*"

While we were left by ourselves, after the Dutchman had gone to bed, Dr. Johnson talked of that studied behaviour which many have recommended and practised. He disapproved of it; and said, "I never considered whether I should be a grave man, or a merry man, but just let inclination, for the time, have its course."

He flattered me with some hopes that he would, in the course of the following summer, come over to Holland, and accompany me in a tour through the Netherlands.

I teased him with fanciful apprehensions of unhappiness. A moth having fluttered round the candle, and burnt itself, he laid hold of this little incident to admonish me; saying, with a sly look, and in a solemn but a quiet tone, "That creature was its own tormentor, and I believe its name was BOSWELL."

Next day we got to Harwich, to dinner; and my passage in the packet-boat to Helvoetsluys being secured, and my baggage put on board, we dined at our inn by ourselves. I happened to say, it would be terrible if he should not find a speedy opportunity of returning to London, and be confined in so dull a place. JOHNSON. "Don't, Sir, accustom yourself to use big words for little matters. It would *not* be *terrible*, though I *were* to be detained some time here." The practice of using words of dispro portionate magnitude, is, no doubt, too frequent every where; but, I think, most remarkable among the French, of which, all who have travelled in France must have been struck with innumerable instances.

We went and looked at the church, and having gone into it, and walked up to the altar, Johnson, whose piety was constant and fervent, sent me to my knees, saying, "Now that you are going to leave your native country, recommend yourself to the protection of your CREATOR and REDEEMER."

After we came out of the church, we stood talking for some time together of Bishop Berkeley's ingenious sophistry to prove the non-existence of matter, and that every thing in the universe is merely ideal. I observed, that though we are satisfied his doctrine is not true, it is impossible to refute it. I never shall forget the alacrity with which Johnson answered, striking his foot with mighty force against a large stone, till he rebounded from it,—"I refute it *thus*." This was a stout exemplification of the *first truths of Pere Bouffier,* or the *original principles* of Reid and of Beattie; without admitting which, we can no more argue in metaphysics, than we can argue in mathematicks without axioms. To me it is not conceivable how Berkeley can be answered by pure reasoning; but I know that the nice and difficult task was to have been undertaken by one of the most luminous minds of the present age, had not politicks "turned him from calm philosophy aside." What an admirable display of subtility, united with brilliance, might his contending with Berkeley have afforded us! How must we, when we reflect on the loss of

such an intellectual feast, regret that he should be characterised as the man,

"Who born for the universe narrow'd his mind,
And to party gave up what was meant for mankind?"

My revered friend walked down with me to the beach, where we embraced and parted with tenderness, and engaged to correspond by letters. I said, "I hope, Sir, you will not forget me in my absence." JOHNSON. "Nay, Sir, it is more likely you should forget me, than that I should forget you." As the vessel put out to sea, I kept my eyes upon him for a considerable time, while he remained rolling his majestic frame in his usual manner; and at last I perceived him walk back into the town, and he disappeared.

Utrecht seeming at first very dull to me, after the animated scenes of London, my spirits were grievously affected; and I wrote to Johnson a plaintive and desponding letter, to which he paid no regard. Afterwards, when I had acquired a firmer tone of mind, I wrote him a second letter, expressing much anxiety to hear from him. At length I received the following epistle, which was of important service to me, and I trust, will be so to many others.

A Mr. BOSWELL, *à la Cour de l'Empereur,*
UTRECHT.

DEAR SIR,

You are not to think yourself forgotten, or criminally neglected, that you have had yet no letter from me. I love to see my friends, to hear from them, to talk to them, and to talk of them; but it is not without a considerable effort of resolution that I prevail upon myself to write. I would not, however, gratify my own indolence by the omission of any important duty, or any office of real kindness.

To tell you that I am or am not well, that I have or have not been in the country, that I drank your health in the room in which we last sat together, and that your acquaintance continue to speak of you with their former kindness, topicks with which those letters are commonly filled which are written only for the sake of writing, I seldom shall think worth communicating; but if I can have it in my power to calm any harassing disquiet, to excite any virtuous desire, to rectify any important opinion, or fortify any generous resolution, you need not doubt but I shall at least wish to prefer the pleasure of gratifying a friend much less esteemed than yourself, before the gloomy calm of idle vacancy. Whether I shall easily arrive at an exact punctuality of correspondence, I cannot tell. I shall, at present, expect that you will receive this in return for two which I have had from you. The first, indeed, gave me an account so hopeless of the state of your mind, that it hardly admitted or deserved an answer; by the second I was much better pleased; and the pleasure will still be increased by such a narrative of the progress of your studies, as may evince the continuance of an equal and rational application of your mind to some useful enquiry.

You will, perhaps, wish to ask, what study I would recommend. I shall not speak of theology, because it ought not to be considered as a question whether you shall endeavour to know the will of GOD.

I shall, therefore, consider only such studies as we are at liberty to pursue or to neglect; and of these I know not how you will make a better choice, than by studying the civil law as your father advises, and the ancient languages, as you had determined for yourself; at least resolve, while you remain in any settled residence, to spend a certain number of hours every day amongst your books. The dissipation of thought of which you complain, is nothing more than the vacillation of a mind suspended between different motives, and changing its direction as any motive gains or loses strength. If you can but kindle in your mind any strong desire, if you can but keep predominant any wish for some particular excellence or attainment, the gusts of imagination will break away, without any effect upon your conduct, and commonly without any traces left upon the memory.

There lurks, perhaps, in every human heart a desire of distinction, which inclines every man first to hope, and then to believe, that nature has given him something peculiar to himself. This vanity makes one mind nurse aversion, and another actuate desires, till they rise by art much above their original state of power; and as affectation in time improves to habit, they at last tyrannise over him who at first encouraged them only for show. Every desire is a viper in the bosom, who, while he was chill, was harmless; but when warmth gave him strength, exerted it in poison. You know a gentleman, who, when first he set his foot in the gay world, as he prepared himself to whirl in the vortex of pleasure, imagined a total indifference and universal negligence to be the most agreeable concomitants of youth, and the strongest indication of an airy temper and a quick apprehension. Vacant to every object, and sensible of every impulse, he thought that all appearance of diligence would deduct something from the reputation of genius; and hoped that he should appear to attain, amidst all the ease of carelessness, and all the tumult of diversion, that knowledge and those accomplishments which mortals of the common fabrick obtain only by mute abstraction and solitary drudgery. He tried this scheme of life awhile, was made weary of it by his sense and his virtue; he then wished to return to his studies; and finding long habits of idleness and pleasure harder to be cured than he expected, still willing to retain his claim to some extraordinary prerogatives, resolved the common consequences of irregularity into an unalterable decree of destiny, and concluded that Nature had originally formed him incapable of rational employment.

Let all such fancies, illusive and destructive, be banished hence-forward from your thoughts for ever. Resolve, and keep your resolution; choose, and pursue your choice. If you spend this day in study, you will find yourself still more able to study to-morrow; not that you are to expect that you shall at once obtain a complete victory. Depravity is not very easily overcome. Resolution will sometimes relax, and diligence will sometimes be interrupted; but let no accidental surprise or deviation, whether short or long, dispose you to despondency. Consider these failings as incident to all mankind. Begin again where you left off, and endeavour to avoid the seducements that prevailed over you before.

This, my dear Boswell, is advice which, perhaps, has been often given you, and given you without effect. But this advice, if you will not take from others, you must take from your own reflections, if you purpose to do the duties of the station to which the bounty of Providence has called you.

Let me have a long letter from you as soon as you can. I hope you continue your Journal, and enrich it with many observations upon the country in which you reside. It will be a favour if you can get me any books in the Frisick language, and can enquire how the poor are maintained in the Seven Provinces. I am, dear Sir,
Your most affectionate servant,
SAM JOHNSON

London, Dec. 8, 1763.

I am sorry to observe, that neither in my own minutes, nor in my letters to Johnson which have been preserved by him, can I find any information how the poor are maintained in the Seven Provinces. But I shall extract from one of my letters what I learnt concerning the other subject of his curiosity.

I have made all possible enquiry with respect to the Frisick language, and find that it has been less cultivated than any other of the northern dialects; a certain proof of which is their deficiency of books. Of the old Frisick there are no remains, except some ancient laws preserved by Schotanus in his *"Beschryvinge van die Heerlykheid van Friesland;"* and his *"Historia Frisica."* I have not yet been able to find these books. Professor Trotz, who formerly was of the University of Vranyken in Friesland, and is at present preparing an edition of all the Frisick laws, gave me this information. Of the modern Frisick, or what is spoken by the boors of this day, I have procured a specimen. It is Gisbert Japix's *"Rymelerie,"* which is the only book that they have. It is amazing that they have no translation of the bible, no treatises of devotion, nor even any of the ballads and story-books which are so agreeable to country people. You shall have Japix by the first convenient opportunity. I doubt not to pick up Schotanus. Mynheer Trotz has promised me his assistance.

———◆———

JOHN LOCKE

1632–1704

John Locke, the most influential of the English philosophers, was born at Wrington in Somerset, and educated at Westminster School and Christ Church, Oxford. After taking his medical degree at Oxford in 1674, he became a friend of the Earl of Shaftesbury and a member of his household. There he seems to have served as personal physician to the Earl, having performed a delicate operation credited with saving his life, and as tutor to the young son of the Earl, who grew up to become the third Earl of Shaftesbury and the author of *Characteristics of Men, Manners, Opinions, Times.* After the Earl of Shaftesbury's political downfall, Locke went to Holland where he resided for a time. Perhaps some of the composition of the *Essay Concerning Human Understanding* took place in Holland. When he returned to England in 1689, after the Whig victory of the Glorious Revolution, Locke, it is said, could have had an important post in the government, but he preferred to remain in a private and advisory position which left him more freedom for his literary work.

He published nothing until he was fifty-seven years old. Then began a brilliantly versatile series of publications. His *Essay Concerning Human Understanding*, perhaps the most important single work in English philosophy, appeared in 1690, after Locke had been thinking and working on the subject for twenty years. After a discussion with some friends one night in 1671, he undertook the next day to expound the nature of ideas on a single sheet of paper; the monumental work which changed the course of European thought in 1690 thus had its inception. The influence and importance of the *Essay* can hardly be overstated. Casting aside all time-hallowed notions about innate ideas, Locke sought to determine the basis of ideas—how we know what we know. In so doing he established a new branch of philosophy which has since been called "theory of knowledge" or "epistemology." His constant emphasis on the experience of the senses gave empiricism an impetus that lasted throughout the eighteenth century, and has even now not completely spent its force. Though the rationalism of his thought unwittingly led to the growth of skepticism and atheism in later generations, Locke himself was a staunch Anglican, perfectly willing to believe in the miracles of Christian revelation as being *above* human reason, not *contrary* to it. His last words are indicative of the breadth of his tolerance and the depth of his sincerity: "I die in perfect charity with all men and in sincere communion with the whole church of Christ by whatever name we followers call ourselves."

Locke's *Two Treatises on Government* (1690) have been particularly influential in the development of constitutional democracy, both in England and in America. As the basis of his political philosophy, he held the unswerving faith that the source of all governmental authority lay in the consent of the governed. The welfare of the people thus in Locke's thought became the highest law. Though his political ideas were perhaps originally and primarily intended to justify the Revolution of 1688, they later contributed to the philosophical basis of the American Revolution, and of a number of other democratic revolutions against absolutism.

The amazing fecundity and versatility of Locke are indicated by a list of his lesser-known publications: *Epistola de Tolerantia* (Holland, 1689); *A Second Letter Concerning Toleration* (1690); *A Third Letter for Toleration* (1692); *Some Considerations of the Consequences of the Lowering of Interest, and Raising the Value of Money* (·1691); *Some Thoughts Concerning Education* (1693); *The Reasonableness of Christianity* (1695); *A Vindication of Christianity* (1696). Thus Locke is not only important in the history of philosophy, but is also a significant figure in psychology, government, economics, and education as well. And because of the clarity of his writing, his treatises also have literary merit.

FURTHER READING

HEFELBOWER, S. G. *The Relation of John Locke to Deism* (Chicago, 1918).
MACLEAN, KENNETH. *John Locke and English Literature of the Eighteenth Century* (New Haven, 1936).

An Essay Concerning Human Understanding

BOOK II

CHAPTER I

Of Ideas in General, and Their Original

1. Every man being conscious to himself that he thinks; and that which his mind is applied about whilst thinking being the *ideas* that are there, it is past doubt that men have in their minds several ideas,—such as are those expressed by the words *whiteness, hardness, sweetness, thinking, motion, man, elephant, army, drunkenness,* and others: it is in the first place then to be inquired, *How he comes by them?*

I know it is a received doctrine, that men have native ideas, and original characters, stamped upon their minds in their very first being. This opinion I have at large examined already; and, I suppose what I have said in the foregoing Book will be much more easily admitted, when I have shown whence the understanding may get all the ideas it has; and by what ways and degrees they may come into the mind;—for which I shall appeal to every one's own observation and experience.

2. Let us then suppose the mind to be, as we say, white paper, void of all characters, without any ideas:—How comes it to be furnished? Whence comes it by that vast store which the busy and boundless fancy of man has painted on it with an almost endless variety? Whence has it all the *materials* of reason and knowledge? To this I answer, in one word, from EXPERIENCE. In that all our knowledge is founded; and from that it ultimately derives itself. Our observation employed either, about external sensible objects, or about the internal operations of our minds perceived and reflected on by ourselves, in that which supplies our understandings with all the *materials* of thinking. These two are the fountains of knowledge, from whence all the ideas we have, or can naturally have, do spring.

3. First, our Senses, conversant about particular sensible objects, do convey into the mind several distinct perceptions of things, according to those various ways wherein those objects do affect them. And thus we come by those *ideas* we have of *yellow, white, heat, cold, soft, hard, bitter, sweet,* and all those which we call sensible qualities; which when I say the senses convey into the mind, I mean, they

from external objects convey into the mind what produces there those perceptions. This great source of most of the ideas we have, depending wholly upon our senses, and derived by them to the understanding, I call SENSATION.

4. Secondly, the other fountain from which experience furnisheth the understanding with ideas is,—the perception of the operations of our own mind within us, as it is employed about the ideas it has got;—which operations, when the soul comes to reflect on and consider, do furnish the understanding with another set of ideas, which could not be had from things without. And such are *perception, thinking, doubting, believing, reasoning, knowing, willing,* and all the different actings of our own minds;—which we being conscious of, and observing in ourselves, do from these receive into our understandings as distinct ideas as we do from bodies affecting our senses. This source of ideas every man has wholly in himself; and though it be not sense, as having nothing to do with external objects, yet it is very like it, and might properly enough be called *internal sense.* But as I call the other Sensation, so I call this REFLECTION, the ideas it affords being such only as the mind gets by reflecting on its own operations within itself. By reflection then, in the following part of this discourse, I would be understood to mean, that notice which the mind takes of its own operations, and the manner of them, by reason whereof there come to be ideas of these operations in the understanding. These two, I say, viz. external material things, as the objects of SENSATION, and the operations of our own minds within, as the objects of REFLECTION, are to me the only originals from whence all our ideas take their beginnings. The term *operations* here I use in a large sense, as comprehending not barely the actions of the mind about its ideas, but some sort of passions arising sometimes from them, such as is the satisfaction of uneasiness arising from any thought.

5. The understanding seems to me not to have the least glimmering of any ideas which it doth not receive from one of these two. *External objects* furnish the mind with the ideas of sensible qualities, which are all those different perceptions they produce in us; and *the mind* furnishes the understanding with ideas of its own operations.

These, when we have taken a full survey of them, and their several modes, combinations, and relations, we shall find to contain all our whole stock of ideas; and that we have nothing in our minds which did not come in one of these two ways. Let any one examine his own thoughts, and thoroughly search into his understanding; and then let him tell me, whether all the original ideas he has there, are any other than of the objects of his senses, or of the operations of his mind, considered as objects of his reflection. And how great a mass of knowledge soever he imagines to be lodged there, he will, upon taking a strict view, see that he has not any idea in his mind but what one of these two have imprinted;—though perhaps, with infinite variety compounded and enlarged by the understanding, as we shall see hereafter.

6. He that attentively considers the state of a child, at his first coming into the world, will have little reason to think him stored with plenty of ideas, that are to be the matter of his future knowledge. It is *by degrees* he comes to be furnished with them. And though the ideas of obvious and familiar qualities imprint themselves before the memory begins to keep a register of time or order, yet it is often so late before some unusual qualities come in the way, that there are few men that cannot recollect the beginning of their acquaintance with them. And if it were worth while, no doubt a child might be so ordered as to have but a very few, even of the ordinary ideas, till he were grown up to a man. But all that are born into the world, being surrounded with bodies that perpetually and diversely affect them, variety of ideas, whether care be taken of it or not, are imprinted on the minds of children. Light and colours are busy at hand everywhere, when the eye is but open; sounds and some tangible qualities fail not to solicit their proper senses, and force an entrance to the mind;—but yet, I think, it will be granted easily, that if a child were kept in a place where he never saw any other but black and white till he were a man, he would have no more ideas of scarlet or green, than he that from his childhood never tasted an oyster, or a pine-apple, has of those particular relishes.

7. Men then come to be furnished with fewer or more simple ideas from without, according as the objects they converse with afford greater or less variety; and from the operations of their minds within, according as they more or less reflect on them. For, though he that contemplates the operations of his mind, cannot but have plain and clear ideas of them; yet, unless he turns his thoughts that way, and considers them *attentively,* he will no more have clear and distinct ideas of all the operations of his mind, and all that may be observed therein, than he will have all the particular ideas of any landscape, or of the parts and motions of a clock, who will not turn his eyes to it, and with

attention heed all the parts of it. The picture, or clock may be so placed, that they may come in his way every day; but yet he will have but a confused idea of all the parts they are made up of, till he applies himself with attention, to consider them each in particular.

8. And hence we see the reason why it is pretty late before most children get ideas of the operations of their own minds; and some have not any very clear or perfect ideas of the greatest part of them all their lives. Because, though they pass there continually, yet, like floating visions, they make not deep impressions enough to leave in their mind clear, distinct, lasting ideas, till the understanding turns inward upon itself, reflects on its own operations, and makes them the objects of its own contemplation. Children when they come first into it, are surrounded with a world of new things, which, by a constant solicitation of their senses, draw the mind constantly to them; forward to take notice of new, and apt to be delighted with the variety of changing objects. Thus the first years are usually employed and diverted in looking abroad. Men's business in them is to acquaint themselves with what is to be found without; and so growing up in a constant attention to outward sensations, seldom make any considerable reflection on what passes within them, till they come to be of riper years; and some scarce ever at all.

9. To ask, at what *time* a man has first any ideas, is to ask, when he begins to perceive;—*having ideas,* and *perception,* being the same thing. I know it is an opinion, that the soul always thinks, and that it has the actual perception of ideas in itself constantly, as long as it exists; and that actual thinking is as inseparable from the soul as actual extension is from the body; which if true, to inquire after the beginning of a man's ideas is the same as to inquire after the beginning of his soul. For, by this account, soul and its ideas, as body and its extension, will begin to exist both at the same time.

10. But whether the soul be supposed to exist antecedent to, or coeval with, or some time after the first rudiments of organization, or the beginnings of life in the body, I leave to be disputed by those who have better thought of that matter. I confess myself to have one of those dull souls, that doth not perceive itself always to contemplate ideas; nor can conceive it any more necessary for the soul always to think, than for the body always to move: the perception of ideas being (as I conceive) to the soul, what motion is to the body; not its essence, but one of its operations. And therefore, though think-

ing be supposed never so much the proper action of the soul, yet it is not necessary to suppose that it should be always thinking, always in action. That, perhaps, is the privilege of the infinite Author and Preserver of all things, who "never slumbers nor sleeps"; but is not competent to any finite being, at least not to the soul of man. We know certainly, by experience that we *sometimes* think; and thence draw this infallible consequence,—that there is something in us that has a power to think. But whether that substance *perpetually* thinks or no, we can be no further assured than experience informs us. For, to say that actual thinking is essential to the soul, and inseparable from it, is to beg what is in question, and not to prove it by reason;—which is necessary to be done, if it be not a self-evident proposition. But whether this, "That the soul always thinks," be a self-evident proposition, that everybody assents to at first hearing, I appeal to mankind. It is doubted whether I thought at all last night or no. The question being about a matter of fact, it is begging it to bring, as a proof for it, an hypothesis, which is the very thing in dispute: by which way one may prove anything, and it is but supposing that all watches, whilst the balance beats, think, and it is sufficiently proved, and past doubt, that my watch thought all last night. But he that would not deceive himself, ought to build his hypothesis on matter of fact, and make it out by sensible experience, and not presume on matter of fact, because of his hypothesis, that is, because he supposes it to be so; which way of proving amounts to this, that I must necessarily think all last night, because another supposes I always think, though I myself cannot perceive that I always do so.

But men in love with their opinions may not only suppose what is in question, but allege wrong matter of fact. How else could any one make it an inference of mine, that a thing is not, because we are not sensible of it in our sleep? I do not say there is no *soul* in a man, because he is not sensible of it in his sleep; but I do say, he cannot *think* at any time, waking or sleeping, without being sensible of it. Our being sensible of it is not necessary to anything but to our thoughts; and to them it is; and to them it always will be necessary, till we can think without being conscious of it.

11. I grant that the soul, in a waking man, is never without thought, because it is the condition of being awake. But whether sleeping without dreaming be not an affection of the whole man, mind as well as body, may be worth a waking man's consideration; it being hard to conceive that any-

thing should think and not be conscious of it. If the soul doth think in a sleeping man without being conscious of it, I ask whether, during such thinking, it has any pleasure or pain, or be capable of happiness or misery? I am sure the man is not; no more than the bed or earth he lies on. For to be happy or miserable without being conscious of it, seems to me utterly inconsistent and impossible. Or if it be possible that the *soul* can, whilst the body is sleeping, have its thinking, enjoyments and concerns, its pleasures or pain, apart, which the *man* is not conscious of nor partakes in,—it is certain that Socrates asleep and Socrates awake is not the same person; but his soul when he sleeps, and Socrates the man, consisting of body and soul, when he is waking, are two persons: since waking Socrates has no knowledge of, or concernment for that happiness or misery of his soul, which it enjoys alone by itself whilst he sleeps, without perceiving anything of it; no more than he has for the happiness or misery of a man in the Indies, whom he knows not. For, if we take wholly away all consciousness of our actions and sensations, especially of pleasure and pain, and the concernment that accompanies it, it will be hard to know wherein to place personal identity.

12. The soul, during sound sleep, thinks, say these men. Whilst it thinks and perceives, it is capable certainly of those of delight or trouble, as well as any other perceptions; and *it* must necessarily be *conscious* of its own perceptions. But it has all this apart: the sleeping *man*, it is plain, is conscious of nothing of all this. Let us suppose, then, the soul of Castor, while he is sleeping, retired from his body; which is no impossible supposition for the men I have here to do with, who so liberally allow life, without a thinking soul, to all other animals. These men cannot then judge it impossible, or a contradiction, that the body should live without the soul; nor that the soul should subsist and think, or have perception, even perception of happiness or misery, without the body. Let us then, I say, suppose the soul of Castor separated during his sleep from his body, to think apart. Let us suppose, too, that it chooses for its scene of thinking the body of another man, v. g. Pollux, who is sleeping without a soul. For, if Castor's soul can think, whilst Castor is asleep, what Castor is never conscious of, it is no matter what *place* it chooses to think in. We have here, then, the bodies of two men with only one soul between them, which we will suppose to sleep and wake by turns; and the soul still thinking in the waking man, whereof the

sleeping man is never conscious, has never the least perception. I ask, then, whether Castor and Pollux, thus with only one soul between them, which thinks and perceives in one what the other is never conscious of, nor is concerned for, are not two as distinct *persons* as Castor and Hercules, or as Socrates and Plato were? And whether one of them might not be very happy, and the other very miserable? Just by the same reason, they make the soul and the man two persons, who make the soul think apart what the man is not conscious of. For, I suppose nobody will make identity of persons to consist in the soul's being united to the very same numerical particles of matter. For if that be necessary to identity, it will be impossible, in that constant flux of the particles of our bodies, that any man should be the same person two days, or two moments, together.

13. Thus, methinks, every drowsy nod shakes their doctrine, who teach that the soul is always thinking. Those, at least, who do at any time *sleep without dreaming,* can never be convinced that their thoughts are sometimes for four hours busy without their knowing of it; and if they are taken in the very act, waked in the middle of that sleeping contemplation, can give no manner of account of it.

14. It will perhaps be said,—That the soul thinks even in the soundest sleep, but the *memory* retains it not. That the soul in a sleeping man should be this moment busy a thinking, and the next moment in a waking man not remember nor be able to recollect one jot of all those thoughts, is very hard to be conceived, and would need some better proof than bare assertion to make it be believed. For who can without any more ado, but being barely told so, imagine that the greatest part of men do, during all their lives, for several hours every day, think of something, which if they were asked, even in the middle of these thoughts, they could remember nothing at all of? Most men, I think, pass a great part of their sleep without dreaming. I once knew a man that was bred a scholar, and had no bad memory, who told me had never dreamed in his life, till he had that fever he was then newly recovered of, which was about the five or six, and twentieth year of his age. I suppose the world affords more such instances: at least every one's acquaintance will furnish him with examples enough of such as pass most of their nights without dreaming.

15. To think often, and never to retain it so much as one moment, is a very useless sort of thinking; and the soul, in such a state of thinking, does very little, if at all, excel that of a looking-glass, which constantly receives variety of images, or ideas, but retains none; they disappear and vanish, and there remain no footsteps of them; the looking-glass is never the better for such ideas, nor the soul for such thoughts. Perhaps it will be said, that in a waking *man* the materials of the body are employed, and made use of, in thinking; and that the memory of thoughts is retained by the impressions that are made on the brain, and the traces there left after such thinking; but that in the thinking of the *soul,* which is not perceived in a sleeping man, there the soul thinks apart, and making no use of the organs of the body, leaves no impressions on it, and consequently no memory of such thoughts. Not to mention again the absurdity of two distinct persons, which follows from this supposition, I answer, further,—That whatever ideas the mind can receive and contemplate without the help of the body, it is reasonable to conclude it can retain without the help of the body too; or else the soul, or any separate spirit, will have but little advantage by thinking. If it has no memory of its own thoughts; if it cannot lay them up for its own use, and be able to recall them upon occasion; if it cannot reflect upon what is past, and make use of its former experiences, reasonings, and contemplations, to what purpose does it think? They who make the soul a thinking thing, at this rate, will not make it a much more noble being than those do whom they condemn, for allowing it to be nothing but the subtilest parts of matter. Characters drawn on dust, that the first breath of wind effaces; or impressions made on a heap of atoms, or animal spirits, are altogether as useful, and render the subject as noble, as the thoughts of a soul that perish in thinking; that, once out of sight, are gone for ever, and leave no memory of themselves behind them. Nature never makes excellent things for mean or no uses: and it is hardly to be conceived that our infinitely wise Creator should make so admirable a faculty as the power of thinking, that faculty which comes nearest the excellency of his own incomprehensible being, to be so idly and uselessly employed, at least a fourth part of its time here, as to think constantly, without remembering any of those thoughts, without doing any good to itself or others, or being any way useful to any other part of the creation. If we will examine it, we shall not find, I suppose, the motion of dull and senseless matter, any where in the universe, made so little use of and so wholly thrown away.

16. It is true, we have sometimes instances of perception whilst we are asleep, and retain the memory of those thoughts: but how extravagant and incoherent for the most part they are; how little conformable to the perfection and order of a rational being, those who are acquainted with dreams need not be told. This I would willingly be satisfied in,—whether the soul, when it thinks thus apart, and as it were separate from the body, acts less rationally than when conjointly with it, or no. If its separate thoughts be less rational, then these men must say, that the soul owes the perfection of rational thinking to the body: if it does not, it is a wonder that our dreams should be, for the most part, so frivolous and irrational; and that the soul should retain none of its more rational soliloquies and meditations.

17. Those who so confidently tell us that the soul always actually thinks, I would they would also tell us, what those ideas are that are in the soul of a child, before or just at the union with the body, before it hath received any by sensation. The dreams of sleeping men are, as I take it, all made up of the waking man's ideas; though for the most part oddly put together. It is strange, if the soul has ideas of its own that it derived not from sensation or reflection, (as it must have, if it thought before it received any impressions from the body,) that it should never, in its private thinking, (so private, that the man himself perceives it not,) retain any of them the very moment it wakes out of them, and then make the man glad with new discoveries. Who can find it reason that the soul should, in its retirement during sleep, have so many hours' thoughts, and yet never light on any of those ideas it borrowed not from sensation or reflection; or at least preserve the memory of none but such, which, being occasioned from the body, must needs be less natural to a spirit? It is strange the soul should never once in a man's whole life recall over any of its pure native thoughts, and those ideas it had before it borrowed anything from the body; never bring into the waking man's view any other ideas but what have a tang of the cask, and manifestly derive their original from that union. If it always thinks, and so had ideas before it was united, or before it received any from the body, it is not to be supposed but that during sleep it recollects its native ideas; and during that retirement from communicating with the body, whilst it thinks by itself, the ideas it is busied about should be, sometimes at least, those more natural and congenial ones which it had in itself, underived from the body, or its own operations about them: which, since the waking man never remembers, we must from this hypothesis conclude either that the soul remembers something that the man does not; or else that memory belongs only to such ideas as are derived from the body, or the mind's operations about them.

18. I would be glad also to learn from these men who so confidently pronounce that the human soul, or, which is all one, that a man always thinks, how they come to know it; nay, how they come to know that they themselves think, when they themselves do not perceive it. This, I am afraid, is to be sure without proofs, and to know without perceiving. It is, I suspect, a confused notion, taken up to serve an hypothesis; and none of those clear truths, that either their own evidence forces us to admit, or common experience makes it impudence to deny. For the most that can be said of it is, that it is possible the soul may always think, but not always retain it in memory. And I say, it is as possible that the soul may not always think; and much more probable that it should sometimes not think, than that it should often think, and that a long while together, and not be conscious to itself, the next moment after, that it had thought.

19. To suppose the soul to think, and the man not to perceive it, is, as has been said, to make two persons in one man. And if one considers well these men's way of speaking, one should be led into a suspicion that they do so. For they who tell us that the *soul* always thinks, do never, that I remember, say that a *man* always thinks. Can the soul think, and not the man? Or a man think, and not be conscious of it? This, perhaps, would be suspected of jargon in others. If they say the man thinks always, but is not always conscious of it, they may as well say his body is extended without having parts. For it is altogether as intelligible to say that a body is extended without parts, as that anything thinks without being conscious of it, or perceiving that it does so. They who talk thus may, with as much reason, if it be necessary to their hypothesis, say that a man is always hungry, but that he does not always feel it; whereas hunger consists in that very sensation, as thinking consists in being conscious that one thinks. If they say that a man is always conscious to himself of thinking, I ask, How they know it? Consciousness is the perception of what passes in a man's own mind. Can another man perceive that I am conscious of anything, when I perceive it not myself? No man's knowledge here can go beyond his experience. Wake a man out of a sound sleep, and ask him what he was that moment thinking of. If he himself be conscious of

nothing he then thought on, he must be a notable diviner of thoughts that can assure him that he was thinking. May he not, with more reason, assure him he was not asleep? This is something beyond philosophy; and it cannot be less than revelation, that discovers to another thoughts in my mind, when I can find none there myself. And they must needs have a penetrating sight who can certainly see that I think, when I cannot perceive it myself, and when I declare that I do not; and yet can see that dogs or elephants do not think, when they give all the demonstration of it imaginable, except only telling us that they do so. This some may suspect to be a step beyond the Rosicrucians; it seeming easier to make one's self invisible to others, than to make another's thoughts visible to me, which are not visible to himself. But it is but defining the soul to be "a substance that always thinks," and the business is done. If such definition be of any authority, I know not what it can serve for but to make many men suspect that they have no souls at all; since they find a good part of their lives pass away without thinking. For no definitions that I know, no suppositions of any sect, are of force enough to destroy constant experience; and perhaps it is the affectation of knowing beyond what we perceive, that makes so much useless dispute and noise in the world.

20. I see no reason, therefore, to believe that the soul thinks before the senses have furnished it with ideas to think on; and as those are increased and retained, so it comes, by exercise, to improve its faculty of thinking in the several parts of it; as well as, afterwards, by compounding those ideas, and reflecting on its own operations, it increases its stock, as well as facility in remembering, imagining, reasoning, and other modes of thinking.

21. He that will suffer himself to be informed by observation and experience, and not make his own hypothesis the rule of nature, will find few signs of a soul accustomed to much thinking in a new-born child, and much fewer of any reasoning at all. And yet it is hard to imagine that the rational soul should think so much, and not reason at all. And he that will consider that infants newly come into the world spend the greatest part of their time in sleep, and are seldom awake but when either hunger calls for the teat, or some pain (the most importunate of all sensations), or some other violent impression on the body, forces the mind to perceive and attend to it;—he, I say, who considers this, will perhaps find reason to imagine that a *foetus* in the mother's womb differs not much from the state of a vegetable, but passes the greatest part of its time without perception or thought; doing very little but sleep in a place where it needs not seek for food, and is surrounded with liquor, always equally soft, and near of the same temper; where the eyes have no light, and the ears so shut up are not very susceptible of sounds; and where there is little or no variety, or change of objects, to move the senses.

22. Follow a child from its birth, and observe the alterations that time makes, and you shall find, as the mind by the senses comes more and more to be furnished with ideas, it comes to be more and more awake; thinks more, the more it has matter to think on. After some time it begins to know the objects which, being most familiar with it, have made lasting impressions. Thus it comes by degrees to know the persons it daily converses with, and distinguishes them from strangers; which are instances and effects of its coming to retain and distinguish the ideas the senses convey to it. And so we may observe how the mind, *by degrees*, improves in these; and *advances* to the exercise of those other faculties of enlarging, compounding, and abstracting its ideas, and of reasoning about them, and reflecting upon all these; of which I shall have occasion to speak more hereafter.

23. If it shall be demanded then, *when* a man *begins* to have any ideas, I think the true answer is,—*when he first has any sensation.* For, since there appear not to be any ideas in the mind before the senses have conveyed any in, I conceive that ideas in the understanding are coeval with *sensation; which is such an impression or motion made in some part of the body, as [produces some perception] in the understanding.* It is about these impressions made on our senses by outward objects that the mind seems *first* to employ itself, in such operations as we call perception, remembering, consideration, reasoning, &c.

24. In time the mind comes to reflect on its own operations about the ideas got by sensation, and thereby stores itself with a new set of ideas, which I call ideas of reflection. These are the impressions that are made on our senses by outward objects that are extrinsical to the mind; and its own operations, proceeding from powers intrinsical and proper to itself, which, when reflected on by itself, become also objects of its contemplation—are, as I have said, the original of all knowledge. Thus the first capacity of human intellect is,—that the mind is fitted to receive the impressions made on it; either through the senses by outward objects, or by its own operations when it reflects on them. This is the first

step a man makes towards the discovery of any-thing, and the groundwork whereon to build all those notions which ever he shall have naturally in this world. All those sublime thoughts which tower above the clouds, and reach as high as heaven itself, take their rise and footing here: in all that great extent wherein the mind wanders, in those remote speculations it may seem to be elevated with, it stirs not one jot beyond those ideas which *sense* or *reflection* have offered for its contemplation.

25. In this part the understanding is merely passive; and whether or no it will have these be-ginnings, and as it were materials of knowledge, is not in its own power. For the objects of our senses do, many of them, obtrude their particular ideas upon our minds whether we will or not; and the operations of our minds will not let us be without, at least, some obscure notions of them. No man can be wholly ignorant of what he does when he thinks. These simple ideas, when offered to the mind, the understanding can no more refuse to have, nor alter when they are imprinted, nor blot them out and make new ones itself, than a mirror can refuse, alter, or obliterate the images or ideas which the objects set before it do therein produce. As the bodies that surround us do diversely affect our organs, the mind is forced to receive the impressions; and cannot avoid the perception of those ideas that are annexed to them.

An Essay Concerning the True Original, Extent and End of Civil Government

CHAPTER II

Of the State of Nature

4. To understand political power aright, and de-rive it from its original, we must consider what estate all men are naturally in, and that is, a state of perfect freedom to order their actions, and dispose of their possessions and persons as they think fit, within the bounds of the law of Nature, without asking leave or depending upon the will of any other man.

A state also of equality, wherein all the power and jurisdiction is reciprocal, no one having more than another, there being nothing more evident than that creatures of the same species and rank, pro-

miscuously born to all the same advantages of Nature, and the use of the same faculties, should also be equal one amongst another, without sub-ordination or subjection, unless the lord and master of them all should, by any manifest declaration of his will, set one above another, and confer on him, by an evident and clear appointment, an undoubted right to dominion and sovereignty.

5. This equality of men by Nature, the judicious Hooker looks upon as so evident in itself, and be-yond all question, that he makes it the foundation of that obligation to mutual love amongst men on which he builds the duties they owe one another, and from whence he derives the great maxims of justice and charity. His words are:

"The like natural inducement hath brought men to know that it is no less their duty to love others than themselves, for seeing those things which are equal, must needs all have one measure; if I cannot but wish to receive good, even as much at every man's hands, as any man can wish unto his own soul, how should I look to have any part of my desire herein satisfied, unless myself be careful to satisfy the like desire, which is undoubtedly in other men weak, being of one and the same nature: to have anything offered them repugnant to this desire must needs, in all respects, grieve them as much as me; so that if I do harm, I must look to suffer, there being no reason that others should show greater measure of love to me than they have by me showed unto them; my desire, therefore, to be loved of my equals in Nature, as much as possible may be, im-poseth upon me a natural duty of bearing to them-ward fully the like affection. From which relation of equality between ourselves and them that are as ourselves, what several rules and canons natural reason hath drawn for direction of life no man is ignorant." (*Eccl. Pol. i.*)

6. But though this be a state of liberty, yet it is not a state of licence; though man in that state have an uncontrollable liberty to dispose of his person or possessions, yet he has not liberty to destroy himself, or so much as any creature in his possession, but where some nobler use than its bare preservation calls for it. The state of Nature has a law of Nature to govern it, which obliges every one, and reason, which is that law, teaches all mankind who will but consult it, that being all equal and independent, no one ought to harm another in his life, health, liberty or possessions; for men being all the work-manship of one omnipotent and infinitely wise Maker; all the servants of one sovereign Master, sent into the world by His order and about His

business; they are His property, whose workmanship they are made to last during His, not one another's pleasure. And, being furnished with like faculties, sharing all in one community of Nature, there cannot be supposed any such subordination among us that may authorise us to destroy one another, as if we were made for one another's uses, as the inferior ranks of creatures are for ours. Every one as he is bound to preserve himself, and not to quit his station wilfully, so by the like reason, when his own preservation comes not in competition, ought he as much as he can to preserve the rest of mankind, and not unless it be to do justice on an offender, take away or impair the life, or what tends to the preservation of the life, the liberty, health, limb, or goods of another.

7. And that all men may be restrained from invading others' rights, and from doing hurt to one another, and the law of Nature be observed, which willeth the peace and preservation of all mankind, the execution of the law of Nature is in that state put into every man's hands, whereby every one has a right to punish the transgressors of that law to such a degree as may hinder its violation. For the law of Nature would, as all other laws that concern men in this world, be in vain if there were nobody that in the state of Nature had a power to execute that law, and thereby preserve the innocent and restrain offenders; and if any one in the state of Nature may punish another for any evil he has done, every one may do so. For in that state of perfect equality, where naturally there is no superiority or jurisdiction of one over another, what any may do in prosecution of that law, every one must needs have a right to do.

8. And thus, in the state of Nature, one man comes by a power over another, but yet no absolute or arbitrary power to use a criminal, when he has got him in his hands, according to the passionate heats or boundless extravagancy of his own will, but only to retribute to him so far as calm reason and conscience dictate, what is proportionate to his transgression, which is so much as may serve for reparation and restraint. For these two are the only reasons why one man may lawfully do harm to another, which is that we call punishment. In transgressing the law of Nature, the offender declares himself to live by another rule than that of reason and common equity, which is that measure God has set to the actions of men for their mutual security, and so he becomes dangerous to mankind; the tie which is to secure them from injury and violence being slighted and broken by him, which

being a trespass against the whole species, and the peace and safety of it, provided for by the law of Nature, every man upon this score, by the right he hath to preserve mankind in general, may restrain, or where it is necessary, destroy things noxious to them, and so may bring such evil on any one who hath transgressed that law, as may make him repent the doing of it, and thereby deter him, and, by his example, others from doing the like mischief. And in this case, and upon this ground, every man hath a right to punish the offender, and be executioner of the law of Nature.

9. I doubt not but this will seem a very strange doctrine to some men; but before they condemn it, I desire them to resolve me by what right any prince or state can put to death or punish an alien for any crime he commits in their country? It is certain their laws, by virtue of any sanction they receive from the promulgated will of the legislature, reach not a stranger. They speak not to him, nor, if they did, is he bound to hearken to them. The legislative authority by which they are in force over the subjects of that commonwealth hath no power over him. Those who have the supreme power of making laws in England, France, or Holland are, to an Indian, but like the rest of the world—men without authority. And therefore, if by the law of Nature every man hath not a power to punish offences against it, as he soberly judges the case to require, I see not how the magistrates of any community can punish an alien of another country, since, in reference to him, they can have no more power than what every man naturally may have over another.

10. Besides the crime which consists in violating the laws, and varying from the right rule of reason, whereby a man so far becomes degenerate, and declares himself to quit the principles of human nature and to be a noxious creature, there is commonly injury done, and some person or other, some other man, receives damage by his transgression: in which case, he who hath received any damage has (besides the right of punishment common to him, with other men) a particular right to seek reparation from him that hath done it. And any other person who finds it just may also join with him that is injured, and assist him in recovering from the offender so much as may make satisfaction for the harm he hath suffered.

11. From these two distinct rights (the one of punishing the crime, for restraint and preventing the like offence, which right of punishing is in everybody, the other of taking reparation, which belongs only to the injured party) comes it to pass

that the magistrate, who by being magistrate hath the common right of punishing put into his hands, can often, where the public good demands not the execution of the law, remit the punishment of criminal offences by his own authority, but yet cannot remit the satisfaction due to any private man for the damage he has received. That he who hath suffered the damage has a right to demand in his own name, and he alone can remit. The damnified person has this power of appropriating to himself the goods or service of the offender by right of self-preservation, as every man has a power to punish the crime to prevent its being committed again, by the right he has of preserving all mankind, and doing all reasonable things he can in order to that end. And thus it is that every man in the state of Nature has a power to kill a murderer, both to deter others from doing the like injury (which no reparation can compensate) by the example of the punishment that attends it from everybody, and also to secure men from the attempts of a criminal who, having renounced reason, the common rule and measure God hath given to mankind, hath, by the unjust violence and slaughter he hath committed upon one, declared war against all mankind, and therefore may be destroyed as a lion or a tiger, one of those wild savage beasts with whom men can have no society nor security. And upon this is grounded the great law of Nature, "Whoso sheddeth man's blood, by man shall his blood be shed." And Cain was so fully convinced that every one had a right to destroy such a criminal, that, after the murder of his brother, he cries out, "Every one that findeth me shall slay me," so plain was it writ in the hearts of all mankind.

12. By the same reason may a man in the state of Nature punish the lesser breaches of that law, it will, perhaps, be demanded, with death? I answer: Each transgression may be punished to that degree, and with so much severity, as will suffice to make it an ill bargain to the offender, give him cause to repent, and terrify others from doing the like. Every offence that can be committed in the state of Nature may, in the state of Nature, be also punished equally, and as far forth, as it may, in a commonwealth. For though it would be beside my present purpose to enter here into the particulars of the law of Nature, or its measures of punishment, yet it is certain there is such a law, and that too as intelligible and plain to a rational creature and a studier of that law as the positive laws of commonwealths, nay, possibly plainer; as much as reason is easier to be understood than the fancies

and intricate contrivances of men, following contrary and hidden interests put into words; for truly so are a great part of the municipal laws of countries, which are only so far right as they are founded on the law of Nature, by which they are to be regulated and interpreted.

13. To this strange doctrine—viz., That in the state of Nature every one has the executive power of the law of Nature—I doubt not but it will be objected that it is unreasonable for men to be judges in their own cases, that self-love will make men partial to themselves and their friends; and, on the other side, ill-nature, passion, and revenge will carry them too far in punishing others, and hence nothing but confusion and disorder will follow, and that therefore God hath certainly appointed government to restrain the partiality and violence of men. I easily grant that civil government is the proper remedy for the inconveniences of the state of Nature, which must certainly be great where men may be judges in their own case, since it is easy to be imagined that he who was so unjust as to do his brother an injury will scarce be so just as to condemn himself for it. But I shall desire those who make this objection to remember that absolute monarchs are but men; and if government is to be the remedy of those evils which necessarily follow from men being judges in their own cases, and the state of Nature is therefore not to be endured, I desire to know what kind of government that is, and how much better it is than the state of Nature, where one man commanding a multitude has the liberty to be judge in his own case, and may do to all his subjects whatever he pleases without the least question or control of those who execute his pleasure? and in whatsoever he doth, whether led by reason, mistake, or passion, must be submitted to? which men in the state of Nature are not bound to do one to another. And if he that judges, judges amiss in his own or any other case, he is answerable for it to the rest of mankind.

14. It is often asked as a mighty objection, where are, or ever were, there any men in such a state of Nature? To which it may suffice as an answer at present, that since all princes and rulers of "independent" governments all through the world are in a state of Nature, it is plain the world never was, nor never will be, without numbers of men in that state. I have named all governors of "independent" communities, whether they are, or are not, in league with others; for it is not every compact that puts an end to the state of Nature between men, but only this one of agreeing together mutu-

ally to enter into one community, and make one body politic; other promises and compacts men may make one with another, and yet still be in the state of Nature. The promises and bargains for truck, etc., between the two men in Soldania, in or between a Swiss and an Indian, in the woods of America, are binding to them, though they are perfectly in a state of Nature in reference to one another for truth, and keeping of faith belongs to men as men, and not as members of society.

15. To those that say there were never any men in the state of Nature, I will not only oppose the authority of the judicious Hooker (*Eccl. Pol.* i. 10) where he says, "the laws which have been hitherto mentioned"—*i.e.,* the laws of Nature—"do bind men absolutely, even as they are men, although they have never any settled fellowship, never any solemn agreement amongst themselves what to do or not to do; but for as much as we are not by ourselves sufficient to furnish ourselves with competent store of things needful for such a life as our Nature doth desire, a life fit for the dignity of man, therefore to supply those defects and imperfections which are in us, as living single and solely by ourselves, we are naturally induced to seek communion and fellowship with others; this was the cause of men uniting themselves as first in politic societies." But I, moreover, affirm that all men are naturally in that state, and remain so till, by their own consents, they make themselves members of some politic society, and I doubt not, in the sequel of this discourse, to make it very clear.

CHAPTER V

Of Property

24. Whether we consider natural reason, which tells us that men, being once born, have a right to their preservation, and consequently to meat and drink and such other things as Nature affords for their subsistence, or "revelation," which gives us an account of those grants God made of the world to Adam, and to Noah and his sons, it is very clear that God, as King David says (Psalm cxv. 16), "has given the earth to the children of men," given it to mankind in common. But, this being supposed, it seems to some a very great difficulty how any one should ever come to have a property in anything, I will not content myself to answer, that, if it be difficult to make out "property" upon a supposition that God gave the world to Adam and his posterity

in common, it is impossible that any man but one universal monarch should have any "property" upon a supposition that God gave the world to Adam and his heirs in succession, exclusive of all the rest of his posterity; but I shall endeavour to show how men might come to have a property in several parts of that which God gave to mankind in common, and that without any express compact of all the commoners.

25. God, who hath given the world to men in common, hath also given them reason to make use of it to the best advantage of life and convenience. The earth and all that is therein is given to men for the support and comfort of their being. And though all the fruits it naturally produces, and beasts it feeds, belong to mankind in common, as they are produced by the spontaneous hand of Nature, and nobody has originally a private dominion exclusive of the rest of mankind in any of them, as they are thus in their natural state, yet being given for the use of men, there must of necessity be a means to appropriate them some way or other before they can be of any use, or at all beneficial, to any particular men. The fruit or venison which nourishes the wild Indian, who knows no enclosure, and is still a tenant in common, must be his, and so his—*i.e.,* a part of him, that another can no longer have any right to it before it can do him any good for the support of his life.

26. Though the earth and all inferior creatures be common to all men, yet every man has a "property" in his own "person." This nobody has any right to but himself. The "labour" of his body and the "work" of his hands, we may say, are properly his. Whatsoever, then, he removes out of his state that Nature hath provided and left it in, he hath mixed his labour with it, and joined to it something that is his own, and thereby makes it his property. It being by him removed from the common state Nature placed it in, it hath by this labour something annexed to it that excludes the common right of other men. For this "labour" being the unquestionable property of the labourer, no man but he can have a right to what that is once joined to, at least where there is enough, and as good left in common for others.

27. He that is nourished by the acorns he picked up under an oak, or the apples he gathered from the trees in the wood, has certainly appropriated them to himself. Nobody can deny but the nourishment is his. I ask, then, when did they begin to be his? when he digested? or when he ate? or when he

boiled? or when he brought them home? or when he picked them up? And it is plain, if the first gathering made them not his, nothing else could. That labour put a distinction between them and common. That added something to them more than Nature, the common mother of all, had done, and so they became his private right. And will any one say he had no right to those acorns or apples he thus appropriated because he had not the consent of all mankind to make them his? Was it robbery thus to assume to himself what belonged to all in common? If such a consent as that was necessary, man had starved, notwithstanding the plenty God had given him. We see in commons, which remain so by compact, that it is the taking any part of what is common, and removing it out of the state Nature leaves it in, which begins the property, without which the common is of no use. And the taking of this or that part does not depend on the express consent of all the commoners. Thus, the grass my horse has bit, the turfs my servant has cut, and the ore I have digged in any place, where I have a right to them in common with others, become my property without the assignation or consent of anybody. The labour that was mine, removing them out of that common state they were in, hath fixed my property in them.

28. By making an explicit consent of every commoner necessary to any one's appropriating to himself any part of what is given in common. Children or servants could not cut the meat which their father or master had provided for them in common without assigning to every one his peculiar part. Though the water running in the fountain be every one's, yet who can doubt but that in the pitcher is his only who drew it out? His labour hath taken it out of the hands of Nature where it was common, and belonged equally to all her children, and hath thereby appropriated it to himself.

29. Thus this law of reason makes the deer that Indian's who hath killed it; it is allowed to be his goods who hath bestowed his labour upon it, though, before, it was the common right of every one. And amongst those who are counted the civilised part of mankind, who have made and multiplied positive laws to determine property, this original law of Nature for the beginning of property, in what was before common, still takes place, and by virtue thereof, what fish any one catches in the ocean, that great and still remaining common of mankind; or what ambergris any one takes up here is by the labour that removes it out of that common

state Nature left it in, made his property who takes that pains about it. And even amongst us, the hare that any one is hunting is thought his who pursues her during the chase. For being a beast that is still looked upon as common, and no man's private possession, whoever has employed so much labour about any of that kind as to find and pursue her has thereby removed her from the state of Nature wherein she was common, and hath begun a property.

30. It will, perhaps, be objected to this, that if gathering the acorns or other fruits of the earth, etc., makes a right to them, then any one may engross as much as he will. To which I answer, Not so. The same law of Nature that does by this means give us property, does also bound that property too. "God has given us all things richly." Is the voice of reason confirmed by inspiration? But how far has He given it us—"to enjoy"? As much as any one can make use of to any advantage of life before it spoils, so much he may by his labour fix a property in. Whatever is beyond this is more than his share, and belongs to others. Nothing was made by God for man to spoil or destroy. And thus considering the plenty of natural provisions there was a long time in the world, and the few spenders, and to how small a part of that provision the industry of one man could extend itself and engross it to the prejudice of others, especially keeping within the bounds set by reason of what might serve for his use, there could be then little room for quarrels or contentions about property so established.

31. But the chief matter of property being now not the fruits of the earth and the beasts that subsist on it, but the earth itself, as that which takes in and carries with it all the rest, I think it is plain that property in that too is acquired as the former. As much land as a man tills, plants, improves, cultivates, and can use the product of, so much is his property. He by his labour does, as it were, enclose it from the common. Nor will it invalidate his right to say everybody else has an equal title to it, and therefore he cannot appropriate, he cannot enclose, without the consent of his fellow-commoners, all mankind. God, when He gave the world in common to all mankind, commanded man also to labour, and the penury of his condition required it of him. God and his reason commanded him to subdue the earth—i.e., improve it for the benefit of life and therein lay out something upon it that was his own, his labour. He that, in obedience to this command of God, subdued, tilled, and sowed any

part of it, thereby annexed to it something that was his property, which another had no title to, nor could without injury take from him.

32. Nor was this appropriation of any parcel of land, by improving it, any prejudice to any other man, since there was still enough and as good left, and more than the yet unprovided could use. So that, in effect, there was never the less left for others because of his enclosure for himself. For he that leaves as much as another can make use of does as good as take nothing at all. Nobody could think himself injured by the drinking of another man, though he took a good draught, who had a whole river of the same water left him to quench his thirst. And the case of land and water, where there is enough of both, is perfectly the same.

33. God gave the world to men in common, but since He gave it them for their benefit and the greatest conveniencies of life they were capable to draw from it, it cannot be supposed He meant it should always remain common and uncultivated. He gave it to the use of the industrious and rational (and labour was to be his title to it); not to the fancy or covetousness of the quarrelsome and contentious. He that had as good left for his improvement as was already taken up needed not complain, ought not to meddle with what was already improved by another's labour; if he did it is plain he desired the benefit of another's pains, which he had no right to, and not the ground which God had given him, in common with others, to labour on, and whereof there was as good left as that already possessed, and more than he knew what to do with, or his industry could reach to.

34. It is true, in land that is common in England or any other country, where there are plenty of people under government who have money and commerce, no one can enclose or appropriate any part without the consent of all his fellow-commoners; because this is left common by compact— i.e., by the law of the land, which is not to be violated. And, though it be common in respect of some men, it is not so to all mankind, but is the joint propriety of this country, or this parish. Besides, the remainder, after such enclosure, would not be as good to the rest of the commoners as the whole was, when they could all make use of the whole; whereas in the beginning and first peopling of the great common of the world it was quite otherwise. The law man was under was rather for appropriating. God commanded, and his wants forced him to labour. That was his property, which could not be taken from him wherever he had fixed it. And hence subduing or cultivating the earth and having dominion, we see, are joined together. The one gave title to the other. So that God, by commanding to subdue, gave authority so far to appropriate. And the condition of human life, which requires labour and materials to work on, necessarily introduced private possessions.

35. The measure of property Nature well set, by the extent of men's labour and the conveniency of life. No man's labour could subdue or appropriate all, nor could his enjoyment consume more than a small part; so that it was impossible for any man, this way, to entrench upon the right of another or acquire to himself a property to the prejudice of his neighbour, who would still have room for as good and as large a possession (after the other had taken out his) as before it was appropriated. Which measure did confine every man's possession to a very moderate proportion, and such as he might appropriate to himself without injury to anybody in the first ages of the world, when men were more in danger to be lost, by wandering from their company, in the then vast wilderness of the earth than to be straitened for want of room to plant in.

36. The same measure may be allowed still, without prejudice to anybody, full as the world seems. For, supposing a man or family, in the state they were at first, peopling of the world by the children of Adam or Noah, let him plant in some inland vacant places of America. We shall find that the possessions he could make himself, upon the measures we have given, would not be very large, nor, even to this day, prejudice the rest of mankind or give them reason to complain or think themselves injured by this man's encroachment, though the race of men have now spread themselves to all the corners of the world, and do infinitely exceed the small number that was at the beginning. Nay, the extent of ground is of so little value without labour that I have heard it affirmed that in Spain itself a man may be permitted to plough, sow, and reap, without being disturbed, upon land he has no other title to, but only his making use of it. But, on the contrary, the inhabitants think themselves beholden to him who, by his industry on neglected, and consequently waste land, has increased the stock of corn, which they wanted. But be this as it will, which I lay no stress on, this I dare boldly affirm, that the same rule of property—viz., that every man should have as much as he could make use of, would hold still in the world, without straitening anybody, since there is land enough in the world to suffice double the inhabitants, had not the inven-

tion of money, and the tacit agreement of men to put a value on it, introduced (by consent) larger possessions and a right to them; which, how it has done, I shall by and by show more at large.

37. This is certain, that in the beginning, before the desire of having more than men needed had altered the intrinsic value of things, which depends only on their usefulness to the life of man, or had agreed that a little piece of yellow metal, which would keep without wasting or decay, should be worth a great piece of flesh or a whole heap of corn, though men had a right to appropriate by their labour, each one to himself, as much of the things of Nature as he could use, yet this could not be much, nor to the prejudice of others, where the same plenty was still left, to those who would use the same industry.

Before the appropriation of land, he who gathered as much of the wild fruit, killed, caught, or tamed as many of the beasts as he could—he that so employed his pains about any of the spontaneous products of Nature as any way to alter them from the state Nature put them in, by placing any of his labour on them, did thereby acquire a propriety in them; but if they perished in his possession without their due use—if the fruits rotted or the venison putrefied before he could spend it, he offended against the common law of Nature, and was liable to be punished: he invaded his neighbour's share, for he had no right farther than his use called for any of them, and they might serve to afford him conveniencies of life.

38. The same measures governed the possession of land, too. Whatsoever he tilled and reaped, laid up and made use of before it spoiled, that was his peculiar right; whatsoever he enclosed, and could feed and make use of, the cattle and product was also his. But if either the grass of his enclosure rotted on the ground, or the fruit of his planting perished without gathering and laying up, this part of the earth, notwithstanding his enclosure, was still to be looked on as waste, and might be the possession of any other. Thus, at the beginning, Cain might take as much ground as he could till and make it his own land, and yet leave enough to Abel's sheep to feed on: a few acres would serve for both their possessions. But as families increased and industry enlarged their stocks, their possessions enlarged with the need of them; but yet it was commonly without any fixed property in the ground they made use of till they incorporated, settled themselves together, and built cities, and then, by consent, they came in time to set out the bounds of their distinct territories and agree on limits between them and their neighbours, and by laws within themselves settled the properties of those of the same society. For we see that in that part of the world which was first inhabited, and therefore like to be best peopled, even as low down as Abraham's time, they wandered with their flocks and their herds, which was their substance, freely up and down—and this Abraham did in a country where he was a stranger; whence it is plain that, at least, a great part of the land lay in common, that the inhabitants valued it not, nor claimed property in any more than they made use of; but when there was not room enough in the same place for their herds to feed together, they, by consent, as Abraham and Lot did (Gen. xiii. 5), separated and enlarged their pasture where it best liked them. And for the same reason, Esau went from his father and his brother, and planted in Mount Seir (Gen. xxxvi. 6).

39. And thus, without supposing any private dominion and property in Adam over all the world, exclusive of all other men, which can no way be proved, nor any one's property be made out from it, but supposing the world, given as it was to the children of men in common, we see how labour could make them distinct titles to several parcels of it for their private uses, wherein there could be no doubt of right, no room for quarrel.

40. Nor is it so strange as, perhaps, before consideration, it may appear, that the property of labour should be able to overbalance the community of land, for it is labour indeed that puts the difference of value on everything; and let any one consider what the difference is between an acre of land planted with tobacco or sugar, sown with wheat or barley, and an acre of the same land lying in common without any husbandry upon it, and he will find that the improvement of labour makes the far greater part of the value. I think it will be but a very modest computation to say, that of the products of the earth useful to the life of man, nine-tenths are the effects of labour. Nay, if we will rightly estimate things as they come to our use, and cast up the several expenses about them—what in them is purely owing to Nature and what to labour—we shall find that in most of them ninety-nine hundredths are wholly to be put on the account of labour.

41. There cannot be a clearer demonstration of anything than several nations of the Americans are of this, who are rich in land and poor in all the comforts of life; whom Nature, having furnished as

liberally as any other people with the materials of plenty—*i.e.*, a fruitful soil, apt to produce in abundance what might serve for food, raiment, and delight; yet, for want of improving it by labour, have not one hundredth part of the conveniencies we enjoy, and a king of a large and fruitful territory there feeds, lodges, and is clad worse than a day labourer in England.

42. To make this a little clearer, let us but trace some of the ordinary provisions of life, through their several progresses, before they come to our use, and see how much they receive of their value from human industry. Bread, wine, and cloth are things of daily use and great plenty; yet notwithstanding acorns, water, and leaves, or skins must be our bread, drink and clothing, did not labour furnish us with these more useful commodities. For whatever bread is more worth than acorns, wine than water, and cloth or silk than leaves, skins or moss, that is wholly owing to labour and industry. The one of these being the food and raiment which unassisted Nature furnishes us with; the other provisions which our industry and pains prepare for us, which how much they exceed the other in value, when any one hath computed, he will then see how much labour makes the far greatest part of the value of things we enjoy in this world; and the ground which produces the materials is scarce to be reckoned in as any, or at most, but a very small part of it; so little, that even amongst us, land that is left wholly to nature, that hath no improvement of pasturage, tillage, or planting, is called, as indeed it is, waste; and we shall find the benefit of it amount to little more than nothing.

43. An acre of land that bears here twenty bushels of wheat, and another in America, which, with the same husbandry, would do the like, are, without doubt, of the same natural, intrinsic value. But yet the benefit mankind receives from one in a year is worth five pounds, and the other possibly not worth a penny; if all the profit an Indian received from it were to be valued and sold here, at least I may truly say, not one thousandth. It is labour, then, which puts the greatest part of value upon land, without which it would scarcely be worth anything; it is to that we owe the greatest part of all its useful products; for all that the straw, bran, bread, of that acre of wheat, is more worth than the product of an acre of as good land which lies waste is all the effect of labour. For it is not barely the ploughman's pains, the reaper's and thresher's toil, and the baker's sweat, is to be counted into the bread we eat; the labour of those

who broke the oxen, who digged and wrought the iron and stones, who felled and framed the timber employed about the plough, mill, oven, or any other utensils, which are a vast number, requisite to this corn, from its sowing to its being made bread, must all be charged on the account of labour, and received as an effect of that; Nature and the earth furnished only the almost worthless materials as in themselves. It would be a strange catalogue of things that industry provided and made use of about every loaf of bread before it came to our use if we could trace them; iron, wood, leather, bark, timber, stone, bricks, coals, lime, cloth, dyeing-drugs, pitch, tar, masts, ropes, and all the materials made use of in the ship that brought any of the commodities made use of by any of the workmen, to any part of the work, all of which it would be almost impossible, at least too long, to reckon up.

44. From all which it is evident, that though the things of Nature are given in common, man (by being master of himself, and proprietor of his own person, and the actions or labour of it) had still in himself the great foundation of property; and that which made up the great part of what he applied to the support or comfort of his being, when invention and arts had improved the conveniences of life, was perfectly his own, and did not belong in common to others.

45. Thus labour, in the beginning, gave a right of property, wherever any one was pleased to employ it, upon what was common, which remained a long while, the far greater part, and is yet more than mankind makes use of. Men at first, for the most part, contented themselves with what unassisted Nature offered to their necessities; and though afterwards, in some parts of the world, where the increase of people and stock, with the use of money, had made land scarce, and so of some value, the several communities settled the bounds of their distinct territories, and, by laws, within themselves, regulated the properties of the private men of their society, and so, by compact and agreement, settled the property which labour and industry began. And the leagues that have been made between several states and kingdoms, either expressly or tacitly disowning all claim and right to the land in the other's possession, have, by common consent, given up their pretences to their natural common right, which originally they had to those countries; and so have, by positive agreement, settled a property amongst themselves, in distinct parts of the world; yet there are still great tracts of ground to be found, which the inhabitants thereof,

not having joined with the rest of mankind in the consent of the use of their common money, lie waste, and are more than the people who dwell on it, do, or can make use of, and so still lie in common; though this can scarce happen amongst that part of mankind that have consented to the use of money.

46. The greatest part of things really useful to the life of man, and such as the necessity of subsisting made the first commoners of the world look after—as it doth the Americans now—are generally things of short duration, such as—if they are not consumed by use—will decay and perish of themselves. Gold, silver, and diamonds are things that fancy or agreement hath put the value on, more than real use and the necessary support of life. Now of those good things Nature hath provided in common, every one has a right (as hath been said) to as much as he could use, and had a property in all he could effect with his labour; all that his industry could extend to, to alter from the state Nature had put it in, was his. He that gathered a hundred bushels of acorns or apples had thereby a property in them; they were his goods as soon as gathered. He was only to look that he used them before they spoiled, else he took more than his share, and robbed others. And, indeed, it was a foolish thing, as well as dishonest, to hoard up more than he could make use of. If he gave away a part to anybody else, so that it perished not uselessly in his possession, these he also made use of. And if he also bartered away plums that would have rotted in a week, for nuts that would last good for his eating a whole year, he did no injury; he wasted not the common stock; destroyed no part of the portion of goods that belonged to others, so long as nothing perished uselessly in his hands. Again, if he would give his nuts for a piece of metal, pleased with its colour, or exchange his sheep for shells, or wool for a sparkling pebble or a diamond, and keep those by him all his life, he invaded not the right of others; he might heap up as much of these durable things as he pleased; the exceeding of the bounds of his just property not lying in the largeness of his possession, but the perishing of anything uselessly in it.

47. And thus came in the use of money; some lasting thing that men might keep without spoiling, and that, by mutual consent, men would take in exchange for the truly useful but perishable supports of life.

48. And as different degrees of industry were apt to give men possessions in different proportions, so this invention of money gave them the opportunity to continue and enlarge them. For supposing an island, separate from all possible commerce with the rest of the world, wherein there were but a hundred families, but there were sheep, horses, and cows, with other useful animals, wholesome fruits, and land enough for corn for a hundred thousand times as many, but nothing in the island, either because of its commonness or perishableness, fit to supply the place of money. What reason could any one have there to enlarge his possessions beyond the use of his family, and a plentiful supply to its consumption, either in what their own industry produced, or they could barter for like perishable, useful commodities with others? Where there is not something both lasting and scarce, and so valuable to be hoarded up, there men will not be apt to enlarge their possessions of land, were it never so rich, never so free for them to take. For I ask, what would a man value ten thousand or an hundred thousand acres of excellent land, ready cultivated and well stocked, too, with cattle, in the middle of the inland parts of America, where he had no hopes of commerce with other parts of the world, to draw money to him by the sale of the product? It would not be worth the enclosing, and we should see him give up again to the wild common of Nature whatever was more than would supply the conveniences of life, to be had there for him and his family.

49. Thus, in the beginning, all the world was America, and more so than that is now; for no such thing as money was anywhere known. Find out something that hath the use and value of money amongst his neighbours, you shall see the same man will begin presently to enlarge his possessions.

50. But since gold and silver, being little useful to the life of man, in proportion to food, raiment, and carriage, has its value only from the consent of men—whereof labour yet makes in great part the measure—it is plain that the consent of men have agreed to a disproportionate and unequal possession of the earth—I mean out of the bounds of society and compact; for in governments the laws regulate it; they having, by consent, found out and agreed in a way how a man may, rightfully and without injury, possess more than he himself can make use of by receiving gold and silver, which may continue long in a man's possession without decaying for the overplus, and agreeing those metals should have a value.

51. And thus, I think, it is very easy to conceive, without any difficulty, how labour could at first

begin a title of property in the common things of Nature, and how the spending it upon our uses bounded it; so that there could then be no reason of quarrelling about title, nor any doubt about the largeness of possession it gave. Right and conveniency went together. For as a man had a right to all he could employ his labour upon, so he had no temptation to labour for more than he could make use of. This left no room for controversy about the title, nor for encroachment on the right of others. What portion a man carved to himself was easily seen; and it was useless, as well as dishonest, to carve himself too much, or take more than he needed.

CHAPTER IX

Of the Ends of Political Society and Government

123. If man in the state of Nature be so free as has been said, if he be absolute lord of his own person and possessions, equal to the greatest and subject to nobody, why will he part with his freedom, this empire, and subject himself to the dominion and control of any other power? To which it is obvious to answer, that though in the state of Nature he hath such a right, yet the enjoyment of it is very uncertain and constantly exposed to the invasion of others; for all being kings as much as he, every man his equal, and the greater part no strict observers of equity and justice, the enjoyment of the property he has in this state is very unsafe, very insecure. This makes him willing to quit this condition which, however free, is full of fears and continual dangers; and it is not without reason that he seeks out and is willing to join in society with others who are already united, or have a mind to unite for the mutual preservation of their lives, liberties and estates, which I call by the general name—property.

124. The great and chief end, therefore, of men uniting into commonwealths, and putting themselves under government, is the preservation of their property; to which in the state of Nature there are many things wanting.

Firstly, there wants an established, settled, known law, received and allowed by common consent to be the standard of right and wrong, and the common measure to decide all controversies between them. For though the law of Nature be plain and intelligible to all rational creatures, yet men, being biased by their interest, as well as ignorant for want

of study of it, are not apt to allow of it as a law binding to them in the application of it to their particular cases.

125. Secondly, in the state of Nature there wants a known and indifferent judge, with authority to determine all differences according to the established law. For every one in that state being both judge and executioner of the law of Nature, men being partial to themselves, passion and revenge is very apt to carry them too far, and with too much heat in their own cases, as well as negligence and unconcernedness, make them too remiss in other men's.

126. Thirdly, in the state of Nature there often wants power to back and support the sentence when right, and to give it due execution. They who by any injustice offended will seldom fail where they are able by force to make good their injustice. Such resistance many times makes the punishment dangerous, and frequently destructive to those who attempt it.

127. Thus mankind, notwithstanding all the privileges of the state of Nature, being but in an ill condition while they remain in it are quickly driven into society. Hence it comes to pass, that we seldom find any number of men live any time together in this state. The inconveniencies that they are therein exposed to by the irregular and uncertain exercises of the power every man has of punishing the transgressions of others, make them take sanctuary under the established laws of government, and therein seek the preservation of their property. It is this makes them so willingly give up every one his single power of punishing to be exercised by such alone as shall be appointed to it amongst them, and by such rules as the community, or those authorised by them to that purpose, shall agree on. And in this we have the original right and rise of both the legislative and executive power as well as of the governments and societies themselves.

128. For in the state of Nature to omit the liberty he has of innocent delights, a man has two powers. The first is to do whatsoever he thinks fit for the preservation of himself and others within the permission of the law of Nature; by which law, common to them all, he and all the rest of mankind are one community, make up one society distinct from all other creatures, and were it not for the corruption and viciousness of degenerate men, there would be no need of any other, no necessity that men should separate from this great and natural community, and associate into lesser combinations.

The other power a man has in the state of Nature is the power to punish the crimes committed against that law. Both these he gives up when he joins in a private, if I may so call it, or particular political society, and incorporates into any commonwealth separate from the rest of mankind.

129. The first power—viz., of doing whatsoever he thought fit for the preservation of himself and the rest of mankind, he gives up to be regulated by laws made by the society, so far forth as the preservation of himself and the rest of that society shall require; which laws of the society in many things confine the liberty he had by the law of Nature.

130. Secondly, the power of punishing he wholly gives up, and engages his natural force, which he might before employ in the execution of the law of Nature, by his own single authority, as he thought fit, to assist the executive power of the society as the law thereof shall require. For being now in a new state, wherein he is to enjoy many conveniencies from the labour, assistance, and society of others in the same community, as well as protection from its whole strength, he is to part also with as much of his natural liberty, in providing for himself, as the good, prosperity, and safety of the society shall require, which is not only necessary but just, since the other members of the society do the like.

131. But though men when they enter into society give up the equality, liberty, and executive power they had in the state of Nature into the hands of the society, to be so far disposed of by the legislative as the good of the society shall require, yet it being only with an intention in every one the better to preserve himself, his liberty and property (for no rational creature can be supposed to change his condition with an intention to be worse), the power of the society or legislative constituted by them can never be supposed to extend farther than the common good, but is obliged to secure every one's property by providing against those three defects above mentioned that made the state of Nature so unsafe and uneasy. And so, whoever has the legislative or supreme power of any commonwealth, is bound to govern by established standing laws, promulgated and known to the people, and not by extemporary decrees, by indifferent and upright judges, who are to decide controversies by those laws; and to employ the force of the community at home only in the execution of such laws, or abroad to prevent or redress foreign injuries and secure the community from inroads and invasion.

And all this to be directed to no other end but the peace, safety, and public good of the people.

———◆———

THOMAS JEFFERSON

1743–1826

Although as third President of the United States Thomas Jefferson was at the same time the best-loved and best-hated public man of his times, in the perspective of years he has become increasingly symbolic of the idealism of American democracy. From that distinguished group of statesmen and political thinkers of the American Enlightenment who founded the Republic, Jefferson has emerged as the happy amalgam of the idealist, the liberal intellectual, and the practical man of affairs that was most urgently needed by the American colonies in their bitter struggle against the encroachments of the Crown. In the wisdom, range, and power of his political understanding, Jefferson perceived that the first principle of American democracy must be the common man's assurance of moral and political freedom against all forms of political and religious tyranny.

Thus it was that when Jefferson arrived in Philadelphia in June, 1775, as a delegate from Virginia to the Second Continental Congress he brought with him not only that "happy talent of composition" commended by John Adams, but as well a broad, liberal conception of egalitarianism which has since become the scripture of American democracy. Indeed, it is not fanciful to see in Jefferson's substitution of "pursuit of happiness" for "property" in the Lockean designation of "life, liberty, and property" the anticipation of the principles of "The Four Freedoms" and of the Atlantic Charter. Some of the principles of The Declaration of Independence had already been stated or implied in the instructions which Jefferson had composed for the Virginia delegates to the First Continental Congress, "A Summary View of the Rights of British America" (1774).

On June 7, 1776, Richard Henry Lee moved in behalf of the Virginia delegates that Congress declare the United Colonies free and independent states. On June 11, a committee consisting of John Adams, Benjamin Franklin, Roger Sherman, Robert R. Livingston, and Thomas Jefferson was appointed to prepare such a declaration. Jefferson observes in his *Autobiography*, "The committee for drawing the Declaration of Independence desired me to do it." The resolution was presented on June 28, and after debating it on July 1, 2, 3, 4, Congress formally ratified on July 4, "A Declaration by the Representatives of the United States of America in General Congress Assembled." The underlying concept of this Declaration, John Locke's doctrine of natural rights, was not original with Jefferson, as all were aware; his intention was "to place before mankind the common sense of the subject, in terms so plain and firm as to command their assent." It shall always remain as Thomas Jefferson's first claim to the gratitude of these United States of America.

FURTHER READING

BOYD, JULIAN P., ed. *The Papers of Thomas Jefferson* (Princeton University Press, 1950).
MALONE, DUMAS. *Thomas Jefferson and His Time* (Boston, 1951).

The Declaration of Independence

WHEN in the Course of human events, it becomes necessary for one people to dissolve the political bands, which have connected them with another, and to assume among the powers of the earth, the separate and equal station to which the Laws of Nature and of Nature's God entitle them, a decent respect to the opinions of mankind requires that they should declare the causes which impel them to the separation.

We hold these truths to be self-evident: that all men are created equal, that they are endowed by their Creator with certain unalienable Rights, that among these are Life, Liberty and the Pursuit of Happiness.—That to secure these rights, Governments are instituted among Men, deriving their just powers from the consent of the governed.—That whenever any Form of Government becomes destructive of these ends, it is the Right of the People to alter or to abolish it, and to institute new Government, laying its foundation on such principles and organizing its powers in such form as to them shall seem most likely to effect their Safety and Happiness. Prudence, indeed, will dictate that Govern-

ments long established should not be changed for light and transient causes; and accordingly all experience hath shewn, that mankind are more disposed to suffer, while evils are sufferable, than to right themselves by abolishing the forms to which they are accustomed. But when a long train of abuses and usurpations, pursuing invariably the same Object evinces a design to reduce them under absolute Despotism, it is their right, it is their duty, to throw off such Government, and to provide new Guards for their future security.—Such has been the patient sufferance of these Colonies; and such is now the necessity which constrains them to alter their former Systems of Government. The history of the present King of Great Britain is a history of repeated injuries and usurpations, all having in direct object the establishment of an absolute Tyranny over these States. To prove this, let Facts be submitted to a candid world.

He has refused his Assent to Laws, the most wholesome and necessary for the public good.

He has forbidden his Governors to pass Laws of immediate and pressing importance, unless suspended in their operation till his Assent should be obtained; and when so suspended, he has utterly neglected to attend to them.

He has refused to pass other Laws for the accommodation of large districts of people, unless those people would relinquish the right of Representation in the Legislature, a right inestimable to them and formidable to tyrants only.

He has called together legislative bodies at places unusual, uncomfortable, and distant from the depository of their public Records, for the sole purpose of fatiguing them into compliance with his measures.

He has dissolved Representative Houses repeatedly, for opposing with manly firmness his invasions on the rights of the people.

He has refused for a long time, after such dissolutions, to cause others to be elected; whereby the Legislative powers, incapable of Annihilation, have returned to the People at large for their exercise; the State remaining in the meantime exposed to all the dangers of invasion from without, and convulsions within.

He has endeavored to prevent the population of these States; for that purpose obstructing the laws for naturalization of foreigners; refusing to pass others to encourage their migration hither, and raising the conditions of new appropriations of lands.

He has obstructed the administration of justice,

by refusing his assent to laws for establishing judiciary powers.

He has made judges dependent on his will alone, for the tenure of their offices, and the amount and payment of their salaries.

He has erected a multitude of new offices, and sent hither swarms of officers to harass our people, and eat out their substance.

He has kept among us, in times of peace, standing armies without the consent of our legislature.

He has affected to render the military independent of and superior to the civil power.

He has combined with others to subject us to a jurisdiction foreign to our constitution, and unacknowledged by our laws; giving his assent to their acts of pretended legislation: for quartering large bodies of armed troops among us; for protecting them, by a mock trial, from punishment for any murders which they should commit on the inhabitants of these States; for cutting off our trade with all parts of the world; for imposing taxes on us without our consent; for depriving us in many cases, of the benefits of trial by jury; for transporting us beyond seas to be tried for pretended offenses; for abolishing the free system of English laws in a neighboring province, establishing therein an arbitrary government, and enlarging its boundaries so as to render it at once an example and fit instrument for introducing the same absolute rule into these Colonies; for taking away our charters, abolishing our most valuable laws, and altering fundamentally the forms of our governments; for suspending our own legislatures, and declaring themselves invested with power to legislate for us in all cases whatsoever.

He has abdicated government here, by declaring us out of his protection and waging war against us.

He has plundered our seas, ravaged our coasts, burned our towns, and destroyed the lives of· our people.

He is at this time transporting large armies of foreign mercenaries to complete the works of death, desolation, and tyranny, already begun with circumstances of cruelty and perfidy scarcely paralleled in the most barbarous ages, and totally unworthy the head of a civilized nation.

He has constrained our fellow citizens taken captive on the high seas to bear arms against their country, to become the executioners of their friends and brethren, or to fall themselves by their hands.

He has excited domestic insurrections amongst us, and has endeavored to bring on the inhabitants of our frontiers, the merciless Indian savages, whose known rule of warfare, is an undistinguished destruction of all ages, sexes, and conditions.

In every stage of these oppressions we have petitioned for redress in the most humble terms: our repeated petitions have been answered only by repeated injury. A prince, whose character is thus marked by every act which may define a tyrant, is unfit to be the ruler of a free people.

Nor have we been wanting in attention to our British brethren. We have warned them from time to time of attempts by their legislature to extend an unwarrantable jurisdiction over us. We have reminded them of the circumstances of our emigration and settlement here. We have appealed to their native justice and magnanimity, and we have conjured them by the ties of our common kindred to disavow these usurpations, which would inevitably interrupt our connections and correspondence. They too have been deaf to the voice of justice and of consanguinity. We must, therefore, acquiesce in the necessity, which denounces our separation, and hold them, as we hold the rest of mankind, enemies in war, in peace friends.

We, therefore, the Representatives of the United States of America, in General Congress assembled, appealing to the Supreme Judge of the world for the rectitude of our intentions, do, in the name, and by authority of the good people of these Colonies, solemnly publish and declare, That these United Colonies are, and of right ought to be Free and Independent States; that they are absolved from all allegiance to the British Crown, and that all political connection between them and the State of Great Britain, is and ought to be totally dissolved; and that as Free and Independent States, they have full power to levy war, conclude peace, contract alliances, establish commerce, and to do all other acts and things which independent states may of right do. And for the support of this Declaration, with a firm reliance on the protection of Divine Providence, we mutually pledge to each other our lives, our fortunes, and our sacred Honor.

THE ROMANTIC WORLD

The
Romantic
World

The Cottage Door by Thomas Gainsborough.

So many divergent traits and tendencies are embraced in the term "Romanticism" that it defies definition. One can only point to each particular manifestation of the Romantic spirit and say, "This is one expression of Romanticism." But it is this very individuality among the Romantics which provides the great fascination of the Romantic world. Of course by adopting a broader definition of the term, one could conceivably say that the Romantic movement began in the fourteenth century and that it continued through the twenties of the present century, interrupted only by the emergence of classicism in the seventeenth and eighteenth centuries. But the Romantic movement proper, that era in which the dominance of the spirit is most clearly indicated and which we call "The Romantic World," extends roughly from 1775 to 1850. There is not one Romanticism, but many Romanticisms, each as valid as any other: there is the revolutionary Romanticism of the early Wordsworth, of Shelley, and of Byron; the primitivistic Romanticism of Rousseau and Chateaubriand; the medieval or Gothic Romanticism of Scott and Bürger; the mystical Romanticism of Blake; and the return-to-nature Romanticism of Wordsworth and Constable. Yet there is in all of them one clearly recognizable Romantic spirit which manifests itself in multiform ways. Consequently, in cataloguing the various expressions of the Romantic spirit, we must never expect to find a combination of more than several of them in any one Romantic artist.

THE DOMINATION OF THE EGO

THE Romantic world exhibits a great many characteristics and tendencies which are rather directly opposed to the tenets of Neo-classicism. Whereas the Neo-classicists placed their primary confidence in reason and the intellect, the Romantics usually believed in a power higher than reason —the intuition and the imagination—and, foregoing Neo-classic decorum, gave free rein to the expression of their emotions. Expression of the individual self became the goal; the terms in which Jean Jacques Rousseau (1712–1778) spoke of his personality, *au moins je suis autre* ("at least I am other") was a universal European theme in the rich literature of subjectivity.

Rousseau, with whom the French Romantic movement may be said to begin, revealed his innermost feelings in his posthumous *Confessions*, though the novels of the Abbé Prévost, like Richardson's and Sterne's in England, prepared the way for the sentiment and sensibility of the *Confessions*. Influenced by the "Sturm und Drang" movement, the youthful Romantic, Goethe (1749–1832)—as distinguished from the aged Goethe who repudiated Romanticism—laid bare his emotions in *The Sorrows of Young Werther* (1774) in which the sensitive hero is blackly pessimistic. Wordsworth (1770–1850) found in himself a wealth of psychologically important material for poetry which he fashioned into the *Prelude*, his autobiographical study of the development of a poet's mind. But perhaps the most egocentric of all was Lord Byron (1788–1824) whose Byronic heroes, created in their author's own image, fascinated all Europe. Though the narcissistic Byron enjoyed many loves, it is doubtful, as Macaulay implied in a famous essay, if he ever completely loved anyone but himself. The subject matter of almost all of his poetry is the exploration and exploitation of his own ego, but it concerned a sad "pageant of the bleeding heart" across Europe. The Byronic hero, that Romantic meteor which flashed across the Continent, is but a projection of Byron's own despairing soul. The Byron of *Manfred* and *Cain* is a lineal descendent of young Werther.

TRANSCENDENTALISM

ONE reason for attaching great importance to the individual was that many Romantics held the religious and almost mystic view that there was a divine perception in every person; it was an intuitive and personal revelation of the voice of God within man that, without intermediation of any religious formalism, told him what was right and wrong. Immanuel Kant (1724–1804) made the chief German contribution to the philosophy of Romanticism in his *Critique of Pure Reason* (1781). Here, since the causes of the phenomena of the natural world lie beyond our ordinary understanding, he rejected the Cartesian and Lockean theories of knowledge based on sensuous perceptions, and enunciated the idea that the logical understanding alone is incapable of reaching ultimate truths—such as belief in God or immortality—and, concomitantly, that since logical understanding is incapable of attaining these ultimate realities, only the divine gift of an intuition transcending logical reason can lead to final truths. This revolt against the primacy of the intellect profoundly influenced Coleridge and the first generation of English Romantics.

Kantian philosophy provides for a development and extension of Locke's theory of knowledge based on sensory perceptions, in that Kant conceived our knowledge to be an outcome of sense impressions and the logical understanding; but in view of the inadequacy of this knowledge in reaching final truths, he establishes faith and intuition as a new basis for religious belief. Thus Kantian philosophy is not at all contradictory to the eighteenth-century revivalist movements, best exemplified in the work of John Wesley (1703–1791), in which all attempts to construct purely rational bases for Christian faith are abandoned in the attempt to found faith squarely on intuitive belief.

Kant's pupil, Johann Gottlieb Fichte (1762–1814), went even a step beyond his master to construct a philosophy of pure idealism, rejecting the phenomena of sensory perception and discovering the only reality in the thinking self and in the "divine idea which lies at the base of all experience." From such premises as these it is an easy passage a generation later, via the writings of Thomas Carlyle (1795–1881), to Ralph Waldo Emerson (1803–1882) and the New England Transcendentalists who believed that every human being participates in the great Oversoul, and that through meditation and self-reliance he could communicate directly with the Infinite. Granting such premises as these, then, self-expression, quite uninhibited, becomes a positive duty.

The attempts of the poet-painter William Blake (1757–1827) to give expression to his mystical, intuitive knowledge of the world of spiritual reality by use of symbolism and allegory is consonant with this element of Romanticism. Blake's painting and engraving is completely antithetical to the classic artistic canons of Sir Joshua Reynolds (1723–1792), who believed all art must emphasize the *ethos,* that is, the fixed universal character, not the incidental emotion, the *pathos.* This was hardly a theory in line with *Songs of Innocence,* and Blake so detested all that Reynolds stood for in art that he maintained that Satan had hired Reynolds to depress art.

So deeply did Romanticism take root in the congenial German temper that it produced the most celebrated writers in all German literature: Goethe, Schiller (1759–1805), and Heine (1797–1856). Indeed, at the risk of oversimplification, we may say that Germany, together with England, set the artistic standards for the Romantic world, just as France had given Neo-classicism to Europe. Though France gave the Romantic movement in Europe a great impetus through the works of Rousseau, whose influence in both Germany and England was profound, the French spirit seemed for a long time to remain antipathetic to the growth of Romantic art. Although in the Baroque era of German music we have the remarkable development of Protestant Baroque in the music of Schütz, Buxtehude, and Bach, in literature the Germans, servilely imitating

Courtesy Pierpont Morgan Library, New York

Satan Before the Throne of God by William Blake.

French Neo-classicism, which they poorly understood as it was never congenial to the Teutonic temperament, did not produce a single monument of world literature. German Romanticism as represented in the von Schlegels and in von Hardenberg (Novalis) was not, however, a revolt against classicism so much as an attempt to supplement it. But now, just as the young French writers turned to England for inspiration and emancipation from Neo-classical restrictions, so in the late eighteenth century a new generation of Germans, destined to be the Fatherland's most illustrious writers, looked to England, and particularly to Shakespeare—England's sublime genius—for inspiration. Shakespeare was made available to Germans by the monumental translation of A. W. von Schlegel (1767–1845), published between 1797 and 1810. Thus during the Romantic period an unusually productive cross-fertilization between Germany and England took place. But perhaps the most important German contribution to Romanticism is Romantic irony, in part the search for the ineffable, the feeling that the

Romantic poet can never quite satisfy his yearning to exhaust the infinite.

In German Romanticism the poet became the seer, a divine creator who mediates between the infinite and society, who strives to communicate the ideal and the ineffable to man. The aim of his poetry was the attempt to achieve the infinite, the absolute, and to free his imagination from the trammels of time and place. The German Romantic felt that poetry could establish a universal harmony between man and nature by suggesting infinitely more than it states; that, like the Kantian intuition, it could reach transcendent truths beyond sense experience. This continual striving after an ever remote infinite, the unattainable world of the ideal, is symbolized in Friedrich von Hardenberg's unfinished novel *Heinrich von Ofterdingen* (to explain "the true essence of poetry") by the famous blue flower. In Schiller's "On Naïve and Sentimental Poetry" it is suggested that the superiority of modern poetry over Greek is due to the striving of the poet to achieve this infinite, and to his creative restlessness in passing from one poetic experiment to another, the poet being never satisfied, never fixed irrevocably by the form of his work, which he must destroy if it prevents him from expressing himself. Thus the poet must ever be able to rise above his own work and remain a free spirit; he must always be in a position to elevate

Courtesy National Gallery of Art (Rosenwald Collection), Washington, D. C.
Seven-Headed Beast of the Apocalypse by William Blake.

himself above all his artistic creation and treat it condescendingly, even with ridicule. This is Romantic irony, clearly perceptible in some of Heine's lyrics.

PRIMITIVISM

THE glorification of common folk and of homely scenes, carried so far by the poet Wordsworth, is a significant Romantic trait. In the *Lyrical Ballads* (1798) Wordsworth turned to cottagers of the Lake District for poetic subject matter because he felt they were closer to nature, that their fundamental human emotions were not veneered or concealed by urban culture and education, nor contaminated by sophistication. Since their emotional springs were pure, they would express their feelings more truly than their city cousins. In the same spirit of discovery, the Romantic painters turned to rural landscapes and to countrymen for their subjects.

The first great Romantic painter is Gainsborough (1727–1788) in his most mature period. (He had,

of course, been one of the portrait painters of the aristocratic society of an earlier era.) No artist has given us a better pictorial record of fashionable life than Gainsborough in his "Georgiana, Duchess of Devonshire," a painting which exhibits all of the sophistication of academic Neo-classic art. Yet his "The Cottage Door" is practically Wordsworthian in subject matter and feeling. No doubt Gainsborough wearied, as Herbert Read has said, of "a silly, selfish, and complacent society that had no better use for great artists than to make them mirror its own vanity and self-satisfaction." In a letter to a friend Gainsborough wrote: "I'm sick of Portraits, and wish very much to take my viol-da-gam and walk off to some sweet village, where I can paint landskips and enjoy the fag end of life in quietness and ease. But these fine ladies and their tea drinkings, dancings, husband-huntings, etc., etc., etc., will fob me out of the last ten years. . . ." And so Gainsborough turned to another type of painting, Romantic in mood. As his biographer Walter Armstrong has said, "Gainsborough was the first to concentrate all his powers on the translation of his own continuing emotion into paint, and to make the vigor, heat, and unity of his own passion the measure of his art." This landscape painting tradition was carried on by John Constable (1776–1837), and by Joseph Mallord William Turner (1775–1851), who gave his country and the world an emotionally inspired depiction of landscapes, perhaps with less tendency than Gainsborough to select the "picturesque" nature setting for his landscapes. No one has ever been more successful in romanticizing the commonplace—witness his "Keelmen Heaving in Coals by Moonlight."

All of this idealization of the common man is actually a part of the philosophy of Primitivism which stems from Rousseau. He maintained that civilization and organized modern society had corrupted the original goodness of human nature. Though he did not actually suggest a return to the state of nature, the popular interpretation of Rousseau held that man in order to be happy would have to slough off completely his sophistication and civilization. The same common view of Rousseau's complex thought conceived that genuine nobility was to be found only in uncontaminated savages—hence the phrase "noble savage." Similarly, in *Émile* (1762) he placed an unusually high value on childhood; for the child, somewhat like the

Courtesy National Gallery of Art (Widener Collection), Washington, D. C.

Keelmen Heaving in Coals by Moonlight by Joseph M. W. Turner.

savage, is much more nearly in the uncorrupted state of nature than is the cultivated adult, a philosophy which inspired English education novels like Thomas Day's *Sandford and Merton* (1789) and Mrs. Inchbald's *Nature and Art* (1796). This apotheosizing of savages, children, peasants, and cottagers would have seemed to Neo-classicists in effect an approbation of ignorance, a complete revolt against the fundamental Neo-classic premise that the good life is obtained through right reason. Though the French Revolution and Napoleonic Empire inhibited the development of French Romanticism (Napoleon's taste was classic), by the turn of the century Rousseauistic primitivism found its most influential disciple in the Vicomte François René de Chateaubriand (1768–1848). He is famed

for two novels, *Atala* (1801) and *René* (1802), both of which appeared early in the French Romantic Movement. *Atala* is an idealized and highly romanticized story of the love of a young Indian couple in America. *René* tells of a young European (generally identified with Chateaubriand), who, overcome by sorrow, flees away to the solitary wildernesses of America. The work embodies the tortured searching for the infinite that we remarked in German literature, and anticipates the romantic *Weltschmerz* that reaches its apogee later in Byron. Both were enthusiastically received by Chateaubriand's contemporaries in France.

The Primitivism of Rousseau, with its belief in the essential nobility of savages, led almost inevitably to a revision of the centuries-old attitude

A View of Salisbury Cathedral by John Constable.

The White Horse by John Constable.

toward human nature. From time immemorial it had been held that man was by nature evil. The Neo-classicists, believing that human nature is essentially evil, maintained that the good life could be attained by right reason. But the Romantic attitude toward man was one of high confidence in his essential goodness: all that people needed was a change; the evil lay in the economic system or in social institutions, not in human nature itself, for that was basically good. Thus the English radical William Godwin (1756–1836) held that man had no soul, that he was merely a part of the physical universe. Since of course all human institutions and laws were based on what he considered completely erroneous psychological assumptions, he believed that all of them must be completely changed. Godwin asserted that if marriage, private property, jails, courts, laws, wars, and organized religion could be entirely abolished, man, thus freed, would assert his innate goodness and human perfection would be

rapidly achieved. His seminal ideas about the perfectibility of man and about the iniquity of social institutions influenced many writers in both England and America, among them Shelley, Byron, and Coleridge. In particular his ideas about perfectibility led to many of the early nineteenth-century schemes for the establishment of utopias, including the New England Transcendental Brook Farm.

One of the most interesting of these projects was the "Pantisocracy" which Coleridge and Southey and some of their friends proposed to establish on the banks of the Susquehanna in Pennsylvania. Incidentally, the Susquehanna was chosen because of the Romantic sound of its name. Here twelve young couples were to lead the ideal life, combining a certain amount of manual labor in order to produce food with the greatest proportion of their time devoted to the intellectual life—contemplating, reading, discussing and writing. All things were to be shared in common, and the repressive social institu-

The Forest of Coubron by Camille Corot.

tions of Europe were to be abrogated. The plan was never effected.

Because the Romantic world believed in the essential goodness of all human beings, it developed and supported all kinds of humanitarian and reform movements. But the greatest and most widespread manifestation of the humanitarian impulse is not to be found in organized movements for social betterment, but rather in the ubiquitous expression of sympathy with humble people. It is eloquently expressed in Gray's "Elegy Written in a Country Churchyard," for example, where Gray declares that only lack of opportunities has kept the villagers in obscurity:

Perhaps in this neglected spot is laid
Some heart once pregnant with celestial fire;
Hands, that the rod of empire might have swayed,
Or waked to ecstasy of the living lyre.

But Knowledge to their eyes her ample page
Rich with the spoils of time did ne'er unroll;
Chill Penury repressed their noble rage,
And froze the genial current of the soul.

The same basic sympathy with the humble extends, but with dozens of variations, through the poetry of Burns, Blake, Cowper, Wordsworth, Whittier, and on down to Whitman; and it appears as well in the novels of George Eliot and Charles Dickens.

THE BREAK WITH TRADITION

THE Romantic world began with a spirit of revolt. The American Revolution and, especially, the French Revolution were not only revolts against haughty and aristocratic governments; they were assertions of the important new concepts of the inalienable rights of man to liberty and to equality with his fellow citizens. This period marks the culmination of a long growth of democratic thought. The egalitarian spirit, the steady belief that one man is just as good as another—unless, of course, a peasant might be a little better than an aristocrat—is one of the many manifestations of the Romantic spirit. During the latter part of the eighteenth century a considerable amount of dissatisfaction, particularly among intellectuals, had been developing against the corruption and abuses of the old aristocratic regimes. Consequently, when the French Revolution commenced it was quite widely hailed on the Continent and in England as the dawning of new opportunity for humanity. Unfortunately, the excesses of the Reign of Terror turned many former supporters of revolutionary principles against the cause, and had the effect of stiffening conservative and reactionary forces all over Europe. Although Wordsworth early embraced the principles of the Revolution, or at least those of the moderate party of revolutionists (the Girondists, for example), he had turned from them by the time he reached his early thirties. But most of the early Romantics, like Blake and Burns, were enthusiastic revolutionists, in their utterances at least. Like Wordsworth, Coleridge (1772–1834), was a revolutionary doctrinaire, though revulsion came as early as 1796. And the second-generation Romantics, Shelley (1792–1822), and Byron, made revolution and freedom their life work (in Italy and Greece, for example); and Byron censured the corruptions and the treacherous hypocrisy of European conservatism in the venomous satire of Don Juan, his last and greatest work.

The Romantic break with tradition was by no means limited to political, social, economic, and religious principles. Whether we call this the Romantic Revolt, or, as many scholars prefer, the Romantic Return (since they view the Romantic movement not so much as a revolt against the limitations of seventeenth- and eighteenth-century Neo-classicism, but as a return to the older traditions of the literary mainstream) it is clearly revealed in a revival of the literary reputations of Shakespeare and Milton. The humble origin of Shakespeare, especially, corresponded perfectly with the Rousseauistic doctrines of the natural man—a somewhat rude, untutored genius, who by his divine intuition could give Nature her supreme expression. As the Romantic evaluation of Shakespeare, Milton, and even Chaucer soared, there appeared a corresponding decline in reverence accorded the Neo-classical high priests, Dryden and Pope. The revolt against early eighteenth-century literary canons is nowhere more clearly seen than in the rather general rejection by the Romantics of the closed heroic couplet (Keats' and Shelley's use of it had the fluidity of blank verse) which had been practically the standard medium of poetic expression for a century and a half. Thus Romantic poets once again utilized with magnificent effect the older poetic forms: blank verse, the Spenserian stanza, the irregular ode, the sonnet, and ballad verse, which so long had been largely neglected.

The break with poetic tradition is explicitly stated by Wordsworth in his Preface to the second edition of *The Lyrical Ballads* (1800), where he clearly defines the intention of the new poetry:

The principal object, then, proposed in these Poems was to choose incidents and situations from common life, and to relate or describe them throughout, as far as was possible, in a selection of the language really used by man, and at the same time, to throw over them a certain colouring of imagination, whereby ordinary things should be presented to the mind in an unusual aspect; and further, and above all, to make these incidents and situations interesting by tracing in them, truly though not ostentatiously, the primary laws of our nature: chiefly, as far as regards the manner in which we associate ideas in a state of excitement. Humble and rustic life was generally chosen, because, in that condition, the essential passions of the heart find a better soil in which they can attain their maturity, are less under restraint, and speak a plainer and more emphatic language; because in that condition of life our elementary feelings co-exist in a state of greater simplicity, and consequently, may be more accurately contemplated, and more forcibly communicated; because the manners of rural life germinate from those elementary feelings, and, from the necessary character of rural occupations, are more easily comprehended, and are more durable; and, lastly, because in that condition the passions of men are incorporated with the beautiful and permanent forms of nature.

Again, in his definition of poetry, Wordsworth reaches the apex of Romanticism: "For all good poetry is the spontaneous overflow of powerful feelings: and though this be true, Poems to which any value can be attached were never produced on any variety of subjects but by a man who, being possessed of more than usual organic sensibility, had also thought long and deeply." Wordsworth consciously revolted against the shackles of typical eighteenth-century poetic diction. He dismisses the use of personifications, stock epithets, periphrases, and all of the other poetic trappings of Pope's followers as not consonant with the language actually spoken by men, and hence unsuitable for his poems: "There will also be found in these volumes little of what is usually called poetic diction; as much pains has been taken to avoid it as is ordinarily taken to produce it."

NATURE

ONE of the most widely pervasive of the Romantic tendencies is a love of nature as a source of wisdom, guidance, consolation, and happiness. Indeed, in some poets like Wordsworth it becomes an almost mystical worship of the world around us, particularly in its more scenic or "picturesque" and rugged aspects. In this particular manifestation of Romanticism, nature becomes the greatest teacher of philosophical truth. Although hostile critics sometimes absurdly raise Wordsworth's momentary poetic intuitions to the status of a "philosophy" in order that they may the better attack them, actually, when taken in its context, the following quotation is understandable and not silly:

> One impulse from a vernal wood
> Can teach us more of man,
> Of moral evil and of good,
> Than all the sages can.

No longer was the countryside viewed through library windows and described in the pale, translated epithets conceived to be the language of Vergil's *Georgics* or in terms borrowed from the pastorals of Theocritus; the Romantics looked directly at the world around them and described what they saw in language somewhat like that actually used by their contemporaries. This love of nature is found throughout the English Romantic movement, from forerunners like Thomson, Burns, Blake, and Cowper to Wordsworth and Shelley and Keats.

Though the revolutionary theme of Shelley's "Ode to the West Wind" is dominant, it is nevertheless a nature poem. And though Keats's great fame is not that of a nature poet, "To Autumn" is one of the most successful nature poems in English literature. Even Byron, by nature akin to Pope in many respects, found a pantheistic solace in nature in the third canto of *Childe Harold*. Later, in France, lyric poetry is reborn in romantic melancholy in

formality of the Italian or French. Axial design was replaced with an asymmetrical carelessness nicely calculated to resemble nature in her "noble wild prospects": the straight canal became a meandering brook; Gothic ruins replaced classic temples; and Chinese bridges and pagodas, and dramatically placed gnarled tree trunks, thickets, and cataracts contributed to the picturesque. Actually in their studied artlessness, they were hardly more natural

Courtesy Osvald Sirén, *China and Gardens of Europe* (copyright, 1950)

Entrance to the Garden at Stourhead Park, Wiltshire.

the midst of the natural scenery of Lamartine's *Les Méditations* (1820). The Neo-classicists had enjoyed the well-cultivated, neatly trimmed countryside, for it had much in common with their formal gardens, but the true Romantic imagination was fired most of all by the wildest natural landscapes.

Changing taste in landscapes, as well as in architecture, brought a revulsion against the regularized Neo-classical beauty of formal gardens. The new style, at first nameless, eventually came to be called "the natural garden," "the Romantic garden," or "the English garden" in contradistinction to the

than old-fashioned formal gardens. But now large numbers of the clipped yews and parterres formerly found all over fashionable Europe were eradicated in keeping with the new English taste (see Hubert Robert's "Felling the Trees at Versailles").

The new reverence of nature contributed greatly to the revolt against Neo-classical artistic canons. John Constable (1776–1837), perhaps the most Wordsworthian of the English painters, thus defined the new artistic objectives:

In art there are two modes by which men aim at distinction. In the one, by a careful application to what

Felling the Trees at Versailles by Hubert Robert.

others have accomplished, the artist imitates their works or selects and combines their various beauties; in the other, he seeks excellence at its primitive source—nature. In the first he forms a style upon the study of pictures and produces either imitative or eclectic art; in the second, by a close observation of nature, he discovers qualities existing in her which have never been portrayed before, and thus forms a style which is original.[1]

Not all painters were content to base their work upon a close observation of nature. Eugene Delacroix (1799–1863), the illegitimate son of Talleyrand, was one of the most influential and significant of the Romantic painters. But Delacroix is Byronic, not Wordsworthian, and there is in his work a genius, a vigor, and even a fury that goes far beyond the quiet rural palette of Constable.

THE MIDDLE AGES AND THE SUPERNATURAL

A<small>N</small> important aspect of Romanticism is its return to the Middle Ages for subject matter and theme. The Neo-classicists had also returned to the past, of course, but to the classic past; the Middle Ages they generally eschewed as dark, barbarous, and unenlightened. The use of medieval themes in

Romantic literature produced a new literary genre, the Gothic novel of mystery and horror, perhaps best exemplified by Horace Walpole's *Castle of Otranto* (1764). In addition to the new type of novel, there was a wide adaptation of medieval themes to Romantic poetry—for example in Coleridge's "Christabel" and in Keats's "The Eve of St.

[1] From *The English Landscape*, 1829.

The Marseillaise, Arc de Triomphe, Paris, by François Rude.

Agnes." The spurious medievalism of the Romantics was closely allied to the cult of the strange and the supernatural; in fact it is sometimes difficult to differentiate between the two; note in Keats's "La Belle Dame Sans Merci" where the two motifs are found in combination. By the time Chateaubriand in France wrote his *Génie du Christianisme* (1802) the medieval and the Gothic had become a Romantic cult.

But the supernatural and weird provinces of Romanticism are unquestionably ruled by Samuel Taylor Coleridge (1772–1834) who consciously chose to work in this area. "It was agreed," he tells us, "that my endeavors should be directed to persons and characters supernatural, or at least romantic; yet so as to transfer from our inward nature a human interest and a semblance of truth sufficient to procure for these shadows of imagination that willing suspension of disbelief for the moment, which constitutes poetic faith. Mr. Wordsworth, on the other hand was to propose to himself as his object, to give the charm of novelty to things of every day, and to excite a feeling analogous to the supernatural, by awakening the mind's attention to the lethargy of custom, and directing it to the loveliness and the wonders of the world before us; an inexhaustible treasure, but for which, in consequence of the film of familiarity and selfish solicitude, we have eyes,

Death of Sardanapalus by Eugène Delacroix.

yet see not, ears that hear not, and hearts that neither feel nor understand." As Byron was later boisterously to remark, Coleridge took a pixie for his muse.

The return to the Middle Ages brought with it a considerable interest in ancient balladry and folk poetry, which manifested itself in the collecting and editing of texts. Gottfried August Bürger (1747–1794) is an early example of the poet-scholar interested in collecting and imitating medieval folk poetry. He advocated a poetry addressed to the folk as a whole, to all classes of humanity. "Poetry," he said, "should speak a human language and not try to stammer with the tongues of the Gods." Bürger's "Lenore," perhaps the most successful imitation of a folk ballad ever achieved, was responsible for starting Scott on his poetical career. Two lines from "Lenore" so fired his interest that Scott sent to Hamburg for a copy of Bürger's poems in order to make a translation of the ballad for himself. The result, "William and Helen," was Scott's first published poem.

In 1778–1779 Herder published his *Volkslieder*, an extremely important collection of German balladry, but the English antiquarian, Thomas Percy, had antedated Herder considerably with the publication in 1765 of his *Reliques of Ancient English Poetry*, the first great landmark in the long history of English ballad collecting. So popular did such compilations become that by 1808, in both Germany and England, there was a wave of publications dealing with folk literature which turned poetic style toward simplicity and naïve spontaneity.

The medievalism of Scott in turn influenced Victor Hugo (1802–1885) in the direction which led to his *Notre Dame de Paris* and may have had some effect upon the Catholic revival as reflected in the work of the Italian novelist and dramatist Alessandro Manzoni (1785–1873) and of the German lyrist and novelist Baron Friedrich von Hardenberg, better known as Novalis (1772–1801), the author of the unfinished novel *Heinrich von Ofterdingen*, which

The Four Continents, Fountain of the Luxembourg, Paris, by J. B. Carpeaux.

concerns the formative years of a medieval minnesinger.

The return to medieval themes in literature was accompanied by a revival of Gothic architecture. Horace Walpole (1717–1797) started the fashion when he built his country home "Strawberry Hill" in what he conceived to be the Gothic style. The pseudo-medieval architecture rapidly caught the public fancy, and the Palladian style gave ground to the late eighteenth-century Gothic, even in churches. As the nineteenth century advanced, this spurious medievalism led our Victorian ancestors to commit some of the worst atrocities against architectural taste.

Strawberry Hill, Estate of Horace Walpole.

MUSIC

Nowhere is the German prominence in the Romantic world more strikingly evident than in music. Here the Romantic traits of subjectivity, emotionalism, individualism, interest in the medieval past and in distant lands, and fondness for the weird and the supernatural are all magnificently expressed in the compositions of the great nineteenth-century masters: Beethoven, Brahms, Schumann, Mendelssohn, Schubert, Hugo Wolf, Wagner, and others. When considering Beethoven (1770–1827), however, one must be careful in ascribing Romantic influences. In an age of developing Romanticism, he was a classicist who compelled his musical themes to submit to symphonic logic and who rewrote the Leonora *Overture* because in its free dramatic conception it did not seem to possess the formal recapitulation of the sonata. Although in some of his music, both early and late, Beethoven seems drawn spiritually to Romanticism, his music is closer to a new fusion with eighteenth-century classicism, and his Romantic tendencies are reminiscent rather of the German *sturm und drang* period that preceded German Romanticism. His position is not too far from that of the earliest German Romanticists, like the Schlegels and Novalis, who attempted to supplement classicism, not revolt from it. Neither Goethe (the later Goethe of *Faust*) nor Beethoven is as much a leader of German Romanticism as he is occasionally thought to be.

Although as the arts develop in the various cultural periods there is often a time lag which the reader must be ready to recognize, lest he expect too close a chronological relationship between Romantic music and literature, in this instance there is perhaps a closer chronological parallel. There was a strong anti-sonata movement which was Romantic (the sonata is the cornerstone of musical classicism), and the first signs of Romanticism in music manifested themselves in opposition to the large symphonic forms. In piano music the "character piece," such as the impromptu, rhapsody, and eclogue, appeared and deliberately shunned the sonata form. Although the symphony flourished still,

composers gradually abandoned the principles established by the Neo-classical originators. Certainly some of the composers of the earlier nineteenth century still worked almost wholly in the orbit of the classical symphony, such as Beethoven and Schubert, and even such later ones as Mendelssohn, Schumann, and Brahms continued the tradition; but nevertheless the development of the symphonic poem and program music nearly brought to an end the reign of the symphonic form. Piano music began to monopolize instrumental music, and hence chamber music, another important aspect of Neo-classic music, declined.

Opera, originally developed in seventeenth-century Italy, maintained there an unbroken tradition from Monteverdi (1567–1643) to Verdi (1813–1901), composer of *La Traviata*, *Aïda*, *Otello*.

Courtesy Henry E. Huntington Library and Art Gallery, San Marino, Calif.

Fonthill Abbey, Wiltshire.

Siegfried and the Rhine Maidens by Albert P. Ryder.

Courtesy National Gallery of Art (Mellon Collection), Washington, D. C.

French Romanticism produced, however, a new form—Grand Opera. Under the influence of Eugène Scribe's knowledge and mastery of stage techniques and his skilled dramatic fabrications of "the well-made play," Giacomo Meyerbeer (1791–1864) achieved a combination of music and drama of grand spectacle in his *Robert le Diable* (1831) that to a degree anticipated the later development of the musical drama and opera of Berlioz and Wagner. French Romantic opera is represented, too, in Charles Gounod's (1818–1893) operatic versions of *Faust* and *Roméo et Juliette*.

German Romantic Opera, a fusion of such important elements of German Romanticism as folklore and legend, folksongs and *lieder,* the Romantic conception of nature and the supernatural, is most importantly represented by Carl Maria von Weber

(1786–1826). But the greatest German operatic development was made by Richard Wagner (1813–1883), who achieved a synthesis of the arts of drama, music, and poetry in *Tannhäuser, Lohengrin, Das Rheingold, Der Ring des Nibelungen, Die Walküre, Tristan und Isolde, Die Meistersinger von Nürnberg, Siegfried, Götterdämmerung, Parsifal,* and others. Wagnerian opera gave a tremendous impetus to Romanticism in the other arts—see, for example, Ryder's painting "Siegfried and the Rhine Maidens," which it directly inspired.

The emergence in the nineteenth century of German Romantic lyric poetry is closely related to an important musical development, the solo song, or art song, or *lied.* The greatest composer of *lieder* is Franz Schubert (1797–1828), who gave the world over six hundred Romantic melodies. In this genre, Johannes Brahms (1833–1897) used folk songs extensively, Robert Schumann (1810–1856) represents the quintessence of Romanticism, and Hugo Wolf (1860–1903) expresses wildly Romantic moods.

Though the music of the Romantic world is dominated by the great Germans, contributions were also made by the composers of other countries. We have already seen that the opera was advanced by Italian and French composers. Frédéric François Chopin (1810–1849), son of a French father and a Polish mother, spent most of his mature life in France, and can therefore justifiably be called French. Chopin wrote almost exclusively for the piano and produced some of the greatest piano music of the Romantic era. Described by George Sand in her novel *Lucrezia Floriana* as "a high-flown, consumptive, and exasperating nuisance," he gave the world 55 mazurkas, 13 polonaises, 24 preludes, 27 etudes, 19 nocturnes, and many other lovely works.

Louis Hector Berlioz (1803–1869), also French, almost epitomizes Romanticism in his immensely moving symphony *Harold in Italy*. Though there is no relation to the text of Byron's *Childe Harold*, Berlioz' symphony is deeply indebted to Byron for his concept of the melancholy poet wandering through romantic scenes, for Berlioz himself says of this composition that it was his intention "to write for the orchestra a series of scenes in which the solo viola would figure as a more or less active personage of constantly preserved individuality; I wished to put the viola in the midst of poetic recollections left me by my wanderings in the Abruzzi; and make it a sort of melancholy dreamer, after the manner of Byron's *Childe Harold*. Hence the title, *Harold en Italie*." His *Symphonie Fantastique*, as the name implies, gives expression to another important Romantic trait, the attraction felt toward the weird and the strange.

The brooding melancholy of the Slavic soul is the contribution to Romantic music made by the Russian symphonic composers Tschaikovsky, Rimsky-Korsakov (who occasionally utilized Oriental motifs), Moussorgsky (*Night on Bald Mountain*), and Rachmaninoff, who continued to write piano music in the great Romantic tradition; but these composers come so late in the nineteenth century that they must be treated as post-Romantic.

LIST OF RECORDINGS

Nineteenth-Century Music

1. *Sonata in B-flat Major* ("Hammerklavier"), by Ludwig van Beethoven (1770–1827), recorded for the Beethoven Sonata Society by Arthur Schnabel, and by Horszowski on Vox Long Playing record PL-6750.
2. *Sonata No. 23 in F Minor, Op. 57* ("Appassionata"), by Ludwig van Beethoven, performed by Artur Rubinstein on Victor Long Playing record LM-1071.
3. *Symphony No. 6* ("Pastoral"), by Ludwig van Beethoven, performed by the Philadelphia Orchestra on Columbia Long Playing record ML-4010.
4. *Symphony No. 9* ("Choral"), by Ludwig van Beethoven, performed by the Boston Symphony Orchestra on Victor Long Playing record LM-6001.
5. *Quartet in F Minor for Strings, Op. 74* ("Harp"), by Ludwig van Beethoven, performed by the Budapest String Quartet on Columbia Long Playing record ML-4073.
6. *Serenade in D Major for Flute, Violin, and Viola, Op. 25*, by Ludwig van Beethoven, performed by John Wummer, Alexander Schneider, and Milton Katims on Columbia Long Playing record M-839.
7. *Trio No. 2 in E-Flat Major, Op. 100*, by Franz Schubert (1797–1828), performed by the Alma Trio on Allegro Long Playing record LA-1.
8. *Quintet in A Major* ("The Trout"), by Franz Schubert, performed by Horszowski and the Budapest Quartet on Columbia Long Playing record ML-4317. *Symphony No. 9 in C Major*, by Franz Schubert, recorded by Arturo Toscanini and the NBC Symphony Orchestra on Victor Long Playing record LM-1040.
9. Songs by Franz Schubert are presented on several Long Playing records, including Victor LM-81, Capitol P-8085, Columbia ML-4365.
10. *Der Freischütz*, complete opera by Karl Maria von Weber (1786–1826), is presented on London Long Playing set LLPA-5. German Grammophon set DGS-6 in the 78-rpm records offers substantial excerpts from the same opera.
11. Overture to *Oberon*, by Karl Maria von Weber, recorded by the London Philharmonic Orchestra on Columbia record 69410D (78 rpm). In *Oberon* appear Oberon, Titania, and Puck from Shakespeare's *Midsummer Night's Dream*.
12. Excerpts from *Romeo and Juliet*, by Louis Hector Berlioz (1803–1869), are presented by Arturo Toscanini and the NBC Symphony Orchestra on Victor Long Playing record LM-1019.
13. *Harold in Italy*, by Louis Hector Berlioz, performed by Breitenbach, Moralt, and the Vienna Symphony, is presented on VOX PL-6700.
14. Incidental music for Shakespeare's *Midsummer Night's Dream* by Felix Mendelssohn (1809–1847) is presented on Columbia Long Playing record ML-4032 by the Cleveland Orchestra under the direction of Artur Rodzinski.
15. *Symphony No. 4 in A Major* ("Italian"), by Felix Mendelssohn, performed by George Szell and the Cleveland Orchestra, on Columbia Long Playing record ML-4127.

16. *Overture for Byron's Manfred, Op. 14,* by Robert Schumann (1810–1856), performed by the BBC Symphony Orchestra, on Victor record 11713-4.
17. *Symphony No. 1 in B-Flat, Op. 38* ("Spring"), by Robert Schumann, performed by Eric Leinsdorf and the Cleveland Orchestra, on Columbia Long Playing record ML-2131.
18. Songs by Robert Schumann: "The Two Grenadiers," on Victor record 15825; "You Are Like a Flower," on Victor record 1859; "Lorelei," on Victor record 1764; "Wanderlied," on Victor 7473. The *Dichterliebe,* on Columbia Long Playing record ML-2183, sung by Lotte Lehmann, contains sixteen songs to lyrics by Heine.
19. *Etudes,* by Frédéric François Chopin (1810–1849), performed by Alexander Brailowsky, on Victor Long Playing record LM-6000.
20. *Sonata No. 2 in B-flat Minor, Op. 35,* by Frédéric François Chopin, performed by Vladimir Horowitz on Victor Long Playing record LM-1113.

21. *Les Préludes,* by Franz von Liszt (1811–1886), performed by Eugene Ormandy and the Philadelphia Orchestra on Columbia Long Playing record ML-4132.
22. *Faust,* by Charles Gounod (1818–1893), complete opera performed by the Metropolitan Opera Company, on Columbia Long Playing set SL-112.
23. *Academic Festival Overture,* by Johannes Brahms 1833–1897), containing the "Gaudeamus Igitur," performed by Barbirolli and the New York Philharmonic Orchestra on Columbia Long Playing record ML-2075.
24. *Symphony No. 1 in C Minor,* by Johannes Brahms, recorded by Artur Rodzinski and the New York Philharmonic Orchestra on Columbia Long Playing record ML-4016.
25. *Quintet in B Minor for Clarinet and Strings, Op. 115,* by Johannes Brahms, performed by Gallodoro and the Stuyvesant Quartet on Concert Hall Society Long Playing record CHC-4.
26. *Clair de Lune,* by Gabriel Fauré (1845–1924), on Columbia record (78 rpm) 4164M. This work is suggestive of Verlaine's "Clair de Lune."

HEINRICH HEINE

1797–1856

Heine was one of the most gifted of the German poets of the nineteenth century. His *Book of Songs,* 1827, was immediately recognized as an important contribution to German poetry. His work reflects many of the conflicts and contradictions which characterized and influenced his life. He was sentimental and pessimistic, naïve and skeptical, an aristocrat and a revolutionist at the same time. Although a Romantic, on occasion he violently attacked the new movement. His work, however, has a quality of brilliance and wit seldom found in German literature. Much of it has a lightness and clarity typical of French literature which he admired so much, although it sometimes is lacking in basic balance. His prose style became a model for later writers, but his poetry surpasses his prose in excellence. Heine was the poet of moods, and was greatly affected by folk songs. He is able to evoke a delicate, exquisite mood in a few simple words. It is no wonder that his poetry has inspired numerous musical compositions. The *Romantic School* (1836) was intended to instruct the French

in German Romanticism. It contains some errors of fact and judgment, but it presents many acute observations and characterizations.

FURTHER READING

ATKINS, H. G. *Heine* (New York, 1929).
BROWNE, L. *That Man Heine* (New York, 1927).
UNTERMEYER, L. *Heinrich Heine, Paradox and Poet* (New York, 1937).

The Romantic School *

BUT what was the Romantic School in Germany? It was nothing else but the reawakening of the poetry of the Middle Ages, as it had shown itself in its songs, images, and architecture, in art and in life. But this poetry had risen from Christianity; it was a passion-flower which had sprung from the blood of Christ. I do not know whether the melancholy passion-flower of Germany is known by that name in France, or whether popular legend attributes to it the same mystical origin. It is a strange, unpleasantly colored blossom, in whose calyx we see set forth the implements which were used in the crucifixion of Christ, such as the ham-

* Translated by Charles Godfrey Leland. By permission of William Heinemann, Ltd.

mer, pincers, and nails—a flower which is not so much ugly as ghostly, and even whose sight awakens in our soul a shuddering pleasure, like the convulsively agreeable sensations which come from pain itself. From this view the flower was indeed the fittest symbol for Christianity itself, whose most thrilling chain was the luxury of pain.

Though in France only Roman Catholicism is understood by the word Christianity, I must specially preface that I speak only of the latter. I speak of that religion in whose first dogmas there is a damnation of all flesh, and which not only allows to the spirit power over the flesh, but will also kill this to glorify the spirit. I speak of that religion by whose unnatural requisitions sin and hypocrisy really came into the world, in that by the condemnation of the flesh the most innocent sensuous pleasures became sins, and because the impossibility of a man's becoming altogether spiritual naturally created hypocrisy. I speak of that religion which, by teaching the doctrine of the casting away of all earthly goods and of cultivating a dog-like, abject humility and angelic patience, became the most approved support of despotism. Men have found out the real life and meaning (*Wesen*) of this religion, and do not now content themselves with promises of supping in Paradise; they know that matter has also its merits, and is not all the devil's, and they now defend the delights of this world, this beautiful garden of God, our inalienable inheritance. And therefore, because we have grasped so entirely all the consequences of that absolute spiritualism, we may believe that the Christian Catholic view of the world has reached its end. Every age is a sphinx, which casts itself into the abyss when man has guessed its riddle.

Yet we do in no wise deny the good results which this Christian Catholic view of the world established in Europe. It was necessary as a wholesome reaction against the cruelly colossal materialism which had developed itself in the Roman realm and threatened to destroy all spiritual human power. As the lascivious memoirs of the last century form the *pièces justificatives* of the French Revolution, as the terrorism of a *comité du salut public* seems to be necessary physic when we read the confessions of the aristocratic world of France, so we recognize the wholesomeness of ascetic spiritualism when we read Petronius or Apuleius, which are to be regarded as the *pièces justificatives* of Christianity. The flesh had become so arrogant in this Roman world that it required Christian discipline to chasten it. After the banquet of a Trimalchion,

such a hunger-cure as Christianity was a necessity.

Or was it that as lascivious old men seek by being whipped to excite new power of enjoyment, so old Rome endured monkish chastisement to find more exquisite delight in torture and voluptuous rapture in pain? Evil excess of stimulant! it took from the body of the state of Rome its last strength. It was not by division into two realms that Rome perished. On the Bosphorus, as by the Tiber, Rome was devoured by the same Jewish spiritualism, and here, as there, Roman history was that of a long dying agony which lasted for centuries. Did murdered Judea, in leaving to Rome its spiritualism, wish to revenge itself on the victorious foe, as did the dying centaur who craftily left to the son of Hercules the deadly garment steeped in his own blood? Truly Rome, the Hercules among races, was so thoroughly devoured by Jewish poison that helm and harness fell from its withered limbs, and its imperial war-voice died away into the wailing cadences of monkish prayer and the soft trilling of castrated boys.

But what weakens old age strengthens youth. That spiritualism had a healthy action on the too sound and strong races of the North; the too full-blooded barbarous bodies were spiritualized by Christianity, and European civilization began. The Catholic Church has in this respect the strongest claims on our regard and admiration, for it succeeded by subduing with its great genial institutions the bestiality of Northern barbarians and by mastering brutal matter.

The Art-work of the Middle Ages manifests this mastery of mere material by mind, and it is very often its only mission. The epic poems of this period may be easily classed according to the degree of this subjection or influence. There can be no discussion here of lyrical and dramatic poems, for the latter did not exist, and the former are as like in every age as are the songs of nightingales in spring.

Although the epic poetry of the Middle Ages was divided into sacred and profane, both were altogether Christian according to their kind; for if sacred poesy sang of the Jewish race and its history, the only race which was regarded as holy, or of the heroes and legends of the Old and New Testaments, and, in brief, the Church—still all the life of the time was reflected in profane poetry with its Christian views and action. The flower of the religious poetic art in the German Middle Ages is perhaps *Barlaam and Josaphat,* in which the doctrine of abnegation, of abstinence, and the denial and contempt of all worldly glory, is set forth most consistently. Next to this I would class the *The Eulogium of St. Hanno (Lobgesang auf den heiligen Anno)* as the best of the religious kind; but this is of a far more secular character, differing from the first as the portrait of a Byzantine saint differs from an old German one. As in those Byzantine pictures, so we see in *Barlaam and Josaphat* the utmost simplicity; there is no perspective sidework, and the long, lean, statue-like forms and the idealistic serious faces come out strongly drawn, as if from a mellow gold ground. On the other hand, in the song of praise of St. Hanno, the sidework or accessories are almost the subject, and, notwithstanding the grandeur of the plan, the details are treated in the minutest manner, so that we know not whether to admire in it the conception of a giant or the patience of a dwarf. But the evangel-poem of Ottfried, which is generally praised as the masterpiece of sacred poetry, is far less admirable than the two which I have mentioned.

In profane poetry we find, as I have already signified, first the cycle of sagas of the *Nibelungen* and the *Heldenbuch,* or *Book of Heroes.* In them prevails all the pre-Christian manner of thought and of feeling; in them rude strength has not as yet been softened by chivalry. There the stern Kempewarriors of the North stand like stone images, and the gentle gleam and the more refined breath of Christianity have not as yet penetrated their iron armor. But little by little a light dawns in the old Teutonic forest; the ancient idolatrous oak-trees are felled, and we see a brighter field of battle where Christ wars with the heathen. This appears in the saga-cycle of Charlemagne, in which what we really see is the Crusades reflecting themselves with their religious influences. And now from the spiritualizing power of Christianity, chivalry, the most characteristic feature of the Middle Ages, unfolds itself, and is at last sublimed into a spiritual knighthood. This secular knighthood appears most attractively glorified in the saga cycle of King Arthur, in which the sweetest gallantry, the most refined courtesy, and the most adventurous passion for combat prevail. Among the charmingly eccentric arabesques and fantastic flower-pictures of this poem we are greeted by the admirable Iwain, the all-surpassing Lancelot du Lac, and the bold, gallant, and true, but somewhat tiresome, Wigalois. Nearly allied and interwoven with this cyclus of sagas is that of the Holy Grail, in which the spiritual knighthood is glorified; and in this epoch we meet three

of the grandest poems of the Middle Ages, the *Titurel,* the *Parsifal,* and the *Lohengrin.* Here indeed we find ourselves face to face with Romantic Poetry. We look deeply into her great sorrowing eyes; she twines around us, unsuspectingly, her fine scholastic nets, and draws us down into the bewildering, deluding depths of medieval mysticism.

At last, however, we come to poems of that age which are not unconditionally devoted to Christian spiritualism; nay, it is often indirectly reflected on, where the poet disentangles himself from the bonds of abstract Christian virtues and plunges delighted into the world of pleasure and of glorified sensuousness; and it is not the worst poet, by any means, who has left us the principal work thus inspired. This is *Tristan and Isolde;* and I must declare that Gottfried von Strassburg, the composer of this most beautiful poem of the Middle Ages, is perhaps also its greatest poet, towering far above all the splendor of Wolfram von Eschenbach, whom we so admire in *Parsifal* and the fragments of *Titurel.* We are at last permitted to praise Gottfried unconditionally, though in his own time his book was certainly regarded as godless, and similar works, among them the *Lancelot,* were considered dangerous. And some very serious results did indeed ensue. The fair Francesca da Polenta and her handsome friend had to pay dearly for the pleasure of reading on a summer day in such a book; but the trouble came not from the reading, but from their suddenly ceasing to read.

There is in all these poems of the Middle Ages a marked character which distinguishes them from those of Greece and Rome. We characterize this difference by calling the first Romantic and the other Classic. Yet these appellations are only uncertain rubrics, and have led hitherto to the most discouraging, wearisome entanglements, which become worse since we give to antique poetry the designation of "Plastic," instead of "Classic." From this arose much misunderstanding; for, justly, all poets should work their material plastically, be it Christian or heathen; they should set it forth in clear outlines; in short, plastic form should be the main desideratum in modern Romantic art, quite as much as in the ancient. And are not the figures in the *Divina Commedia* of Dante or in the pictures of Raphael as plastic as those in Virgil? The difference lies in this, that the plastic forms in ancient art are absolutely identical with the subject or the idea which the artist would set forth, as, for example, that the wanderings of Ulysses mean noth-

ing else than the journeyings of a man named
Odysseus, who was son of Laërtes and husband of
Penelope; and further, that the Bacchus which we
see in the Louvre is nothing else than the graceful,
winsome son of Semele, with audacious melancholy
in his eyes and sacred voluptuousness on his soft
and arching lips. It is quite otherwise in Romantic
art, in which the wild wanderings of a knight have
ever an esoteric meaning, symbolizing perhaps the
erring course of life. The dragon whom he overcomes is sin; the almond which from afar casts comforting perfume to the traveler is the Trinity, God
the Father, God the Son, and God the Holy Ghost,
which are three in one, as shell, fibre, and kernel
make one nut. When Homer describes the armor
of a hero, it is a good piece of work, worth such
and such a number of oxen; but when a monk of
the Middle Ages describes in his poems the garments of the Mother of God, one may be sure that
by this garb he means as many virtues, and a
peculiar significance lies hidden under this holy
covering of the immaculate virginity of Maria, who,
as her son is the almond-kernel, is naturally sung
as the almond-flower. That is the character of the
medieval poetry which we call Romantic.

Classic art had only to represent the finite or
determined, and its forms could be one and the
same with the idea of the artist. Romantic art had
to set forth, or rather signify, the infinite and
purely spiritual, and it took refuge in a system of
traditional, or rather of parabolistic symbols, as
Christ himself had sought to render clear his spiritu-
alistic ideas by all kinds of beautiful parables.
Hence the mystical, problematic, marvelous, and
transcendental in the art-work of the Middle Ages,
in which fantasy makes her most desperate efforts
to depict the purely spiritual by means of sensible
images, and invents colossal follies, piling Pelion
on Ossa and *Parsifal* on *Titurel* to attain to heaven.

Among other races where poetry attempted to
display the infinite, and where monstrous fancies
appeared, as, for instance, among the Scandina-
vians and Indians, we find poems which, being
romantic, are given that classification.

We cannot say much as to the music of the
Middle Ages, for original documents, which might
have served for our guidance, are wanting. It was
not till late in the sixteenth century that the masterpieces of Catholic church music, which cannot
be too highly praised, appeared. These express in
the most exquisite manner pure Christian spirituality. The recitative arts, which are spiritual from
their very nature, could indeed flourish fairly in

Christianity, yet it was less favorable to those of
design, for as these had to represent the victory of
mind over matter, and yet must use matter as the
means wherewith to work, they had to solve a
problem against Nature. Hence we find in sculpture and painting those revolting subjects—martyr-
doms, crucifixions, dying saints, and the flesh
crushed in every form. Such themes were martyrdom for sculpture; and when I contemplate those
distorted images in which Christian asceticism and
renunciation of the senses are expressed by distorted, pious heads, long thin arms, starveling legs,
and awkwardly fitting garments, I feel an indescribable compassion for the artists of that time. The
painters were indeed more favored, for the material
for their work, because of its susceptivity to varied
play of color, did not antagonize spirituality so
obstinately as the material of the sculptors, and yet
they were obliged to load the sighing canvas with
the most repulsive forms of suffering. In truth,
when we regard many galleries which contain
nothing but scenes of bloodshed, scourging, and
beheading, one might suppose that the old masters
had painted for the collection of an executioner.

But human genius can transform and glorify
even the unnatural; many painters solved this problem of making what was revolting beautiful and
elevating—the Italians, especially, succeeding in
paying tribute to beauty at the expense of spirituality, and in rising to that ideality which attained
perfection in so many pictures of the Madonna. As
regards this subject the Catholic clergy always made
some concession to the physical. This image of immaculate beauty which is glorified by maternal love
and suffering had the privilege of being made
famous by poets and painters, and adorned with all
charms of the sense, for it was a magnet which
could attract the multitude to the lap of Christianity. Madonna Maria was the beautiful *dame du
comptoir* of the Catholic Church, who, with her
beautiful eyes, attracted and held fast its customers,
especially the barbarians of the North.

Architecture had in the Middle Ages the same
character as the other arts, as indeed all the manifestations of life then harmonized so marvelously
with one another. The tendency to parable shows
itself here, as in poetry. When we now enter a
Gothic cathedral, we hardly suspect the esoteric
sense of its stone symbolism; only a general impression pierces our soul; we realize an elevation of
feeling and mortification of the flesh. The interior
is a hollow cross, and we wander among the instruments of martyrdom itself; the variegated windows

cast on us red and green light, like blood and corruption; funeral songs wail about us; under our feet are mortuary tablets and decay; and the soul soars with the colossal columns in a giddy height, tearing itself with pain from the body, which falls like a weary, worn-out garment to the ground. But when we behold the exteriors of these Gothic cathedrals, these enormous buildings which are wrought so aërially, so finely, delicately, transparently, cut as it were into such open work that one might take them for Brabant lace in marble, then we feel truly the power of that age which could so master stone itself that it seems spectrally transfused with spiritual life, and thus even the hardest material declares Christian spirituality.

But arts are only the mirror of life, and, as Catholicism died away, so its sounds grew fainter and its lights dimmer in art. During the Reformation Catholic song gradually disappeared in Europe, and in its place we see the long-slumbering poetry of Greece re-awakening to life. But it was only an artificial spring, a work of the gardener, not of the sun, and the trees and flowers were in close pots, and a glass canopy protected them from cold and northern winds.

In the world's history no event is the direct result of another; all events rather exert a mutual influence. It was by no means due only to the Greek scholars who emigrated to Europe after the fall of Byzantium that a love for Grecian culture and the desire to imitate it became so general among us; a similar Protestantism prevailed then in art as well as in life. Leo X., that splendid Medici, was as zealous a Protestant as Luther, and as there was a Latin prose protest in Wittenberg, so they protested poetically in Rome in stone, color, and *ottaverime*. And do not the mighty marble images of Michelangelo, the laughing nymphs of Giulio Romano, and the joyous intoxication of life in the verses of Ludovico Ariosto form a protesting opposition to the old, gloomy, worn-out Catholicism? The painters of Italy waged a polemic against priestdom which was perhaps more effective than that of the Saxon theologian. The blooming rosy flesh in the pictures of Titian is all Protestantism. The limbs of his Venus are more thorough *theses* than those which the German monk pasted on the church door of Wittenberg. Then it was that men felt as if suddenly freed from the force and pressure of a thousand years; the artists, most of all, again breathed freely as the nightmare of Christianity seemed to spin whirling from their breasts, and they threw themselves with enthusiasm into the sea of Greek joyousness from whose foam rose to them goddesses of beauty. Painters once more limned the ambrosial joys of Olympus; sculptors carved, with the joy of yore, old heroes from the marble; poets again sang the house of Atreus and Laius; and so the age of new classic poetry began.

As modern life was most perfectly developed in France under Louis XIV, so the new classic poetry received there its most finished perfection, and, in a measure, an independent originality. Through the political influence of that great king this poetry spread over Europe; in Italy, its home, it assumed a French color, and thence the heroes of French tragedy went with the Anjous to Spain; it passed with Henrietta Maria to England, and we Germans, as a matter of course, built our clumsy temples to the powdered Olympus of Versailles. The most famous high-priest of this religion was Gottsched, that wonderful long wig whom our dear Goethe has so admirably described in his memoirs.

Lessing was the literary Arminius who delivered our theatre from this foreign rule. He showed us the nothingness, the laughableness, the flat and faded folly of those imitations of the French theatre, which were in turn imitated from the Greek. But he became the founder of modern German literature, not only by his criticism, but by his own works of art. This man pursued with enthusiasm and sincerity art, theology, antiquity, and archaeology, the art of poetry, history—all with the same zeal and to the same purpose. There lives and breathes in all his works the same great social idea, the same progressive humanity, the same religion of reason, whose John he was, and whose Messiah we await. This religion he always preached, but, alas! too often alone and in the desert. And there was one art only of which he knew nothing—that of changing stones into bread, for he consumed the greatest part of his life in poverty and under hard pressure— a curse which clings to nearly all great German geniuses, and will last, it may be, till ended by political freedom. Lessing was more inspired by political feelings than men supposed, a peculiarity which we do not find among his contemporaries, and we can now see for the first time what he meant in sketching the duo-despotism in *Emilia Galotti*. He was regarded then as a champion of freedom of thought and against clerical intolerance; for his theological writings were better understood. The fragments *On the Education of the Human Race*, which Eugène Rodrigue has translated into French, may give an idea of the vast comprehensiveness of Lessing's mind. The two critical works which exercised the most influence on art are his *Hamburg Dramatic Art (Hamburgische Dramaturgie)*, and his *Laokoon, or the Limits of Painting and Poetry.* His most remarkable theatrical pieces are *Emilia Galotti, Minna von Barnhelm,* and *Nathan the Wise.*

Gotthold Ephraim Lessing was born at Camenz in Lausitz, January 22, 1729, and died in Brunswick, February 15, 1781. He was a thorough-going man who, when he destroyed something old in a battle, at the same time always created something new and better. "He was," says a German author, "like those pious Jews, who, during the second building of the Temple, were often troubled by attacks of the enemy, and so fought with one hand while with the other they worked at the house of God." This is not the place where I can say more of Lessing, but I cannot refrain from remarking that he is, of all who are recorded in the whole history of literature, the writer whom I love best.

I will here mention another author who worked in the same spirit, with the same object, as Lessing, and who may be regarded as his successor. It is true that his eulogy is here also out of place, since he occupies an altogether peculiar position in literature, and a unique relation to his time and to his contemporaries. It is Johann Gottfried Herder, born in 1744 at Mohrungen, in East Prussia, and who died at Weimar in the year 1803.

Literary history is the great "Morgue" where every one seeks his dead, those whom he loves or to whom he is related. When I see there, among so many dead who were of little interest, a Lessing or a Herder, with their noble, manly countenances, my heart throbs; I cannot pass them by without hastily kissing their dead lips.

Yet if Lessing did so much to destroy the habit of imitating French second-hand Greekdom, he still, by calling attention to the true works of art of Greek antiquity, gave an impulse to a new kind of ridiculous imitations. By his battling with religious superstition he advanced the sober search for clearer views which spread widely in Berlin, which had in the late blessed Nicolai its chief organ, and in the General German Library its arsenal. The most deplorable mediocrity began to show itself more repulsively than ever, and flatness and insipidity blew themselves up like the frog in the fable.

It is a great mistake to suppose that Goethe, who had already come before the world, was at once universally recognized as a writer of commanding genius. His *Götz von Berlichingen* and his *Werther* were received with a degree of enthusiasm, to be sure; but so, too, were the works of common bunglers, and Goethe had but a small niche in the temple of literature. As I have said, *Götz* and *Werther* had a spirited reception, but more on account of the subject-matter than their artistic merits, which very few appreciated in these masterworks. *Götz* was a dramatized romance of chivalry, and such writings were then the rage. In *Werther* the world saw the reproduction of a true story, that of young Jerusalem, who shot himself dead for love, and thereby, in those dead-calm days, made a great noise. People read with tears his touching letters; some shrewdly observed that the manner in which Werther had been banished from aristocratic society had increased his weariness of life. The discussion of suicide caused the book to be still more discussed; it occurred to several fools on this occasion to make away with themselves, and the book, owing to its subject, went off like a shot. The novels of August Lafontaine were just as much read, and, as this author wrote incessantly, he was more famous than Wolfgang von Goethe. Wieland was the great poet then, with whom perhaps might be classed the ode-maker, Rambler of Berlin. Wieland was honored idolatrously, far more at that time than Goethe. Iffland ruled the theatre with his dreary *bourgeois* dramas, and Kotzebue with his flat and frivolously witty jests.

It was in opposition to this literature that there sprang up in Germany, at the end of the last century, a school which we call the Romantic, and of which August Wilhelm and Friedrich Schlegel have presented themselves as managing agents. Jena, where these and many other souls in like accord found themselves "off and on," was the centre from which the new esthetic doctrine spread. I say doctrine, for this school began with judgments of the art-works of the past and recipes for art-works of the future, and in both directions the Schlegel school rendered great service to esthetic criticism. By judging of such works of art as already existed, either their faults and failures were indicated, or their merits and beauties brought to light. In controversy and in indicating artistic shortcomings, the Schlegels were entirely imitators of old Lessing; they obtained possession of his great battle-blade, but the arm of August Wilhelm Schlegel was too tenderly weak and the eyes of his brother Friedrich too mystically clouded for the former to strike so strongly and the latter so keenly and accurately as Lessing. True, in descriptive criticism where the beauties of poetry were concerned and where it came to a delicate detection of its characteristics and bringing them home to our intelligence—then, compared to the Schlegels, old Lessing was nowhere. But what shall I say as to their recipes for preparing works of art? There we find in the Schlegels a weakness which we think may also be detected in Lessing; for the latter is as weak in affirming as he is strong in denying. He rarely succeeds in laying down a fundamental principle, still more seldom a correct one. He wants the firm basis of a philosophy or of a philosophical system. And this is still more sadly the case with the brothers Schlegel.

Much is fabled as to the influence of Fichtean Idealism and Schelling's Philosophy of Nature on the Romantic school, which is even declared to have sprung from it. But I see here, at the most, only the influence of certain fragments of thoughts from Fichte and Schelling, and not at all that of a philosophy. This may be explained on the simple ground that Fichte's philosophy had lost its hold, and Fichte himself had made it lose its interest by a mingling of tenets and ideas from Schelling; and because, on the other hand, Schelling had never set forth a philosophy, but only a vague philosophizing, an unsteady, vacillating improvisation of poetical philosophemes. It may be that it was from the Fichtean Idealism—that deeply ironical system, where the I is opposed to the not-I and annihilates it—that the Romantic school took the doctrine of irony which the late Solger especially developed, and which the Schlegels at first regarded as the soul of art, but which they subsequently found to be fruitless and exchanged for the more positive axioms of the Theory of Identity of Schelling. Schelling, who then taught in Jena, had indeed a great personal influence on the Romantic school; he is, what is not generally known in France, also a bit of a poet; and it is said that he was in doubt whether he should not deliver all his philosophical doctrines in a poetic or even metrical form. This doubt characterizes the man.

———◆———

JEAN JACQUES ROUSSEAU

1712–1778

Musician, philosopher, and writer, Rousseau was born at Geneva, the son of a watchmaker. After an escapade the nature of which we do not know, Rousseau was forced to leave Geneva. He was taken under the protection of a wealthy lady who subsequently sent him to Turin in Italy to study. He later became a lackey in the household of a prominent family, but was again forced to flee after falling in love with the daughter of that family. He again became the companion of the same wealthy lady who had sent him to Turin, but after a quarrel with her he went to Paris to participate in its literary life. He there became involved in a liaison with one Thérèse Levasseur, an ignorant servant-girl, who eventually presented him with five children whom he placed in an orphans' home. The qualities which characterize Rousseau as a person and which emerge in most of his writings are sensitivity, egotism, individualism, instability, and fickleness. A victim of persecution mania, he was perennially at war with himself and with all around him. He is the incarnation of the true revolutionary, regarding the reforms which men like Voltaire were trying to bring about as useless. According to Rousseau, the entire structure of society needed to be destroyed so that a completely fresh start could be made. The course of action which he advocated was a return to a state wherein man would be uncontaminated by vices of a social order considered decadent. He demanded the free play of the human heart; the unfettered development of the individual, who was by nature good, should be the paramount achievement of the body politic and social. Thus in Rousseau we find a doctrine of equalitarianism, totally lacking in Voltaire, which supplied an incendiary stimulus for the political and social outlook which eventually produced the French Revolution. From the literary point of view, it is the emphasis which he places on emotion and on the wild, exotic aspects of nature that is important, for it stamps him as a forerunner of the nineteenth-century Romantics. His *Nouvelle Héloïse* (1761) is a tearfully sentimental novel of interminable length in an epistolary form derived from the English novelist Richardson. *Émile* (1762) presents a pedagogical Utopia based on the principle that children should be allowed the free play of their instincts in a seclusion providing protection against the corrupting influence of books, civilization, and society. The *Social Contract* (1762) advocated a sort of democratic society based on mutual consent of the governed within the framework of a state in which each individual is at once subject and citizen-ruler under a cabinet ministry controlled through popular referendums. The *Confessions* (1781–1788), one of the world's great autobiographies, was written to defend his own character against the manifold attacks to which he was continually subjected and to prove that a better man than Jean Jacques Rousseau did not exist. The *Reveries of a Solitary Walker* is a series of sketches each complete in itself, synthesizing the majority of the views already expressed in the earlier works. These ideas, not entirely original with Rousseau, but collected from the philosophical ambient submerged by Neo-classicism, had a tremendous popular appeal throughout eighteenth-century Europe. They fundamentally motivated not only the French Revolution and nineteenth-century Romanticism, but are still exerting a tremendous influence on Western thought.

FURTHER READING

BABBITT, IRVING. *Rousseau and Romanticism* (Boston and New York, 1919).
FAIRCHILD, H. N. *The Noble Savage* (New York, 1928).
HENDEL, C. W. *Jean Jacques Rousseau, Moralist* (London and New York, 1934).
JOSEPHSON, M. *Jean Jacques Rousseau* (London, 1932).

Reverie of a Solitary Walker *

PROMENADE V

OF ALL the places I have lived in (and I have been in some that were delightful), none ever rendered me so truly happy or left such pleasing impressions on my memory as the island of Saint Pierre in the Lake of Bienne. This little island which is called at Neufchâtel the Isle de la Motte, is not well known, even in Switzerland. No traveller, so far as I know, has mentioned it. However it is very agreeable and peculiarly well situated to create the happiness of a man who loves to keep to himself; for though I am perhaps the only one in the world for whom Destiny has made a law of it, I can not believe that I am the only person who possesses so natural an inclination in spite of the fact that to the present moment I have never happened to meet any one of similar disposition.

The banks of the Lake of Bienne are wilder and more romantic than those of the Lake of Geneva, since the rocks and woods approach nearer to the

* Anonymous translation, revised.

edge of the water, but they are not less delightful. While well cultivated meadows and vineyards are not so numerous and while there are fewer towns and houses, there is more natural verdure, more meadows, more shady retreats and groves; in a word, agreeable and well-contrasted terrain is much more often encountered. As there is no suitable road on these happy shores for carriages, the country is not much frequented by travellers; but is highly interesting to the contemplative philosopher who likes to intoxicate himself at his leisure on the charms of Nature, who likes to retire into a silence broken only by the cries of eagles, by the mingled warbling of various song birds, or by the rushing of torrents which fall from the surrounding mountains. This beautiful basin, almost round in form, contains near its center, two small islands. One, inhabited and cultivated, about a half league in circumference, the other smaller, deserted and fallow, will in time be totally destroyed because of the continual removal of earth from it to repair the devastation made by the waves and storms on the larger one. Thus, in every instance, the substance of the weak is employed to the profit of the powerful.

There is on the island but one house, large, agreeable and comfortable, belonging to the hospital of Berne as does the entire island. The house is inhabited by the steward of the estate with his family and servants. He has poultry in abundance, a dovehouse, and fish ponds. The island, though small, is so diversified in its terrain and aspect that it offers a variety of scenery and undergoes every sort of cultivation. You see alternately fields, vineyards, orchards, and rich pastures shaded by groves of trees and bordered with shrubs of all kinds which the proximity of the water maintains in a perpetually fresh condition. A high terrace, planted with two rows of trees, runs the entire length of the island, and in the middle of this terrace a pretty hall has been erected where the inhabitants of the neighboring shores meet and dance on Sundays during the vintage season.

On this island I took refuge after the stoning at Motiers.[1] I found its situation so delightful and the life I led there so much in conformity to my humor, that, having resolved to end my days there, I was troubled by no thought other than that I would not be permitted to carry out that resolution which was not in accord with the project of dragging me off to

[1] Rousseau says in Book XII of the *Confessions* that he was violently attacked in September, 1765, by the citizens of Motiers, stones being thrown through the windows of his house. Authorities disagree on the seriousness of this attack.

England.[2] In the presentments which were disturbing me, I would have liked for this asylum to be made into a perpetual prison for me; I would have been glad to be confined in it for life; and I might have wished that all power and hope of leaving it be taken from me and that I should have been forbidden to have any kind of communication with the mainland. Being unaware of the happenings in the world, I could then forget its existence and it could forget mine.

I was hardly permitted to pass as much as two months on this island, but I could have passed two years, two centuries, a whole eternity there without a moment's weariness, though, except for my wife, I had no company other than the steward, his wife and servants, who were all a very good sort of people and nothing more, but they were precisely what I needed. I reckon these two months as the happiest time of my life, so truly happy, that I would have been satisfied with it during the whole of my existence without a single wish arising in my soul to exchange it for a different state.

What then was this happiness and what did the enjoyment of it consist of? I leave that to be guessed by the present generation from the description which I shall give of it. The precious *far niente* was the first and principal one of these enjoyments which I wanted to enjoy in all their sweetness, and all I did during my residence there was but the pleasant and necessary activity of a man who is devoted to indolence.

The hope that nothing more could be devised by my enemies than to leave me in that lonely spot where I had willingly become entirely wrapped up in myself, which it was impossible for me to leave without help or without being seen, and where I could have neither communication or correspondence except through the medium of those who surrounded me. This inspired me with the hope of concluding my days in greater tranquillity than I had hitherto passed them, and the idea that I should have time to settle all at leisure, occasioned me to neglect everything. Having been taken there suddenly naked and alone, I successively sent for my wife, my books, and my luggage which I never had the pleasure of unpacking, but left my chests and trunks as they arrived, living on the spot where I hoped to end my life as I would in an inn which I intended to leave the next day. I found everything here so perfectly suited to my mind that to have made any change at all would have spoiled it. One

of my greatest pleasures above all was to leave those books well packed, and to have no writing desk. When troublesome letters forced me to take up my pen to answer, I grumblingly borrowed the steward's desk which I hastened to return vainly hoping that I would not need to borrow it again. Instead of melancholy manuscripts and musty books, I filled my apartment with flowers and plants, for I was then in the first fervor of botany, which taste Doctor D'Ivernois had lately inspired me with and which presently became a passion for me. Rejecting, therefore, all laborious work, I occupied myself only with studies suited to an indolent life and furnishing amusement without causing much trouble. I undertook to compose the *Flora Petrinsularis* and to describe all the plants of the island, without omitting a single one, in sufficient detail to keep me busy for the rest of my days.

It is said that a certain German wrote a book on a lemon peel; I should have written one on each herb the field produced, on each kind of moss that adhered to the trees, on each weed that covered and adorned the rocks; in short, I wished not to leave a single blade of grass or vegetable atom without an ample description.

In consequence of this noble resolution, every morning after breakfast (which we all took together) I went, with a magnifying glass in my hand, and my *systema naturae* under my arm, to visit a portion of the island which I had for that purpose divided into small squares, intending to explore each of them in turn in each season of the year. Nothing can be more singular than the delight and ecstasy which I experienced on each observation I made on the vegetable structure and organization, and on the action of the sexual parts in the fructification, the system of which was at that time entirely new to me. The distinction of the generic characteristics, of which I had not the least idea before, charmed me as I verified them on the common species as I waited until rarer ones should be presented to me. The fork of the two long stamens of the prunella, the springing of those of the nettle and the parietary, the explosion of the fruit of the balsam and the bud of the boxwood, many little acts of fructification which I observed for the first time, all filled me with delight; I went about asking people if they had seen the horns of the prunella, just as Fontaine[3] inquired if anyone had ever read Habakkuk. In two or three hours, I usually returned with an ample harvest— material to keep me amused during the afternoon

---

[2] Hume had invited Rousseau to come to England, and he was being urged to do so by some of his friends.

[3] Fontaine is La Fontaine the celebrated seventeenth-century poet and philosopher.

at home in case of rain. I employed the rest of the morning in going with the steward, his wife, and Teresa to see the workmen and their harvest, usually putting my hand to the work along with them; and frequently when people from Berne came to visit me, they found me perched up in a great tree, girded about with a sack that I was filling with fruit and which I afterwards let down by a cord. The exercise I had taken in the morning and the good humor which accompanied it, rendered rest at dinner-time very agreeable, but when it was too long and the fine weather invited me outside, I could not spare so much time, and while others were yet at table, I stole away and, leaping into a boat, rowed it to the middle of the lake; and when the water was calm; and there, lying stretched out in the bottom of the boat with my eyes towards Heaven, let it drift slowly with the waters, sometimes for several hours, enjoying a delicious though confused revery which, without any particular and fixed object were, in my opinion a hundred times preferable to all I have ever found to be most delightful in what are called the pleasures of life. Sometimes warned by the sun's going down that it was time to return home, I found myself so far from the island that I was obliged to labor with my utmost strength to reach it before nightfall. At other times, instead of passing my time on the water, I took delight in walking along the verdant banks of the island, where the limpid waters and refreshing shade frequently invited me to have a swim in them. But one of my most usual excursions was a voyage to the small island where I used to disembark and spend the afternoon in closely circumscribed walks either in the midst of the willows, alders, persicaria and shrubs of every kind, or else sometimes reposing on the top of a sandy hillock covered with grass, wild thyme, flowers and even sainfoin and clover which possibly had been sown there a long time before and provided very proper nourishment for rabbits who might multiply there in peace, without fear for themselves and without harming anything. I made this remark to the steward, who sent to Neufchâtel for some male and female rabbits, and we went with great ceremony, he, his wife, one of his sisters, Teresa and myself, to settle them on the little island, which they began to people before my departure and where doubtless they have continued to increase if they could sustain the rigor of the winters. The planting of this little colony was a holiday. The pilot of the Argonauts could not have been prouder of his office than I was on that occasion, triumphantly leading the company

and the rabbits from the large to the small island; and I noted with pride that the steward's wife, who was excessively apprehensive of water, embarked with confidence under my care, and showed no sign of fear during the crossing.

When the lake was too much agitated to permit my navigating it with safety, I passed the afternoon walking through the island, herbalizing in all parts or sitting in the pleasantest and most solitary nooks to dream at ease either about the charm of the terraces and hillocks or else choosing a spot on the terraces and hillocks to enjoy the superb view of the lake and its shores bounded on one side by the near-by mountains and on the other by rich and fertile meadows over which could be seen bluish mountains in the distance along the horizon.

On the approach of night, I descended from these eminences and sitting on the sands of the lake shore in some hidden asylum, where the roaring of the waves and the movement of the water captured my attention and chased every other agitation from my soul, plunging it into delicious reverie in which night frequently stole on me unperceived. The ebb and flow of the water, its continual noise, increased from time to time by the wind, perpetually striking on my ears and my eyes, took the place of those inward sensations which my reveries almost dispelled and were enough to make me feel my existence with pleasure without my having to take the trouble to think. At times there came to me some weak and brief thought about the instability of worldly things which were reflected upon the surface of the waters; but soon these fleeting impressions were effaced by the uniformity of the continual movement which lulled me and which, without active aid from my soul, did not fail to absorb me to such an extent that when summoned by the hour and by the signal agreed upon, I could not tear myself away without a great effort.

After supper, when the evening was fine, we walked all together on the terrace, and breathed the fresh air of the lake; or, seated in the pavilion, laughed, chatted, or sang some of the good old songs which were preferable to the labored composition of our modern ones; and, at length, we retired to rest pleased with our day and desiring nothing more than a similar one for the next day.

Thus passed my time, during my residence on that island when it was not interrupted by unforeseen and troublesome visitors. But what was there in all this sufficiently attractive to excite in my heart regrets so keen, tender and durable that after fifteen years it is impossible for me to think of that beloved spot without feeling myself in a manner carried there by the intensity of my wishes?

I have noted, during the vicissitudes of a long life that the periods of sweetest enjoyment and of keenest pleasure are not, however, those whose remembrance wins and delights me most. Those short moments of delirium and passion, however intense they might be, are, because of their intensity itself, nothing more than pin points thinly spaced along the line of life. They are too rare and too fleeting to constitute any permanent idea of happiness; and the felicity which my heart looks back upon with regret is not composed of fugitive moments, but is a simple and lasting condition which has no intensity in itself but the durability of which increases its charm till at length it becomes supreme happiness.

Everything fluctuates on earth; nothing remains in a constant and lasting form, and those affections of ours which are attached to external things necessarily pass and change with their object. Ever before or behind us, they remind us of the past which exists no longer or they anticipate for us a future which often never arrives; there is nothing solid to which the heart can attach itself. Likewise we have in this world hardly any pleasures that are lasting. Permanent happiness is, I fear, unknown. Scarcely is there in our keenest enjoyments an instant when the heart can truly say, "May this moment last forever!"—How then can we call happiness a state so fleeting, one which leaves an uneasy void in the heart, which ever prompts us to regret something that is past, or desire something for the future?

But if there is a state where the soul can find a hold strong enough to lean on securely, to attach its whole being to, without any need to recall the past or anticipate the future, where time is of no importance, where the present lasts forever without marking its duration in any way and without any trace of succession, without any other feeling of privation or enjoyment, of pleasure or pain, of desire or fear than the one of our existence and which this feeling alone can fill entirely; so long as this state lasts, he who is in it may be called happy, not with an imperfect happiness, poor and relative, such as the one which is found in the pleasures of life, but with a sufficing happiness, perfect and full, which does not leave in the soul any void which it feels the need of filling. Such is the state in which I frequently found myself on the island of Saint Pierre, in my solitary reveries; whether stretched in my boat which I let float at the whim of the waters, or seated on the banks of the agitated lake, or elsewhere on the banks of a beautiful river, or by a brook murmuring over its pebbled bottom.

What does one enjoy in such a situation? Nothing outside of oneself, nothing except oneself and one's own existence, for while this state lasts, one is sufficient for oneself, like God. The consciousness of existence divested of every other affection is in itself a precious feeling of contentment and peace, which alone would suffice to render this existence dear and sweet to the one who can put away from oneself those sensual and earthly affections which perpetually distract us and disturb happiness here below. But the greater part of mankind, agitated by continual passions are not well acquainted with this state, and having enjoyed it only imperfectly for a few instants, they keep of it an obscure and confused idea which prevents their feeling its charm. Perhaps it might not be convenient, in the present order of things, that lost in pleasant ecstasies, mankind should be disgusted with the active life, since their multiplied wants have prescribed it as a duty. But an unfortunate man, cut off from human society, and who can no longer perform anything useful or good here below, either for himself or for others, may find in this state a pleasing consolation which neither fortune nor men can deprive him of.

It is true that these consolations cannot be felt by all minds nor in all situations. It is necessary that the heart should be at peace, that no passion should arise to disturb this calm. It requires not only a disposition adapted to it on the part of the person who is to experience this felicity, but also assistance from surrounding objects. There must be neither absolute repose nor too much agitation, but a uniform and moderate disposition, not subject to sudden gusts of passion or utter despondency.—Without emotion, life is but a lethargy. If the emotion is unequal or too violent, it disturbs; in recalling us to surrounding objects, it destroys the pleasure of the reverie, and tearing us from ourselves, instantly replacing us under the yoke of fortune and mankind and giving us back the sensation of our misfortunes. Absolute silence is productive of melancholy. It presents an image of death: then the assistance of a cheerful imagination is necessary, and it is naturally given to those whom Heaven has gratified with it. The emotion which does not come from the outside then arises within us. This lessens our repose, it is true, but it is also more pleasant when sweet ideas lightly touch the surface of the soul without disturbing its depths. Only enough of them are necessary for one to remember oneself and forget all misfortune. This kind of reverie may be enjoyed wherever we can be calm; and I have often thought that in the Bastille, or even in a dungeon where I could see no object, I could enjoy agreeable dreams.

It must be admitted that all is achieved more easily and more pleasantly in a fertile and solitary island, naturally circumscribed and detached from the rest of the world, where nothing but smiling objects were visible, where nothing reminded one of painful memories and where the society of a small number of local people was pleasant and sweet, without being sufficiently interesting to occupy all of my time; where, in fine, I could either give myself up for the whole day without obstacle and without concern to those occupations which were most in conformity with my disposition, or to the most luxurious indolence. The opportunity doubtless was splendid for a dreamer who, knowing how to take his nourishment from agreeable chimeras set in the midst of the most unpleasant objects, could satiate himself on them at his ease, adding to them everything that could really strike his senses. Awaking from a long and charming reverie, beholding myself surrounded by verdure, flowers, and birds, letting my eyes wander to the distant romantic shores along a vast extent of crystalline waters, I connected all those pleasing objects with my fictitious enjoyments, and finding myself brought back by degrees to myself, I could scarcely distinguish the point of separation between ideal and real delights; so much did everything contribute to the happiness of that quiet solitary life which I led in that charming abode! Would that it might begin again! Why cannot I go and finish my days on that dear island, without ever leaving it or seeing any person from the continent who might bring in mind all those calamities which they have taken delight in showering upon me for so many years? They would soon be forgotten forever: undoubtedly they would not forget me, but what would it matter if they could not come and disturb my repose? Delivered from all earthly passions which are engendered by the tumults of social life, my soul would frequently bound above this atmosphere, and anticipate its communion with those celestial intelligences whose numbers it shortly hopes to augment. I know mankind will beware of affording me so quiet an asylum where they have not been willing to leave me. But they can not prevent me from transporting myself each day on the wings of imagination to that happy spot and from enjoying for a few hours the same pleasure as if I still lived there. The sweetest thing I could do there would be to dream at my ease. If I dream that I am there am I not doing the same thing? I am even doing more; to the charm of abstract and monotonous reverie, I add a charming picture which gives it life. Their objects often escaped my senses in my ecstasies; and now the deeper my reverie the more sharply it paints them for me. I am often more with them and even more pleasantly so than I was when I was really there. The unfortunate thing about it is that as the imagination cools, all that comes back to me with more difficulty and does not last so long. Alas! it is when one begins to leave one's own carcass that one is most hindered by it.

———◆———

JOHANN WOLFGANG VON GOETHE

1749-1832

Goethe, a great man and a great poet by any standard, represents the transition from rationalistic Neo-classicism to individualistic Romanticism; and, in his later work, he achieves a synthesis of the best elements of the two. He was a precocious youth, son of a rather severe lawyer who had sufficient wealth to enable him to devote his time to manifold hobbies. From early training of a liberal and humane character given him at home by his father, the young Goethe proceeded to the study of law at the University of Leipzig. Finding the courses stultifyingly dull and having greater interest in poetry and in languages, he zestfully joined in the activities of the theatrical and literary society then flourishing in Leipzig. Having already composed a number of lively lyrics together with a short play, Goethe returned home in 1768 after a long illness. During his convalescence, he read quite widely in chemistry, alchemy, theosophy, and mysticism. He later completed his study of law at Strasbourg, even practicing for a time in Frankfurt, but soon gave it up in favor of other pursuits.

The comprehensive and versatile genius of Goethe approaches ideal universality more closely than that of any figure in modern times, for, through unceasing labor, he developed to the fullest the wonderful intellectual gifts with which he had been endowed. He dealt effectively with almost every phase of intellectual activity, and in most of them he was far in advance of his time. Besides being one of the greatest figures in all literary history, he was a painter of note, an illustrious statesman who rose to the highest administrative posts in the government of Duke Karl August of Saxe-Weimar, a distinguished scientist who performed significant work in biology, geology, and in the theory of colors. He was, in addition, both an actor and a theater manager. But perhaps most of all he was a great humanitarian dedicated to an enlightened liberalism as opposed to the authoritarianism which generally characterized the Neo-classic period. His tremendous literary production, accomplished concurrently with his other multifarious activities, comprises love lyrics, ballads, philosophical poems and plays, novels, epics, tragedies, satires, short stories, and operettas, all characterized by sincerity, simplicity, warmth of feeling, transcendent beauty of form as well as by profundity of thought and conception. His writings, intensely personal and very often autobiographical, were intended to interpret for his contemporaries the great spiritual, moral, and philosophical issues of his time. Strongly in accord with and stimulated by the pantheism of Spinoza, Goethe's works reflect his own personal unity with God which he achieved through love and understanding of the beauties of nature.

Goethe's literary work is represented in this volume by selections from his novel *The Sorrows of Young Werther* (1774), and by Part I of his monumental *Faust* (1808). *Werther,* a product of Goethe's youth, immediately won him a vast reputation as a writer. It is the story of a typical Romantic hero who becomes the victim of a hopeless passion for a married woman. Werther is moody, melancholy, oversensitive, mystical, incapable of adapting himself to the exigencies of harsh reality. He obtains a diplomatic post abroad in a desperate effort to forget his stormy passion, but he soon has a quarrel with his not so sensitive superior, and resigns. At the end, bewildered, restless, profoundly unhappy, he commits suicide. In addition to the character of the hero, the novel contains such other Romantic characteristics as the glorification of the self, comprehension through the heart rather than through the mind, worship of nature even in its most awesome aspects, an inordinate admiration for

the simple life of peasants and children, and a generally tearful atmosphere. The sentimentality which pervades the book, based at least in part on Goethe's own emotional experiences, made a great appeal to the people of the time. While the modern reader might find it difficult to accept the melancholy emotionalism of the novel, his contemporaries, living as they did at the beginning of the Romantic movement, found in it an expression of their own feelings. Its success was unparalleled, not only in Germany but in other countries also, for it was immediately translated into almost every civilized tongue, including Chinese, and was widely imitated, more or less successfully, by a host of other writers.

Faust, Goethe's greatest work, is perhaps the highest point ever reached by the modern poetic imagination. This poem of epic proportions, the fruit of sixty years of labor, thought, and observation, sets forth the doctrine of creative evolution. The first part was published in 1808 and the second in 1832, just after his death. It is based on a legend concerning a sixteenth-century scholar, one Dr. Johann Faust, whose thirst for knowledge of supernatural things reputedly led him to make a pact with the devil. This apostasy eventually brought about his downfall and eternal damnation. But Goethe, by saving his hero, makes a great deal more than that out of the old legend. With Goethe the story is a vehicle for a profound treatment of such fundamental and eternal human problems as love and its responsibilities, the purpose and manner of human learning, indeed, the entire mystery of human existence. But even more, *Faust* is the supreme glorification of striving and perseverance. As the eminent critic John Macy has said: "Our highest achievement is a noble striving, a tireless creative living. That it is which saves Faust and defeats Mephistopheles." Thus Faust, though constantly swayed by earthly passion, remains an earnest striver after Truth and self-realization. The powers of good and evil test his staying power and eventually prove his moral worth. Mephistopheles is the representation of the evil which besets man in this life. Faust enters into a pact with him, but ultimately finds (in Part II) that the highest degree of self-realization lies in selfless service to mankind. At the end of the poem, although he has often erred as does any human being who acts, his soul is snatched away from the devil and is carried to paradise, for he has persisted in his quest. *Faust* is therefore both a warning against the shortcomings of human nature and a monument to the hopes and aspirations of every man, giving assurance that, though man may sin and stumble, he will, if he perseveres, reach the highest goal.

FURTHER READING

BRANDES, G. *Goethe* (New York, 1924).
LUDWIG, E. *Goethe* (Stuttgart and London, 1929).
MEEK, G. J. *Faust, the Man and the Myth* (Oxford, 1930).
ROBERTSON, J. G. *Goethe* (London, 1932).

The Sorrows of Young Werther *

June 21st.

MY DAYS are as happy as those reserved by God for his elect, and whatever be my fate hereafter, I can never say that I have not tasted joy,—the purest joy of life. You know Walheim. I am now completely settled there. In that spot I am only half a league from Charlotte, and there I enjoy myself, and taste all the pleasure which can fall to the lot of man.

Little did I imagine when I selected Walheim for my pedestrian excursions, that all heaven lay so near it. How often in my wanderings from the hill-side or from the meadows across the river, have I beheld this hunting-lodge, which now contains within it all the joy of my heart!

I have often, my dear Wilhelm, reflected on the eagerness men feel to wander and make new discoveries, and upon that secret impulse which afterwards inclines them to return back to their narrow circle, to conform to the laws of custom, and to embarrass themselves no longer with what passes around them.

It is so strange how, when I came here first and gazed upon that lovely valley from the hill-side, I felt charmed with the entire scene around me. The little wood opposite,—how delightful to sit under its shade! How fine the view from that point of rock! Then that delightful chain of hills and the exquisite valleys at their feet! Could I but wander and lose myself amongst them! I went and returned without finding what I wished. Distance, my friend, is like futurity. A dim vastness is spread before our souls; the perceptions of our mind are as obscure as those of our vision, and we desire earnestly to sur-

* Translated by R. D. Boylan.

render up our whole being, that it may be filled with the complete and perfect bliss of one glorious emotion. But, alas! when we have attained our object, when the distant *there* becomes the present *here,* all is changed again; we are as poor and circumscribed as ever, and our souls still languish for unattainable happiness.

So the restless traveller pants for his native soil, and finds in his own cottage, in the arms of his wife, in the affections of his children, and in the labour necessary for their support, that happiness which he had sought in vain through the wide world.

When I go out at sunrise in the morning to Walheim, and with my own hands gather the peas in the garden, which are to serve for my dinner, when I sit down to shell them and read my Homer during the intervals, and then selecting a saucepan from the kitchen, fetch my own butter, put my mess on the fire, cover it up, and sit down to stir it as occasion requires, I figure to myself the illustrious suitors of Penelope, killing, dressing, and preparing their own oxen and swine. Nothing fills me with a more pure and genuine sense of happiness than those traits of patriarchal life which, thank Heaven! I can imitate without affectation. Happy is it, indeed, for me that my heart is capable of feeling the same simple and innocent pleasure as the peasant, whose table is covered with food of his own rearing, and who not only enjoys his meal, but remembers with delight the happy days and sunny mornings when he planted it, the soft evenings when he watered it, and the pleasure he experienced in watching its daily growth.

June 29th.

The day before yesterday, the physician came from the town to pay a visit to the Judge. He found me on the floor playing with Charlotte's children. Some of them were scrambling over me, and others romped with me, and as I caught and tickled them they made a great noise. The Doctor is a formal sort of personage; he adjusts the plaits of his ruffles, and continually settles his frill whilst he speaks with you, and he thought my conduct beneath the dignity of a sensible man. I could perceive this by his countenance. But I did not suffer myself to be disturbed. I allowed him to continue his wise conversation whilst I rebuilt the children's card-houses for them as fast as they threw them down. He went about the town, afterwards, complaining that the Judge's children were spoiled enough before, but that now Werther was completely ruining them.

Nothing on this earth, my dear Wilhelm, affects my heart so much as children. When I consider them, when I mark in the little creatures the seeds of all those virtues and qualities which they will one day find so indispensable; when I behold in the obstinate all the future firmness and constancy of a noble character; in the capricious, that levity and gaiety of temper which will carry them lightly over the dangers and troubles of life, their whole nature simple and unpolluted; then I call to mind the golden words of the Great Teacher of mankind, "If you become not like one of these!" And now, my friend, these children, who are our equals, whom we ought to consider as our models, we treat them as subjects. They are allowed no will of their own! And have we then none ourselves? Whence comes our exclusive right? Is it because we are older and more experienced? Great God! from the height of thy heaven, thou beholdest great children and little children, and no others; and thy Son has long since declared which afford Thee greatest pleasure. But they believe in Him, and hear Him not,—that too is an old story; and they train their children after their own image, &c.

Adieu, Wilhelm, I will not further bewilder myself with this subject.

———

August 18th.

Must it ever be thus—that the source of our happiness must also be the fountain of our misery? The full and ardent sentiment which animated my heart with the love of nature, overwhelming me with a torrent of delight, and which brought all paradise before me, has now become an insupportable torment—a demon which perpetually pursues and harasses me. When in bye-gone days I gazed from these rocks upon yonder mountains across the river, and upon the green flowery valley before me, and saw all nature budding and bursting around—the hills clothed from foot to peak with tall, thick forest trees—the valleys in all their varied windings, shaded with the loveliest woods, and the soft river gliding along amongst the lisping reeds, mirroring the beautiful clouds which the soft evening breeze wafted across the sky,—when I heard the groves about me melodious with the music of birds, and saw the million swarms of insects dancing in the last golden beams of the sun, whose setting rays awoke the humming beetles from their grassy beds, whilst the subdued tumult around directed my attention to the ground, and I there observed the arid rock compelled to yield nutriment to the dry moss, whilst the heath flourished upon the barren sands below me,—all this displayed to me the inner warmth which animates all nature, and filled and glowed within my heart. I felt myself exalted by this overflowing fullness to the perception of the Godhead, and the glorious forms of an infinite universe became visible to my soul! Stupendous mountains encompassed me, abysses yawned at my feet, and cataracts fell headlong down before me; impetuous rivers rolled through the plain, and rocks and mountains resounded from afar. In the depths of the earth I saw innumerable powers in motion, and multiplying to infinity, whilst upon its surface, and beneath the heavens, there teemed ten thousand varieties of living creatures. Everything around is alive with an infinite number of forms, while mankind fly for security to their petty houses, from the shelter of which they rule in their imaginations over the wide-extended universe. Poor fool! in whose petty estimation all things are little. From the inaccessible mountains, across the desert which no mortal foot has trod, far as the confines of the unknown ocean, breathes the spirit of the eternal Creator, and every atom to which he has given existence finds favour in his sight. Ah, how often at that time has the flight of a bird, soaring above my head, inspired me with the desire of being transported to the shores of the immeasurable waters, there to quaff the pleasures of life from the foaming goblet of the Infinite; and, to partake, if but for a moment, even with the confined powers of my soul, the beatitude of that Creator, who accomplishes all things in himself, and through himself.

My dear friend, the bare recollection of those hours still consoles me. Even this effort to recall those ineffable sensations, and give them utterance, exalts my soul above itself, and makes me doubly feel the intensity of my present anguish.

It is as if a curtain had been drawn from before my eyes; and, instead of prospects of eternal life, the abyss of an ever open grave yawned before me. Can we say of anything that it exists when all passes away—when time, with the speed of a storm, carries all things onward—and our transitory existence, hurried along by the torrent, is either swallowed up by the waves or dashed against the rocks. There is not a moment but preys upon you, and upon all around you—not a moment in which you do not yourself become a destroyer. The most innocent walk deprives of life thousands of poor insects; one step destroys the fabric of the industrious ant, and converts a little world into chaos. No; it is not the great and rare calamities of the world, the floods which sweep away whole villages, the earthquakes which swallow up our towns, that affect me. My heart is wasted by the thought of that destructive power which lies concealed in every part of universal nature. Nature has formed nothing that does not consume itself, and every object near it; so that, surrounded by earth and air, and all the active powers, I wander on my way with aching heart, and the universe is to me a fearful monster, for ever devouring its own offspring.

November 3rd.

Witness Heaven how often I lie down in my bed, with a wish, and even a hope, that I may never awaken again! and in the morning, when I open my eyes, I behold the sun once more, and am wretched. If I were whimsical, I might blame the weather, or an acquaintance, or some personal disappointment, for my discontented mind, and then this insupportable load of trouble would not rest entirely upon myself. But, alas! I feel it too sadly. I am alone the cause of my own woe,—am I not? Truly, my own bosom contains the source of all my sorrow, as it previously contained the source of all my pleasure. Am I not the same being who once enjoyed an excess of happiness—who, at every step, saw Paradise open before him, and whose heart was ever expanded towards the whole world? And this heart is now dead; no sentiment can revive it: my eyes are dry, and my senses, no more refreshed by the influence of soft tears, wither and consume my brain. I suffer much, for I have lost the only charm of life; that active sacred power which created worlds around me,—it is no more. When I look from my window at the distant hills, and behold the morning sun breaking through the mists, and illuminating the country around, which is still wrapt in silence, whilst the soft stream winds gently through the willows which have shed their leaves; when glorious Nature displays all her beauties before me, and her wondrous prospects are ineffectual to extract one tear of joy from my withered heart; I feel that in such a moment I stand like a reprobate before Heaven, hardened, insensible, and unmoved. Oftentimes do I then bend my knee to the earth, and implore God for the blessing of tears, as the desponding labourer, in some scorching climate, prays for the dews of heaven to moisten his parched corn.

But I feel that God does not grant sunshine or rain to our importunate entreaties. And O those bygone days, whose memory now torments me, why were they so fortunate? Because I then waited with patience for the blessings of the Eternal, and received his gifts with the grateful feelings of a thankful heart.

December 12th.

Dear Wilhelm! I am reduced to the condition of those unfortunate wretches who believe they are pursued by an evil spirit. Sometimes I am oppressed—not by apprehension or fear—but by an inexpressible internal sensation, which weighs upon my heart and impedes my breath! Then I wander forth at night, even in this tempestuous season, and feel pleasure in surveying the dreadful scenes around me.

Yesterday evening I went forth. A rapid thaw had suddenly set in; I had been informed that the river had risen, that the brooks had all overflowed their banks, and that the whole vale of Walheim was under water! Upon the stroke of twelve I hastened forth. I beheld a fearful sight. The foaming torrents rolled from the mountains in the moonlight,—fields and meadows, trees and hedges, were confounded together, and the entire valley was converted into a deep lake, which was agitated by the roaring wind! And when the moon shone forth and tinged the black clouds with silver, and the impetuous torrent at my feet foamed and resounded with awful and grand impetuosity, I was overcome by a mingled sensation of apprehension and delight. With extended arms I looked down into the yawning abyss and cried "Plunge!" For a moment my senses forsook me, in the intense delight of ending my sorrows and my sufferings by a plunge into that gulph! And then I felt as if I were rooted to the earth, and incapable of seeking an end to my woes! But my hour is not yet come; I feel it is not. O Wilhelm, how willingly could I abandon my existence to ride the whirlwind or to embrace the torrent! and then might not rapture perchance be the portion of this liberated soul?

I turned my sorrowful eyes towards a favourite spot, where I was accustomed to sit with Charlotte beneath a willow, after a fatiguing walk. Alas! it was covered with water, and with difficulty I found even the meadow. And the fields around the hunting-lodge, thought I!—has our dear bower been destroyed by this unpitying storm? And a beam of past happiness streamed upon me, as the mind of a captive is illumined by dreams of flocks and herds and bygone joys of home! But I am free from blame. I have courage to die! Perhaps I have—but I still sit here, like a wretched pauper who collects faggots and begs her bread from door to door, that she may prolong for a few days a miserable existence, which she is willing to resign.

Faust *

DEDICATION [1]

Again ye come, ye hovering Forms! I find ye,
As early to my clouded sight ye shone!
Shall I attempt, this once, to seize and bind ye?
Still o'er my heart is that illusion thrown?
Ye crowd more near! Then, be the reign assigned
　　ye,
And sway me from your misty, shadowy zone!
My bosom thrills, with youthful passion shaken,
From magic airs that round your march awaken.

Of joyous days ye bring the blissful vision;
The dear, familiar phantoms rise again,　　　　10
And, like an old and half-extinct tradition,
First Love returns, with Friendship in his train.
Renewed is Pain: with mournful repetition
Life tracks his devious, labyrinthine chain,
And names the Good, whose cheating fortune tore
　　them
From happy hours, and left me to deplore them.

They hear no longer these succeeding measures,
The souls, to whom my earliest songs I sang:
Dispersed the friendly troop, with all its pleas-
　　ures
And still, alas! the echoes first that rang!　　　20
I bring the unknown multitude my treasures;
Their very plaudits give my heart a pang,
And those beside, whose joy my Song so flattered,
If still they live, wide through the world are scat-
　　tered.

And grasps me now a long-unwonted yearning
For that serene and solemn Spirit-Land:
My song, to faint Aeolian murmurs turning,
Sways like a harp-string by the breezes fanned.
I thrill and tremble; tear on tear is burning,
And the stern heart is tenderly unmanned.　　　30
What I possess, I see far distant lying,
And what I lost, grows real and undying.

* Translated by Bayard Taylor. By permission of Houghton Mifflin Company.
[1] Written late in life by Goethe to express his regret at
the absence of the many friends to whom he had recited
earlier versions of *Faust*.

PRELUDE ON THE STAGE

MANAGER.　　DRAMATIC POET.　　MERRY-ANDREW.

MANAGER

You two, who oft a helping hand
Have lent, in need and tribulation,
Come, let me know your expectation
Of this, our enterprise, in German land!
I wish the crowd to feel itself well treated,
Especially since it lives and lets me live;
The posts are set, the booth of boards completed,
And each awaits the banquet I shall give.
Already there, with curious eyebrows raised,
They sit sedate, and hope to be amazed.　　　10
I know how one the People's taste may flatter,
Yet here a huge embarrassment I feel:
What they're accustomed to, is no great matter.
But then, alas! they've read an awful deal.
How shall we plan, that all be fresh and new,—
Important matter, yet attractive too?
For 't is my pleasure to behold them surging,
When to our booth the current sets apace,
And with tremendous, oft-repeated urging,
Squeeze onward through the narrow gate of
　　grace:　　　20
By daylight even, they push and cram in
To reach the seller's box, a fighting host,
And as for bread, around a baker's door, in famine,
To get a ticket break their necks almost.
This miracle alone can work the Poet
On men so various: now, my friend, pray show it.

POET

Speak not to me of yonder motley masses,
Whom but to see, puts out the fire of Song!
Hide from my view the surging crowd that passes,
And in its whirlpool forces us along!　　　30
No, lead me where some heavenly silence glasses
The purer joys that round the Poet throng,—
Where Love and Friendship still divinely fashion
The bonds that bless, the wreaths that crown his
　　passion!

Ah, every utterance from the depths of feeling
The timid lips have stammeringly expressed,—
Now failing, now, perchance, success revealing,—
Gulps the wild Moment in its greedy breast;
Or oft, reluctant years its warrant sealing,
Its perfect stature stands at last confessed!　　　40
What dazzles, for the Moment spends its spirit:
What's genuine, shall Posterity inherit.

MERRY-ANDREW

Posterity! Don't name the word to me!
If *I* should choose to preach Posterity,
Where would you get cotemporary fun?
That men *will* have it, there's no blinking:
A fine young fellow's presence, to my thinking,
Is something worth, to every one.
Who genially his nature can outpour,
Takes from the People's moods no irritation;   50
The wider circle he acquires, the more
Securely works his inspiration.
Then pluck up heart, and give us sterling coin
Let Fancy be with her attendants fitted,—
Sense, Reason, Sentiment, and Passion join,—
But have a care, lest Folly be omitted!

MANAGER

Chiefly, enough of incident prepare!
They come to look, and they prefer to stare.
Reel off a host of threads before their faces,
So that they gape in stupid wonder: then   60
By sheer diffuseness you have won their graces,
And are, at once, most popular of men.
Only by mass you touch the mass; for any
Will finally, himself, his bit select:
Who offers much, brings something unto many,
And each goes home content with the effect.
If you've a piece, why, just in pieces give it:
A hash, a stew, will bring success, believe it!
'T is easily displayed, and easy to invent.
What use, a Whole compactly to present?   70
Your hearers pick and pluck, as soon as they receive
    it!

POET

You do not feel, how such a trade debases;
How ill it suits the Artist, proud and true!
The botching work each fine pretender traces
Is, I perceive, a principle with you.

MANAGER

Such a reproach not in the least offends;
A man who some result intends
Must use the tools that best are fitting.
Reflect, soft wood is given to you for splitting,
And then, observe, for whom you write!   80
If one comes bored, exhausted quite,
Another, satiate, leaves the banquet's tapers,
And, worst of all, full many a wight

Is fresh from reading of the daily papers.
Idly to us they come, as to a masquerade,
Mere curiosity their spirits warming:
The ladies with themselves, and with their finery,
    aid,
Without a salary their parts performing.
What dreams are yours in high poetic places?
You're pleased, forsooth, full houses to behold?   90
Draw near, and view your patrons' faces!
The half are coarse, the half are cold.
One, when the play is out, goes home to cards;
A wild night on a wench's breast another chooses:
Why should you rack, poor, foolish bards,
For ends like these, the gracious Muses?
I tell you, give but more—more, ever more, they
    ask:
Thus shall you hit the mark of gain and glory.
Seek to confound your auditory!
To satisfy them is a task.—   100
What ails you now? Is 't suffering, or pleasure?

POET

Go, find yourself a more obedient slave!
What! shall the Poet that which Nature gave,
The highest right, supreme Humanity,
Forfeit so wantonly, to swell your treasure?
Whence o'er the heart his empire free?
The elements of Life how conquers he?
Is 't not his heart's accord, urged outward far and
    dim,
To wind the world in unison with him?
When on the spindle, spun to endless distance, 110
By Nature's listless hand the thread is twirled,
And the discordant tones of all existence
In sullen jangle are together hurled,
Who, then, the changeless orders of creation
Divides, and kindles into rhythmic dance?
Who brings the One to join the general ordination,
Where it may throb in grandest consonance?
Who bids the storm to passion stir the bosom?
In brooding souls the sunset burn above?
Who scatters every fairest April blossom   120
Along the shining path of Love?
Who braids the noteless leaves to crowns, requiting
Desert with fame, in Action's every field?
Who makes Olympus sure, the Gods uniting?
The might of Man, as in the Bard revealed.

MERRY-ANDREW

So, these fine forces, in conjunction,
Propel the high poetic function,

As in a love-adventure they might play!
You meet by accident; you feel, you stay,
And by degrees your heart is tangled;　　130
Bliss grows apace, and then its course is jangled;
You're ravished quite, then comes a touch of woe,
And there's a neat romance, completed ere you
　　know!
Let us, then, such a drama give!
Grasp the exhaustless life that all men live!
Each shares therein, though few may comprehend:
Where'er you touch, there's interest without end.
In motley pictures little light,
Much error, and of truth a glimmering mite,
Thus the best beverage is supplied,　　140
Whence all the world is cheered and edified.
Then, at your play, behold the fairest flower
Of youth collect, to hear the revelation!
Each tender soul, with sentimental power,
Sucks melancholy food from your creation;
And now in this, now that, the leaven works,
For each beholds what in his bosom lurks.
They still are moved at once to weeping or to laugh-
　　ter,
Still wonder at your flights, enjoy the show they
　　see:
A mind, once formed, is never suited after;　　150
One yet in growth will ever grateful be.

POET

Then give me back that time of pleasures,
While yet in joyous growth I sang,—
When, like a fount, the crowding measures
Uninterrupted gushed and sprang!
Then bright mist veiled the world before me,
In opening buds a marvel woke,
As I the thousand blossoms broke,
Which every valley richly bore me!
I nothing had, and yet enough for youth—　　160
Joy in Illusion, ardent thirst for Truth.
Give, unrestrained, the old emotion,
The bliss that touched the verge of pain,
The strength of Hate, Love's deep devotion,—
O, give me back my youth again!

MERRY-ANDREW

Youth, good my friend, you certainly require
When foes in combat sorely press you;
When lovely maids, in fond desire,
Hang on your bosom and caress you;
When from the hard-won goal the wreath　　170
Beckons afar, the race awaiting;
When, after dancing out your breath,

You pass the night in dissipating:—
But that familiar harp with soul
To play,—with grace and bold expression,
And towards a self-erected goal
To walk with many a sweet digression,—
This, aged Sirs, belongs to you,
And we no less revere you for that reason:
Age childish makes, they say, but 't is not true;　　180
We're only genuine children still, in Age's season!

MANAGER

The words you've bandied are sufficient;
'T is deeds that I prefer to see:
In compliments you're both proficient,
But might, the while, more useful be.
What need to talk of Inspiration?
'T is no companion of Delay.
If Poetry be your vocation,
Let Poetry your will obey!
Full well you know what here is wanting;　　190
The crowd for strongest drink is panting,
And such, forthwith, I'd have you brew.
What's left undone to-day, To-morrow will not do.
Waste not a day in vain digression:
With resolute, courageous trust
Seize every possible impression,
And make it firmly your possession;
You'll then work on, because you must.
Upon our German stage, you know it,
Each tries his hand at what he will;　　200
So, take of traps and scenes your fill,
And all you find, be sure to show it!
Use both the great and lesser heavenly light,—
Squander the stars in any number,
Beasts, birds, trees, rocks, and all such lumber,
Fire, water, darkness, Day and Night!
Thus, in our booth's contracted sphere,
The circle of Creation will appear,
And move, as we deliberately impel,
From Heaven, across the World, to Hell!　　210

PROLOGUE IN HEAVEN

THE LORD. THE HEAVENLY HOSTS. *Afterwards*

MEPHISTOPHELES [2]

(*The* THREE ARCHANGELS *come forward.*)

RAPHAEL

The sun-orb sings, in emulation,
'Mid brother-spheres, his ancient round:

[2] In medieval demonology, one of the seven chief devils.

His path predestined through Creation
He ends with step of thunder-sound.
The angels from his visage splendid
Draw power, whose measure none can say;
The lofty works, uncomprehended,
Are bright as on the earliest day.

GABRIEL

And swift, and swift beyond conceiving,
The splendor of the world goes round,   10
Day's Eden-brightness still relieving
The awful Night's intense profound:
The ocean-tides in foam are breaking,
Against the rocks' deep bases hurled,
And both, the spheric race partaking,
Eternal, swift, are onward whirled!

MICHAEL

And rival storms abroad are surging
From sea to land, from land to sea.
A chain of deepest action forging
Round all, in wrathful energy.   20
There flames a desolation, blazing
Before the Thunder's crashing way:
Yet, Lord, Thy messengers are praising
The gentle movement of Thy Day.

THE THREE

Though still by them uncomprehended,
From these the angels draw their power,
And all Thy works, sublime and splendid,
Are bright as in Creation's hour.

MEPHISTOPHELES

Since Thou, O Lord, deign'st to approach again
And ask us how we do, in manner kindest,   30
And heretofore to meet myself wert fain,
Among Thy menials, now, my face Thou findest.
Pardon, this troop I cannot follow after
With lofty speech, though by them scorned and
    spurned,
My pathos certainly would move Thy laughter,
If Thou hadst not all merriment unlearned.
Of suns and worlds I've nothing to be quoted;
How men torment themselves, is all I've noted.
The little god o' the world sticks to the same old
    way,
And is as whimsical as on Creation's day.   40
Life somewhat better might content him,
But for the gleam of heavenly light which Thou
    hast lent him:
He calls it Reason—thence his power's increased,
To be far beastlier than any beast.

Saving Thy Gracious Presence, he to me
A long-legged grasshopper appears to be,
That springing flies, and flying springs,
And in the grass the same old ditty sings.
Would he still lay among the grass he grows in!
Each bit of dung he seeks, to stick his nose in.   50

THE LORD

Hast thou, then, nothing more to mention?
Com'st ever, thus, with ill intention?
Find'st nothing right on earth, eternally?

MEPHISTOPHELES

No, Lord! I find things, there, still bad as they
    can be.
Man's misery even to pity moves my nature;
I've scarce the heart to plague the wretched crea-
    ture.

THE LORD

Know'st Faust?

MEPHISTOPHELES

    The Doctor Faust?

THE LORD

          My servant, he!

MEPHISTOPHELES

Forsooth! He serves you after strange devices:
No earthly meat or drink the fool suffices:
His spirit's ferment far aspireth;   60
Half conscious of his frenzied, crazed unrest,
The fairest stars from Heaven he requireth,
From Earth the highest raptures and the best,
And all the Near and Far that he desireth
Fails to subdue the tumult of his breast.

THE LORD

Though still confused his service unto Me,
I soon shall lead him to a clearer morning.
Sees not the gardener, even while buds his tree,
Both flower and fruit the future years adorning?

MEPHISTOPHELES

What will you bet? There's still a chance to gain
    him,   70
If unto me full leave you give,
Gently upon *my* road to train him!

THE LORD

As long as he on earth shall live,
So long I make no prohibition.

He is about 50
but she is about 20
after witches cut 30
years off.

While Man's desires and aspirations stir,
He cannot choose but err.

MEPHISTOPHELES

My thanks! I find the dead no acquisition,
And never cared to have them in my keeping.
I much prefer the cheeks where ruddy blood is
    leaping,
And when a corpse approaches, close my house: 80
It goes with me, as with the cat the mouse.

THE LORD

Enough! What thou hast asked is granted.
Turn off this spirit from his fountain-head;
To trap him, let thy snares be planted,
And him, with thee, be downward led;
Then stand abashed, when thou art forced to
    say:
A good man, through obscurest aspiration,
Has still an instinct of the one true way.

MEPHISTOPHELES

Agreed! But 't is a short probation.
About my bet I feel no trepidation. 90
If I fulfil my expectation,
You'll let me triumph with a swelling breast:
Dust shall he eat, and with a zest,
As did a certain snake, my near relation.

THE LORD

Therein thou 'rt free, according to thy merits;
The like of thee have never moved My hate.
Of all the bold, denying Spirits,
The waggish knave least trouble doth create.
Man's active nature, flagging, seeks too soon the
    level;
Unqualified repose he learns to crave; 100
Whence, willingly, the comrade him I gave,
Who works, excites, and must create, as Devil.
But ye, God's sons in love and duty,
Enjoy the rich, the ever-living Beauty!
Creative Power, that works eternal schemes,
Clasp you in bonds of love, relaxing never,
And what in wavering apparition gleams
Fix in its place with thoughts that stand forever!

(*Heaven closes: the* ARCHANGELS *separate.*)

MEPHISTOPHELES (*solus*)

I like, at times, to hear The Ancient's word,
And have a care to be most civil: 110
It's really kind of such a noble Lord
So humanly to gossip with the Devil!

FIRST PART OF THE TRAGEDY

I

NIGHT

(*A lofty-arched, narrow, Gothic chamber.* FAUST,
in a chair at his desk, restless.)

FAUST

I've studied now Philosophy
And jurisprudence, Medicine,—
And even, alas! Theology,—
From end to end, with labor keen;
And here, poor fool! with all my lore
I stand, no wiser than before:
I'm Magister—yea, Doctor—hight,
And straight or cross-wise, wrong or right,
These ten years long, with many woes,
I've led my scholars by the nose,— 10
And see, that nothing can be known!
That knowledge cuts me to the bone.
I'm cleverer, true, than those fops of teachers,
Doctors and Magisters, Scribes and Preachers;
Neither scruples nor doubts come now to smite me,
Nor Hell nor Devil can longer affright me.
For this, all pleasure am I foregoing;
I do not pretend to aught worth knowing,
I do not pretend I could be a teacher
To help or convert a fellow-creature. 20
Then, too, I've neither lands nor gold,
Nor the world's least pomp or honor hold—
No dog would endure such a curst existence!
Wherefore, from Magic I seek assistance,
That many a secret perchance I reach
Through spirit-power and spirit-speech,
And thus the bitter task forego
Of saying the things I do not know,—
That I may detect the inmost force
Which binds the world, and guides its course; 30
Its germs, productive powers explore,
And rummage in empty words no more!

O full and splendid Moon, whom I
Have, from this desk, seen climb the sky
So many a midnight,—would thy glow
For the last time beheld my woe!
Ever thine eye, most mournful friend,
O'er books and papers saw me bend;
But would that I, on mountains grand,
Amid thy blessed light could stand, 40
With spirits through mountain-caverns hover,
Float in thy twilight the meadows over,
And, freed from the fumes of lore that swathe me,
To health in thy dewy fountains bathe me!

Ah, me! this dungeon still I see,
This drear, accursed masonry,
Where even the welcome daylight strains
But duskly through the painted panes.
Hemmed in by many a toppling heap
Of books worm-eaten, gray with dust,   50
Which to the vaulted ceiling creep,
Against the smoky papers thrust,—
With glasses, boxes, round me stacked,
And instruments together hurled,
Ancestral lumber, stuffed and packed—
Such is my world: and what a world!

And do I ask, wherefore my heart
Falters, oppressed with unknown needs?
Why some inexplicable smart
All movement of my life impedes?   60
Alas! in living Nature's stead,
Where God His human creature set,
In smoke and mould the fleshless dead
And bones of beasts surround me yet!

Fly! Up and seek the broad, free land!
And this one Book of Mystery
From Nostradamus' [3] very hand,
Is 't not sufficient company?
When I the starry courses know,
And Nature's wise instruction seek,   70
With light of power my soul shall glow,
As when to spirits spirits speak.
'T is vain, this empty brooding here,
Though guessed the holy symbols be:
Ye, Spirits, come—ye hover near—
Oh, if you hear me, answer me!

(*He opens the Book, and perceives the sign of the
Macrocosm.*)[4]

Ha! what a sudden rapture leaps from this
I view, through all my senses swiftly flowing!
I feel a youthful, holy, vital bliss
In every vein and fibre newly glowing.   80
Was it a God, who traced this sign,
With calm across my tumult stealing,
My troubled heart to joy unsealing,
With impulse, mystic and divine,
The powers of Nature here, around my path, re-
     vealing?
Am I a God?—so clear mine eyes!
In these pure features I behold
Creative Nature to my soul unfold.

[3] Author of a book of prophecies entitled *Centuries*,
1555. He wrote no such work as Goethe attributes to him
here.

[4] The Universe as compared with the microcosm, Man,
who is conceived as a small universe within a large one.

What says the sage, now first I recognize:
"The spirit-world no closures fasten;   90
Thy sense is shut, thy heart is dead:
Disciple, up! untiring, hasten
To bathe thy breast in morning-red!"

(*He contemplates the sign.*)

How each the Whole its substance gives,
Each in the other works and lives!
Like heavenly forces rising and descending,
Their golden urns reciprocally lending,
With wings that winnow blessing
From Heaven through Earth I see them pressing,
Filling the All with harmony unceasing!   100
How grand a show! but, ah! a show alone.
Thee, boundless Nature, how make thee my own?
Where you, ye breasts? Founts of all Being, shin-
     ing,
Whereon hang Heaven's and Earth's desire,
Whereto our withered hearts aspire,—
Ye flow, ye feed: and am I vainly pining?

(*He turns the leaves impatiently, and perceives the
sign of the Earth-Spirit.*)[5]

How otherwise upon me works this sign!
Thou, Spirit of the Earth, art nearer:
Even now my powers are loftier, clearer;
I glow, as drunk with new-made wine: 110
New strength and heart to meet the world incite
     me,
The woe of earth, the bliss of earth, invite me,
And though the shock of storms may smite me,
No crash of shipwreck shall have power to fright
     me!
Clouds gather over me—
The moon conceals her light—
The lamp's extinguished!—
Mists rise,—red, angry rays are darting
Around my head!—There falls
A horror from the vaulted roof,   120
And seizes me!
I feel thy presence, Spirit I invoke!
Reveal thyself!
Ha! in my heart what rending stroke!
With new impulsion
My senses heave in this convulsion!
I feel thee draw my heart, absorb, exhaust me:
Thou must! thou must! and though my life it cost
     me!

(*He seizes the book, and mysteriously pronounces
the sign of the Spirit. A ruddy flame flashes: the
Spirit appears in the flame.*)

[5] The personification of Nature, giver of all things.

SPIRIT

Who calls me?

FAUST (*with averted head*)
Terrible to see!

SPIRIT

Me hast thou long with might attracted,   130
Long from my sphere thy food exacted,
And now—

FAUST

Woe! I endure not thee!

SPIRIT

To view me is thine aspiration,
My voice to hear, my countenance to see;
Thy powerful yearning moveth me,
Here am I!—what mean perturbation
Thee, superhuman, shakes? Thy soul's high calling,
where?
Where is the breast, which from itself a world did
bear,
And shaped and cherished—which with joy ex-
panded,
To be our peer, with us, the Spirits, banded?   140
Where art thou, Faust, whose voice has pierced to
me,
Who towards me pressed with all thine energy?
He art thou, who, my presence breathing, seeing,
Trembles through all the depths of being,
A writhing worm, a terror-stricken form?

FAUST

Thee, form of flame, shall I then fear?
Yes, I am Faust: I am thy peer!

SPIRIT

In the tides of Life, in Action's storm,
A fluctuant wave,
A shuttle free,   150
Birth and the Grave,
An eternal sea,
A weaving, flowing
Life, all-glowing,
Thus at Time's humming loom 't is my hand pre-
pares
The garment of Life [6] which the Deity wears!

FAUST

Thou, who around the wide world wendest,
Thou busy Spirit, how near I feel to thee!

[6] The visible forms of nature.

SPIRIT

Thou 'rt like the Spirit which thou comprehendest,
Not me!   160

(*Disappears.*)

FAUST (*overwhelmed*)

Not thee!
Whom then?
I, image of the Godhead!
Not even like thee!

(*A knock.*)

O Death!—I know it—'t is my Famulus! [7]
My fairest luck finds no fruition:
In all the fulness of my vision
The soulless sneak disturbs me thus!

(*Enter* WAGNER, *in dressing-gown and night-cap, a
lamp in his hand.* FAUST *turns impatiently.*)

WAGNER

Pardon, I heard your declamation;
'T was sure an old Greek tragedy you read?   170
In such an art I crave some preparation,
Since now it stands one in good stead.
I 've often heard it said, a preacher
Might learn, with a comedian for a teacher.

FAUST

Yes, when the priest comedian is by nature,
As haply now and then the case may be.

WAGNER

Ah, when one studies thus, a prisoned creature,
That scarce the world on holidays can see,—
Scarce through a glass, by rare occasion,
How shall one lead it by persuasion?   180

FAUST

You'll ne'er attain it, save you know the feeling,
Save from the soul it rises clear,
Serene in primal strength, compelling
The hearts and minds of all who hear.
You sit forever gluing, patching;
You cook the scraps from others' fare;
And from your heap of ashes hatching
A starveling flame, ye blow it bare!
Take children's, monkeys' gaze admiring,
If such your taste, and be content;   190
But ne'er from heart to heart you'll speak inspiring,
Save your own heart is eloquent!

[7] Assistant to a professor, usually living in the professor's
home and performing menial services.

WAGNER

Yet through delivery orators succeed;
I feel that I am far behind, indeed.

FAUST

Seek thou the honest recompense!
Beware, a tinkling [8] fool to be!
With little art, clear wit and sense
Suggest their own delivery;
And if thou 'rt moved to speak in earnest,
What need, that after words thou yearnest? 200
Yes, your discourses, with their glittering show,
Where ye for men twist shredded thought like
  paper,
Are unrefreshing as the winds that blow
The rustling leaves through chill autumnal vapor!

WAGNER

Ah, God! but Art is long,
And Life, alas! is fleeting.
And oft, with zeal my critic-duties meeting,
In head and breast there 's something wrong.
How hard it is to compass the assistance
Whereby one rises to the source! 210
And, haply, ere one travels half the course
Must the poor devil quit existence.

FAUST

Is parchment, then, the holy fount before thee,
A draught wherefrom thy thirst forever slakes?
No true refreshment can restore thee,
Save what from thine own soul spontaneous
  breaks.

WAGNER

Pardon! a great delight is granted
When, in the spirit of the ages planted,
We mark how, ere our time, a sage has thought,
And then, how far his work, and grandly, we have
  brought. 220

FAUST

O yes, up to the stars at last!
Listen, my friend: the ages that are past
Are now a book with seven seals protected:
What you the Spirit of the Ages call
Is nothing but the spirit of you all,
Wherein the Ages are reflected.
So, oftentimes, you miserably mar it!
At the first glance who sees it runs away.
An offal-barrel and a lumber-garret,
Or, at the best, a Punch-and-Judy play, 230

[8] Court jesters often wore tiny bells on their costumes.

With maxims most pragmatical and hitting,
As in the mouths of puppets are befitting!

WAGNER

But then, the world—the human heart and brain!
Of these one covets some slight apprehension.

FAUST

Yes, of the kind which men attain!
Who dares the child's true name in public mention?
The few, who thereof something really learned,
Unwisely frank, with hearts that spurned conceal-
  ing,
And to the mob laid bare each thought and feeling,
Have evermore been crucified and burned. 240
I pray you, Friend, 't is now the dead of night;
Our converse here must be suspended.

WAGNER

I would have shared your watches with delight,
That so our learned talk might be extended.
To-morrow, though, I 'll ask, in Easter leisure,
This and the other question, at your pleasure.
Most zealously I seek for erudition:
Much do I know—but to know all is my ambition.
  [Exit.

FAUST (solus)

That brain, alone, not loses hope, whose choice is
To stick in shallow trash forevermore,— 250
Which digs with eager hand for buried ore,
And, when it finds an angle-worm, rejoices!

Dare such a human voice disturb the flow,
Around me here, of spirit-presence fullest?
And yet, this once my thanks I owe
To thee, of all earth's sons the poorest, dullest!
For thou hast torn me from that desperate state
Which threatened soon to overwhelm my senses:
The apparition was so giant-great,
It dwarfed and withered all my soul's pretences! 260

I, image of the Godhead, who began—
Deeming Eternal Truth secure in nearness—
To sun myself in heavenly light and clearness,
And laid aside the earthly man;—
I, more than Cherub, whose free force had planned
To flow through Nature's veins in glad pulsation,
To reach beyond, enjoying in creation
The life of Gods, behold my expiation!
A thunder-word hath swept me from my stand.

With thee I dare not venture to compare me. 270
Though I possessed the power to draw thee near
  me,

The power to keep thee was denied my hand.
When that ecstatic moment held me,
I felt myself so small, so great;
But thou hast ruthlessly repelled me
Back upon Man's uncertain fate.
What shall I shun? Whose guidance borrow?
Shall I accept that stress and strife?
Ah! every deed of ours, no less than every sorrow,
Impedes the onward march of life.   280
Some alien substance more and more is cleaving
To all the mind conceives of grand and fair;
When this world's Good is won by our achieving,
The Better, then, is named a cheat and snare.
The fine emotions, whence our lives we mould,
Lie in the earthly tumult dumb and cold.
If hopeful Fancy once, in daring flight,
Her longings to the Infinite expanded,
Yet now a narrow space contents her quite,
Since Time's wild wave so many a fortune
    stranded.   290
Care at the bottom of the heart is lurking:
Her secret pangs in silence working,
She, restless, rocks herself, disturbing joy and rest:
In newer masks her face is ever drest,
By turns as house and land, as wife and child,
    presented,—
As water, fire, as poison, steel:
We dread the blows we never feel,
And what we never lose is yet by us lamented!
I am not like the Gods! That truth is felt too deep:
The worm am I, that in the dust doth creep,—   300
That, while in dust it lives and seeks its bread,
Is crushed and buried by the wanderer's tread.
Is not this dust, these walls within them hold,
The hundred shelves, which cramp and chain me,
The frippery, the trinkets thousand-fold,
That in this mothy den restrain me?
Here shall I find the help I need?
Shall here a thousand volumes teach me only
That men, self-tortured, everywhere must bleed,—
And here and there one happy man sits lonely?   310
What mean'st thou by that grin, thou hollow skull,
Save that thy brain, like mine, a cloudy mirror,
Sought once the shining day, and then, in twilight
    dull,
Thirsting for Truth, went wretchedly to Error?
Ye instruments, forsooth, but jeer at me
With wheel and cog, and shapes uncouth of won-
    der;
I found the portal, you the keys should be;
Your wards are deftly wrought, but drive no bolts
    asunder!

Mysterious even in open day,
Nature retains her veil, despite our clamors: 320
That which she doth not willingly display
Cannot be wrenched from her with levers, screws,
    and hammers.
Ye ancient tools, whose use I never knew,
Here, since my father used ye, still ye moulder:
Thou, ancient scroll, hast worn thy smoky hue
Since at this desk the dim lamp wont to smoulder.
'T were better far, had I my little idly spent,
Than now to sweat beneath its burden, I confess it!
What from your fathers' heritage is lent,
Earn it anew, to really possess it!   330
What serves not, is a sore impediment:
The Moment's need creates the thing to serve and
    bless it!
Yet, wherefore turns my gaze to yonder point so
    lightly?
Is yonder flask a magnet for mine eyes?
Whence, all around me, glows the air so brightly,
As when in woods at night the mellow moonbeam
    lies?

I hail thee, wondrous, rarest vial!
I take thee down devoutly, for the trial:
Man's art and wit I venerate in thee.
Thou summary of gentle slumber-juices,   340
Essence of deadly finest powers and uses,
Unto thy master show thy favor free!
I see thee, and the stings of pain diminish;
I grasp thee, and my struggles slowly finish:
My spirit's flood-tide ebbeth more and more.
Out on the open ocean speeds my dreaming;
The glassy flood before my feet is gleaming,
A new day beckons to a newer shore!

A fiery chariot,[9] borne on buoyant pinions,
Sweeps near me now! I soon shall ready be   350
To pierce the ether's high, unknown dominions,
To reach new spheres of pure activity!
This godlike rapture, this supreme existence,
Do I, but now a worm, deserve to track?
Yes, resolute to reach some brighter distance,
On Earth's fair sun I turn my back!
Yes, let me dare those gates to fling asunder,
Which every man would fain go slinking by!
'T is time, through deeds this word of truth to
    thunder:
That with the height of Gods Man's dignity may
    vie!   360
Nor from that gloomy gulf to shrink affrighted,

[9] Elijah's chariot in II Kings 2:11.

Where Fancy doth herself to self-born pangs com-
   pel,—
To struggle toward that pass benighted,
Around whose narrow mouth flame all the fires of
   Hell,—
To take this step with cheerful resolution,
Though Nothingness should be the certain, swift
   conclusion!

And now come down, thou cup of crystal clearest!
Fresh from thine ancient cover thou appearest,
So many years forgotten to my thought!
Thou shon'st at old ancestral banquets cheery,   370
The solemn guests thou madest merry,
When one thy wassail to the other brought.
The rich and skilful figures o'er thee wrought,
The drinker's duty, rhyme-wise to explain them,
Or in one breath below the mark to drain them,
From many a night of youth my memory caught.
Now to a neighbor shall I pass thee never,
Nor on thy curious art to test my wit endeavor:
Here is a juice whence sleep is swiftly born.
It fills with browner flood thy crystal hollow;   380
I chose, prepared it: thus I follow,—
With all my soul the final drink I swallow,
A solemn festal cup, a greeting to the morn!

(*He sets the goblet to his mouth.*)

(*Chime of bells and choral song.*)

CHORUS OF ANGELS

Christ is arisen!
Joy to the Mortal One,
Whom the unmerited,
Clinging, inherited
Needs did imprison.

FAUST

What hollow humming, what a sharp, clear stroke,
Drives from my lip the goblet's, at their meet-
   ing?   390
Announce the booming bells already woke
The first glad hour of Easter's festal greeting?
Ye choirs, have ye begun the sweet, consoling chant,
Which, through the night of Death, the angels
   ministrant
Sang, God's new Covenant repeating?

CHORUS OF WOMEN

With spices and precious
Balm, we arrayed him;
Faithful and gracious,
We tenderly laid him:
Linen to bind him   400
Cleanlily wound we: [10]
Ah! when we would find him,
Christ no more found we!

CHORUS OF ANGELS

Christ is ascended
Bliss hath invested him,
Woes that molested him,
Trials that tested him,
Gloriously ended!

FAUST

Why, here in dust, entice me with your spell,
Ye gentle, powerful sounds of Heaven?   410
Peal rather there, where tender natures dwell.
Your messages I hear, but faith has not been given;
The dearest child of Faith is Miracle.
I venture not to soar to yonder regions
Whence the glad tidings hither float;
And yet, from childhood up familiar with the note,
To Life it now renews the old allegiance.
Once Heavenly Love sent down a burning kiss
Upon my brow, in Sabbath silence holy;
And, filled with mystic presage, chimed the church-
   bell slowly,   420
And prayer dissolved me in a fervent bliss.
A sweet, uncomprehended yearning
Drove forth my feet through woods and meadows
   free,
And while a thousand tears were burning,
I felt a world arise for me.
These chants, to youth and all its sports appealing,
Proclaimed the Spring's rejoicing holiday;
And Memory holds me now, with childish feeling,
Back from the last, the solemn way.
Sound on, ye hymns of Heaven, so sweet and
   mild!   430
My tears gush forth: the Earth takes back her child!

CHORUS OF DISCIPLES

Has He, victoriously,
Burst from the vaulted
Grave, and all-gloriously
Now sits exalted?
Is He, in glow of birth,
Rapture creative near?
Ah! to the woe of earth
Still are we native here.

[10] This, according to the New Testament, was their intention, but they were not able to find the Christ.

We, His aspiring   440
Followers, Him we miss;
Weeping, desiring,
Master, Thy bliss!

CHORUS OF ANGELS

Christ is arisen,
Out of Corruption's womb:
Burst ye the prison,
Break from your gloom!
Praising and pleading Him,
Lovingly needing Him,
Brotherly feeding Him,   450
Preaching and speeding Him.
Blessing, succeeding Him,
Thus is the Master near,—
Thus is He here!

II

BEFORE THE CITY-GATE

(*Pedestrians of all kinds come forth.*)

SEVERAL APPRENTICES

Why do you go that way?

OTHERS

We 're for the Hunter's-lodge, today.

THE FIRST

We'll saunter to the Mill, in yonder hollow.

AN APPRENTICE

Go to the River Tavern, I should say.

SECOND APPRENTICE

But then, it 's not a pleasant way.

THE OTHERS

And what will *you*?

A THIRD

        As goes the crowd, I follow.

A FOURTH

Come up to Burgdorf? There you 'll find good
        cheer,
The finest lasses and the best of beer,
And jolly rows and squabbles, trust me!   10

A FIFTH

You swaggering fellow, is your hide
A third time itching to be tried?
I won't go there, your jolly rows disgust me!

SERVANT-GIRL

No,—no! I'll turn and go to town again.

ANOTHER

We'll surely find him by those poplars yonder.

THE FIRST

That's no great luck for me, 't is plain.
You'll have him, when and where you wander:
His partner in the dance you'll be,—
But what is all your fun to me?

THE OTHER

He's surely not alone to-day: 20
He'll be with Curly-head, I heard him say.

A STUDENT

Deuce! how they step, the buxom wenches!
Come, Brother! we must see them to the benches.
A strong, old beer, a pipe that stings and bites,
A girl in Sunday clothes,—these three are my de-
        lights.

CITIZEN'S DAUGHTER

Just see those handsome fellows, there!
It's really shameful, I declare;—
To follow servant-girls, when they
Might have the most genteel society to-day!

SECOND STUDENT (*to* THE FIRST)

Not quite so fast! Two others come behind,—   30
Those, dressed so prettily and neatly.
My neighbor's one of them, I find,
A girl that takes my heart, completely.
They go their way with looks demure,
But they'll accept us, after all, I'm sure.

THE FIRST

No, Brother! not for me their formal ways.
Quick! lest our game escape us in the press:
The hand that wields the broom on Saturdays
Will best, on Sundays, fondle and caress.

CITIZEN

He suits me not at all, our new-made Burgomas-
        ter!   40
Since he's installed, his arrogance grows faster.

How has he helped the town, I say?
Things worsen,—what improvement names he?
Obedience, more than ever, claims he,
And more than ever we must pay!

BEGGAR (sings)

Good gentlemen and lovely ladies,
So red of cheek and fine of dress,
Behold, how needful here your aid is,
And see and lighten my distress!
Let me not vainly sing my ditty; 50
He's only glad who gives away:
A holiday, that shows your pity,
Shall be for me a harvest-day!

ANOTHER CITIZEN

On Sundays, holidays, there's naught I take delight in,
Like gossiping of war, and war's array,
When down in Turkey,[11] far away,
The foreign people are a-fighting.
One at the window sits, with glass and friends,
And sees all sorts of ships go down the river gliding:
And blesses then, as home he wends 60
At night, our times of peace abiding.

THIRD CITIZEN

Yes, Neighbor! that's my notion, too:
Why, let them break their heads, let loose their passions,
And mix things madly through and through,
So, here, we keep our good old fashions!

OLD WOMAN (to the CITIZEN'S DAUGHTER)

Dear me, how fine! So handsome, and so young!
Who wouldn't lose his heart, that met you?
Don't be so proud! I'll hold my tongue,
And what you'd like I'll undertake to get you.

CITIZEN'S DAUGHTER

Come, Agatha! I shun the witch's sight 70
Before folks, lest there be misgiving:
'T is true, she showed me, on Saint Andrew's Night,[12]
My future sweetheart, just as he were living.

[11] There was a Russo-Turkish War (1767-1774) during Goethe's youth.

[12] November 29. On this date German girls went to fortune tellers to ask about their future husbands. The fortune tellers caused the girls to look into crystal balls and persuaded them that they were seeing what they wanted to see.

THE OTHER

She showed me mine, in crystal clear,
With several wild young blades, a soldier-lover:
I seek him everywhere, I pry and peer,
And yet, somehow, his face I can't discover.

SOLDIERS

Castles, with lofty
Ramparts and towers,
Maidens disdainful 80
In Beauty's array,
Both shall be ours!
Bold is the venture,
Splendid the pay!
Lads, let the trumpets
For us be suing,—
Calling to pleasure
Calling to ruin.
Stormy our life is;
Such is its boon! 90
Maidens and castles
Capitulate soon.
Bold is the venture,
Splendid the pay!
And the soldiers go marching,
Marching away!

FAUST AND WAGNER

FAUST

Released from ice are brook and river
By the quickening glance of the gracious Spring
The colors of hope to the valley cling,
And weak old Winter himself must shiver, 100
Withdrawn to the mountains, a crownless king:
Whence, ever retreating, he sends again
Impotent showers of sleet that darkle
In belts across the green o' the plain.
But the sun will permit no white to sparkle;
Everywhere form in development moveth;
He will brighten the world with the tints he loveth,
And, lacking blossoms, blue, yellow, and red,
He takes these gaudy people instead.
Turn thee about, and from this height 110
Back on the town direct thy sight.
Out of the hollow, gloomy gate,
The motley throngs come forth elate:
Each will the joy of the sunshine hoard,
To honor the Day of the Risen Lord!
They feel, themselves, their resurrection:
From the low, dark rooms, scarce habitable;
From the bonds of Work, from Trade's restriction;
From the pressing weight of roof and gable;

From the narrow, crushing streets and alleys;   120
From the churches' solemn and reverend night,
All come forth to the cheerful light.
How lively, see! the multitude sallies,
Scattering through gardens and fields remote,
While over the river, that broadly dallies,
Dances so many a festive boat;
And overladen, nigh to sinking,
The last full wherry takes the stream.
Yonder afar, from the hill-paths blinking,
Their clothes are colors that softly gleam.   130
I hear the noise of the village, even;
Here is the People's proper Heaven;
Here high and low contented see!
Here I am Man,—dare man to be!

WAGNER

To stroll with you, Sir Doctor, flatters;
'T is honor, profit, unto me.
But I, alone, would shun these shallow matters,
Since all that's coarse provokes my enmity.
This fiddling, shouting, ten-pin rolling
I hate,—these noises of the throng: 140
They rave, as Satan were their sports controlling,
And call it mirth, and call it song!

PEASANTS, UNDER THE LINDEN-TREE

(Dance and Song.)

All for the dance the shepherd dressed,
In ribbons, wreath, and gayest vest
    Himself with care arraying:
Around the linden lass and lad
Already footed it like mad:
    Hurrah! hurrah!
    Hurrah—tarara-la!
    The fiddle-bow was playing.   150

He broke the ranks, no whit afraid,
And with his elbow punched a maid,
    Who stood, the dance surveying:
The buxom wench, she turned and said:
"Now, you I call a stupid-head!"
    Hurrah! hurrah!
    Hurrah—tarara-la!
    "Be decent while you're staying!"

Then round the circle went their flight,
They danced to left, they danced to right: 160
    Their kirtles all were playing.
They first grew red, and then grew warm,
And rested, panting, arm in arm,—
    Hurrah! hurrah!
    Hurrah—tarara-la!
    And hips and elbows straying.

Now, don't be so familiar here!
How many a one has fooled his dear,
    Waylaying and betraying!
And yet, he coaxed her soon aside,   170
And round the linden sounded wide:
    Hurrah! hurrah!
    Hurrah—tarara-la!
    And the fiddle-bow was playing.

OLD PEASANT

Sir Doctor, it is good of you,
That thus you condescend, to-day,
Among this crowd of merry folk,
A highly-learned man, to stray.
Then also take the finest can,
We fill with fresh wine, for your sake: 180
I offer it, and humbly wish
That not alone your thirst it slake,—
That, as the drops below its brink,
So many days of life you drink!

FAUST

I take the cup you kindly reach,
With thanks and health to all and each.

(The People gather in a circle about him.)

OLD PEASANT

In truth, 't is well and fitly timed,
That now our day of joy you share,
Who heretofore, in evil days,
Gave us so much of helping care.   190
Still many a man stands living here,
Saved by your father's skilful hand,
That snatched him from the fever's rage
And stayed the plague in all the land.
Then also you, though but a youth,
Went into every house of pain:
Many the corpses carried forth,
But you in health came out again.
No test or trial you evaded:
A Helping God the helper aided.   200

ALL

Health to the man, so skilled and tried,
That for our help he long may bide!

FAUST

To Him above bow down, my friends,
Who teaches help, and succor sends!

(He goes on with WAGNER.)

WAGNER

With what a feeling, thou great man, must thou
Receive the people's honest veneration!
How lucky he, whose gifts his station
With such advantages endow!
Thou 'rt shown to all the younger generation:
Each asks, and presses near to gaze;   210
The fiddle stops, the dance delays.
Thou goest, they stand in rows to see,
And all the caps are lifted high;
A little more, and they would bend the knee
As if the Holy Host came by.

FAUST

A few more steps ascend, as far as yonder stone!—
Here from our wandering will we rest contented.
Here, lost in thought, I've lingered oft alone,
When foolish fasts and prayers my life tormented.
Here, rich in hope and firm in faith,   220
With tears, wrung hands and sighs, I've striven,
The end of that far-spreading death
Entreating from the Lord of Heaven!
Now like contempt the crowd's applauses seem:
Couldst thou but read, within mine inmost spirit,
How little now I deem
That sire or son such praises merit!
My father's was a sombre, brooding brain,
Which through the holy spheres of Nature groped
    and wandered,
And honestly, in his own fashion, pondered   230
With labor whimsical, and pain:
Who, in his dusky work-shop bending,
With proved adepts in company,
Made, from his recipes unending,
Opposing substances agree.
There was a Lion red, a wooer daring,[13]
Within the Lily's tepid bath espoused,
And both, tormented then by flame unsparing,
By turns in either bridal chamber housed.
If then appeared, with colors splendid,   240
The young Queen in her crystal shell,
This was the medicine—the patient's woes soon
    ended,
And none demanded: who got well?
Thus we, our hellish boluses compounding,
Among these vales and hills surrounding,

[13] This and the following lines are couched in the jargon
of alchemy. The theory was that a panacea would be produced from the mixture of two substances in a warm medium and then heated. The chemical union is here presented as a marriage and the panacea as the offspring. The
father is the lion, the mother the lily and the young queen
is the panacea produced.

Worse than the pestilence, have passed.
Thousands were done to death from poison[14] of my
    giving;
And I must hear, by all the living,
The shameless murderers praised at last!

WAGNER

Why, therefore, yield to such depression?   250
A good man does his honest share
In exercising, with the strictest care,
The art bequeathed to his possession!
Dost thou thy father honor, as a youth?
Then may his teaching cheerfully impel thee:
Dost thou, as man, increase the stores of truth?
Then may thine own son afterwards excel thee.

FAUST

O happy he, who still renews
The hope, from Error's deeps to rise forever!
That which one does not know, one needs to
    use;   260
And what one knows, one uses never.
But let us not, by such despondence, so
The fortune of the hour embitter!
Mark how, beneath the evening sunlight's glow,
The green-embosomed houses glitter!
The glow retreats, done is the day of toil,
It yonder hastes, new fields of life exploring;
Ah, that no wing can lift me from the soil,
Upon its track to follow, follow soaring!
Then would I see eternal Evening gild   270
The silent world beneath me glowing,
On fire each mountain-peak, with peace each valley
    filled,
The silver brook to golden rivers flowing.
The mountain-chain, with all its gorges deep,
Would then no more impede my godlike motion;
And now before mine eyes expands the ocean
With all its bays, in shining sleep!
Yet, finally, the weary god is sinking;
The new-born impulse fires my mind,—
I hasten on, his beams eternal drinking,   280
The Day before me and the Night behind,
Above me heaven unfurled, the floor of waves
    beneath me,—
A glorious dream! though now the glories fade.
Alas! the wings that lift the mind no aid
Of wings to lift the body can bequeath me.
Yet in each soul is born the pleasure
Of yearning onward, upward and away,
When o'er our heads, lost in the vaulted azure,

[14] Since mercury was often used as a component of these
experiments, the cure-all was indeed poison.

The lark sends down his flickering lay,—
When over crags and piny highlands   290
The poising eagle slowly soars,
And over plains and lakes and islands
The crane sails by to other shores.

WAGNER

I've had, myself, at times, some odd caprices,
But never yet such impulse felt, as this is.
One soon fatigues, on woods and fields to look,
Nor would I beg the bird his wing to spare us:
How otherwise the mental raptures bear us
From page to page, from book to book!
Then winter nights take loveliness untold,   300
As warmer life in every limb had crowned you;
And when your hands unroll some parchment rare
      and old,
All Heaven descends, and opens bright around you!

FAUST

One impulse art thou conscious of, at best;
O, never seek to know the other!
Two souls, alas! reside within my breast,
And each withdraws from, and repels, its brother.
One with tenacious organs holds in love
And clinging lust the world in its embraces;
The other strongly sweeps, this dust above,   310
Into the high ancestral spaces.
If there be airy spirits near,
'Twixt Heaven and Earth on potent errands fleeing,
Let them drop down the golden atmosphere,
And bear me forth to new and varied being!
Yea, if a magic mantle once were mine,
To waft me o'er the world at pleasure,
I would not for the costliest stores of treasure—
Not for a monarch's robe—the gift resign.

WAGNER

Invoke not thus the well-known throng,   320
Which through the firmament diffused is faring,
And danger thousand-fold, our race to wrong,
In every quarter is preparing.
Swift from the North the spirit-fangs so sharp
Sweep down, and with their barbéd points assail
      you;
Then from the East they come, to dry and warp
Your lungs, till breath and being fail you:
If from the Desert sendeth them the South,
With fire on fire your throbbing forehead crowning,
The West leads on a host, to cure the drouth   330
Only when meadow, field, and you are drowning.
They gladly hearken, prompt for injury,—
Gladly obey, because they gladly cheat us;

From Heaven they represent themselves to be,
And lisp like angels, when with lie they meet us
But, let us go! 'T is gray and dusky all:
The air is cold, the vapors fall.
At night, one learns his house to prize:—
Why stand you thus, with such astonished eyes?
What, in the twilight, can your mind so trouble? 340

FAUST

Seest thou the black dog coursing there, through
      corn and stubble?

WAGNER

Long since: yet deemed him not important in the
      least.

FAUST

Inspect him close: for what tak'st thou the beast?

WAGNER

Why, for a poodle who has lost his master,
And scents about, his track to find.

FAUST

Seest thou the spiral circles, narrowing faster,
Which he, approaching, round us seems to wind?
A streaming trail of fire, if I see rightly,
Follows his path of mystery.

WAGNER

It may be that your eyes deceive you slightly;   350
Naught but a plain black poodle do I see.

FAUST

It seems to me that with enchanted cunning
He snares our feet, some future chain to bind.

WAGNER

I see him timidly, in doubt, around us running,
Since, in his master's stead, two strangers doth he
      find.

FAUST

The circle narrows: he is near!

WAGNER

A dog thou seest, and not a phantom, here!
Behold him stop—upon his belly crawl—
His tail set wagging: canine habits, all!

FAUST

Come, follow us! Come here, at least!   360

WAGNER

'T is the absurdest, drollest beast.
Stand still, and you will see him wait;
Address him, and he gambols straight;
If something's lost, he'll quickly bring it,—
Your cane, if in the stream you fling it.

FAUST

No doubt you're right: no trace of mind, I own,
Is in the beast: I see but drill, alone.

WAGNER

The dog, when he's well educated,
Is by the wisest tolerated.
Yes, he deserves your favor thoroughly,—   370
The clever scholar of the students, he!

(*They pass in the city-gate.*)

III

THE STUDY

FAUST

(*Entering, with the poodle.*)

Behind me, field and meadow sleeping,
I leave in deep, prophetic night,
Within whose dread and holy keeping
The better soul awakes to light.
The wild desires no longer win us,
The deeds of passion cease to chain;
The love of Man revives within us,
The love of God revives again.

Be still, thou poodle! make not such racket and riot!
Why at the threshold wilt snuffing be?   10
Behind the stove repose thee in quiet!
My softest cushion I give to thee.
As thou, up yonder, with running and leaping
Amused us hast, on the mountain's crest,
So now I take thee into my keeping,
A welcome, but also a silent, guest.

Ah, when, within our narrow chamber
The lamp with friendly lustre glows,
Flames in the breast each faded ember,
And in the heart, itself that knows.   20
Then Hope again lends sweet assistance,
And Reason then resumes her speech:
One yearns, the rivers of existence,
The very founts of Life, to reach.[15]

[15] For this Biblical imagery, see Psalms 36:9; Jeremiah 17:13; Revelation 21:6.

Snarl not, poodle! To the sound that rises,
The sacred tones that my soul embrace,
This bestial noise is out of place.
We are used to see, that Man despises
What he never comprehends,
And the Good and the Beautiful vilipends,   30
Finding them often hard to measure:
Will the dog, like man, snarl *his* displeasure?

But ah! I feel, though will thereto be stronger,
Contentment flows from out my breast no longer.
Why must the stream so soon run dry and fail us,
And burning thirst again assail us?
Therein I've borne so much probation!
And yet, this want may be supplied us;
We call the Supernatural to guide us;
We pine and thirst for Revelation,   40
Which nowhere worthier is, more nobly sent,
Than here, in our New Testament.
I feel impelled, its meaning to determine,—
With honest purpose, once for all,
The hallowed Original
To change to my beloved German.

(*He opens a volume, and commences.*)

'T is written: "In the Beginning was the *Word*."
Here am I balked: who, now, can help afford?
The *Word*?[16]—impossible so high to rate it;
And otherwise must I translate it,   50
If by the Spirit I am truly taught.
Then thus: "In the Beginning was the *Thought*."
The first line let me weigh completely,
Lest my impatient pen proceed too fleetly.
Is it the *Thought* which works, creates, indeed?
"In the Beginning was the *Power*," I read.
Yet, as I write, a warning is suggested,
That I the sense may not have fairly tested.
The Spirit aids me: now I see the light!
"In the Beginning was the *Act*," I write.   60

If I must share my chamber with thee,
Poodle, stop that howling, prithee!
Cease to bark and bellow!
Such a noisy, disturbing fellow
I'll no longer suffer near me.
One of us, dost hear me!
Must leave, I fear me.
No longer guest-right I bestow;
The door is open, art free to go.
But what do I see in the creature?   70
Is that in the course of nature?
Is't actual fact? or Fancy's shows?
How long and broad my poodle grows!

[16] See John 1:1.

He rises mightily:
A canine form that cannot be!
What a spectre I've harbored thus!
He resembles a hippopotamus.
With fiery eyes, teeth terrible to see:
O, now am I sure of thee!
For all of thy half-hellish brood   80
The Key of Solomon [17] is good.

SPIRITS (*in the corridor*)

Some one, within, is caught!
Stay without, follow him not!
Like the fox in a snare,
Quakes the old hell-lynx there.
Take heed—look about!
Back and forth hover,
Under and over,
And he'll work himself out.
If your aid can avail him,   90
Let it not fail him;
For he, without measure,
Has wrought for our pleasure.

FAUST

First, to encounter the beast,
The Words of the Four be addressed:
Salamander, shine glorious!
Wave, Undine, as bidden!
Sylph, be thou hidden!
Gnome, be laborious!

Who knows not their sense   100
(These elements),—
Their properties
And power not sees,—
No mastery he inherits
Over the Spirits.

Vanish in flaming ether,
Salamander!
Flow foamingly together,
Undine!
Shine in meteor-sheen,   110
Sylph!
Bring help to hearth and shelf,
Incubus! Incubus!
Step forward, and finish thus!

Of the Four, no feature
Lurks in the creature.
Quiet he lies, and grins disdain:
Not yet, it seems, have I given him pain.

[17] A magician's book containing formulae for the evocation and exorcism of spirits.

Now, to undisguise thee,
Hear me exorcise thee!   120
Art thou, my gay one,
Hell's fugitive stray-one?
The sign witness now,
Before which they bow,
The cohorts of Hell!

With hair all bristling, it begins to swell.

Base Being, hearest thou?
Knowest and fearest thou
The One, unoriginate,
Named inexpressibly,   130
Through all Heaven impermeate,
Pierced irredressibly!

Behind the stove still banned,
See it, an elephant, expand!
It fills the space entire,
Mist-like melting, ever faster.
'T is enough: ascend no higher,—
Lay thyself at the feet of the Master!
Thou seest, not vain the threats I bring thee:
With holy fire I'll scorch and sting thee!   140
Wait not to know
The threefold dazzling glow! [18]
Wait not to know
The strongest art within my hands!

MEPHISTOPHELES

(*while the vapor is dissipating, steps forth from behind the stove in the costume of a Traveling Scholar*)

Why such a noise? What are my lord's commands?

FAUST

This was the poodle's real core,
A traveling scholar,[19] then? The *casus* is diverting.

MEPHISTOPHELES

The learned gentleman I bow before:
You've made me roundly sweat, that's certain!

FAUST

What is thy name?   150

[18] The Holy Trinity. Holy symbols bring Mephistopheles out.
[19] Many medieval students went from university to university leading an idle and usually gay life. *Cf.* the Goliards, Vol. I, pp. 311 and 404.

MEPHISTOPHELES

A question small, it seems,
For one whose mind the Word so much despises;
Who, scorning all external gleams,
The depths of being only prizes.

FAUST

With all you gentlemen, the name's a test,
Whereby the nature usually is expressed.
Clearly the latter implies
In names like Beelzebub, Destroyer,[20] Father of
    Lies.[21]
What art thou, then?

MEPHISTOPHELES

Part of that Power, not understood,
Which always wills the Bad, and always works the
    Good.   160

FAUST

What hidden sense in this enigma lies?

MEPHISTOPHELES

I am the Spirit that Denies!
And justly so: for all things, from the Void
Called forth, deserve to be destroyed:
'T were better, then, were naught created.
Thus, all which you as Sin have rated,—
Destruction,—aught with Evil blent,—
That is my proper element.

FAUST

Thou nam'st thyself a part, yet show'st complete to
    me?

MEPHISTOPHELES

The modest truth I speak to thee.   170
If Man, that microcosmic fool, can see
Himself a whole so frequently,
Part of the Part am I, once All, in primal Night,—
Part of the Darkness which brought forth the Light,
The haughty Light, which now disputes the space,
And claims of Mother Night her ancient place.
And yet, the struggle fails; since Light, howe'er it
    weaves,
Still, fettered, unto bodies cleaves:
It flows from bodies, bodies beautifies;
By bodies is its course impeded;   180
And so, but little time is needed,
I hope, ere, as the bodies die, it dies!

[20] See Revelation 9:11.
[21] See John 8:44.

FAUST

I see the plan thou art pursuing:
Thou canst not compass general ruin,
And hast on smaller scale begun.

MEPHISTOPHELES

And truly 'tis not much, when all is done.
That which to Naught is in resistance set,—
The Something of this clumsy world,—has yet,
With all that I have undertaken,
Not been by me disturbed or shaken: 190
From earthquake, tempest, wave, volcano's brand,
Back into quiet settle sea and land!
And that damned stuff, the bestial, human brood,—
What use, in having that to play with?
How many have I made away with!
And ever circulates a newer, fresher blood.
It makes me furious, such things beholding:
From Water, Earth, and Air unfolding,
A thousand germs break forth and grow,
In dry, and wet, and warm, and chilly;   200
And had I not the Flame reserved, why, really,
There's nothing special of my own to show!

FAUST

So, to the actively eternal
Creative force, in cold disdain
You now oppose the fist infernal,
Whose wicked clench is all in vain!
Some other labor seek thou rather,
Queer Son of Chaos, to begin!

MEPHISTOPHELES

Well, we'll consider: thou canst gather
My views, when next I venture in.   210
Might I, perhaps, depart at present?

FAUST

Why thou shouldst ask, I don't perceive.
Though our acquaintance is so recent,
For further visits thou hast leave.
The window's here, the door is yonder;
A chimney, also, you behold.

MEPHISTOPHELES

I must confess that forth I may not wander,
My steps by one slight obstacle controlled,—
The wizard's-foot,[22] that on your threshold made is.

[22] The pentagram, or five-pointed star. Evil spirits sup-
posedly could not pass over it unless all the points were
completely closed.

FAUST

The pentagram prohibits thee?   220
Why, tell me now, thou Son of Hades,
If that prevents, how cam'st thou in to me?
Could such a spirit be so cheated?

MEPHISTOPHELES

Inspect the thing: the drawing's not completed.
The outer angle, you may see,
Is open left—the lines don't fit it.

FAUST

Well,—Chance, this time, has fairly hit it!
And thus, thou'rt prisoner to me?
It seems the business has succeeded.

MEPHISTOPHELES

The poodle naught remarked, as after thee he
    speeded;   230
But other aspects now obtain:
The Devil can't get out again.

FAUST

Try, then, the open window-pane!

MEPHISTOPHELES

For Devils and for spectres this is law:
Where they have entered in, there also they with-
    draw.
The first is free to us; we're governed by the second.

FAUST

In Hell itself, then, laws are reckoned?
That's well! So might a compact be
Made with you gentlemen—and binding,—surely?

MEPHISTOPHELES

All that is promised shall delight thee purely;   240
No skinflint bargain shalt thou see.
But this is not of swift conclusion;
We'll talk about the matter soon.
And now, I do entreat this boon—
Leave to withdraw from my intrusion.

FAUST

One moment more I ask thee to remain,
Some pleasant news, at least, to tell me.

MEPHISTOPHELES

Release me, now! I soon shall come again;
Then thou, at will, mayst question and compel me.

FAUST

I have not snares around thee cast;   250
Thyself hast led thyself into the meshes.
Who traps the Devil, hold him fast!
Not soon a second time he'll catch a prey so pre-
    cious.

MEPHISTOPHELES

An't please thee, also I'm content to stay,
And serve thee in a social station;
But stipulating, that I may
With arts of mine afford thee recreation.

FAUST

Thereto I willingly agree,
If the diversion pleasant be.

MEPHISTOPHELES

My friend, thou 'lt win, past all pretences,   260
More in this hour to soothe thy senses,
Than in the year's monotony.
That which the dainty spirits sing thee,
The lovely pictures they shall bring thee,
Are more than magic's empty show.
Thy scent will be to bliss invited;
Thy palate then with taste delighted,
Thy nerves of touch ecstatic glow!
All unprepared, the charm I spin:
We're here together, so begin!   270

SPIRITS

Vanish, ye darkling
Arches above him!
Loveliest weather,
Born of blue ether,
Break from the sky!
O that the darkling
Clouds had departed!
Starlight is sparkling,
Tranquiller-hearted
Suns are on high.   280
Heaven's own children
In beauty bewildering,
Waveringly bending,
Pass as they hover;
Longing unending
Follows them over.
They, with their glowing
Garments, out-flowing,
Cover, in going,
Landscape and bower,   290
Where, in seclusion,

Lovers are plighted,
Lost in illusion.
Bower on bower!
Tendrils unblighted!
Lo! in a shower
Grapes that o'ercluster
Gush into must, or
Flow into rivers
Of foaming and flashing   300
Wine, that is dashing
Gems, as it boundeth
Down the high places,
And spreading, surroundeth,
With crystalline spaces,
In happy embraces,
Blossoming forelands,
Emerald shore-lands!
And the winged races
Drink, and fly onward—   310
Fly ever sunward
To the enticing
Islands, that flatter,
Dipping and rising
Light on the water!
Hark, the inspiring
Sound of their quiring!
See, the entrancing
Whirl of their dancing!
All in the air are   320
Freer and fairer.
Some of them scaling
Boldly the highlands,
Others are sailing,
Circling the islands;
Others are flying;
Life-ward all hieing,—
All for the distant
Star of existent
Rapture and Love!   30

MEPHISTOPHELES

He sleeps! Enough, ye fays! your airy number
Have sung him truly into slumber:
For this performance I your debtor prove.—
Not yet art thou the man, to catch the Fiend and
     hold him!—
With fairest images of dreams infold him,
Plunge him in seas of sweet untruth!
Yet, for the threshold's magic which controlled him,
The Devil needs a rat's quick tooth.
I use no lengthened invocation:
Here rustles one that soon will work my libera-
     tion.   340

The lord of rats and eke of mice,[23]
Of flies and bed-bugs, frogs and lice,
Summons thee hither to the door-sill,
To gnaw it where, with just a morsel
Of oil, he paints the spot for thee:—
There com'st thou, hopping on to me!
To work, at once! The point which made me craven
Is forward, on the ledge, engraven.
Another bite makes free the door:
So, dream thy dreams, O Faust, until we meet once
     more!   350

FAUST (*awaking*)

Am ı again so foully cheated?
Remains there naught of lofty spirit-sway,
But that a dream the Devil counterfeited,
And that a poodle ran away?

IV

THE STUDY

FAUST. MEPHISTOPHELES.

FAUST

A knock? Come in! Again my quiet broken?

MEPHISTOPHELES

'T is I!

FAUST

Come in!

MEPHISTOPHELES

Thrice must the words be spoken.

FAUST

Come in, then!

MEPHISTOPHELES

Thus thou pleasest me.
I hope we'll suit each other well;
For now, thy vapors to dispel,
I come, a squire of high degree,
In scarlet coat, with golden trimming,
A cloak in silken lustre swimming,
A tall cock's-feather in my hat,
A long, sharp sword for show or quarrel,—   10
And I advise thee, brief and flat,
To don the self-same gay apparel,
That, from this den released, and free,
Life be at last revealed to thee!

[23] Folklore has always associated the devil with these animals and insects.

FAUST

This life of earth, whatever my attire,
Would pain me in its wonted fashion.
Too old am I to play with passion;
Too young, to be without desire.
What from the world have I to gain?
Thou shalt abstain—renounce—refrain!   20
Such is the everlasting song
That in the ears of all men rings,—
That unrelieved, our whole life long,
Each hour, in passing, hoarsely sings.
In very terror I at morn awake,
Upon the verge of bitter weeping,
To see the day of disappointment break,
To no one hope of mine—not one—its promise keep-
        ing:—
That even each joy's presentiment
With wilful cavil would diminish,   30
With grinning masks of life prevent
My mind its fairest work to finish!
Then, too, when night descends, how anxiously
Upon my couch of sleep I lay me:
There, also, comes no rest to me,
But some wild dream is sent to fray me.
The God that in my breast is owned
Can deeply stir the inner sources;
The God, above my powers enthroned,
He cannot change external forces.   40
So, by the burden of my days oppressed,
Death is desired, and Life a thing unblest!

MEPHISTOPHELES

And yet is never Death a wholly welcome guest.

FAUST

O fortunate, for whom, when victory glances,
The bloody laurels on the brow he bindeth!
Whom, after rapid, maddening dances,
In clasping maiden-arms he findeth!
O would that I, before that spirit-power,
Ravished and rapt from life, had sunken!

MEPHISTOPHELES

And yet, by some one, in that nightly hour,   50
A certain liquid was not drunken.

FAUST

Eavesdropping, ha! thy pleasure seems to be.

MEPHISTOPHELES

Omniscient am I not; yet much is known to me.

FAUST

Though some familiar tone, retrieving
My thoughts from torment, led me on,
And sweet, clear echoes came, deceiving
A faith bequeathed from Childhood's dawn,
Yet now I curse whate'er entices
And snares the soul with visions vain;
With dazzling cheats and dear devices   60
Confines it in this cave of pain!
Cursed be, at once, the high ambition
Wherewith the mind itself deludes!
Cursed be the glare of apparition
That on the finer sense intrudes!
Cursed be the lying dream's impression
Of name, and fame, and laurelled brow!
Cursed, all that flatters as possession,
As wife and child, as knave and plow!
Cursed Mammon be, when he with treasures   70
To restless action spurs our fate!
Cursed when, for soft, indulgent leisures,
He lays for us the pillows straight!
Cursed be the vine's transcendent nectar,—
The highest favor Love lets fall!
Cursed, also, Hope!—cursed Faith, the spectre!
And cursed be Patience most of all!

CHORUS OF SPIRITS (*invisible*)

Woe! woe!
Thou hast it destroyed,
The beautiful world,   80
With powerful fist:
In ruin 't is hurled,
By the blow of a demigod shattered!
The scattered
Fragments into the Void we carry,
Deploring
The beauty perished beyond restoring.
Mightier
For the children of men,
Brightlier   90
Build it again,
In thine own bosom build it anew!
Bid the new career
Commence,
With clearer sense,
And the new songs of cheer
Be sung thereto!

MEPHISTOPHELES

These are the small dependants
Who give me attendance.
Hear them, to deeds and passion   100

Counsel in shrewd old-fashion!
Into the world of strife,
Out of this lonely life
That of senses and sap has betrayed thee,
They would persuade thee.
This nursing of the pain forego thee,
That, like a vulture, feeds upon thy breast!
The worst society thou find'st will show thee
Thou art a man among the rest.
But 't is not meant to thrust 110
Thee into the mob thou hatest!
I am not one of the greatest,
Yet, wilt thou to me entrust
Thy steps through life, I'll guide thee,—
Will willingly walk beside thee,—
Will serve thee at once and forever
With best endeavor,
And, if thou art satisfied,
Will as servant, slave, with thee abide.

FAUST

And what shall be my counter-service therefor? 120

MEPHISTOPHELES

The time is long: thou need'st not now insist.

FAUST

No—no! The Devil is an egotist,
And is not apt, without a why or wherefore,
"For God's sake," [24] others to assist.
Speak thy conditions plain and clear!
With such a servant danger comes, I fear.

MEPHISTOPHELES

Here, an unwearied slave, I'll wear thy tether,
And to thine every nod obedient be:
When *There* again we come together,
Then shalt thou do the same for me. 130

FAUST

The *There* my scruples naught increases.
When thou hast dashed this world to pieces,
The other, then, its place may fill.
Here, on this earth, my pleasures have their sources;
Yon son beholds my sorrows in his courses;
And when from these my life itself divorces,
Let happen all that can or will!
I'll hear no more: 't is vain to ponder
If there we cherish love or hate,
Or, in the spheres we dream of yonder, 140
A High and Low our souls await.

[24] Gratuitously.

MEPHISTOPHELES

In this sense, even, canst thou venture.
Come, bind thyself by prompt indenture,
And thou mine arts with joy shalt see:
What no man ever saw, I'll give to thee.

FAUST

Canst thou, poor Devil, give me whatsoever?
When was a human soul, in its supreme endeavor,
E'er understood by such as thou?
Yet, hast thou food which never satiates, now,—
The restless, ruddy gold hast thou, 150
That runs, quicksilver-like, one's fingers through,—
A game whose winnings no man ever knew,—
A maid, that, even from my breast,
Beckons my neighbor with her wanton glances,
And Honor's godlike zest,
The meteor that a moment dances,—
Show me the fruits that, ere they're gathered, rot,
And trees that daily with new leafage clothe them!

MEPHISTOPHELES

Such a demand alarms me not:
Such treasures have I, and can show them. 160
But still the time may reach us, good my friend,
When peace we crave and more luxurious diet.

FAUST

When on an idler's bed I stretch myself in quiet,
There let, at once, my record end!
Canst thou with lying flattery rule me,
Until, self-pleased, myself I see,—
Canst thou with rich enjoyment fool me,
Let that day be the last for me!
The bet I offer.

MEPHISTOPHELES

Done!

FAUST

And heartily!
When thus I hail the Moment flying: 170
"Ah, still delay—thou art so fair!"
Then bind me in thy bonds undying,
My final ruin then declare!
Then let the death-bell chime the token,
Then art thou from thy service free!
The clock may stop, the hand be broken,
Then Time be finished unto me!

MEPHISTOPHELES

Consider well: my memory good is rated.

FAUST

Thou hast a perfect right thereto.
My powers I have not rashly estimated: 180
A slave am I, whate'er I do—
If thine, or whose? 't is needless to debate it.

MEPHISTOPHELES

Then at the Doctors'-banquet I, to-day,
Will as a servant wait behind thee.
But one thing more! Beyond all risk to bind thee,
Give me a line or two, I pray.

FAUST

Demand'st thou, Pedant, too, a document?
Hast never known a man, nor proved his word's
    intent?
Is 't not enough, that what I speak to-day
Shall stand, with all my future days agreeing?   190
In all its tides sweeps not the world away,
And shall a promise bind my being?
Yet this delusion in our hearts we bear:
Who would himself therefrom deliver?
Blest he, whose bosom Truth makes pure and fair!
No sacrifice shall he repent of ever.
Nathless a parchment, writ and stamped with care,
A spectre is, which all to shun endeavor.
The word, alas! dies even in the pen,
And wax and leather keep the lordship then.   200
What wilt from me, Base Spirit, say?—
Brass, marble, parchment, paper, clay?
The terms with graver, quill, or chisel, stated?
I freely leave the choice to thee.

MEPHISTOPHELES

Why heat thyself, thus instantly,
With eloquence exaggerated?
Each leaf for such a pact is good;
And to subscribe thy name thou 'lt take a drop of
    blood.

FAUST

If thou therewith art fully satisfied,
So let us by the farce abide.   210

MEPHISTOPHELES

Blood is a juice of rarest quality.

FAUST

Fear not that I this pact shall seek to sever!
The promise that I make to thee
Is just the sum of my endeavor.
I have myself inflated all too high;

My proper place is thy estate:
The Mighty Spirit deigns me no reply,
And Nature shuts on me her gate.
The thread of Thought at last is broken,
And knowledge brings disgust unspoken.   220
Let us the sensual deeps explore,
To quench the fervors of glowing passion!
Let every marvel take form and fashion
Through the impervious veil it wore!
Plunge we in Time's tumultuous dance,
In the rush and roll of Circumstance!
Then may delight and distress,
And worry and success,
Alternately follow, as best they can:
Restless activity proves the man!   230

MEPHISTOPHELES

For you no bound, no term is set.
Whether you everywhere be trying,
Or snatch a rapid bliss in flying,
May it agree with you, what you get!
Only fall to, and show no timid balking.

FAUST

But thou hast heard, 't is not of joy we're talking.
I take the wildering whirl, enjoyment's keenest
    pain,
Enamored hate, exhilarant disdain.
My bosom, of its thirst for knowledge sated,
Shall not, henceforth, from any pang be wrested, 240
And all of life for all mankind created
Shall be within mine inmost being tested:
The highest, lowest forms my soul shall borrow,
Shall heap upon itself their bliss and sorrow,
And thus, my own sole self to all their selves ex-
    panded
I too, at last, shall with them all be stranded!

MEPHISTOPHELES

Believe me, who for many a thousand year
The same tough meat have chewed and tested.
That from the cradle to the bier
No man the ancient leaven has digested!   250
Trust one of us, this Whole supernal
Is made but for a God's delight!
He dwells in splendor single and eternal,
But *us* he thrusts in darkness, out of sight,
And *you* he dowers with Day and Night.

FAUST

Nay, but I will!

MEPHISTOPHELES

A good reply!
One only fear still needs repeating:
The art is long, the time is fleeting.
Then let thyself be taught, say I!
Go, league thyself with a poet,   260
Give the rein to his imagination,
Then wear the crown, and show it,
Of the qualities of his creation,—
The courage of the lion's breed.
The wild stag's speed,
The Italian's fiery blood,
The North's firm fortitude!
Let him find for thee the secret tether
That binds the Noble and Mean together,
And teach thy pulses of youth and pleasure   270
To love by rule, and hate by measure!
I'd like, myself, such a one to see:
Sir Microcosm his name should be.

FAUST

What am I, then, if 't is denied my part
The crown of all humanity to win me,
Whereto yearns every sense within me?

MEPHISTOPHELES

Why, on the whole, thou 'rt—what thou art.
Set wigs of million curls upon thy head, to raise
    thee.
Wear shoes an ell in height,—the truth betrays thee,
And thou remainest—what thou art.   280

FAUST

I feel, indeed, that I have made the treasure
Of human thought and knowledge mine, in vain;
And if I now sit down in restful leisure,
No fount of newer strength is in my brain:
I am no hair's-breadth more in height,
Nor nearer to the Infinite.

MEPHISTOPHELES

Good Sir, you see the facts precisely
As they are seen by each and all.
We must arrange them now, more wisely,
Before the joys of life shall pall.   290
Why, Zounds! Both hands and feet are, truly—
And head and virile forces—thine:
Yet all that I indulge in newly,
Is 't thence less wholly mine?
If I've six stallions in my stall,
Are not their forces also lent me?
I speed along, completest man of all,
As though my legs were four-and-twenty.

Take hold, then! let reflection rest,
And plunge into the world with zest!   300
I say to thee, a speculative wight
Is like a beast on moorlands lean,
That round and round some fiend misleads to evil
    plight,
While all about lie pastures fresh and green.

FAUST

Then how shall we begin?

MEPHISTOPHELES

                    We'll try a wider sphere.
What place of martyrdom is here!
Is 't like, I ask, is 't even prudence,
To bore thyself and bore the students?
Let Neighbor Paunch to that attend!
Why plague thyself with threshing straw for-
    ever?   310
The best thou learnest, in the end
Thou dar'st not tell the youngsters—never!
I hear one's footsteps, hither steering.

FAUST

To see him now I have no heart.

MEPHISTOPHELES

So long the poor boy waits a hearing,
He must not unconsoled depart.
Thy cap and mantle straightway lend me!
I'll play the comedy with art.

(He disguises himself.)

My wits, be certain, will befriend me.
But fifteen minutes' time is all I need;   320
For our fine trip, meanwhile, prepare thyself with
    speed!

(Exit FAUST.)

MEPHISTOPHELES

(In FAUST's long mantle.)

Reason and Knowledge only thou despise,
The highest strength in man that lies!
Let but the Lying Spirit bind thee
With magic works and shows that blind thee,
And I shall have thee fast and sure!
Fate such a bold, untrammelled spirit gave him,
As forwards, onwards, ever must endure;
Whose over-hasty impulse drave him
Past earthly joys he might secure.   330
Dragged through the wildest life, will I enslave
    him,

Through flat and stale indifference;
With struggling, chilling, checking, so deprave him
That, to his hot, insatiate sense,
The dream of drink shall mock, but never lave him:
Refreshment shall his lips in vain implore—
Had he not made himself the Devil's, naught could
    save him,
Still were he lost forevermore!

(A STUDENT *enters.)*

STUDENT

A short time, only, am I here,
And come, devoted and sincere,   340
To greet and know the man of fame,
Whom men to me with reverence name.

MEPHISTOPHELES

Your courtesy doth flatter me:
You see a man, as others be.
Have you, perchance, elsewhere begun?

STUDENT

Receive me now, I pray, as one
Who comes to you with courage good,
Somewhat of cash, and healthy blood:
My mother was hardly willing to let me;
But knowledge worth having I fain would get
    me.   350

MEPHISTOPHELES

Then you have reached the right place now.

STUDENT

I'd like to leave it, I must avow;
I find these walls, these vaulted spaces
Are anything but pleasant places.
'T is all so cramped and close and mean;
One sees no tree, no glimpse of green,
And when the lecture-halls receive me,
Seeing, hearing, and thinking leave me.

MEPHISTOPHELES

All that depends on habitude.
So from its mother's breasts a child   360
At first, reluctant, takes its food,
But soon to seek them is beguiled.
Thus, at the breasts of Wisdom clinging,
Thou 'lt find each day a greater rapture bringing.

STUDENT

I'll hang thereon with joy, and freely drain them;
But tell me, pray, the proper means to gain them.

MEPHISTOPHELES

Explain, before you further speak,
The special faculty you seek.

STUDENT

I crave the highest erudition;
And fain would make my acquisition   370
All that there is in Earth and Heaven,
In Nature and in Science too.

MEPHISTOPHELES

Here is the genuine path for you;
Yet strict attention must be given.

STUDENT

Body and soul thereon I'll wreak;
Yet, truly, I've some inclination
On summer holidays to seek
A little freedom and recreation.

MEPHISTOPHELES

Use well your time! It flies so swiftly from us;
But time through order may be won, I promise. 380
So, Friend, (my views to briefly sum,)
First, the *collegium logicum.*[25]
There will your mind be drilled and braced,
As if in Spanish boots [26] 't were laced,
And thus, to graver paces brought,
'T will plod along the path of thought,
Instead of shooting here and there,
A will-o'-the-wisp in murky air.
Days will be spent to bid you know,
What once you did at a single blow,   390
Like eating and drinking, free and strong,—
That one, two, three! thereto belong.
Truly the fabric of mental fleece
Resembles a weaver's masterpiece,
Where a thousand threads one treadle throws,
Where fly the shuttles hither and thither,
Unseen the threads are knit together,
And an infinite combination grows.
Then, the philosopher steps in
And shows, no otherwise it could have been: 400
The first was so, the second so,
Therefore the third and fourth are so;
Were not the first and second, then
The third and fourth had never been.
The scholars are everywhere believers,
But never succeed in being weavers.

[25] Course in logic.
[26] An instrument of torture used by the Spanish Inquisition.

He who would study organic existence,
First drives out the soul with rigid persistence;
Then the parts in his hand he may hold and class,
But the spiritual link is lost, alas!   410
Encheiresin naturae,[27] this Chemistry names,
Nor knows how herself she banters and blames!

STUDENT

I cannot understand you quite.

MEPHISTOPHELES

Your mind will shortly be set aright,
When you have learned, all things reducing,
To classify them for your using.

STUDENT

I feel as stupid, from all you've said,
As if a mill-wheel whirled in my head!

MEPHISTOPHELES

And after—first and foremost duty—
Of Metaphysics learn the use and beauty!   420
See that you most profoundly gain
What does not suit the human brain!
A splendid word to serve, you'll find
For what goes in—or won't go in—your mind.
But first, at least this half a year,
To order rigidly adhere;
Five hours a day, you understand,
And when the clock strikes, be on hand!
Prepare beforehand for your part
With paragraphs all got by heart,   430
So you can better watch, and look
That naught is said but what is in the book:
Yet in thy writing as unwearied be,
As did the Holy Ghost dictate to thee!

STUDENT

No need to tell me twice to do it!
I think, how useful 't is to write;
For what one has, in black and white,
One carries home and then goes through it.

MEPHISTOPHELES

Yet choose thyself a faculty!

STUDENT

I cannot reconcile myself to Jurisprudence.   440

MEPHISTOPHELES

Nor can I therefore greatly blame you students:
I know what science this has come to be.

[27] The handling of nature.

All rights and laws are still transmitted
Like an eternal sickness of the race,—
From generation unto generation fitted,
And shifted round from place to place.
Reason becomes a sham, Beneficence a worry:
Thou art a grandchild, therefore woe to thee!
The right born with us, ours in verity,
This to consider, there's, alas! no hurry.   450

STUDENT

My own disgust is strengthened by your speech.
O lucky he, whom you shall teach!
I've almost for Theology decided.

MEPHISTOPHELES

I should not wish to see you here misguided:
For, as regards this science, let me hint
'T is very hard to shun the false direction;
There's so much secret poison lurking in 't,
So like the medicine, it baffles your detection.
Hear, therefore, one alone, for that is best, in sooth,
And simply take your master's words for truth.   460
On *words* let your attention centre!
Then through the safest gate you'll enter
The temple-halls of Certainty.

STUDENT

Yet in the word must some idea be.

MEPHISTOPHELES

Of course! But only shun too over-sharp a tension,
For just where fails the comprehension,
A word steps promptly in as deputy.
With words 't is excellent disputing;
Systems to words 't is easy suiting;
On words 't is excellent believing;   470
No word can ever lose a jot from thieving.

STUDENT

Pardon! With many questions I detain you,
Yet must I trouble you again.
Of Medicine I still would fain
Hear one strong word that might explain you.
Three years is but a little space,
And, God! who can the field embrace?
If one some index could be shown,
'T were easier groping forward, truly.

MEPHISTOPHELES (*aside*)

I'm tired enough of this dry tone,—   480
Must play the Devil again, and fully.

(*Aloud.*)

To grasp the spirit of Medicine is easy:
Learn of the great and little world your fill,
To let it go at last, so please ye,
Just as God will!
In vain that through the realms of science you may
    drift;
Each one learns only—just what learn he can:
Yet he who grasps the Moment's gift,
He is the proper man.
Well-made you are, 't is not to be denied,   490
The rest a bold address will win you;
If you but in yourself confide,
At once confide all others in you.
To lead the women, learn the special feeling!
Their everlasting aches and groans,
In thousand tones,
Have all one source, one mode of healing;
And if your acts are half discreet,
You'll always have them at your feet.
A title first must draw and interest them,   500
And show that yours all other arts exceeds;
Then, as a greeting, you are free to touch and test
    them,
While, thus to do, for years another pleads.
You press and count the pulse's dances,
And then, with burning sidelong glances,
You clasp the swelling hips to see
If tightly laced her corsets be.

STUDENT

That's better, now! The How and Where, one sees.

MEPHISTOPHELES

My worthy friend, gray are all theories,
And green alone Life's golden tree.   510

STUDENT

I swear to you, 't is like a dream to me.
Might I again presume, with trust unbounded,
To hear your wisdom thoroughly expounded?

MEPHISTOPHELES

Most willingly, to what extent I may.

STUDENT

I cannot really go away:
Allow me that my album first I reach you,—
Grant me this favor, I beseech you!

MEPHISTOPHELES

Assuredly.

(*He writes, and returns the book.*)

STUDENT (*reads*)

Eritis sicut Deus, scientes bonum et malum.[28]

(*Closes the book with reverence, and withdraws.*)

MEPHISTOPHELES

Follow the ancient text, and the snake thou wast
    ordered to trample!
With all thy likeness to God, thou 'lt yet be a sorry
    example!   520

(FAUST *enters.*)

FAUST

Now, whither shall we go?

MEPHISTOPHELES

                      As best it pleases thee.
The little world, and then the great, we'll see.
With what delight, what profit winning,
Shalt thou sponge through the term beginning!

FAUST

Yet with the flowing beard I wear,
Both ease and grace will fail me there.
The attempt, indeed, were a futile strife;
I never could learn the ways of life.
I feel so small before others, and thence
Should always find embarrassments.   530

MEPHISTOPHELES

My friend, thou soon shalt lose all such misgiving:
Be thou but self-possessed, thou hast the art of
    living!

FAUST

How shall we leave the house, and start?
Where hast thou servant, coach and horses?

MEPHISTOPHELES

We'll spread this cloak with proper art,
Then through the air direct our courses.
But only, on so bold a flight,
Be sure to have thy luggage light.
A little burning air, which I shall soon prepare us,
Above the earth will nimbly bear us,   540
And, if we're light, we'll travel swift and clear:
I gratulate thee on thy new career!

[28] Genesis 3:5.

V

AUERBACH'S CELLAR IN LEIPZIG

CAROUSAL OF JOLLY COMPANIONS

FROSCH

Is no one laughing? no one drinking?
I'll teach you how to grin, I'm thinking.
To-day you're like wet straw, so tame;
And usually you're all aflame.

BRANDER

Now that's your fault; from you we nothing see,
No beastliness and no stupidity.

FROSCH

(*Pours a glass of wine over* BRANDER's *head.*)

There's both together!

BRANDER

Twice a swine!

FROSCH

You wanted them: I've given you mine.

SIEBEL

Turn out who quarrels—out the door!
With open throat sing chorus, drink and roar!   10
Up! holla! ho!

ALTMAYER

Woe's me, the fearful bellow!
Bring cotton, quick! He's split my ears, that fellow.

SIEBEL

When the vault echoes to the song,
One first perceives the bass is deep and strong.

FROSCH

Well said! and out with him that takes the least
offence!
Ah, tara, lara, da!

ALTMAYER

Ah, tara, lara, da!

FROSCH

The throats are tuned, commence!

(*Sings.*)

*The dear old holy Roman realm,
How does it hold together?*   20

BRANDER

A nasty song! Fie! a political song—
A most offensive song! Thank God, each morning,
therefore,
That you have not the Roman realm to care for!
At least, I hold it so much gain for me,
That I nor Chancellor nor Kaiser be.
Yet also we must have a ruling head, I hope,
And so we'll choose ourselves a Pope.
You know the quality that can
Decide the choice, and elevate the man.

FROSCH (*sings*)

Soar up, soar up, Dame Nightingale!   30
Ten thousand times my sweetheart hail!

SIEBEL

No, greet my sweetheart not! I tell you, I'll resent it.

FROSCH

My sweetheart greet and kiss! I dare you to prevent
it!

(*Sings.*)

*Draw the latch! the darkness makes:
Draw the latch! the lover wakes.
Shut the latch! the morning breaks.*

SIEBEL

Yes, sing away, sing on, and praise, and brag of her!
I'll wait my proper time for laughter:
Me by the nose she led, and now she'll lead you
after.
Her paramour should be an ugly gnome,   40
Where four roads cross, in wanton play to meet her:
An old he-goat, from Blocksberg coming home,
Should his good-night in lustful gallop bleat her!
A fellow made of genuine flesh and blood
Is for the wench a deal too good.
Greet her? Not I: unless, when meeting,
To smash her windows be a greeting!

BRANDER (*pounding on the table*)

Attention! Hearken now to me!
Confess, Sirs, I know how to live.
Enamored persons here have we,   50
And I, as suits their quality,
Must something fresh for their advantage give.
Take heed! 'T is of the latest cut, my strain,
And all strike in at each refrain!

(*He sings.*)

There was a rat in the cellar-nest,
Whom fat and butter made smoother:
He had a paunch beneath his vest
Like that of Doctor Luther.
The cook laid poison cunningly,
And then as sore oppressed was he   60
As if he had love in his bosom.

CHORUS (*shouting*)

As if he had love in his bosom!

BRANDER

He ran around, he ran about,
His thirst in puddles laving;
He gnawed and scratched the house throughout,
But nothing cured his raving.
He whirled and jumped, with torment mad,
And soon enough the poor beast had,
As if he had love in his bosom.

CHORUS

As if he had love in his bosom!   70

BRANDER

And driven at last, in open day,
He ran into the kitchen,
Fell on the hearth, and squirming lay,
In the last convulsion twitching.
Then laughed the murderess in her glee:
"Ha! ha! he's at his last gasp," said she.
"As if he had love in his bosom!"

CHORUS

As if he had love in his bosom!

SIEBEL

How the dull fools enjoy the matter!
To me it is a proper art   80
Poison for such poor rats to scatter.

BRANDER

Perhaps you'll warmly take their part?

ALTMAYER

The bald-pate pot-belly I have noted:
Misfortune tames him by degrees;
For in the rat by poison bloated
His own most natural form he sees.

FAUST AND MEPHISTOPHELES.

MEPHISTOPHELES

Before all else, I bring thee hither
Where boon companions meet together,
To let thee see how smooth life runs away.
Here, for the folk, each day's a holiday: 90
With little wit, and ease to suit them,
They whirl in narrow, circling trails,
Like kittens playing with their tails;
And if no headache persecute them
So long the host may credit give,
They merrily and careless live.

BRANDER

The fact is easy to unravel,
Their air's so odd, they've just returned from travel:
A single hour they've not been here.

FROSCH

You've verily hit the truth! Leipzig to me is dear: 100
Paris in miniature, how it refines its people!

SIEBEL

Who are the strangers, should you guess?

FROSCH

Let me alone! I'll set them first to drinking,
And then, as one a child's tooth draws, with clever-
    ness,
I'll worm their secret out, I'm thinking.
They're of a noble house, that's very clear:
Haughty and discontented they appear.

BRANDER

They're mountebanks, upon a revel.

ALTMAYER

Perhaps.

FROSCH

Look out, I'll smoke them now!

MEPHISTOPHELES (*to* FAUST)

Not if he had them by the neck, I vow,   110
Would e'er these people scent the Devil!

FAUST

Fair greeting, gentlemen!

SIEBEL

                    Our thanks: we give the same.

(*Murmurs, inspecting* MEPHISTOPHELES *from the side.*)

In one foot is the fellow lame? [29]

MEPHISTOPHELES

Is it permitted that we share your leisure?
In place of cheering drink, which one seeks vainly
   here,
Your company shall give us pleasure.

ALTMAYER

A most fastidious person you appear.

FROSCH

No doubt 't was late when you from Rippach [30]
   started?
And supping there with Hans occasioned your
   delay?

MEPHISTOPHELES

We passed, without a call, to-day.   120
At our last interview, before we parted
Much of his cousins did he speak, entreating
That we should give to each his kindly greeting.

(*He bows to* FROSCH.)

ALTMAYER (*aside*)

You have it now! he understands.

SIEBEL

                        A knave sharp-set!

FROSCH

Just wait awhile: I'll have him yet.

MEPHISTOPHELES

If I am right, we heard the sound
Of well-trained voices, singing chorus;
And truly, song must here rebound
Superbly from the arches o'er us.

FROSCH

Are you, perhaps, a virtuoso?   130

MEPHISTOPHELES

O no! my wish is great, my power is only so-so.

ALTMAYER

Give us a song!

[29] He has one human foot and one horse's hoof.
[30] "Small village": the word in German is used much as
"Podunk" in America, and indicates a certain rusticity.

MEPHISTOPHELES

If you desire, a number.

SIEBEL

So that it be a bran-new strain!

MEPHISTOPHELES

We've just retraced our way from Spain,
The lovely land of wine, and song, and slumber.

(*Sings.*)

There was a king once reigning,
Who had a big black flea—

FROSCH

Hear, hear! A flea! D' ye rightly take the jest?
I call a flea a tidy guest.

MEPHISTOPHELES (*sings*)

There was a king once reigning,   140
Who had a big black flea,
And loved him past explaining,
As his own son were he.
He called his man of stitches;
The tailor came straightway:
Here, measure the lad for breeches,
And measure his coat, I say!

BRANDER

But mind, allow the tailor no caprices:
Enjoin upon him, as his head is dear,
To most exactly measure, sew and shear,   150
So that the breeches have no creases!

MEPHISTOPHELES

In silk and velvet gleaming
He now was wholly drest—
Had a coat with ribbons streaming,
A cross upon his breast.
He had the first of stations,
A minister's star and name;
And also all his relations
Great lords at court became.

And the lords and ladies of honor   160
Were plagued, awake and in bed;
The queen she got them upon her,
The maids were bitten and bled.
And they did not dare to brush them,
Or scratch them, day or night:
We crack them and we crush them,
At once, whene'er they bite.

CHORUS (*shouting*)

We crack them and we crush them,
At once, whene'er they bite!

FROSCH

Bravo! bravo! that was fine.   170

SIEBEL

Every flea may it so befall!

BRANDER

Point your fingers and nip them all!

ALTMAYER

Hurrah for Freedom! Hurrah for wine!

MEPHISTOPHELES

I fain would drink with you, my glass to Freedom
      clinking,
If 't were a better wine that here I see you drinking.

SIEBEL

Don't let us hear that speech again!

MEPHISTOPHELES

Did I not fear the landlord might complain,
I'd treat these worthy guests, with pleasure,
To some from out our cellar's treasure.

SIEBEL

Just treat, and let the landlord me arraign!   180

FROSCH

And if the wine be good, our praises shall be
      ample.
But do not give too very small a sample;
For, if its quality I decide,
With a good mouthful I must be supplied.

ALTMAYER (*aside*)

They 're from the Rhine! I guessed as much, before.

MEPHISTOPHELES

Bring me a gimlet here!

BRANDER

                  What shall therewith be done?
You 've not the casks already at the door?

ALTMAYER

Yonder, within the landlord's box of tools, there 's
      one!

MEPHISTOPHELES (*takes the gimlet*)
(*To* FROSCH.)

Now, give me of your taste some intimation.

FROSCH

How do you mean? Have you so many kinds?   190

MEPHISTOPHELES

The choice is free: make up your minds.

ALTMAYER (*to* FROSCH)

Aha! you lick your chops, from sheer anticipation.

FROSCH

Good! if I have the choice, so let the wine be
      Rhenish!
Our Fatherland can best the sparkling cup replen-
      ish.

MEPHISTOPHELES

(*boring a hole in the edge of the table, at the place
            where* FROSCH *sits*)

Get me a little wax, to make the stoppers, quick!

ALTMAYER

Ah! I perceive a juggler's trick.

MEPHISTOPHELES (*to* BRANDER)

And you?

BRANDER

            Champagne shall be my wine.
And let it sparkle fresh and fine!

MEPHISTOPHELES

(*bores: in the mean time one has made the wax
      stoppers, and plugged the holes with them*)

BRANDER

What 's foreign one can't always keep quite clear of,
For good things, oft, are not so near;   200
A German can't endure the French to see or hear of,
Yet drinks their wines with hearty cheer.

SIEBEL

(*as* MEPHISTOPHELES *approaches his seat*)

For me, I grant, sour wine is out of place;
Fill up my glass with sweetest, will you?

MEPHISTOPHELES (*boring*)

Tokay shall flow at once, to fill you!

ALTMAYER

No—look me, Sirs, straight in the face!
I see you have your fun at our expense.

MEPHISTOPHELES

O no! with gentlemen of such pretence,
That were to venture far, indeed.
Speak out, and make your choice with speed!   210
With what a vintage can I serve you?

ALTMAYER

With any—only satisfy our need.

(After the holes have been bored and plugged.)

MEPHISTOPHELES

(with singular gestures)

Grapes the vine-stem bears,
Horns the he-goat wears!
The grapes are juicy, the vines are wood,
The wooden table gives wine as good!
Into the depths of Nature peer,—
Only believe, there's a miracle here!

Now draw the stoppers, and drink your fill!

ALL

(as they draw out the stoppers, and the wine which
has been desired flows into the glass of each)

O beautiful fountain, that flows at will!   220

MEPHISTOPHELES

But have a care, that you nothing spill!

(They drink repeatedly.)

ALL (sing)

As 't were five hundred hogs, we feel
So cannibalic jolly!

MEPHISTOPHELES

See, now, the race is happy—it is free!

FAUST

To leave them is my inclination.

MEPHISTOPHELES

Take notice, first! their bestiality
Will make a brilliant demonstration.

SIEBEL

(drinks carelessly: the wine spills upon the earth,
and turns to flame)

Help! Fire! Help! Hell-fire is sent!

MEPHISTOPHELES

(charming away the flame)

Be quiet, friendly element!

(To the revellers.)

A bit of purgatory 't was for this time, merely.   230

SIEBEL

What mean you? Wait!—you 'll pay for 't dearly!
You 'll know us, to your detriment.

FROSCH

Don't try that game a second time upon us!

ALTMAYER

I think we 'd better send him packing quietly.

SIEBEL

What, Sir! you dare to make so free,
And play your hocus-pocus on us!

MEPHISTOPHELES

Be still, old wine-tub.

SIEBEL

Broomstick, you!
You face it out, impertinent and heady?

BRANDER

Just wait! a shower of blows is ready.

ALTMAYER

(draws a stopper out of the table: fire flies in
his face)

I burn! I burn!

SIEBEL

'T is magic! Strike—   240
The knave is outlawed! Cut him as you like!

(They draw their knives, and rush upon
MEPHISTOPHELES.)

MEPHISTOPHELES

(with solemn gestures)

False word and form of air,
Change place, and sense ensnare!
Be here—and there!

(They stand amazed and look at each other.)

ALTMAYER

Where am I? What a lovely land!

FROSCH

Vines? Can I trust my eyes?

SIEBEL

And purple grapes at hand!

BRANDER

Here, over this green arbor bending,
See, what a vine! what grapes depending!

(*He takes* SIEBEL *by the nose: the others do the
same reciprocally, and raise their knives.*)

MEPHISTOPHELES (*as above*)

Loose, Error, from their eyes the band,
And how the Devil jests, be now enlightened! 250

(*He disappears with* FAUST: *the revellers start and
separate.*)

SIEBEL

What happened?

ALTMAYER

How?

FROSCH

Was that your nose I tightened?

BRANDER (*to* SIEBEL)

And yours that still I have in hand?

ALTMAYER

It was a blow that went through every limb!
Give me a chair! I sink! my senses swim.

FROSCH

But what has happened, tell me now?

SIEBEL

Where is he? If I catch the scoundrel hiding,
He shall not leave alive, I vow.

ALTMAYER

I saw him with these eyes upon a wine-cask riding
Out of the cellar-door, just now.
Still in my feet the fright like lead is weighing. 260

(*He turns towards the table.*)

Why! If the fount of wine should still be playing?

SIEBEL

'T was all deceit, and lying, false design!

FROSCH

And yet it seemed as I were drinking wine.

BRANDER

But with the grapes how was it, pray?

ALTMAYER

Shall one believe no miracles, just say!

VI

WITCHES' KITCHEN

*Upon a low hearth stands a great caldron, under
which a fire is burning. Various figures appear in
the vapors which rise from the caldron. An ape
sits beside it, skims it, and watches lest it boil
over. The he-ape, with the young ones, sits near
and warms himself. Ceiling and walls are covered
with the most fantastic witch-implements.*

FAUST. MEPHISTOPHELES.

FAUST

These crazy signs of witches' craft repel me!
I shall recover, dost thou tell me,
Through this insane, chaotic play?
From an old hag shall I demand assistance?
And will her foul mess take away
Full thirty years from my existence?
Woe 's me, canst thou naught better find!
Another baffled hope must be lamented:
Has Nature, then, and has a noble mind
Not any potent balsam yet invented? 10

MEPHISTOPHELES

Once more, my friend, thou talkest sensibly.
There is, to make thee young, a simpler mode and
apter;
But in another book 't is writ for thee,
And is a most eccentric chapter.

FAUST

Yet will I know it.

MEPHISTOPHELES

Good! the method is revealed
Without or gold or magic or physician.
Betake thyself to yonder field,
There hoe and dig, as thy condition;
Restrain thyself, thy sense and will
Within a narrow sphere to flourish; 20
With unmixed food thy body nourish;

Live with the ox as ox, and think it not a theft
That thou manur'st the acre which thou reapest;—
That, trust me, is the best mode left,
Whereby for eighty years thy youth thou keepest!

FAUST

I am not used to that; I cannot stoop to try it—
To take the spade in hand, and ply it.
The narrow being suits me not at all.

MEPHISTOPHELES

Then to thine aid the witch must call.

FAUST

Wherefore the hag, and her alone?   30
Canst thou thyself not brew the potion?

MEPHISTOPHELES

That were a charming sport, I own:
I 'd build a thousand bridges meanwhile, I 've a
    notion.
Not Art and Science serve, alone;
Patience must in the work be shown.
Long is the calm brain active in creation;
Time, only, strengthens the fine fermentation.
And all, belonging thereunto,
Is rare and strange, howe'er you take it:
The Devil taught the thing, 't is true,   40
And yet the Devil cannot make it.

(Perceiving the Animals.)

See, what a delicate race they be!
That is the maid! the man is he!

(To the Animals.)

It seems the mistress has gone away?

THE ANIMALS

Carousing, to-day!
Off and about,
By the chimney out!

MEPHISTOPHELES

What time takes she for dissipating?

THE ANIMALS

While we to warm our paws are waiting.

MEPHISTOPHELES (to FAUST)

How findest thou the tender creatures?   50

FAUST

Absurder than I ever yet did see.

MEPHISTOPHELES

Why, just such talk as this, for me,
Is that which has the most attractive features!

(To the Animals.)

But tell me now, ye curséd puppets,
Why do ye stir the porridge so?

THE ANIMALS

We 're cooking watery soup for beggars.

MEPHISTOPHELES

Then a great public you can show.

THE HE-APE

(comes up and fawns on MEPHISTOPHELES)

O cast thou the dice!
Make me rich in a trice,
Let me win in good season!   60
Things are badly controlled,
And had I but gold,
So had I my reason.

MEPHISTOPHELES

How would the ape be sure his luck enhances,
Could he but try the lottery's chances!

(In the mean time the young apes have been playing with a large ball, which they now roll forward.)

THE HE-APE

The world 's the ball:
Doth rise and fall,
And roll incessant:
Like glass doth ring,
A hollow thing,—   70
How soon will 't spring,
And drop, quiescent?
Here bright it gleams,
Here brighter seems:
I live at present!
Dear son, I say,
Keep thou away!
Thy doom is spoken!
'T is made of clay,
And will be broken.   80

MEPHISTOPHELES

What means the sieve?

THE HE-APE (taking it down)

Wert thou the thief,
I'd know him and shame him.

(He runs to the SHE-APE, *and lets her look through it.)*

> Look through the sieve! [31]
> Know'st thou the thief,
> And darest not name him?

MEPHISTOPHELES *(approaching the fire)*

And what's this pot?

HE-APE AND SHE-APE

> The fool knows it not!
> He knows not the pot,
> He knows not the kettle!   90

MEPHISTOPHELES

Impertinent beast!

THE HE-APE

> Take the brush here, at least,
> And sit down on the settle!

(He invites MEPHISTOPHELES *to sit down.)*

FAUST

(who during all this time has been standing before a mirror, now approaching and now retreating from it)

What do I see? What heavenly form revealed
Shows through the glass from Magic's fair domin-
        ions!
O lend me, Love, the swiftest of thy pinions,
And bear me to her beauteous field!
Ah, if I leave this spot with fond designing,
If I attempt to venture near,
Dim, as through gathering mist, her charms ap-
        pear!—   100
A woman's form, in beauty shining!
Can woman, then, so lovely be?
And must I find her body, there reclining,
Of all the heavens the bright epitome?
Can Earth with such a thing be mated?

MEPHISTOPHELES

Why, surely, if a God first plagues Himself six days,
Then, self-contented, *Bravo!* says,
Must something clever be created.
This time, thine eyes be satiate!
I 'll yet detect thy sweetheart and ensnare her, 110

[31] In Germany during the sixteenth and seventeenth centuries, a fortune teller would take a sieve between the middle fingers of her two hands and read the list of those suspected of crime. At the right name, the sieve was supposed to begin to turn.

And blest is he, who has the lucky fate,
Some day, as bridegroom, home to bear her.

*(*FAUST *gazes continually in the mirror.* MEPHIS-
TOPHELES *stretching himself out on the settle,
and playing with the brush, continues to speak.)*

So sit I, like the King upon his throne:
I hold the sceptre, here,—and lack the crown alone.

THE ANIMALS

*(who up to this time have been making all kinds of
fantastic movements together, bring a crown to
MEPHISTOPHELES with great noise)*

> O be thou so good
> With sweat and with blood
> The crown to belime!

*(They handle the crown awkwardly and break it
into two pieces, with which they spring around.)*

> 'T is done, let it be!
> We speak and we see,
> We hear and we rhyme!   120

FAUST *(before the mirror)*

Woe 's me! I fear to lose my wits.

MEPHISTOPHELES *(pointing to the Animals)*

My own head, now, is really nigh to sinking.

THE ANIMALS

> If lucky our hits,
> And everything fits,
> 'T is thoughts, and we 're thinking!

FAUST *(as above)*

My bosom burns with that sweet vision;
Let us, with speed, away from here!

MEPHISTOPHELES *(in the same attitude)*

One must, at least, make this admission—
They 're poets, genuine and sincere.

(The caldron, which the SHE-APE *has up to this
time neglected to watch, begins to boil over: there
ensues a great flame, which blazes out the chimney. The* WITCH *comes careering down through
the flame, with terrible cries.)*

THE WITCH

> Ow! ow! ow! ow!   130
> The damnéd beast—the curséd sow!
> To leave the kettle, and singe the Frau!
> Accurséd fere!

(*Perceiving* FAUST *and* MEPHISTOPHELES.)

    What is that here?
    Who are you here?
    What want you thus?
    Who sneaks to us?
    The fire-pain
    Burn bone and brain!

(*She plunges the skimming-ladle into the caldron,
and scatters flames towards* FAUST, MEPHISTOPH-
ELES, *and the Animals. The Animals whimper.*)

MEPHISTOPHELES

(*reversing the brush, which he has been holding in
his hand, and striking among the jars and glasses*)

    In two! in two!   140
    There lies the brew!
    There lies the glass!
    The joke will pass,
    As time, foul ass!
    To the singing of thy crew.

(*As the* WITCH *starts back, full of wrath and
horror:*)

Ha! know'st thou me? Abomination, thou!
Know'st thou, at last, thy Lord and Master?
What hinders me from smiting now
Thee and thy monkey-sprites with fell disaster?
Hast for the scarlet coat no reverence?   150
Dost recognize no more the tall cock's-feather?
Have I concealed this countenance?—
Must tell my name, old face of leather?

THE WITCH

O pardon, Sir, the rough salute!
Yet I perceive no cloven foot;
And both your ravens, where are *they* now?

MEPHISTOPHELES

This time, I 'll let thee 'scape the debt;
For since we two together met,
'T is verily full many a day now.
Culture, which smooth the whole world licks,   160
Also unto the Devil sticks.
The days of that old Northern phantom now are
    over:
Where canst thou horns and tail and claws discover?
And, as regards the foot, which I can't spare, in
    truth,
'T would only make the people shun me;
Therefore I 've worn, like many a spindly youth,
False calves these many years upon me.

THE WITCH (*dancing*)

Reason and sense forsake my brain,
Since I behold Squire Satan here again!

MEPHISTOPHELES

Woman, from such a name refrain!   170

THE WITCH

Why so? What has it done to thee?

MEPHISTOPHELES

It 's long been written in the Book of Fable;
Yet, therefore, no whit better men we see:
The Evil One has left, the evil ones are stable.
Sir Baron call me thou, then is the matter good;
A cavalier am I, like others in my bearing.
Thou hast no doubt about my noble blood:
See, here 's the coat-of-arms that I am wearing!

(*He makes an indecent gesture.*)

THE WITCH (*laughs immoderately*)

Ha! ha! That 's just your way, I know:
A rogue you are, and you were always so.   180

MEPHISTOPHELES (*to* FAUST)

My friend, take proper heed, I pray!
To manage witches, this is just the way.

THE WITCH

Wherein, Sirs, can I be of use?

MEPHISTOPHELES

Give us a goblet of the well-known juice!
But, I must beg you, of the oldest brewage;
The years a double strength produce.

THE WITCH

With all my heart! Now, here 's a bottle,
Wherefrom, sometimes, I wet my throttle,
Which, also, not the slightest, stinks;
And willingly a glass I'll fill him.   190

(*Whispering.*)

Yet, if this man without due preparation drinks,
As well thou know'st, within an hour 't will kill
    him.

MEPHISTOPHELES

He is a friend of mine, with whom it will agree,
And he deserves thy kitchen's best potation:
Come, draw thy circle, speak thine adjuration,
And fill thy goblet full and free!

THE WITCH

(*with fantastic gestures draws a circle and places mysterious articles therein; meanwhile the glasses begin to ring, the caldron to sound, and make a musical accompaniment. Finally she brings a great book, and stations in the circle the Apes, who are obliged to serve as reading-desk, and to hold the torches. She then beckons* FAUST *to approach*)

FAUST (*to* MEPHISTOPHELES)

Now, what shall come of this? the creatures antic,
The crazy stuff, the gestures frantic,—
All the repulsive cheats I view,—
Are known to me, and hated, too.   200

MEPHISTOPHELES

O, nonsense! That's a thing for laughter;
Don't be so terribly severe!
She juggles you as doctor now, that, after,
The beverage may work the proper cheer.

(*He persuades* FAUST *to step into the circle.*)

THE WITCH

(*begins to declaim, with much emphasis, from the book*)

> See, thus it's done!
> Make ten of one,
> And two let be,
> Make even three,
> And rich thou 'lt be.
> Cast o'er the four!   210
> From five and six
> (The witch's tricks)
> Make seven and eight,
> 'T is finished straight!
> And nine is one,
> And ten is none.
> This is the witch's once-one's-one!

FAUST

She talks like one who raves in fever.

MEPHISTOPHELES

Thou 'lt hear much more before we leave her.
'T is all the same: the book I can repeat,   220
Such time I 've squandered o'er the history:
A contradiction thus complete
Is always for the wise, no less than fools, a mystery.
The art is old and new, for verily
All ages have been taught the matter,—
By Three and One, and One and Three,
Error instead of Truth to scatter.

They prate and teach, and no one interferes;
All from the fellowship of fools are shrinking.
Man usually believes, if only words he hears,   230
That also with them goes material for thinking!

THE WITCH (*continues*)

> The lofty skill
> Of Science, still
> From all men deeply hidden!
> Who takes no thought,
> To him 't is brought,
> 'T is given unsought, unbidden!

FAUST

What nonsense she declaims before us!
My head is nigh to split, I fear:
It seems to me as if I hear   240
A hundred thousand fools in chorus.

MEPHISTOPHELES

O Sibyl excellent, enough of adjuration!
But hither bring us thy potation,
And quickly fill the beaker to the brim!
This drink will bring my friend no injuries:
He is a man of manifold degrees,
And many draughts are known to him.

(*The* WITCH, *with many ceremonies, pours the drink into a cup; as* FAUST *sets it to his lips, a light flame arises.*)

Down with it quickly! Drain it off!
'T will warm thy heart with new desire:
Art with the Devil hand and glove,   250
And wilt thou be afraid of fire?

(*The* WITCH *breaks the circle:* FAUST *steps forth.*)

MEPHISTOPHELES

And now, away! Thou dar'st not rest.

THE WITCH

And much good may the liquor do thee!

MEPHISTOPHELES (*to the* WITCH)

Thy wish be on Walpurgis Night expressed;
What boon I have, shall then be given unto thee.

THE WITCH

Here is a song, which, if you sometimes sing,
You 'll find it of peculiar operation.

MEPHISTOPHELES (*to* FAUST)

Come, walk at once! A rapid occupation
Must start the needful perspiration,

And through thy frame the liquor's potence
    fling.   260
The noble indolence I 'll teach thee then to treasure,
And soon thou 'lt be aware, with keenest thrills of
    pleasure,
How Cupid stirs and leaps, on light and restless
    wing.

FAUST

One rapid glance within the mirror give me,
How beautiful that woman-form!

MEPHISTOPHELES

No, no! The paragon of all, believe me,
Thou soon shalt see, alive and warm.

(Aside.)

Thou 'lt find, this drink thy blood compelling,
Each woman beautiful as Helen!

VII

A STREET

FAUST. MARGARET (*passing by*).

FAUST

Fair lady, let it not offend you,
That arm and escort I would lend you!

MARGARET

I 'm neither lady, neither fair,
And home I can go without your care.

(*She releases herself, and exit.*)

FAUST

By Heaven, the girl is wondrous fair!
Of all I 've seen, beyond compare;
So sweetly virtuous and pure,
And yet a little pert, be sure!
The lip so red, the cheek's clear dawn,
I 'll not forget while the world rolls on!   10
How she cast down her timid eyes,
Deep in my heart imprinted lies:
How short and sharp of speech was she,
Why, 't was a real ecstasy!

(MEPHISTOPHELES *enters.*)

FAUST

Hear, of that girl I 'd have possession!

MEPHISTOPHELES

Which, then?

FAUST

The one who just went by.

MEPHISTOPHELES

She, there? She 's coming from confession,
Of every sin absolved; for I,
Behind her chair, was listening nigh.
So innocent is she, indeed,   20
That to confess she had no need.
I have no power o'er souls so green.

FAUST

And yet, she 's older than fourteen.

MEPHISTOPHELES

How now! You 're talking like Jack Rake,
Who every flower for himself would take,
And fancies there are no favors more,
Nor honors, save for him in store;
Yet always does n't the thing succeed.

FAUST

Most Worthy Pedagogue, take heed!
Let not a word of moral law be spoken!   30
I claim, I tell thee, all my right;
And if that image of delight
Rest not within mine arms to-night,
At midnight is our compact broken.

MEPHISTOPHELES

But think, the chances of the case!
I need, at least, a fortnight's space,
To find an opportune occasion.

FAUST

Had I but seven hours for all,
I should not on the Devil call,
But win her by my own persuasion.   40

MEPHISTOPHELES

You almost like a Frenchman prate;
Yet, pray, don't take it as annoyance!
Why, all at once, exhaust the joyance?
Your bliss is by no means so great
As if you 'd use, to get control,
All sorts of tender rigmarole,
And knead and shape her to your thought,
As in Italian tales 't is taught.

FAUST

Without that, I have appetite.

MEPHISTOPHELES

But now, leave jesting out of sight!   50
I tell you, once for all, that speed
With this fair girl will not succeed;
By storm she cannot captured be;
We must make use of strategy.

FAUST

Get me something the angel keeps!
Lead me thither where she sleeps!
Get me a kerchief from her breast,—
A garter that her knee has pressed!

MEPHISTOPHELES

That you may see how much I 'd fain
Further and satisfy your pain,   60
We will no longer lose a minute;
I 'll find her room to-day, and take you in it.

FAUST

And shall I see—possess her?

MEPHISTOPHELES

          No!
Unto a neighbor she must go,
And meanwhile thou, alone, mayst glow
With every hope of future pleasure,
Breathing her atmosphere in fullest measure.

FAUST

Can we go thither?

MEPHISTOPHELES

          'T is too early yet.

FAUST

A gift for her I bid thee get!   (Exit.)

MEPHISTOPHELES

Presents at once? That 's good: he 's certain to get
     at her!   70
Full many a pleasant place I know,
And treasures, buried long ago:
I must, perforce, look up the matter.   (Exit.)

VIII

EVENING

A SMALL, NEATLY KEPT CHAMBER

MARGARET

(plaiting and binding up the braids of her hair)

I 'd something give, could I but say
Who was that gentleman, to-day.

Surely a gallant man was he,
And of a noble family;
So much could I in his face behold,—
And he would n't, else, have been so bold!

          (Exit.)

MEPHISTOPHELES.   FAUST.

MEPHISTOPHELES

Come in, but gently: follow me!

FAUST (after a moment's silence)

Leave me alone, I beg of thee!

MEPHISTOPHELES (prying about)

Not every girl keeps things so neat.

FAUST (looking around)

O welcome, twilight soft and sweet,   10
That breathes throughout this hallowed shrine!
Sweet pain of love, bind thou with fetters fleet
The heart that on the dew of hope must pine!
How all around a sense impresses
Of quiet, order, and content
This poverty what bounty blesses!
What bliss within this narrow den is pent!

(He throws himself into a leather arm-chair near
     the bed.)

Receive me, thou, that in thine open arms
Departed joy and pain wert wont to gather!
How oft the children, with their ruddy charms,   20
Hung here, around this throne, where sat the
     father!
Perchance my love, amid the childish band,
Grateful for gifts the Holy Christmas gave her,
Here meekly kissed the grandsire's withered hand.
I feel, O maid! thy very soul
Of order and content around me whisper,—
Which leads thee with its motherly control,
The cloth upon thy board bids smoothly thee unroll,
The sand beneath thy feet makes whiter, crisper.
O dearest hand, to thee 't is given   30
To change this hut into a lower heaven!
And here!

(He lifts one of the bed-curtains.)
          What sweetest thrill is in my blood!
Here could I spend whole hours, delaying:
Here Nature shaped, as if in sportive playing,
The angel blossom from the bud.

Here lay the child, with Life's warm essence
The tender bosom filled and fair,

And here was wrought, through holier, purer presence.
The form diviner beings wear!

And I? What drew me here with power? 40
How deeply am I moved, this hour!
What seek I? Why so full my heart, and sore?
Miserable Faust! I know thee now no more.

Is there a magic vapor here?
I came, with lust of instant pleasure,
And lie dissolved in dreams of love's sweet leisure!
Are we the sport of every changeful atmosphere?

And if, this moment, came she in to me,
How would I for the fault atonement render!
How small the giant lout would be, 50
Prone at her feet, relaxed and tender!

MEPHISTOPHELES

Be quick! I see her there, returning.

FAUST

Go! go! I never will retreat.

MEPHISTOPHELES

Here is a casket, not unmeet,
Which elsewhere I have just been earning.
Here, set it in the press, with haste!
I swear, 't will turn her head, to spy it:
Some baubles I therein had placed,
That you might win another by it.
True, child is child, and play is play. 60

FAUST

I know not, should I do it?

MEPHISTOPHELES

　　　　　　　　Ask you, pray?
Yourself, perhaps, would keep the bubble?
Then I suggest, 't were fair and just
To spare the lovely day your lust,
And spare to me the further trouble.
You are not miserly, I trust?
I rub my hands, in expectation tender—

(*He places the casket in the press and locks it
again.*)

Now quick, away!
The sweet young maiden to betray,
So that by wish and will you bend her; 70
And you look as though
To the lecture-hall you were forced to go,—
As if stood before you, gray and loath,

Physics and Metaphysics both!
But away!

　　　　　　　　(*Exeunt.*)

MARGARET (*with a lamp*)

It is so close, so sultry, here!

(*She opens the window.*)

And yet 't is not so warm outside.
I feel, I know not why, such fear!—
Would mother came!—where can she bide?
My body 's chill and shuddering,— 80
I 'm but a silly, fearsome thing!

(*She begins to sing, while undressing.*)

　　There was a King in Thule,
　　Was faithful till the grave,—
　　To whom his mistress, dying,
　　A golden goblet gave.

　　Naught was to him more precious;
　　He drained it at every bout:
　　His eyes with tears ran over.
　　As oft as he drank thereout.

　　When came his time of dying, 90
　　The towns in his land he told,
　　Naught else to his heir denying
　　Except the goblet of gold.

　　He sat at the royal banquet
　　With his knights of high degree,
　　In the lofty hall of his fathers
　　In the Castle by the Sea.

　　There stood the old carouser,
　　And drank the last life-glow;
　　And hurled the hallowed goblet 100
　　Into the tide below.

　　He saw it plunging and filling,
　　And sinking deep in the sea:
　　Then fell his eyelids forever,
　　And never more drank he!

(*She opens the press in order to arrange her clothes,
and perceives the casket of jewels.*)

How comes that lovely casket here to me?
I locked the press, most certainly.
'T is truly wonderful! What can within it be?
Perhaps 't was brought by some one as a pawn,
And mother gave a loan thereon? 110
And here there hangs a key to fit:
I have a mind to open it.
What is that? God in Heaven! Whence came

Such things? Never beheld I aught so fair!
Rich ornaments, such as a noble dame
On highest holidays might wear!
How would the pearl-chain suit my hair?
Ah, who may all this splendor own?

(*She adorns herself with the jewelry, and steps before the mirror.*)

Were but the ear-rings mine, alone!
One has at once another air.   120
What helps one's beauty, youthful blood?
One may possess them, well and good;
But none the more do others care.
They praise us half in pity, sure:
To gold still tends,
On gold depends
All, all! Alas, we poor!

IX

PROMENADE

(FAUST, *walking thoughtfully up and down. To him* MEPHISTOPHELES.)

MEPHISTOPHELES

By all love ever rejected! By hell-fire hot and unsparing!
I wish I knew something worse, that I might use it for swearing!

FAUST

What ails thee? What is 't gripes thee, elf?
A face like thine beheld I never.

MEPHISTOPHELES

I would myself unto the Devil deliver,
If I were not a Devil myself!

FAUST

Thy head is out of order, sadly:
It much becomes thee to be raving madly.

MEPHISTOPHELES

Just think, the pocket of a priest should get
The trinkets left for Margaret!   10
The mother saw them, and, instanter,
A secret dread began to haunt her.
Keen scent has she for tainted air;
She snuffs within her book of prayer,
And smells each article, to see
If sacred or profane it be;
So here she guessed, from every gem,
That not much blessing came with them.

"My child," she said, "ill-gotten good
Ensnares the soul, consumes the blood.   20
Before the Mother of God we 'll lay it;
With heavenly manna she 'll repay it!"
But Margaret thought, with sour grimace,
"A gift-horse is not out of place,
And, truly! godless cannot be
The one who brought such things to me."
A parson came, by the mother bidden:
He saw, at once, where the game was hidden,
And viewed it with a favor stealthy.
He spake: "That is the proper view,—   30
Who overcometh, winneth too.
The Holy Church has a stomach healthy:
Hath eaten many a land as forfeit,
And never yet complained of surfeit:
The Church alone, beyond all question,
Has for ill-gotten goods the right digestion."

FAUST

A general practice is the same,
Which Jew and King may also claim.

MEPHISTOPHELES

Then bagged the spangles, chains, and rings,
As if but toadstools were the things,   40
And thanked no less, and thanked no more
Than if a sack of nuts he bore,—
Promised them fullest heavenly pay,
And deeply edified were they.

FAUST

And Margaret?

MEPHISTOPHELES

                    Sits unrestful still,
And knows not what she should, or will;
Thinks on the jewels, day and night,
But more on him who gave her such delight.

FAUST

The darling's sorrow gives me pain.
Get thou a set for her again!   50
The first was not a great display.

MEPHISTOPHELES

O yes, the gentleman finds it all child's-play!

FAUST

Fix and arrange it to my will;
And on her neighbor try thy skill!
Don't be a Devil stiff as paste,
But get fresh jewels to her taste!

MEPHISTOPHELES

Yes, gracious Sir, in all obedience!

(*Exit* FAUST.)

Such an enamored fool in air would blow
Sun, moon, and all the starry legions,
To give his sweetheart a diverting show.   60

(*Exit.*)

X

THE NEIGHBOR'S HOUSE

MARTHA (*solus*)

God forgive my husband, yet he
Has n't done his duty by me!
Off in the world he went straightway,—
Left me lie in the straw where I lay,
And, truly, I did naught to fret him:
God knows I loved, and can't forget him!

(*She weeps.*)

Perhaps he 's even dead! Ah, woe!—
Had I a certificate to show!

MARGARET (*comes*)

Dame Martha!

MARTHA

Margaret! what 's happened thee?

MARGARET

I scarce can stand, my knees are trembling!   10
I find a box, the first resembling,
Within my press! Of ebony,—
And things, all splendid to behold,
And richer far than were the old.

MARTHA

You must n't tell it to your mother!
'T would go to the priest, as did the other.

MARGARET

Ah, look and see—just look and see!

MARTHA (*adorning her*)

O, what a blessed luck for thee!

MARGARET

But, ah! in the streets I dare not bear them,
Nor in the church be seen to wear them.   20

MARTHA

Yet thou canst often this way wander,
And secretly the jewels don,
Walk up and down an hour, before the mirror
    yonder,—
We'll have our private joy thereon.
And then a chance will come, a holiday,
When, piece by piece, can one the things abroad
    display,
A chain at first, then other ornament:
Thy mother will not see, and stories we'll invent.

MARGARET

Whoever could have brought me things so precious?
That something's wrong, I feel suspicious.   30

(*A knock.*)

Good Heaven! My mother can that have been?

MARTHA (*peeping through the blind*)

'T is some strange gentleman.—Come in!

(MEPHISTOPHELES *enters.*)

MEPHISTOPHELES

That I so boldly introduce me,
I beg you, ladies, to excuse me.

(*Steps back reverently, on seeing* MARGARET.)

For Martha Schwerdtlein I'd inquire!

MARTHA

I'm she: what does the gentleman desire?

MEPHISTOPHELES (*aside to her*)

It is enough that you are she:
You 've a visitor of high degree.
Pardon the freedom I have ta'en,—
Will after noon return again.   40

MARTHA (*aloud*)

Of all things in the world! Just hear—
He takes thee for a lady, dear!

MARGARET

I am a creature young and poor:
The gentleman's too kind, I'm sure.
The jewels don't belong to me.

MEPHISTOPHELES

Ah, not alone the jewelry!
The look, the manner, both betray—
Rejoiced am I that I may stay!

MARTHA

What is your business? I would fain—

MEPHISTOPHELES

I would I had a more cheerful strain!   50
Take not unkindly its repeating:
Your husband's dead, and sends a greeting.

MARTHA

Is dead? Alas, that heart so true!
My husband dead! Let me die, too!

MARGARET

Ah, dearest dame, let not your courage fail!

MEPHISTOPHELES

Hear me relate the mournful tale!

MARGARET

Therefore I'd never love, believe me!
A loss like this to death would grieve me.

MEPHISTOPHELES

Joy follows woe, woe after joy comes flying.

MARTHA

Relate his life's sad close to me!   60

MEPHISTOPHELES

In Padua buried, he is lying
Beside the good Saint Antony,
Within a grave well consecrated,
For cool, eternal rest created.

MARTHA

He gave you, further, no commission?

MEPHISTOPHELES

Yes, one of weight, with many sighs:
Three hundred masses buy, to save him from perdition!
My hands are empty, otherwise.

MARTHA

What! Not a pocket-piece? no jewelry?
What every journeyman within his wallet spares,   70
And as a token with him bears,
And rather starves or begs, than loses?

MEPHISTOPHELES

Madam, it is a grief to me;
Yet, on my word, his cash was put to proper uses.

Besides, his penitence was very sore,
And he lamented ill fortune all the more.

MARGARET

Alack, that men are so unfortunate!
Surely for his soul's sake full many a prayer I'll
proffer.

MEPHISTOPHELES

You well deserve a speedy marriage-offer:
You are so kind, compassionate.   80

MARGARET

O, no! As yet, it would not do.

MEPHISTOPHELES

If not a husband, then a beau for you!
It is the greatest heavenly blessing,
To have a dear thing for one's caressing.

MARGARET

The country's custom is not so.

MEPHISTOPHELES

Custom, or not! It happens, though.

MARTHA

Continue, pray!

MEPHISTOPHELES

I stood beside his bed of dying.
'T was something better than manure,—
Half-rotten straw: and yet, he died a Christian, sure,
And found that heavier scores to his account were
lying.   90
He cried: "I find my conduct wholly hateful!
To leave my wife, my trade, in manner so ungrateful!
Ah, the remembrance makes me die!
Would of my wrong to her I might be shriven!"

MARTHA (weeping)

The dear, good man! Long since was he forgiven.

MEPHISTOPHELES

"Yet she, God knows! was more to blame than I."

MARTHA

He lied! What! On the brink of death he slandered?

MEPHISTOPHELES

In the last throes his senses wandered,
If I such things but half can judge.

He said: "I had no time for play, for gaping free-
    dom: 100
First children, and then work for bread to feed
    'em,—
For bread, in the widest sense, to drudge,
And could not even eat my share in peace and
    quiet!"

MARTHA

Had he all love, all faith forgotten in his riot?
My work and worry, day and night?

MEPHISTOPHELES

Not so: the memory of it touched him quite.
Said he: "When I from Malta went away
My prayers for wife and little ones were zealous,
And such a luck from Heaven befell us,
We made a Turkish merchantman our prey,   110
That to the Soldan bore a mighty treasure.
Then I received, as was most fit,
Since bravery was paid in fullest measure,
My well-apportioned share of it."

MARTHA

Say, how? Say, where? If buried, did he own it?

MEPHISTOPHELES

Who knows, now, whither the four winds have
    blown it?
A fair young damsel took him in her care,
As he in Naples wandered round, unfriended;
And she much love, much faith to him did bear,
So that he felt it till his days were ended.   120

MARTHA

The villain! From his children thieving!
Even all the misery on him cast
Could not prevent his shameful way of living!

MEPHISTOPHELES

But see! He's dead therefrom, at last.
Were I in *your* place, do not doubt me,
I'd mourn him decently a year,
And for another keep, meanwhile, my eyes about
    me.

MARTHA

Ah, God! another one so dear
As was my first, this world will hardly give me.
There never was a sweeter fool than mine,   130
Only he loved to roam and leave me,
And foreign wenches and foreign wine,
And the damned throw of dice, indeed.

MEPHISTOPHELES

Well, well! That might have done, however,
If he had only been as clever,
And treated *your* slips with as little heed.
I swear, with this condition, too,
I would, myself, change rings with you.

MARTHA

The gentleman is pleased to jest.

MEPHISTOPHELES (*aside*)

I'll cut away, betimes, from here: 140
She 'd take the Devil at his word, I fear.

(*To* MARGARET.)

How fares the heart within your breast?

MARGARET

What means the gentleman?

MEPHISTOPHELES (*aside*)

               Sweet innocent, thou art!

(*Aloud.*)

Ladies, farewell!

MARGARET

Farewell!

MARTHA

               A moment, ere we part!
I'd like to have a legal witness,
Where, how, and when he died, to certify with
    fitness.
Irregular ways I've always hated;
I want his death in the weekly paper stated.

MEPHISTOPHELES

Yes, my good dame, a pair of witnesses
Always the truth establishes.   150
I have a friend of high condition,
Who'll also add his deposition.
I'll bring him here.

MARTHA

           Good Sir, pray do!

MEPHISTOPHELES

And this young lady will be present, too?
A gallant youth! has travelled far:
Ladies with him delighted are.

MARGARET

Before him I should blush, ashamed.

MEPHISTOPHELES

Before no king that could be named!

MARTHA

Behind the house, in my garden, then,
This eve we'll expect the gentlemen.   160

XI

STREET

FAUST. MEPHISTOPHELES.

FAUST

How is it? under way? and soon complete?

MEPHISTOPHELES

Ah, bravo! Do I find you burning?
Well, Margaret soon will still your yearning:
At Neighbor Martha's you'll this evening meet.
A fitter woman ne'er was made
To ply the pimp and gypsy trade!

FAUST

'T is well.

MEPHISTOPHELES

Yet something is required from us.

FAUST

One service pays the other thus.

MEPHISTOPHELES

We've but to make a deposition valid
That now her husband's limbs, outstretched and
    pallid,   10
At Padua rest, in consecrated soil.

FAUST

Most wise! And first, of course, we'll make the jour-
    ney thither?

MEPHISTOPHELES

Sancta simplicitas! no need of such a toil;
Depose, with knowledge or without it, either!

FAUST

If you've naught better, then, I'll tear your pretty
    plan!

MEPHISTOPHELES

Now, there you are! O holy man!
Is it the first time in your life you're driven
To bear false witness in a case?
Of God, the world and all that in it has a place,
Of Man, and all that moves the being of his race, 20
Have you not terms and definitions given
With brazen forehead, daring breast?
And, if you'll probe the thing profoundly,
Knew you so much—and you'll confess it roundly!—
As here of Schwerdtlein's death and place of rest?

FAUST

Thou art, and thou remain'st, a sophist, liar.

MEPHISTOPHELES

Yes, knew I not more deeply thy desire.
For wilt thou not, no lover fairer,
Poor Margaret flatter, and ensnare her,
And all thy soul's devotion swear her?   30

FAUST

And from my heart.

MEPHISTOPHELES

                'T is very fine!
Thine endless love, thy faith assuring,
The one almighty force enduring,—
Will that, too, prompt this heart of thine?

FAUST

Hold! hold! It will!—If such my flame,
And for the sense and power intense
I seek, and cannot find, a name;
Then range with all my senses through creation,
Craving the speech of inspiration,
And call this ardor, so supernal,   40
Endless, eternal and eternal,—
Is that a devilish lying game?

MEPHISTOPHELES

And yet I'm right!

FAUST

                Mark this, I beg of thee!
And spare my lungs henceforth: whoever
Intends to have the right, if but his tongue be clever,
Will have it, certainly.
But come: the further talking brings disgust,
For thou art right, especially since I must.

XII

GARDEN

(MARGARET *on* FAUST'S *arm.* MARTHA *and* MEPHIS-
TOPHELES *walking up and down.*)

MARGARET

I feel, the gentleman allows for me,
Demeans himself, and shames me by it;
A traveller is so used to be
Kindly content with any diet.
I know too well that my poor gossip can
Ne'er entertain such an experienced man.

FAUST

A look from thee, a word, more entertains
Than all the lore of wisest brains.

(*He kisses her hand.*)

MARGARET

Don't incommode yourself! How could you eve
    kiss it!
It is so ugly, rough to see!   10
What work I do,—how hard and steady is it!
Mother is much too close with me.
                        (*They pass.*)

MARTHA

And you, Sir, travel always, do you not?

MEPHISTOPHELES

Alas, that trade and duty us so harry!
With what a pang one leaves so many a spot,
And dares not even now and then to tarry!

MARTHA

In young, wild years it suits your ways,
This round and round the world in freedom sweep-
    ing;
But then come on the evil days,
And so, as bachelor, into his grave a-creeping,   20
None ever found a thing to praise.

MEPHISTOPHELES

I dread to see how such a fate advances.

MARTHA

Then, worthy Sir, improve betimes your chances!
                        (*They pass.*)

MARGARET

Yes, out of sight is out of mind!
Your courtesy an easy grace is;
But you have friends in other places,
And sensibler than I, you'll find.

FAUST

Trust me, dear heart! what men call sensible
Is oft mere vanity and narrowness.

MARGARET

                        How so?

FAUST

Ah, that simplicity and innocence ne'er know   30
Themselves, their holy value, and their spell!
That meekness, lowliness, the highest graces
Which Nature portions out so lovingly—

MARGARET

So you but think a moment's space on me,
All times I'll have to think on you, all places!

FAUST

No doubt you're much alone?

MARGARET

Yes, for our household small has grown,
Yet must be cared for, you will own.
We have no maid: I do the knitting, sewing, sweep-
    ing,
The cooking, early work and late, in fact;   40
And mother, in her notions of housekeeping,
Is so exact!
Not that she needs so much to keep expenses down:
We, more than others, might take comfort, rather:
A nice estate was left us by my father,
A house, a little garden near the town.
But now my days have less of noise and hurry;
My brother is a soldier,
My little sister's dead.
True, with the child a troubled life I led,   50
Yet I would take again, and willing, all the worry,
So very dear was she.

FAUST

                    An angel, if like thee!

MARGARET

I brought it up, and it was fond of me.
Father had died before it saw the light,
And mother's case seemed hopeless quite,
So weak and miserable she lay;

And she recovered, then, so slowly, day by day.
She could not think, herself, of giving
The poor wee thing its natural living;
And so I nursed it all alone   60
With milk and water: 't was my own.
Lulled in my lap with many a song,
It smiled, and tumbled, and grew strong.

FAUST

The purest bliss was surely then thy dower.

MARGARET

But surely, also, many a weary hour.
I kept the baby's cradle near
My bed at night: if 't even stirred, I'd guess it,
And waking, hear.
And I must nurse it, warm beside me press it,
And oft, to quiet it, my bed forsake,   70
And dandling back and forth the restless creature
    take,
Then at the wash-tub stand, at morning's break;
And then the marketing and kitchen-tending,
Day after day, the same thing, never-ending.
One's spirits, Sir, are thus not always good,
But then one learns to relish rest and food.

                        (They pass.)

MARTHA

Yes, the poor women are bad off, 't is true:
And stubborn bachelor there's no converting.

MEPHISTOPHELES

It but depends upon the like of you,
And I should turn to better ways than flirting.   80

MARTHA

Speak plainly, Sir, have you no one detected?
Has not your heart been anywhere subjected?

MEPHISTOPHELES

The proverb says: One's own warm hearth
And a good wife, are gold and jewels worth.

MARTHA

I mean, have you not felt desire, though ne'er so
    slightly?

MEPHISTOPHELES

I've everywhere, in fact, been entertained politely.

MARTHA

I meant to say, were you not touched in earnest,
    ever?

MEPHISTOPHELES

One should allow one's self to jest with ladies never.

MARTHA

Ah, you don't understand!

MEPHISTOPHELES

                    I'm sorry I'm so blind:
But I am sure—that you are very kind.   90

                        (They pass.)

FAUST

And me, thou angel! didst thou recognize,
As through the garden-gate I came?

MARGARET

Did you not see it? I cast down my eyes.

FAUST

And thou forgiv'st my freedom, and the blame
To my impertinence befitting,
As the Cathedral thou wert quitting?

MARGARET

I was confused, the like ne'er happened me;
No one could ever speak to my discredit.
Ah, thought I, in my conduct has he read it—
Something immodest or unseemly free?   100
He seemed to have the sudden feeling
That with this wench 't were very easy dealing.
I will confess, I knew not what appeal
On your behalf, here, in my bosom grew;
But I was angry with myself, to feel
That I could not be angrier with you.

FAUST

Sweet darling!

MARGARET

                    Wait a while!

(She plucks a star-flower, and pulls off the leaves,
    one after the other.)

FAUST

                    Shall that a nosegay be?

MARGARET

No, it is just in play.

FAUST

                    How?

MARGARET

Go! you'll laugh at me.

(*She pulls off the leaves and murmurs.*)

FAUST

What murmurest thou?

MARGARET (*half aloud*)

He loves me—loves me not.

FAUST

Thou sweet, angelic soul!   110

MARGARET (*continues*)

Loves me—not—loves me—not—

(*plucking the last leaf, she cries with frank delight:*)

He loves me!

FAUST

Yes, child! and let this blossom-word
For thee be speech divine! He loves thee!
Ah, know'st thou what it means? He loves thee!

(*He grasps both her hands.*)

MARGARET

I'm all a-tremble!

FAUST

O tremble not! but let this look,
Let this warm clasp of hands declare thee
What is unspeakable!
To yield one wholly, and to feel a rapture
In yielding, that must be eternal!
Eternal!—for the end would be despair.   120
No, no—no ending! no ending!

MARTHA (*coming forward*)

The night is falling.

MEPHISTOPHELES

Ay! we must away.

MARTHA

I'd ask you, longer here to tarry,
But evil tongues in this town have full play.
It's as if nobody had nothing to fetch and carry,
Nor other labor,
But spying all the doings of one's neighbor:
And one becomes the talk, do whatsoe'er one may.
Where is our couple now?

MEPHISTOPHELES

Flown up the alley yonder,
The wilful summer-birds!

MARTHA

He seems of her still fonder.   130

MEPHISTOPHELES

And she of him. So runs the world away!

XIII

A GARDEN-ARBOR

(MARGARET *comes in, conceals herself behind the door, puts her finger to her lips, and peeps through the crack.*)

MARGARET

He comes!

FAUST (*entering*)

Ah, rogue! a tease thou art:
I have thee!

(*He kisses her.*)

MARGARET
(*clasping him, and returning the kiss*)

Dearest man! I love thee from my heart.

(MEPHISTOPHELES *knocks.*)

FAUST (*stamping his foot*)

Who's there?

MEPHISTOPHELES

A friend!

FAUST

A beast!

MEPHISTOPHELES

'T is time to separate.

MARTHA (*coming*)

Yes, Sir, 't is late.

FAUST

May I not, then, upon you wait?

MARGARET

My mother would—farewell!

FAUST

> Ah, can I not remain?

Farewell!

MARTHA

> Adieu!

MARGARET

> And soon to meet again!

(*Exeunt* FAUST *and* MEPHISTOPHELES.)

MARGARET

Dear God! However is it, such
A man can think and know so much?
I stand ashamed and in amaze,
And answer "Yes" to all he says,   10
A poor, unknowing child! and he—
I can't think what he finds in me!

> (*Exit.*)

XIV

FOREST AND CAVERN

FAUST (*solus*)

Spirit sublime, thou gav'st me, gav'st me all
For which I prayed. Not unto me in vain
Hast thou thy countenance revealed in fire.
Thou gav'st me Nature as a kingdom grand,
With power to feel and to enjoy it. Thou
Not only cold, amazed acquaintance yield'st,
But grantest, that in her profoundest breast
I gaze, as in the bosom of a friend.
The ranks of living creatures thou dost lead
Before me, teaching me to know my brothers   10
In air and water and the silent wood.
And when the storm in forests roars and grinds,
The giant firs, in falling, neighbor boughs
And neighbor trunks with crushing weight bear
    down,
And falling, fill the hills with hollow thunders,—
Then to the cave secure thou leadest me,
Then show'st me mine own self, and in my breast
The deep, mysterious miracles unfold.
And when the perfect moon before my gaze
Comes up with soothing light, around me float   20
From every precipice and thicket damp
The silvery phantoms of the ages past,
And temper the austere delight of thought.

That nothing can be perfect unto Man
I now am conscious. With this ecstasy,
Which brings me near and nearer to the Gods,

Thou gav'st the comrade, whom I now no more
Can do without, though, cold and scornful, he
Demeans me to myself, and with a breath,
A word, transforms thy gifts to nothingness.   30
Within my breast he fans a lawless fire,
Unwearied, for that fair and lovely form:
Thus in desire I hasten to enjoyment,
And in enjoyment pine to feel desire.

(MEPHISTOPHELES *enters.*)

MEPHISTOPHELES

Have you not led this life quite long enough?
How can a further test delight you?
'T is very well, that once one tries the stuff,
But something new must then requite you.

FAUST

Would there were other work for thee!
To plague my day auspicious thou returnest.   40

MEPHISTOPHELES

Well! I'll engage to let thee be:
Thou darest not tell me so in earnest.
The loss of thee were truly very slight,—
A comrade crazy, rude, repelling:
One has one's hands full all the day and night;
If what one does, or leaves undone, is right,
From such a face as thine there is no telling.

FAUST

There is, again, thy proper tone!—
That thou hast bored me, I must thankful be!

MEPHISTOPHELES

Poor Son of Earth, how couldst thou thus alone   50
Have led thy life, bereft of me?
I, for a time, at least, have worked thy cure;
Thy fancy's rickets plague thee not at all:
Had I not been, so hadst thou, sure,
Walked thyself off this earthly ball.
Why here to caverns, rocky hollows slinking,
Sit'st thou, as 't were an owl a-blinking?
Why suck'st, from sodden moss and dripping stone,
Toad-like, thy nourishment alone?
A fine way, this, thy time to fill!   60
The Doctor's in thy body still.

FAUST

What fresh and vital forces, canst thou guess,
Spring from my commerce with the wilderness?
But, if thou hadst the power of guessing,
Thou wouldst be devil enough to grudge my soul
    the blessing.

MEPHISTOPHELES

A blessing drawn from supernatural fountains!
In night and dew to lie upon the mountains;
All Heaven and Earth in rapture penetrating;
Thyself to Godhood haughtily inflating;
To grub with yearning force through Earth's dark   70
      marrow,
Compress the six days' work within thy bosom nar-
      row,—
To taste, I know not what, in haughty power,
Thine own ecstatic life on all things shower,
Thine earthly self behind thee cast,
And then the lofty instinct, thus—

(*With a gesture:*)

                                    at last,—
I dare n't say how—to pluck the final flower!

FAUST

Shame on thee!

MEPHISTOPHELES

                Yes, thou findest that unpleasant!
Thou hast the moral right to cry me "shame!" at
      present.
One dares not that before chaste ears declare,
Which chaste hearts, notwithstanding, cannot
      spare;   80
And, once for all, I grudge thee not the pleasure
Of lying to thyself in moderate measure.
But such a course thou wilt not long endure;
Already art thou o'er-excited,
And, if at last, wilt soon be plighted
To madness and to horror, sure.
Enough of that! Thy love sits lonely yonder,
By all things saddened and oppressed;
Her thoughts and yearnings seek thee, tenderer,
      fonder,—
A mighty love is in her breast.   90
First came thy passion's flood and poured around
      her
As when from melted snow a streamlet overflows;
Thou hast therewith so filled and drowned her,
That now *thy* stream all shallow shows.
Methinks, instead of in the forests lording,
The noble Sir should find it good,
The love of this young silly blood
At once to set about rewarding.
Her time is miserably long;
She haunts her window, watching clouds that
      stray   100
O'er the old city-wall, and far away.
"Were I a little bird!" so runs her song,

Day long, and half night long.
Now she is lively, mostly sad,
Now, wept beyond her tears;
Then again quiet she appears,—
Always love-mad.

FAUST

Serpent! serpen'

MEPHISTOPHELES (*aside*)

Ha! do I trap thee!

FAUST

Get thee away with thine offences,   110
Reprobate! Name not that fairest thing.
Nor the desire for her sweet body bring
Again before my half-distracted senses!

MEPHISTOPHELES

What wouldst thou, then? She thinks that thou art
      flown;
And half and half thou art, I own.

FAUST

Yet am I near, and love keeps watch and ward;
Though I were ne'er so far, it cannot falter:
I envy even the Body of the Lord
The touching of her lips, before the altar.

MEPHISTOPHELES

'T is very well! *My* envy oft reposes   120
On your twin-pair, that feed among the roses.

FAUST

Away, thou pimp!

MEPHISTOPHELES

                You rail, and it is fun to me.
The God, who fashioned youth and maid,
Perceived the noblest purpose of His trade,
And also made their opportunity.
Go on! It is a woe profound!
'T is for your sweetheart's room you're bound,
And not for death, indeed.

FAUST

What are, within her arms, the heavenly blisses?
Though I be glowing with her kisses,   130
Do I not always share her need?
I am the fugitive, all houseless roaming,
The monster without aim or rest,
That like a cataract, down rocks and gorges foam-
      ing,

Leaps, maddened, into the abyss's breast!
And side-wards she, with unwakened senses,
Within her cabin on the Alpine field
Her simple, homely life commences,
Her little world therein concealed.
And I, God's hate flung o'er me,   140
Had not enough, to thrust
The stubborn rocks before me
And strike them into dust!
She and her peace I yet must undermine:
Thou, Hell, hast claimed this sacrifice as thine!
Help, Devil! through the coming pangs to push me;
What must be, let it quickly be!
Let fall on me her fate, and also crush me,—
One ruin whelm both her and me!

MEPHISTOPHELES

Again it seethes, again it glows!   150
Thou fool, go in and comfort her!
When such a head as thine no outlet knows,
It thinks the end must soon occur.
Hail him, who keeps a steadfast mind!
Thou, else, dost well the devil-nature wear:
Naught so insipid in the world I find
As is a devil in despair.

XV

MARGARET'S ROOM

MARGARET

(at the spinning-wheel, alone)

My peace is gone,
My heart is sore:
I never shall find it
Ah, nevermore!

Save I have him near,
The grave is here;
The world is gall
And bitterness all.

My poor weak head
Is racked and crazed;   10
My thought is lost,
My senses mazed.

My peace is gone,
My heart is sore:
I never shall find it,
Ah, nevermore!

To see him, him only,
At the pane I sit;

To meet him, him only,
The house I quit.   20

His lofty gait,
His noble size,
The smiles of his mouth,
The power of his eyes,

And the magic flow
Of his talk, the bliss
In the clasp of his hand,
And, ah! his kiss!

My peace is gone
My heart is sore: 30
I never shall find it,
Ah, nevermore!

My bosom yearns
For him alone;
Ah, dared I clasp him,
And hold, and own!

And kiss his mouth,
To heart's desire,
And on his kisses
At last expire!   40

XVI

MARTHA'S GARDEN

MARGARET. FAUST.

MARGARET

Promise me, Henry!—

FAUST

What I can!

MARGARET

How is 't with thy religion, pray?
Thou art a dear, good-hearted man,
And yet, I think, dost not incline that way.

FAUST

Leave that, my child! Thou know'st my love is
        tender;
For love, my blood and life would I surrender,
And as for Faith and Church, I grant to each his
        own.

MARGARET

That's not enough: we must believe thereon.

FAUST

Must we?

MARGARET

Would that I had some influence!
Then, too, thou honorest not the Holy Sacraments.   10

FAUST

I honor them.

MARGARET

Desiring no possession.
'T is long since thou hast been to mass or to con-
fession,
Believest thou in God?

FAUST

My darling, who shall dare
"I believe in God!" to say?
Ask priest or sage the answer to declare,
And it will seem a mocking play,
A sarcasm on the asker.

MARGARET

Then thou believest not!

FAUST

Hear me not falsely, sweetest countenance!
Who dare express Him?
And who profess Him,   20
Saying: I believe in Him!
Who, feeling, seeing,
Deny His being,
Saying: I believe Him not!
The All-enfolding,
The All-upholding,
Folds and upholds he not
Thee, me, Himself?
Arches not there the sky above us?
Lies not beneath us, firm, the earth?   30
And rise not, on us shining,
Friendly, the everlasting stars?
Look I not, eye to eye, on thee,
And feel'st not, thronging
To head and heart, the force,
Still weaving its eternal secret,
Invisible, visible, round thy life?
Vast as it is, fill with that force thy heart,
And when thou in the feeling wholly blessed art,
Call it, then, what thou wilt,—   40
Call it Bliss! Heart! Love! God!
I have no name to give it!

Feeling is all in all:
The Name is sound and smoke,
Obscuring Heaven's clear glow.

MARGARET

All that is fine and good, to hear it so:
Much the same way the preacher spoke,
Only with slightly different phrases.

FAUST

The same thing, in all places,
All hearts that beat beneath the heavenly day—   50
Each in its language—say;
Then why not I, in mine, as well?

MARGARET

To hear it thus, it may seem passable;
And yet, some hitch in 't there must be
For thou hast no Christianity.

FAUST

Dear love!

MARGARET

I've long been grieved to see
That thou art in such company.

FAUST

How so?

MARGARET

The man who with thee goes, thy mate.
Within my deepest, inmost soul I hate.
In all my life there's nothing   60
Has given my heart so keen a pang of loathing,
As his repulsive face has done.

FAUST

Nay, fear him not, my sweetest one!

MARGARET

I feel his presence like something ill.
I've else, for all, a kindly will,
But, much as my heart to see thee yearneth,
The secret horror of him returneth;
And I think the man a knave, as I live!
If I do him wrong, may God forgive!

FAUST

There must be such queer birds, however.   70

MARGARET

Live with the like of him, may I never!
When once inside the door comes he,
He looks around so sneeringly,

And half in wrath:
One sees that in nothing no interest he hath:
'T is written on his very forehead
That love to him, is a thing abhorréd.
I am so happy on thine arm,
So free, so yielding, and so warm,
And in his presence stifled seems my heart.   80

FAUST

Foreboding angel that thou art!

MARGARET

It overcomes me in such degree,
That wheresoe'er he meets us, even,
I feel as though I'd lost my love for thee.
When he is by, I could not pray to Heaven.
That burns within me like a flame,
And surely, Henry, 't is with thee the same.

FAUST

There, now, is thine antipathy!

MARGARET

But I must go.

FAUST

Ah, shall there never be
A quiet hour, to see us fondly plighted,   90
With breast to breast, and soul to soul united?

MARGARET

Ah, if I only slept alone!
I'd draw the bolts to-night, for thy desire;
But mother's sleep so light has grown,
And if we were discovered by her,
'T would be my death upon the spot!

FAUST

Thou angel, fear it not!
Here is a phial: in her drink
But three drops of it measure,
And deepest sleep will on her senses sink.   100

MARGARET

What would I not, to give thee pleasure?
It will not harm her, when one tries it?

FAUST

If 't would, my love, would I advise it?

MARGARET

Ah, dearest man, if but thy face I see,
I know not what compels me to thy will:

So much have I already done for thee,
That scarcely more is left me to fulfil.

(*Exit.*)

(*Enter* MEPHISTOPHELES.)

MEPHISTOPHELES

The monkey [32]! Is she gone?

FAUST

Hast played the spy again?

MEPHISTOPHELES

I've heard, most fully, how she drew thee.
The Doctor has been catechised, 't is plain;   110
Great good, I hope, the thing will do thee.
The girls have much desire to ascertain
If one is prim and good, as ancient rules compel:
If there he's led, they think, he'll follow them as
     well.

FAUST

Thou, monster, wilt nor see nor own
How this pure soul, of faith so lowly,
So loving and ineffable,—
The faith alone
That her salvation is,—with scruples holy
Pines, lest she hold as lost the man she loves so
     well!   120

MEPHISTOPHELES

Thou, full of sensual, super-sensual desire,
A girl by the nose is leading thee.

FAUST

Abortion, thou, of filth and fire!

MEPHISTOPHELES

And then, how masterly she reads physiognomy!
When I am present she's impressed, she knows not
     how;
She in my mask a hidden sense would read:
She feels that surely I'm a genius now,—
Perhaps the very Devil, indeed!
Well, well,—to-night—?

FAUST

What's that to thee?

MEPHISTOPHELES

Yet my delight 't will also be!   130

[32] A term of endearment. "Kitten" might have been a
more adequate translation of the German *Grasaffe*.

XVII

AT THE FOUNTAIN

MARGARET *and* LISBETH *with pitchers.*

LISBETH

Hast nothing heard of Barbara?

MARGARET

No, not a word. I go so little out.

LISBETH

It's true, Sibylla said, to-day.
She's played the fool at last, there's not a doubt.
Such taking on of airs!

MARGARET

How so?

LISBETH

It stinks!
She's feeding two, whene'er she eats and drinks.

MARGARET

Ah!

LISBETH

And so, at last, it serves her rightly.
She clung to the fellow so long and tightly!
That was a promenading!
At village and dance parading!   10
As the first they must everywhere shine,
And he treated her always to pies and wine,
And she made a to-do with her face so fine;
So mean and shameless was her behavior,
She took all the presents the fellow gave her.
'T was kissing and coddling, on and on!
So now, at the end, the flower is gone.

MARGARET

The poor, poor thing!

LISBETH

Dost pity her, at that?
When one of us at spinning sat,
And mother, nights, ne'er let us out the door   20
She sported with her paramour.
On the door-bench, in the passage dark,
The length of the time they'd never mark.
So now her head no more she'll lift,
But do church-penance in her sinner's shift!

MARGARET

He'll surely take her for his wife.

LISBETH

He'd be a fool! A brisk young blade
Has room, elsewhere, to ply his trade.
Besides, he's gone.

MARGARET

That is not fair!

LISBETH

If him she gets, why let her beware!   30
The boys shall dash her wreath on the floor,
And we'll scatter chaff before her door!

(*Exit.*)

MARGARET (*returning home*)

How scornfully I once reviled,
When some poor maiden was beguiled!
More speech than any tongue suffices
I craved, to censure others' vices.
Black as it seemed, I blackened still,
And blacker yet was in my will;
And blessed myself, and boasted high,—
And now—a living sin am I!   40
Yet—all that drove my heart thereto,
God! was so good, so dear, so true!

XVIII

DONJON

(*In a niche of the wall a shrine, with an image of
the Mater Dolorosa. Pots of flowers before it.*)

MARGARET

(*putting fresh flowers in the pots*)

Incline, O Maiden,
Thou sorrow-laden,
Thy gracious countenance upon my pain!

The sword Thy heart in,
With anguish smarting,
Thou lookest up to where Thy Son is slain!

Thou seest the Father;
Thy sad sighs gather,
And bear aloft Thy sorrow and His pain!

Ah, past guessing,   10
Beyond expressing,
The pangs that wring my flesh and bone!

Why this anxious heart so burneth,
Why it trembleth, why it yearneth,
Knowest Thou, and Thou alone!

Where'er I go, what sorrow,
What woe, what woe and sorrow
Within my bosom aches!
Alone, and ah! unsleeping,
I'm weeping, weeping, weeping,   20
The heart within me breaks.

The pots before my window,
Alas! my tears did wet,
As in the early morning
For thee these flowers I set.

Within my lonely chamber
The morning sun shone red:
I sat, in utter sorrow,
Already on my bed.

Help! rescue me from death and stain!   30
O Maiden!
Thou sorrow-laden,
Incline Thy countenance upon my pain!

XIX

NIGHT

STREET BEFORE MARGARET'S DOOR.

VALENTINE

(*a soldier*, MARGARET'S *brother*)

When I have sat some carouse,
Where each to each his brag allows,
And many a comrade praised to me
His pink of girls right lustily,
With brimming glass that spilled the toast,
And elbows planted as in boast:
I sat in unconcerned repose,
And heard the swagger as it rose.
And stroking then my beard, I 'd say,
Smiling, the bumper in my hand: 10
"Each well enough in her own way,
But is there one in all the land
Like sister Margaret, good as gold,—
One that to her can a candle hold?"
Cling! clang! "Here 's to her!" went around
The board: "He speaks the truth!" cried some;
"In her the flower o' the sex is found!"
And all the swaggerers were dumb.
And now!—I could tear my hair with vexation,
And dash out my brains in desperation!   20
With turned-up nose each scamp may face me,

With sneers and stinging taunts disgrace me,
And, like a bankrupt debtor sitting,
A chance-dropped word may set me sweating!
Yet, though I thresh them all together,
I cannot call them liars, either.

But what comes sneaking, there, to view?
If I mistake not, there are two.
If *he's* one, let me at him drive!
He shall not leave the spot alive.   30

FAUST. MEPHISTOPHELES.

FAUST

How from the window of the sacristy
Upward th' eternal lamp sends forth a glimmer,
That, lessening side-wards, fainter grows and dim-
    mer,
Till darkness closes from the sky!
The shadows thus within my bosom gather.

MEPHISTOPHELES

I'm like a sentimental tom-cat, rather,
That round the tall fire-ladders sweeps,
And stealthy, then, along the coping creeps:
Quite virtuous, withal, I come,
A little thievish and a little frolicsome.   40
I feel in every limb the presage
Forerunning the grand Walpurgis-Night:
Day after to-morrow brings its message,
And one keeps watch then with delight.

FAUST

Meanwhile, may not the treasure risen be,
Which there, behind, I glimmering [33] see?

MEPHISTOPHELES

Shalt soon experience the pleasure,
To lift the kettle with its treasure.
I lately gave therein a squint—
Saw splendid lion-dollars in 't.   50

FAUST

Not even a jewel, not a ring,
To deck therewith my darling girl?

MEPHISTOPHELES

I saw, among the rest, a thing
That seemed to be a chain of pearl.

[33] According to German folklore, a phosphorescent light
hovered over buried treasure.

FAUST

That's well, indeed! For painful is it
To bring no gift when her I visit.

MEPHISTOPHELES

Thou shouldst not find it so annoying,
Without return to be enjoying.
Now, while the sky leads forth its starry throng,
Thou 'lt hear a masterpiece, no work completer: 60
I'll sing her, first, a moral song,
The surer, afterwards, to cheat her.

(*Sings* [34] *to the cither.*)

What dost thou here
In daybreak clear,
Kathrina dear,
Before thy lover's door?
Beware! the blade
Lets in a maid,
That out a maid
Departeth nevermore! 70

The coaxing shun
Of such an one!
When once 't is done
Good-night to thee, poor thing!
Love's time is brief:
Unto no thief
Be warm and lief,
But with the wedding-ring!

VALENTINE (*comes forward*)

Whom wilt thou lure? God's-element!
Rat-catching piper, thou!—perdition!
To the Devil, first, the instrument!
To the Devil, then, the curst musician!

MEPHISTOPHELES

The cither's smashed! For nothing more 't is fitting.

VALENTINE

There's yet a skull I must be splitting!

MEPHISTOPHELES (*to* FAUST)

Sir Doctor, don't retreat, I pray!
Stand by: I'll lead, if you'll but tarry:
Out with your spit, without delay!
You've but to lunge, and I will parry.

VALENTINE

Then parry that!

[34] Adapted from Ophelia's song in *Hamlet*, Act IV,
Scene 5.

MEPHISTOPHELES

Why not? 't is light.

VALENTINE

That too!

MEPHISTOPHELES

Of course.

VALENTINE

I think the Devil must fight! 90
How is it, then? my hand's already lame.

MEPHISTOPHELES (*to* FAUST)

Thrust home!

VALENTINE (*falls*)

O God!

MEPHISTOPHELES

Now is the lubber tame!
But come, away! 'T is time for us to fly;
For there arises now a murderous cry.
With the police 't were easy to compound it,
But here the penal court [35] will sift and sound it.

(*Exit with* FAUST)

MARTHA (*at the window*)

Come out! come out!

MARGARET (*at the window*)

Quick, bring a light!

MARTHA (*as above*)

They swear and storm, they yell and fight!

PEOPLE

Here lies one dead already—see!

MARTHA (*coming from the house*)

The murderers, whither have they run? 100

MARGARET (*coming out*)

Who lies here?

PEOPLE

'T is thy mother's son!

[35] The Penal Court derived its power, according to legend, from God. Therefore Mephistopheles could do nothing about it, though he could control the police.

MARGARET

Almighty God! what misery!

VALENTINE

I'm dying! That is quickly said,
And quicker yet 't is done.
Why howl, you women there? Instead,
Come here and listen, every one!

(*All gather around him.*)

My Margaret, see! still young thou art,
But not the least bit shrewd or smart,
Thy business thus to slight:
So this advice I bid thee heed—   110
Now that thou art a whore indeed,
Why, be one then, outright!

MARGARET

My brother! God! such words to me?

VALENTINE

In this game let our Lord God be!
What's done's already done, alas!
What follows it, must come to pass.
With one begin'st thou secretly,
Then soon will others come to thee,
And when a dozen thee have known,
Thou 'rt also free to all the town.   120

When Shame is born and first appears,
She is in secret brought to light,
And then they draw the veil of night
Over her head and ears;
Her life, in fact, they 're loath to spare her.
But let her growth and strength display,
She walks abroad unveiled by day,
Yet is not grown a whit the fairer.
The uglier she is to sight,
The more she seeks the day's broad light.   130
The time I verily can discern
When all the honest folk will turn
From thee, thou jade! and seek protection
As from a corpse that breeds infection.
Thy guilty heart shall then dismay thee,
When they but look thee in the face:—
Shalt not in a golden chain array thee,
Nor at the altar take thy place!
Shalt not, in lace and ribbons flowing,
Make merry when the dance is going!   140
But in some corner, woe betide thee!
Among the beggars and cripples hide thee;
And so, though even God forgive,
On earth a damned existence live!

MARTHA

Commend your soul to God for pardon,
That you your heart with slander harden!

VALENTINE

Thou pimp most infamous, be still!
Could I thy withered body kill,
'T would bring, for all my sinful pleasure,
Forgiveness in the richest measure.   150

MARGARET

My brother! This is Hell's own pain!

VALENTINE

I tell thee, from thy tears refrain!
When thou from honor didst depart
It stabbed me to the very heart.
Now through the slumber of the grave
I go to God as a soldier brave.
(*Dies.*)

XX

CATHEDRAL

SERVICE, ORGAN AND ANTHEM.

(MARGARET *among much people: the* EVIL SPIRIT
behind MARGARET.)

EVIL SPIRIT

How otherwise was it, Margaret,
When thou, still innocent,
Here at the altar cam'st,
And from the worn and fingered book
Thy prayers didst prattle,
Half sport of childhood,
Half God within thee!
Margaret!
Where tends thy thought?
Within thy bosom   10
What hidden crime?
Pray'st thou for mercy on thy mother's soul,
That fell asleep to long, long torment, and through
    thee?
Upon thy threshold whose the blood?
And stirreth not and quickens
Something beneath thy heart,
Thy life disquieting
With most foreboding presence?

MARGARET

Woe! woe!
Would I were free from the thoughts   20

That cross me, drawing hither and thither,
Despite me!

CHORUS

Dies irae, dies illa,
Solvet saeclum in favilla! [36]
(Sound of the organ.)

EVIL SPIRIT

Wrath takes thee!
The trumpet peals!
The graves tremble!
And thy heart
From ashy rest
To fiery torments   30
Now again requickened,
Throbs to life!

MARGARET

Would I were forth!
I feel as if the organ here
My breath takes from me,
My very heart
Dissolved by the anthem!

CHORUS

Judex ergo cum sedebit,
Quidquid latet, adparebit,
Nil inultum remanebit. [37]   40

MARGARET

I cannot breathe!
The massy pillars
Imprison me!
The vaulted arches
Crush me!—Air!

EVIL SPIRIT

Hide thyself! Sin and shame
Stay never hidden.
Air? Light?
Woe to thee!

CHORUS

Quid sum miser tunc dicturus,   50
Quem patronum rogaturus,
Cum vix justus sit securus? [37]

EVIL SPIRIT

They turn their faces,
The glorified, from thee:

[36] See Vol. I, p. 400, for a translation of this celebrated hymn.
[37] Other stanzas from the *Dies Irae.*

The pure, their hands to offer,
Shuddering, refuse thee!
Woe!

CHORUS

Quid sum miser tunc dicturus?

MARGARET

Neighbor! your cordial! [38]
(She falls in a swoon.)

XXI

WALPURGIS-NIGHT

THE HARTZ [39] MOUNTAINS.

District of Schierke and Elend.

FAUST. MEPHISTOPHELES.

MEPHISTOPHELES

Dost thou not wish a broomstick-steed's assistance?
The sturdiest he-goat I would gladly see:
The way we take, our goal is yet some distance.

FAUST

So long as in my legs I feel the fresh existence,
This knotted staff suffices me.
What need to shorten so the way?
Along this labyrinth of vales to wander,
Then climb the rocky ramparts yonder,
Wherefrom the fountain flings eternal spray,
Is such delight, my steps would fain delay.   10
The spring-time stirs within the fragrant birches,
And even the fir-tree feels it now:
Should then our limbs escape its gentle searches?

MEPHISTOPHELES

I notice no such thing, I vow!
'T is winter still within my body:
Upon my path I wish for frost and snow.
How sadly rises, incomplete and ruddy,
The moon's lone disk, with its belated glow,
And lights so dimly, that, as one advances,
At every step one strikes a rock or tree!   20
Let us, then, use a Jack-o'-lantern's [40] glances:
I see one yonder, burning merrily.
Ho, there! my friend! I'll levy thine attendance:
Why waste so vainly thy resplendence?
Be kind enough to light us up the steep!

[38] Smelling salts.
[39] This scene takes place on the Brocken, the highest of the Hartz Mountains.
[40] In German folklore, an evil spirit which lures travelers from their way and leads them to destruction.

WILL-O'-THE-WISP

My reverence, I hope, will me enable
To curb my temperament unstable;
For zigzag courses we are wont to keep.

MEPHISTOPHELES

Indeed? he'd like mankind to imitate!
Now, in the Devil's name, go straight,   30
Or I'll blow out his being's flickering spark!

WILL-O'-THE-WISP

You are the master of the house, I mark,
And I shall try to serve you nicely.
But then, reflect: the mountain's magic-mad to-day,
And if a will-o'-the-wisp must guide you on the way,
You must n't take things too precisely.

FAUST, MEPHISTOPHELES, WILL-O'-THE-WISP
(in alternating song)

We, it seems, have entered newly
In the sphere of dreams enchanted.
Do thy bidding, guide us truly,
That our feet be forwards planted   40
In the vast, the desert spaces!

See them swiftly changing places,
Trees on trees beside us trooping,
And the crags above us stooping,
And the rocky snouts, outgrowing,—
Hear them snoring, hear them blowing!
O'er the stones, the grasses, flowing
Stream and streamlet seek the hollow.
Hear I noises? songs that follow?
Hear I tender love-petitions?   50
Voices of those heavenly visions?
Sounds of hope, of love undying!
And the echoes, like traditions
Of old days, come faint and hollow.

Hoo-hoo! Shoo-hoo! Nearer hover
Jay and screech-owl, and the plover,—
Are they all awake and crying?
Is 't the salamander pushes,
Bloated-bellied, through the bushes?
And the roots, like serpents twisted,   60
Through the sand and boulders toiling,
Fright us, weirdest links uncoiling
To entrap us, unresisted:
Living knots and gnarls uncanny
Feel with polypus-antennae
For the wanderer. Mice are flying,
Thousand-colored, herd-wise hieing
Through the moss and through the heather!

And the fire-flies wink and darkle,
Crowded swarms that soar and sparkle,   70
And in wildering escort gather!

Tell me, if we still are standing
Or if further we're ascending?
All is turning, whirling, blending,
Trees and rocks with grinning faces,
Wandering lights that spin in mazes,
Still increasing and expanding!

MEPHISTOPHELES

Grasp my skirt with heart undaunted!
Here a middle-peak is planted,
Whence one seëth, with amaze,   80
Mammon in the mountain blaze.

FAUST

How strangely glimmers through the hollows
A dreary light,[41] like that of dawn!
Its exhalation tracks and follows
The deepest gorges, faint and wan.
Here steam, there rolling vapor sweepeth;
Here burns the glow through film and haze:
Now like a tender thread it creepeth,
Now like a fountain leaps and plays.
Here winds away, and in a hundred   90
Divided veins the valley braids:
There, in a corner pressed and sundered,
Itself detaches, spreads and fades.
Here gush the sparkles incandescent
Like scattered showers of golden sand;—
But, see! in all their height, at present,
The rocky ramparts blazing stand.

MEPHISTOPHELES

Has not Sir Mammon grandly lighted
His palace for this festal night?
'T is lucky thou hast seen the sight;   100
The boisterous guests approach that were invited.

FAUST

How raves the tempest through the air!
With what fierce blows upon my neck 't is beating!

MEPHISTOPHELES

Under the old ribs of the rock retreating,
Hold fast, lest thou be hurled down the abysses
      there!
The night with the mist is black;
Hark! how the forests grind and crack!
Frightened, the owlets are scattered:
Hearken! the pillars are shattered,

[41] See note 33, above.

The evergreen palaces shaking!   110
Boughs are groaning and breaking,
The tree-trunks terribly thunder,
The roots are twisting asunder!
In frightfully intricate crashing
Each on the other is dashing,
And over the wreck-strewn gorges
The tempest whistles and surges!
Hear'st thou voices higher ringing?
Far away, or nearer singing?
Yes, the mountain's side along,   120
Sweeps an infuriate glamouring song!

WITCHES (*in chorus*)

The witches ride to the Brocken's top,
The stubble is yellow, and green the crop.
There gathers the crowd for carnival;
Sir Urian [42] sits over all.
And so they go over stone and stock;
The witch she —s, and —s the buck.

A VOICE

Alone, old Baubo's [43] coming now;
She rides upon a farrow-sow.

CHORUS

Then honor to whom the honor is due!   130
Dame Baubo first, to lead the crew!
A tough old sow and the mother thereon,
Then follow the witches, every one.

A VOICE

Which way com'st thou hither?

VOICE

O'er the Ilsen-stone. [44]
I peeped at the owl in her nest alone:
How she stared and glared!

VOICE

Betake thee to Hell!
Why so fast and so fell?

VOICE

She has scored and has flayed me:
See the wounds she has made me!   140

WITCHES (*chorus*)

The way is wide, the way is long:
See, what a wild and crazy throng!

[42] One of the names of the Devil.
[43] Goethe presents her elsewhere as a leader in ribald revelry.
[44] A high rock a few miles northeast of the Brocken.

The broom it scratches, the fork it thrusts,
The child is stifled, the mother bursts.

WIZARDS (*semichorus*)

As doth the snail in shell, we crawl:
Before us go the women all.
When towards the Devil's House we tread,
Woman's a thousand steps ahead.

OTHER SEMICHORUS

We do not measure with such care:
Woman in thousand steps is there,   150
But howsoe'er she hasten may,
Man in one leap has cleared the way.

VOICE (*from above*)

Come on, come on, from Rocky Lake!

VOICE (*from below*)

Aloft we'd fain ourselves betake.
We've washed, and are bright as ever you will,
Yet we're eternally sterile still.

BOTH CHORUSES

The wind is hushed, the star shoots by,
The dreary moon forsakes the sky;
The magic notes, like spark on spark,
Drizzle, whistling through the dark.   160

VOICE (*from below*)

Halt, there! Ho, there!

VOICE (*from above*)

Who calls from the rocky cleft below there?

VOICE (*below*)

Take me, too! take me, too!
I'm climbing now three hundred years,
And yet the summit cannot see:
Among my equals I would be.

BOTH CHORUSES

Bears the broom and bears the stock,
Bears the fork and bears the buck:
Who cannot raise himself to-night
Is evermore a ruined wight.   170

HALF-WITCH (*below*)

So long I stumble, ill bestead,
And the others are now so far ahead!
At home I've neither rest nor cheer,
And yet I cannot gain them here.

CHORUS OF WITCHES

To cheer the witch will salve avail;
A rag will answer for a sail;
Each trough a goodly ship supplies;
He ne'er will fly, who now not flies.

BOTH CHORUSES

When round the summit whirls our flight
Then lower, and on the ground alight;   180
And far and wide the heather press
With witchhood's swarms of wantonness!
(*They settle down.*)

MEPHISTOPHELES

They crowd and push, they roar and clatter!
They whirl and whistle, pull and chatter!
They shine, and spirt, and stink, and burn!
The true witch-element we learn.
Keep close! or we are parted, in our turn.
Where art thou?

FAUST (*in the distance*)
Here!

MEPHISTOPHELES

What! whirled so far astray!
Then house-right I must use and clear the way.
Make room! Squire Voland [45] comes! Room, gentle
    rabble, room!   190
Here, Doctor, hold to me: in one jump we'll resume
An easier space, and from the crowd be free:
It's too much, even for the like of me.
Yonder, with special light, there's something shining
    clearer
Within those bushes; I've a mind to see
Come on! we'll slip a little nearer.

FAUST

Spirit of Contradiction! On! I'll follow straight.
'T is planned most wisely, if I judge aright:
We climb the Brocken's top in the Walpurgis-
    Night,
That arbitrarily, here, ourselves we isolate.   200

MEPHISTOPHELES

But see, what motley flames among the heather!
There is a lively club together:
In smaller circles one is not alone.

FAUST

Better the summit, I must own:
There fire and whirling smoke I see.

[45] Another name for the Devil.

They seek the Evil One in wild confusion:
Many enigmas there might find solution.

MEPHISTOPHELES

But there enigmas also knotted be.
Leave to the multitude their riot!
Here will we house ourselves in quiet.   210
It is an old, transmitted trade,
That in the greater world the little worlds are made.
I see stark-nude young witches congregate,
And old ones, veiled and hidden shrewdly:
On my account be kind, nor treat them rudely!
The trouble's small, the fun is great.
I hear the noise of instruments attuning,—
Vile din! yet one must learn to bear the crooning.
Come, come along! It *must* be, I declare!
I'll go ahead and introduce thee there,   220
Thine obligation newly earning.
That is no little space: what say'st thou, friend?
Look yonder! thou canst scarcely see the end:
A hundred fires along the ranks are burning.
They dance, they chat, they cook, they drink, they
    court:
Now where, just tell me, is there better sport?

FAUST

Wilt thou, to introduce us to the revel,
Assume the part of wizard or of devil?

MEPHISTOPHELES

I'm mostly used, 't is true, to go incognito,
But on a gala-day one may his orders show.   230
The Garter does not deck my suit,
But honored and at home is here the cloven foot.
Perceiv'st thou yonder snail? It cometh, slow and
    steady;
So delicately its feelers pry,
That it hath scented me already:
I cannot here disguise me, if I try.
But come! we'll go from this fire to a newer:
I am the go-between, and thou the wooer.
(*To some, who are sitting around dying embers:*)
Old gentlemen, why at the outskirts? Enter!
I'd praise you if I found you snugly in the
    centre,   240
With youth and revel round you like a zone:
You each, at home, are quite enough alone.

GENERAL

Say, who would put his trust in nations,
Howe'er for them one may have worked and
    planned?

For with the people, as with women,
Youth always has the upper hand.

MINISTER

They're now too far from what is just and sage.
I praise the old ones, not unduly:
When we were all-in-all, then, truly,
Then was the real golden age.   250

PARVENU

We also were not stupid, either,
And what we should not, often did;
But now all things have from their bases slid,
Just as we meant to hold them fast together.

AUTHOR

Who, now, a work of moderate sense will read?
Such works are held as antiquate and mossy;
And as regards the younger folk, indeed,
They never yet have been so pert and saucy.

MEPHISTOPHELES

(who all at once appears very old)

I feel that men are ripe for Judgment-Day,
Now for the last time I've the witches'-hill as-
    cended: 260
Since to the lees *my* cask is drained away,
The world's, as well, must soon be ended.

HUCKSTER-WITCH

Ye gentlemen, don't pass me thus!
Let not the chance neglected be!
Behold my wares attentively:
The stock is rare and various.
And yet, there's nothing I've collected—
No shop, on earth, like this you'll find—
Which has not, once, sore hurt inflicted
Upon the world, and on mankind.   270
No dagger's here, that set not blood to flowing;
No cup, that hath not once, within a healthy frame
Poured speedy death, in poison glowing:
No gems, that have not brought a maid to shame;
No sword, but severed ties for the unwary,
Or from behind struck down the adversary.

MEPHISTOPHELES

Gossip! the times thou badly comprehendest:
What's done has happened—what haps, is done!
'T were better if for novelties thou sendest:
By such alone can we be won.   280

FAUST

Let me not lose myself in all this pother!
This is a fair as never was another!

MEPHISTOPHELES

The whirlpool swirls to get above:
Thou 'rt shoved thyself, imagining to shove.

FAUST

But who is that?

MEPHISTOPHELES

                    Note her especially,
'T is Lilith.

FAUST

    Who?

MEPHISTOPHELES

                    Adam's first wife is she.[46]
Beware the lure within her lovely tresses,
The splendid sole adornment of her hair!
When she succeeds therewith a youth to snare,
Not soon again she frees him from her jesses.   290

FAUST

Those two, the old one with the young one sitting,
They've danced already more than fitting.

MEPHISTOPHELES

No rest to-night for young or old!
They start another dance: come now, let us take
    hold!

FAUST *(dancing with the young witch)*

A lovely dream once came to me;
I then beheld an apple-tree,
And there two fairest apples shone:
They lured me so, I climbed thereon.

THE FAIR ONE

Apples have been desired by you,
Since first in Paradise they grew;   300
And I am moved with joy, to know
That such within my garden grow.

MEPHISTOPHELES *(dancing with the old one)*

A dissolute dream once came to me:
Therein I saw a cloven tree,
Which had a —— —— ——;
Yet, —— as 't was, I fancied it.

[46] According to Jewish tradition, after having been superseded by Eve, she took great delight in seducing men and
in injuring children.

THE OLD ONE

I offer here my best salute
Unto the knight with cloven foot!
Let him a —— —— prepare,
If him —— —— —— does not scare.   310

PROKTOPHANTASMIST [47]

Accurséd folk! How dare you venture thus?
Had you not, long since, demonstration
That hosts can't stand on ordinary foundation?
And now you even dance, like one of us!

THE FAIR ONE (*dancing*)

Why does he come, then, to our ball?

FAUST (*dancing*)

O, everywhere on him you fall!
When others dance, he weighs the matter:
If he can't every step bechatter,
Then 't is the same as were the step not made;
But if you forwards go, his ire is most displayed. 320
If you would whirl in regular gyration
As he does in his dull old mill,
He'd show, at any rate, good-will,—
Especially if you heard and heeded his hortation.

PROKTOPHANTASMIST

You still are here? Nay, 't is a thing unheard!
Vanish, at once! We've said the enlightening word.
The pack of devils by no rules is daunted:
We are so wise, and yet is Tegel [48] haunted.
To clear the folly out, how have I swept and stirred!
'T will ne'er be clean: why, 't is a thing un-
          heard!   330

THE FAIR ONE

Then cease to bore us at our ball!

PROKTOPHANTASMIST

I tell you, spirits, to your face,
I give to spirit-despotism no place;
My spirit cannot practise it at all.

FAUST

(*The dance continues.*)

Naught will succeed, I see, amid such revels;
Yet something from a tour I always save
And hope, before my last step to the grave,
To overcome the poets and the devils.

[47] Allusion to Christoph Friedrich Nicolai (1733–1811),
German critic, book-dealer and writer, regarded by Goethe
as the personification of pedantry and tediousness.
[48] A town near Berlin. Nicolai wrote a paper about a
ghost which appeared here in 1797.

MEPHISTOPHELES

He now will seat him in the nearest puddle;
The solace thus, whereof he's most assured: 340
And when upon his rump the leeches [49] hang and
          fuddle,
He'll be of spirits and of Spirit cured.

(*To* FAUST, *who has left the dance:*)

Wherefore forsaketh thou the lovely maiden,
That in the dance so sweetly sang?

FAUST

Ah! in the midst of it there sprang
A red mouse from her mouth [50]—sufficient reason!

MEPHISTOPHELES

That's nothing! One must not so squeamish be;
So the mouse was not gray, enough for thee.
Who'd think of that in love's selected season?

FAUST

Then saw I—

MEPHISTOPHELES

                    What?

FAUST

                    Mephisto, seest thou there, 350
Alone and far, a girl most pale and fair?
She falters on, her way scarce knowing,
As if with fettered feet that stay her going.
I must confess, it seems to me
As if my kindly Margaret were she.

MEPHISTOPHELES

Let the thing be! All thence have evil drawn:
It is a magic shape, a lifeless eidolon.[51]
Such to encounter is not good:
Their blank, set stare benumbs the human blood,
And one is almost turned to stone.   360
Medusa's [52] tale to thee is known.

FAUST

Forsooth, the eyes they are of one whom, dying,
No hand with loving pressure closed;
That is the breast whereon I once was lying,—
The body sweet, beside which I reposed!

[49] Nicolai was once treated for hallucinations by having
leeches placed on his rump.
[50] In German folklore, red mice sometimes jumped from
the mouths of sleeping witches.
[51] Phantom (Greek).
[52] Her eyes turned to stone all who looked into them.

MEPHISTOPHELES

'T is magic all, thou fool, seduced so easily!
Unto each man his love she seems to be.

FAUST

The woe, the rapture, so ensnare me,
That from her gaze I cannot tear me!
And, strange! around her fairest throat   370
A single scarlet band is gleaming,
No broader than a knife-blade seeming!

MEPHISTOPHELES

Quite right! The mark I also note.
Her head beneath her arm she'll sometimes carry;
'T was Perseus lopped it, her old adversary.
Thou crav'st the same illusion still!
Come, let us mount this little hill;
The Prater [53] shows no livelier stir,
And, if they've not bewitched my sense,
I verily see a theatre.   380
What's going on?

SERVIBILIS

                'T will shortly recommence:
A new performance—'t is the last of seven.
To give that number is the custom here:
'T was by a Dilettante written,
And Dilettanti in the parts appear.
That now I vanish, pardon, I entreat you!
As Dilettante I the curtain raise.

MEPHISTOPHELES

When I upon the Blocksberg meet you,
I find it good: for that's your proper place.

XXII

WALPURGIS-NIGHT'S DREAM

OBERON AND TITANIA'S GOLDEN WEDDING

INTERMEZZO

MANAGER

Sons of Mieding, rest to-day!
Needless your machinery:
Misty vale and mountain gray,
That is all the scenery.

HERALD

That the wedding golden be,
Must fifty years be rounded:

[53] A famous park in Vienna.

But *the Golden* give to me,
When the strife's compounded.

OBERON

Spirits, if you're here, be seen—
Show yourselves, delighted!   10
Fairy king and fairy queen,
They are newly plighted.

PUCK

Cometh Puck, and, light of limb,
Whisks and whirls in measure:
Come a hundred after him,
To share with him the pleasure.

ARIEL

Ariel's song is heavenly-pure,
His tones are sweet and rare ones:
Though ugly faces he allure,
Yet he allures the fair ones.   20

OBERON

Spouses, who would fain agree,
Learn how we were mated!
If your pairs would loving be,
First be separated!

TITANIA

If her whims the wife control,
And the man berate her,
Take him to the Northern Pole,
And her to the Equator!

ORCHESTRA. TUTTI.

Fortissimo

Snout of fly, mosquito-bill,
And kin of all conditions,   30
Frog in grass, and cricket-trill,—
These are the musicians!

SOLO

See the bagpipe on our track!
'T is the soap-blown bubble:
Hear the *schnecke-schnicke-schnack*
Through his nostrils double!

SPIRIT, JUST GROWING INTO FORM

Spider's foot and paunch of toad,
And little wings—we know 'em!
A little creature 't will not be,
But yet, a little poem.   40

A LITTLE COUPLE

Little step and lofty leap
Through honey-dew and fragrance:
You'll never mount the airy steep
With all your tripping vagrance.

INQUISITIVE TRAVELLER

Is 't but masquerading play?
See I with precision?
Oberon, the beauteous fay,
Meets, to-night, my vision!

ORTHODOX

Not a claw, no tail I see!
And yet, beyond a cavil,   50
Like "the Gods of Greece," must he
Also be a devil.

NORTHERN ARTIST

I only seize, with sketchy air,
Some outlines of the tourney;
Yet I betimes myself prepare
For my Italian journey.

PURIST

My bad luck brings me here, alas!
How roars the orgy louder!
And of the witches in the mass,
But only two wear powder.   60

YOUNG WITCH

Powder becomes, like petticoat,
A gray and wrinkled noddy;
So I sit naked on my goat,
And show a strapping body.

MATRON

We've too much tact and policy
To rate with gibes a scolder;
Yet, young and tender though you be,
I hope to see you moulder.

LEADER OF THE BAND

Fly-snout and mosquito-bill,
Don't swarm so round the Naked!   70
Frog in grass and cricket-trill,
Observe the time, and make it!

WEATHERCOCK (*towards one side*)

Society to one's desire!
Brides only, and the sweetest!
And bachelors of youth and fire,
And prospects the completest!

WEATHERCOCK (*towards the other side*)

And if the Earth don't open now
To swallow up each ranter,
Why, then will I myself, I vow,
Jump into hell instanter!   80

XENIES

Us as little insects see!
With sharpest nippers flitting,
That our Papa Satan we
May honor as is fitting.

HENNINGS

How, in crowds together massed,
They are jesting, shameless!
They will even say, at last,
That their hearts are blameless.

MUSAGETES

Among this witches' revelry
His way one gladly loses;   90
And, truly, it would easier be
Than to command the Muses.

CI-DEVANT GENIUS OF THE AGE

The proper folks one's talents laud:
Come on, and none shall pass us!
The Blocksberg has a summit broad,
Like Germany's Parnassus.

INQUISITIVE TRAVELLER

Say, who's the stiff and pompous man?
He walks with haughty paces:
He snuffles all he snuffle can:
"He scents the Jesuits' traces."   100

CRANE

Both clear and muddy streams, for me
Are good to fish and sport in:
And thus the pious man you see
With even devils consorting.

WORLDLING

Yes, for the pious, I suspect,
All instruments are fitting;
And on the Blocksberg they erect
Full many a place of meeting.

DANCER

A newer chorus now succeeds!
I hear the distant drumming.   110
"Don't be disturbed! 't is, in the reeds,
The bittern's changeless booming."

DANCING-MASTER

How each his legs in nimble trip
Lifts up, and makes a clearance!
The crooked jump, the heavy skip,
Nor care for the appearance.

GOOD FELLOW

The rabble by such hate are held,
To maim and slay delights them:
As Orpheus' lyre the brutes compelled,
The bagpipe here unites them.   120

DOGMATIST

I'll not be led by any lure
Of doubts or critic-cavils:
The Devil must be something, sure,—
Or how should there be devils?

IDEALIST

This once, the fancy wrought in me
Is really too despotic:
Forsooth, if I am all I see,
I must be idiotic!

REALIST

This racking fuss on every hand,
It gives me great vexation;   130
And, for the first time, here I stand
On insecure foundation.

SUPERNATURALIST

With much delight I see the play,
And rant to these their merits,
Since from the devils I also may
Infer the better spirits.

SCEPTIC

The flame they follow, on and on,
And think they're near the treasure:
But *Devil* rhymes with *Doubt* alone,
So I am here with pleasure.   140

LEADER OF THE BAND

Frog in green, and cricket-trill,
Such dilettants!—perdition!
Fly-snout and mosquito-bill,—
Each one's a fine musician!

THE ADROIT

Sanssouci, we call the clan
Of merry creatures so, then;
Go a-foot no more we can
And on our heads we go, then.

THE AWKWARD

Once many a bit we sponged; but now,
God help us! that is done with: 150
Our shoes are all danced out, we trow,
We've but naked soles to run with.

WILL-O'-THE-WISPS

From the marshes we appear,
Where we originated;
Yet in the ranks, at once, we're here
As glittering gallants rated.

SHOOTING-STAR

Darting hither from the sky,
In star and fire light shooting,
Cross-wise now in grass I lie:
Who'll help me to my footing?   160

THE HEAVY FELLOWS

Room! and round about us, room!
Trodden are the grasses:
Spirits also, spirits come,
And they are bulky masses.

PUCK

Enter not so stall-fed quite,
Like elephant-calves about one!
And the heaviest weight to-night
Be Puck, himself, the stout one!

ARIEL

If loving Nature at your back,
Or Mind, the wing uncloses,   170
Follow up my airy track
To the mount of roses!

ORCHESTRA

Pianissimo

Cloud and trailing mist o'erhead
Are now illuminated:
Air in leaves, and wind in reed,
And all is dissipated.

XXIII

DREARY DAY

A FIELD

FAUST. MEPHISTOPHELES.

FAUST

In misery! In despair! Long wretchedly astray
on the face of the earth, and now imprisoned! That
gracious, ill-starred creature shut in a dungeon as a

criminal, and given up to fearful torments! To this has it come! to this!—Treacherous, contemptible spirit, and thou hast concealed it from me!—Stand, then—stand! Roll the devilish eyes wrathfully in thy head! Stand and defy me with thine intolerable presence! Imprisoned! In irretrievable misery! Delivered up to evil spirits and to condemning, 10 unfeeling Man! And thou hast lulled me, meanwhile, with the most insipid dissipations, hast concealed from me her increasing wretchedness, and suffered her to go helplessly to ruin!

MEPHISTOPHELES

She is not the first.

FAUST

Dog! Abominable monster! Transform him, thou Infinite Spirit! transform the reptile again into his dog-shape, in which it pleased him often at night to scamper on before me, to roll himself at the feet of the unsuspecting wanderer, and hang upon his 20 shoulders when he fell! Transform him again into his favorite likeness, that he may crawl upon his belly in the dust before me,—that I may trample him, the outlawed, under foot! Not the first! O woe! woe which no human soul can grasp, that more than one being should sink into the depths of this misery,—that the first, in its writhing death-agony under the eyes of the Eternal Forgiver, did not expiate the guilt of all others! The misery of this single one pierces to the very marrow of my life; 30 and thou art calmly grinning at the fate of thousands!

MEPHISTOPHELES

Now we are already again at the end of our wits, where the understanding of you men runs wild. Why didst thou enter into fellowship with us, if thou canst not carry it out? Wilt fly, and art not secure against dizziness? Did we thrust ourselves upon thee, or thou thyself upon us?

FAUST

Gnash not thus thy devouring teeth at me! It fills me with horrible disgust. Mighty, glorious 40 Spirit, who hast vouchsafed to me Thine apparition, who knowest my heart and my soul, why fetter me to the felon-comrade, who feeds on mischief and gluts himself with ruin?

MEPHISTOPHELES

Hast thou done?

FAUST

Rescue her, or woe to thee! The fearfullest curse be upon thee for thousands of ages!

MEPHISTOPHELES

I cannot loosen the bonds of the Avenger, nor undo his bolts. Rescue her? Who was it that plunged her into ruin? I, or thou? 50

(FAUST *looks around wildly*)

Wilt thou grasp the thunder? Well, that it has not been given to you, miserable mortals! To crush to pieces the innocent respondent—that is the tyrant-fashion of relieving one's self in embarrassments.

FAUST

Take me thither! She shall be free!

MEPHISTOPHELES

And the danger to which thou wilt expose thyself? Know that the guilt of blood, from thy hand, still lies upon the town! Avenging spirits hover over the spot where the victim fell, and lie in wait for the returning murderer. 60

FAUST

That, too, from thee? Murder and death of a world upon thee, monster! Take me thither, I say, and liberate her!

MEPHISTOPHELES

I will convey thee there; and hear, what I can do! Have I all the power in Heaven and on Earth? I will becloud the jailer's senses: get possession of the key, and lead her forth with human hand! I will keep watch: the magic steeds are ready, I will carry you off. So much is in my power.

FAUST

Up and away! 70

XXIV

NIGHT

OPEN FIELD

(FAUST *and* MEPHISTOPHELES *speeding onward on black horses.*)

FAUST

What weave they there round the raven-stone? [54]

[54] Place of execution.

MEPHISTOPHELES

I know not what they are brewing and doing.

FAUST

Soaring up, sweeping down, bowing and bending!

MEPHISTOPHELES

A witches'-guild.

FAUST

They scatter, devote and doom!

MEPHISTOPHELES

On! on!

XXV
DUNGEON

FAUST

(*with a bunch of keys and a lamp, before an iron door*)

A shudder, long unfelt, comes o'er me;
Mankind's collected woe o'erwhelms me, here.
She dwells within the dark, damp walls before me,
And all her crime was a delusion dear!
What! I delay to free her?
I dread, once again to see her?
On! my shrinking but lingers Death more near.

(*He grasps the lock: the sound of singing is heard inside.*)

    My mother, the harlot,
    Who put me to death;
    My father, the varlet,   10
    Who eaten me hath!
    Little sister, so good,
    Laid my bones in the wood,
    In the damp moss and clay:
    Then was I a beautiful bird o' the wood;
    Fly away! Fly away! [55]

FAUST (*unlocking*)

She does not dream her lover listens near;
That he the rattling chain, the rustling straw, can hear.

(*He enters.*)

MARGARET (*hiding herself on the pallet*)

Woe! woe!
They come. O death of bitterness!   20

[55] This song refers to the folk tale of a wicked woman who served her stepson as a meal to her husband. The boy's little sister later gathered the bones and buried them under a juniper tree whence they became the bird in the song.

FAUST (*whispering*)

Hush! hush! The hour is come that frees thee.

MARGARET (*throwing herself before him*)

Art thou a man, then pity my distress!

FAUST

Thy cries will wake the guards, and they will seize thee!

(*He takes hold of the fetters to unlock them.*)

MARGARET (*on her knees*)

Who, headsman! unto thee such power
Over me could give?
Thou 'rt come for me at midnight-hour:
Have mercy on me, let me live!
Is 't not soon enough when morning chime has rung?

(*She rises.*)

And I am yet so young, so young!
And now Death comes, and ruin!   30
I, too, was fair, and that was my undoing.
My love was near, but now he's far;
Torn lies the wreath, scattered the blossoms are.
Seize me not thus so violently!
Spare me! What have I done to thee?
Let me not vainly entreat thee!
I never chanced, in all my days, to meet thee!

FAUST

Shall I outlive this misery?

MARGARET

Now am I wholly in thy might.
But let me suckle, first, my baby!   40
I blessed it all this livelong night;
They took 't away, to vex me, maybe,
And now they say I killed the child outright.
And never shall I be glad again.
They sing songs about me! 't is bad of the folk to do it!
There's an old story has the same refrain;
Who bade them so construe it?

FAUST (*falling upon his knees*)

Here lieth one who loves thee ever,
The thraldom of thy woe to sever.

MARGARET (*flinging herself beside him*)

O let us kneel, and call the Saints to hide us!   50
Under the steps beside us,

The threshold under,
Hell heaves in thunder!
The Evil One
With terrible wrath
Seeketh a path
His prey to discover!

FAUST (*aloud*)

Margaret! Margaret!

MARGARET (*attentively listening*)

That was the voice of my lover!

(*She springs to her feet: the fetters fall off.*)

Where is he? I heard him call me.   60
I am free! No one shall enthrall me.
To his neck will I fly,
On his bosom lie!
On the threshold he stood, and *Margaret!* calling.
Midst of Hell's howling and noises appalling,
Midst of the wrathful, infernal derision,
I knew the sweet sound of the voice of the vision!

FAUST

'T is I!

MARGARET

'T is thou! O, say it once again!

(*Clasping him.*)

'T is he! 't is he! Where now is all my pain?
The anguish of the dungeon, and the chain?   70
'T is thou! Thou comest to save me,
And I am saved!—
Again the street I see
Where first I looked on thee;
And the garden, brightly blooming,
Where I and Martha wait thy coming.

FAUST (*struggling to leave*)

Come! Come with me!

MARGARET

Delay, now!
So fain I stay, when thou delayest!

(*Caressing him.*)

FAUST

Away, now!
If longer here thou stayest,   80
We shall be made to dearly rue it.

MARGARET

Kiss me!—canst no longer do it?
My friend, so short a time thou 'rt missing,
And hast unlearned thy kissing?
Why is my heart so anxious, on thy breast?
Where once a heaven thy glances did create me,
A heaven thy loving words expressed,
And thou didst kiss, as thou wouldst suffocate me—
Kiss me!
Or I'll kiss thee!   90

(*She embraces him.*)

Ah, woe! thy lips are chill,
And still.
How changed in fashion
Thy passion!
Who has done me this ill?

(*She turns away from him.*)

FAUST

Come, follow me! My darling, be more bold:
I'll clasp thee, soon, with warmth a thousand-fold;
But follow now! 'T is all I beg of thee.

MARGARET (*turning to him*)

And is it thou? Thou, surely, certainly?

FAUST

'T is I! Come on!

MARGARET

Thou wilt unloose my chain,   100
And in thy lap wilt take me once again.
How comes it that thou dost not shrink from me?—
Say, dost thou know my friend, whom thou mak'st
free?

FAUST

Come! come! The night already vanisheth.

MARGARET

My mother have I put to death;
I've drowned the baby born to thee.
Was it not given to thee and me?
Thee, too!—'T is thou! It scarcely true doth seem—
Give me thy hand! 'T is not a dream!
Thy dear, dear hand!—But, ah, 't is wet!   110
Why, wipe it off! Methinks that yet
There's blood thereon.
Ah, God! what hast thou done?
Nay, sheathe thy sword at last!
Do not affray me!

FAUST

O, let the past be past!
Thy words will slay me!

MARGARET

No, no! Thou must outlive us.
Now I'll tell thee the graves to give us:
Thou must begin to-morrow   120
The work of sorrow!
The best place give to my mother,
Then close at her side my brother,
And me a little away.
But not too very far, I pray!
And here, on my right breast, my baby lay!
Nobody else will lie beside me!—
Ah, within thine arms to hide me,
That was a sweet and a gracious bliss,
But no more, no more can I attain it!   130
I would force myself on thee and constrain it,
And it seems thou repellest my kiss:
And yet 't is thou, so good, so kind to see!

FAUST

If thou feel'st it is I, then come with me!

MARGARET

Out yonder?

FAUST

To freedom.

MARGARET

        If the grave is there,
Death lying in wait, then come!
From here to eternal rest:
No further step—no, no!
Thou goest away! O Henry, if I could go!   140

FAUST

Thou canst! Just will it! Open stands the door.

MARGARET

I dare not go: there's no hope any more.
Why should I fly? They'll still my steps waylay!
It is so wretched, forced to beg my living,
And a bad conscience sharper misery giving!
It is so wretched, to be strange, forsaken,
And I'd still be followed and taken!

FAUST

I'll stay with thee.

MARGARET

Be quick! Be quick!
Save thy perishing child!   150
Away! Follow the ridge
Up by the brook,
Over the bridge,
Into the wood,
To the left, where the plank is placed
In the pool!
Seize it in haste!
'T is trying to rise,
'T is struggling still!
Save it! Save it!   160

FAUST

Recall thy wandering will!
One step, and thou art free at last!

MARGARET

If the mountain we had only passed!
There sits my mother upon a stone,—
I feel an icy shiver!
There sits my mother upon a stone,
And her head is wagging ever.
She beckons, she nods not, her heavy head falls o'er;
She slept so long that she wakes no more.
She slept, while we were caressing: 170
Ah, those were the days of blessing!

FAUST

Here words and prayers are nothing worth;
I'll venture, then, to bear thee forth.

MARGARET

No—let me go! I'll suffer no force!
Grasp me not so murderously!
I've done, else, all things for the love of thee.

FAUST

The day dawns: Dearest! Dearest!

MARGARET

Day? Yes, the day comes,—the last day breaks for
        me!
My wedding-day it was to be!
Tell no one thou hast been with Margaret!   180
Woe for my garland! The chances
Are over—'t is all in vain!
We shall meet once again,
But not at the dances!
The crowd is thronging, no word is spoken:
The square below

And the streets overflow:
The death-bell tolls,[56] the wand is broken.
I am seized, and bound, and delivered—
Shoved to the block—they give the sign!   190
Now over each neck has quivered
The blade that is quivering over mine.
Dumb lies the world like the grave!

FAUST

O had I ne'er been born!

MEPHISTOPHELES (*appears outside*)

Off! or you're lost ere morn.
Useless talking, delaying and praying!
My horses are neighing:
The morning twilight is near.

MARGARET

What rises up from the threshold here?
He! he! suffer him not!   200
What does he want in this holy spot?
He seeks me!

[56] It was once the practice to toll church bells as a convicted criminal was being led to execution. A white wand was also broken over his head to show that his life was rightfully being taken by the law.

FAUST

Thou shalt live.

MARGARET

Judgment of God! myself to thee I give.

MEPHISTOPHELES (*to* FAUST)

Come! or I'll leave her in the lurch, and thee!

MARGARET

Thine am I, Father! rescue me!
Ye angels, holy cohorts, guard me,
Camp around, and from evil ward me!
Henry! I shudder to think of thee.

MEPHISTOPHELES

She is judged!

VOICE (*from above*)

She is saved!

MEPHISTOPHELES (*to* FAUST)

Hither to me!

(*He disappears with* FAUST.)

VOICE (*from within, dying away*)

Henry! Henry!   210

German Lyric Poetry

GOETHE

For an introduction to the life and works of Goethe see page 249.

Mignon

Know'st thou the land where the fair citron blows,
Where the bright orange midst the foliage glows,
Where soft winds greet us from the azure skies,
Where silent myrtles, stately laurels rise,
Know'st thou it well?
　　　　　'Tis there, 'tis there,
That I with thee, beloved one, would repair!

Know'st thou the house? On columns rests its pile,
Its halls are gleaming, and its chambers smile,
And marble statues stand and gaze on me:
"Poor child! what sorrow hath befallen thee?"
Know'st thou it well?
　　　　　'Tis there, 'tis there,
That I with thee, protector, would repair!

Know'st thou the mountain, and its cloudy bridge?
The mule can scarcely find the misty ridge;
In caverns dwells the dragon's olden brood,
The frowning crag obstructs the raging flood.
Know'st thou it well?
　　　　　'Tis there, 'tis there,
Our path lies—Father—thither, oh repair!

(*trans. by Edgar H. Bowring*)

To a Golden Heart, Worn Round His Neck

Remembrancer of joys long passed away,
  Relic, from which as yet I cannot part,
O, hast thy power to lengthen love's short day?
  Stronger thy chain than that which bound the
    heart?

Lili, I fly!—yet still thy fetters press me
  In distant valley, or far lonely wood.
Still with a struggling sigh of pain confess thee
  The mistress of my soul in every mood.

The bird may burst the silken chain that bound
    him,
  Flying to the green home, which fits him best;
But, ah! he hears the prisoner's badge around him,
  Still by the piece about his neck distressed.
He ne'er can breathe his free wild notes again;
  They're stifled by the pressure of his chain.

(trans. by Margaret Fuller Ossoli)

The Shepherd's Lament

Up yonder on the mountain
  A thousand times I stand,
Leant on my crook, and gazing
  Down on the valley-land.

I follow the flock to the pasture;
  My little dog watches them still.
I have come below, but I know not
  How I descended the hill.

The beautiful meadow is covered
  With blossoms of every hue;
I pluck them, alas! without knowing
  Whom I shall give them to.

I seek, in the rain and the tempest,
  A refuge under the tree:
Yonder the doors are fastened,
  And all is a dream to me.

Right over the roof of the dwelling
  I see a rainbow stand;
But she has departed forever,
  And gone far out in the land.

Far out in the land, and farther,—
  Perhaps to an alien shore:
Go forward, ye sheep! go forward,—
  The heart of the shepherd is sore.

(trans. by Bayard Taylor)

The Rose

Once a boy beheld a bright
  Rose in dingle growing;
Far, far off it pleased his sight;
Near he viewed it with delight:
  Soft it seemed and glowing,
Lo! the rose, the rose so bright,
  Rose so brightly blowing!

Spake the boy, "I'll pluck thee, grand
  Rose all wildly blowing."
Spake the rose, "I'll wound thy hand,
Thus the scheme thy wit hath planned
  Deftly overthrowing."
O! the rose, the rose so grand,
  Rose so grandly glowing.

But the stripling plucked the red
  Rose in glory growing,
And the thorn his flesh hath bled,
And the rose's pride is fled,
  And her beauty's going.
Woe! the rose, the rose once red
  Rose once redly glowing.

(trans. by James Clarence Mangan)

Wanderer's Night-Songs

I

Thou that from the heavens art,
Every pain and sorrow stillest,
And the doubly wretched heart
Doubly with refreshment fillest,
I am weary with contending!
Why this rapture and unrest?
Peace descending
Come, ah, come into my breast!

II

O'er all the hill-tops
Is quiet now,
In all the tree-tops
Hearest thou
Hardly a breath;
The birds are asleep in the trees:
Wait; soon like these
Thou too shalt rest.

(trans. by Henry Wadsworth Longfellow)

An Irish Lamentation

O! raise the woeful *Pillalu*,
    And let your tears in streams be shed;
Och, orro, orro, ollalu!
    The Master's eldest hope is dead!

Ere broke the morning dim and pale
    The owlet flapped his heavy wing:
We heard the winds at evening wail,
    And now our dirge of death we sing,
        Och, orro, orro, ollalu!

Why wouldst thou go? How couldst thou die?
    Why hast thou left thy parents dear?
Thy friends, thy kindred far and nigh,
    Whose cries, *mo vrone!* thou dost not hear?
        Och, orro, orro, ollalu!

Thy mother, too!—how could she part
    From thee, her darling fair and sweet,
The heart that throbbed within her heart,
    The pulse, the blood that bade it beat?
        Och, orro, orro, ollalu!

Oh! lost to her and all thy race,
    Thou sleepest in the House of Death;
She sees no more thy cherub face,
    She drinks no more thy violet breath;
        Och, orro, orro, ollalu!

By strand and road, by field and fen,
    The sorrowing clans come thronging all;
From camp and dun, from hill and glen,
    They crowd around the castle wall.
        Och, orro, orro, ollalu!

From East and West, from South and North,
    To join the funeral train they hie;
And now the mourners issue forth,
    And far they spread the keening cry,
        Och, orro, orro, ollalu!

Then raise the woeful *Pillalu*,
    And let your tears in streams be shed,
Och, orro, orro, ollalu!
    The Chieftain's pride, his heir, is dead.

                    (trans. by James Clarence Mangan)

A Voice from the Invisible World

High o'er his moldering castle walls
    The warrior's phantom glides,
And loudly to the skiff it calls
    That on the billow rides—

"Behold! these arms once vaunted might,
    This heart beat wild and bold—
Behold! these ducal veins ran bright
    With wine-red blood of old.

"The noon in storm, the eve in rest,
    So sped my life's brief day.
What then? *Young bark on Ocean's breast,
    Cleave thou thy destined way!"*

                    (trans. by James Clarence Mangan)

The Erl-King

O who rides by night thro' the woodland so wild?
It is the fond father embracing his child;
And close the boy nestles within his loved arm.
To hold himself fast, and to keep himself warm.

"O father, see yonder! see yonder!" he says;
"My boy, upon what dost thou fearfully gaze?"
"O, 'tis the Erl-King with his crown and his shroud."
"No, my son, it is but a dark wreath of the cloud."

(The Erl-King speaks)

"O come and go with me, thou loveliest child;
By many a gay sport shall thy time be beguiled;
My mother keeps for thee full many a fair toy,
And many a fine flower shall she pluck for my boy."

"O father, my father, and did you not hear
The Erl-King whisper so low in my ear?"
"Be still, my heart's darling—my child, be at ease;
It was but the wild blast as it sung thro' the trees."

Erl-King

"O wilt thou go with me, thou loveliest boy?
My daughter shall tend thee with care and with joy;
She shall bear thee so lightly thro' wet and thro'
        wild,
And press thee, and kiss thee, and sing to my child."

"O father, my father, and saw you not plain
The Erl-King's pale daughter glide past thro' the
        rain?"
"O yes, my loved treasure, I knew it full soon;
It was the gray willow that danced to the moon."

Erl-King

"O come and go with me, no longer delay,
Or else, silly child, I will drag thee away."
"O father! O father! now, now, keep your hold,
The Erl-King has seized me—his grasp is so cold!"

Sore trembled the father; he spurr'd thro' the wild,
Clasping close to his bosom his shuddering child;
He reaches his dwelling in doubt and in dread,
But, clasp'd to his bosom, the infant was dead.

(trans. by Sir Walter Scott)

JOHANN GOTTFRIED VON HERDER

1744–1803

Herder was the leading German pre-Romantic philosopher who did much to promulgate new irrational trends which were entering into a struggle to the death with the previous Neo-classical ideals of form and content imported from France. He was the German exponent of Rousseau's back-to-nature movement and the leading folklorist of his age. Herder was one of the earliest advocates of the so-called "organic" interpretation of history which holds that historical periods develop like organisms from birth through maturity to decay, each cycle marking a step forward in the progress toward a perfect humanity. His preoccupation with folklore and with primitive peoples in their Romantic aspects is reflected in the ballad "Sir Olaf."

FURTHER READING

GILLIES, A. *Herder* (New York, 1947).

Sir Olaf

Sir Olaf he rideth west and east
To bid the folk to his bridal feast.

On the wold are dancing an elvish band,
And Erl-king's daughter proffers her hand.

"Now welcome, Sir Olaf: what haste's with thee?
Step into our circle and dance with me."

"To dance I neither will nor may,
To-morrow's dawn is my bridal-day."

"Nay, stay, Sir Olaf, and dance with me,
And golden spurs will I give to thee."   10

"To dance I neither will nor may,
To-morrow's dawn is my bridal-day."

"Nay, stay, Sir Olaf, and dance with me,
A heap of gold will I give to thee."

"For all thy gold I will not stay,
And dance I neither will nor may."

"If thou wilt nor dance, Sir Olaf, with me,
Then Pest and Sickness shall follow thee."

She touched Sir Olaf upon the heart—
Ne'er in his life had he felt such smart.   20

She lifted him up on his steed that tide,
"Ride home! ride fast to thy troth-plight bride!"

And when he came to his castle-door,
His mother stood there, and trembled sore.

"Now say, sweet son, right speedilie
Why art thou wan, and white of blee?"

"Well may my face be wan and white.
I was in Erl-king's realm last night."

"Now tell me, my son so true and tried,
What thing shall I say to thy plighted bride!"   30

"Say that I hunt in the good greenwood,
With hound and horse as a good knight should."

When scarce the dawn in heaven shone red,
Came the train with the bride Sir Olaf should wed.

They sat at meat, they sat at wine;
"Now where is Sir Olaf, bridegroom of mine?"

"Sir Olaf rode out to the greenwood free,
With horse and hound to the hunt rode he."

The bride she lifted a cloth of red:
Beneath, Sir Olaf was dying dead.   40

(trans. by Elizabeth Craigmyle)

JOHANN CHRISTOPH FRIEDRICH VON SCHILLER

1759–1805

Schiller's early life was a continuous struggle against despotic parental authority, against financial want, and against disease (tuberculosis). The great achievement which he was able to make in literature is a monument to his indomitable will power and to his triumph over need and suffering.

The ideal which runs through much of his work, his lyric poetry as well as his drama, is that of liberty: first personal liberty, then later somewhat idealized spiritual liberty. His lyric production is small in amount, range, and variety when compared with that of Goethe, but in their own field the quality of his poems is of equal excellence. Schiller was master, particularly, of the longer lyric based on philosophic themes, such as we find in the "Song of the Bell," and of ballad poetry, which he used as a vehicle for moral ideas. His drama may well be his best work, for he closely approaches Shakespeare in the boldness and scope of his conceptions. Particularly noteworthy for their excellence are his historical tragedies such as *Wallenstein*. Schiller's style is refined, melodious, majestic, yet full of feeling and enriched with appropriate figures of speech.

FURTHER READING

GARLAND, HENRY B. *Schiller* (New York, 1950).
WITTE, WILLIAM. *Schiller* (New York, 1949).

Thekla's Song
(From *The Piccolomini*)

The cloud doth gather, the green wood roar,
The damsel paces along the shore;
The billows they tumble with might, with might;
And she flings out her voice to the darksome night;
  Her bosom is swelling with sorrow;
The world it is empty, the heart will die,
There's nothing to wish for beneath the sky:
Thou Holy One, call thy child away!
I've lived and loved, and that was to-day—
  Make ready my grave-clothes to-morrow.

(trans. by Samuel Taylor Coleridge)

Song of the Bell*

Fastened deep in firmest earth
  Stands the mould of well burnt clay.
Now we'll give the bell its birth;
  Quick, my friends, no more delay!
    From the heated brow
    Sweat must freely flow,
If to your master praise be given:
But the blessing comes from Heaven.

* Translated by S. A. Eliot.

To the work we now prepare
  A serious thought is surely due;   10
And cheerfully the toil we'll share,
  If cheerful words be mingled too.
Then let us still with care observe
  What from our strength, yet weakness, springs;
For he respect can ne'er deserve
  Who hands alone to labor brings.
'T is only this which honors man;
  His mind with heavenly fire was warmed,
That he with deepest thought might scan
  The work which his own hand has formed.   20

With splinters of the driest pine
  Now feed the fire below;
Then the rising flame shall shine,
  And the melting ore shall flow.
    Boils the brass within,
    Quickly add the tin;
That the thick metallic mass
Rightly to the mould may pass.

What with the aid of fire's dread power
  We in the dark, deep pit now hide,   30
Shall, on some lofty, sacred tower,
  Tell of our skill and form our pride.
And it shall last to days remote,
  Shall thrill the ear of many a race;
Shall sound with sorrow's mournful note,
  And call to pure devotion's grace.
Whatever to the sons of earth
  Their changing destiny brings down,
To the deep, solemn clang gives birth,
  That rings from out this metal crown.   40

See, the boiling surface whitening,
  Shows the whole is mixing well;
Add the salts, the metal brightening,
  Ere flows out the liquid bell.
    Clear from foam or scum
    Must the mixture come,
That with a rich metallic note
The sound aloft in air may float.
Now with joy and festive mirth
  Salute that loved and lovely child,   50
Whose earliest moments on the earth
  Are passed in sleep's dominion mild.
While on Time's lap he rests his head,
The fatal sisters spin their thread;
  A mother's love, with softest rays,
  Gilds o'er the morning of his days.—
But years with arrowy haste are fled.
His nursery bonds he proudly spurns;
  He rushes to the world without;

After long wandering, home he turns,
   Arrives a stranger and in doubt.
There, lovely in her beauty's youth,
   A form of heavenly mould he meets,
Of modest air and simple truth;
   The blushing maid he bashful greets.
A nameless feeling seizes strong
   On his young heart. He walks alone;
To his moist eyes emotions throng;
   His joy in ruder sports has flown.
He follows, blushing, where she goes;   70
   And should her smile but welcome him,
The fairest flower, the dewy rose,
   To deck her beauty seems too dim.
O tenderest passion! Sweetest hope!
   The golden hours of earliest love!
Heaven's self to him appears to ope;
   He feels a bliss this earth above.
O, that it could eternal last!
That youthful love were never past!

See how brown the liquid turns!   80
   Now this rod I thrust within;
If it's glazed before it burns,
   Then the casting may begin.
     Quick, my lads, and steady,
     If the mixture's ready!
When the strong and weaker blend,
Then we hope a happy end:
Whenever strength with softness joins,
When with the rough and mild combines,
   Then all is union sweet and strong.   90
Consider, ye who join your hands,
If hearts are twined in mutual bands;
   For passion's brief, repentance long.
How lovely in the maiden's hair
   The bridal garland plays!
And merry bells invite us there,
   Where mingle festive lays.
Alas! that all life's brightest hours
   Are ended with its earliest May!
That from those sacred nuptial bowers   100
   The dear deceit should pass away!
     Though passion may fly,
       Yet love will endure
     The flower must die,
       The fruit to insure.
     The man must without,
       Into struggling life;
       With toiling and strife,
     He must plan and contrive;
     Must be prudent to thrive;   110
       With boldness must dare,
       Good fortune to share.

'Tis by means such as these, that abundance is   60
   poured
In a full, endless stream, to increase all his hoard,
   While his house to a palace spreads out.

     Within doors governs
     The modest, careful wife,
     The children's kind mother;
     And wise is the rule
     Of her household school.   120
     She teaches the girls,
     And she warns the boys;
     She directs all the bands
     Of diligent hands,
     And increases their gain
     By her orderly reign.
And she fills with her treasure her sweet-scented
   chests;
From the toil of her spinning-wheel scarcely she
   rests;
And she gathers in order, so cleanly and bright,
The softest of wool, and the linen snow-white: 130
The useful and pleasant she mingles ever,
     And is slothful never.
   The father, cheerful, from the door,
     His wide-extended homestead eyes;
   Tells all his smiling fortunes o'er;
   The future columns in his trees,
   His barn's well furnished stock he sees,
   His granaries e'en now o'erflowing,
   While yet the waving corn is growing.
     He boasts with swelling pride,   140
     "Firm as the mountain's side
     Against the shock of fate
     Is now my happy state."
   Who can discern futurity?
   Who can insure prosperity?
   Quick misfortune's arrow flies.

Now we may begin to cast;
   All is right and well prepared:
Yet, ere the anxious moment's past,
   A pious hope by all be shared.   150
     Strike the stopper clear!
     God preserve us here!
Sparkling, to the rounded mould
It rushes hot, like liquid gold.
How useful is the power of flame,
If human skill control and tame!
And much of all that man can boast,
Without this child of Heaven, were lost.
But frightful is her changing mien,
When, bursting from her bonds, she's seen   160
To quit the safe and quiet hearth,

And wander lawless o'er the earth.
Woe to those whom then she meets!
   Against her fury who can stand?
Along the thickly peopled streets
   She madly hurls her fearful brand.
Then the elements, with joy,
Man's best handiwork destroy.
      From the clouds
      Falls amain   170
      The blessed rain:
      From the clouds alike
      Lightenings strike.
Ringing loud the fearful knell,
      Sounds the bell.
      Dark blood-red
      Are all the skies;
But no dawning light is spread.
      What wild cries
      From the streets arise!   180
      Smoke dims the eyes.
Flickering mounts the fiery glow
Along the street's extended row,
Fast as fiercest winds can blow.
Bright, as with a furnace glare,
And scorching, is the heated air;
Beams are falling, children crying,
Windows breaking, mothers flying,
Creatures moaning, crushed and dying,—
All is uproar, hurry, flight,   190
And light as day the dreadful night.
Along the eager living lane,
      Though all in vain,
Speeds the bucket. The engine's power
Sends the artificial shower.
But see, the heavens still threatening lower!
The winds rush soaring to the flame.
Cinders on the store-house frame,
And its drier stores, fall thick;
While kindling, blazing, mounting quick,   200
As though it would, at one fell sweep,
   All that on the earth is found
   Scatter wide in ruin round,
Swells the flame to heaven's blue deep,
      With giant size.
      Hope now dies.
   Man must yield to Heaven's decrees.
   Submissive, yet appalled, he sees
His fairest works in ashes sleep.

      All burnt over   210
      Is the place,
The storm's wild home. How changed its face!
   In the empty, ruined wall
   Dwells dark horror;

While heaven's clouds in shadow fall
   Deep within.

      One look,
      In memory sad,
      Of all he had,
      The unhappy sufferer took,—   220
Then found his heart might yet be glad.
   However hard his lot to bear,
His choicest treasures still remain:
He calls for each with anxious pain,
   And every loved one's with him there.

To the earth it's now committed.
   With success the mould is filled.
To skill and care alone's permitted
   A perfect work with toil to build.
      Is the casting right?   230
      Is the mould yet tight?
Ah! while now with hope we wait,
Mischance, perhaps, attends its fate.
   To the dark lap of mother earth
      We now confide what we have made;
      As in earth too the seed is laid,
   In hope the seasons will give birth
      To fruits that soon may be displayed.
   And yet more precious seed we sow
      With sorrow in the world's wide field;   240
   And hope, though in the grave laid low,
      A flower of heavenly hue 'twill yield.

      Slow and heavy
         Hear it swell!
      'Tis the solemn
         Passing bell!
Sad we follow, with these sounds of woe,
Those who on this last, long journey go.
   Alas! the wife,—it is the dear one,—
   Ah! it is the faithful mother,   250
Whom the shadowy king of fear
Tears from all that life holds dear;—
From the husband,—from the young,
The tender blossoms, that have sprung
From their mutual, faithful love,
'T was hers to nourish, guide, improve.
Ah! the chain which bound them all
      Is for ever broken now;
She cannot hear their tender call,
      Nor see them in affliction bow.   260
Her true affection guards no more;
      Her watchful care wakes not again:
O'er all the once loved orphan's store
      The indifferent stranger now must reign.

Till the bell is safely cold,
  May our heavy labor rest;
Free as the bird, by none controlled,
  Each may do what pleases best.
    With approaching night,
    Twinkling stars are bright.   270
Vespers call the boys to play;
The master's toils end not with day.

Cheerful in the forest gloom,
  The wanderer turns his weary steps
To his loved, though lowly home.
  Bleating flocks draw near the fold;
    And the herds,
Wide-horned, and smooth, slow-pacing come
  Lowing from the hill,
  The accustomed stall to fill.   280
    Heavy rolls
    Along the wagon,
    Richly loaded.
    On the sheaves,
    With the gayest leaves
    They form the wreath;
And the youthful reapers dance
    Upon the heath.
Street and market all are quiet,
And round each domestic light   290
Gathers now a circle fond,
While shuts the creaking city-gate.
    Darkness hovers
    O'er the earth.
Safety still each sleeper covers
    As with light,
That the deeds of crime discovers;
  For wakes the law's protecting might.

Holy Order! rich with all
The gifts of Heaven, that best we call,— 300
Freedom, peace, and equal laws,—
Of common good the happy cause!
She the savage man has taught
What the arts of life have wrought;
Changed the rude hut to comfort, splendor,
And filled fierce hearts with feelings tender
And yet a dearer bond she wove,—
Our home, our country, taught to love.

A thousand active hands, combined
  For mutual aid, with zealous heart,   310
In well apportioned labor find
Master and workmen all agree,
  Their power increasing with their art.
  Under sweet Freedom's holy care,

And each, content in his degree,
  Warns every scorner to beware.
Labor is the poor man's pride,—
  Success by toil alone is won.
Kings glory in possessions wide,—
  We glory in our work well done.   320

    Gentle peace!
    Sweet union!
    Linger, linger,
Kindly over this our home!
  Never may the day appear,
  When the hordes of cruel war
Through this quiet vale shall rush;
    When the sky,
  With the evening's softened air,
    Blushing red,   330
Shall reflect the frightful glare
  Of burning towns in ruin dread.

Now break up the useless mould:
  Its only purpose is fulfilled.
May our eyes, well pleased, behold
  A work to prove us not unskilled.
    Wield the hammer, wield,
    Till the frame shall yield!
That the bell to light may rise,
The form in thousand fragments flies.   340

The master may destroy the mould
  With careful hand, and judgment wise.
But, woe!—in streams of fire, if rolled,
  The glowing metal seek the skies!
Loud bursting with the crash of thunder,
  It throws aloft the broken ground;
Like a volcano rends asunder,
  And spreads in burning ruin round.
When reckless power by force prevails,
  The reign of peace and art is o'er;   350
And when a mob e'en wrong assails,
  The public welfare is no more.
Alas! when in the peaceful state
  Conspiracies are darkly forming;
The oppressed no longer patient wait;
  With fury every breast is storming.
Then whirls the bell with frequent clang;
  And Uproar, with her howling voice,
Has changed the note, that peaceful rang,
  To wild confusion's dreadful noise.   360

Freedom and equal rights they call,—
  And peace gives way to sudden war;
The street is crowded, and the hall,—
  And crime is unrestrained by law:

E'en woman, to a fury turning,
  But mocks at every dreadful deed;
Against the hated madly burning,
  With horrid joy she sees them bleed.
Now naught is sacred;—broken lies
  Each holy law of honest worth;   370
The bad man rules, the good man flies,
  And every vice walks boldly forth.

There's danger in the lion's wrath,
  Destruction in the tiger's jaw;
But worse than death to cross the path
  Of man, when passion is his law.
Woe, woe to those who strive to light
  The torch of truth by passion's fire!
It guides not;—it but glares through night
  To kindle freedom's funeral pyre.   380

God has given us joy to-night!
  See how, like the golden grain
From the husk, all smooth and bright,
  The shining metal now is ta'en!
    From top to well formed rim,
    Not a spot is dim;
E'en the motto, neatly raised,
Shows a skill may well be praised.

          Around, around,
Companions all, take your ground,   390
And name the bell with joy profound!
CONCORDIA is the word we've found
Most meet to express the harmonious sound,
That calls to those in friendship bound.

Be this henceforth the destined end
To which the finished work we send
High over every meaner thing,
  In the blue canopy of heaven,
Near to the thunder let it swing,
  A neighbour to the stars be given.   400
Let its clear voice above proclaim,
  With brightest troops of distant suns,
The praise of our Creator's name,
  While round each circling season runs.
To solemn thoughts of heart-felt power
  Let its deep note full oft invite,
And tell, with every passing hour,
  Of hastening time's unceasing flight.
Still let it mark the course of fate;
  Its cold, unsympathizing voice   410
Attend on every changing state
  Of human passions, griefs, and joys.

And as the mighty sound it gives
  Dies gently on the listening ear,

We feel how quickly all that lives
  Must change, and fade, and disappear.

Now, lads, join your strength around!
  Lift the bell to upper air!
And in the kingdom wide of sound
  Once placed, we'll leave it there.   420
    All together! heave!
    Its birth-place see it leave!—
Joy to all within its bound!
Peace its first, its latest sound!

To My Friends *

Belovèd friends! More glorious times than ours
Of old existed: men of loftier powers
  Then we can boast have flourished:—who shall
    doubt it?
A million stones dug from the depths of Earth
Will bear this witness for the ancient worth,
  If History's chronicles be mute about it.
    But, all are gone—those richly-gifted souls—
      That constellation of illustrious names:
    For Us, for Us, the current moment rolls,
      And We, We live, and have our claims.   10

My friends! The wanderer tells us—and we own—
That Earth shows many a more luxuriant zone
  Than that whereunder we sedately live;
But, if denied a paradise, our hearts
Are still the home of science and the arts,
  And glow and gladden in the light they give;
    And if beneath our skies the laurel pines,
      And winter desolates our myrtle boughs,
    The curling tendrils of our joyous vines
      Shed freshest greenness round our brows. 20

May burn more feverish life, more maddening pleas-
  ures,
Where four assembled worlds exchange their treas-
  ures,
  At London, in the world's Commercial Hall;
A thousand stately vessels come and go,
And costly sights are there, and pomp and show,
  And Gold is lord and idolgod of all!
    But will the sun be mirrored in the stream
      Sullied and darkened by the flooding rains?
    No! On the still smooth lake alone his beam
      Is brightly imaged, and remains.   30

The beggar at St. Angelo's might gaze
With scorn upon our North, for he surveys
  The one, lone, only, everliving Rome—

* Translated by James Clarence Mangan.

All shapes of beauty fascinate his eye;
He sees a brilliant heaven below the sky
  Shine in Saint Peter's wonderwaking dome.
    But, even while beaming with celestial glory,
      Rome is the grave of long-departed years;
    It is the green young plant and not the hoary
      And time-worn trunk that blooms and
        cheers.   40

Prouder achievements may perchance appear
Elsewhere than signalize our humble sphere,
  But newer nowhere underneath the sun.
We see in pettier outlines on our stage,
Which miniatures the world of every age,
  The storied feats of bypassed eras done.
    All things are but redone, reshown, retold,
      Fancy alone is ever young and new;
    Man and the universe shall both grow old,
      But not the forms her pencil drew!   50

HEINRICH HEINE

For an introduction to the life and works of
Heine, see page 238.

My Child, We Were Children

My child, we were two children,
Small, merry by childhood's law;
We used to creep to the henhouse,
And hide ourselves in the straw.

We crowed like cocks, and whenever
The passers near us drew—
"Cock-a-doodle!" they thought
'Twas a real cock that crew.

The boxes about our courtyard
We carpeted to our mind,
And lived there both together—
Kept house in a noble kind.

The neighbor's old cat often
Came to pay us a visit;
(We have made the very same speeches
Each with a compliment in it.)

After her health we asked,
Our care and regard to evince—
(We have made the very same speeches
To many an old cat since.)

We also sat and wisely
Discoursed, as old folks do,
Complaining how all went better
In those good old times we knew;—

How love, and truth, and believing
Had left the world to itself,
And how so dear was the coffee,
And how so rare was the pelf.

The children's games are over,
The rest is over with youth—
The world, the good games, the good times,
The belief, and the love, and the truth.

              (trans. by Elizabeth Barrett Browning)

Upon My Darling's Beaming Eyes

Upon my darling's beaming eyes
  I plied my rhyming trade;
Upon my darling's cherry lips
  An epigram I made;
My darling has a blooming cheek,
  I penn'd a song upon it;
And if she had but had a heart,
  Her heart had had a sonnet.

              (trans. by Richard Garnett)

The Violets Blue of Her Eyes

The violets blue of the eyes divine,
And the rose of the cheeks as red as wine,
And the lilies white of the hands so fine,
They flourish and flourish from year to year,
And only the heart is withered and sere.

              (trans. by James Thomson)

A Pine Tree Standeth Lonely

A Pine-Tree standeth lonely
  In the North on an upland bare;
It standeth whitely shrouded
  With snow, and sleepeth there.

It dreameth of a Palm Tree
  Which far in the East alone,
In mournful silence standeth
  On its ridge of burning stone.

              (trans. by James Thomson)

My Heart Is Mournful

My heart, my heart is mournful,
    Yet joyously shines the May;
I stand by the linden leaning,
    High on the bastion gray.

The blue town-moat thereunder
    Glides peacefully along;
A boy in a boat is angling,
    And whistling a careless song.

Beyond, like a well-known picture,
    All small and fair, are strewed
Houses and gardens and people,
    Oxen and meadows and wood.

The maidens bleach the linen,
    And dance in the grass for glee;
The mill-wheel scatters diamonds,
    Its far hum reaches me.

Upon the hoary tower
    A sentry-box stands low;
A youth in his coat of scarlet
    There passes to and fro.

He trifles with his musket,
    Which gleams in the sunshine red,
He shoulders and presents it–
    I would he shot me dead!

                (trans. by James Thomson)

The Moon Is Risen

The moon is fully risen,
    And shineth o'er the sea;
And I embrace my darling,
    Our hearts are swelling free.

In the arms of the lovely maiden
    I lie alone on the strand;—
"What sounds in the breezes sighing?
    Why trembles your white hand?"

"That is no breeze's sighing,
    That is the mermaiden's song,
The singing of my sisters
    Whom the sea hath drowned so long."

                (trans. by James Thomson)

Say, Where Is the Maiden Sweet?

"Say, where is the maiden sweet,
    Whom you once so sweetly sung,

When the flames of mighty heat
    Filled your heart and fired your tongue?"

Ah, those flames no longer burn,
    Cold and drear the heart that fed;
And this book is but the urn
    Of the ashes of love dead.

                (trans. by James Thomson)

Old Time Is Lame and Halt

Old Time is lame and halt,
    The snail can barely crawl:
But how should I find fault,
    Who cannot move at all?

No gleam of cheerful sun!
    No hope my life to save!
I have two rooms, the one
    I die in and the grave.

May be, I've long been dead,
    May be, a giddy train
Of phantoms fills my head,
    And haunts what was my brain.

These dear old gods or devils,
    Who see me stiff and dull,
May like to dance their revels
    In a dead Poet's skull.

Their rage of weird delight
    Is luscious pain to me:
And my bony fingers write
    What daylight must not see.

                (trans. by Lord Houghton)

Enfant Perdu

In Freedom's War, of "Thirty Years" and more,
    A lonely outpost have I held—in vain!
With no triumphant hope or prize in store,
    Without a thought to see my home again.

I watched both day and night: I could not sleep
    Like my well-tented comrades far behind,
Though near enough to let their snoring keep
    A friend awake, if e'er to doze inclined.

And thus, when solitude my spirits shook,
    Or fear—for all but fools know fear sometimes,—
To rouse myself and them, I piped and took
    A gay revenge in all my wanton rhymes.

Yes! there I stood, my musket always ready,
  And when some sneaking rascal showed his head,
My eye was vigilant, my aim was steady,
  And gave his brains an extra dose of lead.

But war and justice have far different laws,
  And worthless acts are often done right well;
The rascals' shots were better than their cause,
  And I was hit—and hit again, and fell!

That outpost was abandoned: while the one
  Lies in the dust, the rest in troops depart;
Unconquered—I have done what could be done,
  With sword unbroken, and with broken heart.

(trans. by Lord Houghton)

You Are Like a Flower

E'en as a lovely flower,
  So fair, so pure thou art;
I gaze on thee, and sadness
  Comes stealing o'er my heart.

My hands I fain had folded
  Upon thy soft brown hair,
Praying that God may keep thee
  So lovely, pure and fair.

(trans. by Kate Freiligrath Kroeker)

Ah! Did But the Flowers Know

Ah! did but the little flowers know
  How deep the wound of my heart,
Their tears would mingle and flow,
  To ease my pain and smart.

Ah! did but the nightingale guess
  How sad and sorry am I,
She would pipe, to soothe my distress,
  A quickening melody.

And did the stars golden and bright
  Know all my sorrow and woe,
They would come from their radiant height,
  And words of peace bestow.

But, alas! my sorrows none share,
  One only guesses my pain,
She for whose love I must wear
  A heart that is rent in twain.

(trans. by Edward Chawner)

The Grenadiers *

Toward France there wandered two grenadiers;
  In Russia they had been taken.
And as they reached the German frontiers,
  Body and spirit were shaken.

For there they learned the tragic tale
  That France had been lost and forsaken;
The Army had suffered to no avail,
  And the Emperor, the Emperor was taken!

They wept together, those two grenadiers;
  To one thing their thoughts kept returning.
"Alas," said one, half choked with tears,
  "That old wound of mine keeps burning."

The other said, "This is the end;
  With you I'd gladly perish.
But there's the homeland to defend,
  And wife and child to cherish."

"What matters wife? What matters child?
  With far greater cares I am shaken.
Let them go and beg, with hunger wild;
  My Emperor, my Emperor is taken!

"And, brother, this my only prayer,
  Now I am dying, grant me:
You'll bear my body to France, and there
  In the soil of France you'll plant me.

"The cross of honor with crimson band
  Lay on my heart that bound me;
Then put the musket in my hand
  And strap my saber round me.

"So I will lie and listen and wait,
  A sentinel, down in the grass there,
Till I hear the roar of the guns and the great
  Thunder of hoofs as they pass there.

"The Emperor will come and the columns will
    wave;
  The swords will be flashing and rending;
And I will arise, full-armed, from the grave,
  My Emperor, my Emperor defending."

Ballad

The sickle moon of autumn
  Peers white through clouds around;
The parsonage by the churchyard
  Lies hushed in rest profound.

* From *Heinrich Heine: Paradox and Poet*, Vol. II, by
Louis Untermeyer. Copyright, 1937 by Harcourt, Brace
and Company, Inc.

The mother reads in the Bible,
    The son at the candle stares,
Sits yawning the elder daughter,
    While the younger thus declares:—

"Alas! for the days we live here!
    How creep they so wearily;
Save when one to the grave is carried,
    What have we here to see?"

The mother says, 'mid her reading,
    "Thou'rt wrong; but four have died
Since that thy father was carried
    To rest by the church-door side."

Then yawneth the elder daughter:
    "I'll not starve here with ye;
I will to the Count to-morrow,—
    He's rich, and he loveth me."

The son breaks forth in laughter:
    "There drink at the Star below
Three who make gold, and who'll teach me
    Their secret gladly, I know."

The mother flings the Bible
    Right in his face so wan:
"And would'st thou, God-accurséd,
    Become a highwayman?"

They hear a knock at the window,
    They see a beckoning hand;
Without, in his black-priest garment,
    Doth their dead father stand.

            (trans. by H. W. Dulcken)

Song

In my life too dark and dreary
    Once gleamed an image bright:
That lovely form is faded,
    And I am wrapped in night.

When children stray in darkness,
    And fears around them throng,
To drive away their terror
    They sing aloud a song.

Thus like a child I'm singing
    As life's dark shades draw near;
And though my lay lack music,
    It drives away my fear.

            (trans. by C. G. Leland)

Anno 1829

I crave an ampler, worthier sphere:
    I'd liefer bleed at every vein
Than stifle 'mid these hucksters here,
    These lying slaves of paltry gain.

They eat, they drink; they're every whit
    As happy as their type, the mole;
Large are their bounties—as the slit
    Through which they drop the poor man's dole.

With pipe in mouth they go their way,
    With hands in pockets; they are blest
With grand digestions: only *they*
    Are such hard morsels to digest!

The hand that's red with some dark deed,
    Some giant crime, were white as wool
Compared with these sleek saints, whose creed
    Is paying all their debts in full.

Ye clouds that sail to far-off lands,
    O waft me to what clime ye will!
To Lapland's snows, to Lybia's sands,
    To the world's end—but onward still!

Take me, O clouds! They ne'er look down;
    But (proof of a discerning mind)
One moment hung o'er Hamburg town,
    The next they leave it leagues behind.

        (trans. by Charles Stuart Calverley)

The Lorelei

I know not whence it rises,
    This thought so full of woe;
But a tale of times departed
    Haunts me, and will not go.

The air is cool, and it darkens,
    And calmly flows the Rhine,
The mountain-peaks are sparkling
    In the sunny evening-shine.

And yonder sits a maiden,
    The fairest of the fair;
With gold in her garment glittering,
    And she combs her golden hair:

With a golden comb she combs it;
    And a wild song singeth she,
That melts the heart with a wondrous
    And powerful melody.

The boatman feels his bosom
    With a nameless longing move;

He sees not the gulfs before him,
  His gaze is fixed above,

Till over boat and boatman
  The Rhine's deep waters run:
And this, with her magic singing,
  The Lorelei has done!

(trans. anonymous)

The Sea Hath Its Pearls

The sea hath its pearls
  The heaven hath its stars;

But my heart, my heart,
  My heart hath its love.

Great are the sea, and the heaven;
  Yet greater is my heart,
And fairer than pearls or stars
  Flashes and beams my love.

Thou little, youthful maiden,
  Come unto my great heart;
My heart, and the sea and the heaven
  Are melting away with love!

(trans. by Henry Wadsworth Longfellow)

English Lyric Poetry

WILLIAM BLAKE

1757–1827

William Blake, the painter, engraver, and poet, was the son of a London hosier. He received no formal education because his father, who had whipped him for telling about the visions he saw (e.g., "God looked in the window at me"), observed his son's terrible anger aroused by corporal punishment and feared to send the boy to school. He was therefore apprenticed to an engraver instead. Blake, who rebelled against Neo-classical values more completely than did any of the other Romantics, might very well have come to represent the crucial point in literary history instead of Wordsworth and Coleridge, if in his own day his poetry had received any wide attention or following. But in his own time, although gradually his engravings came to be highly regarded, his poetry remained unknown; not until the middle of the nineteenth century did it gain real recognition.

Blake was a mystic, a man who could perceive truth directly and intuitively without any intermediary. As he walked through the fields he saw the prophet Isaiah sitting under a tree, and beheld visions of angels ascending to and descending from heaven. He saw sights beyond the power of ordinary mortals, which he has preserved for us in his symbolic, mystical paintings and copperplate engravings. His communion with the spiritual world was not limited to the visual, for as he walked through his earthly life, sometimes in the beautiful English countryside, but much more often through the squalid streets of London slums, he heard voices; and the revelation of their truth he has transmitted to us in his incomparable lyrics, which, although superficially simple, are often actually subtle and profound.

A complete rebel against the institutions of society, as well as against all organized religions, he often speaks in righteous fury with the voice of an Old Testament prophet against the injustices and social wrongs, the sham and the hypocrisy that he observed around him. Because of his fondness for symbols, often of so personal and private a kind as to make his work incomprehensible to the general reader, he has assumed a tremendous importance among our own contemporary poets. For example, A. E. Housman has said:

For me the most poetical of all poets is Blake. I find his lyrical note as beautiful as Shakespeare's and more beautiful than anyone else's; and I call him more poetical than Shakespeare, even though Shakespeare has so much more poetry, because poetry in him preponderates more than in Shakespeare over everything else, and instead of being confounded in a great river can be drunk pure from a slender channel of its own.

Many of his later and longer poems—such as *The Four Zoas, Milton, Jerusalem, The Book of Urizen* —are based on such an esoteric symbolism and such a complicated structure of allegory as to form a complete Blake mythology, unintelligible save to a few experts.

Blake's two books of short lyrics, the part of his poetic work best known and loved, are his *Songs of Innocence* (1789) and *Songs of Experience* (1794), from which all of the lyrics here presented except one ("Stanzas from *Milton*") are taken. These two books were not originally set in type but were engraved on copper plates by Blake himself, and the pages were bound into books by his wife.

FURTHER READING

SAURAT, D. *Blake and Modern Thought* (London, 1929).
SCHORER, M. *William Blake, The Politics of Vision* (New York, 1946).

Songs of Innocence: Introduction

Piping down the valleys wild,
  Piping songs of pleasant glee,
On a cloud I saw a child,
  And he laughing said to me:

"Pipe a song about a Lamb!"
  So I piped with merry cheer.
"Piper, pipe that song again";
  So I piped: he wept to hear.

"Drop thy pipe, thy happy pipe;
  Sing thy songs of happy cheer!"
So I sang the same again,
  While he wept with joy to hear.

"Piper, sit thee down and write
  In a book, that all may read."
So he vanished from my sight,
  And I plucked a hollow reed,

And I made a rural pen,
  And I stained the water clear,
And I wrote my happy songs
  Every child may joy to hear.

The Lamb

Little Lamb, who made thee?
  Dost thou know who made thee?
Gave thee life, and bid thee feed,

By the stream and o'er the mead;
Gave thee clothing of delight,
Softest clothing, woolly, bright;
Gave thee such a tender voice,
Making all the vales rejoice?
  Little Lamb, who made thee?
  Dost thou know who made thee?

Little Lamb, I'll tell thee,
Little Lamb, I'll tell thee:
He is callèd by thy name,
For He calls Himself a Lamb,
He is meek, and He is mild;
He became a little child.
I a child, and thou a lamb,
We are callèd by His name.
  Little Lamb, God bless thee!
  Little Lamb, God bless thee!

The Little Black Boy

My mother bore me in the southern wild,
  And I am black, but O my soul is white!
White as an angel is the English child,
  But I am black, as if bereaved of light.

My mother taught me underneath a tree,
  And, sitting down before the heat of day,
She took me on her lap and kissèd me,
  And, pointing to the east, began to say:

"Look on the rising sun;—there God does live,
  And gives His light, and gives His heat away;
And flowers and trees and beasts and men receive
  Comfort in morning, joy in the noonday.

"And we are put on earth a little space,
  That we may learn to bear the beams of love;
And these black bodies and this sunburnt face
  Is but a cloud, and like a shady grove.

"For when our souls have learned the heat to bear,
  The cloud will vanish, we shall hear His voice,
Saying: 'Come out from the grove, my love and
    care,
  And round my golden tent like lambs rejoice.'"

Thus did my mother say, and kissèd me;
  And thus I say to little English boy.
When I from black, and he from white cloud free,
  And round the tent of God like lambs we joy,

I'll shade him from the heat, till he can bear
  To lean in joy upon our Father's knee;
And then I'll stand and stroke his silver hair,
  And be like him, and he will then love me.

The Tiger

Tiger! Tiger! burning bright
In the forests of the night,
What immortal hand or eye
Could frame thy fearful symmetry?

In what distant deeps or skies
Burnt the fire of thine eyes?
On what wings dare he aspire?
What the hand dare seize the fire?

And what shoulder, and what art,
Could twist the sinews of thy heart?
And when thy heart began to beat,
What dread hand and what dread feet?

What the hammer? what the chain?
In what furnace was thy brain?
What the anvil? what dread grasp
Dare its deadly terrors clasp?

When the stars threw down their spears,
And watered heaven with their tears,
Did He smile his work to see?
Did He who made the Lamb make thee?

Tiger! Tiger! burning bright
In the forests of the night,
What immortal hand or eye
Dare frame thy fearful symmetry?

The Clod and the Pebble

"Love seeketh not itself to please,
    Nor for itself hath any care,
But for another gives its ease,
    And builds a Heaven in Hell's despair."

So sung a little clod of clay,
    Trodden with the cattle's feet,
But a pebble of the brook
    Warbled out these meters meet:

"Love seeketh only Self to please,
    To bind another to its delight,
Joys in another's loss of ease,
    And builds a Hell in Heaven's despite."

Holy Thursday

Is this a holy thing to see
In a rich and fruitful land—
Babes reduced to misery,
Fed with cold and usurous hand?

Is that trembling cry a song?
Can it be a song of joy?
And so many children poor?
It is a land of poverty!

And their sun does never shine,
And their fields are bleak and bare,
And their ways are filled with thorns:
It is eternal winter there.

For where'er the sun does shine,
And where'er the rain does fall,
Babe can never hunger there,
Nor poverty the mind appall.

A Poison Tree

I was angry with my friend:
I told my wrath, my wrath did end.
I was angry with my foe:
I told it not, my wrath did grow.

And I watered it in fears
Night and morning with my tears,
And I sunnéd it with smiles
And with soft deceitful wiles.

And it grew both day and night,
Till it bore an apple bright,
And my foe beheld it shine,
And he knew that it was mine—

And into my garden stole
When the night had veiled the pole;
In the morning, glad, I see
My foe outstretched beneath the tree.

The Garden of Love

I went to the Garden of Love,
And saw what I never had seen:
A chapel was built in the midst,
Where I used to play on the green.

And the gates of this chapel were shut,
And "Thou shalt not" writ over the door;
So I turned to the Garden of Love,
That so many sweet flowers bore:

And I saw it was filléd with graves,
And tombstones where flowers should be;
And priests in black gowns were walking their
    rounds,
And binding with briars my joys and desires.

London

I wander through each chartered street,
Near where the chartered Thames does flow,
And mark in every face I meet
Marks of weakness, marks of woe.

In every cry of every man,
In every infant's cry of fear,
In every voice, in every ban,
The mind-forged manacles I hear:

How the chimney-sweeper's cry
Every blackening church appalls,
And the hapless soldier's sigh
Runs in blood down palace walls.

But most, through midnight streets I hear
How the youthful harlot's curse
Blasts the new-born infant's tear,
And blights with plagues the marriage hearse.

The Chimney-Sweeper

A little black thing among the snow,
Crying "'weep! 'weep!" in notes of woe!
"Where are thy father and mother? Say!"
"They are both gone up to the church to pray.

"Because I was happy upon the heath,
And smiled among the winter's snow,
They clothed me in the clothes of death,
And taught me to sing the notes of woe.

"And because I am happy, and dance and sing,
They think they have done me no injury,
And are gone to praise God and his priest and king,
Who make up a heaven of our misery."

Stanzas from *Milton*

And did those feet in ancient time
Walk upon England's mountains green?
And was the holy Lamb of God
On England's pleasant pastures seen?

And did the Countenance Divine
Shine forth upon our clouded hills?
And was Jerusalem builded here
Among these dark Satanic mills?

Bring me my bow of burning gold!
Bring me my arrows of desire!
Bring me my spear! O clouds, unfold!
Bring me my chariot of fire!

I will not cease from mental fight,
Nor shall my sword sleep in my hand,
Till we have built Jerusalem
In England's green and pleasant land.

WILLIAM WORDSWORTH

1770–1850

William Wordsworth, whom Matthew Arnold ranked only below Shakespeare and Milton, was born at Cockermouth in the Lake Country, which he grew up to love and where he spent the greater part of his life. His education was received at the grammar school at Hawkshead and at St. John's College, Cambridge, where he was but an indifferent student, since he preferred to spend his time in solitary walks and in reading. In 1790, while still an undergraduate, he and a college friend went on a walking tour of France, the Rhine Valley, and Switzerland. After taking his degree in 1791, he spent more than a year in France at Orléans and Blois. There he met Captain Beaupuy, a French army officer, whose zeal for the French Revolution fired Wordsworth with enthusiasm for the cause and with a tremendous sympathy with the humble, downtrodden, and oppressed common people. During his French sojourn he met and fell in love with Annette Vallon, a pretty girl of good French family. Why they never married has never been satisfactorily explained. In 1792 she gave birth to their daughter Caroline, and Wordsworth returned to England. He did, however, make some financial provisions for his daughter and kept in infrequent touch with both mother and child.

Returning to England, he soon became somewhat disillusioned by the atrocities of the Terror, although when England declared war on France in 1793 his sympathies still were with the French. In 1795 he received a small legacy and thereupon decided to dedicate the rest of his life to poetry. He settled down with his talented sister Dorothy in a house at Racedown. She, incidentally, devoted most of her life to the encouragement of his genius. In this year he met Samuel Taylor Coleridge, and the three became daily, inseparable companions. In order to be nearer Coleridge, the Wordsworths moved to Alfoxden. Thus began one of the most fruitful collaborations in literature. These two geniuses, although of different poetic orders, mutually stimulated and complemented each other. Together they planned and published in 1798 the truly epochal *Lyrical Ballads,* the publication of which marks the conscious beginning of the Romantic movement in English literature. Two years later a second edition was issued together with a *Preface,* written by Wordsworth, which may be regarded as the critical manifesto of the Romantic movement in England. In this work Wordsworth explicitly stated his intention in the new poetry:

The principal object, then, proposed in these Poems, was to choose incidents and situations from common life, and to relate or describe them throughout, as far as was possible, in a selection of the language really used by men, and, at the same time, to throw over them a certain coloring of imagination, whereby ordinary things should be presented to the mind in an unusual aspect, and further, and above all, to make these incidents and situations interesting by tracing in them, truly though not ostentatiously, the primary laws of our nature. . . . Humble and rustic life was generally chosen, because in that condition the essential passions of the heart find a better soil in which they can attain their maturity, are less under restraint, and speak a plainer and more emphatic language; because in that condition of life our elementary feelings co-exist in a state of greater simplicity, and, consequently, may be more accurately contemplated, and more forcibly communicated. . . . The language, too, of these men is adopted (purified indeed from what appears to be its real defects, from all lasting and rational causes of dislike or disgust), because such men hourly communicate with the best objects from which the best part of language is originally derived. . . .

In 1798 the Wordsworths and Coleridge went to Germany, where Wordsworth wrote the hauntingly beautiful *Lucy* poems. The identity of Lucy, although never discovered, has long fascinated students of literature. It is now rather generally held that Lucy is a nostalgic idealization of an English girl, written by a Wordsworth perhaps a bit homesick. Upon return from Germany, William and Dorothy rented Dove Cottage, near Grasmere, and Coleridge took up residence nearby. Much of Wordsworth's best work was written in this humble home, now a literary shrine. In 1802 Wordsworth married his childhood friend Mary Hutchinson.

Shortly after the birth of their first child in 1803, Wordsworth, accompanied by Dorothy and Coleridge, set out for a tour of Scotland. During their Scottish journey some difference of opinion developed between Wordsworth and Coleridge and they parted; the poets thereafter were never in really intimate association.

Wordsworth lived eighty years, but his best work was done before 1807, or by the time he was thirty-seven. He grew more conservative as he grew older; abandoning the revolutionary ideas of his youth, he now opposed any attempt to alter the status quo in politics, economics, or social structure of his country, and he even looked with disdain upon the younger generation of Romantics—Byron, Shelley, Keats—all of whom he outlived. He continued to write, but the youthful inspiration was spent, and nothing written after 1807 really augmented his poetic reputation. In 1813 he moved into the comfortable estate of Rydal Mount near Grasmere, where he sought and obtained a government sinecure, the Distributorship of Stamps for Westmoreland. He died in 1850, and is buried in the churchyard at Grasmere.

Some of Wordsworth's finest poems do not strictly conform to standards that he himself laid down; among these are *Tintern Abbey* and the *Intimations* ode, in neither of which is the language that used by common men. Wordsworth is generally called a "nature" poet, but he is not primarily a descriptive poet of nature. Rather he gives the philosophy which nature has taught him, as in *Tintern Abbey* where, after telling what nature meant to him as a thoughtless youth, and then as a passionate young man, he states the meaning of nature to him now in maturity as

a sense sublime
Of something far more deeply interfused,
Whose dwelling is the light of setting suns,
And the round ocean and the living air,
And the blue sky, and in the mind of man;
A motion and a spirit, that impels
All thinking things, all objects of all thought,
And rolls through all things.

Wordsworth's Rousseauistic exaltation of the common man and of humble, rustic life often produced poetry of truly immortal beauty, such as "The Solitary Reaper." Though there is much excellent poetry in *The Prelude,* his long poetic autobiography, and in his other extensively ambitious works, it is chiefly upon his fresh and effortless simple lyrics that Wordsworth's great reputation rests. And certainly Wordsworth deserves to be ranked among the four greatest sonnet writers in all English literature.

FURTHER READING

BERNBAUM, ERNEST. *Guide Through the Romantic Movement* (2d ed., New York, 1949).

HARPER, G. M. *William Wordsworth: His Life, Works, and Influence* (New York, 1929).

HAVENS, R. D. *The Mind of a Poet* (Baltimore, 1941).

LEGOUIS, EMILE. *The Early Life of Wordsworth, 1770–1798* (rev. ed., London, 1932).

My Heart Leaps Up When I Behold

My heart leaps up when I behold
  A rainbow in the sky:
So was it when my life began;
So is it now I am a man:
So be it when I shall grow old,
  Or let me die!
The Child is father of the Man;
And I could wish my days to be
Bound each to each by natural piety.

Lines

COMPOSED A FEW MILES ABOVE
TINTERN ABBEY

Five years have past; five summers, with the length
Of five long winters! and again I hear
These waters, rolling from their mountain-springs
With a soft inland murmur.—Once again
Do I behold these steep and lofty cliffs,
That on a wild secluded scene impress
Thoughts of more deep seclusion; and connect
The landscape with the quiet of the sky.
The day is come when I again repose
Here, under this dark sycamore, and view   10
These plots of cottage-ground, these orchard-tufts,
Which at this season, with their unripe fruits,
Are clad in one green hue, and lose themselves
Mid groves and copses. Once again I see
These hedgerows, hardly hedgerows, little lines
Of sportive wood run wild: these pastoral farms,
Green to the very door; and wreaths of smoke
Sent up, in silence, from among the trees!

With some uncertain notice, as might seem
Of vagrant dwellers in the houseless woods,   20
Or of some Hermit's cave, where by his fire
The Hermit sits alone.
           These beauteous forms,
Through a long absence, have not been to me
As is a landscape to a blind man's eye:
But oft, in lonely rooms, and 'mid the din
Of towns and cities, I have owed to them,
In hours of weariness, sensations sweet,
Felt in the blood, and felt along the heart;
And passing even into my purer mind,
With tranquil restoration—feelings too   30
Of unremembered pleasure: such, perhaps,
As have no slight or trivial influence
On that best portion of a good man's life,
His little, nameless, unremembered acts
Of kindness and of love. Nor less, I trust,
To them I may have owed another gift,
Of aspect more sublime; that blessèd mood,
In which the burthen of the mystery,
In which the heavy and the weary weight
Of all this unintelligible world,   40
Is lightened—that serene and blessèd mood,
In which the affections gently lead us on—
Until, the breath of this corporeal frame
And even the motion of our human blood
Almost suspended, we are laid asleep
In body, and become a living soul:
While with an eye made quiet by the power
Of harmony, and the deep power of joy,
We see into the life of things.
                If this
Be but a vain belief, yet, oh! how oft—   50
In darkness and amid the many shapes
Of joyless daylight; when the fretful stir
Unprofitable, and the fever of the world,
Have hung upon the beatings of my heart—
How oft, in spirit, have I turned to thee,
O sylvan Wye! thou wanderer through the woods,
How often has my spirit turned to thee!
  And now, with gleams of half-extinguished thought,
With many recognitions dim and faint,
And somewhat of a sad perplexity,   60
The picture of the mind revives again:
While here I stand, not only with the sense
Of present pleasure, but with pleasing thoughts
That in this moment there is life and food
For future years. And so I dare to hope,
Though changed, no doubt, from what I was when first
I came among these hills; when like a roe

I bounded o'er the mountains, by the sides
Of the deep rivers, and the lonely streams,
Wherever nature led: more like a man 70
Flying from something that he dreads than one
Who sought the thing he loved. For nature then
(The coarser pleasures of my boyish days,
And their glad animal movements all gone by)
To me was all in all.—I cannot paint
What then I was. The sounding cataract
Haunted me like a passion: the tall rock,
The mountain, and the deep and gloomy wood,
Their colors and their forms, were then to me
An appetite; a feeling and a love, 80
That had no need of a remoter charm,
By thought supplied, nor any interest
Unborrowed from the eye.—That time is past,
And all its aching joys are now no more,
And all its dizzy raptures. Not for this
Faint I, nor mourn nor murmur; other gifts
Have followed; for such loss, I would believe,
Abundant recompense. For I have learned
To look on nature, not as in the hour
Of thoughtless youth; but hearing oftentimes 90
The still, sad music of humanity,
Nor harsh nor grating, though of ample power
To chasten and subdue. And I have felt
A presence that disturbs me with the joy
Of elevated thoughts; a sense sublime
Of something far more deeply interfused,
Whose dwelling is the light of setting suns,
And the round ocean and the living air,
And the blue sky, and in the mind of man:
A motion and a spirit, that impels 100
All thinking things, all objects of all thought,
And rolls through all things. Therefore am I still
A lover of the meadows and the woods,
And mountains; and of all that we behold
From this green earth; of all the mighty world
Of eye, and ear—both what they half create,
And what perceive; well pleased to recognize
In nature and the language of the sense
The anchor of my purest thoughts, the nurse,
The guide, the guardian of my heart, and soul 110
Of all my moral being.
                              Nor perchance,
If I were not thus taught, should I the more
Suffer my genial spirits to decay:
For thou art with me here upon the banks
Of this fair river; thou my dearest Friend,[1]
My dear, dear Friend; and in thy voice I catch
The language of my former heart, and read
My former pleasures in the shooting lights

[1] His sister Dorothy.

Of thy wild eyes. Oh! yet a little while
May I behold in thee what I was once, 120
My dear, dear Sister! and this prayer I make,
Knowing that Nature never did betray
The heart that loved her; 'tis her privilege,
Through all the years of this our life, to lead
From joy to joy: for she can so inform
The mind that is within us, so impress
With quietness and beauty, and so feed
With lofty thoughts, that neither evil tongues,
Rash judgments, nor the sneers of selfish men,
Nor greetings where no kindness is, nor all 130
The dreary intercourse of daily life,
Shall e'er prevail against us, or disturb
Our cheerful faith, that all which we behold
Is full of blessings. Therefore let the moon
Shine on thee in thy solitary walk;
And let the misty mountain-winds be free
To blow against thee: and, in after years,
When these wild ecstasies shall be matured
Into a sober pleasure; when thy mind
Shall be a mansion for all lovely forms, 140
Thy memory be as a dwelling-place
For all sweet sounds and harmonies; oh! then,
If solitude, or fear, or pain, or grief,
Should be thy portion, with what healing thoughts
Of tender joy wilt thou remember me,
And these my exhortations! Nor, perchance—
If I should be where I no more can hear
Thy voice, nor catch from thy wild eyes these gleams
Of past existence—wilt thou then forget
That on the banks of this delightful stream 150
We stood together; and that I, so long
A worshiper of Nature, hither came
Unwearied in that service: rather say
With warmer love—oh! with far deeper zeal
Of holier love. Nor wilt thou then forget
That after many wanderings, many years
Of absence, these steep woods and lofty cliffs,
And this green pastoral landscape, were to me
More dear, both for themselves and for thy sake!

Strange Fits of Passion Have I Known

This and the four following poems comprise the so-called "Lucy Poems."

Strange fits of passion have I known:
And I will dare to tell,
But in the Lover's ear alone,
What once to me befell.

When she I loved looked every day
Fresh as a rose in June,
I to her cottage bent my way,
Beneath an evening-moon.

Upon the moon I fixed my eye,
All over the wide lea;
With quickening pace my horse drew nigh
Those paths so dear to me.

And now we reached the orchard-plot;
And, as we climbed the hill,
The sinking moon to Lucy's cot
Came near, and nearer still.

In one of those sweet dreams I slept,
Kind Nature's gentlest boon!
And all the while my eyes I kept
On the descending moon.

My horse moved on; hoof after hoof
He raised, and never stopped:
When down behind the cottage roof,
At once, the bright moon dropped.

What fond and wayward thoughts will slide
Into a Lover's head!
"O mercy!" to myself I cried,
"If Lucy should be dead!"

She Dwelt Among the Untrodden Ways

She dwelt among the untrodden ways
    Beside the springs of Dove,
A Maid whom there were none to praise
    And very few to love:

A violet by a mossy stone
    Half hidden from the eye!
—Fair as a star, when only one
    Is shining in the sky.

She lived unknown, and few could know
    When Lucy ceased to be;
But she is in her grave, and, oh,
    The difference to me!

I Traveled Among Unknown Men

I traveled among unknown men,
    In lands beyond the sea;
Nor, England! did I know till then
    What love I bore to thee.

'Tis past, that melancholy dream!
    Nor will I quit thy shore
A second time; for still I seem
    To love thee more and more.

Among thy mountains did I feel
    The joy of my desire;
And she I cherished turned her wheel
    Beside an English fire.

Thy mornings showed, thy nights concealed
    The bowers where Lucy played;
And thine too is the last green field
    That Lucy's eyes surveyed.

Three Years She Grew in Sun and Shower

Three years she grew in sun and shower,
Then Nature said, "A lovelier flower
On earth was never sown;
This Child I to myself will take;
She shall be mine, and I will make
A Lady of my own.

"Myself will to my darling be
Both law and impulse: and with me
The Girl, in rock and plain,
In earth and heaven, in glade and bower,
Shall feel an overseeing power
To kindle or restrain.

"She shall be sportive as the fawn
That wild with glee across the lawn,
Or up the mountain springs;
And hers shall be the breathing balm,
And hers the silence and the calm
Of mute insensate things.

"The floating clouds their state shall lend
To her; for her the willow bend;
Nor shall she fail to see
Even in the motions of the Storm
Grace that shall mold the Maiden's form
By silent sympathy.

"The stars of midnight shall be dear
To her; and she shall lean her ear
In many a secret place
Where rivulets dance their wayward round,
And beauty born of murmuring sound
Shall pass into her face.

"And vital feelings of delight
Shall rear her form to stately height,

Her virgin bosom swell;
Such thoughts to Lucy I will give
While she and I together live
Here in this happy dell."

Thus Nature spake.—The work was done.—
How soon my Lucy's race was run!
She died, and left to me
This heath, this calm, and quiet scene;
The memory of what has been,
And never more will be.

'A Slumber Did My Spirit Seal

A slumber did my spirit seal;
    I had no human fears:
She seemed a thing that could not feel
    The touch of earthly years.

No motion has she now, no force;
    She neither hears nor sees;
Rolled round in earth's diurnal course,
    With rocks, and stones, and trees.

Composed upon Westminster Bridge

Earth has not anything to show more fair:
Dull would he be of soul who could pass by
A sight so touching in its majesty:
This City now doth like a garment wear
The beauty of the morning; silent, bare,
Ships, towers, domes, theaters, and temples lie
Open unto the fields, and to the sky;
All bright and glittering in the smokeless air.
Never did sun more beautifully steep
In his first splendor valley, rock, or hill;
Ne'er saw I, never felt, a calm so deep!
The river glideth at his own sweet will:
Dear God! the very houses seem asleep;
And all that mighty heart is lying still!

It Is a Beauteous Evening, Calm and Free

It is a beauteous evening, calm and free.
The holy time is quiet as a Nun,
Breathless with adoration: the broad sun
Is sinking down in its tranquillity;
The gentleness of heaven broods o'er the sea;
Listen! the mighty Being is awake,

And doth with his eternal motion make
A sound like thunder—everlastingly.
Dear Child! dear Girl! that walkest with me here,
If thou appear untouched by solemn thought,
Thy nature is not therefore less divine:
Thou liest in Abraham's bosom all the year,
And worship'st at the Temple's inner shrine,
God being with thee when we know it not.

On the Extinction of the Venetian Republic

Once did she hold the gorgeous east in fee;
And was the safeguard of the west: the worth
Of Venice did not fall below her birth,
Venice, the eldest Child of liberty.
She was a maiden City, bright and free;
No guile seduced, no force could violate;
And when she took unto herself a Mate,
She must espouse the everlasting Sea!
And what if she had seen those glories fade,
Those titles vanish, and that strength decay;
Yet shall some tribute of regret be paid
When her long life hath reached its final day:
Men are we, and must grieve when even the Shade
Of that which once was great is passed away.

London, 1802

Milton! thou shouldst be living at this hour:
England hath need of thee: she is a fen
Of stagnant waters: altar, sword, and pen,
Fireside, the heroic wealth of hall and bower,
Have forfeited their ancient English dower
Of inward happiness. We are selfish men:
Oh! raise us up, return to us again;
And give us manners, virtue, freedom, power.
Thy soul was like a Star, and dwelt apart:
Thou hadst a voice whose sound was like the sea,
Pure as the naked heavens, majestic, free;
So didst thou travel on life's common way
In cheerful godliness; and yet thy heart
The lowliest duties on herself did lay.

The World Is Too Much with Us

The world is too much with us; late and soon,
Getting and spending, we lay waste our powers:
Little we see in Nature that is ours;
We have given our hearts away, a sordid boon!

The sea that bares her bosom to the moon;
The winds that will be howling at all hours,
And are up-gathered now like sleeping flowers;
For this, for everything, we are out of tune;
It moves us not.—Great God! I'd rather be
A Pagan suckled in a creed outworn;
So might I, standing on this pleasant lea,
Have glimpses that would make me less forlorn;
Have sight of Proteus rising from the sea;
Or hear old Triton blow his wreathéd horn.

Ode

INTIMATIONS OF IMMORTALITY FROM RECOLLECTIONS OF EARLY CHILDHOOD

————

The Child is father of the man;
And I could wish my days to be
Bound each to each by natural piety.

————

1

There was a time when meadow, grove, and stream,
    The earth, and every common sight,
        To me did seem
        Appareled in celestial light,
The glory and the freshness of a dream. *unreal existence*
It is not now as it hath been of yore;—
        Turn wheresoe'er I may,
            By night or day,
The things which I have seen I now can see no more.

2

        The Rainbow comes and goes,   10
        And lovely is the Rose;
        The Moon doth with delight
    Look round her when the heavens are bare;
        Waters on a starry night
        Are beautiful and fair;
    The sunshine is a glorious birth;
    But yet I know, where'er I go,
That there hath passed away a glory from the earth.

3

Now, while the birds thus sing a joyous song,
    And while the young lambs bound   20
        As to the tabor's sound,
To me alone there came a thought of grief:

A timely utterance gave that thought relief,
        And I again am strong:
The cataracts blow their trumpets from the steep;
No more shall grief of mine the season wrong;
I hear the Echoes through the mountains throng,
The Winds come to me from the fields of sleep,
        And all the earth is gay;
            Land and sea   30
        Give themselves up to jollity,
            And with the heart of May
        Doth every Beast keep holiday;—
            Thou Child of Joy,
Shout round me, let me hear thy shouts, thou happy
        Shepherd-boy!

4

Ye blessèd Creatures, I have heard the call
        Ye to each other make; I see
The heavens laugh with you in your jubilee;
        My heart is at your festival,
        My head hath its coronal,   40
The fulness of your bliss, I feel—I feel it all.
        Oh, evil day! if I were sullen
        While Earth herself is adorning,
            This sweet May-morning,
        And the Children are culling
            On every side,
        In a thousand valleys far and wide,
Fresh flowers; while the sun shines warm,
And the Babe leaps up on his Mother's arm—
        I hear, I hear, with joy I hear!   50
        —But there's a Tree, of many, one,
A single Field which I have looked upon,
Both of them speak of something that is gone:
        The Pansy at my feet
        Doth the same tale repeat:
Whither is fled the visionary gleam?
Where is it now, the glory and the dream?

5

Our birth is but a sleep and a forgetting:
The Soul that rises with us, our life's Star,
        Hath had elsewhere its setting,   60
            And cometh from afar:
        Not in entire forgetfulness,
        And not in utter nakedness,
But trailing clouds of glory do we come
        From God, who is our home:
Heaven lies about us in our infancy!
Shades of the prison-house begin to close
        Upon the growing Boy,
But he beholds the light, and whence it flows
        He sees it in his joy;   70

Child has a perception denied to the man.

Child is in communion with God more than man

The Youth, who daily farther from the east
    Must travel, still is Nature's priest,
    And by the vision splendid
    Is on his way attended;
At length the Man perceives it die away,
And fade into the light of common day.

6

Earth fills her lap with pleasures of her own;
Yearnings she hath in her own natural kind,
And even with something of a Mother's mind,
    And no unworthy aim,   80
    The homely Nurse doth all she can
To make her Foster-child, her Inmate Man,
    Forget the glories he hath known,
And that imperial palace whence he came.

7

Behold the Child among his new-born blisses,
A six years' Darling of a pigmy size!
See, where 'mid work of his own hand he lies,
Fretted by sallies of his mother's kisses,
With light upon him from his father's eyes!
See, at his feet, some little plan or chart,   90
Some fragment from his dream of human life,
Shaped by himself with newly-learnéd art;
    A wedding or a festival,
    A mourning or a funeral,
    And this hath now his heart,
    And unto this he frames his song:
    Then will he fit his tongue
To dialogues of business, love, or strife;
    But it will not be long
    Ere this be thrown aside,   100
    And with new joy and pride
The little Actor cons another part;
Filling from time to time his "humorous stage"
With all the Persons, down to palsied Age,
That Life brings with her in her equipage;
    As if his whole vocation
    Were endless imitation.

8

Thou, whose exterior semblance doth belie
    Thy Soul's immensity;
Thou best Philosopher, who yet dost keep   110
Thy heritage, thou Eye among the blind,
That, deaf and silent, read'st the eternal deep,
Haunted forever by the eternal mind—
    Mighty Prophet! Seer blest!
    On whom those truths do rest,
Which we are toiling all our lives to find.

In darkness lost, the darkness of the grave;
Thou, over whom thy Immortality
Broods like the Day, a Master o'er a Slave,
A Presence which is not to be put by;   120
Thou little Child, yet glorious in the might
Of heaven-born freedom on thy being's height,
Why with such earnest pains dost thou provoke
The years to bring the inevitable yoke,
Thus blindly with thy blessedness at strife?
Full soon thy Soul shall have her earthly freight,
And custom lie upon thee with a weight,
Heavy as frost, and deep almost as life!

9

    Oh, joy! that in our embers
    Is something that doth live,   130
    That nature yet remembers
    What was so fugitive!
The thought of our past years in me doth breed
Perpetual benediction: not indeed
For that which is most worthy to be blest;
Delight and liberty, the simple creed
Of Childhood, whether busy or at rest,
With new-fledged hope still fluttering in his breast—
    Not for these I raise
    The song of thanks and praise;   140
    But for those obstinate questionings
    Of sense and outward things,
    Falling from us, vanishings;
    Blank misgivings of a Creature
Moving about in worlds not realized,
High instincts before which our mortal nature
Did tremble like a guilty thing surprised:
    But for those first affections,
    Those shadowy recollections,
    Which, be they what they may,   150
Are yet the fountain light of all our day,
Are yet a master light of all our seeing;
    Uphold us, cherish, and have power to make
Our noisy years seem moments in the being
Of the eternal Silence: truths that wake,
    To perish never;
Which neither listlessness, nor mad endeavor,
    Nor Man nor Boy,
Nor all that is at enmity with joy,
Can utterly abolish or destroy!   160
    Hence in a season of calm weather
    Though inland far we be,
Our Souls have sight of that immortal sea
    Which brought us hither,
    Can in a moment travel thither,
And see the Children sport upon the shore,
And hear the mighty waters rolling evermore.

10

Then sing, ye Birds, sing, sing a joyous song!
    And let the young Lambs bound
    As to the tabor's sound!   170
We in thought will join your throng,
    Ye that pipe and ye that play,
    Ye that through your hearts today
    Feel the gladness of the May!
What though the radiance which was once so bright
Be now forever taken from my sight,
   Though nothing can bring back the hour
Of splendor in the grass, of glory in the flower;
    We will grieve not, rather find
    Strength in what remains behind;   180
    In the primal sympathy
    Which having been must ever be;
    In the soothing thoughts that spring
    Out of human suffering;
    In the faith that looks through death,
In years that bring the philosophic mind.

11

And O, ye Fountains, Meadows, Hills, and Groves,
Forebode not any severing of our loves!
Yet in my heart of hearts I feel your might;
I only have relinquished one delight   190
To live beneath your more habitual sway.
I love the Brooks which down their channels fret,
Even more than when I tripped lightly as they;
The innocent brightness of a new-born Day
    Is lovely yet;
The Clouds that gather round the setting sun
Do take a sober coloring from an eye
That hath kept watch o'er man's mortality.
Another race hath been, and other palms are won.
Thanks to the human heart by which we live, 200
Thanks to its tenderness, its joys, and fears,
To me the meanest flower that blows can give
Thoughts that do often lie too deep for tears.

The Solitary Reaper

Behold her, single in the field,
Yon solitary Highland lass!
Reaping and singing by herself;
Stop here, or gently pass!
Alone she cuts and binds the grain,
And sings a melancholy strain;
O listen! for the vale profound
Is overflowing with the sound.

No nightingale did ever chaunt
More welcome notes to weary bands
Of travelers in some shady haunt,
Among Arabian sands:
A voice so thrilling ne'er was heard
In springtime from the cuckoo-bird,
Breaking the silence of the seas
Among the farthest Hebrides.

Will no one tell me what she sings?—
Perhaps the plaintive numbers flow
For old, unhappy, far-off things,
And battles long ago:
Or is it some more humble lay,
Familiar matter of today?
Some natural sorrow, loss, or pain,
That has been, and may be again?

Whate'er the theme, the maiden sang
As if her song could have no ending;
I saw her singing at her work,
And o'er the sickle bending;—
I listened, motionless and still;
And, as I mounted up the hill,
The music in my heart I bore,
Long after it was heard no more.

———◆———

SAMUEL TAYLOR COLERIDGE

1772–1834

Samuel Taylor Coleridge, perhaps the greatest genius among the English Romantics, was born in Devonshire, the son of a country clergyman. An extremely precocious youth—it is said he read the Bible at three—he was encouraged by his father to read widely. At the age of ten, after his father's death, he entered Christ's Hospital in London, a charity school for the education of bright boys. Later he was a scholarship student at Jesus College, Cambridge. Here he first began to take opium to gain relief from ailments that troubled him, for he could not endure pain. The excitement of international affairs in 1793—Louis XVI was beheaded, and England declared war on France—was not conducive to quiet study in the university, so Coleridge, who had accumulated a good many college debts, ran away and joined the Fifteenth Dragoons under the improbably fanciful name of Silas Tomkyn

Comberbacke. He detested army life—he did not even like horses—so he was quite unhappy in his military career. A brother secured his release after a time, and Coleridge returned to Cambridge, but left in 1794 without taking a degree.

In this year he met Robert Southey, already a disciple of the revolutionary William Godwin, who interested him in Pantisocracy, a utopian scheme. According to the plan, twelve young men and their wives were to sail for America where, on the banks of the Susquehanna, they were to establish an ideal community in which absolute equality was to prevail and all the social ills and all the decaying social institutions of Europe were to be abrogated in favor of a communal, intellectual life. In order to earn money for their passage, Southey and Coleridge decided to write poetry which they hoped to have published. One other difficulty stood between Coleridge and the promise of a new life in America: the members of the community were to be married, and he had no wife. Southey, however, solved this difficulty by introducing Coleridge to Sarah Fricker, whose sister Edith he had just secretly married. The Fricker sisters, who kept a millinery shop, were pretty but not very intellectual. Nevertheless Coleridge, always a strongly suggestible person, married Sarah, with whom he never seems to have been in love and from whom he soon became estranged.

In 1795 Coleridge met Wordsworth and his lovely and gifted sister Dorothy. The three became fast friends, inseparable companions, and poetical collaborators. It was a great tragedy for Coleridge and for literature that he had already espoused Sarah Fricker, for certainly if ever woman was intended for man, Dorothy Wordsworth was meant for Coleridge. Together the three planned *The Lyrical Ballads*, which they published in 1798, a monumental date in literary history. Coleridge's most important contribution to the volume was "The Rime of the Ancient Mariner," a long supernatural poem in ballad form. The theme of the poem is spiritual isolation, and, as Irving Babbitt has observed, it is the finest treatment in literature of the main Romantic motif of solitude. Perhaps its only artistic flaw is the moral, which Wordsworth insisted upon having attached.

Also in 1798 he was granted an annuity by the Wedgwoods, makers of Wedgwood ware, which enabled him to go to Germany, where within six weeks he had learned enough German to translate one of Schiller's works into English. At the University of Göttingen he studied philosophy and commenced his lifelong preoccupation with the German philosophers.

The collaboration with Wordsworth was continued until 1803 when a coolness developed between Coleridge and Wordsworth while the two were on a tour of Scotland. Coleridge's greatest poetry was written between 1797 and 1803. Seeking a change of climate because his health was not good and his use of opium increasing, he went as secretary to the Governor of Malta, where he resided for almost a year, after which he visited Naples and Rome. He returned to England and made his living by lecturing on philosophy and literature, and occasionally preaching in Unitarian chapels. Coleridge the poet almost ceased to exist, but Coleridge the critic had been born. And truly it may be said that poetry's loss was criticism's gain, for the critical work of Coleridge is, in the opinion of R. P. Blackmur, second in importance only to that of Aristotle. His two most important critical works are *Biographia Literaria* (1817) and *Anima Poetae*, his poetical notebook.

Besides "The Ancient Mariner," Coleridge's two most widely read poems are "Kubla Khan" and "Christabel." "Kubla Khan" is in many ways the most nearly perfect poem in English literature, for it is all sheer, undiluted poetry. According to Coleridge, the vision which it embodies came to him in an opium dream after he had fallen asleep reading volumes of Elizabethan voyages. The poem we have is a fragment, for after Coleridge had started to write down his vision, he was interrupted by a bill collector from his tailor, and the rest was irretrievably lost. The beauty of the weird and the Romanticism of the supernatural here have their most hauntingly lovely expression. "Christabel," a poem in ballad form, returns to the Middle Ages for setting and plot; there is a completely successful blending of medievalism with the supernatural.

FURTHER READING

CHAMBERS, SIR EDMUND. *Samuel Taylor Coleridge* (Oxford, 1938).

LOWES, J. L. *The Road to Xanadu: a Study in the Ways of the Imagination* (rev. ed., Boston, 1930).

RICHARDS, I. A. *Coleridge on Imagination* (New York, 1935).

The Rime of the Ancient Mariner

IN SEVEN PARTS

ARGUMENT

How a Ship having passed the Line was driven by storms to the cold Country towards the South Pole; and how from thence she made her course to the tropical Latitude of the Great Pacific Ocean; and of the strange things that befell: and in what manner the Ancyent Marinere came back to his own Country.

PART I

It is an ancient Mariner,   *An ancient Mariner*
And he stoppeth one of three.   *meeteth three Gal-*
"By thy long gray beard and glit-   *lants bidden to a*
    tering eye,   *wedding-feast, and*
Now wherefore stopp'st thou me?   *detaineth one.*

"The Bridegroom's doors are opened wide,
And I am next of kin,
The guests are met, the feast is set:
May'st hear the merry din."

He holds him with his skinny hand;
"There was a ship," quoth he.   10
"Hold off! unhand me, gray-beard loon!"
Eftsoons his hand dropt he.

He holds him with his glittering eye—
The Wedding-Guest stood still,
And listens like a three years' child.
The Mariner hath his will.

The Wedding-Guest sat on a   *The Wedding-Guest*
    stone: *is spell-bound by the*
He cannot choose but hear;   *eye of the old seafar-*
And thus spake on that ancient   *ing man and con-*
    man,   *strained to hear his*
The bright-eyed Mariner.   20   *tale.*

"The ship was cheered, the harbor cleared,
Merrily did we drop
Below the kirk, below the hill,
Below the light-house top.

"The sun came up upon the left,   *The Mariner tells*
Out of the sea came he!   *how the ship sailed*
And he shone bright, and on the   *southward with a*
    right   *good wind and fair*
Went down into the sea.   *weather, till it*
     reached the Line.

"Higher and higher every day,
Till over the mast at noon—"   30
The Wedding-Guest here beat his breast,
For he heard the loud bassoon.

The bride hath paced into the hall,
Red as a rose is she;   *The Wedding-Guest*
Nodding their heads before her   *heareth the bridal*
    goes   *music; but the*
The merry minstrelsy.   *Mariner continueth*
     his tale.

The Wedding-Guest he beat his breast,
Yet he cannot choose but hear;
And thus spake on that ancient man,
The bright-eyed Mariner.   40

"And now the Storm-blast came   *The ship driven by a*
    and he   *storm toward the*
Was tyrannous and strong: *South Pole.*
He struck with his o'ertaking wings,
And chased us south along.

"With sloping masts and dipping prow,
As who pursued with yell and blow
Still treads the shadow of his foe,
And forward bends his head,
The ship drove fast, loud roared the blast,
And southward aye we fled.   50

"And now there came both mist and snow,
And it grew wondrous cold:
And ice, mast-high, came floating by,
As green as emerald.

"And through the drifts the snowy   *The land of ice, and*
    clifts   *of fearful sounds*
Did send a dismal sheen: *where no living thing*
Nor shapes of men nor beasts we ken—   *was to be seen.*
The ice was all between.

"The ice was here, the ice was there,
The ice was all around: 60
It cracked and growled, and roared and howled,
Like noises in a swound!

"At length did cross an Albatross,   *Till a great sea-bird,*
Thorough the fog it came;   *called the Albatross,*
As if it had been a Christian soul,   *came through the*
We hailed it in God's name.   *snow-fog, and was re-*
     ceived with great
     joy and hospitality.

"It ate the food it ne'er had eat,
And round and round it flew.
The ice did split with a thunder-fit;
The helmsman steered us through!   70

"And a good south wind sprung   *And lo! the Albatross*
    up behind;   *proveth a bird of*
The Albatross did follow,   *good omen, and fol-*
And every day, for food or play,   *loweth the ship as it*
Came to the mariners' hollo!   *returned northward*
     through fog and float-
     ing ice.

"In mist or cloud, on mast or shroud,
It perched for vespers nine;
Whiles all the night, through fog-smoke white,
Glimmered the white moon-shine."   78

"God save thee, ancient Mariner! *The ancient mariner*
From the fiends, that plague thee *inhospitably killeth*
    thus!— *the pious bird of*
Why look'st thou so?"—"With my cross-bow *good omen.*
I shot the Albatross!"

PART II

"The Sun now rose upon the right:
Out of the sea came he,
Still hid in mist, and on the left
Went down into the sea.

"And the good south wind still blew behind,
But no sweet bird did follow,
Nor any day for food or play
Came to the mariners' hollo!   90

"And I had done a hellish thing, *His shipmates cry*
And it would work 'em woe: *out against the*
For all averred, I had killed the *ancient Mariner, for*
    bird *killing the bird of*
That made the breeze to blow. *good luck.*
Ah, wretch! said they, the bird to slay,
That made the breeze to blow!

"Nor dim nor red, like God's own *But when the fog*
    head, *cleared off they jus-*
The glorious Sun uprist: *tify the same, and*
Then all averred, I had killed the *thus make themselves*
    bird *accomplices in the*
That brought the fog and mist. *crime.*   100
'Twas right, said they, such birds to slay,
That bring the fog and mist.

"The fair breeze blew, the white *The fair breeze con-*
    foam flew, *tinues; the ship*
The furrow followed free; *enters the Pacific*
We were the first that ever burst *Ocean, and sails*
Into that silent sea. *northward, even till it*
reaches the Line.

"Down dropt the breeze, the sails *The ship hath been*
    dropt down, *suddenly becalmed.*
'Twas sad as sad could be;
And we did speak only to break
The silence of the sea!   110

"All in a hot and copper sky,
The bloody Sun, at noon,
Right up above the mast did stand,
No bigger than the Moon.

"Day after day, day after day,
We stuck, nor breath nor motion;
As idle as a painted ship
Upon a painted ocean.   118

"Water, water, everywhere, *And the Albatross*
And all the boards did shrink; *begins to be avenged.*
Water, water, everywhere,
Nor any drop to drink.

"The very deep did rot: O Christ!
That ever this should be!
Yea, slimy things did crawl with legs
Upon the slimy sea.   126

"About, about, in reel and rout *A Spirit had fol-*
The death-fires [1] danced at night; *lowed them; one of*
The water, like a witch's oils, *the invisible inhab-*
Burnt green, and blue and white. *itants of this planet,*
neither departed
souls nor angels;
"And some in dreams assurèd were *concerning whom the*
Of the Spirit that plagued us so; *learned Jew, Jose-*
Nine fathom deep he had fol- *phus, and the Pla-*
    lowed us *tonic Constantinopol-*
From the land of mist and snow. *itan, Michael*
Psellus, may be con-
sulted. They are very
numerous, and there
is no climate or ele-
ment without one or
more.

"And every tongue, through utter *The shipmates, in*
    drought, *their sore distress,*
Was withered at the root; *would fain throw the*
We could not speak, no more than *whole guilt on the*
    if *ancient Mariner: in*
We had been choked with soot. *sign whereof they*
hang the dead sea-
bird round his neck.
"Ah! well-a-day! what evil looks
Had I from old and young!   140
Instead of the cross, the Albatross
About my neck was hung.

PART III

"There passed a weary time. Each throat
Was parched, and glazed each eye.
A weary time! a weary time!
How glazed each weary eye,
When looking westward, I beheld *The ancient Mariner*
A something in the sky. *beholdeth a sign in*
the element afar off.

"At first it seemed a little speck,
And then it seemed a mist;   150
It moved and moved, and took at last
A certain shape, I wist.

"A speck, a mist, a shape, I wist!
And still it neared and neared:
As if it dodged a water-sprite,
It plunged and tacked and veered.

[1] phosphorescent lights, considered omens of disaster.

"With throats unslaked, with black lips baked, *At its nearer approach, it seemeth him to be a ship; and at a dear ransom he freeth his speech from the bonds of thirst.*
We could nor laugh nor wail;
Through utter drought all dumb
    we stood!
I bit my arm, I sucked the blood,   160
And cried, A sail! a sail!

"With throats unslaked, with black lips baked,
Agape they heard me call:
Gramercy! they for joy did grin,   *A flash of joy;*
And all at once their breath drew in,
As they were drinking all.

"See! see! (I cried) she tacks no   *And horror follows. For can it be a ship that comes onward without wind or tide?*
    more!
Hither to work us weal—
Without a breeze, without a tide,
She steadies with upright keel!   170

"The western wave was all aflame,
The day was well nigh done!
Almost upon the western wave
Rested the broad bright Sun;
When that strange shape drove suddenly
Betwixt us and the Sun.

"And straight the Sun was flecked   *It seemeth him but the skeleton of a ship.*
    with bars,
(Heaven's Mother send us grace!)
As if through a dungeon-grate he peered
With broad and burning face.   180

"Alas! (thought I, and my heart beat loud)
How fast she nears and nears!
Are those her sails that glance in the Sun,
Like restless gossameres?

"Are those her ribs through which   *And its ribs are seen as bars on the face of the setting Sun.*
    the Sun
Did peer, as through a grate?
And is that Woman all her crew?   *The Specter-Woman and her Deathmate, and no other on board the skeleton-ship.*
Is that a Death? and are there two?
Is Death that woman's mate?

"Her lips were red, her looks were free,   190
Her locks were yellow as gold: *Like vessel, like crew!*
Her skin was as white as leprosy,
The Night-mare Life-in-Death was she,
Who thicks man's blood with cold.

"The naked hulk alongside came,   *Death and Life-in-Death have diced for the ship's crew, and she (the latter) winneth the ancient Mariner.*
And the twain were casting dice;
'The game is done! I've won! I've
    won!'
Quoth she, and whistles thrice.

"The Sun's rim dips; the stars rush   *No twilight within the courts of the Sun.*
    out:
At one stride comes the dark;   200
With far-heard whisper, o'er the sea,
Off shot the specter-bark.

"We listened and looked sideways   *At the rising of the Moon,*
    up!
Fear at my heart, as at a cup,
My life-blood seemed to sip!
The stars were dim, and thick the night,
The steersman's face by his lamp gleamed white;
From the sails the dew did drip—
Till clomb above the eastern bar
The hornéd Moon, with one bright star   210
Within the nether tip.

"One after one, by the star-dogged   *One after another,*
    Moon,
Too quick for groan or sigh,
Each turned his face with a ghastly pang,
And cursed me with his eye.

"Four times fifty living men,   *His shipmates drop down dead.*
(And I heard nor sigh nor groan)
With heavy thump, a lifeless lump,
They dropt down one by one.   219

"The souls did from their bodies   *But Life-in-Death begins her work on the ancient Mariner.*
    fly—
They fled to bliss or woe!
And every soul, it passed me by
Like the whizz of my cross-bow!"

PART IV

"I fear thee, ancient Mariner!   *The Wedding-Guest feareth that a Spirit is talking to him;*
I fear thy skinny hand!
And thou art long, and lank, and brown,
As is the ribbed sea-sand.

"I fear thee and thy glittering eye,
And thy skinny hand, so brown."—   229
"Fear not, fear not, thou   *But the ancient Mariner assureth him of his bodily life, and proceedeth to relate his horrible penance.*
    Wedding-Guest!
This body dropt not down.

"Alone, alone, all, all alone,
Alone on a wide, wide sea!
And never a saint took pity on
My soul in agony.

"The many men, so beautiful!   *He despiseth the creatures of the calm.*
And they all dead did lie:
And a thousand thousand slimy things
Lived on; and so did I.   239

"I looked upon the rotting sea,   *And envieth that*
And drew my eyes away;   *they should live and*
I looked upon the rotting deck,   *so many lie dead.*
And there the dead men lay.

"I looked to heaven, and tried to pray;
But or ever a prayer had gusht,
A wicked whisper came, and made
My heart as dry as dust.

"I closed my lids, and kept them close,
And the balls like pulses beat;
For the sky and the sea, and the sea and the sky 250
Lay like a load on my weary eye,
And the dead were at my feet.

"The cold sweat melted from their   *But the curse liveth*
    limbs,   *for him in the eye*
Nor rot nor reek did they: *of the dead men.*
The look with which they looked on me
Had never passed away.

"An orphan's curse would drag to hell
A spirit from on high;   *In his loneliness*
But oh! more horrible than that   *and fixedness he*
Is a curse in a dead man's eye!   *yearneth towards the*
Seven days, seven nights, I saw that *journeying Moon,*
    curse,   *and the stars that*
And yet I could not die.   *still move onward; and*
                                   everywhere the blue
"The moving Moon went up the   *sky belongs to them,*
    sky,   *and is their ap-*
And nowhere did abide: *pointed rest, and*
Softly she was going up,   *their native country*
And a star or two beside—   *and their own nat-*
                                   ural homes, which
                                   they enter unan-
                                   nounced, as lords
                                   that are certainly
                                   expected, and yet
                                   there is a silent joy
                                   at their arrival.

"Her beams bemocked the sultry main,
Like April hoar-frost spread;
But where the ship's huge shadow lay,
The charméd water burnt alway   270
A still and awful red.

"Beyond the shadow of the ship,   *By the light of the*
I watched the water-snakes: *Moon he beholdeth*
They moved in tracks of shining   *God's creatures of*
    white,   *the great calm.*
And when they reared, the elfish light
Fell off in hoary flakes.

"Within the shadow of the ship
I watched their rich attire:
Blue, glossy green, and velvet black,
They coiled and swam; and every track 280
Was a flash of golden fire.

"O happy living things! no tongue   *Their beauty and*
Their beauty might declare: *their happiness.*
A spring of love gushed from my heart,

And I blessed them unaware;   *He blesseth them in*
Sure my kind saint took pity on   *his heart.*
    me,
And I blessed them unaware.   *The spell begins*
                                    to break.

"The selfsame moment I could pray;
And from my neck so free
The Albatross fell off, and sank   290
Like lead into the sea."

PART V

"Oh sleep! it is a gentle thing,
Beloved from pole to pole!
To Mary Queen the praise be given!
She sent the gentle sleep from Heaven,
That slid into my soul.

"The silly buckets on the deck,   *By grace of the holy*
That had so long remained,   *Mother, the ancient*
I dreamt that they were filled with *Mariner is refreshed*
    dew;   *with rain.*
And when I awoke, it rained.   300

"My lips were wet, my throat was cold,
My garments all were dank;
Sure I had drunken in my dreams,
And still my body drank.

"I moved, and could not feel my limbs:
I was so light—almost
I thought that I had died in sleep,
And was a blessèd ghost.   308

"And soon I heard a roaring wind: *He heareth sounds*
It did not come anear;   *and seeth strange*
But with its sound it shook the   *sights and commo-*
    sails,   *tions in the sky and*
That were so thin and sere.   *the elements.*

"The upper air burst into life!
And a hundred fire-flags sheen,
To and fro they were hurried about!
And to and fro, and in and out,
The wan stars danced between.

"And the coming wind did roar more loud,
And the sails did sigh like sedge;
And the rain poured down from one black cloud; 320
The Moon was at its edge.

"The thick black cloud was cleft, and still
The Moon was at its side:
Like waters shot from some high crag,
The lightning fell with never a jag,
A river steep and wide.

"The loud wind never reached the ship,
Yet now the ship moved on!
Beneath the lightning and the Moon
The dead men gave a groan.   330

The bodies of the ship's crew are inspired, and the ship moves on;

"They groaned, they stirred, they all uprose,
Nor spake, nor moved their eyes;
It had been strange, even in a dream,
To have seen those dead men rise.

"The helmsman steered, the ship moved on;
Yet never a breeze up blew;
The mariners all 'gan work the ropes,
Where they were wont to do;
They raised their limbs like lifeless tools—
We were a ghastly crew.   340

"The body of my brother's son
Stood by me, knee to knee:
The body and I pulled at one rope,
But he said nought to me."

"I fear thee, ancient Mariner!"
"Be calm thou Wedding-Guest!
'Twas not those souls that fled in pain,
Which to their corses came again,
But a troop of spirits blest:

But not by the souls of the men, nor by demons of earth or middle air, but by a blessed troop of angelic spirits, sent down by the invocation of the guardian saint.

"For when it dawned—they dropped their arms,   350
And clustered round the mast;
Sweet sounds rose slowly through their mouths,
And from their bodies passed.

"Around, around, flew each sweet sound,
Then darted to the Sun;
Slowly the sounds came back again,
Now mixed, now one by one.

"Sometimes a-dropping from the sky
I heard the skylark sing;
Sometimes all little birds that are,   360
How they seemed to fill the sea and air
With their sweet jargoning!

"And now 'twas like all instruments,
Now like a lonely flute;
And now it is an angel's song,
That makes the heavens be mute.

"It ceased; yet still the sails made on
A pleasant noise till noon,
A noise like of a hidden brook
In the leafy month of June,   370
That to the sleeping woods all night
Singeth a quiet tune.

"Till noon we quietly sailed on,
Yet never a breeze did breathe:
Slowly and smoothly went the ship,
Moved onward from beneath.

"Under the keel nine fathom deep,
From the land of mist and snow,
The Spirit slid: and it was he
That made the ship to go.
The sails at noon left off their tune,
And the ship stood still also.   382

The lonesome Spirit from the South Pole carries on the ship as far as the Line, in obedience to the angelic troop, but still requireth vengeance.

"The Sun, right up above the mast,
Had fixed her to the ocean:
But in a minute she 'gan stir,
With a short uneasy motion—
Backwards and forwards half her length
With a short uneasy motion.

"Then like a pawing horse let go,
She made a sudden bound: 390
It flung the blood into my head,
And I fell down in a swound.

"How long in that same fit I lay,
I have not to declare;
But ere my living life returned,
I heard, and in my soul discerned,
Two voices in the air.

The Polar Spirit's fellow demons, the invisible inhabitants of the element, take part in his wrong; and two of them relate, one to the other, that penance long and heavy for the ancient Mariner hath been accorded to the Polar Spirit, who returneth southward.

"'Is it he?' quoth one, 'Is this the man?
By Him who died on cross,
With his cruel bow he laid full low   400
The harmless Albatross.

"'The Spirit who bideth by himself
In the land of mist and snow,
He loved the bird that loved the man
Who shot him with his bow.'

"The other was a softer voice,
As soft as honey-dew:
Quoth he, 'The man hath penance done,
And penance more will do.'"

PART VI

FIRST VOICE

"'But tell me, tell me! speak again,   410
Thy soft response renewing—
What makes that ship drive on so fast?
What is the ocean doing?'

SECOND VOICE

"'Still as a slave before his lord,
The ocean hath no blast;
His great bright eye most silently
Up to the Moon is cast—

"'If he may know which way to go;
For she guides him smooth or grim.
See, brother, see! how graciously   420
She looketh down on him.'

FIRST VOICE

"'But why drives on that ship so   *The Mariner hath*
    fast,   *been cast into a*
                                      trance; for the an-
Without or wave or wind?'   *gelic power causeth*
                                      the vessel to drive
                                      northward faster
                                      than human life
                                      could endure.

SECOND VOICE

"'The air is cut away before,
And closes from behind."

"'Fly, brother, fly! more high, more high!
Or we shall be belated:
For slow and slow that ship will go,
When the Mariner's trance is abated.'   429

"I woke, and we were sailing on   *The supernatural*
As in a gentle weather: *motion is retarded;*
                                      the Mariner awakes,
'Twas night, calm night, the moon   *and his penance*
    was high;   *begins anew.*
The dead men stood together.

"All stood together on the deck,
For a charnel-dungeon fitter:
All fixed on me their stony eyes,
That in the Moon did glitter.

"The pang, the curse, with which they died,
Had never passed away:
I could not draw my eyes from theirs,   440
Nor turn them up to pray.

"And now this spell was snapt: *The curse is finally*
    once more   *expiated.*
I viewed the ocean green,
And looked far forth, yet little saw
Of what had else been seen—

"Like one, that on a lonesome road
Doth walk in fear and dread,
And having once turned round, walks on,
And turns no more his head;
Because he knows, a frightful fiend   450
Doth close behind him tread.

"But soon there breathed a wind on me,
Nor sound nor motion made:

Its path was not upon the sea,
In ripple or in shade.

"It raised my hair, it fanned my cheek
Like a meadow-gale of spring—
It mingled strangely with my fears,
Yet it felt like a welcoming.

"Swiftly, swiftly flew the ship,   460
Yet she sailed softly too:
Sweetly, sweetly blew the breeze—
On me alone it blew.

"Oh! dream of joy! is this indeed   *And the ancient*
The light-house top I see?   *Mariner beholdeth*
                                      his native country.
Is this the hill? is this the kirk?
Is this mine own countree?

"We drifted o'er the harbor-bar,
And I with sobs did pray—
O let me be awake, my God!   470
Or let me sleep alway.

"The harbor-bay was clear as glass,
So smoothly it was strewn!
And on the bay the moonlight lay,
And the shadow of the Moon.

"The rock shone bright, the kirk no less,
That stands above the rock:
The moonlight stepped in silentness
The steady weathercock.

"And the bay was white with silent light   480
Till, rising from the same,
Full many shapes, that shadows   *The angelic spirits*
    were,   *leave the dead*
                                      bodies,
In crimson colors came.

"A little distance from the prow
Those crimson shadows were:
I turned my eyes upon the deck—
Oh, Christ! what saw I there!

"Each corse lay flat, lifeless and flat,   488
And, by the holy rood!
A man all light, a seraph-man,   *And appear in their*
On every corse there stood.   *own forms of light.*

"This seraph-band, each waved his hand:
It was a heavenly sight!
They stood as signals to the land,
Each one a lovely light;

"This seraph-band, each waved his hand,
No voice did they impart—
No voice; but oh! the silence sank
Like music on my heart.

"But soon I heard the dash of oars,   500
I heard the Pilot's cheer;
My head was turned perforce away,
And I saw a boat appear.

"The Pilot and the Pilot's boy,
I heard them coming fast:
Dear Lord in Heaven! it was a joy
The dead men could not blast.

"I saw a third—I heard his voice:
It is the Hermit good!
He singeth loud his godly hymns   510
That he makes in the wood.
He'll shrieve my soul, he'll wash away
The Albatross's blood."

PART VII

"This Hermit good lives in that *The Hermit of*
    wood   *the wood,*
Which slopes down to the sea.
How loudly his sweet voice he rears!
He loves to talk with marineres
That come from a far countree.

"He kneels at morn, and noon, and eve—
He hath a cushion plump: 520
It is the moss that wholly hides
The rotted old oak-stump.

"The skiff-boat neared: I heard them talk,
'Why, this is strange, I trow!
Where are those lights so many and fair,
That signal made but now?'

"'Strange, by my faith!' the Her- *Approacheth the ship*
   mit said—   *with wonder.*
'And they answered not our cheer!
The planks looked warped! and see those sails,
How thin they are and sere!   530
I never saw aught like to them,
Unless perchance it were

"'Brown skeletons of leaves that lag
My forest-brook along;
When the ivy-tod is heavy with snow,
And the owlet whoops to the wolf below,
That eats the she-wolf's young.'

"'Dear Lord! it hath a fiendish look—
(The Pilot made reply)
I am a-feared'—'Push on, push on!'   540
Said the Hermit cheerily.

"The boat came closer to the ship,
But I nor spake nor stirred;
The boat came close beneath the ship,
And straight a sound was heard.

"Under the water it rumbled on, *The ship suddenly*
Still louder and more dread: *sinketh.*
It reached the ship, it split the bay;
The ship went down like lead.   549

"Stunned by that loud and dread- *The ancient Mariner*
   ful sound,   *is saved in the*
Which sky and ocean smote,   *Pilot's boat.*
Like one that hath been seven days drowned
My body lay afloat;
But swift as dreams, myself I found
Within the Pilot's boat.

"Upon the whirl, where sank the ship,
The boat spun round and round;
And all was still, save that the hill
Was telling of the sound.

"I moved my lips—the Pilot shrieked   560
And fell down in a fit;
The holy Hermit raised his eyes,
And prayed where he did sit.

"I took the oars: the Pilot's boy,
Who now doth crazy go,
Laughed loud and long, and all the while
His eyes went to and fro.
'Ha! ha!' quoth he, 'full plain I see,
The Devil knows how to row.'

"And now, all in my own countree,   570
I stood on the firm land!
The Hermit stepped forth from the boat,
And scarcely he could stand.

"'O shrieve me, shrieve me, holy man!'
The Hermit crossed his brow. *The ancient Mariner*
'Say quick,' quoth he, 'I bid thee *earnestly entreateth*
   say—   *the Hermit to*
What manner of man art thou?'   *shrieve him; and the*
            penance of life falls
            on him.

"Forthwith this frame of mine was wrenched
With a woful agony,
Which forced me to begin my tale;   580
And then it left me free.

"Since then, at an uncertain hour, *And ever and anon*
That agony returns;   *throughout his*
And till my ghastly tale is told,   *future life an agony*
This heart within me burns.   *constraineth him to*
            travel from land to
            land,

"I pass, like night, from land to land;
I have strange power of speech;
That moment that his face I see,
I know the man that must hear me:
To him my tale I teach.   590

"What loud uproar bursts from that door!
The wedding-guests are there:
But in the garden-bower the bride
And bride-maids singing are:
And hark the little vesper bell,
Which biddeth me to prayer!

"O Wedding-Guest! this soul hath been
Alone on a wide, wide sea:
So lonely 'twas, that God himself
Scarce seeméd there to be.   600

"Oh sweeter than the marriage-feast,
'Tis sweeter far to me,
To walk together to the kirk
With a goodly company!—

"To walk together to the kirk,
And all together pray,
While each to his great Father bends,
Old men, and babes, and loving friends,
And youths and maidens gay!   609

"Farewell, farewell! but this I tell   *And to teach by his*
To thee, thou Wedding-Guest!   *own example love*
He prayeth well, who loveth well   *and reverence to all*
Both man and bird and beast.   *things that God*
                                            made and loveth.

"He prayeth best, who loveth best
All things both great and small;
For the dear God who loveth us,
He made and loveth all."

The Mariner, whose eye is bright,
Whose beard with age is hoar,
Is gone: and now the Wedding-Guest   620
Turned from the bridegroom's door.

He went like one that hath been stunned,
And is of sense forlorn:
A sadder and a wiser man,
He rose the morrow morn.

Kubla Khan; or, a Vision in a Dream

"In the summer of the year 1797, the author, then in ill health, had retired to a lonely farmhouse between Porlock and Linton, on the Exmoor confines of Somerset and Devonshire. In consequence of a slight indisposition, an anodyne had been prescribed, from the effects of which he fell asleep in his chair at the moment he was reading the following sentence, or words of the same substance, in *Purchas's Pilgrimage*: 'Here the Khan Kubla commanded a palace to be built, and a stately garden thereunto. And thus ten miles of fertile ground were inclosed with a wall.' The author continued for about three hours in a profound sleep, at least of the external senses, during which time he has the most vivid confidence that he could not have composed less than from two to three hundred lines; if that indeed can be called composition in which all the images rose up before him as *things,* with a parallel production of the correspondent expressions, without any sensation or consciousness of effort. On awaking he appeared to himself to have a distinct recollection of the whole, and taking his pen, ink, and paper, instantly and eagerly wrote down the lines that are here preserved. At this moment he was unfortunately called out by a person on business from Porlock, and detained by him above an hour, and on his return to his room, found, to his no small surprise and mortification, that though he still retained some vague and dim recollection of the general purport of the vision, yet, with the exception of some eight or ten scattered lines and images, all the rest had passed away like the images on the surface of a stream into which a stone had been cast, but, alas! without the after restoration of the latter!"—COLERIDGE.

In Xanadu [1] did Kubla Khan [2]
A stately pleasure-dome decree:
Where Alph, the sacred river, ran
Through caverns measureless to man
    Down to a sunless sea.
So twice five miles of fertile ground
With walls and towers were girdled round:
And here were gardens bright with sinuous rills,
Where blossomed many an incense-bearing tree;
And here were forests ancient as the hills,
Enfolding sunny spots of greenery.
But oh! that deep romantic chasm which slanted
Down the green hill athwart a cedarn cover!
A savage place! as holy and enchanted
As e'er beneath a waning moon was haunted
By woman wailing for her demon-lover!
And from this chasm, with ceaseless turmoil seeth-
        ing,
As if this earth in fast thick pants were breathing
A mighty fountain momently was forced;
Amid whose swift half-intermittent burst
Huge fragments vaulted like rebounding hail,
Or chaffy grain beneath the thresher's flail:
And 'mid these dancing rocks at once and ever

[1] A region in Tartary.
[2] Cham or Emperor Kubla founded the Mogul dynasty in China in the thirteenth century.

It flung up momently the sacred river.
Five miles meandering with a mazy motion
Through wood and dale the sacred river ran,
Then reached the caverns measureless to man,
And sank in tumult to a lifeless ocean:
And 'mid this tumult Kubla heard from far
Ancestral voices prophesying war!

　　The shadow of the dome of pleasure
　　Floated midway on the waves;
　　Where was heard the mingled measure
　　From the fountain and the caves.
It was a miracle of rare device,
A sunny pleasure-dome with caves of ice!
　　A damsel with a dulcimer
　　In a vision once I saw:
　　It was an Abyssinian maid,
　　And on her dulcimer she played,
　　Singing of Mount Abora.
　　Could I revive within me,
　　Her symphony and song,
　　To such a deep delight 'twould win me,
That with music loud and long,
I would build that dome in air,
That sunny dome! those caves of ice!
And all who heard should see them there,
And all should cry, Beware! Beware!
His flashing eyes, his floating hair!
Weave a circle round him thrice,
And close your eyes with holy dread,
For he on honey-dew hath fed,
And drunk the milk of Paradise.

———◆———

PERCY BYSSHE SHELLEY

1792–1822

Percy Bysshe Shelley, poet of ideal beauty and of the perfectibility of man, was born at Field Place, an eighteenth-century mansion near Horsham, Sussex, of a long line of country squires. He was sent for a few years to an academy, and then to Eton where he remained until he was eighteen. Here he detested the hazing and fagging, the discipline of the school, and the required attendance at religious exercises, all of which he regarded as outmoded and corrupt. Thus, even as a schoolboy, Shelley gave promise of his later zeal for reforming the social

order and of the rebellious fury against human oppression which marks so much of his mature work. At Eton he read William Godwin's *Political Justice,* a radical treatise which unquestionably did much to direct his entire life toward the quest of human perfectibility.

He proceeded to University College, Oxford, where he pursued his strong interest in the natural sciences and his study of skeptical authors. Here he met Thomas Jefferson Hogg, who afterwards became his biographer, and who has given us a striking picture of Shelley at eighteen:

His figure was slight and fragile, and yet his bones and joints were large and strong. He was tall, but he stooped so much that he seemed of a low stature. His clothes were expensive, and made according to the most approved mode of the day; but they were tumbled, rumpled, unbrushed. His gestures were abrupt, and sometimes violent, occasionally even awkward, yet more frequently gentle and graceful. His complexion was delicate and almost feminine, of the purest red and white; yet he was tanned and freckled by the sun. . . . His features, his whole face, and particularly his head, were in fact, unusually small; yet the last appeared of a remarkable bulk, for his hair was long and bushy. . . .

His stay at Oxford was very short: he was expelled for publishing at his own expense a pamphlet entitled *The Necessity of Atheism.* He then went to London, where his sisters were attending school. They introduced him to Harriet Westbrook, with whom he eloped a few months later because he felt she was being oppressed by her family and the school. The young couple—he was nineteen and she sixteen—received some allowance from both families, which enabled them to spend their honeymoon in Ireland. Here they devoted part of their time to the surreptitious distribution of a pamphlet entitled *Declaration of Rights,* which Shelley had written against the government of Ireland. When they returned to England, Shelley formed a platonic friendship with Elizabeth Hitchener, a vegetarian schoolteacher who was interested in idealistic schemes. In 1813 he published *Queen Mab,* his first important poem; it was an attack on Christianity, a plea for atheism, and an advocacy of political anarchy. This work was an obvious result of Godwinian influences. The main hope for mankind which he expressed was that, freed from the shackles of restrictive and decadent religious and political systems, man would learn to live by Reason alone. Thus some kind of golden age was to be reached.

Soon after this publication he met William Godwin himself, under whose shadow his mind had long been, and Godwin's daughter, Mary Wollstonecraft Godwin, a girl of seventeen. Shelley and Mary felt the strongest mutual attraction, and he thereupon decided that Harriet and he were no longer compatible. He talked the situation over with Harriet, suggesting that he bring Mary into the household as his "wife," and that Harriet, now the mother of two children, remain as a friend. When she refused this arrangement, Shelley eloped with Mary to Switzerland. About this time Shelley's grandfather died, leaving him an income of approximately one thousand pounds a year. Shelley very generously divided it with Harriet. After living in Switzerland with Mary Godwin, with her half-sister Clara Jane Clairmont and Byron as their guests, Shelley returned to England. Soon thereafter, Harriet committed suicide by drowning herself in the Serpentine River. After her death he legitimized his common-law marriage with Mary. The Lord Chancellor thereupon deprived Shelley of the custody of his children, on the ground that he was morally unworthy to bring them up. Some of the evidence presented in the case consisted of quotations from *Queen Mab*. At this verdict Shelley was incensed, for he felt that he had been dealt with very unjustly. He therefore determined to go into voluntary exile, and accordingly, in 1818, he left England forever.

The Shelleys went to Italy, where at first they visited Byron at his villa near Venice. A little later they lived in Rome and Florence. After the death of his small daughter Clara, Shelley wrote "Lines Written Among the Euganean Hills." His *Prometheus Unbound*, which he had begun in England and completed at this time, is a closet drama in which he attempts to reconcile neo-Platonic philosophy with Godwinian radicalism. Its greatness lies in the magnificence of many of its lyrics. At Rome he started *The Cenci*, a powerful drama based on a sixteenth-century story of incest and murder. During 1819–1820 he met Teresa Emilia Viviani, a beautiful Italian girl whom he idealized in platonic friendship, and who inspired the poem *Epipsychidion*. In 1821 Edward Williams and his wife Jane arrived in Italy, and Shelley formed a platonic attachment with Jane, for whom he wrote the cherished lyrics, "One Word Is Too Often Profaned" and "With a Guitar to Jane." Most of his greatest work was composed in 1819–1820. In 1821 he visited Byron at Ravenna. The following year, the Shelleys and the Williamses moved to a villa near Lerici, on the bay of Spezzia. Shelley and Captain Williams were drowned in the bay of Spezzia when Shelley's boat, the "Ariel," capsized on July 8, 1822. The bodies were not washed ashore for almost two weeks, and according to Italian sanitary laws, they were burned on the beach. Shelley's ashes are buried in the Protestant Cemetery outside the old Roman walls.

Shelley is one of the greatest of the English lyric poets, and it is chiefly upon his incomparable lyric gift that his reputation rests. *Adonais*, his elegy in the great pastoral tradition on the untimely death of Keats, is one of his major accomplishments. John Addington Symonds has called it "an elegy only equalled in our language by *Lycidas*, and in the point of passionate eloquence even superior to Milton's youthful lament for his friend." Actually it is more than a lament for Keats alone; more broadly viewed it is a lament for all poets and artists.

Shelley is, above all, the poet of love, ideal love, by which he confidently believed that human society might be regenerated into something a great deal more nearly ideal than the one he knew. Out of the radicalism of Godwin and the revolutionary currents of his time he distilled a lyric fire of great intensity, but it is chiefly as a portrayer of nature in all her mystic beauty that we esteem him, for, as he wrote of Keats, we feel that

> He is made one with Nature: there is heard
> His voice in all her music, from the moan
> Of thunder to the song of night's sweet bird;
> He is a presence to be felt and known
> In darkness and in light.

FURTHER READING

BAKER, C. H. *Shelley's Major Poetry* (Princeton, 1948).

LEAVIS, F. R. "Shelley" in *Critiques and Essays in Criticism, 1920–1948*, edited by R. W. Stallman (New York, 1949).

WHITE, N. I. *Shelley* (New York, 1940).

WINWAR, F. *The Romantic Rebels: Byron, Shelley, and Keats* (Boston, 1935).

Hymn to Intellectual Beauty

1

The awful shadow of some unseen Power
  Floats though unseen among us, visiting
  This various world with as inconstant wing
As summer winds that creep from flower to flower;
Like moonbeams that behind some piny mountain
      shower,
    It visits with inconstant glance
    Each human heart and countenance;
Like hues and harmonies of evening,
    Like clouds in starlight widely spread,
    Like memory of music fled,   10
    Like aught that for its grace may be
Dear, and yet dearer for its mystery.

2

Spirit of BEAUTY, that dost consecrate
  With thine own hues all thou dost shine upon
  Of human thought or form, where art thou gone?
Why dost thou pass away, and leave our state,
This dim vast vale of tears, vacant and desolate?
    Ask why the sunlight not forever
    Weaves rainbows o'er yon mountain river;
Why aught should fail and fade that once is
      shown;   20
    Why fear and dream and death and birth
    Cast on the daylight of this earth
    Such gloom; why man has such a scope
For love and hate, despondency and hope.

3

No voice from some sublimer world hath ever
  To sage or poet these responses given;
  Therefore the names of Demon, Ghost, and
      Heaven,
Remain the records of their vain endeavor,
Frail spells, whose uttered charm might not avail
      to sever,
    From all we hear and all we see,   30
    Doubt, chance, and mutability.
Thy light alone, like mist o'er mountains driven,
    Or music by the night wind sent
    Through strings of some still instrument,
    Or moonlight on a midnight stream,
Gives grace and truth to life's unquiet dream.

4

Love, Hope, and Self-esteem, like clouds, depart
  And come, for some uncertain moments lent.
  Man were immortal and omnipotent,
Didst thou, unknown and awful as thou art,   40

Keep with thy glorious train firm state within his
      heart.
    Thou messenger of sympathies
    That wax and wane in lovers' eyes!
Thou, that to human thought art nourishment,
    Like darkness to a dying flame,
    Depart not as thy shadow came,
    Depart not, lest the grave should be,
Like life and fear, a dark reality!

5

While yet a boy I sought for ghosts, and sped
  Through many a listening chamber, cave and
      ruin,   50
  And starlight wood, with fearful steps pursuing
Hopes of high talk with the departed dead;
I called on poisonous names with which our youth
      is fed.
    I was not heard—I saw them not—
    When, musing deeply on the lot
Of life, at that sweet time when winds are wooing
    All vital things that wake to bring
    News of birds and blossoming,—
    Sudden, thy shadow fell on me;
I shrieked, and clasped my hands in ecstasy!   60

6

I vowed that I would dedicate my powers
  To thee and thine—have I not kept the vow?
  With beating heart and streaming eyes, even now
I call the phantoms of a thousand hours
Each from his voiceless grave: they have in visioned
      bowers
    Of studious zeal or love's delight
    Outwatched with me the envious night—
They know that never joy illumed my brow
    Unlinked with hope that thou wouldst free
    This world from its dark slavery,   70
    That thou, O awful LOVELINESS,
Wouldst give whate'er these words cannot express.

7

The day becomes more solemn and serene
  When noon is past; there is a harmony
  In autumn, and a luster in its sky,
Which through the summer is not heard or seen,
As if it could not be, as if it had not been!
    Thus let thy power, which like the truth
    Of nature on my passive youth
Descended, to my onward life supply   80
    Its calm,—to one who worships thee,
    And every form containing thee,
    Whom, SPIRIT fair, thy spells did bind
To fear himself, and love all humankind.

Ozymandias

I met a traveler from an antique land
Who said: "Two vast and trunkless legs of stone
Stand in the desert. Near them, on the sand,
Half sunk, a shattered visage lies, whose frown,
And wrinkled lip, and sneer of cold command,
Tell that its sculptor well those passions read
Which yet survive, stamped on these lifeless things,
The hand[1] that mocked them, and the heart that
    fed:[2]
And on the pedestal these words appear:
'My name is Ozymandias, King of Kings:
Look on my works, ye Mighty, and despair!'
Nothing beside remains. Round the decay
Of that colossal wreck, boundless and bare
The lone and level sands stretch far away."

Ode to the West Wind

1

O wild West Wind, thou breath of Autumn's being,
Thou, from whose unseen presence the leaves dead
Are driven, like ghosts from an enchanter fleeing,

Yellow, and black, and pale, and hectic red,
Pestilence-stricken multitudes! O thou
Who chariotest to their dark wintry bed

The wingèd seeds, where they lie cold and low,
Each like a corpse within its grave, until
Thine azure sister of the Spring shall blow

Her clarion o'er the dreaming earth, and fill   10
(Driving sweet buds like flocks to feed in air)
With living hues and odors plain and hill:

Wild Spirit, which art moving everywhere;
Destroyer and Preserver; hear, oh hear!

2

Thou on whose stream, 'mid the steep sky's commo-
    tion,
Loose clouds like earth's decaying leaves are shed,
Shook from the tangled boughs of heaven and
    ocean,

Angels[3] of rain and lightning! there are spread
On the blue surface of thine airy surge,
Like the bright hair uplifted from the head   20

Of some fierce Maenad,[4] even from the dim verge
Of the horizon to the zenith's height,
The locks of the approaching storm. Thou dirge

Of the dying year, to which this closing night
Will be the dome of a vast sepulchre,
Vaulted with all thy congregated might

Of vapors, from whose solid atmosphere
Black rain, and fire, and hail, will burst: Oh hear!

3

Thou who didst waken from his summer dreams
The blue Mediterranean, where he lay,   30
Lulled by the coil of his crystalline streams,

Beside a pumice isle in Baiae's bay,
And saw in sleep old palaces and towers
Quivering within the wave's intenser day,

All overgrown with azure moss, and flowers
So sweet, the sense faints picturing them! Thou
For whose path the Atlantic's level powers

Cleave themselves into chasms, while far below
The sea-blooms and the oozy woods which wear
The sapless foliage of the ocean know   40

Thy voice, and suddenly grow gray with fear
And tremble and despoil themselves: Oh hear!

4

If I were a dead leaf thou mightest bear;
If I were a swift cloud to fly with thee;
A wave to pant beneath thy power, and share

The impulse of thy strength, only less free
Than Thou, O uncontrollable! If even
I were as in my boyhood, and could be

The comrade of thy wanderings over heaven,
As then, when to outstrip thy skyey speed   50
Scarce seemed a vision; I would ne'er have striven

As thus with thee in prayer in my sore need.
Oh! lift me as a wave, a leaf, a cloud!
I fall upon the thorns of life! I bleed!

A heavy weight of hours has chained and bowed
One too like thee—tameless, and swift, and proud.

5

Make me thy lyre, ev'n as the forest is:
What if my leaves are falling like its own!
The tumult of thy mighty harmonies

[1] The sculptor's.
[2] The king's heart, which nursed the passions.
[3] Messengers.

[4] An attendant of Bacchus.

Will take from both a deep, autumnal tone,   60
Sweet though in sadness. Be thou, Spirit fierce,
My spirit! be thou me, impetuous one!

Drive my dead thoughts over the universe,
Like withered leaves, to quicken a new birth!
And, by the incantation of this verse,

Scatter, as from an unextinguished hearth
Ashes and sparks, my words among mankind!
Be through my lips to unawakened earth

The trumpet of a prophecy! O wind,
If Winter comes, can Spring be far behind?   70

Song to the Men of England

Men of England, wherefore plow
For the lords who lay ye low?
Wherefore weave with toil and care
The rich robes your tyrants wear?

Wherefore feed, and clothe, and save,
From the cradle to the grave,
Those ungrateful drones who would
Drain your sweat—nay, drink your blood?

Wherefore, bees of England, forge
Many a weapon, chain, and scourge,
That these stingless drones may spoil
The forced produce of your toil?

Have ye leisure, comfort, calm,
Shelter, food, love's gentle balm?
Or what is it ye buy so dear
With your pain and with your fear?

The seed ye sow, another reaps;
The wealth ye find, another keeps;
The robes ye weave, another wears;
The arms ye forge, another bears.

Sow seed—but let no tyrant reap;
Find wealth—let no impostor heap;
Weave robes—let not the idle wear;
Forge arms—in your defense to bear.

Shrink to your cellars, holes, and cells;
In halls ye deck another dwells.
Why shake the chains ye wrought? Ye see
The steel ye tempered glance on ye.

With plow and spade, and hoe and loom,
Trace your grave, and build your tomb,
And weave your winding-sheet, till fair
England be your sepulcher.

The Cloud

I bring fresh showers for the thirsting flowers,
    From the seas and the streams;
I bear light shade for the leaves when laid
    In their noonday dreams.
From my wings are shaken the dews that waken
    The sweet buds every one,
When rocked to rest on their mother's breast,
    As she dances about the sun.
I wield the flail of the lashing hail,
    And whiten the green plains under,   10
And then again I dissolve it in rain,
    And laugh as I pass in thunder.

I sift the snow on the mountains below,
    And their great pines groan aghast;
And all the night 'tis my pillow white,
    While I sleep in the arms of the blast.
Sublime on the towers of my skyey bowers,
    Lightning my pilot sits;
In a cavern under is fettered the thunder,
    It struggles and howls at fits;   20
Over earth and ocean, with gentle motion,
    This pilot is guiding me,
Lured by the love of the genii that move
    In the depths of the purple sea;
Over the rills, and the crags, and the hills,
    Over the lakes and the plains,
Wherever he dream, under mountain or stream,
    The Spirit he loves remains;
And I all the while bask in Heaven's blue smile,
    Whilst he is dissolving in rains.   30

The sanguine Sunrise, with his meteor eyes,
    And his burning plumes outspread,
Leaps on the back of my sailing rack,
    When the morning star shines dead;
As on the jag of a mountain crag,
    Which an earthquake rocks and swings,
An eagle alit one moment may sit
    In the light of its golden wings.
And when Sunset may breathe, from the lit sea
        beneath,
    Its ardors of rest and of love,   40
And the crimson pall of eve may fall
    From the depth of Heaven above,
With wings folded I rest, on mine airy nest,
    As still as a brooding dove.

That orbèd maiden with white fire laden,
    Whom mortals call the Moon,
Glides glimmering o'er my fleece-like floor,
    By the midnight breezes strewn;

And wherever the beat of her unseen feet,
  Which only the angels hear,   50
May have broken the woof of my tent's thin roof,
  The stars peep behind her and peer;
And I laugh to see them whirl and flee,
  Like a swarm of golden bees,
When I widen the rent in my wind-built tent,
  Till the calm rivers, lakes, and seas,
Like strips of the sky fallen through me on high,
  Are each paved with the moon and these.

I bind the Sun's throne with a burning zone,
  And the Moon's with a girdle of pearl;   60
The volcanoes are dim, and the stars reel and swim
  When the whirlwinds my banner unfurl.
From cape to cape, with a bridge-like shape,
  Over a torrent sea,
Sunbeam-proof, I hang like a roof,—
  The mountains its columns be.
The triumphal arch, through which I march,
  With hurricane, fire, and snow,
When the Powers of the air are chained to my chair,
  Is the million-colored bow;   70
The sphere-fire above its soft colors wove,
  While the moist Earth was laughing below.

I am the daughter of Earth and Water,
  And the nursling of the Sky;
I pass through the pores of the ocean and shores,
  I change, but I cannot die.
For after the rain when with never a stain
  The pavilion of Heaven is bare,
And the winds and sunbeams with their convex
    gleams
  Build up the blue dome of air,   80
I silently laugh at my own cenotaph,
  And out of the caverns of rain,
Like a child from the womb, like a ghost from the
    tomb,
  I arise and unbuild it again.

To a Skylark

Hail to thee, blithe Spirit!
  Bird thou never wert,
That from Heaven, or near it,
  Pourest thy full heart
In profuse strains of unpremeditated art.

Higher still and higher
  From the earth thou springest

Like a cloud of fire;
  The blue deep thou wingest,
And singing still dost soar, and soaring ever sing-
    est.   10

In the golden lightning
  Of the sunken sun,
O'er which clouds are bright'ning,
  Thou dost float and run;
Like an unbodied joy whose race is just begun.

The pale purple even
  Melts around thy flight;
Like a star of Heaven,
  In the broad daylight
Thou art unseen,—but yet I hear thy shrill de-
    light,   20

Keen as are the arrows
  Of that silver sphere,
Whose intense lamp narrows
  In the white dawn clear
Until we hardly see—we feel that it is there;

All the earth and air
  With thy voice is loud,
As, when night is bare,
  From one lonely cloud
The moon rains out her beams, and Heaven is
    overflowed.   30

What thou art we know not;
  What is most like thee?
From rainbow clouds there flow not
  Drops so bright to see
As from thy presence showers a rain of melody.

Like a Poet hidden
  In the light of thought,
Singing hymns unbidden,
  Till the world is wrought
To sympathy with hopes and fears it heeded not: 40

Like a high-born maiden
  In a palace-tower,
Soothing her love-laden
  Soul in secret hour
With music sweet as love,—which overflows her
    bower:

Like a glowworm golden
  In a dell of dew,
Scattering unbeholden
  Its aërial hue
Among the flowers and grass which screen it from
    the view: 50

Like a rose embowered
   In its own green leaves,
By warm winds deflowered,
   Till the scent it gives
Makes faint with too much sweet those heavy
      wingèd thieves.

Sound of vernal showers
   On the twinkling grass,
Rain-awakened flowers,
   All that ever was
Joyous and clear and fresh, thy music doth sur-
      pass.   60

Teach us, Sprite or Bird,
   What sweet thoughts are thine;
I have never heard
   Praise of love or wine
That panted forth a flood of rapture so divine.

Chorus Hymeneal,
   Or triumphal chant,
Matched with thine, would be all
   But an empty vaunt,
A thing wherein we feel there is some hidden
      want.   70

What objects are the fountains
   Of thy happy strain?
What fields or waves or mountains?
   What shapes of sky or plain?
What love of thine own kind? what ignorance of
      pain?

With thy clear keen joyance
   Languor cannot be;
Shadow of annoyance
   Never came near thee;
Thou lovest—but ne'er knew love's sad satiety.   80

Waking or asleep,
   Thou of death must deem
Things more true and deep
   Than we mortals dream—
Or how could thy notes flow in such a crystal
      stream?

We look before and after,
   And pine for what is not;
Our sincerest laughter
   With some pain is fraught;
Our sweetest songs are those that tell of saddest
      thought.   90

Yet if we could scorn
   Hate, and pride, and fear;

If we were things born
   Not to shed a tear,
I know not how thy joy we ever should come near.

Better than all measures
   Of delightful sound,
Better than all treasures
   That in books are found,
Thy skill to poet were, thou scorner of the
      ground!   100

Teach me half the gladness
   That thy brain must know,
Such harmonious madness
   From my lips would flow
The world should listen then—as I am listening
   now.

Lines: When the Lamp is Shattered

1

When the lamp is shattered,
The light in the dust lies dead;
   When the cloud is scattered,
The rainbow's glory is shed.
   When the lute is broken,
Sweet tones are remembered not;
   When the lips have spoken,
Loved accents are soon forgot.

2

   As music and splendor
Survive not the lamp and the lute,
   The heart's echoes render
No song when the spirit is mute:
   No song but sad dirges,
Like the wind through a ruined cell,
   Or the mournful surges
That ring the dead seaman's knell.

3

   When hearts have once mingled,
Love first leaves the well-built nest;
   The weak one is singled
To endure what it once possessed.
   O Love! who bewailest
The frailty of all things here,
   Why choose you the frailest
For your cradle, your home, and your bier?

4

   Its passions will rock thee,
As the storms rock the ravens on high;

Bright reason will mock thee,
Like the sun from a wintry sky.
From thy nest every rafter
Will rot, and thine eagle home
Leave thee naked to laughter,
When leaves fall and cold winds come.

Final Chorus from *Hellas*

The world's great age begins anew,
    The golden years return,
The earth doth like a snake renew
    Her winter weeds outworn;
Heaven smiles, and faiths and empires gleam,
Like wrecks of a dissolving dream.

A brighter Hellas rears its mountains
    From waves serener far;
A new Peneus[1] rolls his fountains
    Against the morning star.
Where fairer Tempes[2] bloom, there sleep
Young Cyclads[3] on a sunnier deep.

A loftier Argo[4] cleaves the main,
    Fraught with a later prize;
Another Orpheus sings again,
    And loves, and weeps, and dies.
A new Ulysses leaves once more
Calypso[5] for his native shore.

Oh, write no more the tale of Troy,
    If earth Death's scroll must be!
Nor mix with Laian[6] rage the joy
    Which dawns upon the free;
Although a subtler Sphinx renew
Riddles of death Thebes never knew.

Another Athens shall arise,
    And to remoter time
Bequeath, like sunset to the skies,
    The splendor of its prime;
And leave, if nought so bright may live,
All earth can take or Heaven can give.

Saturn and Love their long repose
    Shall burst, more bright and good
Than all who fell, than One who rose,
    Than many unsubdued;
Not gold, not blood, their altar dowers,
But votive tears and symbol flowers.

[1] A river in Greece.
[2] Beautiful vales.
[3] Cyclades, islands in the Aegean.
[4] The ship in which Jason sailed to get the golden fleece.
[5] See Volume I, pp. 48 ff.
[6] See Volume I, pp. 97 ff.

Oh, cease! must hate and death return?
    Cease! must men kill and die?
Cease! drain not to its dregs the urn
    Of bitter prophecy.
The world is weary of the past,
Oh, might it die or rest at last!

To ——

1

One word is too often profaned
    For me to profane it,
One feeling too falsely disdained
    For thee to disdain it;
One hope is too like despair
    For prudence to smother,
And pity from thee more dear
    Than that from another.

2

I can give not what men call love,
    But wilt thou accept not
The worship the heart lifts above
    And the Heavens reject not,—
The desire of the moth for the star,
    Of the night for the morrow,
The devotion to something afar
    From the sphere of our sorrow?

———————

JOHN KEATS

1795–1821

John Keats, the author of perhaps the most sensuously beautiful poetry in English literature, was born above his father's livery stable at the Swan and Hoop Inn, the son of the head keeper of the stable and the daughter of the innkeeper. Though of lowly stock, the Keats family was not poor, and John Keats received an excellent education at the Clarke School at Enfield, an obscure institution of high quality. Here he came under the lasting influence of Charles Cowden Clarke, the headmaster's son, an instructor who was only eight years his senior. From this teacher and friend, who later wrote the poet's biography, we learn that Keats, though small of stature—even as an adult he was little more than five feet tall—was popular at school, and always ready to tussle or fight. He is also described by his sister-in-law Georgiana as having beautiful brown eyes and red hair.

Keats's father was killed in a fall from his horse when Keats was nine, and when he was fifteen his mother died of tuberculosis. Thereafter his guardians removed him from the Clarke School, and, destining him for a career as an apothecary-surgeon, apprenticed him to a surgeon at Edmonton. Keats applied himself diligently and passed his examinations creditably. However, Edmonton was within walking distance of Enfield, and he kept up his friendship with Charles Cowden Clarke. On one of his visits to Clarke he borrowed a copy of Spenser, thereby making a great literary discovery, for Spenser was to be one of the chief influences upon all of his poetry. Clarke had read him Spenser's *Epithalamion*. "That night," Clarke says, "he took away with him the *Faerie Queene* and went through it . . . as a young horse would through a spring meadow—ramping." Later he worked and studied in Guy's and St. Thomas's Hospitals, and passed his examination to practice. About this time, however, he met Leigh Hunt and his circle, under whose influence he composed two fairly long poems. His guardian thought Keats was foolhardy when he learned that the youth was not going to become an apothecary. But Keats steadfastly replied, "I know that I possess abilities greater than most men, and therefore I am determined to gain my living by exercising them." In 1817, with the help of Shelley, he published a small volume entitled *Poems*, and in April, 1818, he published *Endymion*. The latter was harshly attacked in a critical review in *Blackwood's Magazine* and actually ridiculed in the *Quarterly Review*. For a long time it was popular to suppose that these adverse reviews snuffed out Keats's life, a point of view flippantly expressed in Lord Byron's satirical lyric "Who Killed John Keats?":

> "Who killed John Keats?"
> "I," says the *Quarterly*,
> So savage and Tartarly;
> "'Twas one of my feats."

Actually, Keats reacted to these attacks, unfair though they were, in a very sensible and manly fashion by proceeding to write a better poem, *Hyperion*.

In the year 1818 he experienced two great emotional crises: he nursed his brother Tom, and watched him die of tuberculosis, and he fell in love with Fanny Brawne. Though Fanny was something of a flirt, who made Keats upon some occasions suffer agonies of jealousy, she nevertheless did sincerely reciprocate his passion. But he was too poor to support a wife, and too proud to marry her under the circumstances, though she was the one person in all the world he most desired. The prospect of marriage was also darkened by his own developing tuberculosis. Nevertheless in spite of all of these complicating emotional hindrances, or perhaps because of them, the first nine months of the year 1819 were the most productive of his entire life. To this time belong all the great odes, "Lamia," "Isabella," "The Eve of St. Agnes," and other poems, which appeared in the 1820 volume, his last publication.

During 1820 his health grew progressively worse. After six months in the Brawne household, where he was nursed by Fanny and her mother, Keats set out in the company of a friend for the milder climate of Italy. In the eternal city of Rome, in a house by the Old Spanish Stairs, the man who had written so many poignantly beautiful poems on the related themes of the shortness of life and the permanence of artistic beauty died, aged only twenty-five years, three months, and twenty-six days. His body is buried in the Protestant Cemetery outside the ancient walls of Rome, where his simple marker bears the epitaph he had composed: "Here lies one whose name was writ in water." Yet before he died Keats knew that though tuberculosis was to bring his early death, he, too, had achieved an immortality through the beauty of his incomparable lines, for he said: "I think I shall be among the English poets." Certainly there is in all English literature no greater tragedy than the death of Keats just as he was coming into full possession of his mature powers; but even so, it was not before his pen had gleaned from his inspired mind and spirit enough magnificent lines to place the one-time Finsbury stable boy among the major English poets.

Keats's poems depict sensuous beauty. His Romanticism is a blend of medievalism ("The Eve of St. Agnes" and "Isabella"), the inspiration of Greek plastic art ("On a Grecian Urn," "On Seeing the Elgin Marbles"), Spenserian color and sensuousness, the supernatural and the weird ("Lamia," "La Belle Dame Sans Merci," which Coventry Patmore called "the very finest lyric in the English language") with his own passionately subjective personality. Among his greatest themes are the transiency of human life and the permanence of artistic beauty ("On a Grecian Urn," "On Seeing the Elgin Marbles," and "Ode to the Nightingale," which Swinburne called "one of the final masterpieces of human work in all time and for all ages"), love and fame ("When I Have Fears That I May Cease to Be") and high romantic young love ("The Eve of St. Agnes"). The lesson he learned of the Grecian Urn is his testament to posterity:

> "Beauty is truth, truth Beauty"—That is all
> Ye know on earth, and all ye need to know.

FURTHER READING

COLVIN, SIR SIDNEY. *John Keats* (London, 1925).
FINNEY, C. L. *The Evolution of Keats's Poetry* (Cambridge, Mass., 1936).
LOWELL, AMY. *John Keats* (Boston, 1925).
MURRY, J. M. *Studies in Keats* (rev. ed., Oxford, 1938).

On First Looking into Chapman's *Homer*

Much have I traveled in the realms of gold,
And many goodly states and kingdoms seen;
Round many western islands have I been
Which bards in fealty to Apollo hold.
Oft of one wide expanse had I been told,
That deep-browed Homer ruled as his demesne:
Yet did I never breathe its pure serene
Till I heard Chapman speak out loud and bold:
Then felt I like some watcher of the skies
When a new planet swims into his ken;
Or like stout Cortez when with eagle eyes
He stared at the Pacific—and all his men
Looked at each other with a wild surmise—
Silent, upon a peak in Darien.

On Seeing the Elgin Marbles

My spirit is too weak—mortality
Weighs heavily on me like unwilling sleep,
And each imagined pinnacle and steep
Of godlike hardship tells me I must die
Like a sick eagle looking at the sky.

Yet 'tis a gentle luxury to weep
That I have not the cloudy winds to keep,
Fresh for the opening of the morning's eye.
Such dim-conceivèd glories of the brain
Bring round the heart an undescribable feud;
So do these wonders a most dizzy pain,
That mingles Grecian grandeur with the rude
Wasting of old Time—with a billowy main—
A sun—a shadow of a magnitude.

Credo from *Endymion*

A thing of beauty is a joy for ever:
Its loveliness increases; it will never
Pass into nothingness; but still will keep
A bower quiet for us, and a sleep
Full of sweet dreams, and health, and quiet breathing.
Therefore, on every morrow, are we wreathing
A flowery band to bind us to the earth.
Spite of despondence, of the inhuman dearth
Of noble natures, of the gloomy days,
Of all the unhealthy and o'er-darkened ways   10
Made for our searching: yes, in spite of all,
Some shape of beauty moves away the pall
From our dark spirits. Such the sun, the moon,
Trees old and young, sprouting a shady boon
For simple sheep; and such are daffodils
With the green world they live in; and clear rills
That for themselves a cooling covert make
'Gainst the hot season; the mid-forest brake,
Rich with a sprinkling of fair musk-rose blooms:
And such too is the grandeur of the dooms   20
We have imagined for the mighty dead;
All lovely tales that we have heard or read:
An endless fountain of immortal drink,
Pouring unto us from the heaven's brink.

Nor do we merely feel these essences
For one short hour; no, even as the trees
That whisper round a temple become soon
Dear as the temple's self, so does the moon,
The passion poesy, glories infinite,
Haunt us till they become a cheering light   30
Unto our souls, and bound to us so fast,
That, whether there be shine, or gloom o'ercast,
They always must be with us, or we die.

Therefore, 'tis with full happiness that I
Will trace the story of Endymion.
The very music of the name has gone
Into my being, and each pleasant scene
Is growing fresh before me as the green
Of our own valleys: so I will begin

Now while I cannot hear the city's din;   40
Now while the early budders are just new,
And run in mazes of the youngest hue
About old forests; while the willow trails
Its delicate amber; and the dairy pails
Bring home increase of milk. And, as the year
Grows lush in juicy stalks, I'll smoothly steer
My little boat, for many quiet hours,
With streams that deepen freshly into bowers.
Many and many a verse I hope to write,
Before the daisies, vermeil rimm'd and white,   50
Hide in deep herbage; and ere yet the bees
Hum about globes of clover and sweet peas,
I must be near the middle of my story.
O may no wintry season, bare and hoary,
See it half finished: but let Autumn bold,
With universal tinge of sober gold,
Be all about me when I make an end.
And now at once, adventuresome, I send
My herald thought into a wilderness:
There let its trumpet blow, and quickly dress   60
My uncertain path with green, that I may speed
Easily onward, thorough flowers and weed.

When I Have Fears That I May Cease to be

When I have fears that I may cease to be
Before my pen has gleaned my teeming brain,
Before high-pilèd books, in charact'ry,
Hold like rich garners the full-ripened grain;
When I behold, upon the night's starred face,
Huge cloudy symbols of a high romance,
And think that I may never live to trace
Their shadows, with the magic hand of chance;
And when I feel, fair creature of an hour!
That I shall never look upon thee more,
Never have relish in the faery power
Of unreflecting love;—then on the shore
Of the wide world I stand alone, and think,
Till Love and Fame to nothingness do sink.

La Belle Dame Sans Merci

Ah, what can ail thee, knight-at-arms,
    Alone and palely loitering?
The sedge has withered from the lake,
    And no birds sing.

Ah, what can ail thee, wretched wight,
    So haggard and so woe-begone?
The squirrel's granary is full,
    And the harvest's done.

I see a lily on thy brow
    With anguish moist and fever dew,   10
And on thy cheeks a fading rose
    Fast withereth too.

I met a lady in the meads,
    Full beautiful—a faery's child,
Her hair was long, her foot was light,
    And her eyes were wild.

I made a garland for her head,
    And bracelets too, and fragrant zone;
She looked at me as she did love,
    And made sweet moan.   20

I set her on my pacing steed
    And nothing else saw all day long,
For sideways would she bend, and sing
    A faery's song.

She found me roots of relish sweet,
    And honey wild, and manna dew,
And sure in language strange she said—
    "I love thee true!"

She took me to her elfin grot,
    And there she wept and sighed full sore, 30
And there I shut her wild, wild eyes
    With kisses four.

And there she lullèd me asleep,
    And there I dreamed—ah, woe betide!
The latest dream I ever dreamed
    On the cold hill side.

I saw pale kings, and princes too,
    Pale warriors, death-pale were they all;
They cried—"La Belle Dame sans Merci
    Hath thee in thrall!"   40

I saw their starved lips in the gloam,
    With horrid warning gapèd wide,
And I awoke and found me here,
    On the cold hill's side.

And this is why I sojourn here,
    Alone and palely loitering,
Though the sedge is withered from the lake,
    And no birds sing.

Fame

Fame, like a wayward Girl, will still be coy
    To those who woo her with too slavish knees,
But makes surrender to some thoughtless Boy,
    And dotes the more upon a heart at ease;

She is a Gipsy, will not speak to those
  Who have not learned to be content without her;
A Jilt, whose ear was never whispered close,
  Who thinks they scandal her who talk about her;
A very Gipsy is she, Nilus-born,
  Sister-in-law to jealous Potiphar;
Ye love-sick Bards, repay her scorn for scorn,
  Ye Artists lovelorn, madmen that ye are!
Make your best bow to her and bid adieu,
Then, if she likes it, she will follow you.

Sonnet

Bright star, would I were steadfast as thou art—
  Not in lone splendor hung aloft the night
And watching, with eternal lids apart,
  Like Nature's patient, sleepless Eremite,
The moving waters at their priestlike task
  Of pure ablution round earth's human shores,
Or gazing on the new soft fallen mask
  Of snow upon the mountains and the moors—
No—yet still steadfast, still unchangeable,
  Pillowed upon my fair love's ripening breast,
To feel forever its soft fall and swell,
  Awake forever in a sweet unrest,
Still, still to hear her tender-taken breath,
And so live ever—or else swoon to death.

Ode on a Grecian Urn

Thou still unravished bride of quietness,
  Thou foster-child of silence and slow time,
Sylvan historian, who canst thus express
  A flowery tale more sweetly than our rhyme:
What leaf-fringed legend haunts about thy shape
  Of deities or mortals, or of both,
    In Tempe or the dales of Arcady?
    What men or gods are these? What maidens
      loath?
What mad pursuit? What struggle to escape?
    What pipes and timbrels? What wild ec-
      stasy?   10

Heard melodies are sweet, but those unheard
  Are sweeter; therefore, ye soft pipes, play on;
Not to the sensual ear, but, more endeared,
  Pipe to the spirit ditties of no tone:
Fair youth, beneath the trees, thou canst not leave
  Thy song, nor ever can those trees be bare;
    Bold Lover, never, never canst thou kiss,

Though winning near the goal—yet, do not grieve;
    She cannot fade, though thou hast not thy
      bliss,
  For ever wilt thou love, and she be fair!   20

Ah, happy, happy boughs! that cannot shed
  Your leaves, nor ever bid the Spring adieu;
And, happy melodist, unwearièd,
  For ever piping songs for ever new;
More happy love! more happy, happy love!
  For ever warm and still to be enjoyed,
    For ever panting and for ever young;
All breathing human passion far above,
  That leaves a heart high-sorrowful and cloyed,
    A burning forehead, and a parching tongue.   30

Who are these coming to the sacrifice?
  To what green altar, O mysterious priest,
Lead'st thou that heifer lowing at the skies,
  And all her silken flanks with garlands dressed?
What little town by river or sea-shore,
  Or mountain-built with peaceful citadel,
    Is emptied of this folk, this pious morn?
And, little town, thy streets for evermore
  Will silent be; and not a soul to tell
    Why thou art desolate, can e'er return.   40

O Attic shape! Fair attitude! with brede
  Of marble men and maidens overwrought,
With forest branches and the trodden weed;
  Thou, silent form, dost tease us out of thought
As doth eternity: Cold Pastoral!
  When old age shall this generation waste,
    Thou shalt remain, in midst of other woe
    Than ours, a friend to man, to whom thou say'st,
"Beauty is truth, truth beauty,"—that is all
    Ye know on earth, and all ye need to know.   50

Ode to a Nightingale

My heart aches, and a drowsy numbness pains
  My sense, as though of hemlock [1] I had drunk,
Or emptied some dull opiate to the drains
  One minute past, and Lethe-wards had sunk:
'Tis not through envy of thy happy lot,
  But being too happy in thine happiness—
    That thou, light-wingèd Dryad [2] of the trees,
    In some melodious plot
  Of beechen green, and shadows numberless,
  Singest of summer in full-throated ease.   10

[1] A poison.
[2] Tree-nymph.

O for a draught of vintage! that hath been
   Cooled a long age in the deep-delvèd earth,
Tasting of Flora and the country-green,
   Dance, and Provençal song, and sunburnt mirth!
O for a beaker full of the warm South,
   Full of the true, the blushful Hippocrene,[3]
      With beaded bubbles winking at the brim,
         And purple-stainèd mouth;
   That I might drink, and leave the world unseen,
      And with thee fade away into the forest dim: 20

Fade far away, dissolve, and quite forget
   What thou among the leaves hast never known,
The weariness, the fever, and the fret
   Here, where men sit and hear each other groan;
Where palsy shakes a few, sad, last gray hairs,
   Where youth grows pale, and specter-thin, and
         dies;
      Where but to think is to be full of sorrow
         And leaden-eyed despairs;
   Where beauty cannot keep her lustrous eyes,
      Or new Love pine at them beyond tomorrow. 30

Away! away! for I will fly to thee,
   Not charioted by Bacchus and his pards,
But on the viewless wings of Poesy,
   Though the dull brain perplexes and retards:
Already with thee! tender is the night,
   And haply the Queen-Moon is on her throne,
      Clustered around by all her starry Fays;
         But here there is no light,
   Save what from heaven is with the breezes blown
      Through verdurous glooms and winding mossy
         ways.   40

I cannot see what flowers are at my feet,
   Nor what soft incense hangs upon the boughs,
But, in embalmèd darkness, guess each sweet
   Wherewith the seasonable month endows
The grass, the thicket, and the fruit-tree wild;
   White hawthorn, and the pastoral eglantine;
      Fast-fading violets covered up in leaves;
         And mid-May's eldest child,
   The coming musk-rose, full of dewy wine,
      The murmurous haunt of flies on summer
         eves.   50

Darkling I listen; and, for many a time
   I have been half in love with easeful Death,
Called him soft names in many a musèd rhyme,
   To take into the air my quiet breath—
Now more than ever seems it rich to die,

[3] Spring of the Muses located on Mount Helicon.

To cease upon the midnight with no pain,
   While thou art pouring forth thy soul abroad
      In such an ecstasy!
Still wouldst thou sing, and I have ears in vain—
   To thy high requiem become a sod.   60

Thou wast not born for death, immortal Bird!
   No hungry generations tread thee down;
The voice I hear this passing night was heard
   In ancient days by emperor and clown:
Perhaps the self-same song that found a path
   Through the sad heart of Ruth, when, sick for
         home,
      She stood in tears amid the alien corn;
         The same that oft-times hath
   Charmed magic casements, opening on the foam
      Of perilous seas, in faery lands forlorn.   70

Forlorn! the very word is like a bell
   To toll me back from thee to my sole self.
Adieu! the fancy cannot cheat so well
   As she is famed to do, deceiving elf.
Adieu! adieu! thy plaintive anthem fades
   Past the near meadows, over the still stream,
      Up the hill-side; and now 'tis buried deep
         In the next valley-glades:
   Was it a vision, or a waking dream?
      Fled is that music:—do I wake or sleep?   80

To Autumn

Season of mists and mellow fruitfulness,
   Close bosom-friend of the maturing sun;
Conspiring with him how to load and bless
   With fruit the vines that round the thatch-eaves
      run;
To bend with apples the mossed cottage-trees,
   And fill all fruit with ripeness to the core;
      To swell the gourd, and plump the hazel shells
   With a sweet kernel; to set budding more,
And still more, later flowers for the bees,
Until they think warm days will never cease,
      For Summer has o'er-brimmed their clammy
         cells.

Who hath not seen thee oft amid thy store?
   Sometimes whoever seeks abroad may find
Thee sitting careless on a granary floor,
   Thy hair soft-lifted by the winnowing wind;
Or on a half-reaped furrow sound asleep,
   Drowsed with the fumes of poppies, while thy
      hook
      Spares the next swath and all its twinèd flowers;

And sometimes like a gleaner thou dost keep
   Steady thy laden head across a brook;
  Or by a cider-press, with patient look,
    Thou watchest the last oozings, hours by hours.

Where are the songs of Spring? Ay, where are they?
   Think not of them, thou hast thy music too,
While barrèd clouds bloom the soft dying day,
   And touch the stubble-plains with rosy hue;
Then in a wailful choir, the small gnats mourn
  Among the river sallows, borne aloft
   Or sinking as the light wind lives or dies;
And full-grown lambs loud bleat from hilly bourn;
  Hedge-crickets sing; and now with treble soft
  The redbreast whistles from a garden-croft;
   And gathering swallows twitter in the skies.

GEORGE GORDON, LORD BYRON

1788–1824

The son of "Mad Jack" Byron, a wastrel who ran through two fortunes, and an emotionally unstable and immature mother who beat him on some days and caressed him on others, the poet Byron liked to feel that he had "bad blood" in his veins. Somewhat lame from a slight clubfoot, Byron also developed feelings of inferiority during his childhood. He was sent to Harrow to school, and while there he inherited, at the age of ten, his title from a collateral branch of the family. At Harrow also he fell in love with his cousin, Mary Anne Chaworth, his first love affair. He proceeded to Trinity College, Cambridge, in 1805, whence he was graduated in 1808. Thereafter he took his seat in the House of Lords. From 1809 to 1811 he toured Europe with a friend but avoided the itinerary of the fashionable Grand Tour, preferring rather to seek out the less-visited and more romantic countries of Spain, Portugal, Greece, Turkey, and the Balkans. Returning to England, he published the first two cantos of *Childe Harold's Pilgrimage* in 1812.

Overnight a brilliant literary reputation was made, and Byron awoke on the morning of March 10, 1812, to find himself famous. He occupied part of his time at his estate Newstead Abbey and in the House of Lords, where his first speech in extenuation of workingmen who had smashed power looms shocked almost all Englishmen but the followers of William Godwin. But most of his time was spent in a brilliant social life in which he was lionized by London hostesses. So gay was his life dashing from one entertainment to another—for he was a lord, a literary celebrity, and one of the handsomest men who ever lived, and hence extremely sought after by the ladies—that he was too busy to compose poetry except while dressing and undressing. Perhaps he felt the need of greater stability in his life, for in 1815 he married the beautiful Anne Isabella Milbanke, a student of mathematics and a moralist. The two were almost totally incompatible, and a year later (after bearing him a daughter), Anne left him, publicly on the ground of incompatibility but actually because of his intolerable drunkenness, abusiveness, and incestuous relation with his half sister, Mrs. Augusta Leigh. Byron never forgave his wife for deserting him, however, and he felt himself disgraced. He therefore left England in 1816, never to return.

Going to Switzerland he spent some time with Shelley and Mary Godwin, the second Mrs. Shelley, and with her half sister, Claire Claremont. Byron and Claire Claremont immediately were attracted to each other, and in time she bore him a daughter, Allegra. In 1817 he proceeded to Venice, where he took a villa and lived a life which scandalized Europe. In 1819 he met the young countess Teresa Guiccioli, who became his mistress until his death; Byron himself referred to her as "my only, and my last love." In 1823 Byron went to aid the cause of the Greek revolution, and in a miasmal swamp near Missolonghi, during a tremendous rainstorm which provided enough thunder and lightning for the exit of the original Byronic hero himself, he died in 1824 of a fever at the age of thirty-six, a martyr to the cause of freedom.

Byron, arch-rebel against conventional society and implacable foe of tyranny, created a new type of literary hero and a new attitude toward life, an attitude which swept every European country and reflected itself in all Continental literatures. According to this pose, the Byronic hero is a sensitive young man, satiated with sensual pleasures, bored with life, furious at the hypocrisy and abuses of society, who roams friendless and alone from country to country, beyond hope and beyond despair, yet cherishing at the core of his existence the noble ideals of honesty, courage, and love of liberty. Many of Byron's longer works depict such a hero, among them *Manfred* and *Sardanapalus*. But the poems of Byron which today are most highly esteemed are *Childe Harold*, the best philosophical travelogue in poetry; "The Prisoner of Chillon," a passionate indictment of tyranny, and, in the "Sonnet on Chillon," a most eloquent plea for justice and liberty; his short lyric poems; and *Don Juan*.

The latter is a burlesque epic satire of sixteen cantos, mostly in *ottava rima*. Here, as in "English Bards and Scotch Reviewers," Byron most adequately demonstrates that he is the legitimate heir of Alexander Pope's satiric mantle. Certainly no one since the Augustans had been able to write such satire, witty in the best Neo-classical sense, nor has anyone since Byron's time produced its equal. Here, and elsewhere too, Byron indicates that he has nothing but the deepest contempt for the first generation of Romantics, the Lake poets Wordsworth, Coleridge, and Southey. Although he himself is wildly Romantic, his spiritual and intellectual affinity is with the aristocratic writers of the age of Queen Anne.

FURTHER READING

MAYNE, E. C. *Byron* (London, 1924).
NICHOLSON, H. G. *Byron, the Last Journey* (Boston, 1924).
QUENNELL, PETER. *Byron: The Years of Fame* (London, 1935).

She Walks in Beauty

She walks in beauty, like the night
   Of cloudless climes and starry skies;
And all that's best of dark and bright
   Meet in her aspect and her eyes:
Thus mellow'd to that tender light
   Which heaven to gaudy day denies.

One shade the more, one ray the less,
   Had half impair'd the nameless grace
Which waves in every raven tress,
   Or softly lightens o'er her face;
Where thoughts serenely sweet express
   How pure, how dear their dwelling-place.

And on that cheek, and o'er that brow,
   So soft, so calm, yet eloquent,
The smiles that win, the tints that glow,
   But tell of days in goodness spent,
A mind at peace with all below,
   A heart whose love is innocent!

When We Two Parted

When we two parted
   In silence and tears,
Half broken-hearted
   To sever for years,
Pale grew thy cheek and cold,
   Colder thy kiss;
Truly that hour foretold
   Sorrow to this.

The dew of the morning
   Sunk chill on my brow—
It felt like the warning
   Of what I feel now.
Thy vows are all broken,
   And light is thy fame:
I hear thy name spoken,
   And share in its shame.

They name thee before me,
   A knell to mine ear;
A shudder comes o'er me—
   Why wert thou so dear?
They know not I knew thee,
   Who knew thee too well:—
Long, long shall I rue thee,
   Too deeply to tell.

In secret we met—
   In silence I grieve,
That thy heart could forget,
   Thy spirit deceive.
If I should meet thee
   After long years,
How should I greet thee?—
   With silence and tears.

Sonnet on Chillon

Eternal Spirit of the chainless Mind!
Brightest in dungeons, Liberty! thou art,
For there thy habitation is the heart—
The heart which love of thee alone can bind;
And when thy sons to fetters are consigned—
To fetters, and the damp vault's dayless gloom,

Their country conquers with their martyrdom,
And Freedom's fame finds wings on every wind.
Chillon! thy prison is a holy place,
And thy sad floor an altar—for 'twas trod,
Until his very steps have left a trace
Worn, as if thy cold pavement were a sod,
By Bonnivard! May none those marks efface!
For they appeal from tyranny to God.

Don Juan

CANTO THE SECOND

I

Oh ye! who teach the ingenuous youth of nations,
    Holland, France, England, Germany, or Spain,
I pray ye flog them upon all occasions—
    It mends their morals, never mind the pain:
The best of mothers and of educations
    In Juan's case were but employed in vain,
Since, in a way that 's rather of the oddest, he
Became divested of his native modesty.

II

Had he but been placed at a public school,
    In the third form, or even in the fourth,
His daily task had kept his fancy cool,
    At least, had he been nurtured in the North;
Spain may prove an exception to the rule,
    But then exceptions always prove its worth—
A lad of sixteen causing a divorce
Puzzled his tutors very much, of course.

III

I can't say that it puzzles me at all,
    If all things be considered: first, there was
His lady-mother, mathematical,
    A —— never mind;—his tutor, an old ass;
A pretty woman—(that 's quite natural,
    Or else the thing had hardly come to pass)
A husband rather old, not much in unity
With his young wife—a time, and opportunity.

IV

Well—well; the World must turn upon its axis,
    And all Mankind turn with it, heads or tails,
And live and die, make love and pay our taxes,
    And as the veering wind shifts, shift our sails;
The King commands us, and the Doctor quacks us,
    The Priest instructs, and so our life exhales,
A little breath, love, wine, ambition, fame,
Fighting, devotion, dust,—perhaps a name.

V

I said that Juan had been sent to Cadiz—
    A pretty town, I recollect it well—
'T is there the mart of the colonial trade is,
    (Or was, before Peru learned to rebel),
And such sweet girls!—I mean, such graceful ladies,
    Their very walk would make your bosom swell;
I can't describe it, though so much it strike,
Nor liken it—I never saw the like:

VI

An Arab horse, a stately stag, a barb
    New broke, a camelopard, a gazelle,
No—none of these will do;—and then their garb,
    Their veil and petticoat—Alas! to dwell
Upon such things would very near absorb
    A canto—then their feet and ankles,—well,
Thank Heaven I've got no metaphor quite ready,
(And so, my sober Muse—come, let's be steady—

VII

Chaste Muse!—well,—if you must, you must)—the
        veil
    Thrown back a moment with the glancing hand,
While the o'erpowering eye, that turns you pale,
    Flashes into the heart:—All sunny land
Of Love! when I forget you, may I fail
    To——say my prayers—but never was there
        planned
A dress through which the eyes give such a volley,
Excepting the Venetian Fazzioli.[1]

VIII

But to our tale: the Donna Inez sent
    Her son to Cadiz only to embark;
To stay there had not answered her intent,
    But why?—we leave the reader in the dark—
'T was for a voyage the young man was meant,
    As if a Spanish ship were Noah's ark,
To wean him from the wickedness of earth,
And send him like a Dove of Promise forth.

IX

Don Juan bade his valet pack his things
    According to direction, then received
A lecture and some money: for four springs
    He was to travel; and though Inez grieved
(As every kind of parting has its stings),
    She hoped he would improve—perhaps believed:
A letter, too, she gave (he never read it)
Of good advice—and two or three of credit. . . .

[1] Little handkerchiefs.

XI

Juan embarked—the ship got under way,
    The wind was fair, the water passing rough;
A devil of a sea rolls in that bay,
    As I, who've crossed it oft, know well enough;
And, standing on the deck, the dashing spray
    Flies in one's face, and makes it weather-tough:
And there he stood to take, and take again,
His first—perhaps his last—farewell of Spain.

XII

I can't but say it is an awkward sight
    To see one's native land receding through
The growing waters; it unmans one quite,
    Especially when life is rather new:
I recollect Great Britain's coast looks white,
    But almost every other country 's blue,
When gazing on them, mystified by distance,
We enter on our nautical existence. . . .

XVII

And Juan wept, and much he sighed and thought,
    While his salt tears dropped into the salt sea,
"Sweets to the sweet;" (I like so much to quote;
    You must excuse this extract,—'t is where she,
The Queen of Denmark, for Ophelia brought
    Flowers to the grave;) and, sobbing often, he
Reflected on his present situation,
And seriously resolved on reformation.

XVIII

"Farewell, my Spain! a long farewell!" he cried,
    "Perhaps I may revisit thee no more,
But die, as many an exiled heart hath died,
    Of its own thirst to see again thy shore:
Farewell, where Guadalquivir's waters glide!
    Farewell, my mother! and since all is o'er,
Farewell, too, dearest Julia!—(here he drew
Her letter out again, and read it through.)

XIX

"And oh! if e'er I should forget, I swear—
    But that 's impossible, and cannot be—
Sooner shall this blue Ocean melt to air,
    Sooner shall Earth resolve itself to sea,
Than I resign thine image, oh, my fair!
    Or think of anything, excepting thee;
A mind diseased no remedy can physic—
(Here the ship gave a lurch, and he grew sea-sick.)

XX

"Sooner shall Heaven kiss earth—(here he fell
    sicker)
    Oh, Julia! what is every other woe?—

(For God's sake let me have a glass of liquor;
    Pedro, Battista, help me down below.)
Julia, my love!—(you rascal, Pedro, quicker)—
    Oh, Julia!—(this curst vessel pitches so)—
Belovéd Julia, hear me still beseeching!"
(Here he grew inarticulate with retching.)

XXI

He felt that chilling heaviness of heart,
    Or rather stomach, which, alas! attends,
Beyond the best apothecary's art,
    The loss of Love, the treachery of friends,
Or death of those we dote on, when a part
    Of us dies with them as each fond hope ends:
No doubt he would have been much more pathetic,
But the sea acted as a strong emetic. . . .

XXV

His suite consisted of three servants and
    A tutor, the licentiate Pedrillo,
Who several languages did understand,
    But now lay sick and speechless on his pillow
And, rocking in his hammock, longed for land,
    His headache being increased by every billow;
And the waves oozing through the port-hole made
His berth a little damp, and him afraid.

XXVI

'T was not without some reason, for the wind
    Increased at night, until it blew a gale;
And though 't was not much to a naval mind,
    Some landsmen would have looked a little pale,
For sailors are, in fact, a different kind:
    At sunset they began to take in sail,
For the sky showed it would come on to blow,
And carry away, perhaps, a mast or so.

XXVII

At one o'clock the wind with sudden shift
    Threw the ship right into the trough of the sea,
Which struck her aft, and made an awkward rift,
    Started the stern-post, also shattered the
Whole of her stern-frame, and, ere she could lift
    Herself from out her present jeopardy,
The rudder tore away: 't was time to sound
The pumps, and there were four feet water
    found. . . .

XLIX

'T was twilight, and the sunless day went down
    Over the waste of waters; like a veil,
Which, if withdrawn, would but disclose the frown
    Of one whose hate is masked but to assail.

Thus to their hopeless eyes the night was shown,
   And grimly darkled o'er the faces pale,
And the dim desolate deep: twelve days had Fear
Been their familiar, and now Death was here.

L

Some trial had been making at a raft,
   With little hope in such a rolling sea,
A sort of thing at which one would have laughed,
   If any laughter at such times could be,
Unless with people who too much have quaffed,
   And have a kind of wild and horrid glee,
Half epileptical, and half hysterical:—
Their preservation would have been a miracle.

LI

At half-past eight o'clock, booms, hencoops, spars,
   And all things, for a chance, had been cast loose,
That still could keep afloat the struggling tars,
   For yet they strove, although of no great use:
There was no light in heaven but a few stars,
   The boats put off o'ercrowded with their crews;
She gave a heel, and then a lurch to port,
And, going down head foremost—sunk, in short.

LII

Then rose from sea to sky the wild farewell—
   Then shrieked the timid, and stood still the
     brave,—
Then some leaped overboard with dreadful yell,
   As eager to anticipate their grave;
And the sea yawned around her like a hell,
   And down she sucked with her the whirling
     wave,
Like one who grapples with his enemy,
And strives to strangle him before he die.

LIII

And first one universal shriek there rushed,
   Louder than the loud Ocean, like a crash
Of echoing thunder; and then all was hushed,
   Save the wild wind and the remorseless dash
Of billows; but at intervals there gushed,
   Accompanied by a convulsive splash,
A solitary shriek, the bubbling cry
Of some strong swimmer in his agony. . . .

LVI

Juan got into the long-boat, and there
   Contrived to help Pedrillo to a place;
It seemed as if they had exchanged their care,
   For Juan wore the magisterial face

Which courage gives, while poor Pedrillo's pair
   Of eyes were crying for their owner's case:
Battista, though, (a name called shortly Tita),
Was lost by getting at some aqua-vita.

LVII

Pedro, his valet, too, he tried to save,
   But the same cause, conducive to his loss,
Left him so drunk, he jumped into the wave,
   As o'er the cutter's edge he tried to cross,
And so he found a wine-and-watery grave;
   They could not rescue him although so close,
Because the sea ran higher every minute,
And for the boat—the crew kept crowding in it. . . .

CIII

As they drew nigh the land, which now was seen
   Unequal in its aspect here and there,
They felt the freshness of its growing green,
   That waved in forest-tops, and smoothed the air,
And fell upon their glazed eyes like a screen
   From glistening waves, and skies so hot and
     bare—
Lovely seemed any object that should sweep
Away the vast—salt—dread—eternal Deep.

CIV

The shore looked wild, without a trace of man,
   And girt by formidable waves; but they
Were mad for land, and thus their course they ran,
   Though right ahead the roaring breakers lay:
A reef between them also now began
   To show its boiling surf and bounding spray,
But finding no place for their landing better,
They ran the boat for shore,—and overset her.

CV

But in his native stream, the Guadalquivir,
   Juan to lave his youthful limbs was wont;
And having learnt to swim in that sweet river,
   Had often turned the art to some account:
A better swimmer you could scarce see ever,
   He could, perhaps, have passed the Hellespont,
As once (a feat on which ourselves we prided)
Leander, Mr. Ekenhead, and I did.

CVI

So here, though faint, emaciated, and stark,
   He buoyed his boyish limbs, and strove to ply
With the quick wave, and gain, ere it was dark,
   The beach which lay before him, high and dry.

The greatest danger here was from a shark,
   That carried off his neighbour by the thigh;
As for the other two, they could not swim,
So nobody arrived on shore but him. . . .

CXI

How long in his damp trance young Juan lay
   He knew not, for the earth was gone for him,
And Time had nothing more of night nor day
   For his congealing blood, and senses dim;
And how this heavy faintness passed away
   He knew not, till each painful pulse and limb,
And tingling vein, seemed throbbing back to life,
For Death, though vanquished, still retired with
    strife.

CXII

His eyes he opened, shut, again unclosed,
   For all was doubt and dizziness; he thought
He still was in the boat, and had but dozed,
   And felt again with his despair o'erwrought,
And wished it Death in which he had reposed,
   And then once more his feelings back were
    brought,
And slowly by his swimming eyes was seen
A lovely female face of seventeen.

CXIII

'T was bending close o'er his, and the small mouth
   Seemed almost prying into his for breath;
And chafing him, the soft warm hand of youth
   Recalled his answering spirits back from Death:
And, bathing his chill temples, tried to soothe
   Each pulse to animation, till beneath
Its gentle touch and trembling care, a sigh
To these kind efforts made a low reply.

CXIV

Then was the cordial poured, and mantle flung
   Around his scarce-clad limbs; and the fair arm
Raised higher the faint head which o'er it hung;
   And her transparent cheek, all pure and warm,
Pillowed his death-like forehead; then she wrung
   His dewy curls, long drenched by every storm;
And watched with eagerness each throb that drew
A sigh from his heaved bosom—and hers, too.

CXV

And lifting him with care into the cave,
   The gentle girl, and her attendant,—one
Young, yet her elder, and of brow less grave,
   And more robust of figure,—then begun

To kindle fire, and as the new flames gave
   Light to the rocks that roofed them, which the
    sun
Had never seen, the maid, or whatsoe'er
She was, appeared distinct, and tall, and fair.

CXVI

Her brow was overhung with coins of gold,
   That sparkled o'er the auburn of her hair—
Her clustering hair, whose longer locks were rolled
   In braids behind; and though her stature were
Even of the highest for a female mould,
   They nearly reached her heel; and in her air
There was a something which bespoke command,
As one who was a Lady in the land.

CXVII

Her hair, I said, was auburn; but her eyes
   Were black as Death, their lashes the same hue,
Of downcast length, in whose silk shadow lies
   Deepest attraction; for when to the view
Forth from its raven fringe the full glance flies,
   Ne'er with such force the swiftest arrow flew;
'T is as the snake late coiled, who pours his length,
And hurls at once his venom and his strength.

CXVIII

Her brow was white and low, her cheek's pure dye
   Like twilight rosy still with the set sun;
Short upper lip—sweet lips! that make us sigh
   Ever to have seen such; for she was one
Fit for the model of a statuary
   (A race of mere impostors, when all 's done—
I 've seen much finer women, ripe and real,
Than all the nonsense of their stone ideal). . . .

CXXIV

I 'll tell you who they were, this female pair,
   Lest they should seem Princesses in disguise;
Besides, I hate all mystery, and that air
   Of clap-trap, which your recent poets prize;
And so, in short, the girls they really were
   They shall appear before your curious eyes,
Mistress and maid; the first was only daughter
Of an old man, who lived upon the water.

CXXV

A fisherman he had been in his youth,
   And still a sort of fisherman was he;
But other speculations were, in sooth,
   Added to his connection with the sea,
Perhaps not so respectable, in truth:
   A little smuggling, and some piracy,

Left him, at last, the sole of many masters
Of an ill-gotten million of piastres.

CXXVI

A fisher, therefore, was he,—though of men,
　　Like Peter the Apostle, and he fished
For wandering merchant-vessels, now and then,
　　And sometimes caught as many as he wished;
The cargoes he confiscated, and gain
　　He sought in the slave-market too, and dished
Full many a morsel for that Turkish trade,
By which, no doubt, a good deal may be made.

CXXVII

He was a Greek, and on his isle had built
　　(One of the wild and smaller Cyclades)
A very handsome house from out his guilt,
　　And there he lived exceedingly at ease;
Heaven knows what cash he got, or blood he spilt,
　　A sad old fellow was he, if you please;
But this I know, it was a spacious building,
Full of barbaric carving, paint, and gilding.

CXXVIII

He had an only daughter, called Haidée,
　　The greatest heiress of the Eastern Isles;
Besides, so very beautiful was she,
　　Her dowry was as nothing to her smiles:
Still in her teens, and like a lovely tree
　　She grew to womanhood, and between whiles
Rejected several suitors, just to learn
How to accept a better in his turn. . . .

CXXXV

Young Juan slept all dreamless:—but the maid,
　　Who smoothed his pillow, as she left the den
Looked back upon him, and a moment stayed,
　　And turned, believing that he called again.
He slumbered; yet she thought, at least she said
　　(The heart will slip, even as the tongue and
　　　pen),
He had pronounced her name—but she forgot
That at this moment Juan knew it not.

CXXXVI

And pensive to her father's house she went,
　　Enjoining silence strict to Zoe, who
Better than her knew what, in fact, she meant,
　　She being wiser by a year or two:
A year or two 's an age when rightly spent,
　　And Zoe spent hers, as most women do,
In gaining all that useful sort of knowledge
Which is acquired in Nature's good old college. . . .

CXLII

And down the cliff the island virgin came,
　　And near the cave her quick light footsteps drew,
While the Sun smiled on her with his first flame,
　　And young Aurora kissed her lips with dew,
Taking her for a sister; just the same
　　Mistake you would have made on seeing the
　　　two,
Although the mortal, quite as fresh and fair,
Had all the advantage, too, of not being air.

CXLIII

And when into the cavern Haidée stepped
　　All timidly, yet rapidly, she saw
That like an infant Juan sweetly slept;
　　And then she stopped, and stood as if in awe
(For sleep is awful), and on tiptoe crept
　　And wrapped him closer, lest the air, too raw,
Should reach his blood, then o'er him still as Death
Bent, with hushed lips, that drank his scarce-drawn
　　breath.

CXLIV

And thus like to an Angel o'er the dying
　　Who die in righteousness, she leaned; and there
All tranquilly the shipwrecked boy was lying,
　　As o'er him lay the calm and stirless air:
But Zoe the meantime some eggs was frying,
　　Since, after all, no doubt the youthful pair
Must breakfast—and, betimes, lest they should ask
　　it,
She drew out her provision from the basket. . . .

CLII

And Juan gazed as one who is awoke
　　By a distant organ, doubting if he be
Not yet a dreamer, till the spell is broke
　　By the watchman, or some such reality,
Or by one's early valet's curséd knock;
　　At least it is a heavy sound to me,
Who like a morning slumber—for the night
Shows stars and women in a better light.

CLIII

And Juan, too, was helped out from his dream,
　　Or sleep, or whatsoe'er it was, by feeling
A most prodigious appetite; the steam
　　Of Zoe's cookery no doubt was stealing
Upon his senses, and the kindling beam
　　Of the new fire, which Zoe kept up, kneeling,
To stir her viands, made him quite awake
And long for food, but chiefly a beef-steak. . . .

CLVIII

He ate, and he was well supplied; and she,
  Who watched him like a mother, would have fed
Him past all bounds, because she smiled to see
  Such appetite in one she had deemed dead:
But Zoe, being older than Haidée,
  Knew (by tradition, for she ne'er had read)
That famished people must be slowly nurst,
And fed by spoonfuls, else they always burst. . . .

CLXIII

And now, by dint of fingers and of eyes,
  And words repeated after her, he took
A lesson in her tongue; but by surmise,
  No doubt, less of her language than her look:
As he who studies fervently the skies
  Turns oftener to the stars than to his book,
Thus Juan learned his *alpha beta* better
From Haidée's glance than any graven letter.

CLXIV

'T is pleasing to be schooled in a strange tongue
  By female lips and eyes—that is, I mean,
When both the teacher and the taught are young,
  As was the case, at least, where I have been;
  They smile so when one 's right, and when one 's
    wrong
  They smile still more, and then there intervene
Pressure of hands, perhaps even a chaste kiss;—
I learned the little that I know by this: . . .

CLXVIII

And every day by daybreak—rather early
  For Juan, who was somewhat fond of rest—
She came into the cave, but it was merely
  To see her bird reposing in his nest;
And she would softly stir his locks so curly,
  Without disturbing her yet slumbering guest,
Breathing all gently o'er his cheek and mouth,
As o'er a bed of roses the sweet South. . . .

CLXX

While Venus fills the heart, (without heart really
  Love, though good always, is not quite so good,)
Ceres presents a plate of vermicelli,—
  For Love must be sustained like flesh and blood,—
While Bacchus pours out wine, or hands a jelly:
  Eggs, oysters, too, are amatory food;
But who is their purveyor from above
Heaven knows,—it may be Neptune, Pan, or Jove.

CLXXI

When Juan woke he found some good things ready,
  A bath, a breakfast, and the finest eyes
That ever made a youthful heart less steady,
  Besides her maid's, as pretty for their size;
But I have spoken of all this already—
  A repetition 's tiresome and unwise,—
Well—Juan, after bathing in the sea,
Came always back to coffee and Haidée.

CLXXII

Both were so young, and one so innocent,
  That bathing passed for nothing; Juan seemed
To her, as 't were, the kind of being sent,
  Of whom these two years she had nightly
    dreamed,
A something to be loved, a creature meant
  To be her happiness, and whom she deemed
To render happy; all who joy would win
Must share it,—Happiness was born a Twin.

CLXXIII

It was such pleasure to behold him, such
  Enlargement of existence to partake
Nature with him, to thrill beneath his touch,
  To watch him slumbering, and to see him wake:
To live with him for ever were too much;
  But then the thought of parting made her quake;
He was her own, her ocean-treasure cast
Like a rich wreck—her first love, and her last. . . .

CLXXV

Then came her freedom, for she had no mother,
  So that, her father being at sea, she was
Free as a married woman, or such other
  Female, as where she likes may freely pass,
Without even the encumbrance of a brother,
  The freest she that ever gazed on glass:
I speak of Christian lands in this comparison,
Where wives, at least, are seldom kept in garrison.

CLXXVI

Now she prolonged her visits and her talk
  (For they must talk), and he had learnt to say
So much as to propose to take a walk,—
  For little had he wandered since the day
On which, like a young flower snapped from the
    stalk,
  Drooping and dewy on the beach he lay,—
And thus they walked out in the afternoon,
And saw the sun set opposite the moon.

CLXXVII

It was a wild and breaker-beaten coast,
  With cliffs above, and a broad sandy shore,
Guarded by shoals and rocks as by an host,
  With here and there a creek, whose aspect wore
A better welcome to the tempest-tost;
  And rarely ceased the haughty billow's roar,
Save on the dead long summer days, which make
The outstretched Ocean glitter like a lake.

CLXXVIII

And the small ripple split upon the beach
  Scarcely o'erpassed the cream of your champagne,
When o'er the brim the sparkling bumpers reach,
  That spring-dew of the spirit! the heart's rain!
Few things surpass old wine; and they may preach
  Who please,—the more because they preach in
     vain,—
Let us have Wine and Woman, Mirth and Laugh-
   ter,
Sermons and soda-water the day after.

CLXXIX

Man, being reasonable, must get drunk;
  The best of Life is but intoxication:
Glory, the Grape, Love, Gold, in these are sunk
  The hopes of all men, and of every nation;
Without their sap, how branchless were the trunk
  Of Life's strange tree, so fruitful on occasion!
But to return,—Get very drunk, and when
You wake with headache—you shall see what then!

CLXXX

Ring for your valet—bid him quickly bring
  Some hock and soda-water, then you 'll know
A pleasure worthy Xerxes the great king;
  For not the blest sherbet, sublimed with snow,
Nor the first sparkle of the desert-spring,
  Nor Burgundy in all its sunset glow,
After long travel, Ennui, Love, or Slaughter,
Vie with that draught of hock and soda-water!

CLXXXI

The coast—I think it was the coast that I
  Was just describing—Yes, it *was* the coast—
Lay at this period quiet as the sky,
  The sands untumbled, the blue waves untossed,
And all was stillness, save the sea-bird's cry,
  And dolphin's leap, and little billow crossed
By some low rock or shelve, that made it fret
Against the boundary it scarcely wet.

CLXXXII

And forth they wandered, her sire being gone,
  As I have said, upon an expedition;
And mother, brother, guardian, she had none,
  Save Zoe, who, although with due precision
She waited on her lady with the Sun,
  Thought daily service was her only mission,
Bringing warm water, wreathing her long tresses,
And asking now and then for cast-off dresses.

CLXXXIII

It was the cooling hour, just when the rounded
  Red sun sinks down behind the azure hill,
Which then seems as if the whole earth it bounded,
  Circling all Nature, hushed, and dim, and still.
With the far mountain-crescent half surrounded
  On one side, and the deep sea calm and chill
Upon the other, and the rosy sky
With one star sparkling through it like an eye.

CLXXXIV

And thus they wandered forth, and hand in hand,
  Over the shining pebbles and the shells,
Glided along the smooth and hardened sand,
  And in the worn and wild receptacles
Worked by the storms, yet worked as it were
     planned
  In hollow halls, with sparry roofs and cells,
They turned to rest; and, each clasped by an arm,
Yielded to the deep Twilight's purple charm.

CLXXXV

They looked up to the sky, whose floating glow
  Spread like a rosy Ocean, vast and bright;
They gazed upon the glittering sea below,
  Whence the broad Moon rose circling into sight;
They heard the waves' splash, and the wind so low,
  And saw each other's dark eyes darting light
Into each other—and, beholding this,
Their lips drew near, and clung into a kiss;

CLXXXVI

A long, long kiss, a kiss of Youth, and Love,
  And Beauty, all concentrating like rays
Into one focus, kindled from above;
  Such kisses as belong to early days,
Where Heart, and Soul, and Sense, in concert
     move,
  And the blood 's lava, and the pulse a blaze,
Each kiss a heart-quake,—for a kiss's strength,
I think, it must be reckoned by its length.

CLXXXVII

By length I mean duration; theirs endured
  Heaven knows how long—no doubt they never
    reckoned;
And if they had, they could not have secured
  The sum of their sensations to a second:
They had not spoken, but they felt allured,
  As if their souls and lips each other beckoned,
Which, being joined, like swarming bees they
    clung—
Their hearts the flowers from whence the honey
    sprung.

CLXXXVIII

They were alone, but not alone as they
  Who shut in chambers think it loneliness;
The silent Ocean, and the starlight bay,
  The twilight glow, which momently grew less,
The voiceless sands, and dropping caves, that lay
  Around them, made them to each other press,
As if there were no life beneath the sky
Save theirs, and that their life could never die.

CLXXXIX

They feared no eyes nor ears on that lone beach;
  They felt no terrors from the night; they were
All in all to each other: though their speech
  Was broken words, they *thought* a language
    there,—
And all the burning tongues the Passions teach
  Found in one sigh the best interpreter
Of Nature's oracle—first love,—that all
Which Eve has left her daughters since her fall.

CXC

Haidée spoke not of scruples, asked no vows,
  Nor offered any; she had never heard
Of plight and promises to be a spouse,
  Or perils by a loving maid incurred;
She was all which pure Ignorance allows,
  And flew to her young mate like a young bird;
And, never having dreamt of falsehood, she
Had not one word to say of constancy.

CXCI

She loved, and was belovéd—she adored,
  And she was worshipped after Nature's fashion—
Their intense souls, into each other poured,
  If souls could die, had perished in that passion,—
But by degrees their senses were restored,
  Again to be o'ercome, again to dash on;
And, beating 'gainst *his* bosom, Haidée's heart
Felt as if never more to beat apart. . . .

CXCIII

Alas! for Juan and Haidée! they were
  So loving and so lovely—till then never,
Excepting our first parents, such a pair
  Had run the risk of being damned for ever:
And Haidée, being devout as well as fair,
  Had, doubtless, heard about the Stygian river,
And Hell and Purgatory—but forgot
Just in the very crisis she should not.

CXCIV

They look upon each other, and their eyes
  Gleam in the moonlight; and her white arm
    clasps
Round Juan's head, and his around her lies
  Half buried in the tresses which it grasps;
She sits upon his knee, and drinks his sighs,
  He hers, until they end in broken gasps;
And thus they form a group that 's quite antique,
Half naked, loving, natural, and Greek.

CXCV

And when those deep and burning moments passed,
  And Juan sunk to sleep within her arms,
She slept not, but all tenderly, though fast,
  Sustained his head upon her bosom's charms;
And now and then her eye to Heaven is cast,
  And then on the pale cheek her breast now
    warms,
Pillowed on her o'erflowing heart, which pants
With all it granted, and with all it grants. . . .

CXCIX

Alas! the love of Women! it is known
  To be a lovely and a fearful thing;
For all of theirs upon that die is thrown,
  And if 't is lost, Life hath no more to bring
To them but mockeries of the past alone,
  And their revenge is as the tiger's spring,
Deadly, and quick, and crushing; yet, as real
Torture is theirs—what they inflict they feel.

CC

They are right; for Man, to man so oft unjust,
  Is always so to Women: one sole bond
Awaits them—treachery is all their trust;
  Taught to conceal their bursting hearts despond
Over their idol, till some wealthier lust
  Buys them in marriage—and what rests beyond?
A thankless husband—next, a faithless lover—
Then dressing, nursing, praying—and all 's over.

CCI

Some take a lover, some take drams or prayers,
  Some mind their household, others dissipation,
Some run away, and but exchange their cares,
  Losing the advantage of a virtuous station;
Few changes e'er can better their affairs,
  Theirs being an unnatural situation,
From the dull palace to the dirty hovel:
Some play the devil, and then write a novel.

CCII

Haidée was Nature's bride, and knew not this;
  Haidée was Passion's child, born where the Sun
Showers triple light, and scorches even the kiss
  Of his gazelle-eyed daughters; she was one
Made but to love, to feel that she was his
  Who was her chosen: what was said or done
Elsewhere was nothing. She had nought to fear,
Hope, care, nor love, beyond,—her heart beat *here*.

CCIII

And oh! that quickening of the heart, that beat!
  How much it costs us! yet each rising throb
Is in its cause as its effect so sweet,
  That Wisdom, ever on the watch to rob
Joy of its alchemy, and to repeat
  Fine truths; even Conscience, too, has a tough
    job
To make us understand each good old maxim,
So good—I wonder Castlereagh don't tax 'em.

CCIV

And now 't was done—on the lone shore were
    plighted
  Their hearts; the stars, their nuptial torches, shed
Beauty upon the beautiful they lighted:
  Ocean their witness, and the cave their bed,
By their own feelings hallowed and united,
  Their priest was Solitude, and they were wed:
And they were happy—for to their young eyes
Each was an angel, and earth Paradise. . . .

CCVIII

But Juan! had he quite forgotten Julia?
  And should he have forgotten her so soon?
I can't but say it seems to me most truly a
  Perplexing question; but, no doubt, the moon
Does these things for us, and whenever newly a
  Strong palpitation rises, 't is her boon,
Else how the devil is it that fresh features
Have such a charm for us poor human creatures?

CCIX

I hate inconstancy—I loathe, detest,
  Abhor, condemn, abjure the mortal made
Of such quicksilver clay that in his breast
  No permanent foundation can be laid;
Love, constant love, has been my constant guest,
  And yet last night being at a masquerade,
I saw the prettiest creature, fresh from Milan,
Which gave me some sensations like a villain.

CCX

But soon Philosophy came to my aid,
  And whispered, "Think of every sacred tie!"
"I will, my dear Philosophy!" I said,
  "But then her teeth, and then, oh, Heaven! her
    eye!
I 'll just inquire if she be wife or maid,
  Or neither—out of curiosity."
"Stop!" cried Philosophy, with air so Grecian,
(Though she was masqued then as a fair Venetian;)

CCXI

"Stop!" so I stopped.—But to return: that which
  Men call inconstancy is nothing more
Than admiration due where Nature's rich
  Profusion with young beauty covers o'er
Some favoured object; and as in the niche
  A lovely statue we almost adore,
This sort of adoration of the real
Is but a heightening of the *beau ideal*.

CCXII

'T is the perception of the Beautiful,
  A fine extension of the faculties,
Platonic, universal, wonderful,
  Drawn from the stars, and filtered through the
    skies,
Without which Life would be extremely dull;
  In short, it is the use of our own eyes,
With one or two small senses added, just
To hint that flesh is formed of fiery dust. . . .

CCXIV

The Heart is like the sky, a part of Heaven,
  But changes night and day, too, like the sky;
Now o'er it clouds and thunder must be driven,
  And Darkness and Destruction as on high:
But when it hath been scorched, and pierced, and
    riven,
  Its storms expire in water-drops; the eye
Pours forth at last the Heart's blood turned to tears,
Which make the English climate of our years.

CCXV

The liver is the lazaret of bile,
    But very rarely executes its function,
For the first passion stays there such a while,
    That all the rest creep in and form a junction,
Like knots of vipers on a dunghill's soil—
    Rage, fear, hate, jealousy, revenge, compunc-
      tion—
So that all mischiefs spring up from the entrail,
Like Earthquakes from the hidden fire called "cen-
      tral."

CCXVI

In the meantime, without proceeding more
    In this anatomy, I 've finished now
Two hundred and odd stanzas as before,
    That being about the number I 'll allow
Each canto of the twelve, or twenty-four;
    And, laying down my pen, I make my bow,
Leaving Don Juan and Haidée to plead
For them and theirs with all who deign to
    read.

American Lyric Poetry

WILLIAM CULLEN BRYANT

1794–1878

William Cullen Bryant, the first American poet to receive major recognition abroad, was born in the Berkshire Mountains of Massachusetts. His father was a Calvinist of conservative political and economic opinions, which the young poet at first accepted. After one year at Williams College and some study of law, he practiced with fair success in several Massachusetts towns. But after the publication of "Thanatopsis" in 1817, he bravely gave up the security of law for the hazards of literature. In 1821 he published a slender volume of *Poems*. Removing his family—he was happily married to Fanny Fairchild, whom he had described as "fairest of the rural maids"—he took up residence in New York in 1825 and formed a connection with the *Evening Post*. Four years later he became editor-in-chief, and later part owner of the paper. His life, as calm and secure and prosperous as Poe's was tempestuous, was happy and busy. During the following years he made six trips to Europe with his family, and died wealthy.

Bryant, who began as a Calvinist and a conservative, developed into a Unitarian and a political and social liberal. He espoused such advanced causes as workingmen's rights to organize and the abolition of slavery. In his poetry, he began with imitations of Pope and the Neo-classical poets of the eighteenth century and gradually developed through imitations of such Romantic precursors as Thomson and Cowper to a Romanticism most nearly resembling that of Wordsworth. In his love of nature, which sometimes is almost pantheistic, and simplicity of diction he is almost the American counterpart of Wordsworth. His attitude toward American subject matter helped to free youthful American literature from the shackles of imitating European models, for he strongly insisted on the equal worth and dignity of American material. In this practice, both his precept and example were salutary.

FURTHER READING

McDowell, Tremaine. *William Cullen Bryant* (Cincinnati, 1935).

Thanatopsis

To him who in the love of Nature holds
Communion with her visible forms, she speaks
A various language; for his gayer hours
She has a voice of gladness, and a smile
And eloquence of beauty, and she glides
Into his darker musings, with a mild
And healing sympathy, that steals away
Their sharpness, ere he is aware. When thoughts
Of the last bitter hour come like a blight

Over thy spirit, and sad images   10
Of the stern agony, and shroud, and pall,
And breathless darkness, and the narrow house,
Make thee to shudder, and grow sick at heart;—
Go forth, under the open sky, and list
To Nature's teachings, while from all around—
Earth and her waters, and the depths of air—
Comes a still voice—
              Yet a few days, and thee
The all-beholding sun shall see no more
In all his course; nor yet in the cold ground,
Where thy pale form was laid with many tears,   20
Nor in the embrace of ocean, shall exist
Thy image. Earth, that nourished thee, shall claim
Thy growth, to be resolved to earth again,
And, lost each human trace, surrendering up
Thine individual being, shalt thou go
To mix forever with the elements,
To be a brother to the insensible rock
And to the sluggish clod, which the rude swain
Turns with his share, and treads upon. The oak
Shall send his roots abroad, and pierce thy mould. 30
   Yet not to thine eternal resting-place
Shalt thou retire alone, nor couldst thou wish
Couch more magnificent. Thou shalt lie down
With patriarchs of the infant world—with kings,
The powerful of the earth—the wise, the good,
Fair forms, and hoary seers of ages past,
All in one mighty sepulchre. The hills
Rock-ribbed and ancient as the sun,—the vales
Stretching in pensive quietness between;
The venerable woods—rivers that move   40
In majesty, and the complaining brooks
That make the meadows green; and, poured round
    all,
Old Ocean's gray and melancholy waste,—
Are but the solemn decorations all
Of the great tomb of man. The golden sun,
The planets, all the infinite host of heaven,
Are shining on the sad abodes of death,
Through the still lapse of ages. All that tread
The globe are but a handful to the tribes
That slumber in its bosom.—Take the wings   50
Of morning, pierce the Barcan wilderness,
Or lose thyself in the continuous woods
Where rolls the Oregon, and hears no sound
Save his own dashings—yet the dead are there:
And millions in those solitudes, since first
The flight of years began, have laid them down
In their last sleep—the dead reign there alone.
So shalt thou rest; and what if thou withdraw
In silence from the living, and no friend
Take note of thy departure? All that breathe   60

Will share thy destiny. The gay will laugh
When thou art gone, the solemn brood of care
Plod on, and each one as before will chase
His favorite phantom; yet all these shall leave
Their mirth and their employments, and shall come
And make their bed with thee. As the long train
Of ages glide away, the sons of men,
The youth in life's fresh spring, and he who goes
In the full strength of years, matron and maid,
The speechless babe, and the gray-headed man— 70
Shall one by one be gathered to thy side,
By those, who in their turn shall follow them.
   So live, that when thy summons comes to join
The innumerable caravan, which moves
To that mysterious realm, where each shall take
His chamber in the silent halls of death,
Thou go not, like the quarry-slave at night,
Scourged to his dungeon, but, sustained and soothed
By an unfaltering trust, approach thy grave
Like one who wraps the drapery of his couch   80
About him, and lies down to pleasant dreams.

To a Waterfowl

  Whither, midst falling dew,
While glow the heavens with the last steps of day,
Far, through their rosy depths, dost thou pursue
    Thy solitary way?

  Vainly the fowler's eye
Might mark thy distant flight to do thee wrong,
As, darkly seen against the crimson sky,
    Thy figure floats along.

  Seek'st thou the plashy brink
Of weedy lake, or marge of river wide,   10
Or where the rocking billows rise and sink
    On the chafed ocean-side?

  There is a Power whose care
Teaches thy way along that pathless coast—
The desert and illimitable air—
    Lone wandering, but not lost.

  All day thy wings have fanned,
At that far height, the cold, thin atmosphere,
Yet stoop not, weary, to the welcome land,
    Though the dark night is near.   20

  And soon that toil shall end;
Soon shalt thou find a summer home, and rest,
And scream among thy fellows; reeds shall bend,
    Soon, o'er thy sheltered nest.

Thou'rt gone, the abyss of heaven
Hath swallowed up thy form; yet, on my heart
Deeply has sunk the lesson thou hast given,
   And shall not soon depart.

He who, from zone to zone,
Guides through the boundless sky thy certain
   flight,   30
In the long way that I must tread alone,
   Will lead my steps aright.

Inscription for the Entrance to a Wood

Stranger, if thou hast learned a truth which needs
No school of long experience, that the world
Is full of guilt and misery, and hast seen
Enough of all its sorrows, crimes, and cares,
To tire thee of it, enter this wild wood
And view the haunts of Nature. The calm shade
Shall bring a kindred calm, and the sweet breeze
That makes the green leaves dance, shall waft a
   balm
To thy sick heart. Thou wilt find nothing here
Of all that pained thee in the haunts of men,   10
And made thee loathe thy life. The primal curse
Fell, it is true, upon the unsinning earth,
But not in vengeance. God hath yoked to guilt
Her pale tormentor, misery. Hence, these shades
Are still the abodes of gladness; the thick roof
Of green and stirring branches is alive
And musical with birds, that sing and sport
In wantonness of spirit; while below
The squirrel, with raised paws and form erect,
Chirps merrily. Throngs of insects in the shade 20
Try their thin wings and dance in the warm beam
That waked them into life. Even the green trees
Partake the deep contentment; as they bend
To the soft winds, the sun from the blue sky
Looks in and sheds a blessing on the scene.
Scarce less the cleft-born wild-flower seems to enjoy
Existence, than the wingèd plunderer
That sucks its sweets. The mossy rocks themselves,
And the old and ponderous trunks of prostrate trees
That lead from knoll to knoll a causey rude   30
Or bridge the sunken brook, and their dark roots,
With all their earth upon them, twisting high,
Breathe fixed tranquillity. The rivulet
Sends forth glad sounds, and tripping o'er its bed
Of pebbly sands, or leaping down the rocks,
Seems, with continuous laughter, to rejoice
In its own being. Softly tread the marge,
Lest from her midway perch thou scare the wren

That dips her bill in water. The cool wind,
That stirs the stream in play, shall come to thee, 40
Like one that loves thee nor will let thee pass
Ungreeted, and shall give its light embrace.

EDGAR ALLAN POE

1809–1849

Edgar Allan Poe, important American poet, critic, and short-story writer, was born in Boston, the son of impoverished actors. Brought up, but never legally adopted, by John Allan, a rich tobacco merchant of Richmond, he received his education in England and at the University of Virginia. From this institution he was dismissed because of circumstances connected with certain debts. His expulsion led to quarrels with Mr. Allan. Thereupon Poe enlisted in the army and soon after entered West Point, from which he was expelled for insubordination. This event produced a final break with his foster father, and Poe's life, already off to a bad start, continued for the most part to be a sad, unhappy one, cursed by frustration and poverty. Before this break, Poe had already published three slender volumes of poetry. He now lived for a time in Baltimore with a distant cousin, Mrs. Clemm, whose thirteen-year-old daughter, Virginia, he married.

Unable to support himself by poetry, Poe turned to journalism and to the short story. Approaching the problem of the short story by a coldly scientific analysis, he decided that there was a market for a tale of terror with a single effect. Having discovered this formula, he turned it to good effect in all of his best-known stories, now classics of American literature. Indubitably Poe did much to advance the art of fiction in America, for all his stories are based upon a careful structure, attention to which greatly increases the reader's appreciation.

Poe supported himself and his young wife by a career as editor or staff-member of a number of magazines: *The Southern Literary Messenger, Burton's Gentleman's Magazine, Graham's Magazine,* and the New York *Evening Mirror.* Cursed by poverty, for all of his literary industry was poorly remunerated, he could not properly provide for his family's needs. To escape drabness, poverty, and frustration—for Poe realized his genius and felt it should be better rewarded—he resorted to the solace of drink. Frequent sprees alternated with periods of deep penitence. His wife died amid distressing conditions in 1847. During the two years remaining to him, he lectured and wrote some of his finest poetry, including "Ulalume" (1847), written on the death of his wife; "Annabel Lee" (1849); and "Eldorado" (1849). He died in Baltimore in 1849, in rather mysterious circumstances, either ill or drunk.

Evaluation of Poe by literary critics has been far from unanimous. Lowell, his contemporary, says for example in *A Fable for Critics*,

There comes Poe, with his raven, like Barnaby Rudge,
Three fifths of him genius and two fifths sheer
    fudge . . .

Fortunately others have had a much truer perception of his poetic achievement. Baudelaire, the French Symbolist, discovered in Poe's super-rational sensations and approximation of musical effects a poetic development that had gone beyond the late Romanticism then current. Thus Poe's poetry, and especially his critical writings, became immensely popular among the French Symbolists and were read almost as the handbook of the Symbolist movement. Poe has in this way exerted a major influence on the development of modern French literature, which has in turn significantly given the direction to contemporary English and American poetry.

FURTHER READING

ALLEN, HERVEY. *Israfel: The Life and Times of Edgar Allan Poe* (New York, 1926).
QUINN, A. H. *Edgar Allan Poe* (New York, 1941).

To Helen

Helen, thy beauty is to me
    Like those Nicaean barks of yore,
That gently, o'er a perfumed sea,
    The weary, wayworn wanderer bore
    To his own native shore.

On desperate seas long wont to roam,
    Thy hyacinth hair, thy classic face,

Thy Naiad airs have brought me home
    To the glory that was Greece
    And the grandeur that was Rome.

Lo! in yon brilliant window-niche
    How statue-like I see thee stand,
The agate lamp within thy hand!
    Ah, Psyche, from the regions which
    Are Holy Land!

Ulalume

The skies they were ashen and sober;
    The leaves they were crispèd and sere—
    The leaves they were withering and sere:
It was night, in the lonesome October
    Of my most immemorial year;
It was hard by the dim lake of Auber,
    In the misty mid region of Weir—
It was down by the dank tarn of Auber,
    In the ghoul-haunted woodland of Weir.

Here once, through an alley Titanic,   10
    Of cypress, I roamed with my Soul—
    Of cypress, with Psyche, my Soul.
These were days when my heart was volcanic
    As the scoriac rivers that roll—
    As the lavas that restlessly roll
Their sulphurous currents down Yaanek
    In the ultimate climes of the Pole—
That groan as they roll down Mount Yaanek
    In the realms of the Boreal Pole.

Our talk had been serious and sober,   20
    But our thoughts they were palsied and sere—
    Our memories were treacherous and sere—
For we knew not the month was October,
    And we marked not the night of the year—
    (Ah, night of all nights in the year!)
We noted not the dim lake of Auber,
    (Though once we had journeyed down here)
Remembered not the dank tarn of Auber,
    Nor the ghoul-haunted woodland of Weir.

And now, as the night was senescent   30
    And star-dials pointed to morn—
    As the star-dials hinted of morn—
At the end of our path a liquescent
    And nebulous luster was born,
Out of which a miraculous crescent
    Arose with a duplicate horn—
Astarte's bediamonded crescent
    Distinct with its duplicate horn.

And I said—"She is warmer than Dian;
   She rolls through an ether of sighs—   40
   She revels in a region of sighs:
She has seen that the tears are not dry on
   These cheeks, where the worm never dies,
And has come past the stars of the Lion
   To point us the path to the skies—
   To the Lethean peace of the skies—
Come up, in despite of the Lion,
   To shine on us with her bright eyes—
Come up through the lair of the Lion,
   With love in her luminous eyes."   50

But Psyche, uplifting her finger,
   Said—"Sadly this star I mistrust—
   Her pallor I strangely mistrust—
Oh, hasten!—oh, let us not linger!
   Oh, fly!—let us fly!—for we must."
In terror she spoke, letting sink her
   Wings till they trailed in the dust—
In agony sobbed, letting sink her
   Plumes till they trailed in the dust—
   Till they sorrowfully trailed in the dust.   60

I replied—"This is nothing but dreaming:
   Let us on by this tremulous light!
   Let us bathe in this crystalline light!
Its sibyllic splendor is beaming
   With Hope and in Beauty to-night:—
   See! it flickers up the sky through the night!
Ah, we safely may trust to its gleaming,
   And be sure it will lead us aright:
We safely may trust to a gleaming
   That cannot but guide us aright,   70
   Since it flickers up to Heaven through the night."

Thus I pacified Psyche and kissed her,
   And tempted her out of her gloom—
   And conquered her scruples and gloom;
And we passed to the end of a vista,
   But were stopped by the door of a tomb—
   By the door of a legended tomb;
And I said—"What is written, sweet sister,
   On the door of this legended tomb?"
She replied—"Ulalume—Ulalume!—   80
   'Tis the vault of thy lost Ulalume!"

Then my heart it grew ashen and sober
   As the leaves that were crispèd and sere—
   As the leaves that were withering and sere;
And I cried—"It was surely October
   On *this* very night of last year
   That I journeyed—I journeyed down here—
   That I brought a dread burden down here!
   On this night of all nights in the year,

Ah, what demon has tempted me here?   90
Well I know, now, this dim lake of Auber—
   This misty mid region of Weir—
Well I know, now, this dank tarn of Auber—
   This ghoul-haunted woodland of Weir."

Israfel [1]

In Heaven a spirit doth dwell
   "Whose heart-strings are a lute";
None sing so wildly well
As the angel Israfel,
And the giddy stars (so legends tell),
Ceasing their hymns, attend the spell
   Of his voice, all mute.

Tottering above
   In her highest noon,
   The enamored moon   10
Blushes with love,
   While, to listen, the red levin
   (With the rapid Pleiads, even,
   Which were seven)
   Pauses in Heaven.

And they say (the starry choir
   And the other listening things)
That Israfeli's fire
Is owing to that lyre
   By which he sits and sings—   20
The trembling living wire
   Of those unusual strings.

But the skies that angel trod,
   Where deep thoughts are a duty,
Where Love's a grown-up God,
   Where the Houri glances are
Imbued with all the beauty
   Which we worship in a star.

Therefore, thou art not wrong,
   Israfeli, who despisest   30
An unimpassioned song;
To thee the laurels belong,
   Best bard, because the wisest!
Merrily live, and long!

The ecstasies above
   With thy burning measures suit—
Thy grief, thy joy, thy hate, thy love,
   With the fervor of thy lute—
   Well may the stars be mute!

[1] Poe prefaced the poem with the following: "And the angel Israfel, whose heart-strings are a lute, and who has the sweetest voice of all God's creatures.—Koran."

Yes, Heaven is thine; but this   40
  Is a world of sweets and sours;
    Our flowers are merely—flowers,
And the shadow of thy perfect bliss
  Is the sunshine of ours.

If I could dwell
Where Israfel
  Hath dwelt, and he where I,
He might not sing so wildly well
  A mortal melody,
While a bolder note than this might swell   50
  From my lyre within the sky.

The City in the Sea

Lo! Death has reared himself a throne
In a strange city lying alone
Far down within the dim West,
Where the good and the bad and the worst and the
      best
Have gone to their eternal rest.
There shrines and palaces and towers
(Time-eaten towers that tremble not!)
Resemble nothing that is ours.
Around, by lifting winds forgot,
Resignedly beneath the sky   10
The melancholy waters lie.

No rays from the holy heaven come down
On the long night-time of that town;
But light from out the lurid sea
Streams up the turrets silently—
Gleams up the pinnacles far and free—
Up domes—up spires—up kingly halls—
Up fanes [2]—up Babylon-like walls—
Up shadowy long-forgotten bowers
Of sculptured ivy and stone flowers—   20
Up many and many a marvellous shrine
Whose wreathéd friezes intertwine
The viol, the violet, and the vine.
Resignedly beneath the sky
The melancholy waters lie.
So blend the turrets and shadows there
That all seem pendulous in air,
While from a proud tower in the town
Death looks gigantically down.

There open fanes and gaping graves   30
Yawn level with the luminous waves
But not the riches there that lie
In each idol's diamond eye—

[2] Temples.

Not the gaily-jewelled dead
Tempt the waters from their bed;
For no ripples curl, alas!
Along that wilderness of glass—
No swellings tell that winds may be
Upon some far-off happier sea—
No heavings hint that winds have been   40
On seas less hideously serene.

But lo, a stir is in the air!
The wave—there is a movement there!
As if the towers had thrust aside,
In slightly sinking, the dull tide—
As if their tops had feebly given
A void within the filmy Heaven.
The waves have now a redder glow—
The hours are breathing faint and low—
And when, amid no earthly moans,   50
Down, down that town shall settle hence,
Hell, rising from a thousand thrones,
Shall do it reverence.

Eldorado

        Gayly bedight,
        A gallant knight,
In sunshine and in shadow,
        Had journeyed long,
        Singing a song,
In search of Eldorado.

        But he grew old—
        This knight so bold—
And o'er his heart a shadow
        Fell as he found
        No spot of ground
That looked like Eldorado.

        And, as his strength
        Failed him at length,
He met a pilgrim shadow—
        "Shadow," said he,
        "Where can it be—
This land of Eldorado?"

        "Over the Mountains
        Of the Moon,
Down the Valley of the Shadow,
        Ride, boldly ride,"
        The shade replied—
"If you seek for Eldorado!"

HENRY WADSWORTH LONGFELLOW

1807–1882

Henry Wadsworth Longfellow, easily the most popular American poet of his generation, was born of good family in Portland, Maine. Educated at Bowdoin College, after study abroad he returned to become Professor of Modern Languages. After further study in Europe, he became Professor of Modern Languages at Harvard, a position he held until his resignation in 1854. His life in Cambridge, where he lived in beautiful old Craigie House with its admirable view of the Charles River, was a comfortable, well-upholstered, upper-class existence. His early life was, however, desperately saddened by the death of his first wife in 1835. As his second wife he married the beautiful Frances Appleton, a socially prominent and proper Bostonian.

Immensely popular in the nineteenth century for such sentimental poems as *Hiawatha* and *Evangeline,* for the platitudinous moralizing of poems like "A Psalm of Life," and for easy narratives like *The Courtship of Miles Standish,* Longfellow's works had a phenomenal sale. During his European trip in 1868, which was practically a triumphal journey, he was given honorary doctorates at both Oxford and Cambridge. But the literary reputation of Longfellow has greatly declined, until in our time, in an age which dislikes sentimentality and easy moralizing, most critical opinion is adverse. The old schoolroom poems are no longer highly regarded, but in the mass of his writing a relatively few good poems can be selected which, despite the fatuousness of the many, will always be worth a place in any collection of American literature. In addition to his original poems, Longfellow, who was widely read in a dozen literatures, translated a large number of works by European authors, many of which are of considerable distinction.

FURTHER READING

BROOKS, VAN WYCK. *The Flowering of New England* (New York, 1936).
THOMPSON, LAWRANCE. *Young Longfellow* (New York, 1938).

Mezzo Cammin *

WRITTEN AT BOPPARD ON THE RHINE AUGUST 25, 1842, JUST BEFORE LEAVING FOR HOME

Half of my life is gone, and I have let
The years slip from me and have not fulfilled
The aspiration of my youth, to build
Some tower of song with lofty parapet.
Not indolence, nor pleasure, nor the fret
Of restless passions that would not be stilled,
But sorrow, and a care that almost killed,
Kept me from what I may accomplish yet;
Though, half-way up the hill, I see the Past
Lying beneath me with its sounds and sights,—
A city in the twilight dim and vast,
With smoking roofs, soft bells, and gleaming lights,—
And hear above me on the autumnal blast
The cataract of Death far thundering from the heights.

Nuremberg

In the valley of the Pegnitz, where across broad meadow-lands
Rise the blue Franconian mountains, Nuremberg, the ancient, stands.

Quaint old town of toil and traffic, quaint old town of art and song,
Memories haunt thy pointed gables, like the rooks that round them throng:

Memories of the Middle Ages, when the emperors, rough and bold,
Had their dwelling in thy castle, time-defying, centuries old;

And thy brave and thrifty burghers boasted, in their uncouth rhyme,
That their great imperial city stretched its hand through every clime.

In the court-yard of the castle, bound with many an iron band,
Stands the mighty linden planted by Queen Cunigunde's hand;   10

On the square the oriel window, where in old heroic days
Sat the poet Melchior singing Kaiser Maximilian's praise.

* The title, which means "Midway the journey of this life," is from the first line of Dante's *Divine Comedy.*

Everywhere I see around me rise the wondrous
    world of Art:
Fountains wrought with richest sculpture standing
    in the common mart;

And above cathedral doorways saints and bishops
    carved in stone,
By a former age commissioned as apostles to our
    own.

In the church of sainted Sebald sleeps enshrined
    his holy dust,
And in bronze the Twelve Apostles guard from age
    to age their trust;

In the church of sainted Lawrence stands a pix of
    sculpture rare,
Like the foamy sheaf of fountains, rising through
    the painted air. 20

Here, when Art was still religion, with a simple,
    reverent heart,
Lived and labored Albrecht Dürer, the Evangelist
    of Art;

Hence in silence and in sorrow, toiling still with
    busy hand,
Like an emigrant he wandered, seeking for the Bet-
    ter Land.

Emigravit is the inscription on the tombstone where
    he lies;
Dead he is not, but departed,—for the artist never
    dies.

Fairer seems the ancient city, and the sunshine
    seems more fair,
That he once has trod its pavement, that he once
    has breathed its air!

Through these streets so broad and stately, these
    obscure and dismal lanes,
Walked of yore the Mastersingers, chanting rude
    poetic strains. 30

From remote and sunless suburbs came they to the
    friendly guild,
Building nests in Fame's great temple, as in spouts
    the swallows build.

As the weaver plied the shuttle, wove he too the
    mystic rhyme,
And the smith his iron measures hammered to the
    anvil's chime;

Thanking God, whose boundless wisdom makes the
    flowers of poesy bloom

In the forge's dust and cinders, in the tissues of the
    loom.

Here Hans Sachs, the cobbler-poet, laureate of the
    gentle craft,
Wisest of the Twelve Wise Masters, in huge folios
    sang and laughed.

But his house is now an ale-house, with a nicely
    sanded floor,
And a garland in the window, and his face above
    the door; 40

Painted by some humble artist, as in Adam Pusch-
    man's song,
As the old man gray and dove-like, with his great
    beard white and long.

And at night the swart mechanic comes to drown
    his cark and care,
Quaffing ale from pewter tankards, in the master's
    antique chair.

Vanished is the ancient splendor, and before my
    dreamy eye
Wave these mingled shapes and figures, like a faded
    tapestry.

Not thy Councils, not thy Kaisers, win for thee the
    world's regard;
But thy painter, Albrecht Dürer, and Hans Sachs
    thy cobbler bard.

Thus, O Nuremberg, a wanderer from a region far
    away,
As he paced thy streets and court-yards, sang in
    thought his careless lay: 50

Gathering from the pavement's crevice, as a floweret
    of the soil,
The nobility of labor,—the long pedigree of toil.

The Jewish Cemetery at Newport

How strange it seems! These Hebrews in their
    graves,
    Close by the street of this fair seaport town,
Silent beside the never-silent waves,
    At rest in all this moving up and down!

The trees are white with dust, that o'er their sleep
    Wave their broad curtains in the south-wind's
    breath,
While underneath these leafy tents they keep
    The long, mysterious Exodus of Death.

And these sepulchral stones, so old and brown,
  That pave with level flags their burial-place,
Seem like the tablets of the Law, thrown down
  And broken by Moses at the mountain's base.

The very names recorded here are strange,
  Of foreign accent, and of different climes;
Alvares and Rivera interchange
  With Abraham and Jacob of old times.

"Blessed be God, for he created Death!"
  The mourners said, "and Death is rest and peace;"
Then added, in the certainty of faith,
  "And giveth Life that nevermore shall cease."

Closed are the portals of their Synagogue,
  No Psalms of David now the silence break,
No Rabbi reads the ancient Decalogue
  In the grand dialect the Prophets spake.

Gone are the living, but the dead remain,
  And not neglected; for a hand unseen,
Scattering its bounty, like a summer rain,
  Still keeps their graves and their remembrance
    green.

How came they here? What burst of Christian hate,
  What persecution, merciless and blind,
Drove o'er the sea—that desert desolate—
  These Ishmaels and Hagars of mankind?

They lived in narrow streets and lanes obscure,
  Ghetto and Judenstrass, in mirk and mire;
Taught in the school of patience to endure
  The life of anguish and the death of fire.

All their lives long, with the unleavened bread
  And bitter herbs of exile and its fears,
The wasting famine of the heart they fed,
  And slaked its thirst with marah of their tears.

Anathema maranatha! was the cry
  That rang from town to town, from street to
    street:
At every gate the accursed Mordecai
  Was mocked and jeered, and spurned by Chris-
    tian feet.

Pride and humiliation hand in hand
  Walked with them through the world where'er
    they went;
Trampled and beaten were they as the sand,
  And yet unshaken as the continent.

For in the background figures vague and vast
  Of patriarch and of prophets rose sublime,
And all the great traditions of the Past
  They saw reflected in the coming time.

And thus forever with reverted look
  The mystic volume of the world they read,
Spelling it backward, like a Hebrew book,
  Till life became a Legend of the Dead.

But ah! what once has been shall be no more!
  The groaning earth in travail and in pain
Brings forth its races, but does not restore,
  And the dead nations never rise again.

Divina Commedia

I

Oft have I seen at some cathedral door
A laborer, pausing in the dust and heat,
Lay down his burden, and with reverent feet
Enter, and cross himself, and on the floor
Kneel to repeat his paternoster o'er;
Far off the noises of the world retreat;
The loud vociferations of the street
Become an undistinguishable roar.
So, as I enter here from day to day,
And leave my burden at this minster gate,
Kneeling in prayer, and not ashamed to pray,
The tumult of the time disconsolate
To inarticulate murmurs dies away,
While the eternal ages watch and wait.

II

How strange the sculptures that adorn these towers!
This crowd of statues, in whose folded sleeves
Birds build their nests; while canopied with leaves
Parvis and portal bloom like trellised bowers,
And the vast minster seems a cross of flowers!
But fiends and dragons on the gargoyled eaves
Watch the dead Christ between the living thieves,
And, underneath, the traitor Judas lowers!
Ah! from what agonies of heart and brain,
What exultations trampling on despair,
What tenderness, what tears, what hate of wrong,
What passionate outcry of a soul in pain,
Uprose this poem of the earth and air,
This mediaeval miracle of song!

III

I enter, and I see thee in the gloom
Of the long aisles, O poet saturnine!
And strive to make my steps keep pace with thine.
The air is filled with some unknown perfume;
The congregation of the dead make room
For thee to pass; the votive tapers shine;
Like rooks that haunt Ravenna's groves of pine

The hovering echoes fly from tomb to tomb.
From the confessionals I hear arise
Rehearsals of forgotten tragedies,
And lamentations from the crypts below;
And then a voice celestial that begins
With the pathetic words, "Although your sins
As scarlet be," and ends with "as the snow."

IV

With snow-white veil and garments as of flame,
She stands before thee, who so long ago
Filled thy young heart with passion and the woe
From which thy song and all its splendors came;
And while with stern rebuke she speaks thy name,
The ice about thy heart melts as the snow
On mountain heights, and in swift overflow
Comes gushing from thy lips in sobs of shame.
Thou makest full confession; and a gleam,
As of the dawn on some dark forest cast,
Seems on thy lifted forehead to increase;
Lethe and Eunoë [1]—the remembered dream
And the forgotten sorrow—bring at last
That perfect pardon which is perfect peace.

V

I lift mine eyes, and all the windows blaze
With forms of Saints and holy men who died,
Here martyred and hereafter glorified;
And the great Rose [2] upon its leaves displays
Christ's Triumph, and the angelic roundelays,
With splendor upon splendor multiplied;
And Beatrice again at Dante's side
No more rebukes, but smiles her words of praise.
And then the organ sounds, and unseen choirs
Sing the old Latin hymns of peace and love
And benedictions of the Holy Ghost;
And the melodious bells among the spires
O'er all the house-tops and through heaven above
Proclaim the elevation of the Host!

VI

O star of morning and of liberty!
O bringer of the light, whose splendor shines
Above the darkness of the Apennines,
Forerunner of the day that is to be!
The voices of the city and the sea,
The voices of the mountains and the pines,

[1] At the top of the Mountain of Purgatory Dante drinks of Lethe, the river of forgetfulness, and of Eunoë, the river of the memory of good.

[2] At the conclusion of his journey (PARADISO, XXXI), Dante beholds the Trinity and the blessed in the form of a rose, the blessed being seated in order in the petals of the rose.

Repeat thy song, till the familiar lines
Are footpaths for the thought of Italy!
Thy flame is blown abroad from all the heights,
Through all the nations, and a sound is heard,
As of a mighty wind, and men devout,
Strangers of Rome, and the new proselytes,
In their own language hear the wondrous word,
And many are amazed and many doubt.

Chaucer

An old man in a lodge within a park;
The chamber walls depicted all around
With portraitures of huntsman, hawk, and hound,
And the hurt deer. He listeneth to the lark,
Whose song comes with the sunshine through the
  dark
Of painted glass in leaden lattice bound;
He listeneth and he laugheth at the sound,
Then writeth in a book like any clerk.
He is the poet of the dawn, who wrote
The Canterbury Tales, and his old age
Made beautiful with song; and as I read
I hear the crowing cock, I hear the note
Of lark and linnet, and from every page
Rise odors of ploughed field or flowery mead.

———◆———

RALPH WALDO EMERSON

1803–1882

Ralph Waldo Emerson was the son of a Unitarian minister, and the descendant of seven generations of Puritan divines. After working his way through Harvard College and studying at Harvard Divinity School, he took up the pastorate of the Unitarian Second Church of Boston in 1829. His increasing doubts over doctrinal matters finally induced him to take the momentous step of giving up his pastorate in 1832. This decision was reinforced by his European journey, wherein he met Wordsworth, Coleridge, and Carlyle and became intensely interested in the transcendental movement and in German idealism. By the time he delivered his *Divinity School Address* to the senior class at Harvard Divinity School in 1838, Emerson had discovered in German transcendentalism the philosophic basis for his rejection of church dogma: no one could impart spiritual experience second hand, and the dependence upon past revelation limits the direct exploration of one's moral nature by transcendental intuition, the sole means of perceiving truth.

New England was well prepared by the eighteen thirties to receive these transcendental ideas. Edward Everett had studied in Germany from 1815–1819, and George Ticknor (later Harvard's first professor of modern languages) in 1815–1817 at Göttingen. The first class in the German language had been taught at Harvard by Karl Follen, a German republican refugee, who introduced the reading of Goethe and Schiller. By 1830, Follen had a class of sixty students, one quarter of the total college enrollment. Carlyle's essays on Richter, Goethe, Schiller, and "The State of German Literature" were read widely in New England, and intellectual Boston discussed Carlyle's somewhat gifted amateur handling of the distinction between the Kantian Practical Reason and the logical understanding. When Carlyle could not publish his *Sartor Resartus* in book form in England, Emerson recognized the value of its embodiment of German idealism and secured its publication in Boston in 1836. In 1829 President James Marsh of the University of Vermont edited Coleridge's *Aids to Reflection,* a statement of the transcendental doctrines of Schelling. New England was thus prepared for the transcendental movement and the rejection of Unitarian adherence to the philosophy of John Locke. No doubt the German idealism merely fertilized certain seeds in Emerson's mind rather than planted them there; there are evidences of a transcendental frame of mind in Emerson's early "The Present State of Ethical Philosophy" (1821).

Generally, transcendentalism was a belief that man possesses a divine faculty permitting him to perceive spiritual truths directly, by intuition; he thus becomes conscious of his integrity as a man, as a creature in whom alone there is an immanence of divinity. The divine intuition penetrates to truths unsuspected by the logical understanding, which can know only the material world. The transcendentalist is therefore the idealist who looks beyond the world of sense to the only Reality, a pervasive and indestructible spiritual essence for which the material, sensuous world is merely a cloak, an outward raiment. This essence is Emerson's Oversoul, and the god-immanence in man is the basis for his self-reliance. All noble works of man, Emerson believed, come directly from God, as "The Problem" indicates. From Emerson stemmed the transcendental doctrines of the spiritual nature of reality and the evolutionary progress of man to a higher individualism.

During the greater part of his life, Emerson spread these ideas in his lyceum lectures and published them as collections of essays. Today there is a general tendency to evaluate Emerson more highly as a poet than an essayist. Robert Frost admires Emerson the poet deeply; Edward Arlington Robinson regarded him as the greatest American poet. His best poems are the result of intense intuitive experience in which his nobility of character, ethical insight, and skill in expression combine to give us some of the finest poems in American literature, such as "Brahma," "The Concord Hymn," and "The Problem" exemplify. It is unjust to assert, however, that his essays are poorly organized. His prose style abounds in memorable aphorisms and strikingly illuminating single sentences which often conceal the essential unity of his structure. Part of this scintillating style is of course due to the adaptation to the platform lecture and to the need to strike his readers by absolute, sweeping statements.

The sources of Emerson's thought in these essays are many—the Oriental mystics, the German idealists, Plotinus, and Plato may be enumerated among many; Emerson rephrased their wisdom and modified it for his less well-informed audiences. For more than thirty years Emerson inculcated his noble ethical and spiritual ideas into American lyceum audiences; it was just for Arnold to recognize him as a great man, if not a great poet or philosopher. He has been attacked for his optimism, for his trusting to reverie and for his impulse to spontaneity, but the high and noble ethical individualism of Emerson is still significant to us in an American democracy of the twentieth century.

FURTHER READING

BROOKS, VAN WYCK. *The Flowering of New England* (New York, 1936).
CARPENTER, F. I. *Emerson and Asia* (Cambridge, 1930).
PERRY, BLISS. *Emerson Today* (Princeton, 1931).

The Rhodora:

ON BEING ASKED, WHENCE IS THE FLOWER?

In May, when sea-winds pierced our solitudes,
I found the fresh Rhodora in the woods,
Spreading its leafless blooms in a damp nook,
To please the desert and the sluggish brook.
The purple petals, fallen in the pool,
Made the black water with their beauty gay;
Here might the red-bird come his plumes to cool,
And court the flower that cheapens his array.
Rhodora! if the sages ask thee why
This charm is wasted on the earth and sky,
Tell them, dear, that if eyes were made for seeing,
Then Beauty is its own excuse for being:
Why thou wert there, O rival of the rose!
I never thought to ask, I never knew;
But, in my simple ignorance, suppose
The self-same Power that brought me there brought
    you.

The Apology

Think me not unkind and rude
    That I walk alone in grove and glen;
I go to the god of the wood
    To fetch his word to men.

Tax not my sloth that I
    Fold my arms beside the brook;
Each cloud that floated in the sky
    Writes a letter in my book.

Chide me not, laborious band,   .
    For the idle flowers I brought;
Every aster in my hand
    Goes home loaded with a thought.

There was never mystery
    But 'tis figured in the flowers;
Was never secret history
    But birds tell it in the bowers.

One harvest from thy field
    Homeward brought the oxen strong;
A second crop thine acres yield,
    Which I gather in a song.

The Humble Bee

Burly, dozing humble bee,
Where thou art is clime for me.
Let them sail for Porto Rique,

Far-off heats through seas to seek;
I will follow thee alone,
Thou animated torrid-zone!
Zigzag steerer, desert cheerer,
Let me chase thy waving lines:
Keep me nearer, me thy hearer,
Singing over shrubs and vines.   10

Insect lover of the sun
Joy of thy dominion!
Sailor of the atmosphere;
Swimmer through the waves of air;
Voyager of light and noon;
Epicurean of June;
Wait, I prithee, till I come
Within earshot of thy hum,—
All without is martyrdom.
When the south-wind, in May days,   20
With a net of shining haze
Silvers the horizon wall,
And with softness touching all,
Tints the human countenance
With a color of romance,
And infusing subtle heats,
Turns the sod to violets,
Thou, in sunny solitudes,
Rover of the underwoods,
The green silence dost displace   30
With thy mellow, breezy bass.

Hot midsummer's petted crone,
Sweet to me thy drowsy tone
Tells of countless sunny hours,
Long days, and solid banks of flowers;
Of gulfs of sweetness without bound
In Indian wildernesses found;
Of Syrian peace, immortal leisure,
Firmest cheer, and bird-like pleasure.

Aught unsavory or unclean   40
Hath my insect never seen;
But violets and bilberry bells,
Maple-sap and daffodils,
Grass with green flag half-mast high,
Succory to match the sky,
Columbine with horn of honey,
Scented fern, and agrimony,
Clover, catchfly, adder's-tongue
And brier-roses, dwelt among;
All beside was unknown waste,   50
All was picture as he passed.

Wiser far than human seer,
Yellow-breeched philosopher!
Seeing only what is fair,

Sipping only what is sweet,
Thou dost mock at fate and care,
Leave the chaff, and take the wheat.
When the fierce northwestern blast
Cools sea and land so far and fast,
Thou already slumberest deep;   60
Woe and want thou canst outsleep;
Want and woe, which torture us,
Thy sleep makes ridiculous.

Each and All

Little thinks, in the field, yon red-cloaked clown
Of thee from the hill-top looking down;
The heifer that lows in the upland farm,
Far-heard, lows not thine ear to charm;
The sexton, tolling his bell at noon,
Deems not that great Napoleon
Stops his horse, and lists with delight,
Whilst his files sweep round yon Alpine height;
Nor knowest thou what argument
Thy life to thy neighbor's creed has lent.   10
All are needed by each one;
Nothing is fair or good alone.
I thought the sparrow's note from heaven,
Singing at dawn on the alder bough;
I brought him home, in his nest, at even;
He sings the song, but it cheers not now,
For I did not bring home the river and sky;—
He sang to my ear,—they sang to my eye.
The delicate shells lay on the shore;
The bubbles of the latest wave   20
Fresh pearls to their enamel gave;
And the bellowing of the savage sea
Greeted their safe escape to me.
I wiped away the weeds and foam,
I fetched my sea-born treasures home;
But the poor, unsightly, noisome things
Had left their beauty on the shore,
With the sun, and the sand, and the wild uproar.
The lover watched his graceful maid,
As mid the virgin train she strayed,   30
Nor knew her beauty's best attire
Was woven still by the snow-white choir.
At last she came to his hermitage,
Like the bird from the woodlands to the cage;—
The gay enchantment was undone,
A gentle wife, but fairy none.
Then I said, "I covet truth;
Beauty is unripe childhood's cheat;
I leave it behind with the games of youth."—
As I spoke, beneath my feet   40
The ground-pine curled its pretty wreath,

Running over the club-moss burrs;
I inhaled the violet's breath;
Around me stood the oaks and firs;
Pine-cones and acorns lay on the ground;
Over me soared the eternal sky,
Full of light and of deity;
Again I saw, again I heard,
The rolling river, the morning bird;—
Beauty through my senses stole;   50
I yielded myself to the perfect whole.

The Problem

I like a church; I like a cowl;
I love a prophet of the soul;
And on my heart monastic aisles
Fall like sweet strains, or pensive smiles;
Yet not for all his faith can see
Would I that cowled churchman be.

Why should the vest on him allure,
Which I could not on me endure?

Not from a vain or shallow thought
His awful Jove young Phidias brought,   10
Never from lips of cunning fell
The thrilling Delphic oracle;
Out from the heart of nature rolled
The burdens of the Bible old;
The litanies of nations came,
Like the volcano's tongue of flame,
Up from the burning core below,—
The canticles of love and woe;
The hand that rounded Peter's dome,
And groined the aisles of Christian Rome,   20
Wrought in a sad sincerity;
Himself from God he could not free;
He builded better than he knew;—
The conscious stone to beauty grew.

Know'st thou what wove yon woodbird's nest
Of leaves, and feathers from her breast?
Or how the fish outbuilt her shell,
Painting with morn each annual cell?
Or how the sacred pine-tree adds
To her old leaves new myriads?   30
Such and so grew these holy piles,
Whilst love and terror laid the tiles.
Earth proudly wears the Parthenon,
As the best gem upon her zone;
And Morning opes with haste her lids,
To gaze upon the Pyramids;
O'er England's abbeys bends the sky,
As on its friends, with kindred eye;

For, out of Thought's interior sphere,
These wonders rose to upper air;   40
And Nature gladly gave them place,
Adopted them into her race,
And granted them an equal date
With Andes and with Ararat.

These temples grew as grows the grass;
Art might obey, but not surpass.
The passive Master lent his hand
To the vast soul that o'er him planned;
And the same power that reared the shrine
Bestrode the tribes that knelt within.   50
Ever the fiery Pentecost
Girds with one flame the countless host,
Trances the heart through chanting choirs,
And through the priest the mind inspires.
The word unto the prophet spoken
Was writ on tables yet unbroken;
The word by seers or sibyls told,
In groves of oak, or fanes of gold,
Still floats upon the morning wind,
Still whispers to the willing mind.   60
One accent of the Holy Ghost
The heedless world hath never lost.
I know what say the fathers wise,—
The Book itself before me lies,
Old Chrysostom, best Augustine,
And he who blent both in his line,
The younger *Golden Lips* or mines,
Taylor, the Shakspeare of divines.
His words are music in my ear,
I see his cowled portrait dear;   70
And yet, for all his faith could see,
I would not the good bishop be.

Threnody *

The South-wind brings
Life, sunshine and desire,
And on every mount and meadow
Breathes aromatic fire;
But over the dead he has no power,
The lost, the lost, he cannot restore;
And, looking over the hills, I mourn
The darling who shall not return.
I see my empty house,
I see my trees repair their boughs;   10
And he, the wondrous child,
Whose silver warble wild
Outvalued every pulsing sound

* Emerson composed this elegy on the death of his son
Waldo in 1842.

Within the air's cerulean round,—
The hyacinthine boy, for whom
Morn well might break and April bloom,——
The gracious boy, who did adorn
The world whereinto he was born,
And by his countenance repay
The favor of the loving Day,—   20
Has disappeared from the Day's eye;
Far and wide she cannot find him;
My hopes pursue, they cannot bind him.
Returned this day, the south-wind searches,
And finds young pines and budding birches;
But finds not the budding man;
Nature who lost, cannot remake him;
Fate let him fall, Fate can't retake him;
Nature, Fate, men, him seek in vain.
And whither now, my truant wise and sweet,   30
O, whither tend thy feet?
I had the right, few days ago,
Thy steps to watch, thy place to know:
How have I forfeited the right?
Hast thou forgot me in a new delight?
I hearken for thy household cheer,
O eloquent child!
Whose voice, an equal messenger,
Conveyed thy meaning mild.
What though the pains and joys   40
Whereof it spoke were toys
Fitting his age and ken,
Yet fairest dames and bearded men,
Who heard the sweet request,
So gentle, wise and grave,
Bended with joy to his behest,
And let the world's affairs go by,
A while to share his cordial game,
Or mend his wicker wagon-frame,
Still plotting how their hungry ear   50
That winsome voice again might hear;
For his lips could well pronounce
Words that were persuasions.

Gentlest guardians marked serene
His early hope, his liberal mien;
Took counsel from his guiding eyes
To make this wisdom earthly wise.
Ah, vainly do these eyes recall
The school-march, each day's festival,
When every morn my bosom glowed   60
To watch the convoy on the road;
The babe in willow wagon closed,
With rolling eyes and face composed;
With children forward and behind,
Like Cupids studiously inclined;

And he the chieftain paced beside,
The centre of the troop allied,
With sunny face of sweet repose,
To guard the babe from fancied foes.
The little captain innocent   70
Took the eye with him as he went;
Each village senior paused to scan
And speak the lovely caravan.
From the window I look out
To mark thy beautiful parade,
Stately marching in cap and coat
To some tune by fairies played;—
A music heard by thee alone
To works as noble led thee on.
Now Love and Pride, alas! in vain,   80
Up and down their glances strain.
The painted sled stands where it stood;
The kennel by the corded wood;
His gathered sticks to stanch the wall
Of the snow-tower, when snow should fall;
The ominous hole he dug in the sand,
And childhood's castles built or planned;
His daily haunts I well discern,—
The poultry-yard, the shed, the barn,—
And every inch of garden ground   90
Paced by the blessed feet around,
From the roadside to the brook
Whereinto he loved to look.
Step the meek fowls where erst they ranged;
The wintry garden lies unchanged;
The brook into the stream runs on;
But the deep-eyed boy is gone.

On that shaded day,
Dark with more clouds than tempests are,
When thou didst yield thy innocent breath   100
In birdlike heavings unto death,
Night came, and Nature had not thee;
I said, "We are mates in misery."
The morrow dawned with needless glow;
Each snowbird chirped, each fowl must crow;
Each tramper started; but the feet
Of the most beautiful and sweet
Of human youth had left the hill
And garden,—they were bound and still.
There's not a sparrow or a wren.   110
There's not a blade of autumn grain,
Which the four seasons do not tend,
And tides of life and increase lend;
And every chick of every bird,
And weed and rock-moss is preferred.

O ostrich-like forgetfulness!
O loss of larger in the less!

Was there no star that could be sent,
No watcher in the firmament,
No angel from the countless host   120
That loiters round the crystal coast,
Could stoop to heal that only child,
Nature's sweet marvel undefiled,
And keep the blossom of the earth,
Which all her harvests were not worth?
Not mine,—I never called thee mine,
But Nature's heir,—if I repine,
And seeing rashly torn and moved
Not what I made, but what I loved,
Grow early old with grief that thou   130
Must to the wastes of Nature go,—
'Tis because a general hope
Was quenched, and all must doubt and grope.
For flattering planets seemed to say
This child should ills of ages stay,
By wondrous tongue, and guided pen,
Bring the flown Muses back to men.
Perchance not he but Nature ailed,
The world and not the infant failed.
It was not ripe yet to sustain   140
A genius of so fine a strain,
Who gazed upon the sun and moon
As if he came unto his own,
And, pregnant with his grander thought,
Brought the old order into doubt.
His beauty once their beauty tried;
They could not feed him, and he died,
And wandered backward as in scorn,
To wait an aeon to be born.
Ill day which made this beauty waste,   150
Plight broken, this high face defaced!
Some went and came about the dead;
And some in books of solace read;
Some to their friends the tidings say;
Some went to write, some went to pray;
One tarried here, there hurried one;
But their heart abode with none.
Covetous death bereaved us all,
To aggrandize one funeral.
The eager face which carried thee   160
Took the largest part of me:
For this losing is true dying;
This is lordly man's down-lying,
This his slow but sure reclining,
Star by star his world resigning.
O that child of paradise,
Boy who made dear his father's home,
In whose deep eyes
Men read the welfare of the times to come,
I am too much bereft.   170

The world dishonored thou hast left.
O truth's and nature's costly lie!
O trusted broken prophecy!
O richest fortune sourly crossed!
Born for the future, to the future lost!

The deep Heart answered, "Weepest thou?
Worthier cause for passion wild
If I had not taken the child.
And deemest thou as those who pore,
With aged eyes, short way before,—   180
Think'st Beauty vanished from the coast
Of matter, and thy darling lost?
Taught he not thee—the man of eld,
Whose eyes within his eyes beheld
Heaven's numerous hierarchy span
The mystic gulf from God to man?
To be alone wilt thou begin
When worlds of lovers hem thee in?
To-morrow, when the masks shall fall
That dizen Nature's carnival,   190
The pure shall see by their own will,
Which overflowing Love shall fill,
'Tis not within the force of fate
The fate-conjoined to separate.
But thou, my votary, weepest thou?
I gave thee sight—where is it now?
I taught thy heart beyond the reach
Of ritual, bible, or of speech;
Wrote in thy mind's transparent table,
As far as the incommunicable;   200
Taught thee each private sign to raise
Lit by the supersolar blaze.
Past utterance, and past belief,
And past the blasphemy of grief,
The mysteries of Nature's heart;
And though no Muse can these impart,
Throb thine with Nature's throbbing breast,
And all is clear from east to west.

"I came to thee as to a friend;
Dearest, to thee I did not send   210
Tutors, but a joyful eye,
Innocence that matched the sky,
Lovely locks, a form of wonder,
Laughter rich as woodland thunder,
That thou might'st entertain apart
The richest flowering of all art:
And, as the great all-loving Day
Through smallest chambers takes its way,
That thou might'st break thy daily bread
With prophet, savior and head;   220
That thou might'st cherish for thine own
The riches of sweet Mary's Son,

Boy-Rabbi, Israel's paragon.
And thoughtest thou such guest
Would in thy hall take up his rest?
Would rushing life forget her laws,
Fate's glowing revolution pause?
High omens ask diviner guess;
Not to be conned to tediousness
And know my higher gifts unbind   230
The zone that girds the incarnate mind.
When the scanty shores are full
With Thought's perilous, whirling pool;
When frail Nature can no more,
Then the Spirit strikes the hour:
My servant Death, with solving rite,
Pours finite into infinite.

"Wilt thou freeze love's tidal flow,
Whose streams through Nature circling go?
Nail the wild star to its track   240
On the half-climbed Zodiac?
Light is light which radiates,
Blood is blood which circulates,
Life is life which generates,
And many-seeming life is one,—
Wilt thou transfix and make it none?
Its onward force too starkly pent
In figure, bone and lineament?
Wilt thou, uncalled, interrogate,
Talker! the unreplying Fate?   250
Nor see the genius of the whole
Ascendant in the private soul,
Beckon it when to go and come,
Self-announced its hour of doom?
Fair the soul's recess and shrine,
Magic-built to last a season;
Masterpiece of love benign,
Fairer that expansive reason
Whose omen 'tis, and sign.
Wilt thou not ope thy heart to know   260
What rainbows teach, and sunsets show?
Verdict which accumulates
From lengthening scroll of human fates,
Voice of earth to earth returned,
Prayers of saints that inly burned,—
Saying, *What is excellent,
As God lives, is permanent;
Hearts are dust, hearts' loves remain;
Heart's love will meet thee again.*
Revere the Maker; fetch thine eye   270
Up to his style, and manners of the sky.
Not of adamant and gold
Built he heaven stark and cold;
No, but a nest of bending reeds,

Flowering grass, and scented weeds;
Or like a traveller's fleeing tent,
Or bow above the tempest bent;
Built of tears and sacred flames,
And virtue reaching to its aims;
Built of furtherance and pursuing,
Not of spent deeds, but of doing.
Silent rushes the swift Lord
Through ruined systems still restored,
Broadsowing, bleak and void to bless,
Plants with worlds the wilderness;
Waters with tears of ancient sorrow
Apples of Eden ripe to-morrow.
House and tenant go to ground,
Lost in God, in Godhead found."

Days

Daughters of Time, the hypocritic Days,
Muffled and dumb like barefoot dervishes,
And marching single in an endless file,
Bring diadems and fagots in their hands.
To each they offer gifts after his will,
Bread, kingdoms, stars, and sky that holds them all.
I, in my pleachéd garden, watched the pomp,

Forgot my morning wishes, hastily
Took a few herbs and apples, and the Day
Turned and departed silent. I, too late,
Under her solemn fillet saw the scorn.

280

Brahma

If the red slayer think he slays,
Or if the slain think he is slain,
They know not well the subtle ways
I keep, and pass, and turn again.

Far or forgot to me is near;
Shadow and sunlight are the same;
The vanished gods to me appear;
And one to me are shame and fame.

They reckon ill who leave me out;
When me they fly, I am the wings;
I am the doubter and the doubt,
And I the hymn the Brahmin sings.

The strong gods pine for my abode,
And pine in vain the sacred Seven;
But thou, meek lover of the good!
Find me, and turn thy back on heaven.

———◆———

American Fiction

EDGAR ALLAN POE

For an introduction to the life and works of Poe, see page 384.

The Masque of the Red Death *

THE "Red Death" had long devastated the country. No pestilence had ever been so fatal, or so hideous. Blood was its avatar and its seal—the redness and the horror of blood. There were sharp pains, and sudden dizziness, and then profuse bleeding at the pores, with dissolution. The scarlet stains upon the body, and especially upon the face, of the victim were the pest ban which shut him out from the aid

* From the *Broadway Journal*, July 19, 1845.

and from the sympathy of his fellow men. And the whole seizure, progress, and termination of the disease were the incidents of half an hour.

But the Prince Prospero was happy and dauntless and sagacious. When his dominions were half depopulated he summoned to his presence a thousand hale and light-hearted friends from among the knights and dames of his court, and with these retired to the deep seclusion of one of his castellated abbeys. This was an extensive and magnificent structure, the creation of the prince's own eccentric yet august taste. A strong and lofty wall girdled it in. This wall had gates of iron. The courtiers, having entered, brought furnaces and massy hammers, and welded the bolts. They resolved to leave means neither of ingress or egress to the sudden impulses of despair or of frenzy from within. The abbey was amply provisioned. With such precau-

The external world could take care of itself. In the
meantime it was folly to grieve, or to think. The
prince had provided all the appliances of pleasure.
There were buffoons, there were improvisatori,
there were ballet-dancers, there were musicians,
there was Beauty, there was wine. All these and
security were within. Without was the "Red
Death."

It was toward the close of the fifth or sixth month
of his seclusion, and while the pestilence raged
most furiously abroad, that the Prince Prospero entertained his thousand friends at a masked ball of
the most unusual magnificence.

It was a voluptuous scene, that masquerade. But
first let me tell of the rooms in which it was held.
There were seven—an imperial suite. In many palaces, however, such suites form a long and straight
vista, while the sliding doors slide back nearly to
the walls on either hand, so that the view of the
whole extent is scarcely impeded. Here the case
was very different, as might have been expected
from the prince's love of the bizarre. The apartments were so irregularly disposed that the vision
embraced but little more than one at a time. There
was a sharp turn at every twenty or thirty yards,
and at each turn a novel effect. To the right and
left, in the middle of each wall, a tall and narrow
Gothic window looked out upon a closed corridor
which pursued the windings of the suite. These
windows were of stained glass, whose color varied
in accordance with the prevailing hue of the decorations of the chamber into which it opened. That
at the eastern extremity was hung, for example, in
blue—and vividly blue were its windows. The second chamber was purple in its ornaments and
tapestries, and here the panes were purple. The
third was green throughout, and so were the casements. The fourth was furnished and lighted with
orange, the fifth with white, the sixth with violet.
The seventh apartment was closely shrouded in
black velvet tapestries that hung all over the ceiling
and down the walls, falling in heavy folds upon a
carpet of the same material and hue. But, in this
chamber only, the color of the windows failed to
correspond with the decorations. The panes here
were scarlet—a deep blood-color. Now in no one of
the seven apartments was there any lamp or candela-
brum, amid the profusion of golden ornaments that
lay scattered to and fro or depended from the roof.
There was no light of any kind emanating from
lamp or candle within the suite of chambers. But
in the corridors that followed the suite there stood,

opposite to each window, a heavy tripod, bearing a
brazier of fire, that projected its rays through the
tinted glass and so glaringly illumined the room.
And thus were produced a multitude of gaudy and
fantastic appearances. But in the western or black
chamber the effect of the firelight that streamed
upon the dark hanging through the blood-tinted
panes was ghastly in the extreme, and produced so
wild a look upon the countenances of those who
entered that there were few of the company bold
enough to set foot within its precincts at all.

It was in this apartment, also, that there stood
against the western wall a gigantic clock of ebony.
Its pendulum swung to and fro with a dull, heavy,
monotonous clang; and when the minute hand made
the circuit of the face and the hour was to be
stricken there came from the brazen lungs of the
clock a sound which was clear and loud and deep
and exceedingly musical, but of so peculiar a note
and emphasis that, at each lapse of an hour, the
musicians of the orchestra were constrained to pause,
momentarily, in their performance, to hearken to
the sound; and thus the waltzers perforce ceased
their evolutions; and there was a brief disconcert
of the whole gay company; and, while the chimes
of the clock yet rang, it was observed that the
giddiest grew pale, and the more aged and sedate
passed their hands over their brows as if in confused
revery or meditation. But when the echoes had
fully ceased, a light laughter at once pervaded the
assembly; the musicians looked at each other and
smiled as if at their own nervousness and folly, and
made whispering vows, each to the other, that the
next chiming of the clock should produce in them
no similar emotion and then, after the lapse of sixty
minutes (which embrace three thousand and six
hundred seconds of the Time that flies) there came
yet another chiming of the clock, and then were the
same disconcert and tremulousness and meditation
as before.

But, in spite of these things, it was a gay and
magnificent revel. The tastes of the prince were
peculiar. He had a fine eye for colors and effects.
He disregarded the *decora* of mere fashion. His
plans were bold and fiery, and his conceptions
glowed with barbaric luster. There are some who
would have thought him mad. His followers felt
that he was not. It was necessary to hear and see
and touch him to be *sure* that he was not.

He had directed, in great part, the movable embellishments of the seven chambers, upon occasion
of this great fete; and it was his own guiding taste
which had given character to the masqueraders.

Be sure they were grotesque. There were much glare and glitter and piquancy and phantasm—much of what has been since seen in *Hernani*. There were arabesque figures with unsuited limbs and appointments. There were delirious fancies such as the madman fashions. There was much of the beautiful, much of the wanton, much of the bizarre, something of the terrible, and not a little of that which might have excited disgust. To and fro in the seven chambers there stalked, in fact, a multitude of dreams. And these—the dreams—writhed in and about, taking hue from the rooms, and causing the wild music of the orchestra to seem as the echo of their steps. And, anon, there strikes the ebony clock which stands in the hall of the velvet. And then, for a moment, all is still, and all is silent save the voice of the clock. The dreams are stiff frozen as they stand. But the echoes of the chime die away—they have endured but an instant—and a light, half-subdued laughter floats after them as they depart. And now again the music swells, and the dreams live, and writhe to and fro more merrily than ever, taking hue from the many-tinted windows through which stream the rays from the tripods. But to the chamber which lies most westwardly of the seven, there are now none of the maskers who venture; for the night is waning away, and there flows a ruddier light through the blood-colored panes; and the blackness of the sable drapery appals; and to him whose foot falls upon the sable carpet, there comes from the near clock of ebony a muffled peal more solemnly emphatic than any which reaches their ears who indulge in the more remote gayeties of the other apartments.

But these other apartments were densely crowded, and in them beat feverishly the heart of life. And the revel went whirlingly on, until at length there commenced the sounding of midnight upon the clock. And then the music ceased, as I have told; and the evolutions of the waltzers were quieted; and there was an uneasy cessation of all things as before. But now there were twelve strokes to be sounded by the bell of the clock; and thus it happened, perhaps, that before the last echoes of the last chime had utterly sunk into silence, there were many individuals in the crowd who had found leisure to become aware of the presence of a masked figure which had arrested the attention of no single individual before. And the rumor of this new presence having spread itself whisperingly around, there arose at length from the whole company a buzz, or murmur, expressive of disapprobation and surprise —then, finally, of terror, of horror, and of disgust.

In an assembly of phantasms such as I have painted, it may well be supposed that no ordinary appearance could have excited such sensation. In truth the masquerade license of the night was nearly unlimited; but the figure in question had out-Heroded Herod, and gone beyond the bound of even the prince's indefinite decorum. There are chords in the hearts of the most reckless which cannot be touched without emotion. Even with the utterly lost, to whom life and death are equally jests, there are matters of which no jest can be made. The whole company, indeed, seemed now deeply to feel that in the costume and bearing of the stranger neither wit nor propriety existed. The figure was tall and gaunt, and shrouded from head to foot in the habiliments of the grave. The mask which concealed the visage was made so nearly to resemble the countenance of a stiffened corpse that the closest scrutiny must have had difficulty in detecting the cheat. And yet all this might have been endured, if not approved, by the mad revelers around. But the mummer had gone so far as to assume the type of the Red Death. His vesture was dabbled in *blood*—and his broad brow, with all the features of the face, was besprinkled with the scarlet horror.

When the eyes of Prince Prospero fell upon this spectral image (which with a slow and solemn movement, as if more fully to sustain its role, stalked to and fro among the waltzers) he was seen to be convulsed, in the first moment, with a strong shudder either of terror or distaste; but, in the next, his brow reddened with rage.

"Who dares?" he demanded hoarsely of the courtiers who stood near him—"who dares insult us with this blasphemous mockery? Seize him and unmask him—that we may know whom we have to hang at sunrise, from the battlements!"

It was in the eastern or blue chamber in which stood the Prince Prospero as he uttered these words. They rang throughout the seven rooms loudly and clearly—for the prince was a bold and robust man, and the music had become hushed at the waving of his hand.

It was in the blue room where stood the prince, with a group of pale courtiers by his side. At first, as he spoke, there was a slight rushing movement of this group in the direction of the intruder, who at the moment was also near at hand, and now, with deliberate and stately step, made closer approach to the speaker. But from a certain nameless awe with which the mad assumptions of the mummer had inspired the whole party, there were found none who put forth hand to seize him; so that, unimpeded, he passed within a yard of the prince's person; and while the vast assembly as if with one impulse, shrank from the centers of the rooms to the walls, he made his way uninterruptedly, but with the same solemn and measured step which had distinguished him from the first, through the blue chamber to the purple—through the purple to the green—through the green to the orange—through this again to the white—and even thence to the violet, ere a decided movement had been made to arrest him. It was then, however, that the Prince Prospero, maddening with rage and the shame of his own momentary cowardice, rushed hurriedly through the six chambers, while none followed him on account of a deadly terror that had seized upon all. He bore aloft a drawn dagger, and had approached, in rapid impetuosity, to within three or four feet of the retreating figure, when the latter, having attained the extremity of the velvet apartment, turned suddenly and confronted his pursuer. There was a sharp cry—and the dagger dropped gleaming upon the sable carpet, upon which, instantly afterwards, fell prostrate in death the Prince Prospero. Then, summoning the wild courage of despair, a throng of the revelers at once threw themselves into the black apartment, and, seizing the mummer, whose tall figure stood erect and motionless within the shadow of the ebony clock, gasped in unutterable horror at finding the grave cerements and corpselike mask, which they handled with so violent a rudeness, untenanted by any tangible form.

And now was acknowledged the presence of the Red Death. He had come like a thief in the night. And one by one dropped the revelers in the blood-bedewed halls of their revel, and died each in the despairing posture of his fall. And the life of the ebony clock went out with that of the last of the gay. And the flames of the tripods expired. And Darkness and Decay and the Red Death held illimitable dominion over all.

———◆———

NATHANIEL HAWTHORNE

1804–1864

Nathaniel Hawthorne was born in Salem, Massachusetts, of a once distinguished colonial family whose fortunes were in decline. One of his ancestors had been Judge Hathorne, one of the judges presiding at the Salem witchcraft trials, whom he drew as Colonel Pyncheon in *The House of the Seven Gables*. After graduation from Bowdoin College in 1825, Hawthorne returned to Salem, where he lived in seclusion for twelve years. In 1828 he published anonymously his first novel, *Fanshawe*, of no real importance to his development as a writer. A number of his short stories were published in Samuel Goodrich's *The Token*, Hawthorne collecting them finally into his first significant work, *Twice-Told Tales*, 1837. In these tales Hawthorne attempted to create a legend of the New England past through historical narratives. These short stories deal with his favorite themes of secret guilt and the repressions of a harsh and stubborn pride; in them he dramatized imaginatively and critically what he conceived to be the Puritan inheritance of nineteenth-century New England.

After his experience as a member of the Brook Farm experiment in 1841, Hawthorne married Sophia Peabody in 1842. This domestic relationship was an eminently happy one, for Sophia's influence was important in changing Hawthorne's habits of "cursed solitude" to social normality and geniality. In 1846, through the aid of his friends, Hawthorne became the head of the Customhouse in Salem, only to lose the position through the intervention of the Reverend Charles Upham. This was a blessing in disguise, however, since he now was able to finish *The Scarlet Letter*, which was published in 1850. Long retarded fame now came to him, and within the next ten years all the rest of his finest work was written: *The House of the Seven Gables* (1851), *The Blithedale Romance* (1852), and *The Marble Faun* (1860). After serving as consul at Liverpool (1853–1856), he spent several years in Italy and returned to write *The Marble Faun*. Thereafter his creative powers declined until his death in 1864.

Although Hawthorne came to maturity as an artist in the American Romantic transcendental period, he could never agree with the optimistic transcendental religion of Emerson. His own moral sensibility could not accept Emerson's belief that evil was merely negative, and there was too much of the Puritan inheritance in Hawthorne to permit him to disregard the tragic imperfections of human nature. His Romanticism is best shown in his handling of the Gothic elements in his short tales and in *The Scarlet Letter* and *The House of the Seven Gables*; but whether it concerned a portrait, witchcraft, or the mythical appearance of Satan, Hawthorne invests the Gothic property with a moral symbolism which takes it completely out of the realm of the merely sensational. The use of the witches' sabbath to mark the moral deterioration of Young Goodman Brown is a case in point. His best short stories and his finest novel, *The Scarlet Letter*, move against a background of New England history and legend; but at the same time symbolic overtones give the narratives a universality that transcends the historical time and place. While Hawthorne preferred to regard his stories as romances because he liked artistic freedom from realistic notation of surface detail, he sometimes felt the lack of such background in the thinness of some of his allegorical tales, as the carefully noted observations in his notebooks and his admiration for the realistic Dutch painters reveal. For us, Hawthorne remains the first American artist as novelist, and the one writer in American literature who has evaluated imaginatively the significance of the Puritan tradition in American culture.

FURTHER READING

MATTHIESSEN, F. O. *American Renaissance* (New York, 1941).
STEWART, RANDALL. *Nathaniel Hawthorne* (New York, 1948).
VAN DOREN, MARK. *The Best of Hawthorne* (New York, 1951).

Young Goodman Brown

YOUNG Goodman Brown came forth at sunset into the street at Salem village; but put his head back, after crossing the threshold, to exchange a parting kiss with his young wife. And Faith, as the wife was aptly named, thrust her own pretty head into the street, letting the wind play with the pink ribbons of her cap while she called to Goodman Brown.

"Dearest heart," whispered she, softly and rather sadly, when her lips were close to his ear, "prithee put off your journey until sunrise and sleep in your own bed to-night. A lone woman is troubled with such dreams and such thoughts that she's afeard of herself sometimes. Pray tarry with me this night, dear husband, of all nights in the year."

"My love and my Faith," replied young Goodman Brown, "of all nights in the year, this one night must I tarry away from thee. My journey, as thou callest it, forth and back again, must needs be done 'twixt now and sunrise. What, my sweet, pretty wife, dost thou doubt me already, and we but three months married?"

"Then God bless you!" said Faith, with the pink ribbons; "and may you find all well when you come back."

"Amen!" cried Goodman Brown. "Say thy prayers, dear Faith, and go to bed at dusk, and no harm will come to thee."

So they parted; and the young man pursued his way until, being about to turn the corner by the meeting-house, he looked back and saw the head of Faith still peeping after him with a melancholy air, in spite of her pink ribbons.

"Poor little Faith!" thought he, for his heart smote him. "What a wretch am I to leave her on such an errand! She talks of dreams, too. Methought as she spoke there was trouble in her face, as if a dream had warned her what work is to be done to-night. But no, no; 'twould kill her to think it. Well, she's a blessed angel on earth; and after this one night I'll cling to her skirts and follow her to heaven."

With this excellent resolve for the future, Goodman Brown felt himself justified in making more haste on his present evil purpose. He had taken a dreary road, darkened by all the gloomiest trees of the forest, which barely stood aside to let the narrow path creep through, and closed immediately behind. It was all as lonely as could be; and there is this peculiarity in such a solitude, that the traveller knows not who may be concealed by the innumerable trunks and the thick boughs overhead; so that with lonely footsteps he may yet be passing through an unseen multitude.

"There may be a devilish Indian behind every tree," said Goodman Brown to himself; and he glanced fearfully behind him as he added, "What if the devil himself should be at my very elbow!"

His head being turned back, he passed a crook of the road, and, looking forward again, beheld the figure of a man, in grave and decent attire, seated at the foot of an old tree. He arose at Goodman Brown's approach and walked onward side by side with him.

"You are late, Goodman Brown," said he. "The clock of the Old South was striking as I came through Boston, and that is full fifteen minutes agone."

"Faith kept me back a while," replied the young

man, with a tremor in his voice, caused by the sudden appearance of his companion, though not wholly unexpected.

It was now deep dusk in the forest, and deepest in that part of it where these two were journeying. As nearly as could be discerned, the second traveller was about fifty years old, apparently in the same rank of life as Goodman Brown, and bearing a considerable resemblance to him, though perhaps more in expression than features. Still they might have been taken for father and son. And yet, though the elder person was as simply clad as the younger, and as simple in manner too, he had an indescribable air of one who knew the world, and who would not have felt abashed at the governor's dinner table or in King William's court, were it possible that his affairs should call him thither. But the only thing about him that could be fixed upon as remarkable was his staff, which bore the likeness of a great black snake, so curiously wrought that it might almost be seen to twist and wriggle itself like a living serpent. This, of course, must have been an ocular deception, assisted by the uncertain light.

"Come, Goodman Brown," cried his fellow-traveller, "this is a dull pace for the beginning of a journey. Take my staff, if you are so soon weary."

"Friend," said the other, exchanging his slow pace for a full stop, "having kept covenant by meeting thee here, it is my purpose now to return whence I came. I have scruples touching the matter thou wot'st of."

"Sayest thou so?" replied he of the serpent, smiling apart. "Let us walk on, nevertheless, reasoning as we go; and if I convince thee not thou shalt turn back. We are but a little way in the forest yet."

"Too far! too far!" exclaimed the goodman, unconsciously resuming his walk. "My father never went into the woods on such an errand, nor his father before him. We have been a race of honest men and good Christians since the days of the martyrs; and shall I be the first of the name of Brown that ever took this path and kept"—

"Such company, thou wouldst say," observed the elder person, interpreting his pause. "Well said, Goodman Brown! I have been as well acquainted with your family as with ever a one among the Puritans; and that's no trifle to say. I helped your grandfather, the constable, when he lashed the Quaker woman so smartly through the streets of Salem; and it was I that brought your father a pitch-pine knot, kindled at my own hearth, to set fire to an Indian village, in King Philip's war. They were my good friends, both; and many a pleasant walk

have we had along this path, and returned merrily after midnight. I would fain be friends with you for their sake."

"If it be as thou sayest," replied Goodman Brown, "I marvel they never spoke of these matters; or, verily, I marvel not, seeing that the least rumor of the sort would have driven them from New England. We are a people of prayer, and good works to boot, and abide no such wickedness."

"Wickedness or not," said the traveller with the twisted staff, "I have a very general acquaintance here in New England. The deacons of many a church have drunk the communion wine with me; the selectmen of divers towns make me their chairman; and a majority of the Great and General Court [1] are firm supporters of my interest. The governor and I, too— But these are state secrets."

"Can this be so?" cried Goodman Brown, with a stare of amazement at his undisturbed companion. "Howbeit, I have nothing to do with the governor and council; they have their own ways, and are no rule for a simple husbandman like me. But, were I to go on with thee, how should I meet the eye of that good old man, our minister, at Salem village? Oh, his voice would make me tremble both Sabbath day and lecture day." [2]

Thus far the elder traveller had listened with due gravity; but now burst into a fit of irrepressible mirth, shaking himself so violently that his snake-like staff actually seemed to wriggle in sympathy.

"Ha! ha! ha!" shouted he again and again; then composing himself, "Well, go on, Goodman Brown, go on; but, prithee, don't kill me with laughing."

"Well, then, to end the matter at once," said Goodman Brown, considerably nettled, "there is my wife, Faith. It would break her dear little heart; and I'd rather break my own."

"Nay, if that be the case," answered the other, "e'en go thy ways, Goodman Brown. I would not for twenty old women like the one hobbling before us that Faith should come to any harm."

As he spoke he pointed his staff at a female figure on the path, in whom Goodman Brown recognized a very pious and exemplary dame, who had taught him his catechism in youth, and was still his moral and spiritual adviser, jointly with the minister and Deacon Gookin.

"A marvel, truly, that Goody Cloyse should be so far in the wilderness at nightfall," said he. "But with your leave, friend, I shall take a cut through the woods until we have left this Christian woman

[1] The Colonial legislature of Massachusetts.
[2] Thursday.

behind. Being a stranger to you, she might ask whom I was consorting with and whither I was going."

"Be it so," said his fellow-traveller. "Betake you to the woods, and let me keep the path."

Accordingly the young man turned aside, but took care to watch his companion, who advanced softly along the road until he had come within a staff's length of the old dame. She, meanwhile, was making the best of her way, with singular speed for so aged a woman, and mumbling some indistinct words—a prayer, doubtless—as she went. The traveller put forth his staff and touched her withered neck with what seemed the serpent's tail.

"The devil!" screamed the pious old lady.

"Then Goody Cloyse[3] knows her old friend?" observed the traveller, confronting her and leaning on his writhing stick.

"Ah, forsooth, and is it your worship indeed?" cried the good dame. "Yea, truly it is, and in the very image of my old gossip, Goodman Brown, the grandfather of the silly fellow that now is. But— would your worship believe it?—my broomstick hath strangely disappeared, stolen, as I suspect, by that unhanged witch, Goody Cory, and that, too, when I was all anointed with the juice of smallage,[4] and cinquefoil, and wolf's bane—"

"Mingled with fine wheat and the fat of a new-born babe," said the shape of old Goodman Brown.

"Ah, your worship knows the recipe," cried the old lady, cackling aloud. "So, as I was saying, being all ready for the meeting, and no horse to ride on, I made up my mind to foot it; for they tell me there is a nice young man to be taken into communion to-night. But now your good worship will lend me your arm, and we shall be there in a twinkling."

"That can hardly be," answered her friend. "I may not spare you my arm, Goody Cloyse; but here is my staff, if you will."

So saying, he threw it down at her feet, where, perhaps, it assumed life, being one of the rods which its owner had formerly lent to the Egyptian magi. Of this fact, however, Goodman Brown could not take cognizance. He had cast up his eyes in astonishment, and, looking down again, beheld neither Goody Cloyse nor the serpentine staff, but his fellow-traveller alone, who waited for him as calmly as if nothing had happened.

[3] An historical character sentenced to death for witchcraft by Hawthorne's great-great-grandfather in 1692, as were Goody Cory and Martha Carrier mentioned below.

[4] Parsley.

"That old woman taught me my catechism," said the young man; and there was a world of meaning in this simple comment.

They continued to walk onward, while the elder traveller exhorted his companion to make good speed and persevere in the path, discoursing so aptly that his arguments seemed rather to spring up in the bosom of his auditor than to be suggested by himself. As they went, he plucked a branch of maple to serve for a walking stick, and began to strip it of the twigs and little boughs, which were wet with evening dew. The moment his fingers touched them they became strangely withered and dried up as with a week's sunshine. Thus the pair proceeded, at a good free pace, until suddenly, in a gloomy hollow of the road, Goodman Brown sat himself down on the stump of a tree and refused to go any farther.

"Friend," said he, stubbornly, "my mind is made up. Not another step will I budge on this errand. What if a wretched old woman do choose to go to the devil when I thought she was going to heaven: is that any reason why I should quit my dear Faith and go after her?"

"You will think better of this by and by," said his acquaintance, composedly. "Sit here and rest yourself a while; and when you feel like moving again, there is my staff to help you along."

Without more words, he threw his companion the maple stick, and was as speedily out of sight as if he had vanished into the deepening gloom. The young man sat a few moments by the roadside, applauding himself greatly, and thinking with how clear a conscience he should meet the minister in his morning walk, nor shrink from the eye of good old Deacon Gookin. And what calm sleep would be his that very night, which was to have been spent so wickedly, but so purely and sweetly now, in the arms of Faith! Amidst these pleasant and praiseworthy meditations, Goodman Brown heard the tramp of horses along the road, and deemed it advisable to conceal himself within the verge of the forest, conscious of the guilty purpose that had brought him thither, though now so happily turned from it.

On came the hoof tramps and the voices of the riders, two grave old voices, conversing soberly as they drew near. These mingled sounds appeared to pass along the road, within a few yards of the young man's hiding-place; but, owing doubtless to the depth of the gloom at that particular spot, neither the travellers nor their steeds were visible. Though their figures brushed the small boughs by the wayside, it could not be seen that they intercepted, even for a moment, the faint gleam from the strip of bright sky athwart which they must have passed. Goodman Brown alternately crouched and stood on tiptoe, pulling aside the branches and thrusting forth his head as far as he durst without discerning so much as a shadow. It vexed him the more, because he could have sworn, were such a thing possible, that he recognized the voices of the minister and Deacon Gookin, jogging along quietly, as they were wont to do, when bound to some ordination or ecclesiastical council. While yet within hearing, one of the riders stopped to pluck a switch.

"Of the two, reverend sir," said the voice like the deacon's, "I had rather miss an ordination dinner than to-night's meeting. They tell me that some of our community are to be here from Falmouth and beyond, and others from Connecticut and Rhode Island, besides several of the Indian powwows, who, after their fashion, know almost as much deviltry as the best of us. Moreover, there is a goodly young woman to be taken into communion."

"Mighty well, Deacon Gookin!" replied the solemn old tones of the minister. "Spur up, or we shall be late. Nothing can be done, you know, until I get on the ground."

The hoofs clattered again; and the voices, talking so strangely in the empty air, passed on through the forest, where no church had ever been gathered or solitary Christian prayed. Whither, then, could these holy men be journeying so deep into the heathen wilderness? Young Goodman Brown caught hold of a tree for support, being ready to sink down on the ground, faint and overburdened with the heavy sickness of his heart. He looked up to the sky, doubting whether there really was a heaven above him. Yet there was the blue arch, and the stars brightening in it.

"With heaven above and Faith below, I will yet stand firm against the devil!" cried Goodman Brown.

While he still gazed upward into the deep arch of the firmament and had lifted his hands to pray, a cloud, though no wind was stirring, hurried across the zenith and hid the brightening stars. The blue sky was still visible, except directly overhead, where this black mass of cloud was sweeping swiftly northward. Aloft in the air, as if from the depths of the cloud, came a confused and doubtful sound of voices. Once the listener fancied that he could distinguish the accents of townspeople of his own, men and women, both pious and ungodly, many

of whom he had met at the communion table, and had seen others rioting at the tavern. The next moment, so indistinct were the sounds, he doubted whether he had heard aught but the murmur of the old forest, whispering without a wind. Then came a stronger swell of those familiar tones, heard daily in the sunshine at Salem village, but never until now from a cloud of night. There was one voice of a young woman, uttering lamentations, yet with an uncertain sorrow, and entreating for some favor, which, perhaps, it would grieve her to obtain; and all the unseen multitude, both saints and sinners, seemed to encourage her onward.

"Faith!" shouted Goodman Brown, in a voice of agony and desperation; and the echoes of the forest mocked him, crying, "Faith! Faith!" as if bewildered wretches were seeking her all through the wilderness.

The cry of grief, rage, and terror was yet piercing the night, when the unhappy husband held his breath for a response. There was a scream, drowned immediately in a louder murmur of voices, fading into far-off laughter, as the dark cloud swept away, leaving the clear and silent sky above Goodman Brown. But something fluttered lightly down through the air and caught on the branch of a tree. The young man seized it, and beheld a pink ribbon.

"My Faith is gone!" cried he, after one stupefied moment. "There is no good on earth; and sin is but a name. Come, devil; for to thee is this world given."

And, maddened with despair, so that he laughed loud and long, did Goodman Brown grasp his staff and set forth again, at such a rate that he seemed to fly along the forest path rather than to walk or run. The road grew wilder and drearier and more faintly traced, and vanished at length, leaving him in the heart of the dark wilderness, still rushing onward with the instinct that guides mortal man to evil. The whole forest was peopled with frightful sounds—the creaking of the trees, the howling of wild beasts, and the yell of Indians; while sometimes the wind tolled like a distant church bell, and sometimes gave a broad roar around the traveller, as if all Nature were laughing him to scorn. But he was himself the chief horror of the scene, and shrank not from its other horrors.

"Ha! ha! ha!" roared Goodman Brown when the wind laughed at him. "Let us hear which will laugh loudest. Think not to frighten me with your deviltry. Come witch, come wizard, come Indian powwow, come devil himself, and here comes Goodman Brown. You may as well fear him as he fear you."

In truth, all through the haunted forest there could be nothing more frightful than the figure of Goodman Brown. On he flew among the black pines, brandishing his staff with frenzied gestures, now giving vent to an inspiration of horrid blasphemy, and now shouting forth such laughter as set all the echoes of the forest laughing like demons around him. The fiend in his own shape is less hideous than when he rages in the breast of man. Thus sped the demoniac on his course, until, quivering among the trees, he saw a red light before him, as when the felled trunks and branches of a clearing have been set on fire, and throw up their lurid blaze against the sky, at the hour of midnight. He paused, in a lull of the tempest that had driven him onward, and heard the swell of what seemed a hymn, rolling solemnly from a distance with the weight of many voices. He knew the tune; it was a familiar one in the choir of the village meetinghouse. The verse died heavily away, and was lengthened by a chorus, not of human voices, but of all the sounds of the benighted wilderness pealing in awful harmony together. Goodman Brown cried out, and his cry was lost to his own ear by its unison with the cry of the desert.

In the interval of silence he stole forward until the light glared full upon his eyes. At one extremity of an open space, hemmed in by the dark wall of the forest, arose a rock, bearing some rude, natural resemblance either to an altar or a pulpit, and surrounded by four blazing pines, their tops aflame, their stems untouched, like candles at an evening meeting. The mass of foliage that had overgrown the summit of the rock was all on fire, blazing high into the night and fitfully illuminating the whole field. Each pendent twig and leafy festoon was in a blaze. As the red light arose and fell, a numerous congregation alternately shone forth, then disappeared in shadow, and again grew, as it were, out of the darkness, peopling the heart of the solitary woods at once.

"A grave and dark-clad company," quoth Goodman Brown.

In truth they were such. Among them, quivering to and fro between gloom and splendor, appeared faces that would be seen next day at the council board of the province, and others which, Sabbath after Sabbath, looked devoutly heavenward, and benignantly over the crowded pews, from the holiest pulpits in the land. Some affirm that the lady of the governor was there. At least there were high dames well known to her, and wives of honored husbands, and widows, a great multitude, and ancient maidens, all of excellent repute, and fair young girls, who trembled lest their mothers should espy them. Either the sudden gleams of light flashing over the obscure field bedazzled Goodman Brown, or he recognized a score of the church members of Salem village famous for their especial sanctity. Good old Deacon Gookin had arrived, and waited at the skirts of that venerable saint, his revered pastor. But, irreverently consorting with these grave, reputable, and pious people, these elders of the church, these chaste dames and dewy virgins, there were men of dissolute lives and women of spotted fame, wretches given over to all mean and filthy vice, and suspected even of horrid crimes. It was strange to see that the good shrank not from the wicked, nor were the sinners abashed by the saints. Scattered also among their pale-faced enemies were the Indian priests, or powwows, who had often scared their native forest with more hideous incantations than any known to English witchcraft.

"But where is Faith?" thought Goodman Brown; and, as hope came into his heart, he trembled.

Another verse of the hymn arose, a slow and mournful strain, such as the pious love, but joined to words which expressed all that our nature can conceive of sin, and darkly hinted at far more. Unfathomable to mere mortals is the lore of fiends. Verse after verse was sung; and still the chorus of the desert swelled between like the deepest tone of a mighty organ; and with the final peal of that dreadful anthem there came a sound, as if the roaring wind, the rushing streams, the howling beasts, and every other voice of the unconcerted wilderness were mingling and according with the voice of guilty man in homage to the prince of all. The four blazing pines threw up a loftier flame, and obscurely discovered shapes and visages of horror on the smoke wreaths above the impious assembly. At the same moment the fire on the rock shot redly forth and formed a glowing arch above its base, where now appeared a figure. With reverence be it spoken, the figure bore no slight similitude, both in garb and manner, to some grave divine of the New England churches.

"Bring forth the converts!" cried a voice that echoed through the field and rolled into the forest.

At the word, Goodman Brown stepped forth from the shadow of the trees and approached the congregation, with whom he felt a loathful brotherhood by the sympathy of all that was wicked in his heart. He could have well-nigh sworn that the shape of his own dead father beckoned him to advance, looking downward from a smoke wreath, while a woman, with dim features of despair, threw out her hand to warn him back. Was it his mother? But he had no power to retreat one step, nor to resist, even in thought, when the minister and good old Deacon Gookin seized his arms and led him to the blazing rock. Thither came also the slender form of a veiled female, led between Goody Cloyse, that pious teacher of the catechism, and Martha Carrier, who had received the devil's promise to be queen of hell. A rampant hag was she. And there stood the proselytes beneath the canopy of fire.

"Welcome, my children," said the dark figure, "to the communion of your race. Ye have found thus young your nature and your destiny. My children, look behind you!"

They turned; and flashing forth, as it were, in a sheet of flame, the fiend worshippers were seen; the smile of welcome gleamed darkly on every visage.

"There," resumed the sable form, "are all whom ye have reverenced from youth. Ye deemed them holier than yourselves, and shrank from your own sin, contrasting it with their lives of righteousness and prayerful aspirations heavenward. Yet here are they all in my worshipping assembly. This night it shall be granted you to know their secret deeds: how hoary-bearded elders of the church have whispered wanton words to the young maids of their households; how many a woman, eager for widows' weeds, has given her husband a drink at bedtime and let him sleep his last sleep in her bosom; how beardless youths have made haste to inherit their fathers' wealth; and how fair damsels—blush not, sweet ones—have dug little graves in the garden, and bidden me, the sole guest, to an infant's funeral. By the sympathy of your human hearts for sin ye shall scent out all the places—whether in church, bed-chamber, street, field, or forest—where crime has been committed, and shall exult to behold the whole earth one stain of guilt, one mighty blood spot. Far more than this. It shall be yours to penetrate, in every bosom, the deep mystery of sin, the fountain of all wicked arts, and which inexhaustibly supplies more evil impulses than human power—than my power at its utmost—can make manifest in deeds. And now, my children, look upon each other."

They did so; and, by the blaze of the hell-kindled torches, the wretched man beheld his Faith, and the wife her husband, trembling before that unhallowed altar.

"Lo, there ye stand, my children," said the figure, in a deep and solemn tone, almost sad with its despairing awfulness, as if his once angelic nature could yet mourn for our miserable race. "Depending upon one another's hearts, ye had still hoped that virtue were not all a dream. Now are ye undeceived. Evil is the nature of mankind. Evil must be your only happiness. Welcome again, my children, to the communion of your race."

"Welcome," repeated the fiend worshippers, in one cry of despair and triumph.

And there they stood, the only pair, as it seemed, who were yet hesitating on the verge of wickedness in this dark world. A basin was hollowed, naturally, in the rock. Did it contain water, reddened by the lurid light? or was it blood? or, perchance a liquid flame? Herein did the shape of evil dip his hand and prepare to lay the mark of baptism upon their foreheads, that they might be partakers of the mystery of sin, more conscious of the secret guilt of others, both in deed and thought, than they could now be of their own. The husband cast one look at his pale wife, and Faith at him. What polluted wretches would the next glance show them to each other, shuddering alike at what they disclosed and what they saw!

"Faith! Faith!" cried the husband, "look up to heaven, and resist the wicked one."

Whether Faith obeyed he knew not. Hardly had he spoken when he found himself amid calm night and solitude, listening to a roar of the wind which died heavily away through the forest. He staggered against the rock, and felt it chill and damp; while a hanging twig, that had been all on fire, besprinkled his cheek with the coldest dew.

The next morning young Goodman Brown came slowly into the street of Salem village, staring around him like a bewildered man. The good old minister was taking a walk along the graveyard to get an appetite for breakfast and meditate his sermon, and bestowed a blessing, as he passed, on Goodman Brown. He shrank from the venerable saint as if to avoid an anathema. Old Deacon Gookin was at domestic worship, and the holy words of his prayer were heard through the open window. "What God doth the wizard pray to?" quoth Goodman Brown. Goody Cloyse, the excellent old Christian, stood in the early sunshine at her own lattice, catechizing a little girl who had brought her a pint of morning's milk. Goodman Brown snatched away the child as from the grasp of the fiend himself. Turning the corner by the meeting-house, he spied the head of Faith, with the pink ribbons, gazing anxiously forth, and bursting into such joy at sight of him that she skipped along the street and almost kissed her husband before the whole village. But Goodman Brown looked sternly and sadly into her face, and passed on without a greeting.

Had Goodman Brown fallen asleep in the forest and only dreamed a wild dream of a witch-meeting?

Be it so if you will; but, alas! it was a dream of evil omen for young Goodman Brown. A stern, a sad, a darkly meditative, a distrustful, if not a desperate man did he become from the night of that fearful dream. On the Sabbath day, when the congregation were singing a holy psalm, he could not listen because an anthem of sin rushed loudly upon his ear and drowned all the blessed strain. When the minister spoke from the pulpit with power and fervid eloquence, and, with his hand on the open Bible, of the sacred truths of our religion, and of saint-like lives and triumphant deaths, and of future bliss or misery unutterable, then did Goodman Brown turn pale, dreading lest the roof should thunder down upon the gray blasphemer and his hearers. Often, awaking suddenly at midnight, he shrank from the bosom of Faith; and at morning or eventide, when the family knelt down at prayer, he scowled and muttered to himself, and gazed sternly at his wife, and turned away. And when he had lived long, and was borne to his grave a hoary corpse, followed by Faith, an aged woman, and children and grandchildren, a goodly procession, besides neighbors not a few, they carved no hopeful verse upon his tombstone, for his dying hour was gloom.

The Minister's Black Veil

A PARABLE

Another clergyman in New England, Mr. Joseph Moody, of York, Maine, who died about eighty years since, made himself remarkable by the same eccentricity that is here related of the Reverend Mr. Hooper. In his case, however, the symbol had a different import. In early life he had accidentally killed a beloved friend; and from that day till the hour of his own death, he hid his face from men.

THE sexton stood in the porch of Milford meeting-house, pulling busily at the bell-rope. The old people of the village came stooping along the street.

Children, with bright faces, tripped merrily beside their parents, or mimicked a graver gait, in the conscious dignity of their Sunday clothes. Spruce bachelors looked sidelong at the pretty maidens, and fancied that the Sabbath sunshine made them prettier than on week days. When the throng had mostly streamed into the porch, the sexton began to toll the bell, keeping his eye on the Reverend Mr. Hooper's door. The first glimpse of the clergyman's figure was the signal for the bell to cease its summons.

"But what has good Parson Hooper got upon his face?" cried the sexton in astonishment.

All within hearing immediately turned about, and beheld the semblance of Mr. Hooper, pacing slowly his meditative way towards the meeting-house. With one accord they started, expressing more wonder than if some strange minister were coming to dust the cushions of Mr. Hooper's pulpit.

"Are you sure it is our parson?" inquired Goodman Gray of the sexton.

"Of a certainty it is good Mr. Hooper," replied the sexton. "He was to have exchanged pulpits with Parson Shute, of Westbury; but Parson Shute sent to excuse himself yesterday, being to preach a funeral sermon."

The cause of so much amazement may appear sufficiently slight. Mr. Hooper, a gentlemanly person, of about thirty, though still a bachelor, was dressed with due clerical neatness, as if a careful wife had starched his band, and brushed the weekly dust from his Sunday's garb. There was but one thing remarkable in his appearance. Swathed about his forehead, and hanging down over his face, so low as to be shaken by his breath, Mr. Hooper had on a black veil. On a nearer view it seemed to consist of two folds of crape, which entirely concealed his features, except the mouth and chin, but probably did not intercept his sight, further than to give a darkened aspect to all living and inanimate things. With this gloomy shade before him, good Mr. Hooper walked onward, at a slow and quiet pace, stooping somewhat, and looking on the ground, as is customary with abstracted men, yet nodding kindly to those of his parishioners who still waited on the meeting-house steps. But so wonder-struck were they that his greeting hardly met with a return.

"I can't really feel as if good Mr. Hooper's face was behind that piece of crape," said the sexton.

"I don't like it," muttered an old woman, as she hobbled into the meeting-house. "He has changed himself into something awful, only by hiding his face."

"Our parson has gone mad!" cried Goodman Gray, following him across the threshold.

A rumor of some unaccountable phenomenon had preceded Mr. Hooper into the meeting-house, and set all the congregation astir. Few could refrain from twisting their heads towards the door; many stood upright, and turned directly about; while several little boys clambered upon the seats, and came down again with a terrible racket. There was a general bustle, a rustling of the women's gowns and shuffling of men's feet, greatly at variance with that hushed repose which should attend the entrance of the minister. But Mr. Hooper appeared not to notice the perturbation of his people. He entered with an almost noiseless step, bent his head mildly to the pews on each side, and bowed as he passed his oldest parishioner, a white-haired great-grandsire, who occupied an armchair in the centre of the aisle. It was strange to observe how slowly this venerable man became conscious of something singular in the appearance of his pastor. He seemed not fully to partake of the prevailing wonder, till Mr. Hooper had ascended the stairs, and showed himself in the pulpit, face to face with his congregation, except for the black veil. That mysterious emblem was never once withdrawn. It shook with his measured breath, as he gave out the psalm; it threw its obscurity between him and the holy page, as he read the Scriptures; and while he prayed, the veil lay heavily on his uplifted countenance. Did he seek to hide it from the dread Being whom he was addressing?

Such was the effect of this simple piece of crape, that more than one woman of delicate nerves was forced to leave the meeting-house. Yet perhaps the pale-faced congregation was almost as fearful a sight to the minister, as his black veil to them.

Mr. Hooper had the reputation of a good preacher, but not an energetic one: he strove to win his people heavenward by mild, persuasive influences, rather than to drive them thither by the thunders of the Word. The sermon which he now delivered was marked by the same characteristics of style and manner as the general series of his pulpit oratory. But there was something, either in the sentiment of the discourse itself, or in the imagination of the auditors, which made it greatly the most powerful effort that they had ever heard from their pastor's lips. It was tinged, rather more darkly than usual, with the gentle gloom of Mr. Hooper's temperament. The subject had reference to secret sin, and those sad mysteries which we hide from our nearest and dearest, and would fain conceal from our own consciousness, even forgetting that the Omniscient can detect them. A subtle power was breathed into his words. Each member of the congregation, the most innocent girl, and the man of hardened breast, felt as if the preacher had crept upon them, behind his awful veil, and discovered their hoarded iniquity of deed or thought. Many spread their clasped hands on their bosoms. There was nothing terrible in what Mr. Hooper said, at least, no violence; and yet, with every tremor of his melancholy voice, the hearers quaked. An unsought pathos came hand in hand with awe. So sensible were the audience of some unwonted attribute in their minister that they longed for a breath of wind to blow aside the veil, almost believing that a stranger's visage would be discovered, though the form, gesture, and voice were those of Mr. Hooper.

At the close of the services, the people hurried out with indecorous confusion, eager to communicate their pent-up amazement, and conscious of lighter spirits the moment they lost sight of the black veil. Some gathered in little circles, huddled closely together, with their mouths all whispering in the centre; some went homeward alone, wrapt in silent meditation; some talked loudly, and profaned the Sabbath day with ostentatious laughter. A few shook their sagacious heads, intimating that they could penetrate the mystery; while one or two affirmed that there was no mystery at all, but only that Mr. Hooper's eyes were so weakened by the midnight lamp, as to require a shade. After a brief interval, forth came good Mr. Hooper also, in the rear of his flock. Turning his veiled face from one group to another, he paid due reverence to the hoary heads, saluted the middle aged with kind dignity as their friend and spiritual guide, greeted the young with mingled authority and love, and laid his hands on the little children's heads to bless them. Such was always his custom on the Sabbath day. Strange and bewildered looks repaid him for his courtesy. None, as on former occasions, aspired to the honor of walking by their pastor's side. Old Squire Saunders, doubtless by an accidental lapse of memory, neglected to invite Mr. Hooper to his table, where the good clergyman had been wont to bless the food almost every Sunday since his settlement. He returned, therefore, to the parsonage, and, at the moment of closing the door, was observed to look back upon the people, all of whom had their eyes fixed upon the minister. A sad smile gleamed faintly from beneath the black veil, and flickered about his mouth, glimmering as he disappeared.

"How strange," said a lady, "that a simple black veil, such as any woman might wear on her bonnet, should become such a terrible thing on Mr. Hooper's face.

"Something must surely be amiss with Mr. Hooper's intellects," observed her husband, the physician of the village. "But the strangest part of the affair is the effect of this vagary, even on a sober-minded man like myself. The black veil, though it covers only our pastor's face, throws its influence over his whole person, and makes him ghostlike from head to foot. Do you not feel it so?"

"Truly do I," replied the lady; "and I would not be alone with him for the world. I wonder he is not afraid to be alone with himself!"

"Men sometimes are so," said her husband.

The afternoon service was attended with similar circumstances. At its conclusion, the bell tolled for the funeral of a young lady. The relatives and friends were assembled in the house, and the more distant acquaintances stood about the door, speaking of the good qualities of the deceased, when their talk was interrupted by the appearance of Mr. Hooper, still covered with his black veil. It was now an appropriate emblem. The clergyman stepped into the room where the corpse was laid, and bent over the coffin, to take a last farewell of his deceased parishioner. As he stooped, the veil hung straight down from his forehead, so that, if her eyelids not been closed forever, the dead maiden might have seen his face. Could Mr. Hooper be fearful of her glance, that he so hastily caught back the black veil? A person who watched the interview between the dead and living scrupled not to affirm, that, at the instant when the clergyman's features were disclosed, the corpse had slightly shuddered, rustling the shroud and muslin cap, though the countenance retained the composure of death. A superstitious old woman was the only witness of this prodigy. From the coffin Mr. Hooper passed into the chamber of the mourners, and thence to the head of the staircase, to make the funeral prayer. It was a tender and heart-dissolving prayer, full of sorrow, yet so imbued with celestial hopes, that the music of a heavenly harp, swept by the fingers of the dead, seemed faintly to be heard among the saddest accents of the minister. The people trembled, though they but darkly understood him when he prayed that they, and himself, and all of mortal race, might be ready, as he trusted this

young maiden had been, for the dreadful hour that should snatch the veil from their faces. The bearers went heavily forth, and the mourners followed, saddening all the street, with the dead before them, and Mr. Hooper in his black veil behind.

"Why do you look back?" said one in the procession to his partner.

"I had a fancy," replied she, "that the minister and the maiden's spirit were walking hand in hand."

"And so had I, at the same moment," said the other.

That night, the handsomest couple in Milford village were to be joined in wedlock. Though reckoned a melancholy man, Mr. Hooper had a placid cheerfulness for such occasions, which often excited a sympathetic smile where livelier merriment would have been thrown away. There was no quality of his disposition which made him more beloved than this. The company at the wedding awaited his arrival with impatience, trusting that the strange awe, which had gathered over him throughout the day, would now be dispelled. But such was not the result. When Mr. Hooper came, the first thing that their eyes rested on was the same horrible black veil, which had added deeper gloom to the funeral, and could portend nothing but evil to the wedding. Such was its immediate effect on the guests that a cloud seemed to have rolled duskily from beneath the black crape, and dimmed the light of the candles. The bridal pair stood up before the minister. But the bride's cold fingers quivered in the tremulous hand of the bridegroom, and her deathlike paleness caused a whisper that the maiden who had been buried a few hours before was come from her grave to be married. If ever another wedding were so dismal, it was that famous one where they tolled the wedding knell. After performing the ceremony, Mr. Hooper raised a glass of wine to his lips, wishing happiness to the new-married couple in a strain of mild pleasantry that ought to have brightened the features of the guests, like a cheerful gleam from the hearth. At that instant, catching a glimpse of his figure in the looking-glass, the black veil involved his own spirit in the horror with which it overwhelmed all others. His frame shuddered, his lips grew white, he spilt the untasted wine upon the carpet, and rushed forth into the darkness. For the Earth, too, had on her Black Veil.

The next day, the whole village of Milford talked of little else than Parson Hooper's black veil. That, and the mystery concealed behind it, supplied a topic for discussion between acquaintances meeting in the street, and good women gossiping at their open windows. It was the first item of news that the tavern-keeper told to his guests. The children babbled of it on their way to school. One imitative little imp covered his face with an old black handkerchief, thereby so affrighting his playmates that the panic seized himself, and he well-nigh lost his wits by his own waggery.

It was remarkable that of all the busybodies and impertinent people in the parish, not one ventured to put the plain question to Mr. Hooper, wherefore he did this thing. Hitherto, whenever there appeared the slightest call for such interference, he had never lacked advisers, nor shown himself averse to be guided by their judgment. If he erred at all, it was by so painful a degree of self-distrust, that even the mildest censure would lead him to consider an indifferent action as a crime. Yet, though so well acquainted with this amiable weakness, no individual among his parishioners chose to make the black veil a subject of friendly remonstrance. There was a feeling of dread, neither plainly confessed nor carefully concealed, which caused each to shift the responsibility upon another, till at length it was found expedient to send a deputation of the church, in order to deal with Mr. Hooper about the mystery before it should grow into a scandal. Never did an embassy so ill discharge its duties. The minister received them with friendly courtesy, but became silent, after they were seated, leaving to his visitors the whole burden of introducing their important business. The topic, it might be supposed, was obvious enough. There was the black veil swathed round Mr. Hooper's forehead, and concealing every feature above his placid mouth, on which, at times, they could perceive the glimmering of a melancholy smile. But that piece of crape, to their imagination, seemed to hang down before his heart, the symbol of a fearful secret between him and them. Were the veil but cast aside, they might speak freely of it, but not till then. Thus they sat a considerable time, speechless, confused, and shrinking uneasily from Mr. Hooper's eye, which they felt to be fixed upon them with an invisible glance. Finally, the deputies returned abashed to their constituents, pronouncing the matter too weighty to be handled, except by a council of the churches, if, indeed, it might not require a general synod.

But there was one person in the village unappalled by the awe with which the black veil had impressed all beside herself. When the deputies returned without an explanation, or even venturing to demand one, she, with the calm energy of her character, determined to chase away the strange cloud that appeared to be settling round Mr. Hooper, every moment more darkly than before. As his plighted wife, it should be her privilege to know what the black veil concealed. At the minister's first visit, therefore, she entered upon the subject with a direct simplicity, which made the task easier both for him and her. After he had seated himself, she fixed her eyes steadfastly upon the veil, but could discern nothing of the dreadful gloom that had so overawed the multitude: it was but a double fold of crape, hanging down from his forehead to his mouth, and slightly stirring with his breath.

"No," said she aloud, and smiling, "there is nothing terrible in this piece of crape, except that it hides a face which I am always glad to look upon. Come, good sir, let the sun shine from behind the cloud. First lay aside your black veil: then tell me why you put it on."

Mr. Hooper's smile glimmered faintly.

"There is an hour to come," said he, "when all of us shall cast aside our veils. Take it not amiss, beloved friend, if I wear this piece of crape till then."

"Your words are a mystery, too," returned the young lady. "Take away the veil from them, at least."

"Elizabeth, I will," said he, "so far as my vow may suffer me. Know, then, this veil is a type and a symbol, and I am bound to wear it ever, both in light and darkness, in solitude and before the gaze of multitudes, and as with strangers, so with my familiar friends. No mortal eye will see it withdrawn. This dismal shade must separate me from the world: even you, Elizabeth, can never come behind it!"

"What grievous affliction hath befallen you," she earnestly inquired, "that you should thus darken your eyes forever?"

"If it be a sign of mourning," replied Mr. Hooper, "I, perhaps, like most other mortals, have sorrows dark enough to be typified by a black veil."

"But what if the world will not believe that it is the type of an innocent sorrow?" urged Elizabeth. "Beloved and respected as you are, there may be whispers that you hide your face under the consciousness of secret sin. For the sake of your holy office, do away this scandal!"

The color rose into her cheeks as she intimated the nature of the rumors that were already abroad in the village. But Mr. Hooper's mildness did not forsake him. He even smiled again—that same sad smile, which always appeared like a faint glimmering of light, proceeding from the obscurity beneath the veil.

"If I hide my face for sorrow, there is cause enough," he merely replied; "and if I cover it for secret sin, what mortal might not do the same?"

And with this gentle, but unconquerable obstinacy did he resist all her entreaties. At length Elizabeth sat silent. For a few moments she appeared lost in thought, considering, probably, what new methods might be tried to withdraw her lover from so dark a fantasy, which, if it had no other meaning, was perhaps a symptom of mental disease. Though of a firmer character than his own, the tears rolled down her cheeks. But, in an instant, as it were, a new feeling took the place of sorrow: her eyes were fixed insensibly on the black veil, when, like a sudden twilight in the air, its terrors fell around her. She arose, and stood trembling before him.

"And do you feel it then, at last?" said he mournfully.

She made no reply, but covered her eyes with her hand, and turned to leave the room. He rushed forward and caught her arm.

"Have patience with me, Elizabeth!" cried he passionately. "Do not desert me, though this veil must be between us here on earth. Be mine, and hereafter there shall be no veil over my face, no darkness between our souls! It is but a mortal veil—it is not for eternity! O! you know not how lonely I am, and how frightened, to be alone behind my black veil. Do not leave me in this miserable obscurity forever!"

"Lift the veil but once, and look me in the face," said she.

"Never! It cannot be!" replied Mr. Hooper.

"Then farewell!" said Elizabeth.

She withdrew her arm from his grasp, and slowly departed, pausing at the door, to give one long, shuddering gaze, that seemed almost to penetrate the mystery of the black veil. But, even amid his grief, Mr. Hooper smiled to think that only a material emblem had separated him from happiness, though the horrors which it shadowed forth must be drawn darkly between the fondest of lovers.

From that time no attempts were made to remove Mr. Hooper's black veil, or, by a direct appeal, to discover the secret which it was supposed to hide. By persons who claimed a superiority to popular prejudice, it was reckoned merely an eccentric whim, such as often mingles with the sober actions of men otherwise rational, and tinges them all with its own semblance of insanity. But with the multitude, good Mr. Hooper was irreparably a bugbear. He could not walk the street with any peace of mind, so conscious was he that the gentle and timid would turn aside to avoid him, and that others would make it a point of hardihood to throw themselves in his way. The impertinence of the latter class compelled him to give up his customary walk at sunset to the burial ground; for when he leaned pensively over the gate, there would always be faces behind the gravestones, peeping at his black veil. A fable went the rounds that the stare of the dead people drove him thence. It grieved him, to the very depth of his kind heart, to observe how the children fled from his approach, breaking up their merriest sports, while his melancholy figure was yet afar off. Their instinctive dread caused him to feel more strongly than aught else, that a preternatural horror was interwoven with the threads of the black crape. In truth, his own antipathy to the veil was known to be so great, that he never willingly passed before a mirror, nor stooped to drink at a still fountain, lest, in its peaceful bosom, he should be affrighted by himself. This was what gave plausibility to the whispers, that Mr. Hooper's conscience tortured him for some great crime too horrible to be entirely concealed, or otherwise than so obscurely intimated. Thus, from beneath the black veil, there rolled a cloud into the sunshine, an ambiguity of sin or sorrow, which enveloped the poor minister, so that love or sympathy could never reach him. It was said that ghost and fiend consorted with him there. With self-shudderings and outward terrors, he walked continually in its shadow, groping darkly within his own soul, or gazing through a medium that saddened the whole world. Even the lawless wind, it was believed, respected his dreadful secret, and never blew aside the veil. But still good Mr. Hooper sadly smiled at the pale visages of the worldly throng as he passed by.

Among all its bad influences, the black veil had the one desirable effect of making its wearer a very efficient clergyman. By the aid of his mysterious emblem—for there was no other apparent cause—he became a man of awful power over souls that were in agony for sin. His converts always regarded him with a dread peculiar to themselves, affirming, though but figuratively, that, before he brought them to celestial light, they had been with him behind the black veil. Its gloom, indeed, enabled him to sympathize with all dark affections. Dying sinners cried aloud for Mr. Hooper, and would not yield their breath till he appeared; though ever, as he stooped to whisper consolation, they shuddered at the veiled face so near their own. Such were the terrors of the black veil, even when Death had bared his visage! Strangers came for long distances to attend service at his church, with the mere idle purpose of gazing at his figure, because it was forbidden them to behold his face. But many were made to quake ere they departed! Once, during Governor Belcher's administration, Mr. Hooper was appointed to preach the election sermon. Covered with his black veil, he stood before the chief magistrate, the council, and the representatives, and wrought so deep an impression, that the legislative measures of that year were characterized by all the gloom and piety of our earliest ancestral sway.

In this manner Mr. Hooper spent a long life, irreproachable in outward act, yet shrouded in dismal suspicions; kind and loving, though unloved and dimly feared; a man apart from men, shunned in their health and joy, but ever summoned to their aid in mortal anguish. As years wore on, shedding their snows above his sable veil, he acquired a name throughout the New England churches, and they called him Father Hooper. Nearly all his parishioners who were of mature age when he was settled had been borne away by many a funeral: he had one congregation in the church, and a more crowded one in the churchyard; and having wrought so late into the evening, and done his work so well, it was now good Father Hooper's turn to rest.

Several persons were visible by the shaded candlelight, in the death chamber of the old clergyman. Natural connections he had none. But there was the decorously grave, though unmoved physician, seeking only to mitigate the last pangs of the patient whom he could not save. There were the deacons, and other eminently pious members of his church. There, also, was the Reverend Mr. Clark, of Westbury, a young and zealous divine, who had ridden in haste to pray by the bedside of the expiring minister. There was the nurse, no hired handmaiden of death, but one whose calm affection had endured thus long in secrecy, in solitude, amid the chill of age, and would not perish, even at the dying hour. Who, but Elizabeth! And there lay the hoary head of good Father Hooper upon the death pillow, with the black veil still swathed about his brow, and reaching down over his face, so that each more difficult gasp of his faint breath caused it to stir. All through life that piece of crape had hung between him and the world: it had separated him from cheerful brotherhood and

woman's love, and kept him in that saddest of all prisons, his own heart; and still it lay upon his face, as if to deepen the gloom of his darksome chamber, and shade him from the sunshine of eternity.

For some time previous, his mind had been confused, wavering doubtfully between the past and the present, and hovering forward, as it were, at intervals, into the indistinctness of the world to come. There had been feverish turns, which tossed him from side to side, and wore away what little strength he had. But in his most convulsive struggles, and in the wildest vagaries of his intellect, when no other thought retained its sober influence, he still showed an awful solicitude lest the black veil should slip aside. Even if his bewildered soul could have forgotten, there was a faithful woman at his pillow, who, with averted eyes, would have covered that aged face, which she had last beheld in the comeliness of manhood. At length the death-stricken old man lay quietly in the torpor of mental and bodily exhaustion, with an imperceptible pulse, and breath that grew fainter and fainter, except when a long, deep, and irregular inspiration seemed to prelude the flight of his spirit.

The minister of Westbury approached the bedside.

"Venerable Father Hooper," said he, "the moment of your release is at hand. Are you ready for the lifting of the veil that shuts in time from eternity?"

Father Hooper at first replied merely by a feeble motion of his head; then, apprehensive, perhaps, that his meaning might be doubtful, he exerted himself to speak.

"Yea," said he, in faint accents, "my soul hath a patient weariness until that veil be lifted."

"And is it fitting," resumed the Reverend Mr. Clark, "that a man so given to prayer, of such a blameless example, holy in deed and thought, so far as mortal judgment may pronounce; is it fitting that a father in the church should leave a shadow on his memory, that may seem to blacken a life so pure? I pray you, my venerable brother, let not this thing be! Suffer us to be gladdened by your triumphant aspect as you go to your reward. Before the veil of eternity be lifted, let me cast aside this black veil from your face!"

And thus speaking, the Reverend Mr. Clark bent forward to reveal the mystery of so many years. But, exerting a sudden energy, that made all the beholders stand aghast, Father Hooper snatched both his hands from beneath the bedclothes, and pressed them strongly on the black veil, resolute to struggle, if the minister of Westbury would contend with a dying man.

"Never!" cried the veiled clergyman. "On earth, never!"

"Dark old man!" exclaimed the affrighted minister, "with what horrible crime upon your soul are you now passing to the judgment?"

Father Hooper's breath heaved; it rattled in his throat; but, with a mighty effort, grasping forward with his hands, he caught hold of life, and held it back till he should speak. He even raised himself in bed; and there he sat, shivering with the arms of death around him, while the black veil hung down, awful, at that last moment, in the gathered terrors of a lifetime. And yet the faint, sad smile, so often there, now seemed to glimmer from its obscurity, and linger on Father Hooper's lips.

"Why do you tremble at me alone?" cried he, turning his veiled face round the circle of pale spectators. "Tremble also at each other! Have men avoided me, and women shown no pity, and children screamed and fled, only for my black veil? What, but the mystery which it obscurely typifies, has made this piece of crape so awful? When the friend shows his inmost heart to his friend; the lover to his best beloved; when man does not vainly shrink from the eye of his Creator, loathsomely treasuring up the secret of his sin; then deem me a monster, for the symbol beneath which I have lived, and die! I look around me, and, lo! on every visage a Black Veil!"

While his auditors shrank from one another, in mutual affright, Father Hooper fell back upon his pillow, a veiled corpse, with a faint smile lingering on the lips. Still veiled, they laid him in his coffin, and a veiled corpse they bore him to the grave. The grass of many years has sprung up and withered on that grave, the burial stone is moss-grown, and good Mr. Hooper's face is dust; but awful is still the thought that it mouldered beneath the Black Veil.

———◆———

HERMAN MELVILLE

1819–1891

Herman Melville was born in New York City of New England and Dutch patroon ancestry, his mother being a Gansevoort. His early life was unhappy and poverty-stricken, since his father died in bankruptcy and left his wife with seven children to care for. At the age of seventeen Melville shipped as a cabin boy on the *Highlander* to Liverpool. When he returned he taught school in East Albany and Pittsfield, giving this up to ship once more on an eighteen-month voyage to the South Seas on the whaler *Acushnet*. In 1842 he jumped ship at the Marquesas and lived there for a month, later going to Tahiti, where he worked in the fields. After service on the U. S. frigate *United States* for a year, he was discharged in Boston in 1844. His first bids for fame came with the publication of *Typee* (1846) and *Omoo* (1847), romantic and adventurous chronicles of his experience in the South Seas. These works were well accepted, and Melville seemed to be launched on a successful career as a novelist.

In 1849 he and his wife moved to a Massachusetts farm near Pittsfield, where he formed a close friendship with Hawthorne and where he wrote his greatest work, *Moby Dick* (1851). This is perhaps one of the greatest novels in the world ("broiled in hellfire," Melville wrote in describing it to Hawthorne) in its conception of the sense of diabolism in the universe as embodied in the brute energies and inscrutable purposes of the white whale, Moby Dick. The far-ranging symbolism of the novel has caused much discussion and disagreement; the whole matter is admirably presented in Howard P. Vincent's *The Trying-Out of Moby Dick* (1949). After the tortured metaphysical complexities of his next novel, *Pierre* (1852), Melville's small public deserted him. It is doubtful that the romantic legend started by Melville's biographers in the 1920's that the failure of *Pierre* struck him into silence is true, as the correspondence with Hawthorne does not display any sensitive shirking by the artist. His finest collection of short narratives is the *Piazza Tales* (1856), where "Bartleby" was first published.

Melville passed the last years of his life in complete obscurity, writing some poetry, but only one prose work, the novel *Billy Budd*, which he finished just before he died in 1891 and which was published posthumously. After 1920, Melville's fame began to increase astronomically, and his fiction, such as *Billy Budd* and *Pierre*, has been carefully edited with excellent introductions; the Melville revival has included the reprinting of *Piazza Tales* and *The Confidence Man*, not published since 1857.

Melville the poet has also received belated recognition in F. O. Matthiessen's edition of the poems. In the twentieth century Herman Melville has thus emerged as (with Hawthorne and Henry James) one of the three greatest American novelists of the nineteenth century.

FURTHER READING

ARVIN, NEWTON. *Herman Melville* (New York, 1950).
CHASE, RICHARD. *Herman Melville: A Critical Study* (New York, 1949).

Bartleby the Scrivener

I AM a rather elderly man. The nature of my avocations, for the last thirty years, has brought me into more than ordinary contact with what would seem an interesting and somewhat singular set of men, of whom, as yet, nothing, that I know of, has ever been written—I mean, the law-copyists, or scriveners. I have known very many of them, professionally and privately, and, if I pleased, could relate divers histories, at which good-natured gentlemen might smile, and sentimental souls might weep. But I waive the biographies of all other scriveners, for a few passages in the life of Bartleby, who was a scrivener, the strangest I ever saw, or heard of. While, of other law-copyists, I might write the complete life, of Bartleby nothing of that sort can be done. I believe that no materials exist, for a full and satisfactory biography of this man. It is an irreparable loss to literature. Bartleby was one of those beings of whom nothing is ascertainable, except from the original sources, and, in his case, those are very small. What my own astonished eyes saw of Bartleby, *that* is all I know of him, except, indeed, one vague report, which will appear in the sequel.

Ere introducing the scrivener, as he first appeared to me, it is fit I make some mention of myself, my *employés*, my business, my chambers, and general surroundings; because some such description is indispensable to an adequate understanding of the chief character about to be presented. Imprimis: I am a man who, from his youth upwards, has been filled with a profound conviction that the easiest way of life is the best. Hence, though I belong to a profession proverbially energetic and nervous, even to turbulence, at times, yet nothing of that sort have I ever suffered to invade my peace. I am one of those unambitious lawyers who never addresses a jury, or in any way draws down public applause; but, in the cool tranquillity of a snug retreat, do a snug business among rich men's bonds, and mortgages, and title-deeds. All who know me, consider me an eminently *safe* man. The late John Jacob Astor, a personage little given to poetic enthusiasm, had no hesitation in pronouncing my first grand point to be prudence; my next, method. I do not speak it in vanity, but simply record the fact, that I was not unemployed in my profession by the late John Jacob Astor; a name which, I admit, I love to repeat; for it hath a rounded and orbicular sound to it, and rings like unto bullion. I will freely add, that I was not insensible to the late John Jacob Astor's good opinion.

Some time prior to the period at which this little history begins, my avocations had been largely increased. The good old office, now extinct in the State of New York, of a Master in Chancery, had been conferred upon me. It was not a very arduous office, but very pleasantly remunerative. I seldom lose my temper; much more seldom indulge in dangerous indignation at wrongs and outrages; but I must be permitted to be rash here and declare, that I consider the sudden and violent abrogation of the office of Master in Chancery, by the new Constitution, as a premature act; inasmuch as I had counted upon a life-lease of the profits, whereas I only received those of a few short years. But this is by the way.

My chambers were up stairs, at No. — Wall Street. At one end, they looked upon the white wall of the interior of a spacious sky-light shaft, penetrating the building from top to bottom.

This view might have been considered rather tame than otherwise, deficient in what landscape painters call "life." But, if so, the view from the other end of my chambers offered, at least, a contrast, if nothing more. In that direction, my windows commanded an unobstructed view of a lofty brick wall, black by age and everlasting shade; which wall required no spy-glass to bring out its lurking beauties, but, for the benefit of all near-sighted spectators, was pushed up to within ten feet of my window-panes. Owing to the great height of the surrounding buildings, and my chambers being on the second floor, the interval between this wall and mine not a little resembled a huge square cistern.

At the period just preceding the advent of Bartleby, I had two persons as copyists in my employment, and a promising lad as an office-boy. First,

Turkey; second, Nippers; third, Ginger Nut. These may seem names, the like of which are not usually found in the Directory. In truth, they were nicknames, mutually conferred upon each other by my three clerks, and were deemed expressive of their respective persons or characters. Turkey was a short, pursy Englishman, of about my own age—that is, somewhere not far from sixty. In the morning, one might say, his face was of a fine florid hue, but after twelve o'clock, meridian—his dinner hour —it blazed like a grate full of Christmas coals; and continued blazing—but, as it were, with a gradual wane—till six o'clock, P.M., or thereabouts; after which, I saw no more of the proprietor of the face, which, gaining its meridian with the sun, seemed to set with it, to rise, culminate, and decline the following day, with the like regularity and undiminished glory. There are many singular coincidences I have known in the course of my life, not the least among which was the fact, that, exactly when Turkey displayed his fullest beams from his red and radiant countenance, just then, too, at that critical moment, began the daily period when I considered his business capacities as seriously disturbed for the remainder of the twenty-four hours. Not that he was absolutely idle, or averse to business then; far from it. The difficulty was, he was apt to be altogether too energetic. There was a strange, inflamed, flurried, flighty recklessness of activity about him. He would be incautious in dipping his pen into his inkstand. All his blots upon my documents were dropped there after twelve o'clock, meridian. Indeed, not only would he be reckless, and sadly given to making blots in the afternoon, but, some days, he went further, and was rather noisy. At such times, too, his face flamed with augmented blazonry, as if cannel coal had been heaped on anthracite. He made an unpleasant racket with his chair; spilled his sand-box; in mending his pens, impatiently split them all to pieces, and threw them on the floor in a sudden passion; stood up, and leaned over his table, boxing his papers about in a most indecorous manner, very sad to behold in an elderly man like him. Nevertheless, as he was in many ways a most valuable person to me, and all the time before twelve o'clock, meridian, was the quickest, steadiest creature, too, accomplishing a great deal of work in a style not easily to be matched —for these reasons I was willing to overlook his eccentricities, though, indeed, occasionally, I remonstrated with him. I did this very gently, however, because, though the civilest, nay, the blandest and most reverential of men in the morning, yet, in the afternoon, he was disposed, upon provocation, to be slightly rash with his tongue—in fact, insolent. Now, valuing his morning services as I did, and resolved not to lose them—yet, at the same time, made uncomfortable by his inflamed ways after twelve o'clock—and being a man of peace, unwilling by my admonitions to call forth unseemly retorts from him, I took upon me, one Saturday noon (he was always worse on Saturdays) to hint to him, very kindly, that, perhaps, now that he was growing old, it might be well to abridge his labors; in short, he need not come to my chambers after twelve o'clock, but dinner over, had best go home to his lodgings, and rest himself till tea-time. But no; he insisted upon his afternoon devotions. His countenance became intolerably fervid, as he oratorically assured me—gesticulating with a long ruler at the other end of the room—that if his services in the morning were useful, how indispensable, then, in the afternoon?

"With submission, sir," said Turkey, on this occasion, "I consider myself your right-hand man. In the morning I but marshal and deploy my columns; but in the afternoon I put myself at their head, and gallantly charge the foe, thus"—and he made a violent thrust with the ruler.

"But the blots, Turkey," intimated I.

"True; but, with submission, sir, behold these hairs! I am getting old. Surely, sir, a blot or two of a warm afternoon is not to be severely urged against gray hairs. Old age—even if it blot the page—is honorable. With submission, sir, we *both* are getting old."

This appeal to my fellow-feeling was hardly to be resisted. At all events, I saw that go he would not. So, I made up my mind to let him stay, resolving, nevertheless, to see to it that, during the afternoon, he had to do with my less important papers.

Nippers, the second on my list, was a whiskered, sallow, and, upon the whole, rather piratical-looking young man, of about five-and-twenty. I always deemed him the victim of two evil powers—ambition and indigestion. The ambition was evinced by a certain impatience of the duties of a mere copyist, an unwarrantable usurpation of strictly professional affairs, such as the original drawing up of legal documents. The indigestion seemed betokened in an occasional nervous testiness and grinning irritability, causing the teeth to audibly grind together over mistakes committed in copying; unnecessary maledictions, hissed, rather than spoken, in the heat of business; and especially by a continual discontent with the height of the table where he worked. Though of a very ingenious mechanical turn, Nippers could never get this table to suit him. He put chips under it, blocks of various sorts, bits of pasteboard, and at last went so far as to attempt an exquisite adjustment, by final pieces of folded blotting-paper. But no invention would answer. If, for the sake of easing his back, he brought the table-lid at a sharp angle well up towards his chin, and wrote there like a man using the steep roof of a Dutch house for his desk, then he declared that it stopped the circulation in his arms. If now he lowered the table to his waistbands, and stooped over it in writing, then there was a sore aching in his back. In short, the truth of the matter was, Nippers knew not what he wanted. Or, if he wanted anything, it was to be rid of a scrivener's table altogether. Among the manifestations of his diseased ambition was a fondness he had for receiving visits from certain ambiguous-looking fellows in seedy coats, whom he called his clients. Indeed, I was aware that not only was he, at times, considerable of a ward-politician, but he occasionally did a little business at the Justices' courts, and was not unknown on the steps of the Tombs. I have good reason to believe, however, that one individual who called upon him at my chambers, and who, with a grand air, he insisted was his client, was no other than a dun, and the alleged title-deed, a bill. But, with all his failings, and the annoyances he caused me, Nippers, like his compatriot Turkey, was a very useful man to me; wrote a neat, swift hand; and, when he chose, was not deficient in a gentlemanly sort of deportment. Added to this, he always dressed in a gentlemanly sort of way; and so, incidentally, reflected credit upon my chambers. Whereas, with respect to Turkey, I had much ado to keep him from being a reproach to me. His clothes were apt to look oily, and smell of eating-houses. He wore his pantaloons very loose and baggy in summer. His coats were execrable; his hat not to be handled. But while the hat was a thing of indifference to me, inasmuch as his natural civility and deference, as a dependent Englishman, always led him to doff it the moment he entered the room, yet his coat was another matter. Concerning his coats, I reasoned with him; but with no effect. The truth was, I suppose, that a man with so small an income could not afford to sport such a lustrous face and a lustrous coat at one and the same time. As Nippers once observed, Turkey's money went chiefly for red ink. One winter day, I presented Turkey with a highly respectable-looking coat of my own—a padded gray coat, of a most comfortable warmth, and which buttoned straight up from the knee to the neck. I thought Turkey would appreciate the favor, and abate his rashness and obstreperousness of afternoons. But no; I verily believe that buttoning himself up in so downy and blanket-like a coat had a pernicious effect upon him —upon the same principle that too much oats are bad for horses. In fact, precisely as a rash, restive horse is said to feel his oats, so Turkey felt his coat. It made him insolent. He was a man whom prosperity harmed.

Though, concerning the self-indulgent habits of Turkey, I had my own private surmises, yet touching Nippers, I was well persuaded that, whatever might be his faults in other respects, he was, at least, a temperate young man. But, indeed, nature herself seemed to have been his vintner, and, at his birth, charged him so thoroughly with an irritable, brandy-like disposition, that all subsequent potations were needless. When I consider how, amid the stillness of my chambers, Nippers would sometimes impatiently rise from his seat, and stooping over his table, spread his arms wide apart, seize the whole desk, and move it, and jerk it, with a grim, grinding motion on the floor, as if the table were a perverse voluntary agent, intent on thwarting and vexing him, I plainly perceive that, for Nippers, brandy-and-water were altogether superfluous.

It was fortunate for me that, owing to its peculiar cause—indigestion—the irritability and consequent nervousness of Nippers were mainly observable in the morning, while in the afternoon he was comparatively mild. So that, Turkey's paroxysms only coming on about twelve o'clock, I never had to do with their eccentricities at one time. Their fits relieved each other, like guards. When Nippers's was on, Turkey's was off; and *vice versa*. This was a good natural arrangement, under the circumstances.

Ginger Nut, the third on my list, was a lad, some twelve years old. His father was a carman, ambitious of seeing his son on the bench instead of a cart, before he died. So he sent him to my office, as student at law, errand-boy, cleaner and sweeper, at the rate of one dollar a week. He had a little desk to himself, but he did not use it much. Upon inspection, the drawer exhibited a great array of the shells of various sorts of nuts. Indeed, to this quick-witted youth, the whole noble science of the law was contained in a nutshell. Not the least among the employments of Ginger Nut, as well as one which he discharged with the most alacrity, was his duty as cake and apple purveyor for Turkey and Nippers. Copying law-papers being proverbially a dry, husky sort of business, my two scriveners were fain to moisten their mouths very often with Spitzenbergs, to be had at the numerous stalls nigh the Custom House and Post Office. Also, they sent Ginger Nut very frequently for that peculiar cake—small, flat, round, and very spicy—after which he had been named by them. Of a cold morning, when business was but dull, Turkey would gobble up scores of these cakes, as if they were mere wafers—indeed, they sell them at the rate of six or eight for a penny—the scrape of his pen blending with the crunching of the crisp particles in his mouth. Rashest of all the fiery afternoon blunders and flurried rashnesses of Turkey, was his once moistening a ginger-cake between his lips, and clapping it on to a mortgage, for a seal. I came within an ace of dismissing him then. But he mollified me by making an oriental bow, and saying—

"With submission, sir, it was generous of me to find you in stationery on my own account."

Now my original business—that of a conveyancer and title hunter, and drawer-up of recondite documents of all sorts—was considerably increased by receiving the master's office. There was now great work for scriveners. Not only must I push the clerks already with me, but I must have additional help.

In answer to my advertisement, a motionless young man one morning stood upon my office threshold, the door being open, for it was summer. I can see that figure now—pallidly neat, pitiably respectable, incurably forlorn! It was Bartleby.

After a few words touching his qualifications, I engaged him, glad to have among my corps of copyists a man of so singularly sedate an aspect, which I thought might operate beneficially upon the flighty temper of Turkey, and the fiery one of Nippers.

I should have stated before that ground-glass folding-doors divided my premises into two parts, one of which was occupied by my scriveners, the other by myself. According to my humor, I threw open these doors, or closed them. I resolved to assign Bartleby a corner by the folding-doors, but on my side of them, so as to have this quiet man within easy call, in case any trifling thing was to be done. I placed his desk close up to a small side-window in that part of the room, a window which originally had afforded a lateral view of certain grimy backyards and bricks, but which, owing to

subsequent erections, commanded at present no view at all, though it gave some light. Within three feet of the panes was a wall, and the light came down from far above, between two lofty buildings, as from a very small opening in a dome. Still further to a satisfactory arrangement, I procured a high green folding screen, which might entirely isolate Bartleby from my sight, though not remove him from my voice. And thus, in a manner, privacy and society were conjoined.

At first, Bartleby did an extraordinary quantity of writing. As if long famishing for something to copy, he seemed to gorge himself on my documents. There was no pause for digestion. He ran a day and night line, copying by sunlight and by candle-light. I should have been quite delighted with his application, had he been cheerfully industrious. But he wrote on silently, palely, mechanically.

It is, of course, an indispensable part of a scrivener's business to verify the accuracy of his copy, word by word. Where there are two or more scriveners in an office, they assist each other in this examination, one reading from the copy, the other holding the original. It is a very dull, wearisome, and lethargic affair. I can readily imagine that, to some sanguine temperaments, it would be altogether intolerable. For example, I cannot credit that the mettlesome poet, Byron, would have contentedly sat down with Bartleby to examine a law document of, say five hundred pages, closely written in a crimpy hand.

Now and then, in the haste of business, it had been my habit to assist in comparing some brief document myself, calling Turkey or Nippers for this purpose. One object I had, in placing Bartleby so handy to me behind the screen, was, to avail myself of his services on such trivial occasions. It was on the third day, I think, of his being with me, and before any necessity had arisen for having his own writing examined, that, being much hurried to complete a small affair I had in hand, I abruptly called to Bartleby. In my haste and natural expectancy of instant compliance, I sat with my head bent over the original on my desk, and my right hand sideways, and somewhat nervously extended with the copy, so that, immediately upon emerging from his retreat, Bartleby might snatch it and proceed to business without the least delay.

In this very attitude did I sit when I called to him, rapidly stating what it was I wanted him to do—namely, to examine a small paper with me. Imagine my surprise, nay, my consternation, when, without moving from his privacy, Bartleby, in a singularly mild, firm voice, replied, "I would prefer not to."

I sat awhile in perfect silence, rallying my stunned faculties. Immediately it occurred to me that my ears had deceived me, or Bartleby had entirely misunderstood my meaning. I repeated my request in the clearest tone I could assume; but in quite as clear a one came the previous reply, "I would prefer not to."

"Prefer not to," echoed I, rising in high excitement, and crossing the room with a stride. "What do you mean? Are you moon-struck? I want you to help me compare this sheet here—take it," and I thrust it towards him.

"I would prefer not to," said he.

I looked at him steadfastly. His face was leanly composed; his gray eye dimly calm. Not a wrinkle of agitation rippled him. Had there been the least uneasiness, anger, impatience or impertinence in his manner; in other words, had there been anything ordinarily human about him, doubtless I should have violently dismissed him from the premises. But as it was, I should have as soon thought of turning my pale plaster-of-paris bust of Cicero out of doors. I stood gazing at him awhile, as he went on with his own writing, and then reseated myself at my desk. This is very strange, thought I. What had one best do? But my business hurried me. I concluded to forget the matter for the present, reserving it for my future leisure. So, calling Nippers from the other room, the paper was speedily examined.

A few days after this, Bartleby concluded four lengthy documents, being quadruplicates of a week's testimony taken before me in my High Court of Chancery. It became necessary to examine them. It was an important suit, and great accuracy was imperative. Having all things arranged, I called Turkey, Nippers and Ginger Nut, from the next room, meaning to place the four copies in the hands of my four clerks, while I should read from the original. Accordingly, Turkey, Nippers, and Ginger Nut had taken their seats in a row, each with his document in his hand, when I called to Bartleby to join this interesting group.

"Bartleby! quick, I am waiting."

I heard a slow scrape of his chair legs on the uncarpeted floor, and soon he appeared standing in the entrance of his hermitage.

"What is wanted?" said he, mildly.

"The copies, the copies," said I, hurriedly. "We are going to examine them. There"—and I held towards him the fourth quadruplicate.

"I would prefer not to," he said, and gently disappeared behind the screen.

For a few moments I was turned into a pillar of salt, standing at the head of my seated column of clerks. Recovering myself, I advanced towards the screen, and demanded the reason for such extraordinary conduct.

"*Why* do you refuse?"

"I would prefer not to."

With any other man I should have flown outright into a dreadful passion, scorned all further words, and thrust him ignominiously from my presence. But there was something about Bartleby that not only strangely disarmed me, but, in a wonderful manner, touched and disconcerted me. I began to reason with him.

"These are your own copies we are about to examine. It is labor saving to you, because one examination will answer for your four papers. It is common usage. Every copyist is bound to help examine his copy. Is it not so? Will you not speak? Answer!"

"I prefer not to," he replied in a flute-like tone. It seemed to me that, while I had been addressing him, he carefully revolved every statement that I made; fully comprehended the meaning; could not gainsay the irresistible conclusion; but, at the same time, some paramount consideration prevailed with him to reply as he did.

"You are decided then, not to comply with my request—a request made according to common usage and common sense?"

He briefly gave me to understand that, on that point my judgment was sound. Yes: his decision was irreversible.

It is not seldom the case that, when a man is browbeaten in some unprecedented and violently unreasonable way, he begins to stagger in his own plainest faith. He begins, as it were, vaguely to surmise that, wonderful as it may be, all the justice and all the reason is on the other side. Accordingly, if any disinterested persons are present, he turns to them for some reinforcement for his own faltering mind.

"Turkey," said I, "what do you think of this? Am I not right?"

"With submission, sir," said Turkey, in his blandest tone, "I think that you are."

"Nippers," said I, "what do *you* think of it?"

"I think I should kick him out of the office."

(The reader of nice perceptions will here perceive that, it being morning, Turkey's answer is couched in polite and tranquil terms, but Nippers replies in ill-tempered ones. Or, to repeat a previous sentence, Nippers's ugly mood was on duty, and Turkey's off.)

"Ginger Nut," said I, willing to enlist the smallest suffrage in my behalf, "what do *you* think of it?"

"I think, sir, he's a little *luny*," replied Ginger Nut, with a grin.

"You hear what they say," said I, turning towards the screen, "come forth and do your duty."

But he vouchsafed no reply. I pondered a moment in sore perplexity. But once more business hurried me. I determined again to postpone the consideration of this dilemma to my future leisure. With a little trouble we made out to examine the papers without Bartleby, though at every page or two Turkey deferentially dropped his opinion, that this proceeding was quite out of the common; while Nippers, twitching in his chair with a dyspeptic nervousness, ground out, between his set teeth, occasional hissing maledictions against the stubborn oaf behind the screen. And for his (Nippers's) part, this was the first and the last time he would do another man's business without pay.

Meanwhile Bartleby sat in his hermitage, oblivious to everything but his own peculiar business there.

Some days passed, the scrivener being employed upon another lengthy work. His late remarkable conduct led me to regard his ways narrowly. I observed that he never went to dinner; indeed, that he never went anywhere. As yet I had never, of my personal knowledge, known him to be outside of my office. He was a perpetual sentry in the corner. At about eleven o'clock though, in the morning, I noticed that Ginger Nut would advance toward the opening in Bartleby's screen, as if silently beckoned thither by a gesture invisible to me where I sat. The boy would then leave the office, jingling a few pence, and reappear with a handful of ginger-nuts, which he delivered in the hermitage, receiving two of the cakes for his trouble.

He lives, then, on ginger-nuts, thought I; never eats a dinner, properly speaking; he must be a vegetarian, then; but no; he never eats even vegetables, he eats nothing but ginger-nuts. My mind then ran on in reveries concerning the probable effects upon the human constitution of living entirely on ginger-nuts. Ginger-nuts are so called, because they contain ginger as one of their peculiar constituents, and the final flavoring one. Now, what was ginger? A hot, spicy thing. Was Bartleby hot and spicy? Not at all. Ginger, then, had no effect upon Bartleby. Probably he preferred it should have none.

Nothing so aggravates an earnest person as a passive resistance. If the individual so resisted be of a not inhuman temper, and the resisting one perfectly harmless in his passivity, then, in the better moods of the former, he will endeavor charitably to construe to his imagination what proves impossible to be solved by his judgment. Even so, for the most part, I regarded Bartleby and his ways. Poor fellow! thought I, he means no mischief; it is plain he intends no insolence; his aspect sufficiently evinces that his eccentricities are involuntary. He is useful to me. I can get along with him. If I turn him away, the chances are he will fall in with some less indulgent employer, and then he will be rudely treated, and perhaps driven forth miserably to starve. Yes. Here I can cheaply purchase a delicious self-approval. To befriend Bartleby; to humor him in his strange wilfulness, will cost me little or nothing, while I lay up in my soul what will eventually prove a sweet morsel for my conscience. But this mood was not invariable with me. The passiveness of Bartleby sometimes irritated me. I felt strangely goaded on to encounter him in new opposition— to elicit some angry spark from him answerable to my own. But, indeed, I might as well have essayed to strike fire with my knuckles against a bit of Windsor soap. But one afternoon the evil impulse in me mastered me, and the following little scene ensued:

"Bartleby," said I, "when those papers are all copied, I will compare them with you."

"I would prefer not to."

"How? Surely you do not mean to persist in that mulish vagary?"

No answer.

I threw open the folding-doors near by, and, turning upon Turkey and Nippers, exclaimed:

"Bartleby a second time says, he won't examine his papers. What do you think of it, Turkey?"

It was afternoon, be it remembered. Turkey sat glowing like a brass boiler; his bald head steaming; his hands reeling among his blotted papers.

"Think of it?" roared Turkey. "I think I'll just step behind his screen, and black his eyes for him!"

So saying, Turkey rose to his feet and threw his arms into a pugilistic position. He was hurrying away to make good his promise, when I detained him, alarmed at the effect of incautiously rousing Turkey's combativeness after dinner.

"Sit down, Turkey," said I, "and hear what Nippers has to say. What do you think of it, Nippers?

Would I not be justified in immediately dismissing Bartleby?"

"Excuse me, that is for you to decide, sir. I think his conduct quite unusual, and, indeed, unjust, as regards Turkey and myself. But it may only be a passing whim."

"Ah," exclaimed I, "you have strangely changed your mind, then—you speak very gently of him now."

"All beer," cried Turkey; "gentleness is effects of beer—Nippers and I dined together to-day. You see how gentle I am, sir. Shall I go and black his eyes?"

"You refer to Bartleby, I suppose. No, not to-day, Turkey," I replied; "pray, put up your fists."

I closed the doors, and again advanced towards Bartleby. I felt additional incentives tempting me to my fate. I burned to be rebelled against again. I remembered that Bartleby never left the office.

"Bartleby," said I, "Ginger Nut is away; just step around to the Post Office, won't you?" (it was but a three minutes' walk) "and see if there is anything for me."

"I would prefer not to."

"You *will* not?"

"I *prefer* not."

I staggered to my desk, and sat there in a deep study. My blind inveteracy returned. Was there any other thing in which I could procure myself to be ignominiously repulsed by this lean, penniless wight?—my hired clerk? What added thing is there, perfectly reasonable, that he will be sure to refuse to do?

"Bartleby!"

No answer.

"Bartleby," in a louder tone.

No answer.

"Bartleby," I roared.

Like a very ghost, agreeably to the laws of magical invocation, at the third summons, he appeared at the entrance of his hermitage.

"Go to the next room, and tell Nippers to come to me."

"I prefer not to," he respectfully and slowly said, and mildly disappeared.

"Very good, Bartleby," said I, in a quiet sort of serenely-severe self-possessed tone, intimating the unalterable purpose of some terrible retribution very close at hand. At the moment I half intended something of the kind. But upon the whole, as it was drawing towards my dinner-hour, I thought it best to put on my hat and walk home for the day, suffering much from perplexity and distress of mind.

Shall I acknowledge it? The conclusion of this whole business was, that it soon became a fixed fact of my chambers, that a pale young scrivener, by the name of Bartleby, had a desk there; that he copied for me at the usual rate of four cents a folio (one hundred words); but he was permanently exempt from examining the work done by him, that duty being transferred to Turkey and Nippers, out of compliment, doubtless, to their superior acuteness; moreover, said Bartleby was never, on any account, to be dispatched on the most trivial errand of any sort; and that even if entreated to take upon him such a matter, it was generally understood that he would "prefer not to"—in other words, that he would refuse point-blank.

As days passed on, I became considerably reconciled to Bartleby. His steadiness, his freedom from all dissipation, his incessant industry (except when he chose to throw himself into a standing revery behind his screen), his great stillness, his unalterableness of demeanor under all circumstances, made him a valuable acquisition. One prime thing was this—*he was always there*—first in the morning, continually through the day, and the last at night. I had a singular confidence in his honesty. I felt my most precious papers perfectly safe in his hands. Sometimes, to be sure, I could not, for the very soul of me, avoid falling into sudden spasmodic passions with him. For it was exceeding difficult to bear in mind all the time those strange peculiarities, privileges, and unheard-of exemptions, forming the tacit stipulations on Bartleby's part under which he remained in my office. Now and then, in the eagerness of dispatching pressing business, I would inadvertently summon Bartleby, in a short, rapid tone, to put his finger, say, on the incipient tie of a bit of red tape with which I was about compressing some papers. Of course, from behind the screen the usual answer, "I prefer not to," was sure to come; and then, how could a human creature, with the common infirmities of our nature, refrain from bitterly exclaiming upon such perverseness—such unreasonableness? However, every added repulse of this sort which I received only tended to lessen the probability of my repeating the inadvertence.

Here it must be said, that, according to the custom of most legal gentlemen occupying chambers in densely-populated law buildings, there were several keys to my door. One was kept by a woman residing in the attic, which person weekly scrubbed and daily swept and dusted my apartments. Another was kept by Turkey for convenience sake. The third I sometimes carried in my own pocket. The fourth I knew not who had.

Now, one Sunday morning I happened to go to Trinity Church, to hear a celebrated preacher, and finding myself rather early on the ground I thought I would walk round to my chambers for a while. Luckily I had my key with me; but upon applying it to the lock, I found it resisted by something inserted from the inside. Quite surprised, I called out; when to my consternation a key was turned from within; and thrusting his lean visage at me, and holding the door ajar, the apparition of Bartleby appeared, in his shirt-sleeves, and otherwise in a strangely tattered *déshabillé,* saying quietly that he was sorry, but he was deeply engaged just then, and—preferred not admitting me at present. In a brief word or two, he moreover added, that perhaps I had better walk round the block two or three times, and by that time he would probably have concluded his affairs.

Now, the utterly unsurmised appeareance of Bartleby, tenanting my law-chambers of a Sunday morning, with his cadaverously gentlemanly *nonchalance,* yet withal firm and self-possessed, had such a strange effect upon me, that incontinently I slunk away from my own door, and did as desired. But not without sundry twinges of impotent rebellion against the mild effrontery of this unaccountable scrivener. Indeed, it was his wonderful mildness chiefly, which not only disarmed me, but unmanned me, as it were. For I consider that one, for the time, is a sort of unmanned when he tranquilly permits his hired clerk to dictate to him, and order him away from his own premises. Furthermore, I was full of uneasiness as to what Bartleby could possibly be doing in my office in his shirt-sleeves, and in an otherwise dismantled condition of a Sunday morning. Was anything amiss going on? Nay, that was out of the question. It was not to be thought of for a moment that Bartleby was an immoral person. But what could he be doing there?—copying? Nay again, whatever might be his eccentricities, Bartleby was an eminently decorous person. He would be the last man to sit down to his desk in any state approaching to nudity. Besides, it was Sunday; and there was something about Bartleby that forbade the supposition that he would by any secular occupation violate the proprieties of the day.

Nevertheless, my mind was not pacified; and full of a restless curiosity, at last I returned to the door. Without hindrance I inserted my key, opened it, and entered. Bartleby was not to be seen. I looked round anxiously, peeped behind his screen; but it was very plain that he was gone. Upon more closely examining the place, I surmised that for an indefinite period Bartleby must have eaten, dressed, and slept in my office, and that too without plate, mirror, or bed. The cushioned seat of a rickety old sofa in one corner bore the faint impress of a lean, reclining form. Rolled away under his desk, I found a blanket; under the empty grate, a blacking box and brush; on a chair, a tin basin, with soap and a ragged towel; in a newspaper a few crumbs of ginger-nuts and a morsel of cheese. Yes, thought I, it is evident enough that Bartleby has been making his home here, keeping bachelor's hall all by himself. Immediately then the thought came sweeping across me, what miserable friendlessness and loneliness are here revealed! His poverty is great; but his solitude, how horrible! Think of it. Of a Sunday, Wall Street is deserted as Petra; and every night of every day it is an emptiness. This building, too, which of week-days hums with industry and life, at nightfall echoes with sheer vacancy, and all through Sunday is forlorn. And here Bartleby makes his home; sole spectator of a solitude which he has seen all populous—a sort of innocent and transformed Marius brooding among the ruins of Carthage!

For the first time in my life a feeling of overpowering stinging melancholy seized me. Before, I had never experienced aught but a not unpleasing sadness. The bond of a common humanity now drew me irresistibly to gloom. A fraternal melancholy! For both I and Bartleby were sons of Adam. I remembered the bright silks and sparkling faces I had seen that day, in gala trim, swan-like sailing down the Mississippi of Broadway; and I contrasted them with the pallid copyist, and thought to myself, Ah, happiness courts the light, so we deem the world is gay; but misery hides aloof, so we deem that misery there is none. These sad fancyings—chimeras, doubtless, of a sick and silly brain—led on to other and more special thoughts, concerning the eccentricities of Bartleby. Presentiments of strange discoveries hovered round me. The scrivener's pale form appeared to me laid out, among uncaring strangers, in its shivering winding-sheet.

Suddenly I was attracted by Bartleby's closed desk, the key in open sight left in the lock.

I mean no mischief, seek the gratification of no heartless curiosity, thought I; besides, the desk is mine, and its contents, too, so I will make bold to look within. Everything was methodically arranged, the papers smoothly placed. The pigeon-holes were deep, and removing the files of documents, I groped into their recesses. Presently I felt something there, and dragged it out. It was an old bandanna handkerchief, heavy and knotted. I opened it, and saw it was a saving's bank.

I now recalled all the quiet mysteries which I had noted in the man. I remembered that he never spoke but to answer; that, though at intervals he had considerable time to himself, yet I had never seen him reading—no, not even a newspaper; that for long periods he would stand looking out, at his pale window behind the screen, upon the dead brick wall; I was quite sure he never visited any refectory or eating-house; while his pale face clearly indicated that he never drank beer like Turkey, or tea and coffee even, like other men; that he never went anywhere in particular that I could learn; never went out for a walk, unless, indeed, that was the case at present; that he had declined telling who he was, or whence he came, or whether he had any relatives in the world; that though so thin and pale, he never complained of ill-health. And more than all, I remembered a certain unconscious air of pallid —how shall I call it?—of pallid haughtiness, say, or rather an austere reserve about him, which had positively awed me into my tame compliance with his eccentricities, when I had feared to ask him to do the slightest incidental thing for me, even though I might know, from his long-continued motionlessness, that behind his screen he must be standing in one of those dead-wall reveries of his.

Revolving all these things, and coupling them with the recently discovered fact, that he made my office his constant abiding place and home, and not forgetful of his morbid moodiness; revolving all these things, a prudential feeling began to steal over me. My first emotions had been those of pure melancholy and sincerest pity; but just in proportion as the forlornness of Bartleby grew and grew to my imagination, did that same melancholy merge into fear, that pity into repulsion. So true it is, and so terrible, too, that up to a certain point the thought or sight of misery enlists our best affections; but, in certain special cases, beyond that point it does not. They err who would assert that invariably this is owing to the inherent selfishness of the human heart. It rather proceeds from a certain hopelessness of remedying excessive and organic ill. To a sensitive being, pity is not seldom pain. And when at last it is perceived that such pity cannot lead to effectual succor, common sense bids the soul be rid of it. What I saw that morning persuaded me that the scrivener was the victim of innate and incurable disorder. I might give alms to his body;

but his body did not pain him; it was his soul that suffered, and his soul I could not reach.

I did not accomplish the purpose of going to Trinity Church that morning. Somehow, the things I had seen disqualified me for the time from churchgoing. I walked homeward, thinking what I would do with Bartleby. Finally, I resolved upon this—I would put certain calm questions to him the next morning, touching his history, etc., and if he declined to answer them openly and unreservedly (and I supposed he would prefer not), then to give him a twenty dollar bill over and above whatever I might owe him, and tell him his services were no longer required; but that if in any other way I could assist him, I would be happy to do so, especially if he desired to return to his native place, wherever that might be, I would willingly help to defray the expenses. Moreover, if, after reaching home, he found himself at any time in want of aid, a letter from him would be sure of a reply.

The next morning came.

"Bartleby," said I, gently calling to him behind his screen.

No reply.

"Bartleby," said I, in a still gentler tone, "come here; I am not going to ask you to do anything you would prefer not to do—I simply wish to speak to you."

Upon this he noiselessly slid into view.

"Will you tell me, Bartleby, where you were born?"

"I would prefer not to."

"Will you tell me *anything* about yourself?"

"I would prefer not to."

"But what reasonable objection can you have to speak to me? I feel friendly towards you."

He did not look at me while I spoke, but kept his glance fixed upon my bust of Cicero, which, as I then sat, was directly behind me, some six inches above my head.

"What is your answer, Bartleby?" said I, after waiting a considerable time for a reply, during which his countenance remained immovable, only there was the faintest conceivable tremor of the white attenuated mouth.

"At present I prefer to give no answer," he said, and retired into his hermitage.

It was rather weak in me I confess, but his manner, on this occasion, nettled me. Not only did there seem to lurk in it a certain calm disdain, but his perverseness seemed ungrateful, considering the undeniable good usage and indulgence he had received from me.

Again I sat ruminating what I should do. Mortified as I was at his behavior, and resolved as I had been to dismiss him when I entered my office, nevertheless I strangely felt something superstitious knocking at my heart, and forbidding me to carry out my purpose, and denouncing me for a villain if I dared to breathe one bitter word against this forlornest of mankind. At last, familiarly drawing my chair behind his screen, I sat down and said: "Bartleby, never mind, then, about revealing your history; but let me entreat you, as a friend, to comply as far as may be with the usages of this office. Say now, you will help to examine papers to-morrow or next day: in short, say now, that in a day or two you will begin to be a little reasonable: —say so, Bartleby."

"At present I would prefer not to be a little reasonable," was his mildly cadaverous reply.

Just then the folding-doors opened, and Nippers approached. He seemed suffering from an unusually bad night's rest, induced by severer indigestion than common. He overheard those final words of Bartleby.

"*Prefer not,* eh?" gritted Nippers—"I'd *prefer* him, if I were you, sir," addressing me—"I'd *prefer* him; I'd give him preferences, the stubborn mule! What is it, sir, pray, that he *prefers* not to do now?"

Bartleby moved not a limb.

"Mr. Nippers," said I, "I'd prefer that you would withdraw for the present."

Somehow, of late, I had got into the way of involuntarily using this word "prefer" upon all sorts of not exactly suitable occasions. And I trembled to think that my contact with the scrivener had already and seriously affected me in a mental way. And what further and deeper aberration might it not yet produce? This apprehension had not been without efficacy in determining me to summary measures.

As Nippers, looking very sour and sulky, was departing, Turkey blandly and deferentially approached.

"With submission, sir," said he, "yesterday I was thinking about Bartleby here, and I think that if he would but prefer to take a quart of good ale every day, it would do much towards mending him, and enabling him to assist in examining his papers."

"So you have got the word, too," said I, slightly excited.

"With submission, what word, sir?" asked Turkey, respectfully crowding himself into the contracted space behind the screen, and by so doing, making me jostle the scrivener. "What word, sir?"

"I would prefer to be left alone here," said Bartleby, as if offended at being mobbed in his privacy.

"*That's* the word, Turkey," said I—"*that's* it."

"Oh, *prefer?* oh yes—queer word. I never use it myself. But, sir, as I was saying, if he would but prefer—"

"Turkey," interrupted I, "you will please withdraw."

"Oh certainly, sir, if you prefer that I should."

As he opened the folding-door to retire, Nippers at his desk caught a glimpse of me, and asked whether I would prefer to have a certain paper copied on blue paper or white. He did not in the least roguishly accent the word "prefer." It was plain that it involuntarily rolled from his tongue. I thought to myself, surely I must get rid of a demented man, who already has in some degree turned the tongues, if not the heads of myself and clerks. But I thought it prudent not to break the dismission at once.

The next day I noticed that Bartleby did nothing but stand at his window in his dead-wall revery. Upon asking him why he did not write, he said that he had decided upon doing no more writing.

"Why, how now? what next?" exclaimed I, "do no more writing?"

"No more."

"And what is the reason?"

"Do you not see the reason for yourself?" he indifferently replied.

I looked steadfastly at him, and perceived that his eyes looked dull and glazed. Instantly it occurred to me, that his unexampled diligence in copying by his dim window for the first few weeks of his stay with me might have temporarily impaired his vision.

I was touched. I said something in condolence with him. I hinted that of course he did wisely in abstaining from writing for a while; and urged him to embrace that opportunity of taking wholesome exercise in the open air. This, however, he did not do. A few days after this, my other clerks being absent, and being in a great hurry to dispatch certain letters by the mail, I thought that, having nothing else earthly to do, Bartleby would surely be less inflexible than usual, and carry these letters to the postoffice. But he blankly declined. So, much to my inconvenience, I went myself.

Still added days went by. Whether Bartleby's eyes improved or not, I could not say. To all appearance, I thought they did. But when I asked him if they did, he vouchsafed no answer. At all events, he would do no copying. At last, in reply to my urgings, he informed me that he had permanently given up copying.

"What!" exclaimed I; "suppose your eyes should get entirely well—better than ever before—would you not copy then?"

"I have given up copying," he answered, and slid aside.

He remained as ever, a fixture in my chamber. Nay—if that were possible—he became still more of a fixture than before. What was to be done? He would do nothing in the office; why should he stay there? In plain fact, he had now become a millstone to me, not only useless as a necklace, but afflictive to bear. Yet I was sorry for him. I speak less than truth when I say that, on his own account, he occasioned me uneasiness. If he would but have named a single relative or friend, I would instantly have written, and urged their taking the poor fellow away to some convenient retreat. But he seemed alone, absolutely alone in the universe. A bit of wreck in the mid-Atlantic. At length, necessities connected with my business tyrannized over all other considerations. Decently as I could, I told Bartleby that in six days' time he must unconditionally leave the office. I warned him to take measures, in the interval, for procuring some other abode. I offered to assist him in this endeavor, if he himself would but take the first step towards a removal. "And when you finally quit me, Bartleby," added I, "I shall see that you go not away entirely unprovided. Six days from this hour, remember."

At the expiration of that period, I peeped behind the screen, and lo! Bartleby was there.

I buttoned up my coat, balanced myself; advanced slowly towards him, touched his shoulder, and said, "The time has come; you must quit this place; I am sorry for you; here is money; but you must go."

"I would prefer not," he replied, with his back still towards me.

"You *must*."

He remained silent.

Now I had an unbounded confidence in this man's common honesty. He had frequently restored to me sixpences and shillings carelessly dropped upon the floor, for I am apt to be very reckless in such shirt-button affairs. The proceeding, then, which followed will not be deemed extraordinary.

"Bartleby," said I, "I owe you twelve dollars on account; here are thirty-two; the odd twenty are yours—Will you take it?" and I handed the bills towards him.

But he made no motion.

"I will leave them here, then," putting them under a weight on the table. Then taking my hat and cane and going to the door, I tranquilly turned and added—"After you have removed your things from these offices, Bartleby, you will of course lock the door—since every one is now gone for the day but you—and if you please, slip your key underneath the mat, so that I may have it in the morning. I shall not see you again; so good-bye to you. If, hereafter, in your new place of abode, I can be of any service to you, do not fail to advise me by letter. Good-bye, Bartleby, and fare you well."

But he answered not a word; like the last column of some ruined temple, he remained standing mute and solitary in the middle of the otherwise deserted room.

As I walked home in a pensive mood, my vanity got the better of my pity. I could not but highly plume myself on my masterly management in getting rid of Bartleby. Masterly I call it, and such it must appear to any dispassionate thinker. The beauty of my procedure seemed to consist in its perfect quietness. There was no vulgar bullying, no bravado of any sort, no choleric hectoring, and striding to and fro across the apartment, jerking out vehement commands for Bartleby to bundle himself off with his beggarly traps. Nothing of the kind. Without loudly bidding Bartleby depart—as an inferior genius might have done—I *assumed* the ground that depart he must; and upon that assumption built all I had to say. The more I thought over my procedure, the more I was charmed with it. Nevertheless, next morning, upon awakening, I had my doubts—I had somehow slept off the fumes of vanity. One of the coolest and wisest hours a man has, is just after he awakes in the morning. My procedure seemed as sagacious as ever—but only in theory. How it would prove in practice—there was the rub. It was truly a beautiful thought to have assumed Bartleby's departure; but, after all, that assumption was simply my own, and none of Bartleby's. The great point was, not whether I had assumed that he would quit me, but whether he would prefer so to do. He was more a man of preferences than assumptions.

After breakfast, I walked down town, arguing the probabilities *pro* and *con*. One moment I thought it would prove a miserable failure, and Bartleby would be found all alive at my office as usual; the next moment it seemed certain that I should find his chair empty. And so I kept veering about. At the corner of Broadway and Canal Street, I saw quite an excited group of people standing in earnest conversation.

"I'll take odds he doesn't," said a voice as I passed.

"Doesn't go?—done!" said I, "put up your money."

I was instinctively putting my hand in my pocket to produce my own, when I remembered that this was an election day. The words I had overheard bore no reference to Bartleby, but to the success or non-success of some candidate for the mayoralty. In my intent frame of mind, I had, as it were, imagined that all Broadway shared in my excitement, and were debating the same question with me. I passed on, very thankful that the uproar of the street screened my momentary absent-mindedness.

As I had intended, I was earlier than usual at my office door. I stood listening for a moment. All was still. He must be gone. I tried the knob. The door was locked. Yes, my procedure had worked to a charm; he indeed must be vanished. Yet a certain melancholy mixed with this: I was almost sorry for my brilliant success. I was fumbling under the door mat for the key, which Bartleby was to have left there for me, when accidentally my knee knocked against a panel, producing a summoning sound, and in response a voice came to me from within—"Not yet; I am occupied."

It was Bartleby.

I was thunderstruck. For an instant I stood like the man who, pipe in mouth, was killed one cloudless afternoon long ago in Virginia, by summer lightning; at his own warm open window he was killed, and remained leaning out there upon the dreamy afternoon, till some one touched him, when he fell.

"Not gone!" I murmured at last. But again obeying that wondrous ascendancy which the inscrutable scrivener had over me, and from which ascendancy, for all my chafing, I could not completely escape, I slowly went down stairs and out into the street, and while walking round the block, considered what I should next do in this unheard-of perplexity. Turn the man out by an actual thrusting I could not; to drive him away by calling him hard names would not do; calling in the police was an unpleasant idea; and yet, permit him to enjoy his cadaverous triumph over me—this, too, I could not think of. What was to be done? or, if nothing could be done, was there anything further that I could *assume* in the matter? Yes, as before I had prospectively assumed that Bartleby would depart, so now I might retrospectively assume that departed he was. In the legitimate carrying out of this assumption, I might enter my office in a great hurry, and pretending not to see Bartleby at all, walk straight against him as if he were air. Such a proceeding would in a singular degree have the appearance of a home-thrust. It was hardly possible that Bartleby could withstand such an application of the doctrine of assumptions. But upon second thoughts the success of the plan seemed rather dubious. I resolved to argue the matter over with him again.

"Bartleby," said I, entering the office, with a quietly severe expression, "I am seriously displeased. I am pained, Bartleby. I had thought better of you. I had imagined you of such a gentlemanly organization, that in any delicate dilemma a slight hint would suffice—in short, an assumption. But it appears I am deceived. Why," I added, unaffectedly starting, "you have not even touched that money yet," pointing to it, just where I had left it the evening previous.

He answered nothing.

"Will you, or will you not, quit me?" I now demanded in a sudden passion, advancing close to him.

"I would prefer *not* to quit you," he replied, gently emphasizing the *not*.

"What earthly right have you to stay here? Do you pay any rent? Do you pay my taxes? Or is this property yours?"

He answered nothing.

"Are you ready to go on and write now? Are your eyes recovered? Could you copy a small paper for me this morning? or help examine a few lines? or step round to the post-office? In a word, will you do anything at all, to give a coloring to your refusal to depart the premises?"

He silently retired into his hermitage.

I was now in such a state of nervous resentment that I thought it but prudent to check myself at present from further demonstrations. Bartleby and I were alone. I remembered the tragedy of the unfortunate Adams and the still more unfortunate Colt in the solitary office of the latter; and how poor Colt, being dreadfully incensed by Adams, and imprudently permitting himself to get wildly excited, was at unawares hurried into his fatal act—an act which certainly no man could possibly deplore more than the actor himself. Often it had occurred to me in my ponderings upon the subject that had that altercation taken place in the public street, or at a private residence, it would not have terminated as it did. It was the circumstance of being alone in a solitary office, up stairs, of a building entirely unhallowed by humanizing domestic associations— an uncarpeted office, doubtless, of a dusty, haggard sort of appearance—this it must have been, which greatly helped to enhance the irritable desperation of the hapless Colt.

But when this old Adam of resentment rose in me and tempted me concerning Bartleby, I grappled him and threw him. How? Why, simply by recalling the divine injunction: "A new commandment give I unto you, that ye love one another." Yes, this it was that saved me. Aside from higher considerations, charity often operates as a vastly wise and prudent principle—a great safeguard to its possessor. Men have committed murder for jealousy's sake, and anger's sake, and hatred's sake, and selfishness' sake, and spiritual pride's sake; but no man, that ever I heard of, ever committed a diabolical murder for sweet charity's sake. Mere self-interest, then, if no better motive can be enlisted, should, especially with high-tempered men, prompt all beings to charity and philanthropy. At any rate, upon the occasion in question, I strove to drown my exasperated feelings towards the scrivener by benevolently construing his conduct. Poor fellow, poor fellow! thought I, he don't mean anything; and besides, he has seen hard times, and ought to be indulged.

I endeavored, also, immediately to occupy myself, and at the same time to comfort my despondency. I tried to fancy, that in the course of the morning, at such time as might prove agreeable to him, Bartleby, of his own free accord, would emerge from his hermitage and take up some decided line of march in the direction of the door. But no. Half-past twelve o'clock came; Turkey began to glow in the face, overturn his inkstand, and become generally obstreperous; Nippers abated down into quietude and courtesy; Ginger Nut munched his noon apple; and Bartleby remained standing at his window in one of his profoundest dead-wall reveries. Will it be credited? Ought I to acknowledge it? That afternoon I left the office without saying one further word to him.

Some days now passed, during which, at leisure intervals I looked a little into "Edwards on the Will," and "Priestley on Necessity." Under the circumstances, those books induced a salutary feeling. Gradually I slid into the persuasion that these troubles of mine, touching the scrivener, had been all predestinated from eternity, and Bartleby was billeted upon me for some mysterious purpose of an all-wise Providence, which it was not for a mere mortal like me to fathom. Yes, Bartleby, stay there behind your screen, thought I; I shall persecute you no more; you are harmless and noiseless as any of these old chairs; in short, I never feel so private as when I know you are here. At last I see it, I feel it; I penetrate to the predestinated purpose of my life. I am content. Others may have loftier parts to enact; but my mission in this world, Bartleby, is to furnish you with office-room for such period as you may see fit to remain.

I believe that this wise and blessed frame of mind would have continued with me, had it not been for the unsolicited and uncharitable remarks obtruded upon me by my professional friends who visited the rooms. But thus it often is, that the constant friction of illiberal minds wears out at last the best resolves of the more generous. Though to be sure, when I reflected upon it, it was not strange that people entering my office should be struck by the peculiar aspect of the unaccountable Bartleby, and so be tempted to throw out some sinister observations concerning him. Sometimes an attorney, having business with me, and calling at my office, and finding no one but the scrivener there, would undertake to obtain some sort of precise information from him touching my whereabouts; but without heeding his idle talk, Bartleby would remain standing immovable in the middle of the room. So after contemplating him in that position for a time, the attorney would depart, no wiser than he came.

Also, when a reference was going on, and the room full of lawyers and witnesses, and business driving fast, some deeply-occupied legal gentleman present, seeing Bartleby wholly unemployed, would request him to run round to his (the legal gentleman's) office and fetch some papers for him. Thereupon, Bartleby would tranquilly decline, and yet remain idle as before. Then the lawyer would give a great stare, and turn to me. And what could I say? At last I was made aware that all through the circle of my professional acquaintance, a whisper of wonder was running round, having reference to the strange creature I kept at my office. This worried me very much. And as the idea came upon me of his possibly turning out a long-lived man, and keep occupying my chambers, and denying my authority; and perplexing my visitors; and scandalizing my professional reputation; and casting a general gloom over the premises; keeping soul and body together to the last upon his savings (for doubtless he spent but half a dime a day), and in the end perhaps outlive me, and claim possession of my office by right of his perpetual occupancy: as all these dark anticipations crowded upon me more and more, and my friends continually intruded their relentless remarks upon the apparition in my room; a great change was wrought in me. I resolved to gather all my faculties together, and forever rid me of this intolerable incubus.

Ere revolving any complicated project, however, adapted to this end, I first simply suggested to Bartleby the propriety of his permanent departure. In a calm and serious tone, I commended the idea to his careful and mature consideration. But, having taken three days to meditate upon it, he apprised me, that his original determination remained the same; in short, that he still preferred to abide with me.

What shall I do? I now said to myself, buttoning up my coat to the last button. What shall I do? what ought I to do? what does conscience say I *should* do with this man, or, rather, ghost. Rid myself of him, I must; go, he shall. But how? You will not thrust him, the poor, pale, passive mortal—you will not thrust such a helpless creature out of your door? you will not dishonor yourself by such cruelty? No, I will not, I cannot do that. Rather would I let him live and die here, and then mason up his remains in the wall. What, then, will you do? For all your coaxing, he will not budge. Bribes he leaves under your own paperweight on your table; in short, it is quite plain that he prefers to cling to you.

Then something severe, something unusual must be done. What! surely you will not have him collared by a constable, and commit his innocent pallor to the common jail? And upon what ground could you procure such a thing to be done?—a vagrant, is he? What! he a vagrant, a wanderer, who refuses to budge? It is because he will *not* be a vagrant, then, that you seek to count him *as* a vagrant. That is too absurd. No visible means of support: there I have him. Wrong again: for indubitably he *does* support himself, and that is the only unanswerable proof that any man can show of his possessing the means so to do. No more, then. Since he will not quit me, I must quit him. I will change my offices; I will move elsewhere, and give him fair notice, that if I find him on my new premises I will then proceed against him as a common trespasser.

Acting accordingly, next day I thus addressed him: "I find these chambers too far from the City Hall; the air is unwholesome. In a word, I propose to remove my offices next week, and shall no longer require your services. I tell you this now, in order that you may seek another place."

He made no reply, and nothing more was said.

On the appointed day I engaged carts and men, proceeded to my chambers, and, having but little furniture, everything was removed in a few hours. Throughout, the scrivener remained standing behind the screen, which I directed to be removed the last thing. It was withdrawn; and, being folded up like a huge folio, left him the motionless occupant of a naked room. I stood in the entry watching him a moment, while something from within me upbraided me.

I re-entered, with my hand in my pocket—and—and my heart in my mouth.

"Good-bye, Bartleby; I am going—good-bye, and God some way bless you; and take that," slipping something in his hand. But it dropped upon the floor, and then—strange to say—I tore myself from him whom I had so longed to be rid of.

Established in my new quarters, for a day or two I kept the door locked, and started at every footfall in the passages. When I returned to my rooms, after any little absence, I would pause at the threshold for an instant, and attentively listen, ere applying my key. But these fears were needless. Bartleby never came nigh me.

I thought all was going well, when a perturbed-looking stranger visited me, inquiring whether I was the person who had recently occupied rooms at No. — Wall Street.

Full of forebodings, I replied that I was.

"Then, sir," said the stranger, who proved a lawyer, "you are responsible for the man you left there. He refuses to do any copying; he refuses to do anything; he says he prefers not to; and he refuses to quit the premises."

"I am very sorry, sir," said I, with assumed tranquillity, but an inward tremor, "but, really, the man you allude to is nothing to me—he is no relation or apprentice of mine, that you should hold me responsible for him."

"In mercy's name, who is he?"

"I certainly cannot inform you. I know nothing about him. Formerly I employed him as a copyist; but he has done nothing for me now for some time past."

"I shall settle him, then—good morning, sir."

Several days passed, and I heard nothing more; and, though I often felt a charitable prompting to call at the place and see poor Bartleby, yet a certain squeamishness, of I know not what, withheld me.

All is over with him, by this time, thought I, at

last, when, through another week, no further intelligence reached me. But, coming to my room the day after, I found several persons waiting at my door in a high state of nervous excitement.

"That's the man—here he comes," cried the foremost one, whom I recognized as the lawyer who had previously called upon me alone.

"You must take him away, sir, at once," cried a portly person among them, advancing upon me, and whom I knew to be the landlord of No. — Wall Street. "These gentlemen, my tenants, cannot stand it any longer; Mr. B——," pointing to the lawyer, "has turned him out of his room, and he now persists in haunting the building generally, sitting upon the banisters of the stairs by day, and sleeping in the entry by night. Everybody is concerned; clients are leaving the offices; some fears are entertained of a mob; something you must do, and that without delay."

Aghast at this torrent, I fell back before it, and would fain have locked myself in my new quarters. In vain I persisted that Bartleby was nothing to me —no more than to any one else. In vain—I was the last person known to have anything to do with him, and they held me to the terrible account. Fearful, then, of being exposed in the papers (as one person present obscurely threatened), I considered the matter, and, at length, said, that if the lawyer would give me a confidential interview with the scrivener, in his (the lawyer's) own room, I would, that afternoon, strive my best to rid them of the nuisance they complained of.

Going up stairs to my old haunt, there was Bartleby silently sitting upon the banister at the landing.

"What are you doing here, Bartleby?" said I.

"Sitting upon the banister," he mildly replied.

I motioned him into the lawyer's room, who then left us.

"Bartleby," said I, "are you aware that you are the cause of great tribulation to me, by persisting in occupying the entry after being dismissed from the office?"

No answer.

"Now one of two things must take place. Either you must do something, or something must be done to you. Now what sort of business would you like to engage in? Would you like to re-engage in copying for some one?"

"No; I would prefer not to make any change."

"Would you like a clerkship in a dry-goods store?"

"There is too much confinement about that. No,

I would not like a clerkship; but I am not particular."

"Too much confinement," I cried, "why, you keep yourself confined all the time!"

"I would prefer not to take a clerkship," he rejoined, as if to settle that little item at once.

"How would a bar-tender's business suit you? There is no trying of the eye-sight in that."

"I would not like it at all; though, as I said before, I am not particular."

His unwonted wordiness inspirited me. I returned to the charge.

"Well, then, would you like to travel through the country collecting bills for the merchants? That would improve your health."

"No, I would prefer to be doing something else."

"How, then, would going as a companion to Europe, to entertain some young gentleman with your conversation—how would that suit you?"

"Not at all. It does not strike me that there is anything definite about that. I like to be stationary. But I am not particular."

"Stationary you shall be, then," I cried, now losing all patience, and, for the first time in all my exasperating connection with him, fairly flying into a passion. "If you do not go away from these premises before night, I shall feel bound—indeed, I *am* bound—to—to—to quit the premises myself!" I rather absurdly concluded, knowing not with what possible threat to try to frighten his immobility into compliance. Despairing of all further efforts, I was precipitately leaving him, when a final thought occurred to me—one which had not been wholly unindulged before.

"Bartleby," said I, in the kindest tone I could assume under such exciting circumstances, "will you go home with me now—not to my office, but my dwelling—and remain there till we can conclude upon some convenient arrangement for you at our leisure? Come, let us start now, right away."

"No: at present I would prefer not to make any change at all."

I answered nothing; but, effectually dodging every one by the suddenness and rapidity of my flight, rushed from the building, ran up Wall Street towards Broadway, and, jumping into the first omnibus, was soon removed from pursuit. As soon as tranquillity returned, I distinctly perceived that I had now done all that I possibly could, both in respect to the demands of the landlord and his tenants, and with regard to my own desire and sense of duty, to benefit Bartleby, and shield him from rude persecution. I now strove to be entirely care-free and quiescent; and my conscience justi-fied me in the attempt; though, indeed, it was not so successful as I could have wished. So fearful was I of being again hunted out by the incensed landlord and his exasperated tenants, that, surren-dering my business to Nippers, for a few days, I drove about the upper part of the town and through the suburbs, in my rockaway; crossed over to Jersey City and Hoboken, and paid fugitive visits to Man-hattanville and Astoria. In fact, I almost lived in my rockaway for the time.

When again I entered my office, lo, a note from the landlord lay upon the desk. I opened it with trembling hands. It informed me that the writer had sent to the police, and had Bartleby removed to the Tombs as a vagrant. Moreover, since I knew more about him than any one else, he wished me to appear at the place, and make a suitable state-ment of the facts. These tidings had a conflicting effect upon me. At first I was indignant; but, at last, almost approved. The landlord's energetic, summary disposition, had led him to adopt a pro-cedure which I do not think I would have decided upon myself; and yet, as a last resort, under such peculiar circumstances, it seemed the only plan.

As I afterwards learned, the poor scrivener, when told that he must be conducted to the Tombs, offered not the slightest obstacle, but, in his pale, unmoving way, silently acquiesced.

Some of the compassionate and curious by-stand-ers joined the party; and headed by one of the constables arm-in-arm with Bartleby, the silent pro-cession filed its way through all the noise, and heat, and joy of the roaring thoroughfares at noon.

The same day I received the note, I went to the Tombs, or, to speak more properly, the Halls of Justice. Seeking the right officer, I stated the pur-pose of my call, and was informed that the individual I described was, indeed, within. I then assured the functionary that Bartleby was a per-fectly honest man, and greatly to be compassion-ated, however unaccountably eccentric. I narrated all I knew, and closed by suggesting the idea of letting him remain in as indulgent confinement as possible, till something less harsh might be done—though, indeed, I hardly knew what. At all events, if nothing else could be decided upon, the alms-house must receive him. I then begged to have an interview.

Being under no disgraceful charge, and quite serene and harmless in all his ways, they had per-mitted him freely to wander about the prison, and, especially, in the inclosed grass-platted yards there-of. And so I found him there, standing all alone in the quietest of the yards, his face towards a high wall, while all around, from the narrow slits of the jail windows, I thought I saw peering out upon him the eyes of murderers and thieves.

"Bartleby!"

"I know you," he said, without looking round—"and I want nothing to say to you."

"It was not I that brought you here, Bartleby," said I, keenly pained at his implied suspicion. "And to you, this should not be so vile a place. Nothing reproachful attaches to you by being here. And see, it is not so sad a place as one might think. Look, there is the sky, and here is the grass."

"I know where I am," he replied, but would say nothing more, and so I left him.

As I entered the corridor again, a broad meat-like man, in an apron, accosted me, and, jerking his thumb over his shoulder, said—"Is that your friend?"

"Yes."

"Does he want to starve? If he does, let him live on the prison fare, that's all."

"Who are you?" asked I, not knowing what to make of such an unofficially speaking person in such a place.

"I am the grub-man. Such gentlemen as have friends here, hire me to provide them with some-thing good to eat."

"Is this so?" said I, turning to the turnkey.

He said it was.

"Well, then," said I, slipping some silver into the grub-man's hands (for so they called him), "I want you to give particular attention to my friend there; let him have the best dinner you can get. And you must be as polite to him as possible."

"Introduce me, will you?" said the grub-man, looking at me with an expression which seemed to say he was all impatience for an opportunity to give a specimen of his breeding.

Thinking it would prove of benefit to the scriv-ener, I acquiesced; and, asking the grub-man his name, went up with him to Bartleby.

"Bartleby, this is a friend; you will find him very useful to you."

"Your sarvant, sir, your sarvant," said the grub-man, making a low salutation behind his apron. "Hope you find it pleasant here, sir; nice grounds—cool apartments—hope you'll stay with us some time —try to make it agreeable. What will you have for dinner to-day?"

"I prefer not to dine to-day," said Bartleby, turn-ing away. "It would disagree with me; I am un-used to dinners." So saying, he slowly moved to the other side of the inclosure, and took up a position fronting the dead-wall.

"How's this?" said the grub-man, addressing me with a stare of astonishment. "He's odd, ain't he?"

"I think he is a little deranged," said I, sadly.

"Deranged? deranged is it? Well, now, upon my word, I thought that friend of yourn was a gentleman forger; they are always pale and genteel-like, them forgers. I can't help pity 'em—can't help it, sir. Did you know Monroe Edwards?" he added, touchingly, and paused. Then, laying his hand piteously on my shoulder, sighed, "he died of consumption at Sing-Sing. So you weren't acquainted with Monroe?"

"No, I was never socially acquainted with any forgers. But I cannot stop longer. Look to my friend yonder. You will not lose by it. I will see you again."

Some few days after this, I again obtained admission to the Tombs, and went through the corridors in quest of Bartleby; but without finding him.

"I saw him coming from his cell not long ago," said a turnkey, "may be he's gone to loiter in the yards."

So I went in that direction.

"Are you looking for the silent man?" said another turnkey, passing me. "Yonder he lies—sleeping in the yard there. 'Tis not twenty minutes since I saw him lie down."

The yard was entirely quiet. It was not accessible to the common prisoners. The surrounding walls, of amazing thickness, kept off all sounds behind them. The Egyptian character of the masonry weighed upon me with its gloom. But a soft imprisoned turf grew under foot. The heart of the eternal pyramids, it seemed, wherein, by some strange magic, through the clefts, grass-seed, dropped by birds, had sprung.

Strangely huddled at the base of the wall, his knees drawn up, and lying on his side, his head touching the cold stones, I saw the wasted Bartleby. But nothing stirred. I paused; then went close up to him; stooped over, and saw that his dim eyes were open; otherwise he seemed profoundly sleeping. Something prompted me to touch him. I felt his hand, when a tingling shiver ran up my arm and down my spine to my feet.

The round face of the grub-man peered upon me now. "His dinner is ready. Won't he dine to-day, either? Or does he live without dining?"

"Lives without dining," said I, and closed the eyes.

"Eh!—He's asleep, ain't he?"

"With kings and counselors," murmured I.

.   .   .

There would seem little need for proceeding further in this history. Imagination will readily supply the meagre recital of poor Bartleby's interment. But, ere parting with the reader, let me say, that if this little narrative has sufficiently interested him, to awaken curiosity as to who Bartleby was, and what manner of life he led prior to the present narrator's making his acquaintance, I can only reply, that in such curiosity I fully share, but am wholly unable to gratify it. Yet here I hardly know whether I should divulge one little item of rumor, which came to my ear a few months after the scrivener's decease. Upon what basis it rested, I could never ascertain; and hence, how true it is I cannot now tell. But, inasmuch as this vague report has not been without a certain suggestive interest to me, however sad, it may prove the same with some others; and so I will briefly mention it. The report was this: that Bartleby had been a subordinate clerk in the Dead Letter Office at Washington, from which he had been suddenly removed by a change in the administration. When I think over this rumor, hardly can I express the emotions which seize me. Dead letters! does it not sound like dead men? Conceive a man by nature and misfortune prone to a pallid hopelessness, can any business seem more fitted to heighten it than that of continually handling these dead letters, and assorting them for the flames? For by the cart-load they are annually burned. Sometimes from out the folded paper the pale clerk takes a ring—the finger it was meant for, perhaps, moulders in the grave; a bank-note sent in swiftest charity—he whom it would relieve, nor eats nor hungers any more; pardon for those who died despairing; hope for those who died unhoping; good tidings for those who died stifled by unrelieved calamities. On errands of life, these letters speed to death.

Ah, Bartleby! Ah, humanity!

RALPH WALDO EMERSON

For an introduction to the life and works of Emerson, see page 391.

Self-Reliance

"Ne te quaesiveris extra." [1]

I READ the other day some verses written by an eminent painter which were original and not conventional. The soul always hears an admonition in such lines, let the subject be what it may. The sentiment they instil is of more value than any thought they may contain. To believe your own thought, to believe that what is true for you in your private heart is true for all men,—that is genius. Speak your latent conviction, and it shall be the universal sense; for the inmost in due time becomes the outmost, and our first thought is rendered back to us by the trumpets of the Last Judgment. Familiar as the voice of the mind is to each, the highest merit we ascribe to Moses, Plato, and Milton is that they set at naught books and traditions, and spoke not what men, but what *they* thought. A man should learn to detect and watch that gleam of light which flashes across his mind from within, more than the lustre of the firmament of bards and sages. Yet he dismisses without notice his thought, because it is his. In every work of genius we recognize our own rejected thoughts; they come back to us with a certain alienated majesty. Great works of art have no more affecting lesson for us than this. They teach us to abide by our spontaneous impression with good-humored inflexibility then most when the whole cry of voices is on the other side. Else to-morrow a stranger will say with masterly good sense precisely what we have thought and felt all the time, and we shall be forced to take with shame our own opinion from another.

There is a time in every man's education when he arrives at the conviction that envy is ignorance; that imitation is suicide; that he must take himself, for better for worse, as his portion; that though the wide universe is full of good, no kernel of nourishing corn can come to him but through his toil bestowed on that plot of ground which is given to him to till. The power which resides in him is new in nature, and none but he knows what that is which he can do, nor does he know until he has

[1] Seek not outside thyself.

tried. Not for nothing one face, one character, one fact, makes much impression on him and another none. This sculpture in the memory is not without preëstablished harmony. The eye was placed where one ray should fall, that it might testify of that particular ray. We but half express ourselves, and are ashamed of that divine idea which each of us represents. It may be safely trusted as proportionate and of good issues, so it be faithfully imparted, but God will not have his work made manifest by cowards. A man is relieved and gay when he has put his heart into his work and done his best; but what he has said or done otherwise shall give him no peace. It is a deliverance which does not deliver. In the attempt his genius deserts him; no muse befriends; no invention, no hope.

Trust thyself: every heart vibrates to that iron string. Accept the place the divine providence has found for you, the society of your contemporaries, the connection of events. Great men have always done so, and confided themselves childlike to the genius of their age, betraying their perception that the absolutely trustworthy was seated at their heart, working through their hands, predominating in all their being. And we are now men, and must accept in the highest mind the same transcendent destiny; and not minors and invalids in a protected corner, not cowards fleeing before a revolution, but guides, redeemers and benefactors, obeying the Almighty effort and advancing on Chaos and the Dark.

What pretty oracles nature yields us on this text in the face and behavior of children, babes, and even brutes! That divided and rebel mind, that distrust of a sentiment because our arithmetic has computed the strength and means opposed to our purpose, these have not. Their mind being whole, their eye is as yet unconquered, and when we look in their faces we are disconcerted. Infancy conforms to nobody; all conform to it; so that one babe commonly makes four or five out of the adults who prattle and play to it. So God has armed youth and puberty and manhood no less with its own piquancy and charm, and made it enviable and gracious and its claims not to be put by, if it will stand by itself. Do not think the youth has no force, because he cannot speak to you and me. Hark! in the next room his voice is sufficiently clear and emphatic. It seems he knows how to speak to his contemporaries. Bashful or bold then, he will know how to make us seniors very unnecessary.

The nonchalance of boys who are sure of a dinner, and would disdain as much as a lord to do or say aught to conciliate one, is the healthy attitude of human nature. A boy is in the parlor what the pit is in the playhouse; independent, irresponsible, looking out from his corner on such people and facts as pass by, he tries and sentences them on their merits, in the swift, summary way of boys, as good, bad, interesting, silly, eloquent, troublesome. He cumbers himself never about consequences, about interests; he gives an independent, genuine verdict. You must court him; he does not court you. But the man is as it were clapped into jail by his consciousness. As soon as he has once acted or spoken with *éclat* he is a committed person, watched by the sympathy or the hatred of hundreds, whose affections must now enter into his account. There is no Lethe for this. Ah, that he could pass again into his neutrality! Who can thus avoid all pledges and, having observed, observe again from the same unaffected, unbiased, unbribable, unaffrighted innocence,—must always be formidable. He would utter opinions on all passing affairs, which being seen to be not private but necessary, would sink like darts into the ear of men and put them in fear.

These are the voices which we hear in solitude, but they grow faint and inaudible as we enter into the world. Society everywhere is in conspiracy against the manhood of every one of its members. Society is a joint-stock company, in which the members agree, for the better securing of his bread to each shareholder, to surrender the liberty and culture of the eater. The virtue in most request is conformity. Self-reliance is its aversion. It loves not realities and creators, but names and customs.

Whoso would be a man, must be a non-conformist. He who would gather immortal palms must not be hindered by the name of goodness, but must explore if it be goodness. Nothing is at last sacred but the integrity of your own mind. Absolve you to yourself, and you shall have the suffrage of the world. I remember an answer which when quite young I was prompted to make to a valued adviser who was wont to importune me with the dear old doctrines of the church. On my saying, "What have I to do with the sacredness of traditions, if I live wholly from within?" my friend suggested,— "But these impulses may be from below, not from above." I replied, "They do not seem to me to be such; but if I am the Devil's child, I will live then from the Devil." No law can be sacred to me but that of my nature. Good and bad are but names very readily transferable to that or this; the only right is what is after my constitution; the only wrong what is against it. A man is to carry himself

in the presence of all opposition as if every thing were titular and ephemeral but he. I am ashamed to think how easily we capitulate to badges and names, to large societies and dead institutions. Every decent and well-spoken individual affects and sways me more than is right. I ought to go upright and vital, and speak the rude truth in all ways. If malice and vanity wear the coat of philanthropy, shall that pass? If an angry bigot assumes this bountiful cause of Abolition, and comes to me with his last news from Barbadoes,[2] why should I not say to him, "Go love thy infant; love thy wood-chopper; be good-natured and modest; have that grace; and never varnish your hard, uncharitable ambition with this incredible tenderness for black folk a thousand miles off. Thy love afar is spite at home." Rough and graceless would be such greeting, but truth is handsomer than the affectation of love. Your goodness must have some edge to it,—else it is none. The doctrine of hatred must be preached, as the counteraction of the doctrine of love, when that pules and whines. I shun father and mother and wife and brother when my genius calls me. I would write on the lintels of the door-post, *Whim.* I hope it is somewhat better than whim at last, but we cannot spend the day in explanation. Expect me not to show cause why I seek or why I exclude company. Then again, do not tell me, as a good man did to-day, of my obligation to put all poor men in good situations. Are they *my* poor? I tell thee, thou foolish philanthropist, that I grudge the dollar, the dime, the cent I give to such men as do not belong to me and to whom I do not belong. There is a class of persons to whom by all spiritual affinity I am bought and sold; for them I will go to prison if need be; but your miscellaneous popular charities; the education at college of fools; the building of meeting-houses to the vain end to which many now stand; alms to sots, and the thousand-fold Relief Societies;—though I confess with shame I sometimes succumb and give the dollar, it is a wicked dollar, which by and by I shall have the manhood to withhold.

Virtues are, in the popular estimate, rather the exception than the rule. There is the man *and* his virtues. Men do what is called a good action, as some piece of courage or charity, much as they would pay a fine in expiation of daily non-appearance on parade. Their works are done as an apology or extenuation of their living in the world,— as invalids and the insane pay a high board. Their

[2] Slavery was abolished in the British West Indies in 1834.

virtues are penances. I do not wish to expiate, but to live. My life is for itself and not for a spectacle. I much prefer that it should be of a lower strain, so it be genuine and equal, than that it should be glittering and unsteady. I wish it to be sound and sweet, and not to need diet and bleeding. I ask primary evidence that you are a man, and refuse this appeal from the man to his actions. I know that for myself it makes no difference whether I do or forbear those actions which are reckoned excellent. I cannot consent to pay for a privilege where I have intrinsic right. Few and mean as my gifts may be, I actually am, and do not need for my own assurance or the assurance of my fellows any secondary testimony.

What I must do is all that concerns me, not what the people think. This rule, equally arduous in actual and in intellectual life, may serve for the whole distinction between greatness and meanness. It is the harder because you will always find those who think they know what is your duty better than you know it. It is easy in the world to live after the world's opinion; it is easy in solitude to live after our own; but the great man is he who in the midst of the crowd keeps with perfect sweetness the independence of solitude.

The objection to conforming to usages that have become dead to you is that it scatters your force. It loses your time and blurs the impression of your character. If you maintain a dead church, contribute to a dead Bible-society, vote with a great party either for the government or against it, spread your table like base housekeepers,—under all these screens I have difficulty to detect the precise man you are: and of course so much force is withdrawn from all your proper life. But do your work, and I shall know you. Do your work; and you shall reinforce yourself. A man must consider what a blindman's-buff is this game of conformity. If I know your sect I anticipate your argument. I hear a preacher announce for his text and topic the expediency of one of the institutions of his church. Do I not know beforehand that not possibly can he say a new and spontaneous word? Do I not know that with all this ostentation of examining the grounds of the institution he will do no such thing? Do I not know that he is pledged to himself not to look but at one side, the permitted side, not as a man, but as a parish minister? He is a retained attorney, and these airs of the bench are the emptiest affectation. Well, most men have bound their eyes with one or another handkerchief, and attached themselves to some one of these communities of opinion. This conformity makes them not false in a few particulars, authors of a few lies, but false in all particulars. Their every truth is not quite true. Their two is not the real two, their four not the real four; so that every word they say chagrins us and we know not where to begin to set them right. Meantime nature is not slow to equip us in the prison-uniform of the party to which we adhere. We come to wear one cut of face and figure, and acquire by degrees the gentlest asinine expression. There is a mortifying experience in particular, which does not fail to wreak itself also in the general history; I mean the "foolish face of praise," the forced smile which we put on in company where we do not feel at ease, in answer to conversation which does not interest us. The muscles, not spontaneously moved but moved by a low usurping wilfulness, grow tight about the outline of the face, with the most disagreeable sensation.

For nonconformity the world whips you with its displeasure. And therefore a man must know how to estimate a sour face. The by-standers look askance on him in the public street or in the friend's parlor. If this aversion had its origin in contempt and resistance like his own he might well go home with a sad countenance; but the sour faces of the multitude, like their sweet faces, have no deep cause, but are put on and off as the wind blows and a newspaper directs. Yet is the discontent of the multitude more formidable than that of the senate and the college. It is easy enough for a firm man who knows the world to brook the rage of the cultivated classes. Their rage is decorous and prudent, for they are timid, as being very vulnerable themselves. But when to their feminine rage the indignation of the people is added, when the ignorant and the poor are aroused, when the unintelligent brute force that lies at the bottom of society is made to growl and mow, it needs the habit of magnanimity and religion to treat it godlike as a trifle of no concernment.

The other terror that scares us from self-trust is our consistency; a reverence for our past act or word because the eyes of others have no other data for computing our orbit than our past acts, and we are loath to disappoint them.

But why should you keep your head over your shoulder? Why drag about this corpse of your memory, lest you contradict somewhat you have stated in this or that public place? Suppose you should contradict yourself; what then? It seems to be a rule of wisdom never to rely on your memory alone, scarcely even in acts of pure memory, but to bring the past for judgment into the thousand-eyed present, and live ever in a new day. In your metaphysics you have denied personality to the Deity, yet when the devout motions of the soul come, yield to them heart and life, though they should clothe God with shape and color. Leave your theory, as Joseph his coat in the hand of the harlot, and flee.

A foolish consistency is the hobgoblin of little minds, adored by little statesmen and philosophers and divines. With consistency a great soul has simply nothing to do. He may as well concern himself with his shadow on the wall. Speak what you think now in hard words and to-morrow speak what to-morrow thinks in hard words again, though it contradict every thing you said to-day.—"Ah, so you shall be sure to be misunderstood."—Is it so bad then to be misunderstood? Pythagoras was misunderstood, and Socrates, and Jesus, and Luther, and Copernicus, and Galileo, and Newton, and every pure and wise spirit that ever took flesh. To be great is to be misunderstood.

I suppose no man can violate his nature. All the sallies of his will are rounded in by the law of his being, as the inequalities of Andes and Himmaleh are insignificant in the curve of the sphere. Nor does it matter how you gauge and try him. A character is like an acrostic or Alexandrian stanza,—read it forward, backward, or across, it still spells the same thing. In this pleasing contrite wood-life which God allows me, let me record day by day my honest thought without prospect or retrospect, and, I cannot doubt, it will be found symmetrical, though I mean it not and see it not. My book should smell of pines and resound with the hum of insects. The swallow over my window should interweave that thread or straw he carries in his bill into my web also. We pass for what we are. Character teaches above our wills. Men imagine that they communicate their virtue or vice only by overt actions, and do not see that virtue or vice emit a breath every moment.

There will be an agreement in whatever variety of actions, so they be each honest and natural in their hour. For of one will, the actions will be harmonious, however unlike they seem. These varieties are lost sight of at a little distance, at a little height of thought. One tendency unites them all. The voyage of the best ship is a zigzag line of a hundred tacks. See the line from a sufficient distance, and it straightens itself to the average tendency. Your genuine action will explain itself and will explain your other genuine actions. Your conformity explains nothing. Act singly, and what you have already done singly will justify you now. Greatness appeals to the future. If I can be firm enough to-day to do right and scorn eyes, I must have done so much right before as to defend me now. Be it how it will, do right now. Always scorn appearances and you always may. The force of character is cumulative. All the foregone days of virtue work their health into this. What makes the majesty of the heroes of the senate and the field, which so fills the imagination? The consciousness of a train of great days and victories behind. They shed a united light on the advancing actor. He is attended as by a visible escort of angels. That is it which throws thunder into Chatham's voice, and dignity into Washington's port, and America into Adams's eye. Honor is venerable to us because it is no ephemera. It is always ancient virtue. We worship it to-day because it is not of to-day. We love it and pay it homage because it is not a trap for our love and homage, but is self-dependent, self-derived, and therefore of an old immaculate pedigree, even if shown in a young person.

I hope in these days we have heard the last of conformity and consistency. Let the words be gazetted and ridiculous henceforward. Instead of the gong for dinner, let us hear a whistle from the Spartan fife. Let us never bow and apologize more. A great man is coming to eat at my house. I do not wish to please him; I wish that he would wish to please me. I will stand here for humanity, and though I would make it kind, I would make it true. Let us affront and reprimand the smooth mediocrity and squalid contentment of the times, and hurl in the face of custom and trade and office, the fact which is the upshot of all history, that there is a great responsible Thinker and Actor working wherever a man works; that a true man belongs to no other time or place, but is the centre of things. Where he is there is nature. He measures you and all men and all events. Ordinarily everybody in society reminds us of somewhat else, or of some other person. Character, reality, reminds you of nothing else; it takes place of [3] the whole creation. The man must be so much that he must make all circumstances indifferent. Every true man is a cause, a country, and an age; requires infinite spaces and numbers and time fully to accomplish his design;—and posterity seems to follow his steps as a train of clients. A man Caesar is born, and for ages after we have a Roman Empire. Christ is born, and millions of minds so grow and cleave to his

[3] Takes precedence over.

genius that he is confounded with virtue and the possible of man. An institution is the lengthened shadow of one man; as, Monachism, of the Hermit Antony; the Reformation, of Luther; Quakerism, of Fox; Methodism, of Wesley; Abolition, of Clarkson. Scipio, Milton called "the height of Rome"; and all history resolves itself very easily into the biography of a few stout and earnest persons.

Let a man then know his worth, and keep things under his feet. Let him not peep or steal, or skulk up and down with the air of a charity-boy, a bastard, or an interloper in the world which exists for him. But the man in the street, finding no worth in himself which corresponds to the force which built a tower or sculptured a marble god, feels poor when he looks on these. To him a palace, a statue, or a costly book have an alien and forbidding air, much like a gay equipage, and seem to say like that, "Who are you, Sir?" Yet they all are his, suitors for his notice, petitioners to his faculties that they will come out and take possession. The picture waits for my verdict; it is not to command me, but I am to settle its claims to praise. That popular fable [4] of the sot who was picked up dead-drunk in the street, carried to the duke's house, washed and dressed and laid in the duke's bed, and, on his waking, treated with all obsequious ceremony like the duke, and assured that he had been insane, owes its popularity to the fact that it symbolizes so well the state of man, who is in the world a sort of sot, but now and then wakes up, exercises his reason and finds himself a true prince.

Our reading is mendicant and sycophantic. In history our imagination plays us false. Kingdom and lordship, power and estate, are a gaudier vocabulary than private John and Edward in a small house and common day's work; but the things of life are the same to both; the sum total of both is the same. Why all this deference to Alfred [5] and Scanderbeg and Gustavus? Suppose they were virtuous; did they wear out virtue? As great a stake depends on your private act to-day as followed their public and renowned steps. When private men shall act with original views, the lustre will be transferred from the actions of kings to those of gentlemen.

The world has been instructed by its kings, who

have so magnetized the eyes of nations. It has been taught by this colossal symbol the mutual reverence that is due from man to man. The joyful loyalty with which men have everywhere suffered the king, the noble, or the great proprietor to walk among them by a law of his own, make his own scale of men and things and reverse theirs, pay for benefits not with money but with honor, and represent the law in his person, was the hieroglyphic by which they obscurely signified their consciousness of their own right and comeliness, the right of every man.

The magnetism which all original action exerts is explained when we inquire the reason of self-trust. Who is the Trustee? What is the aboriginal Self, on which a universal reliance may be grounded? What is the nature and power of that science-baffling star, without parallax, without calculable elements, which shoots a ray of beauty even into trivial and impure actions, if the least mark of independence appear? The inquiry leads us to that source, at once the essence of genius, of virtue, and of life, which we call Spontaneity or Instinct. We denote this primary wisdom as Intuition, whilst all later teachings are tuitions. In that deep force, the last fact behind which analysis cannot go, all things find their common origin. For the sense of being which in calm hours rises, we know not how, in the soul, is not diverse from things, from space, from light, from time, from man, but one with them and proceeds obviously from the same source whence their life and being also proceed. We first share the life by which things exist and afterwards see them as appearances in nature and forget that we have shared their cause. Here is the fountain of action and of thought. Here are the lungs of that inspiration which giveth man wisdom and which cannot be denied without impiety and atheism. We lie in the lap of immense intelligence, which makes us receivers of its truth and organs of its activity. When we discern justice, when we discern truth, we do nothing of ourselves, but allow a passage to its beams. If we ask whence this comes, if we seek to pry into the soul that causes, all philosophy is at fault. Its presence or its absence is all we can affirm. Every man discriminates between the voluntary acts of his mind and his involuntary perceptions, and knows that to his involuntary perceptions a perfect faith is due. He may err in the expression of them, but he knows that these things are so, like day and night, not to be disputed. My wilful actions and acquisitions are but roving;—the idlest reverie, the faintest native

[4] For Shakespeare's use of the story see the Induction of *The Taming of the Shrew*.

[5] Alfred the Great, King of England from 871 to 901; Scanderbeg (George Castriota) (1403–1468), an Albanian patriot; Gustavus Adolphus, King of Sweden from 1611 to 1632.

emotion, commanded my curiosity and respect. Thoughtless people contradict as readily the statement of perceptions as of opinions, or rather much more readily; for they do not distinguish between perception and notion. They fancy that I choose to see this or that thing. But perception is not whimsical, but fatal. If I see a trait, my children will see it after me, and in course of time all mankind,—although it may chance that no one has seen it before me. For my perception of it is as much a fact as the sun.

The relations of the soul to the divine spirit are so pure that it is profane to seek to interpose helps. It must be that when God speaketh he should communicate, not one thing, but all things; should fill the world with his voice; should scatter forth light, nature, time, souls, from the centre of the present thought; and new date and new create the whole. Whenever a mind is simple and receives a divine wisdom, old things pass away,—means, teachers, texts, temples fall; it lives now, and absorbs past and future into the present hour. All things are made sacred by relation to it,—one as much as another. All things are dissolved to their centre by their cause, and in the universal miracle petty and particular miracles disappear. If therefore a man claims to know and speak of God and carries you backward to the phraseology of some old mouldered nation in another country, in another world, believe him not. Is the acorn better than the oak which is its fulness and completion? Is the parent better than the child into whom he has cast his ripened being? Whence then this worship of the past? The centuries are conspirators against the sanity and authority of the soul. Time and space are but physiological colors which the eye makes, but the soul is light: where it is, is day; where it was, is night; and history is an impertinence and an injury if it be any thing more than a cheerful apologue or parable of my being and becoming.

Man is timid and apologetic; he is no longer upright; he dares not say "I think," "I am," but quotes some saint or sage. He is ashamed before the blade of grass or the blowing rose. These roses under my window make no reference to former roses or to better ones; they are for what they are; they exist with God to-day. There is no time to them. There is simply the rose; it is perfect in every moment of its existence. Before a leaf-bud has burst, its whole life acts; in the full-blown flower there is no more; in the leafless root there is no less. Its nature is satisfied and it satisfies nature in all moments alike. But man postpones or remembers; he does not live in the present, but with reverted eye laments the past, or heedless of the riches that surround him, stands on tiptoe to foresee the future. He cannot be happy and strong until he too lives with nature in the present, above time.

This should be plain enough. Yet see what strong intellects dare not yet hear God himself unless he speak the phraseology of I know not what David, or Jeremiah, or Paul. We shall not always set so great a price on a few texts, on a few lives. We are like children who repeat by rote the sentences of grandames and tutors, and, as they grow older, of the men of talents and character they chance to see,—painfully recollecting the exact words they spoke; afterwards, when they come into the point of view which those had who uttered these sayings, they understand them and are willing to let the words go; for at any time they can use words as good when occasion comes. If we live truly, we shall see truly. It is as easy for the strong man to be strong, as it is for the weak to be weak. When we have new perception, we shall gladly disburden the memory of its hoarded treasures as old rubbish. When a man lives with God, his voice shall be as sweet as the murmur of the brook and the rustle of the corn.

And now at last the highest truth on this subject remains unsaid; probably cannot be said; for all that we say is the far-off remembering of the intuition. That thought by what I can now nearest approach to say it, is this. When good is near you, when you have life in yourself, it is not by any known or accustomed way; you shall not discern the footprints of any other; you shall not see the face of man; you shall not hear any name;—the way, the thought, the good, shall be wholly strange and new. It shall exclude example and experience. You take the way from man, not to man. All persons that ever existed are its forgotten ministers. Fear and hope are alike beneath it. There is somewhat low even in hope. In the hour of vision there is nothing that can be called gratitude, nor properly joy. The soul raised over passion beholds identity and eternal causation, perceives the self-existence of Truth and Right, and calms itself with knowing that all things go well. Vast spaces of nature, the Atlantic Ocean, the South Sea; long intervals of time, years, centuries, are of no account. This which I think and feel underlay every former state of life and circumstances, as it does underlie my present, and what is called life and what is called death.

Life only avails, not the having lived. Power ceases in the instant of repose; it resides in the moment of transition from a past to a new state, in the shooting of the gulf, in the darting to an aim. This one fact the world hates; that the soul *becomes*; for that forever degrades the past, turns all riches to poverty, all reputation to a shame, confounds the saint with the rogue, shoves Jesus and Judas equally aside. Why then do we prate of self-reliance? Inasmuch as the soul is present there will be power not confident by agent.[6] To talk of reliance is a poor external way of speaking. Speak rather of that which relies because it works and is. Who has more obedience than I masters me, though he should not raise his finger. Round him I must revolve by the gravitation of spirits. We fancy it rhetoric when we speak of eminent virtue. We do not yet see that virtue is Height, and that a man or a company of men, plastic and permeable to principles, by the law of nature must overpower and ride all cities, nations, kings, rich men, poets, who are not.

This is the ultimate fact which we so quickly reach on this, as on every topic, the resolution of all into the ever-blessed ONE. Self-existence is the attribute of the Supreme Cause, and it constitutes the measure of good by the degree in which it enters into all lower forms. All things real are so by so much virtue as they contain. Commerce, husbandry, hunting, whaling, war, eloquence, personal weight, are somewhat, and engage my respect as examples of its presence and impure action. I see the same law working in nature for conservation and growth. Power is, in nature, the essential measure of right. Nature suffers nothing to remain in her kingdoms which cannot help itself. The genesis and maturation of a planet, its poise and orbit, the bended tree recovering itself from the strong wind, the vital resources of every animal and vegetable, are demonstrations of the self-sufficing and therefore self-relying soul.

Thus all concentrates: let us not rove; let us sit at home with the cause. Let us stun and astonish the intruding rabble of men and books and institutions by a simple declaration of the divine fact. Bid the invaders take the shoes from off their feet, for God is here within. Let our simplicity judge them, and our docility to our own law demonstrate the poverty of nature and fortune beside our native riches.

But now we are a mob. Man does not stand in awe of man, nor is his genius admonished to stay

[6] Acting.

at home, to put itself in communication with the internal ocean, but it goes abroad to beg a cup of water of the urns of other men. We must go alone. I like the silent church before the service begins, better than any preaching. How far off, how cool, how chaste the persons look, begirt each one with a precinct or sanctuary! So let us always sit. Why should we assume the faults of our friend, or wife, or father, or child, because they sit around our hearth, or are said to have the same blood? All men have my blood and I all men's. Not for that will I adopt their petulance or folly, even to the extent of being ashamed of it. But your isolation must not be mechanical, but spiritual, that is, must be elevation. At times the whole world seems to be in conspiracy to importune you with emphatic trifles. Friend, climate, child, sickness, fear, want, charity, all knock at once at thy closet door and say,—"Come out unto us." But keep thy state; come not into their confusion. The power men possess to annoy me I give them by a weak curiosity. No man can come near but through my act. "What we love that we have, but by desire we bereave ourselves of the love."

If we cannot at once rise to the sanctities of obedience and faith, let us at least resist our temptations; let us enter into the state of war and wake Thor and Woden, courage and constancy, in our Saxon breasts. This is to be done in our smooth times by speaking the truth. Check this lying hospitality and lying affection. Live no longer to the expectation of these deceived and deceiving people with whom we converse. Say to them, "O father, O mother, O wife, O brother, O friend, I have lived with you after appearances hitherto. Henceforward I am the truth's. Be it known unto you that henceforward I obey no law less than the eternal law. I will have no covenants but proximities. I shall endeavor to nourish my parents, to support my family, to be the chaste husband of one wife,—but these relations I must fill after a new and unprecedented way. I appeal from your customs. I must be myself. I cannot break myself any longer for you, or you. If you can love me for what I am, we shall be the happier. If you cannot, I will still seek to deserve that you should. I will not hide my tastes or aversions. I will so trust that what is deep is holy, that I will do strongly before the sun and moon whatever inly rejoices me and the heart appoints. If you are noble, I will love you; if you are not, I will not hurt you and myself by hypocritical attentions. If you are true, but not in the same truth with me, cleave to your companions; I will seek my own. I do this not selfishly but humbly and truly. It is alike your interest, and mine, and all men's, however long we have dwelt in lies, to live in truth. Does this sound harsh to-day? You will soon love what is dictated by your nature as well as mine, and if we follow the truth it will bring us out safe at last."—But so may you give these friends pain. Yes, but I cannot sell my liberty and my power, to save their sensibility. Besides, all persons have their moments of reason, when they look out into the region of absolute truth; then will they justify me and do the same thing.

The populace think that your rejection of popular standards is a rejection of all standard, and mere antinomianism; [7] and the bold sensualist will use the name of philosophy to gild his crimes. But the law of consciousness abides. There are two confessionals, in one or the other of which we must be shriven. You may fulfil your round of duties by clearing yourself in the *direct* or in the *reflex* way. Consider whether you have satisfied your relations to father, mother, cousin, neighbor, town, cat and dog—whether any of these can upbraid you. But I may also neglect this reflex standard and absolve me to myself. I have my own stern claims and perfect circle. It denies the name of duty to many offices that are called duties. But if I can discharge its debts it enables me to dispense with the popular code. If any one imagines that this law is lax, let him keep its commandment one day.

And truly it demands something godlike in him who has cast off the common motives of humanity and has ventured to trust himself for a taskmaster. High be his heart, faithful his will, clear his sight, that he may in good earnest be doctrine, society, law, to himself, that a simple purpose may be to him as strong as iron necessity is to others!

If any man consider the present aspects of what is called by distinction *society*, he will see the need of these ethics. The sinew and heart of man seem to be drawn out, and we are become timorous, desponding whimperers. We are afraid of truth, afraid of fortune, afraid of death, and afraid of each other. Our age yields no great and perfect persons. We want men and women who shall renovate life and our social state, but we see that most natures are insolvent, cannot satisfy their own wants, have an ambition out of all proportion to their practical force and do lean and beg day and night continually. Our housekeeping is mendicant, our arts, our occupations, our marriages, our religion we have not

[7] Opposition to law.

chosen, but society has chosen for us. We are parlor soldiers. We shun the rugged battle of fate, where strength is born.

If our young men miscarry in their first enterprises they lose all heart. If the young merchant fails, men say he is *ruined*. If the finest genius studies at one of our colleges and is not installed in an office within one year afterwards in the cities or suburbs of Boston or New York, it seems to his friends and to himself that he is right in being disheartened and in complaining the rest of his life. A sturdy lad from New Hampshire or Vermont, who in turn tries all the professions, who *teams it, farms it, peddles,* keeps a school, preaches, edits a newspaper, goes to Congress, buys a township, and so forth, in successive years, and always like a cat falls on his feet, is worth a hundred of these city dolls. He walks abreast with his days and feels no shame in not "studying a profession," for he does not postpone his life, but lives already. He has not one chance, but a hundred chances. Let a Stoic open the resources of man and tell men they are not leaning willows, but can and must detach themselves; that with the exercise of self-trust, new powers shall appear; that a man is the word made flesh, born to shed healing to the nations; that he should be ashamed of our compassion, and that the moment he acts from himself, tossing the laws, the books, idolatries, and customs out of the window, we pity him no more but thank and revere him;— and that teacher shall restore the life of man to splendor and make his name dear to all history.

It is easy to see that a greater self-reliance must work a revolution in all the offices and relations of men; in their religion; in their education; in their pursuits; their modes of living; their association; in their property; in their speculative views.

1. In what prayers do men allow themselves! That which they call a holy office is not so much as brave and manly. Prayer looks abroad and asks for some foreign addition to come through some foreign virtue, and loses itself in endless mazes of natural and supernatural, and mediatorial and miraculous. Prayer that craves a particular commodity, anything less than all good, is vicious. Prayer is the contemplation of the facts of life from the highest point of view. It is the soliloquy of a beholding and jubilant soul. It is the spirit of God pronouncing his works good. But prayer as a means to effect a private end is meanness and theft. It supposes dualism and not unity in nature and consciousness. As soon as the man is at one with God, he will not beg. He will then see prayer in all action. The prayer of the

farmer kneeling in his field to weed it, the prayer of the rower kneeling with the stroke of his oar, are true prayers heard throughout nature, though for cheap ends. Caratach, in Fletcher's *Bonduca,* when admonished to inquire the mind of the god Audate,[8] replies,—

> His hidden meaning lies in our endeavors;
> Our valors are our best gods.

Another sort of false prayers are our regrets. Discontent is the want of self-reliance; it is infirmity of will. Regret calamities if you can thereby help the sufferer; if not, attend your own work and already the evil begins to be repaired. Our sympathy is just as base. We come to them who weep foolishly and sit down and cry for company, instead of imparting to them truth and health in rough electric shocks, putting them once more in communication with their own reason. The secret of fortune is joy in our hands. Welcome evermore to gods and men is the self-helping man. For him all doors are flung wide; him all tongues greet, all honors crown, all eyes follow with desire. Our love goes out to him and embraces him because he did not need it. We solicitously and apologetically caress and celebrate him because he held on his way and scorned our disapprobation. The gods love him because men hated him. "To the persevering mortal," said Zoroaster, "the blessed Immortals are swift."

As men's prayers are a disease of the will, so are their creeds a disease of the intellect. They say with those foolish Israelites, "Let not God speak to us, lest we die. Speak thou, speak any man with us, and we will obey." Everywhere I am hindered of meeting God in my brother, because he has shut his own temple doors and recites fables merely of his brother's, or his brother's brother's God. Every new mind is a new classification. If it prove a mind of uncommon activity and power, a Locke,[9] a Lavoisier, a Hutton, a Bentham, a Fourier, it imposes its classification on other men, and lo! a new system! In proportion to the depth of the thought, and so to the number of the objects it touches and brings within reach of the pupil, is his complacency. But

chiefly is this apparent in creeds and churches, which are also classifications of some powerful mind acting on the elemental thought of duty and man's relation to the Highest. Such is Calvinism, Quakerism, Swedenborgism. The pupil takes the same delight in subordinating every thing to the new terminology as a girl who has just learned botany in seeing a new earth and new seasons thereby. It will happen for a time that the pupil will find his intellectual power has grown by the study of his master's mind. But in all unbalanced minds the classification is idolized, passes for the end and not for a speedily exhaustible means, so that the walls of the system blend to their eye in the remote horizon with the walls of the universe; the luminaries of heaven seem to them hung on the arch their master built. They cannot imagine how you aliens have any right to see,—how you can see; "It must be somehow that you stole the light from us." They do not yet perceive that light, unsystematic, indomitable, will break into any cabin, even into theirs. Let them chirp awhile and call it their own. If they are honest and do well, presently their neat new pinfold will be too strait and low, will crack, will lean, will rot and vanish, and the immortal light, all young and joyful, million-orbed, will beam over the universe as on the first morning.

2. It is for want of self-culture that the superstition of Travelling, whose idols are Italy, England, Egypt, retains its fascination for all educated Americans. They who made England, Italy, or Greece venerable in the imagination, did so by sticking fast where they were, like an axis of the earth. In manly hours we feel that duty is our place. The soul is no traveller; the wise man stays at home, and when his necessities, his duties, on any occasion call him from his house, or into foreign lands, he is at home still and shall make men sensible by the expression of his countenance that he goes, the missionary of wisdom and virtue, and visits cities and men like a sovereign, and not like an interloper or a valet.

I have no churlish objection to the circumnavigation of the globe for the purposes of art, of study, and benevolence, so that the man is first domesticated, or does not go abroad with the hope of finding somewhat greater than he knows. He who travels to be amused, or to get somewhat which he does not carry, travels away from himself, and grows old even in youth among old things. In Thebes, in Palmyra, his will and mind have become old and dilapidated as they. He carries ruins to ruins.

Travelling is a fool's paradise. Our first journeys discover to us the indifference of places. At home I

[8] An unimportant blunder. The deity was the Roman goddess Andate (or Andraste), and the quotation from *Bonduca* actually begins "Her hidden meaning."

[9] See *supra,* pp. 197 ff.; Antoine Laurent Lavoisier (1743–1794), a famous French chemist; Charles Hutton (1737–1823), English mathematician (Emerson may have referred to James Hutton [1726–1797], Scottish geologist); Jeremy Bentham (1748–1832), English philosopher and economist; François Fourier (1772–1837), French sociologist.

dream that at Naples, at Rome, I can be intoxicated with beauty and lose my sadness. I pack my trunk, embrace my friends, embark on the sea and at last wake up in Naples, and there beside me is the stern fact, the sad self, unrelenting, identical, that I fled from. I seek the Vatican and the palaces. I affect to be intoxicated with sights and suggestions, but I am not intoxicated. My giant goes with me wherever I go.

3. But the rage of travelling is a symptom of a deeper unsoundness affecting the whole intellectual action. The intellect is vagabond, and our system of education fosters restlessness. Our minds travel when our bodies are forced to stay at home. We imitate; and what is imitation but the travelling of the mind? Our houses are built with foreign taste; our shelves are garnished with foreign ornaments; our opinions, our tastes, our faculties lean, and follow the Past and the Distant. The soul created the arts wherever they have flourished. It was in his own mind that the artist sought his model. It was an application of his own thought to the thing to be done and the conditions to be observed. And why need we copy the Doric or the Gothic model? Beauty, convenience, grandeur of thought and quaint expression are as near to us as to any, and if the American artist will study with hope and love the precise thing to be done by him, considering the climate, the soil, the length of the day, the wants of the people, the habit and form of the government, he will create a house in which all these will find themselves fitted, and taste and sentiment will be satisfied also.

Insist on yourself; never imitate. Your own gift you can present every moment with the cumulative force of a whole life's cultivation; but of the adopted talent of another you have only an extemporaneous half possession. That which each can do best, none but his Maker can teach him. No man yet knows what it is, nor can, till that person has exhibited it. Where is the master who could have taught Shakespeare? Where is the master who could have instructed Franklin, or Washington, or Bacon, or Newton? Every great man is a unique. The Scipionism of Scipio is precisely that part he could not borrow. Shakespeare will never be made by the study of Shakespeare. Do that which is assigned you, and you cannot hope too much or dare too much. There is at this moment for you an utterance brave and grand as that of the colossal chisel of Phidias, or trowel of the Egyptians, or the pen of Moses or Dante, but different from all these. Not possibly will the soul, all rich, all eloquent, with

thousand-cloven tongue, deign to repeat itself; but if you can hear what these patriarchs say, surely you can reply to them in the same pitch of voice; for the ear and the tongue are two organs of one nature. Abide in the simple and noble regions of thy life, obey thy heart, and thou shalt reproduce the Foreworld again.

4. As our Religion, our Education, our Art look abroad, so does our spirit of society. All men plume themselves on the improvement of society, and no man improves.

Society never advances. It recedes as fast on one side as it gains on the other. It undergoes continual changes; it is barbarous, it is civilized, it is christianized, it is rich, it is scientific; but this change is not amelioration. For every thing that is given something is taken. Society acquires new arts and loses old instincts. What a contrast between the well-clad, reading, writing, thinking American, with a watch, a pencil and a bill of exchange in his pocket, and the naked New Zealander, whose property is a club, a spear, a mat, and an undivided twentieth of a shed to sleep under! But compare the health of the two men and you shall see that the white man has lost his aboriginal strength. If the traveller tell us truly, strike the savage with a broad-axe and in a day or two the flesh shall unite and heal as if you struck the blow into soft pitch, and the same blow shall send the white to his grave.

The civilized man has built a coach, but has lost the use of his feet. He is supported on crutches, but lacks so much support of muscle. He has a fine Geneva watch, but he fails of the skill to tell the hour by the sun. A Greenwich nautical almanac he has, and so being sure of the information when he wants it, the man in the street does not know a star in the sky. The solstice he does not observe; the equinox he knows as little; and the whole bright calendar of the year is without a dial in his mind. His note-books impair his memory; his libraries overload his wit; the insurance-office increases the number of accidents; and it may be a question whether machinery does not encumber; whether we have not lost by refinement some energy; by a Christianity, entrenched in establishments and forms, some vigor of wild virtue. For every Stoic was a Stoic; but in Christendom where is the Christian?

There is no more deviation in the moral standard than in the standard of height or bulk. No greater men are now than ever were. A singular equality may be observed between the great men of the first and of the last ages; nor can all the science, art, religion, and philosophy of the nineteenth century avail to educate greater men than Plutarch's heroes, three or four and twenty centuries ago. Not in time is the race progressive. Phocion,[10] Socrates, Anaxagoras, Diogenes, are great men, but they leave no class. He who is really of their class will not be called by their name, but will be his own man, and in his turn the founder of a sect. The arts and inventions of each period are only its costume and do not invigorate men. The harm of the improved machinery may compensate its good. Hudson [11] and Behring accomplished so much in their fishing-boats as to astonish Parry and Franklin, whose equipment exhausted the resources of science and art. Galileo, with an opera-glass, discovered a more splendid series of celestial phenomena than any one since. Columbus found the New World in an undecked boat. It is curious to see the periodical disuse and perishing of means and machinery which were introduced with loud laudation a few years or centuries before. The great genius returns to essential man. We reckoned the improvements of the art of war among the triumphs of science, and yet Napoleon conquered Europe by the bivouac, which consisted of falling back on naked valor and disencumbering it of all aids. The Emperor held it impossible to make a perfect army, says Las Casas, "without abolishing our arms, magazines, commissaries and carriages, until, in imitation of the Roman custom, the soldier should receive his supply of corn, grind it in his hand-mill and bake his bread himself."

Society is a wave. The wave moves onward, but the water of which it is composed does not. The same particle does not rise from the valley to the ridge. Its unity is only phenomenal. The persons who make up a nation today, next year die, and their experience dies with them.

And so the reliance on Property, including the reliance on governments which protect it, is the want of self-reliance. Men have looked away from themselves and at things so long that they have come to esteem the religious, learned, and civil institutions as guards of property, and they deprecate assaults on these, because they feel them to be assaults on property. They measure their esteem of each other by what each has, and not by what each is. But a cultivated man becomes ashamed of his property, out of new respect for his nature. Espe-

[10] An Athenian statesman; Socrates, Anaxagoras, and Diogenes, Emerson uses as types of Greek philosophers.

[11] The older navigators, Henry Hudson and Vitus Behring, are contrasted with Sir William Edward Parry and Sir John Franklin, both of whom were still living when Emerson wrote.

cially he hates what he has if he sees that it is accidental,—came to him by inheritance, or gift, or crime; then he feels that it is not having; it does not belong to him, has no root in him and merely lies there because no revolution or no robber takes it away. But that which a man is, does always by necessity acquire; and what the man acquires, is living property, which does not wait the beck of rulers, or mobs, or revolutions, or fire, or storm, or bankruptcies, but perpetually renews itself wherever the man breathes. "Thy lot or portion of life," said the Caliph Ali, "is seeking after thee; therefore be at rest from seeking after it." Our dependence on these foreign goods leads us to our slavish respect for numbers. The political parties meet in numerous conventions; the greater the concourse and with each new uproar of announcement, The Delegation from Essex! The Democrats from New Hampshire! The Whigs of Maine! the young patriot feels himself stronger than before by a new thousand of eyes and arms. In like manner the reformers summon conventions and vote and resolve in multitude. Not so, O friends! will the God deign to enter and inhabit you, but by a method precisely the reverse. It is only as a man puts off all foreign support and stands alone that I see him to be strong and to prevail. He is weaker by every recruit to his banner. Is not a man better than a town? Ask nothing of man, and, in the endless mutation, thou only firm column must presently appear the upholder of all that surrounds thee. He who knows that power is inborn, that he is weak because he has looked for good out of him and elsewhere, and, so perceiving, throws himself unhesitatingly on his thought, instantly rights himself, stands in the erect position, commands his limbs, works miracles; just as a man who stands on his feet is stronger than a man who stands on his head.

So use all that is called Fortune. Most men gamble with her, and gain all, and lose all, as her wheel rolls. But do thou leave as unlawful these winnings, and deal with Cause and Effect, the chancellors of God. In the Will work and acquire, and thou hast chained the wheel of Chance, and shall sit hereafter out of fear from her rotations. A political victory, a rise of rents, the recovery of your sick or the return of your absent friend, or some other favorable event raises your spirits, and you think good days are preparing for you. Do not believe it. Nothing can bring you peace but yourself. Nothing can bring you peace but the triumph of principles.

HENRY DAVID THOREAU

1817–1862

Henry David Thoreau was born at Concord, and attended Harvard, from which he graduated in 1837. He returned home to teach school, and then lived for two years (1841–1843) with and as a disciple of Emerson. During this period he became a member of the Transcendental Club and a contributor to Margaret Fuller's *The Dial.* After some experience as a tutor, he built his famous hut at Walden Pond where he lived from July 4, 1845, to September 6, 1847. He wanted leisure to think, observe nature, and indulge the necessities of the soul. He was resolved to find out how much he needed to supply the simple wants of the body, so that he could better calculate the time he might devote to his soul. These wants were astonishingly small— his house cost $28.12 and his food for eight months $8.74. In 1854 Thoreau published the account of this experiment, *Walden,* which the world has come to recognize as a great book in style and content, admired by W. B. Yeats, Tolstoi, and Mahatma Gandhi. In *Walden,* Thoreau expressed his firm and unyielding individualism and his absolute confidence in the moral categorical imperative of the conscience as superior to all government and law. Evidently Thoreau was the most uncompromising of Transcendentalists. Emerson's essay, read on Thoreau's funeral in 1862, paid just tribute to his friend in emphasizing his extraordinary knowledge of nature, his integrity, and his high ideals. The later attacks upon his character by Lowell and R. L. Stevenson, and their condescending reduction of Thoreau to a gentle nature essayist, concealed his real value as a social critic of the American scene. Today, with the constant encroachment of the state upon individual freedom, we recognize the importance and relevance of Thoreau's views— his insistence upon the moral superiority of the individual conscience over all external social and legal pressures, and upon the dignity and complete autonomy of the individual. Living as we do in an urban and migratory society, we, like Thoreau, should wish that we might say of one place, "I have travelled a good deal in Concord."

FURTHER READING

Brooks, Van Wyck. *The Flowering of New England* (New York, 1936).
Canby, H. S. *Thoreau* (Boston, 1939).
Shepard, Odell. *The Heart of Thoreau's Journals* (Boston, 1927).

Civil Disobedience

I heartily accept the motto,—"That government is best which governs least"; and I should like to see it acted up to more rapidly and systematically. Carried out, it finally amounts to this, which also I believe,—"That government is best which governs not at all"; and when men are prepared for it, that will be the kind of government which they will have. Government is at best but an expedient; but most governments are usually, and all governments are sometimes, inexpedient. The objections which have been brought against a standing army, and they are many and weighty, and deserve to prevail, may also at last be brought against a standing government. The standing army is only an arm of the standing government. The government itself, which is only the mode which the people have chosen to execute their will, is equally liable to be abused and perverted before the people can act through it. Witness the present Mexican war, the work of comparatively a few individuals using the standing government as their tool; for, in the outset, the people would not have consented to this measure.

This American government,—what is it but a tradition, though a recent one, endeavoring to transmit itself unimpaired to posterity, but each instant losing some of its integrity? It has not the vitality and force of a single living man; for a single man can bend it to his will. It is a sort of wooden gun to the people themselves. But it is not the less necessary for this; for the people must have some complicated machinery or other, and hear its din, to satisfy that idea of government which they have. Governments show thus how successfully men can be imposed on, even impose on themselves, for their own advantage. It is excellent, we must all allow. Yet this government never of itself furthered any enterprise, but by the alacrity with which it got out of its way. *It* does not keep the country free. *It* does not settle the West. *It* does not educate. The character inherent in the American people has done all that has been accomplished; and it would have done somewhat more, if the government had not sometimes got in its way. For government is an expedient by which men would fain succeed in letting one another alone; and, as has been said, when it is most expedient, the governed are most let alone by it. Trade and commerce, if they were not made of india-rubber, would never manage to bounce over the obstacles which legislators are continually putting in their way; and, if one were to judge these men wholly by the effects of their actions and not partly by their intentions, they would deserve to be classed and punished with those mischievous persons who put obstructions on the railroads.

But, to speak practically and as a citizen, unlike those who call themselves no-government men, I ask for, not at once no government, but *at once* a better government. Let every man make known what kind of government would command his respect, and that will be one step toward obtaining it.

After all, the practical reason why, when the power is once in the hands of the people, a majority are permitted, and for a long period continue, to rule is not because they are most likely to be in the right, nor because this seems fairest to the minority, but because they are physically the strongest. But a government in which the majority rule in all cases cannot be based on justice, even as far as men understand it. Can there be a government in which majorities do not virtually decide right and wrong, but conscience?—in which majorities decide only those questions to which the rule of expediency is applicable? Must the citizen ever for a moment, or in the least degree, resign his conscience to the legislator? Why has every man a conscience, then? I think that we should be men first, and subjects afterward. It is not desirable to cultivate a respect for the law, so much as for the right. The only obligation which I have a right to assume is to do at any time what I think right. It is truly enough said that a corporation has no conscience; but a corporation of conscientious men is a corporation *with* a conscience. Law never made men a whit more just; and, by means of their respect for it, even the well-disposed are daily made the agents of injustice. A common and natural result of an undue respect for law is, that you may see a file of soldiers, colonel, captain, corporal, privates, powder-monkeys, and all, marching in admirable order over hill and dale to the wars, against their wills, ay, against their common sense and consciences, which makes it very steep marching indeed, and produces a palpitation of the heart. They have no doubt that it is a damnable business in which they are concerned; they are all peaceably inclined. Now, what are they? Men at all? or small movable forts and magazines, at the service of some unscrupulous man in power? Visit the Navy-Yard, and behold a marine, such a man as an American government can make, or such as it can make a man with its black arts,—a mere shadow and reminiscence of humanity, a man laid out alive and standing, and already as one may say, buried under arms with funeral accompaniments, though it may be,—

"Not a drum was heard, not a funeral note,
    As his corse to the rampart we hurried;
Not a soldier discharged his farewell shot
    O'er the grave where our hero we buried."

The mass of men serve the state thus, not as men mainly, but as machines, with their bodies. They are the standing army, and the militia, jailers, constables, *posse comitatus,* etc. In most cases there is no free exercise whatever of the judgment or of the moral sense; but they put themselves on a level with wood and earth and stones; and wooden men can perhaps be manufactured that will serve the purpose as well. Such command no more respect than men of straw or a lump of dirt. They have the same sort of worth only as horses and dogs. Yet such as these even are commonly esteemed good citizens. Others—as most legislators, politicians, lawyers, ministers, and office-holders—serve the state chiefly with their heads; and, as they rarely make any moral distinctions, they are as likely to serve the devil, without *intending* it, as God. A very few,— as heroes, patriots, martyrs, reformers in the great sense, and *men*—serve the state with their consciences also, and so necessarily resist it for the most part; and they are commonly treated as enemies by it. A wise man will only be useful as a man, and will not submit to be "clay," and "stop a hole to keep the wind away," but leave that office to his dust at least:—

"I am too high-born to be propertied,
    To be a secondary at control,
    Or useful serving-man and instrument
    To any sovereign state throughout the world."

He who gives himself entirely to his fellow-men appears to them useless and selfish; but he who gives himself partially to them is pronounced a benefactor and philanthropist.

How does it become a man to behave toward this American government to-day? I answer, that he cannot without disgrace be associated with it. I cannot for an instant recognize that political organization as *my* government which is the *slave's* government also.

All men recognize the right of revolution; that is, the right to refuse allegiance to, and to resist, the government, when its tyranny or its inefficiency are great and unendurable. But almost all say that such is not the case now. But such was the case, they think, in the Revolution of '75. If one were to tell me that this was a bad government because it taxed certain foreign commodities brought to its ports, it is most probable that I should not make an ado about it, for I can do without them. All machines have their friction; and possibly this does enough good to counterbalance the evil. At any rate, it is a great evil to make a stir about it. But when the friction comes to have its machine, and oppression and robbery are organized, I say, let us not have such a machine any longer. In other words, when a sixth of the population of a nation which has undertaken to be the refuge of liberty are slaves, and a whole country is unjustly overrun and conquered by a foreign army, and subjected to military law, I think that it is not too soon for honest men to rebel and revolutionize. What makes this duty the more urgent is the fact that the country so overrun is not our own, but ours is the invading army.

Paley, a common authority with many on moral questions, in his chapter on the "Duty of Submission to Civil Government," resolves all civil obligation into expediency; and he proceeds to say "that so long as the interest of the whole society requires it, that is, so long as the established government cannot be resisted or changed without public inconveniency, it is the will of God . . . that the established government be obeyed,—and no longer. This principle being admitted, the justice of every particular case of resistance is reduced to a computation of the quantity of the danger and grievance on the one side, and of the probability and expense of redressing it on the other." Of this, he says, every man shall judge for himself. But Paley appears never to have contemplated those cases to which the rule of expediency does not apply, in which a people, as well as an individual, must do justice, cost what it may. If I have unjustly wrested a plank from a drowning man, I must restore it to him though I drown myself. This, according to Paley, would be inconvenient. But he that would save his life, in such a case, shall lose it. This people must cease to hold slaves, and to make war on Mexico, though it cost them their existence as a people.

In their practice, nations agree with Paley; but does any one think that Massachusetts does exactly what is right at the present crisis?

"A drab of state, a cloth-o'-silver slut,
To have her train borne up, and her soul trail in the dirt."

Practically speaking, the opponents to a reform in Massachusetts are not a hundred thousand politicians at the South, but a hundred thousand merchants and farmers here, who are more interested in commerce and agriculture than they are in humanity, and are not prepared to do justice to the slave and to Mexico, *cost what it may*. I quarrel not with far-off foes, but with those who, near at home, coöperate with, and do the bidding of, those far away, and without whom the latter would be harmless. We are accustomed to say, that the mass of men are unprepared; but improvement is slow, because the few are not materially wiser or better than the many. It is not so important that many should be as good as you, as that there be some absolute goodness somewhere; for that will leaven the whole lump. There are thousands who are *in opinion* opposed to slavery and to the war, who yet in effect do nothing to put an end to them; who, esteeming themselves children of Washington and Franklin, sit down with their hands in their pockets, and say that they know not what to do, and do nothing; who even postpone the question of freedom to the question of free trade, and quietly read the prices-current along with the latest advices from Mexico, after dinner, and, it may be, fall asleep over them both. What is the price-current of an honest man and patriot to-day? They hesitate, and they regret, and sometimes they petition; but they do nothing in earnest and with effect. They will wait, well disposed, for others to remedy the evil, that they may no longer have it to regret. At most, they give only a cheap vote, and a feeble countenance and God-speed, to the right, as it goes by them. There are nine hundred and ninety-nine patrons of virtue to one virtuous man. But it is easier to deal with the real possessor of a thing than with the temporary guardian of it.

All voting is a sort of gaming, like checkers or backgammon, with a slight moral tinge to it, a playing with right and wrong, with moral questions; and betting naturally accompanies it. The character of the voters is not staked. I cast my vote, perchance, as I think right; but I am not vitally concerned that that right should prevail. I am willing to leave it to the majority. Its obligation, therefore, never exceeds that of expediency. Even voting *for the right* is *doing* nothing for it. It is only expressing to men feebly your desire that it should prevail. A wise man will not leave the right to the mercy of chance, nor wish it to prevail through the power of majority. There is but little virtue in the action of masses of men. When the majority shall at length vote for the abolition of slavery, it will be because they are indifferent to slavery, or because there is but little slavery left to be abolished by their vote. *They* will then be only slaves. Only *his* vote can hasten the abolition of slavery who asserts his own freedom by his vote.

I hear of a convention to be held at Baltimore, or elsewhere, for the selection of a candidate for the Presidency, made up chiefly of editors, and men who are politicians by profession; but I think, what is it to any independent, intelligent, and respectable man what decision they may come to? Shall we not have the advantage of his wisdom and honesty, nevertheless? Can we not count upon some independent votes? Are there not many individuals in the country who do not attend conventions? But no: I find that the respectable man, so called, has immediately drifted from his position, and despairs of his country, when his country has more reason to despair of him. He forthwith adopts one of the candidates thus selected as the only *available* one, thus proving that he is himself *available* for any purposes of the demagogue. His vote is of no more worth than that of any unprincipled foreigner or hireling native, who may have been bought. O for a man who is a *man,* and, as my neighbor says, has a bone in his back which you cannot pass your hand through! Our statistics are at fault: the population has been returned too large. How many *men* are there to a square thousand miles in this country? Hardly one. Does not America offer any inducement for men to settle here? The American has dwindled into an Odd Fellow,—one who may be known by the development of his organ of gregariousness, and a manifest lack of intellect and cheerful self-reliance; whose first and chief concern, on coming into the world, is to see that the almshouses are in good repair; and, before yet he has lawfully donned the virile garb, to collect a fund for the support of the widows and orphans that may be; who, in short, ventures to live only by the aid of the Mutual Insurance company, which has promised to bury him decently.

It is not a man's duty, as a matter of course, to devote himself to the eradication of any, even the most enormous, wrong; he may still properly have other concerns to engage him; but it is his duty, at least, to wash his hands of it, and, if he gives it no thought longer, not to give it practically his support. If I devote myself to other pursuits and contemplations, I must first see, at least, that I do not pursue them sitting upon another man's shoulders. I must get off his first, that he may pursue his contemplations too. See what gross inconsistency is tolerated. I have heard some of my townsmen say, "I should like to have them order me out to help put down an insurrection of the slaves, or to march to Mexico;—see if I would go"; and yet these very men have each, directly by their allegiance, and so indirectly, at least, by their money, furnished a substitute. The soldier is applauded who refuses to serve in an unjust war by those who do not refuse to sustain the unjust government which makes the war; is applauded by those whose own act and authority he disregards and sets at naught; as if the state were penitent to that degree that it hired one to scourge it while it sinned, but not to that degree that it left off sinning for a moment. Thus, under the name of Order and Civil Government, we are all made at last to pay homage to and support our own meanness. After the first blush of sin comes its indifference; and from immoral it becomes, as it were, *un*moral, and not quite unnecessary to that life which we have made.

The broadest and most prevalent error requires the most disinterested virtue to sustain it. The slight reproach to which the virtue of patriotism is commonly liable, the noble are most likely to incur. Those who, while they disapprove of the character and measures of a government, yield to it their allegiance and support are undoubtedly its most conscientious supporters, and so frequently the most serious obstacles to reform. Some are petitioning the State to dissolve the Union, to disregard the requisitions of the President. Why do they not dissolve it themselves,—the union between themselves and the State,—and refuse to pay their quota into its treasury? Do not they stand in the same relation to the State that the State does to the Union? And have not the same reasons prevented the State from resisting the Union which have prevented them from resisting the State?

How can a man be satisfied to entertain an opinion merely, and enjoy *it*? Is there any enjoyment in it, if his opinion is that he is aggrieved? If you are cheated out of a single dollar by your neighbor, you do not rest satisfied with knowing that you are cheated, or with saying that you are cheated, or even with petitioning him to pay you your due; but you take effectual steps at once to obtain the full amount, and see that you are never cheated again. Action from principle, the perception and the performance of right, changes things and relations; it is essentially revolutionary, and does not consist wholly with anything which was. It not only divides States and churches, it divides families; ay, it divides the *individual,* separating the diabolical in him from the divine.

Unjust laws exist: shall we be content to obey them, or shall we endeavor to amend them, and obey them until we have succeeded, or shall we transgress them at once? Men generally, under such a government as this, think that they ought to wait until they have persuaded the majority to alter them. They think that, if they should resist, the remedy would be worse than the evil. But it is the fault of the government itself that the remedy *is* worse than the evil. *It* makes it worse. Why is it not more apt to anticipate and provide for reform? Why does it not cherish its wise minority? Why does it cry and resist before it is hurt? Why does it not encourage its citizens to be on the alert to point out its faults, and *do* better than it would have them? Why does it always crucify Christ, and excommunicate Copernicus and Luther, and pronounce Washington and Franklin rebels?

One would think, that a deliberate and practical denial of its authority was the only offense never contemplated by government; else, why has it not assigned its definite, its suitable and proportionate penalty? If a man who has no property refuses but once to earn nine shillings for the State, he is put in prison for a period unlimited by any law that I know, and determined only by the discretion of those who placed him there; but if he should steal ninety times nine shillings from the State, he is soon permitted to go at large again.

If the injustice is part of the necessary friction of the machine of government, let it go, let it go: perchance it will wear smooth,—certainly the machine will wear out. If the injustice has a spring, or a pulley, or a rope, or a crank, exclusively for itself, then perhaps you may consider whether the remedy will not be worse than the evil; but if it is of such a nature that it requires you to be the agent of injustice to another, then, I say, break the law. Let your life be a counter friction to stop the machine. What I have to do is to see, at any rate, that I do not lend myself to the wrong which I condemn.

As for adopting the ways which the State has provided for remedying the evil, I know not of such ways. They take too much time, and a man's life will be gone. I have other affairs to attend to. I came into this world, not chiefly to make this a good place to live in, but to live in it, be it good or bad. A man has not everything to do, but something; and because he cannot do *everything,* it is not necessary that he should do *something* wrong. It is not my business to be petitioning the Governor or the Legislature any more than it is theirs to petition me; and if they should not hear my petition, what should I do then? But in this case the State has provided no way: its very Constitution is the evil. This may seem to be harsh and stubborn and unconciliatory; but it is to treat with the utmost kindness and consideration the only spirit that can appreciate or deserves it. So is all change for the better, like birth and death, which convulse the body.

I do not hesitate to say, that those who call themselves Abolitionists should at once effectually withdraw their support, both in person and property, from the government of Massachusetts, and not wait till they constitute a majority of one, before they suffer the right to prevail through them. I think that it is enough if they have God on their side, without waiting for that other one. Moreover, any man more right than his neighbors constitutes a majority of one already.

I meet this American government, or its representative, the State government, directly, and face to face, once a year—no more—in the person of its tax-gatherer; this is the only mode in which a man situated as I am necessarily meets it; and it then says distinctly, Recognize me; and the simplest, the most effectual, and, in the present posture of affairs, the indispensablest mode of treating with it on this head, of expressing your little satisfaction with and love for it, is to deny it then. My civil neighbor, the tax-gatherer, is the very man I have to deal with,—for it is, after all, with men and not with parchment that I quarrel,—and he has voluntarily chosen to be an agent of the government. How shall he ever know well what he is and does as an officer of the government, or as a man, until he is obliged to consider whether he shall treat me, his neighbor, for whom he has respect, as a neighbor and well-disposed man, or as a maniac and disturber of the peace, and see if he can get over this obstruction to his neighborliness without a ruder and more impetuous thought or speech corresponding with his action. I know this well, that if one thousand, if one hundred, if ten men whom I could name,—if ten *honest* men only,—ay, if *one* HONEST man, in this State of Massachusetts, *ceasing to hold slaves,* were actually to withdraw from this copartnership, and be locked up in the county jail therefor, it would be the abolition of slavery in America. For it matters not how small the beginning may seem to be: what is once well done is done forever. But we love better to talk about it: that we say is our mission. Reform keeps many scores of newspapers in its service, but not one man. If my esteemed neighbor, the State's ambassador, who will devote his days to the settlement of the question of human rights in the Council Chamber, instead of being threatened with the prisons of Carolina, were to sit down the prisoner of Massachusetts, that State which is so anxious to foist the sin of slavery upon her sister,—though at present she can discover only an act of inhospitality to be the ground of a quarrel with her,—the Legislature would not wholly waive the subject the following winter.

Under a government which imprisons any unjustly, the true place for a just man is also a prison. The proper place to-day, the only place which Massachusetts has provided for her freer and less desponding spirits, is in her prisons, to be put out and locked out of the State by her own act, as they have already put themselves out by their principles. It is there that the fugitive slave, and the Mexican prisoner on parole, and the Indian come to plead the wrongs of his race should find them; on that separate, but more free and honorable ground, where the State places those who are not *with* her, but *against* her,—the only house in a slave State in which a free man can abide with honor. If any think that their influence would be lost there, and their voices no longer afflict the ear of the State, that they would not be as an enemy within its walls, they do not know by how much truth is stronger than error, nor how much more eloquently and effectively he can combat injustice who has experienced a little in his own person. Cast your whole vote, not a strip of paper merely, but your whole influence. A minority is powerless while it conforms to the majority; it is not even a minority then; but it is irresistible when it clogs by its whole weight. If the alternative is to keep all just men in prison, or give up war and slavery, the State will not hesitate which to choose. If a thousand men were not to pay their tax-bills this year, that would not be a violent and bloody measure, as it would be to pay them, and enable the State to commit violence and shed innocent blood. This is, in fact, the definition of a peaceable revolution, if

any such is possible. If the tax-gatherer, or any other public officer, asks me, as one has done, "But what shall I do?" my answer is, "If you really wish to do anything, resign your office." When the subject has refused allegiance, and the officer has resigned his office, then the revolution is accomplished. But even suppose blood should flow. Is there not a sort of blood shed when the conscience is wounded? Through this wound a man's real manhood and immortality flow out, and he bleeds to an everlasting death. I see this blood flowing now.

I have contemplated the imprisonment of the offender, rather than the seizure of his goods,—though both will serve the same purpose,—because they who assert the purest right, and consequently are most dangerous to a corrupt State, commonly have not spent much time in accumulating property. To such the State renders comparatively small service, and a slight tax is wont to appear exorbitant, particularly if they are obliged to earn it by special labor with their hands. If there were one who lived wholly without the use of money, the State itself would hesitate to demand it of him. But the rich man—not to make any invidious comparison—is always sold to the institution which makes him rich. Absolutely speaking, the more money, the less virtue; for money comes between a man and his objects, and obtains them for him; and it was certainly no great virtue to obtain it. It puts to rest many questions which he would otherwise be taxed to answer; while the only new question which it puts is the hard but superfluous one, how to spend it. Thus his moral ground is taken from under his feet. The opportunities of living are diminished in proportion as what are called the "means" are increased. The best thing a man can do for his culture when he is rich is to endeavor to carry out those schemes which he entertained when he was poor. Christ answered the Herodians according to their condition. "Show me the tribute-money," said he;—and took one penny out of his pocket;—if you use money which has the image of Caesar on it and which he has made current and valuable, that is, *if you are men of the State,* and gladly enjoy the advantages of Caesar's government, then pay him back some of his own when he demands it. "Render therefore to Caesar that which is Caesar's, and to God those things which are God's,"—leaving them no wiser than before as to which was which; for they did not wish to know.

When I converse with the freest of my neighbors, I perceive that, whatever they may say about the magnitude and seriousness of the question, and their regard for the public tranquillity, the long and the short of the matter is, that they cannot spare the protection of the existing government, and they dread the consequences to their property and families of disobedience to it. For my own part, I should not like to think that I ever rely on the protection of the State. But, if I deny the authority of the State when it presents its tax-bill, it will soon take and waste all my property, and so harass me and my children without end. This is hard. This makes it impossible for a man to live honestly, and at the same time comfortably, in outward respects. It will not be worth the while to accumulate property; that would be sure to go again. You must hire or squat somewhere, and raise but a small crop, and eat that soon. You must live within yourself, and depend upon yourself always tucked up and ready for a start, and not have many affairs. A man may grow rich in Turkey even, if he will be in all respects a good subject of the Turkish government. Confucius said: "If a state is governed by the principles of reason, poverty and misery are subjects of shame; if a state is not governed by the principles of reason, riches and honors are the subjects of shame." No: until I want the protection of Massachusetts to be extended to me in some distant Southern port, where my liberty is endangered, or until I am bent solely on building up an estate at home by peaceful enterprise, I can afford to refuse allegiance to Massachusetts, and her right to my property and life. It costs me less in every sense to incur the penalty of disobedience to the State than it would to obey. I should feel as if I were worth less in that case.

Some years ago, the State met me in behalf of the Church, and commanded me to pay a certain sum toward the support of a clergyman whose preaching my father attended, but never I myself. "Pay," it said, "or be locked up in the jail." I declined to pay. But, unfortunately, another man saw fit to pay it. I did not see why the schoolmaster should be taxed to support the priest, and not the priest the schoolmaster; for I was not the State's schoolmaster, but I supported myself by voluntary subscription. I did not see why the lyceum should not present its tax-bill, and have the State to back its demand, as well as the Church. However, at the request of the selectmen, I condescended to make some such statement as this in writing:—"Know all men by these presents, that I, Henry Thoreau, do not wish to be regarded as a member of any incorporated society which I have not joined." This I gave to the town

clerk; and he has it. The State, having thus learned that I did not wish to be regarded as a member of that church, has never made a like demand on me since; though it said that it must adhere to its original presumption that time. If I had known how to name them, I should then have signed off in detail from all the societies which I never signed on to; but I did not know where to find a complete list.

I have paid no poll-tax for six years. I was put into jail once on this account, for one night; and, as I stood considering the walls of solid stone, two or three feet thick, the door of wood and iron, a foot thick, and the iron grating which strained the light, I could not help being struck with the foolishness of that institution which treated me as if I were mere flesh and blood and bones, to be locked up. I wondered that it should have concluded at length that this was the best use it could put me to, and had never thought to avail itself of my services in some way. I saw that, if there was a wall of stone between me and my townsmen, there was a still more difficult one to climb or break through before they could get to be as free as I was. I did not for a moment feel confined, and the walls seemed a great waste of stone and mortar. I felt as if I alone of all my townsmen had paid my tax. They plainly did not know how to treat me, but behaved like persons who are underbred. In every threat and in every compliment there was a blunder; for they thought that my chief desire was to stand the other side of that stone wall. I could not but smile to see how industriously they locked the door on my meditations, which followed them out again without let or hindrance, and *they* were really all that was dangerous. As they could not reach me, they had resolved to punish my body; just as boys, if they cannot come at some person against whom they have a spite, will abuse his dog. I saw that the State was half-witted, that it was timid as a lone woman with her silver spoons, and that it did not know its friends from its foes, and I lost all my remaining respect for it, and pitied it.

Thus the State never intentionally confronts a man's sense, intellectual or moral, but only his body, his senses. It is not armed with superior wit or honesty, but with superior physical strength. I was not born to be forced. I will breathe after my own fashion. Let us see who is the strongest. What force has a multitude? They only can force me who obey a higher law than I. They force me to become like themselves. I do not hear of *men* being *forced* to live this way or that by masses of men. What sort of life were that to live? When I meet a government which says to me, "Your money or your life," why should I be in haste to give it my money? It may be in a great strait, and not know what to do: I cannot help that. It must help itself; do as I do. It is not worth the while to snivel about it. I am not responsible for the successful working of the machinery of society. I am not the son of the engineer. I perceive that, when an acorn and a chestnut fall side by side, the one does not remain inert to make way for the other, but both obey their own laws, and spring and grow and flourish as best they can, till one, perchance overshadows and destroys the other. If a plant cannot live according to its nature, it dies; and so a man.

The night in prison was novel and interesting enough. The prisoners in their shirt-sleeves were enjoying a chat and the evening air in the doorway, when I entered. But the jailer said, "Come, boys, it is time to lock up"; and so they dispersed, and I heard the sound of their steps returning into the hollow apartments. My room-mate was introduced to me by the jailer as "a first-rate fellow and a clever man." When the door was locked, he showed me where to hang my hat, and how he managed matters there. The rooms were whitewashed once a month; and this one, at least, was the whitest, most simply furnished, and probably the neatest apartment in the town. He naturally wanted to know where I came from, and what brought me there; and, when I had told him, I asked him in my turn how he came there, presuming him to be an honest man, of course; and, as the world goes, I believe he was. "Why," said he, "they accuse me of burning a barn; but I never did it." As near as I could discover, he had probably gone to bed in a barn when drunk, and smoked his pipe there; and so a barn was burnt. He had the reputation of being a clever man, had been there some three months waiting for his trial to come on, and would have to wait as much longer; but he was quite domesticated and contented, since he got his board for nothing, and thought that he was well treated.

He occupied one window, and I the other; and I saw that if one stayed there long, his principal business would be to look out the window. I had soon read all the tracts that were left there, and examined where former prisoners had broken out, and where a grate had been sawed off, and heard the history of the various occupants of that room; for I found that even here there was a history and a gossip which never circulated beyond the walls of the jail. Probably this is the only house in the town where verses are composed, which are afterward printed in circular form, but not published. I was shown quite a long list of verses which were composed by some young men who had been detected in an attempt to escape, who avenged themselves by singing them.

I pumped my fellow-prisoner as dry as I could, for fear I should never see him again; but at length he showed me which was my bed, and left me to blow out the lamp.

It was like traveling into a far country, such as I had never expected to behold, to lie there for one night. It seemed to me that I never had heard the town clock strike before, nor the evening sounds of the village; for we slept with the windows open, which were inside the grating. It was to see my native village in the light of the Middle Ages, and our Concord was turned into a Rhine stream, and visions of knights and castles passed before me. They were the voices of old burghers that I heard in the streets. I was an involuntary spectator and auditor of whatever was done and said in the kitchen of the adjacent village-inn,—a wholly new and rare experience to me. It was a closer view of my native town. I was fairly inside of it. I never had seen its institutions before. This is one of its peculiar institutions; for it is a shire town. I began to comprehend what its inhabitants were about.

In the morning, our breakfasts were put through the hole in the door, in small oblong-square tin pans, made to fit, and holding a pint of chocolate, with brown bread, and an iron spoon. When they called for the vessels again, I was green enough to return what bread I had left; but my comrade seized it, and said that I should lay that up for lunch or dinner. Soon after he was let out to work at haying in a neighboring field, whither he went every day, and would not be back till noon; so he bade me good-day, saying that he doubted if he should see me again.

When I came out of prison,—for some one interfered, and paid that tax,—I did not perceive that great changes had taken place on the common, such as he observed who went in a youth and emerged a tottering and gray-headed man; and yet a change had to my eyes come over the scene,—the town, and State, and country,—greater than any that mere time could effect. I saw yet more distinctly the State in which I lived. I saw to what extent the people among whom I lived could be trusted as good neighbors and friends; that their friendship was for summer weather only; that they did not greatly propose to do right; that they were a distinct race from me by their prejudices and superstitions, as the Chinamen and Malays are; that in their sacrifices to humanity they ran no risks, not even to their property; that after all they were not so noble but they treated the thief as he had treated them, and hoped, by a certain outward observance and a few prayers, and by walking in a particular straight though useless path from time to time, to save their souls. This may be to judge my neighbors harshly; for I believe that many of them are not aware that they have such an institution as the jail in their village.

It was formerly the custom in our village, when a poor debtor came out of jail, for his acquaintances to salute him, looking through their fingers, which were crossed to represent the grating of a jail window, "How do ye do?" My neighbors did not thus salute me, but first looked at me, and then at one another, as if I had returned from a long journey. I was put into jail as I was going to the shoemaker's to get a shoe which was mended. When I was let out the next morning, I proceeded to finish my errand, and, having put on my mended shoe, joined a huckleberry party, who were impatient to put themselves under my conduct; and in half an hour,—for the horse was soon tackled,—was in the midst of a huckleberry field, on one of our highest hills, two miles off, and then the State was nowhere to be seen.

This is the whole history of "My Prisons."

I have never declined paying the highway tax, because I am as desirous of being a good neighbor as I am of being a bad subject; and as for supporting schools, I am doing my part to educate my fellow-countrymen now. It is for no particular item in the tax-bill that I refuse to pay it. I simply wish to refuse allegiance to the State, to withdraw and stand aloof from it effectually. I do not care to trace the course of my dollar, if I could, till it buys a man or a musket to shoot one with,—the dollar is innocent,—but I am concerned to trace the effects of my allegiance. In fact, I quietly declare war with the State, after my fashion, though I will still make what use and get what advantage of her I can, as is usual in such cases.

If others pay the tax which is demanded of me, from a sympathy with the State, they do but what they have already done in their own case, or rather they abet injustice to a greater extent than the State requires. If they pay the tax from a mistaken interest in the individual taxed, to save his property, or prevent his going to jail, it is because they have not considered wisely how far they let their private feelings interfere with the public good.

This, then, is my position at present. But one cannot be too much on his guard in such a case, lest his action be biased by obstinacy or an undue regard for the opinions of men. Let him see that he does only what belongs to himself and to the hour.

I think sometimes, Why, this people mean well, they are only ignorant; they would do better if they knew how: why give your neighbors this pain to treat you as they are not inclined to? But I think again, This is no reason why I should do as they do, or permit others to suffer much greater pain of a different kind. Again, I sometimes say to myself, When many millions of men, without heat, without ill will, without personal feeling of any kind, demand of you a few shillings only, without the possibility, such is their constitution, of retracting or altering their present demand, and without the possibility, on your side, of appeal to any other millions, why expose yourself to this overwhelming brute force? You do not resist cold and hunger, the winds and the waves, thus obstinately; you quietly submit to a thousand similar necessities. You do not put your head into the fire. But just in proportion as I regard this as not wholly a brute force, but partly a human force, and consider that I have relations to those millions as to so many millions of men, and not of mere brute or inanimate things, I see that appeal is possible, first and instantaneously, from them to the Maker of them, and, secondly, from them to themselves. But if I put my head deliberately into the fire, there is no appeal to fire or to the Maker of fire, and I have only myself to blame. If I could convince myself that I have any right to be satisfied with men as they are, and to treat them accordingly, and not according, in some respects, to my requisitions and expectations of what they and I ought to be, then, like a good Mussulman and fatalist, I should endeavor to be satisfied with things as they are, and say it is the will of God. And, above all, there is this difference between resisting this and a purely brute or natural force, that I can resist this with some effect; but I cannot expect, like Orpheus, to change the nature of the rocks and trees and beasts.

I do not wish to quarrel with any man or nation. I do not wish to split hairs, make fine distinctions, or set myself up as better than my neighbors. I seek rather, I may say, even an excuse for conforming to the laws of the land. I am but too ready to conform to them. Indeed, I have reason to suspect myself on this head; and each year, the tax-gatherer comes round, I find myself disposed to review the acts and position of the general and State governments, and the spirit of the people, to discover a pretext for conformity.

> "We must affect our country as our parents,
> And if at any time we alienate
> Our love or industry from doing it honor,
> We must respect effects and teach the soul
> Matter of conscience and religion,
> And not desire of rule or benefit."

I believe that the State will soon be able to take all my work of this sort out of my hands, and then I shall be no better a patriot than my fellow-countrymen. Seen from a lower point of view, the Constitution, with all its faults, is very good; the law and the courts are very respectable; even this State and this American government are, in many respects, very admirable, and rare things, to be thankful for, such as a great many have described them; but seen from a point of view a little higher, they are what I have described them; seen from a higher still, and the highest, who shall say what they are, or that they are worth looking at or thinking of at all?

However, the government does not concern me much, and I shall bestow the fewest possible thoughts on it. It is not many moments that I live under a government, even in this world. If a man is thought-free, fancy-free, imagination-free, that which *is not* never for a long time appearing *to be* to him, unwise rulers or reformers cannot fatally interrupt him.

I know that most men think differently from myself; but those whose lives are by profession devoted to the study of these or kindred subjects content me as little as any. Statesmen and legislators, standing so completely within the institution never distinctly and nakedly behold it. They speak of moving society, but have no resting-place without it. They may be men of a certain experience and discrimination, and have no doubt invented ingenious and even useful systems, for which we sincerely thank them; but all their wit and usefulness lie within certain not very wide limits. They are wont to forget that the world is not governed by policy and expediency. Webster never goes behind government, and so cannot speak with authority about it. His words are wisdom to those legislators who contemplate no essential reform in the existing gov-

ernment; but for thinkers, and those who legislate for all time, he never once glances at the subject. I know of those whose serene and wise speculations on this theme would soon reveal the limits of his mind's range and hospitality. Yet, compared with the cheap professions of most reformers, and the still cheaper wisdom and eloquence of politicians in general, his are almost the only sensible and valuable words, and we thank Heaven for him. Comparatively, he is always strong, original, and, above all, practical. Still, his quality is not wisdom, but prudence. The lawyer's truth is not Truth, but consistency or a consistent expediency. Truth is always in harmony with herself, and is not concerned chiefly to reveal the justice that may consist with wrong-doing. He well deserves to be called, as he has been called, the Defender of the Constitution. There are really no blows to be given by him but defensive ones. He is not a leader, but a follower. His leaders are the men of '87. "I have never made an effort," he says, "and never propose to make an effort; I have never countenanced an effort, and never mean to countenance an effort, to disturb the arrangement as originally made, by which the various States came into the Union." Still thinking of the sanction which the Constitution gives to slavery, he says, "Because it was a part of the original compact,—let it stand." Notwithstanding his special acuteness and ability, he is unable to take a fact out of its merely political relations, and behold it as it lies absolutely to be disposed of by the intellect, —what, for instance, it behooves a man to do here in America to-day with regard to slavery,—but ventures, or is driven, to make some such desperate answer as the following, while professing to speak absolutely, and as a private man,—from which what new and singular code of social duties might be inferred? "The manner," says he, "in which the governments of those States where slavery exists are to regulate it is for their own consideration, under their responsibility to their constituents, to the general laws of propriety, humanity, and justice, and to God. Associations formed elsewhere, springing from a feeling of humanity, or any other cause, have nothing whatever to do with it. They have never received any encouragement from me, and they never will."

They who know of no purer sources of truth, who have traced up its stream no higher, stand, and wisely stand, by the Bible and the Constitution, and drink at it there with reverence and humility; but they who behold where it comes trickling into this lake or that pool, gird up their loins once more, and continue their pilgrimage toward its fountain-head.

No man with a genius for legislation has appeared in America. They are rare in the history of the world. There are orators, politicians, and eloquent men, by the thousand; but the speaker has not yet opened his mouth to speak who is capable of settling the much-vexed question of the day. We love eloquence for its own sake, and not for any truth which it may utter, or any heroism it may inspire. Our legislators have not yet learned the comparative value of free trade and of freedom, of union, and of rectitude, to a nation. They have no genius or talent for comparatively humble questions of taxation and finance, commerce and manufactures and agriculture. If we were left solely to the wordy wit of legislators in Congress for our guidance, uncorrected by the seasonable experience and the effectual complaints of the people, America would not long retain her rank among the nations. For eighteen hundred years, though perchance I have no right to say it, the New Testament has been written; yet where is the legislator who has wisdom and practical talent enough to avail himself of the light which it sheds on the science of legislation?

The authority of government, even such as I am willing to submit to,—for I will cheerfully obey those who know and can do better than I, and in many things even those who neither know nor can do so well,—is still an impure one: to be strictly just, it must have the sanction and consent of the governed. It can have no pure right over my person and property but what I concede to it. The progress from an absolute to a limited monarchy, from a limited monarchy to a democracy, is a progress toward a true respect for the individual. Even the Chinese philosopher was wise enough to regard the individual as the basis of the empire. Is a democracy, such as we know it, the last improvement possible in government? Is it not possible to take a step further towards recognizing and organizing the rights of man? There will never be a really free and enlightened State until the State comes to recognize the individual as a higher and independent power, from which all its own power and authority are derived, and treats him accordingly. I please myself with imagining a State at last which can afford to be just to all men, and to treat the individual with respect as a neighbor; which even would not think it inconsistent with its own repose if a few were to live aloof from it, not meddling with it, nor embraced by it, who fulfilled all the duties of neighbors and fellow-men. A State which bore this kind of fruit, and suffered it to drop off as fast as it ripened, would prepare the way for a still more perfect and glorious State, which also I have imagined, but not yet anywhere seen.

Walden

WHERE I LIVED, AND WHAT I LIVED FOR

At a certain season of our life we are accustomed to consider every spot as the possible site of a house. I have thus surveyed the country on every side within a dozen miles of where I live. In imagination I have bought all the farms in succession, for all were to be bought, and I knew their price. I walked over each farmer's premises, tasted his wild apples, discoursed on husbandry with him, took his farm at his price, at any price, mortgaging it to him in my mind; even put a higher price on it,—took everything but a deed of it,—took his word for his deed, for I dearly love to talk,—cultivated it, and him too to some extent, I trust, and withdrew when I had enjoyed it long enough, leaving him to carry it on. This experience entitled me to be regarded as a sort of real-estate broker by my friends. Wherever I sat, there I might live, and the landscape radiated from me accordingly. What is a house but a *sedes*, a seat?—better if a country seat. I discovered many a site for a house not likely to be soon improved, which some might have thought too far from the village, but to my eyes the village was too far from it. Well, there I might live, I said; and there I did live, for an hour, a summer and a winter life; saw how I could let the years run off, buffet the winter through, and see the spring come in. The future inhabitants of this region, wherever they may place their houses, may be sure that they have been anticipated. An afternoon sufficed to lay out the land into orchard, wood lot, and pasture, and to decide what fine oaks or pines should be left to stand before the door, and whence each blasted tree could be seen to best advantage; and then I let it lie, fallow perchance, for a man is rich in proportion to the number of things which he can afford to let alone.

My imagination carried me so far that I even had the refusal of several farms,—the refusal was all I wanted,—but I never got my fingers burned by actual possession. The nearest that I came to actual possession was when I bought the Hollowell place, and had begun to sort my seeds, and collected materials with which to make a wheelbarrow to carry it on or off with; but before the owner gave me a deed of it, his wife—every man has such a wife—changed her mind and wished to keep it, and he offered me ten dollars to release him. Now, to speak the truth, I had but ten cents in the world, and it surpassed my arithmetic to tell, if I was the man who had ten cents, or who had a farm, or ten dollars, or all together. However, I let him keep the ten dollars and the farm too, for I had carried it far enough; or rather, to be generous, I sold him the farm for just what I gave for it, and, as he was not a rich man, made him a present of ten dollars, and still had my ten cents, and seeds, and materials for a wheelbarrow left. I found thus that I had been a rich man without any damage to my poverty. But I retained the landscape, and I have since annually carried off what it yielded without a wheelbarrow. With respect to landscapes,—

> "I am monarch of all I *survey*,
> My right there is none to dispute."

I have frequently seen a poet withdraw, having enjoyed the most valuable part of a farm, while the crusty farmer supposed that he had got a few wild apples only. Why, the owner does not know it for many years when a poet has put his farm in rhyme, the most admirable kind of invisible fence, has fairly impounded it, milked it, skimmed it, and got all the cream and left the farmer only the skimmed milk.

The real attractions of the Hollowell farm, to me, were, its complete retirement, being about two miles from the village, half a mile from the nearest neighbor, and separated from the highway by a broad field; its bounding on the river, which the owner said protected it by its fogs from frosts in the spring, though that was nothing to me; the gray color and ruinous state of the house and barn, and the dilapidated fences, which put such an interval between me and the last occupant; the hollow and lichen-covered apple trees, gnawed by rabbits, showing what kind of neighbors I should have; but above all, the recollection I had of it from my earliest voyages up the river, when the house was concealed behind a dense grove of red maples, through which I heard the house-dog bark. I was in haste to buy it, before the proprietor finished getting out some rocks, cutting down the hollow apple trees, and grubbing up some young birches which had sprung up in the pasture, or, in short, had made any more of his improvements. To enjoy these advantages, I

was ready to carry it on; like Atlas, to take the world on my shoulders,—I never heard what compensation he received for that,—and do all those things which had no other motive or excuse but that I might pay for it and be unmolested in my possession of it; for I knew all the while that it would yield the most abundant crop of the kind I wanted, if I could only afford to let it alone. But it turned out as I have said.

All that I could say, then, with respect to farming on a large scale (I have always cultivated a garden,) was, that I had had my seeds ready. Many think that seeds improve with age. I have no doubt that time discriminates between the good and the bad; and when at last I shall plant, I shall be less likely to be disappointed. But I would say to my fellows, once for all, As long as possible live free and uncommitted. It makes but little difference whether you are committed to a farm or the county jail.

Old Cato, whose "De Re Rusticâ" is my "cultivator," says, and the only translation I have seen makes sheer nonsense of the passage, "When you think of getting a farm, turn it thus in your mind, not to buy greedily; nor spare your pains to look at it, and do not think it enough to go round it once. The oftener you go there the more it will please you, if it is good." I think I shall not buy greedily, but go round and round it as long as I live, and be buried in it first, that it may please me the more at last.

The present was my next experiment of this kind, which I purpose to describe more at length; for convenience, putting the experience of two years into one. As I have said, I do not propose to write an ode to dejection, but to brag as lustily as chanticleer in the morning, standing on his roost, if only to wake my neighbors up.

When first I took up my abode in the woods, that is, began to spend my nights as well as days there, which, by accident, was on Independence day, or the fourth of July, 1845, my house was not finished for winter, but was merely a defence against the rain, without plastering or chimney, the walls being of rough, weather-stained boards, with wide chinks, which made it cool at night. The upright white hewn studs and freshly planed door and window casings gave it a clean and airy look, especially in the morning, when its timbers were saturated with dew, so that I fancied that by noon some sweet gum would exude from them. To my imagination it retained throughout the day more or less of this auroral character, reminding me of a certain house on a mountain which I had visited a year before. This was an airy and unplastered cabin, fit to entertain a travelling god, and where a goddess might trail her garments. The winds which passed over my dwelling were such as sweep over the ridges of mountains, bearing the broken strains, or celestial parts only, of terrestrial music. The morning wind forever blows, the poem of creation is uninterrupted; but few are the ears that hear it. Olympus is but the outside of the earth every where.

The only house I had been the owner of before, if I except a boat, was a tent, which I used occasionally when making excursions in the summer, and this is still rolled up in my garret; but the boat, after passing from hand to hand, has gone down the stream of time. With this more substantial shelter about me, I had made some progress towards settling in the world. This frame, so slightly clad, was a sort of crystallization around me, and reacted on the builder. It was suggestive somewhat as a picture in outlines. I did not need to go out doors to take the air, for the atmosphere within had lost none of its freshness. It was not so much within doors as behind a door where I sat, even in the rainiest weather. The Harivansa [1] says, "An abode without birds is like a meat without seasoning." Such was not my abode, for I found myself suddenly neighbor to the birds; not by having imprisoned one, but having caged myself near them. I was not only nearer to some of those which commonly frequent the garden and the orchard, but to those wilder and more thrilling songsters of the forest which never, or rarely, serenade a villager,—the wood-thrush, the veery, the scarlet tanager, the field-sparrow, the whippoorwill, and many others.

I was seated by the shore of a small pond, about a mile and a half south of the village of Concord and somewhat higher than it, in the midst of an extensive wood between that town and Lincoln, and about two miles south of that our only field known to fame, Concord Battle Ground; but I was so low in the woods that the opposite shore, half a mile off, like the rest, covered with wood, was my most distant horizon. For the first week, whenever I looked out on the pond it impressed me like a tarn high up on the side of a mountain, its bottom far above the surface of other lakes, and, as the sun arose, I saw it throwing off its nightly clothing of mist, and here and there, by degrees, its soft ripples or its smooth reflecting surface was revealed, while

[1] A Sanskrit poem of over sixteen thousand verses.

the mists, like ghosts, were stealthily withdrawing in every direction into the woods, as at the breaking up of some nocturnal conventicle. The very dew seemed to hang upon the trees later into the day than usual, as on the sides of mountains.

This small lake was of most value as a neighbor in the intervals of a gentle rain storm in August, when, both air and water being perfectly still, but the sky overcast, mid-afternoon had all the serenity of evening, and the wood-thrush sang around, and was heard from shore to shore. A lake like this is never smoother than at such a time; and the clear portion of the air above it being shallow and darkened by clouds, the water, full of light and reflections, becomes a lower heaven itself so much the more important. From a hill top near by, where the wood had been recently cut off, there was a pleasing vista southward across the pond, through a wide indentation in the hills which form the shore there, where their opposite sides sloping toward each other suggested a stream flowing out in that direction through a wooded valley, but stream there was none. That way I looked between and over the near green hills to some distant and higher ones in the horizon, tinged with blue. Indeed, by standing on tiptoe I could catch a glimpse of some of the peaks of the still bluer and more distant mountain ranges in the north-west, those true-blue coins from heaven's own mint, and also of some portion of the village. But in other directions, even from this point, I could not see over or beyond the woods which surrounded me. It is well to have some water in your neighborhood, to give buoyancy to and float the earth. One value even of the smallest well is, that when you look into it you see that earth is not continent but insular. This is as important as that it keeps butter cool. When I looked across the pond from this peak toward the Sudbury meadows, which in time of flood I distinguished elevated perhaps by a mirage in their seething valley, like a coin in a basin, all the earth beyond the pond appeared like a thin crust insulated and floated even by this small sheet of intervening water, and I was reminded that this on which I dwelt was but *dry land*.

Though the view from my door was still more contracted, I did not feel crowded or confined in the least. There was pasture enough for my imagination. The low shrub-oak plateau to which the opposite shore arose, stretched away toward the prairies of the West and the steppes of Tartary, affording ample room for all the roving families of men. "There are none happy in the world but beings who enjoy freely a vast horizon,"—said Damodara,[2] when his herds required new and larger pastures.

Both place and time were changed, and I dwelt nearer to those parts of the universe and to those eras in history which had most attracted me. Where I lived was as far off as many a region viewed nightly by astronomers. We are wont to imagine rare and delectable places in some remote and more celestial corner of the system, behind the constellation of Cassiopeia's Chair, far from noise and disturbance. I discovered that my house actually had its site in such a withdrawn, but forever new and unprofaned, part of the universe. If it were worth the while to settle in those parts near to the Pleiades or the Hyades, to Aldebaran or Altair, then I was really there, or at an equal remoteness from the life which I had left behind, dwindled and twinkling with as fine a ray to my nearest neighbor, and to be seen only in moonless nights by him. Such was that part of creation where I had squatted;—

"There was a shepherd that did live,
    And held his thoughts as high
As were the mounts whereon his flocks
    Did hourly feed him by."

What should we think of the shepherd's life if his flocks always wandered to higher pastures than his thoughts?

Every morning was a cheerful invitation to make my life of equal simplicity, and I may say innocence, with Nature herself. I have been as sincere a worshipper of Aurora as the Greeks. I got up early and bathed in the pond; that was a religious exercise, and one of the best things which I did. They say that characters were engraven on the bathing tub of king Tching-thang to this effect: "Renew thyself completely each day; do it again, and again, and forever again." I can understand that. Morning brings back the heroic ages. I was as much affected by the faint hum of a mosquito making its invisible and unimaginable tour through my apartment at earliest dawn, when I was sitting with door and windows open, as I could be by any trumpet that ever sang of fame. It was Homer's requiem; itself an Iliad and Odyssey in the air, singing its own wrath and wanderings. There was something cosmical about it; a standing advertisement, till forbidden, of the everlasting vigor and fertility of the world. The morning, which is the most memorable season of the day, is the awakening hour. Then there is least somnolence in us; and for an

hour, at least, some part of us awakes which slumbers all the rest of the day and night. Little is to be expected of that day, if it can be called a day, to which we are not awakened by our Genius, but by the mechanical nudgings of some servitor, are not awakened by our own newly-acquired force and aspirations from within, accompanied by the undulations of celestial music, instead of factory bells, and a fragrance filling the air—to a higher life than we fell asleep from; and thus the darkness bear its fruit, and prove itself to be good, no less than the light. That man who does not believe that each day contains an earlier, more sacred, and auroral hour than he has yet profaned, has despaired of life, and is pursuing a descending and darkening way. After a partial cessation of his sensuous life, the soul of man, or its organs rather, are reinvigorated each day, and his Genius tries again what noble life it can make. All memorable events, I should say, transpire in morning time and in a morning atmosphere. The Vedas[3] say, "All intelligences awake with the morning." Poetry and art, and the fairest and most memorable of the actions of men, date from such an hour. All poets and heroes, like Memnon,[4] are the children of Aurora, and emit their music at sunrise. To him whose elastic and vigorous thought keeps pace with the sun, the day is a perpetual morning. It matters not what the clocks say or the attitudes and labors of men. Morning is when I am awake and there is a dawn in me. Moral reform is the effort to throw off sleep. Why is it that men give so poor an account of their day if they have not been slumbering? They are not such poor calculators. If they had not been overcome with drowsiness they would have performed something. The millions are awake enough for physical labor; but only one in a million is awake enough for effective intellectual exertion, only one in a hundred millions to a poetic or divine life. To be awake is to be alive. I have never yet met a man who was quite awake. How could I have looked him in the face?

We must learn to reawaken and keep ourselves awake, not by mechanical aids, but by an infinite expectation of the dawn, which does not forsake us in our soundest sleep. I know of no more encouraging fact than the unquestionable ability of man to elevate his life by a conscious endeavor. It is something to be able to paint a particular

---

[2] Damodara Misra, an eleventh-century Sanskrit poet.

[3] The sacred literature, in four parts, of the Hindus.

[4] Memnon was supposed to be the son of the Dawn, and, when reached by the rays of the rising sun, statues of Memnon gave forth a musical chord.

picture, or to carve a statue, and so to make a few objects beautiful; but it is far more glorious to carve and paint the very atmosphere and medium through which we look, which morally we can do. To affect the quality of the day, that is the highest of arts. Every man is tasked to make his life, even in its details, worthy of the contemplation of his most elevated and critical hour. If we refused, or rather used up, such paltry information as we get, the oracles would distinctly inform us how this might be done.

I went to the woods because I wished to live deliberately, to front only the essential facts of life, and see if I could not learn what it had to teach, and not, when I came to die, discover that I had not lived. I did not wish to live what was not life, living is so dear; nor did I wish to practise resignation, unless it was quite necessary. I wanted to live deep and suck out all the marrow of life, to live so sturdily and Spartan-like as to put to rout all that was not life, to cut a broad swath and shave close, to drive life into a corner, and reduce it to its lowest terms, and, if it proved it to be mean, why then to get the whole and genuine meanness of it, and publish its meanness to the world; or if it were sublime, to know it by experience, and be able to give a true account of it in my next excursion. For most men, it appears to me, are in a strange uncertainty about it, whether it is of the devil or of God, and have *somewhat hastily* concluded that it is the chief end of man here to "glorify God and enjoy him forever."

Still we live meanly, like ants; though the fable tells us that we were long ago changed into men; like pygmies we fight with cranes; it is error upon error, and clout upon clout, and our best virtue has for its occasion a superfluous and evitable wretchedness. Our life is frittered away by detail. An honest man has hardly need to count more than his ten fingers, or in extreme cases he may add his ten toes, and lump the rest. Simplicity, simplicity, simplicity! I say, let your affairs be as two or three, and not a hundred or a thousand; instead of a million count half a dozen, and keep your accounts on your thumb nail. In the midst of this chopping sea of civilized life, such are the clouds and storms and quicksands and thousand-and-one items to be allowed for, that a man has to live, if he would not founder and go to the bottom and not make his port at all, by dead reckoning, and he must be a great calculator indeed who succeeds. Simplify, simplify. Instead of three meals a day, if it be necessary eat but one; instead of a hundred dishes, five; and

reduce other things in proportion. Our life is like a German Confederacy, made up of petty states, with its boundary forever fluctuating, so that even a German cannot tell you how it is bounded at any moment. The nation itself, with all its so-called internal improvements, which, by the way, are all external and superficial, is just such an unwieldy and overgrown establishment, cluttered with furniture and tripped up by its own traps, ruined by luxury and heedless expense, by want of calculation and a worthy aim, as the million households in the land; and the only cure for it as for them is in a rigid economy, a stern and more than Spartan simplicity of life and elevation of purpose. It lives too fast. Men think that it is esential that the *Nation* have commerce, and export ice, and talk through a telegraph, and ride thirty miles an hour, without a doubt, whether *they* do or not; but whether we should live like baboons or like men, is a little uncertain. If we do not get our sleepers, and forge rails, and devote days and nights to the work, but go to tinkering upon our *lives* to improve *them,* who will build railroads? And if railroads are not built, how shall we get to heaven in season? But if we stay at home and mind our business, who will want railroads? We do not ride on the railroad; it rides upon us. Did you ever think what those sleepers are that underlie the railroad? Each one is a man, an Irishman, or a Yankee man. The rails are laid on them, and they are covered with sand, and the cars run smoothly over them. They are sound sleepers, I assure you. And every few years a new lot is laid down and run over; so that, if some have the pleasure of riding on a rail, others have the misfortune to be ridden upon. And when they run over a man that is walking in his sleep, a supernumerary sleeper in the wrong position, and wake him up, they suddenly stop the cars, and make a hue and cry about it, as if this were an exception. I am glad to know that it takes a gang of men for every five miles to keep the sleepers down and level in their beds as it is, for this is a sign that they may sometime get up again.

Why should we live with such hurry and waste of life? We are determined to be starved before we are hungry. Men say that a stitch in time saves nine, and so they take a thousand stitches to-day to save nine to-morrow. As for *work,* we haven't any of any consequence. We have the Saint Vitus' dance, and cannot possibly keep our heads still. If I should only give a few pulls at the parish bell-rope, as for a fire, that is, without setting the bell, there is hardly a man on his farm in the outskirts of Concord, notwithstanding that press of engagements which was his excuse so many times this morning, nor a boy, nor a woman, I might almost say, but would forsake all and follow that sound, not mainly to save property from the flames, but, if we will confess the truth, much more to see it burn, since burn it must, and we, be it known, did not set it on fire,—or to see it put out, and have a hand in it, if that is done as handsomely; yes, even if it were the parish church itself. Hardly a man takes a half hour's nap after dinner, but when he wakes he holds up his head and asks, "What's the news?" as if the rest of mankind had stood his sentinels. Some give directions to be waked every half hour, doubtless for no other purpose; and then, to pay for it, they tell what they have dreamed. After a night's sleep the news is as indispensable as the breakfast. "Pray tell me any thing new that has happened to a man anywhere on this globe,"—and he reads it over his coffee and rolls, that a man has had his eyes gouged out this morning on the Wachito River; never dreaming the while that he lives in the dark unfathomed mammoth cave of this world, and has but the rudiment of an eye himself.

For my part, I could easily do without the post-office. I think that there are very few important communications made through it. To speak critically, I never received more than one or two letters in my life—I wrote this some years ago—that were worth the postage. The penny-post is, commonly, an institution through which you seriously offer a man that penny for his thoughts which is so often safely offered in jest. And I am sure that I never read any memorable news in a newspaper. If we read of one man robbed, or murdered, or killed by accident, or one house burned, or one vessel wrecked, or one steamboat blown up, or one cow run over on the Western Railroad, or one mad dog killed, or one lot of grasshoppers in the winter,— we never need read of another. One is enough. If you are acquainted with the principle, what do you care for a myriad instances and applications? To a philosopher all *news*, as it is called, is gossip, and they who edit and read it are old women over their tea. Yet not a few are greedy after this gossip. There was such a rush, as I hear, the other day at one of the offices to learn the foreign news by the last arrival, that several large squares of plate glass belonging to the establishment were broken by the pressure,—news which I seriously think a ready wit might write a twelvemonth or twelve years beforehand with sufficient accuracy. As for Spain, for instance, if you know how to throw in Don Carlos

and the Infanta and Don Pedro and Seville and Granada, from time to time in the right proportions, —they may have changed the names a little since I saw the papers,—and serve up a bullfight when other entertainments fail, it will be true to the letter, and give us as good an idea of the exact state or ruin of things in Spain as the most succinct and lucid reports under this head in the newspapers: and as for England, almost the last significant scrap of news from that quarter was the revolution of 1649; and if you have learned the history of her crops for an average year, you never need attend to that thing again, unless your speculations are of a merely pecuniary character. If one may judge who rarely looks into the newspapers, nothing new does ever happen in foreign parts, a French revolution not excepted.

What news! how much more important to know what that is which was never old! "Kieou-he-yu (great dignitary of the state of Wei) sent a man to Khoung-tseu to know his news. Khoung-tseu caused the messenger to be seated near him, and questioned him in these terms: What is your master doing? The messenger answered with respect: My master desires to diminish the number of his faults, but he cannot come to the end of them. The messenger being gone, the philosopher remarked: What a worthy messenger! What a worthy messenger!" [5] The preacher, instead of vexing the ears of drowsy farmers on their day of rest at the end of the week, —for Sunday is the fit conclusion of an ill-spent week, and not the fresh and brave beginning of a new one,—with this one other draggle-tail of a sermon, should shout with thundering voice,— "Pause! Avast! Why so seeming fast, but deadly slow?"

Shams and delusions are esteemed for soundest truths, while reality is fabulous. If men would steadily observe realities only, and not allow themselves to be deluded, life, to compare it with such things as we know, would be like a fairy tale and the Arabian Nights' Entertainment. If we respected only what is inevitable and has a right to be, music and poetry would resound along the streets. When we are unhurried and wise, we perceive that only great and worthy things have any permanent and absolute existence,—that petty fears and petty pleasures are but the shadow of the reality. This is always exhilarating and sublime. By closing the eyes and slumbering, and consenting to be deceived by shows, men establish and confirm their daily life of routine and habit every where, which still is built

[5] From the *Analects* of Confucius.

on purely illusory foundations. Children, who play life, discern its true law and relations more clearly than men, who fail to live it worthily, but who think that they are wiser by experience, that is, by failure. I have read in a Hindoo book, that "there was a king's son, who, being expelled in infancy from his native city, was brought up by a forester, and, growing up to maturity in that state, imagined himself to belong to the barbarous race with which he lived. One of his father's ministers having discovered him, revealed to him what he was, and the misconception of his character was removed, and he knew himself to be a prince. So the soul," continues the Hindoo philosopher, "from the circumstances in which it is placed, mistakes its own character, until the truth is revealed to it by some holy teacher, and then it knows itself to be *Brahme*." I perceive that we inhabitants of New England live this mean life that we do because our vision does not penetrate the surface of things. We think that that *is* which *appears* to be. If a man should walk through this town and see only the reality, where, think you, would the "Mill-dam" go to? If he should give us an account of the realities he beheld there, we should not recognize the place in his description. Look at a meeting-house, or a court-house, or a jail, or a shop, or a dwelling-house, and say what that thing really is before a true gaze, and they would all go to pieces in your account of them. Men esteem truth remote, in the outskirts of the system, behind the farthest star, before Adam and after the last man. In eternity there is indeed something true and sublime. But all these times and places and occasions are now and here. God himself culminates in the present moment, and will never be more divine in the lapse of all the ages. And we are enabled to apprehend at all what is sublime and noble only by the perpetual instilling and drenching of the reality that surrounds us. The universe constantly and obediently answers to our conceptions; whether we travel fast or slow, the track is laid for us. Let us spend our lives in conceiving them. The poet or the artist never yet had so fair and noble a design but some of his posterity at least could accomplish it.

Let us spend one day as deliberately as Nature, and not be thrown off the track by every nutshell and mosquito's wing that falls on the rails. Let us rise early and fast, or break fast, gently and without perturbation; let company come and let company go, let the bells ring and the children cry,—determined to make a day of it. Why should we knock under and go with the stream? Let us not be upset

and overwhelmed in that terrible rapid and whirlpool called a dinner, situated in the meridian shallows. Weather this danger and you are safe, for the rest of the way is down hill. With unrelaxed nerves, with morning vigor, sail by it, looking another way, tied to the mast like Ulysses. If the engine whistles, let it whistle till it is hoarse for its pains. If the bell rings, why should we run? We will consider what kind of music they are like. Let us settle ourselves, and work and wedge our feet downward through the mud and slush of opinion, and prejudice, and tradition, and delusion, and appearance, that alluvion which covers the globe, through Paris and London, through New York and Boston and Concord, through church and state, through poetry and philosophy and religion, till we come to a hard bottom and rocks in place, which we can call *reality*, and say, This is, and no mistake; and then begin, having a *point d'appui*, below freshet and frost and fire, a place where you might found a wall or a state, or set a lamp-post safely, or perhaps a gauge, not a Nilometer, but a Realometer, that future ages might know how deep a freshet of shams and appearances had gathered from time to time. If you stand right fronting and face to face to a fact, you will see the sun glimmer on both its surfaces, as if it were a cimeter, and feel its sweet edge dividing you through the heart and marrow, and so you will happily conclude your mortal career. Be it life or death, we crave only reality. If we are really dying, let us hear the rattle in our throats and feel cold in the extremities; if we are alive, let us go about our business.

Time is but the stream I go a-fishing in, I drink at it; but while I drink I see the sandy bottom and detect how shallow it is. Its thin current slides away, but eternity remains. I would drink deeper; fish in the sky, whose bottom is pebbly with stars. I cannot count one. I know not the first letters of the alphabet. I have always been regretting that I was not as wise as the day I was born. The intellect is a cleaver; it discerns and rifts its way into the secret of things. I do not wish to be any more busy with my hands than is necessary. My head is hands and feet. I feel all my best faculties concentrated in it. My instinct tells me that my head is an organ for burrowing, as some creatures use their snout and fore-paws, and with it I would mine and burrow my way through these hills. I think that the richest vein is somewhere hereabouts; so by the divining rod and thin rising vapors I judge; and here I will begin to mine.

French Lyric Poetry

ALPHONSE MARIE LOUIS DE PRAT DE LAMARTINE

1790–1869

The highly successful *Premières Méditations* (1820) of Lamartine, brilliant poet, orator, novelist, and statesman, marks the beginning of French Romantic poetry. Many of his lyrics deal with nature, religion, and love. A disciple of Rousseau in his youth, Lamartine manifests the subjectivity, spontaneity, sensitivity, and melancholy characteristic of the Romantics. The lake, the twilight hour, the moon, the gentle slopes of the surrounding hills, and the tall mournful trees are for him symbols of love and reverie. "The Lake" is one of the famous love songs in French. It has the lofty sentiment, delicate thoughts, and melody which are found in his other lyrics.

FURTHER READING

GUILLEMAIN, H. *Connaissance de Lamartine* (Fribourg, 1942).
GUILLEMAIN, H. *Lamartine, l'Homme et l'Oeuvre* (Paris, 1940).
HAZARD, P. *Lamartine* (Paris, 1925).

The Cedars of Lebanon

Eagles, that wheel above our crests,
Say to the storms that round us blow,
They can not harm our gnarled breasts,
Firm-rooted as we are below.
Their utmost efforts we defy.
They lift the sea-waves to the sky;
But when they wrestle with our arms
Nervous and gaunt, or lift our hair,
Balanced within its cradle fair
The tiniest bird has no alarms.

Sons of the rock, no mortal hand
Here planted us: God-sown we grew.
We are the diadem green and grand
On Eden's summit that He threw.

When waters in a deluge rose,
Our hollow flanks could well enclose
Awhile the whole of Adam's race;
And children of the Patriarch
Within our forest built the Ark
Of Covenant, foreshadowing grace.

We saw the Tribes as captives led.
We saw them back return anon;
As rafters have our branches dead
Cover'd the porch of Solomon;
And later, when the Word, made man,
Came down in God's salvation-plan
To pay for sin the ransom-price,
The beams that form'd the Cross we gave:
These, red in blood of power to save,
Were altars of that Sacrifice.

In memory of such great events,
Men come to worship our remains;
Kneel down in prayer within our tents,
And kiss our old trunks' weather-stains.
The saint, the poet, and the sage,
Hear and shall hear from age to age
Sounds in our foliage like the voice
Of many waters; in these shades
Their burning words are forged like blades,
While their uplifted souls rejoice.

(trans. by Toru Dutt)

The Lake

Still tow'rd new shores we wend our unreturning
        way,
Into th' eternal night borne off before the blast;
May we then never on the ages' ocean cast
        Anchor for one sole day?

The year hath scarce attained its term and now
        alone,
By thy beloved waves, which she should see again,
O lake, behold, I come to sit upon this stone,
        Where she to sit was fain.

Thou murmurest then as now against thy rocky
        steep;
As now thou brok'st in foam upon thy sheltered
        sides;   10

And at her feet adored the breeze, as now, did sweep
    The spray from off thy tides.

One night, rememberest thou? in silence did we float;
Nought in the water heard or air was far and near,
Except the rowers' stroke, whose oars in cadence smote
    Upon thy waters clear;

When accents, all at once, unknown to mortal ear,
Th' enchanted echoes woke, and earth, air, water, all,
Straight hearkened, as the voice of her I held so dear
    These pregnant words let fall;   20

"O Time, suspend thy flight; and you, propitious hours,
    Your course a moment stay!
Let us the swift delights taste of this day of ours,
    Of this our fairest day!

Unfortunates enough on earth implore your power;
    For them alone flow yet!
Bear with their days away the cares that them devour
    And happy folk forget."

But I implore in vain a moment of delay;
    Time 'scapes me, still a-flight;   30
Unto the night I say, 'Be slower!' And the day
    Will soon disperse the night.

Let us then love, love still and haste the hour that flees
    Now to enjoy. Alas!
Man hath no port and Time no shore hath its seas;
    It lapses and we pass.

Can't be, O jealous Time, that these our hours so sweet,
Wherein, by long-drawn draughts, Love pours us happiness,
With the same breathless speed away from us do fleet
    As the days distress?   40

What! May we not avail at least to fix their trace?
Are they, then, wholly past and lost for evermore?
Will time, that gave them us and doth them now efface,
    Them ne'er to us restore?

Death, Past, Eternity, ye black abysmal seas,
What do ye with the days ye swallow thus?

Say, will you give us back those rapturous ecstasies
    That you bear off from us?

O lake, O grottoes dumb, rocks, forests dark and deep,
You that Time spares or young can cause again to be,   50
Keep of this night of ours, O goodly Nature, keep
    At least the memory!

Be't in thy stormy days or in thy restful nights,
Fair lake, in the aspect of those thy bright hillsides,
Or in those somber pines or in those wilding heights,
    That overhang thy tides,

Be't in the breeze that sighs and passes on its way,
In the sounds by thy shores echoed from place to place,
In yonder argent star, that with its dulcet ray
    Silvers thy smiling face.   60

Let, let the wind that moans, let, let the reed that sighs,
The perfumes light that float in thine embalsamed air,
Let all one hears and sees and breathes beneath the skies
    Still "They have loved!" declare.
           (trans. by John Payne)

———————◆———————

ALFRED DE VIGNY

1797–1863

Vigny, poet, dramatist, novelist, at first followed his father in the career of arms, but spent his leisure hours writing verse. His first volume, entitled *Poèmes*, appeared in 1826. In 1828 he resigned his army commission and devoted his time to literature. Vigny is the poet of the inner life who, after a series of disappointments and disillusionments retired into solitude.

Most of Vigny's poems are short narratives which express symbolically some philosophical thought. "The Sound of the Horn," for instance, symbolizes the tragic death of Roland at Roncevaux. Vigny was a proud, sincere, pessimistic, melancholy individual. His poetry tends toward classic simplicity rather than Romantic extravagance. He was the intellectual among the Romantics, the thinker within the movement; accordingly, he avoided the overemphasis and grotesqueness of many of his contemporaries.

FURTHER READING

BONNEFOY, G. F. *La Pensée Réligieuse et Morale d'Alfred de Vigny* (Paris, 1944).
LAUVRIÈRE, E. *Alfred de Vigny, sa Vie et son Oeuvre* (Paris, 1946).

The Sound of the Horn *

I love the sound of the horn in the deep, dim wood-
land,
 Whether it wail with the doe that is nigh to death,
Or cry the hunter's farewell on the echoes waning,
 From leaf to leaf borne on by the north wind's
breath.

How often alone, in the shadow at midnight stray-
ing,
 I have smiled to hear it, how often have wept still
more!
For I seemed to hear the rumor of things foreboding
 The death of the Paladin knights that lived of
yore.

O azure Mountain! O land that my heart is fain of!
 Franzona fells, and summits of Marboré,
Fountains that fall with the drifted snows for a
burden,
 Torrents and brooks of the Pyrenees' chill spray,

Mountains frozen or fertile, throning the seasons,
 Who have ice for crown and the meadows about
your feet,
'Tis there would I dwell, 'tis there would I wait to
hearken
 The far-borne sound of the horn blow sad and
sweet.

A traveler strayed mayhap when the air is stilly,
 Lifts up this brazen voice that the night repeats;
With the sound of his cadenced songs for a while is
blending
 The tiny bell of the tethered lamb that bleats.

A doe that heareth the sound flies not but rather
 Stands still as a stone on the hill-top, while waters
chime
In vast uproar with the music forever calling
 From the old romance of the immemorial time.

* Translated by Wilfrid Thorley. Reprinted from *The French Muse* by permission of Frederick Muller Ltd.

Souls of the Paladins, say, do your ghosts still haunt
us?
 Is it you who speak to us still in the blare of the
horn?
Roncevaux! Roncevaux! deep in thy somber valley
 The shade of the noble Roland is still forlorn!

————◆————

VICTOR HUGO

1802–1885

Hugo—dramatist, novelist, poet, polemist—was, through his strong personality and his longevity, the dominant figure in French letters during the nineteenth century. Many consider him the greatest, or certainly one of the greatest lyric poets, France has produced. He was born at Besançon in 1802, son of a general in Napoleon's army, and spent his early, impressionable years in Spain where his father was stationed. After writing for a literary journal which he founded in collaboration with his brother, and after his conversion to the new Romantic movement, Hugo in 1827 composed the famous play *Cromwell* with his even more famous preface, followed in 1830 by *Hernani*. He spent the years 1852 to 1870 on the islands of Guernsey and Jersey in exile for his outspoken opposition to "Napoléon le Petit." After Napoleon III's defeat by the Germans in 1870, Hugo returned to Paris and reigned over his literary and political salon as a hero, prophet, and demigod. Upon his death he was buried with great pomp in the Pantheon amid almost universal mourning.

In many ways the tremendous fame which Hugo achieved was deserved. He had complete mastery over the technical resources of the French language and a facility in composing verse which has seldom been equaled. He was excessively fond of the grandiose, making use of such terms as *immense, sombre, vaste* and of such figures as lions, titans, and world's wonders. The fantastic and the grotesque figure large throughout the major portion of his writing. Unfortunately, his intellectual and spiritual qualities fell far short of his gifts for expression and imagination. He failed utterly to realize his dream of attaining fame as a great philosopher. Hugo's outlook on life was commonplace, and he exhibited all those qualities of the Romantic school in France which are most in disfavor today. He was a bourgeois and had the love for diligent labor and for order which has always been attributed to the middle-class Frenchman. He had many faults, but he had also many virtues which should be entered in the balance when reckoning the value of his life and work.

Among his poetic works *La Légende des Siècles, Les Chants du Crépuscule, Les Rayons et les Ombres,* and *Les Châtiments* have achieved wide popularity. Among his novels, which have been less popular in France than elsewhere, one might cite *Notre-Dame de Paris* in which the cathedral itself is the hero of a work of epic proportions, *Les Travailleurs de la Mer* which depicts the conflict between human and elemental forces, and *Les Misérables* with its Romantic preoccupation with the problems of the proletariat. The latter, for its excessive breadth and massiveness, is Hugo's most imposing work.

FURTHER READING

BELLESSORT, A. *Victor Hugo; Essai sur son Oeuvre* (Paris, 1930).

DAVIDSON, A. F. *Victor Hugo, His Life and Work* (London, 1912).

ESCHOLIER, R. *Victor Hugo,* translated by Lewis Galantiere (New York, 1930).

GIESE, W. F. *Victor Hugo, The Man and the Poet* (New York, 1926).

The Rose and the Grave

The Grave said to the Rose
   "What of the dews of dawn,
Love's flower, what end is theirs"?
   "And what of spirits flown,
The souls whereon doth close
The tomb's mouth unawares"?
The Rose said to the Grave.

The Rose said: "In the shade
From the dawn's tears is made
   A perfume faint and strange,
     Amber and honey sweet."
     "And all the spirits fleet
   Do suffer a sky-change,
     More strangely than the dew,
     To God's own angels new,"
The Grave said to the Rose.

              (*trans. by Andrew Lang*)

The Djinns *

Town, tower,
Shore, deep,
Where lower
Cliffs steep;
Waves gray,
Where play
Winds gay,—
All sleep.

Hark! a sound,
Far and slight,   10
Breathes around
On the night:
High and higher,
Nigh and nigher,
Like a fire
Roaring bright.

Now on 't is sweeping
With rattling beat,
Like dwarf imp leaping
In gallop fleet: 20
He flies, he prances,
In frolic fancies,
On wave-crest dances
With pattering feet.

Hark, the rising swell,
With each nearer burst!
Like the toll of bell
Of a convent cursed;
Like the billowy roar
On a storm-lashed shore,—   30
Now hushed, now once more
Maddening to its worst.

O God! the deadly sound
Of the Djinns' fearful cry!
Quick, 'neath the spiral round
Of the deep staircase fly!
See, see our lamplight fade!
And of the balustrade
Mounts, mounts the circling shade
Up to the ceiling high!   40

'T is the Djinns' wild streaming swarm
Whistling in their tempest-flight;
Snap the tall yews 'neath the storm,
Like a pine-flame crackling bright.
Swift and heavy, lo, their crowd
Through the heavens rushing loud,
Live a livid thunder-cloud
With its bolt of fiery night!

* Anonymous translation, revised.

Ha! they are on us, close without!
Shut tight the shelter where we lie!   50
With hideous din the monster rout,
Dragon and vampire, fill the sky!
The loosened rafter overhead
Trembles and bends like quivering reed;
Shakes the old door with shuddering dread,
As from its rusty hinge 't would fly!

Wild cries of hell! voices that howl and shriek!
The horrid swarm before the tempest tossed—
O Heaven!—descends my lowly roof to seek:
Bends the strong wall beneath the furious host. 60
Totters the house, as though, like dry leaf shorn
From autumn bough and on the mad blast borne,
Up from its deep foundations it were torn
To join the stormy whirl. Ah! all is lost!

O Prophet! if thy hand but now
Save from these foul and hellish things,
A pilgrim at thy shrine I'll bow,
Laden with pious offerings.
Bid their hot breath its fiery rain
Stream on my faithful door in vain,   70
Vainly upon my blackened pane
Grate the fierce claws of their dark wings!

They have passed!—and their wild legions
Cease to thunder at my door;
Fleeting through night's rayless region,
Hither they return no more.
Clanking chains and sounds of woe
Fill the forests as they go;
And the tall oaks cower low,
Bent their flaming flight before.   80

On! on! the storm of wings
Bears far the fiery fear,
Till scarce the breeze now brings
Dim murmurings to the ear;
Like locusts' humming hail,
Or thrash of tiny flail
Plied by the old pattering hail
On some old roof-tree near.

Fainter now are borne
Fitful mutterings still;   90
As, when Arab horn
Swells its magic peal,
Shoreward o'er the deep
Fairy voices sweep,
And the infant's sleep
Golden visions fill.

Each deadly Djinn,
Dark child of fright,
Of death and sin,
Speeds the wild flight   100
Hark, the dull moan,
Like the deep tone
Of ocean's groan,
Afar, by night!

More and more
Fades it now,
As on the shore
Ripple's flow,—
As the plaint
Far and faint   110
Of a saint
Murmured low.

Hark! hist!
Around,
I list!
The bounds
Of space
All trace
Efface
Of sound.   120

The Children of the Poor

Take heed of this small child of earth;
    He is great: he hath in him God most high.
Children before their fleshly birth
    Are lights alive in the blue sky.

In our light bitter world of wrong
    They come; God gives us them awhile.
His speech is in their stammering tongue,
    And his forgiveness in their smile.

Their sweet light rests upon our eyes.
    Alas! their right to joy is plain.
If they are hungry, Paradise
    Weeps, and, if cold, Heaven thrills with pain.

The want that saps their sinless flower
    Speaks judgment on sin's ministers.
Man holds an angel in his power.
    Ah! deep in Heaven what thunder stirs,

When God seeks out these tender things
    Whom in the shadow where we sleep
He sends us clothed about with wings,
    And finds them ragged babes that weep!

                    (trans. by Algernon Charles Swinburne)

HENRI MURGER

1822–1861

Most of the work of Murger, poet, prose writer, dramatist, and unsuccessful painter, deals picturesquely and affectionately with the life of the poor artists and writers in the Latin Quarter of Paris during the first half of the nineteenth century. Giacomo Puccini used his touching play *Bohemian Life*, 1849, as a basis for his perennially popular opera *La Bohème*.

FURTHER READING

SAINTSBURY, G. E. B. *Essays on French Novelists* (1891).

Spring in the Students' Quarter *

Winter is passing, and the bells
    For ever with their silver lay
Murmur a melody that tells
    Of April and of Easter day.
High in the sweet air the light vane sets,
    The weathercocks all southward twirl;
A sou will buy her violets
    And make Nini a happy girl.

The winter to the poor was sore,
    Counting the weary winter days,
Watching his little fire-wood store,
    The cruel snow-flakes fell always;
And now his last log dimly gleamed,
    Lighting the room with feeble glare,
Half cinder and half smoke it seemed
    That the wind wafted into air.

Pilgrims from ocean and far isles
    See where the east is reddening,
The flocks that fly a thousand miles
    From sunsetting to sunsetting;
Look up, look out, behold the swallows,
    The throats that twitter, the wings that beat,
And on their song the summer follows,
    And in the summer life is sweet.

.   .   .

With the green tender buds that know
    The shoot and sap of lusty spring
My neighbor of a year ago
    Her casement, see, is opening;

* Translated by Andrew Lang. Printed by permission of Longmans, Green, Ltd.

Through all the bitter months that were,
    Forth from her nest she dared not flee,
She was a study for Boucher,
    She now might sit to Gavarni.

———◆———

ALFRED DE MUSSET

1810–1857

French Romantic poet, dramatist, and novelist, Musset expresses the passion of love and youth. He was characterized by the critic Sainte-Beuve as the embodiment of adolescent genius. Probably his most exquisite lyric is the long *May Night*. Musset was neither philosopher nor thinker, and he lacked ability to interpret the purposes of human existence. Some of his best work is to be found in his short lyrics. Musset exhibits many of the tendencies of the Romantic school: its ennui, its complete subjectiveness, its individual expansiveness, its medievalism, its exoticism. He was the "spoiled child" (*enfant gâté*) of his time, frivolous, amorous, sensuous, unfortunate, and unhappy.

FURTHER READING

ALLEM, M. *Alfred de Musset* (Grenoble, 1948).
GASTINAL, P. *Le Romantisme d'Alfred de Musset* (Paris, 1933).
TILLEY, A. *Three French Dramatists* (Cambridge, Eng., 1933).

A Last Word

Thing of a day! Fret out thy little hour;
    Whence thy unceasing plaint, thy bitter cry?
And why in tears consume thy spirit's pow'r?
    Immortal is thy soul, thy tears will dry.

Thy heart is racked and wrung by love betrayed,
    Beneath the strain 't will break, or cease to feel;
Thou prayest God to hasten to thine aid:
    Immortal is thy soul, thy heart will heal.

By longing and regret thy life is torn,
    The past shuts out the future from thine eye;
Grieve not for yesterday,—await the morn;
    Immortal is thy soul, time passes by.

Thy form is bent beneath oppressive thought,
　Thy brow is burdened, and thy limbs give way;
O, bow the knee! fall prostrate, thing of naught!
　Immortal is thy soul, death frees thy clay.

Thy mouldering form its mother-earth will feed,
　Thy glory, name, and memory must die,
But not thy love, if thou hast loved indeed,
　Thy deathless soul will cherish it on high.

　　　　　　　　　　(trans. by S. B. Wister)

Fortunio's Song *

So sweet my love, her face so fair,
　So pure her fame,
Not for a kingdom would I dare
　To tell her name.

We'll sing our loves, each lover his,
　And I'll sing mine,
How blithe she is, how blond she is,
　How blue her eyne.

Whate'er she asks me, I will give
　Without a sigh;
It is for her alone I live,
　For her I'd die.

Though love that worships unconfessed
　Is grievous woe,
Yet will I hide mine in my breast
　And fain die so.

Too fond am I my love to tell
　Lest I should shame
Her whom I love and love too well
　To breathe her name.

Pale Star of Even

Pale star of even, on thy distant quest
　Lifting thy radiant brow from twilight's veil,
From out thy azure palace in the west,
　What seest thou in the dale?
The storm recedes, the winds are lulled to rest,
　The shivering trees weep on the grass beneath,
The evening butterfly, with gilded crest,
　Flits o'er the fragrant heath.
What seekest thou on Nature's sleeping breast?
　Down toward the mountains thou art sinking fast,
Sinking and smiling, sweet and pensive guest;
　Thy tremulous gaze has almost looked its last.

* Translated by William Giese (University of Wisconsin
Press). From Le Chandelier, Act II, Scene 3.

Sad, silvery tear on evening's mantle brown,
　Slow gliding downward to the verdant steep,
The shepherd sees thee, as across the down
　He homeward leads his lingering flock of sheep.
Star, at this silent hour so strangely fair,
　Through boundless night, O, whither dost thou
　　go?
To seek beside the shore a reedy lair,
　Or like a pearl, sink in the gulf below?
O, if thy glowing tresses thou must wet
　In ocean's brine, fair star, if thou must die,
Ere thou forsake us, stay a moment yet;
　Sweet star of love! ah, do not leave the sky!

　　　　　　　　　　(trans. by S. B. Wister)

◆

THÉOPHILE GAUTIER

1811–1872

Poet, journalist, novelist, critic, artist, Gautier attempted to give his poetry the plastic quality of painting which he had extensively practiced during his youth. The restrained, highly polished, appropriately entitled Émaux et Camées (Enamels and Cameos) (1852), which marks a definite turn from the sentimental and personal, is the high point of his poetic achievement. His point of departure is the theory of Art for Art's sake, strongly influenced by painting and sculpture. His poetry, therefore, often suggests the painting of an object rather than the direct vision of it. Like many of his contemporaries, Gautier had complete control over the resources of speech and was always able to find the exact word which would provide greatest preciseness and vividness. His poem "L'Art" epitomizes his artistic theories.

FURTHER READING

PALACHE, JOHN G. Gautier and the Romantics (New
　York, 1926).
SYMONS, A. The Symbolist Movement in Literature (New
　York, 1919).

Love at Sea

We are in love's land to-day;
　Where shall we go?
Love, shall we start or stay,
　Or sail or row?

There's many a wind and way,
And never a May but May;
We are in love's land to-day;
   Where shall we go?

Our landwind is the breath
Of sorrows kissed to death
   And joys that were;
Our ballast is a rose;
Our way lies where God knows
   And love knows where
      We are in love's land to-day—

Our seamen are fledged loves,
Our masts are bills of doves,
   Our decks fine gold;
Our ropes are dead maids' hair,
Our stores are love-shafts fair
   And manifold.
      We are in love's land to-day—

Where shall we land you, sweet?
On fields of strange men's feet,
   Or fields near home?
Or where the fire-flowers blow,
Or where the flowers of snow
   Or flowers of foam?
      We are in love's land to-day—

Land me, she says, where love
Shows but one shaft, one dove,
   One heart, one hand.
—A shore like that, my dear,
Lies where no man will steer,
   No maiden land.
      (*trans. by Algernon Charles Swinburne*)

Art *

All things are doubly fair
If patience fashion them
   And care—
Verse, enamel, marble, gem.

No idle chains endure:
Yet, Muse, to walk aright,
   Lace tight
Thy buskin proud and sure.

Fie on a facile measure,
A shoe where every lout   10
   At pleasure
Slips his foot in and out!

Sculptor, lay by the clay
On which thy nerveless finger
   May linger,
Thy thoughts flown far away.

Keep to Carrara rare,
Struggle with Paros cold,
   That hold
The subtle line and fair.   20

Lest haply nature lose
That proud, that perfect line,
   Make thine
The bronze of Syracuse.

And with a tender dread
Upon an agate's face
   Retrace
Apollo's golden head.

Despise a watery hue
And tints that soon expire.   30
   With fire
Burn thine enamel true.

Twine, twine in artful wise
The blue-green mermaid's arms,
   Mid charms
Of thousand heraldries.

Show in their triple lobe
Virgin and Child, that hold
   Their globe,
Cross-crowned and aureoled.   40

—All things return to dust
Save beauties fashioned well.
   The bust
Outlasts the citadel.

Oft doth the plowman's heel,
Breaking an ancient clod,
   Reveal
A Caesar or a god.

The gods, too, die, alas!
But deathless and more strong   50
   Than brass
Remains the sovereign song.

Chisel and carve and file
Till thy vague dream imprint
   Its smile
On the unyielding flint.

THE MODERN WORLD

The Modern World

Courtesy Museum of Modern Art, New York
(gift of A. Conger Goodyear)
Ile de France by Aristide Maillol.

Courtesy Museum of Modern Art, New York
Seated Man by Jacques Lipchitz.

1850–1950

THE English Victorian Age, Matthew Arnold once observed, was an age of expansion. The description is equally appropriate for Western Europe as a whole, despite evident differences and manifold variations within the patterns of national life. Before his death in 1832, Goethe had recognized clearly that one of the dominant characteristics of the Modern world was to be the continual changing and transforming of society. This development was accelerated in the nineteenth century through industrialization and the expansion of free trade; the great nationalistic movements toward freedom and democracy throughout Europe, such as the revolutions of 1848 and the Italian *Risorgimento*; the imperialistic expansion that brought great empires into being; the growth of the press that accom-

panied the development of the low-priced newspaper; the flourishing of a practical materialism and rationalism consequent to the advances of science. Purely materialistic concepts of history and of biological science were introduced by the publication of Marx and Engels' *Communist Manifesto* (1848) with its declaration that the class struggle was an inevitable historical process, and by Charles Darwin's *The Origin of the Species* (1859) which described scientifically the unremitting struggle of an organism to exist by adapting itself vigorously to new environmental conditions. In England, Sir Charles Lyell's *Principles of Geology* (1833) and *The Geological Evidences of the Antiquity of Man* (1863) suggested that man had existed on earth for a far longer period than the limits ostensibly set by

471

Courtesy Metropolitan Museum of Art, New York

Orpheus and Eurydice Emerging from the Gates of Hell by Auguste Rodin.

a literal interpretation of Biblical chronology. The concept of organic world growth and development which was partly derived from the Hegelian philosophy destroyed the eighteenth-century belief in the stable and fixed mathematical universe of Newton and Deism. Although the doctrine of organic change stressed the continuity and slowly transforming nature of historical processes, the later nineteenth century witnessed a sudden and disrupting transformation of Western civilization which had been gathering force since the decline of the Middle Ages and the beginnings of the Renaissance: the development of a credit economy, the expansion of libertarian political ideals, the curtailing of the influence of religious institutions, and the remarkable discoveries in science, accelerated in the early nineteenth century by the researches into "electric" and

organic chemistry, embryology, and comparative anatomy.

Any interpretation of the literature of the Modern world consequently cannot ignore the immense influence and the repercussions of the various industrial, social, economic, and religious revolutions of the preceding one hundred years. While society was undergoing such profound changes, many writers came forward with nostrums to relieve the growing pains, especially those belonging to the schools of realism and naturalism. Although a consideration of the neuroses and maladjustments of the individual artist in his modern environment must recognize that to a degree the spiritual history of the writer or artist is a measure of how the inner man adapts himself to environmental influences and historical processes, the measure of great literature is still the nature of the artist's tone and temper in confronting his environment, the way he transcends his ordinary self to attain his special vision of the life of man.

Indeed, to see what spiritual course we ourselves must steer in the Modern world, we cannot submerge the writer wholly in the mass movements to which he in part belongs; whatever intellectual, religious, or class influences have helped to form his mature values, these must not be thought solely to account for his development. We cannot accept the Marxian *"Der mensch ist was er isst"* (Man is what he eats); above all, the artist cannot be so simply interpreted. The great writer tries to preserve his spiritual integrity amid the flux of world change in which emergent values are often alien; and, possibly even more in the Modern world than ever before, the great artist, as Schopenhauer observed, is the exceptional man, the principal sign of whose vocation is his infinite capacity for suffering. The law of evolutionary development is often demonstrated in the wisdom and insight of the great artist who can see the ultimate realization of design in the imperfect and latent beginnings, as Walt Whitman envisaged the progress of America. Hence this presentation of the literature of the Modern world attempts to represent the significant literary tendencies, and at the same time seeks to reflect those gropings for spiritual integration that are among the most salient characteristics of modern literature, from Tennyson and Baudelaire to Rilke, T. S. Eliot, and Kafka.

ON A DARKLING PLAIN

THE Romantic conception of the human perfectibility of man, found in Condorcet, William Godwin, and Shelley, died hard. At first, the new theories of biological evolution seem to support the optimistic assumption that evolutionary progress was the unfolding nature of human social development and of Christian morality. The mid-nineteenth-century hope for the social improvement of mankind incorporated in Auguste Comte's "religion of humanity" and implied in the later novels of George Eliot found its sanction in the confident expectation of inevitable progress and in the reliance upon man's reason which could operate ideally under the conditions suggested in John Stuart Mill's *On Liberty* (1859): "absolute freedom of opinion and sentiment on all subjects." It was this assurance that evolution worked for progress that enabled Tennyson to reach that reconciliation in *In Memoriam* between the spiritual needs of his generation and the apparent indifference of the cosmic processes to the survival of humanity:

> Move upward, working out the beast,
> And let the ape and tiger die.

Courtesy Art Institute of Chicago

Village Panorama by Paul Cézanne.

At the same time, however, this new conception of evolution and historical development began to undermine the foundations of nineteenth-century orthodox religious belief. David Friedrich Strauss's *Life of Jesus* (1835) undertook to approach the Bible in the historic spirit of examining an ancient history with the strict criteria of scientific historical criticism, at the same time conceding that "the essence of Christian faith is perfectly independent of this criticism." This attempt to ascertain a "natural" explanation for Biblical miracles and to regard the Christian religion as being, like all religions, the result of an historical evolution which compelled a constant verification of the authenticity of early sacred records amid the progressive enlightenment of man, placed Christianity and revealed religion in a new, panoramic perspective that created consternation among believers.

The elegiac note created in English Victorian poetry by the decline of religious faith is marked in *In Memoriam* and in Matthew Arnold's "Dover Beach" and "Thyrsis," poems which typify what Arnold meant by saying in 1869 that his poems "represent, on the whole, the main movement of mind of the last quarter of a century." In Prussia the advent after 1864 of the *Realpolitik* of Bismarck was paralleled in philosophy by Nietzsche's bold application of the Darwinian conception of the struggle for existence to modern ethics in *Thus Spake Zarathustra* (1883–1885). Nietzsche rejected the meek "slave morality" of Christianity and extolled the superman with a pagan love of the senses who despised altruistic morality and took his stand beyond good and evil. The dynamic operation of history glorifies the will to power (*der Wille zur Macht*) which denounces Christian ethics as a transmutation of weaknesses into virtues. The influence of Nietzsche is reflected in the writings of Richard Dehmel (1863–1920), who praised the sexual impulses of the superman in his poetry, and introduced a self-worshiping projection of the ego into historical characters whose ruthlessness, violence, and licentiousness are viewed as "natural morality." A similar theme is also found in a volume of the early poetry of his outstanding contemporary, Stefan George—*Algabal* (1892).

The period in European history from the defeat of France in 1871 to the turn of the century deepened further into disillusionment and pessimism.

In England, men of letters like Arnold and Carlyle distrusted the passing of the Second Reform Bill in 1867 because it granted the working classes the franchise when, it was believed, this new, vast, unmeasured and sprawling democracy was not ready for the political responsibilities it had to assume. To Thomas Carlyle it was "Shooting Niagara." On the Continent, the rise of the new German Empire, following the victories of Prussia over Austria-Hungary (1866) and France (1871), introduced a disturbingly unscrupulous element into modern diplomacy known as Bismarckism.

The revulsion against the increasingly oppressive materialism of the time was expressed memorably in the shattered idealism of Dostoevski's underground man in *Letters from the Underworld* (1864). In America, Walt Whitman tempered his previous optimism regarding the progress of the American Dream by reproving American materialistic tendencies in *Democratic Vistas* (1871). As the century reached its turning, the concise, exquisitely ordered lyrics of A. E. Housman gave popular currency to the bleak, pessimistic, melancholy tones commenting upon the treachery of the world and lovers, the brevity and unhappiness of life, the certainty of the dark and endless night of the grave. Shropshire, in his poetry, was far more a country of the dead than the living. The drying up of spiritual beliefs and the decline of religious credence in an all-powerful and beneficent Providence was reflected in the late novels of Thomas Hardy, such as *The Mayor of Casterbridge* and *Jude the Obscure,* and in his poems (his "unadjusted impressions"), which he began to publish in 1898 with the *Wessex Poems.*

While yet at Harvard, Edward Arlington Robinson read *The Mayor of Casterbridge* and *The Return of the Native,* and issued thereafter in 1896 his first volume of poems which was greeted in the *Bookman* with reservations about its lugubrious, pessimistic philosophy. It was he who described the world as "a kind of spiritual kindergarten where millions of bewildered infants are trying to spell God with the wrong blocks." It should not be assumed that this decline in religious certitude was symptomatic of the beliefs of the whole body social. Readers of the novels of Anthony Trollope, for example, will be aware that conservatism in religion and morals was on the whole the dominant Victorian trend, and even among the more skeptical writers the will to believe was not wholly lost, as the conclusion to E. A. Robinson's "Credo" demonstrates, and as Thomas Hardy's avowal that he would give ten years of his life to see a ghost reveals. Nevertheless, the blight of fifty years of rationalistic examination of the Bible, with no design on the ical concupiscence, as in the contrast in "Sweeney Among the Nightingales" between the sordid suggestions of intrigue in Sweeney's milieu with the classical and tragic symbol of the doom of the House of Atreus, and in the sterile frustrations of modern love in the section of The Waste Land entitled "A Game of Chess." In the early poems and The

Courtesy Museum of Modern Art, New York (gift of Mrs. Simon Guggenheim)

The Sleeping Gypsy by Henri Rousseau.

critic's part to encourage infidelity, had undermined religious belief and created a spiritual uncertainty without establishing a general climate of skepticism.

At the beginning of the third decade of the twentieth century T. S. Eliot gave the Modern world its most widely heralded symbol of the spiritual dearth and aridity of modern civilization in The Waste Land (1922). The first two volumes of his work—Prufrock and Other Observations (1917) and Poems (1920)—suggest the staleness, ennui, infinite weariness of modern life, the living death of the modern "hollow men" without passion or desire. In the poetry of Eliot love became a mechan-

Waste Land, Eliot obsessively depicted the horror of modern man's agonized frustration, lacking spiritual faith, living in "death's dream kingdom." In seventy years the "darkling plain" of Matthew Arnold's "Dover Beach" had become the arid desert of T. S. Eliot, a dismal perspective which seemed to possess only illimitable horizons of ennui and despair. If, as Eliot observed in praising Baudelaire's perception, we are human only as we do evil or good, then to him the inhabitants of the Modern world had reached a state of complete spiritual unawareness in which they could not even say, like the Sibyl in The Waste Land, "I wish to die."

Ball at the Moulin de la Galette by Auguste Renoir.

THE QUEST FOR UNITY

As the Western world expanded in wealth and prosperity during the nineteenth century, the ugly industrialization of our civilization became increasingly repellent to the writer and to the artist. Art and life grew ever further apart; the new society condescendingly regarded the artist as merely ornamental, his chief function being to please their tastes. The vulgarization of literature through the cheap press, the hideous and lifeless adaptations of Renaissance and Gothic architecture to public buildings, such as railroad stations and libraries, were depressing examples of what that taste could be. The artist's sense of alienation from the main currents of modern life was accentuated by his heightened sensitivity to the feverish fret, divided aims, and the lack of a serene unity and integrity of

purpose in life. The world of the sterile, the commonplace, the vulgarly pretentious encompassed man; it was a world in which it seemed that the possibility of great tragic experience was no longer tenable.

The most eloquent spokesman for the writer's consequent alienation was Charles Baudelaire, whose *The Flowers of Evil* (1857) reflected a profound revulsion against modern bourgeois life that is shown in more tempered fashion by his compatriot Gustave Flaubert in *Madame Bovary* (1857). "Commerce," remarked Baudelaire, "is in essence satanic—give me more than I give to you." His conception of the pervasive ennui of modern life as a negative state of simply striving to desire is fundamental not only to the comprehension of

Baudelaire's place in modern poetry but as well to the understanding of such early poems of Eliot as "The Love Song of J. Alfred Prufrock" and "The Hollow Men." Since this ennui was to Baudelaire a denial of man's belief in good and evil, it is not paradoxical to say that his early Satanism, revealed in his more unsuccessful poems, was an aspect of his religious nature, however in reverse. To Baudelaire, the Romantic conception of the naturally good man was an abomination. Modern man was not merely indifferent to love of God; he was in "The Rebel" violently resistant to the somewhat strong-armed ministrations of his good angel—he shall not love God and his creatures, "never, till I die." The characteristic mood of the poet is "spleen": he sits in his city room in stupefied contemplation of the frustrations of his personality, and without lies the dismal, dark, rainy February that pours its gloom and oppressive cold upon the slums and the "pale inhabitants of the nearby cemetery." The City, creation of a modern industrial civilization, has become symbolically identified with this spleen, this spiritual nadir, as we see in Baudelaire's "Be Thou Sage, O My Sorrow" and in the "Unreal City" of *The Waste Land.*

His poetry, although clearly showing the influence of Poe in his emphasis upon the search for pure beauty and the close identification of sadness and melancholy with beauty, demonstrates as well that in his poetic art Baudelaire found a refuge from the abyss. His poetic art is admirable in its carefully integrated, disciplined form, in which the vagrant imagination of a disordered, psychopathic personality is compensated for by the precisely moulded poetic form in which it is expressed. Nevertheless, it is in content more than in manner

Courtesy National Gallery of Art (Chester Dale Collection), Washington, D.C.

The Old Musician by Édouard Manet.

that Baudelaire exercised an extensive influence upon modern poetry: his unsparing revelation of the morbidity of his own soul, and his stern, vindictive summons to his readers to admit a like soul-state: "hypocritical reader—my fellow—my brother." There are intimations of the doctrine of art for art's sake in Baudelaire's devotion to his craft and in his

Courtesy Museum of Modern Art, New York

Toys of a Prince (Evil Genius of a King) by Giorgio di Chirico.

poems to beauty, but the more significant development came later in the poetry of Paul Verlaine (1844–1896) and Stéphane Mallarmé (1842–1898), to be considered elsewhere in this essay.

The same pervasive European literary preoccupation with the disintegrating and disruptive tendencies of modern life is shown in the poetry of Giacomo Leopardi (1798–1837), who, although he died before 1850, fully anticipates the *mal du siècle* which was to come. Known perhaps most widely for his early, noble adjuration to a supine and subservient Italy under Austrian rule in "Ode to Italy," one of the great patriotic exhortations of the *Risorgimento*, he is more significant here for his poetic

interpretation of modern life as decadent, apathetic, a dead century inhabited by dead. The poet's imagination, in contrast, voyaged to the golden age of the past, to antique Greece with its faith in humanism and its undivided energies devoted to the happiness of humane living. Even in his "Ode to Italy" there is the note of the classical scholar in his contrasting the decline of nineteenth-century Italy with the mute testimony to ancient Roman glories extant in the walls, arches, columns, and statues of her Roman ancestors. His progressive disillusionment turned him away from the eager hope of social regeneration found in his early poetry to a lament upon the meaninglessness of life that makes him akin to Baudelaire and to Schopenhauer, who greatly admired him, and to Byron. Leopardi turned to poetry as a means of cultivating the noble illusions about life; possibly the world could still be redeemed through the active cultivation of the poetic imagination: it might be brought to appreciate once more the values to which the Modern world was becoming increasingly insensible. As with Baudelaire, Leopardi found that the rigorous study of the principles of poetic composition supplied in art an integration, a focus of unity for the poet's being which was denied to him in the outer world, and at its most intense his poetic imagination achieved a kind of timeless projection into a pure poetic state such as is found in "The Dream." In a world of constant flux and change, the perfection of the poetic act becomes a symbol to the poet of permanence of achievement, and compensates for his increasing feeling of isolation in the Modern world.

In the poetry of Leopardi the yearning for the serenity and repose of antiquity is in part a predilection for the Golden Age when the world was young, a motif of "The Setting of the Moon" and even of that splendid imitation of the Theocritan idyll, "The Village Saturday." The same preoccupation with antiquity descended to Stefan George (1868–1933), whose *Book of Eclogues and Eulogies* (1895) glorifies the splendid unity of man, his gods, and his world in ancient Greece. In contrast to the bright clarity of this Hellenic mood (also present in Baudelaire's "Exotic Fragrance") the tedium of the exotic escape is implied in George's "Augury." Some of the poems of the *Book of Eclogues* also approach the charm of the Theocritan idyll, but perhaps the most typical of the general poetic tendencies we have been noting is found in the poem "Come to the Park They Say Is Dead," which symbolizes the withdrawal of the poet from life to the sad autumnal landscape of his soul.

The poet's withdrawal, however, cannot be summarized in the pat phrase of "ivory tower"; it was often impelled by the poet's urgent compulsion to project an unimpaired vision of another place and time that might be a fertilizing influence upon and inspiration to his poetic powers, like George's attempt to delineate the plastic values of Fra Angelico's "Coronation of the Virgin" in his poem, "An Angelico." The necessity is seen too in the significant words of his brilliant contemporary, Rainer Maria Rilke, writing to a friend in 1906: "I am thinking in all seriousness and hardihood of Greece, . . . there are voices in me counseling this unconditionally."

Although Rilke (1875-1926) did not turn to the Hellenic world for inspiration as fully as either Leopardi or Stefan George, its effect upon him is cogently revealed in some of his finest poetry, the late *Sonnets to Orpheus*. Certainly the apotheosis of Orpheus and his music as a majestic, mythic, creative energy of art is not far from Baudelaire's or Leopardi's discovery in the resources of the poetic imagination the only dynamic values in modern life. Of the three German poets of the twentieth century who have had the most influence upon German youth—Richard Dehmel for his Nietzschean naturalism, Stefan George for his aristocratic cultivation of art for art's sake, and Rilke—the last has had the most permanent influence.

There is in both Rilke and Franz Kafka (1883-1924) the intimation of the artist's profound alienation from the Modern world, the feeling for the calamitous frustration and damming up of the artist's creative energies which forms a symbolic motif of Rilke's "The Panther" and Kafka's "The Hunger Artist." It is true that to a degree this alienation was for Rilke, if not for Kafka, a premeditated, self-imposed, artistic discipline. Rilke complained in his letters about the static paralysis of his will, comparing himself to the "heroic workers" like Cézanne and Rodin, and no doubt his advice in *Letters to a Young Poet* to cultivate loneliness as an indispensable condition to creation was partly due to his feeling that "only things speak" to him, "complete things" (legends, myths, works of art, animals, periods of past history), and in part because of the difficult struggle he had had with his father to free himself for a poetic career. To Rilke, as to the other modern poets considered, self-isolation from a world he never made was essential to the poet's finding amid the distraught weariness of modern living a centrality of aim, whether it be the cultivation of his art or the quest of a mystical perception such as we find in the most difficult and untranslatable of Rilke's poems, the *Duino Elegies*.

THE AMERICAN DREAM AND THE EUROPEAN TRADITION

IN THE development of American literature after 1850, the time spirit did not permit the American poet to identify himself with the European artist's feeling of isolation in the Modern world, or with the developing cult of art for art's sake. Such orientation of the poetic sensibility would not have accorded with the native American literary tradition or with the still dynamic potentialities of the American Dream. Writing in the optimistic pattern of this dream, Walt Whitman (1819-1892) envisioned in *Leaves of Grass* (1855) the remarkable achievement of America as a land of the future, with its unlimited vistas of freedom and democratic achievement, its men and women noble, free, united in their comradely mission to destroy the antiquated bonds of feudalism and to attain the ideal of complete equalitarianism.

Under the influence of Emerson, Whitman conceived the need to embody in his poetry typical American scenes and new, fresh American types; for this creation he felt the necessity of devising a new poetic medium, free verse, that might express the divinely intended progress of the evolving age of democracy and science. To express the spirit of the "greatest poem," these United States, Whitman attempted to transcend the limits of the old forms of poetic expression: if the New World was moving into an era of unrevealed potentialities for the good of common humanity, new poetic means of expressing this development must unfold organically to keep pace with it. Hence he expressed complete disdain for the regular poetic meters, as he denied the further usefulness of the "trite" themes and "stock poetic touches" drawn from an outmoded European poetic tradition. No one, remarked Whitman, would understand him who approached his poetry purely from the aesthetic point of view; nor would he discuss it merely in terms of his craft. As a result, therefore, of this direction of Whitman's conception of the militant, bardic role of his poetry, he felt that any cultivation of poetry for poetry's sake, whatever the all-sufficient reason to the European poet, would be futile and empty dilettantism. In his view of the new, vibrantly optimistic, vital America with the vastly spiritualizing and mystic kinship of its peoples, Whitman felt no need of combating in himself that despondent poetic attitude of alienation such as we found in Baudelaire and Leopardi, although he might have agreed that the Old World was finished.

In spite of the cultural affinities of the work of Washington Irving (1783–1859) and Henry Wadsworth Longfellow (1807–1882) for European literary antecedents, the native American tradition had always been fundamentally hostile to European standards of taste as feudal, corrupt, and decadent, inseparably part of an evil past. As Americans moved further from the Atlantic seaboard, writers of the Western literary frontier vigorously repudiated the suave and polished culture of the Old World in glorifying the heroic, anecdotal vagaries of frontiersmen like Davy Crockett and Mike Fink; and the tall tales, the Davy Crockett almanacs, the campfire yarns and barroom anecdotes spawned an original literature of the frontier that reached its supreme achievement in Mark Twain (Samuel Clemens, 1835–1910). Mark Twain's hostility toward Europe is sufficiently demonstrated in *Innocents Abroad* (1869) and in *The Connecticut Yankee in King Arthur's Court* (1889); in *Huckleberry Finn* (1884) we see the positive side—the essential decency, the hatred of hypocrisy, the equalitarian humanity—of that great American democrat. Despite his emergence from a raw and undisciplined society, in his writings the true American possesses an innate dignity and integrity that was felt to be clearly superior to the urbane dissimu-

lations and sophistries of the European. While this characteristic attitude is found in Mark Twain's work, it is also implicit in the novels of Henry James (1843–1916): in the early *The American* (1877) as well as in the late *The Wings of the Dove* (1902) and *The Golden Bow* (1904).

It will not be, however, for his characterization of the American virtues or for his skill as a raconteur that Mark Twain will remain, with Whitman, longest remembered among the authors of the "Gilded Age." In *Huckleberry Finn* the lovely poetic descriptions of the Mississippi as Huck and Jim float down that "monstrous big river," and in both *Huckleberry Finn* and *Life on the Mississippi* the vividly drawn, exactly observed types that thronged the Mississippi Valley in the golden age of nineteenth-century America brought to fulfilment an American literary tradition that owed nothing to European influences. From Walt Whitman and Mark Twain, rather than from Longfellow, Lowell, or even Emerson, the first broadly national tradition in American letters springs.

It was the brawling, expansive vitality of Twain and Whitman (singing of physiology "from top to toe") that helped to confound and dissipate in the twentieth century the severe cultural repressions of a moribund Puritan tradition which, by the eighteen-nineties, had deliquesced into the proprieties of the "genteel tradition." The positive spiritual values of seventeenth-century Puritanism had declined into the narrow inhibitions and the jealously guarded moral sanctions of late nineteenth-century New England society; in his last, masterful period Henry James delineated these oppressive traits of the "genteel tradition" acutely in the short story "Europe" (1899) and in *The Ambassadors* (1903). For James, Europe became the symbolic setting for the artist's achievement of self-fulfilment, or to the unfulfilled American like Lambert Strether in *The Ambassadors* who discovered that his potentialities for a sensitive appreciation and enjoyment of the mature values of Old World civilization had been nearly blighted by puritanized New England influences. In the opinion of James, America was still insensitive to the aesthetic values found in the cultivated European society of well-bred, finely civilized men and women. In accepting these values one did not become merely a servile cosmopolite or an ungrateful expatriate; acceptance was rather an act of faith in life, a declaration of cultural independence that enabled Jane Rimmle in "Europe" to free herself from the stultifying repressions of her mother's Puritan background—a background grim, taut, fatal to the joy and happiness of the complete human being.

In their castigation of the moribund Puritan tradition, both James and Whitman were outsiders; there was more evidence of "treason within the castle" in Emily Dickinson's rebellion against the harsh Calvinistic theology of her ancestors. Her metaphysical poems reveal how eager she was for religious experience, but not of the authoritarian orthodox kind. Although it would be going too far to say that Emily Dickinson (1830–1886) made a

religion of her art in the same way as did Baudelaire, Leopardi, and Stefan George, nevertheless there are intimations of a mood close to theirs in such a poem as "I Died for Beauty," and in the evidence that she found her chief happiness in her poetic craft and transmuted the profound disappointment of her mysterious love affair in the triumphant art of her poetry. Possessed of the fresh intellectual independence and power to communicate directly with nature that was characteristic of Emerson, she found in nature a peace and freedom from society at least momentarily consoling in her objective and precise rendering of nature through the humble bee, the hummingbird, the first robin. The spiritual curiosity about nature in her poetry

Courtesy Museum of Modern Art, New York (Lillie P. Bliss bequest)

Starry Night by Vincent van Gogh.

is akin to Thoreau's and Emerson's feeling for it; her litany of praise to nature and her grave wonder at its ever-miraculous, transcendental renewal in a poem like "I'll Tell You How the Sun Rose" reveal her nearness to the transcendental romantic movement of the mid-century. But the seventeenth-century Puritan had always looked on nature as revelatory of God's providences in somewhat the same awesome tone adopted by Emily Dickinson in contemplating natural phenomena; it may be, therefore, that in spite of her transcendentalism the very intensity of Emily Dickinson's rebellion against Puritan providence shows still the stern influence of the dead hand of Puritan tradition, as Martha Graham interprets the legend of the poet in her choreographed composition, "Letter to the World."

As the nineteenth century passed into the twentieth, the presence of an intense inwardness and introspection of spirit in the poetry of Emily Dickinson and Edwin Arlington Robinson (1869–1935) suggests that the finer moral qualities of the Puritan legacy had not been wholly exhausted. Certainly Robinson reveals an allegiance to the older cultural and spiritual values of America which seemed to him to be vanishing in a society that worshiped money and success. He shared with the poets we have discussed the feeling of alienation from an industrialized, mechanical culture, but unlike such poets as Baudelaire and Rilke, Robinson became under compulsion a regional poet of New England because he perceived the social and spiritual malady that he felt was consuming the moral integrity of his native section. His own acutely painful personal experiences of failure in life made Robinson profoundly aware of the plight of those men who sought spiritual integration, despite a pragmatism which derided as pretentious their efforts to oppose the materialistic tendencies of modern life, and which stigmatized them as failures.

Although he shares Robinson's point of view toward modern life in many respects, Robert Frost (1875–   ) reveals in his poetry less of the melancholy, agonizing introspection so characteristic of Robinson. Somewhat more positively, Frost has preferred to praise the sturdy old New England virtues of individualism and independence that seem to him characteristic of the vanishing farmer and country-

man. These virtues are of course traditional in New England, partly because they are a Puritan heritage, and partly because they have been acquired through generations of rigorous cultivation of scarcely arable New England land. The earth to Frost is the right place to cultivate virtues other than love alone; even in handling human relations a firm tactile sense of earthly realities is useful, as is seen in "Mending Wall." Frost emphasizes the austere cultivation of homely qualities of character in a simple, solitary milieu wherein for him, as for Emily Dickinson, the delights of nature have a not unfriendly reticence and shy taciturnity that often leave the poet wondering. There is a kinship in mood between the two poets in their treatment of the elusive and transitory delights of nature (in Emily Dickinson's "A Route of Evanescence" and in Frost's "Spring Pools," for example), and though the poem is not wholly typical, Frost approaches a dominant mood of modern poetry in "Acquainted with the Night," where we feel symbolically the poet's sense of his aloneness in an alien world.

In giving our attention to the more national tradition of American letters represented by Mark Twain and Walt Whitman, we must not thereby overlook the fact that among these New England regional poets we find some of the most vigorous interpreters of the classic American traits of moral and spiritual integrity, stalwart independence, and Emersonian self-reliance. These traits are part of the American Dream, too. At the same time, none of these New England poets was merely regional; the poetry of Emily Dickinson and Frost especially transcends sectional limitations. The stable set of values that Frost admires in his poetry is not just American, for these qualities would have been admired in ancient Rome. Possibly that is one of the reasons why even his most casual poems of narrative incident possess that universal extension of meaning so often noted. Is it wholly wishful thinking, therefore, for us to believe that in the long view the American Dream may merge with the European tradition, and the Oriental? The splendid hope of a world communion of peoples and a great international brotherhood of poets found in Whitman's "Passage to India" may yet come true. It must be, indeed, passage to more than India.

Sunday on Grande Jatte Island by Georges Seurat.

RISE OF REALISM AND NATURALISM

ALTHOUGH it is not certain whether the term "realism" was first used in French criticism as early as 1834, or not until it was applied by the French art critic Edmond Duranty about 1846, as a critical description of the novel it does not seem to have had a vogue until after 1850. Since "realism" and "naturalism" are sometimes used interchangeably in literary discussion, or at least they are used without careful discrimination, the following differentiation is made to avoid confusion. The definitions, however, are relative rather than absolute.

Realism is here conceived to be the exact, faithful, detailed presentation of the material world and the facts of ordinary life. In realistic fiction, the char-

acters are usually commonplace and lead unexceptional lives; they are delineated in a sober style which does not attempt heightened effects. Realism thus was a reaction from the extraordinary characters, singular adventures, and full-blown lyric style of the romantic novel of the early nineteenth century. Unlike naturalism, which requires a completely dispassionate objectivity (at least in theory), the realistic credo may or may not demand the complete self-effacement of the novelist in the presentation of the social milieu. Realism in the nineteenth century did not so rigorously avoid entertaining the reader or edifying him as did naturalism; nor did the realistic approach eschew the representation of the more spiritual sides of man (naturalism tended

Courtesy the Phillips Gallery, Washington, D. C.

Studio Quai St. Michel by Henri Matisse.

to emphasize his purely animalistic aspects). The realistic novelist usually accepted, too, the desirability of aesthetic form in the novel, since he regarded his writing as an art, not as a science as did the naturalist.

FRANCE. In its confrontation of the romantic illusions of Emma Bovary with reality, Gustave Flaubert's *Madame Bovary* (1857) remains one of the great French realistic novels of the nineteenth century. Flaubert was too good a realistic novelist and observer of life to ascribe Emma Bovary's suicide to either remorse or to just compensation as the "wages of sin"; rather her death was based upon the more plausible inference that as a romantic she could not face the dingy, ugly life of shabby liaisons that lay before her. Flaubert cannot be described as a naturalist, because he is too much the artist; he could never accept Émile Zola's conception of the novel as not art but as creation by a scientific method applied to fiction. The most perfect example of Flaubert's realistic art remains "A Simple Heart" from *Three Stories* (1877); unlike the

misanthropic *Madame Bovary* which contains not a single admirable character, this story presents in the perfection of a cultivated, limpid style the heroic servitude of Félicité, who "remained faithful to her mistress—although the latter was by no means an agreeable person."

As it may now be inferred, naturalism is thus distinguished generally from realism by the deliberate and conscious borrowing of its methods and philosophic basis from the objective research techniques of the physical sciences. Even as early as 1842, Honoré de Balzac (1799–1850), although essentially a realist, reflected the naturalist point of view when he said in the "Preface" to the *Human Comedy* that as a novelist he was interested in man as a "social species" whose character was determined by the physical influence of milieu, race, and climate; and the positivistic philosophy of Auguste Comte (1798–1857) supported the application of the laws of physical science to the analysis of man in society. An equally famous pronouncement demonstrating this scientific influence was Hippolyte Taine's statement in his *History of English Literature* (1859) that vice and virtue were, like vitriol and sugar, the products of purely material causes. Taine's comment implied one of the chief tenets of naturalism, wherein it differs from realism (which grants free will): man, completely impotent in will, is wholly subservient to his physical environment. The influence of environment is more readily demonstrable where man is engaged in a nearly primitive struggle for existence; hence the new naturalistic school of fiction usually chose for its subject matter the life of the workingman, or *ouvrier* (a significant restriction to a class which the realistic novelist does not observe).

The extraordinary development of industrialism in the nineteenth century caused the rise of a proletariat, the depiction of whose lives the novelists Edmond and Jules Goncourt frankly suggested as the future aim of fiction (see their "Preface" to *Germinie Lacerteux,* 1864). It may be said, therefore, that unlike realism, which was a fictional method long before the Industrial Revolution, naturalism is a particular philosophy and technique that has arisen in the modern era, evolving from the methodology of the physical sciences, the development of great mass movements, and the emergence of the working class as subject matter for serious fictional treatment. While realism may make allowance for man's intelligence and spiritual qualities, naturalism regards him as a kind of animated machine controlled by his hereditary instincts and passions and by his environment. Realism permits a character's moral judgment to have some influence on his conduct, but naturalism would consider moral judgment irrelevant and uninfluential; accordingly, his deeds are shaped inexorably by physical factors beyond his control. The naturalistic novelist tends to distrust the imagination much more than the realistic writer: the former relies wholly or nearly wholly upon the scientific method of collecting a complete dossier of information about his characters—their lives, backgrounds, and working conditions. At its most extreme, the naturalistic novel reveals the most pathological aspects of man's actions which the realistic novelist would depict either with more reticence and decorum or else would consider too romantic, that is, atypical of man's normal and customary behavior.

Whatever the excesses of naturalism, however, to its credit it did much to free the nineteenth-century novel of its aura of overdecorous gentility and prudish reticence in the depiction of life. Undoubtedly, the grim determination of the naturalist no longer merely to amuse or edify the tired reader of novels was exasperating to the more conservative reading public. This naturalistic principle was embodied uncompromisingly in the early work of Guy de Maupassant, J. K. Huysmans, and the others who gathered about the greatest of French naturalistic novelists, Émile Zola (1840–1902). These writers insisted upon absolute fidelity to fact and the right to treat in fiction any subject matter uncompromisingly, in the spirit of cool, objective, scientific inquiry.

Zola set forth his theory of naturalism most completely in *The Experimental Novel* (1880), after he had published nine novels in his Rougon-Macquart series. Characteristically he found the basis of his fictional method in the scientific works of Dr. Claude Bernard's *Introduction to Experimental Medicine* (1865) and Dr. Prosper Lucas' studies in heredity. In some respects, Zola's most purely naturalistic novel is *L'Assommoir* (*The Bucket Shop*, 1877), the portrait of Gervaise Macquart, whose passionately generous nature and dismal Parisian environment take her through all stages of decadence from drunkenness to illicit love, thievery, and death through tuberculosis. It is an unsparing demonstration of what the naturalist conceived to be the completely dominating effect of heredity and environment upon the life of a human being, carefully documented with scientific exactitude by Zola's researches into public wash houses, dance halls, tenements, laundries, saloons, marriage feasts, wife beatings, alcoholics. Thereafter Zola's major undertaking as a novelist was his series of twenty novels on the "Natural and Social History of a Family Under the Second Empire," a study of the various forms of disease, vice, and crime manifested by two branches of a family, the Rougon-Macquart. But Zola's use of documentation in the novels often arrests his narrative development, and hence his narrative power is better shown in "The Attack on the Mill." At the same time, of course, this short story does not possess that massed documentary detail of the novels which the critic Ferdinand Brunetière has described scornfully as "erudition in the novel," nor does it exhibit those traits of Zola's extreme naturalism that hostile critics have called "the literature of putridity."

If Zola was the greatest of the French naturalistic novelists, Guy de Maupassant (1850–1893) was the most brilliant of the naturalists in his consummate handling of the short story, or *conte*. As an artist he is closer to Flaubert than to Zola, having served a seven-year apprenticeship under the former; his stories, remarkable illustrations of his stylistic powers of economy, compactness, and skill in ironic understatement, are at their best when he follows the naturalist's bent in writing of simple people, such as the soldiers in the Franco-Prussian War and the peasantry. Perhaps, as Henry James observed, Maupassant was fortunate in finding that his theory of fiction and the limitations of his temperament and experience "exactly" corresponded.

RUSSIA. Russian fiction of the nineteenth century was too interested in presenting the woes of the underdog, of the victim of social oppression, to adopt the objective, dispassionate tone of French naturalism which was characterized less by humanitarian sympathy than by a kind of unpitying irony. In the Russian writers we discover an altruistic compassion, the consciousness of a social mission, a reticence in the treatment of sex, and a wholesome

*Family of Saltimbanques
by Pablo Picasso.*

Courtesy Art Institute of Chicago

respect for the ethical values inherent in the moral nature of man that is wanting in French naturalism. Then, too, the naturalistic novel was the consequence of a western European intellectual and scientific movement which both Tolstoi and Dostoevski distrusted.

Nikolai Gogol (1809–1852) is widely accepted as the founder of Russian realism, but his realistic method is imbued with a poetic fancy and a flair for lyrical digression which clearly removes it from the category of naturalism. His story "The Cloak" is generally considered to be the beginning of Russian realism ("We are all from Gogol's *Overcoat*," said Dostoevski), but the social elements in the story have perhaps been overemphasized as a conscious protest by Gogol against the oppression suffered by the underprivileged, with a consequent lack of attention being given to the humor underlying the pity. His fame as a comic writer is international, though again, as in "The Cloak," the

humor of his *chef d'oeuvre*, *Dead Souls* (1842) is tragicomedy which deepens into fantastic horror in its revelation of the corruptness, the inhumanity, and the greed of provincial Russian society.

The most realistic of the Russian novelists were Ivan Turgenev (1818–1883), and Count Leo N. Tolstoi (1828–1910). Certainly, however, Turgenev is the only Russian novelist of the first rank who belongs in all respects to the tradition of Western world literature. His first book, *A Sportsman's Sketches* (1847–1851), with its fresh, impressionistic sketches of the Russian steppes and the range of provincial Russian types, made him famous. As a realist, Turgenev maintained a cool and dispassionate vision that could at the same time admit a deep if unsentimental sympathy. His fictional method was not likely to lead him into social reform, although he has rightfully been given credit for contributing to the emancipation of the serfs through the influence of *A Sportsman's Sketches*.

There is admirable skill in his simple, direct presentation of facts without the intrusion of the author. Because of these traits, in *On the Eve* and *Fathers and Sons* (1862) he is perhaps the soundest observer and interpreter of the Young Russia on the eve of the eighteen-sixties. The admirable balance and exact nuance of his realism is shown in *Smoke,* wherein he satirizes alike the Westerner who despises all things Russian and those who prostrate themselves before the mysteries of the Russian soul. Turgenev, like Henry James, was a realist rather than a naturalist; he demonstrated the limitations of scientific naturalism in portraying Bazarov in *Fathers and Sons*: after having himself fallen in love, the scientist Bazarov is less sure that "physiologists know" and understand the relations of men and women in love.

Although *War and Peace* (1865–1872) and *Anna Karenina* (1875–1876) are masterpieces of Russian realism, we cannot identify Tolstoi with the main current of either the Western naturalistic or realistic tradition because of his anti-intellectualism, of his efforts to approach closer to moral perfection through following the precepts of the Sermon on the Mount, and, finally, of his embracing the simple, naïve faith of the peasant. Like Dostoevski, he rejected Western materialism and culture and, in his later works of fiction, permitted his social doctrines to dominate his art, and finally to replace it wholly in his interest. Once he had assumed the role of prophet, a literary movement based on Western science could have little revelance for Tolstoi, or for Fëdor Dostoevski (1821–1881), to whom subjective states were far more significant than events in the outer world. To Dostoevski the problem of guilt and expiation, as in *Crime and Punishment* (1866), was too much a profoundly inward spiritual crisis for him to consider it as merely clinical physical experience or to submit the irrational in human conduct to objective scientific measurement. He looked upon man's material environment as unimportant; and there is a respect for the distraught modern individual in Dostoevski's *Letters from the Underworld* that is not entertained in the naturalistic credo.

The culminating tendency of the expansion of the naturalistic novel was often a propagandistic tract or a "proletarian" novel denouncing the sordid plight of the working classes and sometimes urging

Courtesy Museum of Modern Art, New York

Oval Still Life by Georges Braque.

direct revolutionary action. Tolstoi and Dostoevski opposed modern international socialistic trends, preferring to substitute nonviolence and spiritual action for revolution. Anton Chekhov (1860–1904), who comes at the end of a great period of Russian literature, neither sought the mantle of a prophet of the coming Revolution nor urged a return to the ancient mores of Holy Russia. A practicing physician, Chekhov insisted that in his writing "the scientific method always kept" him "on guard," and hence to Tolstoi and other contemporaries his dispassionate irony seemed cruel. He had an uncanny eye for the small, petty, mean spots in people which he conveyed with an admirable art of compression and a delicate irony, unfortunately less perceptible in translation. The realist category, because it approaches the problems of life so seriously, is incapable of encompassing that nuance of pathos and humor which is so characteristic of Chekhov—as it is of Kafka and Charles Chaplin. Tolstoi supposed

*Demoiselles of Avignon
by Pablo Picasso.*

Courtesy Museum of Modern Art, New York (Lillie P. Bliss bequest)

that Chekhov, like himself, was out to attack the shams of life, and therefore believed that he wished "to curse the modern woman" in "The Darling" but had instead made her attractive. Chekhov wished to do neither one thing nor the other, and analysis of the story can stop short with Tolstoi's comment, "I at least cannot read it without tears."

If Chekhov was the "voice of twilight Russia," Maxim Gorky (1868–1936) was the militant spokesman for the new Russia and the official founder of Russian proletarian literature. His early experiences in a brutal environment and his migratory movements through Russia gave him a wide knowledge of the oppressed workers, whose daily lives he described with all their frustrations and economic servitudes. Such conditions are recounted in the opening of "One Autumn Night," but the story reveals as well the strength of Gorky's best stories, in that he never allows his indignation or propa-

gandistic tendencies to conceal his real understanding and pity for these hapless, obscure people, or to impair the veracity with which he renders, if unsubtly, the moving daily incidents and emotions of their lives.

The influence of the realistic and naturalistic movement in fiction became truly international, extending itself to England through the novels of George Moore, George Gissing, and Thomas Hardy, and to America with the work of Stephen Crane in *Maggie: A Girl of the Streets* (1893) and *The Red Badge of Courage* (1895), in Frank Norris's *McTeague* (1899), and in Theodore Dreiser's *Sister Carrie* (1900). Since the passions of man are less sophisticated and more easily studied in the more primitive cultures that still survive, the Wessex novels of Thomas Hardy (1840–1928) and the novels and stories of Giovanni Verga (1840–1922) and Luigi Pirandello (1867–1936) reveal the influence of the realistic movement in another direction. Verga's Sicilians live a culturally retarded, pastoral existence where life is bitter, comic, miserable, treacherous, and suddenly violent. Tempers are quick, struggles are elemental, and death is swift. Such a Sicily, with a ceremoniously observed pattern of social culture, a ritual, emerges in Pirandello's "The Evil Spirit," as a like Spanish social pattern of the relation of man and woman appears in García Lorca's most popular poem "The Faithless Wife." These are regional studies, but it is important to observe that they are not Romantic and not "picturesque." Not the least achievement of the realistic and naturalistic movement has been to give us the opportunity to enlarge our comprehension of the "one world" through the study of such realistic regional works as these.

NEW DIRECTIONS

THE basic assumption of nineteenth-century naturalism could not long prove wholly satisfactory as a literary technique. There was no room in the naturalistic novel for a representation of life that was not the deterministic product of a complex of sociological conditions. In naturalism, the types of characters were psychologically simple, and there was inordinate emphasis upon the purely animal drives in man. The heavy documentation put too much emphasis upon external circumstances and thus inhibited extensive search for value and meaning within the mind of the individual himself. Then, too, the enthusiasm of the naturalist for the unselective "slice of life" and his consequent refusal to organize a novel aesthetically often left it formless in structure. It was all very well for the American novelist Frank Norris (1870–1902), to say of naturalistic aims that "we don't want literature, we want life," but the writer still fundamentally wished to be known as an artist, not a zoologist, the analogy suggested by Zola.

By the early years of the twentieth century it was even doubtful whether the nineteenth-century scientific basis for naturalism had further validity. The naturalist had insisted upon "absolute fidelity to fact and the material world," but one began to wonder what the material world was. The late nineteenth- and early twentieth-century advances in atomic chemistry and mathematical physics tended to disintegrate the solid world of experience that the naturalist had accepted; and the sciences which had been presumably steadily reducing the field of the unknown during the nineteenth century suddenly found themselves humbly ignorant of the immense forces of the universe lately disclosed.

Not only did the material nature of the universe seem to be changing very suddenly, but the confident assumptions that man's mental activity was a mechanical response to outside stimuli had also to be seriously modified. When the naturalistic tradition moved beyond the depiction of simple psychological types, it could not cope with the highly complex, neurotic personalities that increasingly became the interest of the writer of modern fiction. As early as the eighteen-sixties, Dostoevski had been hostile to the current spirit of rationalism and science as failing to consider the spiritual imponderables in man, and therefore his art became more and more preoccupied with the irrational in human nature. He once remarked, "What most people regard as fantastic and lacking in universality, I hold to be the essence of truth"; and it is significant that in "The Grand Inquisitor" when Alyosha wonders at the "fantastic" in his story, Ivan replies, "Take it as the last, if you are so corrupted by modern realism and can't stand anything fantastic."

In the early work of James Joyce (Dubliners, 1914) and of Thomas Mann ("Little Herr Friedemann," 1897) the influence of the naturalistic tradition is still evident, but the subtlety of the psychological analysis in both their stories, "A Little Cloud" and "Little Herr Friedemann," goes well beyond the rather crude analytical devices of nineteenth-century naturalism, as any psychological method must do which (in Joyce) considers the relation of the artistic temperament, however feeble, to bourgeois life and the "City," and (in Mann) presents the stories of sensitive individuals warped by some physical or mental abnormality. Perhaps, as George Moore liked to say about some of his later novels, there is a "naturalism of souls"; but

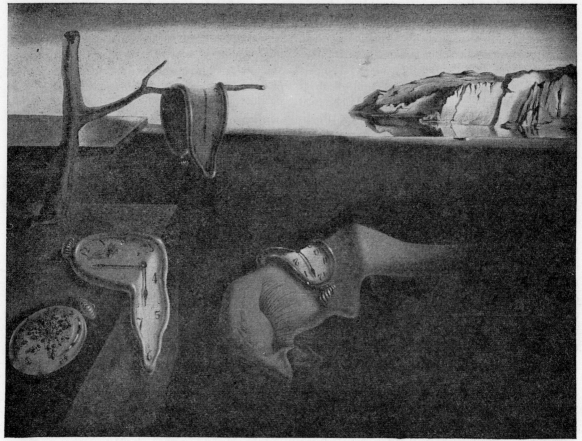

The Persistence of Memory by Salvador Dali.

certainly, at least in both Thomas Mann and James Joyce, there is needed for their purposes a depth psychology not previously comprised within the naturalistic theory, especially in Mann's studies of the relation of the artist to the bourgeois world in such works as *Tonio Kröger* and *The Magic Mountain*. Thomas Mann even anticipated Freudian diagnosis of the psychic conflicts within the subconscious, the night-side of the soul. In "Little Herr Friedemann" we discover suggestions of the conflict between the Ego and the Id, of the relation between psychical and physical aberrations, and of the death wish. Although we may still regard psychoanalysis as a scientific method that is naturalistic, and possibly even deterministic and fatalistic in its acceptance of the dominance of the subconscious, nevertheless its therapeutic technique plumbs man's mind with a profundity quite beyond

the conception and range of nineteenth-century naturalism. More than this, by its emphasis upon the importance of the suprarational in man, it prepared the way for a movement that was completely at odds with naturalism—Surrealism.

In the second decade of the twentieth century this interest in the subconscious became for the surrealists an avenue to the greater mystic force of a higher Reality, or Surreality, which could only be attained by the mastery of man's subconscious. Hence to the surrealist the irrationality of dreams and of hallucinatory states was important in that they revealed aspects of human nature never before observed. The surrealistic development in painting was anticipated in some of the "jungle" painting of Henri Rousseau (1844–1910): his "The Sleeping Gypsy" (1897) suggests a strange, trancelike dream state by the pattern of juxtaposed shape and color alone (the sky is deep blue, and the stripes of the robe are red, pink, yellow, blue, and green). However our conscious minds might reject those fantastic, awesome hallucinatory projections of the dream state in the paintings of Salvador Dali, Paul Klee, and Giorgio di Chirico (as in his "Toys of a Prince," 1915?), the surrealist believed that our subconscious minds rejoiced in them. Chirico's "metaphysical" painting is really surrealistic.

One of the acknowledged spiritual fathers of the surrealistic movement was the French poet Arthur Rimbaud (1854–1891), whose concept of the poet as a seer in his *"Lettre du voyant"* ("letter of a seer," to Paul Demeny, May 15, 1871) and whose startling experiments in breaking up the rational, logical sequence of sense impressions of a reality that has become habitually familiar to us, and in isolating and recreating them into different elements of experience (see *The Drunken Boat*) have had an extensive and fertilizing influence on modern poetry. The modern Spanish poet Federico García Lorca (1899–1936) has shown great sympathy with the surrealist's attempt to achieve a new cosmic reality by detaching material phenomena from their traditional associations and recombining them, as his praise of the surrealist artist in "Ode to Salvador Dali" and his own poetic experiments like "Song to Claudio Guillén" demonstrate.

Courtesy Museum of Modern Art, New York (Philip Goodwin Collection)

Lower Manhattan by John Marin.

ART FOR ART'S SAKE

DURING the later nineteenth century and continuing to the present, painting has taken a course similar to that of literature, from naturalism to impressionism to post-impressionism, expressionism, and surrealism. Of course the term "naturalism" applied to painting is misleading if we conceive it as describing a new movement, because painting has always tended to go to nature for inspiration, and it has been said that Giotto (1276?–1337) was the father of naturalism. We may say, however, that the school of painters that arose in France after the Revolution of 1848 broke with the academic studio tradition and initiated the modern school of naturalism by insisting on looking at nature as it was, and by painting it objectively, ugly or beautiful. The leader of the movement, Gustave Courbet (1819–1877), wanted to paint nature plain, without sentiment or prettiness. There was in Courbet and his fellow artists an impatience with the artificial, "insincere" traditions of academic painting that reminded one of the literary naturalist's similar resentment against mere aesthetic concern for structure and plot, which he regarded as false to the vital depiction of the "slice of life." Indeed, some of the scenes from Courbet's paintings of ugly washerwomen can be paralleled in the opening pages of Zola's *L'Assommoir*. In the same movement, Jean François Millet (1814–1875), possibly influenced by the new interest in the workers that we have noted as a trait of the naturalistic movement, painted harvesters at their work in the famous "Gleaners" with no concession to the older canons that would have prettified the scene, and with no attempt to suggest that it was in the academic tradition of portraying the everyday life of a people, after the genre painting of the Dutch.

Out of this revolution in French painting there grew the more important impressionistic movement led by Edouard Manet (1832–1883) and Claude Monet (1840–1926). The impressionist painters shared Courbet's belief that conventional art did not truly represent nature. To the sensitized eye of the impressionistic painter who refused to accept the academic belief that each object in nature had a fixed form and color, nature had no absolute black, and all scenes of nature were colored. He learned too that yellow sunlight created a complementary bluish shadow, and that shadow was merely a different density of light (Manet's "Olympia" was the beginning of shadow in color.). These artists used a palette of only seven colors (Pissarro had no black in his), and regarded line and form as an intellectual abstraction not to be found in nature, particularly when observed in the open air ("Pleinairisme"). The Impressionists thus rejected all preconceived ideas of nature, for to them painting nature meant the representation of certain aspects of light in which at various times of day different colors dominated. Consequently the impressionists "documented" their paintings somewhat in the naturalistic sense, painting the same subject under all variations of light. The impressionist painted scenes not only from the landscape but

Courtesy Museum of Modern Art, New York
(Mrs. John D. Rockefeller, Jr., Purchase Fund)

Agrarian Leader Zapata by Diego Rivera. (Variant of a fresco in the Palace of Cortez, Cuernavaca, Mexico.)

Courtesy Museum of Modern Art, New York

Portrait of Oriel Ross by Jacob Epstein.

from life, as in Renoir's "Le Moulin de la Galette" ("Ball at the Moulin de la Galette," 1876), wherein, as is typical of the impressionistic technique, even in the black-and-white illustration can be noted the technique of soft blurring of light without the minute distinctions between the figures that the mind knows is there, but the eye does not see.

The influence of impressionism upon literature is shown in the tendency of modern writers to give increased significance to the experience of the single moment, in all its intensity and uniqueness. The method may be demonstrated in the writings of Virginia Woolf, but it is perhaps most clearly evident in the work of Marcel Proust. In the famous passage upon the *madeleine* and the cup of tea from *Swann's Way* we have the epitome of Proust's impressionistic method: he is so aware that the passage of time may deprive him of aesthetic pleas-

ures that he seizes the impressions and images of beauty with an almost pathological intensity of emotion, in which the passage of time (as in painting the lines of form merge, spatially) becomes blurred in the transcendent experience. Such a technique in literature was given psychological justification by the famous chapter in William James's *Principles of Psychology* (1890) entitled "The Stream of Thought," suggesting that "there is no proof that the same bodily sensation is got by us twice," and by Henri Bergson's intimation in *Creative Evolution* (1907) that reality is a continual change of form, and that form is merely a snapshot view of reality in flux. This emphasis upon the significant experience of the moment is also supported by the modern literary technique known as stream-of-consciousness, which in turn is related to the Freudian therapeutics of the free association of ideas: momentary impressions merge swiftly into one another in the way that line, form and silhouette are lost in the pervasive shimmering atmosphere of the impressionistic painter.

Music too began to share with painting and literature the new impressionistic techniques. The aim in impressionistic music was to juxtapose tone harmonies with no clear line of relationship, as the painter arranged the juxtaposition of color and light without the connection of lines. This musical composition ignored the intellectual appeal of the structural elements (such as in the fugue), and by appealing directly to the senses created a lovely, fleeting moment of pure aesthetic pleasure. A languorous, remote, semimystic feeling is created without any clear, logical relation of parts, achieving what the symbolist poet would call the *rêve,* or dream reverie (one notes in this impressionistic music the greater predominance of the harp, flute, and strings with their greater powers of instrumental suggestion).

The outstanding impressionist composer Claude Debussy (1862–1918) was closely associated with a group of poets known as the symbolists, of whom the leaders were Stéphane Mallarmé (1842–1898) and Paul Verlaine 1844–1896). The growing isolation of the artist in the nineteenth century and his consequent hostility to the petty bourgeois world had been partly responsible for the artist's insistence that art need have no utilitarian or didactic aims. Théophile Gautier (1811–1872) stated the doctrine

Courtesy Museum of Modern Art, New York

Fish by Constantin Brancusi.

and in his attempt to arrange the words and tone colors of vowels and consonants in order to give the same experience of sensuous pleasure as the juxtaposition of colors in an impressionistic landscape or of tones in impressionistic music; the delicately and subtly muted strings and muffled snare drums of such music give the same sense of strangeness and dreaminess that we feel in Verlaine's "Clair de Lune." The avoidance of violent dramatic tonal effects in impressionistic music is the background of Verlaine's emphasis upon shade in "Art Poétique":

> Only of shade can the marriage be made
> Of dream with dream and of flute with horn.

This speculation upon the relation of poetry and music owes much of its germinative inspiration to Edgar Allan Poe's aesthetic theories presented in "The Poetic Principle" and in *Marginalia*. The preference of some translators to retain the French titles of translated poems reveals their perception of Baudelaire's and Verlaine's intention to draw upon the resources of music in their titles as well as in their poetry.

of art for art's sake in the preface to his *Mademoiselle de Maupin* (1835) and in his poem "Art." Previously Victor Cousin, in a series of lectures delivered as early as 1818, had argued that art was an end in itself, divorced from a subordination to the useful ends of religion or morality; and the doctrine of Schopenhauer's *The World as Will and Idea*, suggesting that art itself was a legitimate and highly creative escape from the miseries and frustrations of practical human existence, was eagerly accepted with all its implications by the symbolists after 1870.

Interest in the aesthetic form of art (as in Gautier's "Art") took precedence over subject matter, and there followed a natural tendency of poetry to approximate that form of art, music, which it most resembled in poetic devices of sound and harmony, in organization (that is, the medium was temporal, not spatial as in painting), and in aim (not being an imitation of life). This intimate correlation of poetry and music can be seen in Paul Verlaine's apostrophe to music in "Art Poétique,"

Courtesy Museum of Modern Art, New York
(A. Conger Goodyear Fund)

Family Group by Henry Moore.

Debussy wrote music for "Five Poems of Charles Baudelaire" and for Verlaine's poems *Fêtes Galantes,* among them "Mandoline." These musical settings bear an intimate relation to *The Flowers of Evil* and Verlaine's poems. The most famous of these musical poems approximating impressionism in music is Mallarmé's "The Afternoon of a Faun," for which Debussy wrote his *Prelude to the Afternoon of a Faun,* significantly called "a sensuous pastoral rhapsody following no fixed form." The poem should be read with this music, for it creates what Mallarmé called elsewhere a "state of the soul," in which a momentary but dominant mood is presented. Mallarmé's remark that the essential thing in poetry and music was the *impression* (of the *horror* of the forest, for example, not the exact description of the tree and branches) emphasizes the poet's feeling for mood. Even an idea to Mallarmé need not be communicated by direct rational discourse; it could be intuited through direct sensuous impression, as in his comment upon the ballet, "legs like a direct instrument of ideas." Further advocacy of the symbolist position came with the gradual importation of Richard Wagner's influence into France after 1880, since he had insisted that the ideal form of art was best apprehended without reflection, through the feelings, and had introduced in his opera the leitmotif which united drama and music and pointed the way to "the art of the future."

It is of course impossible here to chart the influence of the symbolists upon modern literature. The poet sought freedom to create as he wished, unhampered by any theory that art was a strict imitation of life; he sought unrestricted range of expression free from the previous formal conditions of realistic art; he regarded art as in itself an ideal pursuit that required no apology for its disregard of the didactic or utile. In seeking his new range of expression he disregarded the rules of French syntax, the habitual associations of words, the historical rules of French prosody (see Verlaine's "Art Poétique": "Choose your words, but think not whether/ Each to the other belong"). Possibly the greatest English poet of the twentieth century, William Butler Yeats (1865–1939), was an heir to the symbolist tradition. Since he could not read French readily his conception of symbolism was based upon what his friend Arthur Symons learned from Mallarmé, the ideas of which Yeats summed up in his essay on "Symbolism" (1900): "symbol is indeed the only possible expression of some invisible essence . . ." The important fact about Yeats is that he hated science, and Huxley and Tyndall, with "monkish hate" and in rebellion turned to theosophy, which helped him to believe in the power of certain magical symbols to evoke disembodied cosmic powers. Yeats was not an aesthete like Oscar Wilde so much as a seeker after mystic meanings beyond ordinary human experience and the reach of science. In his famous formulation of his system of metaphysics upon which he based his later poetry, *A Vision* (1925), he describes the mystic communication with the spirits who came to give him these symbols. The seeking out of suprarational intuitions of reality by the modern poet, his attempt to achieve the state of the "voyant," or "seer," is revealed in both the poetry of Yeats and Rilke: the inspiration of Rilke's *Duino Elegies* was the Angel that called to him out of the storm during that winter near Trieste in 1911–1912. In the achievement of the symbolists, of Yeats, and Rilke, the reaction against the rational and the scientific has stimulated an influential modern movement (in the Surrealists as well) which still has immense poetic vitality.

POST-IMPRESSIONISM

THE gradual retreat of poetry from the theory that art was a literal representation of nature and its increasing approximation to music was paralleled in painting. Paul Gauguin (1848–1903) spoke of his painting as "undulating horizontal lines, harmonies of orange and blue," an obvious parallel to music rhythm, and Henri Matisse (1869–   ) described his painting in similar terms. Nevertheless, impressionism seemed formless to many of the younger painters, and hence the movement known as post-impressionism was toward emphasis upon solidity of structure and firmness of planes and horizontal lines, as in the early work of Cézanne and Georges Seurat (in "Sunday on Grande Jatte Island," 1885–1886), achieved without the sacrifice of the intensity of color discovered by the

The Grundtvig "Pipe Organ" Church, Copenhagen, Denmark.

impressionists. These earlier paintings have admirable composition-values without sacrificing verisimilitude completely. But more and more the post-impressionist painters gave up the delineation of subject matter and tried to represent abstractly, in part inspired by Cézanne's advice to look at nature as if it were a cone or cube. No longer was it the painter's ambition to represent a fleeting impression, but to construct paintings which had no relevance to nature as ordinarily perceived. The material objects in the world of common experience were broken up and recombined in a new architectural order to reveal a previously unperceived essence of meaning. Thus one was not to regard the first important Cubist picture, Picasso's "Les Demoiselles d'Avignon" (1907), as a literal transcript of observed nature, but as a remarkably dynamic composition of brilliantly organized planes and sharply

angled lines whose remoteness from photographic reality is also suggested by the imitation of the stylized African Negro masks. The Cubist design of cutting up an object, flattening out its planes, foreshortening the view, assembling different views of the same object is shown in Georges Braque's "Le Violon" (Oval Still Life, 1914).

These post-impressionistic methods of painting are projected into modern literature in "Cubist" poems, like "Zone," of Guillaume Apollinaire, possibly the most influential French poet since Baudelaire, in Rilke's close philosophic interpretation of Picasso's "Les Saltimbanques" (The Mountebanks, 1905) in the Fifth Duino Elegy, and in the experimental novelistic techniques of James Joyce in *Ulysses* and Virginia Woolf in *The Waves*. A close friend of Mrs. Woolf's, Roger Fry, at the time of the post-impressionistic exhibition in London in 1910, had wondered why English novelists were concerned with "the childish problems" of "photographic representations," since Picasso and Cézanne had shown modern writers the way out of such realistic imitations of life. Later André Gide wrote in *The Counterfeiters* (1926) that "the writer's rule is not to hold to nature but to set before himself nothing she can or should promptly copy." In T. S. Eliot's "Burnt Norton" from *Four Quartets* (the title obviously bears upon the assumed relation of poetry and music), the second movement suggests post-impressionistic techniques in the juxtaposition of contraries.

Another influential post-impressionistic movement has been expressionism. Anticipated in the violently insurgent rhythms of Vincent van Gogh (1853–1890), this genre developed early in the twentieth century from the paintings exhibited in the Parisian *Salon D'Automne* in 1905 by a group of artists described satirically as "Les Fauves" (The Wild Beasts). The leader of the group was Henri Matisse (1869–   ), who published what may be described as the "credo" of the expressionistic movement in "Notes of a Painter" (*La Grande Revue*, 1908). In these notes, Matisse declared that what he was after "above all, was expression," and insisted that color should be used solely to express the emotional vision of the artist. This expressionism often became, therefore, the projection of a hallucinatory psychic state or the imposition of a transcendent conception of cosmic forces upon the external world that transformed its normal appearance. This remarkable and startling transformation of everyday reality is seen equally in the extraordinary occult power of Franz Kafka's "The Hunter Gracchus" and in the dynamic rhythms of line and structure in Van Gogh's "Starry Night" (1889) and John Marin's "Lower Manhattan" (1920). There is a close correspondence between Virginia Woolf's insistence that her experimental novels (*To the Lighthouse, The Waves*) reveal their meaning by their structure and arrangement *only* and Matisse's comment in "Notes of a Painter": "A work of art must carry in it its complete significance and impose upon the beholder even before he can identify the subject matter." An illustration of his point of view may be seen in "Studio Quai St. Michel" (1916), wherein the structure, space, and simple drawing (as well as the colors, not perceptible in the illustration) convey the artist's sense of repose, serenity wholly in themselves.

THE "NEW SPIRIT" IN MODERN SCULPTURE AND ARCHITECTURE

SCULPTURE. For a just appreciation of modern sculpture, it is necessary to understand three aesthetic ideas upon which modern sculpture is based. In the first place, we must be willing to judge a piece of sculpture primarily upon its design, its form and structure, and not upon whether it seems to be an exact and faithful copy of forms which we observe in nature, and above all not upon whether it precisely resembles the contours of the human body. Second, we must comprehend the modern sculptor's determination to understand fully both the limitations and the potentialities of the medium in which he works (wood, bronze, stone, wire), and to make his product conform to the nature of that medium. The artist respects his material and allows its structure and grain to control and condition the shape of his sculpture. Third, we must realize that to the modern sculptor the essential tradition in sculpture is not revealed in the exact modeling of materials to the contours of the human body characteristic of the naturalistic Hellenic art, but is rather a development from primitive African, Sumerian, Etruscan, and Greek Archaic art which stressed less the realistic production of natural forms than a method in which the organization of plastic forms is determined by the physical nature of the selected material. In the nineteenth century the artist was not sufficiently aware of the necessity that he be directly in contact with the material in which his design was to be executed; hence one of the chief causes for the decline of sculpture in that century was the artist's inclination to do his work in clay and then to turn over his clay model to others who produced the finished sculpture in marble or in bronze.

Although the sculpture of Auguste Rodin (1840–1917) cannot be called strictly modern, it was he who rescued nineteenth-century sculpture from the decadence into which it had fallen. The tension, the nervous energy, the violent exertion of many of Rodin's sculptured figures revitalized nineteenth-century sculpture. To him the human body became a means of expressing intense human passion. Rodin created his figures under great stress of creative emotion, and when the impulse had passed he often left his work rough and unfinished, frequently with the impression that the figure was just emerging from the stone.

From Rodin to the modern sculptors, the transitional artist was Aristide Maillol (1861–1944). In contrast to the sometimes agonized energy of Rodin's figures, Maillol's sculptures have an ease of posture, a dispassionate objectivity in artistic rendering, a classical serenity that suggests his devoted study of Hellenic art, though he is never merely imitative of it. His female figures have simplicity and repose; at the same time they point the way for the modern sculptor's interest in the rhythm and harmony of significant plastic form in and of itself (note the simplicity of the solidly conceived anatomy in "Ile de France," devoid of the psychological details of sentiment).

The work of the American sculptor Jacob Epstein (b. 1880) may be described as a compromise between the romanticism of Rodin and the modern aesthetic aim to achieve significant form in three dimensions rather than merely to imitate natural forms of the body or of the features. This modern aesthetic aim is revealed in Brancusi's "The Fish" and in Henry Moore's "Family Group." Like

The Bauhaus School, Dessau, Germany; Walter Gropius, architect.

Rodin in France, Epstein broke with the academic traditions of formal beauty, and used his imagination to project his conception in a vivid expressionistic way that he did not fear to make ugly or grotesque. His portrait busts are especially remarkable achievements in the way that Epstein records the psyche of the subject and interprets the complete psychological pattern of emotion as it is revealed in the sitter's face.

Much of the inspiration for modern sculpture came from the Cubist movement of the early twentieth century. In the compositions of Picasso, Modigliani, Braque, and the sculptor Jacques Lipchitz (b. 1891) there is emphasis upon pure plastic form, partly in reaction to nineteenth-century sentimentalism. To these artists, Cézanne's famous pronouncement in his letter to Émile Bernard was significant: "You must see nature in the cylinder, the sphere, the cone." The tendency toward Cubism, we have remarked, was stimulated by

Picasso's "Les Demoiselles d'Avignon" (1907). So it was that Cézanne's dictum influenced not only painting but sculpture and architecture as well. The Cubist stepped inside the frame of the picture and looked at it from all sides: above and below, as well as from the front, once traditionally the only place from which to view the pictorial effects. This artistic conception in painting may be paralleled by the sculptor's seeing his work in three dimensions, a balance of mass and a juxtaposition of planes in space. Modern sculptors like the Romanian Constantin Brancusi (b. 1876) and Henry Moore (b. 1898) conceive their work as a testing of the artist's ability to visualize his sculpture in the round and see volumes and planes of his material in terms of its perspective in space and light. Brancusi's "The Fish," for example, is pivoted in such a way that it can be rotated and seen from all sides (Brancusi takes moving pictures of his work to reveal all its facets from every side).

Only a view of the actual art object can reveal the painstaking attention that Brancusi has given to bringing out the aspects of form that are residual in the gray marble. The architectonic and timeless quality of modern sculpture is indicated in Henry Moore's "Family Group" (1946).

The conception of sculpture as an art whose nature is determined by the relation of plane and mass to space is paralleled in modern dance. This resemblance is particularly to be noted in the dance compositions of the German school of Rudolf Van Laban and Mary Wigman, and of the American school whose leading exponents are Martha Graham and Doris Humphrey. Space is conceived to be a dynamic medium (*Raumkorper* or "space body")

for the dancer's body to work in and to conquer. Modern dance becomes therefore a plastic art form moving in and against three-dimensional space.

ARCHITECTURE. Like sculpture, modern architecture has taken its inspiration from the Cubists. It is significant that the distinguished Swiss architect Le Corbusier (Charles Jeanneret-Gris, *b.* 1887) echoes Cézanne in observing in *New World of Space* (New York, 1948): "Spheres, cones, and cylinders: modern architecture, from reinforced concrete, from steel and glass, combined into appropriate forms, is slowly organizing itself into a symphony." The Cubist emphasis upon presenting an object from several points of view at once, a

From *The Work of Oscar Niemeyer*, Stamo Papadaki, ed. (1950). Courtesy Reinhold Publishing Corp.
Lobby of the Boavista Bank from the Mezzanine, Rio de Janeiro.

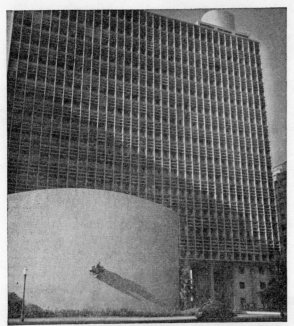

From *The Work of Oscar Niemeyer*, Stamo
Papadaki, ed. (1950). Courtesy Reinhold
Publishing Corp.

Ministry of Education and Health, Rio de Janeiro.

principle defined as *simultaneity,* was, along with associated and derivative movements known as Futurism and Constructivism, the impetus for the architectural creations of Le Corbusier and Walter Gropius (b. 1883). The paintings of Braque and Picasso exhibited the interior and the exterior of an object simultaneously; the Cubist painter tried to see the object from all sides and to go *into* it. In a similar manner, modern architecture, with its extensive use of glass and its exclusion of the traditional posts and beams that once supported the façade, can provide for one's seeing the inside and outside of the building at the same time. If the wall of glass becomes merely a transparent screen separating the space inside the building from the enveloping space in which the building is set, then there is a magnification of spatial effects through the interpenetration of the space inside (now visible) and that outside. As Le Corbusier says, "a miracle of ineffable space" opens up.

One of the most important influences in propagating this new spirit was Walter Gropius' Bauhaus at Dessau (1926). Here is fully developed the doctrine which we have come to know as functional-

ism; that is, the primary aim in architecture is to design the building (or furnishings) for the specific function to be served. The view of the Bauhaus suggests perfect architectural balance of the various units: it seems almost to float in space, and the glass curtain with little visible means of structural support gives a sense of seeing the outside and inside simultaneously.

That such architecture is effectively adapted to modern, machine-age civilization and lends itself to the reorganization of space in modern urban planning may be perceived in a careful study of Rockefeller Center. Here is dynamic functional architecture which severely excludes the meaningless flamboyant decoration so characteristic of the Gothic tower type of skyscraper popular in many of our large cities until recent decades. The functional design is especially noteworthy in the way the rectangular arrangement of the center affords essential light for the allotted space: the respective units are spread out in such relation of height, volume, and plane that their shadows will not affect the lighting space necessary to the modern offices of the individual buildings. That functionalism need not be divorced from beauty is revealed in the creations of the Brazilian architect Oscar Niemeyer

From *The Work of Oscar Niemeyer*, Stamo
Papadaki, ed. (1950). Courtesy Reinhold
Publishing Corp.

The Day Nursery, Gavia Section, Rio de Janeiro.

Courtesy Thomas Airviews

Rockefeller Center, New York City.

(*b.* 1907), especially in the Ministry of Education and Public Health of Rio de Janeiro. Senhor Niemeyer, who designed the Brazilian Pavilion for the New York World's Fair of 1939, has been the consultant for the architectural designs of the new United Nations buildings in New York.

Neither modern sculpture nor modern architecture is in the nineteenth-century tradition of art for art's sake. Jacob Epstein has insisted that sculpture must serve communal man, and Henry Moore's "Family Group" was designed for the cultural center of an English village. Certainly, therefore, both arts subserve the needs of modern man in his communities. Even if one were not to reckon with the great influence of their art concepts upon modern industrial and advertising designs, modern sculpture and architecture are still as characteristic of the twentieth century as Gothic sculpture and architecture were of the twelfth. In their artistic credos are heralded the developments of the arts of the future.

MODERN MUSIC AND "NEW MUSIC"

THE first manifestation of modern music came in the post-Romantic movements of the late nineteenth century: in Germany, Johannes Brahms (1833–1897) signalized the revolt against extreme Romantic subjectivity by returning to the classical form of the sonata and other symphonic forms; in France, this rejection of Romantic emotionalism became the impressionism of Claude Debussy (1862–1918) and Maurice Ravel (1875–1937). After 1910 the "New Music" (*Neue Musik*) arose to break completely with the concepts of nineteenth-century harmony and develop new, experimental, and radical techniques in atonality and in primitive rhythms whose sources (akin to the Cubistic use of African masks) were the violent syncopations of aboriginal music and of ragtime and jazz (in Stravinsky's *L'Histoire du Soldat*, Milhaud's *La Création du Monde*, and Honegger's *Concertino for Piano and Orchestra*). Since 1925, Igor Stravinsky (*b.* 1882) and Paul Hindemith (*b.* 1895), who, with Arnold Schönberg (1874–1951), are perhaps the most influential modern composers, have returned to the music of Bach and his period, thus initiating a movement in music known as Neo-classicism. In America, both jazz and folk music have made significant contributions to serious American music; the use of motifs from American folk music in the compositions of Roy Harris (*b.* 1898) and Aaron Copland (*b.* 1900) suggests a parallel development to the grass roots regional painting of Thomas Benton, John S. Curry, and Grant Wood.

These, then, have been some of the major artistic tendencies in the Modern world. They have been voyages of discovery, in literature, painting, music, and architecture (one recalls Le Corbusier's scrawling over the sketched drawings of Neo-classical buildings in Paris, "This is not architecture"). As in the past, great literature and art are still tireless in their search for a way of life, in their exploration of reality, or perhaps better, realities, in their revaluation and reassessment of traditions. The international scope of modern literary and artistic movements has shown that the ideas common to our Western civilization are without geographical, racial, and political boundaries. Perhaps the way of the imagination remains a potent moral force still, and will grant us, enlarge, and illuminate for us those creative perspectives that shall be needed to solve the spiritual dilemmas characteristic not only of the Western world but as well of the "one world" in this, our Age of Anxiety.

LIST OF RECORDINGS

MODERN MUSIC

1. *Academic Festival Overture,* by Johannes Brahms (1833–1897), containing the "Gaudeamus Igitur," recorded by the New York Philharmonic Orchestra in Columbia Masterworks set X200.
2. *Symphony No. 1 in C Minor,* by Johannes Brahms, recorded by the NBC Symphony Orchestra in Victor Masterworks set 875.
3. *Concerto No. 3 for Piano,* by Béla Bartók (1881–1945), recorded by the Philadelphia Symphony Orchestra in Columbia Long Playing record ML-4239.

4. *Quarter No. 2 in A Minor,* by Béla Bartók, recorded by the Budapest Quartet in Victor Masterworks set 320.

5. *Wozzeck,* by Alban Berg (1885-1935), libretto by Georg Büchner, complete opera recorded by the New York Philharmonic Orchestra in Columbia Long Playing Masterworks set SL-118.

6. *Billy the Kid,* by Aaron Copland (1900-   ), ballet suite recorded by the RCA Victor Symphony Orchestra in Victor Long Playing record LM-1031.

7. *Concerto for Clarinet and Orchestra,* by Aaron Copland, recorded by the Columbia Symphony Orchestra in Columbia Long Playing record ML-4421.

8. *Cinq Poèmes de Charles Baudelaire,* by Claude Debussy (1862-1918), with Jennie Tourel, mezzo-soprano, recorded in Columbia Long Playing record ML-4158.

9. *Prelude to the Afternoon of a Faun,* by Claude Debussy, recorded by the Philadelphia Symphony Orchestra in Victor Long Playing record LM-1154.

10. *Clair de Lune,* by Gabriel Fauré (1845-1924), on Columbia record 4164 M. This work is suggestive of Verlaine's "Clair de Lune."

11. *Symphony for Voices,* by Roy Harris (1898-   ), with texts from Walt Whitman, recorded in Victor Masterworks set 752.

12. *Mathis der Maler,* by Paul Hindemith (1895-   ), recorded by the Philadelphia Symphony Orchestra in Victor Masterworks set 854.

13. *Kammermusik No. 4, Op. 36, No. 3 Violin Concerto,* by Paul Hindemith, recorded by the Winterthur Symphony Orchestra in Westminster Long Playing record WL-5074.

14. *Concertino for Piano and Orchestra,* by Arthur Honegger (1892-   ), recorded by the Columbia Symphony Orchestra in Columbia Long Playing record ML-2156.

15. *La Création du Monde,* ballet by Darius Milhaud (1892-   ), recorded by the Columbia Chamber Orchestra in Columbia Long Playing record ML-4433.

16. *Symphony No. 5,* by Sergei Prokofiev (1891-   ), recorded by the New York Philharmonic Orchestra in Columbia Long Playing record ML-4037.

17. *Daphnis and Chloe, Suite No. 2,* by Maurice Ravel (1875-1937), recorded by the Philadelphia Symphony Orchestra in Columbia Long Playing record ML-4316.

18. *Ma Mere l'Oye,* by Maurice Ravel, recorded by the Boston Symphony Orchestra in Victor Long Playing record LM-1012.

19. *Pierrot Lunaire,* by Arnold Schönberg (1874-1951), recorded by the Columbia Symphony Orchestra in Columbia Long Playing record ML-4471.

20. *Quartet No. 2 in F-sharp Minor,* by Arnold Schönberg, recorded by the Kolisch Quartet in Alco Long Playing record 1005. The music is a voice and string accompaniment to Stefan George's poem, "I Breathe the Air of Other Planets."

21. *Der Rosenkavalier,* by Richard Strauss (1864-1949), libretto by Hugo von Hofmannsthal, abridged recording by the Vienna State Opera in Victor Masterworks set 196.

22. *Elektra,* by Richard Strauss, libretto by Hugo von Hofmannsthal, complete opera recorded by the Florence May Festival Chorus and Orchestra in Cetra Long Playing set LP-1209.

23. *Petrouchka,* by Igor Stravinsky (1882-   ), recorded by the New York Philharmonic Symphony Orchestra in Columbia Long Playing record ML-4438.

24. *L'Histoire du Soldat,* by Igor Stravinsky, recorded by the Boston Symphony Orchestra in Victor Long Playing record LM-1078.

25. *Symphony No. 1 in F,* by Dimitri Shostakovich (1906-   ), recorded by the Cleveland Symphony Orchestra in Columbia Long Playing record ML-4389.

26. *Symphony No. 6,* by Dimitri Shostakovich, recorded by the Pittsburgh Symphony Orchestra in Columbia Long Playing record ML-4249.

27. *Concerto for Oboe and Strings,* by Ralph Vaughan Williams (1872-   ), recorded by the Saidenberg Little Symphony Orchestra, in Mercury Long Playing record 10003.

Italian Poetry

GIACOMO LEOPARDI

1798–1837

Born into a strictly Roman Catholic and highly conservative family, and an invalid from his youth, Leopardi spent a large portion of his life in enforced retirement, devoting himself assiduously to classical and philological studies. He became not only a distinguished scholar but also the finest poet of his generation in Italy. His work is characterized by a classic perfection of form and technique, but possesses at the same time a spirit of melancholy, disillusionment, and pessimism which looks toward the Romantics. As a poet, Leopardi is unsurpassed in modern Italian literature for the depth of thought and sincerity of feeling found throughout his work. In addition to many miscellaneous prose pieces of high literary value, such as his celebrated *Pensieri* and *Operette Morali*, his work includes in particular the renowned ode "To Italy" and others which will continue to be read as long as cultivated people esteem the blending of the best in classical and modern thought.

FURTHER READING

BICKERSTETH, G. L., ed. *The Poems of Leopardi*. With an Introduction and Notes (Cambridge, Eng., 1923).

HEATH-STUBBS, JOHN. *Poems of Giacomo Leopardi* (London, 1946).

HOWELLS, W. D. "Leopardi," in *Modern Italian Poets* (New York, 1887).

ROSSETTI, WILLIAM M. "Leopardi," in *Studies in Comparative Literature* (Oxford, 1900).

The Dream *

'Twas early morning and between the chinks
Of the closed shutters through the window crept
The first faint day-gleam into my dark room,
When at the time that sleep most lightly lies
And gentliest on the eyelids, by my side
Stood gazing down into my countenance
The ghost of her, by whom I first was taught
What love is, and who later left me weeping.

* This and the following two poems from *The Poems of Leopardi*, translated by Geoffrey L. Bickersteth. By permission of the Cambridge University Press.

Not dead, but pale she seemed to me, and like
To theirs who grieve her face was. To my head 10
She stretched her right hand forth and sighing spake:
"Livest thou still? Rememberest thou at all
Our life together?" "Whence," I said, "and how
Com'st thou, my fair belov'd? Much, ah how much
I mourned thee and still mourn: nor ever dreamed
That thou shouldst be aware thereof; and this
Made even sorrow's self more sorrowful.
Yet com'st thou but to leave me once again?
Greatly I fear it. What befell thee? Say;
Art thou as once thou wert? What inward pang 20
Convulses thee?" "Thy thoughts forgetfulness
Encumbereth, and they are swathed in sleep:"
She answered. "I am dead; thou sawest me
For the last time some moons ago." Immense
Anguish o'erwhelmed my spirit at these words.
And she continued: "in the bloom of youth
I died, when life is sweetest, and before
It dawns upon the heart how wholly vain
Is human hope. The sick man hath not far
To travel ere he yearns for one who bears 30
Men forth from all afflictions: but the young
Die unconsoled by death, and hard the fate
Of those whose hope beneath the soil is quenched.
Vain is the knowledge of what nature hides
From the unversed in life, and better far
Than wisdom gained untimely is blind pain,
Pain blind unto itself." "Oh luckless one,
O dearest, hush!" I cried: "hush, or thy words
Will break my heart. Thou art in truth, then, dead,
O my belov'd, and I still live, and heaven 40
Indeed ordained that in its tender youth
My darling's body needs must undergo
The agony of death, while I survive
Still clothed in this vile husk. How oft, alas,
When I remember that thou liv'st no more,
And that on earth I'll find thee ne'er again,
I cannot deem it true. Alas, alas,
What thing is this called death? Ah, would that I
By dying might learn its nature and remove
From fate's fierce hatred my defenseless head. 50
Young am I, yet my youth is all consumed
And blighted like old age, from which I shrink
In horror, though it still lies years away.
But little with life's winter is my spring
Discordant." And she answered me: "we twain
Were born to weep; felicity smiled not

Upon our lives; and in our sorrows heaven
Rejoiced." "Now if these eyes with tears are dim,"
I added, "and if pallor veils my face
That thou must leave me, and if swollen big   60
With anguish is my heart, I pray thee tell
If any spark of pity or of love
For the poor wretch who loved thee fired thy heart,
Whilst thou wert yet alive? My nights and days
I dragged out, half despairing, half in hope.
And now of vain conjecturing my mind
Is weary grown. But if a single pang
Of pity pierced thee for my life of gloom,
I beg thee, tell me and conceal it not;
Let memory be my comforter, since fate   70
Denies us future bliss." And she: "poor soul,
Be comforted. Of pity, whilst I lived,
I was not niggardly, nor am I now,
For I was wretched too. Complain thou not
Of this unhappiest of unhappy maids."
"By our misfortunes, by the love which melts
My yearning heart," I cried, "by that dear name,
The name of youth, and by the vanished hope
Of both our lives, grant me, my only love,
To touch thy hand." And she, with gesture sad   80
And gentle, straightway held it forth. Now while
I cover it with kisses, strain it close
Against my panting bosom, while my heart
Throbbed with delicious pains, and on my brow
And breast broke forth a sweat, and in my throat
The words choked, daylight reeled upon my gaze.
Whereat she, fixing her eyes tenderly
On my eyes: "dear one, dost so soon forget,"
Said she, "that of my beauty I am bare?
And thou, O hapless one, in vain with love   90
Dost burn and moan. Now hear my last farewell.
Our wretched minds are from our bodies now
Sundered for aye. To me thou livest not,
Nor ever shalt live more: now fate hath snapped
The troth thou sworest me." Then struggling hard
To shriek aloud for anguish, shuddering,
My eyelids bursting with unshed, hot tears,
From sleep I started. She before my eyes
Yet stood, and in the Sun's uncertain ray
It seemed to me that I beheld her still.   100

The Village Saturday

The village damsel coming from the fields
At sunset homeward goes
With her truss of hay, and bringing in her hand
A nosegay of the violet and the rose,
Wherewith she doth propose,
As wonted, to adorn

Upon the Sunday morn her breast and hair.
On yonder steps, from where
She faces full towards the dying day,
The beldam sits among the neighbours spinning;   10
And falls to telling tales of her good time,
When she too decked herself for festivals
And, lissom still and gay,
Was wont to dance all evening with the lads
She had for partners of life's lovely May.
'Tis dusk already; soon
The sky turns blue again; again from roof
And hill the shadows creep
Beneath the white beams of the rising moon.
Now the vesper-bell is ringing   20
Of the festival that's coming,
And in that sound 'twould seem
The heart fresh comfort finds.
Shouting the boys run in
To the little market-place,
And raise a merry din,
As they caper here and there.
Meanwhile the ploughman, whistling as he goes
Home to his frugal fare,
Of his repose upon the morrow ponders.   30

When dark are all the other windows round,
And else there is no sound,
Hark to the hammer-stroke, hark to the saw
Of the carpenter, who still
By lamplight labours on in his closed shop
With no rest, no reprieve,
His work to achieve, before the pale dawn glow.

'Tis the most gracious day of all the week,
Full of hope and gladness:
Lassitude and sadness   40
Tomorrow's hours will bring, and each in thought
His wonted labour once again will seek.

Frolicsome little lad,
This season blossom-rife
Is like a day that overflows with joy,
Calm and without annoy,
Coming before the Sunday of your life.
Sport on, my boy; now, while your April blooms,
Now, while it's good to live.
Ah, hush, no more; but do not greatly grieve   50
If it be long still ere your Sunday comes.

The Setting of the Moon

As in the lonely night
O'er lands and waters lit with silvery light,
When softly stirs the air,

And distant shades are weaving
A thousand sense-deceiving
Objects and aspects rare
Mid wavelets, calm and still,
And branch and hedge and farm and little hill;
Poised upon heaven's rim
O'er Apennine or Alp, or where the deep   10
Tyrrhenian heaves in sleep,
Descends the Moon; and all the world grows dim;
The shadows fade, and soon
The dark creeps over all with sombre shoon;
Bereaved the night remains,
And, singing loud in strains of mournful tone,
The waggoner from his road salutes the last
Beams by the radiance cast,
Which, hitherto his guide, now leaves him lone;

   So youth from us is taken,   20
Even so it leaves forsaken
Our mortal years. In flight
The shadows pass and perish
Of loved illusions; catch we rarer sight
Of those far hopes we cherish,
Which lend such strong support to human nature,
Forlorn, and with each feature
Obscure, remaineth life; gazing whereo'er,
The traveller, lost, feels but an idle ranger,
To the long road, which he must yet explore,   30
Seeing no goal, sure only
That earth to him is lonely,
And he to it no more than a mere stranger.

   Too happy seemed to be
Our portion here of pains
Unto the Heavenly Powers, if that our lease

Of youth, whose thousand ills yield but one good,
Through all life should endure without surcease.
Too gracious that decree,
Which to all creatures death for doom ordains,   40
Unless the half of life
Should first be spent in strife
And toil far harder than life's dreaded close.
The eternals Gods designed—
Of immortal intellect
A worthy find—the extremest of all woes,
Old age, that still unchecked
Desire might linger on, when hope had died,
The springs of joy be dried, sorrow not less
But more, and still no hint of happiness.   50

   Ye, little hills and slopes,
Though in the west hath faded now the splendour,
Wherewith the veil of night was silvered o'er,
Shall not be long denied
Your consolation; on the other side
Soon shall ye see once more
Heaven whitening with the tender rays of dawn:
Following whereafter shall the sun arise,
Who, flashing all around
His irresistible beams,   60
Shall inundate with streams
Of light yourselves and all the boundless skies.
But mortal life, when youth has once withdrawn
Its lovely radiance, sees nought else adorning
Its firmament, beholds no second morning.
Dark it remains until the end; and Heaven
As limit to the gloom,
Which shrouds Man's other years, hath set the
   tomb.

English Poetry

ALFRED, LORD TENNYSON

1809-1892

Alfred, Lord Tennyson was poet laureate of the Victorian Age, and hence his poetic reputation has suffered the vagaries of overestimation in his own time and of the underestimation which was accorded the Victorians in the generation that followed his death. The portrait of the grave, bearded, and imperturbable poet laureate in the steel engravings that decorated the parlors of the late Victorian household have done Tennyson a disservice; a reading of *Maud* and the recent biography by his grandson will show us more truthfully the occasionally morbid, brooding, and always sensitive young poet, rugged and shaggy in appearance, who strode across the moors of Somersby shouting his poems to the winds of Lincolnshire. The basic wildness in his nature eventually yielded to the

Victorian love of order and repose, a reaction from Byronic strenuousness that provoked the early pretty, sentimental, and decorous verses to Claribel, Lillian, and his "darling room." Tennyson's greatest fault as a poet was his ready willingness to meet the Victorian compromise more than halfway in its demand for the proprieties and its yearning for the "message" of shallow optimism.

Born at Somersby in Lincolnshire on August 6, 1809, Tennyson attended Trinity College, Cambridge, where he first met Arthur Henry Hallam in a debating and conversation society known as the Apostles. In February, 1831, his father's illness compelled Tennyson to withdraw from Cambridge. His first important volume of poems, published in 1832, contained the early versions of some of his most successful later poems (like the "Lotos Eaters"). The influence of Spenser and of John Keats was especially noteworthy in this volume. The scathing review by John Gibson Lockhart in the *Quarterly Review* struck Tennyson into a ten-years' silence, during which time he revised his poems and prepared them for publication in *Poems,* 1842. This later publication achieved full recognition for Tennyson and reassured him in his poetic career. In 1850 he married Emily Sellwood, published *In Memoriam,* and became poet laureate upon the death of Wordsworth. The remaining years of his life were of undisturbed security, happiness, and increasing poetic fame.

To posterity Tennyson has suffered the fate of a poet, who although not a profound thinker took his social and moral responsibilities seriously in writing "public poetry," and who addressed himself too confidently to the solution of the vexing philosophical questions of the day, such as the reconciliation of theism and science. Tennyson's attempts in *In Memoriam* to justify man's faith in progress seemed shallow to the Edwardian generation; today the undercurrent of misgiving and doubt that runs through that elegy seems to us more the real lyric voice of Tennyson than the more official optimistic pronouncements to his own age.

However dated the Tennysonian message may seem to our generation, his reputation will always remain high as one of the most masterful of English poets in his command of the resources of the poetic art. He was essentially a lyric poet of unrivaled sensibility who could embody in his verse a mood with a subtly evoked background of landscape painting. He was a marvellous artist in words, and possibly the most conscious one in the whole range of English poetry. At his lyric best Tennyson delineated brilliantly the poetic qualities of the Roman poets like Catullus or Vergil, and wrote the perfect lyrics of the *Princess*; at the same time he achieved the grand style in the noble poetic note of "Ulysses" and of that remarkable late achievement of his art, "Rizpah."

FURTHER READING

BAUM, PAULL F. *Tennyson Sixty Years After* (Chapel Hill, 1948).

LOUNSBURY, T. R. *The Life and Times of Tennyson from 1809 to 1850* (New Haven, 1915).

NICOLSON, HAROLD G. *Tennyson* (Boston, 1923).

PADEN, W. D. *Tennyson in Egypt: A Study in the Imagery of His Earlier Work* (Lawrence, Kan., 1942).

TENNYSON, SIR CHARLES. *Alfred Tennyson* (New York, 1949).

The Lotos-Eaters

"Courage!" he said, and pointed toward the land,
"This mounting wave will roll us shoreward soon."
In the afternoon they came unto a land,
In which it seemed always afternoon.
All round the coast the languid air did swoon,
Breathing like one that hath a weary dream.
Full-faced above the valley stood the moon;
And like a downward smoke, the slender stream
Along the cliff to fall and pause and fall did seem.

A land of streams! some, like a downward smoke, 10
Slow-dropping veils of thinnest lawn, did go;
And some through wavering lights and shadows broke,
Rolling a slumbrous sheet of foam below.
They saw the gleaming river seaward flow
From the inner land: far off, three mountain-tops,
Three silent pinnacles of aged snow,
Stood sunset-flush'd: and, dew'd with showery drops,
Up-clomb the shadowy pine above the woven copse.

The charmed sunset linger'd low adown
In the red West: through mountain clefts the dale   20
Was seen far inland, and the yellow down
Border'd with palm, and many a winding vale
And meadow, set with slender galingale;
A land where all things always seem'd the same!
And round about the keel with faces pale,

Dark faces pale against that rosy flame,
The mild-eyed melancholy Lotos-eaters came.

Branches they bore of that enchanted stem,
Laden with flower and fruit, whereof they gave
To each, but whoso did receive of them, 30
And taste, to him the gushing of the wave
Far far away did seem to mourn and rave
On alien shores; and if his fellow spake,
His voice was thin, as voices from the grave;
And deep asleep he seem'd, yet all awake,
And music in his ears his beating heart did make.

They sat them down upon the yellow sand,
Between the sun and moon upon the shore;
And sweet it was to dream of Fatherland,
Of child, and wife, and slave; but evermore 40
Most weary seem'd the sea, weary the oar,
Weary the wandering fields of barren foam.
Then some one said, "We will return no more;"
And all at once they sang, "Our island home
Is far beyond the wave; we will no longer roam."

CHORIC SONG

I

There is sweet music here that softer falls
Than petals from blown roses on the grass,
Or night-dews on still waters between walls
Of shadowy granite, in a gleaming pass;
Music that gentlier on the spirit lies,
Than tir'd eyelids upon tir'd eyes;
Music that brings sweet sleep down from the bliss-
 ful skies.
Here are cool mosses deep,
And through the moss the ivies creep,
And in the stream the long-leaved flowers weep, 10
And from the craggy ledge the poppy hangs in
 sleep.

II

Why are we weigh'd upon with heaviness,
And utterly consum'd with sharp distress,
While all things else have rest from weariness?
All things have rest: why should we toil alone,
We only toil, who are the first of things,
And make perpetual moan,
Still from one sorrow to another thrown:
Nor ever fold our wings,
And cease from wanderings, 20
Nor steep our brows in slumber's holy balm;
Nor harken what the inner spirit sings,
"There is no joy but calm!"

Why should we only toil, the roof and crown of
 things?

III

Lo! in the middle of the wood,
The folded leaf is woo'd from out the bud
With winds upon the branch, and there
Grows green and broad, and takes no care,
Sun-steep'd at noon, and in the moon
Nightly dew-fed; and turning yellow 30
Falls, and floats adown the air.
Lo! sweeten'd with the summer light,
The full-juiced apple, waxing over-mellow,
Drops in a silent autumn night.
All its allotted length of days,
The flower ripens in its place,
Ripens and fades, and falls, and hath no toil,
Fast-rooted in the fruitful soil.

IV

Hateful is the dark-blue sky,
Vaulted o'er the dark-blue sea. 40
Death is the end of life; ah, why
Should life all labour be?
Let us alone. Time driveth onward fast,
And in a little while our lips are dumb.
Let us alone. What is it that will last?
All things are taken from us, and become
Portions and parcels of the dreadful Past.
Let us alone. What pleasure can we have
To war with evil? Is there any peace
In ever climbing up the climbing wave? 50
All things have rest, and ripen toward the grave
In silence; ripen, fall and cease:
Give us long rest or death, dark death, or dreamful
 ease.

V

How sweet it were, hearing the downward stream,
With half-shut eyes ever to seem
Falling asleep in a half-dream!
To dream and dream, like yonder amber light,
Which will not leave the myrrh-bush on the height;
To hear each other's whisper'd speech;
Eating the Lotos day by day, 60
To watch the crisping ripples on the beach,
And tender curving lines of creamy spray;
To lend our hearts and spirits wholly
To the influence of mild-minded melancholy;
To muse and brood and live again in memory,
With those old faces of our infancy.
Heap'd over with a mound of grass,
Two handfuls of white dust, shut in an urn of brass!

VI

Dear is the memory of our wedded lives,
And dear the last embraces of our wives   70
And their warm tears: but all hath suffer'd change;
For surely now our household hearths are cold:
Our sons inherit us: our looks are strange:
And we should come like ghosts to trouble joy.
Or else the island princes over-bold
Have eat our substance, and the minstrel sings
Before them of the ten years' war in Troy,
And our great deeds, as half-forgotten things.
Is there confusion in the little isle?
Let what is broken so remain.   80
The Gods are hard to reconcile:
'Tis hard to settle order once again.
There *is* confusion worse than death,
Trouble on trouble, pain on pain,
Long labour unto aged breath,
Sore task to hearts worn out with many wars
And eyes grown dim with gazing on the pilot-stars.

VII

But propt on beds of amaranth and moly,
How sweet (while warm airs lull us blowing lowly)
With half-dropt eyelids still,   90
Beneath a heaven dark and holy,
To watch the long bright river drawing slowly
His waters from the purple hill—
To hear the dewy echoes calling
From cave to cave through the thick-twined vine—
To watch the emerald-colour'd water falling
Through many a woven acanthus-wreath divine!
Only to hear and see the far-off sparkling brine,
Only to hear were sweet, stretch'd out beneath the
   pine.

VIII

The Lotos blooms below the barren peak: 100
The Lotos blows by every winding creek:
All day the wind breathes low with mellower tone:
Through every hollow cave and alley lone
Round and round the spicy downs the yellow Lotos-
   dust is blown.
We have had enough of action, and of motion we,
Roll'd to starboard, roll'd to larboard, when the
   surge was seething free,
Where the wallowing monster spouted his foam-
   fountains in the sea.
Let us swear an oath, and keep it with an equal
   mind,
In the hollow Lotos-land to live and lie reclined
On the hills like Gods together, careless of man-
   kind.   110

For they lie beside their nectar, and the bolts are
   hurl'd
Far below them in the valleys, and the clouds are
   lightly curl'd
Round their golden houses, girdled with the gleaming world:
Where they smile in secret, looking over wasted
   lands,
Blight and famine, plague and earthquake, roaring
   deeps and fiery sands,
Clanging fights, and flaming towns, and sinking
   ships, and praying hands.
But they smile, they find a music centred in a
   doleful song
Steaming up, lamentation and an ancient tale of
   wrong,
Like a tale of little meaning though the words are
   strong;
Chanted from an ill-used race of men that cleave
   the soil,   120
Sow the seed, and reap the harvest with enduring
   toil,
Storing yearly little dues of wheat, and wine and oil;
Till they perish and they suffer—some, 'tis whis-
   per'd, down in hell
Suffer endless anguish, others in Elysian valleys
   dwell,
Resting weary limbs at last on beds of asphodel.
Surely, surely, slumber is more sweet than toil, the
   shore
Than labour in the deep mid-ocean, wind and wave
   and oar:
O rest ye, brother mariners, we will not wander
   more!

Ulysses

It little profits that an idle king,
By this still hearth, among these barren crags,
Match'd with an aged wife, I mete and dole
Unequal laws unto a savage race,
That hoard, and sleep, and feed, and know not me.
I cannot rest from travel: I will drink
Life to the lees: all times I have enjoy'd
Greatly, have suffer'd greatly, both with those
That loved me, and alone; on shore, and when
Through scudding drifts the rainy Hyades   10
Vext the dim sea: I am become a name;
For always roaming with a hungry heart
Much have I seen and known; cities of men
And manners, climates, councils, governments,
Myself not least but honour'd of them all;

And drunk delight of battle with my peers,
Far on the ringing plains of windy Troy.
I am a part of all that I have met;
Yet all experience is an arch wherethrough
Gleams that untravell'd world, whose margin
     fades   20
For ever and for ever when I move.
How dull it is to pause, to make an end,
To rust unburnish'd, not to shine in use!
As though to breathe were life. Life piled on life
Were all too little, and of one to me
Little remains: but every hour is saved
From that eternal silence, something more,
A bringer of new things; and vile it were
For some three suns to store and hoard myself,
And this gray spirit yearning in desire   30
To follow knowledge, like a sinking star,
Beyond the utmost bound of human thought.
     This is my son, mine own Telemachus,
To whom I leave the sceptre and the isle—
Well-loved of me, discerning to fulfil
This labour, by slow prudence to make mild
A rugged people, and through soft degrees
Subdue them to the useful and the good.
Most blameless is he, centred in the sphere
Of common duties, decent not to fail   40
In offices of tenderness, and pay
Meet adoration to my household gods,
When I am gone. He works his work, I mine.
     There lies the port: the vessel puffs her sail:
There gloom the dark broad seas. My mariners
Souls that have toil'd, and wrought, and thought
     with me—
That ever with a frolic welcome took
The thunder and the sunshine, and opposed
Free hearts, free foreheads—you and I are old;
Old age hath yet his honour and his toil;   50
Death closes all: but something ere the end,
Some work of noble note, may yet be done,
Not unbecoming men that strove with Gods.
The lights begin to twinkle from the rocks:
The long day wanes: the slow moon climbs: the
     deep
Moans round with many voices. Come, my friends,
'Tis not too late to seek a newer world.
Push off, and sitting well in order smite
The sounding furrows; for my purpose holds
To sail beyond the sunset, and the baths   60
Of all the western stars until I die.
It may be that the gulfs will wash us down:
It may be we shall touch the Happy Isles,
And see the great Achilles, whom we knew.
Though much is taken, much abides; and though

We are not now that strength which in old days
Moved earth and heaven, that which we are, we are;
One equal temper of heroic hearts,
Made weak by time and fate, but strong in will
To strive, to seek, to find, and not to yield.   70

Locksley Hall

Comrades, leave me here a little, while as yet 'tis
     early morn;
Leave me here, and when you want me, sound upon
     the bugle-horn.

'Tis the place, and all around it, as of old, the cur-
     lews call,
Dreary gleams about the moorland flying over
     Locksley Hall;

Locksley Hall, that in the distance overlooks the
     sandy tracts,
And the hollow ocean-ridges roaring into cataracts.

Many a night from yonder ivied casement, ere I
     went to rest,
Did I look on great Orion sloping slowly to the
     West.

Many a night I saw the Pleiads, rising through the
     mellow shade,
Glitter like a swarm of fire-flies tangled in a silver
     braid.   10

Here about the beach I wander'd, nourishing a
     youth sublime
With the fairy tales of science, and the long result
     of Time;

When the centuries behind me like a fruitful land
     reposed;
When I clung to all the present for the promise that
     it closed:

When I dipt into the future far as human eye could
     see;
Saw the Vision of the world, and all the wonder
     that would be—

In the spring a fuller crimson comes upon the
     robin's breast;
In the spring the wanton lapwing gets himself
     another crest;

In the spring a livelier iris changes on the burnish'd
     dove;
In the spring a young man's fancy lightly turns to
     thoughts of love.   20

Then her cheek was pale and thinner than should
    be for one so young,
And her eyes on all my motions with a mute
    observance hung.

And I said, "My cousin Amy, speak, and speak the
    truth to me,
Trust me, cousin, all the current of my being sets
    to thee."

On her pallid cheek and forehead came a colour and
    a light,
As I have seen the rosy red flushing in the northern
    night.

And she turn'd—her bosom shaken with a sudden
    storm of sighs—
All the spirit deeply dawning in the dark of hazel
    eyes—

Saying, "I have hid my feelings, fearing they should
    do me wrong;"
Saying, "Dost thou love me, cousin?" weeping, "I
    have loved thee long." 30

Love took up the glass of Time, and turn'd it in his
    glowing hands;
Every moment, lightly shaken, ran itself in golden
    sands.

Love took up the harp of Life, and smote on all the
    chords with might;
Smote the chord of Self, that, trembling, pass'd in
    music out of sight.

Many a morning on the moorland did we hear the
    copses ring,
And her whisper throng'd my pulses with the full-
    ness of the spring.

Many an evening by the waters did we watch the
    stately ships,
And our spirits rush'd together at the touching of
    the lips.

O my cousin, shallow-hearted! O my Amy, mine
    no more!
O the deary, dreary moorland! O the barren, bar-
    ren shore! 40

Falser than all fancy fathoms, falser than all songs
    have sung,
Puppet to a father's threat, and servile to a shrewish
    tongue!

Is it well to wish thee happy? having known me—
    to decline
On a range of lower feelings and a narrower heart
    than mine!

Yet it shall be: thou shalt lower to his level day by
    day,
What is fine within thee growing coarse to sympa-
    thize with clay.

As the husband is, the wife is: thou art mated with
    a clown,
And the grossness of his nature will have weight to
    drag thee down.

He will hold thee, when his passion shall have
    spent its novel force,
Something better than his dog, a little dearer than
    his horse. 50

What is this? his eyes are heavy: think not they are
    glazed with wine.
Go to him: it is thy duty: kiss him: take his hand
    in thine.

It may be my lord is weary, that his brain is over-
    wrought:
Soothe him with thy finer fancies, touch him with
    thy lighter thought.

He will answer to the purpose, easy things to under-
    stand—
Better thou wert dead before me, though I slew thee
    with my hand!—

Better thou and I were lying, hidden from the
    heart's disgrace,
Roll'd in one another's arms, and silent in a last
    embrace.

Cursed be the social wants that sin against the
    strength of youth!
Cursed be the social lies that warp us from the liv-
    ing truth! 60

Cursed be the sickly forms that err from honest
    Nature's rule!
Cursed be the gold that gilds the straiten'd forehead
    of the fool!

Well—'tis well that I should bluster!—Hadst thou
    less unworthy proved—
Would to God—for I had loved thee more than ever
    wife was loved.

Am I mad, that I should cherish that which bears
    but bitter fruit?
I will pluck it from my bosom, though my heart be
    at the root.

Never, though my mortal summers to such length
    of years should come
As the many winter'd crow that leads the clanging
    rookery home.

Where is comfort? in division of the records of the mind?

Can I part her from herself, and love her, as I knew her, kind?   70

I remember one that perish'd: sweetly did she speak and move:

Such a one do I remember, whom to look at was to love.

Can I think of her as dead, and love her for the love she bore?

No—she never loved me truly: love is love for evermore.

Comfort? comfort scorn'd of devils! this is truth the poet sings,

That a sorrow's crown of sorrow is remembering happier things.

Drug thy memories, lest thou learn it, lest thy heart be put to proof,

In the dead unhappy night, and when the rain is on the roof.

Like a dog, he hunts in dreams, and thou art staring at the wall,

Where the dying night-lamp flickers, and the shadows rise and fall.   80

Then a hand shall pass before thee, pointing to his drunken sleep,

To thy widow'd marriage-pillows, to the tears that thou wilt weep.

Thou shalt hear the "Never, never," whisper'd by the phantom years,

And a song from out the distance in the ringing of thine ears;

And an eye shall vex thee, looking ancient kindness on thy pain.

Turn thee, turn thee on thy pillow: get thee to thy rest again.

Nay, but Nature brings thee solace; for a tender voice will cry.

'Tis a purer life than thine; a lip to drain thy trouble dry.

Baby lips will laugh me down: my latest rival brings thee rest.

Baby fingers, waxen touches, press me from the mother's breast.   90

Oh, the child too clothes the father with a dearness not his due.

Half is thine and half is his: it will be worthy of the two.

Oh, I see thee old and formal, fitted to thy petty part,

With a little hoard of maxims preaching down a daughter's heart.

"They were dangerous guides the feelings—she herself was not exempt—

Truly, she herself had suffer'd"—Perish in thy self-contempt!

Overlive it—lower yet—be happy! wherefore should I care?

I myself must mix with action, lest I wither by despair.

What is that which I should turn to, lighting upon days like these?

Every door is barr'd with gold, and opens but to golden keys.   100

Every gate is throng'd with suitors, all the markets overflow.

I have but an angry fancy: what is that which I should do?

I had been content to perish, falling on the foeman's ground,

When the ranks are roll'd in vapour, and the winds are laid with sound.

But the jingling of the guinea helps the hurt that Honour feels,

And the nations do but murmur, snarling at each other's heels.

Can I but relive in sadness? I will turn that earlier page.

Hide me from my deep emotion, O thou wondrous Mother-Age!

Make me feel the wild pulsation that I felt before the strife,

When I heard my days before me, and the tumult of my life;   110

Yearning for the large excitement that the coming years would yield,

Eager-hearted as a boy when first he leaves his father's field,

And at night along the dusky highway near and nearer drawn,

Sees in heaven the light of London flaring like a dreary dawn;

And his spirit leaps within him to be gone before him then,

Underneath the light he looks at, in among the throngs of men:

Men, my brothers, men the workers, ever reaping
    something new:

That which they have done but earnest of the
    things that they shall do:

For I dipt into the future, far as human eye could
    see,

Saw the Vision of the world, and all the wonder
    that would be;   120

Saw the heavens fill with commerce, argosies of
    magic sails,

Pilots of the purple twilight, dropping down with
    costly bales;

Heard the heavens fill with shouting, and there
    rain'd a ghastly dew

From the nations' airy navies grappling in the
    central blue;

Far along the world-wide whisper of the south-wind
    rushing warm,

With the standards of the peoples, plunging
    through the thunder-storm;

Till the war-drum throbb'd no longer, and the bat-
    tle-flags were furl'd

In the Parliament of man, the Federation of the
    world.

There the common sense of most shall hold a fretful
    realm in awe,

And the kindly earth shall slumber, lapt in uni-
    versal law.   130

So I triumph'd, ere my passion sweeping through
    me left me dry,

Left me with the palsied heart, and left me with
    the jaundiced eye;

Eye, to which all order festers, all things here are
    out of joint,

Science moves, but slowly, slowly, creeping on from
    point to point:

Slowly comes a hungry people, as a lion, creeping
    nigher,

Glares at one that nods and winks behind a slowly-
    dying fire.

Yet I doubt not through the ages one increasing
    purpose runs,

And the thoughts of men are widen'd with the
    process of the suns.

What is that to him that reaps not harvest of his
    youthful joys,

Though the deep heart of existence beat for ever
    like a boy's?   140

Knowledge comes, but wisdom lingers, and I linger
    on the shore,

And the individual withers, and the world is more
    and more,

Knowledge comes, but wisdom lingers, and he bears
    a laden breast,

Full of sad experience, moving toward the stillness
    of his rest.

Hark, my merry comrades call me, sounding on the
    bugle-horn,

They to whom my foolish passion were a target for
    their scorn:

Shall it not be scorn to me to harp on such a
    moulder'd string?

I am shamed through all my nature to have loved
    so slight a thing.

Weakness to be wroth with weakness! woman's
    pleasure, woman's pain—

Nature made them blinder motions bounded in a
    shallower brain: 150

Woman is the lesser man, and all thy passions,
    match'd with mine,

Are as moonlight unto sunlight, and as water unto
    wine—

Here at least, where nature sickens, nothing. Ah,
    for some retreat

Deep in yonder shining Orient, where my life
    began to beat;

Where in wild Mahratta-battle fell my father evil-
    starr'd;

I was left a trampled orphan, and a selfish uncle's
    ward.

Or to burst all links of habit—there to wander far
    away,

On from island unto island at the gateways of the
    day.

Larger constellations burning, mellow moons and
    happy skies,

Breadths of tropic shade and palms in cluster, knots
    of Paradise.   160

Never comes the trader, never floats an European
    flag.

Slides the bird o'er lustrous woodland, swings the
    trailer from the crag;

Droops the heavy-blossom'd bower, hangs the heavy-
    fruited tree—

Summer isles of Eden lying in dark-purple spheres
    of sea.

There methinks would be enjoyment more than in
  this march of mind,
In the steamship, in the railway, in the thoughts
  that shake mankind.

There the passions cramp'd no longer shall have
  scope and breathing-space;
I will take some savage woman, she shall rear my
  dusky race.

Iron-jointed, supple-sinew'd, they shall dive, and
  they shall run,
Catch the wild goat by the hair, and hurl their
  lances in the sun;   170

Whistle back the parrot's call, and leap the rainbows
  of the brooks,
Not with blinded eyesight poring over miserable
  books—

Fool, again the dream, the fancy! but I *know* my
  words are wild,
But I count the gray barbarian lower than the Christian child.

I, to herd with narrow foreheads, vacant of our
  glorious gains,
Like a beast with lower pleasures, like a beast with
  lower pains!

Mated with a squalid savage—what to me were sun
  or clime?
I the heir of all the ages, in the foremost files of
  time—

I that rather held it better men should perish one
  by one,
Than that earth should stand at gaze like Joshua's
  moon in Ajalon!   180

Not in vain the distance beacons. Forward, forward
  let us range.
Let the great world spin for ever down the ringing
  grooves of change.

Through the shadow of the globe we sweep into the
  younger day:
Better fifty years of Europe than a cycle of Cathay.

Mother-Age (for mine I knew not) help me as
  when life begun:
Rift the hills, and roll the waters, flash the lightnings, weigh the Sun—

Oh, I see the crescent promise of my spirit hath not
  set.
Ancient founts of inspiration well through all my
  fancy yet.

Howsoever these things be, a long farewell to Locksley Hall!
Now for me the woods may wither, now for me the
  roof-tree fall.   190

Comes a vapour from the margin, blackening over
  heath and holt,
Cramming all the blast before it, in its breast a
  thunderbolt.

Let it fall on Locksley Hall, with rain or hail, or
  fire or snow;
For the mighty wind arises, roaring seaward, and
  I go.

Lyrics from *The Princess*

I

Sweet and low, sweet and low,
  Wind of the western sea,
Low, low, breathe and blow,
  Wind of the western sea!
Over the rolling waters go,
Come from the dying moon, and blow,
  Blow him again to me;
While my little one, while my pretty one, sleeps.

Sleep and rest, sleep and rest,
  Father will come to thee soon;
Rest, rest, on mother's breast,
  Father will come to thee soon;
Father will come to his babe in the nest,
Silver sails all out of the west
  Under the silver moon:
Sleep, my little one, sleep, my pretty one, sleep.

II

The splendour falls on castle walls
  And snowy summits old in story;
The long light shakes across the lakes,
  And the wild cataract leaps in glory.
Blow, bugle, blow, set the wild echoes flying,
Blow, bugle; answer, echoes, dying, dying, dying.

O hark, O hear! how thin and clear,
  And thinner, clearer, farther going!
O sweet and far from cliff and scar
  The horns of Elfland faintly blowing!
Blow, let us hear the purple glens replying:
Blow, bugle; answer, echoes, dying, dying, dying.

O love, they die in yon rich sky;
  They faint on hill or field or river:

Our echoes roll from soul to soul,
    And grow for ever and for ever.
Blow, bugle, blow, set the wild echoes flying,
And answer, echoes, answer, dying, dying, dying.

III

Tears, idle tears, I know not what they mean,
Tears from the depth of some divine despair
Rise in the heart, and gather to the eyes,
In looking on the happy Autumn fields,
And thinking of the days that are no more.

Fresh as the first beam glittering on a sail,
That brings our friends up from the underworld,
Sad as the last which reddens over one
That sinks with all we love below the verge;
So sad, so fresh, the days that are no more.

Ah, sad and strange as in dark summer dawns
The earliest pipe of half-awaken'd birds
To dying ears, when unto dying eyes
The casement slowly grows a glimmering square;
So sad, so strange, the days that are no more.

Dear as remember'd kisses after death,
And sweet as those by hopeless fancy feign'd
On lips that are for others; deep as love,
Deep as first love, and wild with all regret;
O Death in Life, the days that are no more.

IV

O Swallow, Swallow, flying, flying South,
Fly to her, and fall upon her gilded eaves,
And tell her, tell her what I tell to thee.

O tell her, Swallow, thou that knowest each,
That bright and fierce and fickle is the South,
And dark and true and tender is the North.

O Swallow, Swallow, if I could follow, and light
Upon her lattice, I would pipe and trill
And cheep and twitter twenty million loves.

O were I thou that she might take me in
And lay me on her bosom, and her heart
Would rock the snowy cradle till I died.

Why lingereth she to clothe her heart with love,
Delaying as the tender ash delays
To clothe herself, when all the woods are green?

O tell her, Swallow, that thy brood is flown:
Say to her, I do but wanton in the South,
But in the North long since my nest is made.

O tell her, brief is life but love is long,
And brief the sun of summer in the North,
And brief the moon of beauty in the South.

O Swallow, flying from the golden woods,
Fly to her, and pipe and woo her, and make her
    mine,
And tell her, tell her, that I follow thee.

V

Home they brought her warrior dead:
    She nor swoon'd, nor utter'd cry:
All her maidens, watching, said,
    "She must weep, or she will die."

Then they praised him, soft and low,
    Call'd him worthy to be loved,
Truest friend and noblest foe;
    Yet she neither spoke nor moved.

Stole a maiden from her place,
    Lightly to the warrior stept,
Took the face-cloth from the face;
    Yet she neither moved nor wept.

Rose a nurse of ninety years,
    Set his child upon her knee;
Like summer tempest came her tears—
    "Sweet my child, I live for thee."

VI

Ask me no more: the moon may draw the sea;
    The cloud may stoop from heaven and take the
        shape,
    With fold to fold, of mountain or of cape;
But, O too fond, when have I answer'd thee?
        Ask me no more.

Ask me no more: what answer should I give?
    I love not hollow cheek or faded eye:
    Yet, O my friend, I will not have thee die!
Ask me no more, lest I should bid thee live;
        Ask me no more.

Ask me no more: thy fate and mine are seal'd:
    I strove against the stream, and all in vain:
    Let the great river take me to the main:
No more, dear love, for at a touch I yield;
        Ask me no more.

VII

Come down, O maid, from yonder mountain height:
What pleasure lives in height (the shepherd sang),
In height and cold, the splendour of the hills?
But cease to move so near the heavens, and cease
To glide a sunbeam by the blasted pine,
To sit a star upon the sparkling spire;
And come, for Love is of the valley, come,
For Love is of the valley, come thou down

And find him; by the happy threshold, he,
Or hand in hand with Plenty in the maize,　　10
Or red with spirted purple of the vats,
Or foxlike in the vine; nor cares to walk
With Death and Morning on the silver horns,
Nor wilt thou snare him in the white ravine,
Nor find him dropt upon the firths of ice,
That huddling slant in furrow-cloven falls
To roll the torrent out of dusky doors:
But follow; let the torrent dance thee down
To find him in the valley; yet the wild
Lean-headed eagles yelp alone, and leave　　20
The monstrous ledges there to slope, and spill
Their thousand wreaths of dangling water-smoke,
That like a broken purpose waste in air:
So waste not thou; but come; for all the vales
Await thee; azure pillars of the hearth
Arise to thee; the children call, and I
Thy shepherd pipe, and sweet is every sound,
Sweeter thy voice, but every sound is sweet;
Myriads of rivulets hurrying through the lawn,
The moan of doves in immemorial elms,　　30
And murmuring of innumerable bees.

From *In Memoriam A. H. H.*

*This elegy was written in memory of the poet's
closest friend, Arthur Henry Hallam, who died suddenly in Vienna, September 15, 1833.*

PROLOGUE

Strong Son of God, immortal Love,
　　Whom we, that have not seen thy face,
　　By faith, and faith alone, embrace,
Believing where we cannot prove;

Thine are these orbs of light and shade;
　　Thou madest Life in man and brute;
　　Thou madest Death; and lo, thy foot
Is on the skull which thou hast made.

Thou wilt not leave us in the dust:
　　Thou madest man, he knows not why,
　　He thinks he was not made to die;
And thou hast made him: thou art just.

Thou seemest human and divine,
　　The highest, holiest manhood, thou:
　　Our wills are ours, we know not how;
Our wills are ours, to make them thine.

Our little systems have their day;
　　They have their day and cease to be:
　　They are but broken lights of thee,
And thou, O Lord, art more than they.

We have but faith: we cannot know;
　　For knowledge is of things we see;
　　And yet we trust it comes from thee,
A beam in darkness: let it grow.

Let knowledge grow from more to more,
　　But more of reverence in us dwell;
　　That mind and soul, according well,
May make one music as before,

But vaster. We are fools and slight;
　　We mock thee when we do not fear:
　　But help thy foolish ones to bear;
Help thy vain worlds to bear thy light.

Forgive what seemed my sin in me;
　　What seemed my worth since I began;
　　For merit lives from man to man,
And not from man, O Lord, to thee.

Forgive my grief for one removed,
　　Thy creature, whom I found so fair.
　　I trust he lives in thee, and there
I find him worthier to be loved.

Forgive these wild and wandering cries,
　　Confusions of a wasted youth;
　　Forgive them where they fail in truth,
And in thy wisdom make me wise.

I

I held it truth, with him [1] who sings
　　To one clear harp in divers tones,
　　That men may rise on stepping-stones
Of their dead selves to higher things.

But who shall so forecast the years
　　And find in loss a gain to match?
　　Or reach a hand through time to catch
The far-off interest of tears?

Let Love clasp Grief lest both be drown'd,
　　Let darkness keep her raven gloss;
　　Ah, sweeter to be drunk with loss,
To dance with death, to beat the ground,

Than that the victor Hours should scorn
　　The long result of love, and boast:
　　"Behold the man that loved and lost,
But all he was is overworn."

[1] Probably Goethe.

VI

One writes, that "Other friends remain,"
   That "Loss is common to the race"—
   And common is the commonplace,
And vacant chaff well meant for grain.

That loss is common would not make
   My own less bitter, rather more:
   Too common! Never morning wore
To evening, but some heart did break.

O father, wheresoe'er thou be,
   That pledgest now thy gallant son;
   A shot, ere half thy draught be done,
Hath still'd the life that beat from thee.

O mother, praying God will save
   Thy sailor,—while thy head is bow'd,
   His heavy-shotted hammock-shroud
Drops in his vast and wandering grave.

Ye know no more than I who wrought
   At that last hour to please him well;
   Who mused on all I had to tell,
And something written, something thought;

Expecting still his advent home;
   And ever met him on his way
   With wishes, thinking, here to-day,
Or here to-morrow will he come.

O somewhere, meek, unconscious dove,
   That sittest ranging golden hair;
   And glad to find thyself so fair,
Poor child, that waitest for thy love!

For now her father's chimney glows
   In expectation of a guest;
   And thinking "This will please him best,"
She takes a riband or a rose; . . .

VII

Dark house,[2] by which once more I stand
   Here in the long unlovely street,
   Doors, where my heart was used to beat
So quickly, waiting for a hand,

A hand that can be clasp'd no more—
   Behold me, for I cannot sleep,
   And like a guilty thing I creep
At earliest morning to the door.

He is not here; but far away
   The noise of life begins again,
   And ghastly through the drizzling rain
On the bald street breaks the blank day.

[2] Hallam's London residence.

XI

Calm is the morn without a sound,
   Calm as to suit a calmer grief,
   And only through the faded leaf
The chestnut pattering to the ground:

Calm and deep peace on this high wold,
   And on these dews that drench the furze,
   And all the silvery gossamers
That twinkle into green and gold:

Calm and still light on yon great plain
   That sweeps with all its autumn bowers,
   And crowded farms and lessening towers,
To mingle with the bounding main:

Calm and deep peace in this wide air,
   These leaves that redden to the fall;
   And in my heart, if calm at all,
If any calm, a calm despair:

Calm on the seas, and silver sleep,
   And waves that sway themselves in rest,
   And dead calm in that noble breast
Which heaves but with the heaving deep.

XV

To-night the winds begin to rise
   And roar from yonder dropping day;
   The last red leaf is whirl'd away,
The rooks are blown about the skies;

The forest crack'd, the waters curl'd,
   The cattle huddled on the lea;
   And wildly dash'd on tower and tree
The sunbeam strikes along the world:

And but for fancies, which aver
   That all thy motions gently pass
   Athwart a plane of molten glass,
I scarce could brook the strain and stir

That makes the barren branches loud;
   And but for fear it is not so,
   The wild unrest that lives in woe
Would dote and pore on yonder cloud

That rises upward always higher,
   And onward drags a labouring breast,
   And topples round the dreary west,
A looming bastion fringed with fire.

XXVII

I envy not in any moods
   The captive void of noble rage,
   The linnet born within the cage
That never knew the summer woods:

I envy not the beast that takes
   His license in the field of time,
   Unfetter'd by the sense of crime,
To whom a conscience never wakes;

Nor, what may count itself as blest,
   The heart that never plighted troth
   But stagnates in the weeds of sloth,
Nor any want-begotten rest.

I hold it true whate'er befall,
   I feel it when I sorrow most,
   'Tis better to have loved and lost
Than never to have loved at all.

XXVIII

The time draws near the birth of Christ:
   The moon is hid, the night is still;
   The Christmas bells from hill to hill
Answer each other in the mist.

Four voices of four hamlets round,
   From far and near, on mead and moor,
   Swell out and fail, as if a door
Were shut between me and the sound:

Each voice four changes on the wind,
   That now dilate, and now decrease,
   Peace and goodwill, goodwill and peace,
Peace and goodwill, to all mankind.

This year I slept and woke with pain,
   I almost wish'd no more to wake,
   And that my hold on life would break
Before I heard those bells again:

But they my troubled spirit rule,
   For they controll'd me when a boy;
   They bring me sorrow touch'd with joy,
The merry merry bells of Yule.

XXX

With trembling fingers did we weave
   The holly round the Christmas hearth;
   A rainy cloud possess'd the earth,
And sadly fell our Christmas-eve.

At our old pastimes in the hall
   We gamboll'd, making vain pretence
   Of gladness, with an awful sense
Of one mute Shadow watching all.

We paused: the winds were in the beech:
   We heard them sweep the winter land;
   And in a circle hand-in-hand
Sat silent, looking each at each.

Then echolike our voices rang;
   We sung, though every eye was dim,
   A merry song we sang with him
Last year: impetuously we sang:

We ceased: a gentler feeling crept
   Upon us: surely rest is meet:
   "They rest," we said, "their sleep is sweet,"
And silence follow'd, and we wept.

Our voices took a higher range;
   Once more we sang: "They do not die,
   Nor lose their mortal sympathy,
Nor change to us, although they change:

"Rapt from the fickle and the frail
   With gather'd power, yet the same,
   Pierces the keen seraphic flame
From orb to orb, from veil to veil."

Rise, happy morn! rise, holy morn!
   Draw forth the cheerful day from night:
   O Father! touch the east, and light
The light that shone when Hope was born.

LIV

Oh, yet we trust that somehow good
   Will be the final goal of ill,
   To pangs of nature, sins of will,
Defects of doubt, and taints of blood;

That nothing walks with aimless feet;
   That not one life shall be destroy'd,
   Or cast as rubbish to the void
When God hath made the pile complete;

That not a worm is cloven in vain;
   That not a moth with vain desire
   Is shrivell'd in a fruitless fire,
Or but subserves another's gain.

Behold, we know not anything;
   I can but trust that good shall fall
   At last—far off—at last, to all,
And every winter change to spring.

So runs my dream: but what am I?
   An infant crying in the night:
   An infant crying for the light:
And with no language but a cry.

LV

The wish, that of the living whole
   No life may fail beyond the grave,
   Derives it not from what we have
The likest God within the soul?

Are God and Nature then at strife,
   That Nature lends such evil dreams?
   So careful of the type she seems,
So careless of the single life;

That I, considering everywhere
   Her secret meaning in her deeds,
   And finding that of fifty seeds
She often brings but one to bear,

I falter where I firmly trod,
   And falling with my weight of cares
   Upon the great world's altar-stairs
That slope through darkness up to God,

I stretch lame hands of faith, and grope,
   And gather dust and chaff, and call
   To what I feel is Lord of all,
And faintly trust the larger hope.

LVI

"So careful of the type?" but no.
   From scarpèd cliff and quarried stone
   She cries, "A thousand types are gone:
I care for nothing, all shall go.

"Thou makest thine appeal to me:
   I bring to life, I bring to death:
   The spirit does but mean the breath:
I know no more." And he, shall he,

Man, her last work, who seem'd so fair,
   Such splendid purpose in his eyes,
   Who roll'd the psalm to wintry skies,
Who built him fanes of fruitless prayer,

Who trusted God was love indeed,
   And love Creation's final law—
   Though Nature, red in tooth and claw
With ravine, shriek'd against his creed—

Who loved, who suffer'd countless ills,
   Who battled for the True, the Just,
   Be blown about the desert dust,
Or seal'd within the iron hills?

No more? A monster then, a dream,
   A discord. Dragons of the prime,
   That tare each other in their slime,
Were mellow music match'd with him.

O life as futile, then, as frail!
   O for thy voice to soothe and bless!
   What hope of answer, or redress?
Behind the veil, behind the veil.

LXXIII

So many worlds, so much to do,
   So little done, such things to be,
   How know I what had need of thee,
For thou wert strong as thou wert true?

The fame is quench'd that I foresaw,
   The head hath miss'd an earthly wreath:
   I curse not nature; no, nor death,
For nothing is that errs from law.

We pass: the path that each man trod
   Is dim, or will be dim, with weeds:
   What fame is left for human deeds
In endless age? It rests with God.

O Hollow wraith of dying fame,
   Fade wholly, while the soul exults,
   And self-infolds the large results
Of force that would have forged a name.

LXXVIII

Again at Christmas did we weave
   The holly round the Christmas hearth;
   The silent snow possess'd the earth,
And calmly fell our Christmas-eve:

The yule-clog sparkled keen with frost;
   No wing of wind the region swept;
   But over all things brooding slept
The quiet sense of something lost.

As in the winters left behind,
   Again our ancient games had place,
   The mimic picture's breathing grace,
And dance and song and hoodman-blind.

Who show'd a token of distress?
   No single tear, no type of pain:
   O sorrow, then can sorrow wane?
O grief, can grief be changed to less?

O last regret, regret can die!
   No—mixt with all this mystic frame,
   Her deep relations are the same,
But with long use her tears are dry.

LXXXVII

I pass'd beside the reverend walls [3]
   In which of old I wore the gown;
   I roved at random through the town,
And saw the tumult of the halls;

[3] Trinity College, Cambridge.

And heard once more in college fanes
　　The storm their high-built organs make,
　　And thunder-music, rolling, shake
The prophets blazon'd on the panes;

And caught once more the distant shout,
　　The measured pulse of racing oars
　　Among the willows; paced the shores
And many a bridge, and all about

The same gray flats again, and felt
　　The same, but not the same; and last
　　Up that long walk of limes I pass'd
To see the rooms in which he dwelt.

Another name was on the door:
　　I linger'd; all within was noise
　　Of songs, and clapping hands, and boys
That crash'd the glass and beat the floor;

Where once we held debate, a band[4]
　　Of youthful friends, on mind and art,
　　And labour, and the changing mart,
And all the framework of the land;

When one would aim an arrow fair,
　　But send it slackly from the string;
　　And one would pierce an outer ring,
And one an inner, here and there;

And last the master-bowman, he
　　Would cleave the mark. A willing ear
　　We lent him. Who, but hung to hear
The rapt oration flowing free

From point to point, with power and grace,
　　And music in the bounds of law,
　　To those conclusions when we saw
The God within him light his face,

And seem to lift the form, and glow
　　In azure orbits heavenly-wise;
　　And over those ethereal eyes
The bar of Michael Angelo.

XCV

By night we linger'd on the lawn,
　　For underfoot the herb was dry;
　　And genial warmth; and o'er the sky
The silvery haze of summer drawn;

And calm that let the tapers burn
　　Unwavering: not a cricket chirr'd:
　　The brook alone far-off was heard
And on the board the fluttering urn:

[4] "The Apostles," the group to which Tennyson and Hallam belonged.

And bats went round in fragrant skies,
　　And wheel'd or lit the filmy shapes
　　That haunt the dusk, with ermine capes
And woolly breasts and beaded eyes;

While now we sang old songs that peal'd
　　From knoll to knoll, where, couch'd at ease,
　　The white kine glimmer'd, and the trees
Laid their dark arms about the field.

But when those others, one by one,
　　Withdrew themselves from me and night,
　　And in the house light after light
Went out, and I was all alone,

A hunger seized my heart; I read
　　Of that glad year which once had been,
　　In those fall'n leaves which kept their green,
The noble letters of the dead:

And strangely on the silence broke
　　The silent-speaking words, and strange
　　Was love's dumb cry defying change
To test his worth; and strangely spoke

The faith, the vigour, bold to dwell
　　On doubts that drive the coward back,
　　And keen through wordy snares to track
Suggestion to her inmost cell.

So word by word, and line by line,
　　The dead man touch'd me from the past,
　　And all at once it seem'd at last
His living soul was flash'd on mine,

And mine in his was wound, and whirl'd
　　About empyreal heights of thought,
　　And came on that which is, and caught
The deep pulsations of the world,

Aeonian music measuring out
　　The steps of Time—the shocks of Chance—
　　The blows of Death. At length my trance
Was cancell'd, stricken through with doubt.

Vague words! but ah, how hard to frame
　　In matter-moulded forms of speech,
　　Or ev'n for intellect to reach
Through memory that which I became:

Till now the doubtful dusk reveal'd
　　The knolls once more where, couch'd at ease,
　　The white kine glimmer'd, and the trees
Laid their dark arms about the field:

And suck'd from out the distant gloom
　　A breeze began to tremble o'er
　　The large leaves of the sycamore,
And fluctuate all the still perfume;

And gathering freshlier overhead,
   Rock'd the full-foliaged elms, and swung
   The heavy-folded rose, and flung
The lilies to and fro, and said,

"The dawn, the dawn," and died away;
   And East and West, without a breath,
   Mix'd their dim lights, like life and death,
To broaden into boundless day.

CIV

The time draws near the birth of Christ:
   The moon is hid, the night is still;
   A single church below the hill
Is pealing, folded in the mist—

A single peal of bells below,
   That wakens at this hour of rest
   A single murmur in the breast,
That these are not the bells I know.

Like strangers' voices here they sound,
   In lands where not a memory strays.
   Nor landmark breathes of other days,
But all is new unhallow'd ground.

CV

This holly by the cottage-eave,
   To-night, ungather'd, shall it stand:
   We live within the stranger's land,
And strangely falls our Christmas-eve.

Our father's dust is left alone
   And silent under other snows;
   There in due time the woodbine blows,
The violet comes, but we are gone.

No more shall wayward grief abuse
   The genial hour with mask and mime;
   For change of place, like growth of time,
Has broke the bond of dying use.

Let cares that petty shadows cast,
   By which our lives are chiefly proved,
   A little spare the night I loved,
And hold it solemn to the past.

But let no footstep beat the floor,
   Nor bowl of wassail mantle warm;
   For who would keep an ancient form
Through which the spirit breathes no more?

Be neither song, nor game, nor feast,
   Nor harp be touch'd, nor flute be blown;
   No dance, no motion, save alone
What lightens in the lucid east

Of rising worlds by yonder wood.
   Long sleeps the summer in the seed;
   Run out your measured arcs, and lead
The closing cycle rich in good.

CVI

Ring out, wild bells, to the wild sky,
   The flying cloud, the frosty light:
   The year is dying in the night;
Ring out, wild bells, and let him die.

Ring out the old, ring in the new,
   Ring, happy bells, across the snow:
   The year is going, let him go;
Ring out the false, ring in the true.

Ring out the grief that saps the mind,
   For those that here we see no more;
   Ring out the feud of rich and poor,
Ring in redress to all mankind.

Ring out a slowly dying cause,
   And ancient forms of party strife;
   Ring in the nobler modes of life,
With sweeter manners, purer laws.

Ring out the want, the care, the sin,
   The faithless coldness of the times;
   Ring out, ring out my mournful rhymes,
But ring the fuller minstrel in.

Ring out false pride in place and blood,
   The civic slander and the spite;
   Ring in the love of truth and right,
Ring in the common love of good.

Ring out old shapes of foul disease,
   Ring out the narrowing lust of gold;
   Ring out the thousand wars of old,
Ring in the thousand years of peace.

Ring in the valiant man and free,
   The larger heart, the kindlier hand;
   Ring out the darkness of the land,
Ring in the Christ that is to be.

CXV

Now fades the last long streak of snow,
   Now burgeons every maze of quick
   About the flowering squares, and thick
By ashen roots the violets blow.

Now rings the woodland loud and long,
   The distance takes a lovelier hue,
   And drown'd in yonder living blue
The lark becomes a sightless song.

Now dance the lights on lawn and lea,
  The flocks are whiter down the vale,
  And milkier every milky sail
On winding stream or distant sea;

Where now the sea-mew pipes, or dives
  In yonder greening gleam, and fly
  The happy birds, that change their sky
To build and brood, that live their lives

From land to land: and in my breast
  Spring wakens too; and my regret
  Becomes an April violet,
And buds and blossoms like the rest.

CXVIII

Contemplate all this work of Time,
  The giant labouring in his youth;
  Nor dream of human love and truth,
As dying Nature's earth and lime;

But trust that those we call the dead
  Are breathers of an ampler day
  For ever nobler ends. They say
The solid earth whereon we tread

In tracts of fluent heat began,[5]
  And grew to seeming-random forms,
  The seeming prey of cyclic storms,
Till at the last arose the man;

Who throve and branch'd from clime to clime,
  The herald of a higher race,
  And of himself in higher place,
If so he type this work of time

Within himself, from more to more,
  Or, crown'd with attributes of woe
  Like glories, move his course, and show
That life is not as idle ore,

But iron dug from central gloom,
  And heated hot with burning fears,
  And dipt in baths of hissing tears,
And batter'd with the shocks of doom

To shape and use. Arise, and fly
  The reeling Faun, the sensual feast;
  Move upward, working out the beast,
And let the ape and tiger die.

CXXVI

Love is and was my Lord and King,
  And in his presence I attend
  To hear the tidings of my friend,
Which every hour his couriers bring.

[5] Laplace's nebular hypothesis.

Love is and was my King and Lord,
  And will be, though as yet I keep
  Within his court on earth, and sleep
Encompass'd by his faithful guard,

And hear at times a sentinel
  That moves about from place to place
  And whispers to the vast of space
Among the worlds, that all is well.

CXXX

Thy voice is on the rolling air;
  I hear thee where the waters run;
  Thou standest in the rising sun,
And in the setting thou art fair.

What art thou then? I cannot guess;
  But though I seem in star and flower
  To feel thee some diffusive power,
I do not therefore love thee less:

My love involves the love before;
  My love is vaster passion now;
  Though mix'd with God and Nature thou,
I seem to love thee more and more.

Far off thou art, but ever nigh;
  I have thee still, and I rejoice;
  I prosper, circled with thy voice;
I shall not lose thee though I die.

CXXXI

O living will that shalt endure
  When all that seems shall suffer shock,
  Rise in the spiritual rock,
Flow through our deeds and make them pure,

That we may lift from out of dust
  A voice as unto him that hears,
  A cry above the conquer'd years
To one that with us works; and trust,

With faith that comes of self-control,
  The truths that never can be proved
  Until we close with all we loved,
And all we flow from, soul in soul.

"Frater Ave Atque Vale" *

Row us out from Desenzano, to your Sirmione row!
So they rowed, and there we landed—"O venusta
    Sirmio!"
There to me through all the groves of olive in the
    summer glow,

* See Catullus' "On His Brother's Death," Vol. I, p. 289.

There beneath the Roman ruin where the purple
    flowers grow,
Came that "Ave atque Vale" of the Poet's hopeless
    woe,
Tenderest of Roman poets nineteen-hundred years
    ago,
"Frater Ave atque Vale"—as we wandered to and fro
Gazing at the Lydian laughter of the Garda Lake
    below
Sweet Catullus's all-but-island, olive-silvery Sirmio!

To Virgil

WRITTEN AT THE REQUEST OF THE MANTUANS FOR THE NINETEENTH CENTENARY OF VIRGIL'S DEATH

1

Roman Virgil, thou that singest
    Ilion's lofty temples robed in fire,
Ilion falling, Rome arising,
    wars, and filial faith, and Dido's pyre;

2

Landscape-lover, lord of language
    more than he that sang the Works and Days,[1]
All the chosen coin of fancy
    flashing out from many a golden phrase;

3

Thou that singest wheat and woodland,
    tilth and vineyard, hive and horse and herd;
All the charm of all the Muses
    often flowering in a lonely word;

4

Poet of the happy Tityrus[2]
    piping underneath his beechen bowers;
Poet of the poet-satyr
    whom the laughing shepherd bound with flowers;

5

Chanter of the Pollio, glorying
    in the blissful years again to be,
Summers of the snakeless meadow,
    unlaborious earth and oarless sea;

[1] Hesiod.
[2] The references to Tityrus and Pollio (line 17) are to
the *Eclogues*.

6

Thou that seëst Universal
    Nature moved by Universal Mind;[3]
Thou majestic in thy sadness
    at the doubtful doom of human kind;

7

Light among the vanished ages;
    star that gildest yet this phantom shore;
Golden branch amid the shadows,
    kings and realms that pass to rise no more;

8

Now thy Forum roars no longer,
    fallen every purple Caesar's dome—
Though thine ocean-roll of rhythm
    sound for ever of Imperial Rome—

9

Now the Rome of slaves hath perished,
    and the Rome of freemen holds her place,
I, from out the Northern Island
    sundered once from all the human race,

10

I salute thee, Mantovano,
    I that loved thee since my day began,
Wielder of the stateliest measure
    ever moulded by the lips of man.

Rizpah

I

Wailing, wailing, wailing, the wind over land and
    sea—
And Willy's voice in the wind, "O mother come out
    to me."
Why should he call me to-night, when he knows
    that I cannot go?
For the downs are as bright as day, and the full
    moon stares at the snow.

II

We should be seen, my dear; they would spy us out
    of the town.
The loud black nights for us, and the storm rushing
    over the down,
When I cannot see my own hand, but am led by the
    creak of the chain,
And grovel and grope for my son till I find myself
    drenched with the rain.

[3] See the *Aeneid*, Book VI, *ante.*, Vol. I, pp. 265–77.

dramatic monologue

III

Anything fallen again? nay—what was there left to fall?
I have taken them home, I have number'd the bones, I have hidden them all.
What am I saying? and what are *you*? do you come as a spy?
Falls? what falls? who knows? As the tree falls so must it lie.

IV

Who let her in? how long has she been? you—what have you heard?
Why did you sit so quiet? you never have spoken a word.
O—to pray with me—yes—a—lady—none of their spies—
But the night has crept into my heart and begun to darken my eyes.

V

Ah—you, that have lived so soft, what should *you* know of the night,
The blast and the burning shame and the bitter frost and the fright?
I have done it, while you were asleep—you were only made for the day.
I have gather'd my baby together—and now you may go your way.

VI

Nay—for it's kind of you, Madam, to sit by an old dying wife.
But say nothing hard of my boy, I have only an hour of life.
I kiss'd my boy in the prison, before he went out to die.
"They dared me to do it," he said, and he never has told me a lie.
I whipt him for robbing an orchard once when he was but a child—
"The farmer dared me to do it," he said; he was always so wild—
And idle—and couldn't be idle—my Willy—he never could rest.
The King should have made him a soldier, he would have been one of his best.

VII

But he lived with a lot of wild mates, and they never would let him be good;
They swore that he dare not rob the mail, and he swore that he would;

And he took no life, but he took one purse, and when all was done
He flung it among his fellows—"I'll none of it," said my son.

VIII

I came into court to the Judge and the lawyers. I told them my tale,
God's own truth—but they kill'd him, they kill'd him for robbing the mail.
They hang'd him in chains for a show—we had always borne a good name—
To be hang'd for a thief—and then put away—isn't that enough shame?
Dust to dust—low down—let us hide! but they set him so high
That all the ships of the world could stare at him, passing by.
God 'ill pardon the hell-black raven and horrible fowls of the air,
But not the black heart of the lawyer who kill'd him and hang'd him there.

IX

And the jailer forced me away. I had bid him my last goodbye;
They had fasten'd the door of his cell. "O mother!" I heard him cry.
I couldn't get back tho' I tried, he had something further to say,
And now I never shall know it. The jailer forced me away.

X

Then since I couldn't but hear that cry of my boy that was dead,
They seized me and shut me up: they fasten'd me down on my bed.
"Mother, O mother!"—he call'd in the dark to me year after year—
They beat me for that, they beat me—you know that I couldn't but hear;
And then at the last they found I had grown so stupid and still
They let me abroad again—but the creatures had worked their will.

XI

Flesh of my flesh was gone, but bone of my bone was left—
I stole them all from the lawyers—and you, will you call it a theft?—

My baby, the bones that had suck'd me, the bones
   that had laugh'd and had cried—
Theirs? O no! they are mine—not theirs—they had
   moved in my side.

XII

Do you think I was scared by the bones? I kiss'd
   'em, I buried 'em all—
I can't dig deep, I am old—in the night by the
   churchyard wall.
My Willy 'ill rise up whole when the trumpet of
   judgment 'ill sound;
But I charge you never to say that I laid him in
   holy ground.

XIII

They would scratch him up—they would hang him
   again on the cursed tree.
Sin? O yes—we are sinners, I know—let all that be,
And read me a Bible verse of the Lord's good will
   toward men—
"Full of compassion and mercy, the Lord"—let me
   hear it again;
"Full of compassion and mercy—long-suffering."
   Yes, O yes!
For the lawyer is born but to murder—the Saviour
   lives but to bless.
He'll never put on the black cap except for the worst
   of the worst,
And the first may be last—I have heard it in church
   —and the last may be first.
Suffering—O long-suffering—yes, as the Lord must
   know,
Year after year in the mist and the wind and the
   shower and the snow.

XIV

Heard, have you? what? they have told you he never
   repented his sin.
How do they know it? are *they* his mother? are *you*
   of his kin?
Heard! have you ever heard, when the storm on the
   downs began
The wind that 'ill wail like a child and the sea that
   'ill moan like a man?

XV

Election, Election and Reprobation—it's all very
   well,
But I go to-night to my boy, and I shall not find him
   in Hell.

For I cared so much for my boy that the Lord has
   look'd into my care,
And He means me I'm sure to be happy with Willy,
   I know not where.

XVI

And if *he* be lost—but to save *my* soul, that is all
   your desire:
Do you think that I care for *my* soul if my boy be
   gone to the fire?
I have been with God in the dark—go, go, you may
   leave me alone—
You never have borne a child—you are just as hard
   as a stone.

XVII

Madam, I beg your pardon! I think that you mean
   to be kind,
But I cannot hear what you say for my Willy's voice
   in the wind—
The snow and the sky so bright—he used but to call
   in the dark,
And he calls to me now from the church and not
   from the gibbet—for hark!
Nay—you can hear it yourself—it is coming—shaking the walls—
Willy—the moon's in a cloud—Good-night. I am
   going. He calls.

Crossing the Bar

Sunset and evening star,
   And one clear call for me!
And may there be no moaning of the bar,
   When I put out to sea,

But such a tide as moving seems asleep,
   Too full for sound and foam,
When that which drew from out the boundless deep
   Turns again home.

Twilight and evening bell,
   And after that the dark!
And may there be no sadness of farewell,
   When I embark;

For tho' from out our bourne of Time and Place
   The flood may bear me far,
I hope to see my Pilot face to face
   When I have crost the bar.

ROBERT BROWNING

1812–1889

In many respects Robert Browning had an ideal education for a poet. As the son of a Dissenter he was denied entrance to Oxford or Cambridge, but he was privately tutored, and he found his father's admirable library stocked with the classics in literature, art, history, and philosophy. His mother taught him music, and he early fell under the spell of Byron and then of Shelley, declaring at the age of fourteen that like Shelley he would be "an atheist and a vegetarian." His first published volume, *Pauline* (1833), was obscure and incoherent, and consequently was completely neglected.

Being of a social nature, fond of dancing and music and good company, Browning soon made himself known to such distinguished men of letters as Wordsworth, Carlyle, and Dickens. His attempts at writing plays for the manager of Covent Garden, W. C. Macready, were failures, although these plays by no means lacked the dramatic values that were to reside in his dramatic monologues.

Browning discovered his métier as a poet in the dramatic monologues of the third volume of his *Bells and Pomegranates* series, *Dramatic Lyrics* (1842), which contain the "Soliloquy in a Spanish Cloister" and "My Last Duchess." In September, 1846, he eloped with and married Elizabeth Barrett, the culmination of a romance too familiar to rehearse here. The happiness and joy of their life together at the Casa Guidi in Florence helped to mature Browning as a poet in the signal achievement of *Men and Women* (1855), his finest single work outside of *The Ring and the Book*. It contains some of his most famous poems, such as "The Last Ride Together" and "Fra Lippo Lippi."

Mrs. Browning died in Florence in 1861 and Browning, grief-stricken, returned to England. After a period of deep mourning he began again to mix with the world, overseeing his son's education and finding convivial company in a wide circle of friends (it was once remarked that Browning "would die in his dinner jacket"). World acclaim came to him with the publication of *The Ring and the Book* (1868–1869) and helped to make up for the long years in which the public had been indifferent to his poetry. Numerous Browning societies were founded in England and America, and Browning at last became a rival to Tennyson in poetic fame. In 1871 Browning returned to Italy, his "university," and died in Venice in 1889.

Robert Browning's immense energy, physical robustness, intense spirit and passion gave his poetry a range and vitality unequaled in the Victorian Age. His most brilliant original achievement was the development of the poetic genre, the dramatic monologue, to a previously unattained psychological subtlety and complexity in revealing the motivation of human conduct in all the self-deceiving rationalizations and sophistries that underlie it. Though he was not accorded just appreciation in his own time as a poetic technician, Browning was in his way as conscious an artist as Tennyson. His metrical innovations and his deliberate artistic purpose in sacrificing melody to cacophony to achieve poetic effects were not sufficiently recognized. His method in the dramatic monologue and his remarkable command of diction have had an extensive influence upon such modern poets as T. S. Eliot and Ezra Pound. Browning's cheerfulness, high confidence in the ways of God, and general optimism have not appealed to a disillusioned twentieth century. But Browning's optimism never ignored evil or the more crassly materialistic aspects of life, as his numerous characters from the Italian Renaissance testify; it was, however, motivated by a profound religious belief that the will of God would inevitably prevail. He may still have a message for our generation, if only it be the irrepressible wonder and resiliency of the human spirit as a life force that transcends the limitations in time and space of every historical era.

FURTHER READING

CHESTERTON, G. K. *Robert Browning* (London, 1905).
DUCKWORTH, F. R. *Browning, Background and Conflict* (New York, 1932).
PHELPS, WILLIAM LYON. *Robert Browning* (Indianapolis, 1932).
RAYMOND, WILLIAM O. *The Infinite Moment and Other Essays in Robert Browning* (Toronto, 1950).

My Last Duchess

FERRARA

That's my last Duchess painted on the wall,
Looking as if she were alive; I call
That piece a wonder, now: Frà Pandolf's hands

Worked busily a day, and there she stands.
Will't please you sit and look at her? I said
"Frà Pandolf" by design, for never read
Strangers like you that pictured countenance,
The depth and passion of its earnest glance,
But to myself they turned (since none puts by
The curtain I have drawn for you, but I)   10
And seemed as they would ask me, if they durst,
How such a glance came there; so, not the first
Are you to turn and ask thus. Sir, 't was not
Her husband's presence only, called that spot
Of joy into the Duchess' cheek: perhaps
Frà Pandolf chanced to say "Her mantle laps
Over my Lady's wrist too much," or "Paint
Must never hope to reproduce the faint
Half-flush that dies along her throat;" such stuff
Was courtesy, she thought, and cause enough   20
For calling up that spot of joy. She had
A heart . . . how shall I say? . . . too soon made
      glad,
Too easily impressed; she liked whate'er
She looked on, and her looks went everywhere.
Sir, 't was all one! My favour at her breast,
The dropping of the daylight in the West,
The bough of cherries some officious fool
Broke in the orchard for her, the white mule
She rode with round the terrace—all and each
Would draw from her alike the approving speech, 30
Or blush, at least. She thanked men—good; but
      thanked
Somehow . . . I know not how . . . as if she
      ranked
My gift of a nine-hundred-years-old name
With anybody's gift. Who'd stoop to blame
This sort of trifling? Even had you skill
In speech—(which I have not)—to make your will
Quite clear to such an one, and say, "Just this
Or that in you disgusts me; here you miss,
Or there exceed the mark"—and if she let
Herself be lessoned so, nor plainly set   40
Her wits to yours, forsooth, and made excuse,
—E'en then would be some stooping; and I choose
Never to stoop. Oh sir, she smiled, no doubt,
Whene'er I passed her; but who passed without
Much the same smile? This grew; I gave commands;
Then all smiles stopped together. There she stands
As if alive. Will't please you rise? We'll meet
The company below, then. I repeat,
The Count your master's known munificence
Is ample warrant that no just pretence   50
Of mine for dowry will be disallowed;
Though his fair daughter's self, as I avowed
At starting, is my object. Nay, we'll go

Together down, sir. Notice Neptune, though,
Taming a sea-horse, thought a rarity,
Which Claus of Innsbruck cast in bronze for me!

Soliloquy of the Spanish Cloister

I

Gr-r-r—there go, my heart's abhorrence!
      Water your damned flower-pots, do!
If hate killed men, Brother Lawrence,
      God's blood, would not mine kill you!
What? your myrtle-bush wants trimming?
      Oh, that rose has prior claims—
Needs its leaden vase filled brimming?
      Hell dry you up with its flames!

II

At the meal we sit together:
      Salve tibi! I must hear
Wise talk of the kind of weather,
      Sort of season, time of year:
Not a plenteous cork-crop: scarcely
      Dare we hope oak-galls, I doubt:
What's the Latin name for "parsley"?
      What's the Greek name for Swine's Snout?

III

Whew! We'll have our platter burnished,
      Laid with care on our own shelf!
With a fire-new spoon we're furnished,
      And a goblet for ourself,
Rinsed like something sacrificial
      Ere 'tis fit to touch our chaps—
Marked with L. for our initial!
      (He-he! There his lily snaps!)

IV

Saint, forsooth! While brown Dolores
      Squats outside the Convent bank,
With Sanchicha, telling stories,
      Steeping tresses in the tank,
Blue-black, lustrous, thick like horse-hairs,
      —Can't I see his dead eye glow,
Bright as 'twere a Barbary corsair's?
      (That is, if he'd let it show!)

V

When he finishes refection,
      Knife and fork he never lays
Cross-wise, to my recollection,
      As do I, in Jesu's praise.

I, the Trinity illustrate,
  Drinking watered orange-pulp—
In three sips the Arian [1] frustrate;
  While he drains his at one gulp!

VI

Oh, those melons! If he's able
  We're to have a feast; so nice!
One goes to the Abbot's table,
  All of us get each a slice.
How go on your flowers? None double?
  Not one fruit-sort can you spy?
Strange!—And I, too, at such trouble,
  Keep them close-nipped on the sly!

VII

There's a great text in Galatians,
  Once you trip on it, entails
Twenty-nine distinct damnations,
  One sure, if another fails:
If I trip him just a-dying,
  Sure of Heaven as sure as can be,
Spin him round and send him flying
  Off to Hell, a Manichee?

VIII

Or, my scrofulous French novel
  On grey paper with blunt type!
Simply glance at it, you grovel
  Hand and foot in Belial's gripe:
If I double down its pages
  At the woeful sixteenth print,
When he gathers his greengages,
  Ope a sieve and slip it in't?

IX

Or, there's Satan!—one might venture
  Pledge one's soul to him, yet leave
Such a flaw in the indenture
  As he'd miss till, past retrieve,
Blasted lay that rose-acacia
  We're so proud of! *Hy, Zy, Hine* . . .
'St, there's Vespers! *Plena gratiâ*
  Ave, Virgo! Gr-r-r—you swine!

The Bishop Orders His Tomb at Saint Praxed's Church

[ROME, 15—.]

Vanity, saith the preacher, vanity!
Draw round my bed: is Anselm keeping back?
Nephews—sons mine . . . ah God, I know not!
  Well—

[1] Fourth-century heresy of Arius, who denied the Trinity.

She, men would have to be your mother once,
Old Gandolf envied me, so fair she was!
What's done is done, and she is dead beside,
Dead long ago, and I am Bishop since,
And as she died so must we die ourselves,
And thence ye may perceive the world's a dream.
Life, how and what is it? As here I lie   10
In this state-chamber, dying by degrees,
Hours and long hours in the dead night, I ask
"Do I live, am I dead?" Peace, peace seems all.
Saint Praxed's ever was the church for peace;
And so, about this tomb of mine. I fought
With tooth and nail to save my niche, ye know:
—Old Gandolf cozened me, despite my care;
Shrewd was that snatch from out the corner South
He graced his carrion with, God curse the same!
Yet still my niche is not so cramped but thence   20
One sees the pulpit o' the epistle-side,
And somewhat of the choir, those silent seats,
And up into the aery dome where live
The angels, and a sunbeam's sure to lurk:
And I shall fill my slab of basalt there,
And 'neath my tabernacle take my rest,
With those nine columns round me, two and two,
The odd one at my feet where Anselm stands:
Peach-blossom marble all, the rare, the ripe
As fresh-poured red wine of a mighty pulse   30
—Old Gandolf with his paltry onion-stone,
Put me where I may look at him! True peach,
Rosy and flawless: how I earned the prize!
Draw close: that conflagration of my church
—What then? So much was saved if aught were
    missed!
My sons, ye would not be my death? Go dig
The white-grape vineyard where the oil-press stood,
Drop water gently till the surface sinks,
And if ye find . . . Ah, God I know not, I! . . .
Bedded in store of rotten figleaves soft,   40
And corded up in a tight olive-frail,
Some lump, ah God, of *lapis lazuli*,
Big as a Jew's head cut off at the nape,
Blue as a vein o'er the Madonna's breast . . .
Sons, all have I bequeathed you, villas, all,
That brave Frascati villa with its bath,
So, let the blue lump poise between my knees,
Like God the Father's globe on both His hands
Ye worship in the Jesu Church so gay,
For Gandolf shall not choose but see and burst!   50
Swift as a weaver's shuttle fleet our years:
Man goeth to the grave, and where is he?
Did I say basalt for my slab, sons? Black—
'Twas ever antique-black I meant! How else
Shall ye contrast my frieze to come beneath?

The bas-relief in bronze ye promised me,
Those Pans and Nymphs ye wot of, and perchance
Some tripod, thyrsus, with a vase or so,
The Saviour at his sermon on the mount,
Saint Praxed in a glory, and one Pan   60
Ready to twitch the Nymph's last garment off,
And Moses with the tables . . . but I know
Ye mark me not! What do they whisper thee,
Child of my bowels, Anselm? Ah, ye hope
To revel down my villas while I gasp
Bricked o'er with beggar's mouldy travertine
Which Gandolf from his tomb-top chuckles at!
Nay, boys, ye love me—all of jasper, then!
'Tis jasper ye stand pledged to, lest I grieve
My bath must needs be left behind, alas!   70
One block, pure green as a pistachio-nut,
There's plenty jasper somewhere in the world—
And have I not Saint Praxed's ear to pray
Horses for ye, and brown Greek manuscripts,
And mistresses with great smooth marbly limbs?
—That's if ye carve my epitaph aright,
Choice Latin, picked phrase, Tully's [1] every word,
No gaudy ware like Gandolf's second line—
Tully, my masters? Ulpian serves his need!
And then how I shall lie through centuries,   80
And hear the blessed mutter of the mass,
And see God made and eaten all day long,
And feel the steady candle-flame, and taste
Good strong thick stupefying incense-smoke!
For as I lie here, hours of the dead night,
Dying in state and by such slow degrees,
I fold my arms as if they clasped a crook,
And stretch my feet forth straight as stone can point,
And let the bedclothes for a mortcloth drop
Into great laps and folds of sculptor's-work: 90
And as yon tapers dwindle, and strange thoughts
Grow, with a certain humming in my ears,
About the life before I lived this life,
And this life too, Popes, Cardinals and Priests,
Saint Praxed at his sermon on the mount,
Your tall pale mother with her talking eyes,
And new-found agate urns as fresh as day,
And marble's language, Latin pure, discreet,
—Aha, ELUCESCEBAT quoth our friend?
No Tully, said I, Ulpian at the best!   100
Evil and brief hath been my pilgrimage.
All *lapis*, all, sons! Else I give the Pope
My villas: will ye ever eat my heart?
Ever your eyes were as a lizard's quick,
They glitter like your mother's for my soul,
Or ye would heighten my impoverished frieze,
Piece out its starved design, and fill my vase

[1] Marcus Tullius Cicero.

With grapes, and add a vizor and a term,
And to the tripod ye would tie a lynx
That in his struggle throws the thyrsus down,   110
To comfort me on my entablature
Whereon I am to lie till I must ask
"Do I live, am I dead?" There, leave me, there!
For ye have stabbed me with ingratitude
To death—ye wish it—God, ye wish it! Stone—
Gritstone, a-crumble! Clammy squares which sweat
As if the corpse they keep were oozing through—
And no more *lapis* to delight the world!
Well, go! I bless ye. Fewer tapers there,
But in a row: and, going, turn your backs   120
—Ay, like departing altar-ministrants,
And leave me in my church, the church for peace,
That I may watch at leisure if he leers—
Old Gandolf, at me, from his onion-stone,
As still he envied me, so fair she was!

"De Gustibus—"

I

Your ghost will walk, you lover of trees,
    (If our loves remain)
    In an English lane,
By a cornfield-side a-flutter with poppies.
Hark, those two in the hazel coppice—
A boy and a girl, if the good fates please,
    Making love, say,—
    The happier they!
Draw yourself up from the light of the moon,
And let them pass, as they will too soon,   10
    With the beanflowers' boon,
    And the blackbird's tune,
    And May, and June!

II

What I love best in all the world,
Is a castle, precipice-encurled,
In a gash of the wind-grieved Apennine.
Or look for me, old fellow of mine,
(If I get my head from out the mouth
O' the grave, and loose my spirit's bands,
And come again to the land of lands)—   20
In a sea-side house to the farther South,
Where the baked cicala dies of drouth,
And one sharp tree—'tis a cypress—stands,
By the many hundred years red-rusted,
Rough iron-spiked, ripe fruit-o'er-crusted,
My sentinel to guard the sands
To the water's edge. For, what expands
Before the house, but the great opaque

Blue breadth of sea without a break?
While, in the house, for ever crumbles   30
Some fragment of the frescoed walls,
From blisters where a scorpion sprawls.
A girl bare-footed brings, and tumbles
Down on the pavement, green-flesh melons,
And says there's news to-day—the king
Was shot at, touched in the liver-wing,
Goes with his Bourbon arm in a sling:
—She hopes they have not caught the felons.
    Italy, my Italy!
Queen Mary's saying serves for me—   40
    (When fortune's malice
    Lost her, Calais)
Open my heart and you will see
Graved inside of it, "Italy."
Such lovers old are I and she;
So it always was, so shall ever be!

Home-Thoughts, from Abroad

I

Oh, to be in England
Now that April's there,
And whoever wakes in England
Sees, some morning, unaware,
That the lowest boughs and the brushwood sheaf
Round the elm-tree bole are in tiny leaf,
While the chaffinch sings on the orchard bough
In England—now!

II

And after April, when May follows,
And the whitethroat builds, and all the swallows!
Hark, where my blossomed pear-tree in the hedge
Leans to the field and scatters on the clover
Blossoms and dewdrops—at the bent spray's edge—
That's the wise thrush; he sings each song twice
    over,
Lest you should think he never could recapture
The first fine careless rapture!
And though the fields look rough with hoary dew,
All will be gay when noontide wakes anew
The buttercups, the little children's dower
—Far brighter than this gaudy melon-flower!

Fra Lippo Lippi

I am poor brother Lippo, by your leave!
You need not clap your torches to my face.
Zooks, what 's to blame? you think you see a monk!

What, it 's past midnight, and you go the rounds,
And here you catch me at an alley's end
Where sportive ladies leave their doors ajar?
The Carmine 's my cloister: hunt it up,
Do,—harry out, if you must show your zeal,
Whatever rat, there, haps on his wrong hole,
And nip each softling of a wee white mouse,   10
Weke, weke, that 's crept to keep him company!
Aha, you know your betters? Then, you'll take
Your hand away that 's fiddling on my throat,
And please to know me likewise. Who am I?
Why, one, sir, who is lodging with a friend
Three streets off—he 's a certain . . . how d' ye call?
Master—a . . . Cosimo of the Medici,
In the house that caps the corner. Boh! you were
    best!
Remember and tell me, the day you're hanged,
How you affected such a gullet's-gripe!   20
But you, sir, it concerns you that your knaves
Pick up a manner nor discredit you.
Zooks, are we pilchards, that they sweep the streets
And count fair prize what comes into their net?
He 's Judas to a tittle, that man is!
Just such a face! why, sir, you make amends.
Lord, I'm not angry! Bid your hang-dogs go
Drink out this quarter-florin to the health
Of the munificent House that harbours me
(And many more beside, lads! more beside!)   30
And all's come square again. I'd like his face—
His, elbowing on his comrade in the door
With the pike and lantern,—for the slave that holds
John Baptist's head a-dangle by the hair
With one hand ("look you, now," as who should
    say)
And his weapon in the other, yet unwiped!
It 's not your chance to have a bit of chalk,
A wood-coal or the like? or you should see!
Yes, I'm the painter, since you style me so.
What, brother Lippo's doings, up and down,   40
You know them and they take you? like enough!
I saw the proper twinkle in your eye—
'Tell you, I liked your looks at very first.
Let 's sit and set things straight now, hip to haunch.
Here 's spring come, and the nights one makes up
    bands
To roam the town and sing out carnival,
And I've been three weeks shut within my mew,
A-painting for the great man, saints and saints
And saints again. I could not paint all night—
Ouf! I leaned out of window for fresh air.   50
There came a hurry of feet and little feet,
A sweep of lute-strings, laughs, and whifts of song,—
Flower o' the broom,

Take away love, and our earth is a tomb!
Flower o' the quince,
I let Lisa go, and what good 's in life since?
Flower o' the thyme—and so on. Round they went.
Scarce had they turned the corner when a titter
Like the skipping of rabbits by moonlight,—three
    slim shapes—
And a face that looked up . . . zooks, sir, flesh and
    blood,   60
That 's all I'm made of! Into shreds it went,
Curtain and counterpane and coverlet,
All the bed-furniture—a dozen knots,
There was a ladder! down I let myself,
Hands and feet, scrambling somehow, and so
    dropped,
And after them. I came up with the fun
Hard by Saint Laurence, hail fellow, well met,—
Flower o' the rose,
If I've been merry, what matter who knows?
And so as I was stealing back again   70
To get to bed and have a bit of sleep
Ere I rise up to-morrow and go work
On Jerome knocking at his poor old breast
With his great round stone to subdue the flesh,
You snap me of the sudden. Ah, I see!
Though your eye twinkles still, you shake your
    head—
Mine 's shaved,—a monk, you say—the sting 's in
    that!
If Master Cosimo announced himself,
Mum 's the word naturally; but a monk!
Come, what am I a beast for? tell us, now!   80
I was a baby when my mother died
And father died and left me in the street.
I starved there, God knows how, a year or two
On fig skins, melon-parings, rinds and shucks,
Refuse and rubbish. One fine frosty day
My stomach being empty as your hat,
The wind doubled me up and down I went.
Old Aunt Lapaccia trussed me with one hand,
(Its fellow was a stinger as I knew)
And so along the wall, over the bridge,   90
By the straight cut to the convent. Six words, there,
While I stood munching my first bread that month:
"So, boy, you're minded," quoth the good fat father
Wiping his own mouth, 'twas refection-time,—
"To quit this very miserable world?
Will you renounce" . . . The mouthful of bread?
    thought I;
By no means! Brief, they made a monk of me;
I did renounce the world, its pride and greed,
Palace, farm, villa, shop and banking-house,
Trash, such as these poor devils of Medici   100

Have given their hearts to—all at eight years old.
Well, sir, I found in time, you may be sure,
'Twas not for nothing—the good bellyful,
The warm serge and the rope that goes all round,
And day-long blessed idleness beside!
"Let 's see what the urchin's fit for"—that came next.
Not overmuch their way, I must confess.
Such a to-do! they tried me with their books.
Lord, they'd have taught me Latin in pure
    waste!   110
Flower o' the clove,
All the Latin I construe is, "amo" I love!
But, mind you, when a boy starves in the streets
Eight years together, as my fortune was,
Watching folk's faces to know who will fling
The bit of half-stripped grape-bunch he desires,
And who will curse or kick him for his pains—
Which gentleman processional and fine,
Holding a candle to the Sacrament
Will wink and let him lift a plate and catch
The droppings of the wax to sell again,   120
Or holla for the Eight and have him whipped,—
How say I?—nay, which dog bites, which lets drop
His bone from the heap of offal in the street,—
Why, soul and sense of him grow sharp alike,
He learns the look of things, and none the less
For admonitions from the hunger-pinch.
I had a store of such remarks, be sure,
Which, after I found leisure, turned to use:
I drew men's faces on my copy-books,
Scrawled them within the antiphonary's marge,   130
Joined legs and arms to the long music-notes,
Found nose and eyes and chin for A.s and B.s,
And made a string of pictures of the world
Betwixt the ins and outs of verb and noun,
On the wall, the bench, the door. The monks
    looked black.
"Nay," quoth the Prior, "turn him out, d' ye say?
In no wise. Lose a crow and catch a lark.
What if at last we get our man of parts,
We Carmelites, like those Camaldolese
And Preaching Friars, to do our church up fine   140
And put the front on it that ought to be!"
And hereupon they bade me daub away.
Thank you! my head being crammed, their walls
    a blank,
Never was such prompt disemburdening.
First, every sort of monk, the black and white,
I drew them, fat and lean: then, folks at church,
From good old gossips waiting to confess
Their cribs of barrel-droppings, candle-ends,—
To the breathless fellow at the altar-foot,
Fresh from his murder, safe and sitting there   150

With the little children round him in a row
Of admiration, half for his beard and half
For that white anger of his victim's son
Shaking a fist at him with one fierce arm,
Signing himself with the other because of Christ
(Whose sad face on the cross sees only this
After the passion of a thousand years)
Till some poor girl, her apron o'er her head
Which the intense eyes looked through, came at eve
On tip-toe, said a word, dropped in a loaf,   160
Her pair of earrings and a bunch of flowers
The brute took growling, prayed, and then was
        gone.
I painted all, then cried "'tis ask and have—
Choose, for more 's ready!"—laid the ladder flat,
And showed my covered bit of cloister-wall.
The monks closed in a circle and praised loud
Till checked,—taught what to see and not to see,
Being simple bodies,—"that 's the very man!
Look at the boy who stoops to pat the dog!
That woman 's like the Prior's niece who comes   170
To care about his asthma: it 's the life!"
But there my triumph 's straw-fire flared and
        funked—
Their betters took their turn to see and say:
The Prior and the learned pulled a face
And stopped all that in no time. "How? what 's
        here?
Quite from the mark of painting, bless us all!
Faces, arms, legs and bodies like the true
As much as pea and pea! it 's devil's-game!
Your business is not to catch men with show,   180
With homage to the perishable clay,
But lift them over it, ignore it all,
Make them forget there 's such a thing as flesh.
Your business is to paint the souls of men—
Man's soul, and it 's a fire, smoke . . . no it 's
        not . . .
It 's vapour done up like a new-born babe—
(In that shape when you die it leaves your mouth)
It 's . . . well, what matters talking, it 's the soul!
Give us no more of body than shows soul!
Here 's Giotto, with his Saint a-praising God,
That sets you praising,—why not stop with him?   190
Why put all thoughts of praise out of our heads
With wonder at lines, colours, and what not?
Paint the soul, never mind the legs and arms!
Rub all out, try at it a second time.
Oh, that white smallish female with the breasts,
She 's just my niece . . . Herodias, I would say,—
Who went and danced and got men's heads cut off—
Have it all out!" Now, is this sense, I ask?
A fine way to paint soul, by painting body

So ill, the eye can't stop there, must go further   200
And can't fare worse! Thus, yellow does for white
When what you put for yellow 's simply black,
And any sort of meaning looks intense
When all beside itself means and looks nought.
Why can't a partner lift each foot in turn,
Left foot and right foot, go a double step,
Make his flesh liker and his soul more like,
Both in their order? Take the prettiest face,
The Prior's niece . . . patron-saint—is it so pretty
You can't discover if it means hope, fear,   210
Sorrow or joy? won't beauty go with these?
Suppose I've made her eyes all right and blue,
Can't I take breath and try to add life's flash,
And then add soul and heighten them threefold?
Or say there 's beauty with no soul at all—
(I never saw it—put the case the same—)
If you get simple beauty and nought else,
You get about the best thing God invents,—
That 's somewhat. And you'll find the soul you
        have missed,
Within yourself when you return Him thanks,   220
"Rub all out!" Well, well, there 's my life, in short.
And so the thing has gone on ever since.
I'm grown a man no doubt, I've broken bounds—
You should not take a fellow eight years old
And make him swear to never kiss the girls.
I'm my own master, paint now as I please—
Having a friend, you see, in the Corner-house!
Lord, it 's fast holding by the rings in front—
Those great rings serve more purposes than just
To plant a flag in, or tie up a horse!   230
And yet the old schooling sticks, the old grave eyes
Are peeping o'er my shoulder as I work,
The heads shake still—"It 's Art's decline, my son!
You're not of the true painters, great and old;
Brother Angelico's [1] the man, you'll find;
Brother Lorenzo stands his single peer:
Fag on at flesh, you'll never make the third!"
Flower o' the pine,
You keep your mistr . . . manners, and I'll stick
        to mine!
I'm not the third, then: bless us, they must
        know!   240
Don't you think they're the likeliest to know,
They with their Latin? so, I swallow my rage,
Clench my teeth, suck my lips in tight, and paint
To please them—sometimes do, and sometimes don't,
For, doing most, there 's pretty sure to come
A turn, some warm eve finds me at my saints—
A laugh, a cry, the business of the world—
(*Flower o' the peach,*

[1] References to Fra Angelico and Lorenzo Monaco.

Death for us all, and his own life for each!)
And my whole soul revolves, the cup runs over, 250
The world and life 's too big to pass for a dream,
And I do these wild things in sheer despite,
And play the fooleries you catch me at,
In pure rage! the old mill-horse, out at grass
After hard years, throws up his stiff heels so,
Although the miller does not preach to him
The only good of grass is to make chaff.
What would men have? Do they like grass or no—
May they or mayn't they? all I want 's the thing
Settled for ever one way: as it is, 260
You tell too many lies and hurt yourself.
You don't like what you only like too much,
You do like what, if given you at your word,
You find abundantly detestable.
For me, I think I speak as I was taught—
I always see the Garden and God there
A-making man's wife—and, my lesson learned,
The value and significance of flesh,
I can't unlearn ten minutes afterwards.

You understand me: I'm a beast, I know. 270
But see, now—why, I see as certainly
As that the morning-star 's about to shine,
What will hap some day. We've a youngster here
Comes to our convent, studies what I do,
Slouches and stares and lets no atom drop—
His name is Guidi [2]—he'll not mind the monks—
They call him Hulking Tom, he lets them talk—
He picks my practice up—he'll paint apace,
I hope so—though I never live so long,
I know what 's sure to follow. You be judge! 280
You speak no Latin more than I, belike—
However, you're my man, you've seen the world
—The beauty and the wonder and the power,
The shapes of things, their colours, lights and
    shades,
Changes, surprises,—and God made it all!
—For what? do you feel thankful, ay or no,
For this fair town's face, yonder river's line,
The mountain round it and the sky above,
Much more the figures of man, woman, child,
These are the frame to? What 's it all about? 290
To be passed over, despised? or dwelt upon,
Wondered at? Oh, this last of course!—you say.
But why not do as well as say,—paint these
Just as they are, careless what comes of it?
God's works—paint anyone, and count it crime
To let a truth slip. Don't object, "His works
Are here already—nature is complete:
Suppose you reproduce her—(which you can't)

[2] Tommaso Guidi, or Masaccio (1401–1428?).

There 's no advantage! you must beat her, then."
For, don't you mark, we're made so that we love 300
First when we see them painted, things we have
    passed
Perhaps a hundred times nor cared to see;
And so they are better, painted—better to us,
Which is the same thing. Art was given for that—
God uses us to help each other so,
Lending our minds out. Have you noticed, now,
Your cullion's hanging face? A bit of chalk,
And trust me but you should, though! How much
    more,
If I drew higher things with the same truth!
That were to take the Prior's pulpit-place, 310
Interpret God to all of you! oh, oh,
It makes me mad to see what men shall do
And we in our graves! This world's no blot for us,
Nor blank—it means intensely, and means good:
To find its meaning is my meat and drink.
"Ay, but you don't so instigate to prayer!"
Strikes in the Prior: "when your meaning 's plain
It does not say to folks—remember matins,
Or, mind you fast next Friday." Why, for this
What need of art at all? A skull and bones, 320
Two bits of stick nailed cross-wise, or, what 's best,
A bell to chime the hour with, does as well.
I painted a Saint Laurence six months since
At Prato, splashed the fresco in fine style:
"How looks my painting, now the scaffold's down?"
I ask a brother: "Hugely," he returns—
"Already not one phiz of your three slaves
That turn the Deacon off his toasted side,
But 's scratched and prodded to our heart's con-
    tent,
The pious people have so eased their own 330
When coming to say prayers there in a rage:
We get on fast to see the bricks beneath.
Expect another job this time next year,
For pity and religion grow i' the crowd—
Your painting serves its purpose!" Hang the fools!

—That is—you'll not mistake an idle word
Spoke in a huff by a poor monk, God wot,
Tasting the air this spicy night which turns
The unaccustomed head like Chianti wine!
Oh, the church knows! don't misreport me, now! 340
It 's natural a poor monk out of bounds
Should have his apt word to excuse himself:
And hearken how I plot to make amends.
I have bethought me: I shall paint a piece
. . . There 's for you! Give me six months, then
    go, see
Something in Sant' Ambrogio's! Bless the nuns!

They want a cast of my office. I shall paint
God in the midst, Madonna and her babe,
Ringed by a bowery, flowery angel-brood,
Lilies and vestments and white faces, sweet   350
As puff on puff of grated orris-root
When ladies crowd to church at mid-summer.
And then in the front, of course a saint or two—
Saint John, because he saves the Florentines,
Saint Ambrose, who puts down in black and
     white
The convent's friends and gives them a long day,
And Job, I must have him there past mistake,
The man of Uz, (and Us without the z,
Painters who need his patience.) Well, all these
Secured at their devotions, up shall come   360
Out of a corner when you least expect,
As one by a dark stair into a great light,
Music and talking, who but Lippo! I!—
Mazed, motionless and moon-struck—I'm the
     man!
Back I shrink—what is this I see and hear?
I, caught up with my monk's things by mistake,
My old serge gown and rope that goes all round,
I, in this presence, this pure company!
Where's a hole, where's a corner for escape?
Then steps a sweet angelic slip of a thing   370
Forward, puts out a soft palm—"Not so fast!"
—Addresses the celestial presence, "nay—
He made you and devised you, after all,
Though he's none of you! Could Saint John there,
     draw—
His camel-hair make up a painting-brush?
We come to brother Lippo for all that,
Iste perfecit opus!" So, all smile—
I shuffle sideways with my blushing face
Under the cover of a hundred wings
Thrown like a spread of kirtles when you're gay   380
And play hot cockles, all the doors being shut,
Till, wholly unexpected, in there pops
The hothead husband! Thus I scuttle off
To some safe bench behind, not letting go
The palm of her, the little lily thing
That spoke the good word for me in the nick,
Like the Prior's niece . . . Saint Lucy, I would
     say.³
And so all's saved for me, and for the church
A pretty picture gained. Go, six months hence!
Your hand, sir, and good-bye: no lights, no
     lights!   390
The street's hushed, and I know my own way back,
Don't fear me! There's the grey beginning. Zooks!

³ This painting, The Coronation of the Virgin, is in the
Uffizi Galleries, Florence.

The Last Ride Together

I

I said—Then, Dearest, since 'tis so,
Since now at length my fate I know,
Since nothing all my love avails,
Since all, my life seemed meant for, fails,
     Since this was written and needs must be—
My whole heart rises up to bless
Your name in pride and thankfulness!
Take back the hope you gave,—I claim
Only a memory of the same,
—And this beside, if you will not blame,
     Your leave for one more last ride with me.

II

My mistress bent that brow of hers;
Those deep dark eyes where pride demurs
When pity would be softening through,
Fixed me a breathing-while or two
     With life or death in the balance: right!
The blood replenished me again;
My last thought was at least not vain;
I and my mistress, side by side
Shall be together, breathe, and ride,
So one day more am I deified—
     Who knows but the world may end to-night.

III

Hush! if you saw some western cloud
All billowy-bosomed, over-bowed
By many benedictions—sun's
And moon's and evening-star's at once—
     And so, you, looking and loving best,
Conscious grew, your passion drew
Cloud, sunset, moonrise, star-shine too,
Down on you, near and yet more near,
Till flesh must fade for heaven was here!—
Thus leant she and lingered—joy and fear!
     Thus lay she a moment on my breast.

IV

Then we began to ride. My soul
Smoothed itself out—a long-cramped scroll
Freshening and fluttering in the wind.
Past hopes already lay behind.
     What need to strive with a life awry?
Had I said that, had I done this,
So might I gain, so might I miss.
Might she have loved me? just as well
She might have hated,—who can tell?
Where had I been now if the worst befell?
     And here we are riding, she and I.

V

Fail I alone, in words and deeds?
Why, all men strive and who succeeds?
We rode; it seemed my spirit flew,
Saw other regions, cities new,
    As the world rushed by on either side.
I thought,—All labour, yet no less
Bear up beneath their unsuccess.
Look at the end of work, contrast
The petty Done, the Undone vast,
This Present of theirs with the hopeful Past!
    I hoped she would love me: here we ride.

VI

What hand and brain went ever paired?
What heart alike conceived and dared?
What act proved all its thought had been?
What will but felt the fleshly screen?
    We ride and I see her bosom heave.
There 's many a crown for who can reach.
Ten lines, a statesman's life in each!
The flag stuck on a heap of bones,
A soldier's doing! what atones?
They scratch his name on the Abbey-stones.
    My riding is better, by their leave.

VII

What does it all mean, poet? well,
Your brains beat into rhythm—you tell
What we felt only; you expressed
You hold things beautiful the best,
    And pace them in rhyme so, side by side.
'Tis something, nay 'tis much—but then,
Have you yourself what 's best for men?
Are you—poor, sick, old ere your time—
Nearer one whit your own sublime
Than we who never have turned a rhyme?
    Sing, riding 's a joy! For me, I ride.

VIII

And you, great sculptor—so, you gave
A score of years to Art, her slave,
And that 's your Venus—whence we turn
To yonder girl that fords the burn!
    You acquiesce, and shall I repine?
What, man of music, you, grown grey
With notes and nothing else to say,
Is this your sole praise from a friend,
"Greatly his opera's strains intend,
But in music we know how fashions end!"
    I gave my youth—but we ride. in fine.

IX

Who knows what 's fit for us? Had fate
Proposed bliss here should sublimate
My being; had I signed the bond—
Still one must lead some life beyond,
    —Have a bliss to die with, dim-descried.
This foot once planted on the goal,
This glory-garland round my soul,
Could I descry such? Try and test!
I sink back shuddering from the quest—
Earth being so good, would Heaven seem best?
    Now, Heaven and she are beyond this ride.

X

And yet—she has not spoke so long!
What if Heaven be that, fair and strong
At life's best, with our eyes upturned
Whither life's flower is first discerned,
    We, fixed so, ever should so abide?
What if we still ride on, we two,
With life for ever old yet new,
Changed not in kind but in degree,
The instant made eternity,—
And Heaven just prove that I and she
    Ride, ride together, for ever ride?

Prospice

Fear death?—to feel the fog in my throat,
    The mist in my face,
When the snows begin, and the blasts denote
    I am nearing the place,
The power of the night, the press of the storm,
    The post of the foe;
Where he stands, the Arch Fear in a visible form,
    Yet the strong man must go:
For the journey is done and the summit attained,
    And the barriers fall,   10
Though a battle 's to fight ere the guerdon be
        gained,
    The reward of it all.
I was ever a fighter, so—one fight more,
    The best and the last!
I would hate that death bandaged my eyes, and
        forbore,
    And bade me creep past.
No! let me taste the whole of it, fare like my peers
    The heroes of old,
Bear the brunt, in a minute pay glad life's arrears
    Of pain, darkness and cold.   20
For sudden the worst turns the best to the brave,
    The black minute 's at end,

And the element's rage, the fiend-voices that rave,
  Shall dwindle, shall blend,
Shall change, shall become first a peace, then a joy,
  Then a light, then thy breast,
O thou soul of my soul! I shall clasp thee again,
  And with God be the rest!

Epilogue *

At the midnight in the silence of the sleep-time,
  When you set your fancies free,
Will they pass to where—by death, fools think, im-
    prisoned—
Low he lies who once so loved you, whom you loved
    so,
          —Pity me?

Oh to love so, be so loved, yet so mistaken!
  What had I on earth to do
With the slothful, with the mawkish, the unmanly?
Like the aimless, helpless, hopeless, did I drivel
    —Being—who?

One who never turned his back but marched breast
  forward,
  Never doubted clouds would break,
Never dreamed, though right were worsted, wrong
  would triumph,
Held we fall to rise, are baffled to fight better,
    Sleep to wake.

No, at noonday in the bustle of man's work-time
  Greet the unseen with a cheer!
Bid him forward, breast and back as either should
  be,
"Strive and thrive!" cry "Speed,—fight on, fare ever
    There as here!"

————◆————

MATTHEW ARNOLD

1822–1888

The son of Dr. Thomas Arnold, headmaster of
Rugby, Matthew Arnold was born at Laleham on
December 24, 1822. After attending Rugby and
Balliol College, Oxford, where he met Arthur Hugh
Clough, whose death he mourned in "Thyrsis,"

* The last poem in *Asolando,* issued the day Browning
died.

Arnold married Frances Wightman in 1851 and became an inspector of schools. Despite a rigorous
schedule of inspection that left him little free time
for writing much before midnight, Arnold published three volumes of poems, *Empedocles on
Etna* (1852), *Poems* (1853), and *Poems, Second
Series* (1855), by which date the major part of his
poetic work was done. From the time that he visited
the Continent in 1859 as Assistant Commissioner
for the Newcastle Commission to report upon Continental education, when he first met many such
distinguished French intellectuals as Guizot, Sainte-
Beuve, and Victor Cousin, Arnold began to divert
his energies from poetry to social, political, and edu-
cational criticism. He realized that the English
aristocracy was in decline as a political and cultural
force, and he perceived that the unenlightened and
badly educated Philistine middle class which had
taken over the reins of English government was
completely unaware of and insensible to modern
progressive Continental ideas. Arnold thus found
the cultural state of England deplorable, and turned
vigorously to prose in an effort to make "reason and
the will of God prevail" in a middle class that was
stubbornly complacent and insular in its satisfaction
with the material prosperity of England.

Arnold was truly classic in his social criticism in
emphasizing the need for a complete and harmonious development of all the powers of the individual and upon the need of striving for human
perfection; similarly, in his poetic theory Arnold
advocated the use of the Greek writers as models of
discipline for attaining classical qualities of perfect
balance, symmetry, and regard for the total impression of the work. The English Romantic poets
he found lacking in these virtues of discipline and
care for the total effect, and English literary
criticism deficient in sound knowledge and in the
literary principles characteristic of the rigorous
French critical intelligence.

His poetry, Arnold remarked once in a letter to
his mother, would represent, more than either
Tennyson's or Browning's, "the main movement of
mind of the last quarter of century." He meant
that the elegiac, legato note of plaintive melancholy
in his poetry was characteristic of a world failing in
religious belief, of the sick frustration and the futile
scattering of man's energies in a cosmos wherein he
no longer felt at home. The melancholy accents of

"The Scholar Gypsy" and of "Dover Beach" are not calculated to foster the joy and harmonious balance of the whole, integrated human personality, and hence it may be that Arnold deliberately gave up the writing of poetry with the publication of the *New Poems* of 1867, his last volume of verse. Purely personal lamentation did not seem to Arnold great poetry; but his poetic work at its best achieves a union of deep personal emotion with an austere elegiac tone which is the most characteristic English utterance of the spirit of the late Victorian Age as it passes into the modern.

FURTHER READING

BROWN, E. K. *Matthew Arnold: A Study in Conflict* (Chicago, 1948).
PAUL, HERBERT W. *Matthew Arnold* (New York, 1903).
TINKER, C. B., and LOWRY, H. F. *The Poetry of Matthew Arnold* (New York, 1940).
TRILLING, LIONEL. *Matthew Arnold* (New York, 1939).

The Scholar-Gypsy

Go, for they call you, shepherd, from the hill;
  Go, shepherd, and untie the wattled cotes!
    No longer leave thy wistful flock unfed,
  Nor let thy bawling fellows rack their throats,
  Nor the cropped herbage shoot another head.
    But when the fields are still,
  And the tired men and dogs all gone to rest,
  And only the white sheep are sometimes seen
    Cross and recross the strips of moon-blanched green,
  Come, shepherd, and again begin the quest!   10

Here, where the reaper was at work of late—
  In this high field's dark corner, where he leaves
    His coat, his basket, and his earthen cruse,
  And in the sun all morning binds the sheaves,
    Then here, at noon, comes back his stores to use—
    Here will I sit and wait,
  While to my ear from uplands far away
    The bleating of the folded flocks is borne,
    With distant cries of reapers in the corn—
  All the live murmur of a summer's day.   20

Screened in this nook o'er the high, half-reaped field,
  And here till sun-down, shepherd! will I be.
    Through the thick corn the scarlet poppies peep
  And round green roots and yellowing stalks I see

Pale pink convolvulus in tendrils creep;
  And air-swept lindens yield
Their scent, and rustle down their perfumed showers
  Of bloom on the bent grass where I am laid,
  And bower me from the August sun with shade;
  And the eye travels down to Oxford's towers.   30

And near me on the grass lies Glanvil's book—
  Come let me read the oft-read tale again!
    The story of the Oxford scholar poor,
  Of pregnant parts and quick inventive brain,
    Who, tired of knocking at preferment's door,
    One summer-morn forsook
  His friends, and went to learn the gypsy-lore,
    And roamed the world with that wild brotherhood,
    And came, as most men deemed, to little good,
  But came to Oxford and his friends no more.   40

But once, years after, in the country-lanes,
  Two scholars, whom at college erst he knew,
    Met him, and of his way of life inquired;
  Whereat he answered that the gypsy-crew,
    His mates, had arts to rule as they desired
    The workings of men's brains,
  And they can bind them to what thoughts they will.
    "And I," he said, "the secret of their art,
    When fully learned, will to the work impart;
  But it needs heaven-sent moments for this skill."   50

This said, he left them, and returned no more.—
  But rumors hung about the country-side,
    That the lost scholar long was seen to stray,
  Seen by rare glimpses, pensive and tongue-tied,
    In hat of antique shape, and cloak of gray,
    The same the gypsies wore.
  Shepherds had met him on the Hurst in spring;
    At some lone alehouse in the Berkshire moors,
    On the warm ingle-bench, the smock-frocked boors
  Had found him seated at their entering.   60

But 'mid their drink and clatter, he would fly.
  And I myself seem half to know thy looks,
    And put the shepherds, wanderer! on thy trace;
  And boys who in lone wheatfields scare the rooks
    I ask if thou hast passed their quiet place;
    Or in my boat I lie
  Moored to the cool bank in the summer-heats,
    'Mid wide grass meadows which the sunshine fills,

And watch the warm, green-muffled Cumner hills,
And wonder if thou haunt'st their shy retreats. 70

For most, I know, thou lov'st retired ground!
    Thee at the ferry Oxford riders blithe,
        Returning home on summer nights, have met
    Crossing the stripling Thames at Bab-lock-hithe,
        Trailing in the cool stream thy fingers wet,
            As the punt's rope chops round;
    And leaning backward in a pensive dream,
        And fostering in thy lap a heap of flowers
        Plucked in shy fields and distant Wychwood bowers,
    And thine eyes resting on the moonlit stream.   80

And then they land, and thou art seen no more!—
    Maidens, who from the distant hamlets come
        To dance around the Fyfield elm in May,
    Oft through the darkening fields have seen thee roam,
        Or cross a stile into the public way.
            Oft thou hast given them store
    Of flowers—the frail-leafed, white anemone,
        Dark bluebells drenched with dews of summer eves,
        And purple orchises with spotted leaves—
    But none hath words she can report of thee.   90

And, above Godstow Bridge, when hay-time's here
    In June, and many a scythe in sunshine flames,
        Men who through those wide fields of breezy grass
    Where black-winged swallows haunt the glittering Thames,
        To bathe in the abandoned lasher pass,
            Have often passed thee near
    Sitting upon the river bank o'ergrown;
        Marked thine outlandish garb, thy figure spare,
        Thy dark vague eyes, and soft abstracted air—
    But, when they came from bathing, thou wast gone!   100

At some lone homestead in the Cumner hills,
    Where at her open door the housewife darns,
        Thou hast been seen, or hanging on a gate
    To watch the threshers in the mossy barns.
        Children, who early range these slopes and late
            For cresses from the rills,
    Have known thee eying, all an April-day,
        The springing pastures and the feeding kine;
        And marked thee, when the stars come out and shine,
    Through the long dewy grass move slow away.   110

In autumn, on the skirts of Bagley Wood—
    Where most the gypsies by the turf-edged way
        Pitch their smoked tents, and every bush you see
    With scarlet patches tagged and shreds of gray,
        Above the forest-ground called Thessaly—
            The blackbird, picking food,
    Sees thee, nor stops his meal, nor fears at all;
        So often has he known thee past him stray,
        Rapt, twirling in thy hand a withered spray,
    And waiting for the spark from heaven to fall.   120

And once, in winter, on the causeway chill
    Where home through flooded fields foot-travelers go,
        Have I not passed thee on the wooden bridge,
    Wrapped in thy cloak and battling with the snow,
        Thy face tow'rd Hinksey and its wintry ridge?
            And thou hast climbed the hill,
    And gained the white brow of the Cumner range;
        Turned once to watch, while thick the snow-flakes fall,
        The line of festal light in Christ-Church hall—
    Then sought thy straw in some sequestered grange.   130

But what—I dream! Two hundred years are flown
    Since first thy story ran through Oxford halls,
        And the grave Glanvil did the tale inscribe
    That thou wert wandered from the studious walls
        To learn strange arts, and join a gypsy tribe;
            And thou from earth art gone
    Long since, and in some quiet churchyard laid—
        Some country-nook, where o'er thy unknown grave
        Tall grasses and white flowering nettles wave,
    Under a dark, red-fruited yew-tree's shade.   140

—No, no, thou hast not felt the lapse of hours!
    For what wears out the life of mortal men?
        'Tis that from change to change their being rolls;
    'Tis that repeated shocks, again, again,
        Exhaust the energy of strongest souls
            And numb the elastic powers,
    Till having used our nerves with bliss and teen,
        And tired upon a thousand schemes our wit,
        To the just-pausing Genius we remit
    Our worn-out life, and are—what we have been.   150

Thou hast not lived, why should'st thou perish, so?
    Thou hadst *one* aim, *one* business, *one* desire;
        Else wert thou long since numbered with the dead!

Else hadst thou spent, like other men, thy fire!
　The generations of thy peers are fled,
　　And we ourselves shall go;
But thou possessest an immortal lot,
　And we imagine thee exempt from age
　And living as thou liv'st on Glanvil's page,
Because thou hadst—what we, alas! have not.　160

For early didst thou leave the world, with powers
　Fresh undiverted to the world without,
　　Firm to their mark, not spent on other things;
Free from the sick fatigue, the languid doubt,
　Which much to have tried, in much been
　　　baffled, brings.
　　O life unlike to ours!
Who fluctuate idly without term or scope,
　Of whom each strives nor knows for what he
　　　strives,
　And each half lives a hundred different lives;
Who wait like thee, but not, like thee, in
　hope.　170

Thou waitest for the spark from heaven! and we,
　Light half-believers of our casual creeds,
　　Who never deeply felt, nor clearly willed,
Whose insight never has borne fruit in deeds,
　Whose vague resolves never have been ful-
　　　filled;
　　For whom each year we see
Breeds new beginnings, disappointments new;
　Who hesitate and falter life away,
　And lose tomorrow the ground won to-day—
Ah! do not we, wanderer! await it too?　180

Yes, we await it!—but it still delays,
　And then we suffer! and amongst us one,
　　Who most hast suffered, takes dejectedly
His seat upon the intellectual throne;
　And all his store of sad experience he
　　　Lays bare of wretched days;
Tells us his misery's birth and growth and signs,
　And how the dying spark of hope was fed,
　And how the breast was soothed, and how the
　　　head,
And all his hourly varied anodynes.　190

This for our wisest! and we others pine,
　And wish the long unhappy dream would end,
　　And waive all claim to bliss, and try to bear;
With close-lipped patience for our only friend,
　Sad patience, too near neighbor to despair—
　　But none has hope like thine!
Thou through the fields and through the woods
　dost stray,

Roaming the country-side, a truant boy,
　Nursing thy project in unclouded joy,
And every doubt long blown by time away.　200

O born in days when wits were fresh and clear,
　And life ran gayly as the sparkling Thames;
　　Before this strange disease of modern life,
With its sick hurry, its divided aims,
　Its head o'ertaxed, its palsied hearts, was rife—
　　Fly hence, our contact fear!
Still fly, plunge deeper in the bowering wood!
　Averse, as Dido did with gesture stern
　From her false friend's approach in Hades turn,
Wave us away, and keep thy solitude!　210

Still nursing the unconquerable hope,
　Still clutching the inviolable shade,
　　With a free, onward impulse brushing through,
By night, the silvered branches of the glade—
　Far on the forest-skirts, where none pursue,
　　On some mild pastoral slope
Emerge, and resting on the moonlit pales
　Freshen thy flowers as in former years
　With dew, or listen with enchanted ears,
From the dark dingles, to the nightingales!　220

But fly our paths, our feverish contact fly!
　For strong the infection of our mental strife,
　　Which, though it gives no bliss, yet spoils for
　　　rest;
And we should win thee from thy own fair life,
　Like us distracted, and like us unblest.
　　Soon, soon thy cheer would die,
Thy hopes grow timorous, and unfixed thy
　powers,
　And thy clear aims be cross and shifting made;
　And then thy glad perennial youth would fade,
Fade, and grow old at last, and die like ours.　230

Then fly our greetings, fly our speech and smiles!
　—As some grave Tyrian trader, from the sea,
　　Descried at sunrise an emerging prow
Lifting the cool-haired creepers stealthily,
　The fringes of a southward-facing brow
　　Among the Aegean isles;
And saw the merry Grecian coaster come,
　Freighted with amber grapes, and Chian wine,
　Green, bursting figs, and tunnies steeped in
　　　brine—
And knew the intruders on his ancient home, 240

The young light-hearted masters of the waves—
　And snatched his rudder, and shook out more sail;
　　And day and night held on indignantly

O'er the blue Midland waters with the gale,
  Betwixt the Syrtes and soft Sicily,
    To where the Atlantic raves
Outside the western straits; and unbent sails
    There, where down cloudy cliffs, through
      sheets of foam,
    Shy traffickers, the dark Iberians come;
And on the beach undid his corded bales.   250

Thyrsis

A MONODY, TO COMMEMORATE THE AUTHOR'S FRIEND, ARTHUR HUGH CLOUGH, WHO DIED AT FLORENCE, 1861

How changed is here each spot man makes or fills!
  In the two Hinkseys nothing keeps the same;
    The village street its haunted mansion lacks,
  And from the sign is gone Sibylla's name
    And from the roofs the twisted chimney-stacks—
      Are ye too changed, ye hills?
  See, 'tis no foot of unfamiliar men
    Tonight from Oxford up your pathway strays!
    Here came I often, often, in old days—
Thyrsis and I; we still had Thyrsis then.   10

Runs it not here, the track by Childsworth Farm,
  Past the high wood, to where the elm-tree crowns
    The hill behind whose ridge the sunset flames?
  The signal-elm, that looks on Ilsley Downs,
    The Vale, the three lone weirs, the youthful
      Thames?—
      This winter's eve is warm,
  Humid the air! leafless, yet soft as spring,
    The tender purple spray on copse and briers!
  And that sweet city with her dreaming spires,
She needs not June for beauty's heightening. 20

Lovely all times she lies, lovely tonight!—
  Only, methinks, some loss of habit's power
    Befalls me wandering through this upland dim;
  Once passed I blindfold here, at any hour;
    Now seldom come I, since I came with him.
      That single elm tree bright
  Against the west—I miss it! it is gone?
    We prized it dearly; while it stood, we said,
    Our friend, the gypsy-scholar, was not dead;
While the tree lived, he in these fields lived on. 30

Too rare, too rare, grow now my visits here,
  But once I knew each field, each flower, each
    stick;

And with the country folk acquaintance made
  By barn in threshing-time, by new-built rick.
    Here, too, our shepherd-pipes we first assayed.
    Ah me! this many a year
  My pipe is lost, my shepherd's holiday!
    Needs must I lose them, needs with heavy
      heart
    Into the world and wave of men depart;
But Thyrsis of his own will went away. 40

It irked him to be here; he could not rest.
  He loved each simple joy the country yields,
    He loved his mates; but yet he could not keep,
  For that a shadow lowered on the fields,
    Here with the shepherds and the silly sheep.
      Some life of men unblest
  He knew, which made him droop, and filled his
    head.
    He went; his piping took a troubled sound
    Of storms that rage outside our happy ground;
He could not wait their passing, he is dead. 50

So, some tempestuous morn in early June,
  When the year's primal burst of bloom is o'er,
    Before the roses and the longest day—
  When the garden-walks and all the grassy floor
    With blossoms red and white of fallen May
      And chestnut flowers are strewn—
  So have I heard the cuckoo's parting cry,
    From the wet field, through the vexed garden-
    trees,
    Come with the volleying rain and tossing
    breeze:
  The bloom is gone, and with the bloom go I! 60

Too quick despairer, wherefore wilt thou go?
  Soon will the high midsummer pomps come on.
    Soon will the musk carnations break and swell,
  Soon shall we have gold-dusted snapdragon,
    Sweet-William with his homely cottage-smell,
    And stocks in fragrant blow;
  Roses that down the alleys shine afar,
    And open, jasmine-muffled lattices,
    And groups under the dreaming garden-trees,
And the full moon, and the white evening-star. 70

He hearkens not! light comer, he is flown!
  What matters it? next year he will return,
    And we shall have him in the sweet spring
    days,
  With whitening hedges, and uncrumpling fern,
    And bluebells trembling by the forest-ways,
    And scent of hay new-mown.
But Thyrsis never more we swains shall see;
  See him come back, and cut a smoother reed,

And blow a strain the world at last shall heed—
For Time, not Corydon, hath conquered thee! 80

Alack, for Corydon no rival now!—
But when Sicilian shepherds lost a mate,
    Some good survivor with his flute would go,
Piping a ditty sad for Bion's fate;
    And cross the unpermitted ferry's flow,
    And relax Pluto's brow,
And make leap up with joy the beauteous head
Of Proserpine, among whose crownéd hair
Are flowers first opened on Sicilian air,
And flute his friend, like Orpheus, from the
    dead. 90

O easy access to the hearer's grace
When Dorian shepherds sang to Proserpine!
    For she herself had trod Sicilian fields,
She knew the Dorian water's gush divine,
    She knew each lily white which Enna yields,
    Each rose with blushing face;
She loved the Dorian pipe, the Dorian strain.
    But, ah, of our poor Thames she never heard!
    Her foot the Cumner cowslips never stirred;
And we should tease her with our plaint in
    vain! 100

Well! wind-dispersed and vain the words will be,
Yet, Thyrsis, let me give my grief its hour
    In the old haunt, and find our tree-topped hill!
Who, if not I, for questing here hath power?
    I know the wood which hides the daffodil,
    I know the Fyfield tree,
I know what white, what purple fritillaries
    The grassy harvest of the river-fields,
    Above by Ensham, down by Sandford, yields,
And what sedged brooks are Thames's tribu-
    taries; 110

I know these slopes; who knows them if not I?—
But many a dingle on the loved hillside,
    With thorns once studded, old, white-blos-
        somed trees,
Where thick the cowslips grew, and far descried
    High towered the spikes of purple orchises,
    Hath since our day put by
The coronals of that forgotten time;
    Down each green bank hath gone the plow-
        boy's team,
    And only in the hidden brookside gleam
Primroses, orphans of the flowery prime. 120

Where is the girl, who by the boatman's door,
Above the locks, above the boating throng,
    Unmoored our skiff when through the Wy-
        tham flats,

Red loosestrife and blond meadow-sweet among
And darting swallows and light water-gnats,
    We tracked the shy Thames shore?
Where are the mowers, who, as the tiny swell
    Of our boat passing heaved the river-grass,
    Stood with suspended scythe to see us pass?—
They are all gone, and thou art gone as well! 130

Yes, thou art gone! and round me too the night
In ever-nearing circle weaves her shade.
    I see her veil draw soft across the day,
I feel her slowly chilling breath invade
    The cheek grown thin, the brown hair sprent
        with gray;
    I feel her finger light
Laid pausefully upon life's headlong train—
    The foot less prompt to meet the morning dew,
    The heart less bounding at emotion new,
And hope, once crushed, less quick to spring
    again. 140

And long the way appears, which seemed so short
To the less practiced eye of sanguine youth;
    And high the mountain-tops, in cloudy air,
The mountain-tops, where is the throne of Truth,
    Tops in life's morning-sun so bright and bare!
    Unbreachable the fort
Of the long-battered world uplifts its wall;
    And strange and vain the earthly turmoil
        grows,
    And near and real the charm of thy repose,
And night as welcome as a friend would fall. 150

But hush! the upland hath a sudden loss
Of quiet!—Look, adown the dusk hillside,
    A troop of Oxford hunters going home,
As in old days, jovial and talking, ride!
    From hunting with the Berkshire hounds they
        come.
    Quick! let me fly, and cross
Into yon farther field;—'Tis done; and see,
    Backed by the sunset, which doth glorify
    The orange and pale violet evening sky,
Bare on its lonely ridge, the Tree! the Tree! 160

I take the omen! Eve lets down her veil,
The white fog creeps from bush to bush about,
    The west unflushes, the high stars grow bright,
And in the scattered farms the lights come out.
    I cannot reach the signal-tree tonight,
    Yet, happy omen, hail!
Hear it from thy broad lucent Arno-vale
    (For there thine earth-forgetting eyelids keep
    The morningless and unawakening sleep
Under the flowery oleanders, pale), 170

Hear it, O Thyrsis, still our tree is there!—
  Ah, vain! These English fields, this upland dim,
    These brambles pale with mist engarlanded,
That lone, sky-pointing tree, are not for him;
  To a boon southern country he is fled,
    And now in happier air,
Wandering with the great Mother's train divine
  (And purer or more subtle soul than thee,
  I trow, the mighty Mother doth not see)
Within a folding of the Apennine,   180

Thou hearest the immortal chants of old!—
  Putting his sickle to the perilous grain
    In the hot cornfield of the Phrygian king,
For thee the Lityerses-song again
    Young Daphnis with his silver voice doth sing;
      Sings his Sicilian fold,
His sheep, his hapless love, his blinded eyes—
  And how a call celestial round him rang,
  And heavenward from the fountain-brink he
    sprang,
And all the marvel of the golden skies.   190

There thou art gone, and me thou leavest here
  Sole in these fields! yet will I not despair.
    Despair I will not, while I yet descry
    'Neath the mild canopy of English air
    That lonely tree against the western sky.
      Still, still these slopes, 'tis clear,
Our gypsy-scholar haunts, outliving thee!
    Fields where soft sheep from cages pull the hay,
    Woods with anemones in flower till May,
Know him a wanderer still; then why not me? 200

A fugitive and gracious light he seeks,
  Shy to illumine; and I seek it too.
    This does not come with houses or with gold,
With place, with honor, and a flattering crew;
    'Tis not in the world's market bought and
      sold—
      But the smooth-slipping weeks
Drop by, and leave its seeker still untired;
    Out of the heed of mortals he is gone,
    He wends unfollowed, he must house alone;
Yet on he fares, by his own heart inspired.   210

Thou too, O Thyrsis, on like quest wast bound;
  Thou wanderedst with me for a little hour!
    Men gave thee nothing; but this happy quest,
  If men esteemed thee feeble, gave thee power,
    If men procured thee trouble, gave thee rest.
      And this rude Cumner ground,
Its fir-topped Hurst, its farms, its quiet fields,
    Here cam'st thou in thy jocund youthful time,

Here was thine height of strength, thy golden
    prime!
And still the haunt beloved a virtue yields.   220

What though the music of thy rustic flute
  Kept not for long its happy, country tone;
    Lost it too soon, and learned a stormy note
Of men contention-tossed, of men who groan,
    Which tasked thy pipe too sore, and tired thy
      throat—
      It failed, and thou wast mute!
Yet hadst thou always visions of our light,
    And long with men of care thou couldst not
     stay,
    And soon thy foot resumed its wandering way,
Left human haunt, and on alone till night.   230

Too rare, too rare, grow now my visits here!
  'Mid city-noise, not, as with thee of yore,
    Thyrsis! in reach of sheep-bells is my home.
—Then through the great town's harsh, heart-
    wearying roar,
    Let in thy voice a whisper often come,
      To chase fatigue and fear:
Why faintest thou? I wandered till I died.
    Roam on! The light we sought is shining still.
    Dost thou ask proof? Our tree yet crowns the
     hill,
Our scholar travels yet the loved hillside.   240

Dover Beach

The sea is calm tonight,
The tide is full, the moon lies fair
Upon the straits;—on the French coast the light
Gleams and is gone; the cliffs of England stand,
Glimmering and vast, out in the tranquil bay.
Come to the window, sweet is the night-air!

Only, from the long line of spray
Where the sea meets the moon-blanched land,
Listen! you hear the grating roar
Of pebbles which the waves draw back, and fling,
At their return, up the high strand,
Begin, and cease, and then again begin,
With tremulous cadence slow, and bring
The eternal note of sadness in.

Sophocles long ago
Heard it on the Aegean, and it brought
Into his mind the turbid ebb and flow
Of human misery; we
Find also in the sound a thought,
Hearing it by this distant northern sea.

The Sea of Faith
Was once, too, at the full, and round earth's
    shore
Lay like the folds of a bright girdle furled.
But now I only hear
Its melancholy, long, withdrawing roar,
Retreating, to the breath
Of the night-wind, down the vast edges drear
And naked shingles of the world.

Ah, love, let us be true
To one another! for the world, which seems
To lie before us like a land of dreams,
So various, so beautiful, so new,
Hath really neither joy, nor love, nor light,
Nor certitude, nor peace, nor help for pain;
And we are here as on a darkling plain
Swept with confused alarms of struggle and flight,
Where ignorant armies clash by night.

—◆—

American Poetry

WALT WHITMAN

1819–1892

Whitman was born at West Hills, near Huntington, Long Island, on May 31, 1819. His family moved to Brooklyn in the early 1820's, and Whitman became a printer's devil when he was twelve. For the next twenty years he undertook numerous occupations, teaching school, carpentry, typesetting, and journalism. In 1848 he wrote a temperance tract, *Franklin Evans,* but his work in prose and verse was undistinguished until he went to New Orleans in 1848 with his brother Jeff. In the interpretation of his more romantic biographers, Whitman had an "incandescent" love affair with a quadroon beauty during the three months he spent in New Orleans; whatever the truth of this episode, upon his return the dandified aesthete of the frock coat, high hat, small cane, and boutonniere that had been Walter Whitman vanished, and "Walt" Whitman, "one of the roughs . . . eating, drinking, and breeding," appeared and cultivated the ostentatiously masculine dress of the rough shirt, open shirt-collar, and bearded face that we now traditionally associate with him.

The publication of *Leaves of Grass* in 1855 is a landmark in the history of American literature. The "Preface" warmly and passionately announced that the United States is "essentially the greatest poem," and the whole work is full of the wonderful egalitarian hopes, the optimism, the dynamic, creative energy of an expanding, still pioneer America of the mid-nineteenth century. Following the clarion call of Ralph Waldo Emerson in *The American Scholar* (1837) for an emergent indigenous American culture, Whitman was the first to deny the values of the traditional culture of Europe at the time when Longfellow in the Smith professorship of modern languages at Harvard was trying to propagate it. Whitman's ideal of what America was to become was the very antithesis of his conception of feudal European culture; as Emerson rejected the "courtly muses of Europe" so did Whitman call on them to "migrate from Greece and Ionia." This attitude Whitman never abandoned, though he modified it: in his essay, "A Backward Glance O'er Travel'd Roads" (*November Boughs,* 1888) he observed, "Of the great poems received from abroad . . . is there one whose underlying basis is not a denial and an insult to democracy?"

There is a good deal of windy and blatant chest-thumping in *Leaves of Grass*; Whitman's poetic note deepened in sincerity and in emotional power in *Drum-Taps* (1865), the volume of verse which came out of his war experiences as a wound-dresser in the Washington hospitals. In 1873 he had a paralytic stroke, and remained partially incapacitated during the remaining years of his life.

Whitman's poetry has been assailed for its "formlessness" and its frank sensual treatment of sex. We have learned, however, that if we do not expect to read him as we read a sonneteer or a poet of the conventional kinds of verse, Whitman has a mastery of poetic form. His poetry has the structure of the symphony; it possesses a new, free organic verse form because the America which it sought to incorporate is a unique experiment in a new form of government, democracy. So far as his emphasis upon the physical is concerned, he respected the body as the temple of the soul, which is a part of the divine pantheistic Reality pervading the whole universe. There is therefore the intermingling of the spiritual with the physical in Whitman (in the relation of the perpetuation of the species to his theory of transmigration of the soul) that the unwary reader may not always detect.

Whitman strove to embrace all aspects of America and personify in his poetry and in his life the American dream of popular democracy as it came in conflict with the genteel tradition. America was to be a nation of great individuals in a more cosmic sense than ever had been realized before, and the poet who was to celebrate this land must be a great man himself, and identify himself with the trapper, the streetwalker, the Indian bride—he must be bisexual, androgynous. To Whitman, who deplored the materialistic tendencies of the Gilded Age in *Democratic Vistas* (1871), America was the symbol of a great modern spiritual discovery which would lead eventually to the utopian cosmic brotherhood of man, to "passage to more than India." His has been a profound and fertilizing influence upon twentieth-century American literature, in Carl Sandburg, Vachel Lindsay, Hart Crane, and Thomas Wolfe. In the spirit of Whitman, Louis Sullivan and Frank Lloyd Wright have tried to create an indigenous American architecture, and Grant Wood, an American painting. All adjectives derogatory of Whitman's work—strident, formless, vague, sensual, grandiose—all these adjectives fail to dissipate the power and permanence of the Whitman tradition in American letters:

> Camerado, this is no book;
> Who touches this, touches a man.

FURTHER READING

ARVIN, NEWTON. *Whitman* (New York, 1938).
CANBY, HENRY S. *Walt Whitman, An American* (Boston, 1943).
HOLLOWAY, EMORY. *Walt Whitman* (New York, 1926).

Song of Myself

1

I celebrate myself, and sing myself,
And what I asume you shall assume,
For every atom belonging to me as good belongs to you.

I loafe and invite my soul,
I lean and loafe at my ease observing a spear of summer grass.

My tongue, every atom of my blood, form'd from this soil, this air,
Born here of parents born here from parents the same, and their parents the same,
I, now thirty-seven years old in perfect health begin,
Hoping to cease not till death.

Creeds and schools in abeyance,
Retiring back a while sufficed at what they are, but never forgotten,
I harbor for good or bad, I permit to speak at every hazard,
Nature without check with original energy. . . .

6

A child said *What is the grass?* fetching it to me with full hands,
How could I answer the child? I do not know what it is any more than he.

I guess it must be the flag of my disposition, out of hopeful green stuff woven.

Or I guess it is the handkerchief of the Lord,
A scented gift and remembrancer designedly dropt,
Bearing the owner's name someway in the corners, that we may see and remark, and say *Whose?*

Or I guess the grass is itself a child, the produced babe of the vegetation.

Or I guess it is a uniform hieroglyphic,
And it means, Sprouting alike in broad zones and narrow zones,
Growing among black folks as among white,
Kanuck, Tuckahoe, Congressman, Cuff, I give them the same, I receive them the same.

And now it seems to me the beautiful uncut hair of graves.

Tenderly will I use you curling grass,
It may be you transpire from the breasts of young men,
It may be if I had known them I would have loved them,

It may be you are from old people, or from offspring
taken soon out of their mothers' laps,
And here you are the mothers' laps.

This grass is very dark to be from the white heads of
old mothers,
Darker than the colorless beards of old men,
Dark to come from under the faint red roofs of
mouths.
O I perceive after all so many uttering tongues,
And I perceive they do not come from the roofs of
mouths for nothing.

I wish I could translate the hints about the dead
young men and women,
And the hints about old men and mothers, and the
offspring taken soon out of their laps.

What do you think has become of the young and
old men?
And what do you think has become of the women
and children?

They are alive and well somewhere,
The smallest sprout shows there is really no death,
And if ever there was it led forward life, and does
not wait at the end to arrest it,
And ceas'd the moment life appear'd.

All goes onward and outward, nothing collapses,
And to die is different from what any one supposed,
and luckier. . . .

21

I am the poet of the Body and I am the poet of
the Soul,
The pleasures of heaven are with me and the pains
of hell are with me,
The first I graft and increase upon myself, the latter
I translate into a new tongue.

I am the poet of the woman the same as the man,
And I say it is as great to be a woman as to be a
man,
And I say there is nothing greater than the mother
of men.

I chant the chant of dilation or pride,
We have had ducking and deprecating about
enough,
I show that size is only development.

Have you outstript the rest? are you the President?
It is a trifle, they will more than arrive there every
one, and still pass on.

I am he that walks with the tender and growing
night,
I call to the earth and sea half-held by the night.

Press close bare-bosom'd night—press close magnetic
nourishing night!
Night of south winds—night of the large few stars!
Still nodding night—mad naked summer night.

Smile O voluptuous cool-breath'd earth!
Earth of the slumbering and liquid trees!
Earth of departed sunset—earth of the mountains
misty-topt!
Earth of the vitreous pour of the full moon just
tinged with blue!
Earth of shine and dark mottling the tide of the
river!
Earth of the vitreous pour of the full moon just
clearer for my sake!
Far-swooping elbow'd earth—rich apple-blossom'd
earth!
Smile, for your lover comes.

Prodigal, you have given me love—therefore I to
you give love!
O unspeakable passionate love. . . .

31

I believe a leaf of grass is no less than the journey-
work of the stars,
And the pismire is equally perfect, and a grain of
sand, and the egg of the wren,
And the tree-toad is a chef-d'oeuvre for the highest,
And the running blackberry would adorn the parlors of heaven,
And the narrowest hinge in my hand puts to scorn
all machinery,
And the cow crunching with depress'd head surpasses any statue,
And a mouse is miracle enough to stagger sextillions
of infidels.

I find I incorporate gneiss, coal, long-threaded moss,
fruits, grains, esculent roots,
And am stucco'd with quadrupeds and birds all over,
And have distanced what is behind me for good
reasons,
But call any thing back again when I desire it.

In vain the speeding or shyness,
In vain the plutonic rocks send their old heat
against my approach,
In vain the mastodon retreats beneath its own
powder'd bones,

In vain objects stand leagues off and assume manifold shapes,
In vain the ocean settling in hollows and the great
  monsters lying low,
In vain the buzzard houses herself with the sky,
In vain the snake slides through the creepers and
  logs,
In vain the elk takes to the inner passes of the
  woods,
In vain the razor-bill'd auk sails far north to Lab-
  rador,
I follow quickly, I ascend to the nest in the fissure
  of the cliff.

32

I think I could turn and live with animals, they're
  so placid and self-contain'd,
I stand and look at them long and long.

They do not sweat and whine about their condition,
They do not lie awake in the dark and weep for
  their sins,
They do not make me sick discussing their duty to
  God,
Not one is dissatisfied, not one is demented with the
  mania of owning things,
Not one kneels to another, nor to his kind that lived
  thousands of years ago,
Not one is respectable or unhappy over the whole
  earth.

So they show their relations to me and I accept
  them,
They bring me tokens of myself, they evince them
  plainly in their possession.

I wonder where they get those tokens,
Did I pass that way huge times ago and negligently
  drop them?

Myself moving forward then and now and forever,
Gathering and showing more always and with
  velocity,
Infinite and omnigenous, and the like of these
  among them,
Not too exclusive toward the reachers of my remem-
  brances,
Picking out here one that I love, and now go with
  him on brotherly terms.

A gigantic beauty of a stallion, fresh and responsive
  to my caresses,
Head high in the forehead, wide between the ears,
Limbs glossy and supple, tail dusting the ground,
Eyes full of sparkling wickedness, ears finely cut,
  flexibly moving.

His nostrils dilate as my heels embrace him,
His well-built limbs tremble with pleasure as we
  race around and return.
I but use you a minute, then I resign you, stallion,
Why do I need your paces when I myself out-gallop
  them?
Even as I stand or sit passing faster than you. . . .

44

It is time to explain myself—let us stand up.

What is known I strip away,
I launch all men and women forward with me into
  the Unknown.

The clock indicates the moment—but what does
  eternity indicate?

We have thus far exhausted trillions of winters and
  summers,
There are trillions ahead, and trillions ahead of
  them.

Births have brought us richness and variety,
And other births will bring us richness and variety.

I do not call one greater and one smaller,
That which fills its period and place is equal to any.

Were mankind murderous or jealous upon you, my
  brother, my sister?
I am sorry for you, they are not murderous or jealous
  upon me,
All has been gentle with me, I keep no account with
  lamentation,
(What have I to do with lamentation?)

I am an acme of things accomplish'd, and I an
  encloser of things to be.

My feet strike an apex of the apices of the stairs,
On every step bunches of ages, and larger bunches
  between the steps,
All below duly travel'd, and still I mount and
  mount.

Rise after rise bow the phantoms behind me,
Afar down I see the huge first Nothing, I know I
  was even there,
I waited unseen and always, and slept through the
  lethargic mist,
And took my time, and took no hurt from the fetid
  carbon.

Long I was hugg'd close—long and long.

Immense have been the preparations for me,
Faithful and friendly the arms that have help'd me.

Cycles ferried my cradle, rowing and rowing like
    cheerful boatmen,
For room to me stars kept aside in their own rings,
They sent influences to look after what was to hold
    me.

Before I was born out of my mother generations
    guided me,
My embryo has never been torpid, nothing could
    overlay it.

For it the nebula cohered to an orb,
The long slow strata piled to rest it on,
Vast vegetables gave it sustenance,
Monstrous sauroids transported it in their mouths
    and deposited it with care.

All forces have been steadily employ'd to complete
    and delight me,
Now on this spot I stand with my robust soul. . . .

48

I have said that the soul is not more than the body,
And I have said that the body is not more than the
    soul,
And nothing, not God, is greater to one than one's
    self is,
And whoever walks a furlong without sympathy
    walks to his own funeral drest in his shroud,
And I or you pocketless of a dime may purchase the
    pick of the earth,
And to glance with an eye or show a bean in its pod
    confounds the learning of all times,
And there is no trade or employment but the young
    man following it may become a hero,
And there is no object so soft but it makes a hub for
    the wheel'd universe,
And I say to any man or woman, Let your soul stand
    cool and composed before a million universes.

And I say to mankind, Be not curious about God,
For I who am curious about each am not curious
    about God,
(No array of terms can say how much I am at peace
    about God and about death.)

I hear and behold God in every object, yet under-
    stand God not in the least,
Nor do I understand who there can be more won-
    derful than myself.

Why should I wish to see God better than this day?
I see something of God each hour of the twenty-
    four, and each moment then,
In the faces of men and women I see God, and in
    my own face in the glass,

I find letters from God dropt in the street, and
    every one is sign'd by God's name,
And I leave them where they are, for I know that
    wheresoe'er I go
Others will punctually come for ever and ever. . . .

51

The past and present wilt—I have fill'd them, emp-
    tied them,
And proceed to fill my next fold of the future.

Listener up there! what have you to confide to me?
Look in my face while I snuff the sidle of evening,
(Talk honestly, no one else hears you, and I stay
    only a minute longer.)

Do I contradict myself?
Very well then I contradict myself,
(I am large, I contain multitudes.)

I concentrate toward them that are nigh, I wait on
    the door-slab.

Who has done his day's work? who will soonest be
    through with his supper?
Who wishes to walk with me?

Will you speak before I am gone? will you prove
    already too late?

52

The spotted hawk swoops by and accuses me, he
    complains of my gab and my loitering.

I too am not a bit tamed, I too am untranslatable,
I sound my barbaric yawp over the roofs of the
    world.

The last scud of day holds back for me,
It flings my likeness after the rest and true as any
    on the shadow'd wilds,
It coaxes me to the vapor and the dusk.

I depart as air, I shake my white locks at the run-
    away sun,
I effuse my flesh in eddies, and drift it in lacy jags.

I bequeath myself to the dirt to grow from the grass
    I love,
If you want me again look for me under your boot-
    soles.

You will hardly know who I am or what I mean,
But I shall be good health to you nevertheless,
And filter and fibre your blood.

Failing to fetch me at first keep encouraged,
Missing me one place search another,
I stop somewhere waiting for you.

Out of the Cradle Endlessly Rocking *

Out of the cradle endlessly rocking,
Out of the mocking-bird's throat, the musical shuttle,
Out of the Ninth-month midnight,
Over the sterile sands and the fields beyond, where
    the child leaving his bed wander'd alone, bare-
    headed, barefoot,
Down from the shower'd halo,
Up from the mystic play of shadows twining and
    twisting as if they were alive,
Out from the patches of briers and blackberries,
From the memories of the bird that chanted to
    me,
From your memories sad brother, from the fitful
    risings and fallings I heard,
From under that yellow half-moon late-risen and
    swollen as if with tears,   10
From those beginning notes of yearning and love
    there in the mist,
From the thousand responses of my heart never to
    cease,
From the myriad thence-arous'd words,
From the word stronger and more delicious than
    any,
From such as now they start the scene revisiting,
As a flock, twittering, rising, or overhead passing,
Borne hither, ere all eludes me, hurriedly,
A man, yet by these tears a little boy again,
Throwing myself on the sand, confronting the
    waves,
I, chanter of pains and joys, uniter of here and here-
    after,   20
Taking all hints to use them, but swiftly leaping
    beyond them,
A reminiscence sing.

Once Paumanok,
When the lilac-scent was in the air and Fifth-month
    grass was growing,
Up this seashore in some briers,
Two feather'd guests from Alabama, two together,
And their nest, and four light-green eggs spotted
    with brown,
And every day the he-bird to and fro near at hand,
And every day the she-bird crouch'd on her nest,
    silent, with bright eyes,
And every day I, a curious boy, never too close,
    never disturbing them,   30
Cautiously peering, absorbing, translating.

* First published in 1860, now in the section of *Leaves
of Grass* entitled "Sea-Drift."

Shine! shine! shine!
Pour down your warmth, great sun!
While we bask, we two together.

Two together!
Winds blow south, or winds blow north,
Day come white, or day come black,
Home, or rivers and mountains from home,
Singing all time, minding no time,
While we two keep together.   40

Till of a sudden,
May-be kill'd, unknown to her mate,
One forenoon that she-bird crouch'd not on the nest,
Nor return'd that afternoon, nor the next,
Nor ever appear'd again.

And thenceforward all summer in the sound of the
    sea,
And at night under the full of the moon in calmer
    weather,
Over the hoarse surging of the sea,
Or flitting from brier to brier by day,
I saw, I heard at intervals the remaining one, the
    he-bird,   50
The solitary guest from Alabama.

Blow! blow! blow!
Blow up sea-winds along Paumanok's shore;
I wait and I wait till you blow my mate to me.

Yes, when the stars glisten'd,
All night long on the prong of a moss-scallop'd
    stake,
Down almost amid the slapping waves,
Sat the lone singer wonderful causing tears.

He call'd on his mate,
He pour'd forth the meanings which I of all men
    know.   60

Yes my brother I know,
The rest might not, but I have treasur'd every note,
For more than once dimly down to the beach glid-
    ing,
Silent, avoiding the moonbeams, blending myself
    with the shadows,
Recalling now the obscure shapes, the echoes, the
    sounds and sights after their sorts,
The white arms out in the breakers tirelessly tossing,
I, with bare feet, a child, the wind wafting my hair,
Listen'd long and long.

Listen'd to keep, to sing, now translating the notes,
Following you my brother.   70

Soothe! soothe! soothe!
Close on its wave soothes the wave behind,
And again another behind embracing and lapping, every one close,
But my love soothes not me, not me.

Low hangs the moon, it rose late,
It is lagging—O I think it is heavy with love, with love.

O madly the sea pushes upon the land,
With love, with love.

O night! do I not see my love fluttering out among the breakers?
What is that little black thing I see there in the white? 80

Loud! loud! loud!
Loud I call to you, my love!

High and clear I shoot my voice over the waves,
Surely you must know who is here, is here,
You must know who I am, my love.

Low-hanging moon!
What is that dusky spot in your brown yellow?
O it is the shape, the shape of my mate!
O moon do not keep her from me any longer.

Land! land! O land! 90
Whichever way I turn, O I think you could give me my mate back again if you only would,
For I am almost sure I see her dimly whichever way I look.

O rising stars!
Perhaps the one I want so much will rise, will rise with one of you.

O throat! O trembling throat!
Sound clearer through the atmosphere!
Pierce the woods, the earth,
Somewhere listening to catch you must be the one I want.

Shake out carols!
Solitary here, the night's carols! 100
Carols of lonesome love! death's carols!
Carols under that lagging, yellow, waning moon!
O under that moon where she droops almost down into the sea!
O reckless despairing carols.

But soft! sink low!
Soft! let me just murmur,

And do you wait a moment you husky-nois'd sea,
For somewhere I believe I heard my mate responding to me,
So faint, I must be still, be still to listen,
But not altogether still, for then she might not come immediately to me. 110

Hither my love!
Here I am! here!
With this just-sustain'd note I announce myself to you,
This gentle call is for you my love, for you.

Do not be decoy'd elsewhere,
That is the whistle of the wind, it is not my voice,
That is the fluttering, the fluttering of the spray,
Those are the shadows of leaves.

O darkness! O in vain!
O I am very sick and sorrowful. 120
O brown halo in the sky near the moon, drooping upon the sea!
O troubled reflection in the sea!
O throat! O throbbing heart!
And I singing uselessly, uselessly all the night.

O past! O happy life! O songs of joy!
In the air, in the woods, over fields,
Loved! loved! loved! loved! loved!
But my mate no more, no more with me!
We two together no more.

The aria sinking, 130
All else continuing, the stars shining,
The winds blowing, the notes of the bird continuous echoing,
With angry moans the fierce old mother incessantly moaning,
On the sands of Paumanok's shore gray and rustling,
The yellow half-moon enlarged, sagging down, drooping, the face of the sea almost touching,
The boy ecstatic, with his bare feet the waves, with his hair the atmosphere dallying,
The love in the heart long pent, now loose, now at last tumultuously bursting,
The aria's meaning, the ears, the soul, swiftly depositing,
The strange tears down the cheeks coursing,
The colloquy there, the trio, each uttering, 140
The undertone, the savage old mother incessantly crying,
To the boy's soul's questions sullenly timing, some drown'd secret hissing,
To the outsetting bard.

Demon or bird! (said the boy's soul,)
Is it indeed toward your mate you sing? or is it really
    to me?
For I, that was a child, my tongue's use sleeping,
    now I have heard you,
Now in a moment I know what I am for, I awake,
And already a thousand singers, a thousand songs,
    clearer, louder and more sorrowful than yours,
A thousand warbling echoes have started to life
    within me, never to die.

O you singer solitary, singing by yourself, project-
    ing me,   150
O solitary me listening, never more shall I cease
    perpetuating you,
Never more shall I escape, never more the rever-
    berations,
Never more the cries of unsatisfied love be absent
    from me,
Never again leave me to be the peaceful child I was
    before what there in the night,
By the sea under the yellow and sagging moon,
The messenger there arous'd, the fire, the sweet hell
    within,
The unknown want, the destiny of me.

O give me the clew! (it lurks in the night here
    somewhere,)
O if I am to have so much, let me have more!

A word then, (for I will conquer it,)   160
The word final, superior to all,
Subtle, sent up—what is it?—I listen;
Are you whispering it, and have been all the time,
    you sea-waves?
Is that it from your liquid rims and wet sands?

Whereto answering, the sea,
Delaying not, hurrying not,
Whisper'd me through the night, and very plainly
    before daybreak,
Lisp'd to me the low and delicious word death,
And again death, death, death, death,
Hissing melodious, neither like the bird nor like
    my arous'd child's heart,   170
But edging near as privately for me rustling at my
    feet,
Creeping thence steadily up to my ears and laving
    me softly all over,
Death, death, death, death, death.

Which I do not forget,
But fuse the song of my dusky demon and brother,
That he sang to me in the moonlight on Paumanok's
    gray beach,

With the thousand responsive songs at random,
My own songs awaked from that hour,
And with them the key, the word up from the
    waves,
The word of the sweetest song and all songs,   180
That strong and delicious word which, creeping to
    my feet,
(Or like some old crone rocking the cradle, swathed
    in sweet garments, bending aside,)
The sea whisper'd me.

Give Me the Splendid Silent Sun

Give me the splendid silent sun with all his beams
    full-dazzling,
Give me juicy autumnal fruit ripe and red from the
    orchard,
Give me a field where the unmow'd grass grows,
Give me an arbor, give me the trellis'd grape,
Give me fresh corn and wheat, give me serene-
    moving animals teaching content,
Give me nights perfectly quiet as on high plateaus
    west of the Mississippi, and I looking up at the
    stars,
Give me odorous at sunrise a garden of beautiful
    flowers where I can walk undisturb'd,
Give me for marriage a sweet-breath'd woman of
    whom I should never tire,
Give me a perfect child, give me away aside from
    the noise of the world a rural domestic life,
Give me to warble spontaneous songs recluse by
    myself, for my own ears only,   10
Give me solitude, give me Nature, give me again O
    Nature your primal sanities!

These demanding to have them, (tired with cease-
    less excitement, and rack'd by the war-strife,)
These to procure incessantly asking, rising in cries
    from my heart,
While yet incessantly asking still I adhere to my
    city.
Day upon day and year upon year O city, walking
    your streets,
Where you hold me enchain'd a certain time refus-
    ing to give me up,
Yet giving to make me glutted, enrich'd of soul, you
    give me forever faces;
(O I see what I sought to escape, confronting, re-
    versing my cries,
I see my own soul trampling down what it ask'd
    for.)

Keep your splendid silent sun,   20
Keep your woods O Nature, and the quiet places by
    the woods,
Keep your fields of clover and timothy, and your
    cornfields and orchards,
Keep the blossoming buckwheat fields where the
    Ninth-month bees hum;
Give me faces and streets—give me these phantoms
    incessant and endless along the *trottoirs!*
Give me interminable eyes—give me women—give
    me comrades and lovers by the thousand!
Let me see new ones every day—let me hold new
    ones by the hand every day!
Give me such shows—give me the streets of Manhat-
    tan!
Give me Broadway, with the soldiers marching—
    give me the sound of the trumpets and drums!
(The soldiers in companies or regiments—some start-
    ing away, flush'd and reckless,
Some, their time up, returning with thinn'd ranks,
    young, yet very old, worn, marching, noticing
    nothing;)   30
Give me the shores and wharves heavy-fringed with
    black ships!
O such for me! O an intense life, full to repletion
    and varied!
The life of the theatre, bar-room, huge hotel, for me!
The saloon of the steamer! the crowded excursion
    for me! the torchlight procession!
The dense brigade bound for the war, with high
    piled military wagons following;
People, endless, streaming, with strong voices, pas-
    sions, pageants,
Manhattan streets with their powerful throbs, with
    beating drums as now,
The endless and noisy chorus, the rustle and clank
    of muskets, (even the sight of the wounded,)
Manhattan crowds, with their turbulent musical
    chorus!
Manhattan faces and eyes forever for me.   40

When Lilacs Last in the Dooryard Bloom'd

*This famous elegy was published after Lincoln's
assassination in 1865, as a supplement to* Drum Taps.

1

When lilacs last in the dooryard bloom'd,
And the great star early droop'd in the western sky
    in the night,

I mourn'd, and yet shall mourn with ever-returning
    spring.

Ever-returning spring, trinity sure to me you bring,
Lilac blooming perennial and drooping star in the
    west,
And thought of him I love.

2

O powerful western fallen star!
O shades of night—O moody, tearful night!
O great star disappear'd—O the black murk that
    hides the star!
O cruel hands that hold me powerless—O helpless
    soul of me!   10
O harsh surrounding cloud that will not free my
    soul.

3

In the dooryard fronting an old farm-house near the
    white-wash'd palings,
Stands the lilac-bush tall-growing with heart-shaped
    leaves of rich green,
With many a pointed blossom rising delicate, with
    the perfume strong I love,
With every leaf a miracle—and from this bush in
    the dooryard,
With delicate-color'd blossoms and heart-shaped
    leaves of rich green,
A sprig with its flower I break.

4

In the swamp in secluded recesses,
A shy and hidden bird is warbling a song.

Solitary the thrush,   20
The hermit withdrawn to himself, avoiding the
    settlements,
Sings by himself a song.

Song of the bleeding throat,
Death's outlet song of life, (for well dear brother
    I know,
If thou wast not granted to sing thou would'st
    surely die.)

5

Over the breast of the spring, the land, amid cities,
Amid lanes and through old woods, where lately the
    violets peep'd from the ground, spotting the
    gray debris,
Amid the grass in the fields each side of the lanes,
    passing the endless grass,

Passing the yellow-spear'd wheat, every grain from its shroud in the dark-brown fields uprisen,
Passing the apple-tree blows of white and pink in the orchards,   30
Carrying a corpse to where it shall rest in the grave,
Night and day journeys a coffin.

6

Coffin that passes through lanes and streets,
Through day and night with the great cloud darkening the land,
With the pomp of the inloop'd flags with the cities draped in black,
With the show of the States themselves as of crape-veil'd women standing,
With processions long and winding and the flambeaus of the night,
With the countless torches lit, with the silent sea of faces and the unbared heads,
With the waiting depot, the arriving coffin, and the sombre faces,
With dirges through the night, with the thousand voices rising strong and solemn,   40
With all the mournful voices of the dirges pour'd around the coffin,
The dim-lit churches and the shuddering organs—where amid these you journey,
With the tolling tolling bells' perpetual clang,
Here, coffin that slowly passes,
I give you my sprig of lilac.

7

(Nor for you, for one alone,
Blossoms and branches green to coffins all I bring,
For fresh as the morning, thus would I chant a song for you O sane and sacred death.

All over bouquets of roses,
O death, I cover you over with roses and early lilies,   50
But mostly and now the lilac that blooms the first,
Copious I break, I break the sprigs from the bushes,
With loaded arms I come, pouring for you,
For you and the coffins all of you O death.)

8

O western orb sailing the heaven,
Now I know what you must have meant as a month since I walk'd,
As I walk'd in silence the transparent shadowy night,
As I saw you had something to tell as you bent to me night after night,

As you droop'd from the sky low down as if to my side, (while the other stars all look'd on,)
As we wander'd together the solemn night, (for something I know not what kept me from sleep,)   60
As the night advanced, and I saw on the rim of the west how full you were of woe,
As I stood on the rising ground in the breeze in the cool transparent night,
As I watch'd where you pass'd and was lost in the netherward black of the night,
As my soul in its trouble dissatisfied sank, as where you sad orb,
Concluded, dropt in the night, and was gone.

9

Sing on there in the swamp,
O singer bashful and tender, I hear your notes, I hear your call,
I hear, I come presently, I understand you,
But a moment I linger, for the lustrous star has detain'd me,
The star my departing comrade holds and detains me.   70

10

O how shall I warble myself for the dead one there I loved?
And how shall I deck my song for the large sweet soul that has gone?
And what shall my perfume be for the grave of him I love?

Sea-winds blown from east and west,
Blown from the Eastern sea and blown from the Western sea, till there on the prairies meeting,
These and with these and the breath of my chant,
I'll perfume the grave of him I love.

11

O what shall I hang on the chamber walls?
And what shall the pictures be that I hang on the walls,
To adorn the burial-house of him I love?   80

Pictures of growing spring and farms and homes,
With the Fourth-month eve at sundown, and the gray smoke lucid and bright,
With floods of the yellow gold of the gorgeous, indolent, sinking sun, burning, expanding the air,
With the fresh sweet herbage under foot, and the pale green leaves of the trees prolific,
In the distance the flowing glaze, the breast of the river, with a wind-dapple here and there,

With ranging hills on the banks, with many a line
    against the sky, and shadows,
And the city at hand with dwellings so dense, and
    stacks of chimneys,
And all the scenes of life and the workshops, and
    the workmen homeward returning.

12

Lo, body and soul—this land,
My own Manhattan with spires, and the sparkling
    and hurrying tides, and the ships,   90
The varied and ample land, the South and the
    North in the light, Ohio's shores and flashing
    Missouri,
And ever the far-spreading prairies cover'd with
    grass and corn.

Lo, the most excellent sun so calm and haughty,
The violet and purple morn with just-felt breezes,
The gentle soft-born measureless light,
The miracle spreading bathing all, the fulfill'd noon,
The coming eve delicious, the welcome night and
    the stars,
Over my cities shining all, enveloping man and
    land.

13

Sing on, sing on you gray-brown bird,
Sing from the swamps, the recesses, pour your chant
    from the bushes,   100
Limitless out of the dusk, out of the cedars and
    pines.

Sing on dearest brother, warble your reedy song,
Loud human song, with voice of uttermost woe.

O liquid and free and tender!
O wild and loose to my soul—O wondrous singer!
You only I hear—yet the star holds me, (but will
    soon depart,)
Yet the lilac with mastering odor holds me.

14

Now while I sat in the day and look'd forth,
In the close of the day with its light and the fields
    of spring, and the farmers preparing their
    crops,
In the large unconscious scenery of my land with
    its lakes and forests,
In the heavenly aerial beauty, (after the perturb'd
    winds and the storms,)   110
Under the arching heavens of the afternoon swift
    passing, and the voices of children and women,
The many-moving sea-tides, and I saw the ships
    how they sail'd,

And the summer approaching with richness, and
    the fields all busy with labor,
And the infinite separate houses, how they all went
    on, each with its meals and minutia of daily
    usages,
And the streets how their throbbings throbb'd, and
    the cities pent—lo, then and there.
Falling upon them all and among them all, en-
    veloping me with the rest,
Appear'd the cloud, appear'd the long black trail,
And I knew death, its thought, and the sacred
    knowledge of death.

Then with the knowledge of death as walking one
    side of me,   120
And the thought of death close-walking the other
    side of me,
And I in the middle as with companions, and as
    holding the hands of companions,
I fled forth to the hiding receiving night that talks
    not,
Down to the shores of the water, the path by the
    swamp in the dimness,
To the solemn shadowy cedars and ghostly pines
    so still.

And the singer so shy to the rest receiv'd me,
The gray-brown bird I know receiv'd us comrades
    three,
And he sang the carol of death, and a verse for him
    I love.

From deep secluded recesses,
From the fragrant cedars and the ghostly pines so
    still,   130
Came the carol of the bird.

And the charm of the carol rapt me,
As I held as if by their hands my comrades in the
    night,
And the voice of my spirit tallied the song of the
    bird.

Come lovely and soothing death,
Undulate round the world, serenely arriving, arriv-
*   ing,*
In the day, in the night, to all, to each,
Sooner or later delicate death.

Prais'd be the fathomless universe,
For life and joy, and for objects and knowledge
*   curious,*   140
And for love, sweet love—but praise! praise!
*   praise!*
For the sure-enwinding arms of cool-enfolding
*   death.*

Dark mother always gliding near with soft feet,
Have none chanted for thee a chant of fullest wel-
come?
Then I chant it for thee, I glorify thee above all,
I bring thee a song that when thou must indeed
come, come unfalteringly.

Approach strong deliveress,
When it is so, when thou hast taken them, I joy-
ously sing the dead,
Lost in the loving floating ocean of thee,
Laved in the flood of thy bliss O death. 150

From me to thee glad serenades,
Dances for thee I propose saluting thee, adornments
and feastings for thee,
And the sights of the open landscape and the high-
spread sky are fitting,
And life and the fields, and the huge and thought-
ful night.

The night in silence under many a star,
The ocean shore and the husky whispering wave
whose voice I know,
And the soul turning to thee O vast and well-veil'd
death,
And the body gratefully nestling close to thee.

Over the tree-tops I float thee a song,
Over the rising and sinking waves, over the myriad
fields and the prairies wide, 160
Over the dense-pack'd cities all and the teeming
wharves and ways,
I float this carol with joy, with joy to thee O death.

15

To the tally of my soul,
Loud and strong kept up the gray-brown bird,
With pure deliberate notes spreading filling the
night.

Loud in the pines and cedars dim,
Clear in the freshness moist and swamp-perfume,
And I with my comrades there in the night.

While my sight that was bound in my eyes unclosed,
As to long panoramas of visions. 170

And I saw askant the armies,
I saw as in noiseless dreams hundreds of battle-flags,
Borne through the smoke of the battles and pierc'd
with missiles I saw them,
And carried hither and yon through the smoke, and
torn and bloody,

And at last but a few shreds left on the staffs, (and
all in silence,)
And the staffs all splinter'd and broken.

I saw battle-corpses, myriads of them,
And the white skeletons of young men, I saw them,
I saw the debris and debris of all the slain soldiers
of the war,
But I saw they were not as was thought, 180
They themselves were fully at rest, they suffer'd not,
The living remain'd and suffer'd, the mother suf-
fer'd,
And the wife and the child and the musing comrade
suffer'd,
And the armies that remain'd suffer'd.

16

Passing the visions, passing the night,
Passing, unloosing the hold of my comrades' hands,
Passing the song of the hermit bird and the tallying
song of my soul,
Victorious song, death's outlet song, yet varying
ever-altering song,
As low and wailing, yet clear the notes, rising and
falling, flooding the night,
Sadly sinking and fainting, as warning and warn-
ing, and yet again bursting with joy, 190
Covering the earth and filling the spread of the
heaven,
As that powerful psalm in the night I heard from
recesses,
Passing, I leave thee lilac with heart-shaped leaves,
I leave thee there in the door-yard, blooming, returning with spring.

I cease from my song for thee,
From my gaze on thee in the west, fronting the
west, communing with thee,
O comrade lustrous with silver face in the night.

Yet each to keep and all, retrievements out of the
night,
The song, the wondrous chant of the gray-brown
bird,
And the tallying chant, the echo arous'd in my
soul, 200
With the lustrous and drooping star with the
countenance full of woe,
With the holders holding my hand nearing the call
of the bird,
Comrades mine and I in the midst, and their memory ever to keep, for the dead I loved so well,
For the sweetest, wisest soul of all my days and
lands—and this for his dear sake,

Lilac and star and bird twined with the chant of
    my soul,
There in the fragrant pines and the cedars dusk and
    dim.

Passage to India

*The laying of the Atlantic cable (1866) and the com-
pletion of the first transcontinental railroad seemed to
Whitman to bring the unity of East and West closer.*

1

Singing my days,
Singing the great achievements of the present,
Singing the strong light works of engineers,
Our modern wonders, (the antique ponderous
    Seven outvied,)
In the Old World the east the Suez canal,
The new by its mighty railroad spann'd,
The seas inlaid with eloquent gentle wires;
Yet first to sound, and ever sound, the cry with
    thee O soul,
The Past! the Past! the Past!

The Past—the dark unfathom'd retrospect!   10
The teeming gulf—the sleepers and the shadows!
The past—the infinite greatness of the past!

For what is the present after all but a growth out
    of the past?
(As a projectile form'd, impell'd, passing a certain
    line, still keeps on,
So the present, utterly form'd, impell'd by the past.)

2

Passage O soul to India!
Eclaircise the myths Asiatic, the primitive fables.

Not you alone proud truths of the world,
Not you alone ye facts of modern science,
But myths and fables of eld, Asia's, Africa's
    fables,   20
The far-darting beams of the spirit, the unloos'd
    dreams,
The deep diving bibles and legends,
The daring plots of the poets, the elder religions;
O you temples fairer than lilies pour'd over by the
    rising sun!
O you fables spurning the known, eluding the hold
    of the known, mounting to heaven!
You lofty and dazzling towers, pinnacled, red as
    roses, burnish'd with gold!
Towers of fables immortal fashion'd from mortal
    dreams!

You too I welcome and fully the same as the rest!
You too with joy I sing.

Passage to India!   30
Lo, soul, seest thou not God's purpose from the first?
The earth to be spann'd, connected by network,
The races, neighbors, to marry and be given in
    marriage,
The oceans to be cross'd, the distant brought near,
The lands to be welded together.

A worship new I sing,
You captains, voyagers, explorers, yours,
You engineers, you architects, machinists, yours,
You, not for trade or transportation only,
But in God's name, and for thy sake O Soul.   40

3

Passage to India!
Lo soul for thee of tableaus twain.
I see in one the Suez canal initiated, open'd,
I see the procession of steamships, the Empress
    Eugenie's leading the van,
I mark from on deck the strange landscape, the pure
    sky, the level sand in the distance,
I pass swiftly the picturesque groups, the workmen
    gather'd,
The gigantic dredging machines.

In one again, different, (yet thine, all thine, O soul,
    the same,)
I see over my own continent the Pacific railroad
    surmounting every barrier,
I see continual trains of cars winding along the
    Platte carrying freight and passengers,   50
I hear the locomotives rushing and roaring, and the
    shrill steam-whistle,
I hear the echoes reverberate through the grandest
    scenery in the world,
I cross the Laramie plains, I note the rocks in gro-
    tesque shapes, the buttes,
I see the plentiful larkspur and wild onions, the
    barren, colorless, sage-deserts,
I see in glimpses afar or towering immediately above
    me the great mountains, I see the Wind river
    and the Wahsatch mountains,
I see the Monument mountain and the Eagle's Nest,
    I pass the Promontory, I ascend the Nevadas,
I scan the noble Elk mountain and wind around
    its base,
I see the Humboldt range, I thread the valley and
    cross the river,
I see the clear waters of lake Tahoe, I see forests
    of majestic pines,

Or crossing the great desert, the alkaline plains, I
    behold enchanting mirages of waters and
    meadows,   60
Marking through these and after all, in duplicate
    slender lines,
Bridging the three or four thousand miles of land
    travel,
Tying the Eastern to the Western sea,
The road between Europe and Asia.

(Ah Genoese thy dream! thy dream!
Centuries after thou art laid in thy grave,
The shore thou foundest verifies thy dream.)

4

Passage to India!
Struggles of many a captain, tales of many a sailor
    dead,
Over my mood stealing and spreading they come, 70
Like clouds and cloudlets in the unreach'd sky.

Along all history, down the slopes,
As a rivulet running, sinking now, and now again
    to the surface rising,
A ceaseless thought, a varied train—lo, soul, to thee,
    thy sight, they rise,
The plans, the voyages again, the expeditions;
Again Vasco de Gama sails forth,
Again the knowledge gain'd, the mariner's compass,
Lands found and nations born, thou born America,
For purpose vast, man's long probation fill'd,
Thou rondure of the world at last accomplish'd. 80

5

O vast Rondure, swimming in space,
Cover'd all over with visible power and beauty,
Alternate light and day and the teeming spiritual
    darkness,
Unspeakable high processions of sun and moon and
    countless stars above,
Below, the manifold grass and waters, animals,
    mountains, trees,
With inscrutable purpose, some hidden prophetic
    intention,
Now first it seems my thought begins to span thee.

Down from the gardens of Asia descending radiat-
    ing,
Adam and Eve appear, then their myriad progeny
    after them,
Wandering, yearning, curious, with restless explora-
    tions,   90
With questionings, baffled, formless, feverish, with
    never-happy hearts,

With that sad incessant refrain, *Wherefore unsatisfied soul?* and *Whither O mocking life!*

Ah who shall soothe these feverish children?
Who justify these restless explorations?
Who speak the secret of impassive earth?
Who bind it to us? what is this separate Nature so
    unnatural?
What is this earth to our affections? (unloving
    earth, without a throb to answer ours,
Cold earth, the place of graves.)

Yet soul be sure the first intent remains, and shall
    be carried out,
Perhaps even now the time has arrived.   100

After the seas are all cross'd, (as they seem already
    cross'd,)
After the great captains and engineers have accom-
    plish'd their work,
After the noble inventors, after the scientists, the
    chemist, the geologist, ethnologist,
Finally shall come the poet worthy that name,
The true son of God shall come singing his songs.

Then not your deeds only O voyagers, O scientists
    and inventors, shall be justified,
All these hearts as of fretted children shall be
    sooth'd,
All affection shall be fully responded to, the secret
    shall be told,
All these separations and gaps shall be taken up and
    hook'd and link'd together,
The whole earth, this cold, impassive, voiceless
    earth, shall be completely justified,   110
Trinitas divine shall be gloriously accomplish'd and
    compacted by the true son of God, the poet,
(He shall indeed pass the straits and conquer the
    mountains,
He shall double the cape of Good Hope to some
    purpose,)
Nature and Man shall be disjoin'd and diffused no
    more,
The true son of God shall absolutely fuse them.

6

Year at whose wide-flung door I sing!
Year of the purpose accomplish'd!
Year of the marriage of continents, climates and
    oceans!
(No mere doge of Venice now wedding the
    Adriatic,)
I see O year in you the vast terraqueous globe given
    and giving all,   120

Europe to Asia, Africa join'd, and they to the New
World,
The lands, geographies, dancing before you, holding
a festival garland,
As brides and bridegrooms hand in hand.

Passage to India!
Cooling airs from Caucasus, far, soothing cradle of
man,
The river Euphrates flowing, the past lit up again.

Lo soul, the retrospect brought forward,
The old, most populous, wealthiest of earth's lands,
The streams of the Indus and the Ganges and their
many affluents,
(I my shores of America walking to-day behold,
resuming all,) 130
The tale of Alexander on his warlike marches sud-
denly dying,
On one side China and on the other side Persia and
Arabia,
To the south the great seas and the bay of Bengal,
The flowing literatures, tremendous epics, religions,
castes,
Old occult Brahma interminably far back, the ten-
der and junior Buddha,
Central and southern empires and all their belong-
ings, possessors,
The wars of Tamerlane, the reign of Aurungzebe,
The traders, rulers, explorers, Moslems, Venetians,
Byzantium, the Arabs, Portuguese,
The first travelers famous yet, Marco Polo, Batouta
the Moor,
Doubts to be solv'd the map incognita, blanks to be
fill'd, 140
The foot of man unstay'd, the hands never at rest,
Thyself O soul that will not brook a challenge.

The mediaeval navigators rise before me,
The world of 1492, with its awaken'd enterprise,
Something swelling in humanity now like the sap
of the earth in spring,
The sunset splendor of chivalry declining.

And who art thou sad shade?
Gigantic, visionary, thyself a visionary,
With majestic limbs and pious beaming eyes,
Spreading around with every look of thine a golden
world, 150
Enhuing it with gorgeous hues.

As the chief histrion,
Down to the footlights walks in some great scena,
Dominating the rest I see the Admiral himself,
(History's type of courage, action, faith,)

Behold him sail from Palos leading his little fleet,
His voyage behold, his return, his great fame,
His misfortunes, calumniators, behold him a pris-
oner, chain'd,
Behold his dejection, poverty, death.

(Curious in time, I stand, noting the efforts of
heroes, 160
Is the deferment long? bitter the slander, poverty,
death?
Lies the seed unreck'd for centuries in the ground?
lo, to God's due occasion,
Uprising in the night, it sprouts, blooms,
And fills the earth with use and beauty.)

7

Passage indeed O soul to primal thought,
Not lands and seas alone, thy own clear freshness,
The young maturity of brood and bloom,
To realms of budding bibles.

O soul, repressless, I with thee and thou with me,
Thy circumnavigation of the world begin, 170
Of man, the voyage of his mind's return,
To reason's early paradise,
Back, back to wisdom's birth, to innocent intuitions,
Again with fair creation.

8

O we can wait no longer,
We too take ship O soul,
Joyous we too launch out on trackless seas,
Fearless for unknown shores on waves of ecstasy to
sail,
Amid the wafting winds, (thou pressing me to thee,
I thee to me, O soul,)
Caroling free, singing our song of God, 180
Chanting our chant of pleasant exploration.

With laugh and many a kiss
(Let others deprecate, let others weep for sin, re-
morse, humiliation,)
O soul thou pleasest me, I thee.
Ah more than any priest O soul we too believe in
God,
But with the mystery of God we dare not dally.

O soul thou pleasest me, I thee,
Sailing these seas or on the hills, or waking in the
night,
Thoughts, silent thoughts, of Time and Space and
Death, like waters flowing,
Bear me indeed as through the regions infinite, 190
Whose air I breathe, whose ripples hear, lave me
all over,

Bathe me O God in thee, mounting to thee,
I and my soul to range in range of thee.

O Thou transcendent,
Nameless, the fibre and the breath,
Light of the light, shedding forth universes, thou
    centre of them,
Thou mightier centre of the true, the good, the
    loving,
Thou moral, spiritual fountain—affection's source—
    thou reservoir,
(O pensive soul of me—O thirst unsatisfied—waitest
    not there?
Waitest not haply for us somewhere there the Com-
    rade perfect?)   200
Thou pulse—thou motive of the stars, suns, systems,
That, circling, move in order, safe, harmonious,
Athwart the shapeless vastnesses of space,
How should I think, how breathe a single breath,
    how speak, if, out of myself,
I could not launch, to those, superior universes?

Swiftly I shrivel at the thought of God,
At Nature and its wonders, Time and Space and
    Death,
But that I, turning, call to thee O soul, thou actual
    Me,
And lo, thou gently masterest the orbs,
Thou matest Time, smilest content at Death,   210
And fillest, swellest full the vastnesses of Space.

Greater than stars or suns,
Bounding O soul thou journeyest forth;
What love than thine and ours could wider amplify?
What aspirations, wishes, outvie thine and ours O
    soul?
What dreams of the ideal? what plans of purity,
    perfection, strength?
What cheerful willingness for others' sake to give
    up all?
For others' sake to suffer all?

Reckoning ahead O soul, when thou, the time
    achiev'd,
The seas all cross'd, weather'd the capes, the voyage
    done,   220
Surrounded, copest, frontest God, yieldest, the aim
    attain'd,
As fill'd with friendship, love complete, the Elder
    Brother found,
The Younger melts in fondness in his arms.

9

Passage to more than India!
Are thy wings plumed indeed for such far flights?
O soul, voyagest thou indeed on voyages like those?
Disportest thou on waters such as those?
Soundest below the Sanscrit and the Vedas?
Then have thy bent unleash'd.

Passage to you, your shores, ye aged fierce enig-
    mas!   230
Passage to you, to mastership of you, ye strangling
    problems!
You, strew'd with the wrecks of skeletons, that,
    living, never reach'd you.

Passage to more than India!
O secret of the earth and sky!
Of you O waters of the sea! O winding creeks and
    rivers!
Of you O woods and fields! of you strong moun-
    tains of my land!
Of you O prairies! of you gray rocks!
O morning red! O clouds! O rain and snows!
O day and night, passage to you!

O sun and moon and all you stars! Sirius and
    Jupiter!   240
Passage to you!

Passage, immediate passage! the blood burns in my
    veins!
Away O soul! hoist instantly the anchor!
Cut the hawsers—haul out—shake out every sail!
Have we not stood here like trees in the ground long
    enough?
Have we not grovel'd here long enough, eating and
    drinking like mere brutes?
Have we not darken'd and dazed ourselves with
    books long enough?

Sail forth—steer for the deep waters only,
Reckless O soul, exploring, I with thee, and thou
    with me,
For we are bound where mariner has not yet dared
    to go,   250
And we will risk the ship, ourselves and all.

O my brave soul!
O farther farther sail!
O daring joy, but safe! are they not all the seas of
    God?
O farther, farther, farther sail!

EMILY DICKINSON

1830–1886

Emily Dickinson, daughter of a well-known lawyer and treasurer of Amherst College, was born in Amherst, Massachusetts. She was educated in Amherst and for one year in Mount Holyoke Seminary, thence returning home where she passed the rest of an outwardly uneventful life. She sought intellectual companionship with men whom she picturesquely called her tutors, including the Reverend Charles Wadsworth, who (among several other candidates) has been constituted by some of her biographers as the mysterious "lover" of the poems. As a young girl Emily was pleasure-loving and of a sociable disposition, but after the departure of Mr. Wadsworth for San Francisco in 1862, she withdrew into seclusion and remained aloof from all but her closest friends for the rest of her life.

At the time of her withdrawal she began to devote herself seriously to poetry and initiated a literary correspondence with Colonel Thomas W. Higginson, who strongly encouraged her poetic efforts and became her literary adviser. After her death her executors discovered more than twelve hundred poems in manuscript, written on scraps of paper in the poet's almost undecipherable hand, with many variant readings. Three volumes of the poems were published from 1891 to 1896, and were received more favorably than might have been expected. More of her poems were published in 1914, 1929, and 1934, and three biographies in the early 1930's speculated somewhat extraordinarily upon the identity of the lover. The problems of posthumous publication, which have prevented an adequate scholarly editing of Emily Dickinson's poems, are related in Millicent Todd Bingham's *Ancestors' Brocades* (1945).

The poetry of Emily Dickinson is sometimes characterized by perversely quaint irregularities in rhyme and diction, a coy familiarity with philosophic profundity, and a self-pity that occasionally comes close to sentimentality. Nevertheless there is a wonderful gnomic phrasing reminiscent of Emerson, the sharply etched concise images, the metaphysical wit that at first reading seems naïve and on subsequent readings borders upon a profound and moving speculation on the transcendent immensities—immortality, love, death, and God. The remarkable combination of intellectual restraint, of artistic control of her subtly varied simple meters, and of mastery of the approximate rhyme and of assonance, the dramatic shifts in tone that half conceal the most poignant emotions—all these poetic traits disclose one of our most original American poets. Professor Whicher has observed that Emily Dickinson's work reveals the confluence of several currents and traditions of her day, among them especially the spiritual restlessness of Emerson and the Puritan tradition in which she was reared. This consideration of her relation to the thought of her own day is essential for a comprehension of Emily Dickinson, but it will never in itself adequately comprehend her amazing individuality or the vibrant ecstasies of the mind and spirit that comprise the canon of Emily Dickinson's more than one thousand "letters to the world."

FURTHER READING

BINGHAM, M. T. *Ancestors' Brocades: The Literary Début of Emily Dickinson* (New York, 1945).
CHASE, RICHARD. *Emily Dickinson* (New York, 1951).
WELLS, HENRY W. *Introduction to Emily Dickinson* (Chicago, 1942).
WHICHER, GEORGE F. *This Was a Poet* (New York, 1938).

I Taste a Liquor Never Brewed

I taste a liquor never brewed,
From tankards scooped in pearl;
Not all the vats upon the Rhine
Yield such an alcohol!

Inebriate of air am I,
And debauchee of dew,
Reeling, through endless summer days,
From inns of molten blue.

When landlords turn the drunken bee
Out of the foxglove's door,
When butterflies renounce their drams,
I shall but drink the more!

Till seraphs swing their snowy hats,
And saints to windows run,
To see the little tippler
Leaning against the sun!

A Bird Came Down the Walk

A bird came down the walk:
He did not know I saw;
He bit an angle-worm in halves
And ate the fellow, raw.

And then he drank a dew
From a convenient grass,
And then hopped sidewise to the wall
To let a beetle pass.

He glanced with rapid eyes
That hurried all abroad,—
They looked like frightened beads, I thought
He stirred his velvet head

Like one in danger; cautious,
I offered him a crumb,
And he unrolled his feathers
And rowed him softer home

Than oars divide the ocean,
Too silver for a seam,
Or butterflies, off banks of noon,
Leap, plashless, as they swim.

The Soul Selects

The soul selects her own society,
Then shuts the door;
On her divine majority
Obtrude no more.

Unmoved, she notes the chariots pausing
At her low gate;
Unmoved, an emperor is kneeling
Upon her mat.

I've known her from an ample nation
Choose one;
Then close the valves of her attention
Like stone.

I Cannot Live with You

I cannot live with you.
It would be life,
And life is over there
Behind the shelf

The sexton keeps the key to,
Putting up
Our life, his porcelain,
Like a cup

Discarded of the housewife,
Quaint or broken;
A newer Sèvres pleases,
Old ones crack.

I could not die with you,
For one must wait
To shut the other's gaze down,
You could not.

And I, could I stand by
And see you freeze,
Without my right of frost,
Death's privilege?

Nor could I rise with you,
Because your face
Would put out Jesus',
That new grace

Grow plain and foreign
On my homesick eye,
Except that you, than he
Shone closer by.

They'd judge us—how?
For you served Heaven, you know,
Or sought to;
I could not,

Because you saturated sight,
And I had no more eyes
For sordid excellence
As Paradise.

And were you lost, I would be,
Though my name
Rang loudest
On the heavenly fame.

And were you saved,
And I condemned to be
Where you were not,
That self were hell to me.

So we must keep apart,
You there, I here,
With just the door ajar
That oceans are,
And prayer,
And that pale sustenance,
Despair!

I Heard a Fly Buzz When I Died

I heard a fly buzz when I died;
  The stillness round my form
Was like the stillness in the air
  Between the heaves of storm.

The eyes beside had wrung them dry,
  And breaths were gathering sure
For that last onset, when the king
  Be witnessed in his power.

I willed my keepsakes, signed away
  What portion of me I
Could make assignable,—and then
  There interposed a fly,

With blue, uncertain, stumbling buzz,
  Between the light and me;
And then the windows failed, and then
  I could not see to see.

After Great Pain a Formal Feeling Comes

After great pain a formal feeling comes—
The nerves sit ceremonious like tombs;
The stiff heart questions—was it He that bore?
And yesterday—or centuries before?

The feet mechanical go round
A wooden way,
Of ground or air of Ought,
Regardless grown;
A quartz contentment like a stone.

This is the hour of lead
Remembered if outlived
As freezing persons recollect
The snow—
First chill, then stupor, then
The letting go.

The Chariot

Because I could not stop for Death,
He kindly stopped for me;
The carriage held but just ourselves
And Immortality.

We slowly drove, he knew no haste,
And I had put away
My labor, and my leisure too,
For his civility.

We passed the school where children played,
Their lessons scarcely done;
We passed the fields of gazing grain,
We passed the setting sun.

We paused before a house that seemed
A swelling on the ground;
The roof was scarcely visible,
The cornice but a mound.

Since then 'tis centuries; but each
Feels shorter than the day
I first surmised the horses' heads
Were toward eternity.

I'll Tell You How the Sun Rose

I'll tell you how the sun rose,—
A ribbon at a time.
The steeples swam in amethyst,
The news like squirrels ran.

The hills untied their bonnets,
The bobolinks begun.
Then I said softly to myself,
"That must have been the sun!"

. . .

But how he set, I know not.
There seemed a purple stile
Which little yellow boys and girls
Were climbing all the while

Till when they reached the other side,
A dominie in gray
Put gently up the evening bars,
And led the flock away.

A Wife at Daybreak I Shall Be

A wife at daybreak I shall be;
Sunrise, hast thou a flag for me?
At midnight I am yet a maid—
How short it takes to make a bride!

Then, Midnight, ı have passed from thee
Unto the East and Victory.

Midnight, "Good night."
I hear them call.

The angels bustle in the hall,
Softly my Future climbs the stair,
I fumble at my childhood's prayer—
So soon to be a child no more!
Eternity, I'm coming, Sir,—
Master, I've seen that face before.

A Route of Evanescence

A route of evanescence
With a revolving wheel;
A resonance of emerald,
A rush of cochineal;
And every blossom on the bush
Adjusts its tumbled head,—
The mail from Tunis, probably,
An easy morning's ride.

———◆———

American Fiction

SAMUEL L. CLEMENS (MARK TWAIN)

1835–1910

In several respects Samuel Clemens represented Walt Whitman's ideal of what the American man of letters should be. He was the first important author born west of the Mississippi to write in the authentic native idiom of the frontier and to give a firm literary basis to the traditions of frontier realism and Western humor (the other leading American humorists, "Artemus Ward," "Petroleum V. Nasby," and "Josh Billings" were from the East). One would hardly have selected the town of Hannibal, Missouri, on the Mississippi one hundred miles north of St. Louis and just a few miles above Pike County, Missouri, as the place to rear a distinguished man of letters-to-be. Clemens had been born in Florida, Missouri, in 1835, of Virginian and Kentuckian antecedents, and had moved with his family to Hannibal. The frontier in Hannibal was hardly an heroic one, for in Clemens' boyhood the dangers had moved West. The town was quiet and indolent, frequented by the backwash of the frontier—the half-breed Indian, the squatters, the Pike County men in their calico coats, jeans, and yarn suspenders, whittling day by day, sunk in apathy and squalor. It is often assumed that Samuel Clemens was brought up in a Calvinist environment, but on the frontier Calvinism hardly had the admonishing terrors of New England Calvinism, and perhaps had readily lost its hellfire sanctions in the fanning bees, hoedowns, fiddling matches, barbecues, and roof-raisings that were the frequent experiences of the Mississippi river town. There broadhorn and keelboat boys "whooped it up."

In 1847, after the death of his father, Clemens left school, was apprenticed to a printer, and began to write in his brother Orion's paper. After his experience as a journeyman printer he became a steamboat pilot on the Mississippi, to him possibly the most important discipline of his life, although Delancey Ferguson (*Mark Twain: Man and Legend*) rejects the thesis that only on the river did Clemens ever really find himself. The Civil War brought a cessation to the river traffic, and Clemens then went to Nevada with his brother, joining the staff of a Virginia City newspaper and adopting the pseudonym of Mark Twain. He soon began his literary career in the tradition of frontier humor, writing the famous "Jumping Frog of Calaveras County" (1865), one of his most famous anecdotes, along with the narrative of the petrified man who was discovered thumbing his nose at posterity. *Roughing It* (1872) was in the same vein, a vigorous and lusty tale of the frontier, though it reveals his chief defect as an artist, lack of disciplined structure, with very little integration of the tall tales with the narrative. His tour of the Mediterranean and of the Holy Land resulted in *Innocents Abroad*

(1869); this marked a break with the tradition of the earnest American seeker of European culture which had been established by Irving's *Sketch Book* and Longfellow's *Outre-Mer,* his facetious irreverence for European culture (he found the European a dastardly fellow and the topography inferior) establishing him as a leading American writer.

In February, 1870, he married Olivia Langdon of Elmira and settled in Hartford, Connecticut. The thesis that Clemens was a Rabelaisian genius, frustrated by the genteel, repressive influence of his wife and the conservative Eastern society in which he lived, has been overstated. The standards of refinement and delicacy that impelled the revision of his language to more decorous expression were the standards not merely of Mrs. Clemens but of the magazine editors and of the folkways of the Gilded Age. It seems dubious therefore to ascribe the pessimism that we find in his later books such as *The Man That Corrupted Hadleyburg* (1900), *What Is Man* (1906), and *The Mysterious Stranger* (1916) as due to his frustration as an artist, and not to illness, to the loss of his wife, to the failure of his many get-rich-quick schemes, like the Paige typesetter and Grant's *Memoirs,* and his financial debacle in the panic of 1893.

The popularity of Clemens as a humorous lecturer and raconteur did him disservice, because he was not taken seriously by his American audiences as a man of letters until late in his career. Since his death in 1910 we have come to recognize that he gave major literary permanence to the anecdotal narrative and to American frontier realism (as in the backwoods hysteria of the camp meeting in Chapter XX of *Huckleberry Finn*). His humor is often labored and obvious, but at its best it is full of wonderful invention, uninhibited laughter, delight, and sensitivity in rendering the frontier character and talk that is unmatched in American literature. *Life on the Mississippi* (1883) and *Huckleberry Finn* (1884) remain the greatest of Clemens' works in their blending of humor, frontier realism, wonderful exploratory adventure, and deep humanitarian sympathy. These works possess for us the aesthetic distance that in the perspective of time renders life on the Mississippi an American idyll of an age that has now receded relentlessly into the past and become an American myth.

FURTHER READING

BELLAMY, GLADYS CARMEN. *Mark Twain as a Literary Artist* (Norman, Okla., 1950).

DE VOTO, BERNARD. *Mark Twain's America* (Boston, 1932).

Life on the Mississippi

CHAPTER III*

Frescoes from the Past

BY way of illustrating keelboat talk and manners, and that now departed and hardly-remembered raft-life, I will throw in, in this place, a chapter from a book which I have been working at, by fits and starts, during the past five or six years, and may possibly finish in the course of five or six more. The book is a story which details some passages in the life of an ignorant village boy, Huck Finn, son of the town drunkard of my time out West, there. He has run away from his persecuting father, and from a persecuting good widow who wishes to make a nice, truth-telling, respectable boy of him; and with him a slave of the widow's has also escaped. They have found a fragment of a lumber-raft (it is high water and dead summer-time), and are floating down the river by night, and hiding in the willows by day—bound for Cairo, whence the Negro will seek freedom in the heart of the free states. But, in a fog, they pass Cairo without knowing it. By and by they begin to suspect the truth, and Huck Finn is persuaded to end the dismal suspense by swimming down to a huge raft which they have seen in the distance ahead of them, creeping aboard under cover of the darkness, and gathering the needed information by eavesdropping:

But you know [writes Huck] a young person can't wait very well when he is impatient to find a thing out. We talked it over, and by and by Jim said it was such a black night, now, that it wouldn't be no risk to swim down to the big raft and crawl aboard and listen—they would talk about Cairo, because they would be calculating to go ashore there for a spree, maybe; or anyway they would send boats ashore to buy whisky or fresh meat or something. Jim had a wonderful level head, for a nigger: he could most always start a good plan when you wanted one.

* This chapter was written for *Huckleberry Finn,* but never included in that novel.

I stood up and shook my rags off and jumped into the river, and struck out for the raft's light. By and by, when I got down nearly to her, I eased up and went slow and cautious. But everything was all right—nobody at the sweeps. So I swum down along the raft till I was most abreast the camp-fire in the middle, then I crawled aboard and inched along and got in among some bundles of shingles on the weather side of the fire. There was thirteen men there—they was the watch on deck of course. And a mighty rough-looking lot, too. They had a jug, and tin cups, and they kept the jug moving. One man was singing—roaring, you may say; and it wasn't a nice song—for a parlor, anyway. He roared through his nose, and strung out the last word of every line very long. When he was done they all fetched a kind of Injun warwhoop, and then another was sung. It begun:

"There was a woman in our towdn,
    In our towdn did dwed'l [dwell],
She loved her husband dear-i-lee,
    But another man twyste as wed'l.

"Singing too, riloo, riloo, riloo,
    Ri-too, riloo, rilay - - - e,
She loved her husband dear-i-lee,
    But another man twyste as wed'l."

And so on—fourteen verses. It was kind of poor, and when he was going to start on the next verse one of them said it was the tune the old cow died on; and another one said: "Oh, give us a rest!" And another one told him to take a walk. They made fun of him till he got mad and jumped up and begun to cuss the crowd, and said he could lam any thief in the lot.

They was all about to make a break for him, but the biggest man there jumped up and says:

"Set whar you are, gentlemen. Leave him to me; he's my meat."

Then he jumped up in the air three times, and cracked his heels together every time. He flung off a buckskin coat that was all hung with fringes, and says, "You lay thar tell the chawin-up's done"; and flung his hat down, which was all over ribbons, and says, "You lay thar tell his sufferin's is over."

Then he jumped up in the air and cracked his heels together again, and shouted out:

"Whoo-oop! I'm the old original iron-hawed, brass-mounted, copper-bellied corpse-maker from the wilds of Arkansaw! Look at me! I'm the man they call Sudden Death and General Desolation! Sired by a hurricane, dam'd by an earthquake, half-brother to the cholera, nearly related to the small-pox on the mother's side! Look at me! I take nineteen alligators and a bar'l of whisky for breakfast when I'm in robust health, and a bushel of rattlesnakes and a dead body when I'm ailing. I split the everlasting rocks with my glance, and I squench the thunder when I speak! Whoo-oop! Stand back and give me room according to my strength! Blood's my natural drink, and the wails of the dying is music to my ear. Cast your eye on me, gentlemen! and lay low and hold your breath, for I'm about to turn myself loose!"

All the time he was getting this off, he was shaking his head and looking fierce, and kind of swelling around in a little circle, tucking up his wristbands, and now and then straightening up and beating his breast with his fist, saying, "Look at me, gentlemen!" When he got through, he jumped up and cracked his heels together three times, and let off a roaring "Whoo-oop! I'm the bloodiest son of a wildcat that lives!"

Then the man that had started the row tilted his old slouch hat down over his right eye; then he bent stooping forward, with his back sagged and his south end sticking out far, and his fists a-shoving out and drawing in in front of him, and so went around in a little circle about three times, swelling himself up and breathing hard. Then he straightened, and jumped up and cracked his heels together three times before he lit again (that made them cheer), and he began to shout like this:

"Whoo-oop! bow your neck and spread, for the kingdom of sorrow's a-coming! Hold me down to the earth, for I feel my powers a-working! whoo-oop; I'm a child of sin, *don't* let me get a start! Smoked glass, here, for all! Don't attempt to look at me with the naked eye, gentlemen! When I'm playful I use the meridians of longitude and parallels of latitude for a seine, and drag the Atlantic Ocean for whales! I scratch my head with the lightning and purr myself to sleep with the thunder! When I'm cold, I bile the Gulf of Mexico and bathe in it; when I'm hot I fan myself with an equinoctial storm; when I'm thirsty I reach up and suck a cloud dry like a sponge; when I range the earth hungry, famine follows in my tracks! Whoo-oop! Bow your neck and spread! I put my hand on the sun's face and make it night in the earth; I bite a piece out of the moon and hurry the seasons; I shake myself and crumble the mountains! Contemplate me through leather—*don't* use the naked eye! The massacre of isolated communities is the pastime of my idle moments, the destruction of nationalities the serious business of my life! The boundless vastness of the great American desert is my enclosed property, and I bury my dead on my own premises!" He jumped up and cracked his heels together three times before he lit (they cheered him again), and as he come down he shouted out: "Whoo-oop! bow your neck and spread, for the Pet Child of Calamity's a-coming!"

Then the other one went to swelling around and blowing again—the first one—the one they called Bob; next, the Child of Calamity chipped in again, swelling round and round each other and punching their fists most into each other's faces, and whooping and jawing like Injuns; then Bob called the Child names, and the Child called him names back again; next, Bob called him a heap rougher names; and the Child come back at him with the very worst kind of language; next, Bob knocked the Child's hat off, and the Child picked up and kicked Bob's ribbony hat about six foot; Bob went and got it and said never mind, this warn't going to be the last of this thing, because he was a man that never forgot and never forgive, and so the Child better look out, for there was a time a-coming, just as sure as he was a living man, that he would have to answer to him with the best blood in his body. The Child said no man was willinger than he for that time to come, and he would give Bob fair warning, *now*, never to cross his path again, for he could never rest till he had waded in his blood, for such was his nature, though he was sparing him now on account of his family, if he had one.

Both of them was edging away in different directions, growling and shaking their heads and going on about what they was going to do; but a little black-whiskered chap skipped up and says:

"Come back here, you couple of chicken-livered cowards, and I'll thrash the two of ye!"

And he done it, too. He snatched them, he jerked them this way and that, he booted them around, he knocked them sprawling faster than they could get up. Why, it warn't two minutes till they begged like dogs—and how the other lot did yell and laugh and clap their hands all the way through, and shout, "Sail in, Corpse-Maker!" "Hi! at him again, Child of Calamity!" "Bully for you, little Davy!" Well, it was a perfect pow-wow for a while, Bob and the Child had red noses and black eyes when they got through. Little Davy made them own up that they was sneaks and cowards and not fit to eat with a dog or drink with a nigger; then Bob and the Child shook hands with each other, very solemn, and said they had always respected each other and

was willing to let bygones be bygones. So then they washed their faces in the river; and just then there was a loud order to stand by for a crossing, and some of them went forward to man the sweeps there, and the rest went aft to handle the after sweeps.

I lay still and waited for fifteen minutes, and had a smoke out of a pipe that one of them left in reach; then the crossing was finished, and they stumped back and had a drink around and went to talking and singing again. Next they got out an old fiddle, and one played, and another patted juba, and the rest turned themselves loose on a regular old-fashioned keelboat breakdown. They couldn't keep that up very long without getting winded, so by and by they settled around the jug again.

They sung "Jolly, Jolly Raftsman's the Life for Me," with a rousing chorus, and then they got to talking about differences betwixt hogs, and their different kind of habits; and next about women and their different kind of ways; and next about the best ways to put out houses that was afire; and next about what ought to be done with the Injuns; and next what a king had to do, and how much he got; and next about how to make cats fight; and next what to do when a man has fits; and next about the differences betwixt clear-water rivers and muddy-water ones. The man they called Ed said the muddy Mississippi water was wholesomer to drink than the clear water of the Ohio; he said if you let a pint of yaller Mississippi water settle, you would have about a half to three-quarters of an inch of mud in the bottom, according to the stage of the river, and then it warn't no better than Ohio water —what you want to do was to keep it stirred up— and when the river was low, keep mud on hand to put in and thicken the water up the way it ought to be.

The Child of Calamity said that was so; he said there was nutritiousness in the mud, and a man that drunk Mississippi water could grow corn in his stomach if he wanted to. He says:

"You look at the graveyards; that tells the tale. Trees won't grow worth shucks in a Cincinnati graveyard, but in a Sent Louis graveyard they grow upwards of eight hundred foot high. It's all on account of the water the people drunk before they laid up. A Cincinnati corpse don't richen a soil any."

And they talked about how Ohio water didn't like to mix with Mississippi water. Ed said if you take the Mississippi on a rise when the Ohio is low, you'll find a wide band of clear water all the way down the east side of the Mississippi for a hundred mile or more, and the minute you get out a quarter of a mile from shore and pass the line, it is all thick and yaller the rest of the way across. They talked about how to keep tobacco from getting mouldy, and from that they went to ghosts and told about a lot that other folks had seen; but Ed says:

"Why don't you tell something that you've seen yourselves? Now let me have a say. Five years ago I was on a raft as big as this, and right along here it was a bright moonshiny night, and I was on watch and boss of the stabboard oar forrard, and one of my pards was a man named Dick Allbright, and he come along to where I was sitting, forrard— gaping and stretching, he was—and stooped down on the edge of the raft and washed his face in the river, and come and set down by me and got out his pipe, and had just got it filled, when he looks up and says:

"'Why looky-here,' he says, 'ain't that Buck Miller's place, over yander in the bend?'

"'Yes,' says I, 'it is—why?' He laid his pipe down and leaned his head on his hand, and says:

"'I thought we'd be furder down.' I says:

"'I thought it, too, when I went off watch'—we was standing six hours on and six off—'but the boys told me,' I says, 'that the raft didn't seem to hardly move, for the last hour,' says I, 'though she's a-slipping along all right now,' says I. He give a kind of a groan, and says:

"'I seed a raft act so before, along here,' he says, ''pears to me the current has most quit above the head of this bend durin' the last two years,' he says.

"Well, he raised up two or three times, and looked away off and around on the water. That started me at it, too. A body is always doing what he sees somebody else doing, though there mayn't be no sense in it. Pretty soon I see a black something floating on the water away off to stabboard and quartering behind us. I see he was looking at it, too, I says:

"'What's that?' He says, sort of pettish:

"''Tain't nothing but an old empty bar'l.'

"'An empty bar'l!' says I, 'why,' says I, 'a spy-glass is a fool to your eyes. How can you tell it's an empty bar'l?' He says:

"'I don't know; I reckon it ain't a bar'l, but I thought it might be,' says he.

"'Yes,' I says, 'so it might be, and it might be anything else, too; a body can't tell nothing about it, such a distance as that,' I says.

"We hadn't nothing else to do, so we kept on watching it. By and by I says,

"'Why, looky-here, Dick Allbright, that thing's a-gaining on us, I believe.'

"He never said nothing. The thing gained and gained, and I judged it must be a dog that was about tired out. Well, we swung down into the crossing, and the thing floated across the bright streak of the moonshine, and by George, it was a bar'l. Says I:

"'Dick Allbright, what made you think that thing was a bar'l, when it was half a mile off?' says I. Says he:

"'I don't know.' Says I:

"'You tell me, Dick Allbright.' Says he:

"'Well, I knowed it was a bar'l; I've seen it before; lots has seen it; they says it's a ha'nted bar'l.'

"I called the rest of the watch, and they come and stood there, and I told them what Dick said. It floated right along abreast, now, and didn't gain any more. It was about twenty foot off. Some was for having it aboard, but the rest didn't want to. Dick Allbright said rafts that had fooled with it had got bad luck by it. The captain of the watch said he didn't believe in it. He said he reckoned the bar'l gained on us because it was in a little better current than what we was. He said it would leave by and by.

"So then we went to talking about other things, and we had a song, and then a breakdown; and after that the captain of the watch called for another song; but it was clouding up now, and the bar'l stuck right thar in the same place, and the song didn't seem to have much warm-up to it, somehow, and so they didn't finish it, and there warn't any cheers, but it sort of dropped flat, and nobody said anything for a minute. Then everybody tried to talk at once, and one chap got off a joke, but it warn't no use, they didn't laugh, and even the chap that made the joke didn't laugh at it, which ain't usual. We all just settled down glum, and watched the bar'l, and was oneasy and oncomfortable. Well, sir, it shut down black and still, and then the wind began to moan around, and next the lightning began to play and the thunder to grumble. And pretty soon there was a regular storm, and in the middle of it a man that was running aft stumbled and fell and sprained his ankle so that he had to lay up. This made the boys shake their heads. And every time the lightning come, there was that bar'l, with the blue lights winking around it. We was always on the lookout for it. But by and by, toward dawn, she was gone. When the day come we couldn't see her anywhere, and we warn't sorry, either.

"But next night about half past nine, when there was songs and high jinks going on, here she comes again, and took her old roost on the stabboard side. There warn't no more high jinks. Everybody got solemn; nobody talked; you couldn't get anybody to do anything but set around moody and look at the bar'l. It begun to cloud up again. When the watch changed, the off watch stayed up, 'stead of turning in. The storm ripped and roared around all night, and in the middle of it another man tripped and sprained his ankle, and had to knock off. The bar'l left toward day, and nobody see it go.

"Everybody was sober and down in the mouth all day. I don't mean the kind of sober that comes of leaving liquor alone—not that. They was quiet, but they all drunk more than usual—not together, but each man sidled off and took it private, by himself.

"After dark the off watch didn't turn in; nobody sung, nobody talked; the boys didn't scatter around, neither; they sort of huddled together, forrard; and for two hours they set there, perfectly still, looking steady in the one direction, and heaving a sigh once in a while. And then, here comes the bar'l again. She took up her old place. She stayed there all night; nobody turned in. The storm come on again, after midnight. It got awful dark; and the rain poured down; hail, too; the thunder boomed and roared and bellowed; the wind blowed a hurricane; and the lightning spread over everything in big sheets of glare, and showed the whole raft as plain as day; and the river lashed up white as milk as far as you could see for miles, and there was that bar'l jiggering along, same as ever. The captain ordered the watch to man the after sweeps for a crossing, and nobody would go—no more sprained ankles for them, they said. They wouldn't even *walk* aft. Well, then, just then the sky split wide open, with a crash, and the lightning killed two men of the after watch, and crippled two more. Crippled them how, say you? Why, *sprained their ankles!*

"The bar'l left in the dark betwixt lightnings, toward dawn. Well, not a body eat a bite at breakfast that morning. After that the men loafed around in twos and threes, and talked low together. But none of them herded with Dick Allbright. They all give him the cold shake. If he come around where any of the men was, they split up and sidled away. They wouldn't man the sweeps with him. The captain had all the skiffs hauled up on the raft, alongside of his wigwam, and wouldn't let the dead men be took ashore to be planted; he didn't believe a man that got ashore would come back; and he was right.

"After night come, you could see pretty plain that there was going to be trouble if that bar'l come again; there was such a muttering going on. A good many wanted to kill Dick Allbright, because he'd seen the bar'l on other trips, and that had an ugly look. Some wanted to put him ashore. Some said: 'Let's all go ashore in a pile, if the bar'l comes again.'

"This kind of whispers was still going on, the men being bunched together forrard watching for the bar'l, when lo and behold you here she comes again. Down she comes, slow and steady, and settles into her old tracks. You could 'a' heard a pin drop. Then up comes the captain, and says:

"'Boys, don't be a pack of children and fools; I don't want this bar'l to be dogging us all the way to Orleans, and *you* don't: Well, then, how's the best way to stop it? Burn it up—that's the way. I'm going to fetch it aboard,' he says. And before anybody could say a word, in he went.

"He swum to it, and as he come pushing it to the raft, the men spread to one side. But the old man got it aboard and busted in the head, and there was a baby in it! Yes, sir; a stark-naked baby. It was Dick Allbright's baby; he owned up and said so.

"'Yes,' he says, a-leaning over it, 'yes, it is my own lamented darling, my poor lost Charles William Allbright deceased,' says he—for he could curl his tongue around the bulliest words in the language when he was of a mind to, and lay them before you without a jint started anywheres. Yes, he said, he used to live up at the head of this bend, and one night he choked his child, which was crying, not intending to kill it—which was prob'ly a lie—and then he was scared, and buried it in a bar'l, before his wife got home, and off he went, and struck the northern trail and went to rafting; and this was the third year that the bar'l had chased him. He said the bad luck always begun light, and lasted till four men was killed, and then the bar'l didn't come any more after that. He said if the men would stand it one more night—and was a-going on like that—but the men had got enough. They started to get out a boat to take him ashore and lynch him, but he grabbed the little child all of a sudden and jumped overboard with it, hugged up to his breast and shedding tears, and we never see him again, poor old suffering soul, nor Charles William neither."

"*Who* was shedding tears?" says Bob; "was it Allbright or the baby?"

"Why, Allbright, of course; didn't I tell you the baby was dead? Been dead three years—how could it cry?"

"Well, never mind how it could cry—how could it *keep* all that time?" says Davy. "You answer me that."

"I don't know how it done it," says Ed. "It done it, though—that's all I know about it."

"Say—what did they do with the bar'l?" says the Child of Calamity.

"Why, they hove it overboard, and it sunk like a chunk of lead."

"Edward, did the child look like it was choked?" says one.

"Did it have its hair parted?" says another.

"What was the brand on that bar'l, Eddy?" says a fellow they called Bill.

"Have you got the papers for them statistics, Edmund?" says Jimmy.

"Say, Edwin, was you one of the men that was killed by the lightning?" says Davy.

"Him? Oh, no! he was both of 'em," says Bob. Then they all haw-hawed.

"Say, Edward, don't you reckon you'd better take a pill? You look bad—don't you feel pale?" says the Child of Calamity.

"Oh, come, now, Eddy," says Jimmy, "show up; you must 'a' kept part of that bar'l to prove the thing by. Show us the bung-hole—*do*—and we'll all believe you."

"Say, boys," says Bill, "less divide it up. Thar's thirteen of us. I can swaller a thirteenth of the yarn, if you can worry down the rest."

Ed got up mad and said they could all go to some place which he ripped out pretty savage, and then walked off aft, cussing to himself, and they yelling and jeering at him, and roaring and laughing so you could hear them a mile.

"Boys, we'll split a watermelon on that," says the Child of Calamity; and he came rummaging around in the dark amongst the shingle bundles where I was, and put his hand on me. I was warm and soft and naked; so he says "Ouch!" and jumped back.

"Fetch a lantern or a chunk of fire here, boys—there's a snake here as big as a cow!"

So they run there with a lantern, and crowded up and looked in on me.

"Come out of that, you beggar!" says one.

"Who are you?" says another.

"What are you after here? Speak up prompt, or overboard you go."

"Snake him out, boys. Snatch him out by the heels."

I began to beg, and crept out amongst them trembling. They looked me over, wondering, and the Child of Calamity says:

"A cussed thief! Lend me a hand and less heave him overboard!"

"No," says Big Bob, "less get out the paint-pot and paint him a sky-blue all over from head to heel, and *then* heave him over."

"Good! that's it. Go for the paint, Jimmy."

When the paint came, and Bob took the brush and was just going to begin, the others laughing and rubbing their hands, I begun to cry, and that sort of worked on Davy, and he says:

"'Vast there. He's nothing but a cub. I'll paint the man that teches him!"

So I looked around on them, and some of them grumbled and growled, and Bob put down the paint, and the others didn't take it up.

"Come here to the fire, and less see what you're up to here," says Davy. "Now set down there and give an account of yourself. How long have you been aboard here?"

"Not over a quarter of a minute, sir," says I.

"How did you get dry so quick?"

"I don't know, sir, I'm always that way, mostly."

"Oh, you are, are you? What's your name?"

I warn't going to tell my name. I didn't know what to say, so I just says:

"Charles William Allbright, sir."

Then they roared—the whole crowd; and I was mighty glad I said that, because, maybe, laughing would get them in a better humor.

When they got done laughing, Davy says:

"It won't hardly do, Charles William. You couldn't have growed this much in five year, and you was a baby, when you come out of the bar'l, you know, and dead at that. Come now, tell a straight story, and nobody'll hurt you, if you ain't up to anything wrong. What *is* your name?"

"Aleck Hopkins, sir. Aleck James Hopkins."

"Well, Aleck, where did you come from here?"

"From a trading-scow. She lays up the bend yonder. I was born on her. Pap has traded up and down here all his life; and he told me to swim off here, because when you went by he said he would like to get some of you to speak to a Mr. Jonas Turner, in Cairo, and tell him—"

"Oh, come!"

"Yes, sir, it's as true as the world. Pap he says—"

"Oh, your grandmother!"

They all laughed, and I tried again to talk, but they broke in on me and stopped me.

"Now, looky-here," says Davy; "you're scared, and so you talk wild. Honest, now do you live in a scow, or is it a lie?"

"Yes, sir, in a trading-scow. She lays up at the

head of the bend. But I warn't born in her. It's our first trip."

"Now you're talking! What did you come aboard here for? To steal?"

"No, sir, I didn't. It was only to get a ride on the raft. All boys does that."

"Well, I know that. But what did you hide for?"

"Sometimes they drive the boys off."

"So they do. They might steal. Looky-here; if we let you off this time, will you keep out of these kind of scrapes hereafter?"

"'Deed I will, boss. You try me."

"All right, then. You ain't but little ways from shore. Overboard with you, and don't you make a fool of yourself another time this way. Blast it, boy, some raftsmen would rawhide you till you were black and blue!"

I didn't wait to kiss good-by, but went overboard and broke for shore. When Jim come along by and by, the big raft was far away out of sight around the point. I swum out and got aboard, and was mighty glad to see home again.

The boy did not get the information he was after, but his adventure has furnished the glimpse of the departed raftsman and keelboatman which I desire to offer in this place.

CHAPTER IV

The Boys' Ambition

When I was a boy, there was but one permanent ambition among my comrades in our village on the west bank of the Mississippi River. That was, to be a steamboatman. We had transient ambitions of other sorts, but they were only transient. When a circus came and went, it left us all burning to become clowns; the first negro minstrel show that ever came to our section left us all suffering to try that kind of life; now and then we had a hope that, if we lived and were good, God would permit us to be pirates. These ambitions faded out, each in its turn; but the ambition to be a steamboatman always remained.

Once a day a cheap, gaudy packet arrived upward from St. Louis, and another downward from Keokuk. Before these events, the day was glorious with expectancy; after them, the day was a dead and empty thing. Not only the boys, but the whole village, felt this. After all these years I can picture that old time to myself now, just as it was then: the white town drowsing in the sunshine of a summer's morning; the streets empty, or pretty nearly so; one or two clerks sitting in front of the Water Street stores, with their splint-bottomed chairs tilted back against the walls, chins on breasts, hats slouched over their faces, asleep—with shingle-shavings enough around to show what broke them down; a sow and a litter of pigs loafing along the sidewalk, doing a good business in watermelon rinds and seeds; two or three lonely little freight piles scattered about the "levee"; a pile of "skids" on the slope of the stone-paved wharf, and the fragrant town drunkard asleep in the shadow of them; two or three wood flats at the head of the wharf, but nobody to listen to the peaceful lapping of the wavelets against them; the great Mississippi, the majestic, the magnificent Mississippi, rolling its mile-wide tide along, shining in the sun; the dense forest away on the other side; the "point" above the town, and the "point" below, bounding the river-glimpse and turning it into a sort of sea, and withal a very still and brilliant and lonely one. Presently a film of dark smoke appears above one of those remote "points"; instantly a negro drayman, famous for his quick eye and prodigious voice, lifts up the cry, "S-t-e-a-m-boat a-comin'!" and the scene changes! The town drunkard stirs, the clerks wake up, a furious clatter of drays follows, every house and store pours out a human contribution, and all in a twinkling the dead town is alive and moving. Drays, carts, men, boys, all go hurrying from many quarters to a common center, the wharf. Assembled there, the people fasten their eyes upon the coming boat as upon a wonder they are seeing for the first time. And the boat *is* rather a handsome sight, too. She is long and sharp and trim and pretty; she has two tall, fancy-topped chimneys, with a gilded device of some kind swung between them; a fanciful pilot-house, all glass and "gingerbread," perched on top of the "texas" deck behind them; the paddle-boxes are gorgeous with a picture or with gilded rays above the boat's name; the boiler-deck, the hurricane-deck, and the texas deck are fenced and ornamented with clean white railings; there is a flag gallantly flying from the jack-staff; the furnace doors are open and the fires glaring bravely; the upper decks are black with passengers; the captain stands by the big bell, calm, imposing, the envy of all; great volumes of the blackest smoke are rolling and tumbling out of the chimneys—a husbanded grandeur created with a bit of pitch-pine just before arriving at a town; the crew are grouped on the forecastle; the broad stage is run far out over the port bow, and an envied deck-hand stands picturesquely on the end of it with a coil of rope in his hand; the pent steam is screaming through the gauge-cocks; the captain lifts his hand, a bell rings, the wheels stop; then they turn back, churning the water to foam, and the steamer is at rest. Then such a scramble as there is to get aboard, and to get ashore, and to take in freight and to discharge freight, all at one and the same time; and such a yelling and cursing as the mates facilitate it all with! Ten minutes later the steamer is under way again, with no flag on the jack-staff and no black smoke issuing from the chimneys. After ten more minutes the town is dead again, and the town drunkard asleep by the skids once more.

My father was a justice of the peace, and I supposed he possessed the power of life and death over all men, and could hang anybody that offended him. This was distinction enough for me as a general thing; but the desire to be a steamboatman kept intruding, nevertheless. I first wanted to be a cabin-boy, so that I could come out with a white apron on and shake a table-cloth over the side, where all my old comrades could see me; later I thought I would rather be the deck-hand who stood on the end of the stage-plank with the coil of rope in his hand, because he was particularly conspicuous. But these were only day-dreams—they were too heavenly to be contemplated as real possibilities. By and by one of our boys went away. He was not heard of for a long time. At last he turned up as apprentice engineer or "striker" on a steamboat. This thing shook the bottom out of all my Sunday-school teachings. That boy had been notoriously worldly, and I just the reverse; yet he was exalted to this eminence, and I left in obscurity and misery. There was nothing generous about this fellow in his greatness. He would always manage to have a rusty bolt to scrub while his boat tarried at our town, and he would sit on the inside guard and scrub it, where we all could see him and envy him and loathe him. And whenever his boat was laid up he would come home and swell around the town in his blackest and greasiest clothes, so that nobody could help remembering that he was a steamboatman; and he used all sorts of steamboat technicalities in his talk, as if he were so used to them that he forgot common people could not understand them. He would speak of the "lab-board" side of a horse in an easy, natural way that would make one wish he was dead. And he was always talking about "St. Looy" like an old citizen; he would refer casually to occasions when he was "coming down Fourth Street," or when he was "passing by the Planter's House," or when there was a fire and he took a turn on the brakes of "the old Big Missouri"; and then he would go on and lie about how many towns the size of ours were burned down there that day. Two or three of the boys had long been persons of consideration among us because they had been to St. Louis once and had a vague general knowledge of its wonders, but the day of their glory was over now. They lapsed into a humble silence, and learned to disappear when the ruthless "cub"-engineer approached. This fellow had money, too, and hair-oil. Also an ignorant silver watch and a showy brass watch-chain. He wore a leather belt and used no suspenders. If ever a youth was cordially admired and hated by his comrades, this one was. No girl could withstand his charms. He "cut out" every boy in the village. When his boat blew up at last, it diffused a tranquil contentment among us such as we had not known for months. But when he came home the next week, alive, renowned, and appeared in church all battered up and bandaged, a shining hero, stared at and wondered over by everybody, it seemed to us that the partiality of Providence for an undeserving reptile had reached a point where it was open to criticism.

This creature's career could produce but one result, and it speedily followed. Boy after boy managed to get on the river. The minister's son became an engineer. The doctor's and the postmaster's sons became "mud clerks"; the wholesale liquor dealer's son became a barkeeper on a boat; four sons of the chief merchant, and two sons of the county judge, became pilots. Pilot was the grandest position of all. The pilot, even in those days of trivial wages, had a princely salary—from a hundred and fifty to two hundred and fifty dollars a month, and no board to pay. Two months of his wages would pay a preacher's salary for a year. Now some of us were left disconsolate. We could not get on the river—at least our parents would not let us.

So, by and by, I ran away. I said I would never come home again till I was a pilot and could come in glory. But somehow I could not manage it. I went meekly aboard a few of the boats that lay packed together like sardines at the long St. Louis wharf, and humbly inquired for the pilots, but got only a cold shoulder and short words from mates and clerks. I had to make the best of this sort of treatment for the time being, but I had comforting day-dreams of a future when I should be a great and honored pilot, with plenty of money, and could kill some of these mates and clerks and pay for them.

HENRY JAMES

1843–1916

Henry James was born in New York, April 15, 1843. In an age of American progress in business and industrialism, his father, a scholar and a theologian who had written a book upon Swedenborg, allowed his sons little contact with the American business civilization and undertook deliberately to educate them as citizens of the world. As a result, from the time he was six Henry James traveled in Europe, securing a desultory schooling from tutors at Albany, Newport, Geneva, Paris, and other European cities of a cosmopolitan range. In 1869 he made his first adult "passionate pilgrimage" to Europe, and in 1875 settled there permanently, first in Paris and then in London.

During the next forty years, until his death in 1916, James devoted himself with an almost monastic zeal to the cultivation of the art of fiction with a remarkable integrity of purpose. He began with the study of Continental fiction in Flaubert, Balzac, and Turgenev, whom he admired extravagantly, and gradually evolved his own aesthetic of prose fiction which he embodied in permanent critical form in the prefaces to the New York edition of his works, 1907–1909. He found the contemporary novel too crude in structure and method to bear the weight of the psychological analysis he wished to exemplify in his characters; he consequently experimented extensively, particularly in the manipulation of the point of view in fiction. The influence of his fictional techniques has been exerted in the twentieth century upon such novelists of widely diverse tendencies as Virginia Woolf, Edith Wharton, Willa Cather, William Faulkner, and Elizabeth Bowen.

James' fictional subject matter was for the most part the treatment of contrasts between Europeans and Americans, a theme which he adopted as early as the successful *Daisy Miller* (1879), in which he portrays the gaucheries of the American girl and her mother in Europe. He felt strongly the deficiencies of refinement and subtlety in provincial American manners and the lack of traditions in America that seriously handicapped the creative artist in his attempt to utilize American material, as he observed of Hawthorne in his study of that writer in 1879.

James has often been severely criticized for his expatriation (he became an English citizen before he died), but a careful reading throughout the whole range of his fiction, from *The American* (1877) and *The Portrait of a Lady* (1881) to the most difficult novels of his last period, *The Wings of the Dove* (1902) and *The Golden Bowl* (1904), will reveal that he often depicts Americans as far more honest and admirable than their European counterparts. A more just criticism of James is that his work embraces very narrow limits, treating almost wholly the finely tempered and beautifully bred persons of an international society involved in subtle studies of personal betrayals that lurk beneath the seemingly serene and perfectly arranged social relationships of the principals. Nevertheless, within that range his imagination penetrates deeply; and it is capable of encompassing intuitively a stratum of society with which he was not acquainted at all, the anarchists of *The Princess Casamassima* (1886).

The recent revival of Henry James is perhaps in part an indication of his still valid contribution to the return in the fictional trends of the nineteen-forties of an emphasis upon conscience, on moral responsibility of the individual. His short story "Europe" admirably illustrates James' study of this moral responsibility and his regard for Europe as a symbol of the means by which the individual may be brought out, may learn to live the more abundant life.

FURTHER READING

Dupee, F. W. *Henry James* (New York, 1951).
Dupee, F. W. *The Question of Henry James* (New York, 1945).
James, Henry. *Notes of a Son and Brother* (New York, 1914).
Kenyon Review, Vol. V, No. 4 (Autumn, 1943: "The Henry James Number").
Matthiessen, F. O. *Henry James: The Major Phase* (New York, 1944).

"Europe" *

I

"Our feeling is, you know, that Becky should go." The earnest little remark comes back to me, even after long years, as the first note of something that began, for my observation, the day I went with my sister-in-law to take leave of her good friends. It's a memory of the American time, which revives so at present—under some touch that doesn't signify —that it rounds itself off as an anecdote. That walk to say good-bye was the beginning; and the end, so far as I enjoyed a view of it, was not till long after; yet even the end also appears to me now as of the old days. I went, in those days, on occasion, to see my sister-in-law, in whose affairs, on my brother's death, I had had to take a helpful hand. I continued to go indeed after these little matters were straightened out, for the pleasure, periodically, of the impression—the change to the almost pastoral sweetness of the good Boston suburb from the loud longitudinal New York. It was another world, with other manners, a different tone, a different taste; a savour nowhere so mild, yet so distinct, as in the square white house—with the pair of elms, like gigantic wheat-sheaves, in front, the rustic orchard not far behind, the old-fashioned door-lights, the big blue-and-white jars in the porch, the straight bricked walk from the high gate—that enshrined the extraordinary merit of Mrs. Rimmle and her three daughters.

These ladies were so much of the place and the place so much of themselves that from the first of their being revealed to me I felt that nothing else at Brookbridge much mattered. They were what, for me, at any rate, Brookbridge had most to give: I mean in the way of what it was naturally strongest in, the thing we called in New York the New England expression, the air of Puritanism reclaimed and refined. The Rimmles had brought this down to a wonderful delicacy. They struck me even then—all four almost equally—as very ancient and very earnest, and I think theirs must have been the house in all the world in which "culture" first came to the aid of morning calls. The head of the family was the widow of a great public character—as public characters were understood at Brookbridge—whose speeches on anniversaries formed a part of the body of national eloquence spouted in the New England schools by little boys covetous of the most marked, though perhaps the easiest, distinction. He was reported to have been celebrated, and in such fine declamatory connexions that he seemed to gesticulate even from the tomb. He was understood to have made, in his wife's company, the tour of Europe at a date not immensely removed from that of the battle of Waterloo. What was the age then of the bland firm antique Mrs. Rimmle at the period

of her being first revealed to me? That's a point I'm not in a position to determine—I remember mainly that I was young enough to regard her as having reached the limit. And yet the limit for Mrs. Rimmle must have been prodigiously extended; the scale of its extension is in fact the very moral of this reminiscence. She was old, and her daughters were old, but I was destined to know them all as older. It was only by comparison and habit that—however much I recede—Rebecca, Maria and Jane were the "young ladies."

I think it was felt that, though their mother's life, after thirty years of widowhood, had had a grand backward stretch, her blandness and firmness—and this in spite of her extreme physical frailty—would be proof against any surrender not overwhelmingly justified by time. It had appeared, years before, at a crisis of which the waves had not even yet quite subsided, a surrender not justified by anything nameable that she should go to Europe with her daughters and for her health. Her health was supposed to require constant support; but when it had at that period tried conclusions with the idea of Europe it was not the idea of Europe that had been insidious enough to prevail. She hadn't gone, and Becky, Maria and Jane hadn't gone, and this was long ago. They still merely floated in the air of the visit achieved, with such introductions and such acclamations, in the early part of the century; they still, with fond glances at the sunny parlour-walls, only referred, in conversation, to divers pictorial and other reminders of it. The Misses Rimmle had quite been brought up on it, but Becky, as the most literary, had most mastered the subject. There were framed letters—tributes to their eminent father—suspended among the mementoes, and of two or three of these, the most foreign and complimentary, Becky had executed translations that figured beside the text. She knew already, through this and other illumination, so much about Europe that it was hard to believe for her in that limit of adventure which consisted only of her having been twice to Philadelphia. The others hadn't been to Philadelphia, but there was a legend that Jane had been to Saratoga. Becky was a short stout fair person with round serious eyes, a high forehead, the sweetest neatest enunciation, and a miniature of her father—"done in Rome"—worn as a breastpin. She had written the life, she had edited the speeches, of the original of this ornament, and now at last, beyond the seas, she was really to tread in his footsteps.

Fine old Mrs. Rimmle, in the sunny parlour and with a certain austerity of cap and chair—though with a gay new "front" that looked like rusty brown plush—had had so unusually good a winter that the question of her sparing two members of her family for an absence had been threshed as fine, I could feel, as even under that Puritan roof any case of conscience had ever been threshed. They were to make their dash while the coast, as it were, was clear, and each of the daughters had tried—heroically, angelically and for the sake of each of her sisters—not to be one of the two. What I encountered that first time was an opportunity to concur with enthusiasm in the general idea that Becky's wonderful preparation would be wasted if she were the one to stay with their mother. Their talk of Becky's preparation (they had a sly old-maidish humour that was as mild as milk) might have been of some mixture, for application somewhere, that she kept in a precious bottle. It had been settled at all events that, armed with this concoction and borne aloft by their introductions, she and Jane were to start. They were wonderful on their introductions, which proceeded naturally from their mother and were addressed to the charming families that in vague generations had so admired vague Mr. Rimmle. Jane, I found at Brookbridge, had to be described, for want of other description, as the pretty one, but it wouldn't have served to identify her unless you had seen the others. *Her* preparation was only this figment of her prettiness—only, that is, unless one took into account something that, on the spot, I silently divined: the lifelong secret passionate ache of her little rebellious desire. They were all growing old in the yearning to go, but Jane's yearning was the sharpest. She struggled with it as people at Brookbridge mostly struggled with what they liked, but fate, by threatening to prevent what she *dis*liked and what was therefore duty—which was to stay at home instead of Maria—had bewildered her, I judged, not a little. It was she who, in the words I have quoted, mentioned to me Becky's case and Becky's affinity as the clearest of all. Her mother moreover had on the general subject still more to say.

"I positively desire, I really quite insist that they shall go," the old lady explained to us from her stiff chair. "We've talked about it so often, and they've had from me so clear an account—I've amused them again and again with it—of what's to be seen and enjoyed. If they've had hitherto too many duties to leave, the time seems to have come to recognise

that there are also many duties to *seek*. Wherever we go we find them—I always remind the girls of that. There's a duty that calls them to those wonderful countries, just as it called, at the right time, their father and myself—if it be only that of laying-up for the years to come the same store of remarkable impressions, the same wealth of knowledge and food for conversation as, since my return, I've found myself so happy to possess." Mrs. Rimmle spoke of her return as of something of the year before last, but the future of her daughters was somehow, by a different law, to be on the scale of great vistas, of endless aftertastes. I think that, without my being quite ready to say it, even this first impression of her was somewhat upsetting; there was a large placid perversity, a grim secrecy of intention, in her estimate of the ages.

"Well, I'm so glad you don't delay it longer," I said to Miss Becky before we withdrew. "And whoever should go," I continued in the spirit of the sympathy with which the good sisters had already inspired me, "I quite feel, with your family, you know, that *you* should. But of course I hold that every one should." I suppose I wished to attenuate my solemnity; there was, however, something in it I couldn't help. It must have been a faint foreknowledge.

"Have you been a great deal yourself?" Miss Jane, I remembered, enquired.

"Not so much but that I hope to go a good deal more. So perhaps we shall meet," I encouragingly suggested.

I recall something—something in the nature of susceptibility to encouragement—that this brought into the more expressive brown eyes to which Miss Jane mainly owed it that she was the pretty one. "Where, do you think?"

I tried to think. "Well, on the Italian lakes—Como, Bellaggio, Lugano." I liked to say the names to them.

"'Sublime, but neither bleak nor bare—nor misty are the mountains there!'" Miss Jane softly breathed, while her sister looked at her as if her acquaintance with the poetry of the subject made her the most interesting feature of the scene she evoked.

But Miss Becky presently turned to me. "Do you know everything—?"

"Everything?"

"In Europe."

"Oh yes," I laughed, "and one or two things even in America."

The sisters seemed to me furtively to look at each other. "Well, you'll have to be quick—to meet *us*," Miss Jane resumed.

"But surely when you're once there you'll stay on."

"Stay on?"—they murmured it simultaneously and with the oddest vibration of dread as well as of desire. It was as if they had been in presence of a danger and yet wished me, who "knew everything," to torment them with still more of it.

Well, I did my best. "I mean it will never do to cut it short."

"No, that's just what I keep saying," said brilliant Jane. "It would be better in that case not to go."

"Oh, don't talk about not going—at this time!" It was none of my business, but I felt shocked and impatient.

"No, not at *this* time!" broke in Miss Maria, who, very red in the face, had joined us. Poor Miss Maria was known as the flushed one; but she was not flushed—she only had an unfortunate surface. The third day after this was to see them embark.

Miss Becky, however, desired as little as any one to be in any way extravagant. "It's only the thought of our mother," she explained.

I looked a moment at the old lady, with whom my sister-in-law was engaged. "Well—your mother's magnificent."

"*Isn't* she magnificent?"—they eagerly took it up.

She *was*—I could reiterate it with sincerity, though I perhaps mentally drew the line when Miss Maria again risked, as a fresh ejaculation: "I think she's better than Europe!"

"Maria!" they both, at this, exclaimed with a strange emphasis: it was as if they feared she had suddenly turned cynical over the deep domestic drama of their casting of lots. The innocent laugh with which she answered them gave the measure of her cynicism.

We separated at last, and my eyes met Mrs. Rimmle's as I held for an instant her aged hand. It was doubtless only my fancy that her calm cold look quietly accused me of something. Of what *could* it accuse me? Only, I thought, of thinking.

II

I left Brookbridge the next day, and for some time after that had no occasion to hear from my kinswoman; but when she finally wrote there was a passage in her letter that affected me more than all the rest. "Do you know the poor Rimmles never, after all, 'went'? The old lady, at the eleventh hour,

broke down; everything broke down, and all of *them* on top of it, so that the dear things are with us still. Mrs. Rimmle, the night after our call, had, in the most unexpected manner, a turn for the worse—something in the nature (though they're rather mysterious about it) of a seizure; Becky and Jane felt it—dear devoted stupid angels that they are—heartless to leave her at such a moment, and Europe's indefinitely postponed. However, they think they're still going—or *think* they think it—when she's better. They also think—or think they think—that she *will* be better. I certainly pray she may." So did I—quite fervently. I was conscious of a real pang—I didn't know how much they had made me care.

Late that winter my sister-in-law spent a week in New York; when almost my first enquiry on meeting her was about the health of Mrs. Rimmle.

"Oh she's rather bad—she really is, you know. It's not surprising that at her age she should be infirm."

"Then what the deuce *is* her age?"

"I can't tell you to a year—but she's immensely old."

"That of course I saw," I replied—"unless you literally mean so old that the records have been lost."

My sister-in-law thought. "Well, I believe she wasn't positively young when she married. She lost three or four children before these women were born."

We surveyed together a little, on this, the "dark backward." "And they were born, I gather, *after* the famous tour? Well then, as the famous tour was in a manner to celebrate—wasn't it?—the restoration of the Bourbons—" I considered, I gasped. "My dear child, what on earth do you make her out?"

My relative, with her Brookbridge habit, transferred her share of the question to the moral plane—turned it forth to wander, by implication at least, in the sandy desert of responsibility. "Well, you know, we all immensely admire her."

"You can't admire her more than I do. She's awful."

My converser looked at me with a certain fear. "She's *really* ill."

"Too ill to get better?"

"Oh no—we hope not. Because then they'll be able to go."

"And *will* they go if she should?"

"Oh the moment they should be quite satisfied. I mean *really*," she added.

I'm afraid I laughed at her—the Brookbridge "really" was a thing so by itself. "But if she shouldn't get better?" I went on.

"Oh don't speak of it! They want so to go."

"It's a pity they're so infernally good," I mused.

"No—don't say that. It's what keeps them up."

"Yes, but isn't it what keeps *her* up too?"

My visitor looked grave. "Would you like them to kill her?"

I don't know that I was then prepared to say I should—though I believe I came very near it. But later on I burst all bounds, for the subject grew and grew. I went again before the good sisters ever did —I mean I went to Europe. I think I went twice, with a brief interval, before my fate again brought round for me a couple of days at Brookbridge. I had been there repeatedly, in the previous time, without making the acquaintance of the Rimmles; but now that I had had the revelation I couldn't have it too much, and the first request I preferred was to be taken again to see them. I remember well indeed the scruple I felt—the real delicacy—about betraying that *I* had, in the pride of my power, since our other meeting, stood as their phrase went, among romantic scenes; but they were themselves the first to speak of it, and what moreover came home to me was that the coming and going of their friends in general—Brookbridge itself having even at that period one foot in Europe—was such as to place constantly before them the pleasure that was only postponed. They were thrown back after all on what the situation, under a final analysis, had most to give—the sense that, as every one kindly said to them and they kindly said to every one, Europe would keep. Every one felt for them so deeply that their own kindness in alleviating every one's feeling was really what came out most. Mrs. Rimmle was still in her stiff chair and in the sunny parlour, but if *she* made no scruple of introducing the Italian lakes my heart sank to observe that she dealt with them, as a topic, not in the least in the leave-taking manner in which Falstaff babbled of green fields.

I'm not sure that after this my pretexts for a day or two with my sister-in-law weren't apt to be a mere cover for another glimpse of these particulars: I at any rate never went to Brookbridge without an irrepressible eagerness for our customary call. A long time seems to me thus to have passed, with glimpses and lapses, considerable impatience and still more pity. Our visits indeed grew shorter, for, as my companion said, they were more and more of a strain. It finally struck me that the good sisters even shrank from me a little as from one who penetrated their consciousness in spite of himself. It was as if they knew where I thought they ought to be,

and were moved to deprecate at last, by a systematic silence on the subject of that hemisphere, the criminality I fain would fix on them. They were full instead—as with the instinct of throwing dust in my eyes—of little pathetic hypocrisies about Brookbridge interests and delights. I dare say that as time went on my deeper sense of their situation came practically to rest on my companion's report of it. I certainly think I recollect every word we ever exchanged about them, even if I've lost the thread of the special occasions. The impression they made on me after each interval always broke out with extravagance as I walked away with her.

"*She* may be as old as she likes—I don't care. It's the fearful age the 'girls' are reaching that constitutes the scandal. One shouldn't pry into such matters, I know; but the years and the chances are really going. They're all growing old together—it will presently be too late; and their mother meanwhile perches over them like a vulture—what shall I call it?—calculating. Is she waiting for them successively to drop off? She'll survive them each and all. There's something too remorseless in it."

"Yes, but what do you want her to do? If the poor thing *can't* die she can't. Do you want her to take poison or to open a blood vessel? I dare say she'd prefer to go."

"I beg your pardon," I must have replied; "you daren't say anything of the sort. If she'd prefer to go she *would* go. She'd feel the propriety, the decency, the necessity of going. She just prefers *not* to go. She prefers to stay and keep up the tension, and her calling them 'girls' and talking of the good time they'll still have is the mere conscious mischief of a subtle old witch. They won't have *any* time— there isn't any time to have! I mean there's, on her own part, no real loss of measure or of perspective in it. She *knows* she's a hundred and ten, and she takes a cruel pride in it."

My sister-in-law differed with me about this; she held that the old woman's attitude was an honest one and that her magnificent vitality, so great in spite of her infirmities, made it inevitable she should attribute youth to persons who had come into the world so much later. "Then suppose she should die?"—so my fellow student of the case always put it to me.

"Do you mean while her daughters are away? There's not the least fear of that—not even if at the very moment of their departure she should be *in extremis*. They'd find her all right on their return."

"But think how they'd feel not to have been with her!"

"That's only, I repeat, on the unsound assumption. If they'd only go tomorrow—literally make a good rush for it—they'll be with her when they come back. That will give them plenty of time." I'm afraid I even heartlessly added that if she *should,* against every probability, pass away in their absence they wouldn't have to come back at all—which would be just the compensation proper to their long privation. And then Maria would come out to join the two others, and they would be—though but for the too scanty remnant of their career—as merry as the day is long.

I remained ready, somehow, pending the fulfilment of that vision, to sacrifice Maria; it was only over the urgency of the case for the others respectively that I found myself balancing. Sometimes it was for Becky I thought the tragedy deepest—sometimes, and in quite a different manner, I thought it most dire for Jane. It was Jane after all who had most sense of life. I seemed in fact dimly to descry in Jane a sense—as yet undescried by herself or by any one—of all sorts of queer things. Why didn't *she* go? I used desperately to ask; why didn't she make a bold personal dash for it, strike up a partnership with some one or other of the travelling spinsters in whom Brookbridge more and more abounded? Well, there came a flash for me at a particular point of the grey middle desert: my correspondent was able to let me know that poor Jane at last *had* sailed. She had gone of a sudden—I liked my sister-in-law's view of suddenness—with the kind Hathaways, who had made an irresistible grab at her and lifted her off her feet. They were going for the summer and for Mr. Hathaway's health, so that the opportunity was perfect and it was impossible not to be glad that something very like physical force had finally prevailed. This was the general feeling at Brookbridge, and I might imagine what Brookbridge had been brought to from the fact that, at the very moment she was hustled off, the doctor, called to her mother at the peep of dawn, had considered that *he* at least must stay. There had been real alarm—greater than ever before; it actually did seem as if this time the end had come. But it was Becky, strange to say, who, though fully recognising the nature of the crisis, had kept the situation in hand and insisted upon action. This, I remember, brought back to me a discomfort with which I had been familiar from the first. One of the two had sailed, and I was sorry it wasn't the other. But if it had been the other I should have been equally sorry.

I saw with my eyes that very autumn what a fool Jane would have been if she had again backed out. Her mother had of course survived the peril of which I had heard, profiting by it indeed as she had profited by every other; she was sufficiently better again to have come downstairs. It was there that, as usual, I found her, but with a difference of effect produced somehow by the absence of one of the girls. It was as if, for the others, though they hadn't gone to Europe, Europe had come to them: Jane's letters had been so frequent and so beyond even what could have been hoped. It was the first time, however, that I perceived on the old woman's part a certain failure of lucidity. Jane's flight was clearly the great fact with her, but she spoke of it as if the fruit had now been plucked and the parenthesis closed. I don't know what sinking sense of still further physical duration I gathered, as a menace, from this first hint of her confusion of mind.

"My daughter has been; my daughter has been—" She kept saying it, but didn't say where; that seemed unnecessary, and she only repeated the words to her visitors with a face that was all puckers and yet now, save in so far as it expressed an ineffaceable complacency, all blankness. I think she rather wanted us to know how little she had stood in the way. It added to something—I scarce knew what—that I found myself desiring to extract privately from Becky. As our visit was to be of the shortest my opportunity—for one of the young ladies always came to the door with us—was at hand. Mrs. Rimmle, as we took leave, again sounded her phrase, but she added this time: "I'm so glad she's going to have always—"

I knew so well what she meant that, as she again dropped, looking at me queerly and becoming momentarily dim, I could help her out. "Going to have what *you* have?"

"Yes, yes—my privilege. Wonderful experience," she mumbled. She bowed to me a little as if I would understand. "She has things to tell."

I turned, slightly at a loss, to Becky. "She has then already arrived?"

Becky was at that moment looking a little strangely at her mother, who answered my question. "She reached New York this morning—she comes on today."

"Oh then—!" But I let the matter pass as I met Becky's eye—I saw there was a hitch somewhere. It was not she but Maria who came out with us; on which I cleared up the question of their sister's reappearance.

"Oh no, not tonight," Maria smiled; "that's only the way mother puts it. We shall see her about the end of November—the Hathaways are so indulgent. They kindly extend their tour."

"For *her* sake? How sweet of them!" my sister-in-law exclaimed.

I can see our friend's plain mild old face take on a deeper mildness, even though a higher colour, in the light of the open door. "Yes, it's for Jane they prolong it. And do you know what they write?" She gave us time, but it was too great a responsibility to guess. "Why that it has brought her out."

"Oh, I knew it *would!*" my companion sympathetically sighed.

Maria put it more strongly still. "They say we wouldn't know her."

This sounded a little awful, but it was after all what I had expected.

III

My correspondent in Brookbridge came to me that Christmas, with my niece, to spend a week; and the arrangement had of course been prefaced by an exchange of letters, the first of which from my sister-in-law scarce took space for acceptance of my invitation before going on to say: "The Hathaways are back—but without Miss Jane!" She presented in a few words the situation thus created at Brookbridge, but was not yet, I gathered, fully in possession of the other one—the situation created in "Europe" by the presence there of that lady. The two together, however that might be, demanded, I quickly felt, all my attention, and perhaps my impatience to receive my relative was a little sharpened by my desire for the whole story. I had it at last, by the Christmas fire, and I may say without reserve that it gave me all I could have hoped for. I listened eagerly, after which I produced the comment: "Then she simply refused—"

"To budge from Florence? Simply. She had it out there with the poor Hathaways, who felt responsible for her safety, pledged to restore her to her mother's, to her sisters' hands, and showed herself in a light, they mention under their breath, that made their dear old hair stand on end. Do you know what, when they first got back, they said of her—at least it was *his* phrase—to two or three people?"

I thought a moment. "That she had 'tasted blood'?"

My visitor fairly admired me. "How clever of you to guess! It's exactly what he did say. She appeared—she continues to appear, it seems—in a new character."

I wondered a little. "But that's exactly—don't you remember?—what Miss Maria reported to us from them; that we 'wouldn't know her.'"

My sister-in-law perfectly remembered. "Oh yes—she broke out from the first. But when they left her she was worse."

"Worse?"

"Well, different—different from anything she ever *had* been or—for that matter—had had a chance to be." My reporter hung fire a moment, but presently faced me. "Rather strange and free and obstreperous."

"Obstreperous?" I wondered again.

"Peculiarly so, I inferred, on the question of not coming away. She wouldn't hear of it and, when they spoke of her mother, said she had given her mother up. She had thought she should like Europe, but didn't know she should like it so much. They had been fools to bring her if they expected to take her away. She was going to see what she could—she hadn't yet seen half. The end of it at any rate was that they had to leave her alone."

I seemed to see it all—to see even the sacred Hathaways. "So she *is* alone?"

"She told them, poor thing, it appears, and in a tone they'll never forget, that she was in any case quite old enough to be. She cried—she quite went on—over not having come sooner. That's why the only way for her," my companion mused, "*is,* I suppose, to stay. They wanted to put her with some people or other—to find some American family. But she says she's on her own feet."

"And she's still in Florence?"

"No—I believe she was to travel. She's bent on the East."

I burst out laughing. "Magnificent Jane! It's most interesting. Only I feel that I distinctly *should* 'know' her. To my sense, always, I must tell you, she had it in her."

My relative was silent a little. "So it now appears Becky always felt."

"And yet pushed her off? Magnificent Becky!"

My companion met my eyes a moment. "You don't know the queerest part. I mean the way it has *most* brought her out."

I turned it over; I felt I should like to know—to that degree indeed that, oddly enough, I jocosely disguised my eagerness. "You don't mean she has taken to drink?"

My visitor had a dignity—and yet had to have a freedom. "She has taken to flirting."

I expressed disappointment. "Oh she took to *that* long ago. Yes," I declared at my kinswoman's stare, "she positively flirted—with *me!*"

The stare perhaps sharpened. "Then you flirted with *her*?"

"How else could I have been so sure as I wanted to be? But has she means?"

"Means to flirt?"—my friend looked an instant as if she spoke literally. "I don't understand about the means—though of course they have something. But I have my impression," she went on. "I think that Becky—" It seemed almost too grave to say.

But *I* had no doubts. "That Becky's backing her?"

She brought it out. "Financing her."

"Stupendous Becky! So that morally then—"

"Becky's quite in sympathy. But isn't it too odd?" my sister-in-law asked.

"Not in the least. Didn't we know, as regards Jane, that Europe was to bring her out? Well, it has also brought out Rebecca."

"It has indeed!" my companion indulgently sighed. "So what would it do if she were there?"

"I should like immensely to see. And we *shall* see."

"Do you believe then she'll still go?"

"Certainly. She *must*."

But my friend shook it off. "She won't."

"She shall!" I retorted with a laugh. But the next moment I said: "And what does the old woman say?"

"To Jane's behaviour? Not a word—never speaks of it. She talks now much less than she used—only seems to wait. But it's my belief she thinks."

"And—do you mean—knows?"

"Yes, knows she's abandoned. In her silence there she takes it in."

"It's her way of making Jane pay?" At this, somehow, I felt more serious. "Oh dear, dear—she'll disinherit her!"

When in the following June I went on to return my sister-in-law's visit the first object that met my eyes in her little white parlour was a figure that, to my stupefaction, presented itself for the moment as that of Mrs. Rimmle. I had gone to my room after arriving and had come down when dressed; the apparition I speak of had arisen in the interval. Its ambiguous character lasted, however, but a second or two—I had taken Becky for her mother because I knew no one but her mother of that extreme age. Becky's age was quite startling; it had made a great stride, though, strangely enough, irrecoverably seated as she now was in it, she had a wizened brightness that I had scarcely yet seen in her. I remember indulging on this occasion in two silent observations: one on the article of my not having

hitherto been conscious of her full resemblance to the old lady, and the other to the effect that, as I had said to my sister-in-law at Christmas, "Europe," even at reaching her only through Jane's sensibilities, had really at last brought her out. She was in fact "out" in a manner of which this encounter offered to my eyes a unique example: it was the single hour, often as I had been at Brookbridge, of my meeting her elsewhere than in her mother's drawing-room. I surmise that, besides being adjusted to her more marked time of life, the garments she wore abroad, and in particular her little plain bonnet, presented points of resemblance to the close sable sheath and the quaint old headgear that, in the white house behind the elms, I had from far back associated with the eternal image in the stiff chair. Of course I immediately spoke of Jane, showing an interest and asking for news; on which she answered me with a smile, but not at all as I had expected.

"*Those* are not really the things you want to know—where she is, whom she's with, how she manages and where she's going next—oh no!" And the admirable woman gave a laugh that was somehow both light and sad—sad, in particular, with a strange long weariness. "What you do want to know is when she's coming back."

I shook my head very kindly, but out of a wealth of experience that, I flattered myself, was equal to Miss Becky's. "I do know it. Never."

Miss Becky exchanged with me at this a long deep look. "Never."

We had, in silence, a little luminous talk about it, at the end of which she seemed to have told me the most interesting things. "And how's your mother?" I then enquired.

She hesitated, but finally spoke with the same serenity. "My mother's all right. You see she's not alive."

"Oh Becky!" my sister-in-law pleadingly interjected.

But Becky only addressed herself to me. "Come and see if she is. *I* think she isn't—but Maria perhaps isn't so clear. Come at all events and judge and tell me."

It was a new note, and I was a little bewildered. "Ah but I'm not a doctor!"

"No, thank God—you're not. That's why I ask you." And now she said good-bye.

I kept her hand a moment. "*You're* more alive than ever!"

"I'm very tired." She took it with the same smile, but for Becky it was much to say.

IV

"Not alive," the next day, was certainly what Mrs. Rimmle looked when, arriving in pursuit of my promise, I found her, with Miss Maria, in her usual place. Though wasted and shrunken she still occupied her high-backed chair with a visible theory of erectness, and her intensely aged face—combined with something dauntless that belonged to her very presence and that was effective even in this extremity—might have been that of some immemorial sovereign, of indistinguishable sex, brought forth to be shown to the people in disproof of the rumour of extinction. Mummified and open-eyed she looked at me, but I had no impression that she made me out. I had come this time without my sister-in-law, who had frankly pleaded to me—which also, for a daughter of Brookbridge, was saying much—that the house had grown too painful. Poor Miss Maria excused Miss Becky on the score of her not being well—and that, it struck me, was saying most of all. The absence of the others gave the occasion a different note; but I talked with Miss Maria for five minutes and recognised that—save for her saying, of her own movement, anything about Jane—she now spoke as if her mother had lost hearing or sense, in fact both, alluding freely and distinctly, though indeed favourably, to her condition. "She has expected your visit and much enjoys it," my entertainer said, while the old woman, soundless and motionless, simply fixed me without expression. Of course there was little to keep me; but I became aware as I rose to go that there was more than I had supposed.

On my approaching her to take leave Mrs. Rimmle gave signs of consciousness. "Have you heard about Jane?"

I hesitated, feeling a responsibility, and appealed for direction to Maria's face. But Maria's face was troubled, was turned altogether to her mother's. "About her life in Europe?" I then rather helplessly asked.

The old lady fronted me on this in a manner that made me feel silly. "Her life?"—and her voice, with this second effort, came out stronger. "Her death, if you please."

"Her death?" I echoed, before I could stop myself, with the accent of deprecation.

Miss Maria uttered a vague sound of pain, and I felt her turn away, but the marvel of her mother's little unquenched spark still held me. "Jane's dead. We've heard," said Mrs. Rimmle. "We've heard from—where is it we've heard from?" She had quite revived—she appealed to her daughter.

The poor old girl, crimson, rallied to her duty. "From Europe."

Mrs. Rimmle made at us both a little grim inclination of the head. "From Europe." I responded, in silence, by a deflexion from every rigour, and, still holding me, she went on: "And now Rebecca's going."

She had gathered by this time such emphasis to say it that again, before I could help myself, I vibrated in reply. "To Europe—now?" It was as if for an instant she had made me believe it.

She only stared at me, however, from her wizened mask; then her eyes followed my companion. "Has she gone?"

"Not yet, mother." Maria tried to treat it as a joke, but her smile was embarrassed and dim.

"Then where is she?"

"She's lying down."

The old woman kept up her hard queer gaze, but directing it after a minute to me. "She's going."

"Oh some day!" I foolishly laughed; and on this I got to the door, where I separated from my younger hostess, who came no further.

Only, as I held the door open, she said to me under cover of it and very quietly: "It's poor mother's idea."

I saw—it was her idea. Mine was—for some time after this, even after I had returned to New York and to my usual occupations—that I should never again see Becky. I had seen her for the last time, I believed, under my sister-in-law's roof, and in the autumn it was given to me to hear from that fellow admirer that she had succumbed at last to the situation. The day of the call I had just described had been a date in the process of her slow shrinkage—it was literally the first time she had, as they said at Brookbridge, given up. She had been ill for years, but the other state of health in the contemplation of which she had spent so much of her life had left her till too late no margin for heeding it. The power of attention came at last simply in the form of the discovery that it *was* too late; on which, naturally, she had given up more and more. I had heard indeed, for weeks before, by letter, how Brookbridge had watched her do so; in consequence of which the end found me in a manner prepared. Yet in spite of my preparation there remained with me a soreness, and when I was next—it was some six months later— an the scene of her martyrdom I fear I replied with an almost rabid negative to the question put to me in due course by my kinswoman. "Call on them? Never again!"

I went none the less the very next day. Everything was the same in the sunny parlour—everything that most mattered, I mean: the centenarian mummy in the high chair and the tributes, in the little frames on the walls, to the celebrity of its late husband. Only Maria Rimmle was different: if Becky, on my last seeing her, had looked as old as her mother, Maria—save that she moved about—looked older. I remember she moved about, but I scarce remember what she said; and indeed what was there to say? When I risked a question, however, she found a reply.

"But *now* at least—?" I tried to put it to her suggestively.

At first she was vague. "'Now'?"

"Won't Miss Jane come back?"

Oh the headshake she gave me! "Never." It positively pictured to me, for the instant, a well-preserved woman, a rich ripe *seconde jeunesse* by the Arno.

"Then that's only to make more sure of your finally joining her."

Maria Rimmle repeated her headshake. "Never."

We stood so a moment bleakly face to face; I could think of no attenuation that would be particularly happy. But while I heard a hoarse gasp that fortunately relieved me—a signal strange and at first formless from the occupant of the high-backed chair. "Mother wants to speak to you," Maria then said.

So it appeared from the drop of the old woman's jaw, the expression of her mouth opened as if for the emission of sound. It was somehow difficult to me to seem to sympathise without hypocrisy, but, so far as a step nearer could do that, I invited communication. "Have you heard where Becky's gone?" the wonderful witch's white lips then extraordinarily asked.

It drew from Maria, as on my previous visit, an uncontrollable groan, and this in turn made me take time to consider. As I considered, however, I had an inspiration. "To Europe?"

I must have adorned it with a strange grimace, but my inspiration had been right. "To Europe," said Mrs. Rimmle.

◆

Norwegian Drama

HENRIK IBSEN

1828–1906

Although the Scandinavian countries have achieved marked literary distinction in the drama, the novel and philosophy since 1850, it has been the dramatic accomplishment of Henrik Ibsen which has contributed most significantly to the development of modern drama in western Europe. In Scandinavia he must contend for pre-eminence with his contemporaries, August Strindberg (1849–1912) and Björnstjerne Björnson (1832–1910), but it is to Ibsen's plays that the student of the contemporary theater must turn for an anticipation of certain structural aspects of modern drama, for the thematic embodiment of its motivating social ideas, and for the development of symbolic dramatic techniques which are too seldom acknowledged in the acclaim accorded Ibsen as a master of realistic modern drama based upon somewhat parochial themes drawn from small-town Norwegian life.

After an unhappy childhood near the coastal town of Skien on the southeast coast of Norway, in a poverty-stricken and humiliating environment provided for his family by a once-prosperous father, Ibsen at sixteen was apprenticed to an apothecary at Grimstad. He consoled himself for a bitter, isolated existence by writing poetry and a verse tragedy, *Catilina* (1850), which was inspired by the European revolutions of 1848. In 1850 he went to Christiania to prepare himself for university studies which he never undertook; there he devoted himself to various literary and political journalistic activities. In 1851 he accepted a position with the Norwegian National Theater at Bergen, where he remained six years writing a series of romantic national dramas and saga plays based upon Norwegian and Danish legendary materials. None of these plays is significant in his development as a dramatist.

In 1857 he returned to Christiania, where he became for a time director of the theater there. His first significant play, *Love's Comedy* (1862), anticipated the themes of his later plays in the presentation of a social problem: the relation of idealistic love to the marriage of convenience in a conservative and conventional society. The strong public resentment against the play, his failure to obtain a pension from the government, and his disgust with the neutrality of Norway during the Danish-Prussian war of 1864 induced him to seek voluntary exile; for the next twenty-seven years he resided in Germany and Italy (chiefly in Rome).

The publication of *Brand* in 1866 brought him fame in Scandinavia and throughout Europe; his financial independence was established when the Norwegian legislative body, the Storthing, granted him a pension. *Brand* is a profoundly conceived poetic drama about a religious idealist who refuses to make any compromise with a self-righteous society and its mores. The gay verse fantasy *Peer Gynt* (1867), based on Norwegian folklore, is one of his most delightful satirical comments upon some of the benign weaknesses of his countrymen. Although neither *Brand* nor *Peer Gynt* was intended for the theater, both have been produced, the latter with Edvard Grieg's charming score, the *Suites to Peer Gynt*.

With *The League of Youth* (1869) and *The Pillars of Society* (1877) Ibsen the poet became the playwright concerned with the prose social "problem" play and thus established the dominant tradition of late nineteenth-century European drama, as Bernard Shaw pointed out in *The Quintessence of Ibsenism* (1891). The more polemical plays of this second period, *A Doll's House* (1879), *Ghosts* (1881), and *An Enemy of the People* (1882), have now largely an historical value in revealing the late nineteenth-century struggle for the rights of the individual against the overconservative and outmoded traditions of society, especially in the first two plays, wherein is disclosed the sordid status of the conventional marriage rooted in insidious lies and self-deceit. The later plays, *The Wild Duck* (1884), *Rosmersholm* (1886), and *Hedda Gabler* (1890), are less concerned with a social thesis; Ibsen is more interested in revealing the complexities of character motivation and in dramatizing the psychic potentialities of the superior individual.

Rosmersholm lies at a transitional point between the problem plays of the second period and the more mystic and poetic dramas of the last. It is constructed in Ibsen's admirable retrospective dramatic method characteristic of the second period, in which the action is rigorously compressed, the preparation for the crisis is omitted, and the play begun at the crisis; the exposition of the past is introduced throughout the development wherever it will contribute the greatest dramatic value to the suspense. Although *Rosmersholm* is based upon a contemporary political situation, the struggle of the King of Norway and his ministers to dominate the legislative body, is is more concerned with the complex psychological motivation of the characters and with the psychic tensions between individuals of strong personality. The final uncompromising demand of Rosmer that Rebecca West re-establish her integrity and honesty by willing her own death (as did his wife Beate) and their subsequent resolve to die together gladly in preservation of this new-found integrity has a Kierkegaardian absolutism, an "all-or-nothing" quality which anticipates the mysticism of the last period. The recurrent symbols—the portraits of Rosmer's ancestors and the family legend of the White Horse as suggestive of the power of the Rosmer tradition—are more subtle in implication than the rather obvious symbolism in *Ghosts* and *A Doll's House*.

This symbolism received increasing development in the last plays, *The Master Builder* (1892), *John Gabriel Borkman* (1896), and *When We Dead Awaken* (1900); in these the playwright's interest in dramatic technique declined in ratio to his increasingly profound and meditative concern with exalted states of mind and soul, and with the development of new areas of individual psychic experience remote from Ibsen's former preoccupation with social problems.

Henrik Ibsen was the first dramatist to perfect the intensely concentrated dramatic technique for the expression of new social ideas in the theater; for this reason modern drama has always been closely identified with his name. Beyond this achievement, however, he exemplifies the artist who never rests upon his previous accomplishment; from his accomplishment in the drama of ideas Ibsen moved on to anticipate also the development of symbolism in the modern theater, and in his last plays to present cogently some of the more momentous concerns of the modern artist: the nature and personality of the artist, his relation to his art, to his national backgrounds, and to life. *The Master Builder* and *When We Dead Awaken* foreshadow some of the characteristic literary preoccupations of modern writers so diverse in genius as James Joyce, Rainer Maria Rilke, Thomas Mann, and Franz Kafka.

FURTHER READING

BRADBROOK, M. C. *Ibsen the Norwegian* (London, 1948).
DOWNS, BRIAN W. *Ibsen: The Intellectual Background* (Cambridge, Eng., 1948).
SHAW, G. BERNARD. *The Quintessence of Ibsenism* (New York, 1913).

Rosmersholm *

CHARACTERS

JOHANNES ROSMER, *of Rosmersholm, formerly clergyman of the parish*
REBECCA WEST, *in charge of Rosmer's household*
RECTOR [1] KROLL, *Rosmer's brother-in-law*
ULRIC BRENDEL
PETER MORTENSGÅRD [2]
MADAM HELSETH, *housekeeper at Rosmersholm*

The action takes place at Rosmersholm, an old family seat near a small coast town in the west of Norway

ACT ONE

Sitting-room at Rosmersholm; spacious, old-fashioned, and comfortable. In front, on the right, a stove decked with fresh birch-branches and wild flowers. Farther back, on the same side, a door. In the back wall, folding-doors opening into the hall. To the left, a window, and before it a stand with flowers and plants. Beside the stove a table

* Translated by Charles Archer. By permission from *The Collected Works of Henrik Ibsen*, edited by William Archer. Copyright, 1908, by William Heinemann, Ltd.
[1] "Rector" in the Scotch Continental sense of headmaster of a school, not in the English sense of a beneficed clergyman.
[2] Pronounce *Mortensgore.*

with a sofa and easy chairs. On the walls, old and more recent portraits of clergymen, officers and government officials in uniform. The window is open; so are the door into the hall and the house door beyond. Outside can be seen an avenue of fine old trees, leading up to the house. It is a summer evening, after sunset.

REBECCA WEST *is sitting in an easy-chair by the window, and crocheting a large white woollen shawl, which is nearly finished. She now and then looks out expectantly through the leaves of the plants.* MADAM HELSETH *presently enters from the right.*

MADAM HELSETH. I suppose I had better begin to lay the table, Miss?

REBECCA WEST. Yes, please do. The Pastor must soon be in now.

MADAM HELSETH. Don't you feel the draught, Miss, where you're sitting?

REBECCA. Yes, there is a little draught. Perhaps you had better shut the window.

(MADAM HELSETH *shuts the door into the hall and then comes to the window.*)

MADAM HELSETH (*about to shut the window, looks out*). Why, isn't that the Pastor over there?

REBECCA (*hastily*). Where? (*Rises*) Yes, it is he. (*Behind the curtain*) Stand aside—don't let him see us.

MADAM HELSETH (*keeping back from the window*). Only think, Miss—he's beginning to take the path by the mill again.

REBECCA. He went that way the day before yesterday, too. (*Peeps out between the curtains and the window-frame.*) But let us see whether—

MADAM HELSETH. Will he venture across the foot-bridge?

REBECCA. That is what I want to see. (*After a pause*) No, he is turning. He is going by the upper road again. (*Leaves the window*) A long way round.

MADAM HELSETH. Dear Lord, yes. No wonder the Pastor thinks twice about setting foot on that bridge. A place where a thing like that has happened—

REBECCA (*folding up her work*). They cling to their dead here at Rosmersholm.

MADAM HELSETH. Now I would say, Miss, that it's the dead that clings to Rosmersholm.

REBECCA (*looks at her*). The dead?

MADAM HELSETH. Yes, it's almost as if they couldn't tear themselves away from the folk that are left.

REBECCA. What makes you fancy that?

MADAM HELSETH. Well, if it wasn't for that, there would be no White Horse, I suppose.

REBECCA. Now what is all this about the White Horse, Madam Helseth?

MADAM HELSETH. Oh, I don't like to talk about it. And, besides, you don't believe in such things.

REBECCA. Do you believe in it, then?

MADAM HELSETH (goes and shuts the window). Oh, you'd only be for laughing at me, Miss. (Looks out) Why, isn't that Mr. Rosmer on the mill-path again——?

REBECCA (looks out). That man there? (Goes to the window) No, that's the Rector!

MADAM HELSETH. Yes, so it is.

REBECCA. This is delightful. You may be sure he's coming here.

MADAM HELSETH. He goes straight over the foot-bridge, he does. And yet she was his sister, his own flesh and blood. Well, I'll go and lay the table then, Miss West.

(She goes out to the right. REBECCA stands at the window for a short time; then smiles and nods to some one outside. It begins to grow dark.)

REBECCA (goes to the door on the right). Oh, Madam Helseth, you might let us have some little extra dish for supper. You know what the Rector likes best.

MADAM HELSETH (outside). Oh, yes, Miss, I'll see to it.

REBECCA (opens the door to the hall). At last—! How glad I am to see you, my dear Rector.

RECTOR KROLL (in the hall, laying down his stick). Thanks. Then I am not disturbing you?

REBECCA. You? How can you ask?

KROLL (comes in). Amiable as ever. (Looks round) Is Rosmer upstairs in his room?

REBECCA. No, he is out walking. He has stayed out rather longer than usual; but he is sure to be in directly. (Motioning him to sit on the sofa) Won't you sit down till he comes?

KROLL (laying down his hat). Many thanks. (Sits down and looks about him.) Why, how you have brightened up the old room! Flowers everywhere!

REBECCA. Mr. Rosmer is so fond of having fresh, growing flowers about him.

KROLL. And you are too, are you not?

REBECCA. Yes; they have a delightfully soothing effect on me. We had to do without them, though, till lately.

KROLL (nods sadly). Yes, their scent was too much for poor Beata.

REBECCA. Their colours, too. They quite bewildered her——

KROLL. I remember, I remember. (In a lighter tone) Well, how are things going out here?

REBECCA. Oh, everything is going its quiet, jog-trot way. One day is just like another.—And with you? Your wife——?

KROLL. Ah, my dear Miss West, don't let us talk about my affairs. There is always something or other amiss in a family; especially in times like these.

REBECCA (after a pause, sitting down in an easy-chair beside the sofa). How is it you haven't once been near us during the whole of the holidays?

KROLL. Oh, it doesn't do to make oneself a nuisance——

REBECCA. If you knew how we have missed you——

KROLL. And then I have been away——

REBECCA. Yes, for the last week or two. We have heard of you at political meetings.

KROLL (nods). Yes what do you say to that? Did you think I would turn political agitator in my old age, eh?

REBECCA (smiling). Well, you have always been a bit of an agitator, Rector Kroll.

KROLL. Why, yes, just for my private amusement. But henceforth it is to be no laughing matter, I can tell you.—Do you ever see those radical newspapers?

REBECCA. Well yes, my dear Rector, I can't deny that——

KROLL. My dear Miss West, I have nothing to say against it—nothing in your case.

REBECCA. No, surely not. One likes to know what's going on—to keep up with the time——

KROLL. And of course I should not think of expecting you, as a woman, to side actively with either party in the civil contest—I might almost say the civil war—that is raging among us.—But you have seen then, I suppose, how these gentlemen of "the people" have been pleased to treat me? What infamous abuse they have had the audacity to heap on me?

REBECCA. Yes; but it seems to me you gave as good as you got.

KROLL. So I did, though I say it that shouldn't. For now I have tasted blood; and they shall soon find to their cost that I am not the man to turn the other cheek—— (Breaks off) But come come—don't let us get upon that subject this evening—it's too painful and irritating.

REBECCA. Oh no, don't let us talk of it.

KROLL. Tell me now—how do you get on at Rosmersholm, now that you are alone? Since our poor Beata——

REBECCA. Thank you, I get on very well. Of course one feels a great blank in many ways—a great sorrow and longing. But otherwise——

KROLL. And do you think of remaining here?—permanently, I mean.

REBECCA. My dear Rector, I really haven't thought about it, one way or the other. I have got so used to the place now, that I feel almost as if I belonged to it.

KROLL. Why, of course you belong to it.

REBECCA. And so long as Mr. Rosmer finds that I am of any use or comfort to him—why, so long, I suppose, I shall stay here.

KROLL (looks at her with emotion). Do you know,—it is really fine for a woman to sacrifice her whole youth to others as you have done.

REBECCA. Oh, what else should I have had to live for?

KROLL. First, there was your untiring devotion to your paralytic and exacting foster-father——

REBECCA. You mustn't suppose that Dr. West was such a charge when we were up in Finmark. It was those terrible boat-voyages up there that broke him down. But after we came here—well, yes, the two years before he found rest were certainly hard enough.

KROLL. And the years that followed—were they not even harder for you?

REBECCA. Oh, how can you say such a thing? When I was so fond of Beata—and when she, poor dear, stood so sadly in need of care and forbearance.

KROLL. How good it is of you to think of her with so much kindness!

REBECCA (moves a little nearer). My dear Rector, you say that with such a ring of sincerity that I cannot think there is any ill-feeling lurking in the background.

KROLL. Ill-feeling? Why, what do you mean?

REBECCA. Well, it would be only natural if you felt it painful to see a stranger managing the household here at Rosmersholm.

KROLL. Why, how on earth——!

REBECCA. But you have no such feeling? (Takes his hand) Thanks, my dear Rector; thank you again and again.

KROLL. How on earth did you get such an idea into your head?

REBECCA. I began to be a little afraid when your visits became so rare.

KROLL. Then you have been on a totally wrong scent, Miss West. Besides—after all, there has been no essential change. Even while poor Beata was alive—in her last unhappy days—it was you, and you alone, that managed everything.

REBECCA. That was only a sort of regency in Beata's name.

KROLL. Be that as it may——. Do you know, Miss West—for my part, I should have no objection whatever if you——. But I suppose I mustn't say such a thing.

REBECCA. What must you not say?

KROLL. If matters were to shape so that you took the empty place——

REBECCA. I have the only place I want, Rector.

KROLL. In fact yes; but not in——

REBECCA (interrupting gravely). For shame, Rector Kroll. How can you joke about such things?

KROLL. Oh, well, our good Johannes Rosmer very likely thinks he has had more than enough of married life already. But nevertheless——

REBECCA. You are really too absurd, Rector.

KROLL. Nevertheless——. Tell me, Miss West—— if you will forgive the question—what is your age?

REBECCA. I'm sorry to say I am over nine-and-twenty, Rector; I am in my thirtieth year.

KROLL. Indeed. And Rosmer—how old is he? Let me see: he is five years younger than I am, so that makes him well over forty-three. I think it would be most suitable.

REBECCA (rises). Of course, of course; most suitable.—Will you stay to supper this evening?

KROLL. Yes, many thanks; I thought of staying. There is a matter I want to discuss with our good friend.—And I suppose, Miss West, in case you should take fancies into your head again, I had better come out pretty often for the future—as I used to in the old days.

REBECCA. Oh, yes, do—do. (Shakes both his hands) Many thanks—how kind and good you are!

KROLL (gruffly). Am I? Well, that's not what they tell me at home.

(JOHANNES ROSMER enters by the door on the right.)

REBECCA. Mr. Rosmer, do you see who is here?

JOHANNES ROSMER. Madam Helseth told me. (RECTOR KROLL has risen.)

ROSMER (gently and softly, pressing his hands). Welcome back to this house, my dear Kroll. (Lays his hands on Kroll's shoulders and looks into his eyes.) My dear old friend! I knew that sooner or later things would come all right between us.

KROLL. Why, my dear fellow—do you mean to say you too have been so foolish as to fancy there was anything wrong?

REBECCA (*to* ROSMER). Yes, only think,—it was nothing but fancy after all!

ROSMER. Is that really the case, Kroll? Then why did you desert us so entirely?

KROLL (*gravely, in a low voice*). Because my presence would always have been reminding you of the years of your happiness, and of—the life that ended in the mill-race.

ROSMER. Well, it was a kind thought—you were always considerate. But it was quite unnecessary to remain away on that account.—Come, sit here on the sofa. (*They sit down.*) No, I assure you, the thought of Beata has no pain for me. We speak of her every day. We feel almost as if she were still one of the household.

KROLL. Do you really?

REBECCA (*lighting the lamp*). Yes, indeed we do.

ROSMER. It is quite natural. We were both so deeply attached to her. And both Rebec—both Miss West and I know that we did all that was possible for her in her affliction. We have nothing to reproach ourselves with.—So I feel nothing but a tranquil tenderness now at the thought of Beata.

KROLL. You dear, good people! Henceforward, I declare I shall come out and see you every day.

REBECCA (*seats herself in an armchair*). Mind, we shall expect you to keep your word.

ROSMER (*with some hesitation*). My dear Kroll— I wish very much that our intercourse had never been interrupted. Ever since we have known each other, you have seemed predestined to be my adviser—ever since I went to the University.

KROLL. Yes, and I have always been proud of the office. But is there anything particular just now——?

ROSMER. There are many things that I would give a great deal to talk over with you, quite frankly —straight from the heart.

REBECCA. Ah yes, Mr. Rosmer—that must be such a comfort—between old friends——

KROLL. Oh I can tell you I have still more to talk to you about. I suppose you know I have turned a militant politician?

ROSMER. Yes, so you have. How did that come about?

KROLL. I was forced into it in spite of myself. It is impossible to stand idly looking on any longer. Now that the Radicals have unhappily come into power, it is high time something should be done,— so I have got our little group of friends in the town to close up their ranks. I tell you it is high time!

REBECCA (*with a faint smile*). Don't you think it may even be a little late?

KROLL. Unquestionably it would have been bet-ter if we had checked the stream at an earlier point in its course. But who could foresee what was going to happen? Certainly not I. (*Rises and walks up and down.*) But now I have had my eyes opened once for all; for now the spirit of revolt has crept into the school itself.

ROSMER. Into the school? Surely not into your school?

KROLL. I tell you it has—into my own school. What do you think? It has come to my knowledge that the sixth-form boys—a number of them at any rate—have been keeping up a secret society for over six months; and they take in Mortensgård's paper!

REBECCA. The "Beacon"?

KROLL. Yes; nice mental sustenance for future government officials, is it not? But the worst of it is that it's all the cleverest boys in the form that have banded together in this conspiracy against me. Only the dunces at the bottom of the class have kept out of it.

REBECCA. Do you take this so very much to heart, Rector?

KROLL. Do I take it to heart! To be so thwarted and opposed in the work of my whole life! (*Lower*) But I could almost say I don't care about the school —for there is worse behind. (*Looks around*) I suppose no one can hear us?

REBECCA. Oh, no, of course not.

KROLL. Well, then, I must tell you that dissension and revolt have crept into my own house—into my own quiet home. They have destroyed the peace of my family life.

ROSMER (*rises*). What! Into your own house——?

REBECCA (*goes over to the* RECTOR). My dear Rector, what has happened?

KROLL. Would you believe that my own children—— In short, it is Laurits that is the ringleader of the school conspiracy; and Hilda has embroidered a red portfolio to keep the "Beacon" in.

ROSMER. I should certainly never have dreamt that, in your own house——

KROLL. No, who would have dreamt of such a thing? In my house, the very home of obedience and order—where one will, and one only, has always prevailed——

REBECCA. How does your wife take all this?

KROLL. Why, that is the most incredible part of it. My wife, who all her life long has shared my opinions and concurred in my views, both in great things and small—she is actually inclined to side with the children on many points. And she blames me for what has happened. She says I tyrannise over the children. As if it weren't necessary to——.

Well, you see how my house is divided against itself. But of course I say as little about it as possible. Such things are best kept quiet. (*Wanders up the room*) Ah, well, well, well.

(*Stands at the window with his hands behind his back and looks out.*)

REBECCA (*comes up close to* ROSMER *and says rapidly and in a low voice, so that the* RECTOR *does not hear her*). Do it now!

ROSMER (*also in a low voice*). Not this evening.

REBECCA (*as before*). Yes, just this evening.

(*Goes to the table and busies herself with the lamp.*)

KROLL (*comes forward*). Well, my dear Rosmer, now you know how the spirit of the age has overshadowed both my domestic and my official life. And am I to refrain from combating this pernicious, subversive, anarchic spirit, with any weapons I can lay my hands on? Fight it I will, trust me for that; both with tongue and pen.

ROSMER. Have you any hope of stemming the tide in that way?

KROLL. At any rate, I shall have done my duty as a citizen in defense of the State. And I hold it the duty of every right-minded man with an atom of patriotism to do likewise. In fact—that was my principal reason for coming out here this evening.

ROSMER. Why, my dear Kroll, what do you mean——? What can I——?

KROLL. You can stand by your old friends. Do as we do. Lend a hand, with all your might.

REBECCA. But, Rector Kroll, you know Mr. Rosmer's distaste for public life.

KROLL. He must get over his distaste.—You don't keep abreast of things, Rosmer. You bury yourself alive here, with your historical collections. Far be it from me to speak disrespectfully of family trees, and so forth; but, unfortunately, this is no time for hobbies of that sort. You cannot imagine the state things are in, all over the country. There is hardly a single accepted idea that hasn't been turned topsy-turvy. It will be a gigantic task to get all the errors rooted out again.

ROSMER. I have no doubt of it. But I am the last man to undertake such a task.

REBECCA. And besides, I think Mr. Rosmer has come to take a wider view of life than he used to.

KROLL (*with surprise*). Wider?

REBECCA. Yes; or freer, if you like—less one-sided.

KROLL. What is the meaning of this? Rosmer—surely you are not so weak as to be influenced by the accident that the leaders of the mob have won a temporary advantage?

ROSMER. My dear Kroll, you know how little I understand of politics. But I confess it seems to me that within the last few years people are beginning to show greater independence of thought.

KROLL. Indeed! And you take it for granted that that must be an improvement! But in any case you are quite mistaken, my friend. Just inquire a little into the opinions that are current among the Radicals, both out here and in the town. They are neither more nor less than the wisdom that's retailed in the "Beacon."

REBECCA. Yes; Mortensgård has great influence over many people hereabouts.

KROLL. Yes, just think of it! A man of his foul antecedents—a creature that was turned out of his place as a schoolmaster on account on his immoral life! A fellow like that sets himself up as a leader of the people! And succeeds too! Actually succeeds! I hear he is going to enlarge his paper. I know on good authority that he is on the lookout for a capable assistant.

REBECCA. I wonder that you and your friends don't set up an opposition to him.

KROLL. That is the very thing we are going to do. We have to-day bought the "County News"; there was no difficulty about the money question. But—— (*Turns to* ROSMER) Now I came to my real errand. The difficulty lies in the conduct of the paper—the editing—— Tell me, Rosmer,—don't you feel it your duty to undertake it, for the sake of the good cause?

ROSMER (*almost in consternation*). I?

REBECCA. Oh, how can you think of such a thing?

KROLL. I can quite understand your horror of public meetings, and your reluctance to expose yourself to their tender mercies. But an editor's work is less conspicuous, or rather——

ROSMER. No, no, my dear friend, you must not ask me to do this.

KROLL. I should be quite willing to try my own hand at that style of work too; but I couldn't possibly manage it. I have such a multitude of irons in the fire already. But for you, with no profession to tie you down—— Of course the rest of us would give you as much help as we could.

ROSMER. I cannot, Kroll. I am not fitted for it.

KROLL. Not fitted? You said the same thing when your father preferred you to the living here——

ROSMER. And I was right. That was why I resigned it.

KROLL. Oh, if only you are as good an editor as you were a clergyman, we shall not complain.

ROSMER. My dear Kroll—I tell you once for all—I cannot do it.

KROLL. Well, at any rate, you will lend us your name.

ROSMER. My name?

KROLL. Yes, the mere name, Johannes Rosmer, will be a great thing for the paper. We others are looked upon as confirmed partisans—indeed I hear I am denounced as a desperate fanatic—so that if we work the paper in our own names, we can't reckon upon its making much way among the misguided masses. You, on the contrary, have always kept out of the fight. Everybody knows and values your humanity and uprightness—your delicacy of mind—your unimpeachable honour. And then the prestige of your former position as a clergyman still clings to you; and, to crown all, you have your grand old family name!

ROSMER. Oh, my name——

KROLL (points to the portraits). Rosmers of Rosmersholm—clergymen and soldiers; government officials of high place and trust; gentlemen to the finger-tips, every man of them—a family that for nearly two centuries has held its place as the first in the district. (Lays his hand on ROSMER's shoulder.) Rosmer—you owe it to yourself and to the traditions of your race to take your share in guarding all that has hitherto been held sacred in our society. (Turns round) What do you say, Miss West?

REBECCA (laughing softly, as if to herself). My dear Rector—I can't tell you how ludicrous all this seems to me.

KROLL. What do you say? Ludicrous?

REBECCA. Yes, ludicrous. For you must let me tell you frankly——

ROSMER (quickly). No, no—be quiet! Not just now!

KROLL (looks from one to the other). My dear friends, what on earth——? (Interrupting himself) H'm.

(MADAM HELSETH appears in the doorway on the right.)

MADAM HELSETH. There's a man out in the kitchen passage that says he wants to see the Pastor.

ROSMER (relieved). Ah, very well. Ask him to come in.

MADAM HELSETH. Into the sitting-room?

ROSMER. Yes, of course.

MADAM HELSETH. But he looks scarcely the sort of man to bring into the sitting-room.

REBECCA. Why, what does he look like, Madam Helseth?

MADAM HELSETH. Well, he's not much to look at, Miss, and that's a fact.

ROSMER. Did he not give his name?

MADAM HELSETH. Yes—I think he said his name was Hekman or something of the sort.

ROSMER. I know nobody of that name.

MADAM HELSETH. And then he said he was called Uldric, too.

ROSMER (in surprise). Ulric Hetman! Was that it?

MADAM HELSETH. Yes, so it was—Hetman.

KROLL. I've surely heard that name before——

REBECCA. Wasn't that the name he used to write under—that strange being——

ROSMER (to KROLL). It is Ulric Brendel's pseudonym.

KROLL. That black sheep Ulric Brendel's—of course it is.

REBECCA. Then he is still alive.

ROSMER. I heard he had joined a company of strolling players.

KROLL. When last I heard of him, he was in the House of Correction.

ROSMER. Ask him to come in, Madam Helseth.

MADAM HELSETH. Oh, very well.

(She goes out.)

KROLL. Are you really going to let a man like that into your house?

ROSMER. You know he was once my tutor.

KROLL. Yes, I know he went and crammed your head full of revolutionary ideas, until your father showed him the door—with his horsewhip.

ROSMER (with a touch of bitterness). Father was a martinet at home as well as in his regiment.

KROLL. Thank him in his grave for that, my dear Rosmer.—Well!

(MADAM HELSETH opens the door on the right for ULRIC BRENDEL and then withdraws, shutting the door behind him. He is a handsome man, with grey hair and beard; somewhat gaunt, but active and well set up. He is dressed like a common tramp; threadbare frock-coat; worn-out shoes; no shirt visible. He wears an old pair of black gloves, and carries a soft, greasy felt hat under his arm, and a walking-stick in his hand.)

ULRIC BRENDEL (Hesitates at first, then goes quickly up to the Rector, and holds out his hand). Good evening, Johannes!

KROLL. Excuse me——

BRENDEL. Did you expect to see me again? And within these hated walls, too?

KROLL. Excuse me—— (Pointing) There——

BRENDEL (turns). Right. There he is. Johannes—my boy—my best-beloved——!

ROSMER (takes his hand). My old teacher.

BRENDEL. Notwithstanding certain painful memories, I could not pass by Rosmersholm without paying you a flying visit.

ROSMER. You are heartily welcome here now. Be sure of that.

BRENDEL. Ah, this charming lady——? (*Bows*) Mrs. Rosmer, of course.

ROSMER. Miss West.

BRENDEL. A near relation, no doubt. And yonder unknown——? A brother of the cloth, I see.

ROSMER. Rector Kroll.

BRENDEL. Kroll? Kroll? Wait a bit?—Weren't you a student of philology in your young days?

KROLL. Of course I was.

BRENDEL. Why *Donnerwetter*, then I knew you!

KROLL. Pardon me——

BRENDEL. Weren't you——

KROLL. Pardon me——

BRENDEL. ——one of those myrmidons of morality that got me turned out of the Debating Club?

KROLL. Very likely. But I disclaim any closer acquaintanceship.

BRENDEL. Well, well! *Nach Belieben, Herr Doktor*. It's all one to me. Ulric Brendel remains the man he is for all that.

REBECCA. You are on your way into town, Mr. Brendel?

BRENDEL. You have hit it, gracious lady. At certain intervals, I am constrained to strike a blow for existence. It goes against the grain; but—*enfin*—imperious necessity——

ROSMER. Oh, but, my dear Mr. Brendel, you must allow me to help you. In one way or another, I am sure——

BRENDEL. Ha, such a proposal to me! Would you desecrate the bond that unites us? Never, Johannes, never!

ROSMER. But what do you think of doing in town? Believe me, you won't find it easy to——

BRENDEL. Leave that to me, my boy. The die is cast. Simple as I stand here before you, I am engaged in a comprehensive campaign—more comprehensive than all my previous excursions put together. (*To* RECTOR KROLL) Dare I ask the Herr Professor—*unter uns*—have you a tolerably decent, reputable, and commodious Public Hall in your estimable city?

KROLL. The hall of the Workmen's Society is the largest.

BRENDEL. And has the Herr Professor any official influence in this doubtless most beneficent Society?

KROLL. I have nothing to do with it.

REBECCA (*to* BRENDEL). You should apply to Peter Mortensgård.

BRENDEL. Pardon, madame—what sort of an idiot is he?

ROSMER. What makes you take him for an idiot?

BRENDEL. Can't I tell at once by the name that it belongs to a plebeian?

KROLL. I did not expect that answer.

BRENDEL. But I will conquer my reluctance. There is no alternative. When a man stands—as I do—at a turning-point in his career——. It is settled. I will approach this individual—will open personal negotiations——

ROSMER. Are you really and seriously standing at a turning-point?

BRENDEL. Surely my own boy knows that, stand he where he may, Ulric Brendel always stands really and seriously.—Yes, Johannes, I am going to put on a new man—to throw off the modest reserve I have hitherto maintained——

ROSMER. How——?

BRENDEL. I am about to take hold of life with a strong hand; to step forth; to assert myself. We live in a tempestuous, an equinoctial age.—I am about to lay my mite on the altar of Emanicipation.

KROLL. You, too?

BRENDEL (*to them all*). Is the local public at all familiar with my occasional writings?

KROLL. No, I must candidly confess that——

REBECCA. I have read several of them. My adopted father had them in his library.

BRENDEL. Fair lady, then you have wasted your time. For, let me tell you, they are so much rubbish.

REBECCA. Indeed!

BRENDEL. What you have read, yes. My really important works no man or woman knows. No one —except myself.

REBECCA. How does that happen?

BRENDEL. Because they are not written.

ROSMER. But, my dear Mr. Brendel——

BRENDEL. You know, my Johannes, that I am a bit of a Sybarite—a *Feinschmecker*. I have been so all my days. I like to take my pleasures in solitude; for then I enjoy them doubly—tenfold. So, you see when golden dreams descended and enwrapped me—when new, dizzy, far-reaching thoughts were born in me and wafted me aloft on their sustaining pinions—I bodied them forth in poems, visions, pictures—in the rough, as it were, you understand.

ROSMER. Yes, yes.

BRENDEL. Oh, what pleasures, what intoxications I have enjoyed in my time! The mysterious bliss of creation—in the rough, as I said—applause, gratitude, renown, the wreath of bays—all these I have garnered with full hands quivering with joy. I have sated myself, in my secret thoughts, with a rapture—oh! so intense, so inebriating——!

KROLL. H'm.

ROSMER. But you have written nothing down?

BRENDEL. Not a word. The soulless toil of the scrivener has always aroused a sickening aversion in me. And besides, why should I profane my own ideals, when I could enjoy them in their purity by myself? But now they shall be offered up. I assure you I feel like a mother who delivers her tender daughters into their bridegrooms' arms. But I will offer them up, nonetheless. I will sacrifice them on the altar of Emancipation. A series of carefully elaborated lectures—over the whole country——!

REBECCA (with animation). This is noble of you, Mr. Brendel! You are yielding up the dearest thing you possess.

ROSMER. The only thing.

REBECCA (looking significantly at ROSMER). How many are there who do as much—who dare do as much?

ROSMER (returning the look). Who knows?

BRENDEL. My audience is touched. That does my heart good—and steels my will. So now I will proceed to action. Stay—one thing more. (To the RECTOR) Can you tell me, Herr Preceptor,—is there such a thing as a Temperance Society in the town? A Total Abstinence Society? I need scarcely ask.

KROLL. Yes, there is. I am the president, at your service.

BRENDEL. I saw it in your face! Well, it is by no means impossible that I may come to you and enrol myself as a member for a week.

KROLL. Excuse me—we don't receive members by the week.

BRENDEL. A la bonne heure, Herr Pedagogue. Ulric Brendel has never forced himself into that sort of Society. (Turns) But I must not prolong my stay in this house, so rich in memories. I must get on to the town and select a suitable lodging. I presume there is a decent hotel in the place.

REBECCA. Mayn't I offer you anything before you go?

BRENDEL. Of what sort, gracious lady?

REBECCA. A cup of tea, or——

BRENDEL. I thank my bountiful hostess—but I am always loath to trespass on private hospitality. (Waves his hand) Farewell, gentlefolks all! (Goes towards the door, but turns again) Oh, by the way —Johannes—Pastor Rosmer—for the sake of our ancient friendship, will you do your former teacher a service?

ROSMER. Yes, with all my heart.

BRENDEL. Good. Then lend me—for a day or two—a starched shirt—with cuffs.

ROSMER. Nothing else?

BRENDEL. For you see I am travelling on foot—at present. My trunk is being sent after me.

ROSMER. Quite so. But is there nothing else?

BRENDEL. Well, do you know—perhaps you could spare me an oldish, well-worn summer overcoat.

ROSMER. Yes, yes; certainly I can.

BRENDEL. And if a respectable pair of boots happened to go along with the coat——

ROSMER. That we can manage, too. As soon as you let us know your address, we will send the things in.

BRENDEL. Not on any account. Pray do not let me give you any trouble! I will take the bagatelles with me.

ROSMER. As you please. Come upstairs with me then.

REBECCA. Let me go. Madam Helseth and I will see to it.

BRENDEL. I cannot think of suffering this distinguished lady to——

REBECCA. Oh, nonsense! Come along, Mr. Brendel.

(She goes out to the right.)

ROSMER (detaining him). Tell me—is there nothing else I can do for you?

BRENDEL. Upon my word, I know of nothing more. Well, yes, damn it all—now that I think of it——! Johannes, do you happen to have eight crowns in your pocket?

ROSMER. Let me see. (Opens his purse.) Here are two ten-crown notes.

BRENDEL. Well, well, never mind! I can take them. I can always get them changed in the town. Thanks in the meantime. Remember, it was two tenners you lent me. Good-night my own dear boy. Good-night, respected Sir.

(Goes out to the right. ROSMER takes leave of him, and shuts the door behind him.)

KROLL. Merciful Heaven—so that is the Ulric Brendel people once expected such great things of.

ROSMER (quietly). At least he has had the courage to live his life his own way. I don't think that is such a small matter either.

KROLL. What? A life like his! I almost believe he has it in him to turn your head afresh.

ROSMER. Oh, no. My mind is quite clear now, upon all points.

KROLL. I wish I could believe it, my dear Rosmer. You are so terribly impressionable.

ROSMER. Let us sit down. I want to talk to you.

KROLL. Yes, let us.

(*They seat themselves on the sofa.*)

ROSMER (*after a slight pause*). Don't you think we lead a pleasant and comfortable life here?

KROLL. Yes, your life is pleasant and comfortable now—and peaceful. You have found yourself a home, Rosmer. And I have lost mine.

ROSMER. My dear friend, don't say that. The wound will heal again in time.

KROLL. Never; never. The barb will always rankle. Things can never be as they were.

ROSMER. Listen to me, Kroll. We have been fast friends for many and many a year. Does it seem to you conceivable that our friendship should ever go to wreck?

KROLL. I know of nothing in the world that could estrange us. What puts that into your head?

ROSMER. You attach such paramount importance to uniformity of opinions and views.

KROLL. No doubt; but we two are in practical agreement, at any rate, on the great essential questions.

ROSMER (*in a low voice*). No; not now.

KROLL (*tries to spring up*). What is this?

ROSMER (*holding him*). No, you must sit still—I entreat you, Kroll.

KROLL. What can this mean? I don't understand you. Speak plainly.

ROSMER. A new summer has blossomed in my soul. I see with eyes grown young again. And so now I stand——

KROLL. Where—where, Rosmer?

ROSMER. Where your children stand.

KROLL. You? You! Impossible! Where do you say you stand?

ROSMER. On the same side as Laurits and Hilda.

KROLL (*bows his head*). An apostate! Johannes Rosmer an apostate!

ROSMER. I should have felt so happy—so intensely happy, in what you call my apostasy. But, nevertheless, I suffered deeply; for I knew it would be a bitter sorrow to you.

KROLL. Rosmer—Rosmer! I shall never get over this! (*Looks gloomily at him.*) To think that you, too, can find it in your heart to help on the work of corruption and ruin in this unhappy land.

ROSMER. It is the work of emancipation I wish to help on.

KROLL. Oh, yes, I know. That is what both the tempters and their victims call it. But do you think there is any emancipation to be expected from the spirit that is now poisoning our social life?

ROSMER. I am not in love with the spirit that is in the ascendant, nor with either of the contending parties. I will try to bring together men from both sides—as many as I can—and to unite them as closely as possible. I will devote my life and all my energies to this one thing—the creation of a true democracy in this country.

KROLL. So you don't think we have democracy enough already! For my part it seems to me we are all in a fair way to be dragged down into the mire, where hitherto only the mob have been able to thrive.

ROSMER. That is just why I want to awaken the democracy to its true task.

KROLL. What task?

ROSMER. That of making all the people of this country noble——

KROLL. All the people——?

ROSMER. As many as possible, at any rate.

KROLL. By what means?

ROSMER. By freeing their minds and purifying their wills.

KROLL. You are a dreamer, Rosmer. Will you free them? Will you purify them?

ROSMER. No, my dear friend—I will only try to arouse them to their task. They themselves must accomplish it.

KROLL. And you think they can?

ROSMER. Yes.

KROLL. By their own strength?

ROSMER. Yes, precisely by their own strength. There is no other.

KROLL (*rises*). Is this becoming language for a priest?

ROSMER. I am no longer a priest.

KROLL. Well but—the faith of your fathers——?

ROSMER. It is mine no more.

KROLL. No more——!

ROSMER (*rises*). I have given it up. I had to give it up, Kroll.

KROLL (*controlling his agitation*). Oh, indeed—Yes, yes, yes. I suppose one thing goes with another. Was this, then, your reason for leaving the Church?

ROSMER. Yes. As soon as my mind was clear—as soon as I was quite certain that this was no passing attack of scepticism, but a conviction I neither could nor would shake off—then I at once left the Church.

KROLL. So this has been your state of mind all this time! And we—your friends—have heard nothing of it. Rosmer—Rosmer—how could you hide the miserable truth from us!

ROSMER. Because it seemed to me a matter that concerned myself alone. And besides, I did not wish to give you and my other friends any needless pain. I thought I might live on here, as before, quietly, serenely, happy. I wanted to read, to bury myself in all the studies that until then had been sealed books to me. I wanted to make myself thoroughly at home in the great world of truth and freedom that has been revealed to me.

KROLL. Apostate! Every word proves it. But why, then, do you confess your secret apostasy after all? And why just at this time?

ROSMER. You yourself have driven me to it, Kroll.

KROLL. I? Have I driven you——?

ROSMER. When I heard of your violence on the platform—when I read all the rancorous speeches you made—your bitter onslaughts on your opponents—the contemptuous invectives you heaped on them—oh, Kroll, to think that you—you—could come to this!—then my duty stood imperatively before me. Men are growing evil in this struggle. Peace and joy and mutual forbearance must once more enter into our souls. That is why I now intend to step forward and openly avow myself for what I am. I, too, will try my strength. Could not you—from your side—help me in this, Kroll?

KROLL. Never so long as I live will I make peace with the subversive forces in society.

ROSMER. Then at least let us fight with honourable weapons—since fight we must.

KROLL. Whoever is not with me in the essential things of life, him I no longer know. I owe him no consideration.

ROSMER. Does that apply to me, too?

KROLL. It is you that have broken with me, Rosmer.

ROSMER. Is this a breach then?

KROLL. This! It is a breach with all who have hitherto been your friends. You must take the consequences.

(REBECCA WEST *enters from the right, and opens the door wide.*)

REBECCA. There now; he is on his way to his great sacrifice. And now we can go to supper. Will you come in, Rector?

KROLL (*takes up his hat*). Good-night, Miss West. I have nothing more to do here.

REBECCA (*eagerly*). What is this? (*Shuts the door and comes forward.*) Have you spoken?

ROSMER. He knows everything.

KROLL. We will not let you go, Rosmer. We will force you to come back to us.

ROSMER. I can never stand where I did.

KROLL. We shall see. You are not the man to endure standing alone.

ROSMER. I shall not be so completely alone after all.—There are two of us to bear the loneliness together.

KROLL. Ah——. (*A suspicion appears in his face.*) That too! Beata's words——!

ROSMER. Beata's——?

KROLL (*shaking off the thought*). No, no—that was vile. Forgive me.

ROSMER. What? What do you mean?

KROLL. Don't ask. Bah! Forgive me! Good-bye!
(*Goes towards the entrance door.*)

ROSMER (*follows him*). Kroll! Our friendship must not end like this. I will come and see you to-morrow.

KROLL (*in the hall, turns*). You shall never cross my threshold again.
(*He takes up his stick and goes out.*)
(ROSMER *stands for a moment in the doorway; then shuts the door and walks up to the table.*)

ROSMER. It does not matter, Rebecca. We will see it out, we two faithful friends—you [3] and I.

REBECCA. What do you think he meant when he said "That was vile"?

ROSMER. Don't trouble about that, dear. He himself didn't believe what was in his mind. To-morrow I will go and see him. Good-night!

REBECCA. Are you going upstairs so early to-night? After this?

ROSMER. To-night as usual. I feel so relieved, now it is over. You see—I am quite calm, Rebecca. Do you, too, take it calmly. Good-night!

REBECCA. Good-night, dear friend! Sleep well!
(ROSMER *goes out by the hall door; his steps are heard ascending the staircase.*)
(REBECCA *goes and pulls a bell-rope near the stove. Shortly after,* MADAM HELSETH *enters from the right.*)

REBECCA. You can take away the supper things, Madam Helseth. Mr. Rosmer doesn't want anything, and the Rector has gone home.

MADAM HELSETH. Has the Rector gone? What was the matter with him?

REBECCA (*takes up her crochet work*). He said he thought there was a heavy storm brewing——

---

[3] From this point, and throughout when alone, Rosmer and Rebecca use the *du* of intimate friendship in speaking of each other.

MADAM HELSETH. What a strange notion! There's not a cloud in the sky this evening.

REBECCA. Let us hope he mayn't meet the White Horse! I'm afraid we shall soon be hearing something from the bogies now.

MADAM HELSETH. Lord forgive you, Miss! Don't say such awful things.

REBECCA. Well, well, well——

MADAM HELSETH (softly). Do you really think some one is to go soon, Miss?

REBECCA. No; why should I think so? But there are so many sorts of white horses in this world, Madam Helseth.—Well, good-night. I shall go to my room now.

MADAM HELSETH. Good-night, Miss.

(REBECCA goes out to the right, with her crochet work.)

MADAM HELSETH (turns the lamp down, shaking her head and muttering to herself). Lord—Lord! That Miss West! The things she does say!

ACT TWO

JOHANNES ROSMER's study. Entrance door on the left. At the back, a doorway with a curtain drawn aside, leading into ROSMER's bedroom. On the right a window, and in front of it a writing-table covered with books and papers. Book-shelves and cases round the room. The furniture is simple. On the left, an old-fashioned sofa, with a table in front of it.

JOHANNES ROSMER, in an indoor jacket, is sitting in a high-backed chair at the writing-table. He is cutting and turning over the leaves of a pamphlet, and reading a little here and there.

There is a knock at the door on the left.

ROSMER (without moving). Come in.

REBECCA WEST (enters, dressed in a morning gown). Good morning.

ROSMER (turning the leaves of the pamphlet). Good morning, dear. Do you want anything?

REBECCA. I only wanted to hear if you had slept well.

ROSMER. Oh, I have had a beautiful, peaceful night. (Turns.) And you?

REBECCA. Oh, yes, thanks—towards morning——

ROSMER. I don't know when I have felt so light-hearted as I do now. I am so glad I managed to speak out at last.

REBECCA. Yes, it is a pity you remained silent so long, Rosmer.

ROSMER. I don't understand myself how I could be such a coward.

REBECCA. It wasn't precisely cowardice——

ROSMER. Oh, yes, dear—when I think the thing out, I can see there was a touch of cowardice at the bottom of it.

REBECCA. All the braver, then, to make the plunge at last. (Sits on a chair at the writing-table, close to him.) But now I want to tell you of something I have done—and you mustn't be vexed with me about it.

ROSMER. Vexed? How can you think——?

REBECCA. Well, it was perhaps rather indiscreet of me but——

ROSMER. Let me hear what it was.

REBECCA. Yesterday evening, when Ulric Brendel was leaving—I gave him a note to Peter Mortensgård.

ROSMER (a little doubtful). Why, my dear Rebecca—— Well, what did you say?

REBECCA. I said that he would be doing you a service if he would look after that unfortunate creature a little, and help him in any way he could.

ROSMER. Dear, you shouldn't have done that. You have only done Brendel harm. And Mortensgård is not a man I care to have anything to do with. You know of that old episode between us.

REBECCA. But don't you think it would be as well to make it up with him again?

ROSMER. I? With Mortensgård? In what way do you mean?

REBECCA. Well, you know you can't feel absolutely secure now—after this breach with your old friends.

ROSMER (looks at her and shakes his head). Can you really believe that Kroll or any of the others would try to take revenge on me? That they would be capable of——?

REBECCA. In the first heat of anger, dear——. No one can be sure. I think—after the way the Rector took it——.

ROSMER. Oh, you ought surely to know him better than that. Kroll is a gentleman, to the backbone. I am going into town this afternoon to talk to him. I will talk to them all. Oh, you shall see how easily it will all go——

(MADAM HELSETH appears at the door on the left.)

REBECCA (rises). What is it, Madam Helseth?

MADAM HELSETH. Rector Kroll is downstairs in the hall.

ROSMER (rises hastily). Kroll!

REBECCA. The Rector! Is it possible——

MADAM HELSETH. He wants to know if he may come upstairs, Mr. Rosmer.

ROSMER (to REBECCA). What did I tell you?—Of

course he may. (*Goes to the door and calls down the stairs.*) Come up, dear friend! I am delighted to see you.

(ROSMER *stands holding the door open.* MADAM HELSETH *goes out.* REBECCA *draws the curtain before the doorway at the back and then begins arranging things in the room.*)

(RECTOR KROLL *enters, with his hat in his hand.*)

ROSMER (*with quiet emotion*). I knew it couldn't be the last time——

KROLL. I see things to-day in quite a different light from yesterday.

ROSMER. Ah, yes, Kroll; I was sure you would, now that you have had time to reflect.

KROLL. You misunderstand me completely. (*Lays his hat on the table beside the sofa.*) It is of the utmost importance that I should speak to you, alone.

ROSMER. Why may not Miss West——?

REBECCA. No, no, Mr. Rosmer. I will go.

KROLL (*looks at her from head to foot*). And I must ask Miss West to excuse my coming at such an untimely hour—taking her unawares before she has had time to——

REBECCA (*surprised*). What do you mean? Do you see any harm in my wearing a morning gown about the house?

KROLL. Heaven forbid! I know nothing of what may now be customary at Rosmersholm.

ROSMER. Why, Kroll—you are not yourself to-day!

REBECCA. Allow me to wish you good morning, Rector Kroll.

(*She goes out to the left.*)

KROLL. By your leave——

(*Sits on the sofa.*)

ROSMER. Yes, Kroll, sit down, and let us talk things out amicably.

(*He seats himself in a chair directly opposite to the* RECTOR.)

KROLL. I haven't closed an eye since yesterday. I have been lying thinking and thinking all night.

ROSMER. And what do you say to things to-day?

KROLL. It will be a long story, Rosmer. Let me begin with a sort of introduction. I can give you news of Ulric Brendel.

ROSMER. Has he called on you?

KROLL. No. He took up his quarters in a low public-house—in the lowest company of course—and drank and stood treat as long as he had any money. Then he began abusing the whole company as a set of disreputable blackguards—and so far he was quite right—whereupon they thrashed him and pitched him out into the gutter.

ROSMER. So he is incorrigible after all.

KROLL. He had pawned the coat, too; but I am told that has been redeemed for him. Can you guess by whom?

ROSMER. Perhaps by you?

KROLL. No; by the distinguished Mr. Mortensgård.

ROSMER. Ah, indeed.

KROLL. I understand that Mr. Brendel's first visit was to the "idiot" and "plebeian."

ROSMER. Well, it was lucky for him——

KROLL. To be sure it was. (*Leans over the table towards* ROSMER.) And that brings me to a matter it is my duty to warn you about, for our old—for our former friendship's sake.

ROSMER. My dear Kroll, what can that be?

KROLL. It is this: there are things going on behind your back in this house.

ROSMER. How can you think so? Is it Reb—is it Miss West you are aiming at?

KROLL. Precisely. I can quite understand it on her part. She has so long been accustomed to have everything her own way here. But nevertheless——

ROSMER. My dear Kroll, you are utterly mistaken. She and I—we have no concealments from each other on any subject whatever.

KROLL. Has she told you, then, that she has entered into correspondence with the editor of the "Beacon"?

ROSMER. Oh, you are thinking of the few lines she sent by Ulric Brendel?

KROLL. Then you have found it out. And do you approve of her entering into relations with a scurrilous scribbler, who never lets a week pass without holding me up to ridicule, both as a schoolmaster and as a public man?

ROSMER. My dear Kroll, I don't suppose that side of the matter ever entered her head. And besides, of course she has full liberty of action, just as I have.

KROLL. Indeed? Ah, no doubt that follows from your new line of thought. For Miss West presumably shares your present standpoint?

ROSMER. Yes, she does. We two have worked our way forward in faithful comradeship.

KROLL (*looks at him and slowly shakes his head*). Oh, you blind, deluded being!

ROSMER. I? Why do you say that?

KROLL. Because I dare not—I will not think the worst. No no, let me say my say out.—You really do value my friendship, Rosmer? And my respect too? Do you not?

ROSMER. I surely need not answer that question.

KROLL. Well, but there are other questions that do require an answer—a full explanation on your part.—Will you submit to a sort of investigation———?

ROSMER. Investigation?

KROLL. Yes; will you let me question you about certain things it may pain you to be reminded of? You see—this apostasy of yours—well, this emancipation, as you call it—is bound up with many other things that for your own sake you must explain to me.

ROSMER. My dear Kroll, ask what questions you please. I have nothing to conceal.

KROLL. Then tell me—what do you think was the real, the ultimate reason why Beata put an end to her life?

ROSMER. Can you have any doubt on the subject? Or, rather, can you ask for reasons for what an unhappy, irresponsible invalid may do?

KROLL. Are you certain that Beata was completely irresponsible for her actions? The doctors, at any rate, were by no means convinced of it.

ROSMER. If the doctors had ever seen her as I have so often seen her, for days and nights together, they would have had no doubts.

KROLL. I had no doubts either—then.

ROSMER. Oh, no, unhappily, there wasn't the smallest room for doubt. I have told you of her wild frenzies of passion—which she expected me to return. Oh, how they appalled me! And then her causeless, consuming self-reproaches during the last few years.

KROLL. Yes, when she had learnt that she must remain childless all her life.

ROSMER. Yes, just think of that! Such terrible, haunting agony of mind about a thing utterly beyond her control——! How could you call her responsible for her actions?

KROLL. H'm——. Can you remember whether you had any books in the house at that time treating of the rationale of marriage—according to the "advanced" ideas of the day?

ROSMER. I remember Miss West lending me a work of the kind. The Doctor left her his library, you know. But, my dear Kroll, you surely cannot suppose we were so reckless as to let my poor sick wife get hold of any such ideas? I can solemnly assure you that the fault was not ours. It was her own distempered brain that drove her into these wild aberrations.

KROLL. One thing at any rate I can tell you; and that is, that poor, overstrung, tortured Beata put an end to her life in order that you might live happily —live freely, and—after your own heart.

ROSMER (starts half up from his chair). What do you mean by that?

KROLL. Listen to me quietly, Rosmer; for now I can speak of it. In the last year of her life she came to me twice to pour forth all her anguish and despair.

ROSMER. On this same subject?

KROLL. No. The first time she came, it was to declare that you were on the road to perversion— that you were going to break with the faith of your fathers.

ROSMER (eagerly). What you say is impossible, Kroll. Absolutely impossible. You must be mistaken.

KROLL. And why?

ROSMER. Because while Beata was alive I was still wrestling with myself in doubt. And that fight I fought out alone and in utter silence. I don't think even Rebecca——

KROLL. Rebecca?

ROSMER. Oh, well—Miss West. I call her Rebecca for convenience' sake.

KROLL. So I have remarked.

ROSMER. So it is inconceivable to me how Beata could have got hold of the idea. And why did she not speak to me about it? She never did—she never said a single word.

KROLL. Poor creature—she begged and implored me to talk to you.

ROSMER. And why did you not?

KROLL. At that time I never for a moment doubted that she was out of her mind. Such an accusation against a man like you!—And then she came again— about a month later. This time she seemed outwardly calmer; but as she was going she said: "They may soon expect the White Horse at Rosmersholm now."

ROSMER. Yes, yes. The White Horse—she often spoke of it.

KROLL. And when I tried to divert her mind from such melancholy fancies, she only answered: "I have not long to live; for Johannes must marry Rebecca at once."

ROSMER (almost speechless). What do you say? I marry——?

KROLL. That was on a Thursday afternoon——. On the Saturday evening she threw herself from the bridge into the mill-race.

ROSMER. And you never warned us——!

KROLL. You know very well how often she used to say that she felt her end was near.

ROSMER. Yes, I know. But nevertheless—you should have warned us!

KROLL. I did think of it; but not till too late.

ROSMER. But afterwards, why did you not——? Why have you said nothing about all this?

KROLL. What good would it have done for me to come torturing and harassing you still further? I took all she said for mere wild, empty ravings—until yesterday evening.

ROSMER. Then you have now changed your opinion?

KROLL. Did not Beata see quite clearly when she declared you were about to desert the faith of your fathers?

ROSMER (looks fixedly, straight before him). I cannot understand it. It is the most incomprehensible thing in the world.

KROLL. Incomprehensible or not—there it is. And now I ask you, Rosmer,—how much truth is there in her other accusation? The last one, I mean.

ROSMER. Accusation? Was that an accusation?

KROLL. Perhaps you did not notice the way she worded it. She had to go, she said—why?

ROSMER. In order that I might marry Rebecca——

KROLL. These were not precisely her words. Beata used a different expression. She said: "I have not long to live; for Johannes must marry Rebecca at once."

ROSMER (looks at him for a moment; then rises). Now I understand you, Kroll.

KROLL. And what then? What is your answer?

ROSMER (still quiet and self-restrained). To such an unheard-of——? The only fitting answer would be to point to the door.

KROLL (rises). Well and good.

ROSMER (stands in front of him). Listen to me. For more than a year—ever since Beata left us—Rebecca West and I have lived alone here at Rosmersholm. During all that time you have known of Beata's accusation against us. But I have never for a moment noticed that you disapproved of Rebecca's living in my house.

KROLL. I did not know till yesterday evening that it was an unbelieving man who was living with an—emancipated woman.

ROSMER. Ah——! Then you do not believe that purity of mind is to be found among the unbelieving and the emancipated? You do not believe that morality may be an instinctive law of their nature!

KROLL. I have no great faith in the morality that is not founded on the teachings of the Church.

ROSMER. And you mean this to apply to Rebecca and me? To the relation between us two——?

KROLL. Not even out of consideration for you two can I depart from my opinion that there is no unfathomable gulf between free thought and—h'm——

ROSMER. And what?

KROLL. ——and free love,—since you will have it.

ROSMER (in a low voice). And you are not ashamed to say this to me! You, who have known me from my earliest youth!

KROLL. For that very reason. I know how easily you are influenced by the people you associate with. And this Rebecca of yours—well, Miss West then—we really know little or nothing about her. In short, Rosmer—I will not give you up. And you—you must try to save yourself in time.

ROSMER. Save myself? How——?

(MADAM HELSETH peeps in at the door on the left.)

ROSMER. What do you want?

MADAM HELSETH. I wanted to ask Miss West to step downstairs.

ROSMER. Miss West is not up here.

MADAM HELSETH. Isn't she? (Looks round the room.) Well, that's strange.

(She goes.)

ROSMER. You were saying——?

KROLL. Listen to me. I am not going to inquire too closely into the secret history of what went on here in Beata's lifetime—and may still be going on. I know that your marriage was a most unhappy one; and I suppose that must be taken as some sort of excuse——

ROSMER. Oh, how little you really know me——!

KROLL. Don't interrupt me. What I mean is this: if your present mode of life with Miss West is to continue, it is absolutely necessary that the change of views—the unhappy backsliding—brought about by her evil influence, should be hushed up. Let me speak! Let me speak! I say, if the worst comes to the worst, in Heaven's name think and believe whatever you like about everything under the sun. But you must keep your views to yourself. These things are purely personal matters, after all. There is no need to proclaim them from the housetops.

ROSMER. I feel an absolute necessity to get out of a false and equivocal position.

KROLL. But you have a duty towards the traditions of your race, Rosmer! Remember that! Rosmersholm has, so to speak, radiated morality and order from time immemorial—yes and respectful conformity to all that is accepted and sanctioned by the best people. The whole district has taken its stamp from Rosmersholm. It would lead to deplorable, irremediable confusion if it were known that you had broken with what I may call the hereditary idea of the house of Rosmer.

ROSMER. My dear Kroll, I cannot see the matter in that light. I look upon it as my imperative duty to spread a little light and gladness here, where the Rosmer family has from generation to generation been a centre of darkness and oppression.

KROLL (*looks at him severely*). Yes, that would be a worthy life-work for the last of your race! No, Rosmer; let such things alone; you are the last man for such a task. You were born to be a quiet student.

ROSMER. Perhaps so. But for once in a way I mean to bear my part in the battle of life.

KROLL. And do you know what that battle of life will mean for you? It will mean a life-and-death struggle with all your friends.

ROSMER (*quietly*). They cannot all be such fanatics as you.

KROLL. You are a credulous creature, Rosmer. An inexperienced creature, too. You have no conception of the overwhelming storm that will burst upon you.

(MADAM HELSETH *looks in at the door, on the left.*)

MADAM HELSETH. Miss West wants to know——

ROSMER. What is it?

MADAM HELSETH. There's a man downstairs wanting to have a word with the Pastor.

ROSMER. Is it the man who was here yesterday evening?

MADAM HELSETH. No, it's that Mortensgård.

ROSMER. Mortensgård?

KROLL. Aha! So it has come to this, has it?— Already!

ROSMER. What does he want with me? Why didn't you send him away?

MADAM HELSETH. Miss West said I was to ask if he might come upstairs?

ROSMER. Tell him I'm engaged——

KROLL (*to* MADAM HELSETH). Let him come up, Madam Helseth.

(MADAM HELSETH *goes.*)

KROLL (*takes up his hat*). I retire from the field— for the moment. But the main battle has yet to be fought.

ROSMER. On my honour, Kroll—I have nothing whatever to do with Mortensgård.

KROLL. I do not believe you. On no subject and in no relation whatever will I henceforth believe you. It is war to the knife now. We will try whether we cannot disarm you.

ROSMER. Oh, Kroll—how low—how very low you have sunk!

KROLL. I? And you think you have the right to say that to me! Remember Beata!

ROSMER. Still harping upon that?

KROLL. No. You must solve the enigma of the mill-race according to your own conscience—if you have anything of the sort left.

(PETER MORTENSGÅRD *enters softly and quietly from the left. He is a small, wiry man with thin reddish hair and beard.*)

KROLL (*with a look of hatred*). Ah, here we have the "Beacon"—burning at Rosmersholm! (*Buttons his coat.*) Well, now I can no longer hesitate what course to steer.

MORTENSGÅRD (*deferentially*). The "Beacon" may always be relied upon to light the Rector home.

KROLL. Yes; you have long shown your goodwill. To be sure there's a commandment about bearing false witness against your neighbour——

MORTENSGÅRD. Rector Kroll need not instruct me in the commandments.

KROLL. Not even in the seventh?

ROSMER. Kroll——!

MORTENSGÅRD. If I needed instruction, it would rather be the Pastor's business.

KROLL (*with covert sarcasm*). The Pastor's? Oh, yes, unquestionably Pastor Rosmer is the man for that.—Good luck to your conference, gentlemen!

(*Goes out and slams the door behind him.*)

ROSMER (*keeps his eyes fixed on the closed door and says to himself*). Well, well—so be it then. (*Turns.*) Will you be good enough to tell me, Mr. Mortensgård, what brings you out here to me?

MORTENSGÅRD. It was really Miss West I came to see. I wanted to thank her for the friendly note I received from her yesterday.

ROSMER. I know she wrote to you. Have you seen her then?

MORTENSGÅRD. Yes, for a short time. (*Smiles slightly.*) I hear there has been a certain change of views out here at Rosmersholm.

ROSMER. My views are altered in many respects. I might almost say in all.

MORTENSGÅRD. So Miss West told me; and that's why she thought I had better come up and talk things over with the Pastor.

ROSMER. What things, Mr. Mortensgård?

MORTENSGÅRD. May I announce in the "Beacon" that there has been a change in your views—that you have joined the party of freedom and progress?

ROSMER. Certainly you may. In fact, I beg you to make the announcement.

MORTENSGÅRD. Then it shall appear in to-morrow's paper. It will cause a great sensation when it's known that Pastor Rosmer of Rosmersholm is prepared to take up arms for the cause of light, in that sense, too.

ROSMER. I don't quite understand you.

MORTENSGÅRD. I mean that the moral position of our party is greatly strengthened whenever we gain an adherent of serious, Christian principles.

ROSMER (*with some surprise*). Then you do not know——? Did not Miss West tell you that, too?

MORTENSGÅRD. What, Pastor Rosmer? Miss West was in a great hurry. She said I was to go upstairs and hear the rest from yourself.

ROSMER. Well, in that case I may tell you that I have emancipated myself entirely, and on every side. I have broken with all the dogmas of the Church. Henceforth they are nothing to me.

MORTENSGÅRD (*looks at him in amazement*). Well—if the skies were to fall I couldn't be more——! Pastor Rosmer himself announces——.

ROSMER. Yes, I now stand where you have stood for many years. That, too, you may announce in the "Beacon" to-morrow.

MORTENSGÅRD. That too? No, my dear Pastor— excuse me—— I don't think it would be wise to touch on that side of the matter.

ROSMER. Not touch on it?

MORTENSGÅRD. Not at present, I mean.

ROSMER. I don't understand——

MORTENSGÅRD. Well, you see, Pastor Rosmer— you probably don't know the ins and outs of things so well as I do. But, since you have come over to the party of freedom—and, as I hear from Miss West, you intend to take an active share in the movement—I presume you would like to be of as much service as possible, both to the cause in general and to this particular agitation.

ROSMER. Yes, that is my earnest wish.

MORTENSGÅRD. Good. But now I must tell you, Pastor Rosmer, that if you openly declare your defection from the Church, you tie your own hands at the very outset.

ROSMER. Do you think so?

MORTENSGÅRD. Yes, believe me, you won't be able to do much for the cause, in this part of the country at any rate. And besides—we have plenty of free-thinkers already, Pastor Rosmer—I might almost say too many. What the party requires, is a Christian element—something that every one must respect. That is what we are sadly in need of. And, therefore, I advise you to keep your own counsel about what doesn't concern the public. That's my view of the matter, at least.

ROSMER. I understand. Then if I openly confess my apostasy, you dare not have anything to do with me?

MORTENSGÅRD (*shaking his head*). I scarcely like to risk it, Pastor Rosmer. I have made it a rule for some time past not to support any one or anything that is actively opposed to the Church.

ROSMER. Then you have yourself returned to the Church?

MORTENSGÅRD. That concerns no one but myself.

ROSMER. Ah, so that is it. Now I understand you.

MORTENSGÅRD. Pastor Rosmer—you ought to remember that I—I in particular—have not full liberty of action.

ROSMER. What hampers you?

MORTENSGÅRD. The fact that I am a marked man.

ROSMER. Ah—indeed.

MORTENSGÅRD. A marked man, Pastor Rosmer. You, above all men, should remember that; for I have chiefly you to thank for the scandal that branded me.

ROSMER. If I had then stood where I stand now, I should have dealt more gently with your offence.

MORTENSGÅRD. That I don't doubt. But it is too late now. You have branded me once for all— branded me for life. I suppose you can scarcely understand what that means. But now you may perhaps come to feel the smart of it yourself, Pastor Rosmer.

ROSMER. I?

MORTENSGÅRD. Yes. You surely don't suppose that Rector Kroll and his set will ever forgive a desertion like yours? I hear the "County News" is going to be very savage in future. You, too, may find yourself a marked man before long.

ROSMER. In personal matters, Mr. Mortensgård, I feel myself secure from attack. My life is beyond reproach.

MORTENSGÅRD (*with a sly smile*). That's a large word, Mr. Rosmer.

ROSMER. Perhaps; but I have a right to use it.

MORTENSGÅRD. Even if you were to scrutinise your conduct as closely as you once scrutinised mine?

ROSMER. Your tone is very curious. What are you hinting at? Anything definite?

MORTENSGÅRD. Yes, something definite. Only one thing. But that might be bad enough, if malicious opponents got wind of it.

ROSMER. Will you have the kindness to let me hear what it is?

MORTENSGÅRD. Cannot you guess for yourself, Pastor?

ROSMER. No, certainly not. I have not the slightest idea.

MORTENSGÅRD. Well, well, I suppose I must come out with it then.—I have in my possession a strange letter, dated from Rosmersholm.

ROSMER. Miss West's letter, do you mean? Is it so strange?

MORTENSGÅRD. No, there's nothing strange about that. But I once received another letter from this house.

ROSMER. Also from Miss West?

MORTENSGÅRD. No, Mr. Rosmer.

ROSMER. Well then, from whom? From whom?

MORTENSGÅRD. From the late Mrs. Rosmer.

ROSMER. From my wife? You received a letter from my wife!

MORTENSGÅRD. I did.

ROSMER. When?

MORTENSGÅRD. Towards the close of Mrs. Rosmer's life. Perhaps about a year and a half ago. That is the letter I call strange.

ROSMER. I suppose you know that my wife's mind was affected at that time.

MORTENSGÅRD. Yes; I know many people thought so. But I don't think there was anything in the letter to show it. When I call it strange, I mean in another sense.

ROSMER. And what in the world did my poor wife take it into her head to write to you about?

MORTENSGÅRD. I have the letter at home. She begins to the effect that she is living in great anxiety and fear; there are so many malicious people about here, she says; and they think of nothing but causing you trouble and injury.

ROSMER. Me?

MORTENSGÅRD. Yes, so she says. And then comes the strangest part of all. Shall I go on, Pastor Rosmer?

ROSMER. Assuredly! Tell me everything, without reserve.

MORTENSGÅRD. The deceased lady begs and implores me to be magnanimous. She knows, she says, that it was her husband that had me dismissed from my post as teacher; and she conjured me by all that's sacred not to avenge myself.

ROSMER. How did she suppose you could avenge yourself?

MORTENSGÅRD. The letter says that if I should hear rumours of sinful doings at Rosmersholm, I am not to believe them; they are only spread abroad by wicked people who wish to make you unhappy.

ROSMER. Is all that in the letter?

MORTENSGÅRD. You may read it for yourself, sir, when you please.

ROSMER. But I don't understand——! What did she imagine the rumour to be about?

MORTENSGÅRD. Firstly, that the Pastor had deserted the faith of his fathers. Your wife denied that absolutely—then. And next—h'm——

ROSMER. Next?

MORTENSGÅRD. Well, next she writes—rather confusedly—that she knows nothing of any sinful intrigue at Rosmersholm; that she has never been wronged in any way. And if any such rumours should get about, she implores me to say nothing of the matter in the "Beacon."

ROSMER. Is no name mentioned?

MORTENSGÅRD. None.

ROSMER. Who brought you the letter?

MORTENSGÅRD. I have promised not to say. It was handed to me one evening, at dusk.

ROSMER. If you had made inquiries at the time, you would have learnt that my poor, unhappy wife was not fully accountable for her actions.

MORTENSGÅRD. I did make inquiries, Pastor Rosmer. But I must say that was not the impression I received.

ROSMER. Was it not?—But what is your precise reason for telling me now about this incomprehensible old letter?

MORTENSGÅRD. To impress on you the necessity for extreme prudence, Pastor Rosmer.

ROSMER. In my life, do you mean?

MORTENSGÅRD. Yes. You must remember that from today you have ceased to be a neutral.

ROSMER. Then you have quite made up your mind that I must have something to conceal?

MORTENSGÅRD. I don't know why an emancipated man should refrain from living his life out as fully as possible. But, as I said before, be exceedingly cautious in future. If anything should get abroad that conflicts with current prejudices, you may be sure the whole liberal movement will have to suffer for it.—Good-bye, Pastor Rosmer.

ROSMER. Good-bye.

MORTENSGÅRD. I shall go straight to the office and have the great news put into the "Beacon."

ROSMER. Yes; omit nothing.

MORTENSGÅRD. I shall omit nothing that the public need know.

(He bows and goes out. ROSMER remains standing in the doorway while he goes down the stairs. The outer door is heard to close.)

ROSMER (in the doorway, calls softly). Rebecca!

Re— H'm. (*Aloud.*) Madam Helseth,—is Miss West not there?

MADAM HELSETH (*from the hall*). No, Pastor Rosmer, she's not here.

(*The curtain at the back is drawn aside.* REBECCA *appears in the doorway.*)

REBECCA. Rosmer!

ROSMER (*turns*). What! Were you in my room? My dear, what were you doing there?

REBECCA (*goes up to him*). I was listening.

ROSMER. Oh, Rebecca, how could you?

REBECCA. I could not help it. He said it so hatefully—that about my morning gown——

ROSMER. Then you were there when Kroll——?

REBECCA. Yes. I wanted to know what was lurking in his mind.

ROSMER. I would have told you.

REBECCA. You would scarcely have told me all. And certainly not in his own words.

ROSMER. Did you hear everything, then?

REBECCA. Nearly everything, I think. I had to go downstairs for a moment when Mortensgård came.

ROSMER. And then you came back again——?

REBECCA. Don't be vexed with me, dear friend!

ROSMER. Do whatever you think right. You are mistress of your own actions.—But what do you say to all this, Rebecca——? Oh, I seem never to have needed you so much before!

REBECCA. Both you and I have been prepared for what must happen some time.

ROSMER. No, no—not for this.

REBECCA. Not for this?

ROSMER. I knew well enough that sooner or later our beautiful, pure friendship might be misinterpreted and soiled. Not by Kroll—I could never have believed such a thing of him—but by all those other people with the coarse souls and the ignoble eyes. Oh yes—I had reason enough for keeping our alliance so jealously concealed. It was a dangerous secret.

REBECCA. Oh, why should we care what all those people think! We know in our own hearts that we are blameless.

ROSMER. Blameless? I? Yes, I thought so—till today. But now—now, Rebecca——?

REBECCA. Well, what now?

ROSMER. How am I to explain Beata's terrible accusation?

REBECCA (*vehemently*). Oh, don't speak of Beata! Don't think of Beata any more! You were just beginning to shake off the hold she has upon you, even in the grave.

ROSMER. Since I have heard all this, she seems, in a ghastly sort of way, to be alive again.

REBECCA. Oh no—not that, Rosmer! Not that!

ROSMER. Yes, I tell you. We must try to get to the bottom of this. What can possibly have led her to misinterpret things so fatally?

REBECCA. You are surely not beginning to doubt that she was on the very verge of insanity?

ROSMER. Oh yes—that is just what I can't feel quite certain of any longer. And besides—even if she was——

REBECCA. If she was? Well, what then?

ROSMER. I mean—where are we to look for the determining cause that drove her morbid spirit over the borderline of madness?

REBECCA. Oh, why brood over problems no one can solve?

ROSMER. I cannot help it, Rebecca. I cannot shake off these gnawing doubts, however much I may wish to.

REBECCA. But it may become dangerous—this eternal dwelling upon one miserable subject.

ROSMER (*walks about restlessly, in thought*). I must have betrayed myself in one way or another. She must have noticed how happy I began to feel from the time you came to us.

REBECCA. Yes but, dear, even if she did——?

ROSMER. Be sure it didn't escape her that we read the same books—that the interest of discussing all the new ideas drew us together. Yet I cannot understand it! I was so careful to spare her. As I look back, it seems to me I made it the business of my life to keep her in ignorance of all our interests. Did I not, Rebecca?

REBECCA. Yes, yes; certainly you did.

ROSMER. And you, too. And yet——! Oh, it's terrible to think of! She must have gone about here —full of her morbid passion—saying never a word— watching us—noting everything—and misinterpreting everything.

REBECCA (*pressing her hands together*). Oh, I should never have come to Rosmersholm!

ROSMER. To think of all she must have suffered in silence! All the foulness her sick brain must have conjured up around us! Did she never say anything to you to put you at all on the alert?

REBECCA (*as if startled*). To me! Do you think I should have stayed a day longer if she had?

ROSMER. No, no, of course not.—Oh, what a battle she must have fought! And alone, too, Rebecca; desperate and quite alone!—and then, at last, that heart-breaking, accusing victory—in the mill-race.

(*Throws himself into the chair by the writing-table, with his elbows on the table and his face in his hands.*)

REBECCA (*approaches him cautiously from behind*). Listen, Rosmer. If it were in your power to call Beata back—to you—to Rosmersholm—would you do it?

ROSMER. Oh, how do I know what I would or would not do? I can think of nothing but this one thing—that cannot be recalled.

REBECCA. You were just beginning to live, Rosmer. You had begun. You had freed yourself—on every side. You felt so buoyant and happy——

ROSMER. Oh, yes—I did indeed.—And now this crushing blow falls on me.

REBECCA (*behind him, rests her arms on the chair-back*). How beautiful it was when we sat in the twilight, in the room downstairs, helping each other to lay out our new life-plans! You were to set resolutely to work in the world—the living world of to-day, as you said. You were to go as a messenger of emancipation from home to home; to win over minds and wills; to create noble-men around you in wider and wider circles. Noble-men.

ROSMER. Happy noble-men.

REBECCA. Yes—happy.

ROSMER. For it is happiness that ennobles, Rebecca.

REBECCA. Should you not say—sorrow as well? A great sorrow?

ROSMER. Yes—if one can get through it—over it—away from it.

REBECCA. That is what you must do.

ROSMER (*shakes his head gloomily*). I shall never get over this—wholly. There will always be a doubt—a question left. I can never again know that luxury of the soul which makes life so marvellously sweet to live!

REBECCA (*bends over his chair-back, and says more softly*). What is it you mean, Rosmer?

ROSMER (*looking up at her*). Peaceful, happy innocence.

REBECCA (*recoils a step*). Yes. Innocence.

(*A short pause.*)

ROSMER (*with his elbow on the table, leaning his head on his hand, and looking straight before him*). And what extraordinary penetration she showed! How systematically she put all this together! First she begins to doubt my orthodoxy——How could that occur to her? But it did occur to her; and then it grew to a certainty. And then—yes, then of course it was easy for her to think all the rest possible. (*Sits up in his chair and runs his hands through his hair.*) Oh, all these horrible imaginings! I shall never get rid of them. I feel it. I know it. At any moment they will come rushing in upon me, and bring back the thought of the dead!

REBECCA. Like the White Horse of Rosmersholm.

ROSMER. Yes, like that. Rushing forth in the darkness—in the silence.

REBECCA. And because of this miserable figment of the brain, you will let slip the hold you were beginning to take upon the living world?

ROSMER. You may well think it hard. Yes, hard, Rebecca. But I have no choice. How could I ever leave this behind me?

REBECCA (*behind his chair*). By entering into new relations.

ROSMER (*surprised, looks up*). New relations?

REBECCA. Yes, new relations to the outside world. Live, work, act. Don't sit here brooding and groping among insoluble enigmas.

ROSMER (*rises*). New relations? (*Walks across the floor, stops at the door and then comes back.*) One question occurs to me. Has it occurred to you too, Rebecca?

REBECCA (*drawing breath with difficulty*). Let me—hear—what it is.

ROSMER. What form do you think our relations will take after to-day?

REBECCA. I believe our friendship will endure—come what may.

ROSMER. That is not exactly what I meant. The thing that first brought us together, and that unites us so closely—our common faith in a pure comradeship between man and woman——

REBECCA. Yes, yes—what of that?

ROSMER. I mean, that such a relation—as this of ours—does it not presuppose a quiet, happy, peaceful life——?

REBECCA. What then?

ROSMER. But the life I must now look forward to is one of struggle and unrest and strong agitations. For I will live my life, Rebecca! I will not be crushed to earth by horrible possibilities. I will not have my course of life forced upon me, either by the living or by—any one else.

REBECCA. No, no—do not! Be an absolutely free man, Rosmer!

ROSMER. But can you not guess what is in my mind? Do you not know? Don't you see how I can best shake off all gnawing memories—all the unhappy past?

REBECCA. How?

ROSMER. By opposing to it a new, a living reality.

REBECCA (*feeling for the chair-back*). A living—— What do you mean?

ROSMER (*comes nearer*). Rebecca—if I were to ask you—will you be my second wife?

REBECCA (*for a moment speechless, then cries out with joy.*) Your wife! Your——! I!

ROSMER. Come; let us try it. We two will be one. The place of the dead must stand empty no longer.

REBECCA. I—in Beata's place——!

ROSMER. Then she will be out of the saga—completely—for ever and ever.

REBECCA (*softly, trembling*). Do you believe that, Rosmer?

ROSMER. It must be so! It must! I cannot—I will not go through life with a dead body on my back. Help me to cast it off, Rebecca. And let us stifle all memories in freedom, in joy, in passion. You shall be to me the only wife I have ever had.

REBECCA (*with self-command*). Never speak of this again. I will never be your wife.

ROSMER. What! Never! Do you not think you could come to love me? Is there not already a strain of love in our friendship?

REBECCA (*puts her hands over her ears as if in terror*). Don't speak so, Rosmer! Don't say such things!

ROSMER (*seizes her arm*). Yes, yes—there is a growing promise in our relation. Oh, I can see that you feel it, too. Do you not, Rebecca?

REBECCA (*once more firm and calm*). Listen to me. I tell you—if you persist in this, I will go away from Rosmersholm.

ROSMER. Go way! You! You cannot. It is impossible.

REBECCA. It is still more impossible that I should be your wife. Never in this world can I marry you.

ROSMER (*looks at her in surprise*). You say "can"; and you say it so strangely. Why can you not?

REBECCA (*seizes both his hands*). Dear friend—both for your own sake and for mine—do not ask why. (*Lets go his hands.*) Do not, Rosmer.

(*Goes towards the door on the left.*)

ROSMER. Henceforth I can think of nothing but that one question—why?

REBECCA (*turns and looks at him*). Then it is all over.

ROSMER. Between you and me?

REBECCA. Yes.

ROSMER. It will never be all over between us two. You will never leave Rosmersholm.

REBECCA (*with her hand on the door-handle*). No, perhaps I shall not. But if you ask me again— it is all over.

ROSMER. All over? How——?

REBECCA. For then I will go the way that Beata went. Now you know it, Rosmer.

ROSMER. Rebecca——?

REBECCA (*in the doorway, nods slowly*). Now you know it.

(*She goes out.*)

ROSMER (*stares, thunderstruck, at the door, and says to himself*). What—is—this?

ACT THREE

The sitting-room at Rosmersholm. The window and the entrance door are open. The sun is shining outside. Forenoon.

REBECCA WEST, *dressed as in the first Act, stands at the window, watering and arranging the flowers. Her crochet work lies in the armchair.* MADAM HELSETH *is moving about, dusting the furniture with a feather-brush.*

REBECCA (*after a short silence*). I can't understand the Pastor remaining so long upstairs to-day.

MADAM HELSETH. Oh, he often does that. But he'll soon be down now, I should think.

REBECCA. Have you see anything of him?

MADAM HELSETH. I caught a glimpse of him when I went upstairs with his coffee. He was in his bedroom, dressing.

REBECCA. I asked because he was a little out of sorts yesterday.

MADAM HELSETH. He didn't look well. I wonder if there isn't something amiss between him and his brother-in-law.

REBECCA. What do you think it can be?

MADAM HELSETH. I couldn't say. Perhaps it's that Mortensgård that has been setting them against each other.

REBECCA. Likely enough.—Do you know anything of this Peter Mortensgård?

MADAM HELSETH. No indeed. How could you think so, Miss? A fellow like him?

REBECCA. Do you mean because he edits such a low paper?

MADAM HELSETH. Oh, it's not only that.—You must have heard, Miss, that he had a child by a married woman that had been deserted by her husband?

REBECCA. Yes, I have heard of it. But it must have been long before I came here.

MADAM HELSETH. It's true he was very young at the time; and she should have known better. He wanted to marry her, too; but of course he couldn't do that. And I don't say he hasn't paid dear for it.—But, good Lord, Mortensgård has got on in the world since those days. There's a many people run after him now.

REBECCA. Yes, most of the poor people bring their affairs to him when they're in any trouble.

MADAM HELSETH. Ah, and others, too, perhaps, besides the poor folk——

REBECCA (*looks at her furtively*). Indeed.

MADAM HELSETH (*by the sofa, dusting away vigorously*). Perhaps the last people you would think likely to, Miss.

REBECCA (*busy with the flowers*). Come, now, that's only an idea of yours, Madam Helseth. You can't be sure of what you're saying.

MADAM HELSETH. You think I can't, Miss? But I can tell you I am. Why—if you must know it—I once took a letter in to Mortensgård myself.

REBECCA (*turning*). No—did you?

MADAM HELSETH. Yes, indeed I did. And a letter that was written here at Rosmersholm, too.

REBECCA. Really, Madam Helseth?

MADAM HELSETH. Yes, that it was. And it was on fine paper, and there was a fine red seal on it, too.

REBECCA. And it was given to you to deliver? Then, my dear Madam Helseth, it's not difficult to guess who wrote it.

MADAM HELSETH. Well?

REBECCA. It must have been something that poor Mrs. Rosmer, in her morbid state——

MADAM HELSETH. It's you that say that, Miss, not me.

REBECCA. But what was in the letter? Oh, I forgot—you can't know that.

MADAM HELSETH. H'm; what if I did know it, all the same?

REBECCA. Did she tell you what she was writing about?

MADAM HELSETH. No, she didn't exactly do that. But Mortensgård, when he'd read it, he began questioning me backwards and forwards and up and down, so that I soon guessed what was in it.

REBECCA. Then what do you think it was? Oh my dear good Madam Helseth, do tell me.

MADAM HELSETH. Oh no, Miss, Not for the whole world.

REBECCA. Oh you can surely tell me. We two are such good friends.

MADAM HELSETH. Lord preserve me from telling you anything about that, Miss. I can only tell you that it was something horrible that they'd got the poor sick lady to believe.

REBECCA. Who had got her to believe it?

MADAM HELSETH. Wicked people, Miss West. Wicked people.

REBECCA. Wicked——?

MADAM HELSETH. Yes, I say it again. They must have been real wicked people.

REBECCA. And who do you think it could have been?

MADAM HELSETH. Oh, I know well enough what to think. But Lord forbid *I* should say anything. To be sure there's a certain lady in the town—h'm!

REBECCA. I can see that you mean Mrs. Kroll.

MADAM HELSETH. Ah, she's a fine one, she is. She has always been the great lady with me. And she's never had any too much love for you neither.

REBECCA. Do you think Mrs. Rosmer was in her right mind when she wrote that letter to Mortensgård?

MADAM HELSETH. It's a queer thing a person's mind, Miss. Clean out of her mind I don't think she was.

REBECCA. But she seemed to go distracted when she learned that she must always be childless. It was that that unsettled her reason.

MADAM HELSETH. Yes, poor lady, that was a dreadful blow to her.

REBECCA (*takes up her crochet and sits in a chair by the window*). But after all—don't you think it was a good thing for the Pastor, Madam Helseth?

MADAM HELSETH. What, Miss?

REBECCA. That there were no children. Don't you think so?

MADAM HELSETH. H'm, I'm sure I don't know what to say about that.

REBECCA. Oh yes, believe me, it was fortunate for him. Pastor Rosmer is not the man to have crying children about his house.

MADAM HELSETH. Ah, Miss, little children don't cry at Rosmersholm.

REBECCA (*looks at her*). Don't cry?

MADAM HELSETH. No. As long as people can remember, children have never been known to cry in this house.

REBECCA. That's very strange.

MADAM HELSETH. Yes; isn't it? But it runs in the family. And then there's another strange thing. When they grow up, they never laugh. Never, as long as they live.

REBECCA. Why, how extraordinary——

MADAM HELSETH. Have you ever once heard or seen the Pastor laugh, Miss?

REBECCA. No—now that I think of it, I almost believe you are right. But I don't think any one laughs much in this part of the country.

MADAM HELSETH. No, they don't. They say it began at Rosmersholm. And then I suppose it spread round about, as if it was catching-like.

REBECCA. You are a very wise woman, Madam Helseth.

MADAM HELSETH. Oh, Miss, you mustn't sit there and make fun of me. (*Listens.*) Hush, hush—here's the Pastor coming down. He doesn't like to see dusting going on.

(*She goes out to the right.*)
(JOHANNES ROSMER, *with his hat and stick in his hand, enters from the hall.*)

ROSMER. Good morning, Rebecca.

REBECCA. Good morning, dear. (*A moment after —crocheting.*) Are you going out?

ROSMER. Yes.

REBECCA. It's a beautiful day.

ROSMER. You didn't look in on me this morning.

REBECCA. No, I didn't. Not to-day.

ROSMER. Do you not intend to in future?

REBECCA. Oh, I don't know yet, dear.

ROSMER. Has anything come for me?

REBECCA. The "County News" has come.

ROSMER. The "County News"?

REBECCA. There it is on the table.

ROSMER (*puts down his hat and stick*). Is there any thing——?

REBECCA. Yes.

ROSMER. And you didn't send it up?

REBECCA. You will read it soon enough.

ROSMER. Oh, indeed? (*Takes the paper and reads, standing by the table.*)—What!—"We cannot warn our readers too earnestly against unprincipled renegades." (*Looks at her.*) They call me a renegade, Rebecca.

REBECCA. They mention no names.

ROSMER. That makes no difference. (*Reads on.*) "Secret traitors to the good cause."—"Judas-natures, who make brazen confession of their apostasy as soon as they think the most convenient and—profitable moment has arrived." "Ruthless befouling of a name honoured through generations"—"in the confident hope of a suitable reward from the party in momentary power." (*Lays down the paper on the table.*) And they can say such things of me!—Men who have known me so long and so well! Things they themselves don't believe. Things they know there is not a word of truth in—they print them all the same.

REBECCA. That is not all.

ROSMER. (*takes up the paper again*). "Inexperience and lack of judgment the only excuse"—"pernicious influence—possibly extending to matters which, for the present, we do not wish to make subjects of public discussion or accusation." (*Looks at her.*) What is this?

REBECCA. It is aimed at me, plainly enough.

ROSMER (*lays down the paper*). Rebecca,—this is the conduct of dishonourable men.

REBECCA. Yes, they need scarcely be so contemptuous of Mortensgård.

ROSMER (*walks about the room*). Something must be done. All that is good in human nature will go to ruin, if this is allowed to go on. But it shall not go on! Oh, what a joy—what a joy it would be to me to get a little light into all this gloom and ugliness!

REBECCA (*rises*). Ah, yes, Rosmer. In that you have a great and glorious object to live for.

ROSMER. Only think, if I could rouse them to see themselves as they are; teach them to repent and blush before their better natures; bring them together in mutual forbearance—in love, Rebecca!

REBECCA. Yes, put your whole strength into that, and you must succeed.

ROSMER. I think success must be possible. Oh, what a delight it would be then to live one's life! No more malignant wrangling; only emulation. All eyes fixed on the same goal. Every mind, every will pressing forward—upward—each by the path its nature prescribes for it. Happiness for all—through all. (*Happens to look out of the window, starts and says sadly.*) Ah! Not through me.

REBECCA. Not——? Not through you?

ROSMER. Nor for me.

REBECCA. Oh Rosmer, do not let such doubts take hold of you.

ROSMER. Happiness—dear Rebecca—happiness is above all things the calm, glad certainty of innocence.

REBECCA (*looks straight before her*). Yes, innocence——

ROSMER. Oh, you cannot know what guilt means. But I——

REBECCA. You least of all!

ROSMER (*points out of the window*). The mill-race.

REBECCA. Oh Rosmer——!

(MADAM HELSETH *looks in at the door.*)

MADAM HELSETH. Miss West!

REBECCA. Presently, presently. Not now.

MADAM HELSETH. Only a word, Miss.

(REBECCA *goes to the door.* MADAM HELSETH *tells her something. They whisper together for a few moments.* MADAM HELSETH *nods and goes out.*)

ROSMER (*uneasily*). Was it anything for me?

REBECCA. No, only something about the house-work.—You ought to go out into the fresh air, dear Rosmer. You should take a good long walk.

ROSMER (*takes up his hat*). Yes, come. Let us go together.

REBECCA. No, dear, I can't just now. You must go alone. But shake off all these gloomy thoughts. Promise me.

ROSMER. I am afraid I shall never shake them off.

REBECCA. Oh, that such baseless fancies should take so strong a hold of you——!

ROSMER. Not so baseless I am afraid, Rebecca. I lay awake all night thinking it over and over. Perhaps Beata saw clearly after all.

REBECCA. In what?

ROSMER. In her belief that I loved you, Rebecca.

REBECCA. Right in that!

ROSMER (*lays his hat down on the table*). The question that haunts me is this: were we two not deceiving ourselves all the time—when we called our relation friendship?

REBECCA. You mean that it might as well have been called——?

ROSMER. ——love. Yes, Rebecca, that is what I mean. Even while Beata was alive, all my thoughts were for you. It was you alone I longed for. It was when you were by my side that I felt the calm gladness of utter content. If you think it over, Rebecca —did we not feel for each other from the first a sort of sweet, secret child-love—desireless, dreamless? Was it not so with you? Tell me.

REBECCA (*struggling with herself*). Oh—I don't know what to answer.

ROSMER. And it was this close-linked life in and for each other that we took for friendship. No, Rebecca—our bond has been a spiritual marriage— perhaps from the very first. That is why there is guilt on my soul. I had no right to such happiness— it was a sin against Beata.

REBECCA. No right to live happily? Do you believe that, Rosmer?

ROSMER. She looked at our relation with the eyes of her love—judged it after the fashion of her love. Inevitably. Beata could not have judged otherwise than she did.

REBECCA. But how can you accuse yourself because of Beata's delusion?

ROSMER. It was love for me—her kind of love— that drove her into the mill-race. That is an immovable fact, Rebecca. And that is what I can never get over.

REBECCA. Oh, think of nothing but the great, beautiful task you have devoted your life to.

ROSMER (*shakes his head*). It can never be accomplished, dear. Not by me. Not after what I have come to know.

REBECCA. Why not by you?

ROSMER. Because no cause ever triumphs that has its origin in sin.

REBECCA (*vehemently*). Oh, these are only ancestral doubts—ancestral fears—ancestral scruples. They say the dead come back to Rosmersholm in the shape of rushing white horses. I think this shows that it is true.

ROSMER. Be that as it may; what does it matter, so long as I cannnot rid myself of the feeling? And believe me, Rebecca, it is as I tell you. The cause that is to win a lasting victory must have for its champion a happy and innocent man.

REBECCA. Is happiness so indispensable to you, Rosmer?

ROSMER. Happiness? Yes, dear,—it is.

REBECCA. To you, who can never laugh?

ROSMER. Yes, in spite of that. Believe me I have a great capacity for happiness.

REBECCA. Now go for your walk, dear. A good long walk. Do you hear?—See, here is your hat. And your stick, too.

ROSMER (*takes both*). Thanks. And you won't come with me?

REBECCA. No, no; I can't just now.

ROSMER. Very well, then. You are with me nonetheless.

(*He goes out by the entrance door.* REBECCA *waits a moment, cautiously watching his departure from behind the open door; then she goes to the door on the right.*)

REBECCA (*opens the door, and says in a low tone*). Now, Madam Helseth. You can show him in now. (*Goes towards the window.*)

(*A moment after* RECTOR KROLL *enters from the right. He bows silently and formally, and keeps his hat in his hand.*)

KROLL. He has gone out?

REBECCA. Yes.

KROLL. Does he usually stay out long?

REBECCA. Yes, he does. But one cannot count on him to-day. So if you don't care to meet him——

KROLL. No, no. It is you I want to speak to,— quite alone.

REBECCA. Then we had better not lose time. Sit down, Rector.

(*She sits in the easy-chair by the window.* RECTOR KROLL *sits on a chair beside her.*)

KROLL. Miss West—you can scarcely imagine how

deeply and painfully I have taken this to heart—this change in Johannes Rosmer.

REBECCA. We expected it would be so—at first.

KROLL. Only at first?

REBECCA. Rosmer was confident that sooner or later you would join him.

KROLL. I?

REBECCA. You and all his other friends.

KROLL. Ah, there you see! That shows the infirmity of his judgment in all that concerns men and practical life.

REBECCA. But after all—since he feels it a necessity to emancipate himself on all sides——

KROLL. Yes, but wait—that is just what I do not believe.

REBECCA. What do you believe, then?

KROLL. I believe that you are at the bottom of it all.

REBECCA. It is your wife who has put that in your head, Rector Kroll.

KROLL. No matter who has put it in my head. What is certain is that I feel a strong suspicion—an exceedingly strong suspicion—when I think things over and piece together all I know of your behaviour ever since you came here.

REBECCA (looks at him). I seem to recollect a time when you felt an exceedingly strong faith in me, dear Rector. I might almost call it a warm faith.

KROLL (in a subdued voice). Whom could you not bewitch—if you tried?

REBECCA. Did I try——?

KROLL. Yes, you did. I am no longer such a fool as to believe that there was any feeling in the matter. You simply wanted to get a footing at Rosmersholm—to strike root here—and in that I was to serve you. Now I see it.

REBECCA. You seem utterly to have forgotten that it was Beata who begged and implored me to come out here?

KROLL. Yes, when you had bewitched her too. Can the feeling she came to entertain for you be called friendship? It was adoration—almost idolatry. It developed into—what shall I call it?—a sort of desperate passion.—Yes, that is the right word for it.

REBECCA. Be so good as to recollect the state your sister was in. So far as I am concerned, I don't think any one can accuse me of being hysterical.

KROLL. No; that you certainly are not. But that makes you all the more dangerous to the people you want to get into your power. It is easy for you to weigh your acts and calculate consequences—just because your heart is cold.

REBECCA. Cold? Are you so sure of that?

KROLL. I am quite certain of it now. Otherwise you could never have lived here year after year without faltering in the pursuit of your object. Well, well—you have gained your end. You have got him and everything into your power. But in order to do so, you have not scrupled to make him unhappy.

REBECCA. That is not true. It is not I—it is you yourself that have made him unhappy.

KROLL. I?

REBECCA. Yes, when you led him to imagine that he was responsible for Beata's terrible end.

KROLL. Does he feel that so deeply, then?

REBECCA. How can you doubt it? A mind so sensitive as his——

KROLL. I thought that an emancipated man, so-called, was above all such scruples.—But there we have it! Oh yes—I admit I knew how it would be. The descendant of the men that look down on us from these walls—how could he hope to cut himself adrift from all that has been handed down without a break from generation to generation?

REBECCA (looks down thoughtfully). Johannes Rosmer's spirit is deeply rooted in his ancestry. That is very certain.

KROLL. Yes, and you should have taken that fact into consideration, if you had felt any affection for him. But that sort of consideration was no doubt beyond you. There is such an immeasurable difference between your antecedents and his.

REBECCA. What antecedents do you mean?

KROLL. I am speaking of your origin—your family antecedents, Miss West.

REBECCA. Oh, indeed! Yes, it is quite true that I come of very humble folk. Nevertheless——

KROLL. I am not thinking of rank and position. I allude to your moral antecedents.

REBECCA. Moral——? In what sense?

KROLL. The circumstances of your birth.

REBECCA. What do you mean?

KROLL. I only mention the matter because it accounts for your whole conduct.

REBECCA. I do not understand this. You must explain.

KROLL. I really did not suppose you could require an explanation. Otherwise it would have been very odd that you should have let Dr. West adopt you——

REBECCA (rises). Ah! Now I understand.

KROLL. ——and that you should have taken his name. Your mother's name was Gamvik.

REBECCA (*walks across the room*). My father's name was Gamvik, Rector Kroll.

KROLL. Your mother's business must have brought her very frequently into contact with the parish doctor.

REBECCA. Yes, it did.

KROLL. And then he takes you into his house—as soon as your mother dies. He treats you harshly; and yet you stay with him. You know that he won't leave you a half-penny—as a matter of fact, you only got a case full of books—and yet you stay on; you bear with him; you nurse him to the last.

REBECCA (*stands by the table, looking scornfully at him*). And you account for all this by assuming that there was something immoral—something criminal about my birth?

KROLL. I attribute your care for him to involuntary filial instinct. Indeed I believe your whole conduct is determined by your origin.

REBECCA (*vehemently*). But there is not a single word of truth in what you say! And I can prove it! Dr. West did not come to Finmark till after I was born.

KROLL. Excuse me, Miss West. He settled there the year before. I have assured myself of that.

REBECCA. You are mistaken, I say! You are utterly mistaken.

KROLL. You told me the day before yesterday that you were nine-and-twenty—in your thirtieth year.

REBECCA. Indeed! Did I say so?

KROLL. Yes, you did. And I can calculate from that——

REBECCA. Stop! You needn't calculate. I may as well tell you at once: I am a year older than I gave myself out to be.

KROLL (*smiles incredulously*). Really! I am surprised! What can be the reason of that?

REBECCA. When I had passed twenty-five, it seemed to me I was getting altogether too old for an unmarried woman. And so I began to lie about my age.

KROLL. You? An emancipated woman! Have you prejudices about the age for marriage?

REBECCA. Yes, it was idiotic of me—idiotic and absurd. But some folly or other will always cling to us, not to be shaken off. We are made so.

KROLL. Well, so be it; but my calculation may be right, nonetheless. For Dr. West was up there on a short visit the year before he got the appointment.

REBECCA (*with a vehement outburst*). It is not true!

KROLL. Is it not true?

REBECCA. No. My mother never spoke of any such visit.

KROLL. Did she not?

REBECCA. No, never. Nor Dr. West either; not a word about it.

KROLL. Might not that be because they both had reasons for suppressing a year? Just as you have done, Miss West. Perhaps it is a family foible.

REBECCA (*walks about clenching and wringing her hands*). It is impossible. You want to cheat me into believing it. This can never, never be true. It cannot! Never in this world——

KROLL (*rises*). My dear Miss West—why in heaven's name are you so terribly excited? You quite frighten me! What am I to think—to believe——?

REBECCA. Nothing! You are to think and believe nothing.

KROLL. Then you must really tell me how you can take this affair—this possibility—so terribly to heart.

REBECCA (*controlling herself*). It is perfectly simple, Rector Kroll. I have no wish to be taken for an illegitimate child.

KROLL. Indeed! Well, well, let us be satisfied with that explanation—in the meantime. But in that case you must still have a certain—prejudice on that point, too?

REBECCA. Yes, I suppose I have.

KROLL. Ah, I fancy it is much the same with most of what you call your "emancipation." You have read yourself into a number of new ideas and opinions. You have got a sort of smattering of recent discoveries in various fields—discoveries that seem to overthrow certain principles which have hitherto been held impregnable and unassailable. But all this has only been a matter of the intellect, Miss West—a superficial acquisition. It has not passed into your blood.

REBECCA (*thoughtfully*). Perhaps you are right.

KROLL. Yes, look into your own mind, and you will see! And if this is the case with you, one may easily guess how it must be with Johannes Rosmer. It is sheer, unmitigated madness—it is running blindfold to destruction—for him to think of coming openly forward and confessing himself an apostate! Only think—a man of his sensitive nature! Imagine him disowned and persecuted by the circle of which he has always formed a part—exposed to ruthless attacks from all the best people in the community! He is not—he never can be the man to endure all that.

REBECCA. He must endure it! It is too late now for him to retreat.

KROLL. Not at all too late. By no means. What has happened can be hushed up—or at least explained away as a mere temporary aberration, however deplorable. But—one measure is certainly indispensable.

REBECCA. And what is that?

KROLL. You must get him to legalise the position, Miss West.

REBECCA. His position towards me?

KROLL. Yes. You must make him do that.

REBECCA. Then you absolutely cannot clear your mind of the idea, that our position requires to be—legalised, as you call it?

KROLL. I would rather not go into the matter too closely. But I believe I have noticed that it is nowhere easier to break through all so-called prejudices than in—h'm——

REBECCA. In the relation between man and woman, you mean?

KROLL. Yes,—to speak plainly—I think so.

REBECCA (*wanders across the room and looks out at the window*). I could almost say—I wish you were right, Rector Kroll.

KROLL. What do you mean by that? You say it so strangely.

REBECCA. Oh well—please let us drop the subject. Ah,—there he comes.

KROLL. Already! Then I will go.

REBECCA (*goes towards him*). No—please stay. There is something I want you to hear.

KROLL. Not now. I don't feel as if I could bear to see him.

REBECCA. I beg you to stay. Do! If not, you will regret it by-and-by. It is the last time I shall ask you for anything.

KROLL (*looks at her in surprise and puts down his hat*). Very well, Miss West—so be it then.

(*A short silence. Then* JOHANNES ROSMER *enters from the hall.*)

ROSMER (*sees the* RECTOR, *and stops in the doorway*). What!—Are you here?

REBECCA. He did not wish to meet you, dear.[4]

KROLL (*involuntarily*). "Dear!"

REBECCA. Yes, Rector Kroll, Rosmer and I say "dear" to each other. That is one result of our "position."

KROLL. Was that what you wanted me to hear?

REBECCA. That—and a little more.

[4] In the original, Rebecca here addresses Rosmer as "*du*" for the first time in Kroll's presence.

ROSMER (*comes forward*). What is the object of this visit?

KROLL. I wanted to try once more to stop you and win you back to us.

ROSMER (*points to the newspaper*). After what appears in that paper?

KROLL. I did not write it.

ROSMER. Did you make the slightest effort to prevent its appearance?

KROLL. That would have been to betray the cause I serve. And, besides, it was not in my power.

REBECCA (*tears the paper into shreds, crushes up the pieces and throws them behind the stove*). There! Now it is out of sight. And let it be out of mind, too. For there will be nothing more of that sort, Rosmer.

KROLL. Ah, if you could only make sure of that!

REBECCA. Come, let us sit down, dear. All three of us. And then I will tell you everything.

ROSMER (*seats himself mechanically*). What has come over you, Rebecca? This unnatural calmness —what is it?

REBECCA. The calmness of resolution. (*Seats herself*) Pray sit down, too, Rector.

(RECTOR KROLL *seats himself on the sofa.*)

ROSMER. Resolution, you say? What resolution?

REBECCA. I am going to give you back what you require in order to live your life. Dear friend, you shall have your happy innocence back again!

ROSMER. What can you mean?

REBECCA. I have only to tell you something. That will be enough.

ROSMER. Well!

REBECCA. When I came down here from Finmark —along with Dr. West—it seemed to me that a great, wide new world was opening up before me. The Doctor had taught me all sorts of things—all the fragmentary knowledge of life that I possessed in those days. (*With a struggle and in a scarcely audible voice*) And then——

KROLL. And then?

ROSMER. But Rebecca—I know all this.

REBECCA (*mastering herself*). Yes, yes—you are right. You know enough about this.

KROLL (*looks hard at her*). Perhaps I had better go.

REBECCA. No, please stay where you are, my dear Rector. (*To* ROSMER) Well, you see, this was how it was—I wanted to take my share in the life of the new era that was dawning, with all its new ideas.— Rector Kroll told me one day that Ulric Brendel had had great influence over you while you were still a boy. I thought it must surely be possible for me to carry on his work.

ROSMER. You came here with a secret design——?

REBECCA. We two, I thought, should march onward in freedom, side by side. Ever onward. Ever farther and farther to the front. But between you and perfect emancipation there rose that dismal, insurmountable barrier.

ROSMER. What barrier do you mean?

REBECCA. I mean this, Rosmer: You could grow into freedom only in the clear, fresh sunshine—and here you were pining, sickening in the gloom of such a marriage.

ROSMER. You have never before spoken to me of my marriage in that tone.

REBECCA. No, I did not dare to, for I should have frightened you.

KROLL (nods to ROSMER). Do you hear that?

REBECCA (goes on). But I saw quite well where your deliverance lay—your only deliverance. And then I went to work.

ROSMER. Went to work? In what way?

KROLL. Do you mean that——?

REBECCA. Yes, Rosmer—— (Rises.) Sit still. You, too, Rector Kroll. But now it must out. It was not you, Rosmer. You are innocent. It was I that lured —that ended in luring Beata out into the paths of delusion——

ROSMER (springs up). Rebecca!

KROLL (rises from the sofa). The paths of delusion!

REBECCA. The paths—that led to the mill-race. Now you know it both of you.

ROSMER (as if stunned). But I don't understand—— What is it she is saying? I don't understand a word——!

KROLL. Oh yes, Rosmer, I am beginning to understand.

ROSMER. But what did you do? What can you possibly have told her? There was nothing—absolutely nothing to tell!

REBECCA. She came to know that you were working yourself free from all the old prejudices.

ROSMER. Yes, but that was not the case at that time.

REBECCA. I knew that it soon would be.

KROLL (nods to ROSMER). Aha!

ROSMER. And then? What more? I must know all now.

REBECCA. Some time after—I begged and implored her to let me go away from Rosmersholm.

ROSMER. Why did you want to go—then?

REBECCA. I did not want to go; I wanted to stay here, where I was. But I told her that it would be best for us all—that I should go away in time. I gave her to understand that if I stayed here any longer, I could not—I could not tell—what might happen.

ROSMER. Then this is what you said and did!

REBECCA. Yes, Rosmer.

ROSMER. This is what you call "going to work."

REBECCA (in a broken voice). I called it so, yes.

ROSMER (after a pause). Have you confessed all now, Rebecca?

REBECCA. Yes.

KROLL. Not all.

REBECCA (looks at him in fear). What more should there be?

KROLL. Did you not at last give Beata to understand that it was necessary—not only that it would be wisest, but that it was necessary—both for your own sake and Rosmer's that you should go away somewhere—as soon as possible? Well?

REBECCA (low and indistinctly). Perhaps I did say something of the sort.

ROSMER (sinks into the armchair by the window). And this tissue of lies and deceit she—my unhappy, sick wife believed in! Believed in it so firmly! So immovably! (Looks up at REBECCA.) And she never turned to me. Never said one word to me! Oh, Rebecca,—I can see it in your face—you dissuaded her from it!

REBECCA. She had conceived a fixed idea that she, as a childless wife, had no right to be here. And then she imagined that it was her duty to you to efface herself.

ROSMER. And you—you did nothing to disabuse her of the idea?

REBECCA. No.

KROLL. Perhaps you confirmed her in it? Answer me! Did you not?

REBECCA. I believe she may have understood me so.

ROSMER. Yes, yes—and in everything she bowed before your will. And she did efface herself! (Springs up.) How could you—how could you play this ghastly game!

REBECCA. It seemed to me I had to choose between your life and hers, Rosmer.

KROLL (severely and impressively). That choice was not for you to make.

REBECCA (vehemently). You think then that I was cool and calculating and self-possessed all the time! I was not the same woman then that I am now, as I stand here telling it all. Besides, there are two sorts of will in us I believe! I wanted Beata away, by one means or another; but I never really believed that it would come to pass. As I felt my way forward, at each step I ventured, I seemed to hear something within me cry out: No farther! Not a step farther! And yet I could not stop. I had to venture the least little bit farther. Only one hair's-breadth more. And then one more—and always one more.—And then it happened.—That is the way such things come about. (*A short silence.*)

ROSMER (*to* REBECCA). What do you think lies before you now? After this?

REBECCA. Things must go with me as they will. It doesn't greatly matter.

KROLL. Not a word of remorse! Is it possible you feel none?

REBECCA (*coldly putting aside his question*). Excuse me, Rector Kroll—that is a matter which concerns no one but me. I must settle it with myself.

KROLL (*to* ROSMER). And this is the woman you are living under the same roof with—in the closest intimacy! (*Looks round at the pictures.*) Oh, if those that are gone could see us now!

ROSMER. Are you going back to town?

KROLL (*takes up his hat*). Yes. The sooner the better.

ROSMER (*does the same*). Then I will go with you.

KROLL. Will you? Ah, yes, I was sure we had not lost you for good.

ROSMER. Come then, Kroll! Come!

(*Both go out through the hall without looking at* REBECCA.)

(*After a moment,* REBECCA *goes cautiously to the window and looks out through the flowers.*)

REBECCA (*speaks to herself under her breath*). Not over the foot-bridge to-day either. He goes round. Never across the mill-race. Never. (*Leaves window.*) Well, well, well!

(*Goes and pulls the bell-rope; a moment after,* MADAM HELSETH *enters from the right.*)

MADAM HELSETH. What is it, Miss?

REBECCA. Madam Helseth, would you be so good as to have my trunk brought down from the garret?

MADAM HELSETH. Your trunk?

REBECCA. Yes—the brown sealskin trunk, you know.

MADAM HELSETH. Yes, yes. But, Lord preserve us—are you going on a journey, Miss?

REBECCA. Yes—now I am going on a journey, Madam Helseth.

MADAM HELSETH. And immediately!

REBECCA. As soon as I have packed up.

MADAM HELSETH. Well, I've never heard the like

of that! But you'll come back again soon, Miss, of course?

REBECCA. I shall never come back again.

MADAM HELSETH. Never! Dear Lord, what will things be like at Rosmersholm when you're gone, Miss? And the poor Pastor was just beginning to be so happy and comfortable.

REBECCA. Yes, but I have taken fright to-day, Madam Helseth.

MADAM HELSETH. Taken fright! Dear, dear! how was that?

REBECCA. I thought I saw something like a glimpse of white horses.

MADAM HELSETH. White horses! In broad day-light!

REBECCA. Oh, they are abroad early and late—the white horses of Rosmersholm. (*With a change of tone*) Well,—about the trunk, Madam Helseth.

MADAM HELSETH. Yes, yes. The trunk.

(*Both go out to the right.*)

ACT FOUR

The sitting-room at Rosmersholm. Late evening. A lighted lamp, with a shade over it, on the table.

REBECCA WEST *stands by the table, packing some small articles in a hand-bag. Her cloak, hat and the white crocheted shawl are hanging over the back of the sofa.*

MADAM HELSETH *enters from the right.*

MADAM HELSETH (*speaks in a low voice and appears ill at ease*). All your things have been taken down, Miss. They are in the kitchen passage.

REBECCA. Very well. You have ordered the carriage?

MADAM HELSETH. Yes. The coachman wants to know what time he ought to be here.

REBECCA. About eleven o'clock, I think. The steamer starts at midnight.

MADAM HELSETH (*hesitates a little*). But the Pastor? If he shouldn't be home by that time?

REBECCA. I shall go all the same. If I don't see him, you can tell him that I will write to him—a long letter. Tell him that.

MADAM HELSETH. Yes, writing—that may be all very well. But, poor Miss West—I do think you should try to speak to him once more.

REBECCA. Perhaps so. And yet—perhaps not.

MADAM HELSETH. Well—that I should live to see this! I never thought of such a thing.

REBECCA. What did you think then, Madam Helseth?

MADAM HELSETH. Well, I certainly thought Pastor Rosmer was a more dependable man than this.

REBECCA. Dependable?

MADAM HELSETH. Yes, that's what I say.

REBECCA. Why, my dear Madam Helseth, what do you mean?

MADAM HELSETH. I mean what's right and true, Miss. He shouldn't get out of it in this way, that he shouldn't.

REBECCA (looks at her). Come now, Madam Helseth, tell me plainly: what do you think is the reason I am going away?

MADAM HELSETH. Well, Heaven forgive us, I suppose it can't be helped, Miss. Ah, well, well, well! But I certainly don't think the Pastor's behaving handsome-like. Mortensgård had some excuse; for her husband was alive, so that they two couldn't marry, however much they wanted to. But as for the Pastor—h'm!

REBECCA (with a faint smile). Could you have believed such a thing of Pastor Rosmer and me?

MADAM HELSETH. No, never in this world. At least, I mean—not until to-day.

REBECCA. But to-day, then——?

MADAM HELSETH. Well,—after all the horrible things that they tell me the papers are saying about the Pastor——

REBECCA. Aha!

MADAM HELSETH. For the man that can go over to Mortensgård's religion—good Lord, I can believe anything of him.

REBECCA. Oh, yes, I suppose so. But what about me? What have you to say about me?

MADAM HALSETH. Lord preserve us, Miss—I don't see that there's much to be said against you. It's not so easy for a lone woman to be always on her guard, that's certain.—We're all of us human, Miss West.

REBECCA. That's very true, Madam Helseth. We are all of us human.—What are you listening to?

MADAM HELSETH (in a low voice). Oh, Lord,—if I don't believe that's him coming.

REBECCA (starts). After all then——? (Resolutely) Well well; so be it.

(JOHANNES ROSMER enters from the hall.)

ROSMER (sees the hand-bag, etc., turns to REBECCA, and asks). What does this mean?

REBECCA. I am going.

ROSMER. At once?

REBECCA. Yes. (To MADAM HELSETH) Eleven o'clock then.

MADAM HELSETH. Very well, Miss.

(Goes out to the right.)

ROSMER (after a short pause). Where are you going to, Rebecca?

REBECCA. North, by the steamer.

ROSMER. North? What takes you to the North?

REBECCA. It was there I came from.

ROSMER. But you have no ties there now.

REBECCA. I have none here either.

ROSMER. What do you think of doing?

REBECCA. I don't know. I only want to have done with it all.

ROSMER. To have done with it?

REBECCA. Rosmersholm has broken me.

ROSMER (his attention aroused). Do you say that?

REBECCA. Broken me utterly and hopelessly.—I had a free and fearless will when I came here. Now I have bent my neck under a strange law.—From this day forth, I feel as if I had no courage for anything in the world.

ROSMER. Why not? What is the law that you say you have——?

REBECCA. Dear, don't let us talk of that just now.—What happened between you and the Rector?

ROSMER. We have made peace.

REBECCA. Ah yes; so that was the end.

ROSMER. He gathered all our old friends together at his house. They have made it clear to me that the work of ennobling the minds of men—is not for me.—And besides, it is hopeless in itself, Rebecca.—I shall let it alone.

REBECCA. Yes, yes—perhaps it is best so.

ROSMER. Is that what you say now? Do you think so now?

REBECCA. I have come to think so—in the last few days.

ROSMER. You are lying, Rebecca.

REBECCA. Lying——!

ROSMER. Yes, you are lying. You have never believed in me. You have never believed that I was man enough to carry the cause through to victory.

REBECCA. I believed that we two together could do it.

ROSMER. That is not true. You thought that you yourself could do something great in life; and that you could use me to further your ends. I was to be a serviceable instrument to you—that is what you thought.

REBECCA. Listen to me, Rosmer——

ROSMER (seats himself listlessly on the sofa). Oh, what is the use? I see through it all now—I have been like a glove in your hands.

REBECCA. Listen, Rosmer. Hear what I have to

say. It will be for the last time. (*Sits in a chair close to the sofa.*) I intended to write you all about it—when I was back in the North. But I daresay it is best that you should hear it at once.

ROSMER. Have you more confessions to make?

REBECCA. The greatest of all is to come.

ROSMER. The greatest?

REBECCA. What you have never suspected. What gives light and shade to all the rest.

ROSMER (*shakes his head*). I don't understand you at all.

REBECCA. It is perfectly true that I once schemed to gain a footing at Rosmersholm. I thought I could not fail to turn things to good account here. In one way or the other—you understand.

ROSMER. Well, you accomplished your ends.

REBECCA. I believe I could have accomplished anything, anything in the world—at that time. For I had still my fearless, free-born will. I knew no scruples—I stood in awe of no human tie.—But then began what has broken my will—and cowed me so pitiably for all my days.

ROSMER. What began? Do not speak in riddles.

REBECCA. It came over me,—this wild, uncontrollable passion——. Oh, Rosmer——!

ROSMER. Passion? You——! For what?

REBECCA. For you.

ROSMER (*tries to spring up*). What is this?

REBECCA (*stops him*). Sit still, dear; there is more to tell.

ROSMER. And you mean to say—that you have loved me—in that way!

REBECCA. I thought that it should be called love then. Yes, I thought it was love. But it was not. It was what I said. It was a wild, uncontrollable passion.

ROSMER (*with difficulty*). Rebecca, is it really you—you yourself—that you are speaking of?

REBECCA. Yes, would you believe it, Rosmer?

ROSMER. Then it was because of this—under the influence of this—that you—that you "went to work," as you call it?

REBECCA. It came upon me like a storm on the sea. It was like one of the storms we sometimes have in the North in the winter time. It seizes you —and whirls you along with it—wherever it will. There is no resisting it.

ROSMER. And so it swept the unhappy Beata into the mill-race.

REBECCA. Yes; for it was a life-and-death struggle between Beata and me at that time.

ROSMER. Assuredly you were the stronger at Rosmersholm. Stronger than Beata and I together.

REBECCA. I judged you rightly in so far that I was sure I could never reach you until you were a free man, both in circumstances—and in spirit.

ROSMER. But I don't understand you, Rebecca. You—yourself—your whole conduct is an insoluble riddle to me. I am free now—both in spirit and in circumstances. You have reached the very goal you aimed at from the first. And yet——

REBECCA. I have never stood farther from my goal than now.

ROSMER. And yet I say—when I asked you yesterday—begged you to be my wife—you cried out, as if in fear, that it could never be.

REBECCA. I cried out in despair, Rosmer.

ROSMER. Why?

REBECCA. Because Rosmersholm has sapped my strength. My old fearless will has had its wings clipped here. It is crippled! The time is past when I had courage for anything in the world. I have lost the power of action, Rosmer.

ROSMER. Tell me how this has come about.

REBECCA. It has come about through my life with you.

ROSMER. But how? How?

REBECCA. When I was left alone with you here,— and when you had become yourself again——

ROSMER. Yes, yes?

REBECCA. ——for you were never quite yourself so long as Beata lived——

ROSMER. I am afraid you are right there.

REBECCA. But when I found myself sharing your life here,—in quiet—in solitude,—when you showed me all your thoughts without reserve—every tender and delicate feeling, just as it came to you—then the great change came over me. Little by little, you understand. Almost imperceptibly—but at last with such overwhelming force that it reached to the depths of my soul.

ROSMER. Oh, is this true, Rebecca?

REBECCA. All the rest—the horrible sense-intoxicated desire—passed far, far away from me. All the whirling passions settled down into quiet and silence. Rest descended on my soul—a stillness as on one of our northern bird-cliffs under the midnight sun.

ROSMER. Tell me more of this. Tell me all you can.

REBECCA. There is not much more, dear. Only this—it was love that was born in me. The great self-denying love, that is content with life, as we two have lived it together.

ROSMER. Oh, if I had only had the faintest suspicion of all this!

REBECCA. It is best as it is. Yesterday—when you asked me if I would be your wife—I cried out with joy——

ROSMER. Yes, did you not, Rebecca! I thought that was the meaning of your cry.

REBECCA. For a moment, yes. I had forgotten myself. It was my old buoyant will that was struggling to be free. But it has no energy left now—no power of endurance.

ROSMER. How do you account for what has happened to you?

REBECCA. It is the Rosmer view of life—or your view of life, at any rate—that has infected my will.

ROSMER. Infected?

REBECCA. And made it sick. Enslaved it to laws that had no power over me before. You—life with you—has ennobled my mind——

ROSMER. Oh that I could believe it!

REBECCA. You may safely believe it! The Rosmer view of life ennobles. But—— (*Shaking her head*) But—but——

ROSMER. But——? Well?

REBECCA. ——but it kills happiness.

ROSMER. Do you think so, Rebecca?

REBECCA. My happiness, at any rate.

ROSMER. Yes, but are you so certain of that? If I were to ask you again now——? If I were to beg and entreat you——?

REBECCA. Dear,—never speak of this again! It is impossible——! For you must know, Rosmer, I have a—a past behind me.

ROSMER. More than what you have told me?

REBECCA. Yes. Something different and something more.

ROSMER (*with a faint smile*). Is it not strange, Rebecca? Some such idea has crossed my mind now and then.

REBECCA. It has? And yet——? Even so——?

ROSMER. I never believed it. I only played with it—in my thoughts, you understand.

REBECCA. If you wish it, I will tell you all, at once.

ROSMER (*turning it off*). No, no! I will not hear a word. Whatever it may be—I can forget it.

REBECCA. But I cannot.

ROSMER. Oh Rebecca——!

REBECCA. Yes, Rosmer—this is the terrible part of it: that now, when all life's happiness is within my grasp—my heart is changed, and my own past cuts me off from it.

ROSMER. Your past is dead, Rebecca. It has no hold on you any more—it is no part of you—as you are now.

REBECCA. Oh, you know that these are only phrases, dear. And innocence? Where am I to get that from?

ROSMER (*sadly*). Ah,—innocence.

REBECCA. Yes, innocence. That is the source of peace and happiness. That was the vital truth you were to implant in the coming generation of happy noble-men——

ROSMER. Oh, don't remind me of that. It was only an abortive dream, Rebecca—an immature idea, that I myself no longer believe in.—Ah no, we cannot be ennobled from without, Rebecca.

REBECCA (*softly*). Not even by tranquil love, Rosmer?

ROSMER (*thoughtfully*). Yes—that would be the great thing—the most glorious in life, almost—if it were so. (*Moves uneasily.*) But how can I be certain of that? How convince myself?

REBECCA. Do you not believe me, Rosmer?

ROSMER. Oh, Rebecca—how can I believe in you, fully? You who have all this while been cloaking, concealing such a multitude of things!—Now you come forward with something new. If you have a secret purpose in all this, tell me plainly what it is. Is there anything you want to gain by it? You know that I will gladly do everything I can for you.

REBECCA (*wringing her hands*). Oh this killing doubt——! Rosmer—Rosmer——!

ROSMER. Yes, is it not terrible, Rebecca? But I cannot help it. I shall never be able to shake off the doubt. I can never be absolutely sure that you are mine in pure and perfect love.

REBECCA. Is there nothing in the depths of your own heart that bears witness to the transformation in me? And tells you that it is due to you—and you alone?

ROSMER. Oh, Rebecca—I no longer believe in my power of transforming any one. My faith in myself is utterly dead. I believe neither in myself nor in you.

REBECCA (*looks darkly at him*). Then how will you be able to live your life?

ROSMER. That I don't know. I cannot imagine how. I don't think I can live it.—And I know of nothing in the world that is worth living for.

REBECCA. Oh, life—life will renew itself. Let us hold fast to it, Rosmer.—We shall leave it soon enough.

ROSMER (*springs up restlessly*). Then give me my faith again! My faith in you, Rebecca! My faith in your love! Proof! I must have proof!

REBECCA. Proof? How can I give you proof——?

ROSMER. You must! (*Walks across the room.*)

I cannot bear this desolation—this horrible emptiness—this—this——

(*A loud knock at the hall door.*)

REBECCA (*starts up from her chair*). Ah—did you hear that?

(*The door opens.* ULRIC BRENDEL *enters. He has a white shirt on, a black coat and a good pair of boots, with his trousers tucked into them. Otherwise he is dressed as in the first Act. He looks excited.*)

ROSMER. Ah, is it you, Mr. Brendel?

BRENDEL. Johannes, my boy—hail—and farewell!

ROSMER. Where are you going so late?

BRENDEL. Downhill.

ROSMER. How——?

BRENDEL. I am going homewards, my beloved pupil. I am home-sick for the mighty Nothingness.

ROSMER. Something has happened to you, Mr. Brendel! What is it?

BRENDEL. So you observe the transformation? Yes—well you may. When I last set foot in these halls—I stood before you as a man of substance and slapped my breast-pocket.

ROSMER. Indeed! I don't quite understand——

BRENDEL. But as you see me this night, I am a deposed monarch on the ash-heap that was my palace.

ROSMER. If there is anything *I* can do for you——

BRENDEL. You have preserved your childlike heart, Johannes. Can you grant me a loan?

ROSMER. Yes, yes, most willingly!

BRENDEL. Can you spare me an ideal or two?

ROSMER. What do you say?

BRENDEL. One or two cast-off ideals. It would be an act of charity. For I'm cleaned out, my boy. Ruined, beggared.

REBECCA. Have you not delivered your lecture?

BRENDEL. No, seductive lady. What do you think? Just as I am standing ready to pour forth the horn of plenty, I make the painful discovery that I am bankrupt.

REBECCA. But all your unwritten works——?

BRENDEL. For five-and-twenty years I have sat like a miser on his double-locked treasure-chest. And then yesterday—when I open it and want to display the treasure—there's none there! The teeth of time had ground it into dust. There was nix and nothing in the whole concern.

ROSMER. But are you so sure of that?

BRENDEL. There's no room for doubt, my dear fellow. The President has convinced me of it.

ROSMER. The President?

BRENDEL. Well well—His Excellency then. *Ganz nach Belieben.*

ROSMER. What do you mean?

BRENDEL. Peter Mortensgård, of course.

ROSMER. What?

BRENDEL (*mysteriously*). Hush, hush, hush! Peter Mortensgård is the lord and leader of the future. Never have I stood in a more august presence. Peter Mortensgård has the secret of omnipotence. He can do whatever he will.

ROSMER. Oh, don't believe that.

BRENDEL. Yes, my boy! For Peter Mortensgård never wills more than he can do. Peter Mortensgård is capable of living his life without ideals. And that, do you see—that is just the mighty secret of action and of victory. It is the sum of the whole world's wisdom. *Basta!*

ROSMER (*in a low voice*). Now I understand—why you leave here poorer than you came.

BRENDEL. *Bien!* Then take a *Beispiel* by your ancient teacher. Rub out all that he once imprinted on your mind. Build not thy house on shifting sand. And look ahead—and feel your way—before you build on this exquisite creature, who lends sweetness to your life.

REBECCA. Is it me you mean?

BRENDEL. Yes, my fascinating mermaid.

REBECCA. Why am I not to be built on?

BRENDEL (*Comes a step nearer*). I gather that my former pupil has a great cause to carry forward to victory.

REBECCA. What then——?

BRENDEL. Victory is assured. But—mark me well—on one indispensable condition.

REBECCA. Which is——?

BRENDEL (*taking her gently by the wrist*). That the woman who loves him shall gladly go out into the kitchen and hack off her tender, rosy-white little finger—here—just here at the middle joint. Item, that the aforesaid loving woman—again gladly —shall slice off her incomparably-moulded left ear. (*Lets her go, and turns to* ROSMER.) Farewell, my conquering Johannes.

ROSMER. Are you going now? In the dark night?

BRENDEL. The dark night is best. Peace be with you.

(*He goes. There is a short silence in the room.*)

REBECCA (*breathes heavily*). Oh, how close and sultry it is here!

(*Goes to the window, opens it, and remains standing by it.*)

ROSMER (*sits down in the armchair by the stove*).

There is nothing else for it after all, Rebecca. I see it. You must go away.

REBECCA. Yes, I see no choice.

ROSMER. Let us make the most of our last hour. Come here and sit by me.

REBECCA (*goes and sits on the sofa*). What do you want to say to me, Rosmer?

ROSMER. First, I want to tell you that you need not feel any anxiety about your future.

REBECCA (*smiles*). H'm, my future.

ROSMER. I have long ago arranged for everything. Whatever may happen, you are provided for.

REBECCA. That too, my dear one?

ROSMER. You might surely have known that.

REBECCA. It is many a long day since I have given a thought to such things.

ROSMER. Yes, yes—you thought things would always remain as they were between us.

REBECCA. Yes, I thought so.

ROSMER. So did I. But if I were to go——

REBECCA. Oh, Rosmer—you will live longer than I.

ROSMER. Surely my worthless life lies in my own hands.

REBECCA. What is this? You are never thinking of——!

ROSMER. Do you think it would be so strange? After this pitiful, lamentable defeat! I, who was to have borne a great cause on to victory—have I not fled from the battle before it was well begun?

REBECCA. Take up the fight again, Rosmer! Only try—and you shall see, you will conquer. You will ennoble hundreds—thousands of minds. Only try!

ROSMER. Oh, Rebecca—I, who no longer believe in my own mission!

REBECCA. But your mission has stood the test already. You have ennobled one human being at least—me you have ennobled for the rest of my days.

ROSMER. Oh—if I dared believe you.

REBECCA (*pressing her hands together*). Oh, Rosmer,—do you know of nothing—nothing that could make you believe it?

ROSMER (*starts as if in fear*). Don't speak of that! Keep away from that, Rebecca! Not a word more.

REBECCA. Yes, this is precisely what we must speak about. Do you know of anything that would kill the doubt? For *I* know of nothing in the world.

ROSMER. It is well for you that you do not know. —It is well for both of us.

REBECCA. No, no, no.—I will not be put off in this way! If you know of anything that would absolve me in your eyes, I claim as my right to be told of it.

ROSMER (*as if impelled against his will to speak*).

Then let us see. You say that a great love is in you; that through me your mind has been ennobled. Is it so? Is your reckoning just, Rebecca? Shall we try to prove the sum? Say?

REBECCA. I am ready.

ROSMER. At any time?

REBECCA. Whenever you please. The sooner the better.

ROSMER. Then let me see, Rebecca,—if you for my sake—this very evening—— (*Breaks off.*) Oh, no, no, no!

REBECCA. Yes, Rosmer! Yes! Tell me, and you shall see.

ROSMER. Have you the courage—have you the will—gladly, as Ulric Brendel said—for my sake, to-night—gladly—to go the same way that Beata went?

REBECCA (*rises slowly from the sofa; almost voiceless*). Rosmer——!

ROSMER. Yes, Rebecca—this is the question that will for ever haunt me—when you are gone. Every hour in the day it will return upon me. Oh, I seem to see you before my very eyes. You are standing out on the foot-bridge—right in the middle. Now you are bending forward over the railing—drawn dizzily downwards, downwards towards the rushing water! No—you recoil. You have not the heart to do what she dared.

REBECCA. But if I had the heart to do it? And the will to do it gladly? What then?

ROSMER. I should have to believe you then. I should recover my faith in my mission. Faith in my power to ennoble human souls. Faith in the human soul's power to attain nobility.

REBECCA (*takes up her shawl slowly and puts it over her head; says with composure*). You shall have your faith again.

ROSMER. Have you the will and the courage—for this, Rebecca?

REBECCA. That you shall see to-morrow—or afterwards—when they find my body.

ROSMER (*puts his hand to his forehead*). There is a horrible fascination in this——!

REBECCA. For I don't want to remain down there. Not longer than necessary. You must see that they find me.

ROSMER (*springs up*). But all this—is nothing but madness. Go—or stay! I will take your bare word this time too.

REBECCA. Phrases, Rosmer! Let us have no more cowardly subterfuges, dear! How can you believe me on my bare word after this day?

ROSMER. I shrink from seeing your defeat, Rebecca!

REBECCA. It will be no defeat.

ROSMER. Yes, it will. You will never bring yourself to go Beata's way.

REBECCA. Do you think not?

ROSMER. Never. You are not like Beata. You are not under the dominion of a distorted view of life.

REBECCA. But I am under the dominion of the Rosmersholm view of life—now. What I have sinned—it is fit that I should expiate.

ROSMER (*looks at her fixedly*). Is that your point of view?

REBECCA. Yes.

ROSMER (*with resolution*). Well then, I stand firm in our emancipated view of life, Rebecca. There is no judge over us; and therefore we must do justice upon ourselves.

REBECCA (*misunderstanding him*). Yes, that is true—that too. My going away will save what is best in you.

ROSMER. Oh, there is nothing left to save in me.

REBECCA. Yes, there is. But I—after to-day, I should only be a sea-troll dragging down the ship that is to carry you forward. I must go overboard. Why should I remain here in the world, trailing after me my own crippled life? Why brood and brood over the happiness that my past has forfeited for ever? I must give up the game, Rosmer.

ROSMER. If you go—I go with you.

REBECCA (*smiles almost imperceptibly, looks at him, and says more softly*). Yes, come with me—and see——

ROSMER. I go with you, I say.

REBECCA. To the foot-bridge, yes. You know you never dare go out upon it.

ROSMER. Have you noticed that?

REBECCA (*sadly and brokenly*). Yes.—It was that that made my love hopeless.

ROSMER. Rebecca,—now I lay my hand on your head—(*Does so*)—and I wed you as my true wife.

REBECCA (*takes both his hands, and bows her head towards his breast*). Thanks, Rosmer. (*Lets him go.*) And now I will go—gladly.

ROSMER. Man and wife should go together.

REBECCA. Only to the bridge, Rosmer.

ROSMER. Out on to it, too. As far as you go—so far shall I go with you. For now I dare.

REBECCA. Are you absolutely certain—that this way is the best for you?

ROSMER. I am certain that it is the only way.

REBECCA. If you were deceiving yourself? If it were only a delusion? One of those white horses of Rosmersholm.

ROSMER. It may be so. For we can never escape from them—we of this house.

REBECCA. Then stay, Rosmer!

ROSMER. The husband shall go with his wife, as the wife with her husband.

REBECCA. Yes, but first tell me this: Is it you who follow me? Or is it I who follow you?

ROSMER. We shall never think that question out.

REBECCA. But I should like to know.

ROSMER. We go with each other, Rebecca—I with you, and you with me.

REBECCA. I almost think that is the truth.

ROSMER. For now we two are one.

REBECCA. Yes. We are one. Come! We go gladly. (*They go out hand in hand through the hall, and are seen to turn to the left. The door remains open. The room stands empty for a little while. Then the door to the right is opened by* MADAM HELSETH.)

MADAM HELSETH. Miss West—the carriage is—— (*Looks round.*) Not here? Out together at this time of night? Well—I must say——! H'm! (*Goes out into the hall, looks round and comes in again.*) Not on the garden seat. Ah, well, well. (*Goes to the window and looks out.*) Oh, good God! that white thing there——! My soul! They're both of them out on the bridge! God forgive the sinful creatures—if they're not in each other's arms! (*Shrieks aloud.*) Oh—down—both of them! Out into the mill-race! Help! Help! (*Her knees tremble; she holds on to the chair-back, shaking all over; she can scarcely get the words out.*) No. No help here.—The dead wife has taken them.

Russian Fiction

ALEKSANDER PUSHKIN

1799–1837

Aleksander Sergeevich Pushkin was born in Moscow, of an aristocratic family whose fortunes were in decline. Like so many young men who became habitués of the gay, sophisticated, and artificial society of the aristocracy, Pushkin seemed destined for a career in government service. After preparation at the Moscow Lyceum, he entered the Foreign Office in 1817. His strong libertarian tendencies soon revealed themselves in satirical epigrams upon political events; as a consequence he was sent into the virtual exile of a dull provincial existence at Kishinev in South Russia. During this period, the early eighteen-twenties, he fell under the influence of Byron, imitating the latter's Oriental romances and starting his own most brilliant novel in verse, *Eugene Onegin* (1832), under the inspiration of Byron's *Childe Harold's Pilgrimage* and *Don Juan*.

In 1826, after a famous interview with Czar Nicholas I, Pushkin was allowed to return to Moscow, somewhat under the czar's benevolent and despotic patronage. In 1831 he married Natalya Goncharova and settled in St. Petersburg. The acidity of his literary attacks and his bold liberalism antagonized the aristocracy and caused his enemies to circulate scandal about his wife. Their vindictiveness finally involved him in an unsavory court intrigue that resulted in his death from wounds incurred in a duel with his wife's alleged lover.

Pushkin is Russia's first great literary figure, and her greatest poet. His poetry is generally considered untranslatable because its haunting musicality may sound banal in translation; it is astonishingly successful in wresting poetic beauty from the most colloquial Russian diction, and it perfectly fuses classic sobriety of form with the most romantic feeling. Nevertheless, good translations of his poetry evince that melancholy subjectivity (see "The Man I Was of Old" and "Along the Noisy Streets," *post,* p. 663), which is never so wholly despondent as to be

devoid of the life and vitality characteristic of the poet, even in such a lyric as "Abandoning an Alien Country." To some critics, Pushkin is at his best in his lyrics, for they also reflect his hatred of oppression and wrong which was so much a part of his devotion to and belief in the Russian people (see "To Chaadayev" and "With Freedom's Seed").

Despite his liberalism, it is difficult to discover in Pushkin the militant forerunner of the October Revolution of 1917. He is rather the romantic poet, an aristocratic rebel like Byron, who chose for his subject matter contemporary events and political tendencies, and who shared the romantic artist's conviction that he should be free to express himself upon the hypocrisy and illiberality of the venal society about him, in defiance of public opinion and constituted authority.

Pushkin steadily progressed toward artistic maturity as he came to understand his symbolic role as a poet. In this progress he left behind him certain types of poetic experience which he felt he had outgrown. The short lyric, "To Chaadayev," written as early as 1818, anticipates this change, and in *Eugene Onegin* he finally rejects the Byronic egotism and affectation which he had admired. This poem is certainly his masterpiece in the presentation of the varied Russian scene, from the simple country manners to the sophisticated society of St. Petersburg. In his drama *Boris Godunov* (1830) he turns to a nobler source of inspiration, Shakespeare's history plays. Both of these works have been re-created musically by Tchaikovsky and Moussorgsky (*Boris Godunov* is eminently presented in Alexander Kipnis' chorus and orchestra, Victor Set 1000).

The short stories of Pushkin, in their directness and simplicity of style, prepare the way for the development of realism in Russian fiction. In the blending of realistic detail and the macabre which is also characteristic of some of Pushkin's longer poems (like *The Bronze Horseman*), "The Undertaker" anticipates Gogol, who acknowledged Pushkin his master.

Pushkin's strong patriotism and his devotion to the people of Russia never wavered, but at the same time he did not reject or condemn the culture of western Europe. In all respects a good European as well as a good Russian, he was deeply appreciative of all that was admirable and imitable in the literature of the West. He is therefore in a double sense an author of world significance: not only has Pushkin delineated for the Western World the characteristics of the Russian people at a time when their literature was coming into maturity and efflorescence, but he has identified Russian literature as well with the main currents of the literature of Western civilization.

FURTHER READING

SIMMONS, ERNEST J. *Pushkin* (Cambridge, Mass., 1937). TROYAT, HENRI. *Pushkin: His Life and Times* (New York, 1950).

The Undertaker *

Are coffins not beheld each day,
The gray hairs of an aging world?
—DERZHAVIN

THE last of the effects of the undertaker, Adrian Prokhorov, were piled upon the hearse, and a couple of sorry-looking jades dragged themselves along for the fourth time from Basmannaya to Nikitskaya, whither the undertaker was removing with all his household. After locking up the shop, he posted upon the door a placard announcing that the house was for sale or rent, and then made his way on foot to his new abode. On approaching the little yellow house, which had so long captivated his imagination, and which at last he had bought for a considerable sum, the old undertaker was astonished to find that his heart did not rejoice. When he crossed the unfamiliar threshold and found his new home in the greatest confusion, he sighed for his old hovel, where for eighteen years the strictest order had prevailed. He began to scold his two daughters and the servants for their slowness, and then set to work to help them himself. Order was soon established; the ikon-case, the cupboard with the crockery, the table, the sofa, and the bed occupied the corners reserved for them in the back room; in the kitchen and parlor were placed the master's wares— coffins of all colors and of all sizes, together with

* Translated by T. Keane; revised by Avrahm Yarmolinsky. By permission of Random House, Inc., and Avrahm Yarmolinsky.

cupboards containing mourning hats, cloaks and torches.

Over the gate was placed a sign representing a plump Cupid with an inverted torch in his hand and bearing this inscription: "Plain and colored coffins sold and upholstered here; coffins also let out on hire, and old ones repaired."

The girls retired to their bedroom; Adrian made a tour of inspection of his quarters, and then sat down by the window and ordered the samovar to be prepared.

The enlightened reader knows that Shakespeare and Walter Scott have both represented their gravediggers as merry and facetious individuals, in order that the contrast might more forcibly strike our imagination. Out of respect for the truth, we cannot follow their example, and we are compelled to confess that the disposition of our undertaker was in perfect harmony with his gloomy métier. Adrian Prokhorov was usually sullen and pensive. He rarely opened his mouth, except to scold his daughters when he found them standing idle and gazing out of the window at the passers-by, or to ask for his wares an exorbitant price from those who had the misfortune—or sometimes the pleasure—of needing them. And so Adrian, sitting near the window and drinking his seventh cup of tea, was immersed as usual in melancholy reflections. He thought of the pouring rain which, just a week before, had commenced to beat down during the funeral of the retired brigadier. Many of the cloaks had shrunk in consequence of the downpour, and many of the hats had been put quite out of shape. He foresaw unavoidable expenses, for his old stock of funeral apparel was in a pitiable condition. He hoped to compensate himself for his losses by the burial of old Trukhina, the merchant's wife, who for more than a year had been upon the point of death. But Trukhina lay dying in Razgulyay, and Prokhorov was afraid that her heirs, in spite of their promise, would not take the trouble to send so far for him, but would make arrangements with the nearest undertaker.

These reflections were suddenly interrupted by three masonic knocks at the door.

"Who is there?" asked the undertaker.

The door opened, and a man, who at first glance could be recognized as a German artisan, entered the room, and with a jovial air advanced toward the undertaker.

"Pardon me, good neighbor," said he in that Russian dialect which to this day we cannot hear without a smile: "pardon me for disturbing you. . . . I wished to make your acquaintance as soon as possible. I am a shoemaker, my name is Gottlieb Schultz, and I live across the street, in that little house just facing your windows. To-morrow I am going to celebrate my silver wedding, and I have come to invite you and your daughters to dine with us."

The invitation was cordially accepted. The undertaker asked the shoemaker to seat himself and take a cup of tea, and thanks to the open-hearted disposition of Gottlieb Schultz, they were soon engaged in friendly conversation.

"How is business with you?" asked Adrian.

"So so," replied Schultz; "I can't complain. But my wares are not like yours: the living can do without shoes, but the dead cannot do without coffins."

"Very true," observed Adrian; "but if a living person hasn't anything to buy shoes with, he goes barefoot, and holds his peace, if you please; but a dead beggar gets his coffin for nothing."

In this manner the conversation was carried on between them for some time; at last the shoemaker rose and took leave of the undertaker, renewing his invitation.

The next day, exactly at twelve o'clock, the undertaker and his daughters issued from the wicket-door of their newly purchased residence, and went to their neighbor's. I will not stop to describe the Russian *caftan* of Adrian Prokhorov, nor the European toilettes of Akulina and Darya, deviating in this respect from the custom of modern novelists. But I do not think it superfluous to observe that the two girls had on the yellow hats and red shoes, which they were accustomed to don on solemn occasions only.

The shoemaker's little dwelling was filled with guests, consisting chiefly of German artisans with their wives and apprentices. Of the Russian officials there was present but one, Yurko the Finn, a constable, who, in spite of his humble calling, was the special object of the host's attention. Like Pogorelsky's postman, for twenty-five years he had faithfully discharged his duties. The conflagration of 1812, which destroyed the ancient capital, destroyed also his little yellow booth. But immediately after the expulsion of the enemy, a new one appeared in its place, painted gray and with little white Doric columns, and Yurko again began to pace to and fro before it, *with his ax and armor of coarse cloth.* He was known to the greater part of the Germans who lived near the Nikitskaya Gate, and some of them had even spent Sunday night beneath his roof.

Adrian immediately made himself acquainted with him, as with a man whom, sooner or later, he might have need of, and when the guests took their places at the table, they sat down beside each other. Herr Schultz and his wife, and their daughter Lotchen, a young girl of seventeen, did the honors of the table and helped the cook to serve. The beer flowed in streams; Yurko ate like four, and Adrian in no way yielded to him; his daughters, however, stood upon their dignity. The conversation, which was carried on in German, gradually grew more and more noisy. Suddenly the host requested a moment's attention, and uncorking a sealed bottle, he said loudly in Russian:

"To the health of my good Louise!"

The imitation champagne foamed. The host tenderly kissed the fresh face of his partner, and the guests drank noisily to the health of the good Louise.

"To the health of my amiable guests!" exclaimed the host, uncorking a second bottle; and the guests thanked him by draining their glasses once more.

Then followed a succession of toasts. The health of each individual guest was drunk; they drank to Moscow and to a round dozen of little German towns; they drank to the health of all guilds in general and of each in particular; they drank to the health of the masters and apprentices. Adrian drank with assiduity and became so jovial, that he proposed a facetious toast himself. Suddenly one of the guests, a fat baker, raised his glass and exclaimed:

"To the health of those for whom we work, our customers!"

This proposal like all the others, was joyously and unanimously received. The guests began to salute each other; the tailor bowed to the shoemaker, the shoemaker to the tailor, the baker to both, the whole company to the baker, and so on. In the midst of these mutual congratulations, Yurko exclaimed, turning to his neighbor:

"Come, little father! Drink to the health of your corpses!"

Everybody laughed, but the undertaker considered himself insulted, and frowned. Nobody noticed it, the guests continued to drink, and the bells had already rung for vespers when they rose from the table.

The guests dispersed at a late hour, the greater part of them in a very merry mood. The fat baker and the bookbinder, whose face seemed as if bound in red morocco, linked their arms in those of Yurko and conducted him back to his booth, thus observing the proverb: "One good turn deserves another."

The undertaker returned home drunk and angry.

"Why is it," he argued aloud, "why is it that my trade is not as honest as any other? Is an undertaker brother to the hangman? Why did those heathens laugh? Is an undertaker a buffoon? I wanted to invite them to my new house and give them a feast, but now I'll do nothing of the kind. Instead of inviting them, I will invite those for whom I work: the orthodox dead."

"What is the matter, master?" said the servant, who was engaged at that moment in taking off his boots: "why do you talk such nonsense? Make the sign of the cross! Invite the dead to your new house! What nonsense!"

"Yes, by God! I will invite them," continued Adrian, "and that, too, for tomorrow! . . . Do me the favor, my benefactors, to come and feast with me tomorrow evening; I will regale you with what God has sent me."

With these words the undertaker turned into bed and soon began to snore.

It was still dark when Adrian was roused out of his sleep. Trukhina, the merchant's wife, had died during the course of that very night, and a special messenger was sent off on horseback by her clerk to carry the news to Adrian. The undertaker gave him ten copecks to buy brandy with, dressed himself as hastily as possible, took a *droshky* and set out for Razgulyay. At the gate of the house in which the deceased lay, the police had already taken their stand, and the trades-people were busily moving back and forth, like ravens that smell a dead body. The deceased lay upon a table, yellow as wax, but not yet disfigured by decomposition. Around her stood her relatives, neighbors and domestic servants. All the windows were open; tapers were burning; and the priests were reading the prayers for the dead. Adrian went up to the nephew of Trukhina, a young shopman in a fashionable jacket, and informed him that the coffin, wax candles, pall, and the other funeral accessories would be immediately delivered in good order. The heir thanked him in an absent-minded manner, saying that he would not bargain about the price, but would rely upon his acting in everything according to his conscience. The undertaker, in accordance with his custom, swore that he would not charge him too much, exchanged significant glances with the clerk, and then departed to commence operations.

The whole day was spent in passing to and fro between Razgulyay and the Nikitskaya Gate. Toward evening everything was finished, and he returned home on foot, after having dismissed his driver. It was a moonlight night. The undertaker

reached the Nikitskaya Gate in safety. Near the Church of the Ascension he was hailed by our acquaintance Yurko, who, recognizing the undertaker, wished him good night. It was late. The undertaker was just approaching his house, when suddenly he fancied he saw some one approach his gate, open the wicket, and disappear within.

"What does that mean?" thought Adrian. "Who can be wanting me again? Can it be a thief come to rob me? Or have my foolish girls got lovers coming after them? It means no good, I fear!"

And the undertaker thought of calling his friend Yurko to his assistance. But at that moment, another person approached the wicket and was about to enter, but seeing the master of the house hastening toward him, he stopped and took off his three-cornered hat. His face seemed familiar to Adrian, but in his hurry he was not able to examine it closely.

"You are favoring me with a visit," said Adrian, out of breath. "Walk in, I beg of you."

"Don't stand on ceremony, sir," replied the other, in a hollow voice; "you go first, and show your guests the way."

Adrian had no time to spend upon ceremony. The wicket was open; he ascended the steps followed by the other. Adrian thought he could hear people walking about in his rooms.

"What the devil does all this mean?" he thought to himself, and he hastened to enter. But the sight that met his eyes caused his legs to give way beneath him.

The room was full of corpses. The moon, shining through the windows, lit up their yellow and blue faces, sunken mouths, dim, half-closed eyes, and protruding noses. Adrian, with horror, recognized in them people that he himself had buried, and in the guest who had entered with him, the brigadier who had been buried during the pouring rain. They all, ladies and gentlemen, surrounded the undertaker, with bowings and salutations, except one poor man lately buried gratis, who, conscious and ashamed of his rags, did not venture to approach, but meekly kept to a corner. All the others were decently dressed: the female corpses in caps and ribbons, the officials in uniforms, but with their beards unshaven, the tradesmen in their holiday *caftans*.

"You see, Prokhorov," said the brigadier in the name of all the honorable company, "we have all risen in response to your invitation. Only those have stopped at home who were unable to come, who have crumbled to pieces and have nothing left but fleshless bones. But even of these there was one who hadn't the patience to remain behind—so much did he want to come and see you. . . ."

At this moment a little skeleton pushed his way through the crowd and approached Adrian. His skull smiled affably at the undertaker. Shreds of green and red cloth and rotten linen hung on him here and there as on a pole, and the bones of his feet rattled inside his big jackboots, like pestles in mortars.

"You do not recognize me, Prokhorov," said the skeleton. "Don't you remember the retired sergeant of the Guard, Pyotr Petrovich Kurilkin, the same to whom, in the year 1799, you sold your first coffin, and a deal one at that, instead of oak, as agreed?"

With these words the corpse stretched out his bony arms toward him; but Adrian, collecting all his strength, shrieked and pushed him away. Pyotr Petrovich staggered, fell and crumbled to pieces. Among the corpses arose a murmur of indignation; all stood up for the honor of their companion, and they overwhelmed Adrian with such threats and curses, that the poor host, deafened by their shrieks and almost crushed to death, lost his presence of mind, fell upon the bones of the retired sergeant of the Guard, and swooned away.

For some time the sun had been shining upon the bed on which the undertaker lay. At last he opened his eyes and saw before him the servant attending to the samovar. With horror, Adrian recalled all the incidents of the previous day. Trukhina, the brigadier, and the sergeant Kurilkin, rose vaguely before his imagination. He waited in silence for the servant to open the conversation and inform him of the events of the night.

"How you have slept, Adrian Prokhorovich!" said Aksinya, handing him his dressing-gown. "Your neighbor, the tailor, has been here, and the constable also called to inform you that today is his name-day; but you were so sound asleep, that we did not wish to wake you."

"Did anyone come for me from the late Trukhina?"

"The late? Is she dead, then?"

"What a fool you are! Didn't you yourself help me yesterday to prepare the things for her funeral?"

"Have you taken leave of your senses, master, or have you not yet recovered from the effects of yesterday's drinking-bout? What funeral was there yesterday? You spent the whole day feasting at the German's, and then came home drunk and threw yourself upon the bed, and have slept till this hour, when the bells have already rung for mass."

"Really!" said the undertaker, greatly relieved.

"Yes, indeed," replied the servant.

"Well, since that is the case, make tea as quickly as possible and call my daughters."

NIKOLAI VASILIEVICH GOGOL

1809–1852

Nikolai Gogol was born in the Russian Ukraine of a family of landed gentry. After a desultory schooling he went to St. Petersburg, trying his hand at various occupations from acting to teaching. In 1831 he published his first volume of short stories, *Evenings on a Farm near Dikanka,* dealing with the superstitions and the folklore of his native Ukraine. Neither this nor the next two volumes he published are important, despite the humor and fun of *Evenings,* and the romantic Cossack narrative *Taras Bulba.* However, the performance of the amazingly brilliant play, *The Inspector General* (1836), in St. Petersburg brought the name of Gogol before the general public. Although Gogol intended the play as a moral allegory, a dream play which anticipates the expressionistic drama, it was regarded as an attack upon government bureaucracy, and a storm of abuse broke over the author's head. In anger he went into self-exile, devoting his energies to the writing of *Dead Souls* (Part I, 1842) which, though on the surface comedy, carries an undercurrent of scathing satire and indictment of the corruptions and meannesses of Russian provincial society. This was Gogol's last contribution to Russian literature, for he died in February 1852, having destroyed Part II of *Dead Souls* before he died. In "The Cloak" the extraordinarily sympathetic identification of Gogol with his little clerk's futile humility and fantastically resolved, and finally supernatural, passion for his overcoat carries the story to depths that go beyond the mere social criticism which Russian critics have seen in it, and which the Leningradkino film production emphasized.

FURTHER READING

NABAKOV, VLADIMIR. *Nikolai Gogol* (Norfolk, Conn., 1944).

SLONIM, MARC. *The Epic of Russian Literature* (New York, 1950), Chapter VIII, pp. 159–81.

The Cloak *

IN THE department of—but it is better not to mention the department! The touchiest things in the world are departments, regiments, courts of justice —in a word, all branches of public service. Each individual nowadays thinks all society insulted in his person. Quite recently a complaint was received from a district chief of police in which he plainly demonstrated that all the imperial institutions were going to the dogs, and that the Czar's sacred name was being taken in vain; and in proof he appended to the complaint a romance in which the district chief of police is made to appear about once in every ten pages, and sometimes in a downright drunken condition. Therefore, in order to avoid all unpleasantness, it will be better to designate the department in question as A Certain Department.

So, in A Certain Department there was a certain official—not a very notable one, it must be allowed—short of stature, somewhat pock-marked, red-haired, and mole-eyed, with a bald forehead, wrinkled cheeks, and a complexion of the kind known as sanguine; the St. Petersburg climate was responsible for this. As for his official rank—with us Russians the rank comes first—he was what is called a perpetual titular councillor, over which, as is well known, some writers make merry and crack their jokes, obeying the praiseworthy custom of attacking those who can not bite back.

His family name was Bashmachkin. This name is evidently derived from *bashmak*;[1] but when, at what time, and in what manner, is not known. His father and grandfather and all the Bashmachkins always wore boots, which were resoled two or three times a year. His name was Akaky Akakiyevich. It may strike the reader as rather singular and far-fetched; but he may rest assured that it was by no means far-fetched, and that the circumstances were such that it would have been impossible to give him any other.

This is how it came about: Akaky Akakiyevich was born, if my memory fails me not, in the evening on the twenty-third of March. His mother, the wife of a government official, and a very fine woman, made all due arrangements for having the child baptised. She was lying on the bed opposite the door; on her right stood the godfather, Ivan Ivanovich Eroshkin, a most estimable man, who served

as the head clerk of the senate; and the godmother, Arina Semyonovna Bielobrinshkova, the wife of an officer of the quarter, and a woman of rare virtues. They offered the mother her choice of three names, Mokiya, Sossiya, or that the child should be called after the martyr Khozdazat. "No," said the good woman, "all those names are poor." In order to please her, they opened the calendar at another place; three more names appeared, Triphily, Dula, and Varakhasy. "This is awful," said the old woman. "What names! I truly never heard the like. I might have put up with Varadat or Varukh, but not Triphily and Varakhasy!" They turned to another page and found Pavsikakhy and Vakhtisy. "Now I see," said the old woman, "that it is plainly fate. And since such is the case, it will be better to name him after his father. His father's name was Akaky, so let his son's name be Akaky too." In this manner he became Akaky Akakiyevich. They christened the child, whereat he wept, and made a grimace, as though he foresaw that he was to be a titular councillor. In this manner did it all come about. We have mentioned it in order that the reader might see for himself that it was a case of necessity, and that it was utterly impossible to give him any other name.

When and how he entered the department, and who appointed him, no one could remember. However much the directors and chiefs of all kinds were changed, he was always to be seen in the same place, the same attitude, the same occupation —always the letter-copying clerk—so that it was afterwards affirmed that he had been born in uniform with a bald head. No respect was shown him in the department. The porter not only did not rise from his seat when he passed, but never even glanced at him, any more than if a fly had flown through the reception-room. His superiors treated him in coolly despotic fashion. Some insignificant assistant to the head clerk would thrust a paper under his nose without so much as saying, "Copy," or, "Here's an interesting little case," or anything else agreeable, as is customary amongst well-bred officials. And he took it, looking only at the paper, and not observing who handed it to him, or whether he had the right to do so; simply took it, and set about copying it.

The young officials laughed at and made fun of him, so far as their official wit permitted; told in his presence various stories concocted about him, and about his landlady, an old woman of seventy; declared that she beat him; asked when the wedding was to be; and strewed bits of paper over his

* By permission of Random House, Inc. Copyright, 1925, by Modern Library, Inc.
[1] Shoe.

head, calling them snow. But Akaky Akakiyevich answered not a word, any more than if there had been no one there besides himself. It even had no effect upon his work. Amid all these annoyances he never made a single mistake in a letter. But if the joking became wholly unbearable, as when they jogged his hand, and prevented his attending to his work, he would exclaim: "Leave me alone! Why do you insult me?"

And there was something strange in the words and the voice in which they were uttered. There was in it something which moved to pity; so much so that one young man, a newcomer, who, taking pattern by the others, had permitted himself to make sport of Akaky, suddenly stopped short, as though all about him had undergone a transformation, and presented itself in a different aspect. Some unseen force repelled him from the comrades whose acquaintance he had made, on the supposition that they were decent, well-bred men. Long afterwards, in his gayest moments, there recurred to his mind the little official with the bald forehead, with his heart-rending words, "Leave me alone! Why do you insult me?" In these moving words, other words resounded—"I am thy brother." And the young man covered his face with his hand; and many a time afterwards, in the course of his life, shuddered at seeing how much inhumanity there is in man, how much savage coarseness is concealed beneath refined, cultured, worldly refinement, and even, O God! in that man whom the world acknowledges as honorable and upright.

It would be difficult to find another man who lived so entirely for his duties. It is not enough to say that Akaky labored with zeal; no, he labored with love. In his copying, he found a varied and agreeable employment. Enjoyment was written on his face; some letters were even favorites with him; and when he encountered these, he smiled, winked, and worked with his lips, till it seemed as though each letter might be read in his face, as his pen traced it. If his pay had been in proportion to his zeal, he would, perhaps, to his great surprise, have been made even a councillor of state; but he worked, as his companions, the wits, put it, like a horse in a mill.

However, it would be untrue to say that no attention was paid to him. One director, being a kindly man and desirous of rewarding him for his long service, ordered him to be given something more important than mere copying. So he was ordered to make a report, of an already concluded affair, to another department; the duty consisted simply in changing the heading and altering a few words from the first to the third person. This caused him so much toil that he broke into a perspiration, rubbed his forehead, and finally said, "No, give me rather something to copy." After that they let him copy on forever.

Outside this copying, it appeared that nothing existed for him. He gave no thought to his clothes. His uniform was not green, but a sort of rusty-meal color. The collar was low, so that his neck, in spite of the fact that it was not long, seemed inordinately so as it emerged from it, like the necks of the plaster cats which pedlars carry about on their heads. And something was always sticking to his uniform, either a bit of hay or some trifle. Moreover, he had a peculiar knack, as he walked along the street, of arriving beneath a window just as all sorts of rubbish were being flung out of it; hence he always bore about on his hat scraps of melon rinds, and other such articles. Never once in his life did he give heed to what was going on every day in the street; while it is well known that his younger brother officials trained the range of their glances till they could see when anyone's trouser-straps came undone upon the opposite sidewalk, which always brought a malicious smile to their faces. But Akaky Akakiyevich saw in all things the clean, even strokes of his written lines; and only when a horse thrust his nose, from some unknown quarter, over his shoulder, and sent a whole gust of wind down his neck from his nostrils, did he observe that he was not in the middle of a page but in the middle of the street.

On reaching home, he sat down at once at the table, sipped his cabbage-soup up quickly, and swallowed a bit of beef with onions, never noticing their taste, and gulping down everything with flies and anything else which the Lord happened to send at the moment. When he saw that his stomach was beginning to swell, he rose from the table, and copied papers which he had brought home. If there happened to be none, he took copies for himself, for his own gratification, especially if the document was noteworthy, not on account of its style, but of its being addressed to some distinguished person.

Even at the hour when the grey St. Petersburg sky had quite disappeared, and all the official world had eaten or dined, each as he could, in accordance with the salary he received, and his own fancy; when all were resting from the department jar of pens, from running to and fro for their own and other people's indispensable operations, and from all the work that an uneasy man makes willingly for himself rather than what is necessary; when officials hasten to dedicate to pleasure the time that is left to them, one bolder than the rest going to the theater, another into the street looking under the bonnets, another wasting his evening in compliments to some pretty girl, the star of a small official circle, another—and this is the common case of all—visiting his comrades on the third or fourth floor, in two small rooms with an ante-room or kitchen and some pretensions to fashion such as a lamp or some other trifle which has cost many a sacrifice of dinner or pleasure trip; in a word, at the hour when all officials disperse among the contracted quarters of their friends to play whist as they sip their tea from glasses with a kopek's worth [2] of sugar, smoke long pipes, relate at times some bits of gossip which a Russian man can never under any circumstances refrain from, and when there is nothing else to talk about repeat eternal anecdotes about the commandant to whom they had sent word that the tails of the horses on the Falconet Monument had been cut off, when all strive to divert themselves—Akaky Akakiyevich indulged in no kind of diversion. No one could ever say that he had seen him at any kind of evening party. Having written to his heart's content, he lay down to sleep, smiling at the thought of the coming day—of what God might send him to copy on the morrow.

Thus flowed on the peaceful life of the man who, with a salary of four hundred rubles,[3] understood how to be content with his lot; and thus it would have continued to flow on, perhaps, to extreme old age, were it not that there are various ills strewn along the path of life for titular councillors as well as for private, actual, court, and every other species of councillor, even for those who never give any advice or take any themselves.

There exists in St. Petersburg a powerful foe of all who receive a salary of four hundred rubles a year, or thereabouts. This foe is no other than the northern cold, although it is said to be very healthful. At nine o'clock in the morning, at the very hour when the streets are filled with men bound for the various official departments, it begins to bestow such powerful and piercing nips on all noses impartially, that the poor officials really do not know what to do with them. At an hour when the foreheads of even those who occupy exalted positions ache with the cold, and tears start to their eyes, the poor titular councillors are sometimes quite unpro-

tected. Their only salvation lies in traversing as quickly as possible, in their thin little cloaks, five or six streets, and then warming their feet in the porter's room, and so thawing all their talents and qualifications for official service, which had become frozen on their way.

Akaky Akakiyevich had felt for some time that his back and shoulders were paining with peculiar poignancy, in spite of the fact that he tried to traverse the distance with all possible speed. He began finally to wonder whether the fault did not lie in his cloak. He examined it thoroughly at home, and discovered that in two places, namely, on the back and shoulders, it had become thin as gauze. The cloth was worn to such a degree that he could see through it, and the lining had fallen into pieces. You must know that Akaky Akakiyevich's cloak served as an object of ridicule to the officials. They even refused it the noble name of cloak, and called it a cape. In fact, it was of singular make, its collar diminishing year by year to serve to patch its other parts. The patching did not exhibit great skill on the part of the tailor, and was, in fact, baggy and ugly. Seeing how the matter stood, Akaky Akakiyevich decided that it would be necessary to take the cloak to Petrovich, the tailor, who lived somewhere on the fourth floor up a dark staircase, and who, in spite of his having but one eye and pock-marks all over his face, busied himself with considerable success in repairing the trousers and coats of officials and others; that is to say, when he was sober and not nursing some other scheme in his head.

It is not necessary to say much about this tailor, but as it is the custom to have the character of each personage in a novel clearly defined, there is no help for it; so here is Petrovich the tailor: At first he was called, only Grigory, and was some gentleman's serf. He commenced calling himself Petrovich from the time when he received his free papers, and further began to drink heavily on all holidays, at first on the great ones, and then on all church festivals without discrimination, wherever a cross stood in the calendar. On this point he was faithful to ancestral custom; and when quarrelling with his wife, he called her a low female and a German. As we have mentioned his wife, it will be necessary to say a word or two about her. Unfortunately, little is known of her beyond the fact that Petrovich had a wife, who wore a cap and a dress, but could not lay claim to beauty; at least, no one but the soldiers of the guard even looked under her cap when they met her.

[2] Cent's worth.
[3] About two hundred dollars.

Ascending the staircase which led to Petrovich's room—which staircase was all soaked with dish-water and reeked with the smell of spirits which affects the eyes and is an inevitable adjunct to all dark stairways in St. Petersburg houses—ascending the stairs, Akaky Akakiyevich pondered how much Petrovich would ask, and mentally resolved not to give more than two rubles. The door was open; for the mistress, in cooking some fish, had raised such a smoke in the kitchen that not even the beetles were visible. Akaky Akakiyevich passed through the kitchen unperceived, even by the housewife, and at length reached a room where he beheld Petrovich seated on a large unpainted table, with his legs tucked under him like a Turkish pasha. His feet were bare, after the fashion of tailors as they sit at work; and the first thing which caught the eye was his thumb, with a deformed nail thick and strong as a turtle's shell. About Petro-vich's neck hung a skein of silk and thread, and upon his knees lay some old garment. He had been trying unsuccessfully for three minutes to thread his needle, and was enraged at the darkness and even at the thread, growling in a low voice, "It won't go through, the barbarian! You pricked me, you rascal!"

Akaky Akakiyevich was vexed at arriving at the precise moment when Petrovich was angry. He liked to order something of Petrovich when he was a little downhearted, or, as his wife expressed it, "when he had settled himself with brandy, the one-eyed devil!" Under such circumstances Petro-vich generally came down in his price very readily, and even bowed and returned thanks. Afterwards, to be sure, his wife would come, complaining that her husband had been drunk, and so had fixed the price too low; but, if only a ten-kopek piece were added, then the matter would be settled. But now it appeared that Petrovich was in a sober condition, and therefore rough, taciturn, and inclined to de-mand Satan only knows what price. Akaky Akaki-yevich felt this, and would gladly have beat a re-treat; but he was in for it. Petrovich screwed up his one eye very intently at him, and Akaky Akakiyevich involuntarily said, "How do you do, Petrovich?"

"I wish you a good morning, sir," said Petrovich, squinting at Akaky Akakiyevich's hands to see what sort of booty he had brought.

"Ah! I—to you, Petrovich, this—" It must be known that Akaky Akakiyevich expressed himself chiefly by prepositions, adverbs, and scraps of phrases which had no meaning whatever. If the

matter was a very difficult one, he had a habit of never completing his sentences, so that frequently, having begun a phrase with the words, "This, in fact, is quite—" he forgot to go on, thinking he had already finished it.

"What is it?" asked Petrovich, and with his one eye scanned Akaky Akakiyevich's whole uniform from the collar down to the cuffs, the back, the tails, and the button-holes, all of which were well known to him, since they were his own handiwork. Such is the habit of tailors; it is the first thing they do on meeting one.

"But I, here, this—Petrovich—a cloak, cloth—here you see, everywhere, in different places, it is quite strong—it is a little dusty and looks old, but it is new, only here in one place it is a little—on the back, and here on one of the shoulders, it is a little worn; yes, here on this shoulder it is a little—do you see? That is all. And a little work—"

Petrovich took the cloak, spread it out, to begin with, on the table, looked at it hard, shook his head, reached out his hand to the window-sill for his snuff-box adorned with the portrait of some general, though what general is unknown, for the place where the face should have been had been rubbed through by the finger, and a square bit of paper had been pasted over it. Having taken a pinch of snuff, Petrovich held up the cloak, in-spected it against the light, and shook his head once more; then he turned it, lining upwards, and shook his head once more; after which he again lifted the general-adorned lid with its bit of pasted paper, and having stuffed his nose with the snuff, closed and put away the snuff-box, and said finally, "No, it is impossible to mend it; it is a wretched garment!"

Akaky Akakiyevich's heart sank at these words. "Why is it impossible Petrovich?" he said, almost in the pleading voice of a child. "All that ails it is that it is worn on the shoulders. You must have some pieces—"

"Yes, patches could be found—patches are easily found—" said Petrovich, "but there's nothing to sew them to. The thing is completely rotten. If you put a needle to it—see!—it will give way."

"Let it give way, and you can put on another patch at once!"

"But there is nothing to put the patches on to. There's no use in strengthening it; it is too far gone. It's lucky that it's cloth; for, if the wind were to blow, it would fly away!"

"Well, strengthen it again. How's this, in fact—"

"No," said Petrovich decisively, "there is nothing

to be done with it. It's a thoroughly bad job. You'd better, when the cold winter weather comes on, make yourself some gaiters out of it, because stockings are not warm. The Germans invented them in order to make money." Petrovich loved on all occasions to have a fling at the Germans. "But it is plain you must have a new cloak."

At the word "new," all grew dark before Akaky Akakiyevich's eyes, and everything in the room began to whir round. The only thing he saw clearly was the general with the paper face on the lid of Petrovich's snuff-box. "A new one?" said he, as if still in a dream. "Why, I have no money for that!"

"Yes, a new one," said Petrovich, with barbarous composure.

"Well, if it came to a new one, how—it—"

"You mean how much would it cost?"

"Yes."

"Well, you would have to lay out a hundred and fifty or more," said Petrovich, and pursed up his lips significantly. He liked to produce powerful effects, liked to stun utterly and suddenly, and then to glance sideways to see what face the stunned person would put on the matter.

"A hundred and fifty rubles for a cloak!" shrieked poor Akaky Akakiyevich, perhaps for the first time in his life; for his voice had always been distinguished for softness.

"Yes, sir," said Petrovich, "for any kind of cloak. If you have a marten fur on the collar, or a silk-lined hood, it will mount up to two hundred."

"Petrovich, please," said Akaky Akakiyevich in a beseeching tone, not hearing, and not trying to hear, Petrovich's words, and disregarding all his effects, "some repairs, in order that it may wear yet a little longer."

"No, it would only be a waste of time and money," said Petrovich. And Akaky Akakiyevich went away after these words, utterly discouraged. But Petrovich stood for some time after his departure, with significantly compressed lips, and without betaking himself to his work, satisfied that he would not be dropped, and an artistic tailor employed.

Akaky Akakiyevich went out into the street as if in a dream. "Such an affair!" he said to himself. "I did not think it had come to—" and then after a pause, he added, "Well, so it is! See what it has come to at last! And I never imagined that it was so!" Then followed a long silence, after which he exclaimed, "Well, so it is! See what already—nothing unexpected that—it would be nothing—

what a strange circumstance!" So saying, instead of going home, he went in exactly the opposite direction without suspecting it.

On the way, a chimney-sweep bumped up against him, and blackened his shoulder, and a whole hatful of rubbish landed on him from the top of a house which was building. He did not notice it, and only when he ran against a watchman, who, having planted his halberd beside him, was shaking some snuff from his box into his horny hand, did he recover himself a little, and that because the watchman said, "Why are you poking yourself into a man's very face? Haven't you the pavement?" This caused him to look about him, and turn towards home.

There only, he finally began to collect his thoughts, and to survey his position in its clear and actual light, and to argue with himself, sensibly and frankly, as with a reasonable friend, with whom one can discuss private and personal matters. "No," said Akaky Akakiyevich, "it is impossible to reason with Petrovich now. He is that—evidently, his wife has been beating him. I'd better go to him on Sunday morning. After Saturday night he will be a little cross-eyed and sleepy; for he will want to get drunk, and his wife won't give him any money, and at such a time, at ten-kopek piece in his hand will—he will become more fit to reason with, and then the cloak and that—" Thus argued Akaky Akakiyevich with himself, regained his courage, and waited until the first Sunday, when, seeing from afar that Petrovich's wife had left the house, he went straight to him.

Petrovich's eye was indeed very much askew after Saturday. His head drooped, and he was very sleepy; but for all that, as soon as he knew what it was a question of, it seemed as though Satan jogged his memory. "Impossible," said he. "Please to order a new one." Thereupon Akaky Akakiyevich handed over the ten-kopek piece. "Thank you, sir. I will drink your good health," said Petrovich. "But as for the cloak, don't trouble yourself about it; it is good for nothing. I will make you a capital new one, so let us settle about it now."

Akaky Akakiyevich was still for mending it; but Petrovich would not hear of it, and said, "I shall certainly have to make you a new one, and you may depend upon it that I shall do my best. It may even be, as the fashion goes, that the collar can be fastened by silver hooks under a flap."

Then Akaky Akakiyevich saw that it was impossible to get along without a new cloak, and his spirit sank utterly. How, in fact, was it to be done?

Where was the money to come from? He might, to be sure, depend, in part, upon his bonus at Christmas; but that money had long before been allotted. He must have some new trousers, and pay a debt of long standing to the shoemaker for putting new tops to his old boots, and he must order three shirts from the seamstress, and a couple of pieces of linen. In short, all his money must be spent. And even if the director should be so kind as to order him to receive forty-five or even fifty rubles instead of forty, it would be a mere nothing, a mere drop in the ocean towards the funds necessary for a cloak, although he knew that Petrovich was often wrongheaded enough to blurt out some outrageous price, so that even his own wife could not refrain from exclaiming, "Have you lost your senses, you fool?"

At one time he would not work at any price, and now it was quite likely that he had named a higher sum than the cloak would cost. But although he knew that Petrovich would undertake to make a cloak for eighty rubles, still, where was he to get the eighty rubles? He might possibly manage half. Yes, half might be procured; but where was the other half to come from? However, the reader must first be told where the first half came from.

Akaky Akakiyevich had a habit of putting, for every ruble he spent, a groschen into a small box fastened with lock and key and with a slit in the top for the reception of money. At the end of every half-year he counted over the heap of coppers, and changed it for silver. This he had done for a long time; and in the course of years the sum had mounted up to over forty rubles. Thus he had one half on hand—but where was he to find the other half? Where was he to get another forty rubles? Akaky Akakiyevich thought and thought, and decided that it would be necessary to curtail his ordinary expenses for the space of one year at least, to dispense with tea in the evening, to burn no candles, and if there was anything which he must do, to go into his landlady's room, and work by her light. When he went into the street, he must walk as lightly as he could, and as cautiously, upon the stones, almost upon tiptoe, in order not to wear his heels down in too short a time. He must give the laundress as little to wash as possible; and, in order not to wear out his clothes, he must take them off as soon as he got home, and wear only his cotton dressing-gown, which had been long and carefully saved.

To tell the truth, it was a little hard for him at first to accustom himself to these deprivations; but he got used to them at length, after a fashion, and all went smoothly. He even got used to being hungry in the evening; but he made up for it by treating himself, so to say, in spirit, by bearing ever in mind the idea of his future cloak. From that time forth, his existence seemed to become, in some way, fuller, as if he were married, or as if some other man lived in him, as if, in fact, he were not alone, and some pleasant friend had consented to travel along life's path with him—the friend being no other than the cloak with thick wadding and a strong lining incapable of wearing out. He became more lively, and even his character grew firmer, like that of a man who has made up his mind, and set himself a goal. From his face and gait doubt and indecision, all hesitating and wavering, disappeared of themselves. Fire gleamed in his eyes, and occasionally the boldest and most daring ideas flitted through his mind. Why not, for instance, have marten fur on the collar? The thought of this almost made him absent-minded. Once, in copying a letter, he nearly made a mistake, so that he exclaimed almost aloud, "Ugh!" and crossed himself. Once in the course of every month he had a conference with Petrovich on the subject of the cloak—where it would be better to buy the cloth, and the color, and the price. He always returned home satisfied though troubled, reflecting that the time would come at last when it could all be bought, and then the cloak made.

The affair progressed more briskly than he had expected; for beyond all his hopes, the director awarded neither forty nor forty-five rubles for Akaky Akakiyevich's share, but sixty. Whether he suspected that Akaky Akakiyevich needed a cloak, or whether it were merely chance, at all events twenty extra rubles were by this means provided. This circumstance hastened matters. Two or three months more of hunger, and Akaky Akakiyevich had accumulated about eighty rubles. His heart, generally so quiet, began to throb. On the first possible day, he went shopping in company with Petrovich. They bought some very good cloth, and at a reasonable rate, too; for they had been considering the matter for six months, and rarely let a month pass without their visiting the shops to inquire prices. Petrovich himself said that no better cloth could be had. For lining, they selected a cotton stuff, but so firm and thick that Petrovich declared it to be better than silk, and even prettier and more glossy. They did not buy the marten fur, because it was, in fact, dear; but in its stead they picked out the very best of catskin which could be found in the shop, and which might, indeed, be taken for marten at a distance.

Petrovich worked at the cloak two whole weeks, for there was a great deal of quilting; otherwise it would have been finished sooner. He charged twelve rubles for the job; it could not possibly have been done for less. It was all sewed with silk, in small, double seams, and Petrovich went over each seam afterwards with his own teeth, stamping in various patterns.

It was—it is difficult to say precisely on what day, but probably the most glorious one in Akaky Akakiyevich's life, when Petrovich at length brought home the cloak. He brought it in the morning, before the hour when it was necessary to start for the department. Never did a cloak arrive so exactly in the nick of time; for the severe cold had set in, and it seemed to threaten to increase. Petrovich brought the cloak himself as befits a good tailor. On his countenance was a significant expression, such as Akaky Akakiyevich had never beheld there. He seemed fully sensible that he had done no small deed, and crossed a gulf separating tailors who put in linings, and execute repairs, from those who make new things. He took the cloak out of the pocket-handkerchief in which he had brought it. The handkerchief was fresh from the laundress, and he put it in his pocket for use. Taking out the cloak, he gazed proudly at it, held it up with both hands, and flung it skillfully over the shoulders of Akaki Akakiyevich. Then he pulled it and fitted it down behind with his hand, and he draped it around Akaky Akakiyevich without buttoning it. Akaky Akakiyevich, like an experienced man, wished to try the sleeves. Petrovich helped him on with them, and it turned out that the sleeves were satisfactory also. In short, the cloak appeared to be perfect, and most seasonable.

Petrovich did not neglect to observe that it was only because he lived in a narrow street, and had no signboard, and had known Akaky Akakiyevich so long, that he made it so cheaply; but that if he had been in business on the Nevsky Prospect, he would have charged seventy-five rubles for the making alone. Akaky Akakiyevich did not care to argue this point with Petrovich. He paid him, thanked him, and set out at once in his new cloak for the department. Petrovich followed him, and pausing in the street, gazed long at the cloak in the distance, after which he went to one side expressly to run through a crooked alley, and emerge again into the street beyond to gaze once more upon the cloak from another point, namely, directly in front.

Meantime Akaky Akakiyevich went on in holiday mood. He was conscious every second of the time that he had a new cloak on his shoulders, and several times he laughed with internal satisfaction. In fact, there were two advantages; one was its warmth, the other its beauty. He saw nothing of the road, but suddenly found himself at the department. He took off his cloak in the anteroom, looked it over carefully, and confided it to the special care of the attendant. It is impossible to say precisely how it was that every one in the department knew at once that Akaky Akakiyevich had a new cloak, and that the cape no longer existed. All rushed at the same moment into the anteroom to inspect it. They congratulated him, and said pleasant things to him, so that he began at first to smile, and then to grow ashamed. When all surrounded him, and said that the new cloak must be christened, and that he must at least give them all a party, Akaky Akakiyevich lost his head completely, and he did not know where he stood, what to answer, or how to get out of it. He stood blushing all over for several minutes, trying to assure them with great simplicity that it was not a new cloak, that it was in fact the old cape.

At length one of the officials, assistant to the head clerk, in order to show that he was not at all proud, and on good terms with his inferiors, said: "So be it, only I will give the party instead of Akaky Akakiyevich; I invite you all to tea with me tonight. It just happens to be my name-day too."

The officials naturally at once offered the assistant clerk their congratulations, and accepted the invitation with pleasure. Akaky Akakiyevich would have declined; but all declared that it was discourteous, that it was simply a sin and a shame, and that he could not possibly refuse. Besides, the notion became pleasant to him when he recollected that he should thereby have a chance of wearing his new cloak in the evening also.

That whole day was truly a most triumphal festival for Akaky Akakiyevich. He returned home in the most happy frame of mind, took his cloak, and hung it carefully on the wall, admiring afresh the cloth and the lining. Then he brought out his old, worn-out cloak, for comparison. He looked at it, and laughed, so vast was the difference; and long after dinner he laughed again when the condition of the cape returned to his mind. He dined cheerfully, and after dinner wrote nothing, but took his ease for a while on the bed, until it got dark. Then he dressed himself leisurely, put on his cloak, and stepped out into the street.

Where the host lived, unfortunately we can not say. Our memory begins to fail us badly. The houses and streets in St. Petersburg have become so mixed up in our head that it is very difficult to get anything out of it again in proper form. This much is certain: that the official lived in the best part of the city; and therefore it must have been anything but near to Akaky Akakiyevich's residence. Akaky Akakiyevich was first obliged to traverse a kind of wilderness of deserted, dimly lighted streets. But in proportion as he approached the official's quarter, the streets became more lively, more populous, and more brilliantly illuminated. Pedestrians began to appear; handsomely dressed ladies were more frequently encountered; the men had otter-skin collars to their coats; shabby sleigh-men with their wooden, railed sledges, stuck over with brass nails, became rarer; whilst on the other hand, more and more drivers in red velvet caps, lacquered sledges, and bearskin coats began to appear, and carriages with rich hammer-cloths flew swiftly through the streets, their wheels scrunching the snow.

Akaky Akakiyevich gazed upon all this as upon a novel sight. He had not been in the streets during the evening for years. He halted out of curiosity before a shop-window to look at a picture representing a handsome woman who had thrown off her shoe, thereby baring her whole foot in a very pretty way, whilst behind her the head of a man with whiskers and a handsome moustache peeped through the doorway of another room. Akaky Akakiyevich shook his head, and laughed, and then went on his way. Why did he laugh? Either because he had met with a thing utterly unknown, but for which everyone cherishes, nevertheless, some sort of feeling, or else he thought, like many officials, "Well, those French! What is to be said? If they go in for anything of that sort, why—" But possibly he did not think at all.

Akaky Akakiyevich at length reached the house in which the head clerk's assistant lodged. He lived in fine style. The staircase was lit by a lamp, his apartment being on the second floor. On entering the vestibule, Akaky Akakiyevich beheld a whole row of goloshes on the floor. Among them, in the center of the room, stood a samovar, humming and emitting clouds of steam. On the walls hung all sorts of coats and cloaks; among them there were even some with beaver collars or velvet facings. Beyond, the buzz of conversation was

audible, and became clear and loud when the servant came out with a trayful of empty glasses, cream-jugs, and sugar-bowls. It was evident that the officials had arrived long before, and had already finished their first glasses of tea.

Akaky Akakiyevich, having hung up his own cloak, entered the inner room. Before him all at once appeared lights, officials, pipes, and card-tables; and he was bewildered by a sound of rapid conversation rising from all the tables, and the noise of moving chairs. He halted very awkwardly in the middle of the room, wondering what he ought to do. But they had seen him; they received him with a shout, and all thronged at once into the ante-room, and there took another look at his cloak. Akaky Akakiyevich, although somewhat confused, was frank-hearted, and could not refrain from rejoicing when he saw how they praised his cloak. Then, of course, they all dropped him and his cloak, and returned, as was proper, to the tables set out for whist.

All this—the noise, the talk, and the throng of people—was rather overwhelming to Akaky Akakiyevich. He simply did not know where he stood, or where to put his hands, his feet, and his whole body. Finally he sat down by the players, looked at the cards, gazed at the face of one and another, and after a while began to gape and to feel that it was wearisome—the more so as the hour was already long past when he usually went to bed. He wanted to take leave of the host; but they would not let him go, saying that he must not fail to drink a glass of champagne in honor of his new garment.

In the course of an hour, supper, consisting of vegetable salad, cold veal, pastry, confectioner's pies, and champagne, was served. They made Akaky Akakiyevich drink two glasses of champagne, after which he felt things grow livelier. Still, he could not forget that it was twelve o'clock, and that he should have been at home long ago. In order that the host might not think of some excuse for detaining him, he stole out of the room quickly, sought out, in the ante-room, his cloak, which, to his sorrow, he found lying on the floor, brushed it, picked off every speck upon it, put it on his shoulders, and descended the stairs to the street.

In the street all was still bright. Some petty shops, those permanent clubs of servants and all sorts of folks, were open. Others were shut, but, nevertheless, showed a streak of light the whole length of the door-crack, indicating that they were not yet free of company, and that probably some domestics, male and female, were finishing their stories and conversations, whilst leaving their masters in complete ignorance as to their whereabouts. Akaky Akakiyevich went on in a happy frame of mind. He even started to run, without knowing why, after some lady, who flew past like a flash of lightning. But he stopped short, and went on very quietly as before, wondering why he had quickened his pace.

Soon there spread before him those deserted streets which are not cheerful in the daytime, to say nothing of the evening. Now they were even more dim and lonely. The lanterns began to grow rarer; oil, evidently, had been less liberally supplied. Then came wooden houses and fences. Not a soul anywhere; only the snow sparkled in the streets, and mournfully veiled the low-roofed cabins with their closed shutters. He approached the spot where the street crossed a vast square with houses barely visible on its farther side, a square which seemed a fearful desert.

Afar, a tiny spark glimmered from some watchman's-box, which seemed to stand on the edge of the world. Akaky Akakiyevich's cheerfulness diminished at this point in a marked degree. He entered the square, not without an involuntary sensation of fear, as though his heart warned him of some evil. He glanced back, and on both sides it was like a sea about him. "No, it is better not to look," he thought, and went on, closing his eyes. When he opened them, to see whether he was near the end of the square, he suddenly beheld, standing just before his very nose, some bearded individuals of precisely what sort, he could not make out. All grew dark before his eyes, and his heart throbbed.

"Of course, the cloak is mine!" said one of them in a loud voice, seizing hold of his collar.

Akaky Akakiyevich was about to shout "Help!" when the second man thrust a fist, about the size of an official's head, at his very mouth, muttering, "Just you dare to scream!" Akaky Akakiyevich felt them strip off his cloak, and give him a kick. He fell headlong upon the snow, and felt no more.

In a few minutes he recovered consciousness, and rose to his feet, but no one was there. He felt that it was cold in the square, and that his cloak was gone. He began to shout, but his voice did not appear to reach the outskirts of the square. In despair, but without ceasing to shout, he started at a run across the square, straight towards the watchbox, beside which stood the watchman, leaning on his halberd, and apparently curious to know what kind of a customer was running towards him shouting. Akaky Akakiyevich ran up to him, and

began in a sobbing voice to shout that he was asleep, and attended to nothing, and did not see when a man was robbed. The watchman replied that he had seen two men stop him in the middle of the square, but supposed that they were friends of his, and that, instead of scolding vainly, he had better go to the police on the morrow, so that they might make a search for whoever had stolen the cloak.

Akaky Akakiyevich ran home and arrived in a state of complete disorder: his hair, which grew very thinly upon his temples and the back of his head, all tousled, his body, arms and legs, covered with snow. The old woman who was mistress of his lodgings, on hearing a terrible knocking, sprang hastily from her bed, and, with only one shoe on, ran to open the door, pressing the sleeve of her chemise to her bosom out of modesty. But when she had opened it, she fell back on beholding Akaky Akakiyevich in such a condition. When he told her about the affair, she clasped her hands, and said that he must go straight to the district chief of police; for his subordinate would turn up his nose, promise well, and drop the matter there. The very best thing to do, therefore, would be to go to the district chief, whom she knew, because Finnish Anna, her former cook, was now nurse at his house. She often saw him passing the house, and he was at church every Sunday, praying, but the same time gazing cheerfully at everybody; so that he must be a good man, judging from all appearances. Having listened to this opinion, Akaky Akakiyevich betook himself sadly to his room. And how he spent the night there, any one who can put himself in another's place may readily imagine.

Early in the morning, he presented himself at the district chief's, but was told that the official was asleep. He went again at ten, and was again informed that he was asleep; at eleven, and they said, "The superintendent is not at home"; at dinnertime, and the clerks in the ante-room would not admit him on any terms, and insisted upon knowing his business—so that at last, for once in his life, Akaky Akakiyevich felt an inclination to show some spirit, and said curtly that he must see the chief in person, that they ought not to presume to refuse him entrance, that he came from the department of justice, and that when he complained of them they would see.

The clerks dared make no reply to this, and one of them went to call the chief, who listened to the strange story of the theft of the coat. Instead of directing his attention to the principal points of the matter, he began to question Akaky Akakiyevich.

Why was he going home so late? Was he in the habit of doing so, or had he been to some disorderly house? So that Akaky Akakiyevich got thoroughly confused and left him without knowing whether the affair of his cloak was in proper train or not.

All that day, for the first time in his life, he never went near the department. The next day he made his appearance, very pale, and in his old cape, which had become even more shabby. The news of the robbery of the cloak touched many; although there were some officials present who never lost an opportunity, even such a one as the present, of ridiculing Akaky Akakiyevich. They decided to make a collection for him on the spot, but the officials had already spent a great deal in subscribing for the director's portrait, and for some book, at the suggestion of the head of that division, who was a friend of the author; and so the sum was trifling.

One of them, moved by pity, resolved to help Akaky Akakiyevich with some good advice, at least, and told him that he ought not to go to the police; for although it might happen that a police-officer, wishing to win the approval of his superiors, might hunt up the cloak by some means, still, his cloak would remain in the possession of the police if he did not offer legal proof that it belonged to him. The best thing for him, therefore, would be to apply to a certain prominent personage; since this prominent personage, by entering into relation with the proper person, could greatly expedite the matter.

As there was nothing else to be done, Akaky Akakiyevich decided to go to the prominent personage. What was the exact official position of the prominent personage remains unknown to this day. The reader must know that the prominent personage had but recently become a prominent personage, having up to that time been only an insignificant person. Moreover, his present position was not considered prominent in comparison with others still more so; but there is always a circle of people to whom what is insignificant in the eyes of others is important enough. Moreover, he strove to increase his importance by sundry devices: for instance, he managed to have the inferior officials meet him on the staircase when he entered upon his service; no one was to presume to come directly to him, but the strictest etiquette must be observed; the collegiate recorder must make a report to the government secretary, the government secretary to the titular councillor, or whatever other man was proper, and all business must come before him in this manner. In Holy Russia, all is thus contaminated with the love of imitation: every man imitates and copies his superior. They even say that a certain titular councillor, when promoted to be head of some small separate office, immediately partitioned off a private room for himself, called it the audience chamber, and posted at the door a lackey with red collar and braid, who grasped the handle of the door, and opened to all comers, though the audience chamber would hardly hold an ordinary writing-table.

The manners and customs of the prominent personage were grand and imposing, but rather exaggerated. The main foundation of his system was strictness. "Strictness, strictness, and always strictness," he generally said; and at the last word he looked significantly into the face of the person to whom he spoke. But there was no necessity for this; for the half-score of subordinates, who formed the entire force of the office, were properly afraid. On catching sight of him afar off, they left their work, and waited, drawn up in line, until he had passed through the room. His ordinary converse with his inferiors smacked of sternness, and consisted chiefly of three phrases: "How dare you?" "Do you know whom you are speaking to?" "Do you realize who is standing before you?"

Otherwise he was a very kind-hearted man, good to his comrades, and ready to oblige. But the rank of general threw him completely off his balance. On receiving any one of that rank, he became confused, lost his way as it were, and never knew what to do. If he chanced to be amongst his equals, he was still a very nice kind of man, a very good fellow in many respects, and not stupid; but the very moment that he found himself in the society of people but one rank lower than himself, he became silent. And his situation aroused sympathy, the more so, as he felt himself that he might have been making an incomparably better use of his time. In his eyes, there was sometimes visible a desire to join some interesting conversation or group, but he was kept back by the thoughts, "Would it not be a very great condescension on his part? Would it not be familiar? And would he not thereby lose his importance?" And in consequence of such reflections, he always remained in the same dumb state, uttering from time to time a few monosyllabic sounds, and thereby earning the name of the most wearisome of men.

To this prominent personage Akaky Akakiyevich presented himself, and this at the most unfavorable time for himself, though opportune for the prominent personage. The prominent personage was in his cabinet, conversing very gaily with an old acquaintance and companion of his childhood, whom he had not seen for several years, and who had just arrived, when it was announced to him that a person named Bashmachkin had come. He asked abruptly, "Who is he?"

"Some official," he was informed.

"Ah, he can wait! This is no time for him to call," said the important man.

It must be remarked here that the important man lied outrageously. He had said all he had to say to his friend long before, and the conversation had been interspersed for some time with very long pauses, during which they merely slapped each other on the leg, and said, "You think so, Ivan Abramovich!" "Just so, Stepan Varlamovich!" Nevertheless, he ordered that the official should be kept waiting, in order to show his friend, a man who had not been in the service for a long time, but had lived at home in the country, how long officials had to wait in his ante-room.

At length, having talked himself completely out, and more than that, having had his fill of pauses, and smoked a cigar in a very comfortable arm-chair with reclining back, he suddenly seemed to recollect, and said to the secretary, who stood by the door with papers of reports, "So it seems that there is an official waiting to see me. Tell him that he may come in."

On perceiving Akaky Akakiyevich's modest mien and his worn uniform, he turned abruptly to him, and said, "What do you want?" in a curt hard voice, which he had practiced in his room in private, and before the looking-glass, for a whole week before being raised to his present rank.

Akaky Akakiyevich, who was already imbued with a due amount of fear, became somewhat confused, and as well as his tongue would permit, explained, with a rather more frequent addition than usual of the word "that," that his cloak was quite new, and had been stolen in the most inhuman manner; that he had applied to him, in order that he might, in some way, by his intermediation—that he might enter into correspondence with the chief of police, and find the cloak.

For some inexplicable reason, this conduct seemed familiar to the prominent personage. "What, my dear sir!" he said abruptly, "are you not acquainted with etiquette? To whom have you come? Don't you know how such matters are managed? You should first have presented a petition to the office. It would have gone to the head of the department, then to the chief of the division, then it would have been handed over to the secretary, and the secretary would have given it to me."

"But, your excellency," said Akaky Akakiyevich, trying to collect his small handful of wits, and conscious at the same time that he was perspiring terribly, "I, your excellency, presumed to trouble you because secretaries—are an untrustworthy race."

"What, what, what!" said the important personage. "Where did you get such courage? Where did you get such ideas? What impudence towards their chiefs and superiors has spread among the young generation!" The prominent personage apparently had not observed that Akaky Akakiyevich was already in the neighborhood of fifty. If he could be called a young man, it must have been in comparison with some one who was seventy. "Do you know to whom you are speaking? Do you realize who is standing before you? Do you realize it? Do you realize it? I ask you!" Then he stamped his foot, and raised his voice to such a pitch that it would have frightened even a different man from Akaky Akakiyevich.

Akaky Akakiyevich's senses failed him. He staggered, trembled in every limb, and if the porters had not run in to support him, would have fallen to the floor. They carried him out insensible; but the prominent personage, gratified that the effect should have surpassed his expectations, and quite intoxicated with the thought that his word could even deprive a man of his senses, glanced sideways at his friend in order to see how he looked upon this, and perceived, not without satisfaction, that his friend was in a most uneasy frame of mind, and even beginning, on his part, to feel a trifle frightened.

Akaky Akakiyevich could not remember how he descended the stairs, and got into the street. He felt neither his hands nor his feet. Never in his life had he been so rated by any high official, let alone a strange one. He went staggering on through the snow-storm which was blowing in the streets, with his mouth wide open. The wind, in St. Petersburg fashion, darted upon him from all quarters, and down every cross-street. In a twinkling it had blown a quinsy into his throat, and he reached home unable to utter a word. His throat was swollen, and he lay down on his bed. So powerful is sometimes a good scolding!

The next day a violent fever developed. Thanks to the generous assistance of the St. Petersburg climate, the malady progressed more rapidly than could have been expected, and when the doctor arrived, he found, on feeling the sick man's pulse, that there was nothing to be done except to prescribe a poultice so that the patient might not be left entirely without the beneficient aid of medicine; but at the same time he predicted his end in thirty-six hours. After this he turned to the landlady, and said, "And as for you, don't waste your time on him. Order his pine coffin now, for an oak one will be too expensive for him."

Did Akaky Akakiyevich hear these fatal words? And if he heard them, did they produce any overwhelming effect upon him? Did he lament the bitterness of his life? We know not, for he continued in a delirious condition. Visions incessantly appeared to him, each stranger than the other. Now he saw Petrovich, and ordered him to make a cloak, with some traps for robbers, who seemed to him to be always under the bed; and he cried every moment to the landlady to pull one of them from under his coverlet. Then he inquired why his old mantle hung before him when he had a new cloak. Next he fancied that he was standing before the prominent person, listening to a thorough setting-down, and saying, "Forgive me, your excellency!" But at last he began to curse, uttering the most horrible words, so that his aged landlady crossed herself, never in her life having heard anything of the kind from him, and more so as these words followed directly after the words, "your excellency." Later on he talked utter nonsense, of which nothing could be made, all that was evident being that these incoherent words and thoughts hovered ever about one thing—his cloak.

At length poor Akaky Akakiyevich breathed his last. They sealed up neither his room nor his effects, because, in the first place, there were no heirs, and, in the second, there was very little to inherit beyond a bundle of goose-quills, a quire of white official paper, three pairs of socks, two or three buttons which had burst off his trousers, and the mantle already known to the reader. To whom all this fell, God knows. I confess that the person who told me this tale took no interest in the matter. They carried Akaky Akakiyevich out, and buried him; and St. Petersburg was left without Akaky Akakiyevich, as though he had never lived there. A being disappeared, who was protected by none, dear to none, interesting to none, and who never even attracted to himself the attention of those students of human nature who omit no opportunity of thrusting a pin through a common fly and examining it under the microscope; a being who bore meekly the gibes of the department, and went to his grave without having done one unusual deed, but

to whom, nevertheless, at the close of his life, appeared a bright visitant in the form of a cloak, which momentarily cheered his poor life, and upon him, thereafter, an intolerable misfortune descended, just as it descends upon the heads of the mighty of this world!

Several days after his death, the porter was sent from the department to his lodgings, with an order for him to present himself there immediately, the chief commanding it. But the porter had to return unsuccessful, with the answer that he could not come, and to the question, "Why?" replied, "Well, because he is dead; he was buried four days ago!" In this manner did they hear of Akaky Akakiyevich's death at the department. And the next day a new official sat in his place, with a handwriting by no means so upright, but more inclined and slanting.

But who could have imagined that this was not really the end of Akaky Akakiyevich, that he was destined to raise a commotion after death, as if in compensation for his utterly insignificant life? But so it happened, and our poor story unexpectedly gains a fantastic ending.

A rumor suddenly spread through St. Petersburg, that a dead man had taken to appearing on the Kalinkin Bridge, and its vicinity, at night in the form of an official seeking a stolen cloak, and that, under the pretext of its being the stolen cloak, he dragged, without regard to rank or calling, every one's cloak from his shoulders, be it cat-skin, beaver, fox, bear, sable—in a word, every sort of fur and skin which men adopted for their covering. One of the department officials saw the dead man with his own eyes, and immediately recognized in him Akaky Akakiyevich. This, however, inspired him with such terror that he ran off with all his might, and therefore did not scan the dead man closely, but only saw how the latter threatened him from afar with his finger. Constant complaints poured in from all quarters that the backs and shoulders, not only of titular but even of court councillors, were exposed to the danger of a cold, on account of the frequent dragging off of their cloaks.

Arrangements were made by the police to catch the corpse, alive or dead, at any cost, and punish him as an example to others, in the most severe manner. In this they nearly succeeded; for a watchman, on guard in Kirinshkin Lane, caught the corpse by the collar on the very scene of his evil deeds, when attempting to pull off the frieze cloak of a retired musician. Having seized him by the collar, he summoned, with a shout, two of his comrades, whom he enjoined to hold him fast, while he himself felt for a moment in his boot, in order to draw out his snuff-box, and refresh his frozen nose. But the snuff was of a sort which even a corpse could not endure. The watchman having closed his right nostril with his finger, had no sooner succeeded in holding half a handful up to the left, than the corpse sneezed so violently that he completely filled the eyes of all three. While they raised their hands to wipe them, the dead man vanished completely; so that they positively did not know whether they had actually had him in their grip at all. Thereafter the watchmen conceived such a terror of dead men that they were afraid even to seize the living, and only screamed from a distance. "Hey, there! go your way!" So the dead official began to appear even beyond the Kalinkin Bridge, causing no little terror to all timid people.

But we have totally neglected that certain prominent personage who may really be considered as the cause of the fantastic turn taken by this true history. First of all, justice compels us to say, that after the departure of poor, annihilated Akaky Akakiyevich, he felt something like remorse. Suffering was unpleasant to him, for his heart was accessible to many good impulses, in spite of the fact that his rank often prevented his showing his true self. As soon as his friend had left his cabinet, he began to think about Akaky Akakiyevich. And from that day forth, poor Akaky Akakiyevich, who could not bear up under an official reprimand, recurred to his mind almost every day. The thought troubled him to such an extent that a week later he even resolved to send an official to him, to learn whether he really could assist him. And when it was reported to him that Akaky Akakiyevich had died suddenly of fever, he was startled, hearkened to the reproaches of his conscience, and was out of sorts for the whole day.

Wishing to divert his mind in some way and drive away the disagreeable impression, he set out that evening for one of his friends' houses, where he found quite a large party assembled. What was better, nearly every one was of the same rank as himself, so that he need not feel in the least constrained. This had a marvelous effect upon his mental state. He grew expansive, made himself agreeable in conversation—in short, he passed a delightful evening. After supper he drank a couple of glasses of champagne—not a bad recipe for cheerfulness, as every one knows. The champagne inclined him to various adventures, and he determined not to return home, but to go and see a certain well-known lady, of German extraction, Karolina Ivanovna, a lady, it appears, with whom he was on a very friendly footing.

It must be mentioned that the prominent personage was no longer a young man, but a good husband and respected father of a family. Two sons, one of whom was already in the service, and a good-looking, sixteen-year-old daughter, with a slightly arched but pretty little nose, came every morning to kiss his hand and say, "Bon jour, papa." His wife, a still fresh and good-looking woman, first gave him her hand to kiss, and then, reversing the procedure, kissed his. But the prominent personage, though perfectly satisfied in his domestic relations, considered it stylish to have a friend in another quarter of the city. This friend was scarcely prettier or younger than his wife; but there are such puzzles in the world, and it is not our place to judge them.

So the important personage descended the stairs, stepped into his sledge, said to the coachman, "To Karolina Ivanovna's," and, wrapping himself luxuriously in his warm cloak, found himself in that delightful frame of mind than which a Russian can conceive nothing better, namely, when you think of nothing yourself, yet when the thoughts creep into your mind of their own accord, each more agreeable than the other, giving you no trouble either to drive them away, or seek them. Fully satisfied, he recalled all the gay features of the evening just passed and all the *mots* which had made the little circle laugh. Many of them he repeated in a low voice, and found them quite as funny as before; so it is not surprising that he should laugh heartily at them. Occasionally, however, he was interrupted by gusts of wind, which, coming suddenly, God knows whence or why, cut his face, drove masses of snow into it, filled out his cloak-collar like a sail, or suddenly blew it over his head with supernatural force, and thus caused him constant trouble to disentangle himself.

Suddenly the important personage felt some one clutch him firmly by the collar. Turning round, he perceived a man of short stature, in an old, worn uniform, and recognized, not without terror, Akaky Akakiyevich. The official's face was white as snow, and looked just like a corpse's. But the horror of the important personage transcended all bounds when he saw the dead man's mouth open, and heard it utter the following remarks, while it breathed upon him the terrible odor of the grave: "Ah, here you are at last! I have you, that—by the collar! I need your cloak. You took no trouble about mine, but reprimanded me. So now give up your own."

The pallid prominent personage almost died of fright. Brave as he was in the office and in the presence of inferiors generally, and although, at the sight of his manly form and appearance, every one said, "Ugh! how much character he has!" at this crisis, he, like many possessed of an heroic exterior, experienced such terror, that, not without cause, he began to fear an attack of illness. He flung his cloak hastily from his shoulders and shouted to his coachman in an unnatural voice, "Home at full speed!" The coachman, hearing the tone which is generally employed at critical moments, and even accompanied by something much more tangible, drew his head down between his shoulders in case of an emergency, flourished his whip, and flew on like an arrow.

In a little more than six minutes the prominent personage was at the entrance of his own house. Pale, thoroughly scared, and cloakless, he went home instead of to Karolina Ivanovna's, reached his room somehow or other, and passed the night in the direst distress; so that the next morning over their tea, his daughter said, "You are very pale today, papa." But papa remained silent, and said not a word to any one of what had happened to him, where he had been, or where he had intended to go.

This occurrence made a deep impression upon him. He even began to say, "How dare you? Do you realize who is standing before you?" less frequently to the under-officials, and, if he did utter the words, it was only after first having learned the bearings of the matter. But the most noteworthy point was, that from that day forward the apparition of the dead official ceased to be seen. Evidently the prominent personage's cloak just fitted his shoulders. At all events, no more instances of his dragging cloaks from people's shoulders were heard of. But many active and solicitous persons could by no means reassure themselves, and asserted that the dead official still showed himself in distant parts of the city.

In fact, one watchman in Kolomen saw with his own eyes the apparition come from behind a house. But the watchman was not a strong man, so he was afraid to arrest him, and followed him in the dark, until, at length, the apparition looked round, paused, and inquired, "What do you want?" at the same time showing such a fist as is never seen on living men.

The watchman said, "Nothing," and turned back instantly; but the apparition was much too tall, wore huge moustaches, and, directing its steps apparently towards the Obukhov Bridge, disappeared in the darkness of the night.

———◆———

FËDOR MIKHAILOVICH DOSTOEVSKI

1821–1881

Fëdor Dostoevski was born in Moscow of a lower middle-class family. At the age of seventeen he attended a military engineering school at St. Petersburg, which he hated; but away from home he began to cultivate an interest in intellectual studies. Although living in dire poverty, Dostoevski gave up his plans to be a military engineer and in 1844 resolved to be a writer. His first novel, *Poor Folk* (1846), revealed that the fiction of Dostoevski would be directed in paths other than the realism of Turgenev or of Tolstoi, although in the creation of his hero he was undoubtedly influenced by Gogol's "The Cloak." His first literary period ended in 1849 with his arrest for agitating socialistic reforms. Sentenced to Siberia for four years, upon his return he wrote *The House of Death* (1861–1862), a fictional account of his years in the prison at Omsk. His remarkable powers of psychological analysis were revealed for the first time in *Letters from the Underworld* (1864), anticipating in his hero the modern man who is morbidly aware of his own feelings and ceaseless in analyzing them.

In 1866, with *Crime and Punishment*, he entered the major phase of his career during which he wrote his greatest novels: *Crime and Punishment*, *The Possessed* (1871–1872), and *The Brothers Karamazov* (1879–1880). Never the objective realist, Dostoevski passionately identified himself with his characters and with uncanny searching skill revealed in stormy crises of passion the intricate contortions of the psyche of the abnormal, the neurotic, and psychotic. Beyond these traits, his fiction embodies parables of far-reaching ethical and religious implications. The "Grand Inquisitor" passage suggests Dostoevski's religious position (see Ernest J. Simmons, *Dostoevsky*, 1940, pp. 368 ff.).

FURTHER READING

DOSTOYEVSKY, AIMEE. *Fydor Dostoyevsky* (New Haven, 1922).

SIMMONS, ERNEST J. *Dostoevski* (New York, 1940).

YARMOLINSKY, AVRAHM. *Dostoevsky* (New York, 1934).

The Grand Inquisitor *

"Do you know, Alyosha—don't laugh! I made a poem about a year ago. If you can waste another ten minutes on me, I'll tell it to you."

"You wrote a poem?"

"Oh no, I didn't write it," laughed Ivan, "and I've never written two lines of poetry in my life. But I made up this poem in prose and I remembered it. I was carried away when I made it up. You will be my first reader—that is, listener. Why should an author forego even one listener?" smiled Ivan. "Shall I tell it to you?"

"I am all attention," said Alyosha.

"My poem is called the Grand Inquisitor; it's a ridiculous thing, but I want to tell it to you."

"Even this must have a preface—that is, a literary preface," laughed Ivan, "and I am a poor hand at making one. You see, my action takes place in the sixteenth century, and at that time, as you probably learnt at school, it was customary in poetry to bring down heavenly powers on earth. Not to speak of Dante, in France clerks as well as the monks in the monasteries used to give regular performances in which the Madonna, the saints, the angels, Christ, and God Himself were brought on the stage. In those days it was done in all simplicity. In Victor Hugo's *Notre Dame de Paris* an edifying and gratuitous spectacle was provided for the people in the Hotel de Ville of Paris in the reign of Louis XI in honour of the birth of the dauphin. It was called *Le bon jugement de la très sainte et gracieuse Vierge Marie,* and she appears herself on the stage and pronounces her *bon jugement.* Similar plays, chiefly from the Old Testament, were occasionally performed in Moscow too, up to the times of Peter the Great. But besides plays there were all sorts of legends and ballads scattered about the world, in which the saints and angels and all the powers of Heaven took part when required. In our monasteries the monks busied themselves in translating, copying, and even composing such poems—and even under the Tatars. There is, for instance, one such

* From *The Brothers Karamazov,* translated by Constance Garnett. By permission of The Macmillan Company and William Heinemann, Ltd.

poem (of course, from the Greek), *The Wanderings of Our Lady through Hell* with descriptions as bold as Dante's. Our Lady visits Hell, and the Archangel Michael leads her through the torments. She sees the sinners and their punishment. There she sees among others one noteworthy set of sinners in a burning lake; some of them sink to the bottom of the lake so that they can't swim out, and 'these God forgets'—an expression of extraordinary depth and force. And so Our Lady, shocked and weeping, falls before the throne of God and begs for mercy for all in Hell—for all she has seen there, indiscriminately. Her conversation with God is immensely interesting. She beseeches Him, she will not desist, and when God points to the hands and feet of her Son, nailed to the Cross, and asks, 'How can I forgive His tormentors?' she bids all the saints, all the martyrs, all the angels and archangels to fall down with her and pray for mercy on all without distinction. It ends by her winning from God a respite of suffering every year from Good Friday till Trinity day, and the sinners at once raise a cry of thankfulness from Hell, chanting: 'Thou art just, O Lord, in this judgment.' Well, my poem would have been of that kind if it had appeared at that time. He comes on the scene in my poem, but He says nothing, only appears and passes on. Fifteen centuries have passed since He promised to come in His glory, fifteen centuries since His prophet wrote, Behold, I come quickly; Of that day and that hour knoweth no man, neither the Son, but the Father, as He Himself predicted on earth. But humanity awaits him with the same faith and with the same love. Oh, with greater faith, for it is fifteen centuries since man has ceased to see signs from Heaven.

No signs from Heaven come to-day
To add to what the heart doth say.

There was nothing left but faith in what the heart doth say. It is true there were many miracles in those days. There were saints who performed miraculous cures; some holy people, according to their biographies, were visited by the Queen of Heaven herself. But the devil did not slumber, and doubts were already arising among men of the truth of these miracles. And just then there appeared in the north of Germany a terrible new heresy. 'A huge star like to a torch' (that is, to a church) 'fell on the sources of the waters and they became bitter.' These heretics began blasphemously denying miracles. But those who remained faithful were all the more ardent in their faith. The tears of humanity rose up to Him as before, awaited His coming, loved

Him, hoped for Him, yearned to suffer and die for Him as before. And so many ages mankind had prayed with faith and fervour, 'O Lord our God, hasten Thy coming,' so many ages called upon Him, that in His infinite mercy He deigned to come down to His servants. Before that day He had come down, He had visited some holy men, martyrs and hermits, as is written in their Lives. Among us, Tyutchev, with absolute faith in the truth of his words, bore witness that

> Bearing the Cross, in slavish dress
> Weary and worn, the Heavenly King
> Our mother, Russia, came to bless,
> And through our land went wandering.

And that certainly was so, I assure you.

"And behold, He deigned to appear for a moment to the people, to the tortured, suffering people, sunk in iniquity, but loving Him like children. My story is laid in Spain, in Seville, in the most terrible time of the Inquisition, when fires were lighted every day to the glory of God, and 'in the splendid *auto da fé* the wicked heretics were burnt.' Oh, of course, this was not the coming in which He will appear according to His promise at the end of time in all His heavenly glory, and which will be sudden 'as lightning flashing from east to west.' No, He visited His children only for a moment, and there where the flames were crackling round the heretics. In His infinite mercy He came once more among men in that human shape in which He walked among men for three years fifteen centuries ago. He came down to the 'hot pavement' of the southern town in which on the day before almost a hundred heretics had, *ad majorem gloriam Dei,* been burnt by the cardinal, the Grand Inquisitor, in a magnificent *auto da fé,* in the presence of the king, the court, the knights, the cardinals, the most charming ladies of the court, and the whole population of Seville.

"He came softly, unobserved, and yet, strange to say, every one recognised Him. That might be one of the best passages in the poem. I mean, why they recognised Him. The people are irresistibly drawn to Him, they surround Him, they flock about Him, follow Him. He moves silently in their midst with a gentle smile of infinite compassion. The sun of love burns in His heart, light and power shine from His eyes, and their radiance, shed on the people, stirs their hearts with responsive love. He holds out His hands to them, blesses them, and a healing virtue comes from contact with Him, even with His garments. An old man in the crowd, blind from childhood, cries out, 'O Lord, heal me and I shall see Thee!' and, as it were, scales fall from his eyes and the blind man sees Him. The crowd weeps and kisses the earth under His feet. Children throw flowers before Him, sing, and cry hosannah. 'It is He—it is He!' all repeat. 'It must be He, it can be no one but Him!' He stops at the steps of the Seville cathedral at the moment when the weeping mourners are bringing in a little open white coffin. In it lies a child of seven, the only daughter of a prominent citizen. The dead child lies hidden in flowers. 'He will raise your child,' the crowd shouts to the weeping mother. The priest, coming to meet the coffin, looks perplexed, and frowns, but the mother of the dead child throws herself at His feet with a wail. 'If it is Thou, raise my child!' she cries, holding out her hands to Him. The procession halts, the coffin is laid on the steps at His feet. He looks with compassion, and His lips once more softly pronounce, 'Maiden, arise!' and the maiden arises. The little girl sits up in the coffin and looks round, smiling with wide-open wondering eyes, holding a bunch of white roses they had put in her hand.

"There are cries, sobs, confusion among the people, and at that moment the cardinal himself, the Grand Inquisitor, passes by the cathedral. He is an old man, almost ninety, tall and erect, with a withered face and sunken eyes, in which there is still a gleam of light. He is not dressed in his gorgeous cardinal's robes, as he was the day before when he was burning the enemies of the Roman Church—at that moment he was wearing his coarse, old, monk's cassock. At a distance behind him come his gloomy assistants and slaves and the 'holy guard.' He stops at the sight of the crowd and watches it from a distance. He sees everything; he sees them set the coffin down at His feet, sees the child rise up, and his face darkens. He knits his thick grey brows and his eyes gleam with a sinister fire. He holds out his finger and bids the guards take Him. And such is his power, so completely are the people cowed into submission and trembling obedience to him, that the crowd immediately make way for the guards, and in the midst of deathlike silence they lay hands on Him and lead Him away. The crowd instantly bows down to the earth, like one man, before the old Inquisitor. He blesses the people in silence and passes on. The guards lead their prisoner to the close, gloomy vaulted prison in the ancient palace of the Holy Inquisition and shut Him in it. The day passes and is followed by the dark, burning 'breathless' night of Seville. The air is 'fragrant with laurel and lemon.' In the pitch darkness the iron door of the prison is suddenly opened and the Grand Inquisitor himself comes in with a light in his hand. He is alone; the door is closed at once behind him. He stands in the doorway and for a minute or two gazes into His face. At last he goes up slowly, sets the light on the table and speaks,

"'Is it Thou? Thou?' but receiving no answer, he adds at once: 'Don't answer, be silent. What canst Thou say, indeed? I know too well what Thou wouldst say. And Thou hast no right to add anything to what Thou hadst said of old. Why, then, art Thou come to hinder us? For Thou hast come to hinder us, and Thou knowest that. But dost Thou know what will be to-morrow? I know not who Thou art and care not to know whether it is Thou or only a semblance of Him, but to-morrow I shall condemn Thee and burn Thee at the stake as the worst of heretics. And the very people who have to-day kissed Thy feet, to-morrow at the faintest sign from me will rush to heap up the embers of Thy fire. Knowest Thou that? Yes, maybe Thou knowest it,' he added with thoughtful penetration, never for a moment taking his eyes off the Prisoner."

"I don't quite understand, Ivan. What does it mean?" Alyosha, who had been listening in silence, said with a smile. "Is it simply a wild fantasy, or a mistake on the part of the old man—some impossible *qui pro quo*?"

"Take it as the last," said Ivan, laughing, "if you are so corrupted by modern realism and can't stand anything fantastic. If you like it to be a case of mistaken identity, let it be so. It is true," he went on laughing, "the old man was ninety, and he might well be crazy over his set idea. He might have been struck by the appearance of the Prisoner. It might, in fact, be simply his ravings, the delusion of an old man of ninety, over-excited by the *auto da fé* of a hundred heretics the day before. But does it matter to us after all whether it was a mistake of identity or a wild fantasy? All that matters is that the old man should speak out, should speak openly of what he has thought in silence for ninety years."

"And the Prisoner too is silent? Does He look at him and not say a word?"

"That's inevitable in any case," Ivan laughed again. "The old man has told Him He hasn't the right to add anything to what He has said of old. One may say it is the most fundamental feature of Roman Catholicism, in my opinion at least. 'All has been given by Thee to the Pope,' they say, 'and all, therefore, is still in the Pope's hands, and there is no need for Thee to come now at all. Thou must not meddle for the time, at least.' That's how they speak and write too—the Jesuits, at any rate. I have read it myself in the works of their theologians. 'Hast Thou the right to reveal to us one of the mysteries of that world from which Thou hast come?' my old man asks Him, and answers the question for him. 'No, Thou hast not; that Thou mayest not add to what has been said of old, and mayest not take from men the freedom which Thou didst exalt when Thou wast on earth. Whatsoever Thou revealest anew will encroach on men's freedom of faith; for it will be manifest as a miracle, and the freedom of their faith was dearer to Thee than anything in those days fifteen hundred years ago. Didst Thou not often say then: "I will make you free"? But now Thou hast seen these "free" men,' the old man adds suddenly, with a pensive smile. 'Yes, we've paid dearly for it,' he goes on, looking sternly at Him, 'but at last we have completed that work in Thy name. For fifteen centuries we have been wrestling with Thy freedom, but now it is ended and over for good. Dost Thou not believe that it's over for good? Thou lookest meekly at me and deignest not even to be wroth with me. But let me tell Thee that now, to-day, people are more persuaded than ever that they have perfect freedom, yet they have brought their freedom to us and laid it humbly at our feet. But that has been our doing. Was this what Thou didst? Was this Thy freedom?'"

"I don't understand again," Alyosha broke in. "Is he ironical, is he jesting?"

"Not a bit of it! He claims it as a merit for himself and his Church that at last they have vanquished freedom and have done so to make men happy. 'For now' (he is speaking of the Inquisition, of course) 'for the first time it has become possible to think of the happiness of men. Man was created a rebel; and how can rebels be happy? Thou wast warned,' he says to Him. 'Thou hast had no lack of admonitions and warnings, but Thou didst not listen to those warnings; Thou didst reject the only way by which men might be made happy. But, fortunately, departing Thou didst hand on the work to us. Thou hast promised, Thou hast established by Thy word, Thou hast given to us the right to bind and to unbind, and now, of course, Thou canst not think of taking it away. Why, then, hast Thou come to hinder us?'"

"And what's the meaning of 'no lack of admonitions and warnings'?" asked Alyosha.

"Why, that's the chief part of what the old man must say."

"'The wise and dread spirit of self-destruction and non-existence,' the old man goes on, 'the great spirit talked with Thee in the wilderness, and we are told in the books that he "tempted" Thee. Is that so? And could anything truer be said than what he revealed to Thee in three questions and what Thou didst reject, and what in the books is called "the temptation"? And yet if there has ever been on earth a real stupendous miracle, it took place on that day, on the day of the three temptations. The statement of those three questions was itself the miracle. If it were possible to imagine simply for the sake of argument that those three questions of the dread spirit had perished utterly from the books, and that we had to restore them and to invent them anew, and to do so had gathered together all the wise men of the earth—rulers, chief priests, learned men, philosophers, poets—and had set them the task to invent three questions, such as would not only fit the occasion, but express in three words, three human phrases, the whole future history of the world and of humanity—dost Thou believe that all the wisdom of the earth united could have invented anything in depth and force equal to the three questions which were actually put to Thee then by the wise and mighty spirit in the wilderness? From those questions alone, from the miracle of their statement, we can see that we have here to do not with the fleeting human intelligence, but with the absolute and eternal. For in those three questions the whole subsequent history of mankind is, as it were, brought together into one whole, and foretold, and in them are united all the unsolved historical contradictions of human nature. At the time it could not be so clear, since the future was unknown; but now that fifteen hundred years have passed, we see that everything in those three questions was so justly divined and foretold, and has been so truly fulfilled, that nothing can be added to them or taken from them.

"'Judge Thyself who was right—Thou or he who questioned Thee then? Remember the first question; its meaning, in other words, was this: "Thou wouldst go into the world, and art going with empty hands, with some promise of freedom which men in their simplicity and their natural unruliness cannot even understand, which they fear and dread—for nothing has ever been more insupportable for a man and a human society than freedom. But seest Thou these stones in this parched and barren wilderness? Turn them into bread, and mankind will run after Thee like a flock of sheep, grateful and obedient, though for ever trembling, lest Thou withdraw Thy hand and deny them Thy bread." But Thou wouldst not deprive man of freedom and didst reject the offer, thinking, what is that freedom worth if obedience is bought with bread? Thou didst reply that man lives not by bread alone. But dost Thou know that for the sake of that earthly bread the spirit of the earth will rise up against Thee and will strive with Thee and overcome Thee, and all will follow him, crying: "Who can compare with this beast? He has given us fire from heaven!" Dost Thou know that the ages will pass, and humanity will proclaim by the lips of their sages that there is no crime and therefore no sin; there is only hunger? "Feed men, and then ask of them virtue!" that's what they'll write on the banner which they will raise against Thee, and with which they will destroy Thy temple. Where Thy temple stood will rise a new building; the terrible tower of Babel will be built again, and though, like the one of old, it will not be finished, yet Thou mightest have prevented that new tower and have cut short the sufferings of men for a thousand years; for they will come back to us after a thousand years of agony with their tower. They will seek us again, hidden underground in the catacombs, for we shall be again persecuted and tortured. They will find us and cry to us: "Feed us, for those who have promised us fire from heaven haven't given it!" And then we shall finish building their tower, for he finishes the building who feeds them. And we alone shall feed them in Thy name, declaring falsely that it is in Thy name. Oh, never, never can they feed themselves without us! No science will give them bread so long as they remain free. In the end they will lay their freedom at our feet, and say to us: "Make us your slaves, but feed us." They will understand themselves, at last, that freedom and bread enough for all are inconceivable together, for never, never will they be able to share between them! They will be convinced, too, that they can never be free, for they are weak, vicious, worthless and rebellious. Thou didst promise them the bread of Heaven, but, I repeat again, can it compare with earthly bread in the eyes of the weak, ever sinful and ignoble race of man? And if for the sake of the bread of Heaven thousands and tens of thousands shall follow Thee, what is to become of the millions and tens of thousands of millions of creatures who will not have the strength to forego the earthly bread for the sake of the heavenly? Or dost Thou care only for the tens of thousands of the great and strong, while the millions, numerous as the sands of the sea, who are weak but love Thee, must exist only for the sake of the great and strong? No, we care for the weak too. They are sinful and rebellious, but in the end they too will become obedient. They will marvel at us and look on us as gods, because we are ready to endure the freedom which they have found so dreadful and to rule over them—so awful it will seem to them to be free. But we shall tell them that we are Thy servants and rule them in Thy name. We shall deceive them again, for we will not let Thee come to us again. That deception will be our suffering, for we shall be forced to lie.

"'This is the significance of the first question in the wilderness, and this is what Thou hast rejected for the sake of that freedom which Thou hast exalted above everything. Yet in this question lies hid the great secret of this world. Choosing "bread," Thou wouldst have satisfied the universal and everlasting craving of humanity—to find some one to worship. So long as man remains free he strives for nothing so incessantly and so painfully as to find some one to worship. But man seeks to worship what is established beyond dispute, so that all men would agree at once to worship it. For these pitiful creatures are concerned not only to find what one or the other can worship, but to find something that all would believe in and worship; what is essential is that all may be *together* in it. This craving for *community* of worship is the chief misery of every man individually and of all humanity from the beginning of time. For the sake of common worship they've slain each other with the sword. They have set up gods and challenged one another: "Put away your gods and come and worship ours, or we will kill you and your gods!" And so it will be to the end of the world, even when gods disappear from the earth; they will fall down before idols just the same. Thou didst know, Thou couldst not but have known, this fundamental secret of human nature, but Thou didst reject the one infallible banner which was offered Thee to make all men bow down to Thee alone—the banner of earthly bread; and Thou hast rejected it for the sake of freedom and the bread of Heaven. Behold what Thou didst further. And all again in the name of freedom! I tell Thee that man is tormented by no greater anxiety than to find some one quickly to whom he can hand over the gift of freedom with which the ill-fated creature is born. But only one who can appease their conscience can take over their freedom. In bread there was offered Thee an invincible banner; give bread, and man

will worship Thee, for nothing is more certain than bread. But if some one else gains possession of his conscience—oh! then he will cast away Thy bread and follow after him who has ensnared his conscience. In that Thou wast right. For the secret of man's being is not only to live but to have something to live for. Without a stable conception of the object of life, man would not consent to go on living, and would rather destroy himself than remain on earth, though he had bread in abundance. That is true. But what happened? Instead of taking men's freedom from them, Thou didst make it greater than ever! Didst Thou forget that man prefers peace, and even death, to freedom of choice in the knowledge of good and evil? Nothing is more seductive for man than his freedom of conscience, but nothing is a greater cause of suffering. And behold, instead of giving a firm foundation for setting the conscience of man at rest for ever, Thou didst choose all that is exceptional, vague, and enigmatic; Thou didst choose what was utterly beyond the strength of men, acting as though Thou didst not love them at all—Thou who didst come to give Thy life for them! Instead of taking possession of men's freedom, Thou didst increase it, and burdened the spiritual kingdom of mankind with its sufferings for ever. Thou didst desire man's free love, that he should follow Thee freely, enticed and taken captive by Thee. In place of the rigid ancient law, man must hereafter with free heart decide for himself what is good and what is evil, having only Thy image before him as his guide. But didst Thou not know he would at last reject even Thy image and Thy truth, if he is weighed down with the fearful burden of free choice? They will cry aloud at last that the truth is not in Thee, for they could not have been left in greater confusion and suffering than Thou hast caused, laying upon them so many cares and unanswerable problems.

"'So that, in truth, Thou didst Thyself lay the foundation for the destruction of Thy kingdom, and no one is more to blame for it. Yet what was offered Thee? There are three powers, three powers alone, able to conquer and to hold captive for ever the conscience of these impotent rebels for their happiness—those forces are miracle, mystery, and authority. Thou has rejected all three and hast set the example for doing so. When the wise and dread spirit set Thee on the pinnacle of the temple and said to Thee: "If Thou wouldst know whether Thou art the Son of God then cast Thyself down, for it is written: the angels shall hold him up lest he fall and bruise himself, and Thou shalt know then whether Thou art the Son of God and shalt prove then how great is Thy faith in Thy Father." But Thou didst refuse and wouldst not cast Thyself down. Oh! of course, Thou didst proudly and well, like God; but the weak, unruly race of men, are they gods? Oh, Thou didst know then that in taking one step, in making one movement to cast Thyself down, Thou wouldst be tempting God and have lost all Thy faith in Him, and wouldst have been dashed to pieces against that earth which Thou didst come to save. And the wise spirit that tempted Thee would have rejoiced. But I ask again, are there many like Thee? And couldst Thou believe for one moment that men, too, could face such a temptation? Is the nature of men such that they can reject miracle, and at the great moments of their life, the moments of their deepest, most agonising spiritual difficulties, cling only to the free verdict of the heart? Oh, Thou didst know that Thy deed would be recorded in books, would be handed down to remote times and the utmost ends of the earth, and Thou didst hope that man, following Thee, would cling to God and not ask for a miracle. But Thou didst not know that when man rejects miracle he rejects God too; for man seeks not so much God as the miraculous. And as man cannot bear to be without the miraculous, he will create new miracles of his own for himself, and will worship deeds of sorcery and witchcraft, though he might be a hundred times over a rebel, heretic, and infidel. Thou didst not come down from the Cross when they shouted to Thee, mocking and reviling Thee: "Come down from the cross and we will believe that Thou art He." Thou didst not come down, for again Thou wouldst not enslave man by a miracle, and didst crave faith given freely, not based on miracle. Thou didst crave for free love and not the base raptures of the slave before the might that has overawed him for ever. But Thou didst think too highly of men therein, for they are slaves, of course, though rebellious by nature. Look round and judge; fifteen centuries have passed, look upon them. Whom hast Thou raised up to Thyself? I swear, man is weaker and baser by nature than Thou hast believed him! Can he, can he do what Thou didst? By showing him so much respect, Thou didst, as it were, cease to feel for him, for Thou didst ask far too much from him—Thou who hast loved him more than Thyself! Respecting him less, Thou wouldst have asked less of him. That would have been more like love, for his burden would have been lighter. He is weak and vile. What though he is everywhere now rebelling against our power, and

proud of his rebellion? It is the pride of a child and a schoolboy. They are little children rioting and barring out the teacher at school. But their childish delight will end; it will cost them dear. They will cast down temples and drench the earth with blood. But they will see at last, the foolish children, that, though they are rebels, they are impotent rebels, unable to keep up their own rebellion. Bathed in their foolish tears, they will recognise at last that He who created them rebels must have meant to mock at them. They will say this in despair, and their utterance will be a blasphemy which will make them more unhappy still, for man's nature cannot bear blasphemy, and in the end always avenges it on itself. And so unrest, confusion and unhappiness— that is the present lot of man after Thou didst bear so much for their freedom! Thy great prophet tells, in vision and in image, that he saw all those who took part in the first resurrection and that there were of each tribe twelve thousand. But if there were so many of them, they must have been not men but gods. They had borne Thy cross, they had endured scores of years in the barren, hungry wilderness, living upon locusts and roots—and Thou mayest indeed point with pride at those children of freedom, of free love, of free and splendid sacrifice for Thy name. But remember that they were only some thousands; and what of the rest? And how are the other weak ones to blame, because they could not endure what the strong have endured? How is the weak soul to blame that it is unable to receive such terrible gifts? Canst Thou have simply come to the elect and for the elect? But if so, it is a mystery and we cannot understand it. And if it is a mystery, we too have a right to preach a mystery, and to teach them that it's not the free judgment of their hearts, not love that matters, but a mystery which they must follow blindly, even against their conscience. So we have done. We have corrected Thy work and have founded it upon *miracle, mystery,* and *authority.* And men rejoiced that they were again led like sheep, and that the terrible gift that had brought them such suffering, was, at last, lifted from their hearts. Were we right teaching them this? Speak! Did we not love mankind, so meekly acknowledging their feebleness, lovingly lightening their burden, and permitting their weak nature even sin with our sanction? Why hast Thou come now to hinder us? And why dost Thou look silently and searchingly at me with Thy mild eyes? Be angry. I don't want Thy love, for I love Thee not. And what use is it for me to hide anything from Thee? Don't I know to Whom I am speaking?

All that I can say is known to Thee already. And is it for me to conceal from Thee our mystery? Perhaps it is Thy will to hear it from my lips. Listen, then. We are not working with Thee, but with *him*—that is our mystery. It's long—eight centuries—since we have been on *his* side and not on Thine. Just eight centuries ago, we took from him what Thou didst reject with scorn, that last gift he offered Thee, showing Thee all the kingdoms of the earth. We took from him Rome and the sword of Caesar, and proclaimed ourselves sole rulers of the earth, though hitherto we have not been able to complete our work. But whose fault is that? Oh, the work is only beginning, but it has begun. It has long to await completion and the earth has yet much to suffer, but we shall triumph and shall be Caesars, and then we shall plan the universal happiness of man. But Thou mightest have taken even then the sword of Caesar. Why didst Thou reject that last gift? Hadst Thou accepted that last counsel of the mighty spirit, Thou wouldst have accomplished all that man seeks on earth—that is, some one to worship, some one to keep his conscience, and some means of uniting all in one unanimous and harmonious ant-heap, for the craving for universal unity is the third and last anguish of men. Mankind as a whole has always striven to organise a universal state. There have been many great nations with great histories, but the more highly they were developed the more unhappy they were, for they felt more acutely than other people the craving for worldwide union. The great conquerors, Timours and Ghenghis-Khans, whirled like hurricanes over the face of the earth striving to subdue its people, and they too were but the unconscious expression of the same craving for universal unity. Hadst Thou taken the world and Caesar's purple, Thou wouldst have founded the universal state and have given universal peace. For who can rule men if not he who holds their conscience and their bread in his hands. We have taken the sword of Caesar, and in taking it, of course, have rejected Thee and followed *him*. Oh, ages are yet to come of the confusion of free thought, of their science and cannibalism. For having begun to build their tower of Babel without us, they will end, of course, with cannibalism. But then the beast will crawl to us and lick our feet and spatter them with tears of blood. And we shall sit upon the beast and raise the cup, and on it will be written: "Mystery." But then, and only then, the reign of peace and happiness will come for men. Thou art proud of Thine elect, but Thou hast only the elect, while we give rest to all.

And besides, how many of those elect, those mighty ones who could become elect, have grown weary waiting for Thee, and have transferred and will transfer the powers of their spirit and the warmth of their heart to the other camp, and end by raising their *free* banner against Thee. Thou didst Thyself lift up that banner. But with us all will be happy and will no more rebel nor destroy one another as under Thy freedom. Oh, we shall persuade them that they will only become free when they renounce their freedom to us and submit to us. And shall we be right or shall we be lying? They will be convinced that we are right, for they will remember the horrors of slavery and confusion to which Thy freedom brought them. Freedom, free thought, and science will lead them into such straits and will bring them face to face with such marvels and insoluble mysteries that some of them, the fierce and rebellious, will destroy themselves; others, rebellious but weak, will destroy one another; while the rest, weak and unhappy, will crawl fawning to our feet and whine to us: "Yes, you were right, you alone possess His mystery, and we come back to you, save us from ourselves!"

"'Receiving bread from us, they will see clearly that we take the bread made by their hands from them, to give it to them, without any miracle. They will see that we do not change the stones to bread, but in truth they will be more thankful for taking it from our hands than for the bread itself! For they will remember only too well that in old days, without our help, even the bread they made turned to stones in their hands, while since they have come back to us, the very stones have turned to bread in their hands. Too, too well they know the value of complete submission! And until men know that, they will be unhappy. Who is most to blame for their not knowing it, speak? Who scattered the flock and sent it astray on unknown paths? But the flock will come together again and will submit once more, and then it will be once for all. Then we shall give them the quiet humble happiness of weak creatures such as they are by nature. Oh, we shall persuade them at last not to be proud, for Thou didst lift them up and thereby taught them to be proud. We shall show them that they are weak, that they are only pitiful children, but that childlike happiness is the sweetest of all. They will become timid and will look to us and huddle close to us in fear, as chicks to the hen. They will marvel at us and will be awestricken before us, and will be proud at our being so powerful and clever that we have been able to subdue such a turbulent flock of thousands of millions. They will tremble impotently before our wrath, their minds will grow fearful, they will be quick to shed tears like women and children, but they will be just as ready at a sign from us to pass to laughter and rejoicing, to happy mirth and childish song. Yes, we shall set them to work, but in their leisure hours we shall make their life like a child's game, with children's songs and innocent dance. Oh, we shall allow them even sin, they are weak and helpless, and they will love us like children because we allow them to sin. We shall tell them that every sin will be expiated, if it is done with our permission, that we allow them to sin because we love them, and the punishment for these sins we take upon ourselves. And we shall take it upon ourselves, and they will adore us as their saviours who have taken on themselves their sins before God. And they will have no secrets from us. We shall allow or forbid them to live with their wives and mistresses, to have or not to have children —according to whether they have been obedient or disobedient—and they will submit to us gladly and cheerfully. The most painful secrets of their conscience, all, all they will bring to us, and we shall have an answer for all. And they will be glad to believe our answer, for it will save them from the great anxiety and terrible agony they endure at present in making a free decision for themselves. And all will be happy, all the millions of creatures except the hundred thousand who rule over them. For only we, we who guard the mystery, shall be unhappy. There will be thousands of millions of happy babes, and a hundred thousand sufferers who have taken upon themselves the curse of the knowledge of good and evil. Peacefully they will die, peacefully they will expire in Thy name, and beyond the grave they will find nothing but death. But we shall keep the secret, and for their happiness we shall allure them with the reward of heaven and eternity. Though if there were anything in the other world, it certainly would not be for such as they. It is prophesied that Thou wilt come again in victory, Thou wilt come with Thy chosen, the proud and strong, but we will say that they have only saved themselves, but we have saved all. We are told that the harlot who sits upon the beast, and holds in her hands the *mystery*, shall be put to shame, that the weak will rise up again, and will rend her royal purple and will strip naked her loathsome body. But then I will stand up and point out to Thee the thousand millions of happy children who have known no sin. And we who have taken their sins upon us for their happiness will stand up before Thee and say: "Judge us if Thou canst and darest." Know that I fear Thee not. Know that I too have been in the wilderness, I too have lived on roots and locusts, I too prized the freedom with which Thou hast blessed men, and I too was striving to stand among Thy elect, among the strong and powerful, thirsting "to make up the number." But I awakened and would not serve madness. I turned back and joined the ranks of those *who have corrected Thy work*. I left the proud and went back to the humble, for the happiness of the humble. What I say to Thee will come to pass, and our dominion will be built up. I repeat, to-morrow Thou shalt see that obedient flock who at a sign from me will hasten to heap up the hot cinders about the pile on which I shall burn Thee for coming to hinder us. For if any one has ever deserved our fires, it is Thou. To-morrow I shall burn Thee. Dixi.'"

Ivan stopped. He was carried away as he talked and spoke with excitement; when he had finished, he suddenly smiled.

Alyosha had listened in silence; towards the end he was greatly moved and seemed several times on the point of interrupting, but restrained himself. Now his words came with a rush.

"But . . . that's absurd!" he cried, flushing. "Your poem is in praise of Jesus, not in blame of Him—as you meant it to be. And who will believe you about freedom? Is that the way to understand it? That's not the idea of it in the Orthodox Church . . . That's Rome, and not even the whole of Rome, it's false—those are the worst of the Catholics, the Inquisitors, the Jesuits! . . . And there could not be such a fantastic creature as your Inquisitor. What are these sins of mankind they take on themselves? Who are these keepers of the mystery who have taken some curse upon themselves for the happiness of mankind? When have they been seen? We know the Jesuits, they are spoken ill of, but surely they are not what you describe? They are not that at all, not at all. . . . They are simply the Romish army for the earthly sovereignty of the world in the future, with the Pontiff of Rome for Emperor . . . that's their ideal, but there's no sort of mystery or lofty melancholy about it. . . . It's simple lust of power, of filthy earthly gain, of domination—something like a universal serfdom with them as masters—that's all they stand for. They don't even believe in God perhaps. Your suffering inquisitor is a mere fantasy."

"Stay, stay," laughed Ivan, "how hot you are! A fantasy you say, let it be so! Of course it's a fantasy.

But allow me to say: do you really think that the Roman Catholic movement of the last centuries is actually nothing but the lust of power, of filthy earthly gain? Is that Father Païssy's teaching?"

"No, no, on the contrary, Father Païssy did once say something rather the same, as you . . . but of course it's not the same, not a bit the same," Alyosha hastily corrected himself.

"A precious admission, in spite of your 'not a bit the same.' I ask you why your Jesuits and Inquisitors have united simply for vile material gain? Why can there not be among them one martyr oppressed by great sorrow and loving humanity? You see, only suppose that there was one such a man among all those who desire nothing but filthy material gain —if there's only one like my old Inquisitor, who had himself eaten roots in the desert and made frenzied efforts to subdue his flesh to make himself free and perfect. But yet all his life he loved humanity, and suddenly his eyes were opened, and he saw that it is no great moral blessedness to attain perfection and freedom, if at the same time one gains the conviction that millions of God's creatures have been created as a mockery, that they will never be capable of using their freedom, that these poor rebels can never turn into giants to complete the tower, that it was not for such geese that the great idealist dreamt his dream of harmony. Seeing all that he turned back and joined—the clever people. Surely that could have happened?"

"Joined whom, what clever people?" cried Alyosha, completely carried away. "They have no such great cleverness and no mysteries and secrets. . . . Perhaps nothing but Atheism, that's all their secret. Your inquisitor does not believe in God, that's his secret!"

"What if it is so! At last you have guessed it. It's perfectly true that that's the whole secret, but isn't that suffering, at least for a man like that, who has wasted his whole life in the desert and yet could not shake off his incurable love of humanity? In his old age he reached the clear conviction that nothing but the advice of the great dread spirit could build up any tolerable sort of life for the feeble, unruly, 'incomplete, empirical creatures created in jest.' And so, convinced of this, he sees that he must follow the council of the wise spirit, the dread spirit of death and destruction, and therefore accept lying and deception, and lead men consciously to death and destruction, and yet deceive them all the way so that they may not notice where they are being led, that the poor blind creatures may at least on the way think themselves happy. And note, the deception is in the name of Him in Whose ideal the old man had so fervently believed all his life long. Is not that tragic? And if only one such stood at the head of the whole army 'filled with the lust of power only for the sake of filthy gain'—would not one such be enough to make a tragedy? More than that, one such standing at the head is enough to create the actual leading idea of the Roman Church with all its armies and Jesuits, its highest idea. I tell you frankly that I firmly believe that there has always been such a man among those who stood at the head of the movement. Who knows, there may have been some such even among the Roman Popes. Who knows, perhaps the spirit of that accursed old man who loves mankind so obstinately in his own way, is to be found even now in a whole multitude of such old men, existing not by chance but by agreement, as a secret league formed long ago for the guarding of the mystery, to guard it from the weak and the unhappy, so as to make them happy. No doubt it is so, and so it must be indeed. I fancy that even among the Masons there's something of the same mystery at the bottom, and that that's why the Catholics so detest the Masons as their rivals breaking up the unity of the idea, while it is so essential that there should be one flock and one shepherd. . . . But from the way I defend my idea I might be an author impatient of your criticism. Enough of it."

"You are perhaps a Mason yourself!" broke suddenly from Alyosha. "You don't believe in God," he added, speaking this time very sorrowfully. He fancied besides that his brother was looking at him ironically. "How does your poem end?" he asked, suddenly looking down. "Or was it the end?"

"I meant to end it like this. When the Inquisitor ceased speaking he waited some time for his Prisoner to answer him. His silence weighed down upon him. He saw that the Prisoner had listened intently all the time, looking gently in his face and evidently not wishing to reply. The old man longed for Him to say something, however bitter and terrible. But He suddenly approached the old man in silence and softly kissed him on his bloodless aged lips. That was all his answer. The old man shuddered. His lips moved. He went to the door, opened it, and said to Him: 'Go, and come no more . . . come not at all, never, never!' And he let Him out into the dark alleys of the town. The Prisoner went away."

"And the old man?"

"The kiss glows in his heart, but the old man adheres to his idea."

IVAN SERGEEVICH TURGENEV

1818–1883

Ivan Turgenev spent his formative years in Moscow, and thereafter attended universities at Moscow and Berlin. He published some early romantic stories, but he first rose to fame through the narratives and sketches known as *A Sportsman's Sketches,* or *A Sportsman's Notebooks* (1852). These fresh, impressionistic sketches of the Russian steppes made him famous, and the selection in this text is from that work. The work gained contemporary fame because it was conceived to be an attack on the institutions of Russian serfdom. Between 1855 and 1876 he produced a series of notable novels, of which the best are *On the Eve* (1860), *Fathers and Sons* (1862), *Smoke* (1867), and *Virgin Soil* (1877). During the last twenty years of his life he became an expatriate, living in various places of Europe from Paris (where he knew Henry James) to Baden-Baden in Germany (the scene of some of the later novels). His fiction always concerned, however, the problems of Mother Russia from the point of view of a faithful son who was also a good European, and his novels became the chronicles of the political movements of the 1850's and 1860's and the rise of the young Russia. They consequently remain in part the documentary work of the social historian; but beyond this, his admirable clarity of style and presentation and his fine though reticent sympathy for his characters make Turgenev one of the most lasting of the Russian novelists.

FURTHER READING

CECIL, LORD DAVID. "Turgenev," in *Poets and Story-Tellers* (New York, 1949), pp. 123–38.
JAMES, HENRY. *Partial Portraits* (London, 1888).
TURGENEV, IVAN. *The Borzoi Turgenev,* translated by Harry Stevens (New York, 1950).
VOGÜÉ, EUGÈNE. *The Russian Novel,* translated by H. A. Sawyer (New York, 1916).

The District Doctor *

ONE day in autumn on my way back from a remote part of the country I caught cold and fell ill. Fortunately the fever attacked me in the district

* Printed by permission of Random House, Inc. Copyright, 1925, by Modern Library, Inc.

town at the inn; I sent for the doctor. In half-an-hour the district doctor appeared, a thin, dark-haired man of middle height. He prescribed me the usual sudorific, ordered a mustard plaster to be put on, very deftly slid a five-ruble note up his sleeve, coughing drily and looking away as he did so, and then was getting up to go home, but somehow fell into talk and remained. I was exhausted with feverishness; I foresaw a sleepless night, and was glad of a little chat with a pleasant companion. Tea was served. My doctor began to converse freely. He was a sensible fellow, and expressed himself with vigour and some humour. Queer things happen in the world: you may live a long while with some people, and be on friendly terms with them, and never once speak openly with them from your soul; with others you scarcely have time to get acquainted, and all at once you are pouring out to him or he to you—all your secrets, as though you were at confession. I don't know how I gained the confidence of my new friend—anyway, with nothing to lead up to it, he told me a rather curious incident; and here I will report his tale for the information of the indulgent reader. I will try to tell it in the doctor's own words.

"You don't happen to know," he began in a weak and quavering voice (the common result of the use of unmixed Berezov snuff); "you don't happen to know the judge here, Mylov, Pavel Lukich? . . . You don't know him? . . . Well, it's all the same." (He cleared his throat and rubbed his eyes.) "Well, you see, the thing happened, to tell you exactly without mistake, in Lent, at the very time of the thaws. I was sitting at his house—our judge's, you know—playing preference. Our judge is a good fellow, and fond of playing preference. Suddenly" (the doctor made frequent use of this word, suddenly) "they tell me, 'There's a servant asking for you.' I say 'What does he want?' They say 'He has brought a note—it must be from a patient.' 'Give me the note,' I say. So it is from a patient—well and good—you understand—it's our bread and butter. . . . But this is how it was: a lady, a widow, writes to me; she says, 'My daughter is dying. Come, for God's sake!' she says, 'and the horses have been sent for you! . . . Well, that's all right. But she was twenty miles from town, and it was midnight out of doors, and the roads in such a state, my word! And as she was poor herself, one could not expect more than two silver rubles, and even that problematic; and perhaps it might only be a matter of a roll of linen and a sack of oatmeal in payment. However, duty, you know, before everything: a fellow-creature may be dying. I hand over my cards at once to Kalliopin, the member of the provincial commission, and return home. I look; a wretched little trap was standing at the steps, with peasant's horses, fat—too fat—and their coat as shaggy as felt; and the coachman sitting with his cap off out of respect. Well, I think to myself, 'It's clear, my friend, these patients aren't rolling in riches.' . . . You smile; but I tell you, a poor man like me has to take everything into consideration. . . . If the coachman sits like a prince, and doesn't touch his cap, and even sneers at you behind his beard, and flicks his whip—then you may bet on six rubles. But this case, I saw, had a very different air. However, I think there's no help for it; duty before everything. I snatch up the most necessary drugs and set off. Will you believe it? I only just managed to get there at all. The road was infernal: streams, snow, water-courses, and the dyke had suddenly burst there—that was the worst of it! However, I arrived at last. It was a little thatched house. There was a light in the windows; that meant they expected me. I was met by an old lady, very venerable, in a cap. 'Save her!' she says; 'she is dying.' I say, 'Pray don't distress yourself—Where is the invalid?' 'Come this way.' I see a clean little room, a lamp in the corner; on the bed a girl of twenty, unconscious. She was in a burning heat, and breathing heavily—it was fever. There were two other girls, her sisters, scared and in tears. 'Yesterday,' they tell me, 'she was perfectly well and had a good appetite; this morning she complained of her head, and this evening, suddenly, you see, like this.' I say again: 'Pray don't be uneasy.' It's a doctor's duty, you know—and I went up to her and bled her, told them to put on a mustard plaster, and prescribed a mixture. Meantime I looked at her, you know—there, by God! I had never seen such a face!—she was a beauty, in a word! I felt quite shaken by pity. Such lovely features; such eyes! . . . But, thank God! she became easier; she fell into a perspiration, seemed to come to her senses, looked round, smiled, and passed her hand over her face. . . . Her sisters bent over her. They ask, 'How are you?' 'All right,' she says, and turns away. I looked at her; she had fallen asleep. 'Well,' I say, 'now the patient should be left alone.' So we all went out on tiptoe; only a maid remained, in case she was wanted. In the parlour there was a samovar standing on the table, and a bottle of rum; in our profession one can't get on without it. They gave me tea; asked me to stop the night. . . . I consented: where could I go, indeed, at that time of night? The old lady kept groaning. 'What is it?' I say; 'she will live; don't worry yourself; you had

better take a little rest yourself; it is about two o'clock.' 'But will you send to wake me if anything happens?' 'Yes, yes.' The old lady went away, and the girls too went to their own room; they made up a bed for me in the parlour. Well, I went to bed—but I could not get to sleep, for a wonder! for in reality I was very tired. I could not get my patient out of my head. At last I could not put up with it any longer; I got up suddenly; I think to myself, 'I will go and see how the patient is getting on.' Her bedroom was next to the parlour. Well, I got up, and gently opened the door—how my heart beat! I looked in: the servant was asleep, her mouth wide open, and even snoring, the wretch! but the patient lay with her face towards me, and her arms flung wide apart, poor girl! I went up to her . . . when suddenly she opened her eyes and stared at me! 'Who is it? who is it?' I was in confusion. 'Don't be alarmed, madam,' I say; 'I am the doctor; I have come to see how you feel.' 'You the doctor?' 'Yes, the doctor; your mother sent for me from the town; we have bled you, madam; now pray go to sleep, and in a day or two, please God! we will set you on your feet again.' 'Ah, yes, yes, doctor, don't let me die . . . please, please.' 'Why do you talk like that? God bless you!' She is in a fever again, I think to myself; I felt her pulse; yes, she was feverish. She looked at me, and then took me by the hand. 'I will tell you why I don't want to die; I will tell you. . . . Now we are alone; and only, please don't you . . . not to anyone . . . Listen . . . !' I bent down; she moved her lips quite to my ear; she touched my cheek with her hair—I confess my head went round —and began to whisper. . . . I could make out nothing of it. . . . Ah, she was delirious! . . . She whispered and whispered, but so quickly, and as if it were not in Russian; at last she finished, and shivering dropped her head on the pillow, and threatened me with her finger: 'Remember, doctor, to no one.' I calmed her somehow, gave her something to drink, waked the servant, and went away."

At this point the doctor again took snuff with exasperated energy, and for a moment seemed stupefied by its effects.

"However," he continued, "the next day, contrary to my expectations, the patient was no better. I thought and thought, and suddenly decided to remain there, even though my other patients were expecting me. . . . And you know one can't afford to disregard that; one's practice suffers if one does. But, in the first place, the patient was really in danger; and secondly, to tell the truth, I felt strongly drawn to her. Besides, I liked the whole family.

Though they were really badly off, they were singularly, I may say, cultivated people. . . . Their father had been a learned man, an author; he died, of course, in poverty, but he had managed before he died to give his children an excellent education; he left a lot of books too. Either because I looked after the invalid very carefully, or for some other reason; anyway, I can venture to say all the household loved me as one of the family. . . . Meantime the roads were in a worse state than ever; all communications, so to say, were cut off completely; even medicine could with difficulty be got from the town. . . . The sick girl was not getting better. . . . Day after day, and day after day . . . but . . . here . . ." (The doctor made a brief pause.) "I declare I don't know how to tell you." . . . (He again took snuff, coughed, and swallowed a little tea). "I will tell you without beating about the bush. My patient . . . how should I say? . . . Well she had fallen in love with me . . . or, no, it was not that she was in love . . . however . . . really, how should one say?" (The doctor looked down and grew red.) "No," he went on quickly, "in love, indeed! A man should not over-estimate himself. She was an educated girl, clever and well-read, and I had even forgotten my Latin, one may say, completely. As to appearance" (the doctor looked himself over with a smile) "I am nothing to boast of there either. But God Almighty did not make me a fool; I don't take black for white; I know a thing or two; I could see very clearly, for instance, that Aleksandra Andreyevna—that was her name—did not feel love for me, but had a friendly, so to say, inclination—a respect or something for me. Though she herself perhaps mistook this sentiment, anyway this was her attitude; you may form your own judgment of it. But," added the doctor, who had brought out all these disconnected sentences without taking breath, and with obvious embarrassment, "I seem to be wandering rather—you won't understand anything like this. . . . There with your leave, I will relate it all in order."

He drank a glass of tea, and began in a calmer voice.

"Well, then. My patient kept getting worse and worse. You are not a doctor, my good sir; you cannot understand what passes in a poor fellow's heart, especially at first, when he begins to suspect that the disease is getting the upper hand of him. What becomes of his belief in himself? You suddenly grow so timid; it's indescribable. You fancy then that you have forgotten everything you knew, and that the patient has no faith in you, and that other

people begin to notice how distracted you are, and tell you the symptoms with reluctance; that they are looking at you suspiciously, whispering. . . . Ah! it's horrid! There must be a remedy, you think, for this disease, if one could find it. Isn't this it? You try—no, that's not it! You don't allow the medicine the necessary time to do good. . . . You clutch at one thing, then at another. Sometimes you take up a book of medical prescriptions—here it is, you think! Sometimes, by Jove, you pick one out by chance, thinking to leave it to fate. . . . But meantime a fellow creature's dying, and another doctor would have saved him. 'We must have a consultation,' you say; 'I will not take the responsibility on myself.' And what a fool you look at such times! Well, in time you learn to bear it; it's nothing to you. A man has died—but it's not your fault; you treated him by the rules. But what's still more torture to you is to see blind faith in you, and to feel yourself that you are not able to be of use. Well, it was just this blind faith that the whole of Aleksandra Andreyevna's family had in me; they had forgotten to think that their daughter was in danger. I, too, on my side assured them that it is nothing, but meantime my heart sinks into my boots. To add to our troubles, the roads were in such a state that the coachman was gone for whole days together to get medicine. And I never left the patient's room; I could not tear myself away; I tell her amusing stories, you know, and play cards with her. I watch by her side at night. The old mother thanks me with tears in her eyes; but I think to myself, 'I don't deserve your gratitude.' I frankly confess to you—there is no object in concealing it now—I was in love with my patient. And Aleksandra Andreyevna had grown fond of me; she would not sometimes let any one be in her room but me. She began to talk to me, to ask me questions; where I had studied, how I lived, who are my people, whom I go to see. I feel that she ought not to talk; but to forbid her to—to forbid her resolutely, you know—I could not. Sometimes I held my head in my hands, and asked myself, 'What are you doing, villain?' . . . And she would take my hand and hold it, give me a long, long look, and turn away, sigh, and say, 'How good you are!' Her hands were so feverish, her eyes so large and languid. . . . 'Yes,' she says, 'you are a good, kind man; you are not like our neighbours. . . . No, you are not like that. . . . Why did I not know you till now!' 'Aleksandra Andreyevna, calm yourself,' I say. . . . 'I feel, believe me, I don't know how I have gained . . . but there, calm yourself. . . . All will be right; you will be well again.'

And meanwhile I must tell you," continued the doctor, bending forward and raising his eyebrows, "that they associated very little with the neighbours, because the smaller people were not on their level, and pride hindered them from being friendly with the rich. I tell you, they were an exceptionally cultivated family, so you know it was gratifying for me. She would only take her medicine from my hands . . . she would lift herself up, poor girl, with my aid, take it, and gaze at me. . . . My heart felt as if it were bursting. And meanwhile she was growing worse and worse, worse and worse, all the time; she will die, I think to myself; she must die. Believe me, I would sooner have gone to the grave myself; and here were her mother and sisters watching me, looking into my eyes . . . and their faith in me was wearing away. 'Well, how is she?' 'Oh, all right, all right!' All right, indeed! My mind was failing me. Well, I was sitting one night alone again by my patient. The maid was sitting there too, and snoring away in full swing; I can't find fault with the poor girl, though! she was worn out too. Aleksandra Andreyevna had felt very unwell all the evening; she was very feverish. Until midnight she kept tossing about; at last she seemed to fall asleep; at least, she lay still without stirring. The lamp was burning in the corner before the holy image. I sat here, you know, with my head bent; I even dozed a little. Suddenly it seemed as though someone touched me in the side; I turned round. . . . Good God! Aleksandra Andreyevna was gazing with intent eyes at me . . . her lips parted, her cheeks seemed burning. 'What is it?' 'Doctor, shall I die?' 'Merciful Heavens!' 'No, doctor, no; please don't tell me I shall live . . . don't say so. . . . If you knew. . . . Listen! For God's sake don't conceal my real position,' and her breath came so fast. 'If I can know for certain that I must die . . . then I will tell you all—all!' 'Aleksandra Andreyevna, I beg!' 'Listen; I have not been asleep at all . . . I have been looking at you a long while. . . . For God's sake! . . . I believe in you; you are a good man, an honest man; I entreat you by all that is sacred in the world —tell me the truth! If you knew how important it is for me. . . . Doctor, for God's sake tell me. . . . Am I in danger?' 'What can I tell you, Aleksandra Andreyevna pray?' 'For God's sake, I beseech you!' 'I can't conceal from you,' I say, 'Aleksandra Andreyevna; you are certainly in danger; but God is merciful.' 'I shall die, I shall die.' And it seemed as though she were pleased; her face grew so bright; I was alarmed. 'Don't be afraid, don't be afraid! I am not frightened by death at all.' She suddenly sat up and leaned on her elbow. 'Now . . . yes, now I can tell you that I thank you with my whole heart . . . that you are kind and good—that I love you!' I stared at her, like one possessed; it was terrible for me, you know. 'Do you hear, I love you!' 'Aleksandra Andreyevna, how have I deserved—' 'No, no, you don't—you don't understand me.' . . . And suddenly she stretched out her arms, and taking my head in her hands, she kissed it. . . . Believe me, I almost screamed aloud. . . . I threw myself on my knees, and buried my head in the pillow. She did not speak; her fingers trembled in my hair; I listen; she is weeping. I began to soothe her, to assure her. . . . I really don't know what I did say to her. 'You will wake up the girl,' I say to her; 'Aleksandra Andreyevna, I thank you . . . believe me . . . calm yourself.' 'Enough, enough!' she persisted, 'never mind all of them; let them wake, then; let them come in—it does not matter; I am dying, you see. . . . What do you fear? Why are you afraid? Lift up your head. . . . Or, perhaps you don't love me; perhaps I am wrong. . . . In that case, forgive me.' 'Aleksandra Andreyevna, what are you saying! . . . I love you, Aleksandra Andreyevna.' She looked straight into my eyes, and opened her arms wide. 'Then take me in your arms.' I tell you frankly, I don't know how it was I did not go mad that night. I feel that my patient is killing herself; I see that she is not fully herself; I understand, too, that if she did not consider herself on the point of death she would never have thought of me; and, indeed, say what you will, it's hard to die at twenty without having known love; this was what was torturing her; this was why, in despair, she caught at me—do you understand now? But she held me in her arms, and would not let me go. 'Have pity on me, Aleksandra Andreyevna, and have pity on yourself,' I say. 'Why,' she says, 'what is there to think of? You know I must die.' . . . This she repeated incessantly. . . . 'If I knew that I should return to life, and be a proper young lady again, I should be ashamed . . . of course, ashamed . . . but why now?' 'But who has said you will die?' 'Oh, no, leave off! you will not deceive me; you don't know how to lie—look at your face.' . . . 'You shall live, Aleksandra Andreyevna; I will cure you; we will ask your mother's blessing . . . we will be united—we will be happy.' 'No, no, I have your word; I must die . . . you have promised me . . . you have told me.' . . . It was cruel for me—cruel for many reasons. And see what trifling things can do sometimes; it seems nothing at all, but it's painful. It occurred to her to ask me, what is my name;

not my surname, but my first name. I must needs be so unlucky as to be called Trifon. Yes, indeed; Trifon Ivanich. Every one in the house called me doctor. However, there's no help for it. I say, 'Trifon, madam.' She frowned, shook her head, and muttered something in French—ah, something unpleasant, of course!—and then she laughed—disagreeably too. Well, I spent the whole night with her in this way. Before morning I went away, feeling as though I were mad. When I went again into her room it was daytime, after morning tea. Good God! I could scarcely recognise her; people are laid in their grave looking better than that. I swear to you, on my honour, I don't understand—I absolutely don't understand—now, how I lived through that experience. Three days and nights my patient still lingered on. And what nights! What things she said to me! And on the last night—only imagine to yourself—I was sitting near her, and kept praying to God for one thing only: 'Take her,' I said, 'quickly, and me with her.' Suddenly the old mother comes unexpectedly into the room. I had already the evening before told her—the mother—there was little hope, and it would be well to send for a priest. When the sick girl saw her mother she said: 'It's very well you have come; look at us, we love one another—we have given each other our word.' 'What does she say, doctor? what does she say?' I turned livid. 'She is wandering,' I say; 'the fever.' But she: 'Hush, hush; you told me something quite different just now, and have taken my ring. Why do you pretend? My mother is good—she will forgive—she will understand—and I am dying. . . . I have no need to tell lies; give me your hand.' I jumped up and ran out of the room. The old lady, of course, guessed how it was.

"I will not, however, weary you any longer, and to me, too, of course, it's painful to recall all this. My patient passed away the next day. God rest her soul!" the doctor added, speaking quickly and with a sigh. "Before her death she asked her family to go out and leave me alone with her."

"'Forgive me,' she said; 'I am perhaps to blame towards you . . . my illness . . . but believe me, I have loved no one more than you . . . do not forget me . . . keep my ring.'"

The doctor turned away; I took his hand.

"Ah!" he said, "let us talk of something else, or would you care to play preference for a small stake? It is not for people like me to give way to exalted emotions. There's only one thing for me to think of; how to keep the children from crying and the wife from scolding. Since then, you know, I have

had time to enter into lawful wedlock, as they say. . . . Oh . . . I took a merchant's daughter—seven thousand for her dowry. Her name's Akulina; it goes well with Trifon. She is an ill-tempered woman, I must tell you, but luckily she's asleep all day. . . . Well, shall it be preference?"

We sat down to preference for halfpenny points. Trifon Ivanich won two rubles and a half from me, and went home late, well pleased with his success.

———◆———

LEO NIKOLAEVICH TOLSTOI

1828–1910

Count Leo Tolstoi grew up in an aristocratic environment in Moscow and on the family's country estates. After his service in the Crimean War, Tolstoi gradually began to abandon his aristocratic prerogatives and his expected career as the son of a count and a princess. His first important publications were short stories, especially *Three Deaths* (1859). In 1862 he settled down after marriage to the life of a country squire and during the next fifteen years wrote the two novels upon which his literary fame now rests: *War and Peace* (1865–1869) one of the great novels of the world, and *Anna Karenina* (1875–1877).

After 1879 he became a passionate devotee of a primitive Christianity that impelled him to renounce his own property, to urge the abolition of governments, of all nationality, and all church dogma, and to demand nonresistance to evil. He assailed Western materialism and much that was valued in literature and art, including Shakespeare, because it did not promote the true fellowship of man (*What Is Art?*). For Tolstoi the only bearable life was a rural one supported by manual labor. He wrote more fiction like *The Death of Ivan Ilyich* (1886) and *The Kreutzer Sonata* (1890) but these are too doctrinaire to be first-class fiction. The story presented here illustrates one facet of Tolstoi's attempt to propagate and disseminate his faith.

FURTHER READING

KUZMINZKAYA, TATYANA A. *Tolstoy As I Knew Him* (New York, 1948).
MAUDE, AYLMER. *The Life of Tolstoy* (London, 1911).
SIMMONS, ERNEST. *Leo Tolstoy* (Boston, 1946).

God Sees the Truth, but Waits *

In the town of Vladimir lived a young merchant named Ivan Dmitrich Aksionov. He had two shops and a house of his own.

Aksionov was a handsome, fair-haired, curly-headed fellow, full of fun, and very fond of singing. When quite a young man he had been given to drink, and was riotous when he had had too much; but after he married he gave up drinking, except now and then.

One summer Aksionov was going to the Nizhny Fair, and as he bade good-bye to his family, his wife said to him, "Ivan Dmitrich, do not start to-day; I have had a bad dream about you."

Aksionov laughed, and said, "You are afraid that when I go to the fair I shall go on a spree."

His wife replied: "I do not know what I am afraid of; all I know is that I had a bad dream. I dreamt you returned from the town, and when you took off your cap I saw that your hair was quite grey."

Aksionov laughed. "That's a lucky sign," said he. "See if I don't sell out all my goods, and bring you some presents from the fair."

So he said good-bye to his family, and drove away.

When he had travelled half-way, he met a merchant whom he knew, and they put up at the same inn for the night. They had some tea together, and then went to bed in adjoining rooms.

It was not Aksionov's habit to sleep late, and, wishing to travel while it was still cool, he aroused his driver before dawn, and told him to put in the horses.

Then he made his way across to the landlord of the inn (who lived in a cottage at the back), paid his bill, and continued his journey.

When he had gone about twenty-five miles, he stopped for the horses to be fed. Aksionov rested awhile in the passage of the inn, then he stepped out into the porch, and, ordering a samovar to be heated, got out his guitar and began to play.

Suddenly a troika drove up with tinkling bells and an official alighted, followed by two soldiers. He came to Aksionov and began to question him, asking him who he was and whence he came. Aksionov answered him fully, and said, "Won't you have some tea with me?" But the official went on cross-questioning him and asking him, "Where did you spend last night? Were you alone, or with a fellow-

merchant? Did you see the other merchant this morning? Why did you leave the inn before dawn?"

Aksionov wondered why he was asked all these questions, but he described all that had happened, and then added, "Why do you cross-question me as if I were a thief or a robber? I am travelling on business of my own, and there is no need to question me."

Then the official, calling the soldiers, said, "I am the police-officer of this district, and I question you because the merchant with whom you spent last night has been found with his throat cut. We must search your things."

They entered the house. The soldiers and the police-officer unstrapped Aksionov's luggage and searched it. Suddenly the officer drew a knife out of a bag, crying, "Whose knife is this?"

Aksionov looked, and seeing a blood-stained knife taken from his bag, he was frightened.

"How is it there is blood on this knife?"

Aksionov tried to answer, but could hardly utter a word, and only stammered: "I—don't know—not mine."

Then the police-officer said: "This morning the merchant was found in bed with his throat cut. You are the only person who could have done it. The house was locked from inside, and no one else was there. Here is this blood-stained knife in your bag, and your face and manner betray you! Tell me how you killed him, and how much money you stole?"

Aksionov swore he had not done it; that he had not seen the merchant after they had had tea together; that he had no money except eight thousand rubles of his own, and that the knife was not his. But his voice was broken, his face pale, and he trembled with fear as though he were guilty.

The police-officer ordered the soldiers to bind Aksionov and to put him in the cart. As they tied his feet together and flung him into the cart, Aksionov crossed himself and wept. His money and goods were taken from him, and he was sent to the nearest town and imprisoned there. Enquiries as to his character were made in Vladimir. The merchants and other inhabitants of that town said that in former days he used to drink and waste his time, but that he was a good man. Then the trial came on: he was charged with murdering a merchant from Ryazan, and robbing him of twenty thousand rubles.

His wife was in despair, and did not know what to believe. Her children were all quite small; one was a baby at her breast. Taking them all with her,

* By permission of Random House, Inc. Copyright, 1925, by Modern Library, Inc.

she went to the town where her husband was in jail. At first she was not allowed to see him; but after much begging, she obtained permission from the officials, and was taken to him. When she saw her husband in prison-dress and in chains, shut up with thieves and criminals, she fell down, and did not come to her senses for a long time. Then she drew her children to her, and sat down near him. She told him of things at home, and asked about what had happened to him. He told her all, and she asked, "What can we do now?"

"We must petition the Czar not to let an innocent man perish."

His wife told him that she had sent a petition to the Czar, but it had not been accepted.

Aksionov did not reply, but only looked downcast.

Then his wife said, "It was not for nothing I dreamt your hair had turned grey. You remember? You should not have started that day." And passing her fingers through his hair, she said: "Vanya dearest, tell your wife the truth; was it not you who did it?"

"So you, too, suspect me!" said Aksionov, and, hiding his face in his hands, he began to weep. Then a soldier came to say that the wife and children must go away; and Aksionov said good-bye to his family for the last time.

When they were gone, Aksionov recalled what had been said, and when he remembered that his wife also had suspected him, he said to himself, "It seems that only God can know the truth; it is to Him alone we must appeal, and from Him alone expect mercy."

And Aksionov wrote no more petitions; gave up all hope, and only prayed to God.

Aksionov was condemned to be flogged and sent to the mines. So he was flogged with a knot, and when the wounds made by the knot were healed, he was driven to Siberia with other convicts.

For twenty-six years Aksionov lived as a convict in Siberia. His hair turned white as snow, and his beard grew long, thin, and grey. All his mirth went; he stooped; he walked slowly, spoke little, and never laughed, but he often prayed.

In prison Aksionov learnt to make boots, and earned a little money, with which he bought *The Lives of the Saints*. He read this book when there was light enough in the prison; and on Sundays in the prison-church he read the lessons and sang in the choir; for his voice was still good.

The prison authorities liked Aksionov for his meekness, and his fellow-prisoners respected him: they called him "Grandfather," and "The Saint." When they wanted to petition the prison authorities about anything, they always made Aksionov their spokesman, and when there were quarrels among the prisoners they came to him to put things right, and to judge the matter.

No news reached Aksionov from his home, and he did not even know if his wife and children were still alive.

One day a fresh gang of convicts came to the prison. In the evening the old prisoners collected round the new ones and asked them what towns or villages they came from, and what they were sentenced for. Among the rest Aksionov sat down near the newcomers, and listened with downcast air to what was said.

One of the new convicts, a tall, strong man of sixty, with a closely-cropped grey beard, was telling the others what he had been arrested for.

"Well, friends," he said, "I only took a horse that was tied to a sledge, and I was arrested and accused of stealing. I said I had only taken it to get home quicker, and had then let it go; besides, the driver was a personal friend of mine. So I said, 'It's all right.' 'No,' said they, 'you stole it.' But how or where I stole it they could not say. I once really did something wrong, and ought by rights to have come here long ago, but that time I was not found out. Now I have been sent here for nothing at all. . . . Eh, but it's lies I'm telling you; I've been to Siberia before, but I did not stay long."

"Where are you from?" asked some one.

"From Vladimir. My family are of that town. My name is Makar, and they also call me Semyonich."

Aksionov raised his head and said: "Tell me, Semyonich, do you know anything of the merchants Aksionov of Vladimir? Are they still alive?"

"Know them? Of course I do. The Aksionovs are rich, though their father is in Siberia: a sinner like ourselves, it seems! As for you, Gran'dad, how did you come here?"

Aksionov did not like to speak of his misfortune. He only sighed, and said, "For my sins I have been in prison these twenty-six years."

"What sins?" asked Makar Semyonich.

But Aksionov only said, "Well, well—I must have deserved it!" He would have said no more, but his companions told the newcomers how Aksionov came to be in Siberia; how some one had killed a merchant, and had put the knife among Aksionov's things, and Aksionov had been unjustly condemned.

When Makar Semyonich heard this he looked at Aksionov, slapped his own knee, and exclaimed,

"Well, this is wonderful! Really wonderful! But how old you've grown, Gran'dad!"

The others asked him why he was so surprised, and where he had seen Aksionov before; but Makar Semyonich did not reply. He only said: "It's wonderful that we should meet here, lads!"

These words made Aksionov wonder whether this man knew who had killed the merchant; so he said, "Perhaps, Semyonich, you have heard of that affair, or maybe you've seen me before?"

"How could I help hearing? The world's full of rumours. But it's a long time ago, and I've forgotten what I heard."

"Perhaps you heard who killed the merchant?" asked Aksionov.

Makar Semyonich laughed and replied: "It must have been him in whose bag the knife was found! If some one else hid the knife there, 'He's not a thief till he's caught,' as the saying is. How could any one put a knife into your bag while it was under your head? It would surely have woke you up."

When Aksionov heard these words, he felt sure this was the man who had killed the merchant. He rose and went away. All that night Aksionov lay awake. He felt terribly unhappy, and all sorts of images rose in his mind. There was the image of his wife as she was when he parted from her to go to the fair. He saw her as if she were present; her face and her eyes rose before him; he heard her speak and laugh. Then he saw his children, quite little, as they were at that time: one with a little cloak on, another at his mother's breast. And then he remembered himself as he used to be—young and merry. He remembered how he sat playing the guitar in the porch of the inn where he was arrested, and how free from care he had been. He saw, in his mind, the place where he was flogged, the executioner, and the people standing around; the chains, the convicts, all the twenty-six years of his prison life, and his premature old age. The thought of it all made him so wretched that he was ready to kill himself.

"And it's all that villain's doing!" thought Aksionov. And his anger was so great against Makar Semyonich that he longed for vengeance, even if he himself should perish for it. He kept repeating prayers all night, but could get no peace. During the day he did not go near Makar Semyonich, nor even look at him.

A fortnight passed in this way. Aksionov could not sleep at night, and was so miserable that he did not know what to do.

One night as he was walking about the prison he noticed some earth that came rolling out from under one of the shelves on which the prisoners slept. He stopped to see what it was. Suddenly Makar Semyonich crept out from under the shelf, and looked up at Aksionov with frightened face. Aksionov tried to pass without looking at him, but Makar seized his hand and told him that he had dug a hole under the wall, getting rid of the earth by putting it into his high-boots, and emptying it out every day on the road when the prisoners were driven to their work.

"Just you keep quiet, old man, and you shall get out too. If you blab, they'll flog the life out of me, but I will kill you first."

Aksionov trembled with anger as he looked at his enemy. He drew his hand away, saying, "I have no wish to escape, and you have no need to kill me; you killed me long ago! As to telling of you—I may do so or not, as God shall direct."

Next day, when the convicts were led out to work, the convoy soldiers noticed that one or other of the prisoners emptied some earth out of his boots. The prison was searched and the tunnel found. The Governor came and questioned all the prisoners to find out who had dug the hole. They all denied any knowledge of it. Those who knew would not betray Makar Semyonich, knowing he would be flogged almost to death. At last the Governor turned to Aksionov whom he knew to be a just man, and said: "You are a truthful old man; tell me, before God, who dug the hole?"

Makar Semyonich stood as if he were quite unconcerned, looking at the Governor and not so much as glancing at Aksionov. Aksionov's lips and hands trembled, and for a long time he could not utter a word. He thought, "Why should I screen him who ruined my life? Let him pay for what I have suffered. But if I tell, they will probably flog the life out of him, and maybe I suspect him wrongly. And, after all, what good would it be to me?"

"Well, old man," repeated the Governor, "tell me the truth: who has been digging under the wall?"

Aksionov glanced at Makar Semyonich, and said, "I cannot say, your honour. It is not God's will that I should tell! Do what you like with me; I am in your hands."

However much the Governor tried, Aksionov would say no more, and so the matter had to be left.

That night, when Aksionov was lying on his bed and just beginning to doze, some one came quietly and sat down on his bed. He peered through the darkness and recognized Makar.

"What more do you want of me?" asked Aksionov." "Why have you come here?"

Makar Semyonich was silent. So Aksionov sat up and said, "What do you want? Go away, or I will call the guard!"

Makar Semyonich bent close over Aksionov, and whispered, "Ivan Dmitrich, forgive me!"

"What for?" asked Aksionov.

"It was I who killed the merchant and hid the knife among your things. I meant to kill you too, but I heard a noise outside, so I hid the knife in your bag and escaped out of the window."

Aksionov was silent, and did not know what to say. Makar Semyonich slid off the bed-shelf and knelt upon the ground. "Ivan Dmitrich," said he, "forgive me! For the love of God, forgive me! I will confess that it was I who killed the merchant, and you will be released and can go to your home."

"It is easy for you to talk," said Aksionov, "but I have suffered for you these twenty-six years. Where could I go to now? . . . My wife is dead, and my children have forgotten me. I have nowhere to go. . . ."

Makar Semyonich did not rise, but beat his head on the floor. "Ivan Dmitrich, forgive me!" he cried. "When they flogged me with the knot it was not so hard to bear as it is to see you now . . . yet you had pity on me, and did not tell. For Christ's sake forgive me, wretch that I am!" And he began to sob.

When Aksionov heard him sobbing he, too, began to weep. "God will forgive you!" said he. "Maybe I am a hundred times worse than you." And at these words his heart grew light, and the longing for home left him. He no longer had any desire to leave the prison, but only hoped for his last hour to come.

In spite of what Aksionov had said, Makar Semyonich confessed his guilt. But when the order for his release came Aksionov was already dead.

———◆———

ANTON PAVLOVICH CHEKHOV

1860–1904

Anton Chekhov was born of lower middle-class parents in the town of Taganrog. He studied medicine and took his degree at Moscow University in 1884. Since he had to earn his way, his first writings were contributions to Russian humorous magazines, but gradually Chekhov began to write more seriously. In 1886 a letter from the famous critic D. V. Grigorovich praising his talent did much to make Chekhov into a serious artist. His short stories are moments of vision without plot: what has been called the technique of the "frozen moment" in fiction. They may be classed as realistic, for he steadfastly refuses to follow a formula in his writing, but he does manage as well to convey those overtones of lyric emotion which he perhaps best secures in his greatest plays *The Cherry Orchard* and *The Sea Gull*.

The sad, wistful melancholy that lies in Chekhov's manner may be due in part to the effect of the depressing era in which he wrote (he has been called the "voice of twilight Russia"), and in part to the loss of humor that vanishes in translation. His art is seen in his powers of suggestiveness and his skill in conveying much implication by careful brevity of exposition. Chekhov's influence on the twentieth-century short story (on Katherine Mansfield for example) has been profound.

FURTHER READING

GERHARDI, WILLIAM. *Anton Chekhov* (New York, 1923).
HINGLEY, RONALD. *Chekhov* (London, 1950).

The Darling *

OLENKA, the daughter of the retired collegiate assessor Plemyanikov, was sitting on the back-door steps of her house doing nothing. It was hot, the flies were nagging and teasing, and it was pleasant to think that it would soon be evening. Dark rain clouds were gathering from the east, wafting a breath of moisture every now and then.

Kukin, who roomed in the wing of the same house, was standing in the yard looking up at the sky. He was the manager of the Tivoli, an open-air theatre.

"Again," he said despairingly. "Rain again. Rain, rain, rain! Every day rain! As though to spite me. I might as well stick my head into a noose and be done with it. It's ruining me. Heavy losses every day!" He wrung his hands, and continued, addressing Olenka: "What a life, Olga Semyonovna! It's enough to make a man weep. He works, he does his best, his very best, he tortures himself, he passes sleepless nights, he thinks and thinks and thinks how to do everything just right. And what's the result? He gives the public the best operetta, the very best pantomime, excellent artists. But do they want it? Have they the least appreciation of it? The public is rude. The public is a great boor. The public wants a circus, a lot of nonsense, a lot of stuff. And there's the weather. Look! Rain almost every evening. It began to rain on the tenth of May, and it's kept it up through the whole of June. It's simply awful, I can't get any audiences, and don't I have to pay rent? Don't I have to pay the actors?"

The next day towards evening the clouds gathered again, and Kukin said with an hysterical laugh:

"Oh, I don't care. Let it do its worst. Let it drown the whole theatre, and me, too. All right, no luck for me in this world or the next. Let the actors bring suit against me and drag me to court. What's the court? Why not Siberia at hard labour, or even the scaffold? Ha, ha, ha!"

It was the same on the third day.

Olenka listened to Kukin seriously, in silence. Sometimes tears would rise to her eyes. At last Kukin's misfortune touched her. She fell in love with him. He was short, gaunt, with a yellow face, and curly hair combed back from his forehead, and a thin tenor voice. His features puckered all up when he spoke. Despair was ever inscribed on his face. And yet he awakened in Olenka a sincere, deep feeling.

She was always loving somebody. She couldn't get on without loving somebody. She had loved her sick father, who sat the whole time in his armchair in a darkened room, breathing heavily. She had loved her aunt, who came from Brianska once or twice a year to visit them. And before that, when a pupil at the progymnasium, she had loved her French teacher. She was a quiet, kind-hearted, compassionate girl, with a soft gentle way about her. And she made a very healthy, wholesome impression. Looking at her full, rosy cheeks, at her soft white neck with the black mole, and at the good naïve smile that always played on her face when something pleasant was said, the men would think, "Not so bad," and would smile too; and the lady visitors, in the middle of the conversation, would suddenly grasp her hand and exclaim, "You darling!" in a burst of delight.

The house, hers by inheritance, in which she had lived from birth, was located at the outskirts of the city on the Gypsy Road, not far from the Tivoli. From early evening till late at night she could hear the music in the theatre and the bursting of the rockets; and it seemed to her that Kukin was roaring and battling with his fate and taking his chief enemy, the indifferent public, by assault. Her heart melted softly, she felt no desire to sleep, and when Kukin returned home towards morning, she tapped on her window-pane, and through the curtains he saw her face and one shoulder and the kind smile she gave him.

He proposed to her, and they were married. And when he had a good look at her neck and her full vigorous shoulders, he clapped his hands and said: "You darling!"

He was happy. But it rained on their wedding-day, and the expression of despair never left his face.

They got along well together. She sat in the cashier's box, kept the theatre in order, wrote down the expenses, and paid out the salaries. Her rosy cheeks, her kind naïve smile, like a halo around her face, could be seen at the cashier's window, behind the scenes, and in the café. She began to tell her friends that the theatre was the greatest, the most important, the most essential thing in the world, that it was the only place to obtain true enjoyment in and become humanised and educated.

"But do you suppose the public appreciates it?" she asked. "What the public wants is the circus. Yesterday Vanichka and I gave *Faust Burlesqued*, and almost all the boxes were empty. If we had given some silly nonsense, I assure you, the theatre would have been overcrowded. Tomorrow we'll put *Orpheus in Hades* on. Do come."

Whatever Kukin said about the theatre and the actors, she repeated. She spoke, as he did, with contempt of the public, of its indifference to art, of its boorishness. She meddled in the rehearsals, corrected the actors, watched the conduct of the musicians; and when an unfavourable criticism appeared in the local paper, she wept and went to the editor to argue with him.

The actors were fond of her and called her "Vanichka and I" and "the darling." She was sorry for them and lent them small sums. When they bilked her, she never complained to her husband; at the utmost she shed a few tears.

In winter, too, they got along nicely together. They leased a theatre in the town for the whole winter and sublet it for short periods to a Little Russian theatrical company, to a conjuror and to the local amateur players.

Olenka grew fuller and was always beaming with contentment; while Kukin grew thinner and yellower and complained of his terrible losses, though he did fairly well the whole winter. At night he coughed, and she gave him raspberry syrup and lime water, rubbed him with eau de Cologne, and wrapped him up in soft coverings.

"You are my precious sweet," she said with perfect sincerity, stroking his hair. "You are such a dear."

At Lent he went to Moscow to get his company together, and, while without him, Olenka was unable to sleep. She sat at the window the whole time, gazing at the stars. She likened herself to the hens that are also uneasy and unable to sleep when their rooster is out of the coop. Kukin was detained in Moscow. He wrote he would be back during Easter Week, and in his letters discussed arrangements already for the Tivoli. But late one night, before Easter Monday, there was an ill-omened knocking at the wicket-gate. It was like a knocking on a barrel—boom, boom, boom! The sleepy cook ran barefooted, plashing through the puddles, to open the gate.

"Open the gate, please," said some one in a hollow bass voice. "I have a telegram for you."

Olenka had received telegrams from her husband before; but this time, somehow, she was numbed with terror. She opened the telegram with trembling hands and read:

"Ivan Petrovich died suddenly to-day. Awaiting propt orders for wuneral Tuesday."

That was the way the telegram was written —"wuneral"—and another unintelligible word— "propt." The telegram was signed by the manager of the opera company.

"My dearest!" Olenka burst out sobbing. "Vanichka, my dearest, my sweetheart. Why did I ever meet you? Why did I ever get to know and love you? To whom have you abandoned your poor Olenka, your poor, unhappy Olenka?"

Kukin was buried on Tuesday in the Vagankov Cemetery in Moscow. Olenka returned home on Wednesday; and as soon as she entered her house she threw herself on her bed and broke into such loud sobbing that she could be heard in the street and in the neighbouring yards.

"The darling!" said the neighbours, crossing themselves. "How Olga Semyonovna, the poor darling, is grieving!"

Three months afterwards Olenka was returning home from mass, downhearted and in deep mourning. Beside her walked a man also returning from church, Vasily Pustovalov, the manager of the merchant Babakayev's lumber-yard. He was wearing a straw hat, a white vest with a gold chain, and looked more like a landowner than a business man.

"Everything has its ordained course, Olga Semyonovna," he said sedately, with sympathy in his voice. "And if any one near and dear to us dies, then it means it was God's will and we should remember that and bear it with submission."

He took her to the wicket-gate, said good-bye and went away. After that she heard his sedate voice the whole day; and on closing her eyes she instantly had a vision of his dark beard. She took a great liking to him. And evidently he had been impressed by her, too; for, not long after, an elderly woman, a distant acquaintance, came in to have a cup of coffee with her. As soon as the woman was seated at table she began to speak about Pustovalov—how good he was, what a steady man, and any woman could be glad to get him as a husband. Three days later Pustovalov himself paid Olenka a visit. He stayed only about ten minutes, and spoke little, but Olenka fell in love with him, fell in love so desperately that she did not sleep the whole night and burned as with fever. In the morning she sent for the elderly woman. Soon after, Olenka and Pustovalov were engaged, and the wedding followed.

Pustovalov and Olenka lived happily together. He usually stayed in the lumber-yard until dinner, then went out on business. In his absence, Olenka took his place in the office until evening, attending to the book-keeping and despatching the orders.

"Lumber rises twenty per cent every year nowadays," she told her customers and acquaintances. "Imagine, we used to buy wood from our forests here. Now Vasichka has to go every year to the government of Mogilev to get wood. And what a tax!" she exclaimed, covering her cheeks with her hands in terror. "What a tax!"

She felt as if she had been dealing in lumber for ever so long, that the most important and essential thing in life was lumber. There was something touching and endearing in the way she pronounced the words, "beam," "joist," "plank," "stave," "lath," "gun-carriage," "clamp." At night she dreamed of whole mountains of boards and planks, long, endless rows of wagons conveying the wood somewhere, far, far from the city. She dreamed that a whole regiment of beams, 36 ft. x 5 in., were advancing in an upright position to do battle against the lumber-yard; that the beams and joists and clamps were knocking against each other, emitting the sharp crackling reports of dry wood, that they were all falling and then rising again, piling on top of each other. Olenka cried out in her sleep, and Pustovalov said to her gently:

"Olenka my dear, what is the matter? Cross yourself."

Her husband's opinions were all hers. If he thought the room was too hot, she thought so too. If he thought business was dull, she thought business was dull. Pustovalov was not fond of amusements and stayed home on holidays, she did the same.

"You are always either at home or in the office," said her friends. "Why don't you go to the theatre or to the circus, darling?"

"Vasichka and I never go to the theatre," she answered sedately. "We have work to do, we have no time for nonsense. What does one get out of going to theatre?"

On Saturdays she and Pustovalov went to vespers, and on holidays to early mass. On returning home they walked side by side with rapt faces, an agreeable smell emanating from both of them and her silk dress rustling pleasantly. At home they drank tea with milk-bread and various jams, and then ate pie. Every day at noontime there was an appetising odour in the yard and outside the gate of cabbage soup, roast mutton, or duck; and, on fast days, of fish. You couldn't pass the gate without being seized by an acute desire to eat. The samovar was always boiling on the office table, and customers were treated to tea and biscuits. Once a week the married couple went to the baths and returned with red faces, walking side by side.

"We are getting along very well, thank God," said Olenka to her friends. "God grant that all should live as well as Vasichka and I."

When Pustovalov went to the government of Mogilev to buy wood, she was dreadfully homesick for him, did not sleep nights, and cried. Sometimes the veterinary surgeon of the regiment, Smirnov, a young man who lodged in the wing of her house, came to see her evenings. He related incidents, or they played cards together. This distracted her. The most interesting of his stories were those of his own life. He was married and had a son; but he had separated from his wife because she had deceived him, and now he hated her and sent her forty rubles a month for his son's support. Olenka sighed, shook her head, and was sorry for him.

"Well, the Lord keep you," she said, as she saw him off to the door by candlelight. "Thank you for coming to kill time with me. May God give you health. Mother in Heaven!" She spoke very

sedately, very judiciously, imitating her husband. The veterinary surgeon had disappeared behind the door when she called out after him: "Do you know, Vladimir Platonych, you ought to make up with your wife. Forgive her, if only for the sake of your son. The child understands everything, you may be sure."

When Pustovalov returned, she told him in a low voice about the veterinary surgeon and his unhappy family life; and they sighed and shook their heads, and talked about the boy who must be homesick for his father. Then, by a strange association of ideas, they both stopped before the sacred images, made genuflections, and prayed to God to send them children.

And so the Pustovalovs lived for full six years, quietly and peaceably, in perfect love and harmony. But once in the winter Vasily Andreyich, after drinking some hot tea, went out into the lumberyard without a hat on his head, caught a cold and took sick. He was treated by the best physicians, but the malady progressed, and he died after an illness of four months. Olenka was again left a widow.

"To whom have you left me, my darling?" she wailed after the funeral. "How shall I live now without you, wretched creature that I am. Pity me, good people, pity me, fatherless and motherless, all alone in the world!"

She went about dressed in black and weepers, and she gave up wearing hats and gloves for good. She hardly left the house except to go to church and to visit her husband's grave. She almost led the life of a nun.

It was not until six months had passed that she took off the weepers and opened her shutters. She began to go out occasionally in the morning to market with her cook. But how she lived at home and what went on there, could only be surmised. It could be surmised from the fact that she was seen in her little garden drinking tea with the veterinarian while he read the paper out loud to her, and also from the fact that once on meeting an acquaintance at the post-office, she said to her:

"There is no proper veterinary inspection in our town. That is why there is so much disease. You constantly hear of people getting sick from the milk and becoming infected by the horses and cows. The health of domestic animals ought really to be looked after as much as that of human beings."

She repeated the veterinarian's words and held the same opinions as he about everything. It was plain that she could not exist a single year without an attachment, and she found her new happiness in the wing of her house. In any one else this would have been condemned; but no one could think ill of Olenka. Everything in her life was so transparent. She and the veterinary surgeon never spoke about the change in their relations. They tried, in fact, to conceal it, but unsuccessfully; for Olenka could have no secrets. When the surgeon's colleagues from the regiment came to see him, she poured tea, and served the supper, and talked to them about the cattle plague, the foot and mouth disease, and the municipal slaughter houses. The surgeon was dreadfully embarrassed, and after the visitors had left, he caught her hand and hissed angrily:

"Didn't I ask you not to talk about what you don't understand? When we doctors discuss things, please don't mix in. It's getting to be a nuisance."

She looked at him in astonishment and alarm, and asked:

"But, Volodichka, what *am* I to talk about?" And she threw her arms round his neck, with tears in her eyes, and begged him not to be angry. And they were both happy.

But their happiness was of short duration. The veterinary surgeon went away with his regiment to be gone for good, when it was transferred to some distant place almost as far as Siberia, and Olenka was left alone.

Now she was completely alone. Her father had long been dead, and his armchair lay in the attic covered with dust and minus one leg. She got thin and homely, and the people who met her on the street no longer looked at her as they had used to, nor smiled at her. Evidently her best years were over, past and gone, and a new, dubious life was to begin which it were better not to think about.

In the evening Olenka sat on the steps and heard the music playing and the rockets bursting in the Tivoli; but it no longer aroused any response in her. She looked listlessly into the yard, thought of nothing, wanted nothing, and when night came on, she went to bed and dreamed of nothing but the empty yard. She ate and drank as though by compulsion.

And what was worst of all, she no longer held any opinions. She saw and understood everything that went on around her, but she could not form an opinion about it. She knew of nothing to talk about. And how dreadful not to have opinions! For instance, you see a bottle, or you see that it is raining, or you see a muzhik riding by in a wagon. But what the bottle or the rain or the muzhik are

for, or what the sense of them all is, you cannot tell—you cannot tell, not for a thousand rubles. In the days of Kukin and Pustovalov and then of the veterinary surgeon, Olenka had had an explanation for everything, and would have given her opinion freely no matter about what. But now there was the same emptiness in her heart and brain as in her yard. It was as galling and bitter as a taste of wormwood.

Gradually the town grew up all around. The Gypsy Road had become a street, and where the Tivoli and the lumber-yard had been, there were now houses and a row of side streets. How quickly time flies! Olenka's house turned gloomy, the roof rusty, the shed slanting. Dock and thistles overgrew the yard. Olenka herself had aged and grown homely. In the summer she sat on the steps, and her soul was empty and dreary and bitter. When she caught the breath of spring, or when the wind wafted the chime of the cathedral bells, a sudden flood of memories would pour over her, her heart would expand with a tender warmth, and the tears would stream down her cheeks. But that lasted only a moment. Then would come emptiness again, and the feeling, What is the use of living? The black kitten Bryska rubbed up against her and purred softly, but the little creature's caresses left Olenka untouched. That was not what she needed. What she needed was a love that would absorb her whole being, her reason, her whole soul, that would give her ideas, an object in life, that would warm her aging blood. And she shook the black kitten off her skirt angrily, saying:

"Go away! What are you doing here?"

And so day after day, year after year not a single joy, not a single opinion. Whatever Marva, the cook, said was all right.

One hot day in July, towards evening, as the town cattle were being driven by, and the whole yard was filled with clouds of dust, there was suddenly a knocking at the gate. Olenka herself went to open it, and was dumbfounded to behold the veterinarian Smirnov. He had turned grey and was dressed as a civilian. All the old memories flooded into her soul, she could not restrain herself, she burst out crying, and laid her head on Smirnov's breast without saying a word. So overcome was she that she was totally unconscious of how they walked into the house and seated themselves to drink tea.

"My darling!" she murmured, trembling with joy. "Vladimir Platonych, from where has God sent you?"

"I want to settle here for good," he told her. "I

have resigned my position and have come here to try my fortune as a free man and lead a settled life. Besides, it's time to send my boy to the gymnasium. He is grown up now. You know my wife and I have become reconciled."

"Where is she?" asked Olenka.

"At the hotel with the boy. I am looking for lodgings."

"Good gracious, bless you, take my house. Why won't my house do? Oh, dear! Why, I won't ask any rent of you," Olenka burst out in the greatest excitement, and began to cry again. "You live here, and the wing will be enough for me. Oh, Heavens, what a joy!"

The very next day the roof was being painted and the walls whitewashed, and Olenka, arms akimbo, was going about the yard superintending. Her face brightened with her old smile. Her whole being revived and freshened, as though she had awakened from a long sleep. The veterinarian's wife and child arrived. She was a thin, plain woman, with a crabbed expression. The boy Sasha, small for his ten years of age, was a chubby child, with clear blue eyes and dimples in his cheeks. He made for the kitten the instant he entered the yard, and the place rang with his happy laughter.

"Is that your cat, auntie?" he asked Olenka. "When she has little kitties, please give me one. Mama is awfully afraid of mice."

Olenka chatted with him, gave him tea, and there was a sudden warmth in her bosom and a soft gripping at her heart, as though the boy were her own son.

In the evening, when he sat in the dining-room studying his lessons, she looked at him tenderly and whispered to herself:

"My darling, my pretty. You are such a clever child, so good to look at."

"An island is a tract of land entirely surrounded by water," he recited.

"An island is a tract of land," she repeated—the first idea asseverated with conviction after so many years of silence and mental emptiness.

She now had her opinions, and at supper discussed with Sasha's parents how difficult the studies had become for the children at the gymnasium, but how, after all, a classical education was better than a commercial course, because when you graduated from the gymnasium then the road was open to you for any career at all. If you chose to, you could become a doctor, or, if you wanted to, you could become an engineer.

Sasha began to go to the gymnasium. His mother left on a visit to her sister in Kharkov and never came back. The father was away every day inspecting cattle, and sometimes was gone three whole days at a time, so that Sasha, it seemed to Olenka, was utterly abandoned, was treated as if he were quite superfluous, and must be dying of hunger. So she transferred him into the wing along with herself and fixed up a little room for him there.

Every morning Olenka would come into his room and find him sound asleep with his hand tucked under his cheek, so quiet that he seemed not to be breathing. What a shame to have to wake him, she thought.

"Sashenka," she said sorrowingly, "get up, darling. It's time to go to the gymnasium."

He got up, dressed, said his prayers, then sat down to drink tea. He drank three glasses of tea, ate two large cracknels and half a buttered roll. The sleep was not yet out of him, so he was a little cross.

"You don't know your fable as you should, Sashenka," said Olenka, looking at him as though he were departing on a long journey. "What a lot of trouble you are. You must try hard and learn, dear, and mind your teachers."

"Oh, let me alone, please," said Sasha.

Then he went down the street to the gymnasium, a little fellow wearing a large cap and carrying a satchel on his back. Olenka followed him noiselessly.

"Sashenka," she called.

He looked round and she shoved a date or a caramel into his hand. When he reached the street of the gymnasium, he turned around and said, ashamed of being followed by a tall, stout woman: "You had better go home, aunt. I can go the rest of the way myself."

She stopped and stared after him until he had disappeared into the school entrance.

Oh, how she loved him! Not one of her other ties had been so deep. Never before had she given herself so completely, so disinterestedly, so cheerfully as now that her maternal instincts were all aroused. For this boy, who was not hers, for the dimples in his cheeks and for his big cap, she would have given her life, given it with joy and with tears of rapture. Why? Ah, indeed, why?

When she had seen Sasha off to the gymnasium, she returned home quietly, content, serene, overflowing with love. Her face, which had grown younger in the last half year, smiled and beamed. People who met her were pleased as they looked at her.

"How are you, Olga Semyonovna, darling? How are you getting on, darling?"

"The gymnasium course is very hard nowadays," she told at the market. "It's no joke. Yesterday the first class had a fable to learn by heart, a Latin translation, and a problem. How is a little fellow to do all that?"

And she spoke of the teacher and the lessons and the textbooks, repeating exactly what Sasha said about them.

At three o'clock they had dinner. In the evening they prepared the lessons together, and Olenka wept with Sasha over the difficulties. When she put him to bed, she lingered a long time making the sign of the cross over him and muttering a prayer. And when she lay in bed, she dreamed of the far-away, misty future when Sasha would finish his studies and become a doctor or an engineer, have a large house of his own, with horses and a carriage, marry and have children. She would fall asleep still thinking of the same things, and tears would roll down her cheeks from her closed eyes. And the black cat would lie at her side purring: "Mrr, mrr, mrr."

Suddenly there was a loud knocking at the gate. Olenka woke up breathless with fright, her heart beating violently. Half a minute later there was another knock.

"A telegram from Kharkov," she thought, her whole body in a tremble. "His mother wants Sasha to come to her in Kharkov. Oh, great God!"

She was in despair. Her head, her feet, her hands turned cold. There was no unhappier creature in the world, she felt. But another minute passed, she heard voices. It was the veterinarian coming home from the club.

"Thank God," she thought. The load gradually fell from her heart, she was at ease again. And she went back to bed, thinking of Sasha who lay fast asleep in the next room and sometimes cried out in his sleep:

"I'll give it to you! Get away! Quit your scrapping!"

———◆———

MAXIM GORKY

1868–1936

If Anton Chekhov is the "voice of twilight Russia," Aleksei Peshkov (better known by his pen name, Maxim Gorky) is the transitional figure. Gorky lived in three worlds: the underworld of Russian poverty and sullen revolutionary discon-

tent; the uneasy and apprehensive world of the Russian intellectual; and finally the world of the Soviet Union, wherein he was acclaimed as the founder of proletarian literature. The early, brutal experiences of Gorky as an orphan supplied him with ample background and material for his naturalistic fiction: he wrote of the strange nether world of the flophouses, the prisons, the bakers' cellars where drifted the human derelicts whose abject wretchedness was symptomatic of the pitifully inequable state of society in Old Russia. His short stories are the best chronicles of these experiences among the "creatures who once were men," for Gorky rarely attempted longer works, except for his novel *Mother* and his very successful play upon the Russian underworld, *The Lower Depths*, produced by Konstantin Stanislavsky at the Moscow Art Theater in 1902.

In his depiction of the hopeless agony of the Russian masses Gorky had no literary theories; he wrote sincerely, simply, indignantly of the conditions of squalor and repression that maimed the humanity of his fellow countrymen. Gorky was realist enough to recognize that intellectual and ideological convictions concerning the need for social reform may go hand in hand with intellectual snobbery and personal indifference to individual suffering. "One Autumn Night" reveals the awakening of the narrator, an eighteen-year-old boy, to that disinterested pity and deep compassion for the plight of Natasha which is a necessary preliminary step to the individual's more general commitment to the cause of the brotherhood of man.

FURTHER READING

GORKY, MAXIM. *Autobiography*, translated by Isidor Schneider (New York, 1949).
GORKY, MAXIM. *Literature and Life* (London, 1946).
MIRSKY, D. S. *Contemporary Russian Literature* (New York, 1926).
SLONIM, MARC. *The Epic of Russian Literature* (New York, 1950).

One Autumn Night *

ONCE in the autumn I happened to be in a very unpleasant and inconvenient position. In the town where I had just arrived and where I knew not a soul, I found myself without a farthing in my pocket and without a night's lodging.

* By permission of Random House, Inc.

Having sold during the first few days every part of my costume without which it was still possible to go about, I passed from the town into the quarter called "Yste," where were the steamship wharves—a quarter which during the navigation season fermented with boisterous, laborious life, but now was silent and deserted, for we were in the last days of October.

Dragging my feet along the moist sand, and obstinately scrutinising it with the desire to discover in it any sort of fragment of food, I wandered alone among the deserted buildings and warehouses, and thought how good it would be to get a full meal.

In our present state of culture hunger of the mind is more quickly satisfied than hunger of the body. You wander about the streets, you are surrounded by buildings not bad-looking from the outside and—you may safely say it—not so badly furnished inside, and the sight of them may excite within you stimulating ideas about architecture, hygiene, and many other wise and high-flying subjects. You may meet warmly and neatly dressed folks—all very polite, and turning away from you tactfully, not wishing offensively to notice the lamentable fact of your existence. Well, well, the mind of a hungry man is always better nourished and healthier than the mind of the well-fed man; and there you have a situation from which you may draw a very ingenious conclusion in favour of the ill fed.

The evening was approaching, the rain was falling, and the wind blew violently from the north. It whistled in the empty booths and shops, blew into the plastered windowpanes of the taverns, and whipped into foam the wavelets of the river which splashed noisily on the sandy shore, casting high their white crests, racing one after another into the dim distance, and leaping impetuously over one another's shoulders. It seemed as if the river felt the proximity of winter, and was running at random away from the fetters of ice which the north wind might well have flung upon her that very night. The sky was heavy and dark; down from it swept incessantly scarcely visible drops of rain, and the melancholy elegy in nature all around me was emphasised by a couple of battered and misshapen willow-trees and a boat, bottom upwards, that was fastened to their roots.

The overturned canoe with its battered keel and the miserable old trees rifled by the cold wind—everything around me was bankrupt, barren, and dead, and the sky flowed with undryable tears. . . . Everything around was waste and gloomy . . . it

seemed as if everything were dead, leaving me alone among the living, and for me also a cold death waited.

I was then eighteen years old—a good time!

I walked and walked along the cold wet sand, making my chattering teeth warble in honour of cold and hunger, when suddenly, as I was carefully searching for something to eat behind one of the empty crates, I perceived behind it, crouching on the ground, a figure in woman's clothes dank with the rain and clinging fast to her stooping shoulders. Standing over her, I watched to see what she was doing. It appeared that she was digging a trench in the sand with her hands—digging away under one of the crates.

"Why are you doing that?" I asked, crouching down on my heels quite close to her.

She gave a little scream and was quickly on her legs again. Now that she stood there staring at me, with her wide-open grey eyes full of terror, I perceived that it was a girl of my own age, with a very pleasant face embellished unfortunately by three large blue marks. This spoilt her, although these blue marks had been distributed with a remarkable sense of proportion, one at a time, and all were of equal size—two under the eyes, and one a little bigger on the forehead just over the bridge of the nose. This symmetry was evidently the work of an artist well inured to the business of spoiling the human physiognomy.

The girl looked at me, and the terror in her eyes gradually died out. . . . She shook the sand from her hands, adjusted her cotton head-gear, cowered down, and said:

"I suppose you too want something to eat? Dig away then! My hands are tired. Over there"—she nodded her head in the direction of a booth—"there is bread for certain . . . and sausages too. . . . That booth is still carrying on business."

I began to dig. She, after waiting a little and looking at me, sat down beside me and began to help me.

We worked in silence. I cannot say now whether I thought at that moment of the criminal code, of morality, of proprietorship, and all the other things about which, in the opinion of many experienced persons, one ought to think every moment of one's life. Wishing to keep as close to the truth as possible, I must confess that apparently I was so deeply engaged in digging under the crate that I completely forgot about everything else except this one thing: What could be inside that crate?

The evening drew on. The grey, mouldy, cold

fog grew thicker and thicker around us. The waves roared with a hollower sound than before, and the rain pattered down on the boards of that crate more loudly and more frequently. Somewhere or other the night-watchman began springing his rattle.

"Has it got a bottom or not?" softly inquired my assistant. I did not understand what she was talking about, and I kept silence.

"I say, has the crate got a bottom? If it has we shall try in vain to break into it. Here we are digging a trench, and we may, after all, come upon nothing but solid boards. How shall we take them off? Better smash the lock; it is a wretched lock."

Good ideas rarely visit the heads of women, but, as you see, they do visit them sometimes. I have always valued good ideas, and have always tried to utilise them as far as possible.

Having found the lock, I tugged at it and wrenched off the whole thing. My accomplice immediately stooped down and wriggled like a serpent into the gaping-open, four-cornered cover of the crate whence she called to me approvingly, in a low tone:

"You're a brick!"

Nowadays a little crumb of praise from a woman is dearer to me than a whole dithyramb from a man, even though he be more eloquent than all the ancient and modern orators put together. Then, however, I was less amiably disposed than I am now, and, paying no attention to the compliment of my comrade, I asked her curtly and anxiously:

"Is there anything?"

In a monotonous tone she set about calculating our discoveries.

"A basketful of bottles—thick furs—a sunshade—an iron pail."

All this was uneatable. I felt my hopes had vanished. . . . But suddenly she exclaimed vivaciously:

"Aha! here it is!"

"What?"

"Bread . . . a loaf . . . it's only wet . . . take it!"

A loaf flew to my feet and after it herself, my valiant comrade. I had already bitten off a morsel, stuffed it in my mouth, and was chewing it. . . .

"Come, give me some too! . . . And we mustn't stay here. . . . Where shall we go?" she looked inquiringly about on all sides. . . . It was dark, wet, and boisterous.

"Look! there's an upset canoe yonder . . . let us go there."

"Let us go then!" And off we set, demolishing our booty as we went, and filling our mouths with large portions of it. . . . The rain grew more violent, the river roared; from somewhere or other resounded a prolonged mocking whistle—just as if Someone great who feared nobody was whistling down all earthly institutions and along with them this horrid autumnal wind and us its heroes. This whistling made my heart throb painfully, in spite of which I greedily went on eating, and in this respect the girl, walking on my left hand, kept even pace with me.

"What do they call you?" I asked her—why I know not.

"Natasha," she answered shortly, munching loudly.

I stared at her. My heart ached within me; and then I stared into the mist before me, and it seemed to me as if the inimical countenance of my Destiny was smiling at me enigmatically and coldly.

. . .

The rain scourged the timbers of the skiff incessantly, and its soft patter induced melancholy thoughts, and the wind whistled as it flew down into the boat's battered bottom through a rift, where some loose splinters of wood were rattling together—a disquieting and depressing sound. The waves of the river were splashing on the shore, and sounded so monotonous and hopeless, just as if they were telling something unbearably dull and heavy, which was boring them into utter disgust, something from which they wanted to run away and yet were obliged to talk about all the same. The sound of the rain blended with their splashing, and a long-drawn sigh seemed to be floating above the overturned skiff—the endless, labouring sigh of the earth, injured and exhausted by the eternal changes from the bright and warm summer to the cold misty and damp autumn. The wind blew continually over the desolate shore and the foaming river—blew and sang its melancholy songs. . . .

Our position beneath the shelter of the skiff was utterly devoid of comfort; it was narrow and damp, tiny cold drops of rain dribbled through the damaged bottom; gusts of wind penetrated it. We sat in silence and shivered with cold. I remembered that I wanted to go to sleep. Natasha leaned her back against the hull of the boat and curled herself up into a tiny ball. Embracing her knees with her hands, and resting her chin upon them, she stared doggedly at the river with wide-open eyes; on the pale patch of her face they seemed immense, because of the blue marks below them. She never moved, and this immobility and silence—I felt it—

gradually produced within me a terror of my neighbour. I wanted to talk to her, but I knew not how to begin.

It was she herself who spoke.

"What a cursed thing life is!" she exclaimed plainly, abstractedly, and in a tone of deep conviction.

But this was no complaint. In these words there was too much of indifference for a complaint. This simple soul thought according to her understanding—thought and proceeded to form a certain conclusion which she expressed aloud, and which I could not confute for fear of contradicting myself. Therefore I was silent, and she, as if she had not noticed me, continued to sit there immovable.

"Even if we croaked . . . what then . . . ?" Natasha began again, this time quietly and reflectively, and still there was not one note of complaint in her words. It was plain that this person, in the course of her reflections on life, was regarding her own case, and had arrived at the conviction that in order to preserve herself from the mockeries of life, she was not in a position to do anything else but simply "croak"—to use her own expression.

The clearness of this line of thought was inexpressibly sad and painful to me, and I felt that if I kept silence any longer I was really bound to weep. . . . And it would have been shameful to have done this before a woman, especially as she was not weeping herself. I resolved to speak to her.

"Who was it that knocked you about?" I asked. For the moment I could not think of anything more sensible or more delicate.

"Pashka did it all," she answered in a dull and level tone.

"And who is he?"

"My lover. . . . He was a baker."

"Did he beat you often?"

"Whenever he was drunk he beat me. . . . Often!"

And suddenly, turning towards me, she began to talk about herself, Pashka, and their mutual relations. He was a baker with red moustaches and played very well on the banjo. He came to see her and greatly pleased her, for he was a merry chap and wore nice clean clothes. He had a vest which cost fifteen rubles and boots with dress tops. For these reasons she had fallen in love with him, and he became her "creditor." And when he became her creditor he made it his business to take away from her the money which her other friends gave to her for bonbons, and, getting drunk on this money, he would fall to beating her; but that would have been

nothing if he hadn't also begun to "run after" other girls before her very eyes.

"Now, wasn't that an insult? I am not worse than the others. Of course that meant that he was laughing at me, the blackguard. The day before yesterday I asked leave of my mistress to go out for a bit, went to him, and there I found Dimka sitting beside him drunk. And he, too, was half seas over. I said, 'You scoundrel, you!' And he gave me a thorough hiding. He kicked me and dragged me by the hair. But that was nothing to what came after. He spoiled everything I had on—left me just as I am now! How could I appear before my mistress? He spoiled everything . . . my dress and my jacket too—it was quite a new one; I gave a fiver for it . . . and tore my kerchief from my head. . . . Oh, Lord. What will become of me now?" she suddenly whined in a lamentable overstrained voice.

The wind howled, and became ever colder and more boisterous. . . . Again my teeth began to dance up and down, and she, huddled up to avoid the cold, pressed as closely to me as she could, so that I could see the gleam of her eyes through the darkness.

"What wretches all you men are! I'd burn you all in an oven; I'd cut you in pieces. If any one of you was dying I'd spit in his mouth, and not pity him a bit. Mean skunks! You wheedle and wheedle, you wag your tails like cringing dogs, and we fools give ourselves up to you, and it's all up with us! Immediately you trample us underfoot. . . . Miserable loafers!"

She cursed us up and down, but there was no vigour, no malice, no hatred of these "miserable loafers" in her cursing that I could hear. The tone of her language by no means corresponded with its subject-matter, for it was calm enough, and the gamut of her voice was terribly poor.

Yet all this made a stronger impression on me than the most eloquent and convincing pessimistic books and speeches, of which I had read a good many and which I still read to this day. And this, you see, was because the agony of a dying person is much more natural and violent than the most minute and picturesque descriptions of death.

I felt really wretched—more from cold than from the words of my neighbour. I groaned softly and ground my teeth.

Almost at the same moment I felt two little arms about me—one of them touched my neck and the other lay upon my face—and at the same time an anxious, gentle, friendly voice uttered the question:

"What ails you?"

I was ready to believe that someone else was asking me this and not Natasha, who had just declared that all men were scoundrels, and expressed a wish for their destruction. But she it was, and now she began speaking quickly, hurriedly.

"What ails you, eh? Are you cold? Are you frozen? Ah, what a one you are, sitting there so silent like a little owl! Why, you should have told me long ago that you were cold. Come . . . lie on the ground . . . stretch yourself out and I will lie . . . there! How's that? Now put your arms round me? . . . tighter! How's that? You shall be warm very soon now. . . . And then we'll lie back to back. . . . The night will pass so quickly, see if it won't. I say . . . have you too been drinking? . . . Turned out of your place, eh? . . . It doesn't matter."

And she comforted me. . . . She encouraged me.

May I be thrice accursed! What a world of irony was in this single fact for me! Just imagine! Here was I, seriously occupied at this very time with the destiny of humanity, thinking of the re-organisation of the social system, of political revolutions, reading all sorts of devilishly-wise books whose abysmal profundity was certainly unfathomable by their very authors—at this very time. I say, I was trying with all my might to make of myself "a potent active social force." It even seemed to me that I had partially accomplished my object; anyhow, at this time, in my ideas about myself, I had got so far as to recognise that I had an exclusive right to exist, that I had the necessary greatness to deserve to live my life, and that I was fully competent to play a great historical part therein. And a woman was now warming me with her body, a wretched, battered, hunted creature, who had no place and no value in life, and whom I had never thought of helping till she helped me herself, and whom I really would not have known how to help in any way even if the thought of it had occurred to me.

Ah! I was ready to think that all this was happening to me in a dream—in a disagreeable, an oppressive dream.

But, ugh! it was impossible for me to think that, for cold drops of rain were dripping down upon me, the woman was pressing close to me, her warm breath was fanning my face, and—despite a slight odor of vodka—it did me good. The wind howled and raged, the rain smote upon the skiff, the waves splashed, and both of us, embracing each other convulsively, nevertheless shivered with cold. All this was only too real, and I am certain that nobody ever dreamed such an oppressive and horrid dream as that reality.

But Natasha was talking all the time of something or other, talking kindly and sympathetically, as only women can talk. Beneath the influence of her voice and kindly words a little fire began to burn up within me, and something inside my heart thawed in consequence.

Then tears poured from my eyes like a hailstorm, washing away from my heart much that was evil, much that was stupid, much sorrow and dirt which had fastened upon it before that night. Natasha comforted me.

"Come, come, that will do, little one! Don't take on! That'll do! God will give you another chance . . . you will right yourself and stand in your proper place again . . . and it will be all right. . . ."

And she kept kissing me . . . many kisses did she give me . . . burning kisses . . . and all for nothing. . . .

Those were the first kisses from a woman that had ever been bestowed upon me, and they were the best kisses too, for all the subsequent kisses cost me frightfully dear, and really gave me nothing at all in exchange.

"Come, don't take on so, funny one! I'll manage for you to-morrow if you cannot find a place." Her quiet persuasive whispering sounded in my ears as if it came through a dream. . . .

There we lay till dawn. . . .

And when the dawn came, we crept from behind the skiff and went into the town. . . . Then we took friendly leave of each other and never met again, although for half a year I searched in every hole and corner for that kind Natasha, with whom I spent the autumn night just described.

If she be already dead—and well for her if it were so—may she rest in peace! And if she be alive . . . still I say "Peace to her soul!" And may the consciousness of her fall never enter her soul . . . for that would be a superfluous and fruitless suffering if life is to be lived. . . .

Russian Lyric Poetry

ALEKSANDER SERGEEVICH PUSHKIN [1]

To Chaadayev [2]

Not long we basked in the illusions
Of love, of hope, of tranquil fame;
Like morning mist, like dreams' delusions,
Youth's pastimes vanished as they came.
But still, with strong desires burning,
Beneath oppression's fearful hand,
The bidding of the fatherland
We are impatiently discerning;
In hope, in torment, we are turning
Toward freedom, wishing she were near,
As a young lover waits his dear
And looks and longs, consumed with yearning.
While freedom fires the blood, and now
While honor summons us—O hear it!
Friend, to our country let us vow
The noble strivings of the spirit.
Comrade, believe: joy's star will leap
Upon our sight, a radiant token;
Russia will rouse from her long sleep;
And where autocracy lies broken,
Our names shall yet be graven deep.

Grapes

I shall not miss the roses, fading
As soon as spring's fleet days are done;
I love the grapes whose clusters ripen
Upon the hillsides in the sun—
The glory of my fertile valley,

They hang, each lustrous as a pearl,
Gold autumn's joy, oblong, transparent,
Like the slim fingers of a girl.

"With Freedom's Seed"

"Behold, a sower went forth to sow."

With freedom's seed the desert sowing,
I walked before the morning star;
With pure and guiltless fingers throwing—
Where slavish plows had left a scar—
The living seed that should have quickened,
But hope, at last grown weary, sickened
To learn how sad lost labors are. . . .
Graze if you will, you peaceful nations,
Who never rouse at honor's horn!
Should flocks heed freedom's invocations?
Their part is to be slain or shorn,
And wear the bells tame sires have worn
Through whipped and sheeplike generations.

"The Man I Was of Old"

Tel j'étais autrefois et tel je suis encore.[3]

The man I was of old, that man I still remain:
Lighthearted, quick to fall in love. My friends, 'tis vain
To think I can behold the fair without elation
And timid tenderness and secret agitation.
Has love not played with me and teased me quite enough?
In Cytherea's nets wrought of such sturdy stuff,
Like a young hawk have I not struggled long and striven?
Unchastened by the pangs whereby I have been driven,
Unto new idols I my old entreaties bring. . . .

"Along the Noisy Streets"

Along the noisy streets I wander,
A church invites me, it may be,
Or with mad youths my time I squander,
And still these thoughts are haunting me:

[1] The following poems are reprinted from *A Treasury of Russian Verse*, edited by Avrahm Yarmolinsky, The Macmillian Company, New York. Copyright, 1949. By permission of the editor and of Babette Deutsch, the translator. For biographical material on Pushkin, see p. 616.

[2] Peter Chaadayev (1794-1856), aristocrat and friend of Pushkin, was associated with a group of enlightened, humanitarian officers in the Imperial Guard wishing to reform the laws and constitution of Russia. They helped to foster the abortive rising of December, 1825, against the new czar, Nicholas I.

[3] From André Chénier.

This year will fly, the next will follow
As fast, and all whom you see here
Eternity at last will swallow;
For some the hour is drawing near.

When I behold a lone oak thriving
I think: age dooms me to decay,
This patriarch, though, will be surviving
As it survived my fathers' day.

If I caress a babe, I'm thinking:
Farewell, too soon I must make room
For you, and out of sight be sinking—
My time to fade is yours to bloom.

Each day, each year in thought addressing,
I ask in turn ere it flits past
How it will be remembered, guessing
Which shall be reckoned as my last.

And when fate strikes, where will it find me?
In battle, on the road, at sea?
Will that near valley be assigned me
Where my cold clay at home may be?

The witless body's unaffected,
Nor recks where it must rot, 'tis clear,
Yet in my heart I have elected
To lie near places once held dear.

Then, even at the grave's grim portal
Let young life play with careless grace,

And neutral Nature her immortal
Beauty spread round my resting place.

"Abandoning an Alien Country"

Abandoning an alien country,
You have sought your distant native land;
How could I stop the tears at parting
When sorrow was beyond command?
With hands that momently grew colder
I tried to hold you, wordlessly
I begged that our farewells, our anguish,
Might be prolonged eternally.

But from the bitter kiss and clinging
You tore away your lips; and from
The gloomy land of lonely exile
To a new country bade me come.
You said: "When we are reunited,
Beneath a sky of endless blue,
In the soft shadow of the olives,
Then, lip to lip, I'll solace you."

But yonder, where the blue is radiant,
And where the olives from the shore
Cast tender shadows on the waters,
You fell asleep, to wake no more.
Within the funeral urn your beauty
Lies hidden with your suffering now—
But the sweet kiss of our reunion
I wait . . . I hold you to your vow.

French Fiction

HONORÉ DE BALZAC

1799–1850

Balzac, representative of the realistic movement in French literature, was an indefatigable worker who regularly spent twelve to eighteen hours a day at his desk, keeping himself alert by consuming innumerable cups of strong coffee. Within the space of twenty short years he composed *La Comédie Humaine*, a series of novels which together are probably the most powerful work in nineteenth-century French literature. Balzac was by nature vulgar, robust, energetic, exuberant, and controlled by a fundamental need for feverish activity. *The Human Comedy* is a vast panorama of French society at the end of the Empire, under the Restoration, and under the July Monarchy. It is composed of numerous short stories and twenty-four long novels. All environments, all professions, all social classes are given full attention. The whole series is joined together by a system of reappearing characters, each of whom has a well-defined personality and position in life. Although *La Comédie Humaine* was by no means completed, when Balzac died he was literally worn out by his ceaseless labor.

The Human Comedy is the earliest and most conspicuous example of French realism, for it was Balzac's purpose to leave nothing to the imagination of the reader. He felt it was necessary for him to describe everything fully, drawing on his encyclopedic (but often faulty) knowledge of a multitude of subjects. He devoted infinite care and the most elaborate description to the most minute details, but he succeeded as much as anyone ever has in conveying an impression of lifelike reality.

FURTHER READING

BELLESSORT, A. *Balzac et son Oeuvre* (Paris, 1924).
DARGAN, E. P. *Honoré de Balzac, a Force of Nature* (Chicago, 1932).
ZWEIG, STEFAN. *Balzac*, translated by William and Dorothy Rose (New York, 1946).

The Conscript *

(*Le Requisitionnaire*)

[The inner self].......by a phenomenon of vision or of locomotion has been known at times to abolish Space in its two modes of Time and Distance—the one intellectual, the other physical.
—HISTORY OF LOUIS LAMBERT.

ON a November evening in the year 1793 the principal citizens of Carentan were assembled in Mme. de Dey's drawing-room. Mme. de Dey held this reception every night of the week, but an unwonted interest attached to this evening's gathering, owing to certain circumstances which would have passed altogether unnoticed in a great city, though in a small country town they excited the greatest curiosity. For two days before Mme. de Dey had not been at home to her visitors, and on the previous evening her door had been shut, on the ground of indisposition. Two such events at any ordinary time would have produced in Carentan the same sensation that Paris knows on nights when there is no performance at the theatres—existence is in some way incomplete; but in those times when the least indiscretion on the part of an aristocrat might be a matter of life and death, this conduct of Mme. de Dey's was likely to bring about the most disastrous

* Translated by Ellen Marriage.

consequences for her. Her position in Carentan ought to be made clear, if the reader is to appreciate the expression of keen curiosity and cunning fanaticism on the countenances of these Norman citizens, and, what is of most importance, the part that the lady played among them. Many a one during the days of the Revolution had doubtless passed through a crisis as difficult as hers at that moment, and the sympathies of more than one reader will fill in all the coloring of the picture.

Mme. de Dey was the widow of a lieutenant-general, a knight of the Orders of Saint Michael and of the Holy Ghost. She had left the Court when the emigration began, and had taken refuge in the neighborhood of Carentan, where she had large estates, hoping that the influence of the Reign of Terror would be but little felt there. Her calculations, based on a thorough knowledge of the district, proved correct. The Revolution made little disturbance in Lower Normandy. Formerly, when Mme. de Dey had spent any time in the country, her circle of acquaintance had been confined to the noble families of the district; but now, from politic motives, she opened her house to the principal citizens and to the Revolutionary authorities of the town, endeavoring to touch and gratify their social pride without arousing either hatred or jealousy. Gracious and kindly, possessed of the indescribable charm that wins good-will without loss of dignity or effort to pay court to any, she had succeeded in gaining universal esteem; the discreet warnings of exquisite tact enabled her to steer a difficult course among the exacting claims of this mixed society, without wounding the overweening self-love of parvenues on the one hand, or the susceptibilities of her old friends on the other. In a word, Mme. de Dey commanded the respect of all circles of society.

She was about thirty-eight years of age, and still preserved, not the fresh, high-colored beauty of the Basse-Normandes, but a fragile loveliness of what may be called an aristocratic type. Her figure was lissome and slender, her features delicate and clearly cut; the pale face seemed to light up and live when she spoke; but there was a quiet and devout look in the great dark eyes, for all their graciousness of expression—a look that seemed to say that the springs of her life lay without her own existence.

In her early girlhood she had been married to an elderly and jealous soldier. Her false position in the midst of a gay Court had doubtless done something to bring a veil of sadness over a face that must once have been bright with the charms of quick-pulsed life and love. She had been compelled to set constant restraint upon her frank impulses and emotions at an age when a woman feels rather than thinks, and the depths of passion in her heart had never been stirred. In this lay the secret of her greatest charm, a youthfulness of the inmost soul, betrayed at times by her face, and a certain tinge of innocent wistfulness in her ideas. She was reserved in her demeanor, but in her bearing and in the tones of her voice there was still something that told of girlish longings directed toward a vague future. Before very long the least susceptible fell in love with her, and yet stood somewhat in awe of her dignity and high-bred manner. Her great soul, strengthened by the cruel ordeals through which she had passed, seemed to set her too far above the ordinary level, and these men weighed themselves, and instinctively felt that they were found wanting. Such a nature demanded an exalted passion.

Moreover, Mme. de Dey's affections were concentrated in one sentiment—a mother's love for her son. All the happiness and joy that she had not known as a wife, she had found later in her boundless love for him. The coquetry of a mistress, the jealousy of a wife mingled with the pure and deep affection of a mother. She was miserable when they were apart, and nervous about him while he was away; she could never see enough of him, and lived through and for him alone.

Some idea of the strength of this tie may be conveyed to the masculine understanding by stating that this was not only Mme. de Dey's only son, but all she had of kith or kin in the world, the one human being on earth bound to her by all the fears and hopes and joys of her life.

The late Comte de Dey was the last of his race, and she, his wife, was the sole heiress and descendant of her house. So worldly ambitions and family considerations, as well as the noblest cravings of the soul, combined to heighten in the Countess a sentiment that is strong in every woman's heart. The child was all the dearer, because only with infinite care had she succeeded in rearing him to man's estate; medical science had predicted his death a score of times, but she had held fast to her presentiments and her hopes, and had known the inexpressible joy of watching him pass safely through the perils of infancy, of seeing his constitution strengthen in spite of the decrees of the Faculty.

Thanks to her constant care, the boy had grown up and developed so favorably, that at twenty years of age he was regarded as one of the most accomplished gentlemen at the Court of Versailles. One final happiness that does not always crown a

mother's efforts was hers—her son worshipped her; and between these two there was the deep sympathy of kindred souls. If they had not been bound to each other already by a natural and sacred tie, they would instinctively have felt for each other a friendship that is rarely met with between two men.

At the age of eighteen, the young Count had received an appointment as sub-lieutenant in a regiment of dragoons, and had made it a point of honor to follow the emigrant Princes into exile.

Then Mme. de Dey faced the dangers of her cruel position. She was rich, noble, and the mother of an emigrant. With the one desire to look after her son's great fortune, she had denied herself the happiness of being with him; and when she read the rigorous laws in virtue of which the Republic was daily confiscating the property of emigrants at Carentan, she congratulated herself on the courageous course that she had taken. Was she not keeping watch over the wealth of her son at the risk of her life? Later, when news came of the horrible executions ordered by the Convention, she slept, happy in the knowledge that her own treasure was in safety, out of reach of peril, far from the scaffolds of the Revolution. She loved to think that she had followed the best course, that she had saved her darling and her darling's fortunes; and to this secret thought she made such concessions as the misfortunes of the times demanded, without compromising her dignity or her aristocratic tenets, and enveloped her sorrows in reserve and mystery. She had foreseen the difficulties that would beset her at Carentan. Did she not tempt the scaffold by the very fact of going thither to take a prominent place? Yet, sustained by a mother's courage, she succeeded in winning the affection of the poor, ministering without distinction to every one in trouble; and made herself necessary to the well-to-do, by providing amusements for them.

The procureur of the commune might be seen at her house, the mayor, the president of the district, and the public prosecutor, and even the judges of the Revolutionary tribunals went there. The four first-named gentlemen were none of them married, and each paid court to her, in the hope that Mme. de Dey would take him for her husband, either from fear of making an enemy or from a desire to find a protector.

The public prosecutor, once an attorney at Caen, and the Countess' man of business, did what he could to inspire love by a system of devotion and generosity, a dangerous game of cunning! He was the most formidable of all her suitors. He alone knew the amount of the large fortune of his sometime client, and his fervor was inevitably increased by the cupidity of greed, and by the consciousness that he wielded an enormous power, the power of life and death in the district. He was still a young man, and, owing to the generosity of his behavior, Mme. de Dey was unable as yet to estimate him truly. But, in despite of the danger of matching herself against Norman cunning, she used all the craft and inventiveness that nature has bestowed on women to play off the rival suitors one against another. She hoped, by gaining time, to emerge safe and sound from her difficulties at last; for at that time Royalists in the provinces flattered themselves with a hope, daily renewed, that the morrow would see the end of the Revolution—a conviction that proved fatal to many of them.

In spite of difficulties, the Countess had maintained her independence with considerable skill until the day, when, by an inexplicable want of prudence, she took occasion to close her salon. So deep and sincere was the interest that she inspired, that those who usually filled her drawing-room felt a lively anxiety when the news was spread; then, with the frank curiosity characteristic of provincial manners, they went to inquire into the misfortune, grief, or illness that had befallen Mme. de Dey.

To all these questions, Brigitte, the housekeeper, answered with the same formula: her mistress was keeping her room, and would see no one, not even her own servants. The almost claustral lives of dwellers in small towns fosters a habit of analysis and conjectural explanation of the business of everybody else; so strong is it, that when every one had exclaimed over poor Mme. de Dey (without knowing whether the lady was overcome by joy or sorrow), each one began to inquire into the causes of her sudden seclusion.

"If she were ill, she would have sent for the doctor," said gossip number one; now the doctor has been playing chess in my house all day. He said to me, laughing, that in these days there is only one disease, and that, unluckily, it is incurable."

The joke was hazarded discreetly. Women and men, elderly folk and young girls forthwith betook themselves to the vast fields of conjecture. Every one imagined that there was some secret in it, and every head was busy with the secret. Next day the suspicions became malignant. Every one lives in public in a small town, and the womenkind were the first to find out that Brigitte had laid in an extra stock of provisions. The thing could not be disputed. Brigitte had been seen in the market-place betimes that morning, and, wonderful to relate, she had bought the one hare to be had. The whole town knew that Mme. de Dey did not care for game. The hare became a starting-point for endless conjectures.

Elderly gentlemen, taking their constitutional, noticed a sort of suppressed bustle in the Countess' house; the symptoms were the more apparent because the servants were at evident pains to conceal them. The manservant was beating a carpet in the garden. Only yesterday no one would have remarked the fact, but to-day everybody began to build romances upon that harmless piece of household stuff. Every one had a version.

On the following day, that on which Mme. de Dey gave out that she was not well, the magnates of Carentan went to spend the evening at the mayor's brother's house. He was a retired merchant, a married man, a strictly honorable soul; every one respected him, and the Countess held him in high esteem. There all the rich widow's suitors were fain to invent more or less probable fictions, each one thinking the while how to turn to his own advantage the secret that compelled her to compromise herself in such a manner.

The public prosecutor spun out a whole drama to bring Mme. de Dey's son to her house of a night. The mayor had a belief in a priest who had refused the oath, a refugee from La Vendée; but this left him not a little embarrassed how to account for the purchase of a hare on a Friday. The president of the district had strong leaning towards a Chouan chief, or a Vendean leader hotly pursued. Others voted for a noble escaped from the prisons of Paris. In short, one and all suspected that the Countess had been guilty of some piece of generosity that the law of those days defined as a crime, an offence that was likely to bring her to the scaffold. The public prosecutor, moreover, said, in a low voice, that they must hush the matter up, and try to save the unfortunate lady from the abyss towards which she was hastening.

"If you spread reports about," he added, "I shall be obliged to take cognizance of the matter, and to search the house, and then——"

He said no more, but every one understood what was left unsaid.

The Countess' real friends were so much alarmed for her, that on the morning of the third day the Procureur Syndic of the commune made his wife write a few lines to persuade Mme. de Dey to hold her reception as usual that evening. The old merchant took a bolder step. He called that morning upon the lady. Strong in the thought of the service he meant to do her, he insisted that he must see Mme. de Dey, and was amazed beyond expression to find her out in the garden, busy gathering the last autumn flowers in her borders to fill the vases.

"She has given refuge to her lover, no doubt," thought the old man, struck with pity for the charming woman before him.

The Countess' face wore a strange look, that confirmed his suspicions. Deeply moved by the devotion so natural to women, but that always touches us, because all men are flattered by the sacrifices that any woman makes for any one of them, the merchant told the Countess of the gossip that was circulating in the town, and showed her the danger that she was running. He wound up at last with saying that "if there are some of our public functionaries who are sufficiently ready to pardon a piece of heroism on your part so long as it is a priest that you wish to save, no one will show you any mercy if it is discovered that you are sacrificing yourself to the dictates of your heart."

At these words Mme. de Dey gazed at her visitor with a wild excitement in her manner that made him tremble, old though he was.

"Come in," she said, taking him by the hand to bring him to her room, and as soon as she had assured herself that they were alone, she drew a soiled, torn letter from her bodice. "Read it!" she cried, with a violent effort to pronounce the words.

She dropped as if exhausted into her armchair. While the old merchant looked for his spectacles and wiped them, she raised her eyes, and for the first time looked at him with curiosity; then, in an uncertain voice, "I trust in you," she said softly.

"Why did I come but to share in your crime?" the old merchant said simply.

She trembled. For the first time since she had come to the little town her soul found sympathy in another soul. A sudden light dawned meantime on the old merchant; he understood the Countess' joy and her prostration.

Her son had taken part in the Granville expedition; he wrote to his mother from his prison, and the letter brought her a sad, sweet hope. Feeling no doubts as to his means of escape, he wrote that within three days he was sure to reach her, disguised. The same letter that brought these weighty tidings was full of heartrending farewells in case the writer should not be in Carentan by the evening of the third day, and he implored his mother to send a considerable sum of money by the bearer, who had gone through dangers innumerable to deliver it. The paper shook in the old man's hands.

"And to-day is the third day!" cried Mme. de Dey. She sprang to her feet, took back the letter, and walked up and down.

"You have set to work imprudently," the merchant remarked, addressing her. "Why did you buy provisions?" he asked her.

"Why, he may come in dying of hunger, worn out with fatigue, and——" She broke off.

"I am sure of my brother," the old merchant went on; "I will engage him in your interests."

The merchant in this crisis recovered his old business shrewdness, and the advice that he gave Mme. de Dey was full of prudence and wisdom. After the two had agreed together as to what they were to do and say, the old merchant went on various ingenious pretexts to pay visits to the principal houses of Carentan, announcing wherever he went that he had just been to see Mme. de Dey, and that, in spite of her indisposition, she would receive that evening. Matching his shrewdness against Norman wits in the cross-examination he underwent in every family as to the Countess' complaint, he succeeded in putting almost every one who took an interest in the mysterious affair upon the wrong scent.

His very first call worked wonders. He told, in the hearing of a gouty old lady, how that Mme. de Dey had all but died of an attack of gout in the stomach; how that the illustrious Tronchin had recommended her in such a case to put the skin from a live hare on her chest, to stop in bed, and keep perfectly still. The Countess, he sad, had lain in danger of her life for the past two days; but after carefully following out Tronchin's singular prescription, she was now sufficiently recovered to receive visitors that evening.

This tale had an immense success in Carentan. The local doctor, a Royalist *in petto*, added to its effect by gravely discussing the specific. Suspicion, nevertheless, had taken too deep root in a few perverse or philosophical minds to be entirely dissipated; so it fell out that those who had the right of entry into Mme. de Dey's drawing-room hurried thither at an early hour, some to watch her face, some out of friendship, but the greater part attracted by the fame of the marvelous cure.

They found the Countess seated in a corner of the great chimney-piece in her room, which was almost as modestly furnished as similar apartments in Carentan; for she had given up the enjoyment of luxuries to which she had formerly been accustomed, for fear of offending the narrow prejudices of her guests, and she had made no changes in her house. The floor was not even polished. She had left the old sombre hangings on the walls, had kept the old-fashioned country furniture, burned tallow candles, had fallen in with the ways of the place and adopted provincial life without flinching before its cast-iron narrowness, its most disagreeable hardships; but knowing that her guests would forgive her for any prodigality that conduced to their comfort, she left nothing undone where their personal enjoyment was concerned; her dinners, for instance, were excellent. She even went so far as to affect avarice to recommend herself to these sordid natures; and had the ingenuity to make it appear that certain concessions to luxury had been made at the instance of others, to whom she had graciously yielded.

Towards seven o'clock that evening, therefore, the nearest approach to polite society that Carentan could boast was assembled in Mme. de Dey's drawing-room, in a wide circle, about the fire. The old merchant's sympathetic glances sustained the mistress of the house through this ordeal; with wonderful strength of mind, she underwent the curious scrutiny of her guests, and bore with their trivial prosings. Every time there was a knock at the door, at every sound of footsteps in the street, she hid her agitation by raising questions of absorbing interest to the countryside. She led the conversation on to the burning topic of the quality of various ciders, and was so well seconded by her friend who shared her secret, that her guests almost forgot to watch her, and her face wore its wonted look; her self-possession was unshaken. The public prosecutor and one of the judges of the Revolutionary Tribunal kept silence, however; noting the slightest change that flickered over her features, listening through the noisy talk to every sound in the house. Several times they put awkward questions, which the Countess answered with wonderful presence of mind. So brave is a mother's heart!

Mme. de Dey had drawn her visitors into little groups, had made parties of whist, boston, or reversis, and sat talking with some of the young people; she seemed to be living completely in the present moment, and played her part like a consummate actress. She elicited a suggestion of loto, and saying that no one else knew where to find the game, she left the room.

"My good Brigitte, I cannot breathe down there!" she cried, brushing away the tears that sprang to her eyes that glittered with fever, sorrow, and impatience. She had gone up to her son's room, and was looking round it. "He does not come," she said. "Here I can breathe and live. A few minutes more, and he will be here, for he is alive, I am sure that he is alive! My heart tells me so. Do you hear nothing, Brigitte? Oh! I would give the rest of my life to know whether he is still in prison or tramping across the country. I would rather not think."

Once more she looked to see that everything was in order. A bright fire blazed on the hearth, the shutters were carefully closed, the furniture shone with cleanliness, the bed had been made after a fashion that showed that Brigitte and the Countess had given their minds to every trifling detail. It was impossible not to read her hopes in the dainty and thoughtful preparations about the room; love and a mother's tenderest caresses seemed to pervade the air in the scent of flowers. None but a mother could have foreseen the requirements of a soldier and arranged so completely for their satisfaction. A dainty meal, the best of wine, clean linen, slippers—no requisite, no comfort, was lacking for the weary traveler, and all the delights of home heaped upon him should reveal his mother's love.

"Oh, Brigitte!——" cried the Countess, with a heartrending inflexion in her voice. She drew a chair to the table as if to strengthen her illusions and realize her longings.

"Ah! madame, he is coming. He is not far off.—— I haven't a doubt that he is living and on his way," Brigitte answered. "I put a key in the Bible and held it on my fingers while Cottin read the Gospel of St. John, and the key did not turn, madame."

"Is that a certain sign?" the Countess asked.

"Why, yes, madame! everybody knows that. He is still alive; I would stake my salvation on it; God cannot be mistaken."

"If only I could see him here in the house, in spite of the danger."

"Poor Monsieur Auguste!" cried Brigitte; "I expect he is tramping along the lanes!"

"And that is eight o'clock striking now!" cried the Countess in terror.

She was afraid that she had been too long in the room where she felt sure that her son was alive; all those preparations made for him meant that he was alive. She went down, but she lingered a moment in the peristyle for any sound that might waken the sleeping echoes of the town. She smiled at Brigitte's husband, who was standing there on guard; the man's eyes looked stupid with the strain of listening to the faint sounds of the night. She stared into the darkness, seeing her son in every shadow everywhere; but it was only for a moment. Then she went back to the drawing-room with an assumption of high spirits, and began to play at loto with the little girls. But from time to time she complained of feeling unwell, and went to sit in her great chair by the fireside. So things went on in Mme. de Dey's house and in the minds of those beneath her roof.

Meanwhile, on the road from Paris to Cherbourg, a young man, dressed in the inevitable brown *carmagnole* of those days, was plodding his way towards Carentan. When the first levies were made, there was little or no discipline kept up. The exigencies of the moment scarcely admitted of soldiers being equipped at once, and it was no uncommon thing to see the roads thronged with conscripts in their ordinary clothes. The young fellows went ahead of their company to the next halting-place, or lagged behind it; it depended upon their fitness to bear the fatigues of a long march. This particular wayfarer was some considerable distance in advance of a company of conscripts on their way to Cherbourg, whom the mayor was expecting to arrive every hour, for it was his duty to distribute their billets. The young man's footsteps were still firm as he trudged along, and his bearing seemed to indicate that he was no stranger to the rough life of a soldier. The moon shone on the pastureland about Carentan, but he had noticed great masses of white clouds that were about to scatter showers of snow over the country, and doubtless the fear of being overtaken by a storm had quickened his pace in spite of his weariness.

The wallet on his back was almost empty, and he carried a stick in his hand, cut from one of the high, thick box-hedges that surround most of the farms in Lower Normandy. As the solitary wayfarer came into Carentan, the gleaming moonlit outlines of its towers stood out for a moment with ghostly effect against the sky. He met no one in the silent streets that rang with the echoes of his own footsteps, and was obliged to ask the way to the mayor's house of a weaver who was working late. The magistrate was not far to seek, and in a few minutes the conscript was sitting on a stone bench on the mayor's porch waiting for his billet. He was sent for, however, and confronted with that functionary, who scrutinized him closely. The foot-soldier was a good-looking young man, who appeared to be of gentle birth. There was something aristocratic in his bearing and signs in his face of intelligence developed by a good education. These apparent traits gave rise to suspicion.

"What is your name?" asked the mayor, eyeing him shrewdly.

"Julien Jussieu," answered the conscript.

"From?——" queried the official, and an incredulous smile stole over his features.

"From Paris."

"Your comrades must be a good way behind?" remarked the Norman in sarcastic tones.

"I am three leagues ahead of the battalion."

"Some sentiment attracts you to Carentan, of course, citizen conscript," said the mayor astutely. "All right, all right!" he added, with a wave of the hand, seeing that the young man was about to speak. "We know where to send you. There, off with you, *Citizen Jussieu*," and he handed over the billet.

There was a tinge of irony in the stress the magistrate laid on the two last words while he held out a billet on Mme. de Dey. The conscript read the direction curiously.

"He knows quite well that he has not far to go, and when he gets outside he will very soon cross the market-place," said the mayor to himself, as the other went out. "He is uncommonly bold! God guide him!——He has an answer ready for everything. Yes, but if somebody else had asked to see his papers it would have been all up with him!"

The clocks in Carentan struck half-past nine as he spoke. Lanterns were being lit in Mme. de Dey's ante-chamber, servants were helping their masters and mistresses into sabots, greatcoats, and calashes. The card-players settled their accounts, and everybody went out together, after the fashion of all little country towns.

"It looks as if the prosecutor meant to stop," said a lady, who noticed that that important personage was not in the group in the market-place, where they all took leave of one another before going their separate ways home. And, as a matter of fact, that redoubtable functionary was alone with the Countess, who waited tremblingly till he should go. There was something appalling in their long silence.

"Citoyenne," said he at last, "I am here to see that the laws of the Republic are carried out——"

Mme. de Dey shuddered.

"Have you nothing to tell me?"

"Nothing!" she answered, in amazement.

"Ah! madame," cried the prosecutor, sitting down beside her and changing his tone. "At this moment, for lack of a word, one of us—you or I—may carry our heads to the scaffold. I have watched your character, your soul, your manner, too closely to share the error into which you have managed to lead your visitors to-night. You are expecting your son, I could not doubt it."

The Countess made an involuntary sign of denial, but her face had grown white and drawn with the struggle to maintain the composure that she did not feel, and no tremor was lost on the merciless prosecutor.

"Very well," the Revolutionary official went on, "receive him; but do not let him stay under your roof after seven o'clock to-morrow morning; for to-morrow, as soon as it is light, I shall come with a denunciation that I will have made out, and——"

She looked at him, and the dull misery in her eyes would have softened a tiger.

"I will make it clear that the denunciation was false by making a thorough search," he went on in a gentle voice; "my report shall be such that you will be safe from any subsequent suspicion. I shall make mention of your patriotic gifts, your civism, and *all* of us will be safe."

Mme. de Dey, fearful of a trap, sat motionless, her face afire, her tongue frozen. A knock at the door rang through the house.

"Oh!——" cried the terrified mother, falling upon her knees; "save him! save him!"

"Yes, let us save him!" returned the public prosecutor, and his eyes grew bright as he looked at her, "if it costs *us* our lives!"

"Lost!" she wailed. The prosecutor raised her politely.

"Madame," said he with a flourish of eloquence, "to your own free will alone would I owe——"

"Madame, he is——" cried Brigitte, thinking that her mistress was alone. At the sight of the public prosecutor, the old servant's joy-flushed countenance became haggard and impassive.

"Who is it, Brigitte?" the prosecutor asked kindly, as if he too were in the secret of the household.

"A conscript that the mayor has sent here for a night's lodging," the woman replied, holding out the billet.

"So it is," said the prosecutor, when he had read the slip of paper. "A battalion is coming here to-night."

And he went.

The Countess' need to believe in the faith of her sometime attorney was so great, that she dared not entertain any suspicion of him. She fled upstairs; she felt scarcely strength enough to stand; she opened the door, and sprang, half-dead with fear, into her son's arms.

"Oh! my child! my child!" she sobbed, covering him with almost frenzied kisses.

"Madame!" said a stranger's voice.

"Oh! it is not he!" she cried, shrinking away in terror, and she stood face to face with the conscript, gazing at him with haggard eyes.

"*Oh saint bon Dieu!* how like he is!" cried Brigitte.

There was silence for a moment; even the stranger trembled at the sight of Mme. de Dey's face.

"Ah! monsieur," she said, leaning on the arm of Brigitte's husband, feeling for the first time the full extent of a sorrow that had all but killed her at its first threatening; "ah! monsieur, I cannot stay to see you any longer. Permit my servants to supply my place, and to see that you have all that you want."

She went down to her own room, Brigitte and the old serving-man half-carrying her between them. The housekeeper set her mistress in a chair, and broke out—

"What, madame! is that man to sleep in Monsieur Auguste's bed, and wear Monsieur Auguste's slippers, and eat the pastry that I made for Monsieur Auguste? Why, if they were to guillotine me for it, I——"

"Brigitte!" cried Mme. de Dey.

Brigitte said no more.

"Hold your tongue, chatterbox," said her husband, in a low voice; "do you want to kill madame?"

A sound came from the conscript's room as he drew his chair to the table.

"I shall not stay here," cried Mme. de Dey; "I shall go into the conservatory; I shall hear better there if any one passes in the night."

She still wavered between the fear that she had lost her son and the hope of seeing him once more. That night was hideously silent. Once, for the Countess, there was an awful interval, when the battalion of conscripts entered the town, and the men went by, one by one, to their lodgings. Every footfall, every sound in the street, raised hopes to be disappointed; but it was not for long, the dreadful quiet succeeded again. Towards morning the Countess was forced to return to her room. Brigitte, ever keeping watch over her mistress' movements, did not see her come out again; and when she went in she found the Countess lying there dead.

"I expect she heard that conscript," cried Brigitte, "walking about Monsieur Auguste's room, whistling that accursed 'Marseillaise' of theirs while he dressed, as if he had been in a stable! That must have killed her."

But it was a deeper and a more solemn emotion, and doubtless some dreadful vision, that had caused Mme. de Dey's death; for at the very hour when she died at Carentan, her son was shot in le Morbihan.

This tragical story may be added to all the instances on record of the workings of sympathies uncontrolled by the laws of time and space. These observations, collected with scientific curiosity by a few isolated individuals, will one day serve as documents on which to base the foundations of a new science which hitherto has lacked its man of genius.

GUSTAVE FLAUBERT

1821–1880

Flaubert was one of the greatest French prose writers of the nineteenth century. He studied law in Paris unwillingly and unsuccessfully after a rather gloomy youth spent in the hospital at Rouen, where his father was chief surgeon. Most of his life was spent in semiretirement at Croisset, a country estate on the Seine near Rouen, where he devoted himself to literature and to the care of his mother and a niece. In 1851 he began work on his great novels: *Madame Bovary* (1857), *Salammbô* (1862), and *L'Éducation Sentimentale* (1869). His *Trois Contes*, from which "A Simple Heart" is taken, appeared in 1877. Toiling unremittingly at his desk, Flaubert strove to achieve perfection of form and expression with linguistic exactness, harmony, and rhythm. He often spent entire days in the composition of a single paragraph and as many as six years in the writing of one novel. His art had for him the seriousness of a religion so that he both ignored contemporary tastes and fashions and refused to make any concessions whatsoever to the masses of humanity whom he scorned with an abiding passion.

With the publication of *Madame Bovary* in 1857, Flaubert founded the modern school of French realistic fiction. Since then, the term *bovarysme* has been associated with the romantic temperament whose hostility to the ennui of bourgeois society is expressed in a determination to regard the world as always other than it really is. This boredom and disgust with one's environment which was really part of Flaubert's romantic sensibility is under the most admirable artistic discipline in his compassionate treatment of Félicité in "A Simple Heart."

FURTHER READING

STEEGMULLER, F. *Flaubert and Madame Bovary* (New York, 1939).
THIBAUDET, A. *Gustave Flaubert* (Paris, 1935).

A Simple Heart

I

FOR half a century the housewives of Pont-l'Évêque had envied Madame Aubain her servant Félicité.

For a hundred francs a year, she cooked and did the housework, washed, ironed, mended, harnessed the horse, fattened the poultry, made the butter and remained faithful to her mistress—although the latter was by no means an agreeable person.

Madame Aubain had married a handsome young man without money, who had died at the beginning of 1809, leaving her with two young children and a number of debts. She sold all her property excepting the farm of Toucques and the farm of Geffosses, the income of which barely amounted to five thousand francs; then she left her house in Saint-Melaine, and moved into a less pretentious one which had belonged to her ancestors and stood back of the market-place. This house, with its slate-covered roof, was built between a passage-way and a narrow street that led to the river. The interior was so unevenly graded that it caused people to stumble. A narrow hall separated the kitchen from the parlor, where Madame Aubain sat all day in a straw armchair near the window. Eight mahogany chairs stood in a row against the white wainscoting. An old piano, standing beneath a barometer, was covered with a pyramid of old books and boxes. On either side of the yellow marble mantelpiece, in Louis XV style, stood a tapestry armchair. The clock represented a temple of Vesta; and the whole room smelled musty, as it was on a lower level than the garden.

On the first floor was Madame's bed-chamber, a large room papered in a flowered design and containing the portrait of Monsieur dressed in the costume of a dandy. It communicated with a smaller room, in which there were two little cribs, without any mattresses. Next, came the parlor (always closed), filled with furniture covered with sheets. Then a hall, which led to the study, where books and papers were piled on the shelves of a book-case that enclosed three quarters of the big black desk. Two panels were entirely hidden under pen-and-ink sketches, Gouache landscapes and Audran engravings, relics of better times and vanished luxury.

On the second floor, a garret-window lighted Félicité's room, which looked out upon the meadows.

She arose at daybreak, in order to attend mass, and she worked without interruption until night; then, when dinner was over, the dishes cleared away and the door securely locked, she would bury the log under the ashes and fall asleep in front of the hearth with a rosary in her hand. Nobody could bargain with greater obstinacy, and as for cleanliness, the lustre on her brass sauce-pans was the envy and despair of other servants. She was most economical, and when she ate she would gather up crumbs with the tip of her finger, so that nothing should be wasted of the loaf of bread weighing twelve pounds which was baked especially for her and lasted three weeks.

Summer and winter she wore a dimity kerchief fastened in the back with a pin, a cap which concealed her hair, a red skirt, grey stockings, and an apron with a bib like those worn by hospital nurses.

Her face was thin and her voice shrill. When she was twenty-five, she looked forty. After she had passed fifty, nobody could tell her age; erect and silent always, she resembled a wooden figure working automatically.

Like every other woman, she had had an affair of the heart. Her father, who was a mason, was killed by falling from a scaffolding. Then her mother died and her sisters went their different ways; a farmer took her in, and while she was quite small, let her keep cows in the fields. She was clad in miserable rags, beaten for the slightest offense and finally dismissed for a theft of thirty sous which she did not commit. She took service on another farm where she tended the poultry; and as she was well thought of by her master, her fellow-workers soon grew jealous.

One evening in August (she was then eighteen years old), they persuaded her to accompany them to the fair at Colleville. She was immediately dazzled by the noise, the lights in the trees, the brightness of the dresses, the laces and gold crosses, and the crowd of people all hopping at the same time. She was standing modestly at a distance, when presently a young man of well-to-do appearance, who had been leaning on the pole of a wagon and smoking his pipe, approached her, and asked her for a dance. He treated her to cider and cake, bought her a silk shawl, and then, thinking she had guessed his purpose, offered to see her home. When they came to the end of a field he threw her down brutally. But she grew frightened and screamed, and he walked off.

One evening, on the road leading to Beaumont, she came upon a wagon loaded with hay, and when she overtook it, she recognized Théodore. He greeted her calmly, and asked her to forget what had happened between them, as it "was all the fault of the drink."

She did not know what to reply and tried to run away.

Presently he began to speak of the harvest and of the notables of the village; his father had left Colleville and bought the farm of Les Écots, so that now they would be neighbors. "Ah!" she exclaimed. He then added that his parents were looking around for a wife for him, but that he, himself, was not so anxious and preferred to wait for a girl who suited him. She hung her head. He then asked her whether she had ever thought of marrying. She replied, smilingly, that it was wrong of him to make fun of her. "Oh! no, I am in earnest," he said, and put his left arm around her waist while they sauntered along. The air was soft, the stars were bright, and the huge load of hay oscillated in front of them, drawn by four horses whose ponderous hoofs raised clouds of dust. Without a word from their driver they turned to the right. He kissed her again and she went home. The following week, Théodore obtained meetings.

They met in yards, behind walls or under isolated trees. She was not ignorant, as girls of well-to-do families are—for the animals had instructed her;—but her reason and her instinctive sense of honor kept her from falling. Her resistance exasperated Théodore's love and so in order to satisfy it (or perchance ingenuously), he offered to marry her. She would not believe him at first, so he made solemn promises. But, in a short time he mentioned a difficulty; the previous year, his parents had purchased a substitute for him; but any day he might be drafted and the prospect of serving in the army alarmed him greatly. To Félicité his cowardice appeared a proof of his love for her, and her devotion to him grew stronger. When she met him, he would torture her with his fears and his entreaties. At last, he announced that he was going to the prefect himself for information and would let her know everything on the following Sunday, between eleven o'clock and midnight.

When the time drew near, she ran to meet her lover.

But instead of Théodore, one of his friends was at the meeting-place.

He informed her that she would never see her sweetheart again; for, in order to escape the draft, he had married a rich old woman, Madame Lehoussais, of Toucques.

The poor girl's sorrow was frightful. She threw herself on the ground, she cried and called on the Lord, and wandered around desolately until sunrise. Then she went back to the farm, declared her intention of leaving, and at the end of the month, after she had received her wages, she packed all her belongings in a handkerchief and started for Pont-l'Évêque.

In front of the inn, she met a woman wearing widow's weeds, and upon questioning her, learned that she was looking for a cook. The girl did not know very much, but appeared so willing and so modest in her requirements, that Madame Aubain finally said:

"Very well, I will give you a trial."

And half an hour later Félicité was installed in her house.

At first she lived in a constant anxiety that was caused by "the style of the household" and the memory of "Monsieur," that hovered over everything. Paul and Virginia, the one aged seven, and the other barely four, seemed made of some precious material; she carried them pig-a-back, and was greatly mortified when Madame Aubain forbade her to kiss them every other minute.

But in spite of all this, she was happy. The comfort of her new surroundings had obliterated her sadness.

Every Thursday, friends of Madame Aubain dropped in for a game of cards, and it was Félicité's duty to prepare the table and heat the foot-warmers. They arrived at exactly eight o'clock and departed before eleven.

Every Monday morning, the dealer in second-hand goods, who lived under the alley-way, spread out his wares on the sidewalk. Then the city would be filled with a buzzing of voices in which the neighing of horses, the bleating of lambs, the grunting of pigs, could be distinguished, mingled with the sharp sound of wheels on the cobble-stones. About twelve o'clock, when the market was in full swing, there appeared at the front door a tall, middle-aged peasant, with a hooked nose and a cap on the back of his head; it was Robelin, the farmer of Geffosses. Shortly afterwards came Liébard, the farmer of Toucques, short, rotund and ruddy, wearing a grey jacket and spurred boots.

Both men brought their landlady either chickens or cheese. Félicité would invariably thwart their ruses and they held her in great respect.

At various times, Madame Aubain received a visit from the Marquis de Grémanville, one of her uncles, who was ruined and lived at Falaise on the remainder of his estates. He always came at dinner-time and brought an ugly poodle with him, whose paws soiled the furniture. In spite of his efforts to appear a man of breeding (he even went so far as to raise his hat every time he said "My deceased father"), his habits got the better of him, and he would fill his glass a little too often and relate broad stories. Félicité would show him out very politely and say: "You have had enough for this time, Monsieur de Grémanville! Hoping to see you again!" and would close the door.

She opened it gladly for Monsieur Bourais, a retired lawyer. His bald head and white cravat, the ruffling of his shirt, his flowing brown coat, the manner in which he took snuff, his whole person, in fact, produced in her the kind of awe which we feel when we see extraordinary persons. As he managed Madame's estates, he spent hours with her in Monsieur's study; he was in constant fear of being compromised, had a great regard for the magistracy and some pretensions to learning.

In order to facilitate the children's studies, he presented them with an engraved geography which represented various scenes of the world: cannibals with feather head-dresses, a gorilla kidnapping a young girl, Arabs in the desert, a whale being harpooned, etc.

Paul explained the pictures to Félicité. And, in fact, this was her only literary education.

The children's studies were under the direction of a poor devil employed at the town-hall, who sharpened his pocket-knife on his boots and was famous for his penmanship.

When the weather was fine, they went to Geffosses. The house was built in the centre of the sloping yard; and the sea looked like a grey spot in the distance. Félicité would take slices of cold meat from the lunch basket and they would sit down and eat in a room next to the dairy. This room was all that remained of a cottage that had been torn down. The dilapidated wall-paper trembled in the drafts. Madame Aubain, overwhelmed by recollections, would hang her head, while the children were afraid to open their mouths. Then, "Why don't you go and play?" their mother would say; and they would scamper off.

Paul would go to the old barn, catch birds, throw

stones into the pond, or pound the trunks of the trees with a stick till they resounded like drums. Virginia would feed the rabbits and run to pick the wild flowers in the fields, and her flying legs would disclose her little embroidered pantalettes. One autumn evening, they struck out for home through the meadows. The new moon illumined part of the sky and a mist hovered like a veil over the sinuosities of the river. Oxen, lying in the pastures, gazed mildly at the passing persons. In the third field, however, several of them got up and surrounded them. "Don't be afraid," cried Félicité; and murmuring a sort of lament she passed her hand over the back of the nearest ox; he turned away and the others followed. But when they came to the next pasture, they heard frightful bellowing.

It was a bull which was hidden from them by the fog. He advanced towards the two women, and Madame Aubain prepared to flee for her life. "No, no! not so fast," warned Félicité. Still they hurried on, for they could hear the noisy breathing of the bull close behind them. His hoofs pounded the grass like hammers, and presently he began to gallop! Félicité turned around and threw patches of grass in his eyes. He hung his head, shook his horns and bellowed with fury. Madame Aubain and the children, huddled at the end of the field, were trying to jump over the ditch. Félicité continued to back before the bull, blinding him with dirt, while she shouted to them to make haste.

Madame Aubain finally slid into the ditch, after shoving first Virginia and then Paul into it, and though she stumbled several times she managed, with great courage, to climb the other side of it.

The bull had driven Félicité up against a fence; the foam from his muzzle flew in her face and in another minute he would have disembowelled her. She had just time to slip between two bars and the huge animal, thwarted, paused.

For years, this occurrence was a topic of conversation in Pont-l'Évêque. But Félicité took no credit to herself, and probably never knew that she had been heroic.

Virginia occupied her thoughts solely, for the shock she had sustained gave her a nervous affection, and the physician, M. Poupart, prescribed the salt-water bathing at Trouville. In those days, Trouville was not greatly patronised. Madame Aubain gathered information, consulted Bourais, and made preparations as if they were going on an extended trip.

The baggage was sent the day before on Liébard's cart. On the following morning, he brought around two horses, one of which had a woman's saddle with a velveteen back to it, while on the crupper of the other was a rolled shawl that was to be used for a seat. Madame Aubain mounted the second horse, behind Liébard. Félicité took charge of the little girl, and Paul rode M. Lechaptois' donkey, which had been lent for the occasion on the condition that they should be careful of it.

The road was so bad that it took two hours to cover the eight miles. The two horses sank knee-deep into the mud and stumbled into ditches; sometimes they had to jump over them. In certain places, Liébard's mare stopped abruptly. He waited patiently till she started again, and talked of the people whose estates bordered the road, adding his own moral reflections to the outline of their histories. Thus, when they were passing through Toucques, and came to some windows, draped with nasturtiums, he shrugged his shoulders and said: "There's a woman, Madame Lehoussais, who, instead of taking a young man——" Félicité could not catch what followed; the horses began to trot, the donkey to gallop, and they turned into a lane; then a gate swung open, two farm-hands appeared and they all dismounted at the very threshold of the farm-house.

Mother Liébard, seeing her mistress, was prodigal in demonstrations of joy. She served them a lunch of roast beef, tripe, black sausage, a fricassee of chicken, sparkling cider, a fruit tart, and plums in brandy, accompanying the whole with polite observations to madame, who seemed in better health, to mademoiselle, become "magnificent," to Mr. Paul, grown singularly "stout"; without forgetting their late grandparents, whom the Liébards had known, being in the service of the family for several generations. The farm had, like them, an old-time character. The beams of the roof were worm-eaten, the walls black with smoke, the tiles grey with dust. An oak dresser carried all sorts of utensils, jugs, plates, pewter, basins, wolf traps, sheep shears; an enormous syringe made the children laugh. Not a tree in the three courtyards but had mushrooms at its base or in its branches a bunch of mistletoe. The wind had thrown down several. They had sprouted again in the middle, and all were bent under the number of their apples. The thatch roofs, like brown velvet, and all unequal in thickness, resisted the strongest gales. Yet the wagon-shed was falling in ruins. Madame Aubain said she would see about it, and bade them reharness the beasts.

They were half an hour yet before they reached Trouville. The little caravan dismounted to pass the Écores hill. It was a rock overhanging the boats;

and three minutes later, at the end of the quay, they entered the courtyard of the Golden Lamb, Mother David's inn.

Virginia, from the beginning, felt herself more robust because of the change of air and the action of the baths. She took them in her chemise, for lack of a bathing costume; and her maid dressed her afterwards in the shed of a customs official who looked after the bathers.

In the afternoon they would go with the donkey past the Black Rocks in the direction of Hennequeville. The path at first rose between land undulating like the lawns of a gentleman's estate, then reached a plateau where pasture ground alternated with cultivated fields. At the edge of the road, among the clusters of reeds, holly bushes were growing. Here and there a tall dead tree made zigzags with its branches on the blue air.

Almost always they rested in a meadow, with Deauville on their left, Havre on their right, and in front of them the open sea. The latter was brilliant in the sunshine, as smooth as a mirror, so gentle that its murmur could scarcely be heard. Hidden sparrows chirped, and the immense vault of the sky formed a cover for all of them. Madame Aubain worked at her sewing; Virginia, sitting beside her, plaited reeds; Félicité gathered lavender; Paul, who was bored, wanted to leave.

At other times they crossed the Toucques in a boat and looked for shells. The low tide left sea urchins uncovered together with scallops and jellyfish, and the children ran to catch the puffs of foam that the wind cast up. The sleepy waves, falling on the sand, rolled in along the beach; they stretched as far as eyes could see, but on the land side they were stopped by the dunes which separated the sea from the Marais, a wide meadow, shaped like a hippodrome. When they were coming back that way Trouville at the foot of the sloping hill, grew bigger at each step, and with all its different-sized houses, seemed to spread out in gay disorder.

When the heat was too oppressive, they remained in their rooms. The dazzling sunlight cast bars of light between the shutters. Not a sound in the village, not a soul was on the sidewalk. This silence intensified the calmness of everything. In the distance, the hammers of caulkers pounded against the hull of a ship in dry dock, and the sultry breeze brought them an odor of tar.

The principal diversion consisted in watching the return of the fishing-smacks. As soon as they passed the beacons, they began to ply to windward. The sails were lowered to one third of the masts, and

with their fore-sails swelled up like balloons, they glided over the waves and anchored in the middle of the harbor. Then they crept up alongside the dock and the sailors threw the still quivering fish over the side of the boat; a line of carts was waiting for them, and women with white caps sprang forward to receive the baskets and to embrace their men-folk.

One day, one of them spoke to Félicité, who, after a little while, returned to the house gleefully. She had found one of her sisters, and presently Nastasie Barette, wife of Léroux, made her appearance, holding an infant in her arms, another child by the hand, while on her left was a little cabin-boy with his hands in his pockets and his cap on his ear.

At the end of fifteen minutes, Madame Aubain bade her go.

They always hung around the kitchen, or approached Félicité when she and the children were out walking. The husband, however, did not show himself.

Félicité developed a great fondness for them; she bought them a stove, some shirts and a blanket; it was evident that they were exploiting her. Her foolishness annoyed Madame Aubain, who, moreover, did not like the nephew's familiarity, for he called her son "thou";–and, as Virginia began to cough and the season was over, she decided to return to Pont-l'Évêque.

Monsieur Bourais assisted her in the choice of a school. The one at Caen was considered the best. So Paul was sent away and bravely said good-bye to them all, for he was glad to go to live in a house where he would have boy companions.

Madame Aubain resigned herself to the separation from her son because it was unavoidable. Virginia brooded less and less over it. Félicité missed the noise he made, but soon a new occupation diverted her mind; beginning at Christmas, she accompanied the little girl to her catechism lesson every day.

III

After she had made a curtsey at the door, she would walk up the aisle between the double lines of chairs, open Madame Aubain's pew, sit down and look around.

Girls and boys, the former on the right, the latter on the left-hand side of the church, filled the stalls of the choir; the priest stood beside the reading-desk; on one stained window of the side-aisle the Holy Ghost hovered over the Virgin; on another one, Mary knelt before the Child Jesus, and behind the altar, a wooden group represented Saint Michael felling the dragon.

The priest first read a condensed lesson of sacred history. Félicité imagined Paradise, the Flood, the Tower of Babel, the blazing cities, the dying nations, the shattered idols; and out of this she developed a great respect for the Almighty and a great fear of His wrath. Then, when she listened to the Passion, she wept. Why had they crucified Him who loved little children, nourished the people, made the blind see, and who, out of humility, had wished to be born among the poor, in a stable? The sowings, the harvests, the wine-presses, all those familiar things which the Scriptures mention, formed a part of her life; the word of God sanctified them; and she loved the lambs with increased tenderness for the sake of the Lamb, and the doves because of the Holy Ghost.

She found it hard, however, to think of the latter as a person, for was it not a bird, a flame, and sometimes only a breath? Perhaps it is its light that at night hovers over swamps, its breath that propels the clouds, its voice that renders church-bells harmonious. And Félicité worshipped devoutly, while enjoying the coolness and the stillness of the church.

As for the dogma, she could not understand it and did not even try. The priest discoursed, the children recited, and she went to sleep, only to awaken with a start when they were leaving the church and their wooden shoes clattered on the stone pavement.

In this way, she learned her catechism, her religious education having been neglected in her youth; and thenceforth she imitated all Virginia's religious practices, fasted when she did, and went to confession with her. At the Corpus-Christi Day they both decorated an altar.

She worried in advance over Virginia's first communion. She fussed about the shoes, the rosary, the book and the gloves. With what nervousness she helped the mother dress the child!

During the entire ceremony, she felt anguished. Monsieur Bourais hid part of the choir from view, but directly in front of her, the flock of maidens, wearing white wreaths over their lowered veils, formed a snow-white field, and she recognized her darling by the slenderness of the neck and her devout attitude. The bell tinkled. All the heads bent and there was a silence. Then, at the peals of the organ the singers and the worshippers struck up the Agnus Dei; the boys' procession began; behind them came the girls. With clasped hands, they advanced step by step to the lighted altar, knelt at the first step, received one by one the Host, and returned to their seats in the same order. When Vir-

ginia's turn came, Félicité leaned forward to watch her, and through that imagination which springs from true affection, she at once became her child, the child whose face and dress were hers, whose heart beat in her bosom. When Virginia opened her mouth or closed her eye-lids, she did likewise, and came very near fainting.

The following day, she presented herself early at the church so as to be able to receive communion from the curé. She took it with the proper feeling, but did not experience the same delight as on the previous day.

Madame Aubain wished to make an accomplished girl of her daughter; and as Guyot could not teach English nor music, she decided to send her to the Ursulines at Honfleur.

The child made no objection, but Félicité sighed and thought Madame was heartless. Then, she thought that perhaps her mistress was right, as these things were beyond her sphere. Finally, one day, an old *fiacre* stopped in front of the door and a nun stepped out. Félicité put Virginia's luggage on top of the carriage, gave the coachman some instructions, and smuggled six jars of jam, a dozen pears and a bunch of violets under the seat.

At the last minute, Virginia had a fit of sobbing; she embraced her mother again and again, while the latter kissed her on her forehead, and said: "Now, be brave, be brave!" The step was pulled up and the *fiacre* rumbled off.

Then Madame Aubain had a fainting spell, and that evening all her friends, including the two Lormeaus, Madame Lechaptois, the ladies Rochefeuille, Messieurs de Houppeville and Bourais, called on her and tendered their sympathy.

At first the separation proved very painful to her. But her daughter wrote her three times a week and the other days she, herself wrote to Virginia. Then she walked in the garden, read a little, and in this way managed to fill out the emptiness of the hours.

Each morning, out of habit, Félicité entered Virginia's room and gazed at the walls. She missed combing her hair, lacing her shoes, tucking her in her bed, and the bright face and little hand when they used to go out for a walk. In order to occupy herself she tried to make lace. But her clumsy fingers broke the threads; she had no heart for anything, lost her sleep and "wasted away," as she put it.

In order to have some distraction, she asked permission to receive visits from her nephew Victor.

He came on Sundays, after church, with ruddy cheeks and bared chest, bringing with him the scent of the country. She would set the table and they would sit down opposite each other, and eat their dinner. She ate as little as possible herself in order to avoid extra food expense, but she always stuffed him so with food that he finally went to sleep. At the first stroke of vespers, she would wake him up, brush his trousers, tie his cravat and walk to church with him, leaning on his arm with maternal pride.

His parents always told him to get something out of her, either a package of brown sugar, or soap, or brandy, and sometimes even money. He brought her his clothes to mend, and she accepted the task gladly, because it meant another visit from him.

In August, his father took him on a coasting-vessel.

It was vacation time and the arrival of the children was some consolation for Félicité. But Paul was capricious, and Virginia was growing too old to be addressed in the familiar, a fact which seemed to produce a sort of embarrassment in their relations.

Victor went successively to Morlaix, to Dunkirk, and to Brighton; whenever he returned from a trip he would bring her a present. The first time it was a box of shells; the second, a coffee-cup; the third, a big doll of ginger-bread. He was growing handsome; he had a good figure, a small moustache, kind eyes, and a little leather cap that sat jauntily on the back of his head. He amused his aunt by telling her stories filled with nautical expressions.

One Monday, the 14th of July, 1819 (she never forgot the date), Victor announced that he had been employed on a merchant-vessel and that in two days he would take a steamer at Honfleur in order to join his boat which was going to sail from Le Havre very soon. Perhaps he might be away for two years.

The prospect of his departure filled Félicité with despair, and in order to bid him farewell, on Wednesday night, after Madame's dinner, she put on her pattens and trudged the four miles that separated Pont-l'Évêque from Honfleur.

When she reached the Calvary, instead of turning to the right, she turned to the left and lost herself in the coal yards; she had to retrace her steps; some people she spoke to advised her to hasten. She walked helplessly around the harbor filled with vessels, and knocked against hawsers. Presently the ground sloped abruptly, lights flitted to and fro, and she thought all at once that she had gone mad when she saw some horses in the sky.

Others, on the edge of the dock, neighed at the sight of the ocean. A derrick pulled them up in the air and dumped them in a boat, where pas-

sengers were bustling about among barrels of cider, baskets of cheese and bags of meal; chickens cackled, the captain swore and a cabin-boy rested on the railing, apparently indifferent to his surroundings. Félicité, who did not recognize him, kept shouting: "Victor!" He suddenly raised his eyes, but while she was preparing to rush up to him, they withdrew the gangplank.

The packet, towed by singing women, glided out of the harbor. Her hull squeaked and the heavy waves beat up against her sides. The sail had turned and nobody was visible;—and on the ocean, silvered by the light of the moon, the vessel formed a black spot that grew dimmer and dimmer, and finally disappeared.

When Félicité passed the Calvary again, she felt as if she must entrust that which was dearest to her to the Lord; and for a long time she prayed, with uplifted eyes and a face wet with tears. The city was sleeping; some customs officials were taking the air; and the water kept pouring through the holes of the dam with a deafening roar. The town clock struck two.

The parlor of the convent would not open until morning, and surely a delay would annoy Madame; so, in spite of her desire to see the other child, she went home. The maids of the inn were just arising when she reached Pont-l'Évêque.

So the poor boy would be on the ocean for months! His previous trips had not alarmed her. One can come back from England and Brittany; but America, the colonies, the islands, were all lost in an uncertain region at the very end of the world.

From that time on, Félicité thought solely of her nephew. On warm days she feared he would suffer from thirst, and when it stormed, she was afraid he would be struck by lightning. When she harkened to the wind that rattled in the chimney and dislodged the tiles of the roof, she imagined that he was being buffeted by the same storm, perched on top of a shattered mast, with his whole body bent backward and covered with sea-foam; or,—these were recollections of the engraved geography—he was being devoured by savages, or captured in a forest by apes, or dying on some lonely coast. She never mentioned her anxieties, however.

Madame Aubain worried about her daughter.

The sisters thought that Virginia was affectionate but delicate. The slightest emotion enervated her. She had to give up her piano lessons. Her mother insisted upon regular letters from the convent. One morning, when the postman failed to come, she grew impatient and began to pace to and fro from her chair to the window. It was really extraordinary! No news in four days!

In order to console her mistress by her own example, Félicité said:

"Why, Madame, I haven't had any news in six months!—"

"From whom?"

The servant replied gently:

"Why—from my nephew."

"Oh, yes, your nephew!" And shrugging her shoulders, Madame Aubain continued to pace the floor as if to say: "I did not think of it.—Besides, I do not care, a cabin-boy, a pauper!—but my daughter—what a difference! just think of it!—"

Félicité, although she had been reared roughly, was very indignant. Then she forgot all about it.

It appeared quite natural to her that one should lose one's head about Virginia.

The two children were of equal importance; they were united in her heart and their fate was to be the same.

The chemist informed her that Victor's vessel had reached Havana. He had read the information in a newspaper.

Félicité imagined that Havana was a place where people did nothing but smoke, and that Victor walked around among negroes in a cloud of tobacco smoke. Could a person, if he needed to do so, return by land? How far was it from Pont-l'Évêque? In order to learn these things, she questioned Monsieur Bourais. He reached for his map and began explanations concerning longitudes, and he smiled in a superior way at Félicité's bewilderment. At last, he took his pencil and pointed out an imperceptible black point in the scallops of an oval blotch, adding: "There it is." She bent over the map; the maze of colored lines hurt her eyes without enlightening her; and when Bourais asked her what puzzled her, she requested him to show her the house Victor lived in. Bourais threw up his hands, sneezed, and then laughed uproariously; such ignorance delighted his soul; but Félicité failed to understand the cause of his mirth, she whose intelligence was so limited that she perhaps expected to see even the picture of her nephew!

It was two weeks later that Liébard came into the kitchen at market-time, and handed her a letter from her brother-in-law. As neither of them could read, she called upon her mistress.

Madame Aubain, who was counting the stitches of her knitting, laid her work down beside her, opened the letter, started, and in a low tone and with a searching look said: "They tell you of a—misfortune. Your nephew—."

He had died. The letter told nothing more.

Félicité dropped on a chair, leaned her head against the back and closed her eyes. Then, with drooping head, inert hands and staring eyes, she repeated at intervals:

"Poor little chap! poor little chap!"

Liébard watched her and sighed. Madame Aubain was trembling.

She proposed to the girl to go to see her sister in Trouville.

With a single motion, Félicité replied that it was not necessary.

There was a silence. Old Liébard thought it about time for him to take leave.

Then Félicité exclaimed: "They have no sympathy, they do not care!"

Her head fell forward again, and from time to time, mechanically, she toyed with the long knitting needles on the work table.

A few women passed through the yard with baskets of wet clothes.

When Félicité saw them through the window, she suddenly remembered her own wash. As she had soaked it the day before, she must go now and rinse it. So she arose and left the room.

Her tub and her board were on the bank of the Toucques. She threw a heap of clothes on the ground, rolled up her sleeves and grasped her bat; and her loud pounding could be heard in the neighboring gardens. The meadows were empty, the breeze wrinkled the stream, at the bottom of which were long grasses that looked like the hair of corpses floating in the water. She restrained her sorrow and was very brave until night; but, when she had gone to her own room, she gave way to it, burying her face in the pillow and pressing her two fists against her temples.

A long while afterward she learned, through Victor's captain, the circumstances surrounding his death. At the hospital they had bled him too much, treating him for yellow fever. Four doctors held him at one time. He died almost instantly, and the chief surgeon had said:

"Here goes another one!"

His parents had always treated him barbarously; she preferred not to see them again, and they made no advances, either from forgetfulness or from innate hardness.

Virginia was growing weaker.

A cough, continual fever, oppressive breathing and spots on her cheeks indicated some serious trouble. Monsieur Poupart had advised a sojourn in Provence. Madame Aubain decided that they would go, and she would have had her daughter come home at once, had it not been for the climate of Pont-l'Évêque.

She made an arrangement with a livery-stable man who drove her over to the convent every Tuesday. In the garden there was a terrace, from which the view extended to the Seine. Virginia walked in it, leaning on her mother's arm and treading upon the dead vine leaves. Sometimes the sun, shining through the clouds, made her blink her lids when she gazed at the sails in the distance and when she let her eyes roam over the horizon from the Chateau of Tancarville to the lighthouses of Le Havre. Then they rested in the arbor. Her mother had bought a little cask of fine Malaga wine, and Virginia, laughing at the idea of becoming intoxicated, would drink a few drops of it, but never more.

Her strength returned. Autumn passed. Félicité began to reassure Madame Aubain. But, one evening when she returned home after an errand, she met M. Poupart's coach in front of the door; M. Poupart himself was standing in the vestibule and Madame Aubain was tying the strings of her bonnet. "Give me my foot-warmer, my purse and my gloves; and be quick about it," she said.

Virginia had congestion of the lungs; perhaps it was desperate.

"Not yet," said the physician, and both got into the carriage, while the snow fell in thick flakes. It was almost night and very cold.

Félicité rushed to the church to light a candle. Then she ran after the coach which she overtook after an hour's chase, sprang up behind and held on to the straps. But suddenly a thought crossed her mind: "The yard has been left open! Suppose burglars should get in!" And down she jumped.

The next morning, at daybreak, she called at the doctor's. He had been home, but had left again. Then she waited at the inn, thinking that strangers might bring her a letter. At last, at daylight she took the stage coach for Lisieux.

The convent was at the end of a steep and narrow street. When she arrived about the middle of it, she heard strange noises, a funeral knell. "It must be for some one else," she thought, and she pulled the knocker violently.

After several minutes had passed, she heard footsteps, the door was half opened and a nun appeared. The good sister, with an air of compunction, told her that "she had just passed away." And at the same moment the tolling of Saint Léonard's bell increased.

Félicité reached the second floor. Already at the threshold she caught sight of Virginia lying on her back, with clasped hands, her mouth open and her head thrown back, beneath a black crucifix which was leaning toward her and beneath stiff curtains which were less white than her face. Madame Aubain lay at the foot of the couch, clasping it with her arms and uttering groans of agony. The Mother Superior was standing on the right side of the bed. The three candles on the bureau made red blurs, and the windows were dimmed by the fog outside. The nuns carried Madame Aubain from the room.

For two nights, Félicité never left the corpse. She would repeat the same prayers, sprinkle holy water over the sheets, get up, come back to the bed and look at the body. At the end of the first vigil, she noticed that the face had taken on a yellow tinge, the lips grew blue, the nose grew pinched, the eyes became sunken. She kissed them several times and would not have been greatly astonished had Virginia opened them. To souls like this the supernatural is always quite simple. She washed her, wrapped her in a shroud, put her into the casket, laid a wreath of flowers on her head and arranged her curls. They were blond and of an extraordinary length for her age. Félicité cut off a big lock and put half of it into her bosom, resolving never to part with it.

The body was taken to Pont-l'Évêque, according to Madame Aubain's wishes; she followed the hearse in a closed carriage.

After the ceremony it took three quarters of an hour to reach the cemetery. Paul, sobbing, headed the procession; Monsieur Bourais followed, and then came the principal inhabitants of the town, the women covered with black capes, and Félicité. The memory of her nephew, and the thought that she had not been able to render him these honors, made her doubly unhappy, and she felt as if he were being buried with Virginia.

Madame Aubain's grief was uncontrollable. At first she rebelled against God, thinking that he was unjust to have taken away her child—she who had never done anything wrong, and whose conscience was so pure! But no! she ought to have taken her South. Other doctors would have saved her. She accused herself, prayed to be able to join her child, and cried out in her dreams. Of the latter, one in particular haunted her. Her husband, dressed like a sailor, had come back from a long voyage, and with tears in his eyes told her that he had received the order to take Virginia away. Then they both consulted about a hiding-place.

Once she came in from the garden, all upset. A moment before (and she showed the place), the father and daughter had appeared to her, one after the other; they did nothing but look at her.

During several months she remained inert in her room. Félicité scolded her gently; she must keep up for her son and also for the other one, for "her memory."

"Her memory!" replied Madame Aubain, as if she were just awakening. "Oh! yes, yes, you do not forget her!" This was an allusion to the cemetery where she had been expressly forbidden to go.

But Félicité went there every day. At four o'clock exactly, she would go through the town, climb the hill, open the gate and arrive at Virginia's tomb. It was a small column of pink marble with a flat stone at its base, and it was surrounded by a little plot enclosed by chains. The flower beds were bright with blossoms. Félicité watered their leaves, renewed the gravel, and knelt on the ground in order to till the earth properly. When Madame Aubain was able to visit the cemetery she felt very much relieved and consoled.

Years passed, all alike and marked by no other events than the return of the great church holidays: Easter, Assumption, All Saints' Day. Household happenings constituted the only data to which in later years they often referred. Thus, in 1825, workmen painted the vestibule; in 1827, a portion of the roof almost killed a man when it fell into the yard. In the summer of 1828, it was Madame's turn to offer the hallowed bread. At that time, Bourais disappeared mysteriously, and the old acquaintances, Guyot, Liébard, Madame Lechaptois, Robelin, Old Grémanville, paralysed for a long time, passed away one by one. One night, the driver of the mail coach in Pont-l'Évêque announced the July Revolution. A few days later a new sub-prefect was nominated, the Baron de Larsonnière, ex-consul in America, who, besides his wife, had his sister-in-law and her three grown daughters with him. They were often seen on their lawn, dressed in loose blouses, and they had a parrot and a Negro servant. Madame Aubain received a call, which she returned promptly. As soon as she caught sight of them, Félicité would run and notify her mistress. But only one thing was capable of arousing her: a letter from her son.

He could not follow any profession since he devoted himself to drinking. His mother paid his debts and he made fresh ones. The sighs that she heaved while she knitted at the window reached the ears of Félicité who was spinning in the kitchen.

They walked in the garden together, talking always of Virginia, and asking each other if such and such a thing would have pleased her, and what she would probably have said on this or that occasion.

All her little belongings were put away in a closet of the room which held the two little beds. But Madame Aubain looked them over as little as possible. One summer day, however, she resigned herself to the task and when she opened the closet the moths flew out.

Virginia's frocks were hung under a shelf where there were three dolls, some hoops, a doll house and a basin which she had used. Félicité and Madame Aubain also took out the skirts, the handkerchiefs and the stockings, and spread them on the beds before putting them away again. The sun fell on the pathetic things, disclosing their spots and the creases formed by the motions of the body. The atmosphere was warm and blue, and a blackbird trilled in the garden. Everything seemed to live in happiness. They found a little hat of soft brown plush, but it was entirely moth-eaten. Félicité asked for it. Their eyes met and filled with tears; at last the mistress opened her arms and the servant threw herself against her breast and they hugged each other and gave vent to their grief in a kiss which equalized them for a moment.

It was the first time that this had ever happened, for Madame Aubain was not of an expansive nature. Félicité was as grateful for it as if it had been some favor, and thenceforth she loved her with an animal-like devotion and a religious veneration.

Her kind-heartedness developed. When she heard the drums of a marching regiment passing through the street, she would stand in the doorway with a jug of cider and give the soldiers a drink. She nursed cholera victims. She protected Polish refugees, and one of them even declared that he wished to marry her. But they quarrelled, for one morning when she returned from the Angelus she found him in the kitchen coolly eating a dish which he had prepared for himself during her absence.

After the Polish refugees, came Colmiche, an old man who was credited with having committed frightful misdeeds in '93. He lived near the river in the ruins of a pig-sty. The urchins peeped at him through the cracks in the walls and threw stones that fell on his miserable bed, where he lay gasping with catarrh, with long hair, inflamed eyelids, and a tumor as big as his head on one arm.

She got him some linen, tried to clean his hovel

and dreamed of installing him in the bake-house without his being in Madame's way. When the cancer broke, she dressed it every day; sometimes she brought him some cake and placed him in the sun on a bundle of hay; and the poor old creature, trembling and drooling, would thank her in his broken voice, and put out his hands whenever she left him. Finally he died; and she had a mass said for the repose of his soul.

That day a great joy came to her: at dinner-time, Madame de Larsonnière's servant called with the parrot, the cage, and the perch and chain and lock. A note from the baroness told Madame Aubain that as her husband had been promoted to a prefecture, they were leaving that night, and she begged her to accept the bird as a remembrance and a token of her esteem.

For a long time the parrot had been on Félicité's mind, because he came from America, which reminded her of Victor, and she had approached the Negro on the subject.

Once even, she had said:

"How glad Madame would be to have him!"

The man had repeated this remark to his mistress who, not being able to keep the bird, took this means of getting rid of it.

IV

He was called Loulou. His body was green, his head blue, the tips of his wings were pink and his breast was golden.

But he had the tiresome tricks of biting his perch, pulling his feathers out, scattering refuse and spilling the water out of his bath. Madame Aubain grew tired of him and give him to Félicité for good.

Félicité undertook his education, and soon he was able to repeat: "Pretty boy! Your servant, sir! I salute you, Marie!" His perch was placed near the door and several persons were astonished that he did not answer to the name of "Jacquot," for every parrot is called Jacquot. They called him a goose and a log, and these taunts were like so many dagger thrusts to Félicité. Strange stubbornness of the bird which would not talk when people watched him!

Nevertheless, he sought society, for on Sunday when the ladies Rochefeuille, Monsieur de Houppeville and the new habitués, Onfroy the Chemist, Monsieur Varin and Captain Mathieu, dropped in for their game of cards, he struck the window-panes with his wings and made such a racket that it was impossible to talk.

Bourais' face must have appeared very funny to Loulou. As soon as he saw him he would begin to roar. His voice re-echoed in the yard, and the neighbors would come to the windows and begin to laugh. In order that the parrot might not see him, Monsieur Bourais edged along the wall, pushed his hat over his eyes to hide his profile, and entered by the garden door. The looks which he gave the bird lacked affection. Loulou, having thrust his head into the butcher boy's basket, received a slap, and from that time forward he always tried to nip his enemy. Fabu threatened to wring his neck, although he was not inclined to cruelty notwithstanding his big whiskers and his tattooings. On the contrary, he rather liked the bird and, out of deviltry, tried to teach him oaths. Félicité, whom his manner alarmed, put Loulou in the kitchen, took off his chain and let him walk all over the house.

When he went downstairs, he rested his beak on the steps, lifted his right foot and then his left; but his mistress feared that such feats would give him vertigo. He became ill and was unable to eat. There was a small growth under his tongue like those with which chickens are sometimes inflicted. Félicité pulled it off with her finger nails and cured him. One day, Paul was imprudent enough to blow the smoke of his cigar in his face; another time, Madame Lormeau was teasing him with the tip of her umbrella and he swallowed the tip. Finally he got lost.

She had put him on the grass to cool him and went away only for a second; when she returned, she found no parrot! She hunted among the bushes, on the bank of the river, and on the roofs, without paying any attention to Madame Aubain who screamed at her: "Watch out! you must be insane!" Then she searched every garden in Pont-l'Évêque and stopped people in the street to ask: "Haven't you perhaps seen my parrot?" To those who had never seen the parrot, she described him minutely. Suddenly she thought she saw something green fluttering behind the mills at the foot of the hill. But when she got to the top of the hill she could not see it. A hod-carrier told her that he had just seen the bird in Saint-Melaine, in Mother Simon's store. She rushed to the place. The people did not know what she was talking about. At last she came home, exhausted, with her slippers worn to shreds, and despair in her heart. She sat down on the bench near Madame and was telling her of her search when presently a light weight dropped on her shoulder—Loulou! What the deuce had he been doing? Perhaps he had just taken a little walk around town!

She did not easily forget her scare; in fact, she never got over it. In consequence of a cold, she caught a sore throat; and some time afterward she had an earache. Three years later she was stone deaf, and spoke in a very loud voice even in church. Although her sins might have been proclaimed throughout the diocese without any shame to herself, or ill effects to the community, the curé thought it advisable to receive her confession in the vestry-room.

Imaginary buzzings also added to her bewilderment. Her mistress often said to her: "My goodness, how stupid you are!" and she would answer: "Yes, Madame," and look for something.

The narrow circle of her ideas grew more restricted than it already was; the bellowing of the oxen, the chime of the bells no longer reached her intelligence. All things moved silently, like ghosts. Only one noise penetrated her ears; the parrot's voice.

As if to divert her mind, he reproduced for her the tick-tack of the spit in the kitchen, the shrill cry of the fish venders, the saw of the carpenter, who had a shop opposite, and when the door bell rang, he would imitate Madame Aubain: "Félicité go to the front door."

They held conversations together, Loulou repeating the three phrases of his repertory over and over, Félicité replying by words that had no greater meaning, but in which she poured out her feelings. In her isolation, the parrot was almost a son, a lover. He climbed upon her fingers, pecked at her lips, clung to her shawl, and when she rocked her head to and fro like a nurse, the big wings of her cap and the wings of the bird flapped in unison. When clouds gathered on the horizon and the thunder rumbled, Loulou would scream, perhaps because he remembered the storms in his native forests. The drippings of the rain would excite him to frenzy; he flapped around, struck the ceiling with his wings, upset everything, and would finally fly into the garden to play. Then he would come back into the room, light on one of the andirons, and hop around in order to get dry.

One morning during the terrible winter of 1837, when she had put him in front of the fire-place on account of the cold, she found him dead in his cage, hanging to the wire bars with his head down. He had probably died of congestion. But she believed that he had been poisoned, and although she had no proofs whatever, her suspicion rested on Fabu.

She wept so sorely that her mistress said: "Why don't you have him stuffed?"

She asked the advice of the chemist, who had always been kind to the bird.

He wrote to Le Havre for her. A certain man named Fellacher consented to do the work. But, as the stage coach driver often lost parcels entrusted to him, Félicité resolved to take her pet to Honfleur herself.

Leafless apple-trees lined the edges of the road. The ditches were covered with ice. The dogs on the neighboring farms barked; and Félicité, with her hands beneath her cape, her little black sabots and her basket, trotted along nimbly in the middle of the sidewalk. She crossed the forest, passed by the Haut-Chêne and reached Saint Gatien.

Behind her, in a cloud of dust and impelled by the steep incline, a mail-coach drawn by galloping horses advanced like a whirlwind. When he saw a woman in the middle of the road, who did not get out of the way, the driver stood up in his seat and shouted to her and so did the postilion, while the four horses, which he could not hold back, accelerated their pace; the two leaders were almost upon her; with a jerk of the reins he threw them to one side, but, furious at the incident, he lifted his big whip and lashed her from her head to her feet with such violence that she fell to the ground unconscious.

Her first thought, when she recovered her senses, was to open the basket. Loulou was unharmed. She felt a sting on her right cheek. When she took her hand away it was red, for the blood was flowing.

She sat down on a pile of stones, and sopped her cheek with her handkerchief. Then she ate a crust of bread she had put in her basket and consoled herself by looking at the bird.

Arriving at the top of Ecquemanville, she saw the lights of Honfleur shining in the distance like so many stars; further on, the ocean spread out in a confused mass. Then a weakness came over her; the misery of her childhood, the disappointment of her first love, the departure of her nephew, the death of Virginia; all these things came back to her at once, and, rising like a swelling tide in her throat, almost choked her.

Then she wished to speak to the captain of the vessel, and, without stating what she was sending, she gave him some instructions about it.

Fellacher kept the parrot a long time. He always promised that it would be ready for the following week; after six months he announced the shipment of a case, and that was the end of it. Really, it seemed as if Loulou would never come back to his home. "They have stolen him," thought Félicité.

Finally he arrived, sitting bolt upright on a branch which could be screwed into a mahogany pedestal, with his foot in the air, his head on one side, and in his beak a nut which the naturalist, from love of the sumptuous, had gilded. She put him in her room.

This place, to which only a chosen few were admitted, looked like a chapel and a second-hand shop combined, so filled was it with devotional and heterogeneous things. The door could not be opened easily on account of the presence of a large wardrobe. Opposite the window that looked out into the garden, a bull's eye opened on the yard; a table was placed by the cot and held a wash-basin, two combs, and a piece of blue soap in a broken saucer. On the walls were rosaries, medals, a number of Holy Virgins, and a holy-water basin made out of a cocoanut; on the bureau, which was covered with a napkin like an altar, stood the box of shells that Victor had given her; also a watering can and a balloon, writing-books, the engraved geography and a pair of shoes; on the nail which held the mirror, hung Virginia's little plush hat! Félicité carried this sort of respect so far that she even kept one of Monsieur's old coats. All the things which Madame Aubain discarded, Félicité begged for her own room. Thus, she had artificial flowers on the bureau, and the picture of the Comte d'Artois in the recess of the window. By means of a board, Loulou was set on a portion of the chimney which advanced into the room. Every morning when she awoke, she saw him in the dim light of dawn and recalled bygone days and the smallest details of insignificant actions, without any sense of bitterness or grief.

As she was unable to communicate with people, she lived in a sort of somnambulistic torpor. The processions of Corpus-Christi Day seemed to wake her up. She visited the neighbors to beg for candlesticks and mats so as to adorn the temporary altars in the street.

In church, she always gazed at the Holy Ghost, and noticed that there was something about it that resembled a parrot. The likeness appeared even more striking on a colored picture by Espinel, representing the baptism of our Savior. With his scarlet wings and emerald body, it was really the image of Loulou. Having bought the picture, she hung it near the one of the Comte d'Artois so that she could take them in at one glance.

They associated in her mind, the parrot becoming sanctified through the neighborhood of the Holy Ghost, and the latter becoming more lifelike in her eyes and more comprehensive. In all probability the Father had never chosen as messenger a dove, as the latter has no voice, but rather one of Loulou's ances-

tors. And Félicité said her prayers in front of the colored picture, though from time to time she turned slightly toward the bird.

She desired very much to enter the ranks of the "Daughters of the Virgin." But Madame Aubain dissuaded her from it.

A most important event occurred: Paul's marriage.

After being first a notary's clerk, then in business, then in the customs, and a tax collector, and having even applied for a position in the administration of woods and forests, he had at last, when he was thirty-six years old, by a divine inspiration, found his vocation: registrature! and he displayed such a high ability that an inspector had offered him his daughter and his influence.

Paul, who had become quite settled, brought his bride to visit his mother.

But she looked down upon the customs of Pont-l'Évêque, put on airs, and hurt Félicité's feelings. Madame Aubain felt relieved when she left.

The following week they learned of Monsieur Bourais' death in an inn. There were rumors of suicide, which were confirmed; doubts concerning his integrity arose. Madame Aubain looked over her accounts and soon discovered his numerous embezzlements; sales of wood which he had concealed from her, false receipts, etc. Furthermore, he had an illegitimate child, and entertained a friendship for "a person in Dozulé."

These base actions affected her very much. In March 1853, she developed a pain in her chest; her tongue looked as if it were coated with smoke, and the leeches they applied did not relieve her oppression; and on the ninth evening she died, being just seventy-two years old.

People thought that she was younger, because her hair, which she wore in bands framing her pale face, was brown. Few friends regretted her loss, for her manner was so haughty that she did not attract them. Félicité mourned for her as servants seldom mourn for their masters. The fact that Madame should die before her perplexed her mind and seemed contrary to the order of things, and absolutely monstrous and inadmissible. Ten days later (the time to journey from Besançon), the heirs arrived. Her daughter-in-law ransacked the drawers, kept some of the furniture, and sold the rest; then they went back to their own home.

Madame's armchair, foot-warmer, work-table, the eight chairs, everything was gone! The places occupied by the pictures formed yellow squares on the walls. They had taken the two little beds, and the wardrobe had been emptied of Virginia's belongings! Félicité went upstairs, overcome with grief.

The following day a sign was posted on the door; the chemist screamed in her ear that the house was for sale.

For a moment she tottered, and had to sit down.

What hurt her most was to give up her room,—so nice for poor Loulou! She looked at him in despair and implored the Holy Ghost, and it was this way that she contracted the idolatrous habit of saying her prayers kneeling in front of the bird. Sometimes the sun fell through the window on his glass eye, and lighted a great spark in it which sent Félicité into ecstasy.

Her mistress had left her an income of three hundred and eighty francs. The garden supplied her with vegetables. As for clothes, she had enough to last her till the end of her days, and she economised on the light by going to bed at dusk.

She rarely went out in order to avoid passing in front of the second-hand dealer's shop where there was some of the old furniture. Since her fainting spell, she dragged her leg, and as her strength was failing rapidly, old Mother Simon, who had lost her money in the grocery business, came every morning to chop the wood and pump the water.

Her eyesight grew dim. She did not open the shutters after that. Many years passed. But the house did not sell or rent. Fearing that she would be put out, Félicité did not ask for repairs. The laths of the roof were rotting away, and during one whole winter her bolster was wet. After Easter she spit blood.

Then Mother Simon went for a doctor. Félicité wished to know what her complaint was. But, being too deaf to hear, she caught only one word: "Pneumonia." She was familiar with it and gently answered:—"Ah! like Madame," thinking it quite natural that she should follow her mistress.

The time for the altars in the street drew near.

The first one was always erected at the foot of the hill, the second in front of the post-office, and the third in the middle of the street. This position occasioned some rivalry among the women and they finally decided upon Madame Aubain's yard.

Félicité's fever grew worse. She was sorry that she could not do anything for the altar. If she could, at least, have contributed something toward it! Then she thought of the parrot. Her neighbors objected that it would not be proper. But the curé gave his consent and she was so grateful for it that she begged him to accept after her death her only treasure, Loulou. From Tuesday until Saturday, the day before the event, she coughed more frequently. In the evening her face was contracted, her lips stuck to her gums and she began to vomit; and on the following day, she felt so low that she called for a priest.

Three neighbors surrounded her when the dominie administered the Extreme Unction. Afterwards she said that she wished to speak to Fabu.

He arrived in his Sunday clothes, very ill at ease among the funereal surroundings.

"Forgive me," she said, making an effort to extend her arm. "I believed it was you who killed him!"

What did such accusations mean? Suspect a man like him of murder! And Fabu became excited and was about to make trouble.

"Don't you see she is not in her right mind?"

From time to time Félicité spoke to shadows. The women left her and Mother Simon sat down to breakfast.

A little later, she took Loulou and holding him up to Félicité:

"Say good-bye to him, now!" she commanded.

Although he was not a corpse, he was eaten up by worms; one of his wings was broken and the wadding was coming out of his body. But Félicité was blind now, and she took him and laid him against her cheek. Then Mother Simon removed him in order to set him on the altar.

v

The grass exhaled an odor of summer; flies buzzed in the air, the sun shone on the river and warmed the slated roof. Old Mother Simon had returned to Félicité and was peacefully falling asleep.

The ringing of bells awoke her; the people were coming out of church. Félicité's delirium subsided. By thinking of the procession, she was able to see it as if she had taken part in it. All the school-children, the singers and the firemen walked on the sidewalks, while in the middle of the street came first the custodian of the church with his halberd, then the beadle with a large cross, the teacher in charge of the boys and a sister escorting the little girls; three of the smallest ones, with curly heads, threw rose leaves into the air; the deacon with outstretched arms conducted the music; and two incense-bearers turned with each step they took toward the Holy Sacrament, which was carried by M. le Curé, attired in his handsome chasuble and walking under a canopy of red velvet supported by four men. A crowd of people followed, jammed between the walls of the houses hung with white sheets; at last the procession arrived at the foot of the hill.

A cold sweat broke out on Félicité's forehead. Mother Simon wiped it away with a cloth, saying inwardly that some day she would have to go through the same thing herself.

The murmur of the crowd grew louder; it was very distinct for a moment, then died away. A volley of musketry shook the window-panes. It was the postilions saluting the Sacrament. Félicité rolled her eyes and said as loudly as she could:

"Is he all right?" meaning the parrot.

Her death agony began. A rattle that grew more and more rapid shook her body. Froth appeared at the corners of her mouth, and her whole frame trembled. In a little while could be heard the music of the bass horns, the clear voices of the children and the men's deeper notes. At intervals all was still, and their shoes sounded like a herd of cattle passing over the grass.

The clergy appeared in the yard. Mother Simon climbed on a chair to reach the bull's eye, and in this manner could see the altar. It was covered with a lace cloth and draped with green wreaths. In the middle stood a little frame containing relics; at the corners were two little orange-trees, and all along the edge were silver candlesticks, porcelain vases containing sun-flowers, lilies, peonies, and tufts of hydrangeas. This mound of bright colors descended diagonally from the first floor to the carpet that covered the sidewalk. Rare objects arrested one's eye. A golden sugar-bowl was crowned with violets, earrings set with Alençon stones were displayed on green moss, and two Chinese screens with their bright landscapes were near by. Loulou hidden beneath roses, showed nothing but his blue head which looked like a piece of lapis-lazuli.

The singers, the canopy-bearers and the children lined up against the sides of the yard. Slowly the priest ascended the steps and placed his shining sun on the lace cloth. Everybody knelt. There was deep silence; and the censers slipping on their chains were swung high in the air. A blue vapor rose in Félicité's room. She opened her nostrils and inhaled it with a mystic sensuousness; then she closed her lids. Her lips smiled. The beats of her heart grew fainter and fainter, and vaguer like a fountain giving out, like an echo dying away;—and when she exhaled her last breath, she thought she saw in the half-opened heavens a gigantic parrot hovering above her head.

GUY DE MAUPASSANT

1850–1893

Maupassant was a friend and disciple of Flaubert, from whom he learned the value of precision, conciseness and accurate detail. After a great initial success with his novelette *Boule de Suif*, Maupassant produced, in ten years, some thirty large volumes of short stories and novels. He excelled particularly in the short narrative form and in the realistic character portrait which he created by means of a few bold, rapid, and simple strokes. His personages, who seldom attain lasting happiness, are generally victims of worldly materialism. His most popular works are *Pierre et Jean* (1888), *Une Vie* (1883), *Bel-Ami* (1885). The last months of his life were spent in a complete mental breakdown, probably occasioned by the ravages of venereal disease.

The *contes* of Maupassant were written largely for periodicals, and hence most of them are based upon a single incident presented in ironic understatement and with a graphic economy of phrasing that recalls his devotion to Flaubert's doctrine of "le mot juste." It is doubtful that Maupassant possessed the intellectual qualities to be a great writer, but at his best he writes admirably of simple people, such as peasants. Contrary to some critical impressions, he was not so wholly identified with the impersonal method of naturalism as not to regard human suffering sympathetically, as his novel *Pierre et Jean* and "The Two Little Soldiers" reveal.

FURTHER READING

Boyd, E. A. *Guy de Maupassant. A Biographical Study* (New York, 1926).
Dumesnil, R. *Guy de Maupassant* (Paris, 1947).

The Two Little Soldiers *

Every Sunday, as soon as they were free, the two little soldiers started out.

They turned to the right as they left the barracks, passed rapidly through Courbevoie just as if they were on a march. Then, as soon as they had left the

* Translated by L. G. Locke and M. E. Porter.

houses of the town behind, they continued more slowly along the bare, dusty highway which leads to Bezons.

They were small, thin, and lost in their great army coats which were too wide and too long for them, with sleeves covering their hands. They were also hindered by their red breeches which were too big, making them waddle when they walked. And under their stiff high army caps one could see two gentle, calm eyes and a bit of a face, two sallow Breton faces, which had an almost animal naïveté about them.

They never spoke, but marched straight ahead with the same idea in mind. This took the place of conversation, for they had found at the beginning of the little wood of Campioux a spot which reminded them of home. That was the only place where they could feel happy.

When they reached the trees where the Colombes and Chatou roads cross, they took off their caps, which had been crushing their heads, and wiped their foreheads.

They always stopped on the Bezons bridge to look at the Seine. They stayed there for two or three minutes almost bent double over the parapet; or else they ponderingly watched the harbor of Argenteuil where the clippers with white sails were scudding back and forth, reminding them perhaps of the sea in Brittany, of the port of Vannes near which they lived, and of the fishing boats which sailed across the Morbihan toward the open sea.

As soon as they had crossed the Seine, they bought their lunches at the shops of the local sausage-seller, baker, and wine-merchant. A piece of blood pudding, a few cents' worth of bread and a liter of cheap wine, all of which they carried along wrapped in their handkerchiefs, made up their foodstuffs. However, as soon as they left the village, they proceeded very slowly and began to talk to each other.

In front of them a barren plain, broken only by scattered clumps of trees, led to the wood which had seemed to them like that of Kermarivan. Wheat and oats were growing on both sides of their path which was smothered among the growing grain, and Jean Kerderen would always say to Luc Le Ganidec, "It is almost as if we were at Plounivon."

"Yes, exactly."

They went along side by side, their minds filled with vague memories of their homeland, with memories called up by the fancied similarities to their region, mental pictures which were very much like the childish colored prints which can be bought for a penny. They could see a part of a field, a hedge, a bit of marsh, a crossroad or a granite cross.

Each time also they stopped near a stone which marked the entrance to an estate, because it reminded them of the Locneuven dolmen.

When they arrived at the first clump of trees, Luc Le Ganidec every Sunday cut a switch from a hazel tree, and as he stripped the bark off it he thought of the people back home.

Jean Kerderen carried the provisions.

From time to time Luc mentioned a name, recalled an event of their childhood, in just a few words, but it was enough to give them something to think about for a long time. And their own country, their dear country so far away, gradually took hold of their minds, recaptured their imaginations and let them hear and see from so far away her forms, her noises, her familiar views, her odors, the smell of the green marsh land permeated with the salt sea air.

They were no longer conscious of the odors from the Parisian stables from which the surrounding regions are fertilized, but rather of the perfume of the flowering broom which the salty sea air gathers up and carries inland. And the sails of the boats from the river banks seemed just like those of the coasting vessels which they used to see over the great plain extending from their homes down to the sea-shore.

They walked along slowly, Luc Le Ganidec and Jean Kerderen, happy yet sad, haunted by a sweet lingering melancholy like that of an animal in a cage who remembers the time when he was free.

And when Luc had finished stripping the slender switch of its bark, they reached the corner of the wood where they had lunch every Sunday.

They found the two bricks which they had hidden in a thicket, and they lighted a little fire of a few branches to warm their blood pudding on the points of their knives.

And when they had had lunch, eaten their bread to the last crumb, and drunk their wine down to the last drop, they sat in the grass side by side without saying anything, their eyes focussed on the distance, their eyelids heavy, their fingers crossed as at mass, their red legs stretched out alongside the field poppies; and their leather helmets and brass buttons shone in the brilliant sunlight and stopped the larks, that were hovering over their heads, from singing.

About noon they began to turn their glances from time to time in the direction of the village of Bezons, for the girl with the cow was about to come along. She always passed before them on Sundays as she went to milk and lock up her cow for the night. It was the only cow in this region which was on grass, and which was pastured upon a narrow meadow on the edge of the woods a bit further on.

They soon saw the girl, the only human being walking through the countryside, and they felt joy at seeing the flashes cast off by the tin bucket in the light of the sun. They never spoke to each other about her. They were content just to see her, without understanding why.

She was a tall, strong, red-haired girl, and sunburned—a big, muscular wench from the fields around Paris.

Once, seeing them sitting as usual in the same place, she said, "Good morning . . . you always come here?"

Luc Le Ganidec, more daring than his companion, stammered, "Yes, we come here to rest."

That was all. But the following Sunday, she laughed when she saw them; she laughed with the protective benevolence of a shrewd woman sensing their timidity, and she asked, "What are you doing sitting there that way? Are you watching the grass grow?"

Luc smiled gaily, "Maybe."

She replied, "Well! That doesn't go so fast."

He answered, still laughing, "No, it doesn't."

She passed on. But when she returned with her bucket full of milk, she stopped again before them and said, "Do you want a little? That might remind you of home."

With an instinctive feeling of being of the same stock as they, and perhaps also far from home, she had guessed correctly, and put her finger on the spot.

Both of them were touched. Then with some trouble she poured a little of the milk down the neck of the bottle in which they had brought their wine; and Luc drank first with little swallows, continually stopping to see whether he was going beyond his part. Then he gave the bottle to Jean.

She remained standing before them with her hands on her hips, her bucket on the ground at her feet, happy at the pleasure which she was giving them.

Then she went on, crying after her, "Well, goodbye; until next Sunday!"

And they watched as long as they could see her tall silhouette which grew smaller and smaller as she got farther away, until it seemed to merge into the green land.

When they left the barracks the next week, Jean said to Luc, "Should we buy her something good?"

And they were very much at a loss over the problem of choosing a tidbit for the girl with the cow.

Luc was in favor of a piece of chitterling, but Jean preferred candy, for he loved sweets. His opinion won out and they bought at a grocer's two cents' worth of white and red candies.

They ate lunch more quickly than usual in disturbed anticipation.

Jean saw her first. "There she is," he said.

Luc answered, "Yes, there she is."

Laughing from as far as she could see them, she called, "Is everything going as you want it to?"

They replied together, "Are you getting along all right too?"

Then she stopped to chat, talking of the simple things which interested them, of the weather, of the harvest, of her masters.

They did not dare to offer her their candy which was melting in Jean's pocket.

Luc finally summoned his courage and murmured, "We have brought something."

She asked, "What is it?"

Then Jean, red to the ears, reached for the thin sack of paper and held it out to her.

She began to eat the little pieces of sweet which she rolled from one cheek to the other, making humps under the flesh. The two soldiers, sitting in front of her, watched her with emotion and delight.

Then she went to milk her cow, and she again gave them some milk when she returned.

They thought of her all week long, and they spoke of her several times. The following Sunday she sat down beside them to talk more at length, and all three, side by side, with their knees clasped in their hands, told the small doings and the minute details of the villages where they had been born, while the cow seeing the servant girl sitting down, stretched toward her its heavy head with damp nostrils, and lowed long to call her attention.

The girl soon agreed to have some lunch with them and to drink a bit of their wine. She often brought them plums in her pocket, for the plum season had arrived. Her presence enlivened the two little soldiers from Brittany, and they chattered on like two birds.

Now, one Tuesday, Luc Le Ganidec asked for leave, a thing which he had never done before, and he did not return until ten o'clock that night.

Jean, worried, tried to think of some reason for his comrade's going out that way.

The following Friday, Luc, having borrowed ten sous from the man in the next bunk, again asked for leave and was given permission to be absent for a few hours.

And when he started out with Jean for their Sunday walk, he seemed strange, worried, completely different. Kerderen did not understand, but he had a vague suspicion of something, without being able to guess what it might be.

They did not say a word until they reached their usual place where they had worn down the grass from sitting on it so much; and they ate their lunch slowly. Neither one was hungry.

Soon the girl appeared. They watched her coming as they did every Sunday. When she was near, Luc got up and went toward her. She put down her bucket and kissed him. She kissed him impetuously, throwing her arms around his neck, without paying any attention to Jean, without remembering he was there, without seeing him.

And he was dismayed, poor Jean, so dismayed that he did not understand, his mind upset, his heart breaking, not realizing what had happened.

Then the girl sat down beside Luc and they began to chatter.

Jean did not look at them. He guessed now why his friend had left twice during the week, and he felt within himself a poignant grief, a kind of wound, the sort of anguish which is always caused by betrayal.

Luc and the girl got up to go together to put the cow away.

Jean watched them. He saw them go away side by side. His comrade's red breeches made a brilliant spot on the road. It was Luc who picked up the mallet and drove in the stake to which they tied the animal.

The girl bent over to milk while he dreamily caressed the cow's sharp spine. Then they left the bucket in the grass and disappeared into the woods.

Jean could see nothing but the wall of foliage into which they had disappeared; and he felt so disturbed that, if he had tried to get up, he would certainly have fallen back down.

He remained without moving, overcome with astonishment and suffering, a naïve and profound suffering. He wanted to weep, to run away, to hide, to see no one ever again.

All at once he saw them coming out of the thicket. They came back slowly, holding each other by the hand as those who are betrothed do in the villages. Luc was carrying the bucket.

They kissed each other again before parting, and the girl went away after giving Jean an affectionate

"Good evening" with a meaningful smile. She did not think of offering him any milk that day.

The two little soldiers remained side by side, without moving as usual, silent and calm, so that the placidity of their faces betrayed nothing of the disturbance which was in their hearts. The sun was shining down on them. The cow lowed from time to time as she watched them from afar.

At the usual hour, they got up to return to the barracks.

Luc was peeling the bark off a slender branch. Jean was carrying the empty bottle. He left it at the Bezons wine shop. Then they started over the bridge, and as they did each Sunday, they stopped in the middle to watch the water flow for a few minutes.

Jean was leaning, leaning more and more over the iron balustrade, as if he had seen something interesting in the water below. Luc said to him, "Do you want to drink out of it?"

As he uttered the last word, Jean's head carried the rest of him over, his legs described a circle in the air, and the little blue and red soldier fell in a heap, reached the water, and disappeared.

Luc, his throat paralyzed with anxiety, tried in vain to cry out. He saw something move farther on; then his comrade's head came to the surface of the river only to sink back immediately.

Still further on he again saw a hand, a single hand which came up out of the river and sank back again. That was all.

The sailors who came to help did not find the body that day.

Luc returned alone to the barracks at a run, panic stricken; and he told the story of the accident with his eyes and voice filled with tears, continually blowing his nose:

"He leaned—he le-leaned over—so far—so far—that he went head over heels—and he fell—he fell . . ."

He was so choked with emotion that he could not say any more.—If he had only known—

◆

ÉMILE ZOLA

1840–1902

Zola was a novelist, critic, dramatist, social reformer, and leader of the naturalistic school of writing. Son of an Italian engineer and a French mother, he was during his early years a dock hand, then a bookstore employee, when he used his free time for writing. Under the influence of positivism and modern scientific attitudes, Zola reacted strongly against the uncritical Romantic works of imagination. He believed that he could present in novel form profoundly scientific sociological studies which would be true documents of human life and customs. It was his theory that the laws of heredity and the influence of environment could be determined and presented in novel form with mathematical precision. His *Experimental Novel* (1880) outlines his theories. A novel for him was not merely observation of life's fortuitous occurrences but a laboratory in which experiments artificially produce data from which scientific laws may be determined inductively. Thus came into being the series entitled *The Rougon-Macquart,* by which he intended to provide social workers with a series of principles which would aid materially in their task of producing human happiness and well-being. Among the best novels in the series are *L'Assommoir* (1877), *Germinal* (1885), *La Bête Humaine* (1890) and *La Débâcle* (1892).

FURTHER READING

BARBUSSE, H. *Zola* (New York, 1933).
JOSEPHSON, MATTHEW. *Zola and His Time* (New York, 1928).

The Attack on the Mill *

I

IT WAS high holiday at Father Merlier's mill on that pleasant summer afternoon. Three tables had been brought out into the garden and placed end to end in the shadow of the great elm, and now they were awaiting the arrival of the guests. It was known throughout the length and breadth of the land that that day was to witness the betrothal of old Merlier's daughter, Françoise, to Dominique, a young man who was said to be not over fond of work, but whom never a woman for three leagues of the country could look at without sparkling eyes, such a well-favored young fellow was he.

That mill of Father Merlier's was truly a very pleasant spot. It was situated right in the heart of Rocreuse, at the place where the main road makes a sharp bend. The village has but a single street,

* Translated by E. P. Robins.

bordered on either side by a row of low, whitened cottages, but just there where the road curves, there are broad stretches of meadow-land, and huge trees, which follow the course of the Morelle, cover the low grounds of the valley with a most delicious shade. All Lorraine has no more charming bit of nature to show. To right and left dense forests, great monarchs of the wood, centuries old, rise from the gentle slopes and fill the horizon with a sea of verdure, while away towards the south extends the plain, of wondrous fertility and checkered almost to infinity with its small enclosures, divided off from one another by their live hedges. But what makes the crowning glory of Rocreuse is the coolness of this verdurous nook, even in the hottest days of July and August. The Morelle comes down from the woods of Gagny, and it would seem as if it gathered to itself on the way all the delicious freshness of the foliage beneath which it glides for many a league; it brings down with it the murmuring sounds, the glacial, solemn shadows of the forest. And that is not the only source of coolness; there are running waters of all kinds singing among the copses; one cannot take a step without coming on a gushing spring, and as he makes his way along the narrow paths he seems to be treading above subterranean lakes that seek the air and sunshine through the moss above and profit by every smallest crevice, at the roots of trees or among the chinks and crannies of the rocks, to burst forth in fountains of crystalline clearness. So numerous and so loud are the whispering voices of these streams that they silence the song of the bullfinches. It is as if one were in an enchanted park, with cascades falling on every side.

The meadows below are never athirst. The shadows beneath the gigantic chestnut trees are of inky blackness, and along the hedges of the fields long rows of poplars stand like walls of rustling foliage. There is a double avenue of huge plane trees ascending across the fields toward the ancient castle of Gagny, now gone to rack and ruin. In this region, where drought is never known, vegetation of all kinds is wonderfully rank; it is like a flower garden down there in the low ground between those two wooded hills, a natural garden, where the lawns are broad meadows and the giant trees represent colossal beds. When the noonday sun pours down his scorching rays the shadows lie blue upon the ground, the glowing vegetation slumbers in the heat, while every now and then a breath of icy coldness passes under the foliage.

Such was the spot where Father Merlier's mill

enlivened with its cheerful clacking nature run riot. The building itself, constructed of wood and plaster, looked as if it might be coeval with our planet. Its foundations were in part washed by the Morelle, which here expands into a clear pool. A dam, a few feet in height, afforded sufficient head of water to drive the old wheel, which creaked and groaned as it revolved, with the asthmatic wheezing of a faithful servant who has grown old in her place. Whenever Father Merlier was advised to change it, he would shake his head and say that like as not a young wheel would be lazier and not so well acquainted with its duties, and then he would set to work and patch up the old one with anything that came to hand, old hogshead-staves, bits of rusty iron, zinc, or lead. The old wheel only seemed the gayer for it, with its odd profile, all plumed and feathered with tufts of moss and grass, and when the water poured over it in a silvery tide its gaunt black skeleton was decked out with a gorgeous display of pearls and diamonds.

That portion of the mill which was bathed by the Morelle had something of the look of a barbaric arch that had been dropped down there by chance. A good half of the structure was built on piles; the water came in under the floor, and there were deep holes, famous throughout the whole country for the eels and the huge crawfish that were to be caught there. Below the fall the pool was as clear as a mirror, and when it was not clouded by foam from the wheel one could see troops of great fish swimming about in it with the slow, majestic movements of a squadron. There was a broken stairway leading down to the stream, near a stake to which a boat was fastened, and over the wheel was a gallery of wood. Such windows as there were were arranged without any attempt at order. The whole was a quaint conglomeration of nooks and corners, bits of wall, additions made here and there as afterthoughts, beams and roofs, that gave the mill the aspect of an old dismantled citadel; but ivy and all sorts of creeping plants had grown luxuriantly and kindly covered up such crevices as were too unsightly, casting a mantle of green over the old dwelling. Young ladies who passed that way used to stop and sketch Father Merlier's mill in their albums.

The side of the house that faced the road was less irregular. A gateway in stone afforded access to the principal courtyard, on the right and left hand of which were sheds and stables. Beside a well stood an immense elm that threw its shade over half the court. At the farther end, opposite the gate, stood the houses surmounted by a dovecote, the four windows of its first floor in a symmetrical line. The only vanity that Father Merlier ever allowed himself was to paint this façade every ten years. It had just been freshly whitened at the time of our story, and dazzled the eyes of all the village when the sun lighted it up in the middle of the day.

For twenty years Father Merlier had been mayor of Rocreuse. He was held in great consideration on account of his fortune; he was supposed to be worth something like eighty thousand francs, the result of patient saving. When he married Madeleine Guillard, who brought him the mill as her dowry, his entire capital lay in his two strong arms, but Madeleine had never repented of her choice, so manfully had he conducted their joint affairs. Now his wife was dead, and he was left a widower with his daughter Françoise. Doubtless he might have sat himself down to take his rest and suffered the old mill wheel to sleep among its moss, but he would have found idleness too irksome, and the house would have seemed dead to him. He kept on working still for the pleasure of it. In those days Father Merlier was a tall old man, with a long, silent face, on which a laugh was never seen, but beneath which there lay, none the less, a large fund of good humor. He had been elected mayor on account of his money, and also for the impressive air that he knew how to assume when it devolved on him to marry a couple.

Françoise Merlier had just completed her eighteenth year. She was small, and for that reason was not accounted one of the beauties of the country. Until she reached the age of fifteen she had been even homely; the good folks of Rocreuse could not see how it was that the daughter of Father and Mother Merlier, such a hale, vigorous couple, had such a hard time of it in getting her growth. When she was fifteen, however, though still remaining delicate, a change came over her and she took on the prettiest little face imaginable. She had black hair, black eyes, and was red as a rose withal; her mouth was always smiling, there were delicious dimples in her cheeks, and a crown of sunshine seemed to be ever resting on her fair, candid forehead. Although small, as girls went in that region, she was far from being thin; she might not have been able to raise a sack of wheat to her shoulder, but she became quite plump as she grew older, and gave promise of becoming eventually as well-rounded and appetizing as a partridge. Her father's habits of taciturnity had made her reflective while yet a young girl; if she always had a smile on her lips it was in order to give pleasure to others. Her natural disposition was serious.

As was no more than to be expected, she had every young man in the countryside at her heels as a suitor, more even for her money than for her attractiveness, and she had made a choice at last, a choice that had been the talk and scandal of the entire neighborhood.

On the other side of the Morelle lived a strapping young fellow who went by the name of Dominique Penquer. He was not to the manner born; ten years previously he had come to Rocreuse from Belgium to receive the inheritance of an uncle who had owned a small property on the very borders of the forest of Gagny, just facing the mill and distant from it only a few musket-shots. His object in coming was to sell the property, so he said, and return to his own home again; but he must have found the land to his liking, for he made no move to go away. He was seen cultivating his bit of field and gathering the few vegetables that afforded him an existence. He fished, he hunted; more than once he was near coming in contact with the law through the intervention of the keepers. This independent way of living, of which the peasants could not very clearly see the resources, had in the end given him a bad name. He was vaguely looked on as nothing better than a poacher. At all events he was lazy, for he was frequently found sleeping in the grass at hours when he should have been at work. Then, too, the hut in which he lived, in the shade of the last trees of the forest, did not seem like the abode of an honest young man; the old women would not have been surprised at any time to hear that he was on friendly terms with the wolves in the ruins of Gagny. Still, the young girls would now and then venture to stand up for him, for he was altogether a splendid specimen of manhood, was this individual of doubtful antecedents, tall and straight as a young poplar, with a milk-white skin and ruddy hair and moustaches that seemed to be of gold when the sun shone on them. Now one fine morning it came to pass that Françoise told Father Merlier that she loved Dominique, and that never, never would she consent to marry any other young man.

It may be imagined what a knockdown blow it was that Father Merlier received that day! As was his wont, he said never a word; his countenance wore its usual reflective look, only the fun that used to bubble up from within no longer shone in his eyes. Françoise, too, was very serious, and for a

week father and daughter scarcely spoke to each other. What troubled Father Merlier was to know how that rascal of a poacher had succeeded in bewitching his daughter. Dominique had never shown himself at the mill. The miller played the spy a little, and was rewarded by catching sight of the gallant, on the other side of the Morelle, lying among the grass and pretending to be asleep. Françoise could see him from her chamber window. The thing was clear enough; they had been making sheep's eyes at each other over the old mill wheel, and so had fallen in love.

A week slipped by; Françoise became more and more serious. Father Merlier still continued to say nothing. Then, one evening, of his own accord, he brought Dominique to the house, without a word. Françoise was just setting the table. She made no demonstration of surprise; all she did was to add another plate, but her laugh had come back to her, and the little dimples appeared again upon her cheeks. Father Merlier had gone that morning to look for Dominique at his hut on the edge of the forest, and there the two men had had a conference, with closed doors and windows, that lasted three hours. No one ever knew what they said to each other; the only thing certain is that when Father Merlier left the hut he already treated Dominique as a son. Doubtless the old man had discovered that he whom he had gone to visit was a worthy young fellow, even though he did lie in the grass to gain the love of young girls.

All Rocreuse was up in arms. The women gathered at their doors and could not find words strong enough to characterize Father Merlier's folly in thus receiving a ne'er-do-well into his family. He let them talk. Perhaps he thought of his own marriage. Neither had he possessed a penny to his name at the time he married Madeleine and her mill, and yet that had not prevented him from being a good husband to her. Moreover, Dominique put an end to their tittle-tattle by setting to work in such strenuous fashion that all the countryside was amazed. It so happened just then that the boy of the mill drew an unlucky number and had to go as a soldier, and Dominique would not hear of their engaging another. He lifted sacks, drove the cart, wrestled with the old wheel when it took an obstinate fit and refused to turn, and all so pluckily and cheerfully that people came from far and near merely for the pleasure of seeing him. Father Merlier laughed his silent laugh. He was highly elated that he had read the youngster aright. There is nothing like love to hearten up young men.

In the midst of all that laborious toil Françoise and Dominique fairly worshiped each other. They had not much to say, but their tender smiles conveyed a world of meaning. Father Merlier had not said a word thus far on the subject of their marriage, and they had both respected his silence, waiting until the old man should see fit to give expression to his will. At last, one day, toward the middle of July, he had had three tables laid in the courtyard, in the shade of the big elm, and had invited his friends of Rocreuse to come that afternoon and drink a glass of wine with them. When the courtyard was filled with people, and everyone there had a full glass in his hand, Father Merlier raised his own high above his head and said:

"I have the pleasure of announcing to you that Françoise and this lad will be married in a month from now, on Saint Louis's fête-day."

Then there was a universal touching of glasses, attended by a tremendous uproar; everyone was laughing. But Father Merlier, raising his voice above the din, again spoke:

"Dominique, kiss your wife that is to be. It is no more than customary."

And they kissed, very red in the face, both of them, while the company laughed louder still. It was a regular fête; they emptied a small cask. Then, when only the intimate friends of the house remained, conversation went on in a calmer strain. Night had fallen, a starlit night, and very clear. Dominique and Françoise sat on a bench, side by side, and said nothing. An old peasant spoke of the war that the Emperor had declared against Prussia. All the lads of the village were already gone off to the army. Troops had passed through the place only the night before. There were going to be hard knocks.

"Bah!" said Father Merlier, with the selfishness of a man who is quite happy, "Dominique is a foreigner; he won't have to go—and if the Prussians come this way, he will be here to defend his wife."

The idea of the Prussians coming there seemed to the company an exceedingly good joke. The army would give them one good conscientious thrashing, and the affair would be quickly ended.

"I have seen them before, I have seen them before," the old peasant repeated, in a low voice.

There was silence for a little; then they all touched glasses once again. Françoise and Dominique had heard nothing; they had managed to clasp hands behind the bench in such a way as not to be seen by the others, and this condition of affairs seemed so beatific to them that they sat there mute, their gaze lost in the darkness of the night.

What a magnificent, balmy night! The village lay slumbering on either side of the white road as peacefully as a little child. The deep silence was undisturbed save by the occasional crow of a cock in some distant barnyard acting on a mistaken impression that dawn was at hand. Perfumed breaths of air, like long-drawn sighs, came down from the great woods that lay around and above, sweeping softly over the roofs, as if caressing them. The meadows, with their black intensity of shadow, took on a dim, mysterious majesty of their own, while all the springs, all the brooks and watercourses that gurgled in the darkness, might have been taken for the cool and rhythmical breathing of the sleeping country. Every now and then the old dozing mill wheel seemed to be dreaming like a watchdog that barks uneasily in his slumber; it creaked, it talked to itself, rocked by the fall of the Morelle, whose current gave forth the deep, sustained music of an organ pipe. Never was there a more charming or happier nook; never did a deeper peace come down to cover it.

II

One month later, to a day, on the eve of the fête of Saint Louis, Rocreuse was in a state of alarm and dismay. The Prussians had beaten the Emperor, and were advancing on the village by forced marches. For a week past people passing along the road had brought tidings of the enemy: "They are at Lormières, they are at Nouvelles"; and by dint of hearing so many stories of the rapidity of their advance, Rocreuse woke up every morning in the full expectation of seeing them swarming down out of Gagny wood. They did not come, however, and that only served to make the affright the greater. They would certainly fall upon the village in the nighttime and put every soul to the sword.

There had been an alarm the night before, a little before daybreak. The inhabitants had been aroused by a great noise of men tramping upon the road. The women were already throwing themselves upon their knees and making the sign of the cross, when someone, to whom it happily occurred to peer through a half-opened window, caught sight of red trousers. It was a French detachment. The captain had forthwith asked for the mayor, and, after a long conversation with Father Merlier, had remained at the mill.

The sun shone bright and clear that morning,

giving promise of a warm day. There was a golden light floating over the woodland, while in the low grounds white mists were rising from the meadows. The pretty village, so neat and trim, awoke in the cool dawning; and the country, with its streams and its fountains, was as gracious as a freshly plucked bouquet. But the beauty of the day brought gladness to the face of no one; the villagers had watched the captain, and seen him circle round and round the old mill, examine the adjacent houses, then pass to the other bank of the Morelle, and from thence scan the country with a fieldglass; Father Merlier, who accompanied him, appeared to be giving explanations. After that the captain had posted some of his men behind walls, behind trees, or in hollows. The main body of the detachment had encamped in the courtyard of the mill. So there was going to be a fight, then? And when Father Merlier returned they questioned him. He spoke no word, but slowly and sorrowfully nodded his head. Yes, there was going to be a fight.

Françoise and Dominique were there in the courtyard, watching him. He finally took his pipe from his lips and gave utterance to these few words:

"Ah! my poor children, I shall not be able to marry you today!"

Dominique, with lips tight set and an angry frown upon his forehead, raised himself on tiptoe from time to time and stood with eyes bent on Gagny wood, as if he would have been glad to see the Prussians appear and end the suspense they were in. Françoise, whose face was grave and very pale, was constantly passing back and forth, supplying the needs of the soldiers. They were preparing their soup in a corner of the courtyard, joking and chaffing one another while awaiting their meal.

The captain appeared to be highly pleased. He had visited the chambers and the great hall of the mill that looked out on the stream. Now, seated beside the well, he was conversing with Father Merlier.

"You have a regular fortress here," he was saying. "We shall have no trouble in holding it until evening. The bandits are late; they ought to be here by this time."

The miller looked very grave. He saw his beloved mill going up in flame and smoke, but uttered no word of remonstrance or complaint, considering that it would be useless. He only opened his mouth to say: "You ought to take steps to hide the boat; there is a hole behind the wheel fitted to hold it. Perhaps you may find it of use to you."

The captain gave an order to one of his men. This captain was a tall, fine-looking man of about forty, with an agreeable expression of countenance. The sight of Dominique and Françoise seemed to afford him much pleasure; he watched them as if he had forgotten all about the approaching conflict. He followed Françoise with his eyes as she moved about the courtyard, and his manner showed clearly enough that he thought her charming. Then, turning to Dominique: "You are not with the army, I see, my boy?" he abruptly asked.

"I am a foreigner," the young man replied.

The captain did not seem particularly pleased with the answer; he winked his eyes and smiled. Françoise was doubtless a more agreeable companion than a musket would have been. Dominique, noticing his smile, made haste to add: "I am a foreigner, but I can lodge a rifle bullet in an apple at five hundred yards. See, there's my rifle behind you."

"You may find use for it," the captain drily answered.

Françoise had drawn near; she was trembling a little, and Dominique, regardless of the bystanders, took and held firmly clasped in his own the two hands that she held forth to him, as if committing herself to his protection. The captain smiled again, but said nothing more. He remained seated, his sword between his legs, his eyes fixed on space, apparently lost in dreamy reverie.

It was ten o'clock. The heat was already oppressive. A deep silence prevailed. The soldiers had sat down in the shade of the sheds in the courtyard and begun to eat their soup. Not a sound came from the village, where the inhabitants had all barricaded their houses, doors, and windows. A dog, abandoned by his master, howled mournfully upon the road. From the woods and the near-by meadows, that lay fainting in the heat, came a long-drawn, whispering, soughing sound, produced by the union of what wandering breaths of air there were. A cuckoo called. Then the silence became deeper still.

And all at once, upon that lazy, sleepy air, a shot rang out. The captain rose quickly to his feet, the soldiers left their half-emptied plates. In a few seconds all were at their posts; the mill was occupied from top to bottom. And yet the captain, who had gone out through the gate, saw nothing; to right and left the road stretched away, desolate and blindingly white in the fierce sunshine. A second report was heard, and still nothing to be seen, not even so much as a shadow; but just as he was turning to re-enter he chanced to look over toward Gagny and there beheld a little puff of smoke floating away on the tranquil air, like thistledown. The deep peace of the forest was apparently unbroken.

"The rascals have occupied the wood," the officer murmured. "They know we are here."

Then the firing went on and became more and more continuous between the French soldiers posted about the mill and the Prussians concealed among the trees. The bullets whistled over the Morelle without doing any mischief on either side. The firing was irregular; every bush seemed to have its marksman, and nothing was to be seen save those bluish smoke wreaths that hung for a moment on the wind before they vanished. It lasted thus for nearly two hours. The officer hummed a tune with a careless air. Françoise and Dominique, who had remained in the courtyard, raised themselves to look out over a low wall. They were more particularly interested in a little soldier who had his post on the bank of the Morelle, behind the hull of an old boat; he would lie face downward on the ground, watch his chance, deliver his fire, then slip back into a ditch a few steps in his rear to reload, and his movements were so comical, he displayed such cunning and activity, that it was difficult for anyone watching him to refrain from smiling. He must have caught sight of a Prussian, for he rose quickly and brought his piece to his shoulder, but before he could discharge it he uttered a loud cry, whirled completely around in his tracks, and fell backward into the ditch, where for an instant his legs moved convulsively, just as the claws of a fowl do when it is beheaded. The little soldier had received a bullet directly through his heart. It was the first casualty of the day. Françoise instinctively seized Dominique's hand, and held it tight in a convulsive grasp.

"Come away from there," said the captain. "The bullets reach us here."

As if to confirm his words, a slight, sharp sound was heard up in the old elm, and the end of a branch came to the ground, turning over and over as it fell, but the two young people never stirred, riveted to the spot as they were by the interest of the spectacle. On the edge of the wood, a Prussian had suddenly emerged from behind a tree, as an actor comes upon the stage from the wings, beating the air with his arms and falling over upon his back. And beyond that there was no movement; the two dead men appeared to be sleeping in the bright sunshine; there was not a soul to be seen in the fields on which the heat lay heavy. Even the sharp rattle of the musketry had ceased. Only the Morelle kept on whispering to itself with its low, musical murmur.

Father Merlier looked at the captain with an astonished air, as if to inquire whether that were the end of it.

"Here comes their attack," the officer murmured. "Look out for yourself! Don't stand there!"

His words were scarcely out of his mouth when a terrible discharge of musketry ensued. The great elm was riddled, its leaves came eddying down as thick as snowflakes. Fortunately the Prussians had aimed too high. Dominique dragged, almost carried, Françoise from the spot, while Father Merlier followed them, shouting: "Get into the small cellar, the walls are thicker there."

But they paid no attention to him; they made their way to the main hall, where ten or a dozen soldiers were silently waiting, watching events outside through the chinks of the closed shutters. The captain was left alone in the courtyard, where he sheltered himself behind the low wall, while the furious fire was maintained uninterruptedly. The soldiers whom he had posted outside only yielded their ground inch by inch; they came crawling in, however, one after another, as the enemy dislodged them from their positions. Their instructions were to gain all the time they could, taking care not to show themselves, in order that the Prussians might remain in ignorance of the force they had opposed to them. Another hour passed, and as a sergeant came in, reporting that there were now only two or three men left outside, the officer took his watch from his pocket, murmuring: "Half-past two. Come, we must hold out for four hours yet."

He caused the great gate of the courtyard to be tightly secured, and everything was made ready for an energetic defense. The Prussians were on the other side of the Morelle; consequently there was no reason to fear an assault at the moment. There was a bridge indeed, a mile and a quarter away, but they were probably unaware of its existence, and it was hardly to be supposed that they would attempt to cross the stream by fording. The officer, therefore, simply caused the road to be watched; the attack, when it came, was to be looked for from the direction of the fields.

The firing had ceased again. The mill appeared to lie there in the sunlight, void of all life. Not a shutter was open, not a sound came from within. Gradually, however, the Prussians began to show themselves at the edge of Gagny wood. Heads were protruded here and there; they seemed to be mustering up their courage. Several of the soldiers within the mill brought up their pieces to an aim, but the captain shouted: "No, no; not yet; wait. Let them come nearer."

They displayed a great deal of prudence in their advance, looking at the mill with a distrustful air; they seemed hardly to know what to make of the old structure, so lifeless and gloomy, with its curtain of ivy. Still they kept on advancing. When there were fifty of them or so in the open, directly opposite, the officer uttered one word: "Now!"

A crashing, tearing discharge burst from the position, succeeded by an irregular, dropping fire. Françoise, trembling violently, involuntarily raised her hands to her ears. Dominique, from his position behind the soldiers, peered out upon the field, and when the smoke drifted away a little, counted three Prussians extended on their backs in the middle of the meadow. The others had sought shelter among the willows and the poplars. And then commenced the siege.

For more than an hour the mill was riddled with bullets; they beat and rattled on its old walls like hail. The noise they made was plainly audible as they struck the stonework, were flattened, and fell back into the water; they buried themselves in the woodwork with a dull thud. Occasionally a creaking sound would announce that the wheel had been hit. Within the building the soldiers husbanded their ammunition, firing only when they could see something to aim at. The captain kept consulting his watch every few minutes, and as a ball split one of the shutters in halves and then lodged in the ceiling: "Four o'clock," he murmured. "We shall never be able to hold the position."

The old mill, in truth, was gradually going to pieces beneath that terrific fire. A shutter that had been perforated again and again, until it looked like a piece of lace, fell off its hinges into the water, and had to be replaced by a mattress. Every moment, almost, Father Merlier exposed himself to the fire in order to take account of the damage sustained by his poor wheel, every wound of which was like a bullet in his own heart. Its period of usefulness was ended this time for certain; he would never be able to patch it up again. Dominique had besought Françoise to retire to a place of safety, but she was determined to remain with him; she had taken a seat behind a great oaken clothespress, which afforded her protection. A ball struck the press, however, the sides of which gave out a dull hollow sound, whereupon Dominique stationed

himself in front of Françoise. He had as yet taken no part in the firing, although he had his rifle in his hand; the soldiers occupied the whole breadth of the windows, so that he could not get near them. At every discharge the floor trembled.

"Look out! look out!" the captain suddenly shouted.

He had just descried a dark mass emerging from the wood. As soon as they gained the open they set up a telling platoon fire. It struck the mill like a tornado. Another shutter parted company, and the bullets came whistling in through the yawning aperture. Two soldiers rolled upon the floor; one lay where he fell and never moved a limb; his comrades pushed him up against the wall because he was in their way. The other writhed and twisted, beseeching someone to end his agony, but no one had ears for the poor wretch; the bullets were still pouring in, and everyone was looking out for himself and searching for a loophole whence he might answer the enemy's fire. A third soldier was wounded; that one said not a word, but with staring, haggard eyes sank down beneath a table. Françoise, horror-stricken by the dreadful spectacle of the dead and dying men, mechanically pushed away her chair and seated herself on the floor, against the wall; it seemed to her that she would be smaller there and less exposed. In the meantime men had gone and secured all the mattresses in the house; the opening of the window was partially closed again. The hall was filled with debris of every description, broken weapons, dislocated furniture.

"Five o'clock," said the captain. "Stand fast, boys. They are going to make an attempt to pass the stream."

Just then Françoise gave a shriek. A bullet had struck the floor, and, rebounding, grazed her forehead on the ricochet. A few drops of blood appeared. Dominique looked at her, then went to the window and fired his first shot, and from that time kept on firing uninterruptedly. He kept on loading and discharging his piece mechanically, paying no attention to what was passing at his side, only pausing from time to time to cast a look at Françoise. He did not fire hurriedly or at random, moreover, but took deliberate aim. As the captain had predicted, the Prussians were skirting the belt of poplars and attempting the passage of the Morelle, but each time that one of them showed himself he fell with one of Dominique's bullets in his brain. The captain, who was watching the performance, was amazed; he complimented the young man, telling him that he would like to have many more marksmen of his skill. Dominique did not hear a word he said. A ball struck him in the shoulder, another raised a contusion on his arm. And still he kept on firing.

There were two more deaths. The mattresses were torn to shreds and no longer availed to stop the windows. The last volley that was poured in seemed as if it would carry away the mill bodily, so fierce it was. The position was no longer tenable. Still the officer kept repeating: "Stand fast. Another half-hour yet."

He was counting the minutes, one by one, now. He had promised his commanders that he would hold the enemy there until nightfall, and he would not budge a hair's-breadth before the moment that he had fixed on for his withdrawal. He maintained his pleasant air of good humor, smiling at Françoise by way of reassuring her. He had picked up the musket of one of the dead soldiers and was firing away with the rest.

There were but four soldiers left in the room. The Prussians were showing themselves en masse on the other side of the Morelle, and it was evident that they might now pass the stream at any moment. A few moments more elapsed; the captain was as determined as ever, and would not give the order to retreat, when a sergeant came running into the room, saying: "They are on the road; they are going to take us in the rear."

The Prussians must have discovered the bridge. The captain drew out his watch again.

"Five minutes more," he said. "They won't be here within five minutes."

Then exactly at six o'clock he at last withdrew his men through a little postern that opened on a narrow lane, whence they threw themselves into the ditch, and in that way reached the forest of Sauval. The captain took leave of Father Merlier with much politeness, apologizing profusely for the trouble he had caused. He even added: "Try to keep them occupied for a while. We shall return."

While this was occurring Dominique had remained alone in the hall. He was still firing away, hearing nothing, conscious of nothing; his sole thought was to defend Françoise. The soldiers were all gone, and he had not the remotest idea of the fact; he aimed and brought down his man at every shot. All at once there was a great tumult. The Prussians had entered the courtyard from the rear. He fired his last shot, and they fell upon him with his weapon still smoking in his hand.

It required four men to hold him; the rest of them

swarmed about him, vociferating like madmen in their horrible dialect. Françoise rushed forward to intercede with her prayers. They were on the point of killing him on the spot, but an officer came in and made them turn the prisoner over to him. After exchanging a few words in German with his men he turned to Dominique and said to him roughly, in very good French: "You will be shot in two hours from now."

III

It was the standing regulation, laid down by the German staff, that every Frenchman not belonging to the regular army taken with arms in his hands should be shot. Even the *compagnies franches*[1] were not recognized as belligerents. It was the intention of the Germans, in making such terrible examples of the peasants who attempted to defend their firesides, to prevent a rising en masse, which they greatly dreaded.

The officer, a tall, square man about fifty years old, subjected Dominique to a brief examination. Although he spoke French fluently, he was unmistakably Prussian in the stiffness of his manner.

"You are a native of this country?"

"No, I am a Belgian."

"Why did you take up arms? These are matters with which you have no concern."

Dominique made no reply. At this moment the officer caught sight of Françoise where she stood listening, very pale; her slight wound had marked her white forehead with a streak of red. He looked from one to the other of the young people and appeared to understand the situation: he merely added: "You do not deny having fired on my men?"

"I fired as long as I was able to do so," Dominique quietly replied.

The admission was scarcely necessary, for he was black with powder, wet with sweat, and the blood from the wound in his shoulder had trickled down and stained his clothing.

"Very well," the officer repeated. "You will be shot two hours hence."

Françoise uttered no cry. She clasped her hands and raised them above her head in a gesture of mute despair. Her action was not lost upon the officer. Two soldiers had led Dominique away to an adjacent room, where their orders were to guard him and not lose sight of him. The girl had sunk upon a chair; her strength had failed her, her legs refused to support her; she was denied the relief of tears; it seemed as if her emotion was strangling her. The

[1] *compagnies franches*: snipers.

officer continued to examine her attentively, and finally addressed her. "Is that young man your brother?" he inquired.

She shook her head in negation. He was as rigid and unbending as ever, without the suspicion of a smile on his face. Then, after an interval of silence, he spoke again: "Has he been living in the neighborhood long?"

She answered yes, by another motion of the head.

"Then he must be well acquainted with the woods about here?"

This time she made a verbal answer. "Yes, sir," she said, looking at him with some astonishment.

He said nothing more, but turned on his heel, requesting that the mayor of the village should be brought before him. But Françoise had risen from her chair, a faint tinge of color on her cheeks, believing that she had caught the significance of his questions, and with renewed hope she ran off to look for her father.

As soon as the firing had ceased, Father Merlier had hurriedly descended by the wooden gallery to have a look at his wheel. He adored his daughter and had a strong feeling of affection for Dominique, his son-in-law who was to be; but his wheel also occupied a large space in his heart. Now that the two little ones, as he called them, had come safe and sound out of the fray, he thought of his other love, which must have suffered sorely, poor thing, and bending over the great wooden skeleton he was scrutinizing its wounds with a heart-broken air. Five of the buckets were reduced to splinters, the central framework was honeycombed. He was thrusting his fingers into the cavities that the bullets had made to see how deep they were and reflecting how he was ever to repair all that damage. When Françoise found him he was already plugging up the crevices with moss and such debris as he could lay hands on.

"They are asking for you, father," said she.

And at last she wept as she told him what she had just heard. Father Merlier shook his head. It was not customary to shoot people like that. He would have to look into the matter. And he reentered the mill with his usual placid, silent air. When the officer made his demand for supplies for his men, he answered that the people of Rocreuse were not accustomed to be ridden roughshod, and that nothing would be obtained from them through violence; he was willing to assume all the responsibility, but only on condition that he was allowed to act independently. The officer at first appeared to take umbrage at this easy way of viewing matters, but finally gave way before the old man's brief and distinct representations. As the latter was leaving the room the other recalled him to ask: "Those woods there, opposite, what do you call them?"

"The woods of Sauval."

"And how far do they extend?"

The miller looked him straight in the face. "I do not know," he replied.

And he withdrew. An hour later the subvention in money and provisions that the officer had demanded was in the courtyard of the mill. Night was coming on; Françoise followed every movement of the soldiers with an anxious eye. She never once left the vicinity of the room in which Dominique was imprisoned. About seven o'clock she had a harrowing emotion; she saw the officer enter the prisoner's apartment, and for a quarter of an hour heard their voices raised in violent discussion. The officer came to the door for a moment and gave an order in German which she did not understand, but when twelve men came and formed in the courtyard with shouldered muskets, she was seized with a fit of trembling and felt as if she should die. It was all over, then; the execution was about to take place. The twelve men remained there ten minutes; Dominique's voice kept rising higher and higher in a tone of vehement denial. Finally the officer came out, closing the door behind him with a vicious bang and saying:

"Very well; think it over. I give you until tomorrow morning."

And he ordered the twelve men to break ranks by a motion of his hand. Françoise was stupefied. Father Merlier, who had continued to puff away at his pipe while watching the platoon with a simple, curious air, came and took her by the arm with fatherly gentleness. He led her to her chamber.

"Don't fret," he said to her; "try to get some sleep. Tomorrow it will be light and we shall see more clearly."

He locked the door behind him as he left the room. It was a fixed principle with him that women are good for nothing, and that they spoil everything whenever they meddle in important matters. Françoise did not lie down, however; she remained a long time seated on her bed, listening to the various noises in the house. The German soldiers quartered in the courtyard were singing and laughing; they must have kept up their eating and drinking until eleven o'clock, for the riot never ceased for an instant. Heavy footsteps resounded from time to time through the mill itself, doubtless the tramp of the guards as they were relieved. What had most interest for her was the sounds that she could catch in the room that lay directly under her own; several times she threw herself prone upon the floor and applied her ear to the boards. That room was the one in which they had locked up Dominique. He must have been pacing the apartment, for she could hear for a long time his regular, cadenced tread passing from the wall to the window and back again; then there was a deep silence; doubtless he had seated himself. The other sounds ceased too; everything was still. When it seemed to her that the house was sunk in slumber she raised her window as noiselessly as possible and leaned out.

Without, the night was serene and balmy. The slender crescent of the moon, which was just setting behind Sauval wood, cast a dim radiance over the landscape. The lengthening shadows of the great trees stretched far athwart the fields in bands of blackness, while in such spots as were unobscured the grass appeared of a tender green, soft as velvet. But Françoise did not stop to consider the mysterious charm of night. She was scrutinizing the country and looking to see where the Germans had posted their sentinels. She could clearly distinguish their dark forms outlined along the course of the Morelle. There was only one stationed opposite the mill, on the far bank of the stream, by a willow whose branches dipped in the water. Françoise had an excellent view of him; he was a tall young man, standing quite motionless with face upturned toward the sky, with the meditative air of a shepherd.

When she had completed her careful inspection of localities she returned and took her former seat upon the bed. She remained there an hour, absorbed in deep thought. Then she listened again; there was not a breath to be heard in the house. She went again to the window and took another look outside, but one of the moon's horns was still hanging above the edge of the forest, and this circumstance doubtless appeared to her unpropitious, for she resumed her waiting. At last the moment seemed to have arrived; the night was now quite dark; she could no longer discern the sentinel opposite her, the landscape lay before her black as a sea of ink. She listened intently for a moment, then formed her resolve. Close beside her window was an iron ladder made of bars set in the wall, which ascended from the mill wheel to the granary at the top of the building, and had formerly served the miller as a means of inspecting certain portions of the gearing; but a change having been made in the machinery, the ladder had long since become lost to sight beneath the thick ivy that covered all that side of the mill.

Françoise bravely climbed over the balustrade of the little balcony in front of her window, grasped one of the iron bars, and found herself suspended in space. She commenced the descent; her skirts were a great hindrance to her. Suddenly a stone became loosened from the wall and fell into the Morelle with a loud splash. She stopped, benumbed with fear, but reflection quickly told her that the waterfall, with its continuous roar, was sufficient to deaden any noise that she could make, and then she descended more boldly, putting aside the ivy with her foot, testing each round of her ladder. When she was on a level with the room that had been converted into a prison for her lover she stopped. An unforeseen difficulty came near depriving her of all her courage: the window of the room beneath was not situated directly under the window of her bedroom; there was a wide space between it and the ladder, and when she extended her hand it only encountered the naked wall.

Would she have to go back the way she came and leave her project unaccomplished? Her arms were growing very tired; the murmuring of the Morelle, far down below, was beginning to make her dizzy. Then she broke off bits of plaster from the wall and threw them against Dominique's window. He did not hear; perhaps he was asleep. Again she crumbled fragments from the wall, until the skin was peeled from her fingers. Her strength was exhausted; she felt that she was about to fall backward into the stream when at last Dominique softly raised his sash.

"It is I," she murmured. "Take me quick; I am about to fall." Leaning from the window he grasped her and drew her into the room, where she had a paroxysm of weeping, stifling her sobs in order that she might not be heard. Then, by a supreme effort of the will she overcame her emotion.

"Are you guarded?" she asked in a low voice.

Dominique, not yet recovered from his stupefaction at seeing her there, made answer by simply pointing toward his door. There was a sound of snoring audible on the outside; it was evident that the sentinel had been overpowered by sleep and had thrown himself upon the floor close against the door in such a way that it could not be opened without arousing him.

"You must fly," she continued earnestly. "I came here to bid you fly and say farewell."

But he seemed not to hear her. He kept repeating:

"What, is it you, is it you? Oh, what a fright you gave me! You might have killed yourself." He took her hands, he kissed them again and again. "How I love you, Françoise! You are as courageous as you are good. The only thing I feared was that I might die without seeing you again; but you are here, and now they may shoot me when they will. Let me but have a quarter of an hour with you and I am ready."

He had gradually drawn her to him; her head was resting on his shoulder. The peril that was so near at hand brought them closer to each other, and they forgot everything in that long embrace.

"Ah, Françoise!" Dominique went on in low, caressing tones, "today is the fête of Saint Louis, our wedding day, that we have been waiting for so long. Nothing has been able to keep us apart, for we are both here, faithful to our appointment, are we not? It is now our wedding morning."

"Yes, yes," she repeated after him, "our wedding morning."

They shuddered as they exchanged a kiss. But suddenly she tore herself from his arms; the terrible reality arose before her eyes.

"You must fly, you must fly," she murmured breathlessly. "There is not a moment to lose." And as he stretched out his arms in the darkness to draw her to him again, she went on in tender, beseeching tones: "Oh! listen to me, I entreat you. If you die, I shall die. In an hour it will be daylight. Go, go at once; I command you to go."

Then she rapidly explained her plan to him. The iron ladder extended downward to the wheel; once he had got so far he could climb down by means of the buckets and get into the boat, which was hidden in a recess. Then it would be an easy matter for him to reach the other bank of the stream and make his escape.

"But are there no sentinels?" said he.

"Only one, directly opposite here, at the foot of the first willow."

"And if he sees me, if he gives the alarm?"

Françoise shuddered. She placed in his hand a knife that she had brought down with her. They were silent.

"And your father—and you?" Dominique continued. "But no, it is not to be thought of; I must not fly. When I am no longer here those soldiers are capable of murdering you. You do not know them. They offered to spare my life if I would guide them into Sauval forest. When they discover that I have escaped, their fury will be such that they will be ready for every atrocity."

The girl did not stop to argue the question. To all the considerations that he adduced to her one simple answer was: "Fly. For the love of me, fly. If you love me, Dominique, do not linger here a single moment longer."

She promised that she would return to her bedroom; no one should know that she had helped him. She concluded by folding him in her arms and smothering him with kisses in an extravagant outburst of passion. He was vanquished. He put only one more question to her: "Will you swear to me that your father knows what you are doing, and that he counsels my flight?"

"It was my father who sent me to you," Françoise unhesitatingly replied.

She told a falsehood. At that moment she had but one great, overmastering longing, to know that he was in safety, to escape from the horrible thought that the morning's sun was to be the signal for his death. When he should be far away, then calamity and evil might burst upon her head; whatever fate might be in store for her would seem endurable, so that only his life might be spared. Before and above all considerations, the selfishness of her love demanded that he should be saved.

"It is well," said Dominique; "I will do as you desire."

No further word was spoken. Dominique went to the window to raise it again. But suddenly there was a noise that chilled them with affright. The door was shaken violently; they thought that someone was about to open it; it was evidently a party going the rounds who had heard their voices. They stood by the window, close locked in each other's arms, awaiting the event with anguish unspeakable. Again there came the rattling at the door, but it did not open. Each of them drew a deep sigh of relief; they saw how it was. The soldier lying across the threshold had turned over in his sleep. Silence was restored indeed, and presently the snoring began again.

Dominique insisted that Françoise should return to her room first of all. He took her in his arms, he bade her a silent farewell, then helped her to grasp the ladder, and himself climbed out on it in turn. He refused to descend a single step, however, until he knew that she was in her chamber. When she was safe in her room she let fall, in a voice scarce louder than a whisper, the words: "Au revoir. I love you!"

She kneeled at the window, resting her elbows on the sill, straining her eyes to follow Dominique. The night was still very dark. She looked for the sentinel, but could see nothing of him; the willow alone was dimly visible, a pale spot upon the surrounding blackness. For a moment she heard the rustling of the ivy as Dominique descended, then the wheel creaked, and there was a faint splash which told that the young man had found the boat. This was confirmed when a minute later she descried the shadowy outline of the skiff on the gray bosom of the Morelle. Then a horrible feeling of dread seemed to clutch her by the throat. Every moment she thought she heard the sentry give the alarm; every faintest sound among the dusky shadows seemed to her overwrought imagination to be the hurrying tread of soldiers, the clash of steel, the click of musket locks. The seconds slipped by, however; the landscape still preserved its solemn peace. Dominique must have landed safely on the other bank. Françoise no longer had eyes for anything. The silence was oppressive. And she heard the sound of trampling feet, a hoarse cry, the dull thud of a heavy body falling. This was followed by another silence, even deeper than that which had gone before. Then, as if conscious that Death had passed that way, she became very cold in the presence of the impenetrable night.

IV

At early daybreak the repose of the mill was disturbed by the clamor of angry voices. Father Merlier had gone and unlocked Françoise's door. She descended to the courtyard, pale and very calm, but when there, could not repress a shudder upon being brought face to face with the body of a Prussian soldier that lay on the ground beside the well, stretched out upon a cloak.

Around the corpse soldiers were shouting and gesticulating angrily. Several of them shook their fists threateningly in the direction of the village. The officer had just sent a summons to Father Merlier to appear before him in his capacity as mayor of the commune.

"Here is one of our men," he said, in a voice that was almost unintelligible from anger, "who was found murdered on the bank of the stream. The murderer must be found, so that we may make a salutary example of him, and I shall expect you to co-operate with us in finding him."

"Whatever you desire," the miller replied, with his customary impassiveness. "Only it will be no easy matter."

The officer stooped down and drew aside the skirt of the cloak which concealed the dead man's face, disclosing as he did so a frightful wound. The sentinel had been struck in the throat and the weapon had not been withdrawn from the wound. It was a common kitchen knife, with a black handle.

"Look at that knife," the officer said to Father Merlier. "Perhaps it will assist us in our investigation."

The old man had started violently, but recovered himself at once; not a muscle of his face moved as he replied: "Everyone about here has knives like that. Like enough your man was tired of fighting and did the business himself. Such things have happened before now."

"Be silent!" the officer shouted in a fury. "I don't know what it is that keeps me from setting fire to the four corners of your village."

His anger fortunately kept him from noticing the great change that had come over Françoise's countenance. Her feelings had compelled her to sit down upon the stone bench beside the well. Do what she would she could not remove her eyes from the body that lay stretched upon the ground, almost at her feet. He had been a tall, handsome young man in life, very like Dominique in appearance, with blue eyes and yellow hair. The resemblance went to her heart. She thought that perhaps the dead man had left behind him in his German home some sweetheart who would weep for his loss. And she recognized her knife in the dead man's throat. She had killed him.

The officer, meantime, was talking of visiting Rocreuse with some terrible punishment, when two or three soldiers came running in. The guard had just that moment discovered Dominique's escape. The agitation caused by the tidings was extreme. The officer went to inspect the locality, looked out through the still open window, saw at once how the event had happened, and returned in a state of exasperation.

Father Merlier appeared greatly vexed by Dominique's flight. "The idiot!" he murmured; "he has upset everything."

Françoise heard him and was in an agony of suffering. Her father, moreover, had no suspicion of her complicity. He shook his head, saying to her in an undertone: "We are in a nice fix now!"

"It was that scoundrel! It was that scoundrel!" cried the officer. "He has got away to the woods; but he must be found, or the village shall stand the consequences." And addressing himself to the miller: "Come, you must know where he is hiding?"

Father Merlier laughed in his silent way, and pointed to the wide stretch of wooded hills.

"How can you expect to find a man in that wilderness?" he asked.

"Oh! there are plenty of hiding-places that you are acquainted with. I am going to give you ten men; you shall act as guide to them."

"I am perfectly willing. But it will take a week to beat up all the woods of the neighborhood."

The old man's serenity enraged the officer; he saw, indeed, what a ridiculous proceeding such a hunt would be. It was at that moment that he caught sight of Françoise where she sat, pale and trembling, on her bench. His attention was aroused by the girl's anxious attitude. He was silent for a moment, glancing suspiciously from father to daughter and back again.

"Is not that man," he at last coarsely asked the old man, "your daughter's lover?"

Father Merlier's face became ashy pale, and he appeared for a moment as if about to throw himself on the officer and throttle him. He straightened himself up and made no reply. Françoise had hidden her face in her hands.

"Yes, that is how it is," the Prussian continued; "you or your daughter has helped him to escape. You are his accomplices. For the last time, will you surrender him?"

The miller did not answer. He had turned away and was looking at the distant landscape with an air of indifference, just as if the officer were talking to some other person. That put the finishing touch to the latter's wrath.

"Very well, then!" he declared, "you shall be shot in his stead."

And again he ordered out the firing party. Father Merlier was as imperturbable as ever. He scarcely did so much as shrug his shoulders; the whole drama appeared to him to be in very doubtful taste. He probably believed that they would not take a man's life in that unceremonious manner. When the platoon was on the ground he gravely said: "So, then, you are in earnest? Very well, I am willing it should be so. If you feel you must have a victim, it may as well be I as another."

But Françoise arose, greatly troubled, stammering: "Have mercy, sir; do not harm my father. Kill me instead of him. It was I who helped Dominique to escape; I am the only guilty one."

"Hold your tongue, my girl," Father Merlier exclaimed. "Why do you tell such a falsehood? She passed the night locked in her room, sir; I assure you that she does not speak the truth."

"I *am* speaking the truth," the girl eagerly replied. "I got down by the window; I incited Dominique to fly. It is the truth, the whole truth."

The old man's face was very white. He could read in her eyes that she was not lying, and her story terrified him. Ah, those children! those children! how they spoiled everything, with their hearts and their feelings! Then he said angrily: "She is crazy; do not listen to her. It is a lot of trash she is telling you. Come, let us get through with this business."

She persisted in her protestations; she kneeled, she raised her clasped hands in supplication. The officer stood tranquilly by and watched the harrowing scene.

"*Mon Dieu!*" he said at last, "I take your father because the other escaped me. Bring me back the other man, and your father shall have his liberty."

She looked at him for a moment with eyes dilated by the horror which his proposal inspired in her.

"It is dreadful," she murmured. "Where can I look for Dominique now? He is gone; I know nothing beyond that."

"Well, make your choice between them; him or your father."

"Oh, my God! how can I choose? Even if I knew where to find Dominique, I could not choose. You are breaking my heart. I would rather die at once. Yes, it would be more quickly ended thus. Kill me, I beseech you, kill me——"

The officer finally became weary of this scene of despair and tears. He cried: "Enough of this! I wish to treat you kindly; I will give you two hours. If your lover is not here within two hours, your father shall pay the penalty that he has incurred."

And he ordered Father Merlier away to the room that had served as a prison for Dominique. The old man asked for tobacco, and began to smoke. There was no trace of emotion to be descried on his impassive face. Only when he was alone he wept two big tears that coursed slowly down his cheeks. His poor, dear child, what a fearful trial she was enduring!

Françoise remained in the courtyard. Prussian soldiers passed back and forth, laughing. Some of them addressed her with coarse pleasantries which she did not understand. Her gaze was bent upon the door through which her father had disappeared, and with a slow movement she raised her hand to her forehead, as if to keep it from bursting. The officer turned sharply on his heel, and said to her: "You have two hours. Try to make good use of them."

She had two hours. The words kept buzzing, buzzing in her ears. Then she went forth mechanically from the courtyard; she walked straight ahead with no definite end. Where was she to go? What was she to do? She did not even endeavor to arrive at any decision, for she felt how utterly useless were her efforts. And yet she would have liked to see Dominique; they could have come to some understanding together, perhaps they might have hit on some plan to extricate them from their difficulties. And so, amid the confusion of her whirling thoughts, she took her way downward to the bank of the Morelle, which she crossed below the dam by means of some stepping-stones which were there. Proceeding onward, still involuntarily, she came to the first willow, at the corner of the meadow, and stooping down, beheld a sight that made her grow deathly pale—a pool of blood. It was the spot. And she followed the track that Dominique had left in the tall grass; it was evident that he had run, for the footsteps that crossed the meadow in a diagonal line were separated from one another by wide intervals. Then, beyond that point, she lost the trace, but thought she had discovered it again in the adjoining field. It led her onward to the border of the forest, where the trail came abruptly to an end.

Though conscious of the futility of the proceeding, Françoise penetrated into the wood. It was a comfort to her to be alone. She sat down for a moment, then, reflecting that time was passing, rose again to her feet. How long was it since she left the mill? Five minutes, or a half-hour? She had lost all idea of time. Perhaps Dominique had sought concealment in a clearing that she knew of, where they had gone together one afternoon and eaten hazelnuts. She directed her steps toward the clearing; she searched it thoroughly. A blackbird flew out, whistling his sweet and melancholy note; that was all. Then she thought that he might have taken refuge in a hollow among the rocks where he went sometimes with his gun, but the spot was untenanted. What use was there in looking for him? She would never find him, and little by little the desire to discover the hiding-place became a passionate longing. She proceeded at a more rapid pace. The idea suddenly took possession of her that he had climbed into a tree, and thenceforth she went along with eyes raised aloft and called him by name every fifteen or twenty steps, so that he might know she was near him. The cuckoos answered her; a breath of air that rustled the leaves made her think that he was there and was coming down to her. Once she even imagined that she saw him; she stopped with a sense of suffocation, with a desire to run away. What was she to say to him? Had she come there to take him back with her and have him shot? Oh! no, she would not mention those things; she would tell him that he must fly, that he must not remain in the neighborhood. Then she thought of her father

awaiting her return, and the reflection caused her most bitter anguish. She sank upon the turf, weeping hot tears, crying aloud: "My God! My God! why am I here!"

It was a mad thing for her to have come. And as if seized with a sudden panic, she ran hither and thither. She sought to make her way out of the forest. Three times she lost her way and had begun to think she was never to see the mill again when she came out into a meadow, directly opposite Rocreuse. As soon as she caught sight of the village she stopped. Was she going to return alone?

She was standing there when she heard a voice calling her by name, softly: "Françoise! Françoise!"

And she beheld Dominique raising his head above the edge of a ditch. Just God! she had found him.

Could it be, then, that Heaven willed his death? She suppressed a cry that rose to her lips, and slipped into the ditch beside him.

"You were looking for me?" he asked.

"Yes," she replied bewilderedly, scarcely knowing what she was saying.

"Ah! what has happened?"

She stammered, with eyes downcast: "Why, nothing; I was anxious, I wanted to see you."

Thereupon, his fears alleviated, he went on to tell her how it was that he had remained in the vicinity. He was alarmed for them. Those rascally Prussians were not above wreaking their vengeance on women and old men. All had ended well, however, and he added, laughing: "The wedding will be put off for a week, that's all."

He became serious, however, upon noticing that her dejection did not pass away.

"But what is the matter? You are concealing something from me."

"No, I give you my word I am not. I am tired; I ran all the way here."

He kissed her, saying it was imprudent for them both to talk there any longer, and was about to climb out of the ditch in order to return to the forest. She stopped him; she was trembling violently.

"Listen, Dominique; perhaps it will be as well for you to stay here, after all. There is no one looking for you; you have nothing to fear."

"Françoise, you are concealing something from me," he said again.

Again she protested that she was concealing nothing. She only liked to know that he was near her. And there were other reasons still that she gave in stammering accents. Her manner was so strange that no consideration could now have induced him to go away. He believed, moreover, that the French would return presently. Troops had been seen over toward Sauval.

"Ah! let them make haste; let them come as quickly as possible," she murmured fervently.

At that moment the clock of the church at Rocreuse struck eleven; the strokes reached them, clear and distinct. She arose in terror; it was two hours since she had left the mill.

"Listen," she said, with feverish rapidity, "should we need you, I will go up to my room and wave my handkerchief from the window."

And she started off homeward on a run, while Dominique, greatly disturbed in mind, stretched himself at length beside the ditch to watch the mill. Just as she was about to enter the village Françoise encountered an old beggar man, Father Bontemps, who knew everyone and everything in that part of the country. He saluted her; he had just seen the miller, he said, surrounded by a crowd of Prussians; then, making numerous signs of the cross and mumbling some inarticulate words, he went his way.

"The two hours are up," the officer said when Françoise made her appearance.

Father Merlier was there, seated on the bench beside the well. He was smoking still. The young girl again proffered her supplication, kneeling before the officer and weeping. Her wish was to gain time. The hope that she might yet behold the return of the French had been gaining strength in her bosom, and amid her tears and sobs she thought she could distinguish in the distance the cadenced tramp of an advancing army. Oh! if they would but come and deliver them all from their fearful trouble!

"Hear me, sir: grant us an hour, just one little hour. Surely you will not refuse to grant us an hour!"

But the officer was inflexible. He even ordered two men to lay hold of her and take her away, in order that they might proceed undisturbed with the execution of the old man. Then a dreadful conflict took place in Françoise's heart. She could not allow her father to be murdered in that manner; no, no, she would die in company with Dominique rather; and she was just darting away in the direction of her room in order to signal to her fiancé, when Dominique himself entered the courtyard.

The officer and his soldiers gave a great shout of triumph, but he, as if there had been no soul there but Françoise, walked straight up to her; he was perfectly calm, and his face wore a slight expression of sternness.

"You did wrong," he said. "Why did you not bring me back with you? Had it not been for Father Bontemps I should have known nothing of all this. Well, I am here, at all events."

v

It was three o'clock. The heavens were piled high with great black clouds, the tail-end of a storm that had been raging somewhere in the vicinity. Beneath the coppery sky and ragged scud the valley of Rocreuse, so bright and smiling in the sunlight, became a grim chasm, full of sinister shadows. The Prussian officer had done nothing with Dominique beyond placing him in confinement, giving no indication of his ultimate purpose in regard to him. Françoise, since noon, had been suffering unendurable agony; notwithstanding her father's entreaties, she would not leave the courtyard. She was waiting for the French troops to appear, but the hours slipped by; night was approaching, and she suffered all the more since it appeared as if the time thus gained would have no effect on the final result.

About three o'clock, however, the Prussians began to make their preparations for departure. The officer had gone to Dominique's room and remained closeted with him for some minutes, as he had done the day before. Françoise knew that the young man's life was hanging in the balance; she clasped her hands and put up fervent prayers. Beside her sat Father Merlier, rigid and silent, declining, like the true peasant he was, to attempt any interference with accomplished facts.

"Oh! my God! my God!" Françoise exclaimed, "they are going to kill him!"

The miller drew her to him, and took her on his lap as if she had been a little child. At this juncture the officer came from the room, followed by two men conducting Dominique between them.

"Never, never!" the latter exclaimed. "I am ready to die."

"You had better think the matter over," the officer replied. "I shall have no trouble in finding someone else to render us the service which you refuse. I am generous with you; I offer you your life. It is simply a matter of guiding us across the forest to Montredon; there must be paths."

Dominique made no answer.

"Then you persist in your obstinacy?"

"Shoot me, and let's have done with it," he replied.

Françoise, in the distance, entreated her lover with clasped hands; she was forgetful of all considerations save one—she would have had him commit treason. But Father Merlier seized her hands, that the Prussians might not see the wild gestures of a woman whose mind was disordered by her distress.

"He is right," he murmured; "it is best for him to die."

The firing party was in readiness. The officer still had hopes of bringing Dominique over, and was waiting to see him exhibit some signs of weakness. Deep silence prevailed. Heavy peals of thunder were heard in the distance, the fields and the woods lay lifeless beneath the sweltering heat. And it was in the midst of this oppressive silence that suddenly the cry arose: "The French! the French!"

It was a fact; they were coming. The line of red trousers could be seen advancing along the Sauval road, at the edge of the forest. In the mill the confusion was extreme; the Prussian soldiers ran to and fro, giving vent to guttural cries. Not a shot had been fired as yet.

"The French! the French!" cried Françoise, clapping her hands for joy. She was like a woman possessed. She had escaped from her father's embrace and was laughing boisterously, her arms raised high in the air. They had come at last, then, and had come in time, since Dominique was still there, alive!

A crash of musketry that rang in her ears like a thunderclap caused her to turn her head suddenly. The officer had muttered, "We will finish this business first," and with his own hands pushing Dominique up against the wall of a shed, had given the command to the squad to fire. When Françoise turned, Dominique was lying on the ground, pierced by a dozen bullets.

She did not shed a tear; she stood there like one suddenly rendered senseless. Her eyes were fixed and staring, and she went and seated herself beneath the shed, a few steps from the lifeless body. She looked at it wistfully; now and then she would make a movement with her hands in an aimless, childish way. The Prussians had seized Father Merlier as a hostage.

It was a pretty fight. The officer, perceiving that he could not retreat without being cut to pieces, rapidly made the best disposition possible of his men; it was as well to sell their lives dearly. The Prussians were now the defenders of the mill, and the French were the attacking party. The musketry fire began with unparalleled fury; for half an hour there was no lull in the storm. Then a deep report was heard, and a ball carried away a main branch of the old elm. The French had artillery; a battery, in position just beyond the ditch where Dominique had concealed himself, commanded the main street of Rocreuse. The conflict could not last long after that.

Ah! the poor old mill! The cannon balls raked it from wall to wall. Half the roof was carried away; two of the walls fell in. But it was on the side toward the Morelle that the damage was most lamentable. The ivy, torn from the tottering walls, hung in tatters, debris of every description floated away upon the bosom of the stream, and through a great breach Françoise's chamber was visible, with its little bed, the snow-white curtains of which were carefully drawn. Two balls struck the old wheel in quick succession, and it gave one parting groan; the buckets were carried away down stream, the frame was crushed into a shapeless mass. It was the soul of the stout old mill parting from the body.

Then the French came forward to carry the place by storm. There was a mad hand-to-hand conflict with bayonets. Under the dull sky the pretty valley became a huge slaughter pen; the broad meadows looked on in horror, with their great isolated trees and their rows of poplars, dotting them with shade, while to right and left the forest was like the walls of a tilting-ground enclosing the combatants, and in Nature's universal panic the gentle murmur of the springs and watercourses sounded like sobs and wails.

Françoise had not stirred from the shed where she remained hanging over Dominique's body. Father Merlier had met his death from a stray bullet. Then the French captain, the Prussians being exterminated and the mill on fire, entered the courtyard at the head of his men. It was the first success that he had gained since the breaking out of the war; so, all inflamed with enthusiasm, drawing himself up to the full height of his lofty stature, he laughed pleasantly, as a handsome cavalier like him might laugh. Then, perceiving poor idiotic Françoise where she crouched between the corpses of her father and her betrothed, among the smoking ruins of the mill, he saluted her gallantly with his sword, and shouted: "Victory! Victory!"

MARCEL PROUST

1871–1922

Proust was born in 1871, son of a wealthy Parisian physician. Suffering severe asthmatic attacks from his earliest years, he lived in idleness, devoting himself to literature. Until he was thirty-five, he frequented the worldly circles of fashionable French society. Much of this activity was designed to supply him with accurate, factual information concerning society and human psychology. In 1906, suffering a recrudescence of his illness, he withdrew from the world to compose his monumental series of novels *Remembrance of Things Past,* for the most part in bed in a cork-lined, thoroughly sterilized room. The first volume, *Swann's Way,* appeared in 1913.

Proust's hero, a nervous, spoiled young man, grows up in idleness, surrounded by worldly distractions of all sorts which finally come to provide him only with boredom. One day, on tasting a piece of cake dipped into a cup of tea, the protagonist recalls certain people and incidents in his past life associated with such cake and tea. He then devotes himself to reconstituting, clarifying, and explaining as many memories as he can call to mind. A strain of familiar music, the odor of a flower stimulates his memory and permits it to call to mind people and places he has known. The action is often slow, sometimes highly tedious, for Proust wishes to consider in detail each item recalled.

The sixteen volumes of the *Remembrance of Things Past* present a vast panorama of a decadent upper-class society in all of its most subtle psychological aspects. All the snobbery, pretense, unsatisfied love, and fruitless occupations of a society about to be shattered by the first World War find a place on Proust's stupendous canvas. His powers of observation, his psychological insight, and his love for the most minute detail are unparalleled in the modern novel. Proust's work has made of him one of the most discussed and one of the most important novelists of modern times.

FURTHER READING

BELL, CLIVE. *Proust* (London, 1928).

LEMAÎTRE, GEORGES. *Four French Novelists* (London and New York, 1938).

MARCH, HAROLD. *The Two Worlds of Marcel Proust* (Philadelphia, 1948).

The *Madeleine* *

I FEEL that there is much to be said for the Celtic belief that the souls of those whom we have lost are held captive in some inferior being, in an animal, in a plant, in some inanimate object, and so effectively lost to us until the day (which to many never comes) when we happen to pass by the tree or to obtain possession of the object which forms their prison. Then they start and tremble, they call us by our name, and as soon as we have recognised their voice the spell is broken. We have delivered them: they have overcome death and return to share our life.

And so it is with our own past. It is a labour in vain to attempt to recapture it: all the efforts of our intellect must prove futile. The past is hidden somewhere outside the realm, beyond the reach of intellect, in some material object (in the sensation which that material object will give us) which we do not suspect. And as for that object, it depends on chance whether we come upon it or not before we ourselves must die.

Many years had elapsed during which nothing of Combray, save what was comprised in the theatre and the drama of my going to bed there, had any existence for me, when one day in winter, as I came home, my mother, seeing that I was cold, offered me some tea, a thing I did not ordinarily take. I declined at first, and then, for no particular reason, changed my mind. She sent out for one of those short, plump little cakes called "petites madeleines," which look as though they had been moulded in the fluted scallop of a pilgrim's shell. And soon, mechanically, weary after a dull day with the prospect of a depressing morrow, I raised to my lips a spoonful of the tea in which I had soaked a morsel of the cake. No sooner had the warm liquid, and the crumbs with it, touched my palate than a shudder ran through my whole body, and I stopped, intent upon the extraordinary changes that were taking place. An exquisite pleasure had invaded my senses, but individual, detached, with no suggestion of its origin. And at once the vicissitudes of life had become indifferent to me, its disasters innocuous, its brevity illusory—this new sensation having had on me the effect which love has of filling me with a precious essence; or rather this essence was not in me, it was myself. I had ceased now to feel medi-

* From Marcel Proust, *Swann's Way,* translated by C. K. Scott-Moncrieff. Copyright, 1930, by Random House, Inc. By permission of Random House, Inc., and Chatto and Windus.

ocre, accidental, mortal. Whence could it have come to me, this all-powerful joy? I was conscious that it was connected with the taste of tea and cake, but that it infinitely transcended those savours, could not, indeed, be of the same nature as theirs. Whence did it come? What did it signify? How could I seize upon and define it?

I drink a second mouthful, in which I find nothing more than in the first, a third, which gives me rather less than the second. It is time to stop; the potion is losing its magic. It is plain that the object of my quest, the truth, lies not in the cup but in myself. The tea has called up in me, but does not itself understand, and can only repeat indefinitely, with a gradual loss of strength, the same testimony; which I, too, cannot interpret, though I hope at least to be able to call upon the tea for it again and to find it there presently, intact and at my disposal, for my final enlightenment. I put down my cup and examine my own mind. It is for it to discover the truth. But how? What an abyss of uncertainty whenever the mind feels that some part of it has strayed beyond its own borders; when it, the seeker, is at once the dark region through which it must go seeking, where all its equipment will avail it nothing. Seek? More than that: create. It is face to face with something which does not so far exist, to which it alone can give reality and substance, which it alone can bring into the light of day.

And I begin again to ask myself what it could have been, this unremembered state which brought with it no logical proof of its existence, but only the sense that it was a happy, that it was a real state in whose presence other states of consciousness melted and vanished. I decide to attempt to make it reappear. I retrace my thoughts to the moment at which I drank the first spoonful of tea. I find again the same state, illumined by no fresh light. I compel my mind to make one further effort, to follow and recapture once again the fleeting sensation. And that nothing may interrupt it in its course I shut out every obstacle, every extraneous idea, I stop my ears and inhibit all attention to the sounds which come from the next room. And then, feeling that my mind is growing fatigued without having any success to report, I compel it for a change to enjoy that distraction which I have just denied it, to think of other things, to rest and refresh itself before the supreme attempt. And then for the second time I clear an empty space in front of it. I place in position before my mind's eye the still recent taste of that first mouthful, and I feel something start within me, something that leaves its resting-place and attempts to rise, something that has been embedded like an anchor at a great depth; I do not know yet what it is, but I can feel it mounting slowly; I can measure the resistance, I can hear the echo of great spaces traversed.

Undoubtedly what is thus palpitating in the depths of my being must be the image, the visual memory which, being linked to that taste, has tried to follow it into my conscious mind. But its struggles are too far off, too much confused; scarcely can I perceive the colourless reflection in which are blended the uncapturable whirling medley of radiant hues, and I cannot distinguish its form, cannot invite it, as the one possible interpreter, to translate to me the evidence of its contemporary, its inseparable paramour, the taste of cake soaked in tea; cannot ask it to inform me what special circumstance is in question, of what period in my past life.

Will it ultimately reach the clear surface of my consciousness, this memory, this old, dead moment which the magnetism of an identical moment has travelled so far to importune, to disturb, to raise up out of the very depths of my being? I cannot tell. Now that I feel nothing, it has stopped, has perhaps gone down again into its darkness, from which who can say whether it will ever rise? Ten times over I must essay the task, must lean down over the abyss. And each time the natural laziness which deters us from every difficult enterprise, every work of importance, has urged me to leave the thing alone, to drink my tea and to think merely of the worries of to-day and of my hopes for to-morrow, which let themselves be pondered over without effort or distress of mind.

And suddenly the memory returns. The taste was that of the little crumb of madeleine which on Sunday mornings at Combray (because on those mornings I did not go out before church-time), when I went to say good day to her in her bedroom, my aunt Léonie used to give me, dipping it first in her own cup of real or of lime-flower tea. The sight of the little madeleine had recalled nothing to my mind before I tasted it; perhaps because I had so often seen such things in the interval, without tasting them, on the trays in pastry-cooks' windows, that their image had dissociated itself from those Combray days to take its place among others more recent; perhaps because of those memories, so long abandoned and put out of mind, nothing now survived, everything was scattered; the forms of things, including that of the little scallop-shell of pastry, so richly sensual under its severe, religious folds, were either obliterated or had been so long dormant as to have lost the power of expansion which would have allowed them to resume their place in my consciousness. But when from a long-distant past nothing subsists, after the people are dead, after the things are broken and scattered, still, alone, more fragile, but with more vitality, more unsubstantial, more persistent, more faithful, the smell and taste of things remain poised a long time, like souls, ready to remind us, waiting and hoping for their moment, amid the ruins of all the rest; and bear unfaltering, in the tiny and almost impalpable drop of their essence, the vast structure of recollection.

And once I had recognised the taste of the crumb of madeleine soaked in her decoction of lime-flowers which my aunt used to give me (although I did not yet know and must long postpone the discovery of why this memory made me so happy) immediately the old grey house upon the street, where her room was, rose up like the scenery of a theatre to attach itself to the little pavilion, opening on to the garden, which had been built out behind it for my parents (the isolated panel which until that moment had been all that I could see); and with the house the town, from morning to night and in all weathers, the Square where I was sent before luncheon, the streets along which I used to run errands, the country roads we took when it was fine. And just as the Japanese amuse themselves by filling a porcelain bowl with water and steeping in it little crumbs of paper which until then are without character or form, but, the moment they become wet, stretch themselves and bend, take on colour and distinctive shape, become flowers or houses or people, permanent and recognisable, so in that moment all the flowers in our garden and in M. Swann's park, and the water-lilies on the Vivonne and the good folk of the village and their little dwellings and the parish church and the whole of Combray and of its surroundings, taking their proper shapes and growing solid, sprang into being, town and gardens alike, from my cup of tea.

Time Recovered *

[In the final section of Remembrance of Things Past Marcel returns to Paris disillusioned in his seemingly vain quest to discover the source of the inexpressible happiness of recollection that had come to him in the

* From Marcel Proust, The Past Recaptured, translated by Frederick A. Blossom. Copyright, 1930, by Random House, Inc. By permission of Random House, Inc., and Chatto and Windus.

incident of the petite madeleine in Swann's Way. He feels that his creative power as an artist depends upon the discovery of the mystifying cause of this happiness. At his Parisian rooms he finds an invitation to a matinee at the Prince of Guermantes, and he visits the Prince's home. The following passage describes in a vividly dramatic way Marcel's realization that his search for these felicitous images of the past had been mistakenly an act of the intellect. Herein he perceives with a transporting joy of vision that the authentic past is recoverable only through the subconscious, a kind of mémoire involontaire, through a fortuitous association of physical sensation. The aim of the artist becomes, therefore, the communication of the quality of these moments thus recovered from the subconscious memory. They are extra-temporal and extra-spatial in the sense that they exist vividly and intensely, both in the past and in the present at the same time.]

ENGROSSED in the unhappy meditations I described a moment ago, I had entered the court of the Guermantes residence and, in my absorption, failed to notice an automobile that was coming in; at the chauffeur's cry I had barely time to get out of the way and, in stepping back, struck my foot against some unevenly cut flagstones leading to a carriage house. In recovering my balance, I put my foot on a stone that was a little lower than the one next to it; immediately all my discouragement vanished before a feeling of happiness which I had experienced at different moments of my life, at the sight of trees I thought I recognised when driving around Balbec, or the church spires of Martinville, or the savour of a madeleine, dipped in herb tea, or from many other sensations I have mentioned, which had seemed to me to be synthesised in the last works of Vinteuil.[1] Just as when I tasted the madeleine, all anxiety as to the future, all intellectual doubt was dispelled. The misgivings that had been harassing me a moment before concerning the reality of my literary gifts, and even of literature itself, were suddenly banished as if by magic. But this time I made a firm resolve that I would not be satisfied to leave the question unanswered (as I did the day I tasted of a madeleine dipped in herb tea) as to why, without my having worked out any new line of reasoning or found any decisive argument, the difficulties that had seemed insoluble a short time before had now lost all their importance. The feeling of happiness which had just come over me was, indeed, exactly the same as I had experienced while eating the madeleine, but at that time I put off seeking the

[1] A character in Proust's novel, to whose sonata described in La Prisonnière Marcel here refers.

deep-lying causes for it. There was a purely material difference in the mental images evoked. A deep azure blue intoxicated my sight, impressions of coolness and dazzling light hovered near me and, in my eagerness to seize them, not daring to move—just as when I tasted the flavour of the *madeleine* and tried to bring back to my mind what it suggested to me— I stood there, swaying back and forth, as I had done a moment before, one foot on the higher stone and the other on the lower, indifferent to the possible amusement of the large crowd of chauffeurs. Each time that I merely repeated the action physically, the effort was in vain; but if I forgot the Guermantes reception and succeeded in recapturing the sensation I had felt the instant I placed my feet in that position, again the dazzling, elusive vision brushed me with its wings, as if to say, "Seize me in my flight, if you have the power, and try to solve the riddle of happiness I propound to you." And almost immediately I recognised it; it was Venice, about which my efforts at description and the supposed 'snapshots' taken by my memory had never yielded me anything, but which was brought back to me by the sensation I had once felt as I stood on two uneven flagstones in the baptistry of Saint Mark's, and with that sensation came all the others connected with it that day, which had been waiting in their proper place in the series of forgotten days, until a sudden happening had imperiously commanded them to come forth. It was in the same way that the taste of the little *madeleine* had recalled Combray to my mind. But why had the mental images of Combray and Venice at their respective moments given me a joy like a sense of certainty, sufficient, without other proofs, to make me indifferent to death? While I was still putting this question to myself, determined this time to find the answer to it, I entered the Guermantes mansion— for we always put ahead of the subjective task we have to perform the outward rôle we are playing, and mine that day was that of an invited guest. But, when I reached the second story, a butler asked me to step for a moment into a small library adjoining the buffet, until the selection they were playing was finished, the Princess having forbidden that the doors be opened while it was being played. At that very moment a second signal came to reinforce the one I had received from the two uneven flagstones, and urged me to persevere in my task. What happened was that a servant, trying in vain to make no noise, struck a spoon against a plate. The same kind of felicity as I had received from the uneven paving stones now came over me; the sensations were again

those of great heat, but entirely different, mingled with the odour of smoke, tempered by the cool fragrance of a forest setting, and I recognized that what seemed to me so delightful was the very row of trees which I had found it wearisome to study and describe and which, in a sort of hallucination, I thought now stood before me as I uncorked the bottle of beer I had with me in the railway carriage, the sound of the spoon striking the plate having given me—until I came to myself again—the illusion of the very similar noise of the hammer of a workman who had made some repairs to a wheel while our train stopped before that little clump of trees. Then one would have said that the signs which were to lift me out of my discouragement that day and restore my faith in literature had determined to come thick and fast, for when a butler who had been for a long time in the service of the Prince de Guermantes recognised me and, in order to save my going to the buffet, brought to me in the library a small plate of *petits fours* [2] and a glass of orangeade, I wiped my mouth with the napkin he had given me; but immediately, like the character in *The Arabian Nights* who unwittingly performs precisely the rite that calls up before him, visible to his eyes alone, a docile genie, ready to transport him far away, a fresh vision of azure blue passed before my eyes; but this time it was pure and saline and it rounded upward like bluish breasts. The impression was so vivid that the moment I was reliving fused with the real present and, more dazed than on that day when I wondered whether I was really going to be received by the Princesse de Guermantes or was everything going to crash about my head, I thought the servant had just opened the window toward the beach and everything called me to go down and stroll along the embankment at high tide; the napkin which I had taken to wipe my mouth had precisely the same sort of starchy stiffness as the towel with which I had had so much trouble drying myself before the window the first day of my stay at Balbec, and now, in this library of the Guermantes mansion, it spread out in its various folds and creases, like a peacock's tail, the plumage of a green and blue ocean. And I drew enjoyment, not only from those colours, but from a whole moment of my life which had brought them into being and had no doubt been an aspiration toward them, but which perhaps some feeling of fatigue or sadness had prevented me from enjoying at Balbec and which now, pure and disembodied, freed from all the imperfections of objective perception, filled me

[2] Small iced pastries.

with joy. The piece they were playing was likely to finish at any moment and I be obliged to enter the salon. Therefore I made an effort to try as quickly as possible to see clearly into the nature of the identical pleasures I had just felt three separate times within a few minutes, and then to draw from them the lesson they had to give. The great difference there is between the actual impression we received from something and the artificial impression we create for ourselves when we endeavour by an effort of the will to bring the object before us again, I did not pause to consider; remembering only too well the comparative indifference with which Swann used to be able to speak of the period in his life when he was loved (because this expression suggested something so different to him) and the sudden pain caused him by Vinteuil's little phrase, which brought to mind those days themselves just as he had felt them, I understood too clearly that the sensation of the uneven flagstones, the stiffness of the napkin and the savour of the *madeleine* had awakened in me something that had no relation to what I used to endeavour to recall to mind about Venice, Balbec, Combray with the aid of a colourless, undistinguishing memory. And I understood how one can come to judge life to be mediocre, when at certain times it seems so beautiful, because this judgment and this disparaging conclusion are based on something entirely different from life itself, on mental images which have retained no trace of life. At the most, I noted incidentally that the difference between each of these real impressions and the corresponding artificial one—differences which explain why an even-toned painting of life cannot be a true likeness—was probably due to this cause, namely, that the slightest word we have spoken or the most insignificant gesture we have made at a certain moment in our life was surrounded and illumined by things that logically had no relation to it and were separated from it by our intelligence, which had no need of them for reasoning purposes; and yet, in the midst of these irrelevant objects—here, the rosy glow of eventide on the flower-covered wall of a rustic restaurant, the feeling of hunger, the yearning for women, the pleasant sensation of luxury; there, blue volutes of the morning sea, wrapped in spirals around strains of music which only partly emerge, like mermaids' shoulders —the most insignificant gesture, the simplest act remain enclosed, as it were, in a thousand sealed jars, each filled with things of an absolutely different colour, odour and temperature. Furthermore, these jars, ranged along the topmost levels of our

bygone years—years during which we have been constantly changing, if only in our dreams and thoughts—stand at very different altitudes and give us the impression of strangely varied atmospheres. It is true that we have gone through these changes imperceptibly, but between our present state and the memory that suddenly comes back to us, just as between two recollections of different years, places or hours, there is such a wide difference that that fact alone, regardless even of any specific individuality, would suffice to make comparison between them impossible. Yes, if, thanks to our ability to forget, a past recollection has been able to avoid any tie, any link with the present moment, if it has remained in its own place and time, if it has kept its distance, its isolation in the depths of a valley or on the tip of a mountain peak, it suddenly brings us a breath of fresh air—refreshing just because we have breathed it once before—of that purer air which the poets have vainly tried to establish in Paradise, whereas it could not convey that profound sensation of renewal if it had not already been breathed, for the only true paradise is always the paradise we have lost. And, in passing, I noted that the work of art which I already felt myself prepared to undertake, but without my having made any conscious resolution to that effect, would present great difficulties. For I would be obliged to execute the different parts of it in somewhat different mediums. The medium suitable for recalling mornings by the sea would be very different from that required to describe afternoons in Venice, a medium distinct and new, of a very special transparence and sonority, compact, refreshing and rosy-hued. And then, different again would be the medium, if I essayed to depict the evenings at Rivebelle in the dining-room opening on the garden, when the heat seemed to disintegrate, to condense and settle to the ground, while the falling twilight still tinted the roses on the wall of the restaurant and the sky still glowed with the pastel tints of dying day. But I passed quickly over all that, under the more imperious urge which I felt to seek the reason for this feeling of happiness and the air of certainty with which it came over me, a search I had hitherto postponed. I caught an inkling of this reason when I compared these various happy impressions with one another and found that they had this in common, namely, that I felt them as if they were occurring simultaneously in the present moment and in some distant past, which the sound of the spoon against the plate, or the unevenness of the flagstones, or the peculiar savour of the *madeleine* even went so far as to make coincide with the present, leaving me uncertain in which period I was. In truth, the person within me who was at that moment enjoying this impression enjoyed in it the qualities it possessed which were common to both an earlier day and the present moment, qualities which were independent of all considerations of time; and this person came into play only when, by this process of identifying the past with the present, he could find himself in the only environment in which he could live and enjoy the essence of things, that is to say, entirely outside of time. That explained why my apprehensiveness of death vanished the moment I instinctively recognised the savour of the little *madeleine,* because at that moment the person within me was a timeless person, consequently unconcerned with the vicissitudes of the future. That person had never come to me, never manifested himself, except independently of all immediate activity, all immediate enjoyment, whenever the miracle of a resemblance with things past enabled me to escape out of the present. He alone had the power to make me recapture bygone days, times past, which had always balked the efforts of my memory and my intelligence.

And perhaps a moment ago, when I considered that Bergotte had been mistaken in speaking of the satisfactions of the intellectual life, this was because at that time I applied the term 'intellectual life' to logical processes of reasoning which had no connection with it or with what was then taking place within me—just as the reason I found society and even life tiresome was because I appraised them on the basis of false impressions of the past, whereas in reality I had now such an eager desire to live that an actual moment from the past had just been revived within me on three distinct occasions.

Merely a moment from the past? Much more than that, perhaps; something which, common to both past and present, is far more essential than either.

How many times in the course of my life had I been disappointed by reality because, at the time I was observing it, my imagination, the only organ with which I could enjoy beauty, was not able to function, by virtue of the inexorable law which decrees that only that which is absent can be imagined. And now suddenly the operation of this harsh law was neutralised, suspended, by a miraculous expedient of nature by which a sensation—the sound of the spoon and that of the hammer, a similar unevenness in two paving stones—was reflected both in the past (which made it possible for my imagination to take pleasure in it) and in the present, the physical stimulus of the sound or the contact with the stones adding to the dreams of the imagination that which they usually lack, the idea of existence—and this subterfuge made it possible for the being within me to seize, isolate, immobilise for the duration of a lightning flash what it never apprehends, namely, a fragment of time in its pure state. The being that was called to life again in me when, with such a thrill of joy, I heard the sound that characterises both a spoon touching a plate and a hammer striking a car wheel, or when I felt under foot the unevenness of the pavement in the court of the Guermantes residence, similar to that in the baptistry of Saint Mark's, draws its sustenance only from the essence of things, in that alone does it find its nourishment and its delight. It languishes in the contemplation of the present, where the senses cannot furnish this essential substance, or in the study of the past, rendered barren for it by the intelligence, or while awaiting a future which the will constructs out of fragments of the past and the present from which it has withdrawn still more of their reality, retaining only that part of them which is suited to the utilitarian, narrowly human purpose for which it designs them. But let a sound already heard or an odour caught in bygone years be sensed anew, simultaneously in the present and the past, real without being of the present moment, ideal but not abstract, and immediately the permanent essence of things, usually concealed, is set free and our true self, which had long seemed dead but was not dead in other ways, awakes, takes on fresh life as it receives the celestial nourishment brought to it. A single minute released from the chronological order of time has re-created in us the human being similarly released, in order that he may sense that minute. And one comprehends readily how such a one can be confident in his joy; even though the mere taste of a *madeleine* does not seem to contain logical justification for this joy, it is easy to understand that the word "death" should have no meaning for him; situated outside the scope of time, what could he fear from the future?

French Lyric Poetry

PIERRE CHARLES BAUDELAIRE

1821–1867

Poet, critic, and translator, Baudelaire is most famous for *Les Fleurs du Mal* (1857), *Petits Poèmes en Prose* (1869), *Curiosités esthétiques* (1868) and *L'Art Romantique* (1869). Several of the poems in the first work were suppressed upon their appearance as being immoral. In the second volume he developed a new and original literary form in which his genius would have greater freedom and scope. His work is always intensely personal and sincere. It reflects the struggle in him between good and evil, his attempts to escape from bitterness and despair, his worship of beauty as an end in itself. The personal element is often conveyed symbolically and indirectly. Much of his poetry, however, is lurid, many of his descriptions are disgusting and unfit for reading by the young and ignorant. The remainder is couched in a perfection of form which carries it into the regions of the sublime.

Baudelaire's attraction to the experience of sin, his "Satanism," was in part due to his romantic desire to enjoy fully the horror and the ecstasy of life, to his wish to escape ennui and to savor at the same time opposing extremes of emotion, as in the voluptuousness with which the poet tastes sorrow in "Sois Sage, O Ma Douleur." At the same time, this impulse toward spiritual degradation to avoid ennui discloses Baudelaire's recognition of man's inherent sinfulness and exemplifies to T. S. Eliot an attempt "to get into Christianity by the back door." "The Rebel" reveals that this struggle between good and evil is in itself a relief from the insufferable boredom of modern life.

Baudelaire's influence upon symbolism is especially to be remarked in his theory of correspondences: to him the whole visible universe was "a forest of symbols," of analogies to states of mind (see "The Carcass"), and of revelations of a suprasensu-ous world. The poet thus becomes the seer, the *voyant,* who can penetrate to the spiritual through these material symbols: a conception significant in the poetic development of Rimbaud, Rilke, and William Butler Yeats.

FURTHER READING

BENNETT, J. D. *Baudelaire, a Criticism* (Princeton, N. J., 1944).

ELIOT, T. S. "Baudelaire" in *Selected Essays 1917–1932* (New York, 1932).

FERRAN, A. *L'Esthétique de Baudelaire* (Paris, 1933).

GILMAN, M. *Baudelaire the Critic* (New York, 1943).

The Rebel

An Angel swoops, like eagle on his prey,
　　Grips by the hair the unbelieving wight,
　　And furious cries, "O scorner of the right,
'Tis I, thine angel good, who speaks. Obey!
Know thou shalt love without the least distaste
　　The poor, the base, the crooked and the dull;
　　So shall the pageant of thy Lord be graced
With banners by thy love made beautiful.
This is God's love. See that thy soul be fired
　　With its pure flame, or e'er thy heart grow tired,
　　And thou shalt know the bliss that lasts for aye."
Ah! with what ruthless love that Angel grand
　　Tortures and racks the wretch with giant hand!
　　But still he answers "Never, till I die."

(trans. by Cosmo Monkhouse)

Sois Sage, O Ma Douleur

Peace, be at peace, O thou my heaviness,
Thou calledst for the evening, lo! 'tis here,
The City wears a somber atmosphere
That brings repose to some, to some distress.
Now while the heedless throng make haste to press
Where pleasure drives them, ruthless charioteer,
To pluck the fruits of sick remorse and fear,
Come thou with me, and leave their fretfulness.

See how they hang from heaven's high balconies,
The old lost years in faded garments dressed,
And see Regret with faintly smiling mouth;

And while the dying sun sinks in the west,
Hear how, far off, Night walks with velvet tread,
And her long robe trails all about the south.

(trans. by Lord Alfred Douglas)

La Beauté

Fair am I, mortals, as a stone-carved dream,
And all men wound themselves against my breast,
The poet's last desire, the loveliest.
Voiceless, eternal as the world I seem,
In the blue air, strange sphinx, I brood supreme
With heart of snow whiter than swan's white crest,
No movement mars the plastic line—I rest
With lips untaught to laugh or eyes to stream.

Singers who see, in trancèd interludes,
My splendor set with all superb design,
Consume their days, in toilful ecstasy.
To these revealed, the starry amplitudes
Of my great eyes which make all things divine
Are crystal mirrors of eternity.

(trans. by Lord Alfred Douglas)

Harmonie du Soir

Now is the hour when, swinging in the breeze,
Each flower, like a censer, sheds its sweet.
The air is full of scents and melodies,
O languorous waltz! O swoon of dancing feet!

Each flower, like a censer, sheds its sweet,
The violins are like sad souls that cry,
O languorous waltz! O swoon of dancing feet!
A shrine of Death and Beauty is the sky.

The violins are like sad souls that cry,
Poor souls that hate the vast black night of Death;
A shrine of Death and Beauty in the sky.
Drowned in red blood, the Sun gives up his breath.

This soul that hates the vast black night of Death
Takes all the luminous past back tenderly,
Drowned in red blood, the Sun gives up his breath.
Thine image like a monstrance shines in me.

(trans. by Lord Alfred Douglas)

A Carcass *

Recall to mind the sight we saw, my soul,
   That soft, sweet summer day:
Upon a bed of flints a carrion foul,
   Just as we turn'd the way,

* Translated by Richard H. Shepherd.

Its legs erected, wanton-like, in the air,
   Burning and sweating pest,
In unconcern'd and cynic sort laid bare
   To view its noisome breast.

The sun lit up the rottenness with gold,
   To bake it well inclined,   10
And give great Nature back a hundredfold
   All she together join'd.

The sky regarded as the carcass proud
   Oped flower-like to the day;
So strong the odour, on the grass you vow'd
   You thought to faint away.

The flies the putrid belly buzz'd about,
   Whence black battalions throng
Of maggots, like thick liquid flowing out
   The living rags along.   20

And as a wave they mounted and went down,
   Or darted sparkling wide;
As if the body, by a wild breath blown,
   Lived as it multiplied.

From all this life a music strange there ran,
   Like wind and running burns;
Or like the wheat a winnower in his fan
   With rhythmic movement turns.

The forms wore off, and as a dream grew faint,
   An outline dimly shown,   30
And which the artist finishes to paint
   From memory alone.

Behind the rocks watch'd us with angry eye
   A bitch disturbed in theft,
Waiting to take, till we had pass'd her by,
   The morsel she had left.

Yet you will be like that corruption too,
   Like that infection prove—
Star of my eyes, sun of my nature, you,
   My angel and my love!   40

Queen of the graces, you will even be so,
   When, the last ritual said,
Beneath the grass and the fat flowers you go,
   To mould among the dead.

Then, O my beauty, tell the insatiate worm,
   Who wastes you with his kiss,
I have kept the godlike essence and the form
   Of perishable bliss!

Hymn to Beauty

Be thou from Hell upsprung or Heaven descended,
  Beauty! thy look demoniac and divine
Pours good and evil things confusedly blended,
  And therefore art thou likened unto wine.

Thine eye with dawn is filled, with twilight
    dwindles,
  Like winds of night thou sprinklest perfumes
    mild;
Thy kiss, that is a spell, the child's heart kindles,
  Thy mouth, a chalice, makes the man a child.

Fallen from the stars or risen from gulfs of error,
  Fate dogs thy glamoured garments like a slave;
With wanton hands thou scatterest joy and terror,
  And rulest over all, cold as the grave.

Thou tramplest on the dead, scornful and cruel,
  Horror coils like an amulet round thine arms,
Crime on thy superb bosom is a jewel
  That dances amorously among its charms.

The dazzled moth that flies to thee, the candle,
  Shrivels and burns, blessing thy fatal flame;
The lover that dies fawning o'er thy sandal
  Fondles his tomb and breathes the adorèd name.

What if from Heaven or Hell thou com'st,
    immortal
Beauty? O sphinx-like monster, since alone
Thine eye, thy smile, thy hand opens the portal
  Of the Infinite I love and have not known.

What if from God or Satan be the evangel?
  Thou my sole Queen! Witch of the velvet eyes!
Since with thy fragrance, rhythm and light, O
    Angel!
In a less hideous world time swiftlier flies.

               (trans. by W. J. Robertson)

The Spiritual Dawn

When on some wallowing soul the roseate East
  Dawns with the Ideal that awakes and gnaws,
  By vengeful working of mysterious laws
An angel rises in the drowsèd beast.

The inaccessible blue of the soul-sphere
  To him whose grovelling dream remorse doth gall
  Yawns wide as when the gulfs of space enthral.
So, heavenly Goddess, Spirit pure and clear,

Even on the reeking ruins of vile shame
  Thy rosy vision, beautiful and bright,
  For ever floats on my enlargèd sight.

Thus sunlight blackens the pale taper-flame;
  And thus is thy victorious phantom one,
  O soul of splendour, with the immortal Sun!

               (trans. by W. J. Robertson)

Exotic Fragrance

When, with closed eyes in the warm autumn night,
  I breathe the fragrance of thy bosom bare,
  My dream unfurls a clime of loveliest air,
Drenched in the fiery sun's unclouded light.

An indolent island dowered with heaven's delight,
  Trees singular and fruits of savour rare,
  Men having sinewy frames robust and spare,
And women whose clear eyes are wondrous bright.

Led by thy fragrance to those shores I hail
A charmèd harbour thronged with mast and sail,
  Still wearied with the quivering sea's unrest;

What time the scent of the green tamarinds
  That thrills the air and fills my swelling breast
Blends with the mariners' song and the sea-winds.

               (trans. by W. J. Robertson)

STÉPHANE MALLARMÉ

1842–1898

Mallarmé, French symbolist poet and teacher of English, was the author of *Hérodiade,* a drama in verse, and *Igitur ou la Folie d'Elbehnon,* a drama in prose, both left unfinished. Many of Mallarmé's poems present a rather complex drama which is intended to reflect another drama taking place in the poet's mind. Much of his work is extremely difficult because of his disregard of the rules of syntax and his unusual association of words and ideas. It was his purpose to make the reader feel, rather than understand, emotions and impressions which cannot be expressed in words. Like that of Verlaine, Mallarmé's poetry is closely allied to music. Claude Debussy composed in 1892 an orchestral prelude to his "Afternoon of a Faun."

Mallarmé cultivated his vocation as poet with a ritualistic devotion to his craft that suggests the essential spiritual identification of the poet with the religion of art. He eschewed all didactic aims; to him poetry was a pure, mysterious, intuitional evocation of Platonic ideality: "I say: a flower! . . . musically the idea itself arises, the sweet idea that is absent in a bouquet" (*Divagations*). By the "alchemy of the word" in which the musical rhythm, the tenuous symbol, and the word became magical, incantatory, he evoked a world of ideality in which the reader yearns toward an experience that transcends the flux and change of mundane existence. In the symbolic "The Afternoon of a Faun" the outer reality of the Faun's environment merges indistinctly with the inner world of the dream, drowsy, languorous, obscure.

FURTHER READING

NOULET, E. *La Poésie de Stéphane Mallarmé* (Paris, 1940).
SYMONS, A. *The Symbolist Movement in Literature* (New York, 1919).

Sigh

My soul, calm sister, towards thy brow, whereon
    scarce grieves
An autumn strewn already with its russet leaves,
And towards the wandering sky of thine angelic
    eyes,
Mounts, as in melancholy gardens may arise
Some faithful fountain sighing whitely towards the
    blue!
—Towards the blue pale and pure that sad October
    knew,
When, in those depths, it mirrored languors infinite,
And agonising leaves upon the waters white,
Windily drifting, traced a furrow cold and dun,
Where, in one long last ray, lingered the yellow sun.
                (*trans. by Arthur Symons*)

Sonnet

From afar so lov'd and near, so cloudless fair, so
Exquisitely thou, my Mary, that I seem
Breathing rarest balm was never but in dream
From vase-crystal lucent like thee—fain it were so!
Know'st thou? Surely. So all time that I recall, so
Always 'neath thy summer's smile doth bloom for
    aye

This one rose, its gladness wreathing day to day,
Time past one with now—yea, time that cometh,
    also!
My heart searching in the night account to render
How—by what last name to call thee—name most
    tender,
Reacheth but to this but falter'd "sister mine"—
Thou, such treasure in this little head adwelling,
Teachest me the secret—this caressing name of
    thine—
That alone my kiss breath'd on thy hair, is telling.
                (*trans. by Arthur Ellis* [1])

The Afternoon of a Faun [*]

In this poem the reverie of the Faun is in roman type, and his brief, erotic recollections of his encounter with the nymphs are in italics. Nijinsky's ballet (1912) more primitively pantomimed the actual encounter.

I would immortalize these nymphs: so bright
Their sunlit colouring, so airy light,
It floats like drowsing down. Loved I a dream?
My doubts, born of oblivious darkness, seem
A subtle tracery of branches grown
The tree's true self—proving that I have known,
Thinking it love, the blushing of a rose.
But think. These nymphs, their loveliness . . .
    suppose
They bodied forth your senses' fabulous thirst?
Illusion! which the blue eyes of the first,   10
As cold and chaste as is the weeping spring,
Beget: the other, sighing, passioning,
Is she the wind, warm in your fleece at noon?
No; through this quiet, when a weary swoon
Crushes and chokes the latest faint essay
Of morning, cool against the encroaching day,
There is no murmuring water, save the gush
Of my clear fluted notes; and in the hush
Blows never a wind, save that which through my
    reed
Puffs out before the rain of notes can speed   20
Upon the air, with that calm breath of art
That mounts the unwrinkled zenith visibly,
Where inspiration seeks its native sky.
You fringes of a calm Sicilian lake,
The sun's own mirror which I love to take,
Silent beneath your starry flowers, tell
How here I cut the hollow rushes, well
Tamed by my skill, when on the glaucous gold

[1] By permission of Jonathan Cape, Ltd.
[*] Translated by Aldous Huxley. By permission of Chatto and Windus.

Of distant lawns about their fountain cold
A living whiteness stirs like a lazy wave;   30
And at the first slow notes my panpipes gave
These flocking swans, these naiads, rather, fly
Or dive. Noon burns inert and tawny dry,
Nor marks how clean that Hymen slipped away
From me who seek in song the real A.
Wake, then, to the first ardour and the sight,
O lonely faun, of the old fierce white light,
With, lilies, one of you for innocence.
Other than their lips' delicate pretence,
The light caress that quiets treacherous lovers,   40
My breast, I know not how to tell, discovers
The bitten print of some immortal's kiss.
But hush! a mystery so great as this
I dare not tell, save to my double reed,
Which, sharer of my every joy and need,
Dreams down its cadenced monologues that we
Falsely confuse the beauties that we see
With the bright palpable shapes our song creates:
My flute, as loud as passion modulates,
Purges the common dream of flank and breast,   50
Seen through closed eyes and inwardly caressed,
Of every empty and monotonous line.

Bloom then, O Syrinx, in thy flight malign,
A reed once more beside our trysting-lake.
Proud of my music, let me often make
A song of goddesses and see their rape
Profanely done on many a painted shape.
So when the grape's transparent juice I drain,
I quell regret for pleasures past and feign
A new real grape. For holding towards the sky   60
The empty skin, I blow it tight and lie
Dream-drunk till evening, eyeing it.
                  Tell o'er
Remembered joys and plump the grape once more.
Between the reeds I saw their bodies gleam
Who cool no mortal fever in the stream
Crying to the woods the rage of their desire:
And their bright hair went down in jewelled fire
Where crystal broke and dazzled shudderingly.
I check my swift pursuit: for see where lie,   70
Bruised, being twins in love, by languor sweet,
Two sleeping girls, clasped at my very feet.
I seize and run with them, nor part the pair,
Breaking this covert of frail petals, where
Roses drink scent of the sun and our light play
'Mid tumbled flowers shall match the death of day.
I love that virginal fury—ah the wild
Thrill when a maiden body shrinks, defiled,
Shuddering like arctic light, from lips that sear
Its nakedness . . . the flesh in secret fear!   80

Contagiously through my linked pair it flies
Where innocence in either, struggling, dies,
Wet with fond tears or some less piteous dew.
Gay in the conquest of these fears, I grew
So rash that I must needs the sheaf divide
Of ruffled kisses heaven itself had tied.
For as I leaned to stifle in the hair
Of one my passionate laughter (taking care
With a stretched finger, that her innocence
Might stain with her companion's kindling sense   90
To touch the younger little one, who lay
Child-like unblushing) my ungrateful prey
Slips from me, freed by passion's sudden death,
Nor heeds the frenzy of my sobbing breath.

Let it pass! others of their hair shall twist
A rope to drag me to those joys I missed.
See how the ripe pomegranates bursting red
To quench the thirst of the mumbling bees have
          bled;
So too our blood, kindled by some chance fire,
Flows for the swarming legions of desire.   100
At evening, when the woodland green turns gold
And ashen grey, 'mid the quenched leaves, behold!
Red Etna glows, by Venus visited,
Walking the lava with her snowy tread
Whene'er the flames in thunderous slumber die.
I hold the goddess!

              Ah, sure penalty!

But the unthinking soul and body swoon
At last beneath the heavy hush of noon.
Forgetful let me lie where summer's drouth   110
Sifts fine the sand and then with gaping mouth
Dream planet-struck by the grape's round wine-red
          star.

Nymphs, I shall see the shade that now you are.

Sea-Wind

The flesh is sad, alas! and all the books are read.
Flight, only flight! I feel that birds are wild to tread
The floor of unknown foam, and to attain the skies!
Nought, neither ancient gardens mirrored in the
          eyes,
Shall hold this heart that bathes in waters its
          delight,
O nights! nor yet my waking lamp, whose lonely
          light
Shadows the vacant paper, whiteness profits best,
Nor the young wife who rocks her baby on her
          breast.

I will depart. O steamer, swaying rope and spar,
Lift anchor for exotic lands that lie afar!
A weariness, outworn by cruel hopes, still clings
To the last farewell handkerchief's last beckonings!
And are not these, the masts inviting storms, not
    these
That an awakening wind bends over wrecking seas,
Lost, not a sail, a sail, a flowering isle, ere long?
But, O my heart, hear thou, hear thou the sailors'
    song!

                  (trans. by Arthur Symons)

PAUL VERLAINE

1844–1896

French impressionism finds a perfect representative in Paul Verlaine, who even in his first book of verse, *Poèmes Saturniens* (1866), exhibited a passion for both music and the plastic arts, attempting to ally his poetry with them. The precepts outlined in "Poetic Art" are followed in *Romances sans paroles* (1874), where thought, feeling, and recollection are presented in a vague and dreamy manner. Verlaine's later works reflect his efforts to reform his life after a period of imprisonment to which he was sentenced for shooting Rimbaud in the wrist. In 1881 appeared *Sagesse*, which is regarded by some as his masterpiece. Other important works are *Jadis et Naguère* (1884), *Parallèlement* (1889), and *Bonheur* (1891). Verlaine was a poet of great originality, excelling in portrayal of fugitive emotions, the subconscious, the vague. His work is above all musical. The arrangement of vowels and consonants in the words which make up his verses produces something of the same impression created by the color oscillations of the painters and the dissonances of the musicians. With him, French poetry definitively broke away from the classical rules of regularity and approached very near to music.

FURTHER READING

ADAM, A. *Le Vrai Verlaine* (Paris, 1936).
FONTAINE, A. *Verlaine, Homme de Lettres* (Paris, 1937).
NICOLSON, H. G. *Paul Verlaine* (New York, 1921).
SYMONS, A. *The Symbolist Movement in Literature* (New York, 1919).

Il Pleut Doucement sur la Ville

Tears fall within mine heart,
As rain upon the town:
Whence does this languor start,
Possessing all mine heart?

O sweet fall of the rain
Upon the earth and roof,
Unto an heart in pain,
O music of the rain.

Tears that have no reason
Fall in my sorry heart:
What, there was no treason?
This grief hath no reason.

Nay, the more desolate,
Because, I know not why,
(Neither for love nor hate)
Mine heart is desolate.

                  (trans. by Ernest Dowson)

Art Poétique

Music first and foremost of all!
Choose your measure of odd not even,
Let it melt in the air of heaven,
Pose not, poise not, but rise and fall.

Choose your words, but think not whether
Each to other of old belong:
What so dear as the dim gray song
Where clear and vague are joined together?

'Tis veils of beauty for beautiful eyes,
'Tis the trembling light of the naked noon,
'Tis a medley of blue and gold, the moon
And stars in the cool of autumn skies.

Let every shape of its shade be born;
Color, away! come to me, shade!
Only of shade can the marriage be made
Of dream with dream and of flute with horn.

Shun the Point, lest death with it come,
Unholy laughter and cruel wit
(For the eyes of the angels weep at it)
And all the garbage of scullery-scum.

Take Eloquence, and wring the neck of him!
You had better, by force, from time to time,
Put a little sense in the head of Rhyme:
If you watch him not, you will be at the beck of him.

O, who shall tell us the wrongs of Rhyme?
What witless savage or what deaf boy
Has made for us this two-penny toy
Whose bells ring hollow and out of time?

Music always and music still!
Let your verse be the wandering thing
That flutters in the light from a soul on the wing
Towards other skies at a new whim's will.

Let your verse be the luck of the lure
Afloat on the winds that at morning hint
Of the odors of thyme and the savor of mint . . .
And all the rest is literature.

(trans. by Arthur Symons)

Spleen

Around were all the roses red,
The ivy all around was black.

Dear, so thou only move thine head,
Shall all mine old despairs awake.

Too blue, too tender was the sky,
The air too soft, too green the sea.

Always I fear, I know not why,
Some lamentable flight from thee.

I am so tired of holly-sprays
And weary of the bright box-tree,

Of all the endless country ways;
Of everything, alas, save thee.

(trans. by Ernest Dowson)

Clair de Lune

Your soul is a sealed garden, and there go
With masque and bergamasque fair companies
Playing on lutes and dancing and as though
Sad under their fantastic fripperies.

Though they in minor keys go caroling
Of love the conqueror and of live boon
They seem to doubt the happiness they sing
And the song melts into the light of the moon,

The sad light of the moon, so lovely fair
That all the birds dream in the leafy shade
And the slim fountains sob into the air
Among the marble statues in the glade.

(trans. by Arthur Symons)

The Sky Is Up Above the Roof

The sky is up above the roof
 So blue, so soft.
A tree there, up above the roof,
 Swayeth aloft.

A bell within that sky we see,
 Chimes low and faint;
A bird upon that tree we see,
 Maketh complaint.

Dear God, is not the life up there
 Simple and sweet?
How peacefully are borne up there
 Sounds of the street.

What hast thou done, who comest here,
 To weep alway?
Where hast thou laid, who comest here,
 Thy youth away?

(trans. by Ernest Dowson)

———◆———

JEAN ARTHUR RIMBAUD

1854–1891

Jean Nicholas Arthur Rimbaud, a singularly wild prodigy and the evil genius of Verlaine, was born in 1854 at Charleroi, the son of parents who were reluctant to give him the freedom which his tempestuous spirit demanded. He ran away from an unpleasant home life and distasteful school work to spend time in the aesthetic circles of Paris. Somewhat later he made the acquaintance of Verlaine with whom he made a trip to London in 1871, leading there "a stormy and painful life." His relations with Verlaine were characterized by quarrels and were interspersed with several flights from him. After his shooting by Verlaine, he traveled widely, earning his livelihood at small, temporary occupations, spending his time for the most part in one or another of the ports on the Red Sea. He died at Marseilles on November 10, 1891, after the amputation of one of his legs.

All of his strange poetry, composed while he was in his teens, is contained in a few small volumes including *A Season in Hell* and *Illuminations*, a collection of prose poems. His two most famous pieces are "The Drunken Boat" and the "Sonnet on the Vowels." To understand what may seem the incoherence of "The Drunken Boat," the reader should know that the poet, in order to become a seer, must destroy his everyday self and achieve a knowledge of his unknown, "real," subconscious self; that is, he must destroy all familiar patterns of social conduct and logical knowledge to create that "real" self, the *Je* with which the poem begins. The poetic method is by "the derangement of all the senses" in strange, illogical, hallucinatory images. Herein Rimbaud is the progenitor of surrealism.

FURTHER READING

FOWLIE, W. *Rimbaud* (New York, 1946).
STARKIE, E. *Arthur Rimbaud* (London, 1947).
SYMONS, A. *Symbolist Movement in Literature* (New York, 1919).

The Drunken Boat *

As I descended by impassive waterways,
I lost my crew of haulers. They'd been seized by hosts
Of whooping Redskins, and set up as popinjays,
Their naked bodies nailed to multicoloured posts.

Little I cared for any crew I bore, a rover
With Flemish wheat or English cottons in my hold.
When once the tribulations of my crew were over,
The rivers gave me leave to journey uncontrolled.

Amid the fury of the loudly chopping tide,
I, just last winter, with a child's insensate brain,   10
Ah, how I raced! And no Peninsulas untied
Were ever tossed in more triumphant hurricane.

The blessing of the storm on my sea-watch was shed.
More buoyant than a cork I darted for ten nights
Over the waves, those famed old trundlers of the dead,
Nor missed the foolish blink of homely warning lights.

The wash of the green water on my shell of pine,
Sweeter than apples to a child its pungent edge;
It cleansed me of the stains of vomits and blue wine
And carried off with it the rudder and the kedge. 20

* Translated by Norman Cameron. By permission of Hogarth Press, Ltd.

And afterwards down through the poem of the sea,
A milky foam infused with stars, frantic I dive
Down through green heavens where, descending pensively,
Sometimes the pallid remnants of the drowned arrive;

Where suddenly the bluish tracts dissolve, desires
And rhythmic languors stir beneath the day's full glow.
Stronger than alcohol and vaster than your lyres,
The bitter humours of fermenting passion flow!

I know how lightning splits the skies, the current roves;
I know the surf and waterspouts and evening's fall;   30
I've seen the dawn arisen like a flock of doves;
Sometimes I've seen what men believe they can recall.

I've seen the low sun blotched with blasphemies sublime,
Projecting vividly long, violent formations
Which, like tragedians in very ancient mime
Bestride the latticed waves, that speed remote vibrations.

My dreams of green night and its bedazzled snow,
Of kisses slowly mounting up to the sea's eyes,
Of winding courses where unheard-of fluids go,
Flares blue and yellow that from singing phosphors rise.   40

For whole months at a time I've ridden with the surge
That like mad byres a-toss keeps battering the reefs,
Nor thought that the bright touch of Mary's feet could urge
A muzzle on the seas, muting their wheezy griefs.

And, yes, on Florida's beyond belief I've fetched,
Where flowers and eyes of panthers mingle in confusion,
Panthers with human skin, rainbows like bridles stretched
Controlling glaucous herds beneath the sea's horizon.

I've seen fermenting marshes like huge lobster-traps
Where in the rushes rots a whole Leviathan,   50
Or in the midst of calm the water's face collapse
And cataracts pour in from all the distant span.

Glaciers, silver suns, pearl waves and skies afire,
Brown gulfs with loathsome strands in whose profundities

Huge serpents, vermin-plagued, drop down into the
    mire
With black effluvium from the contorted trees!

I longed to show the children how the dolphins
    sport
In the blue waves, these fish of gold, these fish that
    sing.
Flowers of foam have blessed my puttings-out from
    port,
Winds from I know not where at times have lent
    me wing.   60

And often, weary martyr of the poles and zones,
Dark blooms with yellow mouths reached towards
    me from the seas
On which I gently rocked, in time to their soft
    moans;
And I was left there like a woman on her knees.

Trembling peninsula, upon my decks I tossed
The dung of pale-eyed birds and clacking, angry
    sound;
And on I sailed while down through my frail
    cordage crossed
The sleeping, backwards falling bodies of the
    drowned.

I, lost boat in the hair of estuaries caught,
Hurled by the cyclone to a birdless apogee,   70
I, whom the Monitors and Hansamen had thought
Not worth the fishing up—a carcase drunk with sea;

Free, smoking, touched with mists of violet above,
I, who the lurid heavens breached like some rare
    wall
Which boasts—confection that the goodly poets
    love—
Lichens of sunlight on a mucoid azure pall;

Who, with electric moons bedaubed, sped on my
    way,
A plank gone wild, black hippocamps my retinue,
When in July, beneath the cudgels of the day
Down fell the heavens and the craters of the
    blue;   80

I, trembling at the mutter, fifty leagues from me,
Of rutting Behemoths, the turbid Maelstrom's
    threats,
Spinning a motionless and blue eternity
I long for Europe, land of ancient parapets.

Such starry archipelagoes! Many an isle
With heavens fiercely to the wanderer wide-thrown;

Is it these depthless nights that your lone sleep
    beguile,
A million golden birds, O Vigour not yet known?

And yet, I've wept too much. The dawns are sharp
    distress,
All moons are baleful and all sunlight harsh to
    me   90
Swollen by acrid love, sagging with drunkenness—
Oh, that my keel might rend and give me to the sea!

If there's a water in all Europe that I crave,
It is the cold, black pond where 'neath the scented
    sky
Of eve a crouching infant, sorrowfully grave,
Launches a boat as frail as a May butterfly.

Alas, I can no more—steeped, waves, in your long
    trance—
Steal the wind from the lofty cotton-clippers' sails,
Nor venture 'midst the flags' and pennants' arro-
    gance,
Nor swim beneath the frightful eyes of floating
    gaols!   100

———————◆———————

PAUL VALÉRY

1871–1945

Born at Sète in 1871, Valéry came to Paris at the age of twenty-one and made the acquaintance of a number of the poets of the time, including Mallarmé, whose daughter he married in 1917. He published three volumes of writings, then seemed to lose interest in literature, turning instead to the abstraction afforded by mathematics. After an interval of about twenty years away from literature, upon the insistence of friends he returned to writing, celebrating this return with the poem "Cemetery by the Sea." Valéry uses techniques (ellipses, suggestive and musical terminology) learned from Mallarmé, but he goes much further, developing more or less fully his meditations on the great problems concerning being and destiny. His verse is nearly always abstract, sensitive, musical, expressing in elegant form a highly developed thought. His prosody is classic, for he considered free-verse to be anti-artistic.

Valéry's poetry often shifts from the visible, tangible world to one of abstraction in which he attempts to find the absolute. The contrast between these two worlds is his usual subject, as it is in "The Cemetery by the Sea." Stopping in a cemetery at noon, Valéry finds, in the idea which then arises in his mind of the external world, that absolute world of abstraction which he has been seeking so long. But his revery is finally ended by the salt wind which forces him to return to a reality not of his own creation. As Edmund Wilson says: "In such a poem as 'Le Cimetière Marin,' there is no simple second meaning: there is a marvellously close reproduction of the very complex and continually changing relation of human consciousness to the things of which it is conscious. The noonday is inorganic Nature, but it is also the absolute in the poet's mind, it is also his twenty years of inaction— and it is merely the noonday itself, which in a moment will no longer exist, which will be no longer either tranquil or noon." Thus the poet interprets the external world of reality not necessarily as it actually exists, but in accordance with his own varying emotions.

FURTHER READING

BOSANQUET, THEODORA. *Paul Valéry* (London, 1933).
BOWRA, C. M. *The Heritage of Symbolism* (London, 1943).
RODITI, EDOUARD. "Paul Valéry: Poetics as an Exact Science," *Kenyon Review*, VI (Summer, 1944), pp. 398–408.
WILSON, EDMUND. *Axel's Castle* (New York, 1931).

The Cemetery by the Sea *

This tranquil roof, with walking pigeons, looms
Trembling between the pines, beyond the tombs;
Precise mid-day the sea from fire composes—
The sea, the sea, forever re-begun!
What recompense after a thought is one
Look on the calm of gods the sea disposes!

Pure energies of lightning-flash consume
What diamond of evanescent spume!
And how is peace conceived in this pure air!
When the sun rests at noon above the abyss,   10
Pure work of an eternal cause is this,
And dream is knowledge, here in the trembling air.

Thou temple to Athena, quiet curve,
Ponderous calm and visible reserve,

* Translated by Barbara Gibbs. By permission of Barbara Gibbs and Alan Swallow.

Enchanting water, eye so filled with sleep
Beneath a flaming veil, enduring bowl,
O silence! Like a tower within the soul,
A roof of gold, a thousand tiles! thou deep!

Temple of Time that one sigh may resume,
I climb this point and habitude assume,   20
Surrounded by the sea's enclosing sight.
As though an altar flamed and smoke arose,
My offering, the scintillation sows
A sovereign disdain along the height.

And as the hungry mouth obscures the fresh
Contour of fruit, translating thus its flesh
Into enjoyment, which the form abhors,
My future I inhale, in smoke unbound;
And to the soul consumed the heavens sound
The hollow alteration of sea-shores.   30

Fair sky, true sky, consider me who change!
After so much of pride, so much of strange
Indolence, full of power, by deviation
I give myself unto this brilliant space,
Over the tombs my shadow takes its race,
Taming myself to its frail agitation.

My soul exposed to torches of the sun,
I can sustain thee, justice, forthright one,
Implacable light, thou with pitiless arms!
Pure to the place wherein thou art adored   40
I have restored thee . . . But the light restored
Presumes one mournful half the shadow harms.

O for myself, unto myself alone,
Near to the poem's source, against the bone,
Between the void and the pure entity,
I wait the echoing greatness from within,
Like some sonorous, bitter cistern's din,
Sounding some chasm in the soul to be.

Dost thou know, subtle prisoner of leaves,
Devourer of the grills the foliage weaves   50
On my closed eyes, the secret I invite?
What flesh impels me to its slothful end,
What forehead to this bony earth I bend?
My absent ones enter the quick-blown light.

Closed, sacred, filled with fire of nothing spun,
Terrestrial fragment offered to the sun,
This place with torches circled pleases me,
Composed of gold, of stone and sombre glades,
Where so much marble trembles over shades;
Beyond the tombs, asleep, the faithful sea!   60

Resplendent bitch! Keep off the idolator,
While I with shepherd's smile lay out the store
Of earth for these, my white, mysterious sheep,

My tranquil tombs, the strange, white, herded
    things.
Vain dreams, and angels with inquiring wings,
And prudent pigeons at a distance keep!

Once here the future is but idleness;
The clean insect scratches the aridness;
Everything burns and is undone, the sere
Grasses like fire invade the splitting wood . . . 70
Being drunk with absence, life's infinitude,
And bitterness is sweet and wit is clear.

The hidden dead are well within this earth
That warms and re-disposes them to birth.
Mid-day above, high noon-tide without motion,
Thinks in itself and is its proper stem . . .
Thou complete head and perfect diadem,
I am in thee the secret alteration.

Thou hast but me to hold thy fearful taint!
My penitence and doubt and my constraint   80
In thy great diamond comprise the flaw! . . .
But in their night of marble-weighted cold,
A wandering people of the rooted mold,
Slow, hesitating, to thy party draw.

In heavy absence kind with kind is blended,
White species unto the red clay descended;
The gift of life is passing to the flowers.
Where are the well-known phrases of the dead,
The personal art, the souls distinguishèd?
The source of tears the spinning worm devours.   90

Of flattered girls the eager, sharpened cries,
The moistened eyelids and the teeth and eyes,
The charming breasts that parley with the flame,
The shining blood at lips that pleasure rifts,
The fingers that defend the final gifts,
All go beneath the earth, re-join the game.

And you, great soul, hope you to find a dream
Without these colors of a lying scheme
That wave and gold display here to the eye?
When you are changed to breath, then will you
    chant?   100
Fly! my presence is porous! Breath is scant,
And holy eagerness must also die!

You, black and gold, gaunt immortality,
Death's head wreathed with the broken laurel tree,
Who say that where we end we but begin—
O lovely lie! O cunning, pious ruse!
Who does not know them— Who does not refuse
The empty skull and the eternal grin!

Deep fathers, uninhabited heads, now dull
Who, weighted by so many shovelsfull,   110

Become the earth, and who confound our steps,
The undying and unanswerable worm's
Not yours, beneath the table. He confirms
My flesh, he lives on life, he keeps my steps.

What name I call him does not signify,
As love, or self-contempt; his tooth must pry,
Ever, so near my life no name him wrongs!
What matter! He can see, will, dream, and touch!
He likes my flesh, and even on my couch
My passing life to him, who lives, belongs.   120

Ah Zeno! Cruel Zeno [1] of Elea!
Who pierce my body with thy winged idea,
Arrow that flying denies motion's press!
The sound brings me to birth, the arrow slays!
Ah Sun! What shadow of a tortoise stays
The soul, Achilles, running motionless!

No, No! . . . Arise and enter the next state!
This thoughtful pose, my body, dissipate!
Drink, my breast, of the wind, a rising bourne!
A freshness breathed from off the quickening
    sea   130
Gives back my soul . . . Oh salty majesty!
I'll run to the wave and from it be re-born!

Yes! great sea with delirium endowed,
Thou town chlamys and hide of panther proud,
With thousand idols of the sun,
Absolute hydra, drunk with thy blue flesh,
Who tail in mouth eternally enmesh
In turbulence that is with silence one,

The wind awakes! . . . I must presume to live!
The immense air in my book is tentative;   140
The wave dares spout in powder from the rocks!
Flee, dazzled pages! Chase time and the hour!
Break, waves, and shatter with thy wind-bred power
This tranquil roof where jib-sails hunt in flocks.

The Bee [2]

So deadly delicate your sting!
Yet, O golden bee, I place
Over this soft curve, saddening,
Nothing but a dream of lace.

[1] Zeno (ca. 490 B.C.) argued that Achilles could never
overtake the tortoise which continually progresses farther
on as Achilles reaches its starting point. This would seem
a denial of motion, and the imagery here thus concerns the
poet's meditation on the values, respectively, of stasis (the
absolute withdrawal and stillness of the soul in the repose-
ful noonday light) and of surrender to the life of movement, ceaseless mutability (symbolized by the sea).

[2] Translated by Lionel Abel. From *Selected Writings*,
by Paul Valéry. By permission of New Directions, Inc.

Prick the breast's fine gourd and press
Home where love dies, where sleeps his spell!
Thus may some of my rosiness
Rise to the round flesh and rebel!

I need a hurt that's keen and swift.
A torment prompt and soon done with
Is better than one that sleeping lies.

O may my body be made warm
By this tiny gold alarm
Without which love sleeps or dies!

The Rower[3]

Back bent to a great river slowly I pull
Plucking myself away from the smiling shores;
Soul with heavy hands, burdened with these oars
The sky must give way to the slow waters' knell.

Hard in heart, eyes, turned from the beauty I beat,
While the rings around me widening swirled,
My long strokes shall shatter your famous world
Of leaves and of fire that I would celebrate.

Ample iridescence, trees whereon I glide,
Arabesqued water, and fulfilment's peace,
Cleave them, my boat, leave there your trace
So that of great calm no memory abide.

Never, charms of day, never your grace
Has suffered so much from a rebel's blow:
But, as the suns shone and made my childhood
    grow,
I row back to the source where even names cease.

In vain the vast nymph, embracing, infinite,
Restrains with pure arms my harassed hands;
I shall slowly break a thousand frozen bonds
And the silvery ripples of her naked might.

These discreet murmuring waters strangely place
Under a silken bandage my days of gold;
Nothing more blindly frays a joy that was of old
Than the sound of smooth flight, the untroubled
    pace.

Beneath the ringed bridges, borne by waters in spate
I drift where the wind and night-whispers tease,
They straddle a brow they brush with weariness,
But whose arrogant bone is harder than their gate.

[3] Translated by W. J. Strachan. By permission of Mr. Strachan.

Their night is slow to pass. The soul lets through
Its responsive eyelids, its sensitive suns,
When, in the movement that covers me with stones,
I plunge in defiance of all this idle blue.

The Sleeping Beauty [4]

In a palace of pale-rose purity she sleeps,
The princess, in leaf-animated murmurings;
Sometimes a half-heard utterance in coral shapes
Itself, when random birds peck at her golden rings.

She listens neither to the tinkling water-sounds
Of treasure hidden in a wilderness of days,
Nor, on the far-off forests, to flute-blended winds
That tear these ruminations with a horn's clear
    phrase,

Let lingering echoes lull the dawn-stirred sleeper,
She who resembles more and more the soft creeper
That waves and gently beats upon her shrouded
    eyes.

The slow-petalled rose that hangs so close to your
    cheek
Will never squander those in-folded treasuries
That blush in secret when the sun's rays on them
    break.

As on the Shore of the Ocean [5]

As on the shore of the ocean
On the front of separation,
On the pendulous frontier of motion
Time gives, takes back,
Strikes, deploys,
Vomits, gulps back,
Gives and regrets,
Fingers, falls, kisses and moans,
Returns to the mass,
Returns to the ocean . . .   10

I plunge into the interval of two waves.—
Time regretfully
Finite, infinite . . .
What does this time enclose?
What shrinks, what bridles?
What measures, refuses and snatches time away
    from me again?

[4] Translated by James Kirkup. From *Selected Writings*, by Paul Valéry. By permission of New Directions, Inc.
[5] Translated by Louise Varèse. From *Selected Writings*, by Paul Valéry. By permission of New Directions, Inc.

Imposing impotence to go beyond, O wave!
The very sequence of your act is to take back
To flow back so as not to break
The integrity of the water's body!   20

To remain sea and not to cede
The power of motion!
Fated to flow back
Rasping, regretfully,
To be reduced, to be restored,
To be transformed into immutable number.

As idea to the body returns,
As thought from the point falls
Where its secret cause,
Having dared and lifted it   30
It cannot but return
To the pure and simple presence,
To all things less itself,
Even though not itself,
Itself never for long,
Never long enough
Either to be done with all things,
Or to begin other times . . .
It will always be for another time!
For the next and for the other time,   40
An infinity of times!
Disorder of times!

Listen endlessly, hear
The song of waiting and the shock of time,
The constant rocking of the reckoning,
Identity and quantity,
And the voice of the ocean
Reiterating: I win and lose,
I lose and win . . .
Oh! fling a little time outside of time!   50

More than alone on the shore of the ocean,
I give myself like a wave
To the monotonous transmutation
Of water into water,
Myself into myself . . .

GUILLAUME APOLLINAIRE

1880–1918

Wilhelm-Apollinaris de Kostrowitski, of Polish descent, was born near Rome. In 1902 he settled in Paris and assumed the name of Guillaume Apolli-

naire. There he became acquainted with a number of young artists and writers—Pablo Picasso, Georges Braque, Marie Laurencin, Juan Gris, Max Jacob, and Pierre Reverdy—who came to recognize Apollinaire as their spiritual leader in the momentous new developments in literature and the plastic arts which were astir. From discussions of the primitivism of Henri Rousseau, of African Negro art, and of the new aesthetic conceptions of reality, the new movement of Cubism arose. In 1912 Apollinaire published *Les Peintres Cubistes,* the aesthetic apologia of the new movement. His chief works in poetry were *Les Alcools* (1913) and *Calligrammes* (1918). He became a second lieutenant in the French army during the First World War, and was wounded in 1916. His health was so seriously impaired that he became an easy victim of the influenza epidemic in 1918.

"Zone" from *Les Alcools* illustrates the new cubistic techniques in poetry; Apollinaire achieves a new interpretation of reality, the revelation of another world lying beyond the conventional perspective by organizing his poetic structure into astonishing but significant intuitional free associations. The poem embodies as well a Whitmanesque search for self-identity, in which the poet demonstrates his awareness of all the locations, all the places which in his experience have become simultaneously an integral part of his personality, as the cubist painter juxtaposes on his canvas the many-phased aspects of an object, to be encompassed in a single glance. From a reading of his poetry it is not surprising to learn that Apollinaire was the first to use the term *surréaliste* in literature, in describing his play, *Les Mamelles de Tirésias* (1918). In the unbounded freedom of his poetic vision and in his rejection of the restrictions of French prosody and of conventional punctuation, Guillaume Apollinaire has had an extensive influence upon modern French poetry.

FURTHER READING

APOLLINAIRE, GUILLAUME. *Selected Writings,* translated with a Critical Introduction by Roger Shattuck (New York, 1950).
APOLLINAIRE, GUILLAUME. *The Cubist Painters* (New York, 1949).
BOWRA, C. M. *The Creative Experiment* (London, 1949).
SOUPAULT, PHILIPPE. *Guillaume Apollinaire* (Marseilles, 1927).
STRACHAN, W. J., trans. *Apollinaire to Aragon* (London, 1948).

Zone *

You have grown weary of a world effete
This morning Eiffel-tower shepherdess your flocks
    of bridges bleat
Too long you have lived with Roman and Greek
Here even the cars seem pseudo-antique
Religion alone remains religion fresh-revealed
Simple like the hangars on a landing-field

Christ alone in Europe belongs not to ancient men
The most modern European is you Pope Pius Ten
And you whom windows watch and shame restrains
From entering a church to confess your sins   10
You read prospectus catalogue posters which shout
    in rows

This is your morning-poetry newspapers are your
    prose
Numbers at a penny full of crime-adventures
Portraits of the great and a thousand diverse features
This morning I saw a pretty street whose name I
    forget
Fresh and clean with the sun its voice was a trumpet
Directors workmen handsome shorthand-typists
From Monday morning to Saturday night four
    times daily tread this street
Each morning three times you hear the siren moan
And a crazy bell barks each day about noon   20
The inscriptions of the sign-boards and the walls
The plaques and notices like hoarse parrot-calls
I like the beauty of this industrial street
Situated in Paris between rue Aumont-Thieville
    and avenue des Ternes
Once again the youthful street and you a little mite
Whom your Mother still keeps clothed in blue and
    white
You are very pious with your oldest friend René
    Dalize [1]
Loving nothing so much as the Church's mysteries
It is nine o'clock the gas-jet lowered blue from the
    dormitory you steal
You will pray all night in the college chapel   30
While the eternal and adorable depth of amethyst
Turns for ever the flaming glory of Christ
It is the lovely lily before whose shrine we stand
    devout
It is the auburn-haired torch the wind cannot put
    out
It is the pale scarlet son of the Mater Dolorosa

* Translated by W. J. Strachan. From *Apollinaire to
Aragon*, by permission of W. J. Strachan.
[1] Poet, and Apollinaire's school friend, with whom he
founded the literary review, *Les Soirées de Paris*.

It is the tree where prayers sprout ever closer
It is the double rood of honour and eternity
It is the star with six-fold ray
It is God who dies Friday and rises from the dead
    Sunday
It is Christ who soars better than airmen have
    soared   40
It is He who holds the world's altitude record
Pupil Christ of the eye
Twentieth pupil of the centuries He can do it alone
And changed into a bird this century mounts like
    Jesus to a throne
The devils in the pit raise their heads to peer
They say he is imitating Simon Magus of Judea
They shout if he can fly let us call him a "fly" one
The angels fly round the flying-trapeze-man
Icarus Elias Enoch Apollonius of Thyane
Hover around this first aeroplane   50
They divide sometimes for those borne by the Eu-
    charist to clear the coast

Those priests who mount eternally elevating the
    Host
The aeroplane lands at last without folding its
    wings
The sky fills with millions of swallows this spectacle
    brings
Rapidly thither fly falcons owls crows
From Africa Ibis marabous flamingos
The Roc bird of whom poet-fabulists tell
Soars holding in its talons Adam's skull
As the eagle swoops from the sky-line its cry is
    heard
And from America comes the little humming-
    bird   60
From China have come the pihis on long supple
    feather
Their wing-span is one and they fly two together
Here is the dove the immaculate spirit
Lyre-bird and argus-eyed peacock escort it
The phoenix arising from its wing-fanned pyre
Veils all for a moment with its burning fire
The sirens leaving the perilous straits
Arrive all three singing gloriously in the heights
And eagle phoenix pihis of China and condor
Fraternise all with the Flying-wonder   70

You walk now in Paris all alone amid the throng
Herds of lowing buses near you glide along
The tortures of love your throat constrain
As if you were never to be loved again
If you lived of old in a monastery you would seek
    retreat
Now you are ashamed at the prayer you repeat

You rail and your laughter peals like a hellfire of
  sin
The sparks of your laughter gild the life within
It is a picture hanging on a gloomy gallery wall
Whose image at times you with closer eye recall   80
Today you walk in Paris where the women are dyed
  sanguine
It was though I would forget this it was beauty in
  decline
Surrounded with fervent flames Notre-Dame gazed
  up at Chartres
The blood of Sacre-coeur flooded me at Montmartre
The blessed words have robbed me of all ease
The love I suffer from is a shameful disease
And you survive sleepless and anguished in this
  image which possesses
You to whom so close it is this image which passes
Now I find you by the Mediterranean shore
Beneath the lime-trees all the year in flower   90
With some of your friends you take a boat out to sea
One is from Nice one from Mentone and two from
  La Turbie
We watch in a panic the octopus of the deep
Symbols of our Saviour the fish swim among the
  kelp

You are in the tavern-garden in the suburbs of
  Prague
You feel happy and a rose lies before you on the
  table
You observe instead of writing your tale in prose
The canker that lies in the heart of the rose

Terrified you see yourself pictured in the agate of
  Saint Vit
You were mortally sad when your eyes that image
  met   100
You are like Lazarus bewildered by the day
The clock-hands in the ghetto are moving the wrong
  way
And you retreat slowly into your life within
Going up to hear in the taverns at Hradchin
The peasants who sing an ancient Czech song
Here at Marseilles the melons among

Here at Coblenz Hotel Geant your home

Here sitting under a Japanese medlar at Rome

Here at Amsterdam with one you deem lovely but
  is in truth an ugly maiden
She is destined to marry a student at Leyden   110
One can hire rooms in latin *Cubicula locanda*
I remember I spent three days there and as many
  at Gouda

Now in Paris before the judge they attest
While you as a criminal are under arrest [2]
You have made journeys both grievous and happy
Before you were conscious of age and the lie
Of love at twenty and thirty you bitterly tasted
I have lived like a madman and my days were
  wasted
You dare no more behold your hands I can scarce
  restrain my tears
Over you over her I love over all that brought your
  fears   120

You watch with moistened eyes these poor emi-
  grants
They believe in God they pray the mothers suckle
  their infants
They fill with their odour the Hall of Gare Saint-
  Lazare
As in the Wise Kings they have faith in their star
They hope to make money in the Argentine
And their fortune made back home enjoy their gain
A family removes an eiderdown as you would your
  heart
That eiderdown and our dreams are just as unreal
Some of the emigrants stay and find here a roof
In these hovels rue des Rosiers and rue des
  Écouffes   130
I have seen them often in the evening they take
  air in the street
They move as rarely as pieces in chess
There are above all Jews whose wives in their pallor
And wearing wigs sit in the shop back-parlour

You stand against the bar with its filthy counter of
  zinc
Among the down-and-outs taking your simple drink

You are to be found in a big restaurant at night

These women are not bad and their burdens are not
  light
All have brought suffering to their lover even the
  worst "fright"
She is a policeman's daughter in the island of
  Jersey   140
Her hands which I have not seen are hard and
  creasy

I feel a great pity for the stitches of her belly

To a poor wench with a hideous laugh I now humil-
  iate my lips

[2] Probably an allusion to the unjustified arrest of Apollinaire for the theft of the "Mona Lisa" from the Louvre
in 1911.

You are alone the morning will come
The milkmen clatter their milkcans in the street

Night moves off the loveliest of half-breeds
It is Ferdine the false or Leah attentive to my needs

And you drink this alcohol burning like your days
Your days that you drain like a dram to the lees
You walk towards Auteuil weary-footed wend
    home   150
Among your fetishes of Oceania and Guinea lie
    down
They are Christs of different form and faith
Each inferior Christ the false hope of a wraith

Farewell farewell

Sun so soon sunk

PAUL ELUARD

1895–

Paul Eluard, possibly the most gifted lyric poet of his generation in France, has been identified successively with the Dadaist and Surrealistic movements. His poetry is often said to represent "pure poetry," a concept which in part grew out of the surrealistic insistence that poetic images must be "innocent," that is, must neither communicate nor prove anything. The images emerge without premeditation, imponderable in meaning, from a semi-passive state close to automatic writing, sometimes as "Words void of sense" (see "The Poet's Work"). During the Nazi occupation of France, Eluard shared with Louis Aragon the militant task of describing in poetry the anguish, violence, and heroism of the Resistance, but his most distinguished achievement has been as a lyric love poet, both in his earlier surrealist verse and in his more recent postwar volume *Poésie Ininterrompue*. As a love poet Eluard has celebrated the wonderful spiritual and physical union of man with woman (so often associated in his poetry with images of light and dawn) that imparts the extraordinary spontaneity and directness of emotion to such poems as "The Naked Land" and "Marc Chagall." There is in such a poem as "The Naked Land" Eluard's identi-

fication of the transcendant erotic experience of the love of woman with the universal cosmic freedom of the poet in the universe that was so inherent a part of the surrealistic poetic credo. The repose and tranquillity that is the ambient emotional tone of his poetry is the result in part of the luminosity of his style, and in part of his belief that the love of woman may resolve the dissonances and the discordant elements of human experience into a universal harmony that is immediate in its transports, and yet self-renewing, timeless, absolute. Not since the troubadour poetry of the medieval court of love have the ennobling qualities of love been more memorably rendered.

FURTHER READING

Bogan, Louise. "The Poetry of Paul Eluard," *Partisan Review*, VI (Fall, 1939), 76–89.
Eluard, Paul. *Selected Writings* (New York, 1951).
Fowlie, Wallace. *The Age of Surrealism* (New York, 1950).
Read, Herbert, ed. *Surrealism* (London, 1936).

The Poet's Work *

I

How fine to be with the others
On the worn turf in summer
Under white clouds

How fine to be with women
In a house grey and warm
Under a transparent sheet

How fine to be with oneself
Before the white page
Under the threat of impotence
Between two times two spaces

Between boredom and the passion for living

II

What have you come to take
In the accustomed room

A book that is never opened

What have you come to say
To her so indiscreet

What cannot be repeated

* This and the following two poems translated by W. J. Strachan. From *Apollinaire to Aragon*, by permission of W. J. Strachan.

What have you come to see
In this place so unveiled

What the blind see

III

The road is short
Soon one has arrived
Where coloured are stones
Then
Hollow ones

Soon one has arrived
Where words are smooth
Words without weight
Then
Words void of sense

To speak with no message
Dawn is long passed
And it is not day
Nor is it night
Nothing—the echo of an endless step

Marc Chagall [1]

In my arms in my arms to laugh and to weep
My tears have the glow of your moistened lips
I set the world spinning round your pleasure
My garden is haloed round your face

We are the first to dream of flying
Together and the universe
Follows us as the float follows the hooked fish
But the light does not suffer

As you are the most beautiful and the most faithful
I am the most beautiful the most faithful also
Same fire from the same source
The same cool water in the storm

No windows but our windows
Whence life escapes where all things enter
Everywhere being the centre of love
Endlessly the first look

Our birth is perpetual

The Naked Land

The naked land
Where long I shall reside
Tender meadows has
Where your warmth reposes

[1] The poem concerns a painting by Marc Chagall
(1887–   ).

Springs where your breasts
Mirror the day
Roads where your lips
To another's lips smile
Woods where the birds
Raise gently your eyelids
Beneath a sky reflected
By your cloudless brow

Sole universe of mine
Gift lightly accorded
To the rhythm of nature—
Your nakedness will endure

————◆————

LOUIS ARAGON

1898–

Soon after the end of the First World War there came together in Paris a group of young men, André Breton, Philippe Soupault, Blaise Cendrars, Pierre Reverdy, Paul Eluard, and Louis Aragon, who felt that the war had demonstrated the bankruptcy of the old world and its values. Disillusion with human intelligence and rationality was the motivating force that inspired this group to found a Dadaist review, Littérature. Dadaism as a movement was, however, short-lived, and in 1924–1925 Breton, Eluard, and Aragon helped to found the surrealist movement. The period from 1924–1931 was characterized by the strongly polemical activities of the surrealists, signalized especially in 1928 by the publication of Breton's surrealist novel Nadja, Aragon's brilliant Traité de Style, and the release of the first surrealist film, Un Chien Andalou. After 1931 Aragon progressively abandoned his surrealist creed to identify himself with the cultural activities of Communism.

The extraordinary debacle of 1939–1940 must have seemed, in its disordered, phantasmagoric experiences, a surrealist dream come true. Aragon participated in the retreat from Dunkirk, and wrote one of the best poems on that experience to grow out of the Second World War. In recording in his poetry and other writings the retreat, surrender, and occupation of France, Aragon became the outstanding poet of French Resistance.

During the occupation, Aragon arrived at a state of increased moral certainty and social conscience; the poems represented here (with the exception of the lovely and justly famous "Elsa," to his wife, Elsa Triolet) reveal this social conscience and devotion to his fellow countrymen, especially in Aragon's modification of his surrealistic use of language and his consequent increased clarity of expression in his desire to communicate with a wider public.

FURTHER READING

ARAGON, LOUIS. *Aragon, Poet of the French Resistance* (New York, 1945).

ARAGON, LOUIS. *Traité de Style* (Paris, 1928).

RAYMOND, MARCEL. *From Baudelaire to Surrealism* (New York, 1950), Chapter XVI, pp. 300–18.

STRACHAN, W. J., trans. *Apollinaire to Aragon* (London, 1948).

Elsa *

So deep your eyes that as I lean to drink
Their pools the light of all the suns reflect
Lovers in despair plunge from their brink
So deep I lose the power to recollect

Now beneath black wings the ocean heaves
Then sunshine in your eyes and gone the scorn
June clouds are shaken from an angel's sleeves
Never more blue the sky than over corn

The winds dispel the heaven's wrath in vain
Your eyes are still more bright when tears they
    lodge   10
The very sky is jealous of their rain
No glass so blue as at the fragments' edge

Mother of Seven Sorrows tear-drenched rays
Seven swords have pierced the prisms gaily painted
For dawns where tears have flown bring sharper
    days
Bluer the iris when with grief acquainted

Your eyes in sorrow made a double rent
Where through the miracle of the Kings was seen
As by the manger head in reverence bent
They saw the mantle of our Blessed Queen   20

One pair of lips in May can voice the airs
Of all the songs and breathe each sad *alas*
Yet heaven's too small for all the million stars
Lacking your eyes to speak for all that was

  * This and the two following poems translated by W. J. Strachan. From *Apollinaire to Aragon*, by permission of W. J. Strachan.

Child gazing in his picture-book wide-eyed
Imagination fastened by its power
Your open eyes who knows if they have lied
Wild flowers expanding after April shower

What hidden lightning from those beds may stab
O lavender where insects rape their prey   30
I am at the mercy of the weaving web
A sailor drowning in mid-August sea

I have searched pitch-blende where radium lies
My fingers burned at the forbidden fire
Yet I have rediscovered Paradise
Here in your eyes Peru-Golconda of desire

And then one night befell the Crack of Doom
Amid the reefs the wreckers set alight
I saw above the waves in Stygian gloom
Your eyes your eyes O Elsa gleaming bright   40

More Beautiful than Tears

Some people find me too alive it seems
I bring to life discomforting remorse
My brazen rhymes disturb their quiet dreams
With noises that would galvanize a corpse

If grinding tanks should dislocate my verse
If shrill axle cries are far from pleasant
The angel-stops gave way to thunder's curse
And Dunkirk's memory is ever present

In doubtful taste agreed but this is War
And some of us in taste are pretty queer   10
And in our nostrils clings its acrid char
And some of us got drunk on Brussels beer

I speak of love and then my love displeases
When all is fine for me it rains for you
You say my meadows have too many daisies
My night too many stars my sky's too blue

As probes the heart-dissecting medico
Among my words for cheap effects you pried
Have I not seen Pont Neuf and Louvre go
Will vengeance leave you still unsatisfied   20

You may enslave the sea-gull on the wing
You may condemn the poet to be dumb
But take the poet's right his France to sing
And you will try in vain till kingdom come

France fair maid who visitest each door
If ever I forget let it be told
Your eyes are like the sheaves of flowers you bore
Which starred your apron in the Springs of old

Could our love be feigned our passion false
Smile on this brow this sky cloud-torn and grey   30
The understanding smile of County Beauce
Catching the poppied corn on Summer day

Have not her arms the beauty statues have
Here in this land of stone of golden bread
The sweet perfection all her sons can give
Watched by Jean Racine's eternal shade

At Rheims the angel smiles with perfect lips
A glimpse of sun seen at its fair decline
What sure damnation saint or prophet sips
Before that hair so redolent of wine   40

Ingres of Montauban in purest line
The hollow of her shoulder drew wherein
Lingers the long desire as rocks refine
The Peaty water of the mountain burn

O Laura he had loved your later peer
Her for whom murdered we bleed today
Petrarch whom inspired like pointed spear
The doe who from the huntsmen sped away

Evoke Evoke so that the ghosts find haven
The mirage of Arabian-night decor   50
The murals of St. John to Brantome's cavern
From Roncevaux to hillsides of Vercors

Dream-laden winds from Arles were never harsh
Their dreams too deep for heart to put in words
When in Aunis-Saintonge the yellow marsh
Is churned by tanks of ruthless conquering hordes

In tournament each province city town
Vies with the other in their names and flings
Those flowery garlands like a challenge down
That dream and reason in confusion brings   60

O chains which barred the sky and you Durance
O land of shepherds coloured like your fruit
Manosque so loved by François King of France
That on the Arab walls her name he wrote

Beloved madcap jealous without cause
Who fail to recognise yourself in these
My lines—on Naurouze' brow awhile we pause
Our double fate must choose between two seas

No—like a song that lingers in the brain
You wish to haunt again the Mount Ventoux   70
The Seine flows gently here and Lamartine
Dreams of his Madeleine in the orchard row

Woman wine and cradle-song of old
Or scene my wit is slow to celebrate

Are not these fecund breasts and limbs of gold
Like pines and Brittany like suns that set

Breastplate of white where burn my lips with fire
Cider milk of joy satiety
Would not soldiers exiled in Palmyre
Die for their loved and secret Normandy   80

How should I guess what all these charms beget
These names of flesh and blood like Andelys
The image turns and then our cheeks are wet
With tears—stay mute O Paris Paris

Paris home of songs of sudden ire
Whose banners lately overwashed must fade
Metropolis as bright as Polar-star
True Paris only at the barricades

Paris of civil-strife of Cours-la-Reine
Of Blancs-Manteaux of bitter February skies   90
From Saint-Antoine to hill slopes of Suresnes
Paris heart-rending as a glazier's cries

Flee these grim outskirts where all troubles start
Dawn follows dawn as life flows sadly on
The Oise has lost her charm the Marne her heart
Valois deserted with her Sylvie gone

Ramparts of memory we man
With twenty-year-old prayers where clouds have
          frowned
Moulin de Laffaux—Chemin des Dames
Pilgrim do not forget the battleground   100

Over dusty plains your feet move on
Pursuing without pause and undismayed
Over the Meuse and forested Argonne
The dawn of immortal glory but betrayed

Like the wounded hind a coward struck
The pond's blue eye broods over gold-flecked bowers
Halt on the fleeing exile's mountain-track
In Courbet's land where mandragora flowers

Lost is Alsace where when the Rhine o'erflows
From frozen branches drop inert the pheasants   110
Where Werther for a moment quits his woes
To revel with the merry-making peasants

The storm may rage from Dunkirk to Port-Vendre
But voices so beloved can never drown
None has the power to still the tales that wander
Around Ardennes of Aymon's renown

Who from our ears could drive this flute-refrain
Which from our throats for centuries arose
O youthful throng who sang *La Marjolaine*

"The laurels are cut down . . ." and soon our
    foes   120

For now with beat of hooves the forest rings
My brimming heart wells over at the source
Hope speaks at night the language of the springs
Duguesclin comes thundering on his horse

What matter if I die before is seen
The sacred brow which patient waits above
"Dance on my child Dance capucine"
My country is my hunger want and love.

The Night of Dunkirk

France like a stuff our feet have worn and frayed
Has bit by bit refused to bear our tread

Where in the tide weed-woven corpses lie
The boats capsized like Bishops' bonnets rife

Here ends a camp a hundred thousand strong
And Malo beach the sea and sky prolong

Beneath this night where rot the horses slain
Hooves of migratory herds beat in my brain

The level-crossing opens—we depart
To re-discover our unsorted heart   10

A thousand loves throb in John Lackland's breast
Will they at last a thousand times find rest

O arrow-pierced Saint Sebastian
How much how much your fate resembles mine

Assured that they will hear who weakness had
To spare their own and soothe the heart that bled

I at least this confessed love shall cry
Whose flames arising pattern 'gainst the sky

My cries my cries shall shake the burning town
Somnambulists from roofs shall topple down   20

My cries of love shall in your head resound
The Knives O Knives of grinder on his round

My cries my cries in every ear shall ring
O where are you my Sight my precious thing

My cries my cries louder than cannon-shot
Louder than wounded men or drunken sot

My cries will say Your lips are beakers where
I drink the long red draught of love-despair

Your ivy-twining arms can hold me yet
I cannot die—for those who die forget   30

Could I forget the eyes of those who went
Forget Dunkirk—the lover's last lament

I cannot sleep as lights flash in and out
Who could forget the wine of drunken bout

Soldiers have dug their narrow six-foot room
And seem to try the shadow of the tomb

Flintlike faces crazed defiant air
Their slumber is a prescient despair

The scents of Spring this sand has never known
The May is dying in this Northern dune   40

German Fiction

THOMAS MANN

1875–

Born in the northern seaport town of Lübeck in Germany, the son of a wealthy merchant, Thomas Mann is widely considered to be the greatest novelist modern Germany has produced. During the early years of the Nazi regime, Mann came to the United States as a political refugee where he has since resided and become a citizen. Representing an objective trend in literature, Mann's first works were penetrating analytical novels composed in a masterful style and dealing extensively with the decline of the modern bourgeoisie. His early heroes are nearly all overcultured, cosmopolitan figures who exhibit unmistakable signs of decadence. *Buddenbrooks* (1901), one of his more famous novels, is illustrative of decay resulting from excessive refinement. Its hero is an artistic weakling who is the last member of a once vigorous merchant family. *Tonio Kröger* (1903) is the story of an artist of bourgeois origin who, to his great sorrow, discovers the vast gap which separates the artistic temperament from a realistic world. The *Magic Mountain* (1924), which investigates the physical and mental ills of our time, is one of the finest masterpieces of the European novel. Mann's highly artistic style in its wide use of leitmotifs and contrapuntal devices is reminiscent of musical compositions of a symphonic nature. His influence in Germany and abroad has been and still is tremendous.

Thomas Mann has always been a good European, interested in the origins of the traditions of European culture in all its diverse manifestations, as his essays on Goethe and Sigmund Freud demonstrate. His recent *Joseph* novels indicate Mann's study of ancient myths and fertility rites as a means of enriching his narrative with philosophical overtones, and *Dr. Faustus* (1949) returns to a favorite theme, the relation of organic disease to the enhancement of the aesthetic sensibility of the artist. "Little Herr Friedemann" (1897) may seem to anticipate certain discoveries of modern psychology before the advent of Freud; it is not wholly improbable to see in it an indirect allusion to Mann's early interest in the alienation of the artist in a mould of normal social behavior.

FURTHER READING

HATFIELD, HENRY. *Thomas Mann* (New York, 1951).
NEIDER, CHARLES, ed. The *Stature of Thomas Mann* (New York, 1948).

Little Herr Friedemann *

IT WAS the nurse's fault. When they first suspected, Frau Consul Friedemann had spoken to her very gravely about the need of controlling her weakness. But what good did that do? Or the glass of red wine which she got daily besides the beer which was needed for the milk? For they suddenly discovered that she even sank so low as to drink the methylated spirit which was kept for the spirit lamp. Before they could send her away and get someone to take her place, the mischief was done. One day the mother and sisters came home to find that little

* From *Stories of Three Decades*, by permission of Alfred A. Knopf, Inc. Copyright, 1936, by Alfred A. Knopf, Inc.

Johannes, then about a month old, had fallen from the couch and lay on the floor, uttering an appallingly faint little cry, while the nurse stood beside him quite stupefied.

The doctor came and with firm, gentle hands tested the little creature's contracted and twitching limbs. He made a very serious face. The three girls stood sobbing in a corner and the Frau Consul in the anguish of her heart prayed aloud.

The poor mother, just before the child's birth, had already suffered a crushing blow: her husband, the Dutch Consul, had been snatched away from her by sudden and violent illness, and now she was too broken to cherish any hope that little Johannes would be spared to her. But by the second day the doctor had given her hand an encouraging squeeze and told her that all immediate danger was over. There was no longer any sign that the brain was affected. The facial expression was altered, it had lost the fixed and staring look. . . . Of course, they must see how things went on—and hope for the best, hope for the best.

The grey gabled house in which Johannes Friedemann grew up stood by the north gate of the little old commercial city. The front door led into a large flag-paved entry, out of which a stair with a white wooden balustrade led up into the second storey. The faded wall-paper in the living-room had a landscape pattern, and straight-backed chairs and sofas in dark-red plush stood round the heavy mahogany table.

Often in his childhood—Johannes sat here at the window, which always had a fine showing of flowers, on a small footstool at his mother's feet, listening to some fairy-tale she told him, gazing at her smooth grey head, her mild and gentle face, and breathing in the faint scent she exhaled. She showed him the picture of his father, a kindly man with grey side-whiskers—he was now in heaven, she said, and awaiting them there.

Behind the house was a small garden where in summer they spent much of their time, despite the smell of burnt sugar which came over from the refinery close by. There was a gnarled old walnut tree in whose shade little Johannes would sit, on a low wooden stool, cracking walnuts, while Frau Friedemann and her three daughters, now grown women, took refuge from the sun under a grey canvas tent. The mother's gaze often strayed from her embroidery to look with sad and loving eyes at her child.

He was not beautiful, little Johannes, as he

crouched on his stool industriously cracking his nuts. In fact, he was a strange sight, with his pigeon breast, humped back, and disproportionately long arms. But his hands and feet were delicately formed, he had soft red-brown eyes like a doe's, a sensitive mouth, and fine, light-brown hair. His head, had it not sat so deep between his shoulders, might almost have been called pretty.

When he was seven he went to school, where time passed swiftly and uniformly. He walked every day, with the strut deformed people often have, past the quaint gabled houses and shops to the old schoolhouse with the vaulted arcades. When he had done his preparation he would read in his books with the lovely title-page illustrations in colour, or else work in the garden, while his sisters kept house for their invalid mother. They went out too, for they belonged to the best society of the town; but unfortunately they had not married, for they had not much money nor any looks to recommend them.

Johannes too was now and then invited out by his schoolmates, but it is not likely that he enjoyed it. He could not take part in their games, and they were always embarrassed in his company, so there was no feeling of good fellowship.

There came a time when he began to hear certain matters talked about, in the courtyard at school. He listened wide-eyed and large-eared, quite silent, to his companion's raving over this or that little girl. Such things, though they entirely engrossed the attention of these others, were not, he felt, for him; they belonged in the same category as the ball games and gymnastics. At times he felt a little sad. But at length he had become quite used to standing on one side and not taking part.

But after all it came about—when he was sixteen —that he felt suddenly drawn to a girl of his own age. She was the sister of a classmate of his, a blonde, hilarious hoyden, and he met her when calling at her brother's house. He felt strangely embarrassed in her neighbourhood; she too was embarrassed and treated him with such artificial cordiality that it made him sad.

One summer afternoon as he was walking by himself on the wall outside the town, he heard a whispering behind a jasmine bush and peeped cautiously through the branches. There she sat on a bench beside a long-legged, red-haired youth of his acquaintance. They had their arms about each other and he was imprinting on her lips a kiss, which she returned amid giggles. Johannes looked, turned round, and went softly away.

His head was sunk deeper than ever between his shoulders, his hands trembled, and a sharp pain shot upwards from his chest to his throat. But he choked it down, straightening himself as well as he could. "Good," said he to himself. "That is over. Never again will I let myself in for any of it. To the others it brings joy and happiness, for me it can only mean sadness and pain. I am done with it. For me that is all over. Never again."

The resolution did him good. He had renounced, renounced forever. He went home, took up a book, or else played on his violin, which despite his deformed chest he had learned to do.

At seventeen Johannes left school to go into business, like everybody else he knew. He was apprenticed to the big lumber firm of Herr Schlievogt down on the river-bank. They were kind and considerate, he on his side was responsive and friendly, time passed with peaceful regularity. But in his twenty-first year his mother died, after a lingering illness.

This was a sore blow for Johannes Friedemann, and the pain of it endured. He cherished this grief, he gave himself up to it as one gives oneself to a great joy, he fed it with a thousand childhood memories; it was the first important event in his life and he made the most of it.

Is not life in and for itself a good, regardless of whether we may call its content "happiness"? Johannes Friedemann felt that it was so, and he loved life. He, who had renounced the greatest joy it can bring us, taught himself with infinite, incredible care to take pleasure in what it had still to offer. A walk in the springtime in the parks surrounding the town; the fragrance of a flower; the song of a bird—might not one feel grateful for such things as these?

And that we need to be taught how to enjoy, yes, that our education is always and only equal to our capacity for enjoyment—he knew that too, and he trained himself. Music he loved, and attended all the concerts that were given in the town. He came to play the violin not so badly himself, no matter what a figure of fun he made when he did it; and took delight in every beautiful soft tone he succeeded in producing. Also, by much reading he came in time to possess a literary taste the like of which did not exist in the place. He kept up with the new books, even the foreign ones; he knew how to savour the seductive rhythm of a lyric or the ultimate flavour of a subtly told tale—yes, one might almost call him a connoisseur.

He learned to understand that to everything belongs its own enjoyment and that it is absurd to distinguish between an experience which is "happy" and one which is not. With a right good will he accepted each emotion as it came, each mood, whether sad or gay. Even he cherished the unfulfilled desires, the longings. He loved them for their own sakes and told himself that with fulfilment the best of them would be past. The vague, sweet, painful yearning and hope of quiet spring evenings—are they not richer in joy than all the fruition the summer can bring? Yes, he was a connoisseur, our little Herr Friedemann.

But of course they did not know that, the people whom he met on the street, who bowed to him with the kindly, compassionate air he knew so well. They could not know that this unhappy cripple, strutting comically along in his light overcoat and shiny top hat—strange to say, he was a little vain—they could not know how tenderly he loved the mild flow of his life, charged with no great emotions, it is true, but full of a quiet and tranquil happiness which was his own creation.

But Herr Friedemann's great preference, his real passion, was for the theatre. He possessed a dramatic sense which was unusually strong; at a telling theatrical effect or the catastrophe of a tragedy his whole small frame would shake with emotion. He had his regular seat in the first row of boxes at the opera-house; was an assiduous frequenter and often took his sisters with him. Since their mother's death they kept house for their brother in the old home which they all owned together.

It was a pity they were unmarried still; but with the decline of hope had come resignation—Friederike, the eldest, was seventeen years further on than Herr Friedemann. She and her sister Henriette were over-tall and thin, whereas Pfiffi, the youngest, was too short and stout. She had a funny way, too, of shaking herself as she talked, and water came in the corners of her mouth.

Little Herr Friedemann did not trouble himself overmuch about his three sisters. But they stuck together loyally and were always of one mind. Whenever an engagement was announced in their circle they with one voice said how very gratifying that was.

Their brother continued to live with them even after he became independent, as he did by leaving Herr Schlievogt's firm and going into business for himself, in an agency of sorts, which was no great tax on his time. His offices were in a couple of rooms on the ground floor of the house so that at mealtimes he had but the pair of stairs to mount—for he suffered now and then from asthma.

His thirtieth birthday fell on a fine warm June day, and after dinner he sat out in the grey canvas tent, with a new head-rest embroidered by Henriette. He had a good cigar in his mouth and a good book in his hand. But sometimes he would put the latter down to listen to the sparrows chirping blithely in the old nut tree and look at the clean gravel path leading up to the house between lawns bright with summer flowers.

Little Herr Friedemann wore no beard, and his face had scarcely changed at all, save that the features were slightly sharper. He wore his fine light-brown hair parted on one side.

Once, as he left the book fall on his knee and looked up into the sunny blue sky, he said to himself: "Well, so that is thirty years. Perhaps there may be ten or even twenty more, God knows. They will mount up without a sound or a stir and pass by like those that are gone; and I look forward to them with peace in my heart."

Now, it happened in July of the same year that a new appointment to the office of District Commandant had set the whole town talking. The stout and jolly gentleman who had for many years occupied the post had been very popular in social circles and they saw him go with great regret. It was in compliance with goodness knows what regulations that Herr von Rinnlingen and no other was sent hither from the capital.

In any case the exchange was not such a bad one. The new Commandant was married but childless. He rented a spacious villa in the southern suburbs of the city and seemed to intend to set up an establishment. There was a report that he was very rich—which received confirmation in the fact that he brought with him four servants, five riding and carriage horses, a landau and a light hunting-cart.

Soon after their arrival the husband and wife left cards on all the best society, and their names were on every tongue. But it was not Herr von Rinnlingen, it was his wife who was the centre of interest. All the men were dazed, for the moment too dazed to pass judgment; but their wives were quite prompt and definite in the view that Gerda von Rinnlingen was not their sort.

"Of course, she comes from the metropolis, her ways would naturally be different," Frau Hagenström, the lawyer's wife, said, in conversation with Henriette Friedemann. "She smokes, and she rides. That is of course. But it is her manners—they are not only free, they are positively brusque, or even worse. You see, no one could call her ugly, one might even say she is pretty; but she has not a trace of feminine charm in her looks or gestures or her laugh—they completely lack everything that makes a man fall in love with a woman. She is not a flirt—and goodness knows I would be the last to disparage her for that. But it is strange to see so young a woman—she is only twenty-four—so entirely wanting in natural charm. I am not expressing myself very well, my dear, but I know what I mean. All the men are simply bewildered. In a few weeks, you will see, they will be disgusted."

"Well," Fräulein Friedemann said, "she certainly has everything she wants."

"Yes," cried Frau Hagenström, "look at her husband! And how does she treat him? You ought to see it—you will see it! I would be the first to approve of a married woman behaving with a certain reserve towards the other sex. But how does she behave to her own husband? She has a way of fixing him with an ice-cold stare and saying 'My dear friend!' with a pitying expression that drives me mad. For when you look at him—upright, correct, gallant, a brilliant officer and a splendidly preserved man of forty! They have been married four years, my dear."

Herr Friedemann was first vouchsafed a glimpse of Frau von Rinnlingen in the main street of the town, among all the rows of shops, at mid-day, when he was coming from the Bourse, where he had done a little bidding.

He was strolling along beside Herr Stephens, looking tiny and important, as usual. Herr Stephens was in the wholesale trade, a huge stocky man with round side-whiskers and bushy eyebrows. Both of them wore top hats; their overcoats were unbuttoned on account of the heat. They tapped their canes along the pavement and talked of the political situation; but half-way down the street Stephens suddenly said:

"Deuce take it if there isn't the Rinnlingen driving along."

"Good," answered Herr Friedemann in his high, rather sharp voice, looking expectantly ahead. "Because I have never yet set eyes on her. And here we have the yellow cart we hear so much about."

It was in fact the hunting-cart which Frau von Rinnlingen was herself driving today with a pair of thoroughbreds; a groom sat behind her, with folded arms. She wore a loose beige coat and skirt and a small round straw hat with a brown leather band, beneath which her well-waved red-blond hair, a good, thick crop, was drawn into a knot at the nape of her neck. Her face was oval, with a dead-white skin and faint bluish shadows lurking under the close-set eyes. Her nose was short but well-shaped, with a becoming little saddle of freckles; whether her mouth was as good or no could not be told, for she kept it in continual motion, sucking the lower and biting the upper lip.

Herr Stephens, as the cart came abreast of them, greeted her with a great show of deference; little Herr Friedemann lifted his hat too and looked at her with wide-eyed attention. She lowered her whip, nodded slightly, and drove slowly past, looking at the houses and shop-windows.

After a few paces Herr Stephens said:

"She has been taking a drive and was on her way home."

Little Herr Friedemann made no answer, but stared before him at the pavement. Presently he started, looked at his companion, and asked: "What did you say?"

And Herr Stephens repeated his acute remark.

Three days after that Johannes Friedemann came home at midday from his usual walk. Dinner was at half past twelve, and he would spend the interval in his office at the right of the entrance door. But the maid came across the entry and told him that there were visitors.

"In my office?" he asked.

"No, upstairs with the mistresses."

"Who are they?"

"Herr and Frau Colonel von Rinnlingen."

"Ah," said Johannes Friedemann. "Then I will—"

And he mounted the stairs. He crossed the lobby and laid his hand on the knob of the high white door leading into the "landscape room." And then he drew back, turned round, and slowly returned as he had come. And spoke to himself, for there was no one else there, and said: "No, better not."

He went into his office, sat down at his desk, and took up the paper. But after a little he dropped it again and sat looking to one side out of the window. Thus he sat until the maid came to say that luncheon was ready; then he went up into the dining-room where his sisters were already waiting, and sat down in his chair, in which there were three music-books.

As she ladled the soup Henriette said:

"Johannes, do you know who were here?"

"Well?" he asked.

"The new Commandant and his wife."

"Indeed? That was friendly of them."

"Yes," said Pfiffi, a little water coming in the corners of her mouth. "I found them both very agreeable."

"And we must lose no time in returning the call," said Friederike. "I suggest that we go next Sunday, the day after tomorrow."

"Sunday," Henriette and Pfiffi said.

"You will go with us, Johannes?" asked Friederike.

"Of course he will," said Pfiffi, and gave herself a little shake. Herr Friedemann had not heard her at all; he was eating his soup, with a hushed and troubled air. It was as though he were listening to some strange noise he heard.

Next evening *Lohengrin* was being given at the opera, and everybody in society was present. The small auditorium was crowded, humming with voices and smelling of gas and perfumery. And every eye-glass in the stalls was directed towards box thirteen, next to the stage; for this was the first appearance of Herr and Frau von Rinnlingen and one could give them a good looking-over.

When little Herr Friedemann, in flawless dress clothes and glistening white pigeon-breasted shirt-front, entered his box, which was number thirteen, he started back at the door, making a gesture with his hand towards his brow. His nostrils dilated feverishly. Then he took his seat, which was next to Frau von Rinnlingen's.

She contemplated him for a little while, with her under lip stuck out; then she turned to exchange a few words with her husband, a tall, broad-shouldered gentleman with a brown, good-natured face and turned-up moustaches.

When the overture began and Frau von Rinnlingen leaned over the balustrade, Herr Friedemann gave her a quick, searching side glance. She wore a light-coloured evening frock, the only one in the theatre which was slightly low in the neck. Her sleeves were full and her white gloves came up to her elbows. Her figure was statelier than it had looked under the loose coat; her full bosom slowly rose and fell and the knot of red-blond hair hung low and heavy at the nape of her neck.

Herr Friedemann was pale, much paler than usual, and little beads of perspiration stood on his brow beneath the smoothly parted brown hair. He could see Frau von Rinnlingen's left arm, which lay upon the balustrade. She had taken off her glove and the rounded, dead-white arm and ringless hand, both of them shot with pale blue veins, were directly under his eye—he could not help seeing them.

The fiddles sang, the trombones crashed, Telramund was slain, general jubilation reigned in the orchestra, and little Herr Friedemann sat there motionless and pallid, his head drawn in between his shoulders, his forefinger to his lips and one hand thrust into the opening of his waistcoat.

As the curtain fell, Frau von Rinnlingen got up to leave the box with her husband. Johannes Friedemann saw her without looking, wiped his handkerchief across his brow, then rose suddenly and went as far as the door into the foyer, where he turned, came back to his chair, and sat down in the same posture as before.

When the bell rang and his neighbours re-entered the box he felt Frau von Rinnlingen's eyes upon him, so that finally against his will he raised his head. As their eyes met, hers did not swerve aside; she continued to gaze without embarrassment until he himself, deeply humiliated, was forced to look away. He turned a shade paler and felt a strange, sweet pang of anger and scorn. The music began again.

Towards the end of the act Frau von Rinnlingen chanced to drop her fan; it fell at Herr Friedemann's feet. They both stooped at the same time, but she reached it first and gave a little mocking smile as she said: "Thank you."

Their heads were quite close together and just for a second he got the warm scent of her breast. His face was drawn, his whole body twitched, and his heart thumped so horribly that he lost his breath. He sat without moving for half a minute, then he pushed back his chair, got up quietly, and went out.

He crossed the lobby, pursued by the music; got his top hat from the cloak-room, his light overcoat and his stick, went down the stairs and out of doors.

It was a warm, still evening. In the gas-lit street the gabled houses towered towards a sky where stars were softly beaming. The pavement echoed the steps of a few passers-by. Someone spoke to him, but he heard and saw nothing; his head was bowed and his deformed chest shook with the violence of his breathing. Now and then he murmured to himself:

"My God, my God!"

He was gazing horror-struck within himself, beholding the havoc which had been wrought with his tenderly cherished, scrupulously managed feelings. Suddenly he was quite overpowered by the strength of his tortured longing. Giddy and drunken he leaned against a lamp-post and his quivering lips uttered the one word: "Gerda!"

The stillness was complete. Far and wide not a soul was to be seen. Little Herr Friedemann pulled himself together and went on, up the street in which the opera-house stood and which ran steeply down to the river, then along the main street northwards to his home.

How she had looked at him! She had forced him, actually, to cast down his eyes! She had humiliated him with her glance. But was she not a woman and he a man? And those strange brown eyes of hers—had they not positively glittered with unholy joy?

Again he felt the same surge of sensual, impotent hatred mount up in him; then he relived the moment when her head had touched his, when he had breathed in the fragrance of her body—and for the second time he halted, bent his deformed torso backwards, drew in the air through clenched teeth, and murmured helplessly, desperately, uncontrollably:

"My God, my God!"

Then went on again, slowly, mechanically, through the heavy evening air, through the empty echoing streets until he stood before his own house. He paused a minute in the entry, breathing the cool, dank inside air; then he went into his office.

He sat down at his desk by the open window and stared straight ahead of him at a large yellow rose which somebody had set there in a glass of water. He took it up and smelt it with his eyes closed, then put it down with a gesture of weary sadness. No, no. That was all over. What was even that fragrance to him now? What any of all those things that up to now had been the well-springs of his joy?

He turned away and gazed into the quiet street. At intervals steps passed and the sound died away. The stars stood still and glittered. He felt so weak, so utterly tired to death. His head was quite vacant, and suddenly his despair began to melt into a gentle, pervading melancholy. A few lines of a poem flickered through his head, he heard the Lohengrin music in his ears, he saw Frau von Rinnlingen's face and her round white arm on the red velvet—then he fell into a heavy fever-burdened sleep.

Often he was near waking, but feared to do so and managed to sink back into forgetfulness again. But when it had grown quite light, he opened his eyes and looked round him with a wide and painful gaze. He remembered everything, it was as though the anguish had never been intermitted by sleep.

His head was heavy and his eyes burned. But when he had washed up and bathed his head with cologne he felt better and sat down in his place by the still open window. It was early, perhaps only five o'clock. Now and then a baker's boy passed; otherwise there was no one to be seen. In the opposite house the blinds were down. But birds were twittering and the sky was luminously blue. A wonderfully beautiful Sunday morning.

A feeling of comfort and confidence came over little Herr Friedemann. Why had he been distressing himself? Was not everything just as it had been? The attack of yesterday had been a bad one. Granted. But it should be the last. It was not too late, he could still escape destruction. He must avoid every occasion of a fresh seizure; he felt sure he could do this. He felt the strength to conquer and suppress his weakness.

It struck half past seven and Friederike came in with the coffee, setting it on the round table in front of the leather sofa against the rear wall.

"Good morning, Johannes," said she; "here is your breakfast."

"Thanks," said little Herr Friedemann. And then: "Dear Friederike, I am sorry, but you will have to pay your call without me, I do not feel well enough to go. I have slept badly and have a headache—in short, I must ask you—"

"What a pity!" answered Friederike. "You must go another time. But you do look ill. Shall I lend you my menthol pencil?"

"Thanks," said Herr Friedemann. "It will pass." And Friederike went out.

Standing at the table he slowly drank his coffee and ate a croissant. He felt satisfied with himself and proud of his firmness. When he had finished he sat down again by the open window, with a cigar. The food had done him good and he felt happy and hopeful. He took a book and sat reading and smoking and blinking into the sunlight.

Morning had fully come, wagons rattled past, there were many voices and the sound of the bells on passing trams. With and among it all was woven the twittering and chirping; there was a radiant blue sky, a soft mild air.

At ten o'clock he heard his sisters cross the entry; the front door creaked, and he idly noticed that they passed his window. An hour went by. He felt more and more happy.

A sort of hubris mounted in him. What a heavenly air—and how the birds were singing! He felt like taking a little walk. Then suddenly, without any transition, yet accompanied by a terror namelessly sweet came the thought: "Suppose I were to go to her!" And suppressing, as though by actual muscular effort, every warning voice within him, he added with blissful resolution: "I will go to her!"

He changed into his Sunday clothes, took his top hat and his stick, and hurried with quickened breath through the town and into the southern suburbs. Without looking at a soul he kept raising and dropping his head with each eager step, completely rapt in his exalted state until he arrived at the avenue of chestnut trees and the red brick villa with the name of Commandant von Rinnlingen on the gate-post.

But here he was seized by a tremor, his heart throbbed and pounded in his breast. He went across the vestibule and rang at the inside door. The die was cast, there was no retreating now. "Come what come may," thought he, and felt the stillness of death within him.

The door suddenly opened and the maid came towards him across the vestibule; she took his card and hurried away up the red-carpeted stair. Herr Friedemann gazed fixedly at the bright colour until she came back and said that her mistress would like him to come up.

He put down his stick beside the door leading into the salon and stole a look at himself in the glass. His face was pale, the eyes red, his hair was sticking to his brow, the hand that held his top hat kept on shaking.

The maid opened the door and he went in. He found himself in a rather large, half-darkened room, with drawn curtains. At his right was a piano, and about the round table in the centre stood several arm-chairs covered in brown silk. The sofa stood along the left-hand wall, with a landscape painting in a heavy gilt frame hanging above it. The wall-paper too was dark in tone. There was an alcove filled with potted palms.

A minute passed, then Frau von Rinnlingen opened the portières on the right and approached him noiselessly over the thick brown carpet. She wore a simply cut frock of red and black plaid. A ray of light, with motes dancing in it, streamed from the alcove and fell upon her heavy red hair so that it shone like gold. She kept her strange eyes fixed upon him with a searching gaze and as usual stuck out her under lip.

"Good morning, Frau Commandant," began little Herr Friedemann, and looked up at her, for he came only as high as her chest. "I wished to pay you my respects too. When my sisters did so I was unfortunately out . . . I regretted sincerely . . ."

He had no idea at all what else he should say; and there she stood and gazed ruthlessly at him as though she would force him to go on. The blood rushed to his head. "She sees through me," he thought, "she will torture and despise me. Her eyes keep flickering. . . ."

But at last she said, in a very high, clear voice:

"It is kind of you to have come. I have also been sorry not to see you before. Will you please sit down?"

She took her seat close beside him, leaned back, and put her arm along the arm of the chair. He sat bent over, holding his hat between his knees. She went on.

"Did you know that your sisters were here a quarter of an hour ago? They told me you were ill."

"Yes," he answered, "I did not feel well enough to go out, I thought I should not be able to. That is why I am late."

"You do not look very well even now," said she tranquilly, not shifting her gaze. "You are pale and your eyes are inflamed. You are not very strong, perhaps?"

"Oh," said Herr Friedemann, stammering, "I've not much to complain of, as a rule."

"I am ailing a good deal too," she went on, still not turning her eyes from him, "but nobody notices it. I am nervous, and sometimes I have the strangest feelings."

She paused, lowered her chin to her breast, and looked up expectantly at him. He made no reply, simply sat with his dreamy gaze directed upon her. How strangely she spoke, and how her clear and thrilling voice affected him! His heart beat more quietly and he felt as though he were in a dream. She began again:

"I am not wrong in thinking that you left the opera last night before it was over?"

"Yes, madam."

"I was sorry to see that. You listened like a music-lover—though the performance was only tolerable. You are fond of music, I am sure. Do you play the piano?"

"I play the violin, a little," said Herr Friedemann. "That is, really not very much—"

"You play the violin?" she asked, and looked past him consideringly. "But we might play together," she suddenly said. "I can accompany a little. It would be a pleasure to find somebody here—would you come?"

"I am quite at your service—with pleasure," he

said stiffly. He was still as though in a dream. A pause ensued. Then suddenly her expression changed. He saw it alter for one of cruel, though hardly perceptible mockery, and again she fixed him with that same searching, uncannily flickering gaze. His face burned, he knew not where to turn; drawing his head down between his shoulders he stared confusedly at the carpet, while there shot through him once more that strangely sweet and torturing sense of impotent rage.

He made a desperate effort and raised his eyes. She was looking over his head at the door. With the utmost difficulty he fetched out a few words:

"And you are so far not too dissatisfied with your stay in our city?"

"Oh, no," said Frau Rinnlingen indifferently. "No, certainly not; why should I not be satisfied? To be sure, I feel a little hampered, as though everybody's eyes were upon me, but—oh, before I forget it," she went on quickly, "we are entertaining a few people next week, a small, informal company. A little music, perhaps, and conversation. . . . There is a charming garden at the back, it runs down to the river. You and your sisters will be receiving an invitation in due course, but perhaps I may ask you now to give us the pleasure of your company?"

Herr Friedemann was just expressing his gratitude for the invitation when the door-knob was seized energetically from without and the Commandant entered. They both rose and Frau von Rinnlingen introduced the two men to each other. Her husband bowed to them both with equal courtesy. His bronze face glistened with the heat.

He drew off his gloves, addressing Herr Friedemann in a powerful, rather sharp-edged voice. The latter looked up at him with large vacant eyes and had the feeling that he would presently be clapped benevolently on the shoulder. Heels together, inclining from the waist, the Commandant turned to his wife and asked, in a much gentler tone:

"Have you asked Herr Friedemann if he will give us the pleasure of his company at our little party, my love? If you are willing I should like to fix the date for next week and I hope that the weather will remain fine so that we can enjoy ourselves in the garden."

"Just as you say," answered Frau von Rinnlingen, and gazed past him.

Two minutes later Herr Friedemann got up to go. At the door he turned and bowed to her once more, meeting her expressionless gaze still fixed upon him.

He went away, but he did not go back to the town; unconsciously he struck into a path that led away from the avenue towards the old ruined fort by the river, among well-kept lawns and shady avenues with benches.

He walked quickly and absently, with bent head. He felt intolerably hot, as though aware of flames leaping and sinking within him, and his head throbbed with fatigue.

It was as though her gaze still rested on him—not vacantly as it had at the end, but with that flickering cruelty which went with the strange still way she spoke. Did it give her pleasure to put him beside himself, to see him helpless? Looking through and through him like that, could she not feel a little pity?

He had gone along the river-bank under the moss-grown wall; he sat down on a bench within a half-circle of blossoming jasmine. The sweet, heavy scent was all about him, the sun brooded upon the dimpling water.

He was weary, he was worn out; and yet within him all was tumult and anguish. Were it not better to take one last look and then go down into that quiet water; after a brief struggle to be free and safe and at peace? Ah, peace, peace—that was what he wanted! Not peace in an empty and soundless void, but a gentle, sunlit peace, full of good, of tranquil thoughts.

All his tender love of life thrilled through him in that moment, all his profound yearning for his vanished "happiness." But then he looked about him into the silent, endlessly indifferent peace of nature, saw how the river went its own way in the sun, how the grasses quivered and the flowers stood up where they blossomed, only to fade and be blown away; saw how all that was bent submissively to the will of life; and there came over him all at once that sense of acquaintance and understanding with the inevitable which can make those who know it superior to the blows of fate.

He remembered the afternoon of his thirtieth birthday and the peaceful happiness with which he, untroubled by fears or hopes, had looked forward to what was left of his life. He had seen no light and no shadow there, only a mild twilight radiance gently declining into the dark. With what a calm and superior smile had he contemplated the years still to come—how long ago was that?

Then this woman had come, she had to come, it was his fate that she should, for she herself was his fate and she alone. He had known it from the first moment. She had come—and though he had tried his best to defend his peace, her coming had roused in him all those forces which from his youth up he had sought to suppress, feeling, as he did, that they spelled torture and destruction. They had seized upon him with frightful, irresistible power and flung him to the earth.

They were his destruction, well he knew it. But why struggle, then, and why torture himself? Let everything take its course. He would go his appointed way, closing his eyes before the yawning void, bowing to his fate, bowing to the overwhelming, anguishingly sweet, irresistible power.

The water glittered, the jasmine gave out its strong, pungent scent, the birds chattered in the tree-tops that gave glimpses among them of a heavy, velvety-blue sky. Little hump-backed Herr Friedemann sat long upon his bench; he sat bent over, holding his head in his hands.

Everybody agreed that the Rinnlingens entertained very well. Some thirty guests sat in the spacious dining-room, at the long, prettily decorated table, and the butler and two hired waiters were already handing round the ices. Dishes clattered, glasses rang, there was a warm aroma of food and perfumes. Here were comfortable merchants with their wives and daughters; most of the officers of the garrison; a few professional men, lawyers and the popular old family doctor—in short, all the best society.

A nephew of the Commandant, on a visit, a student of mathematics, sat deep in conversation with Fräulein Hagenström, whose place was directly opposite Herr Friedemann's, at the lower end of the table. Johannes Friedemann sat there on a rich velvet cushion, beside the unbeautiful wife of the Colonial Director and not far off Frau von Rinnlingen, who had been escorted to table by Consul Stephens. It was astonishing, the change which had taken place in little Herr Friedemann in these few days. Perhaps the incandescent lighting in the room was partly to blame; but his cheeks looked sunken, he made a more crippled impression even than usual, and his inflamed eyes, with their dark rings, glowed with an inexpressibly tragic light. He drank a great deal of wine and now and then addressed a remark to his neighbour.

Frau von Rinnlingen had not so far spoken to him at all; but now she leaned over and called out: "I have been expecting you in vain these days, you and your fiddle."

He looked vacantly at her for a while before he replied. She wore a light-coloured frock with a low neck that left the white throat bare; a Maréchal Niel rose in full bloom was fastened in her shining hair. Her cheeks were a little flushed, but the same bluish shadows lurked in the corners of her eyes.

Herr Friedemann looked at his plate and forced himself to make some sort of reply; after which the school superintendent's wife asked him if he did not love Beethoven and he had to answer that too. But at this point the Commandant, sitting at the head of the table, caught his wife's eye, tapped on his glass and said:

"Ladies and gentlemen, I suggest that we drink our coffee in the next room. It must be fairly decent out in the garden too, and whoever wants a little fresh air, I am for him."

Lieutenant von Deidesheim made a tactful little joke to cover the ensuing pause, and the table rose in the midst of laughter. Herr Friedemann and his partner were among the last to quit the room; he escorted her through the "old German" smoking-room to the dim and pleasant living-room, where he took his leave.

He was dressed with great care: his evening clothes were irreproachable, his shirt was dazzlingly white, his slender, well-shaped feet were encased in patent-leather pumps, which now and then betrayed the fact that he wore red silk stockings.

He looked out into the corridor and saw a good many people descending the steps into the garden. But he took up a position at the door of the smoking-room, with his cigar and coffee, where he could see into the living-room.

Some of the men stood talking in this room, and at the right of the door a little knot had formed round a small table, the centre of which was the mathematics student, who was eagerly talking. He had made the assertion that one could draw through a given point more than one parallel to a straight line; Frau Hagenström had cried that this was impossible, and he had gone on to prove it so conclusively that his hearers were constrained to behave as though they understood.

At the rear of the room, on the sofa beside the red-shaded lamp, Gerda von Rinnlingen sat in conversation with young Fräulein Stephens. She leaned back among the yellow silk cushions with one knee slung over the other, slowly smoking a cigarette, breathing out the smoke through her nose and sticking out her lower lip. Fräulein Stephens sat stiff as a graven image beside her, answering her questions with an assiduous smile.

Nobody was looking at little Herr Friedemann, so nobody saw that his large eyes were constantly directed upon Frau von Rinnlingen. He sat rather droopingly and looked at her. There was no passion in his gaze nor scarcely any pain. But there was something dull and heavy there, a dead weight of impotent, involuntary adoration.

Some ten minutes went by. Then as though she had been secretly watching him the whole time, Frau von Rinnlingen approached him and paused in front of him. He got up as he heard her say:

"Would you care to go into the garden with me, Herr Friedemann?"

He answered:

"With pleasure, madam."

"You have never seen our garden?" she asked him as they went down the steps. "It is fairly large. I hope that there are not too many people in it; I should like to get a breath of fresh air. I got a headache during supper; perhaps the red wine was too strong for me. Let us go this way." They passed through a glass door, the vestibule, and a cool little courtyard, whence they gained the open air by descending a couple more steps.

The scent of all the flower-beds rose into the wonderful, warm, starry night. The garden lay in full moonlight and the guests were strolling up and down the white gravel paths, smoking and talking as they went. A group had gathered round the old fountain, where the much-loved old doctor was making them laugh by sailing paper boats.

With a little nod Frau von Rinnlingen passed them by, and pointed ahead of her, where the fragrant and well-cared-for garden blended into the darker park.

"Shall we go down this middle path?" asked she. At the beginning of it stood two low, squat obelisks.

In the vista at the end of the chestnut alley they could see the river shining green and bright in the moonlight. All about them was darkness and coolness. Here and there side paths branched off, all of them probably curving down to the river. For a long time there was not a sound.

"Down by the water," she said, "there is a pretty spot where I often sit. We could stop and talk a little. See the stars glittering here and there through the trees."

He did not answer, gazing, as they approached it, at the river's shimmering green surface. You could see the other bank and the park along the city wall. They left the alley and came out on the grassy slope down to the river, and she said:

"Here is our place, a little to the right, and there is no one there."

The bench stood facing the water, some six paces away, with its back to the trees. It was warmer here in the open. Crickets chirped among the grass, which at the river's edge gave way to sparse reeds. The moonlit water gave off a soft light.

For a while they both looked in silence. Then he heard her voice; it thrilled him to recognize the same low, gentle, pensive tone of a week ago, which now as then moved him so strangely:

"How long have you had your infirmity, Herr Friedemann? Were you born so?"

He swallowed before he replied, for his throat felt as though he were choking. Then he said, politely and gently:

"No, gnädige Frau. It comes from their having let me fall, when I was an infant."

"And how old are you now?" she asked again.

"Thirty years old."

"Thirty years old," she repeated. "And these thirty years were not happy ones?"

Little Herr Friedemann shook his head, his lips quivered.

"No," he said, "that was all lies and my imagination."

"Then you have thought that you were happy?" she asked.

"I have tried to be," he replied, and she responded:

"That was brave of you."

A minute passed. The crickets chirped and behind them the boughs rustled lightly.

"I understand a good deal about unhappiness," she told him. "These summer nights by the water are the best thing for it."

He made no direct answer, but gestured feebly across the water, at the opposite bank, lying peaceful in the darkness.

"I was sitting over there not long ago," he said.

"When you came from me?" she asked. He only nodded.

Then suddenly he started up from his seat, trembling all over; he sobbed and gave vent to a sound, a wail which yet seemed like a release from strain, and sank slowly to the ground before her. He had touched her hand with his as it lay beside him on the bench, and clung to it now, seizing the other as he knelt before her, this little cripple, trembling and shuddering; he buried his face in her lap and stammered between his gasps in a voice which was scarcely human:

"You know, you understand . . . let me . . . I can no longer . . . my God, oh, my God!"

She did not repulse him, neither did she bend her face towards him. She sat erect, leaning a little away, and her close-set eyes, wherein the liquid shimmer of the water seemed to be mirrored, stared beyond him into space.

Then she gave him an abrupt push and uttered a short, scornful laugh. She tore her hands from his burning fingers, clutched his arm, and flung him sidewise upon the ground. Then she sprang up and vanished down the wooded avenue.

He lay there with his face in the grass, stunned, unmanned, shudders coursing swiftly through his frame. He pulled himself together, got up somehow, took two steps, and fell again, close to the water. What were his sensations at this moment? Perhaps he was feeling that same luxury of hate which he had felt before when she had humiliated him with her glance, degenerated now, when he lay before her on the ground and she had treated him like a dog, into an insane rage which must at all costs find expression even against himself—a disgust, perhaps of himself, which filled him with a thirst to destroy himself, to tear himself to pieces, to blot himself utterly out.

On his belly he dragged his body a little further, lifted its upper part, and let it fall into the water. He did not raise his head nor move his legs, which still lay on the bank.

The crickets stopped chirping a moment at the noise of the little splash. Then they went on as before, the boughs lightly rustled, and down the long alley came the faint sound of laughter.

———◆———

FRANZ KAFKA

1883–1924

Born in Prague in 1883, of middle-class Jewish parentage, Franz Kafka has since his premature death become one of the most discussed and widely read writers of the modern world. On the surface the fictional method of Kafka is realistic, but the work has overtones and subtle implications of symbolism and allegory that seem to transport the characters and the scenes into a world of almost fantastic surreality. The themes of his fragmentary novels and the short stories seem to represent not only the alienated artist in the modern world ("The Hunger Artist"), but as well the modern man who is distraught and lost in a strangely hostile world which

he can neither comprehend nor find a valid theological explanation for (see *The Castle* and *The Trial*). The essentially religious temperament of Kafka has made him the most forceful spokesman in contemporary fiction upon the tragic plight of modern man, and his work has been compared to the Christian existentialism of Kierkegaard. Kafka possesses as well, especially in *Amerika,* a sad piercing note of philosophic humor.

"The Hunter Gracchus" admirably illustrates the strange suggestive unreality of Kafka's fictional method, and at the same time the implications of allegory and symbolism which hint theological impasse between man and god, a Christlike figure who is forever doomed to wander between two worlds, in neither of which he is assured asylum.

FURTHER READING

BROD, MAX. *Franz Kafka* (New York, 1948).
GOODMAN, PAUL. *Kafka's Prayer* (New York, 1947).
NEIDER, CHARLES. *Kafka: His Mind and Art* (London, 1949).
TAUBER, HERBERT. *Franz Kafka* (New Haven, 1948).

The Hunter Gracchus*

Two boys were sitting on the harbour wall playing with dice. A man was reading a newspaper on the steps of the monument, resting in the shadow of a hero who was flourishing his sword on high. A girl was filling her bucket at the fountain. A fruit-seller was lying beside his scales, staring out to sea. Through the vacant window and door openings of a café one could see two men quite at the back drinking their wine. The proprietor was sitting at a table in front and dozing. A bark was silently making for the little harbour, as if borne by invisible means over the water. A man in a blue blouse climbed ashore and drew the rope through a ring. Behind the boatman two other men in dark coats with silver buttons carried a bier, on which, beneath a great flower-patterned tasselled silk cloth, a man was apparently lying.

Nobody on the quay troubled about the newcomers; even when they lowered the bier to wait for the boatman, who was still occupied with his rope, nobody went nearer, nobody asked them a question, nobody accorded them an inquisitive glance.

* Translated by Willa and Edwin Muir. From *The Great Wall of China,* by permission of Schocken Books, Inc.; copyright, 1948.

The pilot was still further detained by a woman who, a child at her breast, now appeared with loosened hair on the the deck of the boat. Then he advanced and indicated a yellowish two-storeyed house that rose abruptly on the left beside the sea; the bearers took up their burden and bore it to the low but gracefully pillared door. A little boy opened a window just in time to see the party vanishing into the house, then hastily shut the window again. The door too was now shut; it was of black oak, and very strongly made. A flock of doves which had been flying round the belfry alighted in the street before the house. As if their food were stored within, they assembled in front of the door. One of them flew up to the first storey and pecked at the window-pane. They were bright-hued, well-tended, beautiful birds. The woman on the boat flung grain to them in a wide sweep; they ate it up and flew across to the woman.

A man in a top hat tied with a band of crêpe now descended one of the narrow and very steep lanes that led to the harbour. He glanced round vigilantly, everything seemed to displease him, his mouth twisted at the sight of some offal in a corner. Fruit skins were lying on the steps of the monument; he swept them off in passing with his stick. He rapped at the house door, at the same time taking his top hat from his head with his black-gloved hand. The door was opened at once, and some fifty little boys appeared in two rows in the long entry-hall, and bowed to him.

The boatman descended the stairs, greeted the gentleman in black, conducted him up to the first storey, led him round the bright and elegant loggia which encircled the courtyard, and both of them entered, while the boys pressed after them at a respectful distance, a cool spacious room looking towards the back, from whose window no habitation, but only a bare, blackish grey rocky wall was to be seen. The bearers were busied in setting up and lighting several long candles at the head of the bier, yet these did not give light, but only scared away the shadows which had been immobile till then, and made them flicker over the walls. The cloth covering the bier had been thrown back. Lying on it was a man with wildly matted hair, who looked somewhat like a hunter. He lay without motion and, it seemed, without breathing, his eyes closed; yet only his trappings indicated that this man was probably dead.

The gentleman stepped up to the bier, laid his hand on the brow of the man lying upon it, then kneeled down and prayed. The boatman made a sign to the bearers to leave the room; they went out, drove away the boys who had gathered outside, and shut the door. But even that did not seem to satisfy the gentleman, he glanced at the boatman; the boatman understood, and vanished through a side door into the next room. At once the man on the bier opened his eyes, turned his face painfully towards the gentleman, and said: "Who are you?" Without any mark of surprise the gentleman rose from his kneeling posture and answered: "The Burgomaster of Riva."

The man on the bier nodded, indicated a chair with a feeble movement of his arm, and said, after the Burgomaster had accepted his invitation: "I knew that, of course, Burgomaster, but in the first moments of returning consciousness I always forget, everything goes round before my eyes, and it is best to ask about anything even if I know. You too probably know that I am the hunter Gracchus."

"Certainly," said the Burgomaster. "Your arrival was announced to me during the night. We had been asleep for a good while. Then towards midnight my wife cried: 'Salvatore'—that's my name— 'look at that dove at the window.' It was really a dove, but as big as a cock. It flew over to me and said in my ear: 'To-morrow the dead hunter Gracchus is coming; receive him in the name of the city.'"

The hunter nodded and licked his lips with the tip of his tongue: "Yes, the doves flew here before me. But do you believe, Burgomaster, that I shall remain in Riva?"

"I cannot say that yet," replied the Burgomaster. "Are you dead?"

"Yes," said the hunter, "as you see. Many years ago, yes, it must be a great many years ago, I fell from a precipice in the Black Forest—that is in Germany—when I was hunting a chamois. Since then I have been dead."

"But you are alive too," said the Burgomaster.

"In a certain sense," said the hunter, "in a certain sense I am alive too. My death ship lost its way; a wrong turn of the wheel, a moment's absence of mind on the pilot's part, a longing to turn aside towards my lovely native country, I cannot tell what it was; I only know this, that I remained on earth and that ever since my ship has sailed earthly waters. So I, who asked for nothing better than to live among my mountains, travel after my death through all the lands of the earth."

"And you have no part in the other world?" asked the Burgomaster, knitting his brow.

"I am for ever," replied the hunter, "on the great

stair that leads up to it. On that infinitely wide and spacious stair I clamber about, sometimes up, sometimes down, sometimes on the right, sometimes on the left, always in motion. The hunter has been turned into a butterfly. Do not laugh."

"I am not laughing," said the Burgomaster in self-defence.

"That is very good of you," said the hunter. "I am always in motion. But when I make a supreme flight and see the gate actually shining before me I awaken presently on my old ship, still stranded forlornly in some earthly sea or other. The fundamental error of my one-time death grins at me as I lie in my cabin. Julia, the wife of the pilot, knocks at the door and brings me on my bier the morning drink of the land whose coasts we chance to be passing. I lie on a wooden pallet, I wear—it cannot be a pleasure to look at me—a filthy winding sheet, my hair and beard, black tinged with grey, have grown together inextricably, my limbs are covered with a great flower-patterned woman's shawl with long fringes. A sacramental candle stands at my head and lights me. On the wall opposite me is a little picture, evidently of a Bushman who is aiming his spear at me and taking cover as best he can behind a beautifully painted shield. On shipboard one is often a prey to stupid imaginations, but that is the stupidest of them all. Otherwise my wooden case is quite empty. Through a hole in the side wall come in the warm airs of the southern night, and I hear the water slapping against the old boat.

"I have lain here ever since the time when, as the hunter Gracchus living in the Black Forest, I followed a chamois and fell from a precipice. Everything happened in good order. I pursued, I fell, bled to death in a ravine, died, and this ship should have conveyed me to the next world. I can still remember how gladly I stretched myself out on this pallet for the first time. Never did the mountains listen to such songs from me as these shadowy walls did then.

"I had been glad to live and I was glad to die. Before I stepped aboard, I joyfully flung away my wretched load of ammunition, my knapsack, my hunting rifle that I had always been proud to carry, and I slipped into my winding sheet like a girl into her marriage dress. I lay and waited. Then came the mishap."

"A terrible fate," said the Burgomaster, raising his hand defensively. "And you bear no blame for it?"

"None," said the hunter. "I was a hunter; was there any sin in that? I followed my calling as a hunter in the Black Forest, where there were still wolves in those days. I lay in ambush, shot, hit my mark, flayed the skins from my victims: was there any sin in that? My labours were blessed. 'The great hunter of the Black Forest' was the name I was given. Was there any sin in that?"

"I am not called upon to decide that," said the Burgomaster, "but to me also there seems to be no sin in such things. But, then whose is the guilt?"

"The boatman's," said the hunter. "Nobody will read what I say here, no one will come to help me; even if all the people were commanded to help me, every door and window would remain shut, everybody would take to bed and draw the bedclothes over his head, the whole earth would became an inn for the night. And there is sense in that, for nobody knows of me, and if anyone knew he would not know where I could be found, and if he knew where I could be found he would not know how to deal with me, he would not know how to help me. The thought of helping me is an illness that has to be cured by taking to one's bed.

"I know that, and so I do not shout to summon help, even though at moments—when I lose control over myself, as I have done just now, for instance—I think seriously of it. But to drive out such thoughts I need only look round me and verify where I am, and—I can safely assert—have been for hundreds of years."

"Extraordinary," said the Burgomaster, "extraordinary.—And now do you think of staying here in Riva with us?"

"I think not," said the hunter with a smile, and, to excuse himself, he laid his hand on the Burgomaster's knee. "I am here, more than that I do not know, further than that I cannot go. My ship has no rudder, and it is driven by the wind that blows in the undermost regions of death."

German Lyric Poetry

RICHARD DEHMEL

1863-1920

Student of philosophy, sociology, and natural science, Dehmel was a lyric poet who attempted to grapple with fundamental problems of human life. He regarded poetry as a means of expressing man's whole being and attempted to demolish the barriers between the layman and art. Although he placed great importance upon the enjoyment of life, much of his enjoyment is fraught with sorrow. His nature poems defend the beauty and healthfulness of country life as opposed to the drabness and monotony of life in the big cities. Many of his poems in this vein rank among the best socialistic verses of the time. Much, also, of his work is concerned with profound problems of the relationship between man and woman, hence his preoccupation with sex.

In addition to his lyric poetry, Dehmel produced a number of children's stories, an epic, a verse novel, a war diary (he participated as a volunteer in World War I), and a number of plays. In spite of certain erratic qualities in his person and in his poetry, Dehmel is one of the truly great poets produced by modern Germany.

FURTHER READING

Closs, A. *The Genius of the German Lyric* (London, 1938).

Through the Night *

But ever you, this sombre you,
Through all the night this hollow soaring
Of sound—and through the wires a roaring:
The homeward road my steps pursue.

And pace for pace, this sombre you,
As if from pole to pole 'twere soaring;
Of thousand words I hear a roaring,
And dumb my homeward road pursue.

* These three poems are from *A Harvest of German Verse*, by Margarete Münsterberg. By permission of Appleton-Century-Crofts, Inc.

Many a Night

When the night on fields is sinking,
  Then my eyes can see more brightly:
Now my star begins its blinking,
  Crickets' whispers grow more sprightly.

Every sound becomes more glowing,
  Things accustomed now seem queerer,
Paler too the skies are growing
  Near the woods, the tree-tops clearer.

Meditating, never heeding
  Now the myriad lights are showered
Out of darkness, on I'm speeding—
  Till I stop all overpowered.

Wave Dance Song

I tossed a rose into the sea,
A blooming fair rose into the green sea.
Because the sun shone, sun shone bright,
After it leaped the light,
With hundred tremulous toes in glee.
When the first wave came,
Then my rose, my rose began to drown.
When the second wave raised it on shoulders tame,
The light, the light at her feet sank down.
The third snatched it up and then the light
As if in defence, leaped high tremblingly.
But a hundred leaping flower petals
Were rocking red, red, red round me,
And my boat danced about
And my shadow like a spright
On the foam, and the green sea, the sea—

STEFAN GEORGE

1868-1933

The first desire of Stefan George, distinguished lyric poet, was to become a painter. His earlier poetry was symbolistic and impressionistic, more like the work of Hofmannsthal than of his naturalistic contemporaries, in conveying emotions through eye and ear impressions. He later turned to classicism and to the problems of his time, composing poems on World War I and lyrics in imitation of folk songs. It was his aim to produce musical, harmonious beauty in his work, and his results are often magnificently effective. There is, however, in his work frequent obscurity and a certain lack of feeling for popular life which tend to restrict appreciation of his work to small, highly sophisticated circles. He translated into German a number of Shakespeare's sonnets, cantos from Dante's *Divine Comedy*, some of Baudelaire's *Fleurs du Mal*, and numerous poems by French and German writers. Among his significant volumes of poetry are: *Hymnen* (1890); *Pilgarfahrten* (1891), *Algabal* (1892), *Das Jahr der Seele* (1897), *Der Stern des Bundes* (1914), *Das neue Reich* (1928), *Der Teppich des Lebens* (1900).

FURTHER READING

BURKHARD, A. "Stefan George," *German Quarterly*, VII, 1934.
CLOSS, A. *The Genius of the German Lyric* (London, 1938).

The Sounding Journeys You Shall Praise No More *

The sounding journeys you shall praise no more,
Where perilous and false the water leaps,
And where the chasm rears its rugged steeps
Around whose summits heaven's eagles soar.

Learn in these simple fields to apprehend
The breath that all-too frosty spring allays,
And that which renders less its sultry haze,
A willing ear their childish prattle lend!

You find the secret of eternal runes
Within these hills austerely drawn and pure,
Not only seas of stone with magic lure,
"No more the wonder beckons of lagoons,

Of great and ruined Rome, the world-wooed dream,
As vine and bitter scent of oaken grove,
As they who guard your people's treasure-trove:
Your waters, green with life, O surging stream!"

* This and the following three poems translated by Carol North Valhope and Ernst Morwitz. By permission of Pantheon Books, Inc.

Come to the Park They Say Is Dead

Come to the park they say is dead, and view
The shimmer of the smiling shores beyond,
The stainless clouds with unexpected blue
Diffuse a light on motley path and pond.

The tender grey, the burning yellow seize
Of birch and boxwood, mellow is the breeze.
Not wholly do the tardy roses wane,
So kiss and gather them and wreathe the chain.

The purple on the twists of wilding vine,
The last of asters you shall not forget,
And what of living verdure lingers yet,
Around the autumn vision lightly twine.

An Angelico

Above the graceful headings of the story
—Eternal vigil over man who strives,
The ruthless sire's message full of glory—
The deed of glowing grandeur he contrives:

The gold from holy chalices he took,
For yellow hair, the ripened wheaten stalks,
The blue from women washing at the brook,
The pink from children coloring with chalks.

The Lord in kingship's pure and lustrous frame,
Beside Him gentle singers of His fame,
And victors of Medusas, friends of Graces,

The bride whose childish breathing never races,
So meek, and yet with her reward enchanted,
A crown—her very first—by Him is granted.

Augury

White I saw the swallows winging,
Swallows snow- and silver-white,
In the wind I saw them clinging,
In the burning wind and bright.

Jays I saw that slipped and shimmered,
Parakeet and colibri
Through the trees of wonder glimmered,
In the wood of Tusferi.

Huge I saw the ravens slacken,
Daws of black and sombre grey,
Over adders, near the bracken,
Where the magic timber lay.

Now again I see the winging
Snow and silver swallows veer,
In the wind I see them clinging,
In the freezing wind and clear!

———◆———

HUGO VON HOFMANNSTHAL

1874–1929

Poet, dramatist, short-story writer, novelist, and
essayist, Hofmannsthal preferred the symbolist manner of writing to the new naturalism current in
Germany at the turn of the century. In this respect
he may be compared to Stefan George who had a
profound influence upon him. At the age of eighteen, he was recognized as a master of German verse
and, during the next few years, published a number
of lovely poems and a series of excellent plays distinctly lyrical in tone, including *Death and the
Fool* (1913) and the *Marriage of Sobeide* (1913).
His *Elektra* (1903), *Ariadne* (1912), and *Rosenkavalier* (1911) were set to music by Richard
Strauss, for whom Hofmannsthal wrote other plays.
In his poetry he attempted to reveal the subconscious and the irrational in human nature. His
favorite theme, not unlike that of Rilke, was puri-
fication and regeneration through death.

FURTHER READING

GILBERT, M. E. "Hugo von Hofmannsthal and England,"
 German Life and Letters, I, 1937.
GROSS, F. "Hugo von Hofmannsthal," *Contemporary Re-
 view*, CXLIX, 1936.

Ballad of the Outer Life *

And deep-eyed children cannot long be children,
Knowing of nothing they grow up and die,
And all men go their ways upon the earth.

And bitter fruits are sweetened by and by,
And fall at night like dead birds to the floor,
And in a few days rot even where they lie.

* This and the following two poems translated by Jethro
Bithell. By permission of Jethro Bithell.

And ever blows the wind, and evermore
A multitude of words we speak and hear,
And now are happy, and now tired and sore.

And roads run through the grass, and towns uprear
Their torch-filled toils, some menacingly live,
And some cadaverously dry and drear.

Why are these built aloft? And ever strive,
So countless many, not to be the same?
And tears drive laughter out till death arrive?

What profits man this ever-changing game?
Full-grown are we, yet still like chartless ships,
And wandering never follow any aim.

What profit hath he who the furthest roams?
And yet he sayeth much who "evening" saith,
A word from which deep melancholy drips

Like heavy honey out of hollow combs.

Many Indeed Must Perish in the Keel

Many indeed must perish in the keel,
Chained where the heavy oars of vessels smite,
Others direct the rudder on the bridge,
And know the flight of birds and charted stars.

Others with weary limbs lie evermore
By the inextricable roots of life,
For others chairs are with the sibyls set,
The Queens, in whose abode they dwell at home,
With brain untaxed and soft unhampered hands.

But from those lives a shadow falls athwart
On these the lighter, and as to earth and air
The light is with the hard life bound in one.

I cannot free my eyelids from fatigues
Of nations long-forgotten, no, nor guard
My soul in terror from the soundless fall
Of stars remote in deeps of cosmic dark.

Existence plies her shuttle through the woof
Of many fates indissolubly one,
And my own portion of this common life
Is more than taper flame or slender lyre.

Stanzas on Mutability

I

Still on my cheeks I feel their fondling breath:
    How can it be that days so very nigh
Are gone, for ever gone, and merged in death!

This is a thing that no man fathoms quite,
  And far too cruel for complaint or cry,
That all things slip and drip out of men's sight.

And that my own untrammeled I hath found
  Out of a little child its gradual stair,
To me unearthly, dumb, strange as a hound.

Then: that I was a hundred summers ere
  My birth, and that my forebears underground
Are closely kin to me as my own hair.

As much at one with me as my own hair.

II

The hours! when we are gazing at the peerless
  Blue of the sea, and read Death's riddle stark
So easily and solemnly and fearless.

As little pale-faced maidens stand and hark,
  Cold always, with their great eyes opened wide,
Hearken in silence looking into the dark,

Out of their sleep-drunk limbs they feel life glide
  Noiselessly into grass, and trees of the wood,
And smiling tiredly know some little pride,

Even as a holy martyr sheds her blood.

———◆———

RAINER MARIA RILKE

1875–1926

Rilke is one of the most illustrious poets of modern Germany. He traveled widely over Europe and Russia, and was associated in Paris with the great sculptor Rodin, of whom he wrote a biography. His *Duino Elegies* (1923), which is one of the most impressive sequences of great poetry in modern European literature, contains profound philosophic reflection as well as a manifestation of the poet's own nervous sensitivity. In this collection Rilke is preoccupied with a religious crisis within himself and with the theme of death and regeneration through realization of God. In the *Sonnets to Orpheus* (1923) appears the opposite theme, one of joy, affirmation, and praise of life. Rilke was a highly sensitive, mystical poet whose recurrent theme is the precariousness of human life, but who had nevertheless a great trust in death as the final redeemer which will resolve all the discrepancies of this existence.

FURTHER READING

BUTLER, E. M. *Rainer Maria Rilke* (Cambridge, Eng., 1941).

OLIVERO, F. *Rainer Maria Rilke. A Study in Poetry and Mysticism* (Cambridge, Eng., 1931).

RILKE, RAINER MARIA. *Letters*. Translated by Jane Bannard Greene and M. D. Herter Norton (New York, 1948).

Moonlight Night [1]

South German night, spread out beneath the moon,
And mild as if all fairy-tales were there,
The hours fall from the steeple in a swoon
As if into the sea, to some deep lair,—
Now round about a rustling, calling fond,
Then silence hangs but empty in the air;
And then a violin (God knows from where)
Awakes and says quite tranquilly:
                    A blonde—

The Knight

The knight rides forth in blackest mail,
The rustling world to meet.
Out there he finds all: the day and the dale
And the friend and the foe and the castle's pale
And fair May and fair maid and the woods and the grail,
And god Himself doth never fail
To stand upon the street.
        But within the knightly armor yonder,
        Behind that gloomy wringing,
        Cowers Death and has to ponder, ponder:
        When will the blade come springing
        Over the iron wall,
        The stranger, freedom bringing,
        That from my hiding-place shall call
        Me forth, where I for many a day
        Am waiting, crouched and clinging,
        That I may stretch out once for all
        With play
        And singing.

Autumn Day

Lord: it is time. The summer was so grand,
Upon sun-dials now Thy shadow lay,
Set free Thy winds and send them o'er the land.

[1] "Moonlight Night," "The Knight," and "Autumn Day" are from *A Harvest of German Verse*, translated by Margarete Münsterberg, by permission of Appleton-Century-Crofts, Inc.

Command to ripen those last fruits of Thine;
And give them two more southern days of grace
To reach their perfect fullness, and then chase
The final sweetness into the heavy wine.
Who now is homeless, ne'er will build a home.
Who now is lonely, long alone will stay,
Will watch and read and write long letters gray,
And in the lanes he to and fro will roam
All restless, as the drifting fall-leaves stray.

From an April [2]

Again the forest is fragrant.
The soaring larks lift up
aloft with them the sky that to our shoulders was
heavy;
one still saw the day through the branches, indeed,
that it was empty—
but after long, raining afternoons
come the gold-besunned
newer hours,
before which fleeing on far housefronts
all the wounded
windows fearfully beat with wings.

Then it grows still. Even the rain goes softer
over the quietly darkening glint of the stones.
All sounds duck entirely away
in the glistening buds of the brushwood.

Early Apollo

As many a time through the yet unleaved
branches a morn looks through that is already
all in spring: so is there in his head
naught that could hinder the glory of all poems

from falling almost fatally upon us;
for yet no shadow is there in his gaze,
too cool for laurel are his temples still,
and only later from his eyebrows shall

tall-stemmed the rose-garden lift itself,
out of which petals, separately, released
will drift upon the quivering of his mouth,

that yet is quiet, never-used and gleaming
and only drinking something with its smile,
as though its singing were being infused in it.

[2] "From an April," "Early Apollo," "The Panther," "The Swan," and "The Carousel" are from *Translations from the Poetry of Rainer Maria Rilke*, by M. D. Herter Norton, by permission of W. W. Norton & Company, Inc. Copyright, 1938, by W. W. Norton & Company, Inc.

The Panther

JARDIN DES PLANTES, PARIS

His vision from the passing of the bars
is grown so weary that it holds no more.
To him it seems there are a thousand bars
and behind a thousand bars no world.

The padding gait of flexibly strong strides,
that in the very smallest circle turns,
is like a dance of strength around a center
in which stupefied a great will stands.

Only sometimes the curtain of the pupil
soundlessly parts—. Then an image enters,
goes through the tensioned stillness of the limbs—
and in the heart ceases to be.

Nike [3]
(TO AN ANTIQUE FIGURE)

LITTLE NIKE ON THE SHOULDER OF THE HERO

The conqueror bore her. Had she weight? She
swings,
Foreshadowing Fate, upon his shoulder-lace;
Her quickening flight on lightly-outspread wings,
Wakes visions of conquests that fill empty space.

She gathers distance as into a bowl—
That triumphs be not scattered—as clouds move.
She flew to the god—yet delays him from his goal—
Will he be held by Victory or by Love?

The Swan

This toiling to go through something yet
undone, heavily and as though in bonds,
is like the ungainly gait of the swan.

And dying, this no longer grasping
of that ground on which we daily stand,
like his anxious letting-himself-down—:

into the waters, which receive him smoothly
and which, as though happy and bygone,
draw back underneath him, flow on flow;
while he, infinitely still and sure,
ever more maturely and more royally
and more serenely deigns to draw along.

[3] "Nike" and "Sonnet to Orpheus" translated by Jessie Lemont. By permission of Miss Lemont's estate and Columbia University Press.

The Carousel

JARDIN DU LUXEMBOURG

With a roof and its shadow it rotates
a little while, the herd of particolored
horses, all from the land
that lingers long ere it sinks out of sight.
Some it is true are hitched to carriages,
yet all of them have mettle in their mien;
a vicious red lion goes with them
and every now and then a white elephant.

Even a deer is there quite as in the woods,
save that he bears a saddle and on that
a little blue girl buckled up.

And on the lion rides all white a boy
and holds himself with his small hot hand,
the while the lion shows his teeth and tongue.

And every now and then a white elephant.

And on the horses they come passing by,
girls too, bright girls, who almost have outgrown
this leap of horses; midway in their swing
they look up, anywhere, across—

And every now and then a white elephant.

And this goes on and hurries that it may end,
and only circles and turns and has no goal.
A red, a green, a gray being sent by,
some little profile hardly yet begun.
And occasionally a smile, turning this way,
a happy one, that dazzles and dissipates
over this blind and breathless game.

Sonnet to Orpheus

Ripe apple, the banana and the pear,
The gooseberry. . . . How all these things speak
Of Death and Life in the mouth. . . . The magic
    there
Read in a child's face and the meanings seek

When he tastes it. There come slowly from afar,
Namelessly in the mouth yet unsurmised,
Discoveries, where otherwise words are,
From out the fruity flesh, released, surprised.

And for the *apple* what name do you dare
To call this sweetness, gathered up to make
Something you tasted lightly, unaware,

Become clear and transparent and awake,
Significant, sunny, earthy—encompassing—
O Experience, Feeling, Joy—Quickening!

The Fifth Duino Elegy.[4]

*This poem is a philosophic interpretation of Picasso's
"Family of Saltimbanques." See the illustration, ante,
p. 486.*

But tell me, who *are* they, these acrobats, even a
    little
more fleeting than we ourselves,—so urgently, ever
    since childhood,
wrung by an (oh, for the sake of whom?)
never-contented will? That keeps on wringing
    them,
bending them, slinging them, swinging them,
throwing them and catching them back; as though
    from an oily
smoother air, they come down on the threadbare
carpet, thinned by their everlasting
upspringing, this carpet forlornly
lost in the cosmos.   10
Laid on there like a plaster, as though the sub-
    urban
sky had injured the earth.
                        And hardly there,
upright, shown there: the great initial
letter of Thereness,—then even the strongest
men are rolled once more, in sport, by the ever-
returning grasp, as once by Augustus the Strong
a tin platter at table.

Alas, and round this
centre the rose of onlooking   20
blooms and unblossoms. Round this
pestle, this pistil, caught by its own
dust-pollen, and fertilised over again
to a sham-fruit of boredom, their own
never-realised boredom, gleaming with thinnest
lightly sham-smiling surface.

There, the withered wrinkled lifter,
old now and only drumming,
shrivelled up in his mighty skin as though it had
    once contained
two men, and one were already   30
lying in the churchyard, and he had outlasted the
    other,
deaf and sometimes a little
strange in his widowed skin.

[4] From *Duino Elegies* by Rainer Maria Rilke, translated
by J. B. Leishman and Stephen Spender. By permission of
W. W. Norton & Company, Inc. and the Hogarth Press,
Ltd. Copyright 1939 by W. W. Norton & Company, Inc.

And the youngster, the man, like the son of a neck
and a nun: so tautly and smartly filled
with muscle and simpleness.

O you,
a pain that was still quite small
received as a plaything once in one of its
long convalescences . . .   40

You, that fall with the thud
only fruits know, unripe,
daily a hundred times from the tree
of mutually built up motion (the tree that, swifter
        than water,
has spring and summer and autumn in so many
        minutes),
fall and rebound on the grave:
sometimes, in half-pauses, a tenderness tries
to steal out over your face to your seldomly
tender mother, but scatters over your body,
whose surface quickly absorbs the timidly rip-
        pling,   50
hardly attempted look . . . And again
that man is clapping his hands for the downward
        spring, and before
a single pain has got within range of your ever-
galloping heart, comes the tingling
in the soles of your feet, ahead of the spring that it
        springs from,
chasing into your eyes a few physical tears.
And, spite of all, blindly,
your smile . . .

Angel! Oh, take it, pluck it, that small-flowered
        herb of healing!
Shape a vase to preserve it. Set it among those
        joys   60
not yet open to us; in a graceful urn
praise it, with florally-soaring inscription:
                              "Subrisio Saltat."
Then you, my darling,
mutely elided
by all the most exquisite joys. Perhaps
your frills are happy on your behalf,—
or over your tight young breasts
the green metallic silk
feels itself endlessly spoilt and in need of noth-
        ing.   70
You,

time after time, upon all of the quivering scale-pans
        of balance
freshly laid fruit of serenity,
publicly shown among shoulders.

Where, oh where in the world is that place in my
        heart
where they still were far from being able, still fell
        away
from each other like mounting animals, not yet
properly paired;—
where weights are still heavy,
and hoops still stagger   80
away from their vainly
twirling sticks? . . .

And then, in this wearisome nowhere, all of a
        sudden,
the ineffable spot where the pure too-little
incomprehensibly changes,—springs round
into that empty too-much?
Where the many-digited sum
solves into zero?
Squares, o square in Paris, infinite show-place,
where the modiste Madame Lamort   90
winds and binds the restless ways of the world,
those endless ribbons, to ever-new
creations of bow, frill, flower, cockade and fruit,
all falsely-coloured, to deck
the cheap winter-hats of Fate.

Angel: suppose there's a place we know nothing
        about, and there,
on some indescribable carpet, lovers showed all that
        here
they're for ever unable to manage—their daring
lofty figures of heart-flight,
their towers of pleasure, their ladders,   100
long since, where ground never was, just quiver-
        ingly
propped by each other,—suppose they could manage
        it there,
before the spectators ringed round, the countless
        unmurmuring dead:
would not the dead then fling their last, their for
        ever reserved,
ever-concealed, unknown to us, ever-valid
coins of happiness down before the at last
truthfully smiling pair on the quietened
carpet?

Italian Fiction

LUIGI PIRANDELLO

1867–1936

The work of Pirandello, playwright, short-story writer, and novelist, is tinged with a pessimism which was probably caused by an exceedingly unhappy family life. Having achieved world fame by the nineteen-twenties with such plays as his famous *Six Characters in Search of an Author* (1922), he toured Europe and the United States, directing his own troupe in the performance of his plays. He received decorations from the Italian and French governments and won the Nobel prize in 1934. Between the end of World War I and his death he was the outstanding literary figure in Italy. Most of his work is characterized by a humor into which enter philosophical considerations on the meaning and value of this life, which Pirandello considered to be merely a brief interlude between birth and death. Pirandello wrote more than three hundred short stories, presenting in them scenes which he observed in his native Sicily. There is almost always a philosophical basis for his stories in the clash between the cosmic and the actual. "The Evil Spirit" suggests a recurrent theme in Pirandello's work: the impossibility of communicating truth, and the destructive influence of skepticism and disbelief in life.

FURTHER READING

VITTORINI, D. *The Modern Italian Novel* (Philadelphia, 1930).

VITTORINI, D. *The Drama of Luigi Pirandello* (Philadelphia, 1935).

The Evil Spirit *

CARLO NOCCIA had spent seven years of his youth in Algeria, engaged in trade at Bona. He had started in a desperate state of penury, but, after incredible toil and infinite trouble and by running

* Translated by Arthur and Henrie Mayne. By permission of Robert Lantz.

the most daring risks, he had eventually succeeded in accumulating a small capital.

He returned to his native town in Sicily and found himself living among a crowd of merchants who dealt in fruit and sulphur—a dishonest gang who competed so fiercely for the market that they resorted to every kind of fraud and trickery. He was afraid that his fellow-townsmen might regard him as a simpleton, if he admitted that he had made his way by honest work and tireless effort. Consequently he felt that he must disown his reputation as an honest trader and make them think that he had succeeded in his African business by resorting to sharp practices similar to their own. For only in this way could he hope to win their respect. He began to pose as a past-master in rascality, as he moved about amid the noise and bustle of the little seaport. He went every day to the harbour, where steamers of every nationality lay side by side and sailors, interpreters, stevedores, and dockers shouted and quarrelled incessantly—and then on to the beach, where the air was full of sulphur dust from the great mounds of sulphur piled there and a stink arose from the dry heaps of rotting seaweed. He was confused and depressed by it all—the shouts of the harbour boatmen, the clamour of the ever-lasting disputes, the hooting of the sirens, the smoke from the funnels. . . . After a time he began to think that wicked thoughts and the necessity to cheat were actually born in the fermentation of that life of restless activity—that evil grew out of the hatchways of the holds, the harbour water foul with sulphur and coal, and the stinking piles of seaweed. He really came to believe that merely by living in such surroundings and breathing that air, he would inevitably become a rogue in a very short time.

He was overjoyed when he received conclusive proof that his fellow-citizens considered that there was no longer anything they could teach him in the matter of sharp practice. Some time before, he had unexpectedly secured the post of manager of one of the largest concerns in the export of sulphur. The owner of the firm was quite a young man, utterly ignorant of business, who had had to break off his university studies on account of his father's sudden death. He was ambitious to become mayor, and tried hard to ingratiate himself with his fellow-citizens by being always ready to do a good turn and oblige his friends, hoping that they would secure his election. Naturally he at once fell into the clutches of the most rascally speculators in the market. One among them, a man called Grao, took especial advantage of his inexperience, by holding out to him the glittering prospect of founding a huge undertaking with the highly patriotic ideal of freeing the sulphur trade from the clutches of the foreign firms who had branches in the larger towns of the island. Grao assured the young man that, at a modest estimate, he would, in quite a short time, increase his fortune a hundredfold, and also achieve the great distinction of saving the Sicilian sulphur trade from foreign exploitation, so that he would promptly be elected mayor, without a shadow of a doubt.

It happened that Carlo Noccia admired Grao above all men and hung upon his words as though he were an oracle. It may well be that such warm admiration and blind trust were in large measure due to the fact that Grao had a very handsome daughter with whom Noccia had fallen in love. Be that as it may, the result was that when Noccia's young employer was involved by Grao in that huge enterprise, he applied to his manager for explanations and advice as to the speculations proposed by Grao, and Noccia passed on to him (in perfect good faith) the explanations and advice he had picked up from Grao in their private talks. Unfortunately it always happened that if the young owner had speculated on a fall, he found himself face to face with an alarming rise in price when the time for delivery had arrived, and similar losses followed his forward dealings for a rise. In less than a year the unhappy young man was bankrupt.

No one would give Noccia credit for good faith in the transactions. Of course, people said, he must have known that Grao was secretly speculating on the opposite side.

He had not, however, known this. He, too, had firmly believed that the proposed vast commercial enterprise would be sure to lead to a great increase in his employer's fortune—though he did not go so far as to think it would multiply it one hundredfold. When the first, the second, and even the third deal proved a failure, he really believed in Grao's apologies and in his assurance that the next gamble he proposed would redeem the situation and make up for past losses.

Moreover, it was a proof of his good faith that when the transactions ended in his employer's ruin, Noccia found himself ruined too; for he had lost his post as manager and—it was a still more grievous

blow—he had to give up all hope of winning the hand of Grao's daughter. What was his amazement then when Grao came up and embraced him heartily, thanking him for all that he had done and offering him his daughter, together with a dowry of over three hundred thousand lire.

Noccia protested that he was innocent of any deception and had acted in entire good faith, but Grao replied with a sly wink and slapped him on the back, implying that he thought that Noccia was a fit companion to himself and would make a worthy son-in-law. He went on to say that no one would have had a good word for Noccia, if he had failed to take advantage of his position and the game they had played, to line his own pocket. On the contrary, everyone would have looked down upon him as a booby, a good-for-nothing fellow like his employer, only fit to be exploited and then kicked on one side.

・　・　・

To his great surprise, the envy aroused by the wealth brought him from his marriage with the rich speculator's daughter soon led to a bitter hatred of Noccia. People began to speak of him as a Jew, capable of any infamy, any perfidy. This unpopularity went a long way towards ruining the happiness of his married life.

He tried to prove that he was not—no, by God! he was not—the kind of person they thought him. But, alas, on three or four occasions, without his understanding the why or wherefore of the affair, both his actions and his good intentions were suddenly exposed to publicity in exactly the opposite light to what he had meant. Finally, one day, through some inexplicable oversight, he entered a sum of a few hundred lire on the wrong side of the accounts of one of his subordinates. It resulted in a civil suit being brought against him—and this in spite of the fact that he had previously done many a good turn to the man.

Noccia then began to believe in the existence of some kind of evil spirit, born of the envy, hatred and malice of one's enemies, and nourished on their malevolent thoughts and intentions. He believed that this evil spirit always stands close beside us, ready to take advantage of our doubts and perplexities, insinuating ideas into our mind, urging us on, giving suggestions and advice which at the outset have the appearance of being perfectly honest and wise, inspired by the soundest judgment: then all of a sudden, we discover that our ideas are false and that we have been led into a trap, so that our whole behaviour suddenly appears not only in other people's eyes, but even in our own, under a sinister light. We find ourselves caught in a trap and, do what we can, we are unable to escape from it.

Undoubtedly this evil spirit had caused him to make that unfortunate mistake in his accounts, which had made everyone believe him capable of swindling a poor man, merely for the sake of a few hundred lire. From that time onward, they all thought that they could legitimately refuse to pay Noccia his just claims, so that he was frequently compelled to go to law to assert his rights.

One of these law-suits had been dragging on in the courts for some time. Tired of the litigation and despondent as to the result, he would gladly have abandoned the case, if he had not been so annoyed by it. He determined to make one more effort to prove that justice was on his side and journeyed to Rome, to apply personally to the member of Parliament for his constituency to use his influence on his behalf.

. . .

Noccia was now forty-seven. He had the look of a trapped animal—savage, distrustful, suspicious. He was completely soured by years of hostility. His gloomy face, burnt a deep brown on the scorching Sicilian coast, contrasted strangely with his large, restless, pale grey eyes. Every now and then, the deep lines on his face were smoothed away as he stood, lost in wonder at the splendour of the capital —a sensation so novel that it gave him a feeling almost of discomfort.

He had in his breast-pocket a case containing bank-notes for several thousand lire. Perhaps when he left Sicily he had intended to indulge in many of the distractions which a city like Rome could offer, but his suspicion and reserve had become a second nature to him and, though he had already been there four days, he had not yet succumbed to any temptations. He was worried, bored and listless.

He was staying at the *Nuova Roma* hotel, near the station, and travelled several miles a day to return there, even if only to shut himself up in his room for half an hour. After this brief interlude, he would emerge again to resume his aimless wanderings, in a worse temper than ever.

On the morning of his fifth day in Rome, he happened to go into a second-rate café near the station, to while away the time. He found few customers and many flies. He ordered a glass of beer and picked up a newspaper from the adjoining table. The flies however gave him no rest. In driving one

away he tore the newspaper and wanted to pay for it, but the proprietor refused to let him. In hitting at another fly, he nearly upset his glass of beer. With an exclamation of annoyance, he abandoned his attempt to read and stretched out his arms on either side along the leather-padded bench. His right hand touched something and he bent down to see what it was.

It was an old purse, that some customer must have left there. Perhaps there was nothing in it—perhaps some coppers or even a few lire in silver. . . . Noccia hesitated for some moments, wondering whether to pick it up and give it to the landlord to restore to the owner, if claimed. He looked at the landlord and, after a scrutiny of the man, came to the conclusion that he was not at all likely to restore the purse if it had anything in it. Perhaps, thought Noccia, it would be better to find that out first, so he put out his hand cautiously and picked it up. Yes, there seemed to be something in it. He opened it just a little and caught sight of a silver piastre and two small two-centessimi pieces. He had another look at the landlord and felt quite sure that the piastre and the two coppers would end by finding their way into the till behind the bar.

What was he to do? He remembered that, on the previous day, he had happened to see in one of the newspapers a paragraph headed: "A FINE EXAMPLE TO FOLLOW." It told of a telegraph boy who had picked up in the street a pocket-book containing more than a thousand lire, and had gone to the police-station to hand over his find. Should he follow that "fine example"? At the police-station they would ask his name and it would be printed in the papers, if they reported the finding of the purse. He remembered that some of his club acquaintances in Sicily spent their leisure hours reading right through the Roman newspapers, from the leading article to the final advertisement on the sixth page. Those who believed that he was the man to take advantage of anyone for the sake of a few lire would say with a sneer that he had handed in the purse at the police-station because all it contained was a piastre and four centessimi. It really did not seem worth while advertising his honesty for such a trifle. What ought he to do then. . . .

While he was making up his mind, he did not think it wise to keep the purse in his hand, exposed to view, so slipped it into his waistcoat pocket, in order that he could take his time to decide whether it would not be wisest after all to put it back where he had found it. If he did that, however, some other customer, someone with no scruples, might see it and take it without thinking twice about it—in which case the poor fellow who had lost it would . . .

"Come, come!" said Noccia to himself, "It's only a matter of five lire, when all's said and done."

He was on the point of taking the purse out of his pocket when a new customer rushed into the café and made straight for the little table at which he was sitting. The newcomer was an old woman of far from pre-possessing appearance, what with her general dirtiness, her owl-like beak of a nose, and the tufts of grey bristles that sprouted from her face. Her coarse touseled hair escaped in disorder from a tattered bonnet fastened under her chin. She pushed the hair back from her eyes, and panted like a seal as she exclaimed aggressively:

"My purse is here! I left it here . . . my purse!"

At the sudden appearance of this repulsive old woman, Noccia felt horribly alarmed; for, since he had put the purse in his pocket, she would be bound to think that it was his intention to steal it. So he found himself smiling back at her in a silly, meaningless way and pretending complete ignorance. "A purse? Where?" . . . He moved to one side and then stood up to enable her to have a good look for it. The old woman searched on the seat, underneath it and round the legs of the table, with a fretful irritation which shewed him clearly that she suspected him. Then with a savage scowl she peered into his face and asked outright: "You didn't find it?"

His fingers itched to bring the purse out from his pocket and give it back to her, but under the circumstances it was impossible, and the turmoil within him made him blush even to the whites of his eyes and burst out into an indignant protest:

"Are you mad?"

The owner of the café and the few customers present sided with him in the dispute and the old crone left the place grumbling and whimpering. Then they told him that the poor woman was a pitiable case, constantly fuddled with drink and half-witted since her only daughter had died in the hospital.

Noccia now began to feel very uncomfortable: he wanted to pay his bill at once and get out of the place, but unfortunately he had slipped the old woman's purse into the same pocket in which he carried his own. He was afraid that in pulling out his own purse the other one might show. The blood rushed to his head and his eyes glittered feverishly. He drew his fat wallet from his breast-pocket and extracted a bank note for a hundred lire.

"But haven't you got any change?" asked the landlord in surprise.

Noccia shook his head, unable to say a word in answer. One of the customers offered to change the note, and he paid his bill, gave a five-lire tip and left the café.

Once outside, his first impulse was to throw the purse away into some dark corner. He was restrained, however, by the pathetic story he had heard in the shop—that the poor woman had gone half-mad through the death of her daughter. No, it would be a low trick. . . . It was true that the wretched old hag had suspected him of having found her purse and kept it, but after all her suspicion was not without foundation, for he really had acted as if he intended to keep it. Had he not first laughed like a fool—quite against his will—and then moved aside and stood up to let her search the place where he had been sitting? If he now threw the purse away, he would always feel remorse for having taken it. Someone else would pick it up, who would naturally not feel under the same obligation to restore it—an obligation which he felt all the more acutely, now that he knew who the owner was and had denied to her face that he had taken it. No, no! To throw the purse away would be still less creditable than his previous foolish behaviour. What was he to do then? Suddenly the idea occurred to him that the proprietor of the restaurant and the few customers present must have seen that he had a pocket-book full of bank notes and that there was no doubt to them that he was a gentleman, a real gentleman who could well afford the luxury of giving that poor old woman a present of ten or twenty lire as a consolation for the loss of her purse. Yes, that was the thing to do. He would go to the bar and leave a sum of twenty lire for her, in the presence of them all as witnesses, or he would ask the landlord to give him the old woman's address, so that he could trace her and give her the money himself.

With this intention in his mind, Noccia retraced his steps. He was just about to enter the café when he caught sight of the bent figure of the old crone. She was walking slowly about, her eyes glued to the ground, holding back her tangled woolly locks with both her hands, still looking for her purse, and whimpering. Noccia stopped beside her and tapped her gently on the back. He drew a couple of ten-lire notes from his pocket-book and held them out to her. He felt quite nervous about the kind act he was performing, and stammered that he hoped she would accept the sum to make up for the loss she had suffered. To his consternation the old woman promptly clutched hold of him and began to shake him furiously, screaming:

"Thief! Thief! Offering me twenty lire, are you? Only twenty lire! What about the rest of my money —you thief!"

People ran up from every side: among them were two policemen. Noccia had stood still for a moment, stupefied, but when he found himself surrounded by scores of people all struggling to seize him, he made desperate efforts to escape. But it was in vain. He was searched and found to be in possession of the purse, which contained a silver piastre (worth five lire) and two old gold coins worth twenty lire each, not the coppers for which Noccia had mistaken them when he had furtively glanced inside the purse. Forty-five lire in all! So that was why the old hag had made all that outcry for the balance of her money.

Noccia was quite prepared to pay her a hundred lire, two hundred, even as much as a thousand. He pulled out his pocket-book for the money. But, naturally enough, it was held that, quite possibly, the pocket-book also might have been stolen. He was therefore taken to the police-station.

The authorities were puzzled: *prima facie* it seemed safe to assume that a thief would never dream of restoring part of the property he had stolen. But it seemed equally improbable that an honest man would pocket someone else's purse, and deny outright that he had seen it—as Noccia had done. Under the circumstances, it was found necessary to keep him in custody, while enquiries about him were made from Sicily. The police officials naturally refused to pay any serious attention to the alleged persecution by an evil spirit, about which the prisoner raved frantically and incessantly.

Spanish Lyric Poetry

The three modern Spanish poets Antonio Machado (1875–1939), Juan Ramón Jiménez (b. 1881), and Rafael Alberti (b. 1903) represent some of the trends visible in modern Spanish lyric poetry. Machado, who often collaborated in literary work with his famous brother Manuel, was a professor of French in Segovia. His poetry deals extensively with the bare plains of Castile which made a subtle impression upon his sensitive nature. "Poetry for me," he wrote, "consists more in the reaction of a delicate nature to objects than in harmony of words or in color and design."

While the poetry of Juan Ramón Jiménez deals to some extent at least with the subject of nature, he is above all the poet of the inner life, producing mournful, melancholy elegies filled with nostalgic memories. His poems often contain in a highly refined and subtle form an expression of the self-absorption of an unhealthy and solitary life.

Rafael Alberti has brought into Spanish poetry a fresh and original note. However, his career as yet has not been of sufficient scope to determine with accuracy the position he will eventually occupy in the history of Spanish poetry.

Madrigal of Snow-White *

To the seaside went Snow-White:
Now she's melted, quite.

Snow-White, little flower of the north
Went to the shining sea of the south
To bathe her body white:
Now she's melted, quite.

Snow-White, white and cold,
Why did you go so bold
Where the waves so warmly rolled
To bathe your body white?

Now you're melted, quite!

—*Rafael Alberti*

Pirate of Sea and Sky

Pirate of sea and sky:
If I was not before, I shall be by and by.

If I did not steal the dawn from the sea,
If I only passed nigh,
I'll steal it by and by.

* The poems by Alberti, Machado, and Jiménez were translated by Nicholson B. Adams. Reprinted by permission of the authors and the translator.

Pirate of sky and sea,
On a torpedo-chaser,
With six mighty sailors,
Alternate, three by three.

If I did not steal the dawn from the sky,
If I did not steal it,
I'll steal it by and by.

—Rafael Alberti

On the Square's a Building

On the square's a building,
A window in its tower,
At the window a lady,
A lady with a white flower.
A cavalier passed by there:
Who knows why he passed by?
And when he went took with him
Square and building and tower,
With its window and its lady,
Its lady with her white flower.

—Antonio Machado

El Blancor

The scent of the white tube-rose
Is really a naked woman
Who through the dark corridor goes.

—Juan Ramón Jiménez

Renaceré yo

I'll be reborn a stone,
And still, dear, I'll love you.
I'll be reborn a wind,
And still, dear, I'll love you.
I'll be reborn a wave,
And still, dear, I'll love you.
I'll be reborn a man,
And still, dear, I'll love you.

—Juan Ramón Jiménez

La Fusión

When dawn breaks clear,
The fresh world kisses me
With your lips, dear.

—Juan Ramón Jiménez

FEDERICO GARCÍA LORCA

1898–1936

Lorca, one of the finest poets in all modern literature, was born into a wealthy Andalusian family of farmers. He suffered a serious illness during the first months of his life which left him with a permanent physical impediment. Unable to compete with the young people of his own age, he turned to contemplation and imagination. After secondary studies in Granada and a degree in law at the University, he became a distinguished musician. His *Gipsy Ballads (Romancero Gitano)*, 1928, has become the most widely known book of Spanish poetry in the twentieth century. He composed, in addition, several plays and for five years directed a company of actors known as "La Barraca." In August, 1936, he was dragged from the home of friends where he had taken refuge during the first bloody days of the Spanish Civil War, and was murdered by an armed group of Phalangists whose members have remained unidentified.

FURTHER READING

BAREA, ARTURO. *Lorca, the Poet and His People,* translated by Isla Barea (London, 1944).
HONIG, EDWIN. *García Lorca* (Norfolk, Conn., 1944).
NADAL, R. M. *García Lorca: Poems,* with introduction (London, 1939).

Ballad of the Bullfight [1]

(From *Mariana Pineda,* Act I)

In the greatest bullfight
ever seen in Ronda the old,
there were five bulls black as jet
with ribbons of black and green.
All the time I was thinking of you;
I was thinking: if only she were
with me, my sad friend,
my Marianita Pineda!
The girls came shrieking
on painted two-wheeled caleches,   10
with circular fans
embroidered with spangles . . .
And the youths from Ronda
on affected ponies,
the broad grey sombreros
pressed down to their eyebrows.
The bull ring with the crowd

[1] Translated by Stephen Spender and J. L. Gill.

(*calañés* [2] and tall *peinetas* [3])
rotated like a zodiac
of white and black laughs.   20
And when the great Cayetano
crossed the straw-coloured sand
with his apple-coloured suit,
embroidered with silver and silk,
gallantly projected
among the rough people
in front of the vicious bulls
which Spain breeds in her land,
it seemed that the afternoon
became still darker.   30
If you had seen with what
grace he moved his legs!
What grand poise was his
with the cape and the *muleta*!
Better, nor even Pedro Romero
bullfighting with the stars!
Five bulls he killed; five,
with ribbons of black and green.
On the point of his sword
He opened five flowers,   40
and each instant he brushed
the snouts of the beasts,
like a great butterfly
of gold with vermilion wings.
The bull-ring, like the afternoon,
vibrated fiercely, violently,
and between the smell of blood
came the smell of the sierra.
All the time I was thinking of you;
I was thinking: if only she were   50
with me, my sad friend,
my Marianita Pineda!

The Faithless Wife [4]

And I took her to the river
thinking she was a maiden,
but she had a husband.

It was on Saint James's night
and almost as if prearranged.
The lanterns went out
and the crickets lighted up.
In the farthest corners
I touched her sleeping breasts,
and they opened to me suddenly   10
like spikes of hyacinth.

[2] Wide-brimmed, low-crowned Andalusian hat.
[3] High convex comb of Spanish women.
[4] Translated by Stephen Spender and J. L. Gill.

The starch of her petticoat
sounded in my ears
like a piece of silk
torn by ten knives.
Without silver light on their foliage
the trees had grown larger
and a horizon of dogs
barks very far from the river.

Past the blackberries,   20
the reeds and the hawthorn,
underneath her cluster of hair
I made a hollow in the earth.
I took off my tie.
She took off her dress.
I my belt with the revolver.
She her four bodices.
Nor nard nor conch
have skin so fine,
nor did crystals lit by moon   30
shine with this brilliance.
Her thighs escaped me
like startled fish,
half full of fire,
half full of cold.
That night I ran
on the best of the roads
mounted on a mare of nacre
without bridle or stirrups.
As a man, I won't repeat   40
the things she said to me.
The light of understanding
has made me most discreet.
Smeared with sand and kisses
I took her from the river.
With the air battled
the swords of the lilies.

I behaved as the person I am.
Like a proper gipsy.
I gave her a sewing basket, large,   50
of straw-coloured satin,
and I did not want to fall in love
because having a husband
she told me she was a maiden,
when I took her to the river.

Song

To Claudio Guillén, when a boy in Seville [5]

In the laurel branches
I saw two dark pigeons.

[5] Translated by Stephen Spender and J. L. Gill.

One was the sun
the other the moon.
Little neighbours, I said to them,
Where is my grave?
In my tail, said the sun.
In my throat, said the moon.
And I who was walking
with the earth up to my waist   10
saw two eagles of marble
and a naked girl.
One was the other
and the girl was neither.
Little eagles, I said to them,
Where is my grave?
In my tail, said the sun.
In my throat, said the moon.
In the cherry branches
I saw two naked pigeons.   20
One was the other
and both were neither.

The Lament [6]

I have shut my balcony
because I do not want to hear the lament,
but from behind the grey walls
I hear nothing else but the lament.

There are very few angels that sing,
there are very few dogs that bark,
a thousand violins fit into the palm of the hand:
but the lament is an immense angel,
the lament is an immense violin,
the tears muzzle the wind,
and I hear nothing else but the lament.

[6] Translated by Stephen Spender and J. L. Gill.

The Gypsy Nun [7]

Silence deep of white and myrtle.
  Hallows in the deep fine grass,
And the little nun embroiders
  Lilies on straw-colored cloth.
In and out the chandelier
  Fly the seven prismatic birds
And the church grunts in the distance
  Like a bear with belly upward.
What fine stitches! And how graceful
  On the cloth that looks like straw.   10
She would love now to embroider
  Flowers of her own light fancy.
What a sunflower! What magnolias,
  All of sequins and of ribbons,
Tints of saffron and of moonbeams
  Flitting on the altar-cloth.
Five gold shaddocks grow all mellow
  In the nearby fragrant kitchen,
Five bright wounds of Christ the Saviour
  Brought from Almeria's orchards.   20
Through the nun's sweet little eyes
  Two swift horsemen prance and gallop,
Then a noise, both dim and final
  Makes her shrink within her clothing,
And as she sees clouds and mountains
  In the stiff and rigid distance,
Her poor heart is broken, broken,
  Heart of sugar and verbena.
Oh, how tall is yonder plain!
  Tall, with twenty suns above it.   30
How the rivers stand on end
  In the vision of her fancy!
But she still embroiders flowers
  While on tip-toe in the breezes
Light plays at a lofty chess game
  Through the window's jalousie.

[7] Translated by Nicholson B. Adams. By permission of
Mr. Adams.

English Fiction

JAMES JOYCE

1882–1941

James Joyce was born in Dublin on February 2, 1882, and was educated at the Jesuit School of Clongowes Woods (his school life there is reflected in *A Portrait of the Artist as a Young Man*). He then attended Belvedere College and the Royal University at Dublin. Unlike William Butler Yeats and George Moore, he was never an enthusiast for the turn-of-the-century Irish renaissance and the revival of interest in Gaelic folk materials. Disliking Irish parochialism, Joyce felt strongly that the revival of a dead language like Gaelic would cut off Ireland from the central traditions of Western world literature. Possibly, too, his admiration for Ibsen kept him away from the Irish theater movement sponsored by Yeats and Lady Gregory. As early as 1899 he had expressed this admiration for Ibsen in an essay, "Ibsen's New Drama," in the *Fortnightly Review*. When he wrote a pamphlet, *The Day of the Rabblement,* assailing the Irish literary theater in 1901, he was already familiar with Ibsen's opposition to nationalism in literature and with William Archer's essay (1894) which discussed Ibsen's attack on the glorification of the peasant in European literature.

Joyce thus found the atmosphere of Dublin uncongenial to his literary views and exiled himself to Paris in 1902. Although visiting Ireland in 1904 and 1909, he spent the remainder of his life in Europe, especially at Trieste, Paris, and Zurich, where he died in 1941. Like Ibsen before him and like his contemporary, Thomas Mann, Joyce was always interested in the modern problem of the expatriate artist in voluntary exile from his own country, in his deliberate exclusion of himself from the claims of human love, and in his symbolic withdrawal from the social responsibilities of the citizen and man apart from the artist. The theme emerges in his work early and late, from *A Portrait of the Artist as a Young Man* (1916) to his last work, *Finnegans Wake* (1939).

In 1904 and 1905 Joyce wrote a series of naturalistic stories about Dublin which he defined as "a chapter in the moral history of his country." The theme of estrangement and alienation is implicit in many of the stories, especially in Joyce's evident sympathy for the characters who are unhappy and estranged in an uncongenial environment, though the treatment is ironic, as in "The Little Cloud." This collection of stories was published in 1914, and was followed by the publication of his first novel, *A Portrait of the Artist as a Young Man* (1916), first serialized in Ezra Pound's *Egoist*. He then set to work upon what was to be possibly the most influential novel of the twentieth century, *Ulysses* (Paris, 1922), which had been published serially in Margaret Anderson's *Little Review* from 1918 until it was suppressed in 1920. It is impossible here to encompass adequately this extraordinary achievement in naturalism, impressionism, and expressionism: the astoundingly clever parodies, the vast range of learning (such as the knowledge of the history of Hamlet scholarship), the intricate interweaving and integration of themes, the tonal and musical variations on the thematic developments, the epic structure that parallels the events in Leopold Bloom's day to the adventures of Ulysses and the episodes in the novel to various parts of the body and to the various branches of learning. The interested reader will discover an extensive literature that has grown up around *Ulysses*: Stuart Gilbert's *James Joyce's Ulysses* (1930), Paul Jordan Smith's *A Key to Ulysses* (1934), Frank Budgen's *James Joyce and the Making of Ulysses* (1934), Richard Kain's *Fabulous Voyager* (1947).

The last work of Joyce, *Finnegans Wake,* was created over a period of fifteen years. It carried to the degree of nearly complete unintelligibility two of Joyce's chief interests: expressionistic manipulation of language to create new and associated meanings of words; and Giambattista Vico's philosophy of history by means of which, in a dream-state stream of consciousness of H. C. Earwicker, a Dublin tavern keeper, Joyce recapitulates all history and time and space into the present moment. Joyce's experiments in truncating, distorting, lengthening, shortening, and recombining elements of the English language are carried to their expressionistic ultimate. However much the extreme expressionism of *Finnegans Wake* may seem to be a misguided solution of the artist's problem of communication and to have left Joyce talking a private language comprehensible only to himself, nevertheless his dynamic creativeness in *Ulysses* in experimenting with new literary devices has had a vast fertilizing influence upon the modern novel, evident whether one is reading Virginia Woolf's *The Waves*, Thomas Wolfe's *Look Homeward, Angel*, or William Faulkner's *The Sound and the Fury*.

FURTHER READING

See books by Budgen, Gilbert, Kain, and Smith mentioned above, also:

ELIOT, T. S. *"Ulysses,* Order, and Myth" in *Critiques and Essays on Modern Fiction, 1920–1951,* edited by John W. Aldridge (New York, 1952); in the same volume: HENDRY, IRENE, "Joyce's Epiphanies"; LEVIN, HARRY, "Montage"; WILSON, EDMUND, "The Dream of H. C. Earwicker."

A Little Cloud *

EIGHT years before he had seen his friend off at the North Wall and wished him godspeed. Gallaher had got on. You could tell that at once by his travelled air, his well-cut tweed suit, and fearless accent. Few fellows had talents like his and fewer still could remain unspoiled by such success. Gallaher's heart was in the right place and he had deserved to win. It was something to have a friend like that.

Little Chandler's thoughts ever since lunchtime had been of his meeting with Gallaher, of Gallaher's invitation and of the great city London where Gallaher lived. He was called Little Chandler because, though he was but slightly under the average stature, he gave one the idea of being a little man. His hands were white and small, his frame was fragile, his voice was quiet and his manners were refined. He took the greatest care of his fair silken hair and moustache and used perfume discreetly on his handkerchief. The half-moons of his nails were perfect and when he smiled you caught a glimpse of a row of childish white teeth.

* From *Dubliners,* included in *The Portable James Joyce.* Copyright, 1946, 1947, by The Viking Press, Inc. By permission of The Viking Press, Inc.

As he sat at his desk in the King's Inns he thought what changes those eight years had brought. The friend whom he had known under a shabby and necessitous guise had become a brilliant figure on the London Press. He turned often from his tiresome writing to gaze out of the office window. The glow of a late autumn sunset covered the grass plots and walks. It cast a shower of kindly golden dust on the untidy nurses and decrepit old men who drowsed on the benches; it flickered upon all the moving figures—on the children who ran screaming along the gravel paths and on everyone who passed through the gardens. He watched the scene and thought of life; and (as always happened when he thought of life) he became sad. A gentle melancholy took possession of him. He felt how useless it was to struggle against fortune, this being the burden of wisdom which the ages had bequeathed to him.

He remembered the books of poetry upon his shelves at home. He had bought them in his bachelor days and many an evening, as he sat in the little room off the hall, he had been tempted to take one down from the bookshelf and read out something to his wife. But shyness had always held him back; and so the books had remained on their shelves. At times he repeated lines to himself and this consoled him.

When his hour had struck he stood up and took leave of his desk and of his fellow-clerks punctiliously. He emerged from under the feudal arch of the King's Inns, a neat modest figure, and walked swiftly down Henrietta Street. The golden sunset was waning and the air had grown sharp. A horde of grimy children populated the street. They stood or ran in the roadway or crawled up the steps before the gaping doors or squatted like mice upon the thresholds. Little Chandler gave them no thought. He picked his way deftly through all that minute vermin-like life and under the shadow of the gaunt spectral mansions in which the old nobility of Dublin had roystered. No memory of the past touched him, for his mind was full of a present joy.

He had never been in Corless's but he knew the value of the name. He knew that people went there after the theatre to eat oysters and drink liqueurs; and he had heard that the waiters there spoke French and German. Walking swiftly by at night he had seen cabs drawn up before the door and richly dressed ladies, escorted by cavaliers, alight and enter quickly. They wore noisy dresses and many wraps. Their faces were powdered and they caught up their dresses, when they touched earth, like alarmed Atalantas. He had always passed without turning his head to look. It was his habit to walk swiftly in the street even by day and whenever he found himself in the city late at night he hurried on his way apprehensively and excitedly. Sometimes, however, he courted the causes of his fear. He chose the darkest and narrowest streets and, as he walked boldly forward, the silence that was spread about his footsteps troubled him, the wandering, silent figures troubled him; and at times a sound of low fugitive laughter made him tremble like a leaf.

He turned to the right towards Capel Street. Ignatius Gallaher on the London Press! Who would have thought it possible eight years before? Still, now that he reviewed the past, Little Chandler could remember many signs of future greatness in his friend. People used to say that Ignatius Gallaher was wild. Of course, he did mix with a rakish set of fellows at that time, drank freely and borrowed money on all sides. In the end he had got mixed up in some shady affair, some money transaction: at least, that was one version of his flight. But nobody denied him talent. There was always a certain . . . something in Ignatius Gallaher that impressed you in spite of yourself. Even when he was out at elbows and at his wits' end for money he kept up a bold face. Little Chandler remembered (and the remembrance brought a slight flush of pride to his cheek) one of Ignatius Gallaher's sayings when he was in a tight corner:

"Half time now, boys," he used to say lightheartedly. "Where's my considering cap?"

That was Ignatius Gallaher all out; and, damn it, you couldn't but admire him for it.

Little Chandler quickened his pace. For the first time in his life he felt himself superior to the people he passed. For the first time his soul revolted against the dull inelegance of Capel Street. There was no doubt about it: if you wanted to succeed you had to go away. You could do nothing in Dublin. As he crossed Grattan Bridge he looked down the river towards the lower quays and pitied the poor stunted houses. They seemed to him a band of tramps, huddled together along the river-banks, their old coats covered with dust and soot, stupefied by the panorama of sunset and waiting for the first chill of night to bid them arise, shake themselves and begone. He wondered whether he could write a poem to express his idea. Perhaps Gallaher might be able to get it into some London paper for him. Could he write something original? He was not sure what idea he wished to express but the thought that a poetic moment had touched him took life within him like an infant hope. He stepped onward bravely.

Every step brought him nearer to London, farther from his own sober inartistic life. A light began to tremble on the horizon of his mind. He was not so old—thirty-two. His temperament might be said to be just at the point of maturity. There were so many different moods and impressions that he wished to express in verse. He felt them within him. He tried to weigh his soul to see if it was a poet's soul. Melancholy was the dominant note of his temperament, he thought, but it was a melancholy tempered by recurrences of faith and resignation and simple joy. If he could give expression to it in a book of poems perhaps men would listen. He would never be popular: he saw that. He could not sway the crowd but he might appeal to a little circle of kindred minds. The English critics, perhaps, would recognise him as one of the Celtic school by reason of the melancholy tone of his poems; besides that, he would put in allusions. He began to invent sentences and phrases from the notice which his book would get. *"Mr. Chandler has the gift of easy and graceful verse."* . . . *"A wistful sadness pervades these poems."* . . . *"The Celtic note."* It was a pity his name was not more Irish-looking. Perhaps it would be better to insert his mother's name before the surname: Thomas Malone Chandler, or better still: T. Malone Chandler. He would speak to Gallaher about it.

He pursued his revery so ardently that he passed his street and had to turn back. As he came near Corless's his former agitation began to overmaster him and he halted before the door in indecision. Finally he opened the door and entered.

The light and noise of the bar held him at the doorways for a few moments. He looked about him, but his sight was confused by the shining of many red and green wine-glasses. The bar seemed to him to be full of people and he felt that the people were observing him curiously. He glanced quickly to right and left (frowning slightly to make his errand appear serious), but when his sight cleared a little he saw that nobody had turned to look at him: and there, sure enough, was Ignatius Gallaher leaning with his back against the counter and his feet planted far apart.

"Hallo, Tommy, old hero, here you are! What is it to be? What will you have? I'm taking whisky: better stuff than we get across the water. Soda? Lithia? No mineral? I'm the same. Spoils the flavour. . . . Here, *garçon*, bring us two halves of malt whisky, like a good fellow. . . . Well, and how have you been pulling along since I saw you last? Dear God, how old we're getting! Do you see any signs of aging in me—eh, what? A little grey and thin on the top—what?"

Ignatius Gallaher took off his hat and displayed a large closely cropped head. His face was heavy, pale and clean-shaven. His eyes, which were of bluish slate-colour, relieved his unhealthy pallor and shone out plainly above the vivid orange tie he wore. Between these rival features the lips appeared very long and shapeless and colourless. He bent his head and felt with two sympathetic fingers the thin hair at the crown. Little Chandler shook his head as a denial. Ignatius Gallaher put on his hat again.

"It pulls you down," he said, "Press life. Always hurry and scurry, looking for copy and sometimes not finding it: and then, always to have something new in your stuff. Damn proofs and printers, I say, for a few days. I'm deuced glad, I can tell you, to get back to the old country. Does a fellow good, a bit of a holiday. I feel a ton better since I landed again in dear dirty Dublin. . . . Here you are, Tommy. Water? Say when."

Little Chandler allowed his whisky to be very much diluted.

"You don't know what's good for you, my boy," said Ignatius Gallaher. "I drink mine neat."

"I drink very little as a rule," said Little Chandler modestly. "An odd half-one or so when I meet any of the old crowd: that's all."

"Ah, well," said Ignatius Gallaher, cheerfully, "here's to us and to old times and old acquaintance."

They clinked glasses and drank the toast.

"I met some of the old gang to-day," said Ignatius Gallaher. "O'Hara seems to be in a bad way. What's he doing?"

"Nothing," said Little Chandler. "He's gone to the dogs."

"But Hogan has a good sit, hasn't he?"

"Yes; he's in the Land Commission."

"I met him one night in London and he seemed to be very flush. . . . Poor O'Hara! Boose, I suppose?"

"Other things, too," said Little Chandler shortly.

Ignatius Gallaher laughed.

"Tommy," he said, "I see you haven't changed an atom. You're the very same serious person that used to lecture me on Sunday mornings when I had a sore head and a fur on my tongue. You'd want to knock about a bit in the world. Have you never been anywhere even for a trip?"

"I've been to the Isle of Man," said Little Chandler.

Ignatius Gallaher laughed.

"The Isle of Man!" he said. "Go to London or Paris: Paris, for choice. That'd do you good."

"Have you seen Paris?"

"I should think I have! I've knocked about there a little."

"And is it really so beautiful as they say?" asked Little Chandler.

He sipped a little of his drink while Ignatius Gallaher finished his boldly.

"Beautiful?" said Ignatius Gallaher, pausing on the word and on the flavour of his drink. "It's not so beautiful, you know. Of course, it is beautiful. . . . But it's the life of Paris; that's the thing. Ah, there's no city like Paris for gaiety, movement, excitement. . . ."

Little Chandler finished his whisky and, after some trouble, succeeded in catching the barman's eye. He ordered the same again.

"I've been to the Moulin Rouge," Ignatius Gallaher continued when the barman had removed their glasses, "and I've been to all the Bohemian cafés. Hot stuff! Not for a pious chap like you, Tommy."

Little Chandler said nothing until the barman returned with two glasses: then he touched his friend's glass lightly and reciprocated the former toast. He was beginning to feel somewhat disillusioned. Gallaher's accent and way of expressing himself did not please him. There was something vulgar in his friend which he had not observed before. But perhaps it was only the result of living in London amid the bustle and competition of the Press. The old personal charm was still there under this new gaudy manner. And, after all, Gallaher had lived, he had seen the world. Little Chandler looked at his friend enviously.

"Everything in Paris is gay," said Ignatius Gallaher. "They believe in enjoying life—and don't you think they're right? If you want to enjoy yourself properly you must go to Paris. And, mind you, they've a great feeling for the Irish there. When they heard I was from Ireland they were ready to eat me, man."

Little Chandler took four or five sips from his glass.

"Tell me," he said, "is it true that Paris is so . . . immoral as they say?"

Ignatius Gallaher made a catholic gesture with his right arm.

"Every place is immoral," he said. "Of course you

do find spicy bits in Paris. Go to one of the students' balls, for instance. That's lively, if you like, when the *cocottes* begin to let themselves loose. You know what they are, I suppose?"

"I've heard of them," said Little Chandler.

Ignatius Gallaher drank off his whisky and shook his head.

"Ah," he said, "you may say what you like. There's no woman like the Parisienne—for style, for go."

"Then it is an immoral city," said Little Chandler, with timid insistence—"I mean, compared with London or Dublin?"

"London!" said Ignatius Gallaher. "It's six of one and half-a-dozen of the other. You ask Hogan, my boy. I showed him a bit about London when he was over there. He'd open your eye. . . . I say, Tommy, don't make punch of that whisky: liquor up."

"No, really. . . ."

"O, come on, another one won't do you any harm. What is it? The same again, I suppose?"

"Well . . . all right."

"*François*, the same again. . . . Will you smoke, Tommy?"

Ignatius Gallaher produced his cigar-case. The two friends lit their cigars and puffed at them in silence until their drinks were served.

"I'll tell you my opinion," said Ignatius Gallaher, emerging after some time from the clouds of smoke in which he had taken refuge, "it's a rum world. Talk of immorality! I've heard of cases—what am I saying?—I've known them: cases of . . . immorality. . . ."

Ignatius Gallaher puffed thoughtfully at his cigar and then, in a calm historian's tone, he proceeded to sketch for his friend some pictures of the corruption which was rife abroad. He summarised the vices of many capitals and seemed inclined to award the palm to Berlin. Some things he could not vouch for (his friends had told him), but of others he had had personal experience. He spared neither rank nor caste. He revealed many of the secrets of religious houses on the Continent and described some of the practices which were fashionable in high society and ended by telling, with details, a story about an English duchess—a story which he knew to be true. Little Chandler was astonished.

"Ah, well," said Ignatius Gallaher, "here we are in old jog-along Dublin where nothing is known of such things."

"How dull you must find it," said Little Chandler, "after all the other places you've seen!"

"Well," said Ignatius Gallaher, "it's a relaxation to come over here, you know. And, after all, it's the old country, as they say, isn't it? You can't help having a certain feeling for it. That's human nature. . . . But tell me something about yourself. Hogan told me you had . . . tasted the joys of connubial bliss. Two years ago, wasn't it?"

Little Chandler blushed and smiled.

"Yes," he said. "I was married last May twelve months."

"I hope it's not too late in the day to offer my best wishes," said Ignatius Gallaher. "I didn't know your address or I'd have done so at the time."

He extended his hand, which Little Chandler took.

"Well, Tommy," he said, "I wish you and yours every joy in life, old chap, and tons of money, and may you never die till I shoot you. And that's the wish of a sincere friend, an old friend. You know that?"

"I know that," said Little Chandler.

"Any youngsters?" said Ignatius Gallaher.

Little Chandler blushed again.

"We have one child," he said.

"Son or daughter?"

"A little boy."

Ignatius Gallaher slapped his friend sonorously on the back.

"Bravo," he said, "I wouldn't doubt you, Tommy."

Little Chandler smiled, looked confusedly at his glass and bit his lower lip with three childishly white front teeth.

"I hope you'll spend an evening with us," he said, "before you go back. My wife will be delighted to meet you. We can have a little music and——"

"Thanks awfully, old chap," said Ignatius Gallaher, "I'm sorry we didn't meet earlier. But I must leave to-morrow night."

"To-night, perhaps . . .?"

"I'm awfully sorry, old man. You see I'm over here with another fellow, clever young chap he is too, and we arranged to go to a little card-party. Only for that . . ."

"O, in that case. . . ."

"But who knows?" said Ignatius Gallaher considerately. "Next year I may take a little skip over here now that I've broken the ice. It's only a pleasure deferred."

"Very well," said Little Chandler, "the next time you come we must have an evening together. That's agreed now, isn't it?"

"Yes, that's agreed," said Ignatius Gallaher. "Next year if I come, *parole d' honneur*."

"And to clinch the bargain," said Little Chandler, "we'll just have one more now."

Ignatius Gallaher took out a large gold watch and looked at it.

"Is it to be the last?" he said. "Because you know, I have an a.p."

"O, yes, positively," said Little Chandler.

"Very well, then," said Ignatius Gallaher, "let us have another one as a *deoc an doruis*—that's good vernacular for a small whisky, I believe."

Little Chandler ordered the drinks. The blush which had risen to his face a few moments before was establishing itself. A trifle made him blush at any time: and now he felt warm and excited. Three small whiskies had gone to his head and Gallaher's strong cigar had confused his mind, for he was a delicate and abstinent person. The adventure of meeting Gallaher after eight years, of finding himself with Gallaher in Corless's surrounded by lights and noise, of listening to Gallaher's stories and of sharing for a brief space Gallaher's vagrant and triumphant life, upset the equipoise of his sensitive nature. He felt acutely the contrast between his own life and his friend's, and it seemed to him unjust. Gallaher was his inferior in birth and education. He was sure that he could do something better than his friend had ever done, or could ever do, something higher than mere tawdry journalism if he only got the chance. What was it that stood in his way? His unfortunate timidity! He wished to vindicate himself in some way, to assert his manhood. He saw behind Gallaher's refusal of his invitation. Gallaher was only patronising him by his friendliness just as he was patronising Ireland by his visit.

The barman brought their drinks. Little Chandler pushed one glass towards his friend and took up the other boldly.

"Who knows?" he said, as they lifted their glasses. "When you come next year I may have the pleasure of wishing long life and happiness to Mr. and Mrs. Ignatius Gallaher."

Ignatius Gallaher in the act of drinking closed one eye expressively over the rim of his glass. When he had drunk he smacked his lips decisively, set down his glass and said:

"No blooming fear of that, my boy. I'm going to have my fling first and see a bit of life and the world before I put my head in the sack—if I ever do."

"Some day you will," said Little Chandler calmly.

Ignatius Gallaher turned his orange tie and slate-blue eyes full upon his friend.

"You think so?" he said.

"You'll put your head in the sack," repeated Little Chandler stoutly, "like everyone else if you can find the girl."

He had slightly emphasised his tone and he was aware that he had betrayed himself; but, though the colour had heightened in his cheek, he did not flinch from his friend's gaze. Ignatius Gallaher watched him for a few moments and then said:

"If ever it occurs, you may bet your bottom dollar there'll be no mooning and spooning about it. I mean to marry money. She'll have a good fat account at the bank or she won't do for me."

Little Chandler shook his head.

"Why, man alive," said Ignatius Gallaher, vehemently, "do you know what it is? I've only to say the word and to-morrow I can have the woman and the cash. You don't believe it? Well, I know it. There are hundreds—what am I saying?—thousands of rich Germans and Jews, rotten with money, that'd only be too glad. . . . You wait a while, my boy. See if I don't play my cards properly. When I go about a thing I mean business, I tell you. You just wait."

He tossed his glass to his mouth, finished his drink and laughed loudly. Then he looked thoughtfully before him and said in a calmer tone:

"But I'm in no hurry. They can wait. I don't fancy tying myself up to one woman, you know."

He imitated with his mouth the act of tasting and made a wry face.

"Must get a bit stale, I should think," he said.

.   .   .

Little Chandler sat in the room off the hall, holding a child in his arms. To save money they kept no servant but Annie's young sister Monica came for an hour or so in the morning and an hour or so in the evening to help. But Monica had gone home long ago. It was a quarter to nine. Little Chandler had come home late for tea and, moreover, he had forgotten to bring Annie home the parcel of coffee from Bewley's. Of course she was in a bad humour and gave him short answers. She said she would do without any tea but when it came near the time at which the shop at the corner closed she decided to go out herself for a quarter of a pound of tea and two pounds of sugar. She put the sleeping child deftly in his arms and said:

"Here. Don't waken him."

A little lamp with a white china shade stood upon the table and its light fell over a photograph which was enclosed in a frame of crumpled horn. It was Annie's photograph. Little Chandler looked at it, pausing at the thin tight lips. She wore the pale blue summer blouse which he had brought her home as a present one Saturday. It had cost him ten and elevenpence; but what an agony of nervousness it had cost him! How he had suffered that day, waiting at the shop door until the shop was empty, standing at the counter and trying to appear at his ease while the girl piled ladies' blouses before him, paying at the desk and forgetting to take up the odd penny of his change, being called back by the cashier, and finally, striving to hide his blushes as he left the shop by examining the parcel to see if it was securely tied. When he brought the blouse home Annie kissed him and said it was very pretty and stylish; but when she heard the price she threw the blouse on the table and said it was a regular swindle to charge ten and elevenpence for it. At first she wanted to take it back but when she tried it on she was delighted with it, especially with the make of the sleeves, and kissed him and said he was very good to think of her.

Hm! . . .

He looked coldly into the eyes of the photograph and they answered coldly. Certainly they were pretty and the face itself was pretty. But he found something mean in it. Why was it so unconscious and ladylike? The composure of the eyes irritated him. They repelled him and defied him: there was no passion in them, no rapture. He thought of what Gallaher had said about rich Jewesses. Those dark Oriental eyes, he thought, how full they are of passion, of voluptuous longing! . . . Why had he married the eyes in the photograph?

He caught himself up at the question and glanced nervously round the room. He found something mean in the pretty furniture which he had bought for his house on the hire system. Annie had chosen it herself and it reminded him of her. It too was prim and pretty. A dull resentment against his life awoke within him. Could he not escape from his little house? Was it too late for him to try to live bravely like Gallaher? Could he go to London? There was the furniture still to be paid for. If he could only write a book and get it published, that might open the way for him.

A volume of Byron's poems lay before him on the table. He opened it cautiously with his left hand lest he should waken the child and began to read the first poem in the book:

"Hushed are the winds and still the evening gloom,
Not e'en a Zephyr wanders through the grove,
Whilst I return to view my Margaret's tomb
And scatter flowers on the dust I love."

He paused. He felt the rhythm of the verse about him in the room. How melancholy it was! Could he, too, write like that, express the melancholy of his soul in verse? There were so many things he wanted to describe: his sensation of a few hours before on Grattan Bridge, for example. If he could get back again into that mood. . . .

The child awoke and began to cry. He turned from the page and tried to hush it: but it would not be hushed. He began to rock it to and fro in his arms but its wailing cry grew keener. He rocked it faster while his eyes began to read the second stanza:

"Within this narrow cell reclines her clay,
That clay where once . . ."

It was useless. He couldn't read. He couldn't do anything. The wailing of the child pierced the drum of his ear. It was useless, useless! He was a prisoner for life. His arms trembled with anger and suddenly bending to the child's face he shouted:

"Stop!"

The child stopped for an instant, had a spasm of fright and began to scream. He jumped up from his chair and walked hastily up and down the room with the child in his arms. It began to sob piteously, losing its breath for four or five seconds, and then bursting out anew. The thin walls of the room echoed the sound. He tried to soothe it but it sobbed more convulsively. He looked at the contracted and quivering face of the child and began to be alarmed. He counted seven sobs without a break between them and caught the child to his breast in fright. If it died! . . .

The door was burst open and a young woman ran in, panting.

"What is it? What is it?" she cried.

The child, hearing its mother's voice, broke out into a paroxysm of sobbing.

"It's nothing, Annie . . . it's nothing. . . . He began to cry . . ."

She flung her parcels on the floor and snatched the child from him.

"What have you done to him?" she cried, glaring into his face.

Little Chandler sustained for one moment the gaze of her eyes and his heart closed together as he met the hatred in them. He began to stammer:

"It's nothing. . . . He . . . he began to cry. . . . I couldn't . . . I didn't do anything. . . . What?"

Giving no heed to him she began to walk up and down the room, clasping the child tightly in her arms and murmuring:

"My little man! My little mannie! Was 'ou

frightened, love? . . . There now, love! There now!
. . . Lambabaun! Mamma's little lamb of the world!
. . . There now!"

Little Chandler felt his cheeks suffused with
shame and he stood back out of the lamplight. He
listened while the paroxysm of the child's sobbing
grew less and less; and tears of remorse started to his
eyes.

———◆———

VIRGINIA WOOLF

1882–1941

Virginia Woolf was born in London in 1882 and
grew up in the midst of perhaps the finest intellectual environment of the late Victorian age. Her
father, Leslie Stephen, presiding editor of the *Dictionary of National Biography* and historian of the
development of English thought in the eighteenth
century, knew most of the great English writers of
the day intimately. Virginia Woolf may have drawn
the portrait of her father in Mr. Ramsey of *To the
Lighthouse*; certainly her father's revolt from Victorian orthodox religious belief and his espousal of a
then unpopular agnosticism had a great influence
upon his daughter. With her brother, her sister
Vanessa, who married the art critic Clive Bell, and
later her husband, Leonard Woolf, whom she married in 1912, she formed the famous Bloomsbury
group which also included Roger Fry, the Sitwells,
E. M. Forster, Desmond MacCarthy, and the
economist John Maynard Keynes.

Virginia Woolf traveled widely and began her
writing career as a reviewer for the London *Times
Literary Supplement*. When she published her first
novel in 1915, *The Voyage Out,* the preceding
Edwardian generation of brilliant English novelists,
Galsworthy, Wells, and Bennett, had reached full
development and had begun to decline. The way
was prepared for a new generation of writers: James
Joyce was publishing his *Portrait of the Artist as a
Young Man* in the *Egoist*, and D. H. Lawrence had
fully launched himself on his career as a novelist.
Virginia Woolf's first novel and the second, *Night
and Day* (1919), are not important, since they
adopt the themes and structure of the conventional

Edwardian novel, but there are evidences of the
novelist-to-come in the sensitive exploration of the
meaning and significance of personality. In the following years the influence of Joyce, of Proust
(whose first volume of *Remembrance of Things
Past* had been published in 1913), and of the post-
impressionist painters made Virginia Woolf dissatisfied with the conventional plot and structure of the
novel. Her third novel, *Jacob's Room* (1922), fell
short of a successful break with tradition, although
in it she eschews plot and the usual interest in character development to speculate upon a favorite
theme, the meaning of personality and the respects
in which personality may survive after death. There
are also foreshadowings of her later novelistic devices, such as the symbolic juxtaposition of themes
without comment (the juxtaposition of the lovers
and the skull in Chapter I of *Jacob's Room*).

Roger Fry, an intimate friend, became the leading advocate of post-impressionist painting in England, and Mrs. Woolf, discontented with the realistic Edwardian novel of Bennett and Wells, sought
in her next novel to achieve especially that vivid
sense of vibrant life one discovers in the canvases
of Cézanne. As Fry remarked, "in Cézanne a continuous plastic rhythm penetrates the whole composition"; similarly in *Mrs. Dalloway* (1925) Virginia Woolf tried to create a feeling for the
continuous plastic rhythm of Mrs. Dalloway's whole
life in the twelve hours of Mrs. Dalloway's day. In
this way the novel, revealing that all Mrs. Dalloway
had done in her life before shapes her actions and
colors the thoughts of her day, recapitulates the
history of her emotions. Although this technique of
Virginia Woolf is best seen in the novels, "The
New Dress" illustrates it very well in small compass.
In this story the author has placed the inner action
of the reminiscences, the recollection of the heroine
in the foreground, and has evoked the whole history
of her diffident personality.

Virginia Woolf continued her experiments in this
new technique; like the post-impressionists in painting she sought to make the structure and form of
her novel bear the weight of meaning, without overt
comment. Both *To the Lighthouse* (1927), her
finest novel, and *The Waves* (1931) show her profound interest in the manifestations of the life force
through the medium of personality, and the essential unity of all personalities in this life force, what-

ever the diversity (symbolized by the individual waves of the sea in *The Waves*). The purely symbolic pattern of *The Waves*, however, made it difficult reading, and hence Virginia Woolf returned to the more conventional techniques with overtones of symbolism in her last novels, *The Years* (1937) and *Between the Acts* (1941). Her suicide in 1941 in the waves of a Sussex stream was a great loss to the world of modern literature, but not perhaps a complete surprise to the devoted reader of *Mrs. Dalloway*.

FURTHER READING

ANNAN, NOEL G. *Leslie Stephen* (Cambridge, Mass., 1952).

BLACKSTONE, BERNARD. *Virginia Woolf* (New York, 1949).

DAICHES, DAVID. "Virginia Woolf" in *Critiques and Essays on Modern Fiction*, edited by John W. Aldridge (New York, 1952).

DAICHES, DAVID. *Virginia Woolf* (Norfolk, Conn., 1942).

FORSTER, E. M. *Virginia Woolf* (New York, 1941).

The New Dress *

MABEL had her first serious suspicion that something was wrong as she took her cloak off and Mrs. Barnet, while handing her the mirror and touching the brushes and thus drawing her attention, perhaps rather markedly, to all the appliances for tidying and improving hair, complexion, clothes, which existed on the dressing table, confirmed the suspicion—that it was not right, not quite right, which growing stronger as she went upstairs and springing at her, with conviction as she greeted Clarissa Dalloway, she went straight to the far end of the room, to a shaded corner where a looking-glass hung and looked. No! It was not *right*. And at once the misery which she always tried to hide, the profound dissatisfaction—the sense she had had, ever since she was a child, of being inferior to other people— set upon her, relentlessly, remorselessly, with an intensity which she could not beat off, as she would when she woke at night at home, by reading Borrow or Scott; for oh these men, oh these women, all were thinking—"What's Mabel wearing? What a fright she looks! What a hideous new dress!"—their eyelids flickering as they came up and then their lids

* From *A Haunted House and Other Stories*, by Virginia Woolf. Copyright, 1944, by Harcourt, Brace and Company, Inc. By permission of Harcourt, Brace and Company, Inc., and Leonard Woolf.

shutting rather tight. It was her own appalling inadequacy; her cowardice; her mean, water-sprinkled blood that depressed her. And at once the whole of the room where, for ever so many hours, she had planned with the little dressmaker how it was to go, seemed sordid, repulsive; and her own drawing-room so shabby, and herself, going out, puffed up with vanity as she touched the letters on the hall table and said: "How dull!" to show off—all this now seemed unutterably silly, paltry, and provincial. All this had been absolutely destroyed, shown up, exploded, the moment she came into Mrs. Dalloway's drawing-room.

What she had thought that evening when, sitting over the teacups, Mrs. Dalloway's invitation came, was that, of course, she could not be fashionable. It was absurd to pretend it even—fashion meant cut, meant style, meant thirty guineas at least—but why not be original? Why not be herself, anyhow? And, getting up, she had taken that old fashion book of her mother's, a Paris fashion book of the time of the Empire, and had thought how much prettier, more dignified, and more womanly they were then, and so set herself—oh, it was foolish—trying to be like them, pluming herself in fact, upon being modest and old-fashioned and very charming, giving herself up, no doubt about it, to an orgy of self-love, which deserved to be chastised, and so rigged herself out like this.

But she dared not look in the glass. She could not face the whole horror—the pale yellow, idiotically old-fashioned silk dress with its long skirt and its high sleeves and its waist and all the things that looked so charming in the fashion book, but not on her, not among all these ordinary people. She felt like a dressmaker's dummy standing there, for young people to stick pins into.

"But, my dear, it's perfectly charming!" Rose Shaw said, looking her up and down with that little satirical pucker of the lips which she expected—Rose herself being dressed in the height of the fashion, precisely like everybody else, always.

"We are all like flies trying to crawl over the edge of the saucer," Mabel thought, and repeated the phrase as if she were crossing herself, as if she were trying to find some spell to annul this pain, to make this agony endurable. Tags of Shakespeare, lines from books she had read ages ago, suddenly came to her when she was in agony, and she repeated them over and over again. "Flies trying to crawl," she repeated. If she could say that over often enough and make herself see the flies, she would become numb, chill, frozen, dumb. Now she could see flies crawling slowly out of a saucer of milk with their wings stuck together; and she strained and strained (standing in front of the looking-glass, listening to Rose Shaw) to make herself see Rose Shaw and all the other people there as flies, trying to hoist themselves out of something, or into something, meagre, insignificant, toiling flies. But she could not see them like that, not other people. She saw herself like that—she was a fly, but the others were dragon-flies, butterflies, beautiful insects, dancing, fluttering, skimming, while she alone dragged herself up out of the saucer. (Envy and spite, the most detestable of the vices, were her chief faults.)

"I feel like some dowdy, decrepit, horribly dingy old fly," she said, making Robert Haydon stop just to hear her say that, just to reassure herself by furbishing up a poor weak-kneed phrase and so showing how detached she was, how witty, that she did not feel in the least out of anything. And, of course, Robert Haydon answered something quite polite, quite insincere, which she saw through instantly, and said to herself, directly he went (again from some book), "Lies, lies, lies!" For a party makes things either much more real, or much less real, she thought; she saw in a flash to the bottom of Robert Haydon's heart; she saw through everything. She saw the truth. *This* was true, this drawing-room, this self, and the other false. Miss Milan's little work-room was really terribly hot, stuffy, sordid. It smelt of clothes and cabbage cooking; and yet, when Miss Milan put the glass in her hand, and she looked at herself with the dress on, finished, an extraordinary bliss shot through her heart. Suffused with light, she sprang into existence. Rid of cares and wrinkles, what she had dreamed of herself was there—a beautiful woman. Just for a second (she had not dared look longer, Miss Milan wanted to know about the length of the skirt), there looked at her, framed in the scrolloping mahogany, a grey-white, mysteriously smiling, charming girl, the core of herself, the soul of herself; and it was not vanity only, not only self-love that made her think it good, tender, and true. Miss Milan said that the skirt could not well be longer; if anything the skirt, said Miss Milan, puckering her forehead, considering with all her wits about her, must be shorter; and she felt, suddenly, honestly, full of love for Miss Milan, much, much fonder of Miss Milan than of anyone in the whole world, and could have cried for pity that she should be crawling on the floor with her mouth full of pins, and her face red and her eyes bulging—that one human being should be doing this for another, and she saw them all as human

beings merely, and herself going off to her party, and Miss Milan pulling the cover over the canary's cage, or letting him pick a hemp-seed from between her lips, and the thought of it, of this side of human nature and its patience and its endurance and its being content with such miserable, scanty, sordid, little pleasures filled her eyes with tears.

And now the whole thing had vanished. The dress, the room, the love, the pity, the scrolloping looking-glass, and the canary's cage—all had vanished, and here she was in a corner of Mrs. Dalloway's drawing-room, suffering tortures, woken wide awake to reality.

But it was all so paltry, weak-blooded, and petty-minded to care so much at her age with two children, to be still so utterly dependent on people's opinions and not have principles or convictions, not to be able to say as other people did, "There's Shakespeare! There's death! We're all weevils in a captain's biscuit"—or whatever it was that people did say.

She faced herself straight in the glass; she pecked at her left shoulder; she issued out into the room, as if spears were thrown at her yellow dress from all sides. But instead of looking fierce or tragic, as Rose Shaw would have done—Rose would have looked like Boadicea—she looked foolish and self-conscious, and simpered like a schoolgirl and slouched across the room, positively slinking, as if she were a beaten mongrel, and looked at a picture, an engraving. As if one went to a party to look at a picture! Everybody knew why she did it—it was from shame, from humiliation.

"Now the fly's in the saucer," she said to herself, "right in the middle, and can't get out, and the milk," she thought, rigidly staring at the picture, "is sticking its wings together."

"It's so old-fashioned," she said to Charles Burt, making him stop (which by itself he hated) on his way to talk to someone else.

She meant, or she tried to make herself think that she meant, that it was the picture and not the dress, that was old-fashioned. And one word of praise, one word of affection from Charles would have made all the difference to her at the moment. If he had only said, "Mabel, you're looking charming tonight!" it would have changed her life. But then she ought to have been truthful and direct. Charles said nothing of the kind, of course. He was malice itself. He always saw through one, especially if one were feeling particularly mean, paltry, or feeble-minded.

"Mabel's got a new dress!" he said, and the poor

fly was absolutely shoved into the middle of the saucer. Really, he would like her to drown, she believed. He had no heart, no fundamental kindness, only a veneer of friendliness. Miss Milan was much more real, much kinder. If only one could feel that and stick to it, always. "Why," she asked herself—replying to Charles much too pertly, letting him see that she was out of temper, or "ruffled" as he called it ("Rather ruffled?" he said and went on to laugh at her with some woman over there)— "Why," she asked herself, "can't I feel one thing always, feel quite sure that Miss Milan is right, and Charles wrong and stick to it, feel sure about the canary and pity and love and not be whipped all round in a second by coming into a room full of people?" It was her odious, weak, vacillating character again, always giving at the critical moment and not being seriously interested in conchology, etymology, botany, archeology, cutting up potatoes and watching them fructify like Mary Dennis, like Violet Searle.

Then Mrs. Holman, seeing her standing there, bore down upon her. Of course a thing like a dress was beneath Mrs. Holman's notice, with her family always tumbling downstairs or having the scarlet fever. Could Mabel tell her if Elmthorpe was ever let for August and September? Oh, it was a conversation that bored her unutterably!—it made her furious to be treated like a house agent or a messenger boy, to be made use of. Not to have value, that was it, she thought, trying to grasp something hard, something real, while she tried to answer sensibly about the bathroom and the south aspect and the hot water to the top of the house; and all the time she could see little bits of her yellow dress in the round looking-glass which made them all the size of boot-buttons or tadpoles; and it was amazing to think how much humiliation and agony and self-loathing and effort and passionate ups and downs of feeling were contained in a thing the size of a three-penny bit. And what was still odder, this thing, this Mabel Waring, was separate, quite disconnected; and though Mrs. Holman (the black button) was leaning forward and telling her how her eldest boy had strained his heart running, she could see her, too, quite detached in the looking-glass, and it was impossible that the black dot, leaning forward, gesticulating, should make the yellow dot, sitting solitary, self-centred, feel what the black dot was feeling, yet they pretended.

"So impossible to keep boys quiet"—that was the kind of thing one said.

And Mrs. Holman, who could never get enough sympathy and snatched what little there was greedily, as if it were her right (but she deserved much more for there was her little girl who had come down this morning with a swollen knee-joint), took this miserable offering and looked at it suspiciously, grudgingly, as if it were a halfpenny when it ought to have been a pound and put it away in her purse, must put up with it, mean and miserly though it was, times being hard, so very hard; and on she went, creaking, injured Mrs. Holman, about the girl with the swollen joints. Ah, it was tragic, this greed, this clamour of human beings, like a row of cormorants, barking and flapping their wings for sympathy—it was tragic, could one have felt it and not merely pretended to feel it!

But in her yellow dress tonight she could not wring out one drop more; she wanted it all, all for herself. She knew (she kept on looking into the glass, dipping into that dreadfully showing-up blue pool) that she was condemned, despised, left like this in a backwater, because of her being like this a feeble, vacillating creature; and it seemed to her that the yellow dress was a penance which she had deserved, and if she had been dressed like Rose Shaw, in lovely, clinging green with a ruffle of swansdown, she would have deserved that; and she thought that there was no escape for her—none whatever. But it was not her fault altogether, after all. It was being one of a family of ten; never having money enough, always skimping and paring; and her mother carrying great cans, and the linoleum worn on the stair edges, and one sordid little domestic tragedy after another—nothing catastrophic, the sheep farm failing, but not utterly; her eldest brother marrying beneath him but not very much—there was no romance, nothing extreme about them all. They petered out respectably in seaside resorts; every watering-place had one of her aunts even now asleep in some lodging with the front windows not quite facing the sea. That was so like them—they had to squint at things always. And she had done the same—she was just like her aunts. For all her dreams of living in India, married to some hero like Sir Henry Lawrence, some empire builder (still the sight of a native in a turban filled her with romance), she had failed utterly. She had married Hubert, with his safe, permanent underling's job in the Law Courts, and they managed tolerably in a smallish house, without proper maids, and hash when she was alone or just bread and butter, but now and then—Mrs. Holman was off, thinking her the most dried-up, unsympathetic twig she had ever met, absurdly dressed, too, and would tell everyone about Mabel's fantastic appearance—now and then, thought Mabel Waring, left alone on the blue sofa, punching the cushion in order to look occupied, for she would not join Charles Burt and Rose Shaw, chattering like magpies and perhaps laughing at her by the fireplace—now and then, there did come to her delicious moments, reading the other night in bed, for instance, or down by the sea on the sand in the sun, at Easter—let her recall it—a great tuft of pale sand-grass standing all twisted like a shock of spears against the sky, which was blue like a smooth china egg, so firm, so hard, and then the melody of the waves—"Hush, hush," they said, and the children's shouts paddling—yes, it was a divine moment, and there she lay, she felt, in the hand of the Goddess who was the world; rather a hard-hearted, but very beautiful Goddess, a little lamb laid on the altar (one did think these silly things, and it didn't matter so long as one never said them). And also with Hubert sometimes she had quite unexpectedly—carving the mutton for Sunday lunch, for no reason, opening a letter, coming into a room—divine moments, when she said to herself (for she would never say this to anybody else), "This is it. This has happened. This is it!" And the other way about it was equally surprising—that is, when everything was arranged—music, weather, holidays, every reason for happiness was there—then nothing happened at all. One wasn't happy. It was flat, just flat, that was all.

Her wretched self again, no doubt! She had always been a fretful, weak, unsatisfactory mother, a wobbly wife, lolling about in a kind of twilight existence with nothing very clear or very bold, or more one thing than another, like all her brothers and sisters, except perhaps Herbert—they were all the same poor water-veined creatures who did nothing. Then in the midst of this creeping, crawling life, suddenly she was on the crest of a wave. That wretched fly—where had she read the story that kept coming into her mind about the fly and the saucer?

—struggled out. Yes, she had those moments. But now that she was forty, they might come more and more seldom. By degrees she would cease to struggle any more. But that was deplorable! That was not to be endured! That made her feel ashamed of herself!

She would go to the London Library tomorrow. She would find some wonderful, helpful, astonishing book, quite by chance, a book by a clergyman, by an American no one had ever heard of; or she would walk down the Strand and drop, accidentally, into a hall where a miner was telling about the life in the pit, and suddenly she would become a new person. She would be absolutely transformed. She would wear a uniform; she would be called Sister Somebody; she would never give a thought to clothes again. And forever after she would be perfectly clear about Charles Burt and Miss Milan and this room and that room; and it would be always, day after day, as if she were lying in the sun or carving the mutton. It would be it!

So she got up from the blue sofa, and the yellow button in the looking-glass got up too, and she waved her hand to Charles and Rose to show them she did not depend on them one scrap, and the yellow button moved out of the looking-glass, and all the spears were gathered into her breast as she walked towards Mrs. Dalloway and said, "Good night."

"But it's too early to go," said Mrs. Dalloway, who was always so charming.

"I'm afraid I must," said Mabel Waring. "But," she added in her weak, wobbly voice which only sounded ridiculous when she tried to strengthen it, "I have enjoyed myself enormously."

"I have enjoyed myself," she said to Mr. Dalloway, whom she met on the stairs.

"Lies, lies, lies!" she said to herself, going downstairs, and "Right in the saucer!" she said to herself as she thanked Mrs. Barnet for helping her and wrapped herself, round and round and round, in the Chinese cloak she had worn these twenty years.

English Lyric Poetry

A. E. HOUSMAN

1859–1936

There has been perhaps no single book of poetry, unless it be the *Rubáiyát of Omar Khayyám*, that has been more popular than *The Shropshire Lad* (1896) during the last fifty years. Yet on first consideration it is difficult to account for this popularity. The poems are pessimistic: they bewail the brevity of life, the mutual betrayal of lovers, the treachery even of comrades, the transitoriness of fame, the certainty of the survival only of that immortal part, the skeleton, and the eternal dark and hopeless night of the grave, possibly even a desirable refuge from the pain of life. Not all of Housman's poems are so lugubrious, as the reader of the earlier lyrics in *The Shropshire Lad* knows, but the mood is pervasive throughout the first volume and the subsequent ones, *Last Poems* (1922) and *More Poems* (1936).

The personality of Housman offers no clue to the autobiographical background of his poetry. From the time he became in 1911 Professor of Latin at Cambridge after a profoundly disillusioning (though obscure) young manhood, he lived in scholarly seclusion, often inscrutable and inaccessible even to his friends. Possibly the secret of Housman's popularity as a poet in spite of his themes is the admirably chiseled art, the exquisite tact and elegance of his craftsmanship, together with the feeling in the reader that his pessimism is a moral tonic which teaches us to endure stoically the ills of a world we never made—we, like Mithridates, may die old from taking continual doses of the Housman "poison." One may drink his beer, but not cry in it—rather must he "shoulder the sky." Then too, there is a romantic nostalgia in Housman, a pastoral yearning for a mythical Shropshire of lost ideals that imparts a feeling of the Vergilian *"sunt lacrimae rerum."* He remains perhaps a minor poet, but one who memorably reflects the malady of the nineteenth century, the *"mal du siècle"* which carries over into the twentieth.

FURTHER READING

Gow, A. S. F. *A. E. Housman* (New York, 1936).
Housman, Laurence. *My Brother, A. E. Housman* (New York, 1938).
Richards, Grant. *Housman, 1897–1936* (New York, 1942).

With Rue My Heart Is Laden *

With rue my heart is laden
    For golden friends I had,
For many a rose-lipt maiden
    And many a lightfoot lad.

By brooks too broad for leaping
    The lightfoot boys are laid;
The rose-lipt girls are sleeping
    In fields where roses fade.

To an Athlete Dying Young

The time you won your town the race
We chaired you through the market-place;
Man and boy stood cheering by,
And home we brought you shoulder-high.

Today, the road all runners come,
Shoulder-high we bring you home,
And set you at your threshold down,
Townsman of a stiller town.

Smart lad, to slip betimes away
From fields where glory does not stay,
And early though the laurel grows
It withers quicker than the rose.

Eyes the shady night has shut
Cannot see the record cut,
And silence sounds no worse than cheers
After earth has stopped the ears:

Now you will not swell the rout
Of lads that wore their honors out,
Runners whom renown outran
And the name died before the man.

* Poems of A. E. Housman are by permission of The Society of Authors as the literary representative of the Trustees of the Estate of A. E. Housman and Jonathan Cape, Ltd., publishers.

So set, before its echoes fade,
The fleet foot on the sill of shade,
And hold to the low lintel up
The still-defended challenge-cup.

And round that early-laureled head
Will flock to gaze the strengthless dead,
And find unwithered on its curls
The garland briefer than a girl's.

Loveliest of Trees

Loveliest of trees, the cherry now
Is hung with bloom along the bough,
And stands about the woodland ride
Wearing white for Eastertide.

Now, of my threescore years and ten,
Twenty will not come again,
And take from seventy springs a score,
It only leaves me fifty more.

And since to look at things in bloom
Fifty springs are little room,
About the woodlands I will go
To see the cherry hung with snow.

Farewell to Barn and Stack and Tree

"Farewell to barn and stack and tree,
  Farewell to Severn shore.
Terence, look your last at me,
  For I come home no more.

"The sun burns on the half-mown hill,
  By now the blood is dried;
And Maurice amongst the hay lies still
  And my knife is in his side.

"My mother thinks us long away;
  'Tis time the field were mown.
She had two sons at rising day,
  To-night she'll be alone.

"And here's a bloody hand to shake,
  And oh, man, here's good-bye;
We'll sweat no more on scythe and rake,
  My bloody hands and I.

"I wish you strength to bring you pride,
  And a love to keep you clean,
And I wish you luck, come Lammastide,
  At racing on the green.

"Long for me the rick will wait,
  And long will wait the fold,
And long will stand the empty plate,
  And dinner will be cold."

Be Still, My Soul, Be Still

Be still, my soul, be still; the arms you bear are
    brittle,
  Earth and high heaven are fixt of old and
    founded strong.
Think rather,—call to thought, if now you grieve a
    little,
  The days when we had rest, O soul, for they were
    long.

Men loved unkindness then, but lightless in the
    quarry
  I slept and saw not; tears fell down, I did not
    mourn;
Sweat ran and blood sprang out and I was never
    sorry:
  Then it was well with me, in days ere I was born.

Now, and I muse for why and never find the
    reason,
  I pace the earth, and drink the air, and feel the
    sun.
Be still, be still, my soul; it is but for a season:
  Let us endure an hour and see injustice done.

Ay, look: high heaven and earth ail from the prime
    foundation;
  All thoughts to rive the heart are here, and all are
    vain:
Horror and scorn and hate and fear and indigna-
    tion—
  Oh, why did I awake? When shall I sleep again?

The Laws of God, the Laws of Man

The laws of God, the laws of man,
He may keep that will and can;
Not I: let God and man decree
Laws for themselves and not for me;
And if my ways are not as theirs
Let them mind their own affairs.
Their deed I judge and much condemn,
Yet when did I make laws for them?
Please yourselves, say I, and they
Need only look the other way.
But no, they will not; they must still

Wrest their neighbour to their will,
And make me dance as they desire
With jail and gallows and hell-fire.
And how am I to face the odds
Of man's bedevilment and God's?
I, a stranger and afraid
In a world I never made.
They will be master, right or wrong;
Though both are foolish, both are strong.
And since, my soul, we cannot fly
To Saturn nor to Mercury,
Keep we must, if keep we can,
These foreign laws of God and man.

WILLIAM BUTLER YEATS

1865–1939

A few years before the death of William Butler Yeats in 1939, the New York *Times* undertook to select the three most distinguished living men of letters: it named Bernard Shaw, Thomas Mann, and William Butler Yeats. It is not easy to rank Yeats in a lower category. Not only was he mainly instrumental with Lady Augusta Gregory and J. M. Synge in the founding of the Irish Literary Theater in Dublin and promoting the Irish literary renaissance at the beginning of the twentieth century, but he is the most striking modern illustration of a poet who refused to rest in the poetic ideals of his youth, who rather insisted upon his own continually enriched development as a poet to more mature visions—always the test of a great poet, if we may adduce Sophocles, Milton, and Goethe as evidence.

Yeats's hatred of the nineteenth-century scientific materialism, which seemed to spring from the researches of Darwin, Huxley, and Tyndall, was the mainspring of his early poetry and his philosophic attitude generally throughout life. The son of John B. Yeats the artist, William Butler Yeats had been born in Sandymount, Ireland, June 13, 1865. His first poems, romantic and escapist in tone, were published in the *Dublin Review* of 1886. Those in his first serious volume of verse, *The Wanderings of Oisin* (1889), celebrated Irish legends and Celtic landscape. Since his childhood had been spent in the somewhat primitive and romantic county of Sligo, Yeats's early poems revealed that Sligo was the home of his imagination. His most famous and early poem, "The Lake Isle of Innisfree," is a nostalgic yearning for his boyhood dreams in the isle of Lough Gill, in Sligo, near the home of his uncle George Pollexfen. His novelette *John Sherman* (1893) reflects the same attachment to Sligo and Lough Gill. As he turned his youthful energies to poetry, in his reaction against the scientific spirit of the time Yeats was drawn into a fashionable *fin de siècle* aestheticism which we sometimes define as his "Celtic dreaming," his mythologizing of the heroes of Celtic antiquity. The typical aesthetic hostility to the Church and to the middle class was revealed in *The Countess Cathleen* (1892). Yet even in the late 1890's Yeats's attitude toward bourgeois standards was not merely the aesthetic bohemianism of Wilde and Ernest Dowson; to this adherence he added his interest in Irish nationalism and in occultism.

As early as 1886 he had read A. P. Sinnett's *Esoteric Buddhism* and had taken an interest in theosophy and spiritualism. In March, 1890, he joined the occult society of the Hermetic Students of the Golden Dawn, and became more and more interested in attempts to invoke the unseen, mysterious powers of the universe by the use of certain symbols (like the rose) which would be a mystic means of achieving communication with the infinite. Consequently his interest in the contemporary French symbolist movement was avid, and he learned about it from Arthur Symons. To Yeats in his reaction against the material world, that world was chiefly useful as a means of bringing the poet in contact with symbols which had supernatural, spiritual significances. His early poems hence have mysterious, wavering rhythms and occult symbols which Yeats at the time felt would enrich his poetry. From the more modern point of view, these are the least interesting of his poems.

Yeats's involvements in the Irish theater and the Irish political movements rescued him from this dim, remote refuge from reality in a Celtic twilight. He recognized the brute vitality of the Irish peasant; and by the time he wrote his memoirs, *Reveries Over Childhood and Youth* (1915), he had discovered a kind of poetry which eschewed romantic rhetoric and stated his emotions with vigorous exactitude. His poetry was no longer wrapped in nostalgic yearning, vague regret, or frustrated love for Maud Gonne. He now admires (as did the early Joyce) the passionate political symbols of a resurgent Ireland: the proud Parnell, the Fenian movement, the revolutionary man of action such as John O'Leary. Passion and energy and ecstasy must now be the product of bitterness and violence, of intense participation in the crises of one's personal life and of a nation. The Irish, he concluded, were not the traditional sentimental dreamers who reacted against the tyranny of fact by retiring into the Celtic twilight; they were hard-bitten, violent, stubborn realists.

In 1917 Yeats had his revelation as a *voyant*, a poet seer: the disembodied spirits of the universe dictated the symbols he would henceforth use in his poetry, as he describes them in *A Vision* (1925). The period that followed, and was illustrated in three of his finest volumes of poetry, was the "Tower" period (after his new home, the Tower of Ballylee), a poetic achievement of cold disciplined art, classical, yet taut with a suppressed passion which suggests the third period of Beethoven. He began to ponder the relation of the passing of youth to old age, and remarked that "Sex and the dead are the only things that can interest a serious mind." Out of such reflections grew "Sailing to Byzantium" and later "Dialogue Between Self and Soul." Under the influence of Lady Gregory, Yeats was drawn more toward the aristocratic Irish tradition of Jonathan Swift, Edmund Burke, and Bishop Berkeley; he came more and more to admire the Irish tradition of aristocracy represented by Lady Gregory and her home at Coole (see "A Prayer for my Daughter"). Though he became a senator of the Irish Free State, Yeats in the 1930's intensely regretted the dominance in Ireland of the bourgeoisie and the repressive gag of censorship which descended on the Irish state. He came also to believe in a personal theory of the cyclic rise and decline of civilizations not unlike that of Spengler.

But the permanent Yeats does not lie in the obscure meaning and symbolism of his *Vision*; rather Yeats is to us significant because he was a poet who began by taking refuge from reality, and ended by meeting it on its own terms, with an inner dynamism of inspiration that kept him ever moving forward, extracting from each crisis a mastery of himself in which he was never content merely to rest. At every age from twenty to sixty-seven he was pushing on to look at life and reality under a new focus. Living in a society in which religious belief and credence in any kind of pragmatically useful myth was no longer possible, Yeats became a sterling example of the poet who constantly struggled to bring order and coherence out of an intractable world that was constantly in the process of becoming, of changing. That is one of the reasons for the admiration expressed by W. H. Auden in "In Memory of William Butler Yeats." It may be Yeats' chief claim to poetic permanence.

FURTHER READING

BLACKMUR, R. P. "The Later Poetry of W. B. Yeats" in *Critiques and Essays in Criticism, 1920–1948*, edited by R. W. Stallman (New York, 1949).

ELLMAN, RICHARD. *Yeats, The Man and Masks* (New York, 1948).

JEFFARES, NORMAN A. *W. B. Yeats, Man and Poet* (New Haven, 1950).

STAUFFER, D. A. *The Golden Nightingale* (New York, 1949).

The Lake Isle of Innisfree *

I will arise and go now, and go to Innisfree,
And a small cabin build there, of clay and wattles made;
Nine bean rows will I have there, a hive for the honey bee,
    And live alone in the bee-loud glade.

And I shall have some peace there, for peace comes dropping slow,
Dropping from the veils of the morning to where the cricket sings;
There midnight's all a glimmer, and noon a purple glow,
    And evening full of the linnet's wings.

I will arise and go now, for always night and day
I hear lake water lapping with low sounds by the shore;
While I stand on the roadway, or on the pavements gray,
    I hear it in the deep heart's core.

* The poems by William Butler Yeats are by permission of Mrs. Yeats, The Macmillan Company, and The Macmillan Company of Canada, Ltd.

The Wild Swans at Coole

The trees are in their autumn beauty,
The woodland paths are dry,
Under the October twilight the water
Mirrors a still sky;
Upon the brimming water among the stones
Are nine and fifty swans.

The nineteenth Autumn has come upon me
Since I first made my count;
I saw, before I had well finished,
All suddenly mount
And scatter, wheeling, in great broken rings
Upon their clamorous wings.

I have looked upon those brilliant creatures,
And now my heart is sore.
All's changed since I, hearing at twilight,
The first time on this shore,
The bell-beat of their wings above my head,
Trod with a lighter tread.

Unwearied still, lover by lover,
They paddle in the cold,
Companionable streams or climb the air;
Their hearts have not grown old;
Passion or conquest, wander where they will,
Attend upon them still.

But now they drift on the still water
Mysterious, beautiful;
Among what rushes will they build,
By what lake's edge or pool
Delight men's eyes, when I awake some day
To find they have flown away?

A Prayer for My Daughter

Once more the storm is howling, and half hid
Under this cradle-hood and coverlid
My child sleeps on. There is no obstacle
But Gregory's wood and one bare hill
Whereby the hay-stack- and roof-levelling wind,
Bred on the Atlantic, can be stayed;
And for an hour I have walked and prayed
Because of the great gloom that is in my mind.

I have walked and prayed for this young child an
     hour
And heard the sea-wind scream upon the tower,   10
And under the arches of the bridge, and scream
In the elms above the flooded stream;
Imagining in excited reverie
That the future years had come,
Dancing to a frenzied drum,
Out of the murderous innocence of the sea.

May she be granted beauty and yet not
Beauty to make a stranger's eye distraught,
Or hers before a looking-glass, for such,
Being made beautiful overmuch,   20
Consider beauty a sufficient end,
Lose natural kindness and maybe
The heart-revealing intimacy
That chooses right, and never find a friend.

Helen being chosen found life flat and dull
And later had much trouble from a fool,
While that great Queen, that rose out of the spray,
Being fatherless could have her way
Yet chose a bandy-leggèd smith for man.
It's certain that fine women eat   30
A crazy salad with their meat
Whereby the Horn of Plenty is undone.

In courtesy I'd have her chiefly learned;
Hearts are not had as a gift but hearts are earned
By those that are not entirely beautiful;
Yet many, that have played the fool
For beauty's very self, has charm made wise,
And many a poor man that has roved,
Loved and thought himself beloved,
From a glad kindness cannot take his eyes.   40

May she become a flourishing hidden tree
That all her thoughts may like the linnet be,
And have no business but dispensing round
Their magnanimities of sound,
Nor but in merriment begin a chase,
Nor but in merriment a quarrel.
O may she live like some green laurel
Rooted in one dear perpetual place.

My mind, because the minds that I have loved,
The sort of beauty that I have approved,   50
Prosper but little, has dried up of late,
Yet knows that to be choked with hate
May well be of all evil chances chief.
If there's no hatred in a mind
Assault and battery of the wind
Can never tear the linnet from the leaf.

An intellectual hatred is the worst,
So let her think opinions are accursed.
Have I not seen the loveliest woman born
Out of the mouth of Plenty's horn,   60
Because of her opinionated mind
Barter that horn and every good
By quiet natures understood
For an old bellows full of angry wind?

Considering that, all hatred driven hence,
The soul recovers radical innocence
And learns at last that it is self-delighting,
Self-appeasing, self-affrighting,
And that its own sweet will is Heaven's will;
She can, though every face should scowl   70
And every windy quarter howl
Or every bellows burst, be happy still.

And may her bridegroom bring her to a house
Where all's accustomed, ceremonious;
For arrogance and hatred are the wares
Peddled in the thoroughfares.
How but in custom and in ceremony
Are innocence and beauty born?
Ceremony's a name for the rich horn,
And custom for the spreading laurel tree.   80

Sailing to Byzantium

I

That is no country for old men. The young
In one another's arms, birds in the trees,
—Those dying generations—at their song,
The salmon-falls, the mackerel-crowded seas,
Fish, flesh, or fowl, commend all summer long
Whatever is begotten, born, and dies.
Caught in that sensual music all neglect
Monuments of unaging intellect.

II

An aged man is but a paltry thing,
A tattered coat upon a stick, unless
Soul clap its hands and sing, and louder sing
For every tatter in its mortal dress,
Nor is there singing school but studying
Monuments of its own magnificence;
And therefore I have sailed the seas and come
To the holy city of Byzantium.

III

O sages standing in God's holy fire
As in the gold mosaic of a wall,
Come from the holy fire, perne [1] in a gyre,
And be the singing-masters of my soul.
Consume my heart away; sick with desire
And fastened to a dying animal
It knows not what it is; and gather me
Into the artifice of eternity.

[1] Perne: to whirl, movement associated in folklore with the return of the dead.

IV

Once out of nature I shall never take
My bodily form from any natural thing,
But such a form as Grecian goldsmiths make
Of hammered gold and gold enameling
To keep a drowsy Emperor awake;
Or set upon a golden bough to sing
To lords and ladies of Byzantium
Of what is past, or passing, or to come.

A Dialogue of Self and Soul

I

MY SOUL. I summon to the winding ancient stair;
Set all your mind upon the steep ascent,
Upon the broken, crumbling battlement,
Upon the breathless starlit air,
Upon the star that marks the hidden pole;
Fix every wandering thought upon
That quarter where all thought is done:
Who can distinguish darkness from the soul?

MY SELF. The consecrated blade [1] upon my knees
Is Sato's ancient blade, still as it was,   10
Still razor-keen, still like a looking-glass
Unspotted by the centuries;
That flowering, silken, old embroidery, torn
From some court-lady's dress and round
The wooden scabbard bound and wound,
Can, tattered, still protect, faded adorn.

MY SOUL. Why should the imagination of a man
Long past his prime remember things that are
Emblematical of love and war?
Think of ancestral night that can,   20
If but imagination scorn the earth
And intellect its wandering
To this and that and t'other thing,
Deliver from the crime of death and birth.

MY SELF. Montashigi, third of his family, fashioned
      it
Five hundred years ago, about it lie
Flowers from I know not what embroidery—
Heart's purple—and all these I set
For emblems of the day against the tower
Emblematical of the night,   30
And claim as by a soldier's right
A charter to commit the crime once more.

[1] The Japanese sword and the embroidery symbolize the active, vital life on this earth (war and love). The dialogue concerns the desirability of Yeats's reincarnation.

MY SOUL. Such fullness in that quarter overflows
  And falls into the basin of the mind
  That man is stricken deaf and dumb and blind,
  For intellect no longer knows
  Is from the *Ought*, or *Knower* from the *Known*—
  That is to say, ascends to Heaven;
  Only the dead can be forgiven;
  But when I think of that my tongue's a stone.   40

II

MY SELF. A living man is blind and drinks his drop.
  What matter if the ditches are impure?
  What matter if I live it all once more?
  Endure that toil of growing up;
  The ignominy of boyhood; the distress
  Of boyhood changing into man;
  The unfinished man and his pain
  Brought face to face with his own clumsiness;

  The finished man among his enemies?—
  How in the name of Heaven can he escape
  That defiling and disfigured shape
  The mirror of malicious eyes
  Casts upon his eyes until at last
  He thinks that shape must be his shape?
  And what's the good of an escape
  If honour find him in the wintry blast?

  I am content to live it all again
  And yet again, if it be life to pitch
  Into the frog-spawn of a blind man's ditch,
  A blind man battering blind men;   60
  Or into that most fecund ditch of all,
  The folly that man does
  Or must suffer, if he woos
  A proud woman not kindred of his soul.

  I am content to follow to its source,
  Every event in action or in thought;
  Measure the lot; forgive myself the lot!
  When such as I cast out remorse
  So great a sweetness flows into the breast
  We must laugh and we must sing,   70
  We are blest by everything,
  Everything we look upon is blest.

For Anne Gregory

"Never shall a young man,
Thrown into despair
By those great honey-colored
Ramparts at your ear,
Love you for yourself alone
And not your yellow hair."

"But I can get a hair-dye
And set such color there,
Brown, or black, or carrot,
That young men in despair
May love me for myself alone
And not my yellow hair."

"I heard an old religious man
But yesternight declare
That he had found a text to prove
That only God, my dear,
Could love you for yourself alone
And not your yellow hair."

———◆———

W. H. AUDEN

1907–

Wystan Hugh Auden, now an American citizen, was born in York, England, and educated at Christ's Church, Oxford. After teaching school for some years he published his *Poems* in 1930. At first committed to the radical political left in the England which had seemed in the depression to have reached the end of a way of life and a country house tradition, Auden moved gradually to a concern for the problems of modern spiritual estrangement (as in his poetic oratorio, *For the Time Being*, 1944). His poetry has always been an "engaged" poetry, but he has come to be less and less concerned with the strictly Marxist interpretation of society and more and more catholic in his interest in varying attitudes to the modern world; his poems to Freud, Henry James, Yeats, and Voltaire reveal this development clearly. His rather stern exclusion from the *Collected Poems* (1945) of the poems in which his vision failed him suggests a poet who is resolved to grow and mature steadily in the direction of new spiritual values. Auden is perhaps the finest virtuoso writing verse today, secure in his command of a complex variety of verse forms. Without sacrificing the wit and flexibility of this poetry, he has progressed in a period of twenty years from Marxist collectivism to a complete religious conversion to Christianity. In this way he has moved ever closer to the other most influential poet of his time, T. S. Eliot.

FURTHER READING

AUDEN, W. H. *The Enchafèd Flood* (New York, 1950).
HOGGART, RICHARD. *Auden* (London, 1951).
SCHWARTZ, DELMORE. "The Two Audens," *The Kenyon Review,* I (Winter, 1939), 43 ff.
SPEARS, MONROE K. "The Dominant Symbols of Auden's Poetry," *Sewanee Review,* LIX (Summer, 1951), 391–425.

Musée des Beaux Arts *

About suffering they were never wrong,
The Old Masters: how well they understood
Its human position; how it takes place
While someone else is eating or opening a window
    or just walking dully along;
How, when the aged are reverently, passionately
    waiting
For the miraculous birth, there always must be
Children who did not specially want it to happen,
    skating
On a pond at the edge of the wood:
They never forgot
That even the dreadful martyrdom must run its
    course
Anyhow in a corner, some untidy spot
Where the dogs go on with their doggy life and the
    torturer's horse
Scratches its innocent behind on a tree.

In Brueghel's *Icarus,* for instance: how everything
    turns away
Quite leisurely from the disaster; the ploughman
    may
Have heard the splash, the forsaken cry,
But for him it was not an important failure; the sun
    shone
As it had to on the white legs disappearing into the
    green
Water; and the expensive delicate ship that must
    have seen
Something amazing, a boy falling out of the sky,
Had somewhere to get to and sailed calmly on.

In Memory of W. B. Yeats

I

He disappeared in the dead of winter:
The brooks were frozen, the air-ports almost deserted,

And snow disfigured the public statues;
The mercury sank in the mouth of the dying day.
O all the instruments agree
The day of his death was a dark cold day.

Far from his illness
The wolves ran on through the evergreen forests,
The peasant river was untempted by the fashionable
    quays;
By mourning tongues   10
The death of the poet was kept from his poems.

But for him it was his last afternoon as himself,
An afternoon of nurses and rumours;
The provinces of his body revolted,
The squares of his mind were empty,
Silence invaded the suburbs,
The current of his feeling failed: he became his
    admirers.

Now he is scattered among a hundred cities
And wholly given over to unfamiliar affections;
To find his happiness in another kind of wood   20
And be punished under a foreign code of conscience.
The words of a dead man
Are modified in the guts of the living.
But in the importance and noise of to-morrow
When the brokers are roaring like beasts on the
    floor of the Bourse,
And the poor have the sufferings to which they are
    fairly accustomed,
And each in the cell of himself is almost convinced
    of his freedom;
A few thousand will think of this day
As one thinks of a day when one did something
    slightly unusual.

O all the instruments agree   30
The day of his death was a dark cold day.

II

You were silly like us: your gift survived it all;
The parish of rich women, physical decay,
Yourself; mad Ireland hurt you into poetry.
Now Ireland has her madness and her weather still,
For poetry makes nothing happen: it survives
In the valley of its saying where executives
Would never want to tamper; it flows south
From ranches of isolation and the busy griefs,
Raw towns that we believe and die in; it survives, 40
A way of happening, a mouth.

III

Earth, receive an honoured guest;
William Yeats is laid to rest:
Let the Irish vessel lie
Emptied of its poetry.

Time that is intolerant
Of the brave and innocent,
And indifferent in a week
To a beautiful physique,

Worships language and forgives   50
Everyone by whom it lives;
Pardons cowardice, conceit,
Lays its honours at their feet.

Time that with this strange excuse
Pardoned Kipling and his views,
And will pardon Paul Claudel,
Pardons him for writing well.

In the nightmare of the dark
All the dogs of Europe bark,

And the living nations wait,   60
Each sequestered in its hate;

Intellectual disgrace
Stares from every human face,
And the seas of pity lie
Locked and frozen in each eye.

Follow, poet, follow right
To the bottom of the night,
With your unconstraining voice
Still persuade us to rejoice;

With the farming of a verse   70
Make a vineyard of the curse,
Sing of human unsuccess
In a rapture of distress;

In the deserts of the heart
Let the healing fountain start,
In the prison of his days
Teach the free man how to praise.

American Fiction

ERNEST HEMINGWAY

1898–

Although America has been unusually fortunate in possessing so brilliant a generation of novelists as those born near the turn into the twentieth century (John Dos Passos, William Faulkner, F. S. Fitzgerald, Thomas Wolfe), no other writer has had an influence comparable to Ernest Hemingway's upon contemporary literature. All the devices of the famous Hemingway style have been widely imitated—its understatement, deliberate simplification of syntax and sentence structure, its disarming candor, its conscious use of the clichés of feeling that in Hemingway at least are inexplicably transformed into a kind of "fifth dimensional prose" resonant of implication. The clarity, the limpidity, and avoidance of "faking" literary effects made this style seem in the nineteen-twenties just the right medium for Hemingway as the spokesman of the "lost genera-

tion" (in the words of Gertrude Stein). This was the generation which had emerged from the first World War disillusioned with all that the preceding Victorian and Edwardian Ages had admired and idealized, even to the rejection of a cultivated literary style of evident sophistication and artful design.

Ernest Hemingway was born in Oak Park, Illinois, in 1898. After holding numerous miscellaneous jobs, he became a reporter on the Kansas City *Star*. In the first World War he volunteered with an American ambulance unit, and later joined the Italian Arditi, was wounded in Italy, and awarded the *Croce di Guerra*. After the war Hemingway went to Paris as a correspondent for the Hearst newspapers, and there knew Lincoln Steffens, Sherwood Anderson, and Gertrude Stein, who encouraged him to write.

His first important publication was a collection of short stories, *In Our Time* (1925: expanded from the earlier Parisian collection of that title of 1924), the subject matter of which disclosed what were to become two of Hemingway's dominant interests in fiction, war and bullfighting. A number of these stories are obviously autobiographical in their presentation of the experiences of the boy, Nick Adams, and his "initiation" into the violence and evil of the world. *Torrents of Spring* (1926), a literary satire, was followed by the first of his major novels, *The Sun Also Rises* (1926). With an uncanny perception of the mood of his own generation, Hemingway expresses therein the *Zeitgeist*, the time-spirit of Americans expatriated in Paris who had emerged from the war disillusioned, cynical, world-weary, content to live passively from day to day in heroic dissipation and in gallant, heartbreaking, promiscuous love affairs. This mood of romantic pessimism had been anticipated in John Dos Passos' *Three Soldiers* (1921) and in E. E. Cummings' *The Enormous Room* (1922), but both *The Sun Also Rises* and the subsequent *A Farewell to Arms* (1929) seem to embody most memorably the postwar nihilistic mood which found expression in flight to the Parisian Left Bank and to alcoholic solace in the *cafés* of the Montmartre. These novels became the *vade mecums* of all the bewildered and rootless young people, even of those who came of age only in the middle nineteen-twenties.

The origins of this generation's disenchantment are demonstrated in *A Farewell to Arms*, still probably Hemingway's best novel. Despite its saturation with a consciously cultivated nihilism, however, this novel suggests even more evidently than *The Sun Also Rises* the author's admiration for the individual's compliance with his own personal discipline and code of conduct as a substitution for the rejected conventional moral and religious values. Certain characters of Hemingway who have been described as "initiates" (often bullfighters or prizefighters) possess a sensitivity to this personal code and a dogged fidelity in its observance which partially redeem the individual's existence from complete, fatalistic resignation to *nada*, "nothingness." The love affair of Catherine Barkley and Lieutenant Henry in *A Farewell to Arms* begins as a casual, sensual war flirtation and deepens into a profound love which Hemingway deliberately associates with religion to imply the sacred bond between the lovers.

Hemingway's abiding interest in the more "primitive" virtues of man is disclosed once again in *Death in the Afternoon* (1932), regarded even in Spain as possibly the best account of the formal aesthetic conception of bullfighting as an art. To some critics it also embodied one of the more questionably primitive of Hemingway's ideas, that any action is moral after which the participant "feels good." *To Have and Have Not* (1939) added nothing to his reputation as a novelist, but it helped perpetuate the impression that the Hemingway world was a violent, tough, ruthless one in which the inhabitants found only purely physical pleasures in hard drinking and sexual promiscuity. From this novel, and from *The Sun Also Rises,* is often derived the so-called "school of hard-boiled realism." To conceive Hemingway as a naturalist in the nineteenth-century sense is, however, to do him great injustice; and this conception has given way to a sounder recognition of the poetic values residing in his style, and to his use of a discreet symbolism (the high mountains in *A Farewell to Arms* and in "The Snows of Kilimanjaro," for example).

When *For Whom the Bell Tolls* was published in 1940 it became one of the biggest publishing successes of the decade. In his narrative of the death of Robert Jordan fighting for Republican Spain, the novel was hailed as at last a revelation that Hemingway had grown, had developed a social conscience. His recent novel, *Across the River and Into the Trees* (1950), has had such a mixed critical reception that Hemingway's most devoted readers still await the major achievement of his distinguished writing career.

"In Another Country" is not only an excellent illustration of the Hemingway style (the opening suggests *A Farewell to Arms*), but it exemplifies as well the Hemingway hero who typically does not believe in deceitful abstract words like "bravery" but only in knowing simple facts like grammar, in much the same way that Lieutenant Henry cared only for concrete names of towns and rivers, not meaningless words like "glory." The title implies, of course, the deracinated aspects of the characters cut off from their former lives by the war, but it suggests as well the major's code as an initiate which separates him from the others. Here, as in the reference to the high mountains in *A Farewell to Arms,* "Another Country" becomes a symbol for the "clean, well-lighted place" one must strive to create for himself by personal discipline, lest he yield wholly to the fatalism and despair engulfing his war generation.

FURTHER READING

ALDRIDGE, JOHN W. *After the Lost Generation* (New York, 1951).
McCAFFERY, JOHN K. *Ernest Hemingway, the Man and His Work* (Cleveland, 1950).
WARREN, ROBERT PENN. "Ernest Hemingway," in *Critiques and Essays on Modern Fiction, 1920–1951*, edited by John W. Aldridge (New York, 1952).

In Another Country *

IN THE fall the war was always there, but we did not go to it any more. It was cold in the fall in Milan and the dark came very early. Then the electric lights came on, and it was pleasant along the streets looking in the windows. There was much game hanging outside the shops, and the snow powdered in the fur of the foxes and the wind blew their tails. The deer hung stiff and heavy and empty, and small birds blew in the wind and the wind turned their feathers. It was a cold fall and the wind came down from the mountains.

We were all at the hospital every afternoon, and there were different ways of walking across the town through the dusk to the hospital. Two of the ways were alongside canals, but they were long. Always, though, you crossed a bridge across a canal to enter the hospital. There was a choice of three bridges. On one of them a woman sold roasted chestnuts. It was warm, standing in front of her charcoal fire, and the chestnuts were warm afterward in your pocket. The hospital was very old and very beautiful, and you entered through a gate and walked across a courtyard and out a gate on the other side. There were usually funerals starting from the courtyard. Beyond the old hospital were the new brick pavilions, and there we met every afternoon and were all very polite and interested in what was the matter, and sat in the machines that were to make so much difference.

The doctor came up to the machine where I was sitting and said: "What did you like best to do before the war? Did you practice a sport?"

I said: "Yes, football."

"Good," he said. "You will be able to play football again better than ever."

My knee did not bend and the leg dropped straight from the knee to the ankle without a calf, and the machine was to bend the knee and make it move as in riding a tricycle. But it did not bend yet, and instead the machine lurched when it came to the bending part. The doctor said: "That will all pass. You are a fortunate young man. You will play football again like a champion."

In the next machine was a major who had a little hand like a baby's. He winked at me when the doctor examined his hand, which was between two leather straps that bounced up and down and flapped the stiff fingers, and said: "And will I too play football, captain-doctor?" He had been a very great fencer, and before the war the greatest fencer in Italy.

The doctor went to his office in a back room and brought a photograph which showed a hand that had been withered almost as small as the major's, before it had taken a machine course, and after was a little larger. The major held the photograph with his good hand and looked at it very carefully. "A wound?" he asked.

"An industrial accident," the doctor said.

"Very interesting, very interesting," the major said, and handed it back to the doctor.

"You have confidence?"

"No," said the major.

There were three boys who came each day who were about the same age I was. They were all three from Milan, and one of them was to be a lawyer, and one was to be a painter, and one had intended to be a soldier, and after we were finished with the machines, sometimes we walked back together to the Café Cova, which was next door to the Scala. We walked the short way through the communist quarter because we were four together. The people hated us because we were officers, and from a wineshop someone called out, "A basso gli ufficiali!" as we passed. Another boy who walked with us sometimes and made us five wore a black silk handkerchief across his face because he had no nose then and his face was to be rebuilt. He had gone out to the front from the military academy and been wounded within an hour after he had gone into the front line for the first time. They rebuilt his face, but he came from a very old family and they could never get the nose exactly right. He went to South America and worked in a bank. But this was a long time ago, and then we did not any of us know how it was going to be afterward. We only knew then that there was always the war, but that we were not going to it any more.

We all had the same medals, except the boy with the black silk bandage across his face, and he had not been at the front long enough to get any medals. The tall boy with a very pale face who was to be a lawyer had been a lieutenant of Arditi and had three medals of the sort we each had only one of. He had lived a very long time with death and was a little detached. We were all a little detached, and there was nothing that held us together except that we met every afternoon at the hospital. Although, as we walked to the Cova through the tough part of town, walking in the dark, with light and singing coming out of the wine-shops, and sometimes having to walk into the street when the men and women would crowd together on the sidewalk so that we would have had to jostle them to get by, we felt held together by there being something that had happened that they, the people who disliked us, did not understand.

We ourselves all understood the Cova, where it was rich and warm and not too brightly lighted, and noisy and smoky at certain hours, and there were always girls at the tables and the illustrated papers on a rack on the wall. The girls at the Cova were very patriotic, and I found that the most patriotic people in Italy were the café girls—and I believe they are still patriotic.

The boys at first were very polite about my medals and asked me what I had done to get them. I showed them the papers, which were written in very beautiful language and full of *fratellanza* and *abnegazione,* but which really said, with the adjectives removed, that I had been given the medals because I was an American. After that their manner changed a little toward me, although I was their friend against outsiders. I was a friend, but I was never really one of them after they had read the citations, because it had been different with them and they had done very different things to get their medals. I had been wounded, it was true; but we all knew that being wounded, after all, was really an accident. I was never ashamed of the ribbons, though, and sometimes after the cocktail hour, I would imagine myself having done all the things they had done to get their medals; but walking home at night through the empty streets with the cold wind and all the shops closed, trying to keep near the street lights, I knew that I would never have done such things, and I was very much afraid to die, and often lay in bed at night by myself, afraid to die and wondering how I would be when I went back to the front again.

The three with the medals were like hunting-hawks; and I was not a hawk, although I might seem a hawk to those who had never hunted; they, the three, knew better and so we drifted apart. But I stayed good friends with the boy who had been wounded his first day at the front, because he would never know now how he would have turned out; so he could never be accepted either, and I liked him because I thought perhaps he would not have turned out to be a hawk either.

The major, who had been the great fencer, did not believe in bravery, and spent much time while we sat in the machines correcting my grammar. He had complimented me on how I spoke Italian, and we talked together very easily. One day I had said that Italian seemed such an easy language to me that I could not take a great interest in it; everything was so easy to say. "Ah, yes," the major said. "Why, then, do you not take up the use of grammar?" So we took up the use of grammar, and soon Italian was such a difficult language that I was afraid to talk to him until I had the grammar straight in my mind.

The major came very regularly to the hospital. I do not think he ever missed a day, although I am sure he did not believe in the machines. There was a time when none of us believed in the machines, and one day the major said it was all nonsense. The machines were new then and it was we who were to prove them. It was an idiotic idea, he said, "a theory, like another." I had not learned my grammar, and he said I was a stupid impossible disgrace, and he was a fool to have bothered with me. He was a small man and he sat straight up in his chair with his right hand thrust into the machine and looked straight ahead at the wall while the straps thumped up and down with his fingers in them.

"What will you do when the war is over if it is over?" he asked me. "Speak grammatically!"

"I will go to the States."

"Are you married?"

"No, but I hope to be."

"The more of a fool you are," he said. He seemed very angry. "A man must not marry."

"Why, Signor Maggiore?"

"Don't call me 'Signor Maggiore.'"

"Why must not a man marry?"

"He cannot marry. He cannot marry," he said angrily. "If he is to lose everything, he should not place himself in a position to lose that. He should not place himself in a position to lose. He should find things he cannot lose."

He spoke very angrily and bitterly, and looked straight ahead while he talked.

"But why should he necessarily lose it?"

"He'll lose it," the major said. He was looking at the wall. Then he looked down at the machine and jerked his little hand out from between the straps and slapped it hard against his thigh. "He'll lose it," he almost shouted. "Don't argue with me!" Then he called to the attendant who ran the machines. "Come and turn this damned thing off."

He went back into the other room for the light treatment and the massage. Then I heard him ask the doctor if he might use his telephone and he shut the door. When he came back into the room, I was sitting in another machine. He was wearing his cape and had his cap on, and he came directly toward my machine and put his arm on my shoulder.

"I am so sorry," he said, and patted me on the shoulder with his good hand. "I would not be rude. My wife has just died. You must forgive me."

"Oh—" I said, feeling sick for him. "I am *so* sorry."

He stood there biting his lower lip. "It is very difficult," he said. "I cannot resign myself."

He looked straight past me and out through the window. Then he began to cry. "I am utterly unable to resign myself," he said and choked. And then crying, his head up looking at nothing, carrying himself straight and soldierly, with tears on both his cheeks and biting his lips, he walked past the machines and out the door.

The doctor told me that the major's wife, who was very young and whom he had not married until he was definitely invalided out of the war, had died of pneumonia. She had been sick only a few days. No one expected her to die. The major did not come to the hospital for three days. Then he came at the usual hour, wearing a black band on the sleeve of his uniform. When he came back, there were large framed photographs around the wall, of all sorts of wounds before and after they had been cured by the machines. In front of the machine the major used were three photographs of hands like his that were completely restored. I do not know where the doctor got them. I always understood we were the first to use the machines. The photographs did not make much difference to the major because he only looked out of the window.

— ◆ —

WILLIAM FAULKNER

1897–

In the autumn of 1950, the Nobel Prize in literature for 1949 was awarded to William Faulkner, the fourth American writer to be so honored. This international recognition was the culmination of a slowly growing impression of twenty years that in Faulkner America possessed one of the most significant writers of the twentieth century. In turning from the early conception of Faulkner as a kind of Gothic novelist whose chief stock-in-trade was the purveying of terror, shock, and shudder through the depiction of the lives of morbid, repellently moronic characters, recent critical interpretation of his novels has achieved a progressive enlightenment as to the fundamental aims of his fiction. The once popular impression that Faulkner was a Southern writer of horror stories in the tradition of Poe has been supplanted by the discovery of Faulkner the moralist who possesses as orthodox an interest in man's relation to the forces of good and evil as had Hawthorne and Melville.

William Faulkner was born in Mississippi on September 27, 1897, of a distinguished old family, and grew up in Oxford (the "Jefferson" of his fiction) where he still makes his home. After irregular schooling, he joined the Canadian Flying Corps in the first World War, and later the British Royal Air Force. Following the war he attended the University of Mississippi for a year, after which he held a number of jobs of various sorts, including a turn as clerk in a New York bookstore. In 1925 he went on a walking trip in Europe, and then worked as a journalist in New Orleans with Sherwood Anderson, who with Mrs. Anderson encouraged Faulkner to begin his first novel, *Soldiers' Pay*.

Faulkner's earliest published writing was poetry (*The Marble Faun*, 1924) which was largely derivative in style. *Soldiers' Pay* (1926) was, not unlike John Dos Passos' *Three Soldiers*, a narrative of the postwar disillusionment of a returned soldier. *Mosquitoes* (1927) was an uncharacteristic work in the vein of the blasé, sophisticated country-house novel which was having a vogue in Aldous Huxley's *Those Barren Leaves* and *Antic Hay*. This apprenticeship period ended with the publication of

Sartoris (1929), wherein for the first time Faulkner lays his scene in "Jefferson," Mississippi.

His first major novel, *The Sound and the Fury,* which had taken three years to write, also was published in 1929. Despite the obstacles to appreciation occasioned by the perplexing structural organization and the purposely contrived violations of chronological order to achieve certain symbolic effects, this novel is a brilliant accomplishment. It introduces thematically what is to become the characteristic motif of Faulkner's fiction: the decline and the degeneration (1898–1928) of an old, aristocratic Southern family, the Compsons. *As I Lay Dying* (1930), composed in six weeks, is less important, but the next novel, *Sanctuary* (1931) had such a *succès de scandale* that its essential connection with Faulkner's thematic preoccupation with the problem of evil could be seen only belatedly in the publication of the sequel, *Requiem for a Nun* (1951). Of the novels published between these two works, general critical agreement has recognized *Light in August* (1932) and *Absalom, Absalom!* (1936) as his most distinguished fiction.

Readers who have been willing to accept the violence and "degeneration" that brood over the Faulkner scene are still often repelled by the complexity of his style: the sentences that run for pages, interspersed with long, involved parentheses, the repetitions, the affectation that seems to reside in the lush, polysyllabic, heavily Latinized vocabulary. Despite its seeming careless structure and the agonies of its frustrated syntax, however, Faulkner's style has a remarkable power and splendor of imagery and rhythm that are unequaled in contemporary American prose. Then too, it may be too easily forgotten that Faulkner can write with clarity and simplicity when the occasion demands, as in the last section of *The Sound and the Fury* and in the dramatic dialogue of *Requiem for a Nun.*

Since G. M. O'Donnell's essay on "Faulkner's Mythology" (*Kenyon Review*, Summer, 1939) and Malcolm Cowley's "Introduction" to *The Portable Faulkner* (1946), critics have come to perceive in the author's work what Cowley has called Faulkner's "legend or myth" of the Deep South. The Mississippi county of Yoknapatawpha which Faulkner invented and peopled is the microcosm of the South as he conceives it: the center of a struggle between the Sartorises, the aristocrats who settled the South and established its ante-bellum traditions, and the Sutpens, ambitious men of ante-bellum days who were so unaware of the meaning of tradition that they believed it was something to be purchased by success (cf. *Absalom, Absalom!*). The incubus of slavery, the Civil War, and the unhappy circumstances of Reconstruction destroyed the traditional cultural values created by the Sartorises; and their descendants, immersed in the sentimental contemplation of the heroic past and finding refuge from the reality of the present in symbolic withdrawal into an outmoded gentility, became too weak and decadent to do other than surrender abjectly to the class rising to power, the Snopeses, descended from the landless whites of the old days. That Faulkner had clearly in mind some such interpretation of Southern cultural evolution is evinced not only by the care with which he integrates the characters of his individual short stories and novels into the historical frame of reference, but as well by the Appendix[1] which he prepared for *The Portable Faulkner.*

It is important to remember, however, that the Southern regional commitment of Faulkner may be overemphasized. What has concerned him is not a regional problem at all; it is the individual, yet eternal, problem of private spiritual agony, the question of man's experience with guilt and sin and expiation. This meaning may be read in all his work, from Quentin's attitude to his sister's "modern" amour in *The Sound and the Fury* to the discussion of Temple Drake's propensity for evil in *Requiem for a Nun.* From this point of view, the character of Popeye in *Sanctuary* should be read less as a sociological comment upon northern finance capitalism and more as a symbol of evil (we have Faulkner's own authority for this).

As a writer of short stories, William Faulkner has no rival in American literature save Hemingway. This becomes particularly apparent when we consider such admirable collections as *These Thirteen* (1931) and *Go Down Moses* (1942). "A Rose for Emily," from the earlier volume, is certainly one of his most remarkable. Although the story lacks the "folksy" quality of some of his narratives, and the rich vein of his "frontier humor" as well, nevertheless it presents in its most subtle and dreadful

---

[1] Also available in the Modern Library edition of *The Sound and the Fury* (1946).

form the problem of the relation of the traditional past to the rootless present. To Emily as to the Confederate veterans in this story, the past is "not a diminished road, but instead, a huge meadow which no winter ever quite touches." That is her tragedy; but a naïve acceptance of a modernity that possesses no code of humane, man-made values is no substitute. Conceivably the human situation implied here is not merely regional, but belongs to the universal drama of mankind.

FURTHER READING

CAMPBELL, HARRY MODEAN, and FOSTER, RUEL E. *William Faulkner: A Critical Appraisal* (Norman, Okla., 1951).

CHASE, RICHARD. "The Stone and the Crucifixion: Faulkner's *Light in August*" in *Critiques and Essays on Modern Fiction, 1920–1951*, edited by John W. Aldridge (New York, 1952).

COWLEY, MALCOLM. *The Portable Faulkner* (New York, 1946).

COWLEY, MALCOLM. "An Introduction to William Faulkner" in *Critiques and Essays on Modern Fiction, 1920–1951*, edited by John W. Aldridge (New York, 1952).

HOFFMAN, F. J., and VICKERY, OLGA (eds.). *William Faulkner: Two Decades of Criticism* (East Lansing, Mich., 1951).

A Rose for Emily *

I

WHEN Miss Emily Grierson died, our whole town went to her funeral: the men through a sort of respectful affection for a fallen monument, the women mostly out of curiosity to see the inside of her house, which no one save an old manservant— a combined gardener and cook—had seen in at least ten years.

It was a big, squarish frame house that had once been white, decorated with cupolas and spires and scrolled balconies in the heavily lightsome style of the seventies, set on what had once been our most select street. But garages and cotton gins had encroached and obliterated even the august names of that neighborhood; only Miss Emily's house was left, lifting its stubborn and coquettish decay above the cotton wagons and the gasoline pumps—an eyesore among eyesores. And now Miss Emily had gone to join the representatives of those august names where they lay in the cedar-bemused ceme-

* From *These Thirteen*, by William Faulkner. By permission of Random House, Inc., Copyright, 1930, by Forum Magazine.

tery among the ranked and anonymous graves of Union and Confederate soldiers who fell at the battle of Jefferson.

Alive, Miss Emily had been a tradition, a duty, and a care; a sort of hereditary obligation upon the town, dating from that day in 1894 when Colonel Sartoris, the mayor—he who fathered the edict that no Negro woman should appear on the streets without an apron—remitted her taxes, the dispensation dating from the death of her father on into perpetuity. Not that Miss Emily would have accepted charity. Colonel Sartoris invented an involved tale to the effect that Miss Emily's father had loaned money to the town, which the town, as a matter of business, preferred this way of repaying. Only a man of Colonel Sartoris' generation and thought could have invented it, and only a woman could have believed it.

When the next generation, with its more modern ideas, became mayors and aldermen, this arrangement created some little dissatisfaction. On the first of the year they mailed her a tax notice. February came, and there was no reply. They wrote her a formal letter, asking her to call at the sheriff's office at her convenience. A week later the mayor wrote her himself, offering to call or to send his car for her, and received in reply a note on paper of an archaic shape, in a thin, flowing calligraphy in faded ink, to the effect that she no longer went out at all. The tax notice was also enclosed, without comment.

They called a special meeting of the Board of Aldermen. A deputation waited upon her, knocked at the door through which no visitor had passed since she ceased giving china-painting lessons eight or ten years earlier. They were admitted by the old Negro into a dim hall from which a stairway mounted into still more shadow. It smelled of dust and disuse—a close, dank smell. The Negro led them into the parlor. It was furnished in heavy, leather-covered furniture. When the Negro opened the blinds of one window, they could see that the leather was cracked; and when they sat down, a faint dust rose sluggishly about their thighs, spinning with slow motes in the single sun-ray. On a tarnished gilt easel before the fireplace stood a crayon portrait of Miss Emily's father.

They rose when she entered—a small, fat woman in black, with a thin gold chain descending to her waist and vanishing into her belt, leaning on an ebony cane with a tarnished gold head. Her skeleton was small and spare; perhaps that was why what would have been merely plumpness in another was obesity in her. She looked bloated, like a body long submerged in motionless water, and of that pallid hue. Her eyes, lost in the fatty ridges of her face, looked like two small pieces of coal pressed into a lump of dough as they moved from one face to another while the visitors stated their errand.

She did not ask them to sit. She just stood in the door and listened quietly until the spokesman came to a stumbling halt. Then they could hear the invisible watch ticking at the end of the gold chain.

Her voice was dry and cold. "I have no taxes in Jefferson. Colonel Sartoris explained it to me. Perhaps one of you can gain access to the city records and satisfy yourselves."

"But we have. We are the city authorities, Miss Emily. Didn't you get a notice from the sheriff, signed by him?"

"I received a paper, yes," Miss Emily said. "Perhaps he considers himself the sheriff. . . . I have no taxes in Jefferson."

"But there is nothing on the books to show that, you see. We must go by the—"

"See Colonel Sartoris. I have no taxes in Jefferson."

"But, Miss Emily—"

"See Colonel Sartoris." (Colonel Sartoris had been dead almost ten years.) "I have no taxes in Jefferson. Tobe!" The Negro appeared. "Show these gentlemen out."

II

So she vanquished them, horse and foot, just as she had vanquished their fathers thirty years before about the smell. That was two years after her father's death and a short time after her sweetheart —the one we believed would marry her—had deserted her. After her father's death she went out very little; after her sweetheart went away, people hardly saw her at all. A few of the ladies had the temerity to call, but were not received, and the only sign of life about the place was the Negro man—a young man then—going in and out with a market basket.

"Just as if a man—any man—could keep a kitchen properly," the ladies said; so they were not surprised when the smell developed. It was another link between the gross, teeming world and the high and mighty Griersons.

A neighbor, a woman, complained to the mayor, Judge Stevens, eighty years old.

"But what will you have me do about it, madam?" he said.

"Why, send her word to stop it," the woman said. "Isn't there a law?"

"I'm sure that won't be necessary," Judge Stevens said. "It's probably just a snake or a rat that nigger of hers killed in the yard. I'll speak to him about it."

The next day he received two more complaints, one from a man who came in diffident deprecation. "We really must do something about it, Judge. I'd be the last one in the world to bother Miss Emily, but we've got to do something." That night the Board of Aldermen met—three graybeards and one younger man, a member of the rising generation.

"It's simple enough," he said. "Send her word to have her place cleaned up. Give her a certain time to do it in, and if she don't . . ."

"Dammit, sir," Judge Stevens said, "will you accuse a lady to her face of smelling bad?"

So the next night, after midnight, four men crossed Miss Emily's lawn and slunk about the house like burglars, sniffing along the base of the brickwork and at the cellar openings while one of them performed a regular sowing motion with his hand out of a sack slung from his shoulder. They broke open the cellar door and sprinkled lime there, and in all the outbuildings. As they recrossed the lawn, a window that had been dark was lighted and Miss Emily sat in it, the light behind her, and her upright torso motionless as that of an idol. They crept quietly across the lawn and into the shadow of the locusts that lined the street. After a week or two the smell went away.

That was when people had begun to feel really sorry for her. People in our town, remembering how old lady Wyatt, her great-aunt, had gone completely crazy at last, believed that the Griersons held themselves a little too high for what they really were. None of the young men were quite good enough for Miss Emily and such. We had long thought of them as a tableau: Miss Emily a slender figure in white in the background, her father a spraddled silhouette in the foreground, his back to her and clutching a horsewhip, the two of them framed by the back-flung front door. So when she got to be thirty and was still single, we were not pleased exactly, but vindicated; even with insanity in the family she wouldn't have turned down all of her chances if they had really materialized.

When her father died, it got about that the house was all that was left to her; and in a way, people were glad. At last they could pity Miss Emily. Being left alone, and a pauper, she had become humanized. Now she too would know the old thrill and the old despair of a penny more or less.

The day after his death all the ladies prepared to call at the house and offer condolence and aid, as is our custom. Miss Emily met them at the door, dressed as usual and with no trace of grief on her face. She told them that her father was not dead. She did that for three days, with the ministers calling on her, and the doctors, trying to persuade her to let them dispose of the body. Just as they were about to resort to law and force, she broke down, and they buried her father quickly.

We did not say she was crazy then. We believed she had to do that. We remembered all the young men her father had driven away, and we knew that with nothing left, she would have to cling to that which had robbed her, as people will.

III

She was sick for a long time. When we saw her again, her hair was cut short, making her look like a girl, with a vague resemblance to those angels in colored church windows—sort of tragic and serene.

The town had just let the contracts for paving the sidewalks, and in the summer after her father's death they began the work. The construction company came with niggers and mules and machinery, and a foreman named Homer Barron, a Yankee—a big, dark, ready man, with a big voice and eyes lighter than his face. The little boys would follow in groups to hear him cuss the niggers, and the niggers singing in time to the rise and fall of picks. Pretty soon he knew everybody in town. Whenever you heard a lot of laughing anywhere about the square, Homer Barron would be in the center of the group. Presently we began to see him and Miss Emily on Sunday afternoons driving in the yellow-wheeled buggy and the matched team of bays from the livery stable.

At first we were glad that Miss Emily would have an interest, because the ladies all said, "Of course a Grierson would not think seriously of a Northerner, a day laborer." But there were still others, older people, who said that even grief could not cause a real lady to forget *noblesse oblige*—without calling it *noblesse oblige*. They just said, "Poor Emily. Her kinsfolk should come to her." She had some kin in Alabama; but years ago her father had fallen out with them over the estate of old lady Wyatt, the crazy woman, and there was no communication between the two families. They had not even been represented at the funeral.

And as soon as the old people said, "Poor Emily," the whispering began. "Do you suppose it's really so?" they said to one another. "Of course it is.

What else could . . ." This behind their hands; rustling of craned silk and satin behind jalousies closed upon the sun of Sunday afternoon as the thin, swift clop-clop-clop of the matched team passed: "Poor Emily."

She carried her head high enough—even when we believed that she was fallen. It was as if she demanded more than ever the recognition of her dignity as the last Grierson; as if it had wanted that touch of earthiness to reaffirm her imperviousness. Like when she bought the rat poison, the arsenic. That was over a year after they had begun to say "Poor Emily," and while the two female cousins were visiting her.

"I want some poison," she said to the druggist. She was over thirty then, still a slight woman, though thinner than usual, with cold, haughty black eyes in a face the flesh of which was strained across the temples and about the eyesockets as you imagine a lighthouse-keeper's face ought to look. "I want some poison," she said.

"Yes, Miss Emily. What kind? For rats and such? I'd recom—"

"I want the best you have. I don't care what kind."

The druggist named several. "They'll kill anything up to an elephant. But what you want is—"

"Arsenic," Miss Emily said. "Is that a good one?"

"Is . . . arsenic? Yes, ma'am. But what you want—"

"I want arsenic."

The druggist looked down at her. She looked back at him, erect, her face like a strained flag. "Why, of course," the druggist said. "If that's what you want. But the law requires you to tell what you are going to use it for."

Miss Emily just stared at him, her head tilted back in order to look him eye for eye, until he looked away and went and got the arsenic and wrapped it up. The Negro delivery boy brought her the package; the druggist didn't come back. When she opened the package at home there was written on the box, under the skull and bones: "For rats."

IV

So the next day we all said, "She will kill herself"; and we said it would be the best thing. When she had first begun to be seen with Homer Barron, we had said, "She will marry him." Then we said, "She will persuade him yet," because Homer himself had remarked—he liked men, and it was known that he drank with the younger men in the Elks'

Club—that he was not a marrying man. Later we said, "Poor Emily," behind the jalousies as they passed on Sunday afternoon in the glittering buggy, Miss Emily with her head high and Homer Barron with his hat cocked and a cigar in his teeth, reins and whip in a yellow glove.

Then some of the ladies began to say that it was a disgrace to the town and a bad example to the young people. The men did not want to interfere, but at last the ladies forced the Baptist minister—Miss Emily's people were Episcopal—to call upon her. He would never divulge what happened during that interview, but he refused to go back again. The next Sunday they again drove about the streets, and the following day the minister's wife wrote to Miss Emily's relations in Alabama.

So she had blood-kin under her roof again and we sat back to watch developments. At first nothing happened. Then we were sure that they were to be married. We learned that Miss Emily had been to the jeweler's and ordered a man's toilet set in silver, with the letters H.B. on each piece. Two days later we learned that she had bought a complete outfit of men's clothing, including a nightshirt, and we said, "They are married." We were really glad. We were glad because the two female cousins were even more Grierson than Miss Emily had ever been.

So we were not surprised when Homer Barron— the streets had been finished some time since—was gone. We were a little disappointed that there was not a public blowing-off, but we believed that he had gone on to prepare for Miss Emily's coming, or to give her a chance to get rid of the cousins. (By that time it was a cabal, and we were all Miss Emily's allies to help circumvent the cousins.) Sure enough, after another week they departed. And, as we had expected all along, within three days Homer Barron was back in town. A neighbor saw the Negro man admit him at the kitchen door at dusk one evening.

And that was the last we saw of Homer Barron. And of Miss Emily for some time. The Negro man went in and out with the market basket, but the front door remained closed. Now and then we would see her at a window for a moment, as the men did that night when they sprinkled the lime, but for almost six months she did not appear on the streets. Then we knew that this was to be expected too; as if that quality of her father which had thwarted her woman's life so many times had been too virulent and too furious to die.

When we next saw Miss Emily, she had grown fat and her hair was turning gray. During the next few years it grew grayer and grayer until it attained an even pepper-and-salt iron-gray, when it ceased turning. Up to the day of her death at seventy-four it was still that vigorous iron-gray, like the hair of an active man.

From that time on her front door remained closed, save for a period of six or seven years, when she was about forty, during which she gave lessons in china-painting. She fitted up a studio in one of the downstairs rooms, where the daughters and granddaughters of Colonel Sartoris' contemporaries were sent to her with the same regularity and in the same spirit that they were sent on Sundays with a twenty-five cent piece for the collection plate. Meanwhile her taxes had been remitted.

Then the newer generation became the backbone and the spirit of the town, and the painting pupils grew up and fell away and did not send their children to her with boxes of color and tedious brushes and pictures cut from the ladies' magazines. The front door closed upon the last one and remained closed for good. When the town got free postal delivery Miss Emily alone refused to let them fasten the metal numbers above her door and attach a mailbox to it. She would not listen to them.

Daily, monthly, yearly we watched the Negro grow grayer and more stooped, going in and out with the market basket. Each December we sent her a tax notice, which would be returned by the post office a week later, unclaimed. Now and then we would see her in one of the downstairs windows —she had evidently shut up the top floor of the house—like the carven torso of an idol in a niche, looking or not looking at us, we could never tell which. Thus she passed from generation to generation—dear, inescapable, impervious, tranquil, and perverse.

And so she died. Fell ill in the house filled with dust and shadows with only a doddering Negro man to wait on her. We did not even know she was sick; we had long since given up trying to get any information from the Negro. He talked to no one, probably not even to her, for his voice had grown harsh and rusty, as if from disuse.

She died in one of the downstairs rooms, in a heavy walnut bed with a curtain, her gray head propped on a pillow yellow and moldy with age and lack of sunlight.

v

The Negro met the first of the ladies at the front door and let them in, with their hushed, sibilant voices and their quick, curious glances, and then he disappeared. He walked right through the house and out the back and was not seen again.

The two female cousins came at once. They held the funeral on the second day, with the town coming to look at Miss Emily beneath a mass of bought flowers, with the crayon face of her father musing profoundly above the bier and the ladies sibilant and macabre; and the very old men—some in their brushed Confederate uniforms—on the porch and the lawn, talking of Miss Emily as if she had been a contemporary of theirs, believing that they had danced with her and courted her perhaps, confusing time with its mathematical progression, as the old do, to whom all the past is not a diminishing road, but, instead, a huge meadow which no winter ever quite touches, divided from them now by the narrow bottleneck of the most recent decade of years.

Already we knew that there was one room in that region above stairs which no one had seen in forty years, and which would have to be forced. They waited until Miss Emily was decently in the ground before they opened it.

The violence of breaking down the door seemed to fill this room with pervading dust. A thin, acrid pall as of the tomb seemed to lie everywhere upon this room decked and furnished as for a bridal: upon the valance curtains of faded rose color, upon the rose-shaded lights, upon the dressing table, upon the delicate array of crystal and the man's toilet things backed with tarnished silver, silver so tarnished that the monogram was obscured. Among them lay a collar and tie, as if they had just been removed, which, lifted, left upon the surface a pale crescent in the dust. Upon a chair hung the suit, carefully folded; beneath it the two mute shoes and the discarded socks.

The man himself lay in the bed.

For a long while we just stood there, looking down at the profound and fleshless grin. The body had apparently once lain in the attitude of an embrace, but now the long sleep that outlasts love, that conquers even the grimace of love, had cuckolded him. What was left of him, rotted beneath what was left of the nightshirt, had become inextricable from the bed in which he lay; and upon him and upon the pillow beside him lay that even coating of the patient and biding dust.

Then we noticed that in the second pillow was the indentation of a head. One of us lifted something from it, and leaning forward, that faint and invisible dust dry and acrid in the nostrils, we saw a long strand of iron-gray hair.

◆

American Lyric Poetry

EDWIN ARLINGTON ROBINSON

1869–1935

The readers of American poetry in the 1890's were no more ready for Robinson's first volume of poems, *The Torrent and the Night Before*, than they were for those of Emily Dickinson. His own painful experience of failure and his perception of the social and spiritual malady that was consuming the intrinsic integrity of his New England were reflected in this volume and the subsequent one, *The Children of the Night* (1897). Herein is revealed his reading of Thomas Hardy's novels, and certainly the "Credo" anticipated Hardy's pessimistic darkness that was to be evident in the *Wessex* Poems (1899), even to the glimmer of spiritual hope that the end of "Credo" suggests.

Before publishing these volumes Robinson, born and reared in Gardiner, Maine, had studied for two years at Harvard and had worked in menial jobs in New York City. These years of struggle and failure gave him his profoundly sympathetic understanding of the plight of men who endeavored to find spiritual integration or friendship in a hostile modern world, as his long poem *Captain Craig* (1902) and the sharply etched portraits of his characters from "Tilbury Town" show. It is perhaps as the painter of these portraits that Robinson, like Browning, his master in this genre, has made his most significant contribution to literature.

The friendship of President Theodore Roosevelt rescued Robinson from his struggles to earn a pre-

carious living through the offer of a clerkship in the
New York customhouse. There he remained from
1905 to 1910. Upon publishing his two most distinguished volumes of verse, *The Town Down the
River* (1910) and *The Man Against the Sky*
(1916), he achieved at least a *succès d'estime*. In
1911 he left the customhouse and found leisure, at
last, in his summer visitations to the MacDowell
colony at Peterboro, New Hampshire. By the time
the publication of *Tristram* in 1927 and its distribution by a book club secured him popular fame, he
had already won the Pulitzer prize twice. His work
following *Tristram* did not contribute to the further
enhancement of his poetic reputation. Robinson
died in New York, April 6, 1935.

Edwin Arlington Robinson can hardly be aggran-
dized, as he sometimes is, into a penetrating critic
of modern American industrialism, because his perceptions are too fragmentary and lyric. His virtues
of a plain style, his subdued irony (in "Eros Turan-
nos"), and his psychological insight into character
are among the most admirable attributes of his
work. The lack of rich suggestive and connotative
power in his poetic vocabulary and the too strict cast
of his intellectuality are perhaps the most serious
defects in his poetic equipment that the discerning
reader may feel.

FURTHER READING

BARNARD, ELLSWORTH. *Edwin Arlington Robinson* (New
York, 1952).
CESTRE, CHARLES. *An Introduction to Edwin Arlington
Robinson* (New York, 1930).
HAGEDORN, HERMANN. *Edwin Arlington Robinson* (New
York, 1938).
NEFF, EMERY E. *Edwin Arlington Robinson* (New York,
1948).

Credo

I cannot find my way: there is no star
In all the shrouded heavens anywhere;
And there is not a whisper in the air
Of any living voice but one so far
That I can hear it only as a bar
Of lost, imperial music, played when fair
And angel fingers wove, and unaware,
Dead leaves to garlands where no roses are.

No, there is not a glimmer, nor a call,
For one that welcomes, welcomes when he fears,
The black and awful chaos of the night;
But through it all,—above, beyond it all—
I know the far-sent message of the years,
I feel the coming glory of the Light!

Richard Cory

Whenever Richard Cory went down town,
　　We people on the pavement looked at him:
He was a gentleman from sole to crown,
　　Clean favored, and imperially slim.

And he was always quietly arrayed,
　　And he was always human when he talked;
But still he fluttered pulses when he said,
　　"Good-morning," and he glittered when he
　　　　walked.

And he was rich—yes, richer than a king—
　　And admirably schooled in every grace:
In fine, we thought that he was everything
　　To make us wish that we were in his place.

So on we worked, and waited for the light,
　　And went without the meat, and cursed the
　　　　bread;
And Richard Cory, one calm summer night,
　　Went home and put a bullet through his head.

Eros Turannos

She fears him, and will always ask
　　What fated her to choose him;
She meets in his engaging mask
　　All reasons to refuse him;
But what she meets and what she fears
Are less than are the downward years,
Drawn slowly to the foamless weirs
　　Of age, were she to lose him.

Between a blurred sagacity
　　That once had power to sound him,   10
And Love, that will not let him be
　　The Judas that she found him,
Her pride assuages her almost,
As if it were alone the cost.
He sees that he will not be lost;
　　And waits and looks around him.

A sense of ocean and old trees
　　Envelops and allures him;
Tradition, touching all he sees,
　　Beguiles and reassures him;   20

And all her doubts of what he says
Are dimmed with what she knows of days—
Till even prejudice delays
    And fades, and she secures him.

The falling leaf inaugurates
    The reign of her confusion;
The pounding wave reverberates
    The dirge of her illusion;
And home, where passion lived and died,
Becomes a place where she can hide,   30
While all the town and harbor-side
    Vibrate with her seclusion.

We tell you, tapping on our brows,
    The story as it should be,
As if the story of a house
    Were told, or ever could be;
We'll have no kindly veil between
Her visions and those we have seen,—
As if we guessed what hers have been,
    Or what they are or would be.   40

Meanwhile we do no harm; for they
    That with a god have striven,
Not hearing much of what we say,
    Take what the god has given;
Though like waves breaking it may be
Or like a changed familiar tree,
Or like a stairway to the sea
    Where down the blind are driven.

Mr. Flood's Party

Old Eben Flood, climbing alone one night
Over the hill between the town below
And the forsaken upland hermitage
That held as much as he should ever know
On earth again of home, paused warily.
The road was his with not a native near;
And Eben, having leisure, said aloud,
For no man else in Tilbury Town to hear:

"Well, Mr. Flood, we have the harvest moon
Again, and we may not have many more;   10
The bird is on the wing, the poet says,
And you and I have said it here before.
Drink to the bird." He raised up to the light
The jug that he had gone so far to fill,
And answered huskily: "Well, Mr. Flood,
Since you propose it; I believe I will."

Alone, as if enduring to the end
A valiant armor of scarred hopes outworn,

He stood there in the middle of the road
Like Roland's ghost winding a silent horn.[1]   20
Below him, in the town among the trees,
Where friends of other days had honored him,
A phantom salutation of the dead
Rang thinly till old Eben's eyes were dim.

Then, as a mother lays her sleeping child
Down tenderly, fearing it may awake,
He set the jug down slowly at his feet
With trembling care, knowing that most things
    break;
And only when assured that on firm earth
It stood, as the uncertain lives of men   30
Assuredly did not, he paced away,
And with his hand extended paused again:

"Well, Mr. Flood, we have not met like this
In a long time; and many a change has come
To both of us, I fear, since last it was
We had a drop together. Welcome home!"
Convivially returning with himself,
Again he raised the jug up to the light;
And with an acquiescent quaver said:
"Well, Mr. Flood, if you insist, I might.   40

"Only a very little, Mr. Flood—
For auld lang syne. No more, sir; that will do."
So, for the time, apparently it did,
And Eben evidently thought so too;
For soon amid the silver loneliness
Of night he lifted up his voice and sang,
Secure, with only two moons listening,
Until the whole harmonious landscape rang—

"For auld lang syne." The weary throat gave out,
The last word wavered; and the song being done, 50
He raised again the jug regretfully
And shook his head, and was again alone.
There was not much that was ahead of him,
And there was nothing in the town below—
Where strangers would have shut the many doors
That many friends had opened long ago.

Karma

Christmas was in the air and all was well
With him, but for a few confusing flaws
In divers of God's images. Because
A friend of his would neither buy nor sell,
Was he to answer for the axe that fell?
He pondered; and the reason for it was,
Partly, a slowly freezing Santa Claus
Upon the corner, with his beard and bell.

[1] See *Song of Roland*, Vol. I, p. 359, stanza cxxxv.

Acknowledging an improvident surprise,
He magnified a fancy that he wished
The friend whom he had wrecked were here again.
Not sure of that, he found a compromise;
And from the fulness of his heart he fished
A dime for Jesus who had died for men.

———◆———

ROBERT FROST

1875–

Today Robert Frost is one of the most popular of American poets. He has been awarded the Pulitzer prize four times; he has been a professor at Amherst, Michigan, Yale, and Harvard; he has received numerous honorary degrees. Perhaps the most remarkable phenomenon of Frost's career is that a popular poet is at the same time one of our most distinguished poets. In addition to Frost's gnomic, skeptical wisdom of utterance, possibly one of the reasons for this popularity is his poetic treatment of rural settings: to Americans of the present generation the American country life of a few generations ago is the real America; Frost in his poetry has a way of trenchant, dry speaking that suggests the typical canny, wryly humorous countryman of the American tradition, especially the Yankee.

Though descended from eight generations of New Englanders, Frost was born in somewhat alien territory, in San Francisco, on March 26, 1875. After his brief attendance at Dartmouth and Harvard, his occupations during the next twenty years were varied: bobbin boy in a New England mill, shoemaking, editing a country newspaper, schoolteaching, and finally farming. His respect for clean, exact craftsmanship in his poetry probably owes a great deal to his experience. In September, 1912, he went to England with his wife and four children, where he established congenial friendships with a number of the Georgian poets like Edward Thomas, Wilfred Gibson, and Lascelles Abercrombie. His first volumes of poetry were *A Boy's Will* (1913) and *North of Boston* (1914). When the latter volume was reprinted in America, Frost returned to find himself famous. He bought a farm in New Hampshire and undertook, as professor of poetry at Amherst, to teach the young idea how to sprout. No doubt his classes in poetry were very much surprised to hear Frost recommend that they first learn to write a good letter.

Since that time Frost has gone his way writing poetry that is admirably terse, laconic, full of the shrewd appraisal and deceptive diffidence of the Yankee farmer and couched in that language of colloquial and proverbial turns of folk speech. Yet the poems are rich in overtones and symbolic spiritual suggestion, as one may recognize in one of the earliest and most famous, "Mending Wall," and in such later ones as "Acquainted with the Night," which conveys by symbolic indirection the plight of a lonely poet in an indifferent and strange world, a theme to be remarked in such diverse poets as Leopardi and Rilke. Such poems as these should make the reader cautious in observing that Frost is merely a regional New England poet; he is a classicist and a humanist, and regional only in the choice of his poetic materials. One would not dub Vergil a regional poet because of his use of his own Cisalpine country as part of the background for the *Georgics*. Frost has often, and with justice, been compared to Horace; he reads Catullus, Vergil, and Theocritus in the Latin and Greek. There is nevertheless a strong, romantic leavening in his poetry, for Emerson is his favorite poet, as might be expected of a New England inheritor of transcendentalism. Perhaps his genial skepticism regarding systems and his belief in impulse ("Poetry is a little like the course of true love. Both begin with impulse . . .") are Emersonian.

During his later years Frost has turned to a religious poetry which finds expression in the dramatic-didactic poems *A Masque of Reason* (1945) and *A Masque of Mercy* (1947). This new interest is here represented by "Directive" (from *Steeple Bush*, 1947), which is not the retreat into the rural nineteenth century of Grandma Moses and Currier and Ives it may seem on first reading, but a symbolic rendering of the need in the modern world for the curative and restorative ministrations of Christian revelation and God's grace. It is to be hoped that the publication of the *Complete Poems of Robert Frost* (1949) did not mark the *terminus ad quem* of a wise and great American poet.

FURTHER READING

O'DONNELL, W. G. "Robert Frost and New England," *Yale Review*, XXXVII (Summer, 1948), 698 ff.

THOMPSON, LAURENCE R. *Fire and Ice: The Art and Thought of Robert Frost* (New York, 1942).

THORNTON, RICHARD, ed. *Recognition of Robert Frost* (New York, 1937).

Mending Wall *

Something there is that doesn't love a wall,
That sends the frozen-ground-swell under it,
And spills the upper boulders in the sun;
And makes gaps even two can pass abreast.
The work of hunters is another thing:
I have come after them and made repair
Where they have left not one stone on a stone,
But they would have the rabbit out of hiding,
To please the yelping dogs. The gaps I mean,
No one has seen them made or heard them made,
But at spring mending-time we find them there.
I let my neighbour know beyond the hill;
And on a day we meet to walk the line
And set the wall between us once again.
We keep the wall between us as we go.
To each the boulders that have fallen to each.
And some are loaves and some so nearly balls
We have to use a spell to make them balance:
"Stay where you are until our backs are turned!"
We wear our fingers rough with handling them.
Oh, just another kind of out-door game,
One on a side. It comes to little more:
There where it is we do not need the wall:
He is all pine and I am apple orchard.
My apple trees will never get across
And eat the cones under his pines, I tell him.
He only says, "Good fences make good neighbours."
Spring is the mischief in me, and I wonder
If I could put a notion in his head:
"*Why* do they make good neighbours? Isn't it
Where there are cows? But here there are no cows.
Before I built a wall I'd ask to know
What I was walling in or walling out,
And to whom I was like to give offence.
Something there is that doesn't love a wall,
That wants it down." I could say "Elves" to him,
But it's not elves exactly, and I'd rather
He said it for himself. I see him there

Bringing a stone grasped firmly by the top
In each hand, like an old-stone savage armed.
He moves in darkness as it seems to me,
Not of woods only and the shade of trees.
He will not go behind his father's saying,
And he likes having thought of it so well
He says again, "Good fences make good neighbours."

After Apple-Picking

My long two-pointed ladder's sticking through a tree
Toward heaven still,
And there's a barrel that I didn't fill
Beside it, and there may be two or three
Apples I didn't pick upon some bough.
But I am done with apple-picking now.
Essence of winter sleep is on the night,
The scent of apples: I am drowsing off.
I cannot rub the strangeness from my sight
I got from looking through a pane of glass
I skimmed this morning from the drinking trough
And held against the world the hoary grass.
It melted, and I let it fall and break.
But I was well
Upon my way to sleep before it fell,
And I could tell
What form my dreaming was about to take.
Magnified apples appear and disappear,
Stem end and blossom end,
And every fleck of russet showing clear.
My instep arch not only keeps the ache,
It keeps the pressure of a ladder round.
I feel the ladder sway as the boughs bend.
And I keep hearing from the cellar bin
The rumbling sound
Of load on load of apples coming in.
For I have had too much
Of apple-picking: I am overtired
Of the great harvest I myself desired.
There were ten thousand thousand fruit to touch,
Cherish in hand, lift down, and not let fall.
For all
That struck the earth,
No matter if not bruised or spiked with stubble,
Went surely to the cider apple heap
As of no worth.
One can see what will trouble
This sleep of mine, whatever sleep it is.
Were he not gone,
The woodchuck could say whether it's like his
Long sleep, as I describe its coming on,
Or just some human sleep.

Fire and Ice

Some say the world will end in fire,
Some say in ice.
From what I've tasted of desire
I hold with those who favor fire.
But if it had to perish twice,
I think I know enough of hate
To say that for destruction ice
Is also great
And would suffice.

Dust of Snow

The way a crow
Shook down on me
The dust of snow
From a hemlock tree

Has given my heart
A change of mood
And saved some part
Of a day I had rued.

Stopping by Woods on a Snowy Evening

Whose woods these are I think I know.
His house is in the village though;
He will not see me stopping here
To watch his woods fill up with snow.

My little horse must think it queer
To stop without a farmhouse near
Between the woods and frozen lake
The darkest evening of the year.

He gives his harness bells a shake
To ask if there is some mistake.
The only other sound's the sweep
Of easy wind and downy flake.

The woods are lovely, dark and deep,
But I have promises to keep,
And miles to go before I sleep,
And miles to go before I sleep.

Spring Pools

These pools that, though in forests, still reflect
The total sky almost without defect,
And like the flowers beside them, chill and shiver,

Will like the flowers beside them soon be gone,
And yet not out by any brook or river,
But up by roots to bring dark foliage on.

The trees that have it in their pent-up buds
To darken nature and be summer woods—
Let them think twice before they use their powers
To blot out and drink up and sweep away
These flowery waters and these watery flowers
From snow that melted only yesterday.

Acquainted with the Night

I have been one acquainted with the night.
I have walked out in rain—and back in rain.
I have outwalked the furthest city light.

I have looked down the saddest city lane.
I have passed by the watchman on his beat
And dropped my eyes, unwilling to explain.

I have stood still and stopped the sound of feet
When far away an interrupted cry
Came over houses from another street,

But not to call me back or say good-bye;
And further still at an unearthly height,
One luminary clock against the sky

Proclaimed the time was neither wrong nor right.
I have been one acquainted with the night.

Neither Out Far Nor In Deep

The people along the sand
All turn and look one way.
They turn their back on the land.
They look at the sea all day.

As long as it takes to pass
A ship keeps raising its hull;
The wetter ground like glass
Reflects a standing gull.

The land may vary more;
But wherever the truth may be—
The water comes ashore,
And the people look at the sea.

They cannot look out far.
They cannot look in deep.
But when was that ever a bar
To any watch they keep?

Directive

Back out of all this now too much for us,
Back in a time made simple by the loss
Of detail, burned, dissolved, and broken off
Like graveyard marble sculpture in the weather,
There is a house that is no more a house
Upon a farm that is no more a farm
And in a town that is no more a town.
The road there, if you'll let a guide direct you
Who only has at heart your getting lost,
May seem as if it should have been a quarry—   10
Great monolithic knees the former town
Long since gave up pretense of keeping covered.
And there's a story in a book about it:
Besides the wear of iron wagon wheels
The ledges show lines ruled southeast northwest,
The chisel work of an enormous Glacier
That braced his feet against the Arctic Pole.
You must not mind a certain coolness from him
Still said to haunt this side of Panther Mountain.
Nor need you mind the serial ordeal   20
Of being watched from forty cellar holes
As if by eye pairs out of forty firkins.
As for the woods' excitement over you
That sends light rustle rushes to their leaves,
Charge that to upstart inexperience.
Where were they all not twenty years ago?
They think too much of having shaded out
A few old pecker-fretted apple trees.
Make yourself up a cheering song of how
Someone's road home from work this once was,   30
Who may be just ahead of you on foot
Or creaking with a buggy load of grain.
The height of the adventure is the height
Of country where two village cultures faded
Into each other. Both of them are lost.
And if you're lost enough to find yourself
By now, pull in your ladder road behind you
And put a sign up CLOSED to all but me.
Then make yourself at home. The only field
Now left's no bigger than a harness gall.   40
First there's the children's house of make believe,
Some shattered dishes underneath a pine,
The playthings in the playhouse of the children.
Weep for what little things could make them glad.
Then for the house that is no more a house,
But only a belilaced cellar hole,
Now slowly closing like a dent in dough.
This was no playhouse but a house in earnest.
Your destination and your destiny's
A brook that was the water of the house,   50
Cold as a spring as yet so near its source,

Too lofty and original to rage.
(We know the valley streams that when aroused
Will leave their tatters hung on barb and thorn.)
I have kept hidden in the instep arch
Of an old cedar at the waterside
A broken drinking goblet like the Grail
Under a spell so the wrong ones can't find it,
So can't get saved, as Saint Mark says they mustn't.
(I stole the goblet from the children's playhouse.) 60
Here are your waters and your watering place.
Drink and be whole again beyond confusion.

———◆———

T. S. ELIOT

1888–

   T. S. Eliot was born in St. Louis, Missouri, September 26, 1888. He was graduated from Harvard in 1909, and later studied at the Sorbonne and at Oxford. In 1927 he became a British citizen. He has become the most influential poet and critic of his generation. From the time he published his first two volumes of poetry, *Prufrock and Other Observations* (1917) and *Poems* (1920), and his first important critical work, *The Sacred Wood* (1921), his influence upon modern poetry and critical theory has been little less than profound. He has been influential in reviving an interest in Dryden, the Jacobean dramatists, and the metaphysical poets, especially Donne; further, his emphasis upon the value of tradition in criticism and in poetry is one of the most enlightening critical dictums of modern literary criticism, which is amply demonstrated as well in its influence upon his poetry.
   The most significant poem of his 1917 volume of verse, *The Love Song of J. Alfred Prufrock,* written as early as 1911 under the influence of the French symbolist Jules Laforgue and of Dostoevski's *Crime and Punishment,* mirrors the frustration of an introverted psyche, the timidity, the emotional inhibitions, the social impotence of modern man full of self-pity and self-disgust in the environment of inane drawing-room culture. The poem reveals too the nonlogical development in the poetic structure, following the sudden transitions and convolutions

of thought that we have come to associate with his poetry. He attempted to devise a stylistic medium that would communicate the complex experience of the modern world, the sudden contrasts, the dissonances, and at the same time reveal directly to the reader the immediate sensuous impression of this experience. Hence Eliot spoke of his theory of the "objective correlative," of devising a set of material objects which, without intellectual statement, would convey directly to the reader's sensory impression the emotion he wished to evoke. The well-known illustration of this in "Prufrock" is the line, "I have measured out my life with coffee spoons."

The Waste Land (1922) marks the end of Eliot's first period of development in which he sums up the previous attitudes toward the modern world—its spiritual dearth, aridity, the sterile frustrations of modern love that have become mechanical concupiscence. Technically, Eliot sought to give the ideas he had rehearsed in his earlier volumes a more universal context of meaning by adopting as the framework of the poem imagery drawn from Jessie L. Weston's From Ritual to Romance. Here is applied Eliot's insistence that the modern poet must know the tradition of the past, particularly of Western European literature, in order to see a unified pattern of recurrence in certain situations and motifs amid the perplexing complexity of modern life. Surface differences between eras often mask profound underlying resemblances, as there are surprising congruences among the great myths of the human race: in the resemblances between the vegetation myths of antiquity and the rhythm of the seasons, and between the decline and rebirth of potency in the legends of the slain vegetation god (Osiris, Adonis, Orpheus) and the Christian revelation of the death and resurrection of Christ. Thus the modern world becomes the wasteland that is awaiting spiritual rebirth, symbolized by the water which in the fertility rites of ancient cults is always an emblem of rebirth. The method of the poem is free association of ideas and images, and is musical in the manner that it introduces, expands, and repeats the ideas, and in the counterpointing of scenes from the modern world against the myths of the past and against scenes from the great literature of the past (for example, the juxtaposition of such diverse sources as Shakespeare and Wagner).

In 1927 Eliot declared his adherence to classicism in literature, royalism in politics, and Anglo-Catholicism in religion. The steady spiritual progress that one might expect from Eliot after the suggestions of spiritual surrender at the end of The Waste Land ("Give, Sympathize, Control") advanced through the still tormenting spiritual perplexities of Ash Wednesday (1930) to the Four Quartets (1935–1943), possibly in its verse form and range of feeling the finest of his poetry. To a degree, Eliot gradually abandoned the theory of dramatic objectivity which characterized his early poetry (as seen in "Prufrock") and as the protagonist in these poems turned to a mature evaluation of his own spiritual experience and belief. The title Four Quartets suggests the musical analogy which Eliot clearly had in mind (for his indebtedness to music in solving the structure of his poetry see his lecture, "The Music of Poetry" in the Partisan Review, 1945), but as Miss Gardner has pointed out, the analogy must not be carried so far as to find a strict sonata movement in these poems. Perhaps there is an intention to remind the reader of the quartets of Beethoven; there is further evidence here of Eliot's classicism in his effort to submit to the discipline of poetic law (the classical sonata-ideal is implicit here, if not fully illustrated). Burnt Norton, the first of the quartets, is concerned with establishing Eliot's concepts, especially of time and eternity. The scene is a Cotswold manor house and a formal garden, to a degree symbolic of man's attempt to impose an intellectual pattern upon an inchoate natural world. The spiritual experience concerns the religious apprehension in time of a timeless, transcendent reality; it is through spiritual humility ("the way up is the way down") and the passive awaiting of God's grace, Eliot believes, that this profound religious intuition is to be achieved. The poem is a necessary preparation for a reading of the other quartets and for a full understanding of the thematic developments—the problems of human suffering and pain and their mystical resolution in the transcendent awareness of the Revelation.

The quality of Eliot as a dramatist in Murder in the Cathedral (1935), The Family Reunion (1939), and The Cocktail Party (1950), which develop in different ways the theme of sin and expiation, is still to be evaluated. These plays are not, perhaps, his most unquestioned successes, but they have served to accelerate the development of a modern verse drama, a poetic theater, which may still have significant contributions to make to the dramatic history of the twentieth century.

FURTHER READING

DREW, ELIZABETH. *T. S. Eliot: The Design of His Poetry* (New York, 1949).

GARDNER, HELEN. *The Art of T. S. Eliot* (New York, 1950).

GARDNER, HELEN. "*Four Quartets:* A Commentary" in *Critiques and Essays in Criticism, 1920–1948,* edited by R. W. Stallman (New York, 1949).

MATTHIESSEN, F. O. *The Achievement of T. S. Eliot* (2d ed., New York, 1947).

VIVAS, ELISEO. "The Objective Correlative of T. S. Eliot" in *Critiques and Essays in Criticism, 1920–1948,* edited by R. W. Stallman (New York, 1949).

The Love Song of
J. Alfred Prufrock *

*S'io credesse che mia risposta fosse
A persona che mai tornasse al mondo,
Questa fiamma staria senza piu scosse.
Ma perciocche giammai di questo fondo
Non torno vivo alcun, s'i'odo il vero,
Senza tema d'infamia ti rispondo.*[1]

Let us go then, you and I,
When the evening is spread out against the sky
Like a patient etherised upon a table;
Let us go, through certain half-deserted streets,
The muttering retreats
Of restless nights in one-night cheap hotels
And sawdust restaurants with oyster-shells:
Streets that follow like a tedious argument
Of insidious intent
To lead you to an overwhelming question. . . .
Oh, do not ask, "What is it?"
Let us go and make our visit.

In the room the women come and go
Talking of Michelangelo.

[1] "If I thought my answer were to one who could ever return to the world, this flame should shake no more; but since, if what I hear is true, none ever did return alive from this depth, without fear of infamy I answer thee" (Dante, *Inferno*).

The yellow fog that rubs its back upon the window-
panes,
The yellow smoke that rubs its muzzle on the
window-panes
Licked its tongue into the corners of the evening,
Lingered upon the pools that stand in drains,
Let fall upon its back the soot that falls from
chimneys,
Slipped by the terrace, made a sudden leap,
And seeing that it was a soft October night,
Curled once about the house, and fell asleep.

And indeed there will be time
For the yellow smoke that slides along the street,
Rubbing its back upon the window-panes;
There will be time, there will be time
To prepare a face to meet the faces that you meet;
There will be time to murder and create,
And time for all the works and days of hands
That lift and drop a question on your plate;
Time for you and time for me,
And time yet for a hundred indecisions,
And for a hundred visions and revisions,
Before the taking of a toast and tea.

In the room the women come and go
Talking of Michelangelo.

And indeed there will be time
To wonder, "Do I dare?" and, "Do I dare?"
Time to turn back and descend the stair,
With a bald spot in the middle of my hair—
[They will say: "How his hair is growing thin!"]
My morning coat, my collar mounting firmly to the
chin,
My necktie rich and modest, but asserted by a
simple pin—
[They will say: "But how his arms and legs are
thin!"]
Do I dare
Disturb the universe?
In a minute there is time
For decisions and revisions which a minute will
reverse.

For I have known them all already, known them
all:—
Have known the evenings, mornings, afternoons,
I have measured out my life with coffee spoons;
I know the voices dying with a dying fall
Beneath the music from a farther room.
    So how should I presume?

And I have known the eyes already, known them
  all—
The eyes that fix you in a formulated phrase,
And when I am formulated, sprawling on a pin,
When I am pinned and wriggling on the wall,
Then how should I begin
To spit out all the butt-ends of my days and ways?
  And how should I presume?

And I have known the arms already, known them
  all—
Arms that are braceleted and white and bare
[But in the lamplight, downed with light brown
  hair!]
Is it perfume from a dress
That makes me so digress?
Arms that lie along a table, or wrap about a shawl.
  And should I then presume?
  And how should I begin?

. . .

Shall I say, I have gone at dusk through narrow
  streets
And watched the smoke that rises from the pipes
Of lonely men in shirt-sleeves, leaning out of
  windows? . . .

I should have been a pair of ragged claws
Scuttling across the floors of silent seas.

. . .

And the afternoon, the evening, sleeps so peace-
  fully!
Smoothed by long fingers,
Asleep . . . tired . . . or it malingers,
Stretched on the floor, here beside you and me.
Should I, after tea and cakes and ices,
Have the strength to force the moment to its crisis?
But though I have wept and fasted, wept and
  prayed,
Though I have seen my head [grown slightly bald]
  brought in upon a platter,
I am no prophet—and here's no great matter;
I have seen the moment of my greatness flicker,
And I have seen the eternal Footman hold my coat,
  and snicker,
And in short, I was afraid.

And would it have been worth it, after all,
After the cups, the marmalade, the tea,
Among the porcelain, among some talk of you and
  me,
Would it have been worth while,

To have bitten off the matter with a smile,
To have squeezed the universe into a ball
To roll it toward some overwhelming question,
To say: "I am Lazarus, come from the dead,
Come back to tell you all, I shall tell you all"—
If one, settling a pillow by her head,
  Should say: "That is not what I meant at all.
  That is not it, at all."

And would it have been worth it, after all,
Would it have been worth while,
After the sunsets and the dooryards and the sprin-
  kled streets,
After the novels, after the teacups, after the skirts
  that trail along the floor—
And this, and so much more?—
It is impossible to say just what I mean!
But as if a magic lantern threw the nerves in pat-
  terns on a screen:
Would it have been worth while
If one, settling a pillow or throwing off a shawl,
And turning toward the window, should say:
  "That is not it at all,
  That is not what I meant, at all."

. . .

No! I am not Prince Hamlet, nor was meant to be;
Am an attendant lord, one that will do
To swell a progress, start a scene or two,
Advise the prince; no doubt, an easy tool,
Deferential, glad to be of use,
Politic, cautious, and meticulous;
Full of high sentence, but a bit obtuse;
At times, indeed, almost ridiculous—
Almost, at times, the Fool.

I grow old . . . I grow old . . .
I shall wear the bottoms of my trousers rolled.

Shall I part my hair behind? Do I dare to eat a
  peach?
I shall wear white flannel trousers, and walk upon
  the beach.
I have heard the mermaids singing, each to each.

I do not think that they will sing to me.

I have seen them riding seaward on the waves
Combing the white hair of the waves blown back
When the wind blows the water white and black.

We have lingered in the chambers of the sea
By sea-girls wreathed with seaweed red and brown
Till human voices wake us, and we drown.

Sweeney Among the Nightingales

ὤμοι, πέπληγμαι καιρίαν πληγὴν ἔσω.[1]

Apeneck Sweeney spreads his knees
Letting his arms hang down to laugh,
The zebra stripes along his jaw
Swelling to maculate giraffe.

The circles of the stormy moon
Slide westward toward the River Plate,
Death and the Raven drift above
And Sweeney guards the hornèd gate.

Gloomy Orion and the Dog
Are veiled; and hushed the shrunken seas;
The person in the Spanish cape
Tries to sit on Sweeney's knees

Slips and pulls the table cloth
Overturns a coffee-cup,
Reorganised upon the floor
She yawns and draws a stocking up;

The silent man in mocha brown
Sprawls at the window-sill and gapes;
The waiter brings in oranges
Bananas figs and hothouse grapes;

The silent vertebrate in brown
Contracts and concentrates, withdraws;
Rachel *née* Rabinovitch
Tears at the grapes with murderous paws;

She and the lady in the cape
Are suspect, thought to be in league;
Therefore the man with heavy eyes
Declines the gambit, shows fatigue,

Leaves the room and reappears
Outside the window, leaning in,
Branches of wistaria
Circumscribe a golden grin;

The host with someone indistinct
Converses at the door apart,
The nightingales are singing near
The Convent of the Sacred Heart,

And sang within the bloody wood
When Agamemnon cried aloud,
And let their liquid siftings fall
To stain the stiff dishonoured shroud.

[1] "O I am sped—a deep, a mortal blow." See Aeschylus' *Agamemnon*, line 1552, Vol. I, p. 90, for the death of Agamemnon.

The Waste Land

"NAM Sibyllam quidem Cumis ego ipse oculis meis vidi in ampulla pendere, et cum illi pueri dicerent: Σίβυλλα τί θέλεις; respondebat illa: ἀποθανεῖν θέλω."[1]

For Ezra Pound

il miglior fabbro.[2]

I. THE BURIAL OF THE DEAD

April is the cruellest month, breeding
Lilacs out of the dead land, mixing
Memory and desire, stirring
Dull roots with spring rain.
Winter kept us warm, covering
Earth in forgetful snow, feeding
A little life with dried tubers.
Summer surprised us, coming over the Starnber-
gersee
With a shower of rain; we stopped in the colonnade,
And went on in sunlight, into the Hofgarten,   10
And drank coffee, and talked for an hour.
Bin gar keine Russin, stamm' aus Litauen, echt
deutsch.[3]
And when we were children, staying at the arch-
duke's,
My cousin's, he took me out on a sled,
And I was frightened. He said, Marie,
Marie, hold on tight. And down we went.
In the mountains, there you feel free.
I read, much of the night, and go south in the
winter.

What are the roots that clutch, what branches grow
Out of this stony rubbish? Son of man,   20
You cannot say, or guess, for you know only
A heap of broken images, where the sun beats,
And the dead tree gives no shelter, the cricket no
relief,
And the dry stone no sound of water. Only
There is shadow under this red rock,
(Come in under the shadow of this red rock),

[1] "For I saw with my own eyes the Sibyl at Cumae, hanging in a cage, and when the boys said to her, 'Sibyl, what do you want'; she would answer, 'I want to die.'" See *The Satyricon* of Petronius, Trimalchio's dinner (Modern Library edition, p. 72).
[2] "The better craftsman." See Dante's *Purgatorio*, XXVI, line 117, and *The Letters of Ezra Pound* (New York, 1950), pp. 169-71.
[3] "I am not Russian, I come from Lithuania, a true German."

And I will show you something different from
  either
Your shadow at morning striding behind you
Or your shadow at evening rising to meet you;
I will show you fear in a handful of dust.   30

   Frisch weht der Wind
   Der Heimat zu
   Mein Irisch Kind,
   Wo weilest du?

"You gave me hyacinths first a year ago;
"They called me the hyacinth girl."
—Yet when we came back, late, from the Hyacinth
  garden,
Your arms full, and your hair wet, I could not
Speak, and my eyes failed, I was neither
Living nor dead, and I knew nothing,   40
Looking into the heart of light, the silence.
Oed' und leer das Meer.

Madame Sosostris, famous clairvoyante,
Had a bad cold, nevertheless
Is known to be the wisest woman in Europe,
With a wicked pack of cards. Here, said she,
Is your card, the drowned Phoenician Sailor,
(Those are pearls that were his eyes. Look!)
Here is Belladonna, the Lady of the Rocks,
The lady of situations.   50
Here is the man with three staves, and here the
  Wheel,
And here is the one-eyed merchant, and this card,
Which is blank, is something he carries on his back,
Which I am forbidden to see. I do not find
The Hanged Man. Fear death by water.
I see crowds of people, walking round in a ring.
Thank you. If you see dear Mrs. Equitone,
Tell her I bring the horoscope myself:
One must be so careful these days.

Unreal City,   60
Under the brown fog of a winter dawn,
A crowd flowed over London Bridge, so many,
I had not thought death had undone so many.
Sighs, short and infrequent, were exhaled,
And each man fixed his eyes before his feet.
Flowed up the hill and down King William Street,
To where Saint Mary Woolnoth kept the hours
With a dead sound on the final stroke of nine.
There I saw one I knew, and stopped him, crying:
  "Stetson!
"You who were with me in the ships at Mylae!   70
"That corpse you planted last year in your garden,
"Has it begun to sprout? Will it bloom this year?
"Or has the sudden frost disturbed its bed?

"Oh keep the Dog far hence, that's friend to men,
"Or with his nails he'll dig it up again!
"You! hypocrite lecteur!—mon semblable,—mon
  frère!"

II. A GAME OF CHESS

The Chair she sat in, like a burnished throne,
Glowed on the marble, where the glass
Held up by standards wrought with fruited vines
From which a golden Cupidon peeped out   80
(Another hid his eyes behind his wing)
Doubled the flames of sevenbranched candelabra
Reflecting light upon the table as
The glitter of her jewels rose to meet it,
From satin cases poured in rich profusion;
In vials of ivory and coloured glass
Unstoppered, lurked her strange synthetic per-
  fumes,
Unguent, powdered, or liquid—troubled, confused
And drowned the sense in odours; stirred by the air
That freshened from the window, these ascended   90
In fattening the prolonged candle-flames,
Flung their smoke into the laquearia,
Stirring the pattern on the coffered ceiling.
Huge sea-wood fed with copper
Burned green and orange, framed by the coloured
  stone,
In which sad light a carvèd dolphin swam.
Above the antique mantel was displayed
As though a window gave upon the sylvan scene
The change of Philomel, by the barbarous king
So rudely forced; yet there the nightingale   100
Filled all the desert with inviolable voice
And still she cried, and still the world pursues,
"Jug Jug" to dirty ears.
And other withered stumps of time
Were told upon the walls; staring forms
Leaned out, leaning, hushing the room enclosed.
Footsteps shuffled on the stair.
Under the firelight, under the brush, her hair
Spread out in fiery points
Glowed into words, then would be savagely still.   110

"My nerves are bad to-night. Yes, bad. Stay with
  me.
"Speak to me. Why do you never speak. Speak.
  "What are you thinking of? What thinking?
  What?
"I never know what you are thinking. Think."

I think we are in rats' alley
Where the dead men lost their bones.

"What is that noise?"
                    The wind under the door.
"What is that noise now? What is the wind doing?"
                    Nothing again nothing.   120
                              "Do
"You know nothing? Do you see nothing? Do
    you remember
"Nothing?"

      I remember
Those are pearls that were his eyes.
"Are you alive, or not? Is there nothing in your
    head?"
                                          But

O O O O that Shakespeherian Rag—
It's so elegant
So intelligent   130
"What shall I do now? What shall I do?"
"I shall rush out as I am, and walk the street
"With my hair down, so. What shall we do to-
    morrow?
"What shall we ever do?"
                    The hot water at ten.
And if it rains, a closed car at four.
And we shall play a game of chess,
Pressing lidless eyes and waiting for a knock upon
    the door.

When Lil's husband got demobbed, I said—
I didn't mince my words, I said to her myself,   140
Hurry up please its time
Now Albert's coming back, make yourself a bit
    smart.
He'll want to know what you done with that money
    he gave you
To get yourself some teeth. He did, I was there.
You have them all out, Lil, and get a nice set,
He said, I swear, I can't bear to look at you.
And no more can't I, I said, and think of poor
    Albert,
He's been in the army four years, he wants a good
    time,
And if you don't give it him, there's others will, I
    said.
Oh is there, she said. Something o' that, I said. 150
Then I'll know who to thank, she said, and give
    me a straight look.
Hurry up please its time
If you don't like it you can get on with it, I said.
Others can pick and choose if you can't.
But if Albert makes off, it won't be for lack of tell-
    ing.
You ought to be ashamed, I said, to look so antique.
(And her only thirty-one.)

I can't help it, she said, pulling a long face,
It's them pills I took, to bring it off, she said.
(She's had five already, and nearly died of young
    George.)   160
The chemist said it would be all right, but I've
    never been the same.
You *are* a proper fool, I said.
Well, if Albert won't leave you alone, there it is, I
    said,
What you get married for if you don't want chil-
    dren?
Hurry up please its time
Well, that Sunday Albert was home, they had a
    hot gammon,
And they asked me in to dinner, to get the beauty
    of it hot—
Hurry up please its time
Hurry up please its time
Goonight Bill. Goonight Lou. Goonight May.
    Goonight.   170
Ta ta. Goonight. Goonight.
Good night, ladies, good night, sweet ladies, good
    night, good night.

III. THE FIRE SERMON

The river's tent is broken: the last fingers of leaf
Clutch and sink into the wet bank. The wind
Crosses the brown land, unheard. The nymphs are
    departed.
Sweet Thames, run softly, till I end my song.
The river bears no empty bottles, sandwich papers,
Silk handkerchiefs, cardboard boxes, cigarette ends
Or other testimony of summer nights. The nymphs
    are departed.
And their friends, the loitering heirs of city direc-
    tors;   180
Departed, have left no addresses.
By the waters of Leman I sat down and wept . . .
Sweet Thames, run softly till I end my song,
Sweet Thames, runs softly, for I speak not loud or
    long.
But at my back in a cold blast I hear
The rattle of the bones, and chuckle spread from
    ear to ear.
A rat crept softly through the vegetation
Dragging its slimy belly on the bank
While I was fishing in the dull canal
On a winter evening round behind the gas-
    house   190
Musing upon the king my brother's wreck
And on the king my father's death before him.
White bodies naked on the low damp ground

And bones cast in a little low dry garret,
Rattled by the rat's foot only, year to year.
But at my back from time to time I hear
The sound of horns and motors, which shall bring
Sweeney to Mrs. Porter in the spring.
O the moon shone bright on Mrs. Porter
And on her daughter   200
They wash their feet in soda water
Et O ces voix d'enfants, chantant dans la coupole!

Twit twit twit   *nightingale*
Jug jug jug jug jug jug
So rudely forc'd.
Tereu

Unreal City
Under the brown fog of a winter noon
Mr. Eugenides, the Smyrna merchant
Unshaven, with a pocket full of currants   210
C.i.f. London: documents at sight,
Asked me in demotic French
To luncheon at the Cannon Street Hotel
Followed by a weekend at the Metropole.
At the violet hour, when the eyes and back
Turn upward from the desk, when the human en-
    gine waits
Like a taxi throbbing waiting,
I Tiresias, though blind, throbbing between two
    lives,
Old man with wrinkled female breasts, can see
At the violet hour, the evening hour that strives   220
Homeward, and brings the sailor home from sea,
The typist home at teatime, clears her breakfast,
    lights
Her stove, and lays out food in tins.
Out of the window perilously spread
Her drying combinations touched by the sun's last
    rays,
On the divan are piled (at night her bed)
Stockings, slippers, camisoles, and stays.
I Tiresias, old man with wrinkled dugs
Perceived the scene, and foretold the rest—
I too awaited the expected guest.   230
He, the young man carbuncular, arrives,
A small house agent's clerk, with one bold stare,
One of the low on whom assurance sits
As a silk hat on a Bradford millionaire.
The time is now propitious, as he guesses,
The meal is ended, she is bored and tired,
Endeavours to engage her in caresses
Which still are unreproved, if undesired.
Flushed and decided, he assaults at once;
Exploring hands encounter no defence;   240

His vanity requires no response,
And makes a welcome of indifference.
(And I Tiresias have foresuffered all
Enacted on this same divan or bed;
I who have sat by Thebes below the wall
And walked among the lowest of the dead.)
Bestows one final patronising kiss,
And gropes his way, finding the stairs unlit . . .

She turns and looks a moment in the glass,
Hardly aware of her departed lover;   250
Her brain allows one half-formed thought to pass:
"Well now that's done: and I'm glad it's over."
When lovely woman stoops to folly and
Paces about her room again, alone,
She smoothes her hair with automatic hand,
And puts a record on the gramophone.

"This music crept by me upon the waters"
And along the Strand, up Queen Victoria Street.
O City city, I can sometimes hear
Beside a public bar in Lower Thames Street,   260
The pleasant whining of a mandoline
And a clatter and a chatter from within
Where fishmen lounge at noon: where the walls
Of Magnus Martyr hold
Inexplicable splendour of Ionian white and gold.

          The river sweats
          Oil and tar
          The barges drift
          With the turning tide
          Red sails   270
          Wide
          To leeward, swing on the heavy spar.
          The barges wash
          Drifting logs
          Down Greenwich reach
          Past the Isle of Dogs.
                    Weialala leia
                    Wallala leialala

          Elizabeth and Leicester
          Beating oars   280
          The stern was formed
          A gilded shell
          Red and gold
          The brisk swell
          Rippled both shores
          Southwest wind
          Carried down stream
          The peal of bells
          White towers
                    Weialala leia   290
                    Wallala leialala

"Trams and dusty trees.
Highbury bore me. Richmond and Kew
Undid me. By Richmond I raised my knees
Supine on the floor of a narrow canoe."

"My feet are at Moorgate, and my heart
Under my feet. After the event
He wept. He promised 'a new start.'
I made no comment. What should I resent?"

"On Margate Sands.   300
I can connect
Nothing with nothing.
The broken fingernails of dirty hands.
My people humble people who expect
Nothing."
  la la

To Carthage then I came
Burning burning burning burning
O Lord Thou pluckest me out
O Lord Thou pluckest   310

burning

IV. DEATH BY WATER

Phlebas the Phoenician, a fortnight dead,
Forgot the cry of gulls, and the deep sea swell
And the profit and loss.
    A current under sea
Picked his bones in whispers. As he rose and fell
He passed the stages of his age and youth
Entering the whirlpool.
    Gentile or Jew
O you who turn the wheel and look to wind-
  ward,   320
Consider Phlebas, who was once handsome and tall
  as you.

V. WHAT THE THUNDER SAID

After the torchlight red on sweaty faces
After the frosty silence in the gardens
After the agony in stony places
The shouting and the crying
Prison and palace and reverberation
Of thunder of spring over distant mountains
He who was living is now dead
We who were living are now dying
With a little patience   330

Here is no water but only rock
Rock and no water and the sandy road

The road winding above among the mountains
Which are mountains of rock without water
If there were water we should stop and drink
Amongst the rock one cannot stop or think
Sweat is dry and feet are in the sand
If there were only water amongst the rock
Dead mountain mouth of carious teeth that cannot
  spit
Here one can neither stand nor lie nor sit   340
There is not even silence in the mountains
But dry sterile thunder without rain
There is not even solitude in the mountains
But red sullen faces sneer and snarl
From doors of mudcracked houses
      If there were water
And no rock
If there were rock
And also water
And water   350
A spring
A pool among the rock
If there were the sound of water only
Not the cicada
And dry grass singing
But sound of water over a rock
Where the hermit-thrush sings in the pine trees
Drip drop drip drop drop drop drop
But there is no water

Who is the third who walks always beside you?
When I count, there are only you and I together 360*
But when I look ahead up the white road
There is always another one walking beside you
Gliding wrapt in a brown mantle, hooded
I do not know whether a man or a woman
—But who is that on the other side of you?

What is that sound high in the air
Murmur of maternal lamentation
Who are those hooded hordes swarming
Over endless plains, stumbling in cracked earth
Ringed by the flat horizon only   370
What is the city over the mountains
Cracks and reforms and bursts in the violet air
Falling towers
Jerusalem Athens Alexandria
Vienna London
Unreal

A woman drew her long black hair out tight
And fiddled whisper music on those strings
And bats with baby faces in the violet light

* [Editors' note: We are here following line enumeration
as it appears in T. S. Eliot's Collected Poems.]

Whistled, and beat their wings   380
And crawled head downward down a blackened
  wall
And upside down in air were towers
Tolling reminiscent bells, that kept the hours
And voices singing out of empty cisterns and ex-
  hausted wells.

In this decayed hole among the mountains
In the faint moonlight, the grass is singing
Over the tumbled graves, about the chapel
There is the empty chapel, only the wind's home.
It has no windows, and the door swings,
Dry bones can harm no one.   390
Only a cock stood on the rooftree
Co co rico co co rico
In a flash of lightning. Then a damp gust
Bringing rain

Ganga was sunken, and the limp leaves
Waited for rain, while the black clouds
Gathered far distant, over Himavant.
The jungle crouched, humped in silence.
Then spoke the thunder
Da   400
Datta: what have we given?
My friend, blood shaking my heart
The awful daring of a moment's surrender
Which an age of prudence can never retract
By this, and this only, we have existed
Which is not to be found in our obituaries
Or in memories draped by the beneficent spider
Or under seals broken by the lean solicitor
In our empty rooms
Da   410
Dayadhvam: I have heard the key
Turn in the door once and turn once only
We think of the key, each in his prison
Thinking of the key, each confirms a prison
Only at nightfall, aethereal rumours
Revive for a moment a broken Coriolanus
Da
Damyata: The boat responded
Gaily, to the hand expert with sail and oar
The sea was calm, your heart would have re-
  sponded   420
Gaily, when invited, beating obedient
To controlling hands

                          I sat upon the shore
Fishing, with the arid plain behind me
Shall I at least set my lands in order?
London Bridge is falling down falling down falling
  down

Poi s'ascose nel foco che gli affina
Quando fiam uti chelidon—O swallow swallow
Le Prince d'Aquitaine à la tour abolie
These fragments I have shored against my ruins 430
Why then Ile fit you. Hieronymo's mad againe.
Datta. Dayadhvam. Damyata.
        Shantih   shantih   shantih

T. S. ELIOT'S NOTES ON "THE WASTE LAND"

Not only the title, but the plan and a good deal of the incidental symbolism of the poem were suggested by Miss Jessie L. Weston's book on the Grail legend: *From Ritual to Romance* (Cambridge). Indeed, so deeply am I indebted, Miss Weston's book will elucidate the difficulties of the poem much better than my notes can do; and I recommend it (apart from the great interest of the book itself) to any who think such elucidation of the poem worth the trouble. To another work of anthropology I am indebted in general, one which has influenced our generation profoundly; I mean *The Golden Bough*; I have used especially the two volumes *Adonis, Attis, Osiris*. Anyone who is acquainted with these works will immediately recognise in the poem certain references to vegetation ceremonies.

I. THE BURIAL OF THE DEAD

Line 20. Cf. Ezekiel II, i.
23. Cf. Ecclesiastes XII, v.
31. V. *Tristan und Isolde*, I, verses 5–8.
42. *Id.* III, verse 24.
46. I am not familiar with the exact constitution of the Tarot pack of cards, from which I have obviously departed to suit my own convenience. The Hanged Man, a member of the traditional pack, fits my purpose in two ways: because he is associated in my mind with the Hanged God of Frazer, and because I associate him with the hooded figure in the passage of the disciples to Emmaus in Part V. The Phoenician Sailor and the Merchant appear later; also the "crowds of people," and Death by Water is executed in Part IV. The Man with Three Staves (an authentic member of the Tarot pack) I associate, quite arbitrarily, with the Fisher King himself.
60. Cf. Baudelaire:
  "Fourmillante cité, cité pleine de rêves,
  "Où le spectre en plein jour raccroche le passant."
63. Cf. *Inferno*, III, 55–57:
                    "si lunga tratta
      di gente, ch'io non avrei mai creduto
        che morte tanta n'avesse disfatta."
64. Cf. *Inferno*, IV, 25–27:
  "Quivi, secondo che per ascoltare,
  "non avea pianto, ma' che di sospiri,
  "che l'aura eterna facevan tremare."
68. A phenomenon which I have often noticed.
74. Cf. the Dirge in Webster's *White Devil*.
76. V. Baudelaire, Preface to *Fleurs du Mal*.

II. A GAME OF CHESS

77. Cf. *Antony and Cleopatra*, II, ii, l. 190.

92. *Laquearia*. V. *Aeneid*, I, 726:

dependent lychni laquearibus aureis incensi, et noctem flammis funalia vincunt.

98. Sylvan scene. V. Milton, *Paradise Lost*, IV, 140.

99. V. Ovid, *Metamorphoses*, VI, Philomela.

100. Cf. Part III, l. 204.

115. Cf. Part III, l. 195.

118. Cf. Webster: "Is the wind in that door still?"

126. Cf. Part I, l. 37, 48.

138. Cf. the game of chess in Middleton's *Women beware Women*.

III. THE FIRE SERMON

176. V. Spenser, *Prothalamion*.

192. Cf. *The Tempest*, I, ii.

196. Cf. Marvell, *To His Coy Mistress*.

197. Cf. Day, *Parliament of Bees*:

"When of the sudden, listening, you shall hear,
"A noise of horns and hunting, which shall bring
"Actaeon to Diana in the spring,
"Where all shall see her naked skin . . ."

199. I do not know the origin of the ballad from which these lines are taken: it was reported to me from Sydney, Australia.

202. V. Verlaine, *Parsifal*.

210. The currants were quoted at a price "carriage and insurance free to London"; and the Bill of Lading etc. were to be handed to the buyer upon payment of the sight draft.

218. Tiresias, although a mere spectator and not indeed a "character," is yet the most important personage in the poem, uniting all the rest. Just as the one-eyed merchant, seller of currants, melts into the Phoenician Sailor, and the latter is not wholly distinct from Ferdinand Prince of Naples, so all the women are one woman, and the two sexes meet in Tiresias. What Tiresias *sees*, in fact, is the substance of the poem. The whole passage from Ovid is of great anthropological interest:

". . . Cum Iunone iocos et maior vestra profecto est
Quam, quae contingit maribus," dixisse, "voluptas."
Illa negat; placuit quae sit sententia docti
Quaerere Tiresiae: venus huic erat utraque nota.
Nam duo magnorum viridi coeuntia silva
Corpora serpentum baculi violaverat ictu
Deque viro factus, mirabile, femina septem
Egerat autumnos; octavo rursus eosdem
Videt et "est vestrae si tanta potentia plagae,"
Dixit "ut auctoris sortem in contraria mutet,
Nunc quoque vos feriam!" percussis anguibus isdem
Forma prior rediit genetivaque venit imago.
Arbiter hic igitur sumptus de lite iocosa
Dicta Iovis firmat; gravius Saturnia iusto
Nec pro materia fertur doluisse suique
Iudicis aeterna damnavit lumina nocte,
At pater omnipotens (neque enim licet inrita cuiquam
Facta dei fecisse deo) pro lumine adempto
Scire futura dedit poenamque levavit honore.

221. This may not appear as exact as Sappho's lines, but I had in mind the "longshore" or "dory" fisherman, who returns at nightfall.

253. V. Goldsmith, the song of *The Vicar of Wakefield*.

257. V. *The Tempest*, as above.

264. The interior of St. Magnus Martyr is to my mind one of the finest among Wren's interiors. See *The Proposed Demolition of Nineteen City Churches*: (P. S. King & Son, Ltd.).

266. The Song of the (three) Thames-daughters begins here. From line 292 to 306 inclusive they speak in turn. V. *Götterdämmerung* III, i: the Rhine-daughters.

279. V. Froude, *Elizabeth*, Vol. I, ch. iv, letter of De Quadra to Philip of Spain:

"In the afternoon we were in a barge, watching the games on the river. (The queen) was alone with Lord Robert and myself on the poop, when they began to talk nonsense, and went so far that Lord Robert at last said, as I was on the spot there was no reason why they should not be married if the queen pleased."

293. Cf. *Purgatorio*, V, 133:

"Ricorditi di me, che son la Pia;
"Siena mi fe', disfecemi Maremma."

307. V. St. Augustine's *Confessions*: "to Carthage then I came, where a cauldron of unholy loves sang all about mine ears."

308. The complete text of the Buddha's Fire Sermon (which corresponds in importance to the Sermon on the Mount) from which these words are taken, will be found translated in the late Henry Clarke Warren's *Buddhism in Translation* (Harvard Oriental Series). Mr. Warren was one of the great pioneers of Buddhist studies in the Occident.

IV. DEATH BY WATER

312. From St. Augustine's *Confessions* again. The collocation of these two representatives of eastern and western asceticism, as the culmination of this part of the poem, is not an accident.

V. WHAT THE THUNDER SAID

In the first part of Part V three themes are employed: the journey to Emmaus, the approach to the Chapel Perilous (see Miss Weston's book) and the present decay of eastern Europe.

357. This is *Turdus aonalaschkae pallasii*, the hermit-thrush which I have heard in Quebec County. Chapman says (*Handbook of Birds of Eastern North America*) "it is most at home in secluded woodland and thickety retreats. . . . Its notes are not remarkable for variety or volume, but in purity and sweetness of tone and exquisite modulation they are unequalled." Its "water-dripping song" is justly celebrated.

360. The following lines were stimulated by the account of one of the Antarctic expeditions (I forget which, but I think one of Shackleton's): it was related that the party of explorers, at the extremity of their strength, had the constant delusion that there was *one more member* than could actually be counted.

366–76. Cf. Herman Hesse, *Blick ins Chaos*: "Schon ist halb Europa, schon ist zumindest der halbe Osten Europas auf dem Wege zum Chaos, fährt betrunken im heiligem Wahn am Abgrund entlang und singt dazu, singt betrunken und hymnisch wie Dmitri Karamasoff sang. Ueber diese Lieder lacht der Bürger beleidigt, der Heilige und Seher hört si mit Tränen."

401. "Datta, dayadhvam, damyata" (Give, sympathize, control). The fable of the meaning of the Thunder is found in the *Brihadaranyaka—Upanishad*, 5, 1. A translation is found in Deussen's *Sechzig Upanishads des Veda*, p. 489.

407. Cf. Webster, *The White Devil*, V, vi:
". . . they'll remarry
Ere the worm pierce your winding-sheet, ere the spider
Make a thin curtain for your epitaphs."

411. Cf. *Inferno*, XXXIII, 46:
"ed io sentii chiavar l'uscio di sotto
all'orribile torre."
Also F. H. Bradley, *Appearance and Reality*, p. 346. "My external sensations are no less private to myself than are my thoughts or my feelings. In either case my experience falls within my own circle, a circle closed on the outside; and, with all its elements alike, every sphere is opaque to the others which surround it. . . . In brief, regarded as an existence which appears in a soul, the whole world for each is peculiar and private to that soul."

424. V. Weston: *From Ritual to Romance*; chapter on the Fisher King.

427. V. *Purgatorio*, XXVI, 148.
"'Ara vos prec per aquella valor
'que vos guida al som le l'escalina,
'sovegna vos a temps de ma dolor.'
Poi s'ascose nel foco che gli affina."

428. V. *Pervigilium Veneris*. Cf. Philomela in Parts II and III.

429. V. Gerard de Nerval, Sonnet *El Desdichado*.

431. V. Kyd's *Spanish Tragedy*.

433. Shantih. Repeated as here, a formal ending to an Upanishad. "The Peace which passeth understanding" is our equivalent to this word.

Animula

"Issues from the hand of God, the simple soul"
To a flat world of changing lights and noise,
To light, dark, dry or damp, chilly or warm;
Moving between the legs of tables and of chairs,
Rising or falling, grasping at kisses and toys,
Advancing boldly, sudden to take alarm,
Retreating to the corner of arm and knee,
Eager to be reassured, taking pleasure
In the fragrant brilliance of the Christmas tree,
Pleasure in the wind, the sunlight and the sea;
Studies the sunlit pattern on the floor
And running stags around a silver tray;
Confounds the actual and the fanciful,
Content with playing-cards and kings and queens,
What the fairies do and what the servants say.
The heavy burden of the growing soul
Perplexes and offends more, day by day;
Week by week, offends and perplexes more
With the imperatives of "is and seems"
And may and may not, desire and control.
The pain of living and the drug of dreams

Curl up the small soul in the window seat
Behind the *Encyclopædia Britannica*.
Issues from the hand of time the simple soul
Irresolute and selfish, misshapen, lame,
Unable to fare forward or retreat,
Fearing the warm reality, the offered good,
Denying the importunity of the blood,
Shadow of its own shadows, spectre in its own
gloom,
Leaving disordered papers in a dusty room;
Living first in the silence after the viaticum.

Pray for Guiterriez, avid of speed and power,
For Boudin, blown to pieces,
For this one who made a great fortune,
And that one who went his own way.
Pray for Floret, by the boarhound slain between
the yew trees,
Pray for us now and at the hour of our birth.

Burnt Norton *

τοῦ λόγου δ'ἐόντος ξυνοῦ ζώουσιν οἱ πολλοί
ὡς ἰδίαν ἔχοντες φρόνησιν.[1]
I. p. 77. Fr. 2.

ὁδὸς ἄνω κάτω μία καὶ ὡυτή.[2]
I. p. 89. Fr. 60.
Diels: *Die Fragmente der Vorsokratiker* (Herakleitos).

I

Time present and time past
Are both perhaps present in time future,
And time future contained in time past.
If all time is eternally present
All time is unredeemable.
What might have been is an abstraction
Remaining a perpetual possibility
Only in a world of speculation.
What might have been and what has been
Point to one end, which is always present.
Footfalls echo in the memory
Down the passage which we did not take
Towards the door we never opened
Into the rose-garden. My words echo

* From *Four Quartets*. Copyright, 1943, by T. S. Eliot. By permission of Harcourt, Brace & Company, Inc., and Faber and Faber, Ltd.

[1] "Although the word (logos) is in common use for all, most men live as if they each had a private wisdom of his own." For the relation of these quotations from Heraclitus to *Four Quartets*, see Philip Wheelwright, "Eliot's Philosophical Themes," in *T. S. Eliot: A Study of His Writings by Several Hands* (New York, 1948), pp. 96-106, *passim*.

[2] "The way up and the way down are one and the same."

Thus, in your mind.
                    But to what purpose
Disturbing the dust on a bowl of rose-leaves
I do not know.
                    Other echoes
Inhabit the garden. Shall we follow?
Quick, said the bird, find them, find them,
Round the corner. Through the first gate,
Into our first world, shall we follow
The deception of the thrush? Into our first world.
There they were, dignified, invisible,
Moving without pressure, over the dead leaves,
In the autumn heat, through the vibrant air,
And the bird called, in response to
The unheard music hidden in the shrubbery,
And the unseen eyebeam crossed, for the roses
Had the look of flowers that are looked at.
There they were as our guests, accepted and accept-
          ing.
So we moved, and they, in a formal pattern,
Along the empty alley, into the box circle,
To look down into the drained pool.
Dry the pool, dry concrete, brown edged,
And the pool was filled with water out of sunlight,
And the lotos rose, quietly, quietly,
The surface glittered out of heart of light,
And they were behind us, reflected in the pool.
Then a cloud passed, and the pool was empty.
Go, said the bird, for the leaves were full of chil-
          dren,
Hidden excitedly, containing laughter.
Go, go, go, said the bird: human kind
Cannot bear very much reality.
Time past and time future
What might have been and what has been
Point to one end, which is always present.

II

Garlic and sapphires in the mud
Clot the bedded axle-tree.
The trilling wire in the blood
Sings below inveterate scars
And reconciles forgotten wars.
The dance along the artery
The circulation of the lymph
Are figured in the drift of stars
Ascend to summer in the tree
We move above the moving tree
In light upon the figured leaf
And hear upon the sodden floor
Below, the boarhound and the boar
Pursue their pattern as before.
But reconciled among the stars.

At the still point of the turning world. Neither flesh
     nor fleshless;
Neither from nor towards; at the still point, there
     the dance is,
But neither arrest nor movement. And do not call
     it fixity,
Where past and future are gathered. Neither move-
     ment from nor towards,
Neither ascent nor decline. Except for the point,
     the still point,
There would be no dance, and there is only the
     dance.
I can only say, *there* we have been: but I cannot
     say where.
And I cannot say, how long, for that is to place it
     in time.

The inner freedom from the practical desire,
The release from action and suffering, release from
     the inner
And the outer compulsion, yet surrounded
By a grace of sense, a white light still and moving,
Erhebung [3] without motion, concentration
Without elimination, both a new world
And the old made explicit, understood
In the completion of its partial ecstasy,
The resolution of its partial horror.
Yet the enchainment of past and future
Woven in the weakness of the changing body,
Protects mankind from heaven and damnation
Which flesh cannot endure.
                    Time past and time future
Allow but a little consciousness.
To be conscious is not to be in time
But only in time can the moment in the rose-
     garden,
The moment in the arbour where the rain beat,
The moment in the draughty church at smokefall
Be remembered; involved with past and future.
Only through time time is conquered.

III

Here is a place of disaffection
Time before and time after
In a dim light: neither daylight
Investing form with lucid stillness
Turning shadow into transient beauty
With slow rotation suggesting permanence
Nor darkness to purify the soul
Emptying the sensual with deprivation

---

[3] Untranslatable, but very approximately, "spiritual exaltation."

Cleansing affection from the temporal.
Neither plenitude nor vacancy. Only a flicker
Over the strained time-ridden faces
Distracted from distraction by distraction
Filled with fancies and empty of meaning
Tumid apathy with no concentration
Men and bits of paper, whirled by the cold wind
That blows before and after time,
Wind in and out of unwholesome lungs
Time before and time after.
Eructation of unhealthy souls
Into the faded air, the torpid
Driven on the wind that sweeps the gloomy hills of
     London,
Hampstead and Clerkenwell, Campden and Put-
     ney,
Highgate, Primrose and Ludgate. Not here
Not here the darkness, in this twittering world.

Descend lower, descend only
Into the world of perpetual solitude,
World not world, but that which is not world,
Internal darkness, deprivation
And destitution of all property,
Desiccation of the world of sense,
Evacuation of the world of fancy,
Inoperancy of the world of spirit;
This is the one way, and the other
Is the same, not in movement
But abstention from movement; while the world
     moves
In appetency, on its metalled ways
Of time past and time future.

IV

Time and the bell have buried the day,
The black cloud carries the sun away.
Will the sunflower turn to us, will the clematis
Stray down, bend to us; tendril and spray
Clutch and cling?
Chill
Fingers of yew be curled
Down on us? After the kingfisher's wing

Has answered light to light, and is silent, the light is
     still
At the still point of the turning world.

V

Words move, music moves
Only in time; but that which is only living
Can only die. Words, after speech, reach
Into the silence. Only by the form, the pattern,
Can words or music reach
The stillness, as a Chinese jar still
Moves perpetually in its stillness.
Not the stillness of the violin, while the note lasts,
Not that only, but the co-existence,
Or say that the end precedes the beginning,
And the end and the beginning were always there
Before the beginning and after the end.
And all is always now. Words strain,
Crack and sometimes break, under the burden,
Under the tension, slip, slide, perish,
Decay with imprecision, will not stay in place,
Will not stay still. Shrieking voices
Scolding, mocking, or merely chattering,
Always assail them. The Word in the desert
Is most attacked by voices of temptation,
The crying shadow in the funeral dance,
The loud lament of the disconsolate chimera.

The detail of the pattern is movement,
As in the figure of the ten stairs.
Desire itself is movement
Not in itself desirable;
Love is itself unmoving,
Only the cause and end of movement,
Timeless, and undesiring
Except in the aspect of time
Caught in the form of limitation
Between un-being and being.
Sudden in a shaft of sunlight
Even while the dust moves
There rises the hidden laughter
Of children in the foliage
Quick now, here, now, always—
Ridiculous the waste sad time
Stretching before and after.

◆

THE FOUR FREEDOMS AND THE ATLANTIC CHARTER

Whatever may be the final judgment of history upon the administrative policies of President Franklin Delano Roosevelt, the public documents known as "The Four Freedoms" and "The Atlantic Charter" will always constitute landmarks of bright hope for twentieth century humanity in its progress toward the realization of a fuller, richer, more abundant, humane life for the citizen of the One World, and toward the fostering of the fullest spiritual, intellectual, and moral development of the individual, which is the ideal of the democratic way of life. Both these documents form a declaration of human rights and freedom in the most dedicated sense; the Atlantic Charter is in its way a more precise orientation and implementation of the general principles of the "Four Freedoms" to present economic and political realities.

The occasion for the declaration of the "Four Freedoms" was President Roosevelt's Annual Message to Congress on January 6, 1941, to request the passage of the Lend-Lease Bill. The Atlantic Charter was enunciated jointly by President Roosevelt and Prime Minister Winston S. Churchill of Great Britain following their meeting at Argentia, Newfoundland, on August 14, 1941. It was officially signed at Washington on January 1, 1942.

The Four Freedoms

IN THE future days, which we seek to make secure, we look forward to a world founded upon four essential human freedoms.

The first is freedom of speech and expression—everywhere in the world.

The second is freedom of every person to worship God in his own way—everywhere in the world.

The third is freedom from want—which, translated into world terms, means economic understandings which will secure to every nation a healthy peacetime life for its inhabitants—everywhere in the world.

The fourth is freedom from fear—which, translated into world terms, means a world-wide reduction of armaments to such a point and in such a thorough fashion that no nation will be in a position to commit an act of physical aggression against any neighbor—anywhere in the world.

That is no vision of a distant millennium. It is a definite basis for a kind of world attainable in our own time and generation.

The Atlantic Charter

THE President of the United States of America and the Prime Minister, Mr. Churchill, representing His Majesty's Government in the United Kingdom, being met together, deem it right to make known certain common principles in the national policies of their respective countries on which they base their hopes for a better future for the world.

FIRST, their countries seek no aggrandizement, territorial or other;

SECOND, they desire to see no territorial changes that do not accord with the freely expressed wishes of the peoples concerned;

THIRD, they respect the right of all peoples to choose the form of government under which they will live; and they wish to see sovereign rights and self-government restored to those who have been forcibly deprived of them;

FOURTH, they will endeavor, with due respect for their existing obligations, to further the enjoyment by all States, great or small, victor or vanquished, of access, on equal terms, to the trade and to the raw materials of the world which are needed for their economic prosperity;

FIFTH, they desire to bring about the fullest collaboration between all nations in the economic field with the object of securing, for all, improved labor standards, economic advancement, and social security;

SIXTH, after the final destruction of the Nazi tyranny, they hope to see established a peace which will afford to all nations the means of dwelling in safety within their own boundaries, and which will afford assurance that all the men in all the lands may live out their lives in freedom from fear and want;

SEVENTH, such a peace should enable all men to traverse the high seas and oceans without hindrance;

EIGHTH, they believe that all the nations of the world, for realistic as well as spiritual reasons, must come to the abandonment of the use of force. Since no future peace can be maintained if land, sea, or air armaments continue to be employed by nations which threaten, or may threaten, aggression outside of their frontiers, they believe, pending the establishment of a wider and permanent system of general security, that the disarmament of such nations is essential. They will likewise aid and encourage all other practicable measures which will lighten for peace-loving peoples the crushing burden of armaments.

INDEX

The name of an author who is represented by a selection appears in capitals and small capitals. Titles of all selections appear in italic type. Roman type is used for references to material appearing in the editorial matter (introductions and biographies). Boldface numbers are used with an author's name to refer to his biography; with a selection, to refer to the opening page of the selection.